Both David Moore and Philip Williamson have been involved with assessing high quality wine for the best part of 20 years. Both have travelled widely and been exposed to hands-on winemaking from Bordeaux to Australia. During the past 10 years both writers have contributed to a diverse range of wine information media. The authors were influential in the establishment of the Oz Clarke's Wine Guide CD Rom, working in both a consultancy and editing role over several years, and have also contributed to several other Oz Clarke titles. They were also involved with the London based Vinopolis Wine Experience in its inception, ensuring its authenticity as a major Wine tourist attraction. In 2000-2001 they collaborated with Oz Clarke as wine judges for Wine Today Europe for the New York Times.

From 2001 the pair pooled their substantial wine tasting resources to set about creating a wine guide of unprecedented depth and scope. The result, the critically acclaimed Wine behind the label (first edition 2003) covers all the world's top wine producers, and their wines, in a truly global context, in a way no other wine book has before. Rejecting a UK-centred approach to wine writing and assessment, Williamson and Moore actively seek out new producers, travelling extensively to visit them at their wineries or meet them at the most important of the world's major wine fairs. Crucially, David and Philip continue to have no commercial links with wine producers in order to maintain their independent stance and unreserved critical analysis.

For the first edition of French Wines behind the label, further help has been provided by Neville and Sonia Blech. Their considerable restaurant experience (the Crown Inn in Wales prior to Restaurant Mijanou in London) has made it possible to add another dimension to the guide. Sonia's recipes are informed by years of experience as a top chef, being the first woman in the UK to gain a Michelin star. Neville's particular expertise with wine and food matching is backed up by his extensive wine knowledge and tasting experience (a member of Le Grand Jury Européen), in turn enhanced through the establishment of a successful wine importing business.

The first edition of *Wine behind the label* was published in 2003 and elicited an enthusiastic response from the world of wine...

'An incredibly in-depth and addictively readable survey of wines of quality from around the world with intelligent tasting notes and informative background to the producers, plus stockists and UK prices. For me, by far the best of the wine guides'
Steven Spurrier, Decanter Magazine

'I'm a fan.'
Hugh Johnson

'This is Robert Parker territory but succinct and cheaper'
Joanna Simon, Sunday Times

With its championing of authenticity of origin, gifted winemakers, smaller producers, organic and biodynamic winemaking, as well as its wealth of detail, this could well become the annual guide by which all others are judged.'
Fine Wine Magazine

'... a guide that's immediately established itself as more or less indispensable.'
Peter McCombie MW, Restaurant Magazine

'I heartily recommend this book as a thorough independent overview of the world's best wine estates'
Tom Cannavan, wine-pages.com

'As essential to the sommelier as their corkscrew'
Paul Dwyer, BBC Radio 5 Live and BBC Radio Scotland

'If you are passionate about your wine and pay serious attention to sampling the world's finest bottles then this book should be on your shelf... I would strongly recommend this excellent guide'
Dr Edward Fitzgerald, Oxford University Wine Society

'...a tremendously useful and comprehensive reference work...(it) is bang up to date. Any wine nut will have a lot of fun with this book'
Jamie Goode, wineanorak.com

FRENCH WINES
behind
the label

2006 edition

Philip Williamson
& David Moore

W
M
Williamson Moore Publishing Limited
www.winebehindthelabel.com

First published in 2005 by Williamson Moore
13 Rances Way Winchester Hampshire SO22 4PN United Kingdom
Tel/Fax +44 (0)1962 625 539
E-mail: info@williamson-moore.co.uk

A catalogue record for this book is available from the British Library.

ISBN 0-9544097-8-7

Editorial assistance from Bill Evans and Ed Francis

Designed by Davis Wadicci

Printed and bound in Great Britain by Ashford Colour Press Ltd, Fareham, Hants

CONTENTS

A Guide to *Quality* French Wines in English

As the name suggests this new title is devoted to France and her best wine producers. While fine wine production is now associated with more than a dozen different countries around the world not one has quite the same number of top quality producers nor the breadth of excellence across so many different styles. As with our global guide *Wine behind the label* we have endeavoured to produce a reference that is accessible to the novice and learned alike. We believe it will be both a valuable tool for buying wine at home and indispensable for those readers pursuing vinous adventures in France. As well as the extensive catalogue of producers found in *Wine behind the label* we have added information on the the best places to stay, eat and drink. Thanks to Sonia Blech there are also some great regional recipes to try your hand at. The A-Z of producers within each of France's principal regions includes both established names and many of the best new names. For each we have provided a critical assessment of the wines but equally as much pertinent information as possible.

What makes it different?

While there are several good books extolling the qualities of a limited selection of France's best producers, this guide focuses on covering as many of the best and most interesting wines as possible. However rather than just lists of tasting notes and scores we have also tried to bring the producer a little closer to whoever is drinking their wine - providing some background to their method and madness in order to enrich the enjoyment the wine brings. More than 1000 producers are covered in depth. Furthermore every wine is rated and price coded, and there are details on UK Stockists for wines imported to the UK. While some of France's finest wines can be hard to get hold of in many instances there is a first point of contact that will sell direct by mail-order or over the Internet. Alternatives or better value can often be quickly found, not least by using the Author's Choice lists (see Help).

Winemaking and a wine's origins

Whether using this book at home or on your travels hopefully we'll introduce you to many of France' finest. We've tried to provide information about where quality and character come from - the most relevant aspects of winemaking, viticulture and vineyard site that contribute to what's in your glass. There is also information on the extent of a wine's manipulation such as fining or filtration, and whether organic or biodynamic principles are employed. We are also keeping tabs on some on some of the most famous names where the pursuit of profit, lacklustre direction or a change of ownership may have compromised quality. On the hand we point out where a new, often more highly-trained, generation has made a positive impact or where outside investment has resulted in a new lease of life.

Help

There are a number of features we hope will help you find the information you need more quickly. The lists of producers by appellation or region (at the end of each section's introduction) provides an alternative to using the Index. Where possible there are also single page map inserts for quick reference to those numerous appellations. For the many readers who only have time to dip in and out of the book we would encourage you to use the 'Author's Choice' lists at the end of each section. These contain at least one wine from most of a region's best producers and make a useful alternative starting point to discovering new wines. The 'value for money' lists highlight some of the best buys. Given that exciting new producers are emerging all the time we have included a 'Work in progress' list covering those we will be assessing for the next edition.

We'd like as much of your input as possible and will encourage this through our website as we develop it further. Alternatively please write to, or email, us with your constructive criticisms.

Tasting, ratings, and assessing producers

Our Quality Rating (see How to Use this guide) is intended to give a truer assessment of wine quality than a vintage dependent point score. It is nearly always based on scores from a minimum of two recent vintages. Wine shows and competitions encourage the production of wines of flattering first impressions but don't always reward those that show at their best with age. Nor do they address the implications of the vintage characteristics. Rather than a snapshot, consensual tasting mentality we believe in tasting wines again and again (both blind and non-blind) in order to gain a better understanding of a wine's style and when it should be drunk. A rating combined with an understanding of the style is the key to discovering the best wines. A higher rating doesn't necessarily reflect a better wine but one that may develop more complexity, have the structure for greater longevity or simply show greater intensity or persistence in the mouth. Enjoying wine of course has as much to do with context as a rating or score. The question should always be which wine works best now, reflects my mood, personality or other criteria. What flavours do I want? How much flavour? It also depends on whether the wine is drunk immediately (with food or without) or cellared. If it is kept, the character of different vintages of the same wine can be contrasted. Alternatively from a case of the same wine the gradual development and increasing maturity of a specific vintage can be assessed over a decade or more.

Vive la France

It is our hope that this guide will encourage wine lovers to delve deeper into France. No, it doesn't have the ease of recognition of labels in English or a limited palette of grapes and styles to communicate. Thank God! It does require a little more effort to begin to fathom its unequalled vinous riches and wine culture but the return is that much greater too. The best of France embodies complexity, balance, refinement and a sense of place. To discover more choose from the many thousands of wines on these pages, with the certainty of trying wines of dependable quality thanks to our rating system. If you haven't tasted Jurançon or a Cotes du Jura white now is the time. Alternatively buy the best new reds from Languedoc-Roussillon or Provence, try Alsace Grand Cru Riesling or a fine Coteaux du Layon. If you want more of the classics seek out new names from Burgundy, Bordeaux or the Rhône.

nended hotels and restaurants

is book is a *Tour de France* of all the best wine producers there,
ire that some of you will be making your own tour in visiting a
of these estates. Accordingly, we have listed some hotels and
ints in each wine region, which should feature in your itinerary.

ist can hardly be called comprehensive – in fact we have confined it
sting two top and two value for money establishments in each region.
course, if you want to spend lots of money, just stick to the top, but
e value for money entries are not necessarily the cheapest or the plainest
stablishments. Some establishments feature as both restaurant and hotel
and not always in the same category. There are some fairly up market
places which represent excellent value for money for what you get,
although the majority of entries in the value for money sections are
relatively inexpensive. Nearly all of the hotels listed have their restaurant
as well and just because the restaurant for that particular hotel is not
listed only means that we have shown a slight preference for the ones that
are. If both the hotel and the restaurant of a particular establishment is
listed, you are indeed going to get a treat.

So why not have a bit of fun and stay at a top hotel and eat in a value for
money restaurant one day and do the reverse the next. You will have
endless fun experimenting and we look forward to receiving your
feedback on these and on any other discoveries you may find during your
travels.

The establishments are graded by one to five stars for the overall quality
of comfort and satisfaction. The prices for hotels are banded to reflect
the cost of a room without breakfast. The prices for restaurants are
banded to reflect the cost of a three course a la carte meal with half a
bottle of a decent, but not over indulgent wine.

Ratings Hotels
★   Simply furnished, but comfortable bedrooms
★★   More facilities and space in the bedrooms and some public rooms
★★★   Very comfortable rooms with spacious public facilities
★★★★   Luxury rooms with top public facilities
★★★★★ De luxe with every creature comfort

Ratings Restaurants
★   Simple, but tasty regional food
★★   More elaborate cooking and comfort in the restaurant
★★★   A good degree of skill from the chef with greater attention in
        restaurant service
★★★★   Consistently high standards in both cuisine and service
★★★★★ Inventive, innovative, personal and highly skilful cuisine with top
        class service to match

Prices Hotels (per room without breakfast)

£A	<£50 (€75)
£B	£50-£75 (€75-€120)
£C	£75-£100 (€120-€150)

£D	£100-£125 (€150-€190)
£E	£125-£150 (€190-€225)
£F	£150-£175 (€225-€260)
£G	£175-£200 (€260-€300)
£H	over £200 (€300)

Prices Restaurants (per person with wine)

£A	<£20 (€30)
£B	£20-£30 (€30-€45)
£C	£30-£40 (€45-€60)
£D	£40-£50 (€60-€75)
£E	£50-£60 (€75-€90)
£F	£60-£75 (€90-€110)
£G	£75-£100 (€110-€150)
£H	over £100 (€150)

French Regional Recipes

When travelling through France, a notable feature is the regional cuisine you come across, which is very much tied to the local *terroir* and therefore also to the local wines, even if in many areas, these wines are of world class standards. Since the gastronomic regions do not exactly coincide with the wine growing regions, there will not be recipes at the end of every section, but as many as possible that fit in with that particular wine producing region. For the purposes of this book, I have taken a number of traditional French regional recipes and have updated some of them to give them a modern twist, bearing in mind our current obsession with healthy eating. So, in many cases, I have substituted lighter ingredients, such as fromage frais (0% fat), for cream or butter, and kept my hand out of the flour jar wherever possible, except for making pastry, of course.

After you have filled the back of your car with a selection of wines from the top class producers you will find in this book, you can return home and try some of these recipes (they are not particularly difficult) with the wines you have brought back to remind you of those wonderful moments you had touring the vineyards. To assist you, after each recipe, Neville has given you an idea of the type of wine you will need to match the dishes, with a couple of specific recommendations.

Bon Appetit!

Sonia Romano Blech

h section you will find an introduction including, where
intage information. In this edition we have also added a list of
cers, either by region or appellation, that have been profiled
he A-Z that makes up the bulk of the section. At the end of the A-
oducers, is a list of other wines of note from that region. Many are
quality or produce at least one good wine. The best of these are
to be added to the guide in future editions after further assessment.
e in these lists also produce more quality wines than are indicated as
have included only those we have tasted at least once. There is also a
ork in progress' list of producers we will be assessing over the next
velve months. At the very end of each section under Author's Choice we
ave added lists of wines that are a personal selection but are also often
themed by a shared style or grape variety and so should aid navigation and
we have included a value for money selection in each section. For
individual A-Z entries we have provided the winery addresses and
wherever possible we have also provided website addresses. In some
instances we have provided email addresses where there is no website. The
use of CAPS (eg Louis JADOT) indicates the existence of a cross-referenced
entry that can be found from the Index.

Vintages Charts

In those sections where vintages have the greatest significance, Vintage
Charts are also provided (as is text on individual years for the classic wines
of Bordeaux and Burgundy). Specific styles of wine are given an overall
vintage rating between one and five stars for individual years. When to
drink the wines of a given vintage is a largely subjective, personal
judgement and can depend as much on mood or context but the letter (A-
D) following the ratings gives a general indication of their likely
development:

> A - wines to Anticipate, not ready for drinking
>
> B - wines that can be Broached, but with much more to give
>
> C - wines to Consume, at or near their best
>
> D - wines likely to be in Decline, past their best

A-Z Order

The order of the A-Z entries is based on the name they are most
commonly referred to and they appear as they are written but with
priority to surnames. 'Domaine' is ignored but 'Château' is respected as is
the definite article when implicitly part of the name. The only exception
to these principles is in Bordeaux where the name of the château or estate
takes precedent.

UK stockists

'UK stockists' in A-Z producer entries indicates the existence of a UK agent
or stockists of a producer's wines. An exclusive agent appears in **bold**.
Details of these codes can be found in the Agent Codes section. Also given
here is general information on buying wine. Though not all agents can sell
direct to consumers they will at least be able to give details of where the
wines can be bought. In future editions we plan to provide details of agents
and stockists in other markets.

Ownership

Ownership is also given throughout and wherever this appears in *bold* it
refers to a corporate owner rather than an individual or individuals.
Obviously contact with a corporate owner shouldn't be assumed to be
possible via the winery's address that follows it.

Symbols

● red wine   O white wine   ◉ rosé wine

Ratings

★   *a wine of good quality, not just sound but of good fruit and with some character.*

★★   *a wine with more depth, interest and concentration, usually with some aging potential.*

★★★   *a very good, even fine, wine. In the case of many reds repaying lengthy cellaring.*

★★★★   *a wine of very high quality, among the very best even in a top appellation or region.*

★★★★★ *outstanding quality, potentially a classic.*

✪✪✪✪✪ *super 5 stars, restricted to the true classics, out-and-out world class.*

We have rated as many of a producer's wines as possible, but in some instances the wines are too new or, too scarce to have yet received a rating. Such wines are covered in the text only.

Tasting notes and scores

It is not in the style of this guide to provide tasting notes for individual vintages along with their scores. However this information will be provided through our website over the coming year and we intend to give readers the opportunity to receive the scores for currently available vintages by electronic means. Given that scores are vintage specific, they sometimes exceed or fall short of the rating that is based on repeated tastings. (also see 'Tasting, Ratings, and assessing producers' in the Introduction)

Prices

A code is provided which represents an estimated retail price bracket and is based on a standard 75cl bottle size. Price codes for those produced only in 1.5 litre (magnums), 50 cl (half litre) or 37.5 cl (half bottle) formats have been given 75cl equivalents. A half bottle costing £8.95/$16.00 for instance will have a price code of £D.

£A: *less than £5:00 ($9.00)*   £E: *£20 - 30 ($36 - 54)*
£B: *£5 - 10 ($9 - 18)*   £F: *£30 - 50 ($54 - 90)*
£C: *£10 - 15 ($18 - 27)*   £G: *£50 - 75 ($90 - 135)*
£D: *£15 - 20 ($27 - 36)*   £H: *£75 or more ($135 or more)*

The entries follow this simple 'all you need to know' format

|Producer |wine region |website

CH. HAUT-BRION Pessac-Léognan 1er CC www.haut-brion.com
UK stockist: AAA ◀——— Agent or stockist (UK only)

Domaine Clarence Dillon 33608 Pessac Cedex ◀— Owner's name and address
One of the 4 original properties classified as a First Growth in the 1855 Classification of red Bordeaux wines. The vineyards are planted in superbly drained gravel soils that provide an almost ideal supply of moisture to optimise fruit ripening. Red grapes occupy 43ha, while less than 3ha provides a tiny amount of exquisite, subtly barrel-fermented white from Sémillon and Sauvignon Blanc. The property... (DM)   ◀— Individually researched entry

● **Château Haut-Brion** Pessac-Léognan✪✪✪✪✪ £H
● **Le Bahans Haut Brion**★★★ £E
O **Château Haut-Brion** Pessac-Léognan✪✪✪✪✪ £G ◀— Estimated price bracket

↑
Red, white or rosé |Quality rating indicator

In order to make sense of France as a whole we have devoted a section to each of its major wine regions. As an aid to orientation, the major appellations are listed under their respective regions. More detail of each, as well as other exciting smaller appelations, can be found at the start of the individual chapters that follow this Overview.

Bordeaux

For both quality and quantity this is France's most important wine region. Wines vary from simple everyday reds to some of the worlds most expensive classic crus.

Médoc, Graves & Sauternes

The **Médoc** provides all but one of the great Cabernet based Classed-Growths of the Right Bank, the best sites at **Margaux**, **Saint-Julien**, **Pauillac** and **Saint-Estèphe** are found on superbly drained gravel soils. Good wines can also be found in the **Haut-Médoc**, **Listrac** and **Moulis** ACs but the *terroir* is less propitious. **Pessac-Léognan** is a source of not only some great reds but whites which at their best rival the great wines of the Côte de Beaune. **Graves** to the south produces some good wines without the depth or class of Pessac-Léognan. Some of the worlds greatest botryitised sweet wines are produced at **Sauternes** and **Barsac**.

Saint Emilion, Pomerol & other Bordeaux

Almost all the new wave of Bordeaux reds have emerged from the Right Bank. Many top Châteaux have been isolating special crus and bottling them separately and other small volume garage style wines have also emerged. Some are exceptional, some decidedly less so. This revolution has largely occurred in **Saint-Emilion**, rather than the much smaller **Pomerol** AC. Some of the best value has begun to emerge from the lesser and satellite appellations. The vast track of the **Entre-Deux-Mers** to the south of Saint Emilion continues to offer good value whites.

Burgundy

This most famous wine region makes some of the finest examples of both Chardonnay and Pinot Noir. Chardonnay can achieve success almost anywhere but the tricky Pinot Noir achieves rare greatness here.

Chablis & Yonne

One of the wine world's most famous names. Located halfway between Beaune and Paris, these are distinctly cool climate Chardonnays. The white ACs include **Petit Chablis**, **Chablis**, **Chablis Premier Cru** and **Chablis Grand Cru**. The best wines have both a piercing minerality as well as a complex citrus and lees character. Some red is also made as **Bourgogne Irancy**.

Côte d'Or & Côte Chalonnaise

The Côte d'Or is synonymous with Burgundy and includes all its great red wines. It is comprised of two parts. The more northerly Côte de Nuits (mostly red) includes the famous villages of **Gevrey-Chambertin**, **Morey Saint-Denis** and **Vosne-Romanee**. In its southern continuation, the Côte de Beaune, some of the worlds greatest dry whites are produced from **Meursault**, **Chassagne-Montrachet** and **Puligny-Montrachet** as well as some very fine reds, from the likes of **Volnay** and **Pommard**. The Côte

Chalonnaise offers some wines of character and depth both red and white. With a few exceptions the better examples from the Côte d'Or's lesser ACs tend to offer more excitement.

Mâconnais

Perhaps the most exciting of Burgundy's regions, certainly in terms of the number of emerging top quality small producers. Big, full and rich Chardonnay is produced from a number of appellations, pre-eminent among them being **Pouilly-Fuissé**. **Saint-Véran** the various **Macon-Villages**, **Pouilly-Loché** and **Pouilly-Vinzelles** are also important.

Beaujolais

The vast majority of Beaujolais is red and produced from Gamay. Generic examples come mainly from the south of the region. However it is the superior granite soils of the northern sector where the better **Beaujolais-Villages,** the *crus* **Brouilly**, **Chénas**, **Chiroubles**, **Côte de Brouilly**, **Juliénas**, **Régnié**, **Saint-Amour** together with the structured more ageworthy **Fleurie**, **Morgon** and **Moulin-à-Vent** offer wines of sometimes heady strawberry-scented intensity.

Alsace

One of the most northerly of France's regions in the north-east of the country. The warm, dry, sunny climate of the area, enabled through protection by the Vosges Mountains, provides uniquely rich and strikingly aromatic wines which are labelled by grape variety and classified as **Alsace** AC or **Alsace Grand Cru** AC. There is also a spakling wine classification **Crémant d'Alsace**.

Champagne

The world's greatest sparkling wine comes from this exposed marginal climate in northern France. Much of the wine is of potentially very high quality. All is produced from Chardonnay, Pinot Noir and Pinot Meunier and made by the classic Champagne method, emulated almost everywhere else for fine sparkling wines, with a secondary fermentation almost always in bottle.

Loire Valley

An extensive region which stretches from the Atlantic coast at Nantes and follows the Loire River to its source in central France. The Pays Nantais is dominated by just one wine, Muscadet, from a number of ACs. Anjou-Saumur is a source of the great sweet wines of the **Coteaux du Layon**, **Bonnezeaux** and **Quarts de Chaume** as well as some fine dry white from **Savennières**. Good, structured red and white are provided by **Saumur** and Cabernet based reds emanate from **Saumur-Champigny**. Touraine is home to the diverse, ageworthy Chenin Blancs of **Vouvray** and **Montlouis** as well as some fine red based on Cabernet Franc from **Bourgeuil**, **Chinon** and **Saint-Nicolas-de-Bourgeuil**. To the east are the vineyards of **Sancerre** and **Pouilly-Fumé**. Some of finest minerally, gooseberry scented Sauvignon Blanc is made here. The region also stretches south to the Auverne, where some soft easy-drinking red is made.

Jura/Savoie

The Alpine vineyards of Jura and Savoie provide some of the most unusual and strikingly flavoured whites and reds. In the Jura you will also encounter two rare and unusual specialities. *Vin jaune* (yellow wine) a dry

13

white made aged naturally under a yeast film or *voile* (like *flor* in fino sherry) but producing very intense long-lived wines. *Vin de paille* (straw wine) is a sweet wine produced from late-harvested, dried grapes. The key appellations in the Jura are **Arbois**, **L'Etoile** and the **Côtes du Jura**. In Savoie **Vin de Savoie** and **Bugey** are the ACs to note.

Rhône Valley

This huge sprawling area stretches down the narrow river valley of the Rhône towards Provence. The bulk of the regions output is generic **Côtes du Rhône**, almost exclusively from the south. There are also many high quality wines red and white produced throughout the region.

Northern Rhône

Some of the worlds finest red and white wine is produced here. Syrah is the mainstay of the reds including the great wines of **Hermitage, Côte-Rôtie** and **Cornas. Saint-Joseph** and **Crozes-Hermitage** are increasingly important. A small amount of very ageworthy white is made at Hermitage and elsewhere from mainly Marsanne and some Roussanne. The exotically peachy **Condrieu** is the ultimate expression of the aromatic Viognier.

Southern Rhône

As well as the sea of generic red produced here there are some striking and classic reds from the large AC of **Châteauneuf-du-Pape**. As elsewhere in the southern Rhône the wines are based on Grenache, and some of the finest expressions of the variety emanate from here. Its also well worth considering the reds of **Gigondas** and **Vacqueyras** as well as the reds and whites from many of the emerging **Côtes du Rhône Villages**. These are wines that currently offer exciting quality and often great value.

Languedoc-Roussillon

This vast geographical area, still the purveyor of a vast lake of bulk produced vin de table and vin de pays, is also the source of some of the most exciting, newly-emerging wines in France.

Languedoc

Of the two sub-regions, this is much the larger. Key to quality in all the appellations are the isolation of excellent hillside *terroirs* and the planting of Rhône varieties both red and white. The Carignan variety is also proving a valueable resource old bush vines. The **Coteaux du Languedoc** is by far the largest of the appellations with the smaller ACs **Faugeres** and **Saint-Chinian** also providing wines of real substance. The appellations round the coast towards the Roussillon, including **Minervois** and **Corbières** tend to produce softer, lighter wines.

Roussillon

Perhaps the greatest potential in the Midi comes from the vineyards of the Roussillon. The region was best known for the quality of its splendid fortified reds, **Maury**, **Rivesaltes** and **Banyuls**. However many old vine plantings are now providing exceptional raw material for a growing number of high quality light dry reds and a few very impressive whites also. Old Grenache and Carignan are of great importance and increasing amounts of Syrah and Mourvèdre are also being planted. Some wines are classified as vin de pays others are **Côtes du Roussillon** and **Côtes du Roussillon-Villages**.

Provence & Corsica

Provence is becoming justifiably better known for the quality of its reds. Rhône varieties are widely planted in the key appellations. Cabernet Sauvignon is also becoming increasingly important. The top red AC, **Bandol** provides striking, long-lived reds largely based on Mourvèdre. Corsica offers some sound reds from interesting idigenous varieties and fine sweet Muscat.

South-West France

A wide and diverse range of wines are produced in this large area. To the north **Bergerac** produces reds and whites from the Bordeaux varieties. Big structured reds are produced to the south at **Cahors**, largely from Auxerrois (Malbec) and at **Madiran** mainly from Tannat. Some exceptional white is produced at **Jurançon**, including great moelleux, and good whites also emerge from **Pacherenc du Vic-Bilh**. Some of the most unusual and diverse styles come from **Gaillac** to the north-east of Toulouse.

1   Bordeaux
2   Chablis
3   Burgundy
4   Beaujolais
5   Alsace
6   Champagne
7   Loire Valley
8   Northern Rhône   11   Provence
9   Southern Rhône   12   South-West France
10 Languedoc & Roussillon 13   Jura
                            14   Savoie

15

To most people Bordeaux is probably the most well-known of France's great wine regions. In recent years it has enjoyed bountiful harvests, the maintenance of quality – and many improvements too – and until the last couple of years a remarkably buoyant market for its premium wines. The last few years have also seen dynamic changes on the Right Bank of the Gironde in Saint-Emilion, with major investment in established properties and the creation of a number of exciting new labels. The development of the so-called garage *wines, produced in tiny quantities all over the Saint-Emilion appellation, has been welcome in instances where exotic and fine and ageworthy blends have been produced from isolated first-class terroirs. However, where these wines are sourced from lesser sites, they are often over-extracted, lacking in class but nevertheless still marketed and sold at high prices. Perhaps if the current trend towards more realistic pricing in general continues there will be a much-needed reality check. The lesser areas like Fronsac and particularly the Côtes de Castillon continue to forge ahead with exciting developments at prices that mere mortals can afford. It is also important not to lose sight of the fact that there are properties, particularly on the Left Bank in the Médoc, which have consistently been producing some of the world's greatest wines for decades and continue to do so.*

Geography

The Bordeaux region can effectively be looked at in three parts. There are the appellations surrounding Bordeaux itself and stretching to both the north and south. These vineyards are all located on the western side of the Gironde estuary and further south the river Garonne. This is often referred to as the Left Bank. The Right Bank comprises the vineyard areas east of the Gironde and the river Dordogne, particularly the appellations of Saint-Emilion and Pomerol near Libourne. There is another vast tract of vineyard land between the Dordogne and the Garonne. This is neither Left nor Right Bank and is largely dry white wine territory, including the large Entre-Deux-Mers AC. The vast bulk of Bordeaux's commercial wine trade emanates from the city itself. Libourne, though, is also important commercially, with a number of its own *négociants.*

Generic Bordeaux

AC **Bordeaux**, the bottle you're most likely to come across, can be sourced anywhere within the large Bordeaux region, which includes the areas mentioned above and other outlying appellations. The total production is mind-boggling. Some 5.5 to 6 million hectolitres of red and nearly another million of white are produced every year. Around two-thirds of this is generic Bordeaux. This would not be such a huge problem in itself but most of the red is vinified from Merlot, the workhorse grape of the region and often grown in heavy and productive soils. This allied to over-ambitious yields is always going to present a challenge to fully ripening the crop. So much generic Bordeaux not only tastes dilute but can also have a green, vegetal component. Ripening the white grapes here tends to be less of a problem and these wines can often be better bets.

Médoc, Graves and Sauternes

Some of the world's greatest and noblest red wines are produced here as well as benchmark sweet whites and a very small amount of immensely stylish dry white. The **Médoc** AC itself, rather than the area of the Médoc which runs from Bordeaux north to Soulac at the mouth of the Gironde, is centred around the small town of Lesparre-Médoc and is the northernmost of the Left Bank

ACs. There is a higher proportion of clay in the soil rather than the fabled gravel and the wines are generally soft and forward, with a few better examples. The **Haut-Médoc** encompasses all four of the great communal appellations close to the Gironde (Saint-Estèphe, Pauillac, Saint-Julien and Margaux) as well as Listrac and Moulis. There can be a wide variation in quality in the Haut-Médoc AC but a few properties are very serious indeed, producing classic, long-lived cedary reds. Both **Listrac-Médoc** and **Moulis** are located just to the north-west of Margaux. Listrac seems to offer less potential but there are attempts here to fashion some modern *garagiste*-style wines and make the best of the fruit available. Moulis has greater potential, with a number of very good properties.

The northernmost of the great red wine appellations of the Médoc is **Saint-Estèphe**. There are five Classed Growths and the wines are generally the densest, sturdiest examples of the area. Modern winemaking has gone some way to address those firm youthful tannins and the wines are more approachable than they were even a decade ago and are very impressive at their best. **Pauillac** is synonymous with some of the greatest wines of the region. Châteaux Latour, Lafite-Rothschild and Mouton-Rothschild are all here. The deep gravel vineyards provide an ideal base for these strikingly rich styles laden with cassis and spice. The top wines need considerable age. To the south, the wines of **Saint-Julien** are less opulent than Pauillac, more perfumed and with intense cigar box and cedar notes. There are eleven Classed Growths and the extraordinarily refined Léoville-Las-Cases should be a First Growth in many people's books. **Margaux** is just to the north of Bordeaux and contains 21 Classed Growths. At their best these are are the most elegant and refined wines of the Médoc. For a long time Margaux has been an underperforming appellation but change is happening aplenty – new investment, a renewed commitment to quality and, in Marojallia and Clos du Jaugueyron, the first serious *garagiste* wines on the Left Bank. Marojallia is vinified by Jean-Luc Thunevin, owner of Valandraud, one of the first *garagiste* wines in **Saint-Emilion**.

Immediately south of Bordeaux, indeed part of the AC is in the outer suburbs of the city, are the vineyards of **Pessac-Léognan**. Originally part of the larger **Graves** appellation it was granted its own appellation status in 1987 in recognition of the superior quality of its sites. The soil is finely drained deep gravel and all of the properties in the 1959 Classification of the Graves are to be found here. Only Haut-Brion, with its First Growth status in the 1855 Classification, was absent from the list. Some splendid reds are produced here as well as a small number of dry whites. At their best these are rich, complex and very ageworthy and rival the great whites of the Côte de Beaune (see Burgundy). White winemaking in general throughout the Graves has improved immeasurably in recent years. The rest of the region stretches to the east and some way south of the Garonne. It is never as good as Pessac-Léognan but some good red and dry white are regularly produced. There are also a few sweet wines under the **Graves Supérieures** AC, but these are largely pretty dull.

Just north-west of the town of Langon are the great sweet wine appellations of Sauternes and Barsac. A third sweet wine appellation, **Cérons**, is immediately to the north but does not benefit to the same degree as the other two AC's from the remarkable geographical influence of the tiny Ciron river, which creates the conditions for the development of noble rot. Cérons and also the sweet wines from immediately across the Garonne in **Sainte-Croix-du-Mont** and **Loupiac** can be impressive but they never achieve the same intense botrytis quality as **Sauternes**. **Barsac** is one of the five communes of Sauternes and properties here may chose to label their wines Sauternes or Barsac. After a run

17

of very successful vintages in the 1980s these wines are now fetching the kinds of prices that make their production economic and indeed profitable. Fifteen to 20 years ago it was nigh-on impossible for producers to achieve a commercial return. Harvesting is incredibly labour-intensive, with multiple *tris* (passes through the vineyard), and the yield is necessarily tiny. However, major investment has dramatically changed the area. Many wines of truly magnificent concentration and intensity are now being made. In the lesser years cryo-extraction has been used by a number of châteaux to improve quality.

Saint-Emilion, Pomerol and the Rest of Bordeaux

Saint-Emilion and Pomerol are the two great names associated with the Right Bank but there are an increasing number of well-priced, exciting wines emerging from the other ACs. It is also interesting to note that these are all red wine appellations. **Saint-Emilion** itself is the driving force in terms of volume and accounts for some 40 per cent of all wines produced here. As a result it's not surprising that there is a wide variation in quality and very diverse *terroirs*, some exceptional and some, particularly in the southern plains of the AC, distinctly ordinary, with heavy productive soils. Many of Bordeaux's major developments in vinification techniques and the influence of consultant winemakers have their origins in Saint-Emilion. Pre-fermentation cold soaking (or maceration), malolactic fermentation in barrel and micro-oxygenation are now practised all over the world.

Saint-Emilion's Classification was last revised in 1996 and will be again in 2006. There are 13 Premiers Grands Crus Classés with two A-rated properties, Ausone and Cheval-Blanc, as well as 55 properties rated Grand Cru Classé. There have been major investments in recent years in both vineyards and cellars, resulting in some highly priced wines made in very limited quantities. The most notable of these has been La Mondotte, produced at Canon-La-Gaffelière. Many other tiny-production wines or *vins des garagistes* have also emerged. Some have been very impressive, but many are over-extracted and all are expensive.

Pomerol, in contrast, continues to provide some impressive and startlingly opulent wines, full of dark and spicy fruit, generally supple and more approachable than many of the other top wines in Bordeaux. Inevitably there are exceptions to the rule and these tend to occur where there is a higher proportion of Cabernet Franc or Cabernet Sauvignon planted or the soil has more gravel. Pomerol's clay soils suit Merlot very well and provide this uniquely exotic style. Pomerol's wines can also be some of the priciest anywhere on the globe. There has been investment and development here but not on the scale of Saint-Emilion's. The lower tier of the appellation, though, can disappoint. The odd wine of distinction is also beginning to emerge from the lesser Saint-Emilion satellite ACs, **Lussac-Saint-Emilion**, **Montagne-Saint-Emilion**, **Puisseguin-Saint-Emilion** and **Saint-Georges-Saint-Emilion**, as well as **Lalande-de-Pomerol**.

To the north-west of Libourne are the areas of **Côtes de Bourg** and **Côtes de Blaye**. The former produces reds, some decent and some very impressive while dry whites are produced in the latter. To the immediate west of Libourne are **Fronsac** and **Canon-Fronsac**. Good, stylish, well-made dark-fruited styles have been produced here for a decade or so. To the east of Saint-Emilion are the **Côtes de Castillon** and **Bordeaux-Côtes de Francs**. Again these are areas of great potential and the best wines are still well-priced, if becoming less so.

Between the Dordogne and Garonne rivers is a substantial vineyard area comprising some nine appellations. Geographically and physically by far the most important is the **Entre-Deux-Mers,** an appellation devoted to dry whites. A number of properties here are also producing good AC Bordeaux red. The appellation is all about maximising modern white winemaking with some good results, using pre-fermentation skin contact, ageing on lees and, in the more expensive wines, limited barrel-fermentation and ageing with new wood as well. Some well-priced wines have been available for some time now. Vibrant red and rosé is made in the **Premières Côtes de Bordeaux,** just to the east across the Garonne from the city of Bordeaux, and there are good sweet wines on the eastern bank of the river at **Cadillac,** Loupiac and **Sainte-Croix-du-Mont.** In the far east is **Saint-Foy-de-Bordeaux,** where there are reds as well as dry and sweet whites.

A-Z of producers by appellation/region

Médoc, Graves & Sauternes

CH. LA CROIX DU CASSE	69
CLOS L'ÉGLISE	67
DOM. DE L'EGLISE	70
CH. LA CONSEILLANTE	68
CH. LA CROIX-DE-GAY	68
CH. L'ÉGLISE-CLINET	70
CH. L'ÉVANGILE	71
CH. FEYTIT-CLINET	72
CH. LA FLEUR-PÉTRUS	73
CH. FRANC-MAILLET	75
CH. GAZIN	76
CH. LE GAY	76
CH. HOSANNA	80
CH. LAFLEUR	80
CH. LATOUR-À-POMEROL	81
CH. MONTVIEL	84
CH. LE MOULIN	84
CH. PETIT-VILLAGE	86
CH. PÉTRUS	86
CH. LE PIN	87
CH. ROUGET	90
CH. TAILLEFER	91
CH. TROTANOY	93
VIEUX-CHÂTEAU-CERTAN	95
CH. VIEUX-MAILLET	95

Premières Côtes de Blaye

CH. HAUT-BERTINERIE	78
PASSION DU PRIEURÉ MALESAN	85

Premières Côtes de Bordeaux

CH. CARIGNAN	65
CH. CARSIN	65
CH. MONT PÉRAT	84
CH. REYNON	89

Puisseguin-Saint-Emilion

CH. LA MAURIANE	83

Saint-Emilion Grand Cru

CH. L'ARCHANGE	60
CH. ARMENS	61
CLOS BADON	94
CH. BELLEVUE-MONDOTTE	63
CH. LA BIENFAISANCE	63
CH. DESTIEUX	62
CH. FAUGÈRES	72
CH. FLEUR-CARDINAL	73
CH. FOMBRAUGE	73
GRACIA	76
CH. GRAND CORBIN-DESPAGNE	77
CH. LES GRANDES MURAILLES	78
CH. LES GRAVIÈRES	78
LA GOMERIE	
LA MONDOTTE	81
CH. LAFORGE	92
CH. LARCIS-DUCASSE	81

LE DÔME	82
CH. LUCIE	82
CH. LUSSEAU	83
LYNSOLENCE	82
MAGREZ-FOMBRAUGE	74
CH. MONBOUSQUET	84
CH. MOULIN SAINT-GEORGES	85
CH. PEBY-FAUGERES	72
CH. PRIEURÉ LESCOURS	94
CH. QUINAULT	88
CH. RIOU DE THAILLAS	89
CH. ROL VALENTIN	90
CH. TERTRE-RÔTEBOEUF	91
CH. TEYSSIER	92
CH. SANSONNET	91
CLOS DE SARPE	91
CH. DE VALANDRAUD	94
VIRGINIE DE VALANDRAUD	94

Saint-Emilion Grand Cru Classé

CH. ANGÉLUS	60
CH. L'ARROSÉE	60
CH. AUSONE	61
CH. BEAU-SÉJOR-BÉCOT	61
CH. BEAUSÉJOUR	61
CH. BELLEVUE	62
CH. BERLIQUET	63
CH. CANON	64
CH. CANON-LA-GAFFELIÈRE	65
CH. CHAUVIN	66
CH. CHEVAL-BLANC	66
CH. CLOS DES JACOBINS	67
CH. LA CLOTTE	67
CH. LA COUSPAUDE	68
CH. CÔTE DE BALEAU	68
CH. DASSAULT	69
CH. LA DOMINIQUE	70
CH. FIGEAC	72
CLOS FOURTET	74
CH. FRANC-MAYNE	75
CH. LA GAFFELIÈRE	76
CH. GRAND-MAYNE	77
CH. GRAND-PONTET	77
CH. LAROZE	80
CH. MAGDELAINE	83
CLOS DE L'ORATOIRE	85
CH. PAVIE	85
CH. PAVIE-DECESSE	86
CH. PAVIE MACQUIN	86
CLOS SAINT MARTIN	90
CH. TERTRE-DAUGAY	91
CH. LA TOUR FIGEAC	92
CH. TROPLONG-MONDOT	93
CH. TROTTEVIEILLE	94

Sainte-Foy Bordeaux

CH. HOSTENS-PICANT	80

Bordeaux vintages

As in other parts of France Bordeaux has been generally fairly lucky with vintages during the last six or seven years, particularly at the turn of the millenium. There haven't been the number of great years as the Rhône Valley from 1998 but after the disappointments of the early 1990s things have been decidedly better. Winemaking has evolved here and generally for the better. With the top reds, particularly, it is worth bearing in mind if you are purchasing from a fine current vintage that the approach in the cellar is different to that of 20 years ago. The wines are suppler and more approachable but it remains to be seen whether they will be as long-lived as some of their predecessors.

2004: This looks like it could be a good to very good year producing good reds throughout the region. On the Left Bank in particular, the wines are powerful and backward. Many producers are comparing the wines to those of 1998. It was also an abundant year and those who thinned their crops will undoubtedly have achieved much better results. The dry whites look promising wheras Sauternes is likely to be good rather than great.

2003: Marked by a very hot summer this is likely to be a year of very good Left Bank reds, in particular to the north of the Médoc. To the south Graves was more uneven. There are likely to be some exceptional examples from the Right Bank from sites with good moisture retention. Those who picked at optimum ripeness will be very fine. Many though are either under or overipe.. A small amount of very rich Sauternes is likely to emerge.

2002: This looks likely to be a good rather than a great year for reds. The year has turned out to be more successful in the Médoc, particularly Saint-Julien and to the north. It is predominantly a Cabernet Sauvignon year. Earlier-ripening Merlot was most hit by late September rains. Some very good whites were produced and this will be a good year too for Sauternes.

2001: After the magnificent 2000 red vintage this is a good, sometimes very good year for red. The style is sturdy, dense and with firm tannins and notable but not excessive acidity. These are classically structured wines. Look for good wines on both the Left and Right Banks, including some fine examples from the lesser appellations. Sauternes and sweet wines in general look to be very impressive indeed. This could be the best vintage for botrytised wines since 1990. The dry whites were also close to exceptional.

2000: A magnificent year for red Bordeaux. The crop was bountiful and the quality exceptional. The combination of a hot dry August followed by a long even and balmy ripening period throughout September provided the châteaux with perfect late-harvesting conditions. Grapes were picked full of deep colour, super-ripe, fine, supple tannins and intense and heady flavour. This is the best vintage since 1990 for reds throughout Bordeaux. While dry whites enjoyed conditions nearly as good, this was a disappointing year for Sauternes.

1999: A generally impressive year throughout the region with the largest crop of the late 1990s. The summer was good, with warm consistent weather, however early rains in September meant that there was some variation. Those châteaux who went for maximum ripeness and harvested late did well. Whites have generally been good and were harvested before the rain, whereas Sauternes had a successful late harvest and some splendid wines have been produced.

1998: There was a lot of late September rain in the Médoc and quality is variable. To the south Graves fared a little better but it was mainly earlier-ripening Merlot on the Right Bank that did best, producing wines with suppler and riper tannins. Dry whites were good and generally harvested in ideal weather. Sauternes was also very good although the crop was tiny.

1997: A generally trying year, the one exception being Sauternes, which produced its best vintage since 1990. Quantities, though, were small, which kept upward pressure on prices. Indeed, considering the overall quality of the vintage it was surprising that the Bordelais managed to get away with hyping prices as much as they did. The top châteaux, who were rigorous in their selection, produced the best results. The dry whites were generally average to good but some properties harvested grapes lacking in full flavour development and many of these wines should now be drunk.

1996: This was another year when the Bordeaux money men should have been singing the praises of the gods. It was the second very large harvest in a row, a

1	Médoc	12	Barsac
2	Haut-Médoc	13	Sauternes
3	Saint-Estèphe	14	Premières Côtes de Bordeaux
4	Pauillac	15	Loupiac
5	Saint-Julien	16	Sainte-Croix-du-Mont
6	Listrac-Médoc	17	Entre-Deux-Mers
7	Moulis	18	Ste-Foy-Bordeaux
8	Margaux	19	Côtes de Castillon
9	Pessac-Léognan	20	Côtes de Franc
10	Graves	21	Saint-Emilion satellites
11	Cérons	22	Saint-Emilion
		23	Pomerol
		24	Lalande-de-Pomerol
		25	Fronsac & Canon-Fronsac
		26	Côtes de Bourg
		27	Côtes de Blaye / Premières Côtes de Blaye

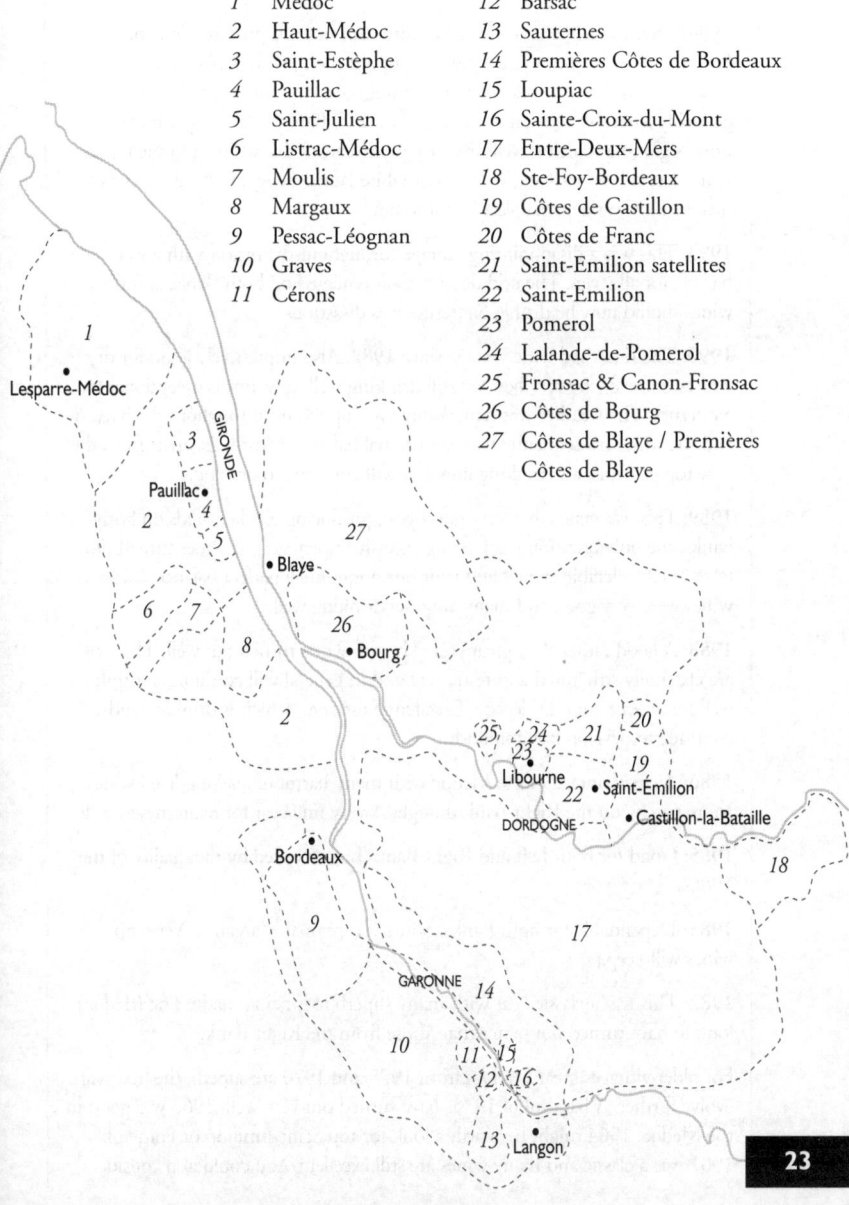

23

trend that was to continue through to the millennium. It was also a year of great wines in the Médoc, particularly in the northern appellations. The Right Bank fared less well, being hit by rain just as the Merlot ripened. Late-harvested Cabernet Sauvignon was consistently more successful. Very good dry whites were produced and the best wines are drinking well now. Sauternes had its best year since 1990. The wines are rich, heady and very intense.

1995: A good, indeed very good year for both Left and Right Bank. The harvest was reasonably consistent and although there was some rain during Setember it was not heavy enough to cause real problems with ripening. The results were very good in Pauillac and Saint-Julien and the wines are not only classically structured but have rich ripe fruit as well. The lesser reds are now beginning to drink well, the top wines need more time. There were some good dry whites and these are now drinking well. However Sauternes was generally disappointing.

1994: After a warm and at times hot, dry summer had promised much, September turned out to be a great disappointment, with persistent rain. Careful control during selection and throughout vinification produced generally agreeable reds on both Right and Left Banks. Many top wines are now beginning to drink well. It was a good year for dry whites and the top wines will still be showing well. Lesser white Pessac-Léognan should now be drunk. This was a dismal year in Sauternes.

1993: This was a disappointing vintage throughout the region with a wet harvest for all styles. The odd decent result emerged on both Banks and these wines should now be drunk. Sauternes was disastrous.

1990: The finest red wine vintage since 1982. Also impressively good for dry whites, some of the very best are still drinking well now. It was exceptional for Sauternes. The weather was remarkably even up to and throughout the harvest and the wines consequently had exceptional balance. Most reds, apart from the very top growths, are drinking now but will continue to develop.

1989: This was generally a very good year, producing excellent reds on both banks, the only question mark being excessive ripeness. The wines turned out to have considerable extract and fruit but not entirely perfect balance. Sweet wines were very good and many are now drinking well.

1988: A good rather than great year. The top wines turned out well. The reds are classically structured and restrained and in general will continue to drink well for at least another decade. Excellent Sauternes, which is drinking and will continue to develop harmoniously.

1986: A great vintage in the Médoc with many harmonious long-lived wines. More patchy on the Right Bank though. A very fine year for Sauternes as well.

1985: Good for both Left and Right Banks but exceeded by the quality of the 1986s.

1983:-Dependable for both Banks. Some exceptional Margaux's. Very top wines will keep.

1982: This was a classic year with many superb reds being made. The Médocs look to have turned out better than those from the Right Bank.

For older vintages great Médocs from 1978 and 1970 are superb, the best will evolve further. A handful of 1975s have turned out very well. 1966 was good in the Médoc. 1964 might be worth a look for top Saint-Emilion or Pomerol. 1961 was a classic and many wines are still excellent. You could also consider

1959, 55, 49, 47, 45 and if you're exceptionally adventurous 35 or 28. Bear in mind that the provenance of the wine is as important as anything if you are acquiring very old vintages.

Bordeaux vintage chart

	Northern Médoc inc Saint-Èstephe, Paulliac, Saint-Julien	Southern Médoc inc Margaux	Red Graves	White Graves
2004	★★★★ A	★★★★ A	★★★/★★★★ A	★★★★ A
2003	★★★★ A	★★★★ A	★★★★ A	★★★★ A
2002	★★★★ A	★★★/★★★★ A	★★★★ A	★★★★ A
2001	★★★/★★★★ A	★★★/★★★★ A	★★★/★★★★ A	★★★★/★★★★★ A
2000	★★★★★ A	★★★★★ A	★★★★★ A	★★★★ B
1999	★★★/★★★★ B	★★★/★★★★ B	★★★/★★★★ B	★★★★ B
1998	★★★/★★★★ A	★★★/★★★★ A	★★★★ A	★★★★/★★★★★ B
1997	★★★ B	★★★ B	★★★ B	★★★★ C
1996	★★★★/★★★★★ A	★★★★ A	★★★★ B	★★★★ C
1995	★★★★ A	★★★★ B	★★★★ B	★★★/★★★★ C
1990	★★★★★ B	★★★★★ B	★★★★ C	★★★★/★★★★★ C
1989	★★★★ C	★★★★ C	★★★★ C	★★★/★★★★ C
1988	★★★★ B	★★★/★★★★ C	★★★★ C	★★★★ D
1986	★★★★/★★★★★ C	★★★★ C	★★★★ C	★★★ D
1985	★★★★ C	★★★★ C	★★★★ C	-
1982	★★★★★ C	★★★★/★★★★★ C	★★★★★ C	-

	Saint-Emilion	Pomerol	Sauternes
2004	★★★★ A	★★★★ A	★★★/★★★★ A
2003	★★★★ A	★★★★ A	★★★★/★★★★★ A
2002	★★★/★★★★ A	★★★/★★★★ A	★★★★/★★★★★ A
2001	★★★★ A	★★★★ A	★★★★/★★★★★ A
2000	★★★★★ A	★★★★★ A	★★ B
1999	★★★/★★★★ B	★★★/★★★★ BA	★★★★ A
1998	★★★★ A	★★★★/★★★★★ A	★★★★ A
1997	★★★ B	★★★ B	★★★★ A
1996	★★★/★★★★ B	★★★/★★★★ B	★★★★/★★★★★ B
1995	★★★★ B	★★★★ B	★★★/★★★★ B
1990	★★★★★ C	★★★★★ C	★★★★ C
1989	★★★★/★★★★★ C	★★★★/★★★★★ C	★★★★ C
1988	★★★★ C	★★★★ C	★★★★★ C
1986	★★★/★★★★ C	★★★/★★★★ C	★★★★/★★★★★ C
1985	★★★★ C	★★★★ C	★★★★ C
1982	★★★★★ C	★★★★★ C	★★★ D

A-Z of producers

Médoc, Graves & Sauternes

CH. D'AGASSAC Haut-Médoc www.agassac.com
Groupama 33290 Ludon-Médoc
UK stockists: AAA

Things are taking a turn for better at this medium-sized operation based in the southern part of the Haut-Médoc and owned by the insurance company Groupama. The wine is now showing good depth and some attractive dark fruit notes and harmonious tannins. A medium-weight style, better with 5 or 6 years' ageing. The rating applies to 1999 onwards. (DM)

● **Château d'Agassac** Haut-Médoc★★ £C

CH. D'ANGLUDET Margaux www.chateau-dangludet.fr
Sichel family 33460 Cantenac
UK stockists: AAA

Well-established Cru Bourgeois with 25-year-old vineyards planted to Cabernet Sauvignon, Merlot and Petit Verdot, which comes from the oldest parcel of vines and adds extra character. The emphasis at the property is to achieve a natural balance in the vineyard and this shows through in the quality of the wine which is medium-weight with refinement and finesse. There is a second label, La Ferme d'Angludet, and a rosé, Clairet d'Angludet. Impressive in 2001 and 00 but the wines have generally shown more class in the late 90s. (DM)

● **Château d'Angludet** Margaux★★★ £D

CH. D'ARCHE Sauternes 2ème CC
Pierre Perromat 33210 Sauternes
UK stockists: AAA

Only around 5,000 cases a year are produced here from 29ha. This is reasonably impressive, full and concentrated Sauternes with a generally good performance in the most favourable vintages over the 2 decades since Pierre Perromat became involved. Harvesting is as selective as necessary, and a portion of new oak is used to age the wine. Good in 2003 and 01, 00; 98 and 97 are also worth seeking out. (DM)

O **Château d'Arche** Sauternes★★★ £E

CH. D'ARMAILHAC Pauillac 5ème CC www.bpdr.com
Baron Philippe de Rothschild SA 33250 Pauillac
UK stockists: AAA

Like its prestigious neighbour MOUTON ROTHSCHILD this château is also owned by Baronne Philippine de Rothschild. At its best, in years like 2000, 99, 98 and 95, this medium-sized property is undoubtedly producing ★★★ Pauillac. When conditions are less favourable, though, the wine struggles a little. Grown in relatively light soils the wine is structured but not overly so, retaining some of the marked cassis and cedar notes of its big brother, and will provide good drinking at 6 or 7 years. (DM)

● **Château d'Armailhac** Pauillac★★★ £D

CH. BASTOR-LAMONTAGNE Sauternes www.bastor-lamontagne.com
Michel Garat 33210 Preignac
UK stockists: BBR, Wai

A consistently fine, small to medium-sized operation which has performed admirably over a long period, providing the essence of Sauternes at an affordable price. As well as Sémillon and Sauvignon Blanc, Michel Garat has just a small amount of Muscadelle to add aroma. The wine is barrel-fermented for an extended 3–4 weeks with around 15% new oak to lend structure and shows classic honeyed, peachy botrytis character even in lesser years. Look out for 1998, 97 and 96. 2001 also looks very promising. The second wine produced from young vines is Les Remparts de Bastor. (DM)

● **Château Bastor-Lamontagne** Sauternes★★★ £E

CH. BATAILLEY   Pauillac 5ème CC

Héritiers Castéja   33250 Pauillac
UK stockists: AAA

A consistently reasonably priced Fifth Growth, Batailly is a wine that has performed reliably throughout the 1990s but never more than that. Good classic blackcurrant and cedar notes can be found, and the wine has sufficient oak with creamy vanilla notes and a supple texture aided by malolactic in barrel. Good without great depth or real complexity. (DM)

● **Château Batailley** Pauillac★★ £D

CH. BEL AIR MARQUIS D'ALIGRE   Margaux

Jean-Pierre Boyer   33460 Soussans
UK stockists: AAA

Cru Bourgeois property that has been performing impressively in recent years. This small château consists of just 13ha with a surprisingly high (35%) proportion of Merlot. Production is low at less than 3,000 cases a year. Low volume, a careful control of yields and meticulously tended vineyards all contribute to the consistently excellent results achieved here. The wine is a refined medium-weight, rather than blockbuster style, a proper Margaux with a real fruit intensity and stylish perfume. Good in the top years since 1990. (DM)

● **Château Bel Air Marquis d'Aligre** Margaux★★★ £D

CH. BELGRAVE   Haut-Médoc 5ème CC

Vignobles Dourthe   33112 Saint-Laurent-de-Médoc
UK stockists: **Dou**,AAA

Purchased by Vignobles Dourthe in 1980, it was only with the 1998 vintage that this property really began to forge ahead. During the past 2 decades the vineyard has been replanted. Cabernet Sauvignon dominates the blend, with a tiny amount of Petit Verdot. Now that the vines are maturing, the wine is evolving from the straightforward, essentially fruit-driven style of the early to mid-1990s to one where there is real depth and refinement. It represents particularly good value for money. (DM)

● **Château Belgrave** Haut-Médoc★★★ £D

CH. BEYCHEVELLE   Saint-Julien 4ème CC   www.beychevelle.com

SC Grands Millésimes de France   33250 Saint-Julien-Beychevelle
UK stockists: AAA

Beychevelle is a sizeable property with 90ha of vineyards planted to Cabernet Sauvignon, Merlot, Cabernet Franc and a little Petit Verdot. It is a Classed Growth with a reasonable, rather than spectacular track record over recent years. At its best the wine shows real finesse, splendid purity of fruit and very subtle oak, not full and powerful but more refined and elegant. Choose your vintage with a bit of caution and avoid lesser years. Amiral de Beychevelle, the second wine, is entitled to the Saint-Julien AC, while Les Brulières-de-Beychevelle is from vineyards in the Haut-Médoc. (DM)

● **Château Beychevelle** Saint-Julien★★★ £E

CH. BOYD-CANTENAC   Margaux 3ème CC   www.boyd-cantenac.fr
Lucien Guillemet   33460 Margaux
UK stockists: AAA

This Third Growth property is turning out very good elegant Margaux. This was not always so. Boyd-Cantenac spent decades in the doldrums and would not have been on anyone's shopping list until the vintages of the late 1990s, which have shown a marked turn for the better. An increasing use of new oak – up to 60% – and, since 1997, no filtration has contributed to this improvement. The wine is fragrant and supple with attractive dark berry fruit and an increasing richness. The rating applies to vintages from 1998 on. (DM)

● **Château Boyd-Cantenac** Margaux★★★ £E

CH. BRANAIRE   Saint-Julien 4ème CC   www.branaire.com
Patrick Maroteaux   33250 Saint-Julien
UK stockists: AAA

For a long time this was a seriously underachieving property. However there has been a significant turnaround here during the last 6 or 7 years. Investment in the cellar, along with a commitment to quality that avoids filtration and employs only limited egg-white fining and racking by gravity, is undoubtedly paying off. The style has moved from light to much fuller and richer. The Cabernet Sauvignon component now really shows and the wines are sturdier and denser with much greater depth and power. Almost all the vintages since 1994 have impressed. 1995, 96, 98 and 99 are all on the cusp of ★★★★. (DM)

● **Château Branaire** Saint-Julien★★★ £F

CH. BRANE-CANTENAC   Margaux 2ème CC   www.lucienlurton.com
Domaines Lucien Lurton & Fils   33460 Margaux
UK stockists: AAA

Since the late 1990s Brane-Cantenac has been showing real evidence of its status as a Second Growth. After 1996 the only vintage which has disappointed has been the 97. The wine is a classic blend of Cabernet Sauvignon, Merlot and Cabernet Franc with intense, cedary Margaux perfume, subtle oak and sheer class and intensity. Domaines Lucien Lurton also own a number of other important châteaux, among them CLIMENS in Barsac, DURFORT-VIVENS in Margaux and BOUSCAUT in Pessac-Léognan. The second wine, Baron de Brane, is of decent quality. (DM)

● **Château Branaire** Margaux★★★★ £F   ● **Baron de Brane**★★ £D

CH. BRANON   Pessac-Léognan CC   www.chateau-haut-bergey.com
Mme. Sylviane Garcin-Cathiard   69 Cours Gambetta, 33850 Léognan

Under the same ownership as HAUT-BERGEY, this boutique winery (4,000 cases) makes a single red wine from equal parts of Cabernet Sauvignon and Merlot. It is a wine of enormous power and concentration with intensely perfumed fruit. The 2ha of vines lie between those of HAUT-BAILLY and MALARTIC-LAGRAVIÈRE and since 2000 Jean-Luc Thunevin of Château de VALANDRAUD has been the consultant winemaker. (NB)

● **Château Branon** Pessac-Léognan★★★★ £G

CH. BROWN   Pessac-Léognan CC
Bernard Barthe   allée John Lewis Brown, 33850 Léognan
UK stockists: N&P

This château has shown considerable improvements over the past few years. There are 23.5ha under vine for the red wine and 4.5 for the white. The white (70% Sauvignon, 30% Sémillon) shows finesse and balance, whilst the red (70% Cabernet Sauvignon, 27% Merlot and 3% Petit Verdot) shares these characteristics along with a degree more upfront fruit than one would normally expect in this appellation. (NB)

● **Château Brown** Pessac-Léognan★★★ £D
O **Château Brown** Pessac-Léognan★★★ £D

CH. CAILLOU Sauternes 2ème CC www.chateaucaillou.fr

Michel & Marie-Josée Pierre 33720 Barsac
UK stockists: AAA

This is one of those confusingly labelled properties which takes the Sauternes AC although it is located in Barsac. There are 2 *cuvées* of the principal wine, the regular Caillou and a barrel selection, La Private Cuvée, produced in top years such as 1995, 97 and 99. Fermentation is in a mix of new oak and *inox* and ageing is between 18 and 24 months with a marked new oak component. This is an intense and heady sweet white but inevitably the regular Caillou suffers in those vintages when La Private Cuvée is released. A second wine, Château Haut-Mayne, is also produced. (DM)

O **Château Caillou** Sauternes★★★ £E

CH. CALON-SÉGUR Saint-Estèphe 2ème CC

Denise Capbern-Gasqueton 33180 Saint-Estèphe
UK stockists: AAA

Like many Bordeaux properties Calon-Ségur has shown a marked upturn in quality during the late 1990s. As well as a more meticulous approach in the vineyard, which has resulted in a reduced crop, the objective in the winemaking has been to produce an altogether suppler, more harmonious style. The wine achieves this and is both opulent and modern with weight, concentration and power. It has a much more velvety texture than of old. Very good since 1996 and seemingly improving with the vintages since 2000. Only below par in 97 and 99. (DM)

● **Château Calon-Ségur** Saint-Estèphe★★★★ £F

CH. CAMBON-LA-PELOUSE Haut Médoc

Thierry & Lorraine Rustmann 5 Chemin de Canteloup, 33460 Macau
UK stockists: AAA

Impressively structured Haut-Médoc that has been on much improved form since 1999. Only the 2002 among recent vintages looks a bit disappointing. The property is fairly substantial with 58ha of vineyards and surprisingly for the Médoc the mix of varieties planted is 65% Merlot to 25% Cabernet Sauvignon, with the remaining 10% Cabernet Franc. As a result, the wine tends to be full, fleshy and relatively forward. Nevertheless, it possesses well-honed tannins and an impressive depth and purity. This wine remains particularly well priced. (DM)

● **Château Cambon-La-Pelouse** Haut-Médoc★★★ £C

CH. CAMENSAC Haut-Médoc 5ème CC www.chateaucamensac.com

Forner family Route de Saint-Julien, 33112 Saint-Laurent-de-Médoc
UK stockists: AAA

The quality of this property has gradually improved since it was acquired in 1964 by the Forner family. Much of the vineyard has been replanted and there is now a relatively high proportion of Merlot (25%) contributing to the style, which is round, forward and accessible. The wine drinks well at 5 years or so. Just a notch up in 1999 and 00. (DM)

● **Château Camensac** Haut-Médoc★★ £D

29

CH. CANTEMERLE Haut-Médoc 5ème CC

Philippe Dambrine   33460 Macau
UK stockists: AAA

The 87ha at Cantemerle are planted to a mix of 50% Cabernet Sauvignon and, unusually for the Left Bank, a whopping 40% Merlot, with the remaining 10% divided evenly between Cabernet Franc and Petit Verdot. Production is sizeable, with 50,000 cases produced annually. After significant replanting 2 decades ago the vine age is beginning to show and this together with the high proportion of Merlot provides a rich, vibrantly dark-fruited Médoc at its best. The very latest vintages are promising and 1998 and 96 are good. It has to be said, though, that the wine has not performed well in lesser years, particularly in the early 1990s. (DM)

● **Château Cantemerle** Haut-Médoc★★ £E

CH. CANTENAC-BROWN Margaux 3ème CC

AXA Millésimes   33460 Cantenac
UK stockists: AAA

Purchased in 1987 by AXA Millésimes, which also owns a number of other prestigious Bordeaux properties including PICHON-LONGUEVILLE and SUDUIRAUT in Sauternes. Quality has been disappointing throughout the 1970s, 80s and, with the exception of 1990, the 90s prior to 96. The rating is for its current performance rather than earlier vintages and, given the performance of other châteaux within the AXA group, one would expect things here to continue to improve. (DM)

● **Château Cantenac-Brown** Margaux★★★ £E

CH. CARBONNIEUX Pessac-Léognan CC

Antony Perrin   33850 Léognan
UK stockists: N&P,Tur

Good rather than memorable red and white Pessac-Léognans. Production is substantial for the appellation at over 30,000 cases a year. The white is good and has performed well throughout the 1990s. Some skin contact is allowed before fermentation in barrel, around half of which is new, and ageing is on lees. The red doesn't quite reach the same level but has also been consistent over recent vintages. Sound, well-crafted and approachable, it is lighter than other Pessac-Léognan reds but displays attractive berry fruit and a fine mineral undercurrent. Both white and red will benefit from 5 years' bottle-ageing. Château Haut-Vigneau is another solid property producing decent red under the AC and there is a second wine, La Tour Léognan, produced in both red and white. The latter can often impress. (DM)

● **Château Carbonnieux** Pessac-Léognan★★ £E
● **Château Haut-Vigneau** Pessac-Léognan★ £D
O **Château Carbonnieux** Pessac-Léognan★★★ £E

CH. LES CARMES HAUT-BRION Pessac-Léognan

Chantecaille-Furt family   197 Avenue Jean Cordier 33600 Pessac
UK stockists: AAA

This a tiny property and, like HAUT-BRION, located amongst the suburbs of Bordeaux. Just 4.5ha are under vine, with an unusually high proportion of 50% Merlot, along with 40% Cabernet Sauvignon amd 10% Cabernet Franc. Dedication to quality has delivered impressive results in the late 1990s. Vinification in small vats enables plots within the vineyard to be fermented separately. Malolactic takes place in barrel and around one-third new wood is used. The wine is supple and rich, with firm but nicely rounded tannins. (DM)

● **Château les Carmes Haut-Brion** Pessac-Léognan★★★ £E

CH. DE CHANTEGRIVE Graves www.chateau-chantegrive.com

Henri Lévèque   33720 Podensac
UK stockists: AAA

This property consists of 50ha of red varieties and 38ha of white, with production now quite substantial at over 40,000 cases a year. Four wines are produced. A good red with a fine balance of dark fruit, cedar and subtle oak is joined by a regular white Graves, an easy, fruit-driven style fermented at low temperatures. There is also the limited production Cuvée Caroline, barrel-fermented in a portion of new oak with regular use of *bâtonnage* to add weight and a rich, creamy texture. The sweet Cérons is a full, fat style with good depth and some honeyed complexity. (DM)

● **Château de Chantegrive** Graves★★ £C
O **Château de Chantegrive** Graves★ £B Cuvée Caroline★★★ £C
O **Château de Chantegrive** Cérons★★ £C

CH. CHARMAIL Haut-Médoc

Olivier Seze   33180 Saint-Seurin-de-Cadourne
UK stockists: AAA

A consistent performer during the last 5 or 6 vintages, located just to the north of Saint-Estèphe. The wine, which has a high proportion of Merlot (55% of the vineyard) is modern and stylish. Neither fined nor filtered, it is marked by supple tannin and attractive, forward, dark berry fruit and hints of cassis, not least as a result of a touch of pre-fermentation maceration. There are none of the often green and herbaceous notes found in some lesser Bordeaux reds dominated by the variety. (DM)

● **Château Charmail** Haut-Médoc★★★ £D

CH. CHASSE-SPLEEN Moulis www.chasse-spleen.com

Céline Villars-Foubet   33480 Moulis-en-Médoc
UK stockists: AAA

Chasse-Spleen, along with POUJEAUX and MAUCAILLOU, is one of the only wines in the Moulis AC really to perform with any consistent class. The property is sizeable, with just under 85ha under vine. The wine is a blend of Cabernet Sauvignon, Merlot and Petit Verdot. With the odd exceptions (1997, 94 and 91) this property has fashioned a rich, concentrated and harmonious red. The 2001, 00 and 99 are noteworthy. It's a shame there aren't more properties turning out wines of this class in the appellation. The second wine, L'Ermitage de Chasse-Spleen, can be better than most. (DM)

● **Château Chasse-Spleen** Moulis★★★ £E

DOM. DE CHEVALIER www.domainedechevalier.com

Olivier Bernard   102 Chemin de Mignoy, 33850 Léognan
UK stockists: AAA

An important and sizeable producer, noted particularly for its splendid white. The production of this is very low, with just 4.5 of the 37.5ha vineyard planted to Sauvignon Blanc and Sémillon. There is a high proportion of Sauvignon (70%) in the blend. Barrel-fermented and aged, it is a remarkably fine and elegant white capable of considerable age. The red has been less impressive than the white in recent years but since 1996 there has been a fair step up in quality and the wine has regularly been of ★★★★ quality. In short, solid and ageworthy and reasonable value. (DM)

● **Domaine de Chevalier** Pessac-Léognan★★★★ £E
O **Domaine de Chevalier** Pessac-Léognan✪✪✪✪✪ £F

31

CH. CISSAC Haut-Médoc www.chateau-cissac.com

Danielle Viallard 33250 Cissac-Médoc
UK stockists: AAA

Cissac is still made in a traditional, firm Médoc style but it is very fairly priced and generally well-crafted. But, although structured and austere when very young, it is increasingly rounder and suppler than of old with a little age. Wooden as well as stainless steel vats are used for fermentation and an increasing amount of new wood (30–40%) is used to age the wine. From the best vintages the wine is undoubtedly complex and harmonious but really needs cellaring for 8–10 years to show at its best. (DM)

● **Château Cissac** Haut-Médoc★★★ £C

CH. CLARKE Listrac-Médoc chateau.clarke@wanadoo.fr

Baron Benjamin de Rothschild 33480 Listrac
UK stockists: AAA

Listrac, like Moulis, is quite a long way inland from the Gironde and the soil here has even less gravel than it does nearer the estuary, which will always hinder the admirable efforts made here. This property with increasingly old vines outclasses almost all of its neighbours but there remains a slightly coarse note. However, since 1995 the wine is more concentrated and harmonious, while retaining its soft and supple, earthy, dark fruit character. (DM)

● **Château Clarke** Listrac-Médoc★★ £C

CH. CLERC-MILON Pauillac 5ème CC www.bpdr.com

Baron Philippe de Rothschild SA 33250 Pauillac
UK stockists: AAA

Moderate-sized property, with some 30ha of vineyards and production running at just under 15,000 cases a year. The Cabernet Sauvignon component is quite low at less than 50% and 35% of the vineyard is planted to Merlot. As a result the style is very rounded and surprisingly approachable for Pauillac. While overshadowed by its sister château and neighbour MOUTON-ROTHSCHILD, Clerc-Milon is nevertheless an excellent, stylish source of the appellation, with a harmonious mix of dark fruits and cedar, all of which is nicely underpinned by its ripe and plummy Merlot component. At its current level since 1995. (DM)

● **Château Clerc-Milon** Pauillac★★★★ £F

CH. CLIMENS Barsac 1er CC www.chateau-climens.fr

Bérénice Lurton 33720 Barsac
UK stockists: AAA

Climens is an exceptional sweet wine and the leading property in the Barsac commune. It is outclassed only by Château d'YQUEM amongst the great botrytised wines of the Sauternes. Production is low at just over 3,000 cases a year and the vineyard, which is just 31ha, is planted solely to Sémillon. Despite the absence of Sauvignon Blanc the wine possesses not only intense and very concentrated honeyed fruit but a marvellously fresh acid balance as well. Best to age it for at least 5 years and it will be better with twice that time in the cellar. The wine was truly great in 2003, 2001,1997, 90, 89. Other very good vintages include 2002, 2000, 1998, 96, 88 and 86. (DM)

● **Château Climens** Barsac✪✪✪✪✪ £G

CLOS FLORIDÈNE Graves www.denisdubourdieu.com

Denis & Florence Dubourdieu 21 Route de Cardan, 33410 Beguey
UK stockists: F&R,Dec

The main focus is on white wine, with 13ha planted as opposed to 5.5ha for red varieties. The white is a particularly impressive example and puts many more exalted Pessac-Léognans to shame. It is barrel-fermented and aged with *bâtonnage* to add richness but it is the citrus and mineral quality of the fruit that really marks it out. It will evolve nicely over the short to medium term. The red is sound and well-crafted but lacks the same excitement. Denis Dubourdieu also produces the wines of Château REYNON. (DM)

● **Clos Floridène** Graves★ £C
O **Clos Floridène** Graves★★★ £C

CH. CLOS HAUT-PEYRAGUEY Sauternes 1er CC

J & J. Pauly   33210 Bommes
UK stockists: AAA

Very small Sauternes property. There are just 12ha of vineyards, 90% of which are Sémillon, the balance Sauvignon Blanc. Quality is good to very good but the wine just lacks the depth and intensity of the best of the other First Growths of the appellation. The style is more one of finesse and elegance than sheer weight and concentration. Very good in 2001, 98, 97, 90 and 88, while other years are not quite of the same order. The second wine is Château Haut Bommes. (DM)

● **Château Clos Haut-Peyraguey** Sauternes★★★ £E

CH. COS D'ESTOURNEL Saint-Estèphe 2ème CC www.estournel.com

Taillan group   33180 Saint-Estèphe
UK stockists: AAA

One of the greatest wines of the Médoc and the premier château in Saint-Estèphe. Purchased from Bruno Prats by the Taillan Group, who also own GRUAUD-LAROSE, in 1998. Jean-Guillaume Prats remains in charge of the property and it is to be hoped that the Prats family's exceptional standards here throughout the 1970s, 80s and 90s will be maintained. After a dip in the late 1990s the wine is right back on form. Using sophisticated vinification including must concentration, malolactic in barrel and new oak for ageing, the wine is very powerful as well as opulent. It should, however, show remarkable depth and harmony with a decade or more in the cellar. The second wine was originally called MARBUZET, which is itself a Cru Bourgeois, but is now labelled Les Pagodes de Cos. The former has regularly been ★ to ★★ throughout the 1990s. (DM)

● **Château Cos d'Estournel** Saint-Estèphe✪✪✪✪✪ £G

CH. COS LABORY Saint-Estèphe 5ème CC cos-labory@wanadoo.fr

Bernard Audoy   33180 Saint-Estèphe
UK stockists: **THt**,AAA

Although overshadowed by its famous neighbour COS D'ESTOURNEL, this property improved greatly in the late 1980s and some of the vintages since have been impressive. 1996, 95, 90 and 88 were all a notch up on what has generally been achieved here over the last 12–15 years. The late 1990s have somewhat disappointingly not maintained this level but the wine looks promising once more in the 2002 and 2003 vintages. At its best the wine is full, marked by impressive blackcurrant fruit and underpinned by a firm, rounded, tannic structure. (DM)

● **Château Cos Labory** Saint-Estèphe★★★ £E

CH. COUHINS-LURTON Pessac-Léognan CC ww.andrelurton.com

Les Vignobles André Lurton   33420 Grézillac
UK stockists: AAA

André Lurton is now a major proprietor in the Graves, Entre-Deux-Mers and Margaux. At this tiny 5.5-ha Pessac property he produces less than 2,000 cases

33

of very stylish white a year from Sauvignon Blanc. No Sémillon is planted here but the wine is barrel-fermented in 50% new wood and aged with *bâtonnage* and has the structure and density to age well in bottle. Both 1999 and 2000 were particularly good examples. (DM)

O **Château Couhins-Lurton** Pessac-Léognan★★★ £E

CH. COUTET   Barsac 1er CC

Baly family   33720 Barsac
UK stockists: AAA

Very good property and near neighbour of CLIMENS, although the wine here doesn't quite reach the same heights. As well as Sémillon, which accounts for 75% of the blend, and Sauvignon Blanc, there is a little Muscadelle, just 3%. There is no doubt that there is a marked aromatic character in the wine in addition to its classic rich vanilla and peach notes. In exceptional years a special super-concentrated Cuvée Madame is released. This is certainly ✪✪✪✪✪. (DM)

O **Château Coutet** Barsac★★★★ £F

CH. DAUZAC   Margaux 5ème CC   www.andrelurton.com

Les Vignobles André Lurton   33460 Labarde
UK stockists: **CRs**

Another André Lurton-controlled property. There are 46ha under vine here and production is just shy of 25,000 cases, so it is a sizeable operation. The style is supple and rich with an emphasis on approachable dark fruit and well-judged oak. The wine is only kept in barrel for 12 months but 50–80% is new. Quality has improved dramatically since the 1990s. (DM)

● **Château Dauzac** Margaux★★★ £E

CH. DOISY-DAËNE   Barsac 2ème CC   www.denisdubourdieu.com

Pierre & Denis Dubourdieu   33720 Barsac
UK stockists: AAA

This is a Barsac marked by its elegance rather than its sheer weight or richness. It can be piercingly aromatic, though, and very intense. Of a completely different order – richer and fuller – is an occasional very limited *cuvée* called L'Extravagance. It is only produced in exceptional vintages, including 2003, 2001, 1997 and 1996. As well as the sweet wines a good dry Bordeaux Blanc is rich and fruity. (DM)

O **Château Doisy-Daëne** Barsac★★★ £E   O **Bordeaux**★★ £C

CH. DOISY-VÉDRINES   Barsac 2ème CC

Pierre Castéja   1 Rue Védrines, 33720 Barsac
UK stockists: AAA

This is the biggest of the 3 Doisy properties with 27ha. In contrast to DOISY-DAENE and most other fine Barsacs, this property tends to produce wine with more overt luscious honeyed fruit. It is very impressive, retaining an elegant finesse in lighter years when the wine carries less sheer weight. There is 5% Muscadelle planted here, which provides an aromatic undercurrent to the wine. (DM)

● **Château Doisy-Védrines** Sauternes★★★★ £E

CH. DUCRU-BEAUCAILLOU   Saint-Julien 2ème CC

Borie family   33250 Saint-Julien-Beychevelle
UK stockists: AAA

One of the greatest wines of Saint-Julien. The 50ha of Ducru based in the south of the appellation are planted to a mix of Cabernet Sauvignon (65%), Merlot (25%), and an equal portion of Cabernet Franc and Petit Verdot. It is a very impressive, classically structured example of the appellation: always elegant, very intense, with subtle cedar and dark fruit underpinned by finely integrated oak. It requires patience and cellaring. From the current crop of excellent vintages 2003, 2000, 1998, 96 and 95 were exemplary but 97 was something of a disappointment. (DM)

● **Château Ducru-Beaucaillou** Saint-Julien✪✪✪✪✪ £H

CH. DUHART-MILON   Pauillac 4ème CC   www.lafite.com
Domaines Barons de Rothschild/Chalone Wine Group   33250 Pauillac
UK stockists: AAA

Intriguingly, this Rothschild property is also part-owned by the Chalone Wine Group from the USA, which established its reputation with the CHALONE winery in Monterey, California. There is no doubt that the 50ha of vineyards have benefited greatly from the Lafite input since the property was purchased in 1962. Fermentation is modern in stainless steel and ageing taking place in barrels, 50% new, that are coopered at Lafite-Rothschild. 1999, 98 and 96 were all nudging ★★★★ quality. (DM)

● **Château Duhart-Milon** Pauillac★★★ £E

CH. DE FARGUES   Sauternes   www.chateau-de-fargues.com
Alexandre de Lur-Saluces   33210 Fargues de Langon
UK stockists: AAA

A rare wine with a price to match. An average of only 15,000 bottles are made annually from 15 hectares of vines owned by the Lur-Saluces family of YQUEM fame. The property did not produce any sweet wine until 1943 but this is one of the finest examples of Sauternes now made and one of the longest-lasting wines in the appellation. (NB)

O **Château de Fargues** Sauternes★★★★★ £F

CH. FERRIÈRE   Margaux 3ème CC   www.ferriere.com
Merlaut family   33460 Margaux
UK stockists:, AAA

Small Classed Growth which has improved dramatically during the 1990s. Production is barely more than 4,000 cases a year and the dedicated commitment to quality here by Claire Villars (aided by the Merlaut family who run the Taillan group, owners of COS D'ESTOURNEL and GRUAUD-LAROSE) has ensured that this is one of the best properties in the Margaux appellation. The wine is rich, intense and concentrated and now shows great harmony and refinement. There is minimal processing with egg-white fining and malolactic in barrel. The wine comfortably absorbs the impact of 60% new oak. (DM)

● **Château Ferrière** Margaux★★★★ £E

CH. DE FIEUZAL   Pessac-Léognan CC   www.fieuzal.com
Lachlann Quinn   124 Avenue de Mont-de-Marsan, 33850 Léognan
UK stockists: THt, AAA

The style here, particularly with the red, is to produce opulent, richly textured, forward, modern and approachable wines, accessible very shortly after release. The white, which unlike the red is not in fact a Cru Classé, also shows rich, forward, honeyed fruit with a solid dose of new oak but with a depth and structure that ensures good, medium-term cellaring and is the more impressive of the 2. These wines, particularly the whites, offer very good value. (DM)

● **Château de Fieuzal** Pessac-Léognan★★★ £E
O **Château de Fieuzal** Pessac-Léognan★★★★ £E

35

CH. FILHOT Sauternes 2ème CC www.filhot.com

Vaucelles family 33210 Sauternes
UK stockists: AAA

A pretty consistent château regularly producing wines with a good balance of sweetness and acidity. It has always been a bit on the light side, probably due to the high proportion of Sauvignon Blanc (36%), but it remains good drinking value for a classed-growth Sauternes. (NB)

● **Château Filhot** Sauternes★★★ £C

CH. DE FRANCE Pessac-Léognan

Bernard Thomassin 33850 Léognan
Inproving medium-sized Pessac property of some 35ha. Just 3ha of the vineyard is so far planted to white varieties, with Sauvignon accounting for 70% and the balance Sémillon. Red grapes are 60% Cabernet Sauvignon and 40% Merlot. The quality of the wines has greatly improved since the late 1990s, particularly the red. In part this is due to the involvement of Michel Rolland who advises on the winemaking. Vinification is traditional with a fermentation temperature in the low 30s celsius and malolactic is conducted in *cuve*. Ageing is for 14–18 months in *barrique*. Medium-weight, with lightly cedary fruit the wine will add flesh with 4 or 5 years' age. The white, which is barrel-fermented with *bâtonnage* and bottled with a light filtration, doesn't have quite the depth of the red. (DM)

● **Château de France** Pessac-Léognan★★ £D
○ **Château de France** Pessac-Léognan★ £C

CH. GISCOURS Margaux 2ème CC www.chateau-giscours.com

Eric Albada Jedgersma 10 Route de Giscours, 33460 Margaux
UK stockists: AAA

Giscours like du TERTRE is now in the ownership of Eric Albada Jedgersma and similarly has been performing at a much improved level in recent vintages. Investment in the vineyard and cellars with reduced yields and careful vinification has produced some impressive examples. The property is sizeable and covers 85ha of vineyards planted to Cabernet Sauvignon (55%), Merlot (40%) and Cabernet Franc. Despite the high proportion of Merlot the wine, at its recent best, is richly textured, powerful and less obviously perfumed than other examples of the appellation. Two secondary wines are produced which both offer some of the character of the Grand Vin. Sirene de Giscours takes the Margaux appellation and there is a budget label, Haut-Médoc de Giscours. The top wine will add increasing richness with 8–10 years' age. (DM)

● **Château Giscours** Margaux★★★★ £E

CH. GLORIA Saint-Julien

Triaud family 33250 Saint-Julien-Beychevelle
UK stockists: AAA

This has been a consistently sound Cru Bourgeois over the years. Gloria has performed admirably throughout the 1970s, 80s and 90s. It is a sizeable property, with widely scattered plots, with some 47ha under vine producing around 25,000 cases a year. The wine is not immensely complex or long-lived but is full of vibrant, dark, brambly blackcurrant fruit, nicely judged oak and an elegant hint of cedar in the background. (DM)

● **Château Gloria** Saint-Julien★★ £D

CH. GRAND-PUY-LACOSTE Pauillac 5ème CC

Borie family   33250 Pauillac
UK stockists: AAA

Under the same ownership as DUCRU-BEAUCAILLOU, this has been an admirable and classic red Bordeaux for the past 3 decades and there have been many admirable vintages since World War II. This is the quintessential example of what you expect from fine Pauillac, a wine loaded with cassis and cedar, refined and elegant but with real power and density. 1990, and more recently 95 and 96, are wines of significant class and 2000 looks very much of the same order, although the most recent vintages are a touch below par (DM)

● **Château Grand-Puy-Lacoste** Pauillac★★★★ £F

CH. GRUAUD-LAROSE Saint-Julien 2ème CC

Taillan group   33250 Saint-Julien-Beychevelle
UK stockists: AAA

Large Saint-Julien property with production approaching 40,000 cases a year, responsible for some formidable and massively structured wines during the 1980s. 1982 and 86 were without a doubt ✪✪✪✪✪, with a number of others on the cusp. Quality generally has remained impressive throughout the 1990s but not at quite the same level. These are powerful, dense and tannic reds in need of at least 8–10 years' cellaring. The second wine, Sarget de Gruaud-Larose, can be good, particularly in better years. (DM)

● **Château Gruaud-Larose** Saint-Julien★★★★ £F

CH. GUIRAUD Sauternes 1er CC www.chateauguiraud.fr

Narby family   33210 Sauternes
UK stockists: AAA

Xavier Planty, in charge of production here, turned out impressive Sauternes in the top vintages of the 1990s. A consistent replanting process has much improved the ratio of Sémillon to Sauvignon Blanc and plantings of the former now account for 70% of the vineyard. The result is wines of sometimes blockbuster proportions, rich, very honeyed and peachy, with spice and vanilla from new oak. It is not to all tastes, and on occasion more refinement would help. (DM)

○ **Château Guiraud** Sauternes★★★★ £F

CH. HAUT-BAILLY Pessac-Léognan CC www.chateau-haut-bailly.com

Robert J Wilmers   Route de Cadaujac, 33850 Léognan
UK stockists: RsW, Las, AAA

A supple, elegant and consistently well-crafted red which is both approachable and refined. In contrast with most neighbouring properties, no white is made here. Haut-Bailly was purchased by Robert Wilmers, an American banker, in 1998 but the original proprietors, the Sanders family, are still involved in the direction and management. Consistent throughout the mid- to late 1990s. The wine ages very well indeed. (DM)

● **Château Haut-Bailly** Pessac-Léognan★★★★ £E

CH. HAUT-BERGEY Pessac-Léognan CC www.chateau-haut-bergey.com

Mme. Sylviane Garcin-Cathiard   69 Cours Gambetta 33850 Léognan
UK stockists:: Gen

Middle-ranking Pessac-Léognan property with 25ha given over to red grapes (54% Cabernet Sauvignon; 46% Merlot) and only 2ha to whites (84% Sauvignon; 18% Sémillon). The white usually shows the better quality, with a great deal of finesse, whilst the red is normally a bit muscular and needs time to

37

come round. Also produces the Pessac super-*cuvée* BRANON. (DM)

● **Château Haut-Bergey** Pessac-Léognan★★ £D
O **Château Haut-Bergey** Pessac-Léognan★★★ £D

CH. HAUT-BATAILLEY   Pauillac 5ème CC   je-borie@je-borie-sa.com

Borie family   33250 Saint-Julien-Beychevelle
UK stockists: AAA

Under the same ownership as DUCRU-BEAUCAILLOU and GRAND-PUY-LACOSTE. Quality here used to be somewhat variable and lesser vintages were light and lacking in substance as well as possessing a hard, at times austerely firm edge. This was surprising given the quality of the other properties owned by the Borie family but the mid-1990s saw an improvement and change in style. The wine is now less aggressive and raw and possesses a fine, more supple and even texture. It is altogether more accessible and harmonious. Significantly more impressive in 1995, 96 and 2000 and 2003 also looks promising. (DM)

● **Château Haut-Batailley** Pauillac★★★ £E

CH. HAUT-BRION   Pessac-Léognan 1er CC   www.haut-brion.com

Domaine Clarence Dillon   33608 Pessac Cedex
UK stockist: AAA

One of the 4 original properties classified as a First Growth in the 1855 Classification of red Bordeaux wines. The vineyards are planted in superbly drained gravel soils that provide an almost ideal supply of moisture to optimise fruit ripening. Red grapes occupy 43ha, while less than 3ha provides a tiny amount of exquisite, subtly barrel-fermented white from Sémillon and Sauvignon Blanc. The property, now surrounded by the ever-encroaching suburbs of Bordeaux, is small in comparison to the other First Growths, producing a total of some 12,500 cases a year. Both red and white have been magnificent through the late 1990s, only the 1997 and 91 red dipping a little. Great older vintages include 1990, 89, 86, 82, 75 and the astonishing 61. The second wine, Le Bahans, can also be very impressive. (DM)

● **Château Haut-Brion** Pessac-Léognan✪✪✪✪✪ £H
● **Le Bahans Haut Brion**★★★ £E
O **Château Haut-Brion** Pessac-Léognan✪✪✪✪✪ £G

CH. HAUT-MARBUZET   Saint-Estèphe

Henri Duboscq   33180 Saint-Estèphe
UK stockists: PBW,Col

Henri Duboscq produces a fleshy, powerful, very rich Saint-Estèphe marked by well-integrated spicy new oak. Not only is this an outstanding Cru Bourgeois but it is only surpassed within the appellation by COS D'ESTOURNEL and MONTROSE. Production is not inconsiderable at close to 30,000 cases a year. The wine has been impressive in recent years, particularly from 2000 and has been performing comfortably out of its class. It offers very good value and there is a decent soft and forward second label, Chambert-Marbuzet. (DM)

● **Château Haut-Marbuzet** Saint-Estèphe★★★★ £E

CH. D'ISSAN   Margaux 3ème CC   www.chateau-issan.com

Cruse family   33460 Cantenac
UK stockists: AAA

This property was often disappointing in the late 1980s and early 90s. However since 1995 things have been looking decidedly better and the wine is once more in the elegant, cedary and perfumed style that represents fine Margaux. Major investment in both vineyard and cellars and input on the winemaking from Jacques Boissenet (one of a number of high-profile Bordeaux consultants, who also advises André Lurton as well as the Napa Valley QUINTESSA operation) are clearly having a positive effect. (DM)

● **Château d'Issan** Margaux★★★ £E

CLOS DU JAUGUEYRON   Margaux

Michel Théron   4 rue de la Halle, 33460 Arsac
UK stockists: **WTs**

Michel Théron is a third-generation *vigneron* and a graduate in viticulture and œnological science. In 1993 he acquired the Clos du Jaugueyron, a 0.4-ha estate in the commune of Cantenac but only entitled to the Haut-Médoc appellation. The grapes have an average age of 50 years and are 60% Cabernet Sauvignon, 20% Merlot, 10% Petit Verdot, 5% Carmenère and 5% "others". There is remarkable quality for the price. Flushed with the success of this wine, he acquired a small parcel of adjoining vines which happened to be in the Margaux appellation. The fact that there are only some 100 cases produced under this appellation, together with the attention given to it by certain influential North American wine writers, has probably made this the ultimate *garagiste* property in the Médoc. (NB)

● **Clos du Jaugueyron** Margaux★★★★ £F
● **Clos du Jaugueyron** Haut-Médoc★★★ £D

CH. KIRWAN   Margaux 3ème CC   www.chateau-kirwan.com

Schÿler family   33460 Cantenac
UK stockists: AAA

The Schÿler family, who also run the Schroder and Schÿler *négociant* operation in Bordeaux, had sold their interest in this small to medium-sized property in the early 1990s but promptly bought it back again a couple of years later. The result has been a real boost for the fortunes of the property and in particular the quality of the wine. Michel Rolland has provided guidance on the winemaking front and quality has been consistently good since 1996,. (DM)

● **Château Kirwan** Margaux★★★ £E

CH. LAFAURIE-PEYRAGUEY   Sauternes 1er CC

Domaines Cordier   33210 Bommes
UK stockists: AAA

From 40ha under vine in the commune of Bommes, with a grape mix of Sémillon (90%), Sauvignon Blanc (8%) and Muscadelle (just 2%), some of the finest Sauternes is now being made at this property. This has only been the case for the last 15 years or so. The 1970s were a disappointment but the wines are now quite exemplary. They combine the intense richness and honeyed concentration of the finest Sauternes with something of the elegance found in CLIMENS. The wines are very stylish and long-lived. The 1999, 98 and 97 are all extraordinarily fine ✪✪✪✪✪ and 2001 may have the potential to be exquisite. (DM)

● **Château Lafaurie-Peyraguey** Sauternes★★★★★ £F

CH. LAFITE-ROTHSCHILD   Pauillac 1er CC   www.lafite.com

Domaines Barons de Rothschild   33250 Pauillac
UK stockists: AAA

One of the world's great wines and a consistent and superlative performer throughout the mid- to late 1990s. The 2000, 98 and 96 are exceptional wines and 2003 shows similar promise, which is not surprising considering the quality of the vintage. However, all has not always been rosy here and 20 or so years ago the quality was much more uneven. The vineyard is planted to some 100ha of Cabernet Sauvignon (75%), Merlot (20%), Cabernet Franc (4%) and

39

Petit Verdot (a mere 1%). A minimum of 15–20 years is required to achieve a harmony between the formidable, powerful tannins and the intense and fragrantly rich cedar and cassis fruit. 1982 marked a real turning point in the quality of the wine and other years of particular note are 1986, 88 and 90. The 53 and 59 were both superb but surprisingly 61 failed to achieve the high quality of that year. The second wine, Les Carruades de Lafite-Rothschild, is very impressive for a second label. (DM)

● **Château Lafite-Rothschild** Pauillac✪✪✪✪✪ £H
● **Les Carruades de Lafite-Rothschild**★★★★ £F

CH. LAFON-ROCHET   Saint-Estèphe 4ème CC

Tesseron family   33180 Saint-Estèphe
UK stockists: AAA

Under the same ownership as PONTET-CANET, Lafon-Rochet has performed well, sometimes very well throughout the mid- to late 1990s. The vintages of the early 1990s did not achieve the same level but that is unsurprising given the difficult conditions of those years. The wine is a great deal more supple and approachable than it used to be and much of the reason has been a progressive replanting of the vineyard with a higher proportion of Merlot, now some 40%. 2003, 01, 00, 98, 96 and 95 stand out. (DM)

● **Château Lafon-Rochet** Saint-Estèphe★★★ £E

CH. LAGRANGE   Saint-Julien 3ème CC   www.chateau-lagrange.com

Suntory   33250 Saint-Julien-Beychevelle
UK stockists:Eno,SsG

The Japanese-owned Suntory company has pushed wine quality at this property forward dramatically since its purchase in the early 1980s and Lagrange is now very well run by Marcel Ducasse. Lagrange is very large, even by the standards of the Médoc, with over 110ha under vine. The wine is rich and concentrated, but in an approachable style, with supple, well-rounded tannin. Consistently good over the last 5 or 6 years, it just needs that extra dimension to take it into the top division. (DM)

● **Château Lagrange** Saint-Julien★★★ £F

CH. LA LAGUNE   Haut-Médoc 3ème CC

Ducellier Family   33290 Ludon-Médoc
UK stockists: AAA

Some great reds were made at this property during the 1970s and 80s but more recently this sizeable 77-ha estate has produced some less exciting wines. The vineyard is mainly Cabernet Sauvignon (60%), Merlot (20%) and the balance Cabernet Franc and Petit Verdot. Under the current ownership things appear to be taking a turn for the better. Some medium-weight, elegant and cedary claret is being made using stainless steel temperature-controlled tanks for vinification, with ageing in an increasing amount of new oak. (DM)

● **Château La Lagune** Haut-Médoc★★ £F

CH. LAMOTHE-GUIGNARD   Sauternes 2ème CC

Philippe & Jacques Guignard   33210 Sauternes
UK stockists: AAA

This is the larger of the 2 Lamothe properties in Sauternes. The other Lamothe, owned by Guy Despujols, does not quite reach the same heights. 90% of the vineyard is planted to Sémillon along with 5% Muscadelle and 5% Sauvignon Blanc. The style is increasingly elegant with luscious botrytis character showing through in the best years. (DM)

○ **Château Lamothe-Guignard** Sauternes★★★ £E

CH. LANESSAN   Haut-Médoc

SCEA Delbos Bouteiller   33460 Cussac-Fort-Médoc
UK stockists: AAA
This is a somewhat old-fashioned style of Médoc located close to Saint-Julien.
Medium- rather than full-bodied or super-rich, the wine can be long-lived,
elegant and intense, particularly in the best vintages when it can really ripen its
at times angular tannins. With time, complex cedar and elegant, evolved
tertiary characters emerge. It was particularly good in 1996 and 2000 shows
real promise also. (DM)
● **Château Lanessan** Haut-Médoc★★ £D

CH. LANGOA-BARTON   Saint-Julien 3ème CC

Anthony Barton   33250 Saint-Julien-Beychevelle
UK stockists: AAA
Sister property to LÉOVILLE-BARTON and in the Barton family for nearly 2
centuries. This has always been a consistent performer, producing elegant Saint-
Julien with attractive dark fruit and some cedary complexity, but inevitably it is
overshadowed by its sibling château, being a mere Third Growth. Both wines
are in fact vinified at Langoa, as Léoville has no winery, and are renowned for
their fair prices. Both also share the same label for the second wine, Réserve de
Léoville-Barton, which can be good. 2001, 00 and 98 stand out among recent
vintages. (DM)
● **Château Langoa-Barton** Saint-Julien★★★ £E

CH. LARRIVET HAUT-BRION   Pessac-Léognan

Société Andros   84 Route de Cadaujac, 33850 Léognan
UK stockists: BBR,F&R,N&P,Sec
There are 52ha of vines planted here, 43ha of which account for an even split
of Cabernet Sauvignon and Merlot. The white varieties are also evenly split,
between Sémillon and Sauvignon Blanc. Both wines are impressive and
consultancy input on the winemaking is provided by Michel Rolland. The
property is worthy of being upgraded to Cru Classé status. Both 1998 and 99
are very good and the potential for 2000 and 01 looks very good also. The red,
particularly, is nudging ★★★★ quality. It is stylish, refined and approachable at
a few years, while the white is an elegant and notably piercing barrel-fermented
style with a harmonious mix of fresh green and citrus fruits and subtle oak.
(DM)
● **Château Larrivet Haut-Brion** Pessac-Léognan★★★ £E
○ **Château Larrivet Haut-Brion** Pessac-Léognan★★★ £E

CH. LASCOMBES   Margaux 2ème CC   www.chateau-lascombes.com

Colony Capital   1, Cours de Verdun, 33460 Margaux
UK stockists: AAA
There has been a sea-change at this château under new ownership. Since 2000
consultant enologist Michel Rolland and the home team of Delphine Barboux,
Cyrille Faure and Miguel da Fonseca have worked wonders. Gone are the
weedy wines produced under the previous regime; in are wines of power and
strength which are nevertheless underscored by Margaux finesse. Without
exception 2001 to 2004 have produced impressively deeply coloured wines
with massive black fruits. Surprisingly, the largest proportion of grapes are
Merlot (50%), with the balance split 45/5 between Cabernet Sauvignon and
Petit Verdot. (NB)
● **Château Lascombes** Margaux★★★★ £E
● **Chevalier de Lascombes** Margaux★★★ £D

41

LA SERÉNITÉ Pessac-Léognan

Bernard Magrez   7. Rue du Professeur-Bernard, 33170 Gradignan

This is a special *garagiste*-style label produced at Château POUMEY. Proprietor Bernard Magrez has also released a number of other similarly styled wines from small, low-yielding properties throughout the region. The wines are sourced from a number of high quality vineyard sites owned by Bernard Magrez and film actor Gérard Depardieu; not only in Bordeaux but also in the Midi, Italy, Morocco and Algeria. La Serénité is a very full, rich and extracted style. Produced from an almost equal blend of Merlot and Cabernet Sauvignon, it is vinified and aged in wood and everything in the cellars is handled by gravity. (DM)

● **La Serénité** Pessac-Léognan★★★ £E

CH. LATOUR Pauillac 1er CC www.chateau-latour.com

François Pinault   Saint-Lambert, 33250 Pauillac
UK stockists: AAA

To many this is the greatest of all the great wines of the Médoc and to some the greatest in the entire region. There is no doubt that it is one of the world's most remarkable reds, which at its magnificent best is both massive and concentrated but at the same time harmonious and very refined. It requires cellaring and you should allow 1 or preferably 2 decades. While the wine performs consistently at a very high level now, a number of vintages in the early to mid-1980s were less impressive, nowhere near its current ✪✪✪✪✪ ranking. Fortunately, with a production of over 30,000 cases a year, the wine is not impossible to find – unlike a number of new 'super' wines being made elsewhere around the world. Recent vintages have all been very striking. Among the great earlier years 82, 71, 66, 61, 59 and 49 are all legendary. Les Forts de Latour is a very impressive second wine. (DM)

● **Château Latour** Pauillac✪✪✪✪✪ £H ● **Les Forts de Latour**★★★★ £F

CH. LA TOUR CARNET Haut-Médoc

Bernard Magrez   33112 Saint-Laurent-Médoc
UK stockists: L&W,BBR,N&P,Tur

A rich, fleshy style of Médoc which is produced from Cabernet Sauvignon (52%), Merlot (42%) and a little Cabernet Franc and Petit Verdot. Michel Rolland consults over the winemaking for which fermentation is carried out in wooden vats with malolactic typically in *barrique*. Around 70% new oak is used and all operations are now carried out by gravity. the wine is ripe and reasonably forward; 4–5 years are required to integrate the fruit and initially dominant oak. The white is a blend of mainly Sauvignon Blanc, Semillon and a touch of Muscadelle. (DM)

● **Château La Tour Carnet** Haut-Médoc★★★ £D
O **Château La Tour Carnet** Bordeaux★★★ £C

CH. LATOUR-MARTILLAC www.latour-martillac.com

Kressmann family   33650 Martillac
UK stockists: AAA

Good to very good white and red Pessac is produced at this property, with around three-quarters of the output red. Increasing vine age is one of the reasons why quality has surged forward during the 1990s. The red varieties now average 30 years and the whites a full 40 years. The red is an approachable, supple wine with refined tannins and nicely judged oak that varies between 30 and 50% depending on the year. The white is rich and honeyed, with a real toasty, creamy character from barrel-fermentation and *bâttonage* underpinned by loads of character and style. Both offer good value for money. (DM)

● **Château Latour-Martillac** Pessac-Léognan★★★ £D
O **Château Latour-Martillac** Pessac-Léognan★★★ £D

CH. LAVILLE HAUT-BRION Pessac-Léognan CC

Domaine Clarence Dillon 33608 Pessac
UK stockists: F&R,C&R

Like HAUT-BRION this property is owned by the Domaine Clarence Dillon. The wine, a blend of Sémillon (70%), Sauvignon Blanc (27%) and just a hint of Muscadelle (at 3%), is produced at LA MISSION HAUT-BRION, as is LA TOUR HAUT-BRION, although all 3 are from separate and distinct vineyard plots. Laville is one of the great Pessac whites, powerfully structured and developing intense honeyed, mineral notes with age. It is barrel-fermented and aged mostly in new oak and requires considerable cellaring to show all its magic – at least 7 or 8 years. (DM)

O **Château Laville Haut-Brion** Pessac-Léognan✪✪✪✪✪ £G

CH. LÉOVILLE-BARTON Saint-Julien 2ème CC

Anthony Barton 33250 Saint-Julien-Beychevelle
UK stockists: AAA

This marvellously consistent red has long been one of Bordeaux's great-value wines. It is produced from 48ha of vineyards planted to a mix of Cabernet Sauvignon (70%), Merlot (22%) and Cabernet Franc (8%). It is vinified at its sister property LANGOA-BARTON as there is no winemaking facility on the Léoville property. The wine is a stylish, cedary, medium-full claret with well-judged oak and a supple but youthfully firm texture that requires time to achieve balance and harmony. It is no blockbuster but very good and long-lived nonetheless. It was seriously nudging ✪✪✪✪✪ in 1996 and potentially 2000 as well. The 89, 86 and 82 were also very fine. (DM)

● **Château Léoville-Barton** Saint-Julien★★★★★ £F

CH. LÉOVILLE-LAS-CASES Saint-Julien 2ème CC

Delon family 33250 Saint-Julien-Beychevelle
UK stockists: AAA

Almost universally regarded now as the finest of the super-seconds, on many occasions this magnificent property outclasses the First Growths. Not surprisingly the wine carries a price to match this performance and has in a number of vintages held up extraordinarily well on auction markets. This is also a fairly significant château, with 97ha under vine. The high standards in place here ensure that a significant amount of the Grand Vin is declassified as Clos du Marquis, which is one of the very best of the Médoc's second labels. The quality was top-notch throughout the 1990s – only 1992 and 91 saw some ground lost, and the wine was a testament to the trying conditions of those years. Recent benchmarks are 2000, 96, 95 and 90, while 86 and 82 are also legendary. The Delon family also own POTENSAC in the Médoc and NENIN at Pomerol. (DM)

● **Château Léoville-las-Cases** Saint-Julien✪✪✪✪✪ £H ● **Clos du Marquis**★★★ £E

CH. LÉOVILLE-POYFERRÉ Saint-Julien 2ème CC

Cuvelier family 33250 Saint-Julien-Beychevelle
UK stockists: AAA

The third among the great Léoville super-seconds. This was originally regarded as the first among equals and today, after a period of relative decline in the 1960s and 70s, it is once more challenging the other 2 Léoville properties. Poyferré, while a serious, dense and powerfully structured wine, is more approachable than the other 2. It has a more vibrant, upfront, dark blackcurrant and mulberry fruit character and is an altogether more opulent style, partly achieved through a portion of the wine being put through malolactic in barrel. Nevertheless it remains very refined and elegant, an excellent expression of its *terroir*. 2000, 96 and 90 were all extremely fine examples of ★★★★★ quality and 2003 looks to have real potential. The second wine, Moulin Riche, is good to very good on occasion. (DM)

● **Château Léoville-Poyferré** Saint-Julien★★★★ £F

CH. LA LOUVIÈRE Pessac-Léognan www.andrelurton.com
Les Vignobles André Lurton 33890 Léognan
UK stockists: AAA

This is one of several property in the André Lurton Graves empire. As well as the wines of La Louvière, 2 other labels are vinified here: Château de CRUZEAU and Château ROCHEMORIN. The La Louvière vineyard comprises some 48ha, of which 33ha are planted to Cabernet Sauvignon and Merlot. The smaller white vineyard holding is dominated by Sauvignon Blanc, which accounts for around 85%, the balance being Sémillon. Both wines are approachable and forward in style but will also age well in the medium term. The red is supple, with refined, nicely rounded tannin and the white ripe and full of citrus and subtle toasted oak. (DM)

● **Château la Louvière** Pessac-Léognan★★★ £E
O **Château la Louvière** Pessac-Léognan★★★ £E

CH. LYNCH-BAGES Pauillac 5ème CC www.lynchbages.com
Jean-Michel Cazes 33250 Pauillac
UK stockists: AAA

Regarded rightly during the 1980s as one of the great super-seconds despite its lower official classification. Talented Jean-Michel Cazes unquestionably had a vast influence on quality here during that period. During the late 1990s he has lost just a touch of the sheen. The wine at its best is still very fine, full of dark cassis and ripe stylish tannin, and is surprisingly approachable. A good straightforward lightly oaked Bordeaux Blanc is also produced, along with the second wine, Haut-Bages-Avérous. Among recent vintages the 2000, 96 and 95 Grand Vin were all very impressive. Among earlier years the trio of 88, 89 and 90 were very fine, as were 85, 82 and 70. (DM)

● **Château Lynch-Bages** Pauillac★★★★★ £F
O **Château Lynch-Bages** Bordeaux★★ £D

CH. LYNCH-MOUSSAS Pauillac 5ème CC
Emile Castéja 33250 Pauillac
UK stockists: AAA

This château has always been considered one of the dullest in the area but recently the wine has become more vibrant and fleshed out. Although it is still a wine for relatively early drinking, it is now producing big tannins with enough fruit underneath to ensure a bit of extra longevity. This is a much improved and improving estate and the prices are still reasonable. (NB)

● **Château Lynch-Moussas** Pauillac★★★ £D

MAGREZ-TIVOLI Médoc
Bernard Magrez c/o Terroirs d'Exception, 33330 Saint-Christophe des Bardes
One of a number of wines including LA SERÉNITÉ, PASSION DU PRIEURÉ MALESAN and LA CROIX DE PEYROLIE that are marketed as part of the Terroirs d'Exception range by Bernard Magrez. This comes from a tiny 2.5-ha plot planted two-thirds/one-third Cabernet Sauvignon and Merlot. The

vineyard is sited on classic Médoc gravel soil and is now 40 years old. Low yields, hand-harvesting, hand-sorting and vinification in small vats all contribute to the impressive quality. The wine is handled entirely by gravity and aged in oak for 22 months. It is both fleshy and concentrated with a pure cedary undercurrent to the fruit as well not inconsiderable new oak. (DM)

● **Magrez-Tivoli** Médoc★★★★ £F

CH. MALARTIC-LAGRAVIÈRE Pessac-Léognan CC

Alfred-Alexandre Bonnie 43 Avenue de Mont-de-Marsan, 33850 Léognan
UK stockists: AAA

This property was sold by Champagne house LAURENT-PERRIER to the Bonnie family in 1997 and since then there has been significant investment with a dramatic raising of standards. Quality since the 1997 vintage has been very good. Prior to this the whites had shown class on occasion but the red was generally a disappointment. The vineyard is now tended organically with reduced yields and a massive renovation of the cellars now means that winery operations are handled where possible by gravity. Michel Rolland consults for the reds. With 20% Sémillon added to the white it offers a ripe and opulent, lightly oaked style with none of the sulphur of old, while the red is rich, ripe and approachable. Both will develop well over the medium term. The second label for both red and white, Le Sillage de Malartic, now offers reliable drinking. (DM)

● **Château Malartic-Lagravière** Pessac-Léognan★★★ £E
○ **Château Malartic-Lagravière** Pessac-Léognan★★★★ £E

CH. MALESCOT-SAINT-EXUPÉRY Margaux 3ème CC

Zuger family 33460 Margaux
UK stockists: AAA

During the 1980s and early 90s this was a reliable if somewhat unexciting Margaux, but reasonably priced. Quality has taken a significant step up in recent vintages and the price has risen but not excessively so. As is so often the case, a new generation has meant progressive moves forward. The wine is now riper and fuller but not at all extracted, retaining a typically elegant, perfumed Margaux character. With the exception of 1997, which was a touch below par, every recent vintage looks pretty good. (DM)

● **Château Malescot-Saint-Exupéry** Margaux★★★★ £F

CH. DE MALLE Sauternes 2ème CC

Comtesse de Bournazel 33210 Preignac
UK stockists: AAA

The Comtesse de Bournazel has been producing consistently fine and elegant Sauternes since the late 1980s. The château itself is registered as a national monument and is open to the public. The wine increasingly shows a rich opulent character as well as an intense fragrance. It perfectly balances weight and finesse. It was very good in 1997 and 98 was of very good ★★★★ quality. 2001 looks equally promising. A decent white Graves, M de Malle, is also made as well as a red, Château de Cardaillan. (DM)

● **Château de Malle** Sauternes★★★★ £E

CH. MARGAUX Margaux 1er CC www.chateau-margaux.com

Mentzelopoulos family 33460 Margaux
UK stockists: AAA

Corinne Mentzelopoulos and general manager Paul Pontallier have crafted truly great red Bordeaux now for upwards of 2 decades. The wine is not only remarkably elegant, with the unmistakably intense perfume of the appellation,

45

but also enormously rich. Loaded with dense but supple tannins, Margaux is remarkably powerful and needs a minimum of 10–12 years' ageing to begin to reveal itself. Meticulous care in the vineyard and at harvest, along with traditional vinification in wooden fermenters, defines the style and quality. The second label, Pavillon Rouge, ensures the integrity of the Grand Vin but is itself regularly very impressive. As well as the 78ha of red varieties planted there are some 12ha of Sauvignon Blanc, which produce an intense floral, grassy and complex white sold under the humble Bordeaux AC. Among the great years are 2000, 99, 96, 95, 90, 86, 83, 82, 79 and 78. It was very uneven prior to this and the Mentzelopoulos family involvement. 1961, good for most other top Bordeaux châteaux, was disappointing. (DM)

● **Château Margaux** Margaux✪✪✪✪✪ £H
● **Pavillon Rouge de Château Margaux**★★★★ £F
O **Pavillon Blanc de Château Margaux** Bordeaux★★★★★ £F

MAROJALLIA   Margaux

Philippe Procheron   33460 Arsac
UK stockists:AAA

Tiny property and vineyard with an exceptional *terroir*, located in the commune of Arsac close to Château du TERTRE. There are just 2.5ha under vine on superbly drained deep gravel soils. Vineyard management includes leaf removal, green-harvesting prior to *veraison* and of course hand-picking and hand-sorting. The Grand Vin is aged solely in new oak and comes from a blend of Cabernet Sauvignon (60%) and Merlot (40%). Very lush and rich, with a sumptuous texture and impressive depth, the wine will drink extremely well with 5 or so years' ageing. The second wine, Clos Margalaine, is also aged in 100% new wood. It is more obviously fleshy and forward and is very impressive as a second label. (DM)

● **Marojallia** Margaux★★★★★ £H ● **Clos Margalaine** Margaux★★★★ £E

CH. MARQUIS DE TERME   Margaux   4ème CC

Sénéclauze family   33460 Margaux
UK stockists:AAA

This château has been in the hands of the Sénéclauze family since 1935 and tradition and loyalty are in full sway, shown by the fact that in the period of their ownership the estate has had only 2 managers. But a continuing programme of modernisation has ensured that the current offerings are holding their own with more overtly progressive operations. This property was in the past considered a bit too butch for the appellation, but its profile is more acceptable to modern tastes and recent vintages have certainly shown plenty of fruit beneath the tannins. Marquis de Terme has always been a slow-maturing wine and needs patient cellaring. (NB)

● **Château Marquis de Terme** Margaux★★★ £D

CLOS MARSALETTE   Pessac-Léognan CC

Comte S. von Neipperg, F. Boutemy & J.P. Sarpoulet 33850 Léognan
UK stockists: AAA

Small, potentially excellent property now with involvement from Stéphan von Neipperg, who also owns CANON-LA-GAFFELIÈRE, d'AIGUILHE and La MONDOTTE. The vineyards have an excellent exposure and are planted in fine, well-drained gravel soils. Just under 3,000 cases a year of red are made and less than 400 cases of a very rare white. The 2004 red seems to be a serious step forward. A 50/50 blend of Merlot and Cabernet Sauvignon aged in 25% new wood, the wine has a rich and supple texture and much finer tannins than many from this AC in the vintage. Expect this to develop very well in the medium term. (DM)

● **Clos Marsalette** Pessac-Léognan★★★★ £E

CH. MAYNE LALANDE   Listrac-Médoc

Bernard Lartigue   33480 Listrac-Médoc
UK stockists: AAA

Small 17 he Listrac property producing increasingly impressive and structured
examples of this lesser appellation. The vineyards are planted to a combination
of Cabernet Sauvignon (45%), Merlot a whopping 45% also and 5% each of
Petit Verdot and Cabernet Franc. Despite this the wine is firm, sturdy and
marked by an intense cedary rather than plummy character. The 2000 here was
particularly good, clearly ★★★, expect recent vintages to develop well in bottle
for 5–7 years. The special limited cuvée Alice-Jeanne offers extra depth and
impressive concentration. (DM)

● **Château Mayne Lalande** Listrac-Médoc★★ £C Alice-Jeanne★★★ £E

MA VÉRITÉ   Haut-Médoc

Gérard Depardieu   c/o Terroirs d'Exception, 33330 Saint-Christophe des Bardes
Produced from a tiny 2-ha vineyard, this is marketed along with a number of
other properties throughout the region including LA SERÉNITÉ, PASSION DU
PRIEURÉ MALESAN and LA CROIX DE PEYROLIE as part of the Terroirs
d'Exception range by Bernard Magrez. The clay and limestone soils are planted
to a mix of 55% Cabernet Sauvignon, 40% Merlot and the balance Cabernet
Franc and Petit Verdot. Yields are kept very low at less than 20hl/ha and leaf
plucking and *vendange vert* are practised in the vineyard. Richly textured with
considerable extract, the wine nevertheless possesses an elegant cedary character
as well as offering copious quantities of ripe cassis and spicy new oak. It will
benefit from 5 or 6 years' ageing. (DM)

● **Ma Vérité** Haut-Médoc★★★★ £F

CH. LA MISSION HAUT-BRION   www.haut-brion.com

Domaine Clarence Dillon   33608 Pessac
UK stockists: AAA

Like HAUT-BRION, LAVILLE HAUT-BRION and LA TOUR-HAUT-BRION this
property is owned by the Domaine Clarence Dillon. La Tour-Haut-Brion used
to be the second wine at La Mission but is now handled as its own separate
vineyard and property. La Mission is only surpassed among Graves reds by
Haut-Brion itself. This is a massive, dense and powerful red. Dark, mineral and
black fruits are underpinned by cedar and oak. While the wine perhaps lacks
the absolute refinement of its illustrious stablemate, it hasn't fallen far short and
is on occasion the more impressive of the 2. 2000, 98 and 95 are recent
benchmarks and 90, 89, 82, 78 and 75 were all of legendary quality. The
second wine, La Chapelle de la Mission Haut-Brion, is a ★★★★ wine in the
ripest years. (DM)

● **Château la Mission Haut-Brion** Pessac-Léognan✪✪✪✪✪ £H

CH. MONTROSE   Saint-Estèphe 2ème CC

Charmolüe family   33180 Saint-Estèphe
UK stockists: AAA

This 68-ha property produces around 28,000 cases of exceptional Saint-
Estèphe a year. The property is second only behind fellow Second Growth COS
D'ESTOURNEL in the appellation hierarchy. These are massive, powerful,
brooding wines – dense, tannic and long-lived. Sometimes the fruit struggles to
emerge through the iron fist in which it is enveloped. Generally though, in the
last decade the wine has become suppler and possesses greater harmony and it

47

was consistently good through the 1990s. 1990 and 95 suggest ✪✪✪✪✪ and 2000 may well turn out the same. La Dame de Montrose is an impressive second wine. (DM)

● **Château Montrose** Saint-Estèphe★★★★★ £F La Dame de Montrose★★★ £E

CH. MOUTON-ROTHSCHILD   Pauillac 1er CC   www.bpdr.com
Baron Philippe de Rothschild SA   33250 Pauillac
UK stockists: AAA

Unique among the First Growths of Bordeaux in that the wine was elevated to its current classification only in 1973, after the successful lobbying of Baron Philippe de Rothschild. The wine is the most opulent and approachable of the top growths, full of dark cassis and cigar box aromas, supported by powerful, supple tannin. Stunning wine was produced in 1982 and 86 but there was some loss of form in the late 80s and early 90s. However, 1996, 98, 99 and 00 have all been back among the very best and 2003 may be of a similar calibre. The second wine is Le Petit Mouton, and a small amount of a premium white Aile d'Argent is also produced. There is a sizeable merchant business owned by Baronne Philippine de Rothschild, producing a range of pretty ordinary generic AC labels along with the dreary Mouton Cadet. Of greater interest are the 2 premium partnerships of OPUS ONE with the ROBERT MONDAVI winery in California, now owned by Constellation and ALMAVIVA with CONCHA Y TORO in Chile. (DM)

● **Château Mouton-Rothschild** Pauillac✪✪✪✪✪ £H

CH. NAIRAC   Barsac 2ème CC
Nicolas Tari-Heeter   33720 Barsac
UK stockists: AAA

A small property of just some 17ha with annual production of barely more than 1,000 cases. The wine often outperforms its Second Growth status. Always picked very ripe, it gains real structure from a high proportion of new oak used for ageing. At times this can seem almost overpowering in its youth but given patience the wine can show a marvellous balance of intense, peachy botrytised fruit and almost sweet vanilla oak. Definitely cellar for 6 or 7 years. (DM)

● **Château Nairac** Barsac★★★★ £E

CH. LES ORMES DE PEZ   Saint-Estèphe   www.ormesdepez.com
Jean-Michel Cazes   33180 Saint-Estèphe
UK stockists: AAA

Les Ormes de Pez is one of the most underrated wines in the Médoc. It is a chunky, dense, plummy wine, normally showing a fair amount of upfront fruit. Jean-Michel Cazes and his team have got just about the maximum potential from this property, the price is fair and it makes solid drinking value. (NB)

● **Château Les Ormes de Pez** Saint-Estèphe★★★ £C

CH. PALMER   Margaux 3ème CC   www.chateau-palmer.com
Mahler Besse/Sichel Families   Cantenac, 33460 Margaux
UK stockists: AAA

This marvellous property is often thought of as a Second Growth and for a period before the Mentzelopoulos years at Château MARGAUX it was also the benchmark for the AC. At its best the wine displays not only the perfume of the appellation but ripe, powerful, almost sumptuous dark fruit. In part this must be down to the very high proportion of Merlot planted, at 47% the same as Cabernet Sauvignon. The second wine, Alter Ego de Palmer, tends to have an even higher proportion of Merlot in the final blend. 2000, 99, 98, 96 and

95 Palmer were of a very high standard and the most recent vintages have similar promise. Of the great years here, 89 and 83 also stand out as do the earlier years of 70, 66 and 61. (DM)

● **Château Palmer** Margaux★★★★★ £G

CH. PAPE-CLÉMENT Pessac-Léognan CC www.pape-clement .com

Léo Montagne/Bernard Magrez 216 Av. du Dr-Nancel-Pénard, 33650 Martillac
UK stockists: AAA

Excellent 32.5-ha property dominated by red vine plantings and like Haut-Brion engulfed by the suburbs of Bordeaux. The white varieties account for a mere 2.5ha with 10% of this being Muscadelle. Both wines are rich and powerful and the red has real density and grip but remains approachable and harmonious. The tiny production of white has an elegant, intense mineral and citrus streak adding to its complexity and all nicely supported by sufficient creamy new oak. Generally very good throughout the 1990s and particularly after 1995. The red in 98, 99 and 2000 was comfortably worth ★★★★★ and 2003 and 2004 have real potential. (DM)

● **Château Pape-Clément** Pessac-Léognan★★★★★ £F
● **Prelude de Pape-Clément** Pessac-Léognan★★★ £C
O **Château Pape-Clément** Pessac-Léognan★★★★ £E

CH. PEYRABON Haut-Médoc

Jacques Babeau 33250 Saint-Sauveur-en-Médoc
UK stockists: BBR,F&R

Sizeable Cru Bourgeois Haut-Médoc property producing close to 30,000 cases a year. Most comes from close to 30ha in the Haut-Médoc but there is also a limited volume of Pauillac. Both represent excellent-value modern, stylish, cedary claret. The Haut-Médoc typically blends Cabernet Sauvignon, Merlot and Cabernet Franc, while the Pauillac often has a hint of Petit Verdot also. The Fleur Peyrabon just has that added dimension with hints of cassis and spice adding a little extra complexity. Both wines are likely to add further complexity with 5 or 6 years' cellaring. (DM)

● **Château Peyrabon** La Fleur Peyrabon Pauillac★★★ £D
● **Château Peyrabon** Haut Médoc★★ £C

CH. PHELAN-SEGUR Saint-Estèphe www.chateauphelansegur.com

Thierry Gardiner 33180 Saint-Estèphe
UK stockists:AAA

One of the most consistent performers in the Médoc, this château was among only 9 upgraded in the 2004 Cru Bourgeois reclassification to Exceptionnel status. The Gardiners have worked hard to put behind them some disastrous vintages in the early 80s and now rate among the best in the *bourgeois* division of the Bordeaux hierarchy. The wine has softer tannins than one would expect from a Saint-Estèphe and is quite elegant if lacking a little in character. (NB)

● **Château Phelan-Segur** Saint-Estèphe★★★ £D

CH. PIBRAN Pauillac

AXA Millésimes 33250 Saint-Sauveur-en-Médoc
UK stockists:AAA

From the same stable as PICHON-LONGUEVILLE, this relatively small Pauillac Cru Bourgeois consists of 17ha and is planted to a mix of 54% Merlot, 45% Cabernet Sauvignon and just 1% Petit Verdot. Quality continues to improve as the vineyard becomes more mature – the current vine age is 30 years. Understandably, given the grape blend here, the wine is sweet-fruited and richly textured with supple, quite soft tannins, but the cassis character of the appellation still shines through. Cellaring for 5 or 6 years will provide increased

49

complexity. (DM)

● **Château Pibran** Pauillac★★★ £E

CH. PICHON-LONGUEVILLE   Pauillac 2ème CC

AXA Millésimes   33250 Pauillac
UK stockists: AAA

Sizeable Second Growth with some 73ha under vine, bought in 1987 by AXA Millésimes – the fine-wine arm of the AXA insurance company. Jean-Michel Cazes, who owns Château LYNCH-BAGES, took over the management of the Bordeaux AXA operation and quality quickly improved with very successful vintages in 1989 and 90. These are world-class, ✪✪✪✪ wines: deep, dark, powerful Pauillac but very finely balanced. Now run and managed by Christian Seely, quality in the late 90s has not been at quite the same heady heights; although the most recent vintages look to be solidly back on form. (DM)

● **Château Pichon-Longueville** Pauillac★★★★★ £F

CH. PICHON-LONGUEVILLE-LALANDE   Pauillac 2ème CC

Lencquesaing family   33250 Pauillac
UK stockists: AAA

A property marked by its rich, elegant, almost sumptuous style of wine. It is no surprise that there are considerable plantings of Merlot (35%). The balance is Cabernet Sauvignon (45%), Cabernet Franc (12%) and a relatively whopping 8% of very old Petit Verdot. The vineyards border Saint-Julien and this also helps contribute to the wine's intense, fragrant and complex style. However, there have been some strange variations in quality over the last couple of decades. Vintages of the late 1990s have been disappointing, whereas 1995 and 96 were magnificent, clear ✪✪✪✪✪ wines. 2000 and 2001 look to be back in the top division. Other exceptional years have included 86, 83 and, of course, the legendary 82. Réserve de la Comtesse is the second wine. (DM)

● **Château Pichon-Longueville-Lalande** Pauillac★★★★★ £G
● **Réserve de la Comtesse**★★ £E

CH. PONTAC MONPLAISIR   Pessac-Léognan CC

Alain Maufras   33140 Villenave d'Ornon

This is a very small estate producing some classy wines. It can be difficult to find but invariably gives good value for money. There are 9ha of red grapes, planted 60% Merlot and 40% Cabernet Sauvignon, and just 2ha of white in the same proportions respectively of Sauvignon and Sémillon. The white shows good, easy-drinking finesse with a good deal of complexity, whilst the red has good fruit and soft tannins, if perhaps lacking a little in weight. Nevertheless, both wines possess excellent balance and are fairly priced. (NB)

● **Château Pontac Monplaisir** Pessac-Léognan★★★ £C
○ **Château Pontac Monplaisir** Pessac-Léognan★★★ £C

CH. PONTET-CANET   Pauillac 5ème CC   www.pontet-canet.com

Tesseron Family   33250 Pauillac
UK stockists: AAA

This property has been in the ownership of the Tesseron Family, who also own Château LAFON-ROCHET, for over 2 decades. They have been responsible for bringing it up to its current level, where it has generally justified its Fifth Growth status. Produced from vineyards planted on some of the best gravel soils of the appellation, at its peak it is exactly what you think of as quintessential Pauillac – big, powerful and dense with supple, well-rounded tannin and an intense fragrance of cassis and cedar. 1989 saw a significant upturn in quality. After the generally poor years between 1991 and 93, really

only 97 has been lighter and less impressive, indeed 00 and 99 clearly rated
★★★★ and 2003 and 2004 look to be equally good. (DM)

● **Château Pontet-Canet** Pauillac★★★ £F

CH. POTENSAC Médoc www.chateau-potensac.com
Delon family   33340 Ordonnac
UK stockists: AAA

Under the same ownership as LÉOVILLE-LAS-CASES, this is without doubt the
finest property sold as Médoc AC and now classified as a Cru Bourgeois
Exceptionnel. The now very old vines are planted on a mix of alluvial gravel
and clay soils. The wine is consistently excellent: ripe but sufficiently firm, with
a hint of new wood (about 20%) providing additional depth. Bottled without
filtration it is better with 5 years' cellaring. Both 2000 and 96 are particularly
impressive. All in all this is a very good-value claret. The second wine is
Chapelle de Potensac. (DM)

● **Château Potensac** Médoc★★★ £D

CH. POUJEAUX Moulis www.chateaupoujeaux.com
Theil family   33480 Moulis-en-Médoc
UK stockists: AAA

Along with CHASSE-SPLEEN, this is one of the 2 best wines in the Moulis AC.
It has performed with an impressive consistency throughout the last 10 years
and more. There are 53ha under vine here, with Cabernet Sauvignon
accounting for slightly more of the vineyard than Merlot. As with most
quality-conscious wine producers, there is a dedication in the vineyard and
cellar which contributes to the final wine. The style is rich and sumptuous with
a hint of vanilla from its 12 months of oak-ageing. Handling is kept to a
minimum, with just egg-white fining and no filtration. A further notch up
from 1996, including 97. (DM)

● **Château Poujeaux** Moulis★★★ £E

CH. PREUILLAC Médoc www.chateau-preuillac.com
Jean-Christophe Mau   33340 Lesparre

Jean-Christophe Mau bought this neglected and run-down château in 1999
and has struggled to bring it back to its former glory despite massive
investment in the vineyard and the winery. The vineyard has 30ha of vines in a
single stretch, with gravelly hilltops planted to 50% Merlot, 48% Cabernet
Sauvignon and 2% Cabernet Franc. The appointment of Stéphane
Derenoncourt as consultant enologist in 2003 has resulted in a quantum leap
in quality. The soft and silky palate now found is a result of the grapes being
picked by hand and sorted in the vineyard. Each varietal and each plot is
separately vinified in 180-hl temperature-controlled vats for up to 5 weeks
before the wine is run off into barrels to be matured for 12 months. A slight
hint of leafiness on the palate shows that there is still further work to be done,
particularly in the vineyards. One to watch. (NB)

● **Château Preuillac** Médoc★★★ £C

CH. PRIEURÉ-LICHINE Margaux 4ème CC prieure.lichine@wanadoo.fr
Ballande family   34 Avenue de la Cinquième République, 33460 Cantenac
UK stockists: AAA

The Ballandes, who run the *négociant* operation the Ballande group, purchased
this property from the Lichine family in 1999. Unusually there are parcels of
vineyard spread throughout the appellation. There has been consultancy input
from Michel Rolland as well as the talented young enologist Stéphane
Derenoncourt. The wine is increasingly sumptuous and supple. This is an

51

ambitious operation and it will be interesting to see how quality develops over the next 5 years or so. The wine showed good potential in 1996, 98 and 00 and this standard looks likely to be maintained. (DM)

● **Château Prieuré-Lichine** Margaux★★★ £E

CH. RABAUD-PROMIS   Sauternes 1er CC

Philippe Dejean   33210 Bommes
UK stockists: AAA

After a long period in the doldrums, this 33-ha property has now been making impressive Sauternes for well more than a decade. This is a full, rich and honeyed wine with not only impressive depth, concentration and the structure to age very well but also real balance and harmony. It can be very intense and stylish, particularly in top years. Very impressive since 1994 and prior to that 90, 89 and 88 are very good indeed. (DM)

O **Château Rabaud-Promis** Sauternes★★★★ £F

CH. RAUZAN-SÉGLA   Margaux 2ème CC

Wertheimer family   33460 Margaux
UK stockists: AAA

This château was acquired by the Wertheimers, who own the Chanel perfume business, in 1994 and a large amount of investment has been put into the property since then. They also now own Château CANON in Saint-Emilion. Prior to the change of ownership the property performed remarkably well in the run of vintages from 1988 to 90 but this wasn't always so. Vinification is now very modern, using temperature-controlled stainless steel, and ageing is in 60% new oak for 18 months. The wine has a fine, elegant texture and displays a complex array of dark fruits and cedar. There is surprising tannin here, though, and the wine will improve with at least 5 or 6 years' cellaring. It has been very consistent since 1995, with the exception of 97 which was a disappointment. (DM)

● **Château Rauzan-Ségla** Margaux ★★★★ £F

CH. RAYMOND-LAFON   Sauternes   www.chateau-raymond-lafon.fr

Meslier family   33210 Sauternes
UK stockists: AAA

The production is tiny at just over 1,600 cases a year from the 18ha of vineyard. The blend is 80% Sémillon with the balance Sauvignon Blanc and no Muscadelle. Not a Classed Growth, Raymond-Lafon is located right next to Yquem and has consistently produced wines in the great years of the last 2 decades which rival all but the absolute best in Sauternes. This has been achieved through a dedicated approach in the vineyard, tiny yields of just 8.5hl/ha, careful and repeated selective harvesting (*tris*) and extensive use of new oak in the cellar. The wine is barrel-fermented and aged for up to 3 years in wood. (DM)

O **Château Raymond-Lafon** Sauternes★★★★★ £F

CH. DE RAYNE-VIGNEAU   Sauternes 1er CC

SC Ch. de Rayne-Vigneau   109. Rue Achard, BP 154, 33042 Bordeaux
UK stockists: **VOC**

This relatively sizeable property has some 80ha of vineyards. It is under the same ownership as Château GRAND-PUY-DUCASSE in Pauillac. The gravel soils here suggest a real potential to the *terroir* that has not yet fully been realised. However, like so many Sauternes châteaux, its reputation has improved over the last 2 decades. The wine is characterised by its elegant and complex botrytised fruit, with a tight, restrained structure. These are not overfull, super-weighty wines but at their best are impressively refined and   intense. (DM)

O **Château de Rayne-Vigneau** Sauternes★★★ £E

CH. RIEUSSEC   Sauternes 1er CC   www.lafite.com

Domaines Baron de Rothschild   33210 Fargues-de-Langon
UK stockists: AAA

Under the same ownership as LAFITE-ROTHSCHILD, this Sauternes is generally regarded as being second only in weight and power to YQUEM. It has generally performed at that level since 1995 and particularly during the trio of great Sauternes years from 88 to 90. Aged in a high proportion of new oak it is almost always a powerful, very rich, opulent but classically structured wine in need of 8–10 years' ageing, often longer in truly great vintages. (DM)

O **Château Rieussec** Sauternes✪✪✪✪✪ £F

CH. ROLLAN-DE-BY   Médoc   www.rollandeby.com

Jean Guyon   7 Route Rollan-de-By, 33340 Bégadan
UK stockists: AAA

This 37-ha property has performed with distinction throughout the past decade and is a shining light for other producers in the outlying areas of the Médoc. The vineyard is planted with a sizeable 70% Merlot and this, allied to the judicious use of new oak, accounts for the ripe, almost lush, plump and approachable fruit style. Haut-Condissas is a premium label with more Cabernet Sauvignon in the blend. (DM)

Château Rollan-de-By
● **Château Rollan-de-By** Médoc★★★ £D
Château Haut-Condissas
● **Château Haut-Condissas** Médoc★★★★ £E

CH. SAINT-PIERRE   Saint-Julien 2ème CC

Triaud family   33250 Saint-Julien-Beychevelle
UK stockists: N&P

This property was purchased in 1981 by the late Henri Martin (the former owner of GLORIA) and is now run by his daughter, Françoise Triaud. Although the wine has been consistently good throughout the last 10 years, it has never quite achieved the potential that its classification suggests. The approach to vinification is always meticulous, with a rigorous selection pre-fermentation and judicious use of new oak. The wine was certainly above average in 1990 and should achieve similar heights again with the fine 2000 vintage. (DM)

● **Château Saint-Pierre** Saint-Julien★★★ £E

CH. SÉNÉJAC   Haut-Médoc

Thierry & Lorraine Rustmann   33290 Pian-Médoc
UK stockists: AAA

Relatively sizeable Haut-Médoc property with 34ha under vine, particularly noted for its now well-established, densely structured special *cuvée* Karolus. The vineyard comprises Cabernet Sauvignon (60%), Merlot (25%), Cabernet Franc (14%) and Petit Verdot (just 1%). The regular bottling has been increasingly good across recent vintages and is produced in a lighter style but with impressive cedary complexity and persistence of fruit. The Karolus is markedly more structured, not least for the use of 100% Cabernet Sauvignon. The new oak is apparent but well integrated and the wine is suppler and better balanced

53

than many a varietal example from the New World. Give it 6 or 7 years. (DM)

● **Château Sénéjac** Haut-Médoc★★★ £D   Haut-Médoc Karolus★★★★ £F

CH. SIGALAS-RABAUD   Sauternes 1er CC

Lambert des Granges family   33210 Bommes
UK stockists: AAA

This is the smaller part of the original Château Rabaud, which was divided nearly a century ago. The other half is RABAUD-PROMIS and both are Sauternes First Growths. The wine is very rich and gloriously honeyed and can show very marked botrytis but it is still refined and very elegant. Indeed the wine has been impressive for years and was one of the few properties to perform well in the 1960s and 70s, a period of recession in the appellation. The great vintages in these decades can at least be approached with some optimism. More recently 2001, 99, 98, 97 and 96 were all on top form and are nudging ★★★★★, as are the great trio of 88, 89 and 90. (DM)

O **Château Sigalas-Rabaud** Sauternes★★★★ £F

CH. SIRAN   Margaux   www.chateausiran.com

William Miailhe   Labarde, 33460 Margaux
UK stockists: AAA

The vineyard of Château Siran consists of 40ha in all, of which 24ha are in Margaux. A further 15ha qualify as Bordeaux Supérieur and 1ha as Haut-Médoc. It is planted to 45% Cabernet Sauvignon, 35% Merlot, 12% Petit Verdot and 8% Cabernet Franc. Since 1995 the winemaking has been guided by Michel Rolland and a fair degree of consistency has been achieved. Typically Margaux, this has never been a blockbuster wine, but one that regularly affords a good price/quality ratio. Recent vintages have shown more suppleness and finesse than previously, which augurs well for the future. Like MOUTON-ROTHSCHILD, the label displays a different painting from a well-known artist each year. The second wine, S de Siran, is made from younger Margaux vines (8–18 year old). (NB)

● **Château Siran** Margaux★★★ £C

CH. SMITH HAUT LAFITTE   Pessac-Léognan CC

Daniel & Florence Cathiard   33650 Martillac
UK stockists: AAA

The wines here under the current ownership are now very good. Around 80% of the production is red, with a mix of 55% Cabernet Sauvignon, 35% Merlot and the balance Cabernet Franc. The white is dominated by Sauvignon Blanc but there is a sprinkling of Sémillon and more unusually Sauvignon Gris (similar in flavour to Sauvignon Blanc but with a slight pink tinge to its skin). The red is lighter in style than some of its neighbours but now possesses impressive depth. The white is fermented relatively cool to retain a marked floral, herbal core and is aged in 50% new oak. Neither wine is filtered and both have performed admirably since 1995, 97 being a touch weak for the red, but 2000 was on the cusp of ★★★★★ for both red and white. (DM)

● **Château Smith Haut Lafitte** Pessac-Léognan★★★★ £F
O **Château Smith Haut Lafitte** Pessac-Léognan★★★★ £F

CH. SOCIANDO-MALLET   Haut-Médoc

Jean Gautreau   33180 Saint-Seurin-de-Cadourne
UK stockists: AAA

This is now undoubtedly the most impressive estate in the Haut-Médoc, a title that at one stage would almost invariably have been given to La LAGUNE. Quality here since 1995 has been good to very good. Perhaps in 97 and 98 it did not quite rate ★★★★ but the wines are impressive dark, powerful and very ageworthy all the same. The style is of a true *vin de garde*, in part due to the well-drained gravel soils, which produce supple but youthfully firm, powerful tannins. Impressive earlier vintages include 1990, 89 and the classic 82. The second wine is Demoiselle, which can be good. (DM)

● **Château Sociando-Mallet** Haut-Médoc★★★★ £E

CH. SUDUIRAUT   Sauternes 1er CC   www.suduiraut.com

AXA Millésimes   33210 Preignac
UK stockists: AAA

More care has been taken with harvesting at this property which neighbours YQUEM since its purchase by AXA in 1992. The fruit is now picked more selectively and late enough to maximise the effect of noble rot. As a result the wine has become increasingly full and rich. It is aged for 18–24 months in barrel, further adding to its impressive depth and concentration. It was very good in 1989 and 90 as well as more recently in 95, 96 and 97. 2003 and particularly 2001 are also extremely promising. The second wine, Castelnau de Suduiraut, can be of sound quality and ensures the integrity of the Grand Vin. (DM)

O **Château Suduiraut** Sauternes★★★★★ £F

CH. TALBOT   Saint-Julien 2ème CC   www.chateau-talbot.com

Lorraine Rustmann & Nancy Bignon   33250 Saint-Julien-Beychevelle
UK stockists: AAA

Originally a Cordier *négociant* property, Talbot has been retained by members of the family and the quality of the Grand Vin has remained reasonably consistent, particularly after 1995. It is now very international in styled and quite different to some of the very firm earlier examples under Cordier ownership. 1998, 00 and 01 were all very good and 03 looks to be promising. The second wine, Connetable Talbot, has been good in the better years and there is a small amount of a white, Caillou Blanc, produced under the Bordeaux AC. This used to be variable with marked sulphur but a more modern approach to its vinification is now undertaken with better results. (DM)

● **Château Talbot** Saint-Julien★★★ £F

CH. DU TERTRE   Margaux 5ème CC

Eric Albada Jedgersma   Chemin de Ligondras, 33460 Arsac
UK stockists: AAA

Eric Albada Jedgersma and his wife also own the revitalised Château GISCOURS, another Classed Growth Margaux property. While not the size of its sister château, du Tertre is by no means small with 50ha under vine, planted in sandy gravel soils in the commune of Arsac. Cabernet Sauvignon accounts for a mere 40% of the vineyard, with 35% Merlot, 20% Cabernet Franc and the balance a small amount of Petit Verdot. Its only since the 1999 vintage that the property has begun to show its true worth but du Tertre is one of the most beguiling and perfumed of all Margaux reds. Cellaring for 6 or more years will result in further complexity. (DM)

● **Château du Tertre** Margaux★★★★ £F

CH. LA TOUR BLANCHE   Sauternes 1er CC

Ministère de l'Agriculture   33210 Bommes
UK stockists: Col

There are a total of some 40ha under vine at this property run by the Ministry of Agriculture and although this is also an agricultural school very high

55

standards are maintained. The vineyards are particularly well sited and result in a big, full-bodied Sauternes produced with marked botrytis and well-judged new oak. The wines have real intensity and power. 1998, 97 and 96 have all been good and the trio of 88, 89 and 90 were also excellent. (DM)

O **Château la Tour Blanche** Sauternes★★★★ £F

CH. LA TOUR HAUT-BRION   Pessac-Léognan CC

Domaine Clarence Dillon   33608 Pessac
UK stockists: BBR,N&P,Sec,Tur

Originally the second wine at LA MISSION HAUT-BRION, this property stands alone with its own identity now that the vineyard is ageing. It neighbours its former big brother and although the wines are still overshadowed by the powerful dense style of La Mission they are becoming increasingly impressive in their own right. Some 80% of the vineyard is planted to Cabernet Sauvignon and Cabernet Franc, resulting in a very sturdy style in the wine's youth. 1995 and 98 were both very impressive and 00 looks to have equal potential. (DM)

● **Château la Tour Haut-Brion** Pessac-Léognan★★★★ £F

VIEUX CHÂTEAU GAUBERT   Graves

Dominique Haverlan   33640 Portets
UK stockists: BBR,CTy

One of the best properties in the Graves AC and a model for many less than perfect performers in the supposedly superior Pessac-Léognan. Both red and white are produced. The red is a 50/50 blend of Cabernet Sauvignon and Merlot and this is emphasised in its vibrant dark plummy fruit character. Structure and depth are lent by an extended fermentation and maceration of 15–20 days and 12 months in 40% new wood. The white, from a roughly equal blend of Sémillon and Sauvignon Blanc, is barrel-fermented in 60% new oak and aged on lees with *bâtonnage*. Nonetheless it is remarkably restrained with intense citrus and lightly grassy aromas subtly supported by sophisticated oak. It will be all the better for 2 or 3 years' ageing in bottle. (DM)

● **Vieux Château Gaubert** Graves★★★ £C
O **Vieux Château Gaubert** Graves★★★ £C

CH. VIEUX ROBIN   Médoc

Maryse Roba   33340 Bégadan
UK stockists: N&P

Vieux Robin is located in the north of the Médoc peninsula and the property has now been classified as a Cru Bourgeois Supérieur. There are 18ha under vine and the vineyard is planted to a combination of Cabernet Sauvignon (60%) and Merlot (35%), with the remaining 5% split between Cabernet Franc and Petit Verdot. The vineyard age of around 40 years is a major contributor to the quality. The regular Médoc is straightforward, a relatively simple fruit-driven style. The Bois de Lunier label is a notch up: the vines are over 40 years old, the wine is aged in new oak (40%) and part of the malolactic takes place in barrel. There is also a limited-release Collection bottling selected from the very best plots. White Blanc de Lunier is produced from old-vine Sauvignon Blanc vinified and matured in 50% new wood. (DM)

● **Château Vieux Robin** Médoc★★ £C Médoc Bois de Lunier★★★ £D

CH. VILLA BEL AIR   Graves   www.villabelair.com

Jean-Michel Cazes   33650 Saint-Morillon
UK stockists: **PFx**,BBR,Far,Sec,F&R

Reliable Graves property producing around 12,000 cases each of red and white Graves. The property was taken over by Jean-Michel Cazes in 1990 and the cellars were modernised and the winemaking brought up to speed. Barrel-fermentation for the white and a red which emphasises attractive dark, black fruit in a supple, approachable style are the keys here. Generally good in 2000, 99 and 98 although prices do seem to be creeping up as well. (DM)

● **Château Villa Bel Air** Graves★★ £C
O **Château Villa Bel Air** Graves★★ £C

CH. D'YQUEM Sauternes 1er GCC

LVMH 33210 Sauternes
UK stockists: **AAA**

Arguably the greatest sweet wine in the world. Owned by the Lur Saluces family for more than 2 centuries, it was purchased by LVMH in 1999. Alexandre de Lur Saluces continues to make the wine. There are 103ha under vine but the vineyards have a superb exposure in the centre of the appellation and enjoy an ideal mix of morning mist and warm sunshine. With a sizeable production of around 8,000 cases a year it is certain that, while occasional TBAs from Germany or SGNs from Alsace might rival it for sheer depth, dimension and fruit intensity, they never will match the volume produced at Yquem. The same remarkable level of attention is spent producing the wine, with harvesting not so much by *tris* but more berry by berry and at a microscopic yield. New oak is used throughout and the wine is bottled without filtration after spending more than 3 years in cask. These are wines of supreme quality that will last for half a century or more, always outstanding in top years. (DM)

O **Château d'Yquem** Sauternes✪✪✪✪✪ £H

OTHER WINES OF NOTE

CH. BEAUMONT ● Haut-Médoc★★ £C
CH. BEL-AIR ● Saint-Estèphe★ £C
CH. BELLE VUE ● Haut-Médoc★ £C
CH. BELLEVUE DE TAYAC ● Margaux★★★ £C
CH. BISTON-BRILLETTE ● Moulis★★ £C
CH. BERNADOTTE ● Haut-Médoc★★ £C
CH. BOURNAC ● Médoc★★ £C
CH. BOUSCAUT ● Pessac-Léognan★★ £E O Pessac-Léognan★★ £D
CH. CANTELYS ● Pessac-Léognan★★ £C O Pessac-Léognan★★ £C
CH. CITRAN ● Haut-Médoc★★ £C
CH. CLAUZET ● Saint-Estèphe★★ £D
CH. CLÉMENT PICHON ● Haut-Médoc★★ £C
CH. CRABITEY ● Graves★★ £C
CH. COUFRAN ● Haut-Médoc★★ £C
CRU BARRÉJATS O Sauternes★★★ £F
CH. DE CRUZEAU ● Pessac-Léognan £D O Pessac-Léognan £D
CH. DESMIRAIL ● Margaux★★★ £E
CH. DURFORT-VIVENS ● Margaux★★★ £E
CH. DES EYRINS ● Margaux★★ £C
CH. FERRAN ● Pessac-Léognan★★ £C O Pessac-Léognan★★ £C
CH. FONBADET ● Pauillac★ £D
CH. FONRÉAUD ● Listrac★ £C
CH. FOURCAS-DUPRÉ ● Listrac★★ £C
CH. FOURCAS-HOSTEN ● Listrac★ £C
CH. LA GARDE ● Pessac-Léognan★ £C O Pessac-Léognan★★ £C
CH. GRAND-PUY-DUCASSE ● Pauillac★★ £E
CH. LES GRANDS CHÊNES ● Médoc★ £D Prestige★★ £D
CH. GREYSAC ● Médoc★★ £C
CH. HAUT-BAGES-LIBÉRAL ● Pauillac★★£D
CH. HAUT BEASÉJOUR ● Saint-Estèphe★★ £C

57

CH. HAUT-BERGERON ○ Sauternes★★ £E
CH. LES JUSTICES ○ Sauternes★★★ £E
CH. LABÉGORCE-ZÉDÉ ● Margaux★★ £E
CH. LALANDE DE GRAVELONGUE ● Médoc★ £C
● **Médoc** Croix de Gravelongue★★ £D
LA PATACHE ● Médoc★★ £C
CH. DE LAMARQUE ● Haut-Médoc★ £C
CH. LA TOUR DE BY ● Médoc★ £C
CH. LILIAN-LADOUYS ● Saint-Estèphe★★ £D
CH. LIOT ○ Barsac★★ £D
CH. LIVERSAN ● Haut-Médoc★★ £C
CH. LOUSTEAUNEUF ● Médoc★★ £C
CH. MALESCASSE ● Haut-Médoc★ £C
CH. MARBUZET ● Saint-Estèphe★★ £C
CH. MAUCAILLOU ● Moulis★★ £C
CH. MEYNEY ● Saint-Estèphe★★ £D
CH. MILLE-ROSES ● Haut-Médoc★★ £C
CH. MONBRISON ● Margaux★★ £D
CH MOULIN DE LA ROSE ● Saint-Julien★★ £E
CH. DU MOULIN ROUGE ● Haut-Médoc★ £C
CH. DE MYRAT ○ Barsac★★ £D
CH. OLIVIER ● Pessac-Léognan★★ £D ○ Pessac-Léognan★★ £D
CH. LES ORMES-SORBET ● Médoc★★ £D
CH. PATACHE D'AUX ● Médoc★★ £D
CH. PETIT-BOCQ ● Saint-Estèphe★★ £D
CH. DE PEZ ● Saint-Estèphe★★ £D
CH. POUMEY ● Pessac-Léognan★★ £D
CH. RAHOUL ● Graves★★ £C ○ Graves★★ £C
CH. RAMAGE-LA-BATISSE ● Haut-Médoc★★ £C
CH. RAUZAN-GASSIES ● Margaux★★★ £E
CH. RESPIDE-MÉDEVILLE ● Graves★★ £D ○ Graves★★ £D
CH. DE ROCHEMORIN ○ Pessac-Léognan £E
CH. ROMER-DU-HAYOT ○ Sauternes★★ £D
CH. DE ROUILLAC ● Pessac-Léognan★★ £D
CH. SÉGUR DE CABANAC ● Saint-Estèphe★★ £D
CH. SOUDARS ● Haut-Médoc★ £C
CH. SUAU ○ Barsac★★ £E
CH. LA TEMPÉRANCE ● Haut-Médoc★★ £C
CH. LE THIL COMTE CLARY ● Pessac-Léognan★★ £C
○ Pessac-Léognan★ £C
CH. TOUR-HAUT-CAUSSAN ● Médoc★★ £C
CH. TOUR DU HAUT-MOULIN ● Haut-Médoc★★ £C
CH. VERDIGNAN ● Haut-Médoc★★ £C
CH. VIEUX ROBIN ● Médoc★★ £C

Work in progress!!

Producers under consideration for the next edition
CLOS DADY (SAUTERNES)
CH. LAMOTHE (SAUTERNES)
CH. LIEUJEAN (MÉDOC)
CH. SAINT-AMAND (SAUTERNES)
CH. SAINT-ROBERT (GRAVES)
CH. GILETTE (SAUTERNES)

Author's choice (DM)

BORDEAUX LEFT BANK

Great cellarworthy Left Bank reds
CH. COS D'ESTOURNEL ● Saint-Estèphe 2ème CC
CH. DUCRU-BEAUCAILLOU ● Saint-Julien 2ème CC
CH. HAUT-BRION ● Pessac-Léognan I er CC
CH. LAFITE-ROTHSCHILD ● Pauillac I er CC
CH. LATOUR ● Pauillac I er CC
CH. LÉOVILLE-LAS-CASES ● Saint-Julien 2ème CC
CH. MARGAUX ● Margaux I er CC
CH. LA MISSION-HAUT-BRION ● Pessac-Léognan CC
CH. MOUTON-ROTHSCHILD ● Pauillac I er CC
CH. PICHON-LONGUEVILLE-LALANDE ● Pauillac 2ème CC

The best of Sauternes and Barsac
CH. CLIMENS O Barsac I er CC
CH. COUTET O Barsac I er CC
CH. GUIRAUD O Sauternes I er CC
CH. LAFAURIE-PEYRAGUEY O Sauternes I er CC
CH. RAYMOND-LAFON O Sauternes
CH. RIEUSSEC O Sauternes I er CC
CH. SIGALAS-RABAUD O Sauternes I er CC
CH. SUDUIRAUT O Sauternes I er CC
CH. LA TOUR BLANCHE O Sauternes I er CC
CH. D'YQUEM O Sauternes I er GCC

Classic dry whites
CH. CARBONNIEUX O Pessac-Léognan CC
DOM. DE CHEVALIER O Pessac-Léognan CC
CLOS FLORIDÈNE O Graves
CH. DE FIEUZAL O Pessac-Léognan
CH. HAUT-BRION O Pessac-Léognan
CH. LAVILLE-HAUT-BRION O Pessac-Léognan CC
CH. LA LOUVIÈRE O Pessac-Léognan
CH. PAPE-CLÉMENT O Pessac-Léognan
PAVILLON BLANC DE MARGAUX O Bordeaux
CH. SMITH-HAUT-LAFITTE O Pessac-Léognan

Good values and fine lesser growths
CH. BEYCHEVELLE ● Saint-Julien 4ème CC
CH. BRANAIRE ● Saint-Julien 4ème CC
CH. CLERC-MILON ● Pauillac 5ème CC
CH. D'ISSAN ● Margaux 3ème CC
CH. LÉOVILLE-POYFERRÉ ● Saint-Julien 2ème CC
CH. PONTET CANET ● Pauillac 5ème CC
CH. POTENSAC ● Médoc
CH. DU TERTRE ● Margaux 5ème CC
VIEUX CH. GAUBERT O Graves
CH. BASTOR-LAMONTAGNE O Sauternes

Saint-Emilion, Pomerol & other Bordeaux

DOM. DE L'A   Côtes de Castillon
Stéphane Derenoncourt   Pavie Nord, 33330 Saint-Emilion
UK stockists: **N&P**
This is the tiny 4-ha home property of winemaking guru Stéphane Derenoncourt. It is planted to old-vine Merlot, Cabernet Franc and a little

59

Cabernet Sauvignon and is farmed biodynamically. The result is remarkably dense and powerful wine from this outlying Bordeaux appellation. The wine is fermented in wood, aged on lees to add weight and texture and afterwards bottled without fining or filtration. Along with a number of other small impressive properties, this is a model for producers from the region's lesser ACs. (DM)

● **Domaine de l'A** Côtes de Castillon★★★ £E

CH. D'AIGUILHE Côtes de Castillon www.neipperg.com
Comte Stéphan von Neipperg 33350 Saint-Philippe-d'Aiguilhe
UK stockists: BBR,N&P,Tur
This very fine Castillon property is under of the same ownership as CANON LA GAFFELIÈRE and LA MONDOTTE. The property consists of 65ha of which 42 are planted to vines on the upper slopes which not only have an excellent southerly exposure but also very well-drained clay/limestone soils. The wine is blended from Merlot (80%) and Cabernet Franc. Fermentation is in oak vats but with temperature control and the wine is aged in a very high proportion (80%) of new oak on its lees. It is neither fined nor filtered. Lushly textured, concentrated and impressively complex, it has a fine tannic structure, firm in its youth, which needs a good 5 or 6 years' ageing. (DM)

● **Château d'Aiguilhe** Côtes de Castillon★★★★ £E

CH. ANGÉLUS Saint-Emilion 1er GCC www.angelus.com
Boüard de Laforest et Fils 33330 Saint-Emilion
UK stockists: AAA
This has consistently been one of the top-performing Saint-Emilion Grands Crus Classés over the last 10 to 15 years. In 1996 the property was upgraded to Premier Grand Cru Classé. These are deeply coloured, concentrated and extracted wines with deep, and dark blackcurrant and plum fruit. They are always produced with well-judged oak treatment but very finely balanced as well. 1995 and 2000 have both been outstanding vintages. Hubert de Boüard de Laforest is also one of the partners in the recently established MASSAYA winery in Lebanon's Bekaa Valley. (DM)

● **Château Angélus** Saint-Emilion Grand Cru Classé★★★★★ £H

CH. AMPÉLIA Côtes de Castillon
François Despagne 21 Allees Robert Boulin, 33500 Libourne
UK stockists: AAA
Yet another example of why this appellation is emerging as one of the most exciting of the Right Bank satellites. The wine is big, full and fleshy but also retains a mineral purity that can now be found in many of the top examples from the AC. Very dominated by Merlot, which accounts for 95% of the vineyard, it also contains a little Cabernet Franc. Give it 3 or 4 years. (DM)

● **Château Ampélia** Côtes de Castillon★★★ £C

CH. L'ARCHANGE Saint-Emilion GC
Pascal Chatonnet 33330 Saint-Emilion
This is the home property of emerging consultant Pascal Chatonnet. The vineyards are located to the west of the town of Saint-Emilion in close proximity to CHEVAL BLANC, ROL VALENTIN and La DOMINIQUE. The wine is marked by its sweet, rich and opulent fruit. Velvety, supple tannins and a relatively soft structure make this a wine for drinking at 3 or 4 years. (DM)

● **Château l'Archange** Saint-Emilion Grand Cru★★★ £E

CH. ARMENS   Saint-Emilion GC

Alexandre de Malet Roquefort   33330, Saint-Emilion
UK stockists: C&B
Alexandre de Malet Roquefort also owns La GAFFELIÈRE and TERTRE-DAUGAY as well as acting as a *négociant* in a small way. This 18-ha property 5km to the south-east of Saint-Emilion is planted to a mix of 90% Merlot and 10% Cabernet Franc. This is reflected in the style of the wine, which is ripe and vibrant with rich and reasonably concentrated forward, brambly, plummy fruit. Drink with 3–4 years' age. (DM)
● **Château Armens** Saint-Emilion Grand Cru★★ £F

CH. L'ARROSÉE   Saint-Emilion GCC

François Rodhain   33330 Saint-Emilion
UK stockists: AAA
Solid and consistent Grand Cru Classé producing ripe, moderately dense and powerful wines. They tend to be marked by their lush and velvety texture and can be broached at around 5 years or so, despite having around 40% Cabernet Sauvignon in the blend. At present this is a good, rather than great property. 2000 was a step up, clearly ★★★, and both 02 and 03 may well turn out the same. (DM)
● **Château l'Arrosée** Saint-Emilion Grand Cru Classé★★ £F

CH. AUSONE   Saint Emilion 1er GCC

Alain Vauthier   33330 Saint-Emilion
UK stockists: AAA
One of the great wines of the Right Bank. Ausone, along with CHEVAL-BLANC, has always been considered to stand out and the 2 are classified Premiers Grands Crus Classés A-grade properties. The wine has been consistently impressive since the late 1980s and in the last half a dozen years has been produced in a rich, supple and immensely velvety style. Very fine and complex, it is now increasingly rich and oaky. Alain Vauthier has gained valuable input on the winemaking approach from Michel Rolland. The blend comprises a roughly equal proportion of Merlot and Cabernet Franc. It has been absolutely top-flight since 1995 with the exception of 97. Approachable at 5 or 6 years, the wine benefits from twice that time. (DM)
● **Château Ausone** Saint Emilion Grand Cru Classé✪✪✪✪✪ £H
● **Chapelle d'Ausone** Saint Emilion Grand Cru★★★★ £E

CH. BARRABAQUE   Fronsac

Noël family   33126, Saint-Emilion
Small 9-ha property planted to Merlot (70%), Cabernet Franc (20%) and Cabernet Sauvignon (10%). The robust, densely structured, plummy Prestige comes from one of the best-exposed sites in the appellation, which stands on a mix of sandy-clay and chalky-clay soils. A straightforward Tradition bottling is also produced. The Prestige, ★★★ in the best recent vintages, gets an extended vatting of up to 3 weeks and is aged in new wood (40%) for up to a year. (DM)
● **Château Barrabaque** Canon-Fronsac Prestige★★★ £C

CH. BEAU-SÉJOUR BÉCOT   Saint-Emilion 1er GCC

Gérard & Dominique Bécot   33330, Saint-Emilion
UK stockists: AAA
This 16.5-ha property was reintroduced to the ranks of the Premiers Grands Crus Classés in 1996. The style is one of considerable extraction and the Bécot brothers seek to produce an opulent, rich, heavily oaked red with sumptuous,

61

plummy fruit. In general they succeed very well. They also make a *garagiste*-style *cuvée* called La Gomerie. Less than a thousand cases are produced of this Merlot aged in 100% new oak. It is sourced from a tiny 2.5-ha plot which is itself unclassified. Both wines need 5 or 6 years to shed the hard edge of their tannins. (DM)

● **Château Beau-Séjour Bécot** Saint-Emilion Grand Cru Classé★★★★ £G
● **La Gomerie** Saint-Emilion Grand Cru★★★★★ £H

CH. BEAUREGARD   Pomerol

Vincent Priou   33500 Pomerol
UK stockists: AAA

One of Pomerol's lesser-known châteaux, this 17.5-ha property has an unusually high proportion of Cabernet Franc planted, around 30%. This is in part because of a high gravel component in the soil. The wine is ripe and forward, with attractively brambly fruit and a hint of oak spice, but with less overtly fleshy, plummy Merlot fruit than some others in the appellation. Very good in 1998 and particularly 2000, which was a clear ★★★★, tight, intense and composed. It is approachable and supple at 4 or 5 years. (DM)

● **Château Beauregard** Pomerol★★★ £E

CH. BEAUSÉJOUR   Saint-Emilion 1er GCC

Héritiers Duffau-Lagarrosse   33330 Saint-Emilion
UK stockists: AAA

Prior to 1985 this property was a notable underperformer among the Premier Grands Crus Classés. Since then the wine has been altogether more impressive. The style is medium to full with a marked black fruit opulence but sufficiently firm tannins to provide the structure needed for real cellaring. 1990 was truly impressive and the property has been consistent throughout the 90s with 2000 again looking like it will provide that additional dimension. (DM)

● **Château Beauséjour** Saint-Emilion Grand Cru Classé★★★★ £E

CH. BEL-AIR LA ROYÈRE   Blaye

Corinne & Xavier Loriaud   Les Ricards, 33390 Cars
UK stockists: C&B

Small, top-class Blaye property with a total of 13ha of vineyards producing not only Blaye but a Premières Côtes de Blaye and a second label called Ricards. Merlot is the major variety (70%) but unusually there is 25% Malbec with the remainder Cabernet Sauvignon. The Blaye is rich, full and impressively concentrated, with a really dark, smoky character. The not inconsiderable oak needs at least 4 or 5 years to fully integrate. Very good in 2000 and 01; 04 shows real promise. (DM)

● **Château Bel-Air La Royère** Blaye★★★ £F

CH. BELLEVUE   Saint-Emilion GCC

SC du Château Bellevue   33330 Saint-Emilion
UK stockists:BBR, Far

Small but increasingly classy Saint-Emilion property run by Nicholas Thienpont with winemaking consultancy from Stéphane Derenoncourt. There are just 6.5ha under vine and Merlot dominates at 85%. The balance is 10/5 Cabernet Franc and Cabernet Sauvignon. This is now a big, powerful and structured wine with rich, dark fruit, well-judged oak and powerful tannins in its youth. As with so many of Derenoncourt's wines, it has impressive depth, purity and impeccable balance. The wine undoubtedly needs 5 or 6 years' cellaring. Very impressive in 2000 and 03, and 04 seems to have all the right hallmarks. (DM)

● **Château Bellevue** Saint-Emilion Grand Cru Classé★★★★ £F

CH. BELLEVUE-MONDOTTE   Saint-Emilion GC

Vignobles Perse   33330 Saint-Laurent-des-Combes
UK stockists:AAA

A tiny-production *cuvée* from Gérard Perse, the owner of PAVIE. From a 2-ha parcel on limestone-based soils, the wine is a blend of 90% Merlot and 5% each of Cabernet Franc and Cabernet Sauvignon. Yields from the 45-years-old vineyard are in fact much lower than at Pavie or Pavie Decesse at just 15hl/ha, which contributes to the rich, concentrated, almost opulent style. This is a big, full and formidably extracted wine with lashings of new oak; very good, if just lacking the depth and purity of the truly great Right Bank reds. Give it 5 years to soften the tannin, although it is quite approachable for a wine at this level. (DM)

● **Château Bellevue** Saint-Emilion Grand Cru★★★★ £H

CH. BERLIQUET   Saint-Emilion GCC

Vicomte Patrick de Lesquen   33330 Saint-Emilion
UK stockists:BBR, N&P

Berliquet is sited on the Saint-Emilion plateau close to CANON and has been a Grand Cru Classé since 1985. The wines are certainly very reasonably made if not yet quite matching the status of some neighbouring properties of a similar classification. Quality has been at least sound since 1998, but there is a slightly aggressive, rugged edge to the tannins, which can often be a touch dry and hard. The wine is aged in a high proportion of new oak (80%) – less would help – and bottled unfiltered. A little more refinement and purity would pull this into the top division. Good but dominated by woody tannins in 2004. (DM)

● **Château Berliquet** Saint-Emilion Grand Cru Classé★★★ £F

CH. LA BIENFAISANCE   Saint-Emilion GC   www.labienfaisance.com

Duval-Fleury family   33330 Saint-Christophe-des-Bardes
UK stockists: F&R

Good small property located on the northern plateau of Saint-Emilion with a total of 16ha planted in limestone, sand and clay/limestone soils across 3 parcels. Merlot dominates plantings at around 80% with 15% Cabernet Franc and a smattering of Cabernet Sauvignon. Vinification for La Bienfaisance is traditional with fermentation in cement and ageing in a small proportion of new oak. A richer and more opulent garage-style wine, Sanctus, is aged in 100% new oak. Produced with consultation from Stéphane Derenoncourt, it is less extracted and better balanced than many of its peers. Consistently good in recent vintages it is a very marked step up on the regular label. (DM)

● **Château La Bienfaisance** Saint-Emilion Grand Cru ★★ £D
● **Sanctus** Saint-Emilion Grand Cru ★★★★ £E

CH. LE BON PASTEUR   Pomerol

Michel Rolland   33500 Pomerol
UK stockists: AAA

Small Pomerol property of less than 7ha owned by roving wine consultant Michel Rolland. The vineyards, planted to a combination of 80% Merlot plus Cabernet Franc, are rigorously maintained and yields tightly harnessed. The wine is inevitably fleshy, rich and characteristic of the Rolland style with malolactic fermentation instigated in barrel. While structured and ageworthy the wine is supple, rounded and approachable with just a few years'

63

cellaring. (DM)

● **Château le Bon Pasteur** Pomerol★★★★ £F

CH. BONALGUE   Pomerol

Pierre Bourotte   33500 Pomerol
UK stockists::AAA

Small Pomerol property which has been in the Bourotte family since 1926.
Pierre Bourotte is also the proprietor at CLOS DU CLOCHER in Pomerol and
du Courlat in Lussac-Saint-Emilion. Here at Bonalgue he has 6.5ha and
Merlot is the dominant variety, accounting for 90% of the vineyard. The
balance is Cabernet Franc. The wine is a typically modern fleshy, supple
example with good depth and well-honed tannins. Expect it to drink well with
4 years' age or so. (DM)

● **Château Bonalgue** Pomerol★★★ £E

CH. BONNET   Entre-Deux-Mers   www.andrelurton.com

André Lurton   33420 Grézillac
UK stockists: **For**,AAA

This now very substantial operation is owned by André Lurton who achieves
first-class results with a number of Châteaux in the Graves and Pessac-Léognan
appellations, including Château La LOUVIÈRE. Output is around 125,000
cases a year and the property has some 122ha of red and 103ha of white
varieties under vine. Red, white and a Bordeaux *clairet* – a lightly coloured style
of rosé – are all produced. The reds take the Bordeaux appellation and include
a Réserve aged partly in new wood. The dry whites, a tank-fermented Classique
and barrel-fermented Réserve, are sold as Entre-Deux-Mers. A new prestige red
cuvée, Divinus, has been added to the range as well as a Lussac Saint-Emilion
Barbe-Blanche. (DM)

● **Château Bonnet** Bordeaux Réserve★★ £B

CH. BOURGNEUF-VAYRON   Pomerol

Xavier Vayron   1. Le Bourg-Neuf, 33500 Pomerol
UK stockists: HHC

Another Pomerol property that offers good value for the appellation with dark
and spicy wines of reasonable depth and concentration. A little more depth and
refinement would lift them into the top division. The 9-ha vineyard close to
TROTANOY is planted mainly to Merlot (90%) with the remainder Cabernet
Franc. Increased complexity can be expected with 4 or 5 years' ageing. 2004
looks promising. (DM)

● **Château Bourgneuf-Vayron** Pomerol★★★ £E

CH. CANON   Saint-Emilion 1er GCC   contact@chateau-canon.com

Wertheimer family   33330 Saint-Emilion
UK stockists:AAA

Now under the same ownership as Château RAUZAN-SEGLA. Historically a
very significant property and one that is now making a welcome return to the
top division of Saint-Emilion estates. The vineyard has recently been extended
with the purchase of Château Curé-Bon, which has been incorporated into
Canon. The cellars have also been cleaned up and modernised after taint
problems. The 1998 was a clear step-up in quality and 2000 and 01 were both
★★★★. The latest vintages look like maintaining this trend. Prior to this you
should tread with caution. At its best this is a taut, restrained style with finely
structured tannin. It is elegant, medium in weight and once more very
ageworthy. (DM)

● **Château Canon** Saint-Emilion Grand Cru Classé★★★ £F

CH. CANON-LA-GAFFELIÈRE Saint Emilion GCC www.neipperg.com

Vignobles von Neipperg   33330 Saint-Emilion
UK stockists:AAA

Canon-la-Gaffelière is now one of a number of striking labels and properties run by Stéphan von Neipperg, who owns the CLOS DE L'ORATOIRE, also in Saint-Emilion, and the outperforming Château D'AIGUILHE in the Côtes de Castillon. The style here, as with all the von Neipperg wines, is opulent, rich and supple, with finely integrated oak and soft, velvety tannin. Canon-la-Gaffelière is itself surprisingly approachable at 3 or 4 years. The property is located on the lower-lying limestone slopes below the town of Saint-Emilion. Dominated by old-vine Cabernet Franc, it has been consistently good over the last 6 or 7 vintages. The *super-cuvée* La MONDOTTE is also now made here. (DM)

● **Château Canon-la-Gaffelière** Saint Emilion Grand Cru Classé★★★★ £F

CH. CARIGNAN   Premières Côtes de Bordeaux

Philippe Pieraerts   33360 Carignan de Bordeaux
UK stockists: C&B

This 25-ha property is producing very good well-priced Bordeaux from one of the outlying appellations. The vineyards are planted on well-sited south-facing slopes in clay-limestone soils covered with stony gravel, which provides excellent drainage. Unlike at CARSIN, only reds are produced from a combination of Merlot (65%), Cabernet Sauvignon (25%) and Cabernet Franc. The splendid château here was originally built in 1452 and the origins of the property date back to the 11th century. Roughly one-third of the vineyard is now over 40 years old and where replanting takes place vine density is being increased. Consultancy advice comes from Louis Mitjaville, whose father owns TERTRE-ROTEBOEUF. The richly textured, dark plum and spice Prima is one of the best examples from the lesser appellations and is aged in 100% new wood for 18 months. An additional premium label, Quator gets 14–18 months in 4 different types of oak. The regular wine is rich, berry-scented and displays very good fruit and the second wine, L'Orangerie de Carignan, ensures the integrity of the top labels. (DM)

● **Château Carignan** Premières Côtes de Bordeaux Prima★★★ £C
● **Château Carignan** Premières Côtes de Bordeaux★★ £B

CH. CARSIN   Premières Côtes de Bordeaux www.carsin.com

Julia Berglund   33410 Rions

A good example of what many properties are now beginning to achieve in the less fashionable outlying appellations of Bordeaux. It is based in the Premières Côtes de Bordeaux and the reds are labelled as such, the whites as Bordeaux AC. The regular bottlings are sound and attractive enough, with nicely developed forward fruit, but it is the white Cuvée Prestige and red Cuvée Noire that particularly stand out here. The white has a touch of barrel-fermentation and is ripe and lightly tropical, with well-judged oak. The red is supple, soft and approachable, with just a hint of vanilla oak underpinning it. Signature l'Etiquette Gris is a limited-production white from Sauvignon Gris and there is also a sweet, moderately intense Cadillac. (DM)

● **Château Carsin** Premières Côtes de Bordeaux Cuvée Noire★★ £C
O **Château Carsin** Bordeaux Cuvée Prestige★★ £B

65

CH. CERTAN-DE-MAY   Pomerol

Mme Barreau-Badar   33500 Pomerol
UK stockists: AAA

Very good, stylish and elegant Pomerol from a tiny holding of vineyards close to PÉTRUS. This is more classically structured than many of its peers and is tight and almost austere when young. Cabernet Franc accounts for 25% of the vineyard, along with a little Cabernet Sauvignon that lends tannin and grip. The wine becomes very harmonious with up to a decade's age. (DM)

● **Château Certan-de-May** Pomerol★★★★ £H

CH. CHAUVIN   Saint-Emilion GCC   www.chateauchauvin.com

Marie-France Février et Beatrice Ondet   1 Cabanne Nord, 33330 Saint-Emilion
UK stockists: BBR,F&R,Tur

This property has been a consistent performer through most of the mid- to late 1990s and continues to be so. Consultancy input comes from Michel Rolland and the style is full, rich and fleshy, with supple, well-rounded tannins and real complexity in 2004, 03, 01, 00, 99 and 98. Needs a minimum of 5 years plus. (DM)

● **Château Chauvin** Saint-Emilion Grand Cru Classé★★★★ £E

CH. CHEVAL BLANC   Saint-Emilion 1er GCC

Bernard Arnault & Albert Frère   33330 Saint-Emilion
UK stockists: AAA

One of the 2 great wines of Saint-Emilion and produced in much greater quantity than AUSONE – some 12,500 cases a year as against barely 2,000. It has also regularly performed at the very highest level throughout the last 2 decades. Cheval Blanc is located close to the appellation boundary with Pomerol. There is a high proportion of Cabernet Franc in the vineyard (over 50%), which makes the wine quite different to those of its near neighbours. Bernault Arnault and Albert Frère purchased the property in the late 1990s and no expense will be spared in attempting to establish Cheval Blanc as the greatest property on Bordeaux's Right Bank. The style is rich, concentrated and opulent, with intensely complex, dark berry fruit and spice all underpinned by a structured velvety texture. To fully appreciate it in all its glory, 10 years or more of ageing is required. A wine of truly legendary proportions in 1990, 83 and 82 and 2000 may yet reach similar heights. (DM)

● **Château Cheval Blanc** Saint-Emilion Grand Cru Classé✪✪✪✪✪ £H
● **Château Petit Cheval** Saint-Emilion Grand Cru★★★ £E

CH. LA CLÉMENCE   Pomerol

Dauriac family   33500 Pomerol
UK stockists:BBR, Sec

The holding here is very small, just 3ha, with 85% Merlot and the balance Cabernet Franc. The Dauriac family also own the Saint-Emilion property DESTIEUX. As well as this they are developing vineyards in South Africa with plantings of Pinotage, Shiraz, Merlot and Cabernet Sauvignon. La Clémence is marked by its opulent, upfront plummy fruit and possesses a rich, supple texture, if a little dominated by new wood in the 2004. It will need time to soften. (DM)

● **Château La Clémence** Pomerol★★★ £F

CLOS DU CLOCHER   Pomerol

Pierre Bourotte   Catusseau, 33500 Pomerol
Small property with just 5.7 hectares under vine, split 80/20 between Merlot and Cabernet Franc. Pierre Bourotte also owns another small Pomerol estate,

Château BONALGUE. Clos du Clocher is a marginally denser and richer wine than its stablemate with generally greater concentration and a firmer, sturdier structure. It is made in a more classical style and as such will benefit from 5 or 6 years' patience. Winemaking input comes from Michel Rolland. (DM)

● **Clos du Clocher** Pomerol★★★ £F

CH. CLINET Pomerol www.wines-uponatime.com

Jean-Louis Laborde 3 Rue Fénelon, 33000 Bordeaux
UK stockists: AAA

Michel Rolland has provided consultancy input at this property for over 10 years, first to the late Jean-Michel Arcaute and now to Jean-Louis Laborde. The style has remained consistent throughout the period. Ripe to very ripe, full, rich and almost opulent with a supple silky texture, the wine is always bottled with neither fining nor filtration and is aged in 100% new oak. Don't be fooled, though, as there is both depth and a firm tannic structure to the young wine. Best with at least 5 years' ageing. (DM)

● **Château Clinet** Pomerol★★★★ £G

CH. CLOS DES JACOBINS Saint-Emilion GCC

Gérard Frydman 33330 Saint-Emilion

Small Saint-Emilion property which has performed admirably in recent years. There are 8.5ha under vine planted to a combination of Merlot (70%), Cabernet Franc (28%) and a mere 2% of Cabernet Sauvignon. Every vintage since 2000 has been on good form. The wine offers rich, dark and plummy fruit with very finely judged oak and impressive purity and intensity. The 2004 was on the cusp of ★★★★. Give it 4 or 5 years at least. (DM)

● **Château Clos des Jacobins** Saint-Emilion Grand Cru Classé★★★ £E

CLOS L'ÉGLISE Pomerol

Sylvain Garcin-Cathiard 33500 Pomerol
UK stockists: **J&B**,AAA

There are just 6ha of vines producing this fine and impressively dense and powerful Pomerol. The wine is lent considerable structure by the inclusion of up to 40% Cabernet Franc. Very rich and fleshy, it is loaded with dark plum and spicy vanilla oak. It was very stylish in 2001, 00, 99 and 98 and will cellar well for up to a decade. There is also a good second wine, L'Esprit de l'Église and other interests now include BRANON, BARDE-HAUT in Pessac-Léognan as well as new wines from POESIA and CLOS DES ANDES in Argentina. (DM)

● **Clos l'Église** Pomerol★★★★★ £H

CH. LA CLOTTE Saint-Emilion GCC

SCEA du Château la Clotte 33330 Saint-Emilion
UK stockists: AAA

The quality at this 4-ha property planted to mainly Merlot with a little Cabernet Franc and less Cabernet Sauvignon was good prior to 1997 but really no more. with vineyards on sand and gravel soils close to PAVIE-MACQUIN there should be real potential here. Things are taking a turn for the better, though. Consultancy is provided by Stéphane Derenoncourt and the style is now more opulent and concentrated with harmonious, well-judged oak and sufficient depth and firm, structured tannin to develop well in bottle over 5 years or so. A property to watch and particularly impressive in 2004. (DM)

● **Château La Clotte** Saint-Emilion Grand Cru Classé★★★★ £E

CH. LA COMMANDERIE DE MAZEYRES Pomerol

Clément Fayat   c/o Château La Dominique, 33330 Saint-Emilion

Under the same ownership as La DOMINIQUE in Saint-Emilion, the vineyard here is slightly under 9ha and is planted to a combination of Merlot (55%) and an unusually large proportion of Cabernet Franc (45%). The finesse and elegance from the Cabernet Franc is evident in a wine that is less upfront and showy than many Pomerols, although there is a lovely depth to the fruit as well as real elegance and intensity. It will achieve greater harmony with 5 years' cellaring. (DM)

● **Château La Commanderie de Mazeyres** Pomerol★★★ £F

CH. LA CONSEILLANTE Pomerol www.la-conseillante.com

Nicolas family   33500 Pomerol
UK stockists: AAA

One of the great Pomerol names, La Conseillante has an excellent vineyard aspect and is located close to L'ÉVANGILE and CHEVAL BLANC across the appellation boundary. With some Cabernet Franc (20%) as well as Merlot (80%) planted in gravel and clay based soils, the wine is both rich, fleshy and full of dark fruit but also firmly structured. The best years show a remarkably complex array of dark fruits and oriental spices. The wine benefits from 6–7 years' ageing at least. 2000 could well be exceptional and of a similar order to the great 89 and 90. Earlier classics were 85 and 82. (DM)

● **Château La Conseillante** Pomerol★★★★★ £G

CH. CÔTE DE BALEAU Saint-Emilion GCC murailles@wanadoo.fr

Reiffers family   33330 Saint-Emilion
UK stockists: AAA

Under the same ownership as Les GRANDES MURAILLES and Clos SAINT MARTIN, this property has been performing well in recent vintages under the management of Sophie Fourcade. There are just under 8ha here and the 35-year-old vineyard is a mix of Merlot (70%) and Cabernet Franc (20%) with the balance Cabernet Sauvignon. The wine offers not only exuberant fruit and some youthfully toasty notes from ageing in 100% new oak but also displays an elegant mineral purity. It is long and persistent and will be better with 5 years' age or so. (DM)

● **Château Côte de Baleau** Saint-Emilion Grand Cru★★★ £E

CH. LA COUSPAUDE Saint-Emilion GCC www.la-couspaude.fr

Vignobles Aubert   33330 Saint-Emilion
UK stockists: AAA

This is now a very impressive property located to the east of the appellation and planted with Merlot and 15% each of Cabernet Sauvignon and Cabernet Franc in limestone soils. The property is another of many benefiting from Michel Rolland's consultancy and the style is characteristically sumptuous and fleshy, with supple, velvety tannin and a complex, dark fruit character with abundant oak spice. Half a decade or so of ageing is needed to throw off the initially firm tannic grip. (DM)

● **Château La Couspaude** Saint-Emilion Grand Cru Classé★★★ £F

CH. LA CROIX-DE-GAY Pomerol

Chantal Lebreton & Alain Raynaud   33500 Pomerol
UK stockists: AAA

This is a good middle-ranking Pomerol with an attractive plump, plummy Merlot character after 3 or fours years of bottle-age but without any great depth or complexity. There are 10ha planted, 90% to Merlot. What marks the property out is the quality of a superior selection called la Fleur-de-Gay. Produced from 100% Merlot, this is dense, opulent, rich and oaky. Not surprisingly it is fairly pricey. (DM)

● **Château La Croix-de-Gay** Pomerol★★★ £E
● **La Fleur-de-Gay** Pomerol★★★★ £H

CH. LA CROIX DU CASSE   Pomerol

Héritiers Arcaute   33500 Pomerol
UK stockists: AAA

This is a dense and powerfully structured Pomerol with a marked cedary, savoury component. The vineyard has a high proportion of Cabernet Franc (some 30%) as well as Merlot and the *terroir* is marked by a high gravel component. The wine is firmly structured and 5 or 6 years' patience will be rewarded with greater complexity. (DM)

● **Château La Croix du Casse** Pomerol★★★ £F

CH. DASSAULT   Saint-Emilion GCC

Laurence Brun   33330 Saint-Emilion
UK stockists: AAA

Since Laurence Brun took over this property in 1995, quality has been consistently good, often very good. The wine offers plenty of depth, in a now very modern, fleshy, supple and oak-dominated style, although the tannin can just have a slightly hard, raw edge to it. The vineyard, planted on chalky siliceous sandy soils and located on the northern slopes of the appellation is relatively sizeable for the area at 24ha. It is planted to a 65/30/5 mix of Merlot, Cabernet Franc and Cabernet Sauvignon. Grand Cru Classé since 1985. Give it 5 years to let the woody tannins integrate. (DM)

● **Château Dassault** Saint-Emilion Grand Cru Classé★★★ £F

CH. DESTIEUX   Saint-Emilion GC

Dauriac family   33330 Saint-Hippolyte
The Dauriac family also own the small Pomerol property La CLÉMENCE. The red here offers a good deal better value both in comparison to its stablemate and when compared to a number of other Saint-Emilion Grands Crus. Quality has been at least good since 1998 and the 2004 wine suggests similar potential. The vineyard is small at just 8ha and the planting is a mix of 70% Merlot and equal holdings of Cabernets Franc and Sauvignon. The wine is rich and supple with a forward, fleshy texture and should drink well at 3 or 4 years of age. (DM)

● **Château Destieux** Saint-Emilion Grand Cru★★★ £E

CH. DE LA DAUPHINE   Fronsac

Jean et Guillaume Halley   33500 Libourne
UK stockists: C&B, Far

Impressive estate formerly owned by the Moueix family's *négociant* arm. Performance here was somewhat erratic during the early 1990s but has shown a significant improvement of late. Four labels come under the La Dauphine estate banner. Both the La Croix Canon, which comes from largest vineyard (13ha), and the La Dauphine are in a fleshy, upfront style with marked dark, spicy blackberry and plum fruit. This contrasts with the Canon-de-Brem, which is more purposefully structured with tannin that can be almost austere when the wine is young. Additional refinement is achieved through limited use of new oak. All the wines have shown impressive depth since 1998. Canon-de-Brem in particular needs 5 years' ageing. A soft, forward rosé La Dauphine is

69

also made. (DM)

Château La Dauphine
● **Château La Dauphine** Fronsac★★★ £C

Château Canon-de-Brem
● **Château Canon-de-Brem** Canon-Fronsac★★★ £C

Château La Croix Canon
● **Château La Croix Canon** Canon-Fronsac★★ £C

CH. DAUPHINÉ-RONDILLON   Loupiac

Vignobles Darriet   33410 Loupiac

The Darriet family pursue a number of interests from their base in Loupiac but it is the splendid Dauphiné-Rondillon that really stands out. This is a very fine alternative to lesser Sauternes from vineyards just the other side of the river Garonne. These are planted in clay and gravel soils and hold 60–80 year old vines, a real rarity in Bordeaux. The harvest is in several *tris* and the yield is comfortably less than 20hl/ha. Maturation is for 18 months and just 20% new wood is used. The wine is characterised by its rich, botrytised, peachy character and excellent balance. Just 3ha of Merlot and Cabernet Sauvignon and 1ha of Sauvignon Blanc produce a pair of fine, essentially fruit-driven Graves. Premières Côtes de Bordeaux, both red and white, is also produced. (DM)

Château Dauphiné-Rondillon
● **Château Dauphiné-Rondillon** La Cuvée d'Or Loupiac★★★ £D

Château Moutin
● **Château Moutin** Graves★★ £C   ● **Château Moutin** Graves★★ £C

CH. LA DOMINIQUE   Saint-Emilion GCC

Clément Fayat   33330 Saint-Emilion
UK stockists: AAA

This property, with an ideal location in very close proximity to CHEVAL BLANC, has been a reasonably consistent performer since the late 1980s. The wine is vinified with consultancy input from Michel Rolland. The style is not only opulent and fleshy with marked new oak and rich, concentrated, spicy, dark fruit but there is an underlying finesse and quality here. The wine is supple but well-structured and very ageworthy. 1998 was very good and 2000 looks set to be in the same mould. The small-volume garage wine, Saint Dominique, is no longer made. (DM)

● **Château La Dominique** Saint-Emilion Grand Cru Classé★★★★ £G

DOM. DE L'EGLISE   Pomerol

Philippe Castéja   33500 Pomerol
UK stockists: AAA

There are just over 7ha here planted mainly to Merlot (95%) with a smattering of Cabernet Franc. The Castéja family are also significant *négociants* and own TROTTEVIEILLE in Saint-Emilion. A rich and sumptuous example of the AC, the wine has a firm mineral structure that will ensure continued development in bottle, particularly in the classic vintages. Youthful oak, very apparent in the 2004, means 4 or 5 years is needed to achieve real balance and harmony. (DM)

● **Domaine de L'Église** Pomerol★★★★ £F

CH. L'ÉGLISE-CLINET   Pomerol

Denis Durantou   33500 Pomerol
UK stockists: AAA

Magnificent small Pomerol property with a holding of just 5.5ha of Merlot and Cabernet Franc. The vineyard is very old, with some of the vines nearing 100 years. The style bears little comparison with those neighbours who opt for modern extracted wines and dollops of new oak. L'Église-Clinet is structured, dense and backward when young. Given 6 or 7 years the result is an elegant, velvety and classically proportioned example of the appellation. Very impressive in 2000, 98, 97, 96 and 95. 2001 should be every bit as good. (DM)

● **Château L'Église-Clinet** Pomerol✪✪✪✪✪ £H

ESSENCE DE DOURTHE Bordeaux

Dourthe 35, rue de Bordeaux, 33290 Parempuyre
UK stockists: **Dou**, AAA

This is the flagship red of the Dourthe *négociant* house. It is unusual for Bordeaux in being the antithesis of *terroir*-driven wines, sourced from 10ha of the best plots of the firm's leading properties throughout the region. These include Château BELGRAVE in the Haut-Médoc, La GARDE in Pessac-Léognan and MARSAU in the Côtes de Francs. A blend of Cabernet Sauvignon (55%) and Merlot, the wine is rich, full and showy. While it is impressively structured with real dimension, it just seems to be missing an element that would move it up among the region's great reds. Give it 4 or 5 years. (DM)

● **Essence de Dourthe** Bordeaux★★★★ £F

CH. L'ÉVANGILE Pomerol www.lafite.com

Domaines Barons de Rothschild 33500 Pomerol
UK stockists: AAA

This is an impressively deep, structured and powerful example of Pomerol. Like L'ÉGLISE-CLINET, it is markedly different from many of its supple, rounded, softly structured contemporaries. Owned since 1990 by the Rothschilds, the wine is traditionally vinified and possesses sturdy, dense, firm tannin when young, along with formidably concentrated levels of complex, dark, spicy fruit. There is oak evident here but its very harmoniously integrated. It has been remarkably good in the best years of the last decade or so; 1990 was of legendary quality – ✪✪✪✪✪ – and 2000 may well end up of a similar stature. (DM)

● **Château l'Évangile** Pomerol★★★★★ £H

EXCELLENCE DE BOIS PERTUIS Bordeaux

Bernard Magrez c/o Ch. Pape Clement, 33607 Pessac

The regular wine here is good, vibrant and forwaed. Rhe Excellence is one of a number of wines released by Bernard Magrez under his Cuvées d'Exception label. Others include LA SERÉNITÉ in Pessac-Léognan and Gérard Depardieu's property MA VERITÉ in the Haut-Médoc. Excellence comes from 2ha planted solely to Merlot which is now 25 years old. Yields are kept very low at just over 20hl/ha and crop thinning is practised. The wine is fermented in wooden vats and ageing is in new wood. It is rich, dense and opulently plummy with marked extract. The initially firm tannins need 3 or 4 years to subside. (DM)

● **Château Bois Pertuis** Bordeaux★ £B
● **Excellence de Bois Pertuis** Bordeaux★★★ £D

CH. FAIZEAU Montagne-Saint-Emilion www.chateau-faizeau.com

Chantal Lebreton 33570 Montagne-Saint-Emilion
UK stockists: N&P

Good Saint-Emilion satellite made from 10ha of Merlot planted in finely drained limestone soils. Quality is boosted by the age of the vines, which are now over 30 years old. This is a ripe, forward style with blackberry and plum fruit and impressive depth and substance. It is not over-extracted and offers firm enough tannin for short-term development in bottle. (DM)

71

● **Château Faizeau** Montagne-Saint-Emilion Vieilles Vignes★★★ £C

CH. FALFAS Côtes de Bourg

Cochran family   33740 Bayon-sur-Gironde
UK stockists: **GWW**,Adm

Decent Bourg property run on biodynamic lines by John Cochran. The winemaking origins of the property go back to 1612. There are 22ha of vines planted, 55% Merlot, 30% Cabernet Sauvignon and unusually 10% of Malbec. The balance is Cabernet Franc. There is a cold soak for 48 hours, traditional fermentation and malolactic in *cuve*, followed by ageing in 30% new wood. The wines are richly textured and full of dark plummy fruit and a marked spicy, tobacco character no doubt emphasised by the inclusion of Malbec. The top label, Le Chevalier, has an added dimension and was on the edge of ★★★ in 2000. (DM)

● **Château Falfas** Côtes de Bourg★★ £B   Côtes de Bourg Le Chevalier★★ £B

CH. FAUGÈRES Saint-Emilion GC   www.chateau-faugères.com

Corinne Guisez   Saint-Étienne-de-Lisse, 33330 Saint-Emilion
UK stockists: AAA

Major investment in both the vineyard and cellars under the current ownership has wrought major change and delivered increasingly impressive wines. The Château Faugères regular Saint-Emilion is a dense, richly concentrated and spicy Grand Cru which is aged in 100% new oak and has the depth and structure to develop well over a decade or more. Since 1998 a super-rich special *cuvée*, Château Péby Faugères, has been produced which is both sumptuously fleshy and very powerful. The Cap de Faugères is a supple, rounded and forward style produced from vineyards owned in the Côtes de Castillon. (DM)

Château Faugères
● **Château Faugères** Saint-Emilion Grand Cru★★★ £E
● **Péby Faugères** Saint-Emilion Grand Cru★★★★ £G
Château Cap de Faugères
● **Château Cap de Faugères** Côtes de Castillon★★★ £C

CH. FEYTIT-CLINET Pomerol

Jérémy Chasseuil   Chemin de Feytit, 33500 Pomerol
UK stockists: AAA

Really characterful and impressive Pomerol is now being made at this well-sited property close to TROTANOY. Merlot is very much the dominant variety, occupying 90% of the 6-ha vineyard, and Cabernet Franc is the only other variety cultivated. The wine offers real style and substance: rich, concentrated dark-berry fruit is underpinned by lots of very well-integrated new oak. It has been good throughout the last 5 or 6 years and 2004 shows equal potential. This is a supple and approachable wine, but give it 4 or 5 years for real balance and harmony. (DM)

● **Château Feytit-Clinet** Pomerol★★★★ £F

CH. FIGEAC Saint-Emilion 1er GCC   www.chateau-figeac.com

Thierry Manoncourt & Eric d'Aramon   33330 Saint-Emilion
UK stockists: AAA

The traditional qualities of this Premier Grand Cru Classé – namely refinement, elegance and a harmonious balance of subtle, dark, spicy fruit and lightly smoky oak – have been apparent in a number of recent vintages but strangely absent in others when one would expect the property to have performed well. The vineyard has an unusually high proportion of Cabernet Sauvignon and Cabernet Franc for Saint-Emilion, mainly because of the marked gravel component of the soil, with just one-third planted to Merlot. The resulting wines are inevitably powerful and structured when at their best and long-lived. Recent vintages look very good, ★★★★ at least, but 1996 and 97 were disappointing. (DM)

● **Château Figeac** Saint-Emilion Grand Cru Classé★★★ £G

CH. LA FLEUR DE BOÜARD   Lalande-de-Pomerol

Hubert de Boüard de Laforest   33500 Pomerol
UK stockists: AAA

One of the benchmark properties from this appellation and, with the Le Plus *cuvée*, one that commands the highest prices. A total of 19ha are planted to Merlot (80%), Cabernet Franc (15%) and Cabernet Sauvignon (5%). The regular label is rich, concentrated and fleshy with opulent, dark, spicy fruit. The brilliantly crafted Le Plus offers layers of flavour and complexity and has a special minerality and fine cedary structure that mark it as one of the region's great reds. The approachable La Fleur will benefit from 4 or 5 years' ageing, while Le Plus really requires 6–8 years' patience. (DM)

● **Château La Fleur de Boüard** Lalande-de-Pomerol★★★ £E
● **Le Plus de La Fleur de Boüard** Lalande-de-Pomerol★★★★ £G

CH. FLEUR-CARDINALE   Saint-Emilion GC

Dominique Decoster   33330 Saint-Emilion
UK stockists: THt

Well-priced and improving Saint-Emilion Grand Cru which has shown a consistent upturn in quality since the late 1990s. Both the 1999 and 2000 were full of rich, fleshy fruit and well-balanced new oak. The 2003 looks certain to be of at least a similar order. The property is situated in the north-east of the appellation and planted to 70% Merlot, the balance equal proportions of Cabernet Sauvignon and Cabernet Franc, in *argilo-calcaire* soils. The average age of the vines is now 35 years and under the insistence of consultant Jean-Luc Thunevin yields are being reduced in a consistent drive for quality. Richly textured, approachable reds are likely to be a regular occurence here. The wine will nonetheless benefit from 3 or 4 years age. (DM)

● **Château Fleur-Cardinale** Saint-Emilion Grand Cru★★★ £D

CH. LA FLEUR-PÉTRUS   Pomerol

Moueix family   33500 Pomerol
UK stockists: AAA

Like PÉTRUS itself this property is owned by the Moueix family. The vineyards have a higher proportion of gravel than is commonly found here and the wine is less opulent and rich than many of its neighbours. It is refined, medium-rather than full-bodied and tightly structured and restrained in its youth. With age it will become very fine and complex and is extraordinarily long-lived. 1975 still seems youthful. Somewhat erratic in the 1980s, the wine has been a model of consistency since the mid- to late 90s. (DM)

● **Château la Fleur-Pétrus** Pomerol★★★★ £G

CH. FOMBRAUGE   St-Emilion GC   www.fombrauge.com

Bernard Magrez   33330 Saint-Christophe des Bardes
UK stockists: AAA

Bernard Magrez, owner of PAPE-CLEMENT in Pessac-Léognan, purchased Fombrauge in 1999. While Fombrauge has been going from strength to strength, particularly throughout the late 1990s, it has achieved new heights under the current ownership. With over 50ha of vineyards and located to the

73

north-east of the appellation, away from the established grandee properties, Fombrauge is proving as elsewhere that the less-fancied plots in this sizeable appellation can provide impressive wines. A limited-production, highly priced special *cuvée,* Magrez-Fombrauge, has also now been released. Massively powerful and extracted, it remains to be seen how this wine will develop, as with other *super-cuvées* from lesser plots, but it has considerable promise. Bernard Magrez has also produced a number of small-scale *garagiste*-style wines of great potential from a number of properties throughout the region and has provided input to actor Gérard Depardieu and actress Carole Bouquet in similar properties in both Bordeaux and the Midi and equally excitingly Spain, Argentina, Morocco and Algeria. (DM)

- **Château Fombrauge** Saint-Emilion Grand Cru★★★ £D
- **Magrez-Fombrauge** Saint-Emilion Grand Cru★★★★★ £G
- O **Château Fombrauge** Bordeaux★★★ £D

CH. FONTENIL   Fronsac
Michel & Dany Rolland   33141 Saillans
UK stockists: **THp**
This small Fronsac property is owned by Michel and Dany Rolland. The 9ha are planted to 90% Merlot, the balance Cabernet Sauvignon. The wine is lushly textured, rich, supple and full of opulence, with just a hint of cassis adding depth and weight to the bramble and dark berry fruit. The new oak so apparent when the wine is young will become more balanced and harmonious with time. One of the better examples of this lesser appellation. A tiny-production *super-cuvée*, Défi de Fontenil, is also now produced. (DM)

- **Château Fontenil** Fronsac★★★★ £D

CH. FOUGAS   Côtes de Bourg
Jean-Yves & Michèle Béchet   33710 Lansac
UK stockists: **F&R,Sec,N&P,Tur**
This is the larger of the 2 properties of the Béchets, who also own the tiny Saint-Emilion property RIOU DE THAILLAS. There are just 11ha under vine here, planted to Merlot (50%) and equal proportions of Cabernet Sauvignon and Cabernet Franc. The site is surrounded by 2 streams which provide excellent natural drainage from its alluvial soils. Each parcel of vines is vinified separately after cold maceration, and the wines spend a small period on their gross lees. The special *cuvée* Maldoror is sourced from the best individual plots on the property and is aged in 100% new oak. Both wines will stand a litle age and the richly textured, dark plum and spice Maldoror demands 2–3 years to integrate the not inconsderable high-toast oak. (DM)

- **Château Fougas** Côtes de Bourg★★ £B Côtes de Bourg Maldoror★★★ £C

CLOS FOURTET   Saint-Emilion 1er GCC   www.premiers-saint-Emilion.com
Philippe Cuvelier   3330 Saint-Emilion
UK stockists: **THt**
Under new ownership since 2001. There are 20ha of vineyards planted to a mix of Merlot (80%), Cabernet Sauvignon (12%) and Cabernet Franc. The resulting wines have generally been big, full and sturdy, particularly during the last decade, which has seen a consistent raising of standards. The wine is densely extracted and sees a high proportion of new oak. Recent vintages have been refined and classy with great intensity. The 2003 has splendid potential, and may turn out to be worthy of ★★★★★ so this trend is likely to continue and the property should move towards greater things. (DM)

- **Clos Fourtet St-Emilion** Grand Cru Classé★★★★ £F

CH. FRANC-MAILLET   Pomerol

Gérard Arpin   10. Maillet, 33500 Pomerol

Very good small producer with less than 10ha spread across 2 vineyards. The Lalande-de-Pomerol, Vieux Château Gachet, is impressively structured at this level and almost restrained in style. Aged in one-third new wood, it is dense and backward and will open out and offer great drinking with 5 years' ageing. The Franc-Maillet is a classically structured Pomerol with subtle cedar as well as dark berry and plum notes. Put this away for at least 5 years, and longer for the Jean Baptiste label. This comes from an older vine parcel of just 0.7 hectares with 90% Merlot. Aged in 90% new oak it is not only remarkably deep and concentrated but offers a piercing minerality to its fruit and great purity. The wines are very well priced and no doubt very scarce. The Arpin family also own the Montage-Saint-Emilion property Château GACHON. (DM)

Château Franc-Maillet
● **Château Franc-Maillet** Pomerol★★★★ £D
● **Château Franc-Maillet Jean Baptiste** Pomerol★★★★ £E
Vieux Château Gachet
● **Vieux Château Gachet** Lalande-de-Pomerol★★★ £C

CH. FRANC-MAYNE   www.chateau-francmayne.com

Georgy Fourcroy   33330 Saint-Emilion
UK stockists: AAA

Relatively tiny Grand Cru Classé property of just 7ha which has produced increasingly good wine in recent vintages. The vineyards are planted in limestone soils to the west of the town of Saint-Emilion, close to neighbouring GRAND-MAYNE. The limited *cuvée* La Gomerie from BEAU-SÉJOUR BÉCOT is also sourced from these slopes. Merlot dominates plantings at 90%; the balance is Cabernet Sauvignon. The wine is richly textured and impressively concentrated with dark spicy fruit and sufficiently supple tannin to drink well with 3 or 4 years' ageing. Michel Rolland provides the winemaking direction and the style of the wine reflects his input. Malolactic is in barrel and copious new oak is used for ageing. Total output is barely 3,000 cases and around a third of this is earmarked for the very decent second label, Les Cèdres de Franc-Mayne. (DM)

● **Château Franc-Mayne** Saint-Emilion Grand Cru Classé★★★ £E

CH. DES FRANCS   Bordeaux Côtes des Francs

Hubert de Boüard & Dominique Hébrard   33570 Francs
Hubert de Boüard, owner of the benchmark Lalande-de-Pomerol property La FLEUR DE BOÜARD, also part-owns this excellent satellite property. There are 31ha under vine and 29 of these are planted to reds – Merlot (80%), Cabernet Franc (10%) and Cabernet Sauvignon (10%). Production is currently about 11,000 cases a year. The regular bottling offers good value and accessible easy drinking. The Les Cerisiers *cuvée* is altogether more serious, offering rich, plummy varietal Merlot character and a fleshy, densely textured palate with impressive depth. It will benefit from at least 4–5 years' patience. (DM)

● **Château de Francs** Bordeaux Côtes de Francs★★ £B
● **Château de Francs** Bordeaux Côtes de Francs Les Cerisiers★★★ £C

CH. GACHON   Montagne-Saint-Emilion

Gérard Arpin   Maillet, 33500 Pomerol
UK stockists:Hal

Gérard Arpin, who also owns Château FRANC-MAILLET in Pomerol, produces one of the best wines from this Saint-Emilion satellite appellation. Part of the

75

quality is contributed by 35-year-old vines planted on south-east facing slopes. The wine is a blend of Merlot (70%), Cabernet Franc (20%) and Cabernet Sauvignon (10%). It is rich and fleshy in a fruit-driven style with an impressively supple structure and minimal oak influence. Four years or so will see real harmony. (DM)

● **Château Gachon** Montage-Saint-Emilion★★★ £C

CH. LA GAFFELIÈRE Saint-Emilion 1er GCC

Comte de Malet Roquefort 33330 Saint-Emilion
UK stockists: AAA

After a period when this 22-ha property was relatively disappointing in the early to mid-1990s the wines appear to be consistently improving. There has been no new ownership or marked change in the style, just, it would appear, a general sharpening of the act. This is very much a classically structured Saint-Emilion: stylish,, medium- rather than full-bodied with a restrained mineral character as well as subtle, smoky, dark fruit. It will add weight with 5 years' cellaring. (DM)

● **Château la Gaffelière** Saint-Emilion Grand Cru Classé★★★ £G

CH. GAZIN Pomerol www.gazin.com

Balliencourt family Le Gazin, 33500 Pomerol
UK stockists: AAA, Las

This is among Pomerol's larger properties, with 23ha under vine, the vast majority being Merlot, with small amounts of Cabernet Sauvignon and Cabernet Franc also planted. The vineyards consist of gravel/clay soils and are sited next to PETRUS and L'EVANGILE. 10,000 cases a year are produced, 8,000 of which are the Grand Vin, the balance being the second wine L'Hospitalet de Gazin. The wines have been cosistently good now for a decade. The 1990s have seen a transformation, with improved management and control in both vineyard and cellar. The vintages of 1998, 99, 00 and particularly 2001 were very good here. The style is rich, forward and opulent with ripe and plummy dark fruit, sufficiently firm and sturdy tannins and an increasing amount of new oak used. (DM)

● **Château Gazin** Pomerol★★★★ £G

CH. LE GAY Pomerol

Catherine Péré-Vergé 33500 Pomerol
UK stockists: AAA

This 10-ha property is now owned by Catherine Péré-Vergé, whose portfolio of interests also includes another Pomerol property, MONTVIEL, and a share in Argentina's CLOS DE LOS SIETE. Le Gay is increasingly impressive and 2004 looks to be maintaining the high standards set of late. The wine is in an opulent, modern, fleshy style laden with rich berry fruit. It has loads of concentration and oak but there is a highly impressive cedary complexity and a finely crafted structure here as well. No doubt 6 or 7 years' patience will be amply rewarded. (DM)

● **Château Le Gay** Pomerol★★★★ £F

GRACIA Saint-Emilion GC

Michel Gracia Rue de Thou, 33330 Saint-Emilion
Small garage operation with facilities in the centre of Saint-Emilion. Michel Gracia produces 2 wines, both aged in new French oak, and his use of wood is well judged. Les Angelots is the lighter and more accessible and comes from a separate 1.25-ha plot of 27-year-old Merlot (80%) and Cabernet Franc (20%). The Gracia label itself is richer and fleshier with loads of dark blackberry fruit

and sweet oak. It offers impressive depth and is supple and well structured. The vine age now averages 30 years and as well as Merlot and Cabernet Franc there is a smattering of Cabernet Sauvignon. (DM)

● **Gracia** Saint-Emilion Grand Cru★★★★ £F
● **Gracia** Saint-Emilion Grand Cru Les Angelots de Gracia★★★ £E

CH. GRAND CORBIN-DESPAGNE Saint-Emilion GC

Despagne family 33330 Saint-Emilion
UK stockists: **Col**,BBR,F&R,Tur
Moderate-sized Grand Cru property with just over 26ha under vine. The Despagne family have been producing good well-priced examples of the appellation since the 1998 vintage. As well as their Grand Vin they also produce a decent second label, Petit Corbin-Despagne. The vineyard, which is a mix of Merlot (75%), Cabernet Franc (24%) and a tiny amount of Cabernet Sauvignon, is planted in sandy-clay soils. The harvest is carefully sorted and with an average vine age of nearly 40 years the wine has no problem handling the 20–30 days of vatting and ageing in 50% new wood for up to 18 months. Rich and fleshy in style, it requires 4–5 years' cellaring to throw the aggressive character of its youthful tannin. (DM)

● **Château Grand Corbin-Despagne** Saint-Emilion Grand Cru★★★ £D
● **Château Grand Corbin-Despagne** Saint-Emilion Petit Corbin-Despagne★ £C

CH. GRAND-MAYNE Saint-Emilion GCC www.grand-mayne.com

Nony family 33330 Saint-Emilion
UK stockists: AAA
Grand-Mayne produces impressively dark, dense and well-structured Saint-Emilions. There are some 17ha under vine and the estate is located towards the western side of the appellation. Quality has much improved in recent vintages and the wine is suppler and has better fruit quality than of old. An increasing use of new oak is helping to underpin the character of the château. While firmly structured when young, the wine avoids austerity. (DM)

● **Château Grand-Mayne** Saint-Emilion Grand Cru Classé★★★★ £F

CH. GRAND ORMEAU Lalande-de-Pomerol

Jean-Claide Beton 33330 Lalande-de-Pomerol
Two *cuvées* are now made at this 11.5-ha property. The vineyards have an aspect facing north to south and are located in the highest part of the appellation. Merlot is inevitably the dominant variety at just under two-thirds of the plantings but both Cabernet Franc and Cabernet Sauvignon are significant, each covering 18% of the *vignoble*. The regular bottling is soft and approachable, while the Cabernet elements are quite apparent in the impressively structured, dark and spicy Madeleine. This in particular should be given 5 years or so to soften and open out. (DM)

● **Château Grand Ormeau** Lalande-de-Pomerol★★ £E
● **Château Grand Ormeau Madeleine** Lalande-de-Pomerol★★★50E

CH. GRAND-PONTET Saint-Emilion GCC

Pourquet-Bécot family 33330 Saint-Emilion
UK stockists: N&P,Tur
There are 14ha of vines here, mainly Merlot with a reasonably high proportion of Cabernet Franc (15%) and Cabernet Sauvignon (10%). The clay-rich soils provide a subtle and elegant style. The wine has been at least good throughout the mid- to late 1990s and this consistency has been continued into the early 2000s. Greater fruit ripeness and suppler tannins have been the keys. (DM)

● **Château Grand-Pontet** Saint-Emilion Grand Cru Classé★★★ £E

77

CH. LES GRANDES MURAILLES   Saint-Emilion GC

Reiffers family   c/o Ch. Côte de Baleau, 33330 Saint-Emilion
From the same ownership as Clos SAINT-MARTIN and CÔTE DE BALEAU, this property is tiny with a mere 2ha, 95% of which is Merlot, the balance Cabernet Franc. The vineyards are now on average 35 years old and this helps in providing rich, dense and concentrated fruit-driven wines. Expect the wine to drink well young although a few years' patience will be rewarded. (DM)

● **Château Les Grandes Murailles** Saint-Emilion Grand Cru★★★ £E

CH. LES GRAVIÈRES   Saint-Emilion GC

Barraud family   33330 Saint Sulpice de Faleyrens
Good and well-priced Saint-Emilion from a small property with barely more than 3ha of vineyards planted on argilo-calcareous soils very close to MONBOUSQUET. Unusually, the wine is 100% Merlot and it is made in a fleshy, lightly plummy style with a hint of herb-spice in the background. Expect it to drink well at 3 or 4 years. (DM)

● **Château Les Gravières** Saint-Emilion Grand Cru★★★ £E

CH. GREE LAROQUE   Bordeaux Supérieur

Benoit de Nyvenheim   Arnaud Laroque, 33910 Saint-Ciers-d'Abzac
This tiny-volume wine sourced from 1.6ha of vineyards to the north of Libourne and Fronsac is a testament to the commitment of Benoit de Nyvenheim and the winemaking skills of consultant Stéphane Derenoncourt. The vines, a mix of Merlot (75%) and Cabernet Franc (20%) as well as a sprinkling of Cabernet Sauvignon, are planted in well-drained gravel, clay and clay/limestone soils. Of equal importance is the age of the vineyard at over 40 years, virtually unheard of in this lesser appellation. Vinification is modern and precise. The harvest is carefully sorted and malolactic takes place in barrel with the wine aged on lees for 12–18 months in one-third new oak. Bottled unfiltered, the wine is impressively deep and concentrated with dark, spicy fruit, opulent oak and just a hint of dark pepper in the background. Give it 3–4 years. (DM)

● **Château Gree Laroque** Bordeaux Supérieur★★★ £D

CH. HAUT-BERTINERIE   www.chateaubertinerie.com

Eric & Frantz Bantegnies   33620 Cubnezais
UK stockists: AAA
Sizeable Blaye operation producing just over 35,000 cases a year in red, white and rosé styles. The top wines from the oldest and best-sited vines – some 30–50 years old – are labelled Haut-Bertinerie. The vineyards here have a higher gravel component than normal and Cabernet Sauvignon accounts for 40% of the 43ha of red plantings. Whites come from 18ha, with Sauvignon at 95% and just 5% of Muscadelle. The high Cabernet Sauvignon component is reflected in the Haut-Bertinerie reds, which have a bigger, firmer structure than most from the appellation. The white Haut-Bertinerie is barrel-fermented with a rich, full texture on the palate and good background acidity. The Bertinerie wines are softer and more approachable. A further label, Manon La Lagune, is used for young-vine red and white. (DM)

● **Château Haut-Bertinerie** Premières Côtes de Blaye★★ £B
● **Château Haut-Bertinerie** Premières Côtes de Blaye Landreau★★★ £D
○ **Château Haut-Bertinerie** Premières Côtes de Blaye★★ £C
● **Château Bertinerie** Premières Côtes de Blaye★★ £B
○ **Château Bertinerie** Premières Côtes de Blaye★ £C

CH. HAUT-CARLES   Fronsac

Antoine Chastenet de Castaing & Stéphane Droulers   33141 Saillans
UK stockists: Tur

Small Fronsac property that has been consistently fine in recent vintages. There are just 8ha under vine with Merlot accounting for 95% of the red plantings and the balance from Cabernet Franc. Two whites are also produced under the Bordeaux AC, including a Blanc de Renouil, and there is a simple, fruit-driven Petit Renouil red as well as a further Fronsac labelled Château du Pavillon. The Haut-Carles red is very good indeed with real style. Marvellously extracted dark, plummy fruit is balanced by subtle, lightly vanilla-scented wood. Expect the wine to continue to develop well over 4 or 5 years or more. (DM)

● **Château Haut Carles** Fronsac★★★ £C

CH. HAUT-CHAIGNEAU   Lalande-de-Pomerol

Jeanine & André Chatonnet   33141 Saillans

Haut-Chaigneau is one of the largest properties in this appellation with some 21ha of vineyards. The Chatonnets also own a 5-ha parcel of 40-year-old vines on finely drained sandy-clay and gravel soils from which they produce La Sergue. Haut-Chaigneau is a blend of Merlot (70%) and 15% each of Cabernet Sauvignon and Cabernet Franc. It is made in a very ripe, sweet style and is supple and approachable young. The more structured and backward La Sergue, which comes from lower yields, is nevertheless rich and very ripe in the house style with more marked new wood. Give it 5 or 6 years' ageing. A second label is also produced, Château Tour Saint-André. (DM)

Château Haut-Chaigneau
● **Château Haut-Chaigneau** Lalande-de-Pomerol★★ £C
Château La Sergue
● **Château La Sergue** Lalande-de-Pomerol★★★ £C

CH. HAUT-MAZERIS   Canon-Fronsac

SCEA du Ch. Haut-Mazeris   33126 Saint-Michel-de-Fronsac
UK stockists: BBR

This 11-ha property offers some of the finest red wine in this small satellite appellation. The wines are deep, dark and concentrated with a real old-vine quality to them, loaded with dark blackberry and herb-spice character. A 2-ha parcel of the oldest vines is retained to produce the richly textured Cuvée Spéciale. Both wines should be given 4 or 5 years' ageing. (DM)

● **Château Haut-Mazeris** Canon-Fronsac★★★ £C
● **Château Haut-Mazeris** Canon-Fronsac Cuvée Spéciale★★★ £D

CH. HAUT-MAZERIS   Fronsac

Mme Ubald-Bocquet   33500 Pomerol
UK stockists: BBR

This property stands on the highest slopes of the Fronsac AC. There are just 5ha here, planted to a mix of Merlot (a mere 65%), Cabernet Sauvignon (20%) and Cabernet Franc (15%) on finely drained clay-limestone soils and the vineyard is now over 35 years of age. The wine has greater structure and grip than those from most neighbouring properties, no doubt aided by the high proportion of the Cabernets in the blend. It is rich, dense and fleshy with just a hint of youthful oak apparent (50% of the barrels are new each year) and it will be better with 5 years' ageing. (DM)

● **Château Haut Mazeros** Fronsac★★★ £C

CH. HOSANNA   Pomerol

Moueix family   33500 Pomerol
UK stockists: AAA, Las
Small Pomerol property showing consistently high-quality over the last 5 or 6
vintages. Hosanna produces just over 1,500 cases a year from 4.5ha of Merlot
(70%) and Cabernet Franc (30%) with a superb exposure close to LAFLEUR
and PÉTRUS. The property was originally known as Certain-Guiraud but the
name was changed by the Moueix family. This is a rich, supple and very elegant
wine with a fine mineral core, no doubt helped by the sizeable proportion of
Cabernet Franc. Give it at least 5 or 6 years. (DM)
● **Château Hosanna** Pomerol★★★★ £C

CH. HOSTENS-PICANT   Sainte-Foy Bordeaux

Yves Picant   33220 Les Levès-et-Thourneyragues
UK stockists: NYg, TPg
Absolute benchmark property for this lesser AC. The Picants have a total of
40ha under vine, three-quarters of which are red. They also produce a decent
white Cuvée des Demoiselles, with a high proportion of Sémillon. Both reds
are modern and fleshy; the regular label is more fruit-driven, while the Lucullus
is bigger and fuller with very marked dark, plummy fruit and spicy oak
undertones but excellent balance too. The Lucullus in particular will evolve
nicely over 4 or 5 years. (DM)
● **Lucullus** Sainte-Foy Bordeaux★★★ £C
● **Château Hostens-Picant** Sainte-Foy Bordeaux★★ £C

CH. JOANIN BÉCOT   Côtes de Castillon

Juliette Bécot   33350 Saint-Philippe d'Aiguilhe
UK stockists: AAA
This small and very fine Castillon property is owned by the Bécot family of
BEAU-SÉJOUR-BÉCOT. There are just over 5ha under vine and production is
tiny at a mere 2,500 cases a year. Merlot is the dominant variety but the
vineyard also has a fair amount of Cabernet Franc, accounting for a quarter of
the plantings. This is a rich, dense Castillon with a hint of new oak, impressive
depth and a subtle mineral purity. Give it 3 or 4 years although its opulent
character suggests the wine will be very attractive in its relative youth. (DM)
● **Château Joanin Bécot** Côtes de Castillon★★★ £C

LA CROIX DE PEYROLIE   Lussac-Saint-Emilion

Carole Bouquet   c/o Terroirs d'Exception, 33330 Saint-Christophe des Bardes
Owned by French film actress Carole Bouquet, a former Bond girl, La Croix
de Peyrolie is marketed under the Terroirs d'Exception label by Bernard
Magrez, owner of FOMBRAUGE. The vineyard is tiny at just 1.3 hectares and
yields a mere 12.5hl/ha, so this is very much a garage-style operation.
Vinification is in wooden barrels with manual *pigeage* and malolactic is
instigated in new oak, where the wine spends 20 months. Rich and very
concentrated, with a fine and firmly tannic structure in its youth it will benefit
from 5 or 6 years' ageing. I feel, as with a number of Magrez wines, that there
can be just a touch too much extract in a lesser year like 2002. Very impressive
nonetheless. (DM)
● **La Croix de Peyrolie** Lussac-Saint-Emilion★★★★ £F

CH. LAFLEUR   Pomerol   *UK stockists:* AAA

Marie Robin   Grand Village, 33240 Mouillac
Tiny Pomerol property consisting of a mere 4.5ha of vines, half surprisingly
planted to Cabernet Franc. This component helps provide the considerable

structure which enables the wine to age gracefully for 2 decades and more. In recent vintages an increasing amount of new oak has been used and the wine possesses not just a finely structured, almost mineral core but a rich, concentrated, black-fruited opulence also. It was remarkably consistent throughout the 1990s and outperformed in the difficult years early in the decade. (DM)

● **Château Lafleur** Pomerol✪✪✪✪✪ £H

CH. LARCIS-DUCASSE Saint-Emilion GC

Gratiot Alphandery family   33330 Saint-Emilion
UK stockists: J&B, Far
This property has 11ha of Merlot, Cabernet Franc and Cabernet Sauvignon planted in south-east facing vineyards on the brilliantly exposed Côte Pavie. The estate is run by Nicolas Thienpont with consultancy input from Stéphane Derenoncourt and recent vintages have been very good. The wine is produced in a supple, accessible style with loads of dark, spicy, fleshy fruit underpinned by fairly high-toast oak. Unlike at a number of other properties the wood is well judged without excessive oak tannins. At present this wine offers great value. Best with 4–5 years. (DM)

● **Château Larcis-Ducasse** Saint-Emilion Grand Cru★★★★ £E

CH. LAROZE Saint-Emilion GCC www.ch-laroze.com

Meslin family   33330 Saint-Emilion
This is another Saint-Emilion property much improved in the late 1990s. Careful grape selection prior to fermentation ensures the wine is crafted in a lush, fleshy and opulent style with supple tannins and a very appealing youthful character. Dark, spicy plummy fruit is very apparent. Part malolactic in barrel helps to underpin the wine. The 27ha of vineyards are located on the western plateau of the appellation and are planted in sandy soils with a chalky/clay bedrock offering good drainage. The estate has been farmed biodynamically since 1991 and the vine age is gradually creeping up although it is still relatively young at 20 years. Certainly it would appear that the best is yet to emerge here. The wine is bottled unfiltered. (DM)

● **Château Laroze** Saint-Emilion Grand Cru★★★ £D

LA MONDOTTE Saint-Emilion www.neipperg.com

Comte Stéphan von Neipperg   33330 Saint-Emilion
UK stockists: AAA
Along with Le DÔME, this is one of the 2 great garage wines to emerge in the last half decade. Produced at CANON-LA-GAFFELIÈRE, the vineyard consists of 4.5ha planted on clay/silt soils over a rocky subsoil. It is superbly drained with an unusually steep south-facing aspect. It is this low-yielding *terroir* that is responsible for a wine of remarkable depth and concentration. Blended from 80% Merlot and 20% Cabernet Franc, it offers a truly opulent and exotic array of dark fruits and oriental spices. It is produced in the classic Derenoncourt style with ageing on lees in new oak for a year and a half and is bottled unfiltered. (DM)

● **La Mondotte** Saint-Emilion Grand Cru★★★★★ £H

CH. LATOUR-À-POMEROL Pomerol

Mme Lacoste-Loubat/Moueix Family   33500 Pomerol
UK stockists: AAA
This is another property under the Moueix family umbrella. These are supple, ripe and at their best richly plummy examples of Pomerol, produced to showcase the more opulent character of the appellation. The wine has generally

performed well during the period from 1994 onwards, with just the odd hint of aggressive tannin sometimes marring the style. It develops well with 6 or 7 years' age. (DM)

● **Château Latour-à-Pomerol**★★★ £H

CH. DE LAUSSAC   Côtes de Castillon

Vignobles Vatelot, Guyon & Roché   33350 Saint-Magne de Castillon
Despite the fact this property has one of the lower lying of the Castillon vineyards it is an excellent big, full-on example of the appellation. While Merlot dominates with 75% of the plantings, Cabernet Franc is also important at 25%. Dark, spicy and plummy Merlot fruit is nicely underpinned by a subtle hint of cedar with a little oak in the background. Impressively long and persistent in 2004. Best with 4 or 5 years. (DM)

● **Château de Laussac** Côtes de Castillon★★★ £C

LE DÔME   Saint-Emilion GC   info@teyssier.fr

Jonathan Maltus   33330 Vignonnet
UK stockists: AAA
This vies with LA MONDOTTE to be first among the garage wines of Saint-Emilion. It is produced by Jonathan Malthus at his property Château TEYSSIER, from a single parcel of 2.85ha which neighbours Château ANGELUS. Cabernet Franc is the main component at 70%, with the balance Merlot. The wine is modern in style with a pre-fermentation maceration and both *pigeage* and pumping over are employed during fermentation. Malolactic is conducted in barrel and then 50% is drawn off and aged in a second series of brand new oak barrels. Yet while it is deep and very concentrated, the wine's fine mineral structure provides exemplary balance. It will require 7 or 8 years' patience to show at its peak. (DM)

● **Le Dôme** Saint-Emilion Grand Cru★★★★★ £G

CH. LUCIE   Saint-Emilion GC

Bortolussi family   316 Grands-Champs, 33330 Saint-Sulpice-de-Faleyrens
A recently established tiny property with less than 2ha under vine. The wines are made with consultancy advice from Stéphane Derenoncourt. The first wines were vinified here in the 1995 vintage although a sizeable proportion of the vines date back over 100 years, which contributes a great deal to the style and quality achieved. The vineyard is planted to Merlot and Cabernet Franc on a mix of sand and clay with a part on clay/limestone. L'ANGÉLUS is a neighbouring property. This is a true garage wine: the vinification takes place in the town of Saint-Emilion but in excellent underground cellar conditions with good ventilation. Malolactic in barrel and ageing in new oak for 12–15 months help create the rich, opulent style. The wine is loaded with dense, dark fruit but there is a real purity and depth often missing in other wines made in a similar style from the region. Accessible from a young age, the wine will nevertheless add further complexity with cellaring. (DM)

● **Lucia** Saint-Emilion Grand Cru★★★★ £E

LYNSOLENCE   Saint-Emilion GC

Denos Barraud   33330 Saint-Sulpice-de-Faleurens
Tiny garage-style operation producing barely more than 500 cases a year from 100% Merlot. Yields are kept low and the vineyard is adjacent to MONBOUSQUET and VALANDRAUD in the south-east of the appellation. Fermentation takes place in small-lot 400-litre barrels and malolactic is in barrel although the wine is not kept on lees. This is very good, rich, fleshy and

concentrated wine and the oak is very well judged. It is a supple, forward style with a velvety texture that will drink well with 3 or 4 years' ageing. (DM)

● **Lynsolence** Saint-Emilion Grand Cru★★★★ £F

CLOS DES LUNELLES   Côtes de Castillon

Vignobles Perse   33350 Saint-Colombe

Very impressive old-vine Castillon from the owner of Château PAVIE. The vineyard is now approaching 40 years of age and yields are deliberately restricted to 20hl/ha. Merlot accounts for 80% of the vineyard with the balance Cabernet Franc and Cabernet Sauvignon. The old-vine character of the wine really shines through with complex, smoky, dark berry and cocoa spice aromas and considerable depth and concentration. Just a hint more purity and elegance would lift this to a different level. Very fine in 2004, on the edge of ★★★★. (DM)

● **Clos des Lunelles** Côtes de Castillon★★★ £D

CH. LUSSEAU   Saint-Emilion GC

Laurent Lusseau   33330 Saint Sulpce de Faleyrens

This tiny Saint-Emilion property is owned by Laurent Lusseau, who is the *regisseur* at Château PAVIE. His holding consists of just 2ha of Merlot (80%) and Cabernet Franc (20%), and the vineyard is now 35 years old. He keeps a tight control on his yields and a green harvest is conducted prior to *veraison* to keep the crop at around 30–35hl/ha. This is a ripe example with piercing dark berry fruit and good depth and fruit intensity. It should drink well from 3 or 4 years. (DM)

● **Château Lusseau** Saint-Emilion Grand Cru★★★ £E

CH. MAGDELAINE   Saint-Emilion 1er GCC

Moueix family   33330 Saint-Emilion
UK stockists: AAA

Another Moueix family property. This is an opulent, richly plummy, Merlot-dominated wine crafted from older vines than is usual for the region. Supple and approachable but nevertheless possessing a fine, well-structured mineral backbone, the wine can be enjoyable with as little as 5 years' cellaring and will keep for much longer. (DM)

● **Château Magdelaine** Saint-Emilion Grand Cru Classé★★★★ £E

CH. MARSAU   Bordeaux Côtes des Francs

Vignobles Dourthe   33570 Francs
UK stockists: AAA

Small stand-out property in this lesser-known AC, along with de FRANCS and PUYGUERAUD. The 8-ha vineyard is planted solely to Merlot and production is barely more than 2,000 cases a year. The vineyard is also one of the sources of Dourthe's top Bordeaux red ESSENCE DE DOURTHE, a blend from appellations on both Left and Right Banks. Marsau is less extracted than the wines from some neighbouring properties and is all the better for that. The wine is dominated by subtle red berry and plum fruit and offers great definition and elegance with impressive length and intensity. Give it 3 or 4 years at least. (DM)

● **Château Marsau** Bordeaux Côtes de Francs★★★ £D

CH. LA MAURIANE   Puisseguin-Saint-Emilion

Pierre Taix   33570 Puisseguin

Tiny 3.5-ha property producing just the *micro-cuvée* La Mauriane, a blend of 85/10/5 Merlot, Cabernet Franc and Cabernet Sauvignon. Output is

83

tiny at barely more than 1,000 cases a year so you'll have to hunt around a bit for this. Pierre Taix is one of those rare producers who are beginning to show the potential of *terroirs* in Saint-Emilion's satellite appellations, particularly where the vines are of considerable age, as is the case with his 45-year-old vineyard. The wine is a modern, fleshy, dark-spiced claret with lots of extract and good depth. Drink it with 3 or 4 years' age. (DM)

● **Château La Mauriane** Puissegiun-Saint-Emilion★★★ £C

CH. MONBOUSQUET   Saint-Emilion GC   www.chateaupavie.com

Vignobles Perse   33330 Saint-Emilion
UK stockists: AAA, Las

A typically modern extractive style of winemaking produces a ripe and bold style of Saint-Emilion here. Michel Rolland is the consultant and his techniques of ripe, late-harvested fruit, deep colour and malolactic in barrel are all on show. The driving force behind the renaissance of this once-mediocre property is Gérard Perse, who also owns PAVIE and PAVIE-DECESSE. Expect the wines to develop well in the medium term. (DM)

● **Château Monbousquet** Saint-Emilion Grand Cru★★★★ £F

CH. MONT PÉRAT   Premieres Côtes de Bordeaux

Despagne family   33550 Capian
As well as the sizeable TOUR DE MIRAMBEAU, the Despagne family also own this much smaller 16-ha property. A typical blend of Merlot and Cabernet Sauvignon, this a dense and muscular red and a benchmark for this appellation along with Château CARIGNAN. The wine is loaded with dark berry fruit and undercurrents of smoke and vanilla. Firmly structured in its youth, it needs 5 years or so. (DM)

● **Château Mont Pérat** Premières Côtes de Bordeaux★★★ £D

CH. MONTVIEL   Pomerol

Catherine Péré-Vergé   33330 Saint-Emilion
Catherine Péré-Vergé, who also now owns Le GAY, is continuing to produce excellent results at this 7.5-ha Pomerol château. Merlot is the dominant variety and the 20% or so of Cabernet Franc lends useful structure to the wine. It is rich and concentrated with a typically fleshy Merlot palate but stands out thanks to a real purity and a mineral quality to the fruit that is often absent in the appellation. The wine deserves 5 or 6 years' patience. (DM)

● **Château Montviel** Pomerol★★★★ £E

CH. LE MOULIN   Pomerol

Catherine Péré-Vergé   33330 Saint-Emilion
Rich and sumptuous, if pricey, Pomerol is produced at this tiny 2.4-ha property. The vineyard is planted to a mix of 80/20 Merlot and Cabernet Franc and the wine displays loads of dark, exotic, plummy, spicy Merlot character. While supple and approachable, it also possesses a depth and persistence so often absent in other examples. Expect this wine to drink very well with medium-term cellaring. (DM)

● **Château le Moulin** Pomerol★★★★ £G

CH. MOULIN HAUT-LAROQUE   www.moulinhautlaroque.fr.st

Jean-Noël Hervé   Le Moulin, 33141 Saillans
UK stockists: N&P

This is one of the more impressive properties in the increasingly fashionable Fronsac appellation. The 15ha are mainly Merlot but there is a significant amount of old-vine Cabernet Franc, along with Cabernet Sauvignon and

Malbec. The style is ripe and full with an element of new oak showing through and a supple, velvety structure. Better with 4–5 years' age. (DM)

● **Château Moulin Haut-Laroque** Fronsac★★ £C

CH. MOULIN PEY-LABRIE   Canon-Fronsac

Bénédicte & Gregoire Hubau   33126 Fronsac
UK stockists: **C&B**

Small property of some 6.5ha producing modern, stylish and ripe reds with a high proportion of Merlot and increasing use of new oak. The approach mirrors that of other quality-minded properties from lesser Bordeaux appellations in emphasising forward, dark and richly plummy fruit in a soft, fleshy, textured style. The rounded, velvety tannin is assisted by completion of the malolactic fermentation in barrel. (DM)

● **Château Moulin Pey-Labrie** Canon-Fronsac★★★ £D

CH. MOULIN SAINT-GEORGES   Saint-Emilion GC

Vauthier Family   33330 Saint-Emilion
UK stockists: AAA

Located in close proximity to AUSONE and in fact owned by the same family. Quality here has been consistently improving in recent vintages, and has rated ★★★★ since 1998. The 8-ha, Merlot-dominated vineyard is meticulously managed and careful vinification produces richly fruity and fleshy wines often high in alcohol with marked new oak. They will be all the better for 4 or 5 years' ageing. (DM)

● **Château Moulin Saint-Georges Saint-Emilion** Grand Cru★★★★ £F

CLOS DE L'ORATOIRE   Saint-Emilion GCC   info@neipperg.com

Vignobles von Neipperg   33330 Saint-Emilion
UK stockists: AAA

Under the same ownership as CANON-LA-GAFFELIÈRE and the *super-cuvée* LA MONDOTTE. As at Stéphan von Neipperg's other properties, the style here is modern and approachable but the wine is neither overripe nor excessively extracted. There is a hallmark of underlying refinement and elegance. The finely crafted tannins need 5 or 6 years to achieve real harmony. Classy and ageworthy. (DM)

● **Clos de l'Oratoire Saint-Emilion** Grand Cru Classé★★★★ £G

PASSION DU PRIEURÉ MALESAN   Premières Côtes de Blaye

Bernard Magrez   c/o Terroirs d'Exception, 33330 Saint-Christophe des Bardes
This is one of a number of wines that Bernard Magrez is now marketing as Terroirs d'Exception. It is a tiny-production garage-style wine from one of Bordeaux's humbler appellations produced from mainly Merlot but also a little Cabernet Franc. The vineyard yields a miserly 20hl/ha or less. The result is a wine which is deeply extracted, rich and concentrated with very evident new oak. It will benefit from 3 or 4 years' ageing. Magrez also works with French film actor and vineyard owner Gérard Depardieu in this project. Similarly impressive reds have been made in the Roussillon along with Depardieu's North African Domaine SAINT AUGUSTIN and LUMIÈRE wines. (DM)

● **Passion du Prieure Malesan** Premières Côtes de Blaye★★★ £D

CH. PAVIE   Saint-Emilion 1er GCC   www.chateaupavie.com

Vignobles Perse   33330 Saint-Emilion
UK stockists: AAA

This property was purchased in 1998 by Gérard Perse who also owns PAVIE-DECESSE, MONBOUSQUET and PETIT-VILLAGE. Quality was formerly variable but substantial investment in the cellars should bring greater consistency. However, the Perse wines and particularly Pavie have become the most controversial of the new wave of late-harvested and highly extracted reds which focus on opulence and concentration perhaps more than elegance or purity. Achieving a balance of the 2 is what marks the greatest of the new wave. Pavie is increasingly very late-harvested and more akin to a full-blown Napa red than a classical Saint-Emilion of the old school. If you are a fan of rich and concentrated reds with massive extract and not inconsiderable alcohol then this will appeal, otherwise you may prefer to look elsewhere. There is no doubting the commitment to quality, with a modern and sophisticated approach to vinification and minimal handling in the cellars. How well the current generation of vintages will age remains to be seen. Prior to 1998 the wines were adequate at best with only the earlier vintages of 1990, 89, 86 and 82 being of real note. (DM)

● **Château Pavie** Saint-Emilion Grand Cru Classé★★★★ £H

CH. PAVIE-DECESSE Saint-Emilion GCC www.chateaupavie.com

Vignobles Perse 33330 Saint-Emilion
UK stockists: AAA

Like PAVIE, owned by Gérard Perse and now producing wines of greater density and power than a few years back. The style, as at Pavie, is for rich and opulent reds but there has always been a tighter, leaner edge to Decesse when compared with its larger, more illustrious neighbour. The wine is reasonably harmonious with copious quantities of sweet, dark fruit and lots of spicy, vanilla-scented oak. Since 1997 it is of a much richer style than of old. It should age reasonably well but is reasonably approachable young. (DM)

● **Château Pavie-Decesse** Saint-Emilion Grand Cru Classé★★★★ £G

CH. PAVIE-MACQUIN Saint-Emilion GCC pavie.macquin@wanadoo.fr

Corre-Macquin family 33330 Saint-Emilion
UK stockists: AAA, Las

Consultancy input here comes from Stéphane Derenoncourt and the property is farmed biodynamically. It shares the same limestone plateau as PAVIE-DECESSE and has an elegant hard, tight and structured mineral edge to its character. In the cellar minimal handling is the order of the day and the results are enormously impressive. The wines are dense, powerful and structured, with seamlessly integrated dark, spicy fruit and oak as well as displaying marvellous purity. They age very well. Only 1992 looks really disappointing. The wines of the late 1990s show a serious hike in quality. (DM)

● **Château Pavie-Macquin** Saint-Emilion Grand Cru Classé★★★★★ £F

CH. PETIT-VILLAGE Pomerol

AXA Millesimes 33500 Pomerol
UK stockists: AAA

This property is part of AXA Millésimes and under the same ownership as PICHON-LONGUEVILLE in Pauillac. The style here has been for fairly sturdy, structured wines with reasonable depth and refinement There has been a step up in quality here since 1998 and the wines are suppler and richer in recent vintages. 2001, 00 and 99 were all impressively dense and concentrated. (DM)

● **Château Petit-Village** Pomerol★★★ £G

CH. PÉTRUS Pomerol

Moueix family 1 Rue Petrus-Arnaud, 33500 Pomerol
UK stockists: AAA

One of the most expensive wines in the world, it used to be the most expensive by a long way but has been challenged in recent years not only by near neighbours but also by limited-production special *cuvées* in California. Much depends on the vagaries of the international auction markets. There is no doubt, though, that Pétrus is one of Bordeaux's truly great reds. A very high proportion of Merlot (95%), with the balance Cabernet Franc, is planted in vineyards that sit upon a plateau of remarkably well-drained clay soils and provide a unique *terroir*. Extraordinary care is taken in both the vineyard and cellars in producing a wine that is immensely rich and concentrated with a bewildering array of dark fruits, oriental spices and seamlessly integrated oak, all supported by very fine supple tannins. It is consistently great and perhaps only struggles very slightly in lesser years, but then so does every other property in the region. (DM)

● **Château Pétrus** Pomerol○○○○○ £H

CH. LE PIN   Pomerol

Jacques Thienpont   Les Grands Champs, 33500 Pomerol
UK stockists: AAA
Production here is tiny at only around 700 cases a year and 2 decades ago the wine was just a hobby of owner Jacques Thienpont. However, it has become an auction favourite and, partly because of its scarcity, has on occasion fetched higher prices than PÉTRUS. The style is for ripe, opulent and approachable wines rather than ones that are overstructured and austere and the vinification reflects this approach. Malolactic is carried out in barrel and the wine sees 100% new oak which is seamlessly integrated. Undoubtedly a very fine and richly opulent example of Pomerol. (DM)

● **Château le Pin** Pomerol○○○○○ £H

CH. LE PIN BEAUSOLEIL   Bordeaux-Supérieur

Elizabeth Leriche & Arnaud Pauchet   Le Pin, 33420 Saint-Vincent-de-Pertignas
UK stockists: Cam,F&R
Small-production, top-quality red from one of the region's humbler appellations. The property is located just the other side of the Dordogne from the Côtes de Castillon and is producing similarly impressive results to some of the better examples of that AC. Less than 2,000 cases a year are made from the 5ha here. The vineyards are planted to Merlot (60%), Cabernet Franc (20%), Cabernet Sauvignon (17%) and a tiny amount of Malbec. Initially backward and firm in structure, it displays an array of dark, spicy almost exotic flavours. Give it 4 or 5 years to round out. (DM)

● **Château Le Pin Beausoleil** Bordeaux Supérieur★★★ £C

CLOS PUY ARNAUD   Côtes de Castillon

Thierry Valette   7 Puy Arnaud, 33350 Belvès de Castillon
UK stockists: F&R
This is one of a handful of really impressive properties from this now excellent satellite appellation. Unlike neighbouring Château d'AIGUILHE, the vineyard area here is small at a mere 7ha. Planted to a mix of 70% Merlot, 20% Cabernet Franc and the balance Cabernet Sauvignon, its aspect is excellent with south facing slopes and the limestone-based soils provide excellent drainage. The vines are also now farmed biodynamically. Clos Puy Arnaud is dense and richly concentrated with dark berry fruit, spicy oak and supple, firmly structured tannin all in evidence. Consultant Stéphane Derenoncourt uses all his techniques during vinification: pre-fermentation maceration, malolactic in barrel and ageing on lees in 50% new oak. The wine is consistently right on the cusp of ★★★★; 2000 was undoubtedly so. Pervenche Puy Arnaud is a very

decent second wine. (DM)

● **Clos Puy Arnaud** Côtes de Castillon★★★★ £D
● **Château Pervenche Puy Arnaud** Côtes de Castillon★ £B

CH. PUYGUERAUD   Bordeaux-Côtes de Francs
Nicolas Thienpont   33570 Saint-Cibard
UK stockists: Sec,F&R

There are a number of impressive producers in this small appellation north-east of Saint-Emilion but Puygueraud particularly stands out. The wine is both refined and surprisingly structured for a lesser appellation and displays an impressive array of cedar, dark fruit and oriental spices, all tightly gripped by firm youthful tannin. The wine will benefit from a few years in the cellar. A special limited production wine, Cuvée Georges, was produced in 2000. (DM)

● **Château Puygueraud** Bordeaux-Côtes de Francs★★★ £C
● **Château Puygueraud** Bordeaux-Côtes de Francs Cuvée Georges★★★ £D

CH. QUINAULT   Saint-Emilion GC   www.chateau-quinault.com
Alain Raynaud   30 Chemin Videlot, 33500 Libourne
UK stockists: CTy,BBR,Sec,N&P,F&R

Alain Raynaud produces around 5,000 cases a year, mainly from some very old Merlot and Cabernet Franc. There are a total of 15ha; Merlot accounts for 65% and Cabernet Sauvignon and Malbec just 15% between them, with the balance Cabernet Franc. Despite being only a regular Saint-Emilion Grand Cru, this is a serious enterprise and the wine bears little resemblance to many of the *garagiste* operations that produce barely more than a few hundred cases a year. Quality is certainly helped by a vineyard with an average age of around 50 years. The style is rich, supple and opulent and is best with 8–10 years' age. A limited-production special bottling has been produced in 2003, Oriel l'Absolu. (DM)

● **Château Quinault L'Enclos** Saint-Emilion Grand Cru★★★★ £F
● **Château Quinault L'Enclos** Saint-Emilion Grand Cru Lafleur de Quinault★★ £D

CH. REIGNAC   Bordeaux-Supérieur   chateau.reignac@wanadoo.fr
Vatelot family   33450 Saint-Loubès
UK stockists: CTy,Tur,F&R

Stéphanie and Yves Vatelot produce some of the very best examples of this lesser appellation and should be a benchmarks for others. They have a sizeable holding of some 76ha of which just 2ha are devoted to whites, producing a good but pricey white Reignac. The red blend has a slightly higher proportion of Merlot than Cabernet Sauvignon and the wine is dense, dark and structured. It should develop very well in the medium term. There is also a special limited-release Reignac, again with a high proportion of Merlot (75%). Modern and fleshy, the wine is cold-macerated before fermentation, with malolactic on lees in barrel. The top label is the Balthus micro-cuvée, which bears all the hallmarks of consultant Michel Rolland. Produced from a tiny yield of 15hl/ha and from nearly 40 year old vines this 100% Merlot is extraordinarily dense and concentrated for Bordeaux. While both the Reignac red and Balthus have the depth and sufficiently finely structured tannin to support considerable development in bottle, both are supple and very approachable with 3 or 4 years. (DM)

Château Reignac
● **Château Reignac** Bordeaux Supérieur★★ £C
● **Château Reignac** Bordeaux Supérieur Reignac★★★ £D
O **Château Reignac** Bordeaux Reignac★★★ £D

Balthus
● **Balthus** Bordeaux Supérieur★★★★ £E

CH. REYNON   Premières Côtes de Bordeaux

Denis & Florence Dubourdieu   21 Route de Cardan, 33410 Beguey
UK stockists:Han

Denis Dubourdieu, the owner of CLOS FLORIDÈNE in the Graves, is an extremely well-known and respected professor of enology in the region. At Château Reynon, he makes some very good dry white and red, along with a little sweet Cadillac from a total of some 57ha of vineyards. The red is good and stylish in a medium-weight style; the regular white is crisp and fresh; and the Vieilles Vignes is classier and subtly barrel-fermented. Both the Vieilles Vignes white and the red will evolve nicely in the short term. (DM)

● **Château Reynon** Premières Côtes de Bordeaux★★ £C
○ **Bordeaux** Vieilles Vignes★★ £B

CH. RIOU DE THAILLAS   Saint-Emilion GC

Jean-Yves Béchet   33330, Saint-Emilion
UK stockists: Jas

The Béchets also own the impressive Château FOUGAS in the Côtes de Bourg. This property is smaller and they make just 1 wine, a dense, powerful and initially tannic Saint-Emilion. There are a total of just 3ha of Merlot set on a hilltop with an aspect facing directly south. At present the vines are just over 20 years old, so more is yet to come. The sandy-clay subsoil and gravelly topsoil provides good drainage. Vinification is partly traditional with fermentation in small wooden vats with manual punching down of the cap. Formidably extracted, the wine is rounded out by malolactic in barrel and maturation in new oak for 18 months. The oak is well integrated although the ferocious nature of the wine in its youth could do with a little taming. Given 6 or 7 years' patience the wine will offer increasing richness and complexity. (DM)

● **Château Riou deThaillas** Saint-Emilion Grand Cru★★★★ £F

CH. DE LA RIVIÈRE   Fronsac   www.chateau-de-la-riviere.com

Jean & Jeanne Le Prince   33126 La Rivière
UK stockists: Cam

A decade ago this substantial Fronsac property was producing wines of somewhat variable quality. There are 59ha under vine, mainly Merlot with Cabernet Sauvignon, Cabernet Franc and a few hectares of Malbec. During the late 1990s some of the quality achieved during the mid-1980s has been replicated, although the wines are now modern and produced in an attractively ripe, dark berry fruit style with soft velvety tannins. A special bottling, Aria, is very good but pricey and a *clairet* is also made. The reds will benefit from 4 or 5 years' aging. (DM)

● **Château la Rivière** Fronsac★★ £D   Fronsac Aria★★★ £E

CH. ROC DE CAMBES   Côtes de Bourg

François Mitjaville   33330 Saint-Laurent-des-Combes
UK stockists: C&B,Sav

This property is not only a serious benchmark for the Côtes de Bourg but also for all the lesser Right Bank appellations. The property is relatively small at 10ha and Merlot dominates the plantings, accounting for 60% of the vineyard. Always harvested as late as possible and from very low yields, the wine is typically rich and ripe, always displaying dense, dark, spicy berry fruit and a hefty dollop of well-integrated oak. It is long, complex, powerful and

89

ageworthy. Minimal cellar handling helps to ensure consistently impressive results. 2000, 99 and 98 were all very impressive. (DM)

● **Château Roc de Cambes** Côtes de Bourg★★★★ £F

CH. ROL VALENTIN   Saint-Emilion GC

Eric & Virginie Prisette   33330, Saint-Emilion
UK stockists: AAA

Former professional footballer Eric Prisette bought Rol Valentin in 1994. Since then the wines have progressively emerged as some of the most exciting of the new wave of reds from the appellation. The property is small with just over 4.5ha planted to Merlot (85%), Cabernet Franc (8%) and Cabernet Sauvignon (7%). Yields are much lower than elsewhere in the region and the vine age is now 35–40 years. All the modern cellar techniques are in evidence: 100% new oak, malolactic in barrel and ageing on lees with micro-oxygenation. This opulent, rich and supple wine will drink well young but has the depth and finely crafted structure to develop well for a decade or more. (DM)

● **Château Rol Valentin** Saint-Emilion Grand Cru★★★★ £F

CH. ROUGET   Pomerol

Jean-Pierre Labrueyère   33330, Saint-Emilion

Sizeable property for the appellation with some 17.5ha, making good, well-priced Pomerol from a well-sited vineyard close to l'ÉGLISE-CLINET. The vines are 85% Merlot with the balance Cabernet Franc. Consultancy input has come from Michel Rolland since 1997 and the wine is crafted in typical Rolland style – rich and plummy with concentrated dark, plummy fruit but real minerality as well. A total of 6,500 cases are produced, half of which are the Grand Vin and half the second wine, Château des Templiers. (DM)

● **Château Rouget** Pomerol★★★ £E

CH. LA ROUSSELLE   Fronsac

Jacques & Viviane Davau   33126 La Rivière

The Davau's tiny property with just 3.5ha under vine is one of the emerging lights of Fronsac. Wine consultant Stéphane Derenoncourt also helps by weaving his own elegant magic on the wine. The vineyard is planted to a mix of Merlot (65%), Cabernet Franc (25%) and the balance Cabernet Sauvignon on finely drained argilo-calcareous soils. Traditionally vinified and aged for around a year in oak, the wine shows marked Merlot character when young as well as impressive purity and depth. Rich, dark plum aromas are underpinned by a subtle leafy character and firm youthful tannin. Four or 5 years' ageing will provide greater richness and weight. (DM)

● **Château La Rousselle** Fronsac★★★ £C

CLOS SAINT MARTIN   Saint-Emilion GCC

Reiffers family c/o Ch. Côte de Baleau, 33330, Saint-Emilion

This tiny 1.3-ha property, the smallest Grand Cru Classé in the appellation, is planted in finely drained clay-limestone soils and has an ideal south-facing exposure. This, along with a vine age of 30 years, provides fruit of tremendous intensity. The wine is a blend of Merlot (65%) and Cabernet Franc (20%) with a fair dollop of Cabernet Sauvignon (15%) adding extra density and structure. It is a full, rich and concentrated red with dark, spicy-plummy fruit and a hint of vanilla and cocoa from 100% new wood. It needs at least 4–5 years, as the tannins can be a bit raw and aggressive in its youth. (DM)

● **Clos Saint Martin** Saint-Emilion Grand Cru Classé★★★★ £F

CH. SANSONNET   Saint-Emilion GC

Patrick d'Aulan   33330 Saint-Emilion
UK stockists: AAA

Sansonnet is a small property with an ancient grand château situated in the north-east of the appellation. Just over 6ha are planted to a mix of Merlot (85%) and Cabernet Franc (15%) and output is only just over 1,500 cases a year, so the wine is fairly scarce. It offers impressive depth and substance, with dark, ripe berry fruit and marked new oak and is supple and finely structured. It will evolve well for a decade and needs half that to hit its stride. (DM)

● **Château Sansonnet** Saint-Emilion Grand Cru★★★ £E

CLOS DE SARPE   Saint-Emilion GC

Beyney family   33330 Saint Christophe des Bardes

Barely 1,000 cases are made a year of this massive and densely textured old-style Bordeaux red. A blend of Merlot and Cabernet Franc, it is sourced from argilo-calcareous soils and from vines cropped at very low yields. The wine is dark when young and marked by an intense, almost overwhelming blackberry fruit character. There is a hint of oak in the background and considerable tannin which demands 7 or 8 years' patience. The second label, Charles de Sarpe, is softer and quite a bit lighter. (DM)

● **Clos de Sarpe** Saint-Emilion Grand Cru★★★★ £G
● **Charles de Sarpe** Saint-Emilion Grand Cru★★★ £E

CH. TAILLEFER   Pomerol

Catherine Moueix   33501 Libourne
UK stockists: Han

This quite grand 12-ha property is to be found in the southern part of the appellation on the edge of Libourne. The vineyards are now around 30 years old and are planted to 80% Merlot with the balance Cabernet Franc. The wine is made in a fairly traditional plummy, earthy style with supple, easy tannins and will drink well with 3 or 4 years' ageing. (DM)

● **Château Taillefer** Pomerol★★★ £E

CH. TERTRE-DAUGAY   Saint-Emilion GCC

Alexandre de Malet-Roquefort   c/o Ch. Armens 33330 Saint-Peu-d'Armens
UK stockists: Tur, C&B, F&R

This property is under the same ownership as Château ARMENS. During the last 3–4 years quality has been increasingly impressive under consultant Stéphane Derenoncourt, who is also responsible for PAVIE-MACQUIN, Clos PUY ARNAUD and the wines of CANON-LA-GAFFELIÈRE. Tertre-Daugay is rich and fleshy but now offers an impressive level of refinement and class too. (DM)

● **Château Tertre-Daugay** Saint-Emilion Grand Cru Classé★★★★ £E

CH. TERTRE-RÔTEBOEUF   Saint-Emilion GC

François Mitjaville   33330, Saint-Laurent-des-Combes
UK stockists: AAA

Although this remarkable Saint-Emilion has not been elevated to Grand Cru Classé status, the property enjoys a highly propitious site for producing fine wine. Low yields, meticulous care in the vineyard and ageing in new oak for a year and a half all contribute to the very high quality of the wine, which has been exemplary for the last 15 years. It is immensely complex with a myriad of dark and spicy fruits and stylish oak. It will age gracefully and requires 6 or 7 years' patience. (DM)

● **Château Tertre-Rôteboeuf** Saint-Emilion Grand Cru★★★★★ £H

CH. TEYSSIER   Saint-Emilion GC

Maltus family   33330 Saint-Emilion
UK stockists: AAA

Englishman Jonathan Maltus purchased this property in 1994 and since then has added a number of other more impressively sited vineyard holdings. Teyssier itself is a soft and attractive, relatively forward, spicy Saint-Emilion full of fleshy, dark, plummy fruit. It is sourced from the low-lying vineyards in the south of the appellation and is a testament to what can be achieved from these lesser sites. Vinification is modern, as with all the wines here, with pre-fermentation maceration, malolactic in barrel and ageing on lees for added richness. Château Laforge is produced from a number of superior Grand Cru sites, including the Le Chatelot vineyard purchased from Château CANON in 2000. The wine is rich and supple, finely structured and with impressive depth and concentration. The high Merlot content (92%) of the blend accounts for its opulent, exotic style. Le DÔME is the top red label and comes from a single parcel neighbouring Château ANGELUS. There is also an excellent barrel-fermented white, Clos Nardian, which blends all 3 white Bordeaux varieties. The Muscadelle comes from vines planted in the mid-1930s. Sourced from 3 tiny, ideally exposed parcels in limestone soils just across the river Dordogne south of the Saint-Emilion AC, this is a rich and complex, subtly oaked white. New for the 2004 vintage were Les Astéries, a super-premium low yielding cuvée and Château Grand Destieu. We will be bringing you ratings and further details in the next edition. Maltus also produces a good red and white Bordeaux, Château LACROIX, both of which are vinified at Teyssier. (DM)

● **Château Teyssier** Saint-Emilion Grand Cru★★★ £D
● **Château Laforge** Saint-Emilion Grand Cru★★★★ £F
O **Clos Nardian** Bordeaux★★★★ £F

CH. TOUR DE MIRAMBEAU   Entre-deux-Mers

Vignobles Despagne   33420 Naujon-et-Posiac
UK stockists: Odd

The Despagne family have a total of nearly 90ha under vine and production is not inconsiderable at nearly 50,000 cases a year. Just over half the land is planted to red varieties and it is these that really stand out here. A decent regular white takes the Bordeaux AC as does a rosé and there is an Entre-deux-Mers white as well. Cuvée Passion white is good and the red version is one of the best wines of the Bordeaux Supérieur AC. The recently produced super-*cuvée* Girolate only takes the humble Bordeaux AC but is a wine of serious depth and structure. Produced from an extraordinarily steep 10-ha site with very low yields, this dark, spicy, almost over-extracted red sets new standards for the area. It is likely to drink well young. The family also own the Premières Côtes de Bordeaux property Château MONT PÉRAT. (DM)

Château Tour de Mirambeau
● **Château Tour de Mirambeau** Bordeaux Supérieur Cuvée Passion★★ £C
● **Château Tour de Mirambeau** Bordeaux Supérieur★ £B
O **Château Tour de Mirambeau** Bordeaux Supérieur Cuvée Passion★★ £C
Girolate
● **Girolate** Bordeaux★★★★ £E

CH LA TOUR FIGEAC   Saint-Emilion GCC

Otto Rettenmaier   33330, Saint-Emilion
UK stockists: AAA

Biodynamically tended 14.6-ha property planted to Merlot (60%) and Cabernet Franc. Low yields are maintained and consultancy comes from

Christine Derenoncourt, wife of roving Bordeaux guru Stéphane. The wine is produced very much in an opulent, forward and showy style and the oak can be just a bit assertive in its youth, but it will offer good drinking within 4 or 5 years. (DM)

● **Château La Tour Figeac** Saint-Emilion Grand Cru Classé★★★★ £F

CH. THIEULEY   Bordeaux
Francis Courselle   La Sauve, 33670 Créon
UK stockists: **CTy**

This is an excellent example of what can be achieved under the humble Bordeaux AC but so very rarely is. Francis Courselle now has some 80ha of vineyard, 45ha of which are planted to red varieties. These go towards the crafting of stylish, straightforward, berry-fruited AC Bordeaux, impressively dense, structured Supérieur Réserve and attractively fruity *clairet.* A Premières Côtes de Bordeaux, Clos Sainte-Anne, is also now produced. The regular white is crisp and fresh and full of grassy green apple fruit, whereas the Cuvée Francis Courselle, which is barrel-fermented and aged with *bâtonnage,* is elegantly toasty and oaky. (DM)

● **Château Thieuley** Bordeaux★ £B
● **Château Thieuley** Bordeaux Supérieur Francis Courselle Réserve★★ £C
O **Château Thieuley** Bordeaux★ £B Bordeaux Cuvée Francis Courselle★★ £C

CH. LES TROIS CROIX   Fronsac
Bertrand Léon   33126 Fronsac

The Léon family purchased this 15-ha estate in 1995. The vineyard is dominated by Merlot (90%) and the balance is Cabernet Franc, which provides a nicely lifted, leafy, cedary quality to the wine. The vineyard is also one of the highest in the appellation and this too tends to result in a lighter, more elegant style than at many neighbouring properties. 2000, 03 and 04, though, all produced wines of depth and intensity as well as impressively deep, dark, rich fruit. Four to 5 years' cellaring is advisable. (DM)

● **Château Les Trois Croix** Fronsac★★★ £C

CH. TROPLONG-MONDOT   Saint-Emilion GCC
Valette family   33330 Saint-Emilion
UK stockists: AAA

This has been a consistently excellent source of top Saint-Emilion over the past decade and longer and is unquestionably a serious candidate for elevation to Premier Grand Cru Classé status. There are some 30ha of vines, the bulk of which are Merlot. This high percentage is reflected in the wine, which is full, rich, plump and fleshy with marked new oak and considerable refinement. The initial firm tannic structure means the wine needs 6 or 7 years' cellaring. Very long and impressive and top-notch in recent vintages. The 2000 was ★★★★★. (DM)

● **Château Troplong-Mondot** Saint-Emilion Grand Cru Classé★★★★ £G

CH. TROTANOY   Pomerol
Moueix family   33500 Pomerol
UK stockists: AAA

Typically small Pomerol property of 7ha, which, like PÉTRUS, is owned by the Moueix family. The wine is dense and very seriously structured, with considerable grip and tannin when young. Seven or 8 years' cellaring will see the evolution of all sorts of opulent black fruit characters and oriental spices all effortlessly wrapped up in very classy new wood. On top form since 1997,

93

although there were a number of disappointing vintages in the 1980s. (DM)
● **Château Trotanoy** Pomerol★★★★★ £H

CH TROTTEVIEILLE Saint-Emilion 1er GCC
Casteja family   33330, Saint-Emilion
UK stockists: AAA
Since 2000 this property has reclaimed its place in the top rank of Saint-Emilion after a period in the relative doldrums in the early to mid-90s. There are a total of 10ha here with Merlot accounting for 50% of the vineyard, Cabernet Franc a very sizeable 45% and the balance Cabernet Sauvignon. The wine is rich and plump with dark, spicy berry fruit and marked new oak, underpinned by a fine mineral purity. This firm and structured wine needs at least 5 or 6 years to bring the fruit, oak and tannin fully into balance. (DM)
● **Château Trottevieille** Saint-Emilion 1er Grand Cru Classé★★★★ £F

CH. DE VALANDRAUD Saint-Emilion GC www.thunevin.com
Jean-Luc Thunevin   6 Rue Guadet, 33330 Saint-Emilion
UK stockists: **Far**,AAA
This is the original *garagiste* wine, first made in 1991. Like most of its kind it was originally produced in limited volumes, although output is increasing following vineyard acquisitions. The property consists of various plots, some of them on the low-lying plain below the town of Saint-Emilion. New sites have been added between 1997 and 1999 and Clos Badon, Virginie de Valandraud and Prieuré Lescours are now produced separately. To help ensure the integrity of the Valandraud labels a second wine, 3 de Valandraud, is also produced. Yields are restricted and the harvest is carefully sorted prior to vinification. The winemaking is modern, with a pre-fermentation cold soak and malolactic in barrel. The wines are neither fined nor filtered and, particularly in the case of Valandraud and Clos Badon, offer dense, fleshy and extracted reds of increasing depth and purity. The style is forward and accessible, yet they possess striking grip and structure. A very impressive Kosher Valandraud red is also produced, although due to the need to make it under strict conditions it doesn't have quite the level of complexity or depth of Valandraud itself. A white Bordeaux is also now being produced in tiny quantities and is labelled No. 1 Blanc de Valandraud. Jean-Luc Thunevin is involved with a number of other small-scale projects, among them GRACIA and Andréas in Saint-Emilion and MAROJALLIA in Margaux. He has also purchased the Margaux property Bellevue de Tayac and has yet to decide how it will be labelled in future. The 2004 vintage shows much promise. (DM)
Château Valandraud
● **Château de Valandraud** Saint-Emilion Grand Cru★★★★★ £F
● **Château de Valandraud Kosher** Saint-Emilion Grand Cru★★★ £F
Clos Badon
● **Clos Badon** Saint-Emilion Grand Cru★★★★ £F
Virginie de Valandraud
● **Virginie de Valandraud** Saint-Emilion Grand Cru★★★ £F
Château Preuré Lescours
● **Château Prieuré Lescours** Saint-Emilion Grand Cru★★★ £F

CH. VEYRY Côtes de Castillon
Christian Veyry   33330 Saint-Laurent des Combes
Tiny 4-ha property planted to Merlot (95%) and Cabernet Franc. The sole wine, a Côtes de Castillon, was first made only in 1997. It has been

consistently good during the last 5 years and 2004 looks set to maintain this record. The wine has a lovely piercing mineral quality to its fruit, with characteristic warm, dark and spicy Merlot flavours and real depth, elegance and class for this level. Up to 5 years' ageing would not go amiss. (DM)

● **Château Veyry** Côtes de Castillon★★★ £C

CH. LA VIEILLE CURE Fronsac www.expressions-de-fronsac.com
Colin Ferenbach Coutreau, 33141 Saillans
UK stockists: N&P,F&R

This is yet another of a number of outperformers in Bordeaux's lesser appellations and money has been pumped into the property to improve quality over the last 15 years. There are 18ha under vine, 75% planted to Merlot. Michel Rolland has provided consultancy input and the wine is typically extracted, ripe and seductive in style. Only the slightest hard edge can occasionally drift into the equation. The wine is a good medium-term ageing prospect. It has been good to very good since the late 1990s. There is also now an impressive second wine, Sacristie de La Vieille Cure, which other more esteemed properties from grander appellations would struggle to emulate. (DM)

● **Château La Vieille Cure** Fronsac★★★ £D

VIEUX-CHÂTEAU-CERTAN Pomerol www.vieuxchateaucertan.com
Thienpont family 33500 Pomerol
UK stockists: AAA

Cabernet Franc and Cabernet Sauvignon account for 40% of the 14ha of vineyard here and this is in part the reason for the surprisingly dense and powerful structure of the wine. The tannin can be very firm in the wine's youth and it really needs a decade to begin to show its true class, when it becomes very refined and harmonious. Excellent from 1998 on – ★★★★★. 1995 and 90 were also very good here. (DM)

● **Vieux-Château-Certan** Pomerol★★★★★ £H

CH. VIEUX MAILLET Pomerol
Griet Laviale-Van Malderen 16. Route de Maillet, 33500 Pomerol
UK stockists: Jas

Small property with barely more than 4ha under vine. This is dominated by Merlot (82%) with the remainder planted to Cabernet Franc. The wine is a traditional, earthy style of Pomerol with some reasonably hard tannins. It offers good depth and intensity but is made in a fairly extracted way and in 2004 this was just a touch overdone. It definitely needs 4 or 5 years' ageing. (DM)

● **Château Vieux Maillet** Pomerol★★★ £F

CH. VILLARS Fronsac
Thierry Gaudrie 33141 Saillans

Decent Fronsac property that has been producing consistently good wine throughout the last 4 or 5 years. The property is relatively large with just under 30ha of vineyards planted to a mix of Merlot (73%), Cabernet Franc (18%) and Cabernet Sauvignon (9%). The wine possesses impressive depth as well as typically dark, berry-scented fruit. The inclusion of the Cabernets gives it a firm tannic grip and it needs 1 or 2 years longer than many others from this AC. (DM)

● **Château Villars** Fronsac★★★ £D

95

OTHER WINES OF NOTE

CH. BALESTARD-LA-TONNELLE ● **Saint-Emilion** Grand Cru Classé★★ £E

CH. BARDE-HAUT ● **Saint-Emilion** Grand Cru★★★ £E

CH. BAUDUC ○ **Bordeaux** Les Trois Hectares★★ £C

CH. BEAULIEU ● **Bordeaux**★★ £C

CH. BEAU-SOLEIL ● **Pomerol**★★ £E

CH. BELLEFONT-BELCIER ● **Saint-Emilion** Grand Cru★★★ £E

CH. BELLEGRAVE ● **Pomerol**★★ £E

CH. BONNES RIVES ● **Lalande-de-Pomerol**★★ £C

CH. BRANDA ● **Puisseguin-Saint-Emilion**★★ £C

CH. BRÛLESÉCAILLE ● **Côtes de Bourg**★★ £B

CH. BRUN DESPAGNE ● **Bordeaux Supérieur**★ £B Quintessence★★ £C

CH. CADET BON ● **Saint-Emilion** Grand Cru Classé★★ £E

CH. CANON ● **Canon-Fronsac**★★ £C

CH. CAP DE MOURLIN ● **Saint Emilion** Grand Cru Classé★★ £D

CH. CASSAGNE HAUT-CANON ● **Canon-Fronsac**★ £B Truffière★★ £C

CH. DE CÉRONS ○ **Cérons**★★ £B

CH. CHADENNE ● **Fronsac**★ £B

CH. LES CHARMES GODARD ○ **Bordeaux Côtes de Francs**★★ £B

CH. CHARRON ○ **Premières Côtes de Blaye** Acacia★★ £B

CH. CLOS CHAUMONT ● **Premières Côtes de Bordeaux**★★ £B

CH. CLOS DE LA TOUR ● **Bordeaux Supérieur**★★ £B

CH. LA COMMANDERIE ● **Saint-Emilion** Grand Cru★★ £D

CH. LA CROIX DE L'ESPÉRANCE ● **Lussac Saint-Emilion**★★ £D

CONFIANCE ● **Premières Côtes de Blaye**★★★ £D

CH. DE LA COUR D'ARGENT ● **Bordeaux**★★ £D

CH. CORBIN MICHOTTE ● **Saint-Emilion** Grand Cru Classé★★ £F

CH. CÔTE MONPEZAT ● **Côtes de Castillon**★★ £C

CH. DU COURLAT ● **Lussac-Saint-Emilion**★ £C

CH. LA COURONNE ● **Montagne-Saint-Emilion** Reclos★★ £C

DOMAINE DE COURTEILLAC ● **Bordeaux Supérieur**★★ £B
○ **Bordeaux Supérieur**★ £B

CH. LA CROIX ● **Pomerol**★★ £D

CH. LA CROIX BELLEVUE ● **Lalande-de-Pomerol**★ £C

CROIX DE LABRIE ● **Saint Emilion** Grand Cru★★★ £F

LA CROIX DU PRIEURÉ ● **Premières Côtes de Blaye**★★ £D

CH. LA CROIX TAILLEFER ● **Pomerol**★★ £D

CH. DU CROS ○ **Loupiac**★★ £C

CH. CROS FIGEAC ● **Saint-Emilion** Grand Cru★★ £E

CH. DALEM ● **Fronsac**★★ £D

CH. LE DOYENNÉ ● **Premières Côtes de Bordeaux**★★ £C

L'EGRÉGORE ● **Bordeaux**★★★ £D

CH. L'ENCLOS ● **Pomerol**★★★ £E

CH. LA FLEUR ● **Saint-Emilion** Grand Cru★★ £D

CH. LA FLEUR-MONGIRON ● **Bordeaux**★★★ £C

CH. DE FONBEL ● **Saint-Emilion** Grand Cru★★ £E

CH. FONPLÉGADE ● **Saint-Emilion** Grand Cru Classé★★ £E

CH. FONROQUE ● **Saint-Emilion** Grand Cru Classé★★ £E

CH. DU GABY ● **Canon-Fronsac**★★ £C

CH. GADRAS ● **Bordeaux**★ £B

CH. LA GRANGERE ● **Saint-Emilion** Grand Cru★★ £D

CH. LA GRAVE À POMEROL ● **Pomerol**★★ £E

CH. HAUT-BALLET ● **Fronsac**★★ £C

CH. HAUT-MACO ● **Côtes de Bourg** Cuvée Jean★ £C

CH. HAUT-MOULEYRE ○ **Bordeaux**★★ £C

CH. HAUT-SEGOTTES ● **Saint-Emilion Grand Cru**★★ £D

HOMMAGE DE MALESAN ● **Bordeaux**★★★ £D

CH. JEAN DE GUÉ ● **Lalande-de-Pomerol**★★ £C Cuvée Prestige★★★ £D

CH. LES JONQUEYRES ● **Premières Côtes de Blaye**★★ £B

CH. LABADIE ● **Côtes de Bourg** Vieilli en Fûts de Chêne★ £C

CH. LAFLEUR-GAZIN ● Pomerol★★ £E

CH. LAGRANGE ● Pomerol★★ £E

CH. LANIOTE ● Saint-Emilion Grand Cru Classé★ £E

CH. LARMANDE ● Saint-Emilion Grand Cru Classé★★★ £E

CH. LA TOUR-DU-PIN-FIGEAC ● Saint-Emilion Grand Cru Classé★★ £E

CH. LA VIOLETTE MANOIR DU GRAVOUX ● Côtes de Castillon★★ £B

CLOS LEO ● Côtes de Castillon★★★ £C

CH. LOUBENS ○ Sainte-Croix-du-Mont★★ £C

CH. DU LYONNAT ● Lussac-Saint-Emilion★★ £C

CH. LA MARZELLE ● Saint-Emilion Grand Cru Classé★★ £E

CH. LA MADELEINE ● Saint-Emilion Grand Cru★★ £E

CH. MAZEYRES ● Pomerol★★★ £E

CH. MERCIER ● Côtes de Bourg Cuvée Prestige★★ £C

CH. MESSILE AUBERT ● Montagne-Saint-Emilion★★ £C

CH. MONGIRON ● Bordeaux La Fleur Mongiron★★★ £C

CH. NÉNIN ● Pomerol★★★ £F

CH. NODOZ ● Côtes de Bourg★ £B

CH. PENIN ● Bordeaux Supérieur Grande Sélection★★ £B

CH. PETIT GRAVE-AINÉ ● Saint-Emilion Grand Cru★★★ £D

CH. LA POINTE ● Pomerol★★ £D

CH. LA PRADE ● Bordeaux Côtes de Francs★★ £C

CH. DE PRESSAC ● Saint-Emilion Grand Cru★★ £D

CH. LA RAME ○ Sainte-Croix-du-Mont Tradition★★ £C Réserve★★★ £E

CH. RAUZAN DESPAGNE ○ Bordeaux Blanc Cuvée Passion★★ £C

RECLOS DE LA COURONNE ● Montagne-Saint-Emilion★★ £C

CH. REMPIMPLET ● Côtes de Bourg★ £B

CH. RICHELIEU ● Fronsac★★ £C

CH. RIPEAU ● Saint-Emilion Grand Cru Classé★★ £E

CH. DE LA ROCHE BEAULIEU ● Côtes de Castillon Amavinum★★ £C
● Bordeaux Rex Bibendi★★★ £D

CH. ROCHEBELLE ● Saint-Emilion Grand Cru★★ £D

CH. ROCHER BELLEVUE FIGEAC ● Saint-Emilion Grand Cru★★ £D

CH. ROLAND LA GARDE ● Premières Côtes de Blaye Grand Vin★★ £C

ROMULUS ● Pomerol★★★ £E

CH. ROYLLAND ● Saint-Emilion Grand Cru★★ £D

CH. SAINTE-COLOMBE ● Côtes de Castillon★★ £C

CH SAINTE-MARIE ● Bordeaux Supérieur★ £B Alios★★ £C
○ Entre-deux-Mers★★ £B Madlys★★ £C

CH. DE SALES ● Pomerol★★★ £E

CH. SEGONZAC ● Premières Côtes de Blaye★ £B

CH. TAYAC ● Côtes de Bourg Cuvée Prestige★★ £C Cuvée Reservée★★ £C

CH. TEYSSIER ● Montagne-Saint-Emilion★★ £C

CH. TRIANON ● Saint-Emilion Grand Cru★★ £D

VILLA MONGIRON ● Bordeaux★★ £B

CH. VILLHARDY ● Saint-Emilion Grand Cru★★ £D

CH. YON FIGEAC ● Saint-Emilion Grand Cru Classé★★★ £E

Work in progress!!

Producers under consideration for the next edition
CH. CANTELAUZE (POMEROL)
CH. DU CHAMP DES TREILLES (SAINTE-FOY BORDEAUX)
CH. CHAPELLE MARACAN (BORDEAUX SUPÉRIEUR)
CH. DE CHELIVETTE (PREMIÈRES CÔTES DE BORDEAUX)
CH. LA CROIX SAINT-GEORGES (POMEROL)
CH. LES CRUZELLES (LALANDE-DE-POMEROL)
CH. GARRAUD (LALANDE-DE-POMEROL)
CH. LA GRAVIÈRE (LALANDE-DE-POMEROL)
CH. LA SERRE (SAINT-EMILION GRAND CRU CLASSÉ)
CH. MÉMOIRES (PREMIÈRES CÔTES DE BORDEAUX)

DOM. MONDÉSIR-GAZIN (PREMIÈRES CÔTES DE BLAYE)
VIEUX CH. CHAMPS DE MARS (CÔTES DE CASTILLON)

Author's choice (DM)

BORDEAUX RIGHT BANK

Great cellarworthy Right Bank reds
CH. AUSONE ● Saint-Emilion I er Grand Cru Classé
CH. CHEVAL-BLANC ● Saint-Emilion I er Grand Cru Classé
CH. LA CONSEILLANT ● Pomerol
CH. L'ÉGLISE-CLINET ● Pomerol
CH. LAFLEUR ● Pomerol
CH. PAVIE-DECESSE ● Saint-Emilion Grand Cru Classé
CH. PÉTRUS ● Pomerol
CH. LE PIN ● Pomerol
CH. TERTRE-RÔTEBOEUF ● Saint-Emilion Grand Cru
CH. TROPLONG-MONDOT ● Saint-Emilion Grand Cru Classé
CH. PAVIE ● Saint-Emilion Grand Cru Classé
CH. CANON ● Saint-Emilion Grand Cru Classé
CH. DE VALANDRAUD ● Saint-Emilion Grand Cru
VIEUX CH. CERTAN ● Pomerol
CH. CHAUVIN ● Saint-Emilion Grand Cru Classé

New Right Bank classics
CH. BEAU-SÉJOUR BÉCOT ● Saint-Emilion La Gomerie Grand Cru
CH. BEAUREGARD ● Pomerol
LE DÔME ● Saint-Emilion Grand Cru
CH. FAUGÈRES ● Saint-Emilion Péby-Faugères Grand Cru
LA FLEUR DU BOÙARD ● Lalande-de-Pomerol
CH. FOMBRAUGE ● Saint-Emilion Magrez-Fombrauge Grand Cru
LA MONDOTTE ● Saint-Emilion Grand Cru
CH. MONBOUSQUET ● Saint-Emilion Grand Cru
CH. QUINAULT ● Saint-Emilion Quinault l'Enclos Grand Cru
CH. GAZIN ● Pomerol
CH. FOMBRAUGE ● Saint-Emilion Magrez-Fombrauge Grand Cru
LA MONDOTTE ● Saint-Emilion Grand Cru

Emerging Right Bank reds
DOM. DE L'A ● Côtes de Castillon
CH. D'AIGUIHE ● Côtes de Castillon
LA CROIX DE PEYROLIE ● Lussac-Saint-Emilion
CH. FONTENIL ● Fronsac
CH. MOULIN PEY-LABRIE ● Canon-Fronsac
CLOS PUY ARNAUD ● Côtes de Castillon
CH. PUYGUERAUD ● Bordeaux-Côtes des Francs
CH. DE LA RIVIÈRE ● Fronsac
CH. ROC DE CAMBES ● Côtes de Bourg
CH. LA VIEILLE CURE ● Fronsac
CH. AMPÉLIA ● Côtes de Castillon
CH. CARIGNAN ● 1er Côtes de Bordeaux Prima
ESSENCE DE DOURTHE ● Bordeaux
CH. MOULIN HAUT-LAROQUE ● Fronsac
CH. GRAND CORBIN_DESPAGNE ● Saint-Emilion Grand Cru

Top Right Bank values
CH. BARRABAQUE ● Fronsac
CH. BEL-AIR LA ROYÈRE ● Côtes de Castillon
CH. BONNET ● Bordeaux Réserve
CH. CARSIN ○ Bordeaux Cuvée Prestige
CH. LA DAUPHINE ● Fronsac

CH. DAUPHINÉ-RONDILLON ● **Loupiac** La Cuvée d'Or

CH. REIGNAC ● **Bordeaux Superieur**

CLOS NARDIAN ○ **Bordeaux**

CH. CAP DE FAUGÈRES ● **Côtes de Castillon**

VIEUX CH. GACHET ● **Lalande-de-Pomerol**

CH. LA MAURIANE ● **Puisseguin-Saint-Emilion**

CH. REYNON ○ **Bordeaux** Vieilles Vignes

RECOMMENDED HOTELS AND RESTAURANTS - BORDEAUX

Top Hotels

★★★★★*Sources de Caudalie*   Chemin de Smith Haut Lafite, Martillac 33650

Tel. 05 57 83 83 83   Fax 05 57 83 83 84

Email sources@sources-caudalie.com   43 rooms   £F/H

★★★★*Relais de Margaux*   Chemin de l'île Vincent, Margaux 33460

Tel. 05 57 88 38 30 Fax 05 57 88 31 73

Email relais-margaux@relais-margaux.fr   58 rooms   £D/F

Top Restaurants

★★★★*Ch. Cordeillan-Bages*   Route des Châteaux, Pauillac 33255

Tel. 05 56 59 24 24 Fax 05 56 59 01 89

Email cordeillan@relaischateaux.fr   £F

★★★★*Pavillon des Boulevards*   120r Croix de Seguey, Bordeaux 33000

Tel. 05 56 81 51 02 Fax 05 56 51 14 58

Email pavillon.des.boulevards@wanadoo.fr   £F

Value for money Hotels

★*Clemenceau*   4 cours Clemenceau, Bordeaux 33000

Tel. 05 56 52 98 98 Fax 05 56 81 24 91

Email clemenceau@hotelbordeaux.com   45 rooms   £A

★★*Les Remparts*   16 rue Château, Gensac 33890

Tel. 05 57 47 43 46 Fax 05 57 47 46 76

Email rempartsgensac@aol.com   7 rooms   £B

Value for money restaurants

★★*Chez Servais*   14 place Decazes, Libourne 33500

Tel. 05 57 51 83 97 Fax 05 57 51 83 97

No email address   £B

★★★*Le Saprien*   14 Rue Principale, Sauternes 33210

Tel. 05 56 76 60 87 Fax 05 56 76 68 92

No email address   £B/C

BORDEAUX RECIPES

SAUCISSE ET HUITRES ET VIN BLANC

Tradition demands that for a fine white wine tasting you first eat a raw oyster,
followed by a small piece of very hot sausage, followed by some bread and butter…
and then start again until you have consumed 12 oysters!!!

RECOMMENDED WINES

*Well, you can probably have almost anything with this, from the humblest Bordeaux Blanc
Sec, to top white Pessac-Léognan, but whatever you do, this dish acts better than go faster
stripes! From the best producers in the book, you can go no wrong than choosing Denis
Dubourdieu's modestly priced Clos Floridène and if you want to up the ante, you could go for*

99

a little Bordeaux Blanc AC called Pavillon Blanc de Château Margaux, but they are both probably too good for just an aperitif!

LOTTE À LA BORDELAISE

Ingredients for 4 people: 500gr. monk tails cut into 2cms. thick slices - some oil for cooking - 400gr. tomatoes, peeled seeded and chopped - 2 good shallots, chopped - thyme and bay leaf - 1dl. Madeira, 1dl. white wine.

Shallow fry the slices of monk fish in the hot oil on both sides and remove; keep warm. Sauté the shallots in the same oil, add the tomatoes, Madeira and white wine, herbs and seasoning, and cook until the sauce is smooth and thick; put the monk fish back in the pan, cook until almost done (a few minutes) and serve sprinkled with parsley and croutons.

RECOMMENDED WINES

Monkfish is a firm, fleshy fish and the Madeira in the sauce will add a touch of sweetness, so good quality Pessac-Léognan is the order of the day here. (Or you could use the Clos Floridène as above – it will go extremely well). Without going into the stratosphere on prices, Ch. Malartic-Lagravière (and for a bit more money and quality) Domaine de Chevalier, would both do admirably.

ENTRECÔTES À LA BORDELAISE

Ingredients for 4 people: 4 entrecôtes (150gr each) - a little oil for shallow frying, one good shallot, a pinch of flour, 2dl. Bordeaux red wine, 2dl. stock, 60gr. of diced raw marrow from a marrowbone, chopped parsley, salt &pepper.

Cook the steaks to taste and remove slightly underdone - to the same pan add the shallot, and a good pinch of flour: stir well, and add the wine and stock and cook until reduced. Add the raw marrow; boil quickly on a high light to integrate the marrow fat to the sauce; season and coat each steak with this sauce and some more marrow (if available, and very quickly poached in boiling water)

RECOMMENDED WINES

I had a bottle of Ch. Pavie Macquin 1999 the other day and it would have been just WONDERFUL with this dish (I am still salivating!) instead of the ham sandwich, but again the choice is so wide with Bordeaux wines, and they are so digestible – ideal food wines – that practically anything with any type of pedigree is going to match. It really depends on your pocket. This dish is not overpowering with strange flavours, so drink the best you can afford – it won't detract from the wine.

CANNELETS DE BORDEAUX:

Ingredients: 1 litre of milk, 100gr. butter, 450gr. sugar, 4 whole eggs and 4 yolks, 300gr flour, two vanilla pods or two teaspoons of vanilla essence, a good dash of Rum, Armagnac or Cognac.

The night before: boil the milk with vanilla pods or essence; then add butter and melt, beat the eggs, egg yolks and the sugar together until light. Put the flour through a sieve and add slowly to sugar & egg mix. Add cool milk slowly and mix very vigorously (always by hand, not machine) until smooth. Add the alcohol (two or three tablespoons) and leave overnight. The next day bake in hot oven until the top is quite dark. Take out of oven let it rest for 2 minutes and unmould.

There are some special moulds for cannelets. The metal ones are individually free standing, whereas there is a new type of tray mould which is fantastic, very pliable and non-stick which you place on a flat tray before filling. If you use the free standing metal ones, butter them extremely well and line with sugar. If using the other type, just sprinkle the insides with sugar; fill three quarters full.

RECOMMENDED WINES

Oh! Cannelets de Bordeaux. Not really a proper dessert dish, but such a more-ish pre- or post- dessert, or a wonderful alternative to petits fours. What better way to finish a meal than with a tray full of cannelets and sipping your favourite Sauternes. Doisy-Védrines is reasonably priced 4 star quality, whilst Ch. Rieussec is super 5 stars without paying the earth

Burgundy can be considered as four distinct entities. In the north lies Chablis, at its heart is the Côte d'Or, next comes the Côte Chalonnaise then, still further south, the Mâconnais. The main appellations for each are given below, with more detail in the individual sections that follow.

Chablis & Yonne

Chablis and the surrounding vineyards are isolated from the heart of Burgundy, being almost halfway to Paris from the Côte d'Or. All Chablis is produced from the Chardonnay grape and is classified by vineyard site as either **Petit Chablis, Chablis, Chablis Premier Cru** or **Chablis Grand Cru**. Other than Chablis there's Sauvignon under the **Saint-Bris** AC and occasional pure cherryish Pinot Noir from **Irancy** AC. Pinot Noir or Chardonnay from other villages in the Yonne is suffixed **Bourgogne**.

Côte d'Or & Côte Chalonnaise

The Côte d'Or is synonymous with Burgundy and includes all its great red wines. The two parts are the more northerly Côte de Nuits (mostly red) and extending southwards, the Côte de Beaune (white and red). The CÔTE DE NUITS is Burgundy's most classic red wine district and based primarily on just one grape variety, Pinot Noir. It runs from **Marsannay** and **Fixin** through the leading communes of **Gevrey-Chambertin** (including leading *grands crus* **Chambertin** and **Clos de Bèze**), **Morey-Saint-Denis** (with *grands crus* **Clos de la Roche, Clos Saint-Denis, Clos des Lambrays** and **Clos de Tart**), **Chambolle Musigny** (with **Bonnes Mares** and **Le Musigny**) and **Vougeot** (for **Clos Vougeot**), Flagey-Echezeaux (for **Echezeaux** and **Grands Echezeaux**), **Vosne-Romanée** (*grands crus* **La Romanée, Romanée-Conti, Richebourg, Romanée-Saint-Vivant, La Grande Rue**, and **La Tâche**) to **Nuits-Saint-Georges**. The CÔTE DE BEAUNE is famous for great white Burgundy made from Chardonnay, although more Pinot Noir is planted. Much of both is at least potentially very high quality. In a confusion of appellations in the north, **Aloxe-Corton** with the famous *grands crus* of **Corton** (mostly red) and **Corton-Charlemagne** (white) stands out. **Beaune, Pernand-Vergelesses** and **Savigny-lès-Beaune** produce fine reds but some good whites too, while the celebrated **Pommard** and **Volnay** are restricted to red. **Monthélie**, and **Auxey-Duresses** provide more affordable red and a little white, while **Saint-Romain** and the often excellent **Saint-Aubin** do better with white. The big three white Burgundy appellations are **Meursault, Puligny-Montrachet** (including *grands crus* **Chevalier-Montrachet, Le Montrachet** and part of **Bâtard-Montrachet**) and **Chassagne-Montrachet**. The latter also produces red as do **Santenay** and **Maranges** in the tail of the Côte d'Or.

The CÔTE CHALONNAISE begins close to this tail. Both the wines and the countryside are distinctly different but the village appellations are again classified for wines from Chardonnay and/or Pinot Noir – with the exception the first village, **Bouzeron**, which is classified for Aligoté. **Rully** makes more white than red, while **Mercurey** and **Givry** produce mostly red. The southernmost appellation, **Montagny**, is for Chardonnay alone. **Crémant de Bourgogne** is for the region's sparkling wine.

Mâconnais

As in the Côte de Beaune here too there is greatness in white wine (from Chardonnay), with a new wave of excellent producers beginning to emerge. Quality wine production is focused on **Pouilly-Fuissé** (with its four communes of Chaintré, Fuissé, Solutré and Vergisson), adjoined at its eastern end by the small **Pouilly-Loché** and **Pouilly-Vinzelles** ACs. Many other vineyards north and south of Pouilly-Fuissé qualify as **Saint-Véran**. There is fine quality too from **Viré-Clessé** and increasingly from several of some 43 villages that can be suffixed to Mâcon (eg **Mâcon-Bussières**).

101

BURGUNDY OVERVIEW

- SEREIN
- 2
- 1 Chablis
- 2 Auxerre
- 2
- •Dijon
- 3
- •Marsannay
- •Fixin
- •Gevrey-Chambertin
- •Morey-Saint-Denis
- • Chambolle-Musigny
- •Vougeot
- 4 •Vosne-Romanée
- •Nuits-Saint-Georges
- •Pernand-Vergelesses
- Savigny-lès-Beaune• 5 •Aloxe-Corton
- 6 •Beaune
- •Pommard
- Volnay•
- •Auxey-Duresses
- 6 •Meursault
- Chassagne-Montrachet• •Puligny-Montrachet
- Santenay• •Chagny
- Bouzeron• •Rully
- •Mercurey
- 7
- Givry• •Chalon-sur-Saône
- •Montagny
- SAÔNE
- 8
- •Viré
- 9
- •Clessé
- Milly-Lamartine• •La Roche Vineuse
- 12
- Vergisson• 10
- 12 •Pouilly •Mâcon
- Fuissé• 11
- •Chaintré
- 10

1 Chablis
2 Yonne (other vineyards)
3 Côte de Nuits
4 Hautes Côtes de Nuits
5 Côtes de Beaune
6 Hautes Côtes de Beaune
7 Côte Chalonnaise
8 Mâcon, Mâcon-Villages
9 Viré-Clessé
10 Pouilly-Fuissé
11 Pouilly-Loché, Pouilly-Vinzelles
12 Saint-Véran

Chablis is one of the great white wines of the world, and partly because the cultivation of the Chardonnay grape in these cool hills is so close to the limit of where obtaining full ripeness is possible. Success rarely comes easily, fraught with an annual battle against frost and rain, demanding constant diligence. The importance of fully ripe fruit cannot be understated. The wines should be vigorous, fresh, suffused with minerality but also with generosity and length of flavour without the greeness, harshness or indeed sulphur that some disciples have been duped into believing was authentic Chablis character.

Chablis

Style

So what defines that unique Chablis character? A fine, subtle gun-flint, smoke or stony mineral character and greengage plum aromas are typical – but these must be ripe plums. Some wines are more floral or appley, citrusy or peachy but there should still be an unmistakable minerally, steely aspect and marvellous depth, with a toasty, nutty (or honeyed) complexity with age. The vintage matters greatly; while the longevity of Chablis should never be underestimated, most wines from a weaker vintage will evolve quite quickly and the leaness, often greeness on the palate will never disappear.

Controversy

Two major areas of debate in the past two decades have been the extension of the *premier cru* vineyard area and the use of new oak but as important to quality are the issues of yield (often too high) and mechanical harvesting, which is widespread. The Union des Grands Crus in Chablis recently banned mechanical harvesting but many *premiers crus* are harvested in this way, in part due to the greater ease of using this method here in contrast to the Côte d'Or, where difficulties are posed by the more fragmented ownership of vineyards. Much of the argument over expansion of the *vignoble* concerns soil types and whether Portlandian and other limestones are capable of the same quality as fossilised Kimmeridgian limestone found in the established *grands* and *premiers crus*. The second area of debate is whether to oak or not to oak. There are now many good exponents of both schools of thought, though the style of each varies significantly. A *grand cru* from Domaine François Raveneau (aged in used oak) is a benchmark but most of the new oak versions from Drouhin or Verget are also of very high quality and have as much validity as those from the unoaked camp. Quality is the key, the question of style is more subjective and unless the oak overwhelms the wine it is down to personal choice. That said, Chablis should always taste of its origins and not be mistaken for something from the Côte de Beaune or further afield.

Classification

Understanding the Chablis classification is straightforward. There are four levels: **Chablis Grand Cru**, **Chablis Premier Cru**, **Chablis** and **Petit Chablis**. The seven *grands crus* that total 106ha of vineyards (the total Chablis vineyard area is now 4,500ha) are Blanchot, Bougros, Les Clos, Grenouilles, Preuses, Valmur and Vaudésir. Arguably the most consistent class comes from Les Clos, Valmur and Vaudésir but the producer is more important and a good producer's best *premiers crus* easily outperform weaker *grand cru* efforts. Seven times the area is designated Chablis Premier Cru, encompassing forty names. Less than half of these are in common usage as the main *premier cru* name is usually taken. This unfortunately causes confusion and better definition of these large vineyard areas might make for easier quality identification. Those

103

premiers crus with the greatest potential to be fine are Fourchaume, Montée de Tonnerre and Mont de Milieu, all lying on the same side (northern, right bank) of the river Serein as the *grand crus* and with similar exposures. But poorer examples of these will be surpassed easily by the best versions of *premiers crus* from the other side of the Serein (left bank), especially Montmains, Vaillons and Vau de Vey. The quality of regular Chablis is very much dependent on the producer whilst Petit Chablis is, for the most part, best avoided.

Yonne - life beyond Chablis

Most of the wines made in the area surrounding Chablis are made from Chardonnay, Pinot Noir or Aligoté. If conditions are generally less favoured in terms of soil and climate than in much of Chablis, it is possible to produce wines of reasonable concentration and sufficient ripeness in both colours from villages such as Coulanges-la-Vineuse and Irancy providing there is a fastidious approach to viticulture – the wines of Anita & Jean-Pierre Colinot are proof enough. **Irancy** is an AC for red in its own right; other villages are suffixed Bourgogne (**Bourgogne Coulanges-la-Vineuse, Bourgogne Chitry**) for red and white. **Bourgogne Côtes d'Auxerre** covers other villages in the vicinity of Auxerre (including Pinot Noir and Chardonnay from Saint-Bris-le-Vineux) while those from around Tonnerre, to the east of Chablis, are labelled **Bourgogne Épineuil**. Some growers are at least as successful with rosé as red. If the cultivation of Sauvignon in the Yonne seems unusual, consider that it's a relatively short hop to the Central Vineyards of the Loire Valley from here. However, few examples of **Saint-Bris** (Sauvignon from around Saint-Bris, Irancy and Chitry) are better than green and edgy, despite its promotion in 2003 to appellation status. Goisot is an exception. Further afield, some Chablis-like white is made some 50 km to the south of Chablis and Auxerre at Vézelay (**Bourgogne Vézelay**).

A-Z of producers by appellation/region

Chablis & Yonne

Chablis vintages

No two vintages in Chablis are quite alike and even from a good producer the choice of vintage can make a significant difference to the quality in your glass. Given the problems of frost, the not uncommon struggle for ripeness in cooler years, the incidence of mildew and rot in wetter years, and, too often, lack of a rigorous grape selection, short of being able to afford Raveneau from every vintage it is important to choose a vintage carefully especially if the wines are intended for cellaring.

Recent vintages in Chablis have been by no means bad though conditions have been highly variable, necessitating a flexible response from producers in their approach to vinification and ageing.

2004★★★/★★★★: This was always going to be a cooler vintage than 2003 and due to a successful flowering it was a large crop but a poor summer and uneven ripening required a rigorous approach in the vineyards prior to picking in early October. Despite some claims of 'quality and quantity' only where yields were kept down and the healthiest, ripest fruit used will the wines be first-rate.

2003★★/★★★★: A hitherto almost inconceivable vintage in Chablis, which suffered the same extreme heat as much of Europe, the like of which had never before been experienced here. With temperatures over 40C, conditions resulted in a small, extremely early harvest (late August!). The wines are atypically rich and ripe yet with surprisingly good structures from the very best producers (and much better than further south in Burgundy). Top examples have also retained classic minerality and are more approachable than usual but will also age well. Some lesser wines from cooler parts are uncharacteristically ripe and drinkable.

2002★★★★/★★★★★: This was a much more complete vintage than 2003 (and a bit closer to normality), despite some swings in the weather. The wines are ripe and concentrated, although just occasionally a little broad and diffuse. From the top echelon of producers there are many outstanding, balanced and ageworthy examples.

2001★★/★★★★: A difficult vintage: the wet and cold conditions of July and September resulted in rot and under-ripeness for many, and even where ripeness was achieved some wines lack balance. Nonetheless where there was a diligent grape selection the wines can be very good and very expressive of terroir (Fèvre for instance).

2000★★★/★★★★: Overall quality was higher than in 2001 with a warm sunny run-in to another early vintage in late September. However yields were generally high (a few producers excepted) and some wines are evolving quite quickly. The best, though, are concentrated, structured and balanced.

1999★★★★: Like 2000, 1999 was also fine. Despite some growers being affected by the late rains there are some excellent wines for drinking now while the best *grands crus* should be kept another 5–10 years.

Of early vintages, there were several other good vintages in the 1990s but (1990 apart) all come from the latter half of the decade. **1995**, **1996** and **1997** all produced good wines, particular the latter despite a very hot August. Due to an adverse growing season (frost, hail, mildew) **1998** Chablis is generally better avoided now as are the vast majority of wines from 1994, 1993, 1992, and 1991. However for a taste of how well Chablis can age consider the best from 1990 (an exceptional vintage), 1988 or even 1986.

A-Z of producers

JEAN-CLAUDE BESSIN

Jean-Claude Bessin   3 Rue de la Planchotte, 89800 Chablis
UK stockist: But, PWa, NYg

One of Chablis' best small domaines. Former architects Jean-Claude Bessin and his wife had the good fortune to inherit (from her family) prime Chablis vineyards. Seven of their 12ha are located in 3 leading *crus*, the *premiers crus* Montmains and Fourchaume, and *grand cru* Valmur; the Fourchaume in particular contains a wealth of fine old vines. Bessin has only been bottling his own wine since 1992 but has already produced plenty of rich, fruit-intense, unoaked Chablis notable for its ripeness. Oak is now employed for the Valmur but doesn't overwhelm its concentrated fruit, instead adding structure that should enhance its longevity. The regular Chablis can be drunk quite young, but the *crus* are better with 3 years' age or more. (PW)

O **Chablis Grand Cru** Valmur★★★ £D
O **Chablis Premier Cru** Montmains★★ £C Fourchaume★★★ £C O **Chablis**★★ £B

BILLAUD-SIMON   www.billaud-simon.com

Billaud-Simon family   Quai de Reugny, BP 46, 89800 Chablis
UK stockist: BBR, CTy, L&W, HHB, IGH, WSc, NYg, Sel

A family domaine dating from 1815 making brilliant, predominantly unoaked Chablis under the winemaking direction of Samuel Billaud. Together with his uncle Bernard Billaud, they have considerably advanced the quality level over the past decade. The estate's 20ha include a little of 3 *grands crus* (Les Clos, Preuses and Vaudésir) and a tiny bit of Blanchots, as well as significant vineyards in the *premiers crus* of Mont de Milieu, Montée de Tonnerre and Vaillons, and a little Fourchaume. Except for Fourchaume, there is a high proportion of old vines – the Mont de Milieu is also made in a Vieilles Vignes bottling. This contributes to the depth and concentration of the wines, which have a distinctive minerally, occasionally smoky, ripe fruit character and great definition and structure. A carefully temperature-controlled vinification in stainless steel is followed by a lengthy low-temperature *débourbage*. Barrel-fermentation and ageing are only employed exceptionally, as in the case of the Les Clos (from 55-year-old vines), where it enhances the structure but takes nothing from the wine's purity. In short, these are quite delicious, graceful, stylish Chablis with extra distinction and depth at the *premier cru* level and wonderful dimension and complexity at the *grand cru* level. If the prices are edging upwards they still represent marvellous value vis-à-vis similar quality from the Côte de Beaune. Even the Petit Chablis is worth considering here. (PW)

O **Chablis Grand Cru** Preuses★★★★ £E Vaudésir★★★★★ £E
O **Chablis Grand Cru** Les Clos★★★★★ £E
O **Chablis Grand Cru** Blanchots Vieilles Vignes★★★★★ £F
O **Chablis Premier Cru** Vaillons★★★★ £C Montée de Tonnerre★★★★ £C
O **Chablis Premier Cru** Mont de Milieu★★★★ £C Fourchaume★★★ £D
O **Chablis**★★ £B Tête d'Or★★★ £C O **Petit Chablis**★ £B

DOMAINE DE BOIS D'YVER

Georges Pico & Eleana Puentes Grande Rue Nicolas Droin, Courgis, 89800 Chablis
UK stockist: JNi, CPp, Hrd

This 22-ha estate at Courgis makes a sound range of Chablis both from its own vineyards and from grapes bought in from another grower. The wines show something of a leesy influence, though this is more pronounced at the lower levels, with added minerality and fruit depth in the Vaillons and Montmains *premiers crus*. Though for the most part machine-harvested, they usually show good ripeness, a certain elegance and good balance. Used oak is employed for ageing the Blanchots, which shows a *grand cru*-like complexity, though wants for greater fruit intensity on the finish for a higher rating. Those from bought-in grapes, which includes the Blanchots, are labelled only as 'mis en bouteille par Domaine de Bois d'Yver'. (PW)

O **Chablis Grand Cru** Blanchots★★★ £E
O **Chablis Premier Cru** Beauregard★★ £C Vaillons★★★ £C Montmains★★★ £C
O **Chablis**★★ £B

A & F BOUDIN/DOM. DE CHANTEMERLE

Adhémar & Francis Boudin 27 Rue de Serein, 89800 Chablis
UK stockist: **L&S**, Rae, IGH, Maj

The Domaine de Chantemerle is an exciting small domaine based in the village of La Chapelle Vaupelteigne, producing ripe, characterful Chablis from 15ha of vineyards close by. Low yields, manual harvesting and vinification in inert vats contribute to a rich, ripe, almost buttery style (yet minerally too) but without any oak influence. Particularly worth seeking out is L'Homme Mort, bottled separately from the rest of Fourchaume – not perhaps an inspiring choice of name but the wine has great vitality and individuality. All the wines can be drunk quite young but if you think their immediacy suggests they won't keep, you are wrong. The depth, structure and concentration of fruit means they'll keep for a decade and that often includes the regular Chablis. (PW)

O **Chablis Premier Cru** Fourchaume★★★ £C L'Homme Mort★★★ £D
O **Chablis**★★ £B

JEAN-MARC BROCARD www.domaine-brocard.fr

Jean-Marc Brocard 3 Route de Chablis, Préhy, 89800 Chablis
UK stockist: **JBa**, Adm, BWC, J&B, Odd

Thirty years ago Jean-Marc Brocard had a single hectare of vines, now he has 96ha and climbing (though not all of it in the Chablis AC). Based at Préhy, on the edge of the Chablis region, he has turned out reasonably consistent, lively, assertive Chablis since the early 1980s. The emphasis is on producing 'typical' Chablis that is minerally and elegant. Though for the most part from mechanically harvested grapes, these stainless steel-vinified Chablis usually deliver adequate fruit and structure, particularly with a couple of years' bottle-age, but they can sometimes be a bit lean and underripe. The most interest and character is to be found among the *premiers* and *grands crus*, which if not first rate can offer decent value for money. They should, however, not be drunk too young (4 years is a minimum). A series of Bourgogne Blancs produced to differentiate between different soil types in the Chablis region are of good Petit Chablis quality, while newer is a series of blended Premier Cru Chablis that go some way to live up to their names: Minéral, Extrème, Sensuel and Paradoxe (the last sees some new oak). Chablis Domaine de la Boisseneuse is a biodynamically produced example. Other Yonne wines include an Irancy from Domaine Sainte Claire. Also produced in 2002 was a refined, intense example of *grand cru* Valmur. All in all, the wines are a good bet in a fine vintage but more variable from lesser years. (PW)

O **Chablis Grand Cru** Bougros★★★ £E Vaudésir★★★★ £E
O **Chablis Premier Cru** Montmains Le Manant★★★ £C Beauregard★★★ £C
O **Chablis Premier Cru** Vaucoupin★★★ £C Montée de Tonnerre★★ £C
O **Chablis Premier Cru** Côte de Jouan★ £C
O **Chablis** Dom. Sainte-Claire★ £B Vieilles Vignes Dom. Sainte-Claire★★ £B
O **Bourgogne Blanc** Jurassique★ £B Kimméridgien★ £B Portlandien★ £B
O **Bourgogne Aligoté**★ £B

107

LA CHABLISIENNE www.chablisienne.com

'Cooperative' 8 Boulevard Pasteur, BP 14, 89800 Chablis
UK stockist: **SsG, Cib,** E&T, Maj, WSc

With 1,100ha of vineyards the La Chablisienne co-op draws on a massive chunk of the Chablis *vignoble*, producing a quarter of all Chablis made. Much of what appears under the labels of the large Beaune *négociants* is sourced from here. The operation is very competently run by Hervé Tucki and considerable sums are spent on renewing a battery of oak barrels. At the village level or lower (Petit Chablis) the wines can be lean and dilute, while some of the *premiers crus* and *grands crus* are excessively oaked despite the intention to bring out the *terroir*. Certainly in weaker vintages there just doesn't seem to be fruit of sufficient quality to achieve this. That said, and while a bad bottle can put you off, *premiers crus* like Vaulorent, Montmains and Montée de Tonnerre can be really good and the Vieilles Vignes with some oak influence is typically concentrated with good balance. The most prized wine is that bottled from the best part of 6ha of Grenouilles as Château Grenouilles, though sadly the oak can be a bit overdone. Most significantly, quality and style depend to a large degree on the requirements of the customer, be it a *négociant* or supermarket chain. If its standards are high then expect a decent Chablis. While a Chablis from a good small grower is still likely to be a better bet, nonetheless there are some fine bottles that may be encountered in top restaurants and elsewhere. Unfortunately, while a co-op can mean great value, prices for Chablisienne-labelled wines are near the top of the hierarchy for their respective appellations. Listed below are the most consistent of the leading *crus*. (PW)

O **Chablis Grand Cru** Blanchots★★★ £E Grenouilles★★★ £E Preuses★★★ £E
O **Chablis Grand Cru** Château Grenouilles★★ £F
O **Chablis Premier Cru** Montmains★★ £D Montée de Tonnerre★★ £D
O **Chablis Premier Cru** Vaulorent★★ £D
O **Chablis** Vieilles Vignes★★ £C

ANITA ET JEAN-PIERRE COLINOT Irancy

Anita et Jean-Pierre Colinot 1 Rue des Chariats, 89290 Irancy

If the pure, pristine, cherry-scented character of very cool-climate Pinot drives you to distraction then this is the place to come. One or 2 others in Irancy can also make enticing red but their wines are let down more often by a lack of complete ripeness. From 10ha (which, typically for this Auxerrois region, includes a little César), Jean-Pierre Colinot and his wife make light but very elegant wines with a gentle charm and good intensity of flavour and length. Of the various *cuvées*, the Côte du Moutier has perhaps the most structure, Palotte slightly more obvious fruit. As well as those below, wines come from other parcels of vines, including Les Mazelots. Unfortunately the wines have a certain following in France and can be difficult to find but it's worth the effort, particularly from a good vintage. Though light in body, the wines are not fragile and will keep well for 5 years. For another intriguing Auxerrois red see Ghislaine et Jean-Hugues GOISOT. (PW)

● **Irancy** Vieilles Vignes★★ £B Palotte★★ £B Côte du Moutier★★ £B

DOM. DU COLOMBIER

Guy Mothe et Fils 42 Grand Rue, Fontenay-près-Chablis, 89800 Chablis
UK stockist: **FMV**

Thierry and his 2 brothers, Jean-Louis and Vincent, are now responsible for this 35-ha estate and are building on the reputation established by their father. All levels of Chablis are produced and all are unwooded. The style is for ripe, intense examples with good minerality and restrained lees influence. *Premier crus* Fourchaume and Vaucoupin are refined with good fruit and length. A richer and more concentrated Bougros is also refined with impressive underlying structure. Petit Chablis and Chablis should be drunk fairly young but both *premiers crus* and Bougros with at least 5 years' age. (PW)

O **Chablis Grand Cru** Bougros★★★★ £E
O **Chablis Premier Cru** Fourchaume★★★ £C Vaucoupin★★★ £C
O **Chablis**★★ £B O **Petit Chablis**★ £B

DANIEL DAMPT   www.dampt-defaix.com

Dampt family   1 Rue des Violettes, Milly, 89800 Chablis
UK stockist: Bal, HHC, NYg

Daniel Dampt married the daughter of Jean Defaix, a respected *vigneron* who little by little reclaimed vineyards abandoned following phylloxera in the late 19th century. The Dampts now make very good Chablis from 26ha of vineyards, including 13ha of *premiers crus* (predominantly Côte de Léchet and Vaillons). The wines are vinified in stainless steel, with the emphasis on a ripe fruit and floral character but retaining firm acidity and a minerally influence. The pride of the domaine are the Côte de Léchet vineyards, which lie close to the winery and produce arguably the most classic, minerally wine, but there is good quality in all the *premiers crus*. If not amongst the top names this is nonetheless a good inexpensive source of Chablis that drinks well with 3 or 4 years' age but will keep for longer in the case of the *premiers crus*. (PW)

O **Chablis Premier Cru** Beauroy★★★ £C Vaillons★★ £C Fourchaume★★★ £C
O **Chablis Premier Cru** Côte de Léchet★★★ £C O **Chablis**★★ £B

RENÉ ET VINCENT DAUVISSAT

René & Vincent Dauvissat   8 Rue Émile Zola, 89800 Chablis
UK stockist: DDr, HHB, J&B, L&S, Tan, IGH, F&M

The Dauvissats have deep roots in the region going back centuries. Vincent's grandfather started domaine bottling in the 1930s and his father René built up and maintains a rich viticultural resource; almost all of the 11.5ha are either *premier* or *grand cru*. In the vineyard, a uniform high average vine age is maintained as old or weak vines are replaced individually, grafted from the best existing vines (*sélection massale*). In addition, all the grapes are manually picked, not just the leading *crus* – a relatively rare occurrence in Chablis. Vincent uses oak, used not new, to ferment and age most of the wines. The resulting Chablis are simply marvellous, characterised by their depth, breadth and body, filled with a gently honeyed ripeness and stylish minerality. All are fine, even the Petit Chablis, but the distinctive minerally yet contrasting *premiers crus* Vaillons and Forest are surpassed by the bigger, more concentrated *grands crus* Preuses and Les Clos. The latter need 6 or 7 years' ageing, *premiers crus* 4 or 5, and even the regular Chablis 3 or 4. The wines can be in short supply, having long been favoured by top Parisian restaurants. (PW)

O **Chablis Grand Cru** Preuses★★★★★ £F Les Clos✪✪✪✪✪ £F
O **Chablis Premier Cru** Séchet★★★★ £E Forest★★★★ £E Vaillons★★★★ £E
O **Chablis** ★★★ £C O **Petit Chablis** ★★ £B

DOM. BERNARD DEFAIX   www.bernard-defaix.com

Sylvain & Didier Defaix   17 Rue du Château, Milly, 89800 Chablis
UK stockist: HrV, F&R

From grape-growing family tradition, Bernard Defaix set up independently in 1959. There are now 25ha run by his sons Sylvain, responsible for the winemaking, and Didier who takes care of the vineyards. Sustainable viticulture is practised and work to maintain and revitalise the soils is ongoing. All the vineyards are on the left bank of the Serein and include a large chunk of *premier cru* Côte de Lechet. This produces a very distinctive floral, mineral and

109

flinty example with good weight and breadth. Other wines are good too, properly ripe with good body in part from lees enrichment; Les Lys is more floral, Vaillons more mineral. There is some use of oak to enhance the structure, such as in a Vieille Vigne (sic) version of Côte de Lechet, but this has not been tasted. In general, while there is not the intensity or definition of the very best examples, these wines show good *typicité*, with the *crus* bringing out the characteristics of their specific *terroirs*, and will keep well. Some Fourchaume and *grand cru* Bougros are produced from bought-in grapes and sold under the Sylvain & Didier Defaix label. (PW)

O **Chablis Premier Cru** Côte de Lechet★★★ £C Les Lys★★★£C Vaillons★★★ £C
O **Chablis** Vieille Vigne★★ £C

DANIEL-ÉTIENNE DEFAIX www.chablisdefaix.com

Daniel Defaix & family   23 Rue de Champlain, Milly, 89800 Chablis
UK stockist: **GFy**, BBR, Con, Tan, Han, IGH

The Defaix lineage goes back centuries in the Chablis region. Even recent history relating to the domaine goes back to the 18th century. The domaine's reputation rests with 3 *premiers crus* of 4ha each, almost half the estate's total of 25ha. Viticulture is effectively organic, though not certified as such, vine age is high and grape selection rigorous. A sustained fermentation and long lees contact also contribute to the character of these wines. There is less of the floral, mineral and pure fruit character of other good producers but there is depth, intensity and complexity. The Les Lys has more mineral, citrus character plus honey with age; in Côte de Léchet and Vaillons there is more of a leesy influence but a little more structure too, particularly in the latter. Rarely seen is a little Bourgogne Rouge from very old vines, successful in the best vintages. A tiny amount of Grand Cru Blanchots is also made. Most of the wines can be drunk soon after their delayed release but will keep for longer. (PW)

O **Chablis Premier Cru** Côte de Léchet★★★ £D Les Lys★★★ £D Vaillons★★★ £D
O **Chablis** Vieilles Vignes★★ £C

JEAN-PAUL & BENOÎT DROIN www.jeanpaul-droin.fr

Jean-Paul Droin   14 bis Rue Jean Jaurès, 89800 Chablis
UK stockist: **RsW, DDr**, BBR, Bib, A&B, IGH, UnC

Jean-Paul Droin and his son Benoît draw from 20ha of vines spread over 5 *grands crus* (with around 1ha each of Vaudésir, Valmur and Les Clos) and 7 *premiers crus*. The range is generally of high quality. At the *premiers* and *grands crus* levels the wines are (to a greater or lesser degree) fermented and aged in oak of varying age and provenance, resulting in rich, ripe (occasionally too ripe), full wines. The use of oak has become gradually more refined over the past decade and, though there are still some oak flavours, these now rarely overwhelm the ripe, minerally fruit. Nearly all the wines can be drunk with just 3 or 4 years' ageing, but will improve for as long again. Try the *crus*, particularly the Montée de Tonnerre, Vaudésir and Les Clos; the regular Chablis and Petit Chablis are more variable. In addition to those below, a little *grand cru* Blanchots and *premiers crus* Côte de Lechet and Vaucoupin are also made. The 2001s are of variable quality, the best being Montée de Tonnerre, Grenouilles and Les Clos. (PW)

O **Chablis Grand Cru** Valmur★★★ £E Grenouilles★★★★ £E Vaudésir★★★★ £E
O **Chablis Grand Cru** Les Clos★★★★ £E
O **Chablis Premier Cru** Vaillons★★★ £C Montmains★★★ £C
O **Chablis Premier Cru** Montée de Tonnerre★★★★ £C
O **Chablis Premier Cru** Fourchaume★★★ £C Vosgros★★★ £C

JOSEPH DROUHIN (CHABLIS) www.drouhin.com

Drouhin family   Moulin de Vaudon, Chichée, 89800 Chablis
UK stockist: **DAy**, Add, MCW, WsB

Under Robert Drouhin, the house of Joseph DROUHIN, an important high-quality Beaune *négociant*, added Chablis vineyards to its holdings in the Côte d'Or in the late 1960s. Though the wines are vinified at the company's headquarters in Beaune, the grapes from more than 40ha are pressed locally. The estate includes 3ha of *grand cru* vineyards spread over 4 *climats,* mostly Vaudésir and Les Clos but a little Bougros and Preuses too. Low yields contribute to ripe, concentrated fruit and, though oak is important to the style, it is only used in the top wines and there is usually a good minerally aspect to their character. As well as *premiers crus* Vaillons and Sécher, some Montmains and a regular Chablis Premier Cru from a blend of other sites are bottled separately. (PW)

O **Chablis Grand Cru** Preuses★★★ £F Vaudésir★★★★ £F Les Clos★★★★★ £F
O **Chablis Premier Cru** Sécher★★★ £E Vaillons★★★ £E
O **Chablis★** £B Domaine de Vaudon★★ £C

GÉRARD DUPLESSIS

Gérard Duplessis   5 Quai de Reugny, 89800 Chablis
UK stockist: **RsW**, A&B, Rae, Maj

This excellent small grower's 7ha of vineyards are mostly in 4 of the very best *premiers crus.* Gérard Duplessis vinifies in stainless steel and matures in old wood for classic Chablis flavours. The wines can start out a little austere but there is that wonderful Chablis combination of underlying richness and a steely, minerally character that can provide wonderful drinking with 5 years' ageing, and is even better with another 5 or 10 in a top vintage. (PW)

O **Chablis Grand Cru** Les Clos★★★★ £E
O **Chablis Premier Cru** Fourchaume★★★ £D Montée de Tonnerre★★★ £D
O **Chablis Premier Cru** Montmains★★★ £D
O **Chablis Premier Cru** Vaillons★★ £D O **Chablis★★** £C

JEAN DURUP ET FILS www.durup-chablis.com

Jean Durup   4 Grande Rue, Maligny, 89800 Chablis
UK stockist: **ABy**, DDr, THt, HRp, Tan, Hrd

Jean Durup led the movement for expansion of the Chablis *vignoble* in direct opposition to WILLIAM FÈVRE in the 1970s and 80s. His estate, partly as a consequence of the authorised expansion, is the largest in the region (much of it regular Chablis but there are also substantial holdings of *premiers crus*). It is very competently run and is increasingly directed by Jean Durup's son, Jean-Paul. While derided by some at the time, Jean has gradually earned greater respect for the quality of his wines. He has also been a leading advocate of unoaked Chablis. The wines are generally well-balanced, with adequate richness if sometimes lacking a little character and extra flair. Most of the wines drink well with 2–5 years' ageing but *premiers crus* can age for up to a decade. The 2001s were rather weak after some good 2000s but much better 2002s. While the most important labels are Jean Durup, Domaine de l'Eglantière and Château de Maligny, the same wines are also bottled under Domaine de la Paulière and Domaine des Valéry labels for some importers. Some *grand cru* Vaudésir and Les Clos have also been made. (PW)

O **Chablis Premier Cru** L'Homme Mort★★★ £C Fourchaume★★ £C
O **Chablis Premier Cru** Montée de Tonnerre★★ £C
O **Chablis Premier Cru** Vau-de-Vey★★ £C
O **Chablis** Vieilles Vignes★★ £B Vigne de la Reine★★ £C Carré de César★★ £C
O **Chablis★** £B

111

WILLIAM FÈVRE www.williamfevre.com

Joseph Henriot (Champagne) 21 Avenue d'Oberwesel, 89800 Chablis
UK stockist: **JEF, HBJ**, BBR, WSc, F&M, Wai

Over the last 5–6 years, the William Fèvre domaine has reassumed the leadership of Chablis – combining both outstanding quality and significant quantity. Its revival followed the takeover by Joseph Henriot (also see HENRIOT Champagne and BOUCHARD PÈRE in the Côte d'Or). The Domaine de la Maladière comprises 47ha and includes an unrivalled collection of *premiers* and *grands crus*. Almost 16ha are *grand cru* and include 6 of the 7 *climats*. In the late 80s and early 90s William Fèvre was the staunchest and most vocal of those opposed to the expansion of the Chablis vineyards. The use of new oak became an increasing theme too, to the point of compromising the inherent fruit character of Chablis. Now, under the direction of Didier Séguier, there has been a return to manual harvesting and much more rigorous grape selection. New oak is still used but the wines are bottled later and there is better concentration and something more of each wine's origin is captured and enhanced by the oak. Though most of the wines are domaine-sourced, some also are made from bought-in grapes. Wines appear also under the Domaine de la Maladière label and the names Ancien Domaine Auffray and Jeanne-Paule Filippi have also been used. Vintages since 1998 (including very good 2003s) and older vintages are highly recommended, but those from the mid-1990s are more variable. (PW)

O **Chablis Grand Cru** Les Clos✪✪✪✪✪ £F Vaudésir✪✪✪✪✪ Valmur✪✪✪✪✪ £F
O **Chablis Grand Cru** Bougros Côte de Bougerots★★★★★ £F Preuses★★★★★ £F
O **Chablis Grand** Bougros★★★★ £E Grenouilles★★★★ £F
O **Chablis Premier Cru** Fourchaume Vignoble de Vaulorent★★★★ £E
O **Chablis Premier Cru** Vaillons★★★★ £D
O **Chablis Premier Cru** Montée de Tonnerre★★★★ £D Mont de Milieu★★★ £D
O **Chablis Premier Cru** Montmains★★★ £D Les Lys★★★ £D Butteaux★★★ £D
O **Chablis Premier Cru** Forêts★★ £D Beauroy★★ £D
O **Chablis**★★ £C O **Petit Chablis**★ £B

GHISLAINE ET JEAN-HUGUES GOISOT Saint-Bris

Ghislaine & Jean-Hugues Goisot, 89530 Saint-Bris-le-Vineux
UK stockist: **DDr**, HHB, Rae

The Goisots' vineyards lie outside the Chablis appellation in the less than glamorous Saint-Bris, which promotes Sauvignon rather than Chardonnay. But both Sauvignon and Chardonnay are produced here (an extremely rare occurrence in France, in contrast to much of the New World) along with Aligoté and Pinot Noir from a total of 27ha of vineyards. Through meticulous and dedicated work in the vineyards and cellars, all the wines are of extremely high quality yet don't command high prices thanks to their lowly appellations. The pure-fruited Chardonnay and perfumed Pinot Noir are sold as Bourgogne Côtes d'Auxerre, the pungent green-pepper Sauvignon now as newly promoted Saint-Bris AC, while the Aligoté appears as humble Bourgogne. The wines are ripe, concentrated and aromatic, with lovely definition and length, and under the Corps de Garde label are worth keeping for 2 or 3 years. Also made but not tasted are prestige *cuvées* from Côtes d'Auxerre whites, Biaumont and Gondonne, and an Irancy, Mazelots. (PW)

O **Bourgogne Côtes d'Auxerre**★★ £B Corps de Garde★★★ £C
O **Saint-Bris**★★ £B Corps de Garde Gourmand★★ £B
O **Bourgogne Aligoté**★ £B ● **Bourgogne** Rouge★ £B Corps de Garde★★ £C

JEAN-PIERRE GROSSOT & CORINNE PERCHAUD

J-P Grossot & C. Perchaud 4 Route de Mont de Milieu, Fleys, 89800 Chablis
UK stockist: **L&W, Lib, Eno,** IGH

This is a great source for Chablis whether labelled Grossot or sold under the label established by his wife, Corinne Perchaud. If initially a little austere, the wines are intensely fruity, with excellent definition, weight and fine perfumes. Though there are no *grands crus*, the 18ha includes some excellent *premiers crus*. Stainless steel dominates their production but some oak is used for the Fourneaux and Mont de Milieu *premiers crus* and the village *cuvée*, 'Grossot' or Fûts de Chênes. Only the latter is obviously oaky, the others properly racy and minerally. While the wines are delicious with 3 or 4 years' ageing, they will keep. Solid quality and reasonable prices too. (PW)

O **Chablis Premier Cru** Fourneaux★★ £C Vaucoupin★★ £C Fourchaume★★★ £C
O **Chablis Premier Cru** Mont de Milieu★★★ £C
O **Chablis★** £B Fûts de Chênes★ £B La Part des Anges★★ £C

DOM. LAROCHE   www.michellaroche.com

Michel Laroche   L'Obédiencerie, 22 Rue Louis Bro, 89800 Chablis
UK stockist: **Bib,** NYg

Michel Laroche is one of Chablis' major players and has recently become almost as well-known for wines made in the South of France (he also has a joint venture with Jorge Coderch in Chile) as for his many prestigious Chablis *crus*. The estate's offices are based in the Obédiencerie in the heart of Chablis, originally a monastery dating back to the ninth century. The Saint-Martin monks here established Chablis' first vines. Though the Laroche domaine dates from the mid-19th century, its major expansion has been only recently, under Michel and his father Henri, and it now covers 100ha of vines. Most of the the wine is exported around the globe. There are 6ha of *grands crus*, mostly Blanchots but also some Les Clos and a little Bouguerots (Bougros), and 29ha of *premiers crus* centred on Fourchaume, Vaillons and Vau de Vey. Lesser wines can be a bit light, but can show typical minerally fruit. In the top wines the style is more unusual, with marked oak influence and sometimes a discernible lactic character in the top *crus*. The wines are supple and gently creamy, without the austerity more characteristic of young Chablis but still retaining a mineral stamp. *Grands crus* can be very good; a small portion of the Blanchots is set apart for the top wine, Réserve de l'Obédience, while the Fourchaumes and Vaillons are labelled Vieilles Vignes for their old vine fruit. Good as the wines can be, the price-for-quality ratio is less convincing. (PW)

O **Chablis Grand Cru** Les Clos★★★★ £F Blanchots★★★ £E
O **Chablis Grand Cru** Blanchots Réserve de l'Obédience★★★★ £F
O **Chablis Premier Cru** Vaillons Vieilles Vignes★★★ £D
O **Chablis Premier Cru** Fourchaumes Vieilles Vignes★★★ £D
O **Chablis Premier Cru** Beauroy★★ £D Montmains★★ £D Vau de Vey★★★ £C
O **Chablis** Saint-Martin★ £B

BERNARD LEGLAND/DOM. DES MARRONNIERS

Bernard Legland   Rue de Chablis, Préhy, 89800 Chablis
UK stockist: **Bib,** GWW

This is a good source of attractive, well-made and relatively inexpensive Chablis. Bernard Legland's 18ha doesn't include much in the way of prime vineyards; 2.5ha of Montmains is the most prized possession. The domaine was established in 1976 and has adhered to a principle of unoaked Chablis. Previously the *premiers crus* (there is also a little Côte de Jouan) were made from relatively young vines but these are now more than 20 years old, giving the wines added richness and depth. (PW)

113

O **Chablis Premier Cru** Côte de Jouan★★ £C Montmains★★★ £C
O **Chablis**★ £B

LONG-DEPAQUIT

Maison Albert Bichot   45 Rue Auxerroise, 89800 Chablis
UK stockist: Bal, BBR

This historic estate dates from the time of the French Revolution. There are
now 65ha but much of it has been acquired in the last 30 years or so. As well as
a sprinkling of wines from *premier* and *grand cru* vineyards, the wine of the
famous La Moutonne vineyard is made here. Acquired in 1791 by Simon
Depaquy, it is a *monopole* of 2.35ha that straddles part of *grands crus* Vaudésir
and Preuses that belonged originally to the monks of the Abbey of Pontigny.
Though most of the wines are both vinified and aged in stainless steel in order
not to compromise the classic, flinty, minerally Chablis style, the *grands crus* see
varying percentages of oak. Quality can be a bit uneven but at their best they
have intensity, style and finesse; the top wines, especially La Moutonne, develop
a gentle honeyed richness with age. The selected *crus* below are the most
consistently fine and ageworthy, lesser wines are more of a gamble but can also
be good. Prices are on the high side for the quality level. (PW)

O **Chablis Grand Cru** La Moutonne★★★★ £E Blanchots★★★ £E
O **Chablis Grand Cru** Vaudésir★★★ £E Les Clos★★★ £E
O **Chablis Premier Cru** Montée de Tonnerre★★★ £D Vaucoupin★★ £C
O **Chablis Premier Cru** Vaillons★★ £C

DOM. DES MALANDES   www.domainedesmalandes.com

Jean-Bernard et Lyne Marchive   63 Rue Auxerroise, 89800 Chablis
UK stockist: **CHk**, H&B, Evg, WSc

Established in 1986 from the family inheritance of Lyne Marchive (*née*
Tremblay), this 26-ha estate has a good following for unoaked Chablis. The
reputation has been built on producing wines from low yields and fully ripe
fruit and a non-interventionist winemaking philosophy. The wines are ripe,
more floral and fruit-driven in the lesser *cuvées* but with more minerally
intensity and complexity, as well as concentration, in the *grands crus*.
Fourchaume and Montmains are perhaps the pick of the *premiers crus* but a
fruit-emphasized Vau de Vey and very mineral, more classically austere Côte de
Lechet are also very good. Both the *grands crus* are very classy, reflecting their
respective terroir but with similar breadth, depth and length. Though all can be
drunk fairly young, these are the wines to keep. (PW)

O **Chablis Grand Cru** Vaudésir★★★★★ £E Les Clos★★★★ £E
O **Chablis Premier Cru** Côte de Léchet★★★ £C Montmains★★★ £C
O **Chablis Premier Cru** Fourchaume★★★ £C Vau de Vey★★★ £C
O **Chablis**★★ £B Vieilles Vignes Tour du Roy★★ £C   O **Petit Chablis**★ £B

DOM. LOUIS MICHEL ET FILS

Jean-Loup Michel   9-11 Boulevard de Ferrières, 89800 Chablis
UK stockist: **OWL, DAy**, BBR, Eno, IGH, Odd, WSc

Fifth-generation Jean-Loup Michel has made the wines here in recent years but
the 23-ha estate's international reputation was established by his father, Louis
Michel, who died in 1999. Much of the production is now exported and
widely available but remarkably without the high prices and compromised
quality of some exporters. For its unoaked style of Chablis this is perhaps the
most lauded producer in the English-speaking press. The wines spend an
extended period of time in stainless steel before a relatively late bottling. Austere
but with an underlying minerally fruit richness when young, the *premiers crus*
are always better with 3–5 years' ageing, the *grands crus* with 5 or more. At their
best these are excellent Chablis with fine *terroir* definition and real elegance and

length on the palate if not the texture or dimension of the very best. That said these are wines to buy from the better vintages only; a cool or wet or generally more difficult vintage (such as 2001) can reveal a lack of full ripeness as well as a tendency to age more rapidly than usual. (PW)

O **Chablis Grand Cru** Les Clos★★★★★ £E Grenouilles★★★★ £E
O **Chablis Grand Cru** Vaudésir★★★★ £E
O **Chablis Premier Cru** Montée de Tonnerre★★★★ £D Vaillons★★★ £C
O **Chablis Premier Cru** Fourchaume★★★ £C Montmains★★★ £C
O **Chablis**★★ £B O **Petit Chablis**★ £B

DOM. LOUIS MOREAU www.domaine-louismoreau.com

Louis Moreau 10 Grande Rue, Beines, 89800 Chablis
UK stockist: **PBW**, ACh

Louis and Anne Moreau control 120ha comprising mostly village Chablis and including the separate estates of Domaine de Biéville and Domaine du Cèdre Doré. The wines should not be confused with those of the *négociant* house, Moreau. Vinified in stainless steel, without recourse to any wood, the wines are quite racy and austere when young but have great reserves of fruit underneath, particularly in the 2 *premiers crus*, Vaulignot (Vau Ligneau) and Fourneaux. Some top *grands crus,* previously leased out, have been produced since the 2002 vintage. These see a little new oak and though only moderately concentrated should add richness with age. Led by a classy Vaudésir, they also include Valmur, Les Clos and, from a plot of vines within Les Clos, Clos des Hospices. (PW)

O **Chablis Grand Cru** Valmur★★★★ £E Vaudésir★★★★ £E
O **Chablis Grand Cru** Les Clos des Hospices★★★★ £E
O **Chablis Premier Cru** Fourneaux★★★ £C Vaulignot★★ £C
O **Chablis**★ £B Domaine du Cèdre D'oré★★ £B Domaine de Biéville★★ £B

MOREAU-NAUDET

Roger et Stéphane Moreau 5 Rue des Fossés, 89800 Chablis
UK stockist: OWL, L&S, SVS, Tan, WSc, Hrd

Stéphane Moreau, not related to the Moreaus of Domaine Louis Moreau, has been running this 21-ha estate since 1999 and the wines are now very good indeed. Machine harvesting is only used for the regular wines yet even at this level, both Petit Chablis and Chablis as well as some special *cuvées,* the fruit is ripe and intense with a mineral aspect. Several excellent *premiers crus,* including a Montée de Tonnerre imbued with smoke, mineral and citrus, give good expression to their origins. Deep, minerally Valmur is long and classy, an excellent and affordable example of this often pricey *grand cru.* Cuvée Les Pargues and an old-vine Charactère will be added with further tastings. (PW)

O **Chablis Grand Cru** Valmur★★★★ £D
O **Chablis Premier Cru** Vaillons★★★ £C Montée de Tonnerre★★★ £C
O **Chablis Premier Cru** Montmains★★★ £C
O **Chablis**★★ £B

DIDIER & PASCAL PICQ

Didier & Pascal Picq 3 Route de Chablis, Chichée, 89800 Chablis
UK stockist: **FMV**, NYg

The small village of Chichée lies some 3km south-east of the town of Chablis. Here the Picqs have 13ha, including a little of Chichée's 2 *premiers crus.* Didier Picq is responsible for the winemaking, while his brother, Pascal maximises grape quality. The grapes are picked as late as possible and both fermentation and ageing are in stainless steel. The wines are crisp and fresh, quite floral and fruity in style but with good intensity in the Vieilles Vignes and extra character and concentration in the *premiers crus.* From most vintages the Vieilles Vignes

115

should be drunk with at least 3 years' ageing, the *premiers crus* with 5 or more. The wines are also labelled Gilbert Picq et Fils. (PW)

O **Chablis Premier Cru** Vaucoupin★★★ £C Vosgros★★★ £C
O **Chablis**★★ £B Vieilles Vignes★★★ £B

DOM. PINSON FRÈRES www.domaine-pinson.com

Laurent & Christophe Pinson 5 Quai Voltaire, 89800 Chablis
UK stockist: A&B, CPp, L&W, NYg

Perpetually rustic would perhaps best describe the atmosphere *chez* Pinson as almost anyone who has visited the estate over the past couple of decades I'm sure would agree. But brothers Laurent and Christophe, the current generation in charge of this small 11.5-ha estate, seem set on a new image while continuing to make Chablis of real depth and character. The parcels of vines are all of the first order, including 2.5ha of Les Clos and nearly 5ha of Mont de Milieu. Used oak is employed in their ageing (only the regular Chablis is unoaked), which contributes to their excellent texture and breadth but only subtly influences flavour, though it is sometimes more apparent on the Montmains. The wines have been a little uneven in terms of their ability to age but quality is often remarkably high. All the wines are better with 5 years' ageing or more, the Les Clos often with 10 or more. A little of the *premiers crus* Vaillons and Vaugiraut are also made. (PW)

O **Chablis Grand Cru** Les Clos★★★★ £D
O **Chablis Premier Cru** La Forêt★★★ £C Mont de Milieu★★★ £C
O **Chablis Premier Cru** Montmains★★★ £C
O **Chablis**★★ £B

DENIS POMMIER www.denis-pommier.com

Denis Pommier 31 Rue de Poinchy, Poinchy, 89800 Chablis
UK stockist: L&S, Han

Denis Pommier started out with just 2.5ha in 1990 but now has 11ha. He is already forging a reputation as a young *vigneron* of some talent. Though he has started fermenting and ageing his *premiers crus* in barrel, apart from the Beauroy, only part of the wine gets this treatment and then only a small percentage of the oak is new. Certainly the quality of the grapes is very good and the wines show concentrated ripe fruit; the mineral and citrus intensity is set against a spicy oak character and a gently buttery texture in the most recent vintages of the Côte de Léchet. The overall balance and oak integration in the Beauroy has been less convincing but it will be interesting to see how the style evolves here. At present the small production quickly sells out. The Vieilles Vignes also shows some oak influence but the regular version sees no oak whatsoever. A very small amount of Fourchaume is also made from relatively young vines. (PW)

O **Chablis Premier Cru** Côte de Léchet★★★ £C Beauroy★★ £C
O **Chablis**★★ £B Croix aux Moines★★ £B Vieilles Vignes★★ £B

DENIS RACE www.chablisrace.com

Laurence & Denis Race 5a Rue de Chichée, 89800 Chablis
UK stockist: FMV, All, Mar, PWa

Denis Race is an exponent of unoaked Chablis. He and his wife have 15ha of vines including 5.5ha of *premier cru* Montmains. There is careful attention to the grapes prior to harvesting (and what is left ready for picking) – the key to quality when the grapes are machine-harvested as so much in Chablis now is. The Montmains appears in 2 bottlings, the Vieilles Vignes version from vines that are 65 years old and there is a marked difference in depth and oomph in the latter. All the wines show good *terroir* definition. A steely, minerally Mont de Milieu contrasts with a softer, more elegant Vaillon. A little *grand cru*

Blanchots is also made. (PW)

O **Chablis Premier Cru** Montmains Vieilles Vignes★★★★ £D   Montmains★★★ £C
O **Chablis Premier Cru** Mont de Milieu★★★ £C Vaillon★★★
O **Chablis**★★ £B

DOM. RAVENEAU

Jean-Marie & Bernard Raveneau   9 Rue de Chichée, 89800 Chablis
UK stockist: JAr, HHC, Sec, Blx

If I had to chosoe 1 source of Chablis above all others this would be it.
Continuing the work of their father, François Raveneau, brothers Jean-Marie
and Bernard Raveneau make superb Chablis from just 7.5ha of *premier* and
grand cru sites. Unquestionably the grape quality is paramount – all are hand-
picked and from low-yielding vines – but if anyone makes the case for the use
of oak and how it should be used, surely this is the model to emulate. The
wines have fabulous structure yet never taste as if they have seen the inside of a
barrel. Typically pure minerally, citrusy, greengage notes prevail on the nose, if
occasionally more floral or with a hint of smoke, while the palate is taut,
intense and steely when young but with wonderful dimension, underlying
concentration and depth that builds in richness and complexity over a decade
or longer. No 2 wines are quite the same but there is fine quality here even in
weaker vintages. The domaine also has small plots in Chapelot, Forest (Forêt)
and Montmains. Prices are surprisingly reasonable unless you buy them second-
or third-hand. (PW)

O **Chablis Grand Cru** Les Clos❍❍❍❍❍ £E   Blanchots★★★★★ £E
O **Chablis Grand Cru** Valmur★★★★★ £E
O **Chablis Premier Cru** Butteaux★★★★ £E Vaillons★★★★ £E
O **Chablis Premier Cru** Montée de Tonnerre★★★★ £E

GÉRARD TREMBLAY   www.chablis-tremblay.com

Tremblay family   12 Rue de Poinchy, 89800 Chablis
UK stockist: Anl, Eno, Cav

This is a well-established family domaine with a good record of producing
classic minerally Chablis. Around 20,000 cases are produced from 33ha of
vineyards. There is some use of oak, around 20% for the *premiers crus* and 40%
for *grands crus*, but it is rarely obvious and as a result of intelligent vinification
and ageing the wines impress most for their structure. They open out with
some bottle age, the mineral, floral aspects apparent when young becoming
allied to a rich, ripe fruit depth, especially with 4–5 years' age from a good
vintage. *Premiers crus* Côte de Lechet, Fourchaume and Montmains all illustrate
the style handsomely. Vaudésir from 0.62ha shows the classic stone-spice-floral
quality of this *grand cru* though was less good than usual in 2001. Some *grand
cru* Valmur is also made. (PW)

O **Chablis Grand Cru** Vaudésir★★★★ £E
O **Chablis Premier Cru** Fourchaume★★★ £C   Montmains★★★ £C
O **Chablis Premier Cru** Côte de Léchet★★★ £C   O **Chablis**★★ £B

DOM. VOCORET   www.vocoret.com

Patrice & Jérôme Vocoret   40 Route d'Auxerre, 89800 Chablis
UK stockist: **HHB**, IGH, Maj

This family domaine of 40ha includes around 4ha of *grands crus* (mostly
Blanchots and Les Clos) and more than 15ha of *premiers crus* (especially
Vaillons and La Forêt). Third-generation Jérôme makes the wines while his
uncle Patrice manages the vineyards. Though much of the fruit is mechanically
harvested, the fruit is generally ripe and concentrated. Vinification is in stainless
steel but the *crus* are aged in large used oak. Quality is generally very good with
an intense, vibrant fruit character and reasonable depth, though the wines can

117

miss a little extra concentration in more difficult vintages. In addition to those below, small quantities of the *grands crus* Valmur and Vaudésir and *premier cru* Mont de Milieu are also made. (PW)

O **Chablis Grand Cru** Blanchot★★★ £D Les Clos★★★ £D
O **Chablis Premier Cru** Côte de Léchet★★ £C La Forêt★★ £C Montmains★★ £C
O **Chablis Premier Cru** Montée de Tonnerre★★ £C Vaillons★★ £C
O **Chablis**★ £B

Also see the following Burgundy *négociants* with an entry in the section *Côte D'Or & Côte Chalonnaise:*

OLIVIER LEFLAIVE FRÈRES
VERGET

OTHER WINES OF NOTE

DOM. DE LA CONCIÈRGERIE O **Chablis Premier Cru** Montmains★★★ £C
DOM. BARAT O **Chablis Premier Cru** Côte de Léchet★★★ £C
O **Chablis Premier Cru** Fourneaux★★★ £C Vaillons★★★ £C
DOM. DU CHARDONNAY O **Chablis Premier Cru** Montée de Tonnerre★★★ £C
O **Chablis Premier Cru** Vaillons★★★ £C Montmains★★★ £C
DOM. JEAN COLLET ET FILS O **Chablis Grand Cru** Valmur★★★★ £E
O **Chablis Premier Cru** Vaillons★★★ £C Montmains★★★ £C O **Chablis**★ £B
DOM. D'ÉLISE O **Chablis**★★ £B
DOM. ALAIN GAUTHERON O **Chablis Premier Cru** Les Fourneaux V V★★★ £D
DOM. ALAIN GEOFFROY O **Chablis Grand Cru** Les Clos★★★★ £F
O **Chablis Premier Cru** Beauroy★★ £C Fourchaume★★ £C
O **Chablis**★ £B Vieilles Vignes★★ £C
DOM. HAMELIN O **Chablis** Vieilles Vignes★★ £B
O **Chablis Premier Cru** Beauroy★★ £C Vau Ligneau★★★ £C
DOM. CHRISTIAN MOREAU O **Chablis Grand Cru** Vaudésir★★★ £E
O **Chablis Grand Cru** Les Clos★★★★ £E
SYLVAIN MOSNIER O **Chablis Premier Cru** Beauroy★★★ £C
O **Chablis Premier Cru** Côte de Léchet★★★ £C
O **Chablis**★ £B Vieilles Vignes★★ £B
DOM. OUDIN O **Chablis** Les Serres★★ £B
O **Chablis Premier Cru** Vaugiraut★★★ £C Vaucoupin★★★ £C
FRANCINE ET OLIVIER SAVARY O **Chablis Premier Cru** Fourchaume★★★ £D
O **Chablis** Vieilles Vignes★★ £C O **Chablis**★★ £C
DOM. LAURENT TRIBUT O **Chablis**★★ £B
O **Chablis Premier Cru** Beauroy★★★ £C Côte de Léchet★★★ £C
DOM. J C & D. TUPINIER O **Chablis Premier Cru** Montée de Tonnerre★★★ £C
O **Chablis Premier Cru** Montmains★★★ £C Vaillons★★ £C O **Chablis**★★ £B
DOM. DE VAUROUX O **Chablis Grand Cru** Bougros★★★ £E
O **Chablis Premier Cru** Montmains★ £C Montée de Tonnerre★★ £C
O **Chablis** Vieilles Vignes★ £C

Author's Choice for Chablis & Yonne (PW)

A selection of classic Chablis
BILLAUD-SIMON O **Chablis** Grand Cru Vaudésir
ADHÉMAR & FRANCIS BOUDIN O **Chablis** Premier Cru L'Homme Mort
DOM. DU COLOMBIER O **Chablis** Grand Cru Bougros
DANIEL DAMPT O **Chablis** Premier Cru Côte de Léchet
RENÉ ET VINCENT DAUVISSAT O **Chablis** Grand Cru Preuses
DOM. BERNARD DEFAIX O **Chablis** Premier Cru Côte de Léchet
JEAN-PAUL DROIN O **Chablis** Premier Cru Montée de Tonnerre
JOSEPH DROUHIN O **Chablis** Grand Cru Les Clos
WILLIAM FEVRE O **Chablis** Grand Cru Valmur
JEAN-PIERRE GROSSOT O **Chablis** Premier Cru Mont de Milieu

DOM. LAROCHE O **Chablis** Grand Cru Blanchots Réserve de l'Obédience
DOM. DES MALANDES O **Chablis** Premier Cru Fourchaume
DOM. LOUIS MICHEL O **Chablis** Premier Cru Montée de Tonnerre
MOREAU-NAUDET O **Chablis** Premier Cru Montée de Tonnerre
DOM. PINSON O **Chablis** Premier Cru Mont de Milieu
DOM. RAVENEAU O **Chablis** Grand Cru Blanchots

Good value Chablis & Yonne whites

JEAN-CLAUDE BESSIN O **Chablis**
BILLAUD-SIMON O **Chablis** Tête d'Or
JEAN-MARC BROCARD O **Chablis** Vieilles Vignes Dom. Sainte-Claire
DOM. DU COLOMBIER O **Chablis**
WILLIAM FEVRE O **Chablis**
GHISLAINE ET JEAN-HUGUES GOISOT O **Bourgogne Côte d'Auxerre**
DOM. DES MALANDES O **Chablis**
DOM. LOUIS MOREAU O **Chablis** Dom. du Cèdre D'oré
DIDIER & PASCAL PICQ O **Chablis** Vieilles Vignes
DENIS RACE O **Chablis**

RECOMMENDED HOTELS AND RESTAURANTS - CHABLIS & YONNE

Top Hotels

★★★★*L'Espérance*   St-Père-sous-Vézeley 89450
Tel. 03 86 33 39 10 Fax 03 86 33 26 15
Email marc.meneau@wanadoo.fr   20 rooms   £C/G

★★★★*Côte St. Jacques*   14fg Paris, Joigny 89300
Tel. 03 86 62 09 70 Fax 03 86 91 49 70
Email. lorain@relaischateaux.com   27 rooms   £D/H

Top Restaurants

★★★★★*L'Espérance*   St-Père-sous-Vézeley 89450
Tel. 03 86 33 39 10 Fax 03 86 33 26 15
Email marc.meneau@wanadoo.fr   £H

★★★★★*Côte St. Jacques*   14fg Paris, Joigny 89300
Tel. 03 86 62 09 70 Fax 03 86 91 49 70
Email. lorain@relaischateaux.com   £H

Value for money Hotels

★*Soleil d'Or*   Montigny-la-Resle 89230
Tel. 03 86 41 81 21 Fax 03 86 41 86 88
No email address   16 rooms   £A

★*Les Tilleuls*   3 rue Decourtive, St. Florentin 89600
Tel. 0386 35 11 86 Fax 05 57 47 46 76
Email alliance.tilleuls@wanadoo.fr   9 rooms   £A

Value for money Restaurants

★★★*Auberge du Pot d'Étain*   24 rue Bouchardat, L'Isle-sur-Serein 89440
Tel. 03 86 33 88 10 Fax 03 86 33 90 93
Email potdetain@ipoint.fr   £B/C

★*Les Tilleuls*   3 rue Decourtive, St. Florentin 89600
Tel. 0386 35 11 86 Fax 05 57 47 46 76
Email alliance.tilleuls@wanadoo.fr   £A/B

What a difference a new generation and a responsive market can make. Younger, highly-trained and talented winemakers have played their part in transforming quality in this the most complex and magical of France's wine regions. No stronger argument can be made for the validity of terroir than in Burgundy, where subtle differences of climate, soil composition and aspect identified over the course of centuries and expressed in individual climats make this region so complex and fascinating. Red Burgundy should enthrall with its perfume, complexity, finesse and textural qualities rather than power, oak and out-and-out concentration. White Burgundy should express complexity in both aroma and flavour, be it more minerally or buttery and nutty, and have a depth, structure and balance proportionate to its origins. Both should be more than just the most noble expression of two grapes, now familiar the world over, Pinot Noir and Chardonnay.

A change of direction

In the Côte d'Or, Burgundy's heart, the fragmentation of the vineyard area is extreme, and a complete contrast to Bordeaux's more coherent, larger patchwork. With a few rows here and a few there and the difficulties of vinifying such small quantities of grapes, it made sense to sell to a *négociant* as almost all growers did in the early 20th century. The cost in terms of quality has been well documented but through buying, trading and marriage a host of new independent growers have formed an important part of the new desire for quality.

Yet as recently as 20 years ago Burgundy was in dire straits. Excessive use of potassium and other chemicals on the soils (especially in the Côte de Nuits) led to reduced natural acidity levels and the dependence on pesticides, in turn leading to generally debilitated vineyard health. The resulting grapes were low in both sugar and acidity. Many producers considered it necessary to both over-chaptalize and acidify, a dual-pronged desperation made illegal in 1987. Whilst one practice or the other may be employed within strict limits there is little doubt that some producers still continue to do both despite some high-profile prosecutions by the authorities. Others, though, have sought to restore the health of their vineyards and obtain grapes of high quality and a new order of producers has emerged, better qualified but more often than not getting back to basics. They have improved the soil and plant health and consequently that of the grapes and wines. A movement towards organic and biodynamic viticulture has been stronger here than probably anywhere else in the wine-producing world. Currently many top estates take the advice of soil scientist Claude Bourguignon to enhance further the quality of their soils. Another consequence of the Burgundy's weak constitution was a tendency towards excessive fining and filtration in order to ensure the wine's stability. Better fruit quality as well as widely expressed criticism of heavy reliance on these practices, mean this trend has been reversed. Much too is made of lower yields, but there is still plenty of argument about how this is best achieved – whether through winter pruning, increasing vine densities, the use of different rootstocks or the use of green harvesting.

The best wines are now cleaner, riper and much more consistent even in more difficult years – though in the 1990s nature seems to have rewarded the many varied efforts – yet the wines are far from standardised. And even though there has been a general trend to ever bigger, oakier and more concentrated wines, at least some succeed admirably in retaining balance without losing the stamp of *terroir*. Where there were pockets of quality and occasional bright spots in some of the larger appellations now there are many producers turning out consistently high-quality wines. Yet from too many of the big merchants or *négociants* the wines continue to be very mediocre and it is why so many of them are missing from the following producer profiles. The ones included are the exception and in some instances are very good indeed. Much of the best wine comes from the smaller growers but an increasing number now also buy in some grapes.

Côte d'Or

The basic hierarchy in the Côte d'Or is of *grands crus* at the top, followed by *premiers crus* – always associated with one of 25 villages (*premiers crus* are often blended together due to fragmentation, so labelled simply Premier Cru) – then the level of the village itself (e.g. Gevrey-Chambertin) before the sub-regional appellations (such as Côte de Nuits-Villages) and finally the regional generics: **Bourgogne Rouge** (Pinot Noir), **Bourgogne Blanc** (Chardonnay) and **Bourgogne Aligoté**. The lowest level is not necessarily the humblest, however, as wine from any level may be sold as a generic (for instance, recently replanted vines that have only just come into production or vines that lie just outside a classified area). It is also worth noting that *premier cru* wine may also be included in part of a village-level bottling. This may be due to insufficient quantities for a separate bottling or a grower's decision not to compromise the integrity of his *premier cru* when faced with unsatisfactory quality in a difficult vintage. Also important to understanding the appellation system in Burgundy is the concept of *climat* or individual vineyard areas. Occasionally only part of a named area may be designated *premier cru* (e.g Chambolle-Musigny la Combe d'Orveaux) while within the unclassified village areas (which may be large, as in Meursault) the named vineyards (*lieux-dits*) may be added to the label (e.g. Meursault Tillets). The best of these will be close to *premier cru* level, just as several *premiers crus* are comparable to some of the less well-defined *grands crus*. Note too that the spelling of a particular vineyard can vary slightly from one producer to another. What follows is a brief breakdown of the most important villages and their most important *crus*.

Côte de Nuits

Production from the more northerly Côte de Nuits is almost exclusively red. **Marsannay** and **Fixin** at the north end of the Côte de Nuits, begin the band of mostly east-facing hills that stretches, with twists and breaks, until Santenay and Maranges in the tail of the Côte de Beaune. Marsannay tends to be light but scented and produces, unusually for the Côte de Nuits, a significant amount of rosé and white. Fixin in contrast, produces quite forceful, earthy Burgundy, including some powerful reds from *premiers crus* on slopes above the village. The wine, like that from the southern end of the Côte de Nuits, can be sold as **Côte de Nuits-Villages**. After the briefest of interludes (around Brochon) begins Burgundy's great rich seam of red.

Gevrey-Chambertin has 26 *premiers crus* including the outstanding Clos Saint-Jacques (*grand cru* in all but name) and Les Cazetiers at the centre of an arc of *premiers crus* on slopes to the east of the town. South of the village itself begins the great chain of *grands crus* that run almost to the southern edge of Vosne-Romanée. Of the nine in Gevrey, the 12.9-ha **Chambertin** and 15-ha **Clos-de-Bèze** are easily the most important. Seven others all append the name Chambertin: **Mazis-Chambertin** and **Ruchottes-Chambertin** are arguably the next best in potential; **Griottes-Chambertin**, **Charmes-Chambertin** (under which much of **Mazoyères-Chambertin** is sold) and **Chapelle-Chambertin** are also capable of greatness; the last, **Latricières-Chambertin**, rarely reaches the quality of the best *premiers crus*. Gevrey at any level should be distinguished by

121

its greater power, concentration and structure than its neighbouring communes. Despite a radical improvement, too much of it remains pretty poor. **Morey-Saint-Denis** undeservedly lacks the lustre of Gevrey and Chambolle, but can combine the muscle of the former with the elegance of the latter, though which prevails to the greater degree depends as much on the grower as the on vineyard site. A tiny amount of white is made here too. While significantly smaller than Gevrey, it still boasts 20 *premiers crus* and four *grands crus* – **Clos de la Roche** (17ha), **Clos Saint-Denis** (6.6ha), **Clos des Lambrays** (8.8ha) and **Clos de Tart** (7.5ha) – as well as a thin slice of the 15-ha **Bonnes Mares** which falls mostly in **Chambolle-Musigny**. Bonnes Mares, with its mixed soils, is of variable style but is usually sturdier when sourced from the Morey end of the vineyards. Then the chain of *grands crus* is broken, before continuing with **Le Musigny** (10.7ha) at the southern end of the commune. Some fine *premier cru* vineyards lie between the two, including Cras, Fuées and Baudes, but closest in style and proximity to Musigny are the often superb Amoureuses and Charmes. Musigny, like no other *cru*, can express the sumptuous elegant beauty of red Burgundy.

The commune of **Vougeot** is dominated by the massive 50-ha *grand cru* of **Clos Vougeot**. Though continuous and walled-in, in its lower, flatter reaches it juts deep into what corresponds to only village-quality land in neighbouring Vosne-Romanée. Arguably it ought to be partitioned into three different levels. Without due care you may find you have paid a *grand cru* price for what is, in effect, only village-level wine, although your choice of grower among the 80 owners of the vineyard counts for as much as the position of the vines. At its highest it adjoins both Musigny and Grands Echezeaux and at its best it is full, rich and complex if less aristocratic than the former. Both of the *grands crus* **Echezeaux** and **Grands Echezeaux** (with 32ha and 9ha respectively in production) fall in the commune of Flagey-Echezeaux. At their best both produce sturdy, characterful Burgundy, though much of Echezeaux lacks the class expected in a *grand cru*. Neighbouring **Vosne-Romanée** is a commune like no other in the Côte de Nuits. Behind the village lie the great vineyards that produce Burgundy's most expensive and sought-after wines. At the heart of 27ha of *grands crus* are **La Romanée** (0.85ha) and **Romanée-Conti** (1.8ha) with **Richebourg** (8ha) to the north, **Romanée-Saint-Vivant** (9.4ha) closer to the village, and **La Grande Rue** (1.65ha) and **La Tache** (6.1ha) to the south. These in turn are flanked by some marvellous *premiers crus* including Malconsorts, Chaumes and Clos des Réas on the southern edge of the commune with Nuits-Saint-Georges; with Brûlées, Suchots and Beaux Monts on the northern side, the latter two pressing up against Echezeaux. The best of these are rich, intense and concentrated but with varying degrees of finesse, opulence or silkiness, dependent as much on producer as location. Village-level Vosne comes from east of the village.

The last major village in the Côtes de Nuits is **Nuits-Saint-Georges** though vineyards continue on south to Comblanchien. Here, the best wines offer power and intensity as well as a degree of finesse in the best of 38 *premiers crus* (which extend into the more southerly commune of Prémeaux). Damodes, Boudots and Murgers are some of the best between Nuits-Saint-Georges (the town) and Vosne-Romanée; Vaucrains, Pruliers and Les Saint-Georges are the most notable to the south of Nuits. There are no *grand crus*. Lesser wine can be flavoursome if chunky but the worst is rough and dilute. The cooler hinterland of the Côte de Nuits contains pockets of vineyards in favourable sites which constitute the **Hautes-Côtes de Nuits**. South of the town of Beaune is the equivalent **Hautes-Côtes de Beaune**. A significant amount of the wine is made by the co-op Les Caves des Hautes-Côtes; these wines or an example from a top grower can be good in an exceptional vintage.

Côte de Beaune

The Côte de Beaune's reputation is more for white than red yet the majority of wines are in fact red. From here south the gradients are lower and the swathe of vineyards wider, occasionally receding into the hills behind the main slopes. It begins in a cluster of villages around the famous hill of Corton. The humble AC of **Ladoix** (with seven *premiers crus*) is not widely seen and some of the wine is sold under the sub-regional appellation of **Côte de Beaune-Villages.** Wine for the latter can also come from another 15 villages, making it much more important than the Nuits equivalent. **Aloxe-Corton** at the foot of the Corton hill includes the famous appellations of Corton and Corton-Charlemagne, though vineyards spill into adjoining Ladoix and Pernand-Vergelesses. Most of the white from Burgundy's largest *grand cru* is sold as **Corton-Charlemagne** (51ha) and most of the red as **Corton** (98ha), though there is a little white Corton too (2.5ha). The trend to planting Chardonnay begun in the mid-19th century continues, the paler soils at the top of the hill being the best site. Great Corton-Charlemagne is full-bodied but slow-developing due to a powerful structure and requires patience. Red Corton (which oftens attaches one of several *lieu-dit* names) can be similarly austere when young but develops a richness and a distinctive minerally elegance with age. Aloxe-Corton AC, almost entirely red, includes 13 *premiers crus* which lie directly below the red Corton vineyards. To the west of the Aloxe-Corton commune lies **Pernand-Vergelesses**, some of it tucked into the folds in the hills. Increasingly good red and white is made under the AC. The best *premier cru*, Ile de Vergelesses, favours reds of finesse rather than power but they add weight with age. To the south, it adjoins **Savigny-lès-Beaune**, which extends east up a little valley to the village itself. The best vineyards lie on both sides, the more northern band of *premiers crus* (including Guettes, Serpentières and Lavières) are more elegant than those from the southern band (including Dominodes, Marconnets, Narbantons and Peuillets), which tend to be fuller and firmer. Importantly, this is a reasonably plentiful source of good-value Burgundy. Rarely exciting is wine from **Chorey-lès-Beaune**, from flat land to the east of the Savigny AC.

Beaune, historically and commercially, is the heart of Burgundy but it is also one of the three leading Côte de Beaune red wine villages and includes some excellent *premiers crus* from the gentle slopes west of the town. Due to diverse soil types, leading *premiers crus* vary from the full and firm to softer, more elegant wines. Marconnets, Fèves and Bressandes are of the first category, Grèves and Teurons are richer and softer, Clos des Mouches full but elegant too. Important vineyard owners such as Jadot, Albert Morot, Bouchard Père and Drouhin all provide the opportunity to compare and contrast some of the best *crus* from a single source. Another major vineyard owner, and one of the most important in the Côte de Beaune, is the Hospices de Beaune, their many (often oaky) *cuvées* (unique blends of predominantly *premiers crus* named for their benefactor) are sold at the famous auction in November. The wines are then 'finished' by the purchasing *négociant*, a factor that has a further bearing on their (variable) quality. The rarely seen **Côte de Beaune** AC is for a few vineyards in the hills behind Beaune AC. **Pommard** is a continuation of Beaune and its reputation for sturdy, full-bodied reds is in part due to more clayey, often iron-rich, soils than its neighbours. Grands Epenots and Rugiens Bas are the finest *premiers crus*. In **Volnay** the soils are lighter and poorer, contributing to the wine's refinement and elegance. Most of the best *premiers crus* come from south of the village, including Taillepieds, Clos des Chênes, Caillerets Dessus and Santenots. Santenots actually lies within the adjacent

123

Meursault but is generally sold as Volnay when made from Pinot Noir, and as Meursault if from Chardonnay. South and west of Volnay an ascending flank of vineyards extends into the hills and includes the villages of **Monthelie**, **Auxey-Duresses** and **Saint-Romain**. The first two can provide excellent reds from several *premiers crus* but also a little good village white, especially in Auxey-Duresses. Good Saint-Romain white can be better than its position in the Hautes-Côtes de Beaune hills might suggest.

Meursault is one of the three biggest communes in the Côte d'Or and is the most important white wine village. But as with Beaune or Gevrey-Chambertin, with size comes variability. At its worst it is heavy and characterless but good examples are full, ripe and fruit-rich. The finest are intense, stylish and in the case of the would-be *grand cru*, Perrières, minerally and refined. There are no *grands crus* but other fine *premiers crus* include the best examples of Genevrières, Charmes, Poruzots and Goutte d'Or. Village *lieux-dits* names of note include Chevalières, Grands Charrons, Narvaux, Tessons and Tillets. **Blagny** is a small red wine outpost nestled against Meursault and **Puligny-Montrachet**. 'Puligny' and 'world's best' often share the same sentence and with good reason. The village includes the *grands crus* **Chevalier-Montrachet** (7.36ha), **Bienvenues-Bâtard-Montrachet** (3.69ha) and half of the 8ha **Le Montrachet** and 6ha of the 11.87-ha **Bâtard-Montrachet**. Le Montrachet is the greatest, and most expensive, of all but is a wine capable of marvellous concentration, sublime proportions and exquisite complexity. Chevalier-Montrachet, from thinner soils above, is potentially the closest in quality but Bâtard-Montrachet, from flatter vineyards, can offer superb richness and intensity too. There are many outstanding *premiers crus* which also command high prices. Caillerets (including Les Demoiselles) and Pucelles, adjoining the *grands crus*, will surpass any *grand cru* not at its full potential. Clavoillon and Folatières and the more elevated Champ Gain and La Garenne can highlight the Puligny finesse and intensity as can Champ-Canet, Combettes and Referts which extend as far as Meursault's Perrières and Charmes. As well as the continuation of *grands crus* Le Montrachet and Bâtard-Montrachet, the village of **Chassagne-Montrachet** adds the tiny 1.57-ha *grand cru* of Criots-Bâtard-Montrachet. The wines sold under the Chassagne AC were once predominantly red but its reputation is now emphatically white. Leading *premiers crus* include Caillerets, Champs Gains, Embrazées, Morgeots, La Romanée and Ruchottes – mostly confined to lighter-coloured soils on the higher slopes. Reds vary from the thin and unripe to full and fleshy and can be a source of good value (they only command around half the price of a white from the same vineyard, thus the trend to white continues). La Boudriotte, Clos Saint-Jean, La Maltroie, Morgeots and Chenevottes are the most noted red *premiers crus*. Behind Chassagne and Puligny lies the commune of **Saint-Aubin**. Some remarkably good white is produced by the best growers from the most worthy *premier cru* vineyards: La Chatenière and those that adjoin Chassagne (Le Charmois) and Puligny (En Remilly and Murgers des Dents de Chien – backing on to the Mont Rachet hill). Reds tend to be relatively light and slightly earthy.

Santenay is the Côte de Beaune's last significant commune for quality as the tail of the vineyard area swings west. From south-facing vineyards red wines dominate, the best of these are both full and stylish. These are likely to come from the *premiers crus* Gravières, La Comme and Clos des Tavannes that extend to the edge of Chassagne. One or two excellent whites are also being produced. While a fast improving AC with some excellent-value wines, Santenay is not so good from a weaker vintage or from a mediocre producer when the wine may be lean and stalky. To the west the vineyards adjoin **Maranges**, more earthy and robust than the best Santenay, though exceptions exist.

Côte Chalonnaise

As a source of quality and value the best Côte Chalonnaise growers provide a real alternative to the lesser villages of the Côte d'Or. To the east of the Santenay and Maranges vineyards, and south of the town of Chagny, lie those of **Bouzeron**, the first of five separate appellations within the Côte Chalonnaise region. This is not a continuation of the Côte d'Or but an area of less sheltered rolling hills where the grapes ripen later and the wines are lighter. Bouzeron is classified for Aligoté only, its Pinot Noir and Chardonnay sold as **Bourgogne Côte Chalonnaise**. **Rully** lies east and south of Bouzeron and makes more white than red – both of which can reveal ripe, attractive fruit in a top example. Less ripe Chardonnay is likely to be made into **Crémant de Bourgogne**. South of Rully is **Mercurey**, the most important Chalonnaise appellation. Most of the wine is a quite structured red, surprisingly rich and intense from a combination of a top year and producer, but often hard and lean when not. A little good white is also produced. Slightly more supple yet stylish reds are produced in **Givry**, where the balance of red and white is similar to that of Mercurey. The southernmost appellation is **Montagny**, where exclusively white wine is made. The wines can be fuller if sometimes less distinguished than those from Rully. The reputable Buxy co-op, La Cave des Vignerons de Buxy, is based here

A-Z of producers by appellation/region

CÔTE D'OR & CÔTE CHALONNAISE

Côte d'Or & Côte Chalonnaise vintages

In general terms red Burgundy doesn't offer the same potential longevity as do Bordeaux or other great Cabernet-based wines. Exceptional wines can, however, be very long-lived, and it is not unusual for the top whites to outlast the best reds. Ageing potential also depends as much on the style favoured by the particular producer or on the origin of the wines. Therefore comments about the character of the vintage made here should be considered against remarks made in the individual producer profiles. The very best estates, aided by a generally fine run of vintages in the past decade or so, now produce consistently high quality. Yet away from the top names and most famous sites the choice of vintage remains crucial, especially at a lower level, given the struggle for ripeness in Burgundy's many more marginal vineyard sites.

2004: Whether 2004 is seen as a counterbalance to 2003 or not, it was certainly cool, wet and grey, despite finishing with a decent September. Worse it was hit by hail and oidium (mildew which attacks the grapes). As in Chablis yields are very high unless the potential crop was constantly cut back in the vineyard. Whites look to be better than reds with fine fruit and good acidities. Reds demanded even greater selection and quality is likely to be very producer-dependent, particularly in the Côte de Beaune.

2003: An extraordinarily hot year that required both intelligence and speed from growers. Quantities are small and much, often raisined, fruit had to be discarded. Yet reds are surprisingly good with plenty of colour, ripe but not raisined fruit, with good if not classic structures. There is good quality too from lesser appellations where in other years the grapes struggle to ripen. With few exceptions whites are disappointing, but variable from grower to grower. Most, at best have a ripe, exotic fruit appeal but many are overblown and such a paucity of structure that they need to be drunk now or within a couple of years.

2002: This is certainly an exciting red wine vintage in Burgundy despite a spell of warm but wet weather in early September. Yields were low, the grapes small but high in sugar, with good colour and acidity that has ensured intense, ripe and ageworthy wines throughout the Côte d'Or. Some of the most exceptional young reds have come from Volnay and Nuits-Saint-Georges. Whites are very good too, including those from the Côte Chalonnaise - the best with concentration, structure, perfectly ripe fruit and good balance to at least equal the high quality from 99 and 2000.

2001: A repeat of 2000 in the sense that the more northerly Côte de Nuits looks better than the Côte de Beaune (with reduced quantities in Volnay and Pommard due to hail). A wet year but with a mostly fine finish, one where only the best-managed vineyards produce ripe, concentrated grapes with good acidities. A good producer is essential but the wines have improved considerably in the bottle and show good terroir expression. The difficult weather also made for variable white wines; some have both good acidity and concentration but others lack ripeness.

2000: In red this was a much better vintage in the Côte de Nuits than the Côte de Beaune. Santenay was particularly badly affected by rain. Not one to cellar but fine quality further up the hierarchy. Generally a very good vintage for whites if slightly less consistent than 1999. Opinions are divided amongst growers as to the better of the two years for white; some have better ripeness, concentration and acidity in the latter, some in the former. Decent quality in the Côte Chalonnaise.

127

1999: A generally excellent large vintage for reds with remarkable colour, good acidity and ripe tannins. The size of the crop encouraged growers to be more rigorous in removing the less promising bunches. These reds, particularly good in the Côte de Beaune, are vigorous and intense and only the generic or more humble village appellations be should be drunk now. Whites were plentiful too, and, though more variable than the reds, are also fine with some outstanding examples from the top estates. An excellent vintage in the Côte Chalonnaise in both colours.

1998: A problematic growing season lowered expectations but this has turned out to be a vintage with more potential than 1997 thanks to better acidity and more stuffing. Quantities were down due to severe Easter frosts. Though generally very good, quality is much more irregular at a lower level, with a lack of full ripeness in the tannins due in part to some very hot August days. Isolated hail hit the volume of whites, especially in Meursault, and quality is variable; some wines lack concentration and others will evolve quite quickly. The best, though, will not disappoint.

1997: A much smaller vintage of more forward reds than 1996 but very attractive and one that has already given much pleasure. The wines have lowish acidities but it is a good vintage for drinking now if not for keeping. Whites can have lowish acidities too but there is no lack of richness or intensity in the top wines. The best in both colours will still keep.

1996: One of the finest red wine vintages of the 1990s, with both quantity and quality at the top level. Among the best growers there is excellent fruit intensity and ripeness in the tannins (although in some cases tannins have not softened) allied to good acidity that will repay further keeping. Many remain closed but more humble appellations from a good grower can be drunk now. Also a vintage in which exceptional reds and whites from the Côte Chalonnaise might still be drinking.

1995: Not a vintage of great richness in the reds but fine nonetheless. The best have added weight with age, are ripe and structured and will still improve. An excellent vintage for whites; good examples can be drunk now but will continue to improve.

1994: Arguably the weakest red wine vintage in the last 15 years but there is not much between this and 1992 in quality. A better bet in the Côte de Nuits than the Côte de Beaune. Whites are merely attractive when from a good producer, others are best left for the unwary.

1993: A very fine red wine vintage with great vigour, structure and intensity. Good village-level examples or those from lesser *climats* should be drunk now but the best will still improve. Much weaker in the whites, though some have both concentration and structure and provide rich, mature drinking now. Only the very best will still improve.

1992: A large red harvest, though not as much as 1990, and some of it full and charming though missing the extra concentration or structure of a really good vintage. Producers noted for their low yields are a safer bet though generally there is a lack of intensity and definition. Whites showed some delicious fruit but only in the top examples can this still be enjoyed.

1991: Many rich, concentrated and structured reds. The best still have plenty of life but some lack harmony and fully ripe tannins. Find a good bottle, though, and it's likely to be much cheaper than the 1990 of the same wine. Good drinking now, though a handful might keep a bit longer. Whites were mostly ordinary at best and should only be bought with extreme care.

1990: A superlative vintage for red wines and unequalled in recent decades for the overall quality of the vintage, though due to vinicultural improvements many individual producers have made wines of higher quality since. A very good vintage for whites too. Many fine bottles, including those from some of the lesser *climats*, and these will last for many years to come.

1989: A warm, plentiful vintage with relatively low acidity in the reds, though it is still good at top level. Whites had particularly good structure and have proved more long-lived than 1988, 90 or 92.

1988: A rather firm, austere vintage with high acidity and tannins in the reds. It has taken a long time to come into its own but the best examples are only now revealing the underlying refinement. Whites are less good though some have aged well.

Earlier years

At the top level 1985 can still provide good drinking, though whites are a safer bet as the once rich, ripe reds are mostly past their best due to low acidity levels. A few of the structured reds from the 1983 vintage can still be vigorous where rot was avoided. Even older vintages might only be considered for an outstanding *cru* from an impeccable source. Vintages from the 1970s include 78, 76 and 71 while the more successful 1960s include 69, 66, 64, 62 and 61. For these and wines from any older vintages, however, consider the advice of a trusted merchant or friend who still has other bottles of the same wine, or consult Michael Broadbent's *Vintage Wine*.

Côte d'Or & Côte Chalonnaise vintage chart

	Côte de Nuits Red	Côte de Beaune Red	Côte Chalonnaise Red	Côte de Beaune White
2004	★★★ A	★★/★★★ A	★★/★★★ A	★★★★A
2003	★★★/★★★★ A	★★★/★★★★ A	★★/★★★★ A	★/★★★ B
2002	★★★★/★★★★★ A	★★★★/★★★★★★ A	★★★★B	★★★★/★★★★★ A
2001	★★★ B	★★★ B	★★/★★★ B	★★★ B
2000	★★★ B	★★ B	★★ C	★★★★/★★★★★ B
1999	★★★★ B	★★★★/★★★★★★ A	★★★★/★★★★★ B	★★★★/★★★★★ B
1998	★★★/★★★★ B	★★★ B	★★★ C	★★/★★★ C
1997	★★★ C	★★/★★★ C	★★/★★★ C	★★★/★★★★ B
1996	★★★/★★★★★ B	★★★/★★★★★ B	★★★★ C	★★★★/★★★★★ B
1995	★★★★ C	★★★★ C	★★★/★★★★ D	★★★★/★★★★★ B
1994	★/★★ C	★/★★ C		★★★ C
1993	★★★★ B	★★★★ C		★★ D
1992	★★ C	★★ C		★★★★ C
1991	★★★/★★★★ C	★★★/★★★★ C		★★/★★★ D
1990	★★★★★ C	★★★★★ C	★★★★/★★★★★ C	★★★/★★★★ C
1989	★★★★ C	★★★★ C		★★★★/★★★★★ C
1988	★★★★ C	★★★★ C		★★★/★★★★ D

STÉPHANE ALADAME   Montagny

Stéphane Aladame   Rue de Lavoir, 71390 Montagny-lès-Buxy
UK stockists: **Goe, Lib**, ACh

This 5.5-ha domaine planted mostly to Chardonnay is one of the few independent estates in Montagny worth investigating. The 2002s are particularly good, combining ripe fruit with weight on the palate and structure so that only now are the wines beginning to open out fully. Les Coères is particularly stylish with a very fine minerality and real persistence on the palate. Cuvée Selection isn't quite at the same level but shows good complexity with a well-integrated lees-derived character. Prices are comparable to other good Chalonnaise whites. In addition to those rated below, *premiers crus* Burnins and Les Platières are also produced. (PW)

O **Montagny** 1er Cru★★ £C   1er Cru Cuvée Selection★★★ £C
O **Montagny** 1er Cru Les Coères★★★ £C

BERTRAND AMBROISE   Nuits-Saint-Georges   www.ambroise.com

Bertrand Ambroise   Prémeaux-Prissey, 21700 Nuits-Saint-Georges
 UK stockists: **CTy, Jas, Bal, BBR, Win**

Ambroise's red Burgundies are at one extreme of the Burgundian spectrum of wine styles. Their colour and strength are virtually unmatched in the Côte d'Or. The biggest reds are bold, oaky and tannic when young but the depth and concentration ensure that both something of the wine's origin and a certain finesse come with age. Of some 20ha of vineyards spread over several communes in the centre of the Côte d'Or, around a quarter is for whites, with some notable Saint-Aubin and Corton-Charlemagne. Whites are rich and not excessively oaky and show a structure and depth worthy of their appellations, often with a real succulence that encourages early drinking. If not to everyone's taste, the wines are consistent and well-priced. Lesser reds (Bourgogne Rouge and Bourgogne Rouge Vieilles Vignes) and whites (Bourgogne Chardonnay and Hautes-Côtes de Nuits) can seem a little coarse but don't lack for fruit or flavour. 2002 Nuits-Saint-Georges *premiers crus* though deep and characterful are over-extracted, even in the context of the style here but 2003s are generally much better including a superb Corton Le Rognet. (PW)

● **Corton Le Rognet**★★★★ £F   ● **Clos de Vougeot**★★★★ £F
● **Nuits-Saint-Georges** 1er Cru Clos des Argillières★★★ £E
● **Nuits-Saint-Georges** 1er Cru Rue de Chaux★★★ £E
● **Nuits-Saint-Georges** 1er Cru Les Vaucrains★★★ £E
● **Nuits-Saint-Georges**★★ £D Vieilles Vignes★★★ £D
● **Côte de Nuits-Villages**★ £C   ● **Vougeot** 1er Cru Les Cras★★ £D
O **Corton-Charlemagne**★★★★ £F
O **Chassagne-Montrachet** 1er Cru Maltroie★★★ £E
O **Saint-Aubin** 1er Cru Murgers Dents de Chien★★ £C

DOM. GUY AMIOT ET FILS   Chassagne-Montrachet

G & T Amiot   13 Rue de Grand-Puits, 21190 Chassagne-Montrachet
 UK stockists: **Bal, Bib, Gen, HRp, L&S, F&R**

Guy Amiot and his son Thierry make a string of white Chassagne-Montrachet *crus*, which have shown increasing refinement and complexity in the most recent vintages. The wines are now bottled later than previously but perhaps more importantly Thierry has made changes in the vineyard resulting in richer, riper fruit from vines with an increasingly high average age (especially Vergers and Caillerets). At least as interesting if not at the same quality level are the red wines, which have very good richness for southern Côte de Beaune reds, with added length and style in the Clos Saint-Jean bottling. All the better reds deserve at least 3 or 4 years' age. Only a very little Puligny-Montrachet Premier Cru Les Demoiselles and Montrachet are made. Lesser whites can be drunk young but the best need at least 3 or 4 years' ageing. (PW)

○ **Puligny-Montrachet** 1er Cru Les Demoiselles★★★★★ £E
○ **Chassagne-Montrachet** 1er Cru Les Caillerets★★★★ £E
○ **Chassagne-Montrachet** 1er Cru Les Vergers★★★★ £E
○ **Chassagne-Montrachet** 1er Cru Les Macharelles★★★★ £E
○ **Chassagne-Montrachet** 1er Cru Clos Saint-Jean★★★ £E
○ **Chassagne-Montrachet** 1er Cru Champgains★★★ £E
○ **Chassagne-Montrachet**★★★ £D 1er Cru Les Baudines★★★ £E
○ **Saint-Aubin** 1er Cru En Remilly★★★ £E
● **Chassagne-Montrachet** 1er Cru Clos Saint-Jean★★★ £E
● **Chassagne-Montrachet** 1er Cru La Maltroie★★★ £E
● **Chassagne-Montrachet**★ £C Les Chaumes★★ £C
● **Santenay** La Comme Dessus★ £C

AMIOT-SERVELLE Chambolle-Musigny www.amiot-servelle.com

Christian & Elizabeth Amiot 21220 Chambolle-Musigny
UK stockists: **CTy**, Add, Jas

Christian and Elizabeth Amiot farm almost 7ha of vines. The wines are sturdy, and can at times be a little too structured to let the fruit sing through. However, when it does, the wines are rich and plump as in 1995, 96 and 97. The 98s and 99s are firmer, more robust and in their youth seemed rather hard, extracted and lacking in generosity. Nevertheless these are fine, often from old vines and as always are beginning to offer more with a few years' bottle-age. As well as a concentrated Chambolle-Musigny Amoureuses, the little known *premier cru* Derrière la Grange (which lies below Les Fuées) can show lots of style and there's some well-sited Clos de Vougeot. After some very good 2001s, some superb 02s have been produced. Bourgogne Rouge and a little Aligoté and Chardonnay are also made. (PW)

● **Clos de Vougeot**★★★★ £F
● **Chambolle-Musigny** 1er Cru Les Amoureuses★★★★★ £F
● **Chambolle-Musigny** 1er Cru Les Charmes★★★★ £F
● **Chambolle-Musigny**★★★ £D 1er Cru Derrière la Grange★★★★ £E

MARQUIS D'ANGERVILLE Volnay

D'Angerville family Volnay, 21190 Meursault
UK stockists: C&B, CTy, JAr, OWL, Maj

The greatly respected Jacques d'Angerville died in 2003 but the legacy of his estate and wines seems certain to continue under Guillaume d'Angerville. These remarkable expressions of Volnay are taut and structured when tasted very young but are classy and refined with concentrated, intense fruit underneath. Production from 13ha is dominated by 4 *premiers crus*, including the prize 2.4ha *monopole* Clos des Ducs. Low yields, with rigorous selection and full destemming are part of the formula and the red-fruits intensity is always well integrated with subdued oak. The wines have been on very good form since the late 1980s. Through a string of very different vintages in the late 90s and early in the new century (superb 2002s and excellent 03s) the wines are wonderfully consistent but in every vintage deserve to be drunk with at least 5 or 6 years' age. All *crus* show the elegance and refinement of Volnay. Of the 4 most important *crus*, the elegant, stylish Frémiets is complemented by a medium-full, fragrant yet quite powerful Champans. Taillepieds combines great refinement and fullness while Clos des Ducs reveals a fabulous structure and superb length and class. There is no Caillerets from current vintages due to replanting. A powerful Meursault-Santenots white has lots of substance and fruit richness. (PW)

● **Volnay** 1er Cru Clos des Ducs✪✪✪✪✪ £F
● **Volnay** 1er Cru Taillepieds★★★★★ £F

● **Volnay** 1er Cru Champans★★★★★ £E 1er Cru Frémiets★★★★ £E
O **Meursault-Santenots** 1er Cru★★★★ £E

DOM. DE L'ARLOT Nuits-Saint-Georges

Jean-Pierre de Smet   Prémeaux-Prissey, 21700 Nuits-Saint-Georges
UK stockists: **ABy, Goe, JAr, L&W, HRp, WSc**

This worthy estate, created in 1987 after the purchase of an existing domain by
French insurance giant AXA Millésimes, has now had 15 years of steady
direction under Jean-Pierre de Smet. Some 14ha includes 2ha of white grapes
and 2 substantial Nuits-Saint-Georges *monopoles*, the 7-ha Clos des Fôrets-
Saint-Georges and 3-ha Clos de l'Arlot. Great care is taken in the vineyards and
there is minimal interference in the vinification and only a moderate use of new
oak. The whites are more consistent than the reds as they do not tend to show
the leanness encountered in lighter vintages for reds. Due at least partly to a
policy of not destemming, there can be a lack of both flesh and depth to the
reds and at times a stemmy quality (as some of the stalks included must still
retain a green aspect, despite careful selection). However, in the ripest vintages
this is rarely a problem and elegance and class shine through. The wines will
always put on weight with age too, losing any sturdiness of youth to become
very refined and harmonious. Recent vintages have been better, though even
the best 1997s and 00s do not compare with the superior 98s and 99s. Nuits-
Saint-Georges was particularly favoured in 2002 and generally this is reflected
here. A regular Nuits-Saint-Georges made from young vines in the Clos des
Fôrets has been redesignated *premier cru* from 2000. (PW)

● **Romanée-Saint-Vivant**★★★★ £G
● **Vosne-Romanée** 1er Cru Les Suchots★★★ £E
● **Nuits-Saint-Georges** 1er Cru★★ £D 1er Cru Clos de l'Arlot★★★ £E
● **Nuits-Saint-Georges** 1er Cru Clos des Fôrets-Saint-Georges★★★ £E
● **Côtes de Nuits-Villages** Clos du Chapeau★★ £C
O **Nuits-Saint-Georges** 1er Cru Clos de l'Arlot★★★ £F
O **Nuits-Saint-Georges** Cuvée Jeunes Vignes★★ £E

COMTE ARMAND www.domaine-des-epeneaux.com

Comte Armand   Place de l'Église, 21630 Pommard
UK stockists: **HRp, GFy, L&S, L&W, FMV, Gau**

The Comte Armand's Domaine des Epeneaux for long produced just 1 wine,
the famous Pommard Clos des Epeneaux from a 5-ha vineyard that forms part
of the *premier cru* Les Grands Epenots. Since 1995 red and white Auxey-
Duresses have been added, as has a very good Volnay Frémiets. Yields are low
and the reds are notable for their colour, structure and depth. In 1999
Benjamin Leroux took over making the wines from Pascal Marchand, who had
firmly established a quality regime here from the mid-1980s. Pascal's minimal
use of chemicals has been taken a stage further - production has been certified
biodynamic since 2001. The Clos continues to be made from 3 separately
vinified parcels of vines differentiated by their age. The wine is always full-
bodied and powerful but balanced and complex. Village Pommard is produced
from some of the younger-vine fruit not used in the Clos. A little Meursault,
Meix-Chavaux has also been produced. Very good 2001s, even better 02s. (PW)

● **Pommard**★★★ £E 1er Cru Clos des Epeneaux★★★★★ £F
● **Volnay** Frémiets★★★★ £E ● **Auxey Duresses** 1er Cru★★★ £D
O **Auxey-Duresses**★★ £C

DOM. ROBERT ARNOUX Vosne-Romanée

Arnoux family   RN3 21700 Vosne-Romanée
UK stockists: **A&B, BWC, Eno, CTy, HRp, JAr, Gau**

Pascal Lachaux is the son-in-law of the late Robert Arnoux and he has been making better and better wines here over the past decade. The top wines, of which there are several, receive 100% new oak treatment but rarely is this obvious. The wines are sturdy, structured with at times almost overwhelming intensity and power. In vintages like 1996, 99 and 02 *premiers crus* such as Corvées Pagets and Suchots show their inherent class to best effect while the *grands crus* reveal great depth and texture but all are also very good in other recent vintages too. Pascal has also been producing a range of *négociant* wines since 2002. (PW)

● **Romanée-Saint-Vivant**✪✪✪✪✪ £H
● **Clos de Vougeot**★★★★★ £F ● **Echezeaux**★★★★★ £F
● **Vosne-Romanée** 1er Cru Aux Reignots★★★★ £F
● **Vosne-Romanée** 1er Cru Les Suchots★★★★ £F
● **Vosne-Romanée** 1er Cru Les Chaumes★★★★ £E
● **Vosne-Romanée**★★★ £D Les Hautes-Maizières★★★ £E
● **Nuits-Saint-Georges** 1er Cru Les Corvées Pagets★★★★ £E
● **Nuits-Saint-Georges** 1er Cru Les Procès★★★ £E
● **Nuits-Saint-Georges**★★★ £D Les Poisets★★★ £E

DOM. D'AUVENAY Saint-Romain

Lalou Bize-Leroy Domaine d'Auvenay, 21190 Meursault
UK stockists: Far, J&B, HRp, F&R

This is the private estate of Madame Lalou Bize and is quite distinct from both the considerably larger Domaine LEROY and the Leroy *négociant* business. Though there are just 3.9ha (farmed biodynamically) there are several exquisite small *crus* which are made to the same exacting standards as Domaine Leroy. While reds dominate the production of Domaine Leroy, apart from a little *grand cru* Bonnes-Mares and Mazis-Chambertin, here it is white magic that prevails. The wines are rich, pure and concentrated – even at the level of Auxey-Duresses or Bourgogne Aligoté. Prices are astoundingly high and though the same general ratings apply (5 stars for the *grands crus*, at least 4 stars for the *premiers crus* and 3 stars for the other wines), I'd find the individuality and grandeur of the Domaine Leroy reds a greater temptation if I had the money to spend. The wines to look out for are: Chevalier-Montrachet, Criots-Bâtard-Montrachet, Puligny-Montrachet (La Richarde, Premier Cru Folatières), Meursault (Narvaux, Premier Cru Goutte d'Or), Auxey-Duresses (Boutonniers, Les Clous) and some Bourgogne Aligoté. A straight village Meursault is sometimes bottled separately as Chaumes de Perrières and Pré de Manche. (PW)

DENIS BACHELET Gevrey-Chambertin

Denis Bachelet 54 Route de Beaune, 21220 Gevrey-Chambertin
UK stockists: HRp, FMV

Denis Bachelet's wines are not that widely seen, such are the small quantities he produces, but they are wines of great finesse and class with lovely fruit intensity and harmony. In fact they might almost be considered atypical for an appellation that delivers up powerful, meaty, sometimes tannic, examples of Pinot. If the rich, intense Premier Cru Les Corbeaux and complex and classy *grand cru* Charmes-Chambertin are hard to find, the village Gevrey-Chambertin Vieilles Vignes is a super example at this level; all 3 are made from old vines. There's also reasonable quantities of a Côte de Nuits-Villages and a Bourgogne Rouge that make delicious red Burgundy seem almost affordable. (PW)

● **Charmes-Chambertin**★★★★★ £F
● **Gevrey-Chambertin** 1er Cru Les Corbeaux★★★★ £E
● **Gevrey-Chambertin** Vieilles Vignes★★★★ £E
● **Côte de Nuits-Villages**★★ £C ● **Bourgogne Rouge**★★ £B

133

GHISLAINE BARTHOD   Chambolle-Musigny

Barthod-Noëllat family   Rue du Lavoir, 21220 Chambolle-Musigny
UK stockists: RsW J&B, FMV, BBR, Rae, Tan, L&W

This small family domaine has just 6.5ha of vineyards but all lie within this pretty commune that epitomises finesse in the Côte de Nuits. Seven small plots of *premiers crus* can all be measured in ares rather than hectares, such is their size. Ghislaine Barthod's wines have grace, finesse and succulence, there is nothing brash or harsh yet they have very good structure and personality. Cras and Charmes are the top 2 wines though the Véroilles (only the family's holding is of *premier cru* status) is also consistently fine. Cras is the most structured and profound, Charmes is concentrated and classy but there are no weak wines here, as even the village Chambolle-Musigny is always an excellent example and the Bourgogne Rouge is attractive, fruity and delicious. Also see Louis BOILLOT for the wines of Ghislaine's husband. (PW)

Ghislaine Barthod:
- **Chambolle-Musigny** 1er Cru Les Cras★★★★★ £E
- **Chambolle-Musigny** 1er Cru Les Véroilles★★★★★ £E
- **Chambolle-Musigny** 1er Cru Les Charmes★★★★★ £E
- **Chambolle-Musigny** 1er Cru Les Fuées★★★★ £E
- **Chambolle-Musigny** 1er Cru Les Chatelots★★★★ £E
- **Chambolle-Musigny** 1er Cru Les Baudes★★★★ £E
- **Chambolle-Musigny**★★★ £D   1er Cru Les Beaux Bruns★★★ £E
- **Bourgogne Rouge**★★ £B

ROGER BELLAND   Santenay   www.domaine-belland-roger.com

Roger Belland   3 Rue de la Chapelle, B P 13, 21590 Santenay
UK stockists: Lib, BBR, BSh, B&T

This is now an excellent source of top white Burgundy. Roger Belland is based in Santenay but a little over 4ha of a total of 23ha of vineyards include fine Chassagne-Montrachet (Morgeot Clos Pitois, a *monopole*), some Puligny and even some of the tiny Criots-Bâtard-Montrachet *grand cru*. In common with many of the great domaines, Belland is a dedicated viticulturalist and goes to great lengths in the vineyard to maximise the quality of the fruit. Whites see new oak – 100% for the *grand cru* Criots – but the intensity and depth of the fruit are only enhanced by it. Red Santenay includes the leading *premiers crus* at the northern end of this sizeable appellation; these are very good examples, full of ripe berry fruits but with good structure and length too. A source of great value Burgundy too. (PW)

- O **Criots-Bâtard-Montrachet**✪✪✪✪✪ £H
- O **Chassagne-Montrachet** 1er Cru Morgeot Clos Pitois★★★★ £E
- O **Puligny-Montrachet** 1er Cru Les Champs Gains★★★★ £F
- O **Santenay**★★ £C   1er Cru Beauregard★★★ £C
- ● **Pommard** Les Cras★★★ £E   ● **Volnay** 1er Cru Santenots★★★ £E
- ● **Chassagne-Montrachet** 1er Cru Morgeot Clos Pitois★★★ £D
- ● **Santenay** 1er Cru Commes★★★ £C   1er Cru Beauregard★★★ £C
- ● **Santenay** Charmes★★ £C   1er Cru Gravières★★★ £C
- ● **Maranges**★ £B   1er Cru La Fussière★★ £C

DOM. BERTAGNA   Vougeot   www.domainebertagna.com

Eva Reh-Siddle   16 Rue de Vieux Château, 21640 Vougeot
UK stockists: **FMV**, BBR

This 30-ha estate has a wide spread of vineyards in the Côte de Nuits, having steadily acquired more parcels since it was bought in 1982 by Günter Reh (of von KESSELSTATT in Germany), father of the current director, Eva Reh-Siddle. Since 1999 the wines have been made by Claire Forrestier and the reds are vigorous, rich and structured. But the *terroir* is emphasised rather than suppressed, especially as the wines age, so there is density and muscle in wines like Vougeot Les Cras, but class and intensity in Vosne-Romanée Les Beaux-Monts and finesse in Clos Saint-Denis. All the best *premiers crus* and *grands crus* need 8–10 years' age. Clos de la Perrière is a *monopole*. Also made are Corton Les Grandes Lolières and a little Chambertin. Two whites, Vougeot Premier Cru and Corton Charlemagne, are classsy and structured but could sometimes use a little better balance and definition. (PW)

● **Clos Saint-Denis**★★★★★ £G   ● **Clos de Vougeot**★★★★ £G
● **Vougeot** 1er Cru Clos de la Perrière★★★★ £F
● **Vougeot** 1er Cru Les Cras★★★ £F   1er Cru Petits Vougeots★★★ £F
● **Vosne-Romanée** 1er Cru Beaux-Monts★★★★ £F
● **Nuits-Saint-Georges** 1er Cru Les Murgers★★★★ £F
● **Chambolle-Musigny** 1er Cru Les Plantes★★★★ £F
O **Corton-Charlemagne**★★★ £F   O **Vougeot Blanc**★★★ £F

DOM. SIMON BIZE ET FILS   Savigny-lès-Beaune

Patrick Bize   12 Rue du Chanoine-Donin, 21420 Savigny-lès-Beaune
UK stockists: ABy, Gen, HRp, JAr, L&W, OWL

This serious and expanding operation, now with 22 ha, is one of the leading exponents of Savigny-lès-Beaune. The wines have greatly improved since 1999 after some rather flat and slightly over-extracted wines in the mid- to late 1990s contrasted starkly with the refinement and class of the likes of Jean-Marc PAVELOT. Long *cuvaison* times and only partial destemming contribute to a bold, sturdy and sometimes gamy style. The best wines show increasing refinement and composure with bottle-age and there is enough fruit and structure for them to improve well beyond 5 years. Best are the *premiers crus*, with good weight and richness in the Marconnets (an extension of Beaune Marconnets) and real intensity in Aux Vergelesses. Whites are good, with plenty of fruit and good structure in both versions of Savigny and additional style in Corton-Charlemagne. Basic Bourgogne Rouge and Blanc made from Les Perrières vineyards and can be every bit as good as the 'lesser' Savignys. A little Latricières-Chambertin is also made. (PW)

● **Savigny-lès-Beaune** 1er Cru Aux Vergelesses★★★ £D
● **Savigny-lès-Beaune** 1er Cru Aux Serpentières★★★ £D
● **Savigny-lès-Beaune** 1er Cru Marconnets★★★ £D
● **Savigny-lès-Beaune** 1er Cru Fourneaux★★★ £D
● **Savigny-lès-Beaune** 1er Cru Aux Guettes★★★ £D
● **Savigny-lès-Beaune** Aux Grands Liards★★ £C   Bourgeots★★ £C
● **Bourgogne Rouge** Les Perrières★★ £B
● **Aloxe-Corton** Le Suchot★ £D   O **Corton-Charlemagne**★★★★ £F
O **Savigny-lès-Beaune**★★ £C   Aux Vergelesses★★★ £D
O **Bourgogne Blanc** Les Perrières★★ £B

BLAIN-GAGNARD   Chassagne-Montrachet

J-M & C Blain-Gagnard   21190 Chassagne-Montrachet
UK stockists: JAr, HHC, Maj, F&R

Jean-Marc and his wife Claudine (whose father is Jacques Gagnard) have a small selection of precious sites, thanks largely to her family. The wines are handled carefully with restrained oak and not overworked, resulting in wines of good richness and structure that remain true to their origins. A ripe, minerally and well-structured regular Chassagne develops nicely with 3–4 years' age. The *premiers crus* add more depth and richness and, although they can be drunk fairly young, deserve 4 or 5 years' age. Considerably more expensive but a big step up in quality is a Bâtard-Montrachet made in reasonable quantities. This has the characteristic Bâtard power and terrific dimension on the palate, becoming marvellously complex with even a little age. A little Criots-Bâtard-

135

Montrachet is also made and a tiny amount of Le Montrachet (from Jacques Gagnard) has also recently been added. *Premier cru* Chassagne red is reasonably elegant if sometimes lean, while Clos Saint-Jean adds a little more depth. Both, as with all the whites, are reasonably priced. Gagnard-Delagrange is Jacques Gagnard's label, which includes La Boudriotte and Morgeots (both ★★★) and outstanding ✪✪✪✪✪ Bâtard-Montrachet and Montrachet. Though the vineyards have been gradually relinquished to the next generation some of the wines have continued to be made in recent vintages. (PW)

O **Bâtard-Montrachet**★★★★★ £F   O **Puligny-Montrachet**★★★ £E
O **Chassagne-Montrachet** 1er Cru Caillerets★★★★ £E
O **Chassagne-Montrachet** 1er Cru Morgeots★★★★ £E
O **Chassagne-Montrachet** 1er Cru La Boudriotte★★★ £E
O **Chassagne-Montrachet**★★★ £D 1er Cru Clos Saint-Jean★★★ £E
● **Chassagne-Montrachet** 1er Cru Clos Saint-Jean★ £C
● **Volnay** 1er Cru Champans★★★ £D
● **Pommard**★★ £D

DOM. JEAN BOILLOT ET FILS   Volnay

Jean Boillot   Rue des Angles, 21190 Volnay
UK stockists: Anl, Eno, CCC, CTy, L&S, F&M, F&R

Henri Boillot, brother of Jean-Marc BOILLOT, is now making the wines on his father's domaine as well as running an expanding *négociant* business, Maison Henri Boillot. Though the domaine is based in Volnay, there's a decent parcel of Puligny vines, including a substantial wholly owned *lieu-dit* within Perrières, Clos de la Mouchère, as well as 1 or 2 other choice *crus*. The fruit is picked very late, the reds 100% destemmed and both reds and whites see a lot of new oak. The wines are rich, even opulent and consequently can be drunk quite young, though the Volnays, particularly the excellent Caillerets, deserve at least 4 or 5 years' aging. The pick of the whites, Les Pucelles, which reflects the class and finesse of that wonderful site, also demands a little patience. The *négociant* Henri Boillot wines includes some top-notch *crus*, and can be very good indeed if slightly less consistent. (PW)

Domaine Jean Boillot:
● **Volnay** 1er Cru Frémiets★★★★ £E 1er Cru Chevrets★★★★ £E
● **Volnay** 1er Cru Caillerets★★★★ £F
● **Beaune** 1er Cru Clos du Roi★★★ £E 1er Cru Epenottes★★★ £E
● **Savigny-lès-Beaune** 1er Cru Les Lavières★★ £D
O **Puligny-Montrachet** 1er Cru Clos de la Mouchère★★★★ £E
O **Puligny-Montrachet** 1er Cru Les Pucelles★★★★ £F
O **Puligny-Montrachet**★★★ £E 1er Cru Les Perrières★★★★ £E
O **Meursault** 1er Cru Les Genevrières★★★★ £F
O **Savigny-lès-Beaune** 1er Cru Les Vergelesses★★★ £D

JEAN-MARC BOILLOT   Pommard

Jean-Marc Boillot   La Pommardière, 21630 Pommard
UK stockists: RsW, BBR, DDr, L&S, Rae, F&R

Jean-Marc Boillot seems equally at ease making both red or white, as indeed he needs to be with half of his 10ha planted to Chardonnay. The wines have a fruit richness and depth to marry with the oak input. The reds range from a full Beaune to more structured Pommards, including a tiny amount of superb rich Rugiens, and a Volnay-like Jarolières (contiguous with Volnay Frémiets) to stylish, perfumed Volnays. Even the village examples are very good. The whites if anything are even better. A string of Puligny *premiers crus* (the SAUZET inheritance) all have an intense pure fruit and great class, nowhere better expressed than in Les Combettes. There is also a little Bâtard-Montrachet. Some Rully and Puligny-Montrachet Les Pucelles have recently been made from bought-in fruit. Jean-Marc Boillot is now also making wine in the Coteaux du Languedoc at Domaine La Truffière (see Languedoc-Roussillon). (PW)

● **Pommard**★★★ £D 1er Cru Jarolières★★★ £E 1er Cru Rugiens★★★★ £F
● **Volnay**★★★ £E 1er Cru Carelle-sous-Chapelle★★★ £E 1er Cru Pitures★★★ £E
● **Volnay**1er Cru Le Ronceret★★★ £E ● **Beaune** 1er Cru Montrevenots★★ £D
○ **Puligny-Montrachet** 1er Cru Champ Canet★★★★ £F
○ **Puligny-Montrachet** 1er Cru Les Combettes★★★★ £F
○ **Puligny-Montrachet** 1er Cru Les Referts★★★★ £F 1er Cru La Truffière★★★★ £F
○ **Puligny-Montrachet**★★★ £E 1er Cru La Garenne★★★ £F

LOUIS BOILLOT

Louis Boillot   Rue du Lavoir, 21220 Chambolle-Musigny
UK stockists: CTy, BBR, L&W

Louis Boillot is the husband of Ghislaine BARTHOD and has recently split with his brother Pierre the estate of Lucien Boillot et Fils (see below) which they used to jointly run. The 7ha of vineyards stretches from Gevrey-Chambertin to Volnay. While many of the same wines are repeated under the new label of Louis Boillot et Fils, not all have been tasted. Whether there will be significant differences in quality or style between the 2 estates remains to be seen. Volnay Les Grand Poisots is a good village -level example - dense, full, more Pommard-like. Also listed here are some of the very reasonably priced wines (including good village *climats* from Gevrey and Morey-Saint-Denis) made under the existing négociant business of Louis Boillot. (PW)

Louis Boillot et Fils:
● **Gevrey-Chambertin**★★★ £E
● **Morey-Saint-Denis**★★★ £E 1er Cru Aux Charmes★★★★ £E
● **Chambolle-Musigny**★★★ £E
● **Volnay** Les Grands Poisots★★★★ £E 1er Cru Les Caillerets★★★★ £E

Maison Louis Boillot:
● **Gevrey-Chambertin**★★★ £E Les Carougeots★★★ £E
● **Morey-Saint-Denis** 1er Cru Les Sorbes★★★★ £E
● **Morey-Saint-Denis**★★★ £D Les Ruchots★★★ £E
● **Chambolle-Musigny**★★★ £E

LUCIEN BOILLOT ET FILS Gevrey-Chambertin

Pierre Boillot   1 Rue Docteur Magnon Pujo, 21220 Gevrey-Chambertin
UK stockists: CTy, Eno BBR, WSc

Though Gevrey-based, this domaine draws half of its grapes from original family vineyards in Volnay and Pommard. The vineyards have recently been split between 'fils' Louis and Pierre and the latter continues to make the wines under the Lucien Boillot label. The grapes are only partially destemmed and an extended maceration is favoured, resulting in wines with structure, breadth and flavour intensity, though not always with the concentration or fullness to match. Some wines from late 1990s can be disappointing but results in 2002 and 2003 show good promise with plenty of intensity and extract without being overdone. For the wines of Louis Boillot, including existing négociant wines, see above. (PW)

● **Gevrey-Chambertin** 1er Cru Les Cherbaudes★★★★ £E
● **Gevrey-Chambertin** 1er Cru Les Corbeaux★★★ £E
● **Gevrey-Chambertin**★★ £D Evocelles★★★ £D
● **Nuits-Saint-Georges** 1er Cru Les Pruliers★★★ £E
● **Beaune** Epenottes★ £C ● **Pommard** 1er Cru Fremiers★★★ £E
● **Pommard**★★ £D 1er Cru Les Croix Noires★★ £E
● **Volnay** 1er Cru Brouillards★★★ £E 1er Cru Caillerets★★★ £E
● **Volnay**★★ £D 1er Cru Angles★★★ £E

137

DOM. BONNEAU DU MARTRAY

Jean-Charles Le Bault de la Morinière   21420 Pernand-Vergelesses
UK stockists: HHC, BBR, L&W, HRp, L&S, JAr, Las, F&R, C&R

An outstanding 11-ha domaine producing just 2 wines. The white Corton-Charlemagne comes from 9.5ha of the best-sited part of the famous vineyard. The red comes from 1.5ha at the base of the Corton hill. As good as the wines are now, the reputation of this domaine has only been fully re-established by Jean-Charles Le Bault de la Morinière, who has made tremendous progress since taking over from his father. The red, in particular, has improved; since 1995 a previously rather dilute, insubstantial wine has taken on greater flesh and extract without sacrificing its finesse. The white has long been a wine of tremendous richness and great depth and character that will keep for many years from the best vintages. It is also one of the few wines made from this large vineyard to show true *grand cru* class. (PW)

O **Corton-Charlemagne** ✪✪✪✪✪ £F   ● **Corton**★★★★ £F

BOUCHARD PÈRE ET FILS   Beaune   www.bouchard-pereetfils.com

Joseph Henriot   15 Rue du Château, 21200 Beaune
UK stockists: **JEF**, AAA

This merchant is one of the best-known names in Burgundy, thanks in part to its substantial holdings. Domaine vineyards total 130ha, including 12ha of *grands crus* and 74ha of *premiers crus* and two-thirds of the vineyards are planted to Pinot Noir. Its decline under family ownership and the scandal of its conviction for flouting legal winemaking practices have been well-documented. Yet from the time of the purchase by the much respected Champenois Joseph Henriot (see HENRIOT) in 1995, quality has dramatically improved. Despite the poor health of the vineyards, almost immediately the reds showed greater richness and better structure and more recently have added more expression and individuality. The ongoing investment in both people and winemaking facilities is backed by a determination to maximise quality and consistency. In more difficult vintages, such as 2000 for red, Bouchard was prepared to sell off a large quantity of wine in order to maintain the progress made in re-establishing the integrity of its label. The best whites show superb fruit combined with excellent structure and concentration and are particularly fine in 2000. As with other leading *négociants* the range is quite vast. Most of the wines below are 'domaine' bottlings though one or two generics are made from purchased grapes as is the very fine Chambertin
Clos-de-Bèze which shows fabulous breadth, depth and complexity. Excellent style and consistency here in 2002 though some will need more time than usual. Good 2003 reds too. (PW)

● **La Romanée**✪✪✪✪ £H   ● **Chambertin Clos-de-Bèze**✪✪✪✪✪ £H
● **Chambertin**★★★★★ £H   ● **Le Corton**★★★★ £G
● **Gevrey-Chambertin**★★ £E   1er Cru Les Cazetiers★★★★ £F
● **Bonnes Mares**★★★★★ £G   ● **Chambolle-Musigny**★★★ £E
● **Clos de Vougeot**★★★★ £G   ● **Echezeaux**★★★ £G
● **Vosne-Romanée** 1er Cru Aux Reignots★★★ £G
● **Nuits Saint-Georges** 1er Cru Clos des Argillières★★★★ £E
● **Nuits Saint-Georges** 1er Cru Les Cailles★★★★ £E
● **Nuits Saint-Georges**★★★ £E   1er Cru Clos Saint-Marc★★★★ £E
● **Savigny-lès-Beaune**★★ £C   1er Cru Les Lavières★★ £C
● **Beaune** 1er Cru Grèves Vigne de L'Enfant Jésus★★★★ £E
● **Beaune** 1er Cru Teurons★★★ £E   1er Cru Clos de la Mousse★★ £E
● **Beaune** 1er Cru Beaune du Château★★★ £D
● **Pommard** 1er Cru Rugiens★★★★ £E   1er Cru Pezerolles★★★★ £E
● **Pommard**★★★ £D   1er Cru Les Chanlins★★★ £E
● **Volnay** 1er Cru Caillerets Ancienne Cuvée Carnot★★★★ £E

● **Volnay** 1er Cru Clos des Chênes★★★★ £E
● **Volnay** 1er Cru Fremiets Clos de la Rougeotte★★★ £E
● **Volnay** 1er Cru Taillepieds★★★ £E
● **Monthelie**★★ £C 1er Cru Les Duresses★★ £D
● **Monthelie** 1er Cru Clos des Champs Fuillot★★★ £D
○ **Le Montrachet**✪✪✪✪ £H ○ **Chevalier-Montrachet**★★★★ £H
○ **Corton-Charlemagne**★★★★ £F
○ **Puligny-Montrachet**★★★ £E 1er Cru Champs Gains★★★★ £F
○ **Meursault** 1er Cru Perrières★★★★★ £F
○ **Meursault** 1er Cru Genevrières★★★★★ £F
○ **Meursault** 1er Cru Les Gouttes d'Or★★★★ £E
○ **Meursault** 1er Cru Les Bouchères★★★★ £E
○ **Meursault**★★★ £E Les Clous★★★ £E
○ **Beaune** 1er Cru Clos Saint-Landry★★★ £C
○ **Beaune** 1er Cru Sur Les Grèves★★★ £C
○ **Beaune** 1er Cru Beaune du Château★★ £C
○ **Montagny** Les Platières★★ £C ○ **Pouilly-Fuissé**★★ £C

RENÉ BOUVIER   Gevrey-Chambertin

Bouvier family   29 B Route de Dijon, 21220 Gevrey-Chambertin
UK stockists: THt, DDr, UnC

This increasingly fine domaine based on 17ha of vineyards has been
transformed from a producer of fine Marsannay to one that includes many
other fine *crus* from the Côtes de Nuits. Working in part in a négociant role
Bernard Bouvier is expanding on his father's achievements. As well as good
Gevrey-Chambertin recently there has been fine Chambolle-Musigny, Vosne-
Romanée and even Echezeaux and Clos de Vougeot. Of the most recent
vintages, the 2001s are atypically good for this vintage while the 02s provide
further endorsement of the consistent high quality obtained. Some of the best
value is at the lower levels: some of the *grands crus* while good aren't up there
with those from the very best growers. In addtition to the wines below,
following on from an excellent Clos Saint-Denis in 2001, very good Echezeaux
and Vosne-Romanée Premier Cru Les Chaumes were made in 2002. (PW)

● **Charmes-Chambertin**★★★ £G ● **Clos de Vougeot**★★★★ £G
● **Gevrey-Chambertin** 1er Cru Petite Chapelle★★★★ £F
● **Gevrey-Chambertin** Jeunes Rois★★★ £D 1er Cru Cazetiers★★★★ £F
● **Gevrey-Chambertin** Racines du Temps Très Vieilles Vignes★★★ £E
● **Morey-Saint-Denis** 1er Cru Genevrières★★★ £E
● **Chambolle-Musigny** 1er Cru Les Noirots★★★ £F
● **Marsannay** Longeroies★★ £C En Ouzeloy★★ £C
● **Marsannay** Champs Salomon★★ £C Clos du Roy★★ £C
● **Fixin** Crais de Chêne★★ £C ● **Côtes de Nuits-Villages**★★ £C
○ **Marsannay** Vieilles Vignes★★ £C Le Clos★★ £C

MICHEL BOUZEREAU ET FILS   Meursault

Michel & Jean-Baptiste Bouzereau 3 Rue de la Planche-Meunière, 21190 Meursault
UK stockists: FMV, BBR, CTy, L&W, F&R

Devotees of white Burgundy will recognise a Michel Bouzereau label as a good
bet for ripe, full yet elegant Meursault and as Michel's son Jean-Baptiste
assumes responsibility it seems certain to remain that way. The domaine
comprises 12ha, more than three-quarters of it white. Stylish and pure, the
whites show good definition with subtle differences between the various *crus*.
Most outstanding is the Meursault-Charmes. Meursault-Blagny can be the
most austere but is deep and minerally, Genevrières is very suggestive of this
cru, and there is plenty of style and fruit in the humbler village-level Grands
Charrons, Limouzin and Les Tessons too. Caillerets is much the better of the 2
Pulignys but this is reflected in the price difference. There's only a little red and

139

if it's not at the same level as the whites it is at least reasonably priced for the quality. Good value, too, are the basic Bourgogne Aligoté and Bourgogne Chardonnay. (PW)

O **Meursault** 1er Cru Charmes★★★★★ £E   1er Cru Blagny★★★★ £E
O **Meursault** Les Tessons★★★ £D   1er Cru Genevrières★★★★ £E
O **Meursault** Grands Charrons★★★ £D   Limouzin★★★ £D
O **Puligny-Montrachet** 1er Cru Cailllerets★★★★ £F
O **Puligny-Montrachet** 1er Cru Champ Gain★★★ £E
O **Bourgogne Aligoté**★ £B   O **Bourgogne Chardonnay**★★ £B
● **Beaune** Epenottes★ £C   1er Cru Vignes Franches★★ £D

BOYER-MARTENOT   Meursault

Yves Boyer   17 Place de l'Europe, 21190 Meursault
UK stockists: CTy, BBR, For, F&R
Yves Boyer who is now assisted by his son Vincent (fourth generation), makes classic rich, plump and full-flavoured Meursault, traditional in the best sense with a measure of restraint when young. A high average vine age in 10ha of vines is maintained as is apparent in wines with plenty of personality and depth but that are also well-balanced with good definition. Les Narvaux vies with Les Tillets as the best of the village Meursault *climats* while Perrières is arguably the finest *premier cru* Meursault, with a little extra breadth and complexity characteristic of the vineyard. This in turn vies with an intense, refined and classy Puligny-Montrachet Le Cailleret as the top wine. All the better *crus* will keep for 6–8 years but can readily be drunk with just 2 or 3. Good Bourgogne Chardonnay can show good fruit and flavour, too, if in a simpler fashion. The 2002s show a classic combination of restraint and stylish complexity. (PW)

O **Meursault** 1er Cru Genevrières★★★★ £F   1er Cru Perrières★★★★ £F
O **Meursault** 1er Cru Charmes★★★★ £F   Narvaux★★★ £E
O **Meursault**★★ £D   En L'Ormeaux★★★ £D   Tillets★★★ £E
O **Puligny-Montrachet** 1er Cru Le Cailleret★★★★ £F
O **Puligny-Montrachet** les Reuchaux★★★ £E
O **Bourgogne Blanc**★ £B

DOM. BRINTET   Mercurey   www.domaine-brintet.com

Luc & Véronique Brintet   Grande Rue, 71640 Mercurey
UK stockists: DDr, Goe, OWL
Luc Brintet's 13ha are mostly red as would be expected in Mercurey but he makes a little white that is every bit as good. Reds are rigorously sorted and totally destemmed and a long *cuvaison* is sought with an extended period of pre-fermentation maceration. Both reds and whites are oakier than some but have ripe succulent fruit underneath and good structure and definition. The *premiers crus* are a definite notch up in quality and are among the best in the appellation. Whites are better with 2 or 3 years' age, reds with 3–5. (PW)

● **Mercurey** 1er Cru Crêts★★ £C   1er Cru Levrières★★★ £C
● **Mercurey** Vieilles Vignes★★ £C   1er Cru Vasées★★ £C
● **Mercurey**★ £B   Charmée★ £B   Perrières★ £B
O **Mercurey**★ £B   Vieilles Vignes★★ £C   1er Cru Crêts★★★ £C

ALAIN BURGUET   Gevrey-Chambertin

Alain Burguet   18 Rue de l'Église, 21220 Gevrey-Chambertin
UK stockists: HRp
Already experienced, Alain Burguet first got a foothold of his own in Gevrey back in 1974 and has now progressed to 6ha. His reputation is for being tough and intransigent both in personality and in his approach to winemaking. Yet there is clearly a mellowing of sorts as he has modified and refined his vinification and ageing methods in the 1990s, including complete destemming

and longer oak ageing. It has taken a couple of vintages to perfect but since 1998 the wines have been more stylish and complete though still with good richness and power. If most of the wines are only village level (there is now a little Premier Cru Champeaux), a Vieilles Vignes bottling (now labelled Mes Favorites) of great depth and richness is consistently of comparable quality to some of the best Gevrey made. All the wines show good classic Gevrey spice, strength and red and black fruit intensity. Older vintages can be slightly tougher, more rustic but can mellow and soften with age, too and are unlikely to disappoint from a good vintage. Bourgogne Rouge is a decent example too. (PW)

● **Gevrey-Chambertin** Vieilles Vignes Mes Favorites★★★★ £E
● **Gevrey-Chambertin** Billard★★★ £D Ier Cru Champeaux★★★ £E
● **Gevrey-Chambertin** Tradition★★ £D Reniard★★★ £D
● **Bourgogne Rouge** Les Pince Vins★ £B

LOUIS CARILLON ET FILS Puligny-Montrachet

Carillon family 21190 Puligny-Montrachet
UK stockists: BBR, CTy, L&W, JNi, Maj, F&R, Las

The wines of Louis Carillon et Fils are widely distributed and with good reason. This is a star Puligny domaine that has been making excellent wines for decades, with a lineage that goes back several centuries. The whites have great vibrancy, expressive fruit and in a way are more direct and easier to appreciate than others of comparable quality – but are not lesser wines for that. Out of a total of 12ha, 3.5ha are planted to Pinot Noir but the fuss is rightly about the Puligny *premiers crus*. Central to the style are low yields and minimal manipulation during both vinification and ageing. Champ Canet is the most elegant and approachable when quite young; Combettes is seductive and more immediate than the bigger, more structured Perrières; the citrusy, minerally Referts fattens up with age and like Perrières will benefit from extra bottle age. The *grand cru* Bienvenues is the most complex and refined of all, and while deserving of the most patience, shows great power and intensity when young. To an extent the prices reflect the high regard in which the wines are held, though the sound reds are much more affordable. (PW)

O **Bienvenues-Bâtard-Montrachet**✪✪✪✪✪ £H
O **Puligny-Montrachet** Ier Cru Perrières★★★★ £F
O **Puligny-Montrachet** Ier Cru Referts★★★★ £E
O **Puligny-Montrachet** Ier Cru Combettes★★★★ £F
O **Puligny-Montrachet**★★★ £E Ier Cru Champ Canet★★★ £F
● **Puligny-Montrachet**★ £C ● **Saint-Aubin** Ier Cru Pitangerets★ £C

DOM. CARRÉ-COURBIN Volnay

Philippe & Maëlle Carré 9 Rue Celer, 21200 Beaune
UK stockists: **FMV**, BBR, P&S

There has been a younger generation in charge here in recent years and the structure and balance in the wines has been steadily improved. There was a tendency for the wines from just over 9ha of vineyards to be too extracted and without a compensating fruit richness. In 2002 they really hit jackpot and made superb, ripe concentrated Volnay with great depth and fine structure. There is classic Volnay perfume, expression and refinement allied to good grip and intensity. Similarly fine 2003s confirm that this estate has really arrived. *Premiers crus* Clos de la Cave des Ducs and Taillepieds are especially fine with weight and breadth to go with the style and intensity. Pommard Grands Épenots is sturdy, powerful and requires the greatest patience. Drink village Volnay and Pommard with 5 years' or more, Volnay premiers crus with 6-10 and Grands Épenots with 10 or more. Some red and white Beaune *premier cru* Les Reversées is also made along some Meursault. (PW)

141

- **Volnay** 1er Cru Taillepieds★★★★★ £F
- **Volnay** 1er Cru Clos de la Cave des Ducs★★★★ £E
- **Volnay** 1er Cru Les Lurets★★★★ £E 1er Cru Robardelle★★★★ £E
- **Volnay**★★★ £D Vieilles Vignes★★★★ £E
- **Pommard**★★★ £D 1er Cru Grands Epenots★★★★ £F

SYLVAIN CATHIARD Vosne-Romanée

Sylvain Cathiard 20 Rue de la Goillotte, 21700 Vosne-Romanée
UK stockists: OWL, FMV, L&W, BBR, HHC, SVS

Sylvain Cathiard makes very refined, super stylish and harmonious wines. In the past some of the lesser wines needed a little more richness and ripeness but this is no longer the case, in fact they are atypically good for generic or village-level wines. All Vosne-Romanée (including an exceptional village example) show marvellous expression, purity as well as breadth, depth and intensity. The inspired *grand cru* Romanée-Saint-Vivant is exquisitely intense, seductive and refined. Of the Vosne *premiers crus*, En Orveaux (nearest to Chambolle-Musigny) is classy and fruit-rich, Aux Reignots has fabulous perfume and a veritable peacock's tail expression on the palate. Suchots and Malconsorts are a little bigger and richer - the purity and intensity of Suchots contrasts with the *grand cru* like breadth and depth of Malconsorts. Nuits-Saint-Georges Aux Murgers has great class, very much the essence of Nuits. A sophisticated Bourgogne Rouge and elegant Chambolle-Musigny apart, all the wines deserve to be kept for at least 5 or 6 years from the vintage date. Recent vintages have been outstanding with superb 2002s and 2003s. (PW)

- **Romanée-Saint-Vivant**✪✪✪✪✪ £H
- **Vosne-Romanée** 1er Cru Les Malconsorts✪✪✪✪✪ £F
- **Vosne-Romanée** 1er Cru Les Suchots★★★★★ £F
- **Vosne-Romanée** 1er Cru En Orveaux★★★★★ £F
- **Vosne-Romanée**★★★ £E 1er Cru Aux Reignots★★★★★ £F
- **Chambolle-Musigny** Clos de L'Orme★★★★ £E
- **Nuits-Saint-Georges** 1er Cru Aux Murgers★★★★ £E
- **Bourgogne Rouge**★★ £C

MAISON CHAMPY Beaune www.champy.com

Meurgey family 5 Rue Grenier à Sel, 21202 Beaune
UK stockists: HHC, Sav, Pol, ThP, F&R

This 280-year-old *négociant* house, the oldest in Burgundy, has been in the hands of the Meurgey family for a little over a decade, but how its fortunes have been revived. Quality has been good since the mid-1990s but the hiring of Dimitri Bazas is providing a further boost. As well as bought-in grapes, around 13ha are now owned. The winemaking hand is light, allowing the individual *terroirs* to shine through. Among the many reds, Vosne-Romanée Les Suchots, from a well-established vineyard (35–40 years), always stands out with fine fruit, lots of class and great length; a Bonnes-Mares is more classy and complex again, as is the Romanée-Saint-Vivant. At a lower level, Beaune Champs Pimont is a consistently plump and approachable red full of raspberry fruit. The 2000 and 02 whites are the best yet and if not yet the equal of the top growers, are well-made and reasonably priced, particularly regular Savigny-lès-Beaune and Pernand-Vergelesses. Puligny Enseignères has nice richness for a village-level example, while Corton-Charlemagne adds more breadth; both can be drunk fairly young but will develop further with age. All in all this is a increasingly good, reliable source of Burgundy. Listed are most of the best wines that are regularly made. Other good examples may be encountered, though the basic generics are of more modest quality. (PW)

- **Bonnes Mares**★★★★ £G ● **Romanée-Saint-Vivant**★★★★ £G
- **Clos de Vougeot**★★★ £F

● **Vosne-Romanée** 1er Cru Les Suchots★★★★ £F
● **Vosne-Romanée** 1er Cru Les Beaumonts★★★ £F
● **Gevrey-Chambertin** 1er Cru Les Cazetiers★★★ £E
● **Beaune** 1er Cru Les Grèves★★ £D
● **Beaune** V.Vignes★★ £D   1er Cru Les Champs Pimont★★ £D
● **Savigny-lès-Beaune** Aux Fourches★ £C   1er Cru Les Peuillets★★ £C
● **Savigny-lès-Beaune** 1er Cru Les Vergelesses★★ £C
● **Aloxe-Corton** 1er Cru Les Vercots★★ £D
● **Volnay** 1er Cru Les Caillerets★★★ £E
○ **Corton-Charlemagne**★★★ £F
○ **Puligny-Montrachet** 1er Cru Les Chalumeaux★★★ £E
○ **Puligny-Montrachet** Les Enseignières★★★ £E
○ **Meursault** Grand Charrons★★★ £E   1er Cru Genevrières★★★ £E
○ Pernand-Vergelesses★★ £C   ○ **Savigny-lès-Beaune**★★ £C
○ **Saint-Aubin** 1er Cru Murgers Dents de Chien★★ £C

CHANDON DE BRIAILLES   Savigny-lès-Beaune

De Nicolay family   Rue Soeur Goby, 21420 Savigny-lès-Beaune
UK stockists: **HHC, CTy, BBR, L&S, L&W, Tan, F&M**
A popular and fine domaine and a leading proponent of Savigny-lès-Beaune, Pernand-Vergelesses and Corton. François de Nicolay and his sister Claude Drouhin work with their mother to produce wines from low yields that favour elegance over power. Corton Clos du Roi is the top red, the most structured and profound. Corton-Bressandes has better dimension, weight and length than Les Maréchaudes, though the latter almost matches it for finesse and style. The Pernand-Vergelesses are only medium-bodied, though the racy, slender but classy and intense Île des Vergelesses adds a little more weight with age. Both Savigny wines can be good value, with a stylish Fourneaux and slightly leaner Les Lavières. 2000 reds were generally lighter as were the 01s if still with the characteristic intensity and style. Well-structured 2002s and supple 03s promises a little more. Whites are very good too, tight and minerally when very young but with real intensity and length, becoming quite rich with a little age. The Corton becomes fuller and broader than a deeper, more minerally Corton-Charlemagne. François de Nicolay also owns a vineyard in his own right, producing an aromatic, plump white Savigny. (PW)

● **Corton Clos du Roi**★★★★ £F   ● **Corton Bressandes**★★★★ £E
● **Corton Les Maréchaudes**★★★★ £E
● **Pernand-Vergelesses** 1er Cru Île des Vergelesses★★★ £D
● **Pernand-Vergelesses** 1er Cru Les Vergelesses★★★ £D
● **Savigny-lès-Beaune** 1er Cru Les Fourneaux★★★ £C
● **Savigny-lès-Beaune** 1er Cru Les Lavières★★ £D
○ **Corton-Charlemagne**★★★★ £F   ○ **Corton** Blanc★★★★ £F
○ **Pernand-Vergelesses** 1er Cru Île des Vergelesses★★★ £D
○ **Savigny-lès-Beaune** 1er Cru Aux Vergelesses★★★ £C

CHANSON PÈRE ET FILS   www.vins-chanson.com

Societé Jacques Bollinger   10 Rue Paul-Chanson, 21200 Beaune
UK stockists: **Cha, Men,** F&R
This is a hugely improved historic Beaune *maison* (dating from 1750) with 10ha of its own vineyards. Since it came under the ownership of Champagne house Bollinger in 1999, richer, better structured wines have been produced from lower yields. Gilles de Courcelles and Jean-Pierre Confuron head a new team that is re-emphasizing differences of *terroir* across some of Beaune's finest *premiers crus*. Red Clos des Mouches is particularly fine with impressive depth and balanced oak, while Clos des Fèves is deep and concentrated. Of the whites, the Meursault Perrières has plenty of class and expression if not amongst the very best examples of this fabulous *cru*. On the other hand

143

Savigny-lès-Beaune Hauts-Marconnets is an excellent example of this *lieu-dit*.
The rated wines only cover a selection of the best domaine wines. (PW)

- ● **Beaune** 1er Cru Grèves★★★ £E 1er Cru Clos des Mouches★★★★ £F
- ● **Beaune** 1er Cru Champs Pimonts★★★★ £E
- ● **Beaune** 1er Cru Bressandes★★★ £E 1er Cru Clos des Fèves★★★★ £F
- ● **Côte de Beaune-Villages★★** £C
- ● **Pernand-Vergelesses** 1er Cru Les Vergelesses★★★ £D
- O **Beaune** 1er Cru Clos des Mouches★★★★ £F
- O **Savigny-lès-Beaune** Hauts Marconnets★★★ £D
- O **Pernand-Vergelesses** Caradeux★★★ £E
- O **Meursault** 1er Cru Perrières★★★★ £F

PHILIPPE CHARLOPIN   Gevrey-Chambertin

Philippe Charlopin   18 Route de Dijon, 21220 Gevrey-Chambertin
UK stockists: IVV

Starting from a meagre 1.8ha of family vineyards in 1976, Philippe Charlopin's
holdings have since mushroomed to more than 15ha. To the more humble
village parcels have been added small segments of several *grands crus*. Harvesting
often very late for Burgundy, Philippe subjects his very ripe grapes to a rigorous
selection. Vinification involves a long maceration followed by minimal racking
(sometimes leading to a measure of reduction in the wines) and quite liberal
helpings of new oak; 100% new oak in the case of the Vieilles Vignes Gevrey-
Chambertin and the 7 *grands crus*. They are also unfined and unfiltered. The
result is usually richly textured, chewy, sometimes tannic wines, a style that does
work (for the most part) and the wines still reflect the general style of their
appellations. The regular village wines have plenty of immediate appeal and are
for relatively early drinking. The top wines will keep for at least a decade. Of
the simpler reds, the Marsannay and Bourgogne Rouge can be good value
while the whites, too, can offer ample fruit and character. Bonnes Mares, Clos
de Vougeot and Echezeaux are the newest of the *grands crus*. (PW)

- ● **Chambertin★★★★** £H ● **Charmes-Chambertin★★★★** £G
- ● **Mazis-Chambertin★★★★** £F ● **Clos Saint-Denis★★★★** £G
- ● **Bonnes Mares★★★★** £G ● **Morey-Saint-Denis★★** £E
- ● **Gevrey-Chambertin** La Justice★★ £E Vieilles Vignes★★★ £F
- ● **Chambolle-Musigny★★★** £F ● **Vosne-Romanée★★★** £F
- ● **Fixin** Clos de Fixey★ £D ● **Marsannay** En Montchenevoy★★ £D
- ● **Bourgogne Rouge★★** £C
- O **Fixin** Blanc★★ £C O **Marsannay** Blanc★★ £C

DOM. DU CH. DE CHOREY   Chorey-lès-Beaune

Germain family   Château de Chorey-lès-Beaune, 21220 Beaune
UK stockists: DDr

The fine château of this domaine provides accomodation for those who have
come in search of good red and white Burgundy. Formerly called Domaine
Germain Père et Fils, the wines of the 17-ha estate have, over the last decade,
increasingly been made by François Germain's son, Benoît, who now runs the
estate with his sister, Aude. The wines are good rather than great, with full-
flavoured, balanced white Pernand-Vergelesses and fairly full, sturdy yet not
inelegant reds. The latter are completely destemmed and subject to a pre-
fermentation maceration. Ratings apply to the best and most recent vintages of
which 2002 is the best to date. Occasionally in the past some of the reds have
been a little too extracted and lacked fully ripe tannins. As well as those listed, 2
other red *premiers crus* Beaunes (Boucherottes and Cent Vignes) and a little
white (Sous les Grèves) are also made. A village Meursault, Les Pellans, has
been made since 1999. (PW)

- ● **Beaune** 1er Cru Vignes Franches★★ £E 1er Cru Cras★★ £E

● **Beaune** 1er Cru Teurons★★ £E
● **Chorey-lès-Beaune**★ £C ○ **Pernand-Vergelesses**★★ £C

CH. DE LA MALTROYE Chassagne-Montrachet

J-P Cournut 16 Rue de la Murée, 21190 Chassagne-Montrachet
UK stockists: Anl, OWL, HRp

In a few short years the fortunes of this 15-ha Chassagne-Montrachet estate have been transformed. Jean-Pierre Cornut now makes some of the best wines in the appellation. The *premier cru* whites are all consistently fine – ripe, concentrated and with terrific fruit intensity and excellent balance. As impressive as the 2002s taste young they'll only really open out with 6 years' age or more. Dents de Chien is probably the best example of this *premier cru* made while La Romanée is minerally and elegant and Grandes Ruchottes is more powerful but also minerally. The more affordable white Santenay is a fine example of the appellation. There is a significant amount of red produced too, including that from part of the 2.5ha Clos du Château de la Maltroye *monopole*. It has depth, intensity and real charm, becoming increasingly silky with age. A little Bâtard-Montrachet is also made. (PW)

○ **Chassagne-Montrachet** 1er Cru Dent de Chien★★★★★ £F
○ **Chassagne-Montrachet** 1er Cru Grandes Ruchottes★★★★ £F
○ **Chassagne-Montrachet** 1er Cru Morgeot Vignes Blanches★★★★ £F
○ **Chassagne-Montrachet** 1er Cru La Romanée★★★★ £F
○ **Chassagne-Montrachet** 1er Cru Chevenottes★★★ £E
○ **Chassagne-Montrachet** 1er Cru Clos Château de Maltroye★★★ £E
○ **Santenay** 1er Cru Comme★★★ £D
● **Santenay** 1er Cru Comme★★ £C
● **Chassagne-Montrachet** 1er Cru Clos Château de Maltroye★★★ £E
● **Chassagne-Montrachet** 1er Cru Clos Saint-Jean★★★ £E

CH. DE PULIGNY-MONTRACHET Puligny-Montrachet

CFF -Groupe Caisse d'Epargne 21190 Puligny-Montrachet
UK stockists: FMV, OWL, BBR

The transformation of this important domaine with 20ha of vineyards is the work of Étienne de Montille (of Domaine de MONTILLE). From the beginning of 2002 he has reduced yields and moved to organic practices, giving whites of much better definition, depth and style. Holdings include significant amounts of Saint Aubin, Monthelie and Chassagne-Montrachet as well as *premiers crus* in Meursault and Puligny-Montrachet. The change in the quality of the whites is evident from 2001 with some excellent 02s and ripe, intense, if less well-structured 03s. Puligny Folatières and both Meursault Poruzots and Perrières combine intensity with class. Of reds tasted, Saint Aubin En Remilly is far better than Monthelie, which still lacks depth and concentration. Very small amounts of Chevalier-Montrachet and Le Montrachet are also made. (PW)

○ **Puligny-Montrachet**★★★ £E 1er Cru Les Folatières★★★★ £F
○ **Meursault** 1er Cru Perrières★★★★ £F
○ **Meursault** 1er Cru Les Poruzots★★★★ £F
○ **Chassagne-Montrachet**★★★ £E
○ **Saint-Aubin** 1er Cru En Remilly★★★ £E ○ **Monthelie**★★ £D
● **Saint-Aubin** 1er Cru En Remilly★★ £D ● **Monthelie**★ £D

GÉRARD CHAVY ET FILS Puligny-Montrachet

Chavy family 12 Rue de Château, 21190 Puligny-Montrachet
UK stockists: BBR, CTy, Eno, HRp, FMV, Lwt, CPp

Alain and Jean-Louis, sons of Gérard, have made many changes at their family's small domaine, with the result that this is now one of the emerging stars of the appellation. Typical of small, well-run family domaines, there are no short cuts

145

taken and every wine is given the same measure of respect. Bourgogne Blanc can be very good while the regular example of Puligny has some substance and style and a good example of Saint-Aubin is made too. But it is the *premiers crus* that are forging the reputation, including a very minerally, full Perrières and an elegant Clavoillons that contrasts with the firmer, more structured Folatières. An intense weighty Champs-Gain first made in 2002 shows real promise too. The wines can be a bit reduced if drunk very young but the generally excellent quality is matched by good prices. (PW)

O **Puligny-Montrachet** Ier Cru Perrières★★★★ £E
O **Puligny-Montrachet** Ier Cru Clavoillons★★★★ £E
O **Puligny-Montrachet** Ier Cru Folatières★★★★ £E
O **Puligny-Montrachet** Ier Cru Champs-Gain★★★★ £E
O **Puligny-Montrachet**★★ £D Charmes★★★ £D
O **Saint-Aubin** Ier Cru En Remilly★★ £C   O **Bourgogne Blanc**★ £B

ROBERT CHEVILLON Nuits-Saint-Georges

Chevillon family 68 Rue Félix Tisserand, 21700 Nuits-Saint-Georges
UK stockists: J&B, Gen, WTs, F&M, Sec, Las, F&R, Maj

Robert Chevillon is one of the celebrated names of this appellation at the southern end of the Côte de Nuits, a village that is synonymous with red Burgundy. Robert is making way for his sons and Bertrand Chevillon now makes the wines from the vines tended by his older brother, Denis. There are no less than 8 different *premiers crus* (6 of them in the central section of Nuits, which has a higher clay content and is south of the town itself), all with a high average vine age. No two taste quite the same, each giving a different expression of its individual *terroir*. With relatively high fermentation temperatures and a small percentage of stems retained, the wines are fairly full-bodied and tannic but with the flesh, depth and fruit intensity to be very rich and satisfying with 8–10 years' age. The regular Nuits, Bousselots and to a lesser extent Chaignots (the Chevillons' 2 *crus* north of Nuits) can be a bit light in lesser vintages but the others regularly deliver the fruit to match their robust structures. The fullest and most structured are the Les Saint-Georges and Vaucrains, followed by Les Cailles. Also made is a little white Nuits-Saint-Georges with a very good reputation and some Bourgogne Rouge. (PW)

● **Nuits-Saint-Georges** Ier Cru Les Vaucrains★★★★ £F
● **Nuits-Saint-Georges** Ier Cru Les Saint-Georges★★★★ £F
● **Nuits-Saint-Georges** Ier Cru Les Cailles★★★★ £F
● **Nuits-Saint-Georges** Ier Cru Les Perrières★★★ £E
● **Nuits-Saint-Georges** Ier Cru Les Pruliers★★★ £E
● **Nuits-Saint-Georges** Ier Cru Les Roncières★★★ £E
● **Nuits-Saint-Georges** Ier Cru Les Chaignots★★★ £E
● **Nuits-Saint-Georges** Ier Cru Les Bousselots★★★ £E
● **Nuits-Saint-Georges** Vieilles Vignes★★ £D

BRUNO CLAIR Marsannay

Bruno Clair 5 Rue du Vieux Collège, 21160 Marsannay-la-Côte
UK stockists: J&B, Col, Tan, WSc, F&R

Bruno Clair has been a style leader for a couple of decades, producing the mostly northern Nuits reds of great balance, harmony and elegance. One of the beneficiaries of the noted Clair-Daü estate (many of the prime vineyards went to Louis JADOT), he now commands 23ha, nearly 5ha of which are planted to Chardonnay. The classics are his Gevrey *premiers crus* Clos Saint-Jacques and Cazetiers, and the *grand cru* Chambertin Clos de Bèze. These are wines with great purity, elegance and with exceptional length of flavour. Not to be overlooked are the *monopole* Clos du Fonteny, a deep, dense Savigny, La Dominode, and an increasingly classy Corton-Charlemagne. The best value lies in the 3 Marsannay reds (though a white can be good too), with the floral, intense Longeroies usually vying with the slightly darker-fruited Grasses Têtes as the best of these. While the reds have been generally less impressive in lighter vintages such as 1997, there are excellent 96s, 98s and 99s, and 00, 01 and 02 all look promising. All the reds can seem a little firm and austere when young and shouldn't be drunk with less than 3 or 4 years' age; 7 or 8 for the top examples. A rare Morey-Saint-Denis white is made from the same vineyard as the red, while a white Pernand-Vergelesses is a recent addition. (PW)

● **Chambertin Clos de Bèze**★★★★★ £G
● **Gevrey-Chambertin** 1er Cru Clos Saint-Jacques★★★★★ £G
● **Gevrey-Chambertin** 1er Cru Les Cazetiers★★★★ £F
● **Gevrey-Chambertin** 1er Cru Petite Chapelle★★★★ £F
● **Gevrey-Chambertin** 1er Cru Clos du Fonteny★★★ £F
● **Morey-Saint-Denis** En La Rue de Vergy★★★ £E
● **Chambolle-Musigny** Véroilles★★ £D
● **Vosne-Romanée** Champs-Perdrix★★★ £E
● **Savigny-lès-Beaune** 1er Cru La Dominode★★★★ £E
● **Marsannay** Grasses Têtes★★★ £C Longeroies★★★ £C
● **Marsannay** Vaudenelles★★ £C
O **Corton-Charlemagne**★★★★ £G O **Pernand-Vergelesses**★★ £C
O **Marsannay** Blanc★ £C

FRANÇOISE ET DENIS CLAIR Santenay

Françoise et Denis Clair 14 Rue de la Chapelle, 21590 Santenay
UK stockists: **HHC**
Denis and his son Jean-Baptiste produce some of the best examples of red Santenay but their 14ha of vineyards also includes fine Saint-Aubin whites. Santenays range from a deep and intense village-level Clos Genet to fine *premiers crus* including rich and structured Clos de Tavannes and classy Clos de la Comme. While prices have risen the red are particularly good in the best vintages (recently 2003, 02, 01 and 99) and provide a good alternative to village-level wines from more famous appellations. In cooler or wet vintages the wines can suffer more than most. Of the Saint-Aubin whites, Murgers des Dents de Chien is particularly good with good structure and concentration in 03. Others are En Remilly, Les Frionnes and Sur le Sentier des Cloux. Also made is some Puligny-Montrachet La Garenne. (PW)

● **Santenay** Clos Genet★★ £C 1er Cru Beaurepaire★★★ £D
● **Santenay** 1er Cru Clos des Tavannes★★★ £D
● **Santenay** 1er Cru Clos des Mouches★★★ £D
● **Santenay** 1er Cru Clos de la Comme★★★ £E
O **Saint-Aubin** 1er Cru Murgers des Dents de Chien★★★ £D

BRUNO CLAVELIER Vosne-Romanée

Bruno Clavelier 6 Route Nationale 74, 21700 Vosne-Romanée
UK stockists: Dec, HRp, OWL, Sav
Bruno Clavelier is a relatively new star who took over his grandfather's vines in 1987 and started bottling wine previously sold in bulk. He has since expanded into other Côte de Nuits communes. The domaine is now fully biodynamic and there has been a steady refinement in the wines while adding greater richness and expression, particularly in the most recent vintages. The amount of new oak used is low and the average vine age very high (most are either 50 or 65 years old), giving wines with delicious fruit, ample concentration and a real sense *terroir*. Of the *premiers crus*, Vosne-Romanée Beaux-Monts has the greater structure, Aux Brulées a touch more refinement. The Nuits-Saint-Georges, lying close to Vosne-Romanée, tastes like a cross between the 2 appellations. The Chambolle-Musigny is even better, combining grace and

147

purity with richness. From 2000 the regular Vosne-Romanée, from some of the highest slopes in the commune, has been bottled as La Combe Brulée and Les Hauts de Beaux Monts. A third of a hectare of Corton Rognets was purchased in 1999 and is also from old vines and has the potential to be the best wine of the lot, while Bruno's old-vine Aligoté is just about as good as it gets. (PW)

- **Vosne-Romanée** 1er Cru Les Beaux Monts★★★★ £F
- **Vosne-Romanée** 1er Cru Aux Brulées★★★★ £F
- **Vosne-Romanée** Les Hauts Maizières★★★ £E
- **Vosne-Romanée** La Montagne★★★ £E La Combe Brulée★★★ £E
- **Vosne-Romanée** Les Hauts de Beaux Monts★★★ £E
- **Gevrey-Chambertin** 1er Cru Les Corbeaux★★★ £E
- **Chambolle-Musigny** 1er Cru Combe d'Orveau★★★★★ £F
- **Nuits-Saint-Georges** 1er Cru Aux Cras★★★★ £E

CLOS SALOMON   Givry

Ludovic du Gardin   Clos Salomon, 71640 Givry
UK stockists: **DDr**

This 8-ha estate is centred on a single vineyard, the walled Clos Salomon which dates from the middle ages. By pursuing very low yields, Ludovic du Gardin (whose family have owned the Clos since 1632) and Fabrice Perrotto produce a powerful, fleshy Burgundy full of wild red fruits. After 12 months in 30% new oak it is bottled unfined and unfiltered. While it can struggle in cooler vintages, it is ripe with real breadth and a vibrant acidity in years like 2002 or 03. A white Montagny Le Clou was first produced in 03. (PW)

- **Givry** 1er Cru★★★ £C

CLOS DE TART   Clos de Tart

Mommessin family   21220 Morey-Saint-Denis
UK stockists: Cas, BBR, HRp, WSc, F&R

Winemaker Sylvain Pitiot has made this 7.53-ha *grand cru monopole* great again. Lying between Bonnes Mares and Clos des Lambrays, Clos de Tart has remained intact since being named by Benedictine monks in the late 12th century. The wine is increasingly adding some of the succulence of Clos des Lambrays to the power and sturdiness of Bonnes Mares. There is greater depth and concentration than previously, together with the complexity, class and elegance of a *grand cru*. Yields are low, the vine age high and being such a large site, different parcels are vinified separately. Spice and red and black cherries are the predominant flavours if drunk fairly young but wait 10 years from a top vintage. While there are many good earlier vintages, buy to cellar from 1996 or later. (PW)

- **Clos de Tart**✪✪✪✪✪ £G

JEAN-FRANÇOIS COCHE-DURY   Meursault

Jean-François Coche-Dury   9 Rue Charles Giraud, 21190 Meursault
UK stockists: BBR, Far, Hrd, Sec, Las, F&R

An outstanding domaine. Jean-François's Meursaults are rivalled only by those from LAFON and perhaps 1 or 2 others. Yet apart from from a little *grand cru* Corton-Charlemagne and *premier cru* Perrières, his reputation has been established with village-level wines, an indication of his talent and dedication. There is great attention to detail in the vineyard and as at many top-quality estates vines are replaced 1 at time when necessary and from the best existing plant material. The approach to vinification is flexible to maximise the potential of each vintage and long fermentations are also favoured. What makes the wines so special? Well, a grace, subtlety and purity allied to a remarkably well-delineated complexity. The depth, length, structure and concentration are givens. The floral, fruit and mineral components, as well as a fine grilled nuts character that comes with age, give the wines extra finesse over most other examples. Of 11ha, almost 2.5 are planted to Pinot Noir and a chance to try the Volnay Premier Cru shouldn't be passed up. A little red Auxey-Duresses and Monthelie are also made. The Meursault Vireuils is now being bottled separately as Vireuils Dessous and Vireuils Dessus. Nearly all the whites deserve 5 years' age but will keep for 10 or more. 2002, 00 and 99 are the best recent vintages but due to the demand, finding any of the wines at reasonable prices will be a minor miracle. (PW)

O **Corton-Charlemagne**✪✪✪✪ £H
O **Meursault** 1er Cru Perrières✪✪✪✪ £H Rougeots★★★★ £F
O **Meursault** Chevalières★★★★ £F Caillerets★★★★ £G
O **Meursault** Vireuils★★★★ £F Narvaux★★★★ £F
O **Puligny-Montrachet** Les Enseignières★★★★ £F
● **Volnay** 1er Cru★★★ £F ● **Bourgogne Pinot Noir**★ £C
O **Bourgogne Aligoté**★ £C ● **Bourgogne Chardonnay**★★ £D

DOM. MARC COLIN ET FILS   Saint-Aubin

Colin family   Gamay, 21190 Saint-Aubin
UK stockists: CCC, RsW, F&R

Marc Colin and his sons, Joseph, Pierre-Yves and Damien manage 20ha and the domaine's reputation is built on its finest whites. These are rich, ripe wines with good complexity and a distinct and attractive minerality in the best examples. Several Chassagne-Montrachets, led by an intense, minerally Caillerets, are made to a high standard and there is a galaxy of really fine Saint-Aubin in both colours (more than a third of the estate is planted to Pinot Noir). A very minerally, stylish En Remilly vies with a slightly more structured La Chatenière and classy Les Charmes as the best Saint-Aubin white, though newish Sentier du Clou from old vines is very rich. For red, the Santenay Vieilles Vignes shows what is possible from that appellation, particularly when from an excellent vintage such as 1999 or 2002. This still-expanding domaine also produces some *négociant* wines, including a Bâtard-Montrachet. (PW)

O **Montrachet**★★★★★ £H
O **Chassagne-Montrachet** 1er Cru Caillerets★★★★ £F
O **Chassagne-Montrachet** 1er Cru Vide Bourse★★★★ £E
O **Chassagne-Montrachet** 1er Cru Champ Gain★★★★ £E
O **Chassagne-Montrachet** Enseignières★★★ £E
O **Puligny-Montrachet** 1er Cru Garennes★★★ £E
O **Saint-Aubin** 1er Cru Les Charmes★★★ £D
O **Saint-Aubin** 1er Cru La Chatenière★★★ £D
O **Saint-Aubin** 1er Cru Sentier du Clou★★★ £D
O **Saint-Aubin** 1er Cru En Remilly★★★ £D
O **Saint-Aubin** 1er Cru En Montceau★★ £D
O **Saint-Aubin** Fontenotte★★ £C 1er Cru Les Combes★★ £D
● **Saint-Aubin**★ £C 1er Cru★★ £C 1er Cru Frionnes★★ £D
● **Chassagne-Montrachet**★★ £D ● **Santenay** Vieilles Vignes★★★ £D

MICHEL COLIN-DELÉGER ET FILS

Colin-Deléger family   21190 Chassagne-Montrachet
UK stockists: BWC, BBR, MCW, HRp, L&W, F&R

As much of the wine here is red as white but, as so often with Chassagne producers, the attention they receive is based almost solely on the quality of the whites. The standard here is very high, with intense, concentrated but beautifully balanced wines produced from low-yielding vines. En Remilly heads a raft of fine Chassagne-Montrachet *premiers crus*. Of the very fine Puligny-Montrachet *premiers crus* made in small quantities, an outstanding Les Demoiselles is tucked up against a tiny amount of *grand cru* Chevalier-

149

Montrachet. The reds used to be a little tough but are now richer with riper tannins, especially from a good red wine vintage such as 2002. Santenay Gravières and Chassagne-Montrachet Morgeots both stand out; Michel Colin is unusual in producing a fine example of both red and white Morgeots. The best reds, like the whites, will benefit from 5 or 6 years' age, sometimes more. Other attractive whites are made on a *négociant* basis. (PW)

○ **Chassagne-Montrachet** 1er Cru Morgeots★★★★ £F
○ **Chassagne-Montrachet** 1er Cru En Remilly★★★★£F
○ **Chassagne-Montrachet** 1er Cru Les Chaumées★★★★ £F
○ **Chassagne-Montrachet** 1er Cru Vergers★★★★ £F
○ **Chassagne-Montrachet** 1er Cru Chevenottes★★★ £F
○ **Chassagne-Montrachet**★★★ £E 1er Cru La Maltroie★★★ £F
○ **Puligny-Montrachet** 1er Cru Les Demoiselles★★★★★ £G
○ **Puligny-Montrachet**★★★ £E 1er Cru La Truffière★★★★ £G
○ **Saint-Aubin** 1er Cru Les Charmois★★★ £C
● **Chassagne-Montrachet** Vieilles Vignes★★ £C Morgeots★★★ £D
● **Santenay**★★ £B 1er Cru Gravières★★★ £C

DOM. JEAN-JACQUES CONFURON   Nuits-Saint-Georges

A & S Meunier   Prémeaux-Prissey, 21700 Nuits-Saint-Georges
UK stockists: Bal, OWL, Eno, BBR, F&R

Alain Meunier and his wife Sophie make increasingly good wines from 7ha of their own vineyards in the heart of the Côte de Nuits. By following organic principles, much has been done to restore the health of the vineyard and yields are low. A cold pre-fermentation maceration is employed, with moderately high temperatures, and a lot of new oak is used in ageing the wines. Quite dense and concentrated when young, the powerful fruit unfurls with 5–10 years' age. The results can be a little uneven and the wines have occasionally suffered from a little reduction or too much oak. But if patience is needed there's great intensity and length of flavour, particularly in the *premiers* and *grands crus*. Alain Meunier also oversees production for the part-domaine, part-*négociant* Domaine Féry/Féry-Meunier label. (PW)

● **Romanée-Saint-Vivant**★★★★★ £G   ● **Clos Vougeot**★★★★ £G
● **Vosne-Romanée** 1er Cru Beaux Monts★★★★ £E
● **Chambolle-Musigny**★★★ £D   1er Cru★★★★ £E
● **Nuits-Saint-Georges** 1er Cru Boudots★★★★ £E
● **Nuits-Saint-Georges** Fleurières★★★ £D Chaboeufs★★★ £E
● **Côte de Nuits-Villages** Les Vignottes★★ £C

DOM. CONFURON-COTÉTIDOT   Vosne-Romanée

Jacky Confuron-Cotétidot   21700 Vosne-Romanée
UK stockists: Gen, L&S, OWL

The Confuron domaine was one of the original private estates in the Côtes de Nuits and Yves Confuron now maintains this fine 11-ha property, further building on his father's considerable achievements. Jacky Confuron's dedication and skill as a *vigneron* has produced healthy vines of a high average age with really low yields. A so-called traditional approach has long been adhered to in the winemaking. There is no destemming (requiring ripe stalks as well as fruit), a long pre-fermentation maceration and lengthy *cuvaison*, while the subsequent ageing utilises a relatively low percentage of new oak, though this has recently been increased. This usually results in intense, deep and, at times, tannic Burgundies but there is more refinement in the latest releases. Across a range of appellations with good *terroir*, the wines show varied character but almost always good colour, body and ripe fruit. While not every wine in every vintage always achieves its full potential, each does require attention on the part of the drinker. These are wines that require assessment and often, patience; wines to devote cellar space to so they can be revisited over a period of years. Cellar some very good 2001s and 02s. A tiny amount of Mazis-Chambertin and only a little Clos de Vougeot are also made. Yves also makes some excellent Pommard at the De COURCEL estate. (PW)

● **Charmes-Chambertin**★★★★ £F   ● **Echezeaux**★★★★ £F
● **Vosne-Romanée**★★★ £E   1er Cru Suchots★★★★ £F
● **Gevrey-Chambertin** 1er Cru Lavaux-Saint-Jacques★★★★ £F
● **Gevrey-Chambertin**★★★ £E   1er Cru Petite Chapelle★★★ £F
● **Chambolle-Musigny**★★★ £E
● **Nuits-Saint-Georges**★★★ £E   1er Cru★★★ £F

DOM. DE COURCEL   Pommard

De Courcel family   Place de l'Église, 21630 Pommard
UK stockists: HRp, Gen, OWL, L&S, P&S, C&C

As at his family's domaine, CONFURON-COTÉTIDOT, winemaker Yves Confuron favours whole-bunch fermentation after having harvested late for fully ripe grapes. Yields are low and the percentage of wine bottled by the domaine has gone from around half to the lion's share of what it grows. At the heart of the estate's 8ha is 5ha of Grand Epenots, supplemented by sometimes brilliant Rugiens and another classy *premier cru*, Fremiers. There were some fine wines made prior to Yves's arrival but the standard is even higher now. Recent vintages have been vigorous, sturdy, concentrated, more oaky than previously and capable of ageing for a decade (both 2002s and 03s are powerful and extracted). Grand Clos des Epenots and the Rugiens need almost that long before they've even started to open up. The elegance and complexity of the Rugiens is only fully apparent with age. Consistently excellent Bourgogne Rouge deserves a couple of years' bottle-age, too. A fine village Pommard, Valmuriens, has only been made since 1999. (PW)

● **Pommard** 1er Cru Grand Clos des Epenots★★★★ £F
● **Pommard** 1er Cru Fremiers★★★ £E   1er Cru Rugiens★★★★ £F
● **Pommard** Les Valmuriens★★★ £E   1er Cru Croix Noires★★★ £E
● **Bourgogne Rouge**★★ £C

DOM. PIERRE DAMOY   www.domaine-pierre-damoy.com

Damoy family   21220 Gevrey-Chambertin
UK stockists: OWL, Dec, JNi, L&W

Under the direction of the young Pierre Damoy (the current generation Damoy who shares the domaine's name), this important 11-ha estate only started to realise its potential in the 1990s. A remarkable 5.3ha are in Chambertin Clos-de-Bèze but as well as a decent chunk (2.2ha) of Chapelle-Chambertin there's some Chambertin and a solely-owned village *lieu-dit*, Clos Tamisot from vineyards surrounding the cellar. The wines are harvested late and the yields are now low, considerably reduced from what they were prior to Pierre's stewardship. The wines are lush, powerful and concentrated, with good breadth and length, but are also oaky with a lot of tannin, particularly in a heavily structured and more austere Chambertin. There has been a lack of consistency, too, in recent years until 1999, which worked more in favour of the style of wines here. 2001s and 02s show promise too, though a little extra harmony and class is still required before the top wines rival the best in their respective *grands crus*. Ripe fruity Bourgogne Blanc and a lightish Bourgogne Rouge are also made. (PW)

● **Chambertin Clos-de-Bèze**★★★★ £H   ● **Chambertin**★★★★ £G
● **Chapelle-Chambertin**★★★★ £G
● **Gevrey-Chambertin**★★ £E   Clos Tamisot★★★ £E

151

DARVIOT-PERRIN Monthelie

Darviot-Perrin family   Grande Rue, 21190 Monthelie
UK stockists: HRp, A&B, JAr, Dec, L&W, T&W

Didier Darviot's cellar is in the quiet pretty village of Monthelie but his 9.5ha estate includes Volnay, Meursault and Chassagne-Montrachet, much of it inherited by his wife. The wines are elegant and racy with fine pure fruit, and are increasingly generous and complex with 5 years' age. *Premiers crus* Charmes and Perrières are excellent examples of their noble *terroirs*. Dark, deep and intense Volnay with classic perfumes and really delicious fruit show similarly sophisticated winemaking. Though not quite at the same level, these wines are, in fact, a very credible alternative if superstars like COCHE-DURY or COMTES LAFON remain out of reach due to the demand-inflated prices. Village-level Meursaults Clos de la Velle and Tesson have only been produced separately from 2000 and an excellent Meursault Premier Cru Genevrières since 01. A little Pommard is also made. (PW)

O **Chassagne-Montrachet** 1er Cru Blanchots-Dessus★★★★ £F
O **Chassagne-Montrachet** La Bergerie★★ £E
O **Meursault** 1er Cru Genevrières★★★★£F 1er Cru Perrières★★★★£F
O **Meursault** 1er Cru Charmes★★★★ £E
O **Meursault** Clos de la Velle★★★ £D Le Tesson★★★ £E
● **Monthelie**★★ £C ● **Volnay** 1er Cru Santenots★★★★ £E
● **Volnay** Les Blanches★★★ £D 1er Cru La Gigotte★★★ £E
● **Chassagne-Montrachet** 1er Cru Les Bondues★★ £D

JEAN-YVES DEVEVEY Hautes-Côtes de Beaune

Jean-Yves Devevey   Rue de Breuil, Demigny, 71150 Chagny
UK stockists: FMV

Although based in the humble Hautes Côtes, Jean-Yves Devevey is an excellent source of inexpensive red and white Burgundy. Two Hautes-Côtes de Beaune white are both fermented and aged in oak - Les Champs Perdrix is atypically full and concentrated with an unusual mix of cool and ripe fruit flavours. Les Chagnots ('XVIII lunes' for 18 months in 15% new oak) is more overly oak enriched but has lots of promise and is likely to be better than a good many basic village Meursault. Also recently produced are a very appealing, fruit expressive Beaune Pertuisots with good purity and length, and a village-level Chassagne-Montrachet of good depth and style. (PW)

O **Hautes-Côtes de Beaune** Les Chagnots XVIII lunes★★★ £C
O **Hautes-Côtes de Beaune** Les Champs Perdrix★★ £B
O **Chassagne-Montrachet**★★★ £E O **Bourgogne Aligoté**★ £B
● **Beaune** 1er Cru Pertuisots★★★ £E

JOSEPH DROUHIN Beaune www.drouhin.com

Drouhin family   7 Rue d'Enfer, 21200 Beaune
UK stockists: DAy, OWL, L&W, Sav, C&R, Las

An excellent high-profile domaine (now 72ha) and *négociant* that combines integrity and know-how. Equally adept at producing red as white, Drouhin delivers good-quality wine at every level. As celebrated as any of the Drouhin wines are the red and white from the Beaune *premier cru* Clos des Mouches. While the red can be good, it can be surpassed by a Grèves bottling, but the white can be superb, with its delicate spice, flavour complexity, real presence on the palate and considerable elegance. Generally the wines are not big or overly powerful yet show good expression and are subtle and elegant. Occasionally wines miss a little extra concentration but it is important not to expect immediate gratification. The wines add weight and their centres usually fill in with the requisite bottle-age. Of the reds, the attractive Côte de Beaune (a Beaune appellation but usually including young-vine Clos des Mouches) and similarly-priced examples usually need 3 years' ageing; Vosne, Chambolle and other village-level wines and the Beaune *premiers crus* around 6; the top *crus* 8–10 years. Not all the *grands crus* are of the same standard but Drouhin's versions of Griotte-Chambertin and Grands-Echezeaux, where good examples can be hard to find, are usually excellent. In Chablis, where Drouhin is an important vineyard owner (see Joseph DROUHIN CHABLIS), there are facilities to press the grapes, though vinification takes place in Beaune. Drouhin also make the wines for the Marquis de Laguiche including the brilliant Montrachet, which comes from the appellation's largest single parcel. DOMAINE DROUHIN is the company's quality outpost in Oregon, run by Veronique, daughter of Robert Drouhin. As well as those listed, a little of the *grands crus* Chambertin, Chambertin Clos de Bèze, Charmes-Chambertin, Clos Saint-Denis, Clos de la Roche, Romanée-Saint-Vivant, Corton and Bâtard-Montrachet are also made, as are generic examples of leading village appellations. (PW)

- **Musigny**✪✪✪✪✪ £H ● **Grands-Echezeaux**★★★★★ £G
- **Griotte-Chambertin**★★★★ £G ● **Bonnes Mares**★★★★ £G
- **Clos de Vougeot**★★★★ £F ● **Echezeaux**★★★ £F
- **Corton Bressandes**★★★★ £F
- **Morey-Saint-Denis** 1er Cru Clos Sorbé★★★ £E
- **Chambolle-Musigny** 1er Cru Amoureuses★★★★ £F
- **Chambolle-Musigny**★★ £E 1er Cru★★★ £E
- **Vosne-Romanée**★★★ £E 1er Cru Petits Monts★★★ £F
- **Beaune** 1er Cru Clos des Mouches★★★ £E 1er Cru Grèves★★★ £E
- **Volnay** 1er Cru Clos des Chênes★★★ £E
- **Volnay**★★★ £D 1er Cru Chevret★★ £E
- **Côte de Beaune**★★ £D ● **Côte de Beaune-Villages**★ £C
- **Savigny-lès-Beaune**★ £C 1er Cru Serpentières★★ £D
- **Chorey-lès-Beaune**★★ £C
- ○ **Montrachet** Marquis de Laguiche✪✪✪✪✪ £H
- ○ **Corton-Charlemagne**★★★★ £G
- ○ **Beaune** 1er Cru Clos des Mouches★★★★ £F
- ○ **Chassagne-Montrachet** Marquis de Laguiche★★★ £F
- ○ **Puligny-Montrachet** 1er Cru Folatières★★★★ £F
- ○ **Meursault**★★★ £E ○ **Côte de Beaune**★★ £D
- ○ **Saint-Aubin**★ £D ○ **Saint-Romain**★ £C ○ **Rully**★ £B

CLAUDE DUGAT Gevrey-Chambertin

Claude Dugat 1 Place de l'église, 21220 Gevrey-Chambertin
UK stockists: Eno, HRp, Hrd, Sec, Las, F&R

There are similarities between Claude Dugat and his cousin Bernard (Bernard DUGAT-PY). Both have small holdings (Claude has just 4 ha) and both make very rich, concentrated wines swaddled in, but not swamped by, new oak. In addition, yields are low, occasionally very low, and there is an intuitive feel for the vine that runs back a generation or 2. Unsurprisingly perhaps, Claude Dugat's wines have gone down a treat in the US and their prices have soared (at first filling the pockets of the middlemen). The wines are rich with, in some instances, old-vine succulence as well as balancing fine ripe tannins and good acidities but how many of these wines get the 6–10 years' ageing they deserve, and occasionally need, I wouldn't hazard a guess at. A tiny amount of Chapelle-Chambertin is also made. As well as the *premiers crus* and *grands crus* there's very good if no longer inexpensive village-level Gevrey and Bourgogne Rouge. Both cousins also have beautiful, restored medieval cellars. (PW)

- **Charmes-Chambertin**✪✪✪✪✪ £H
- **Griottes-Chambertin**✪✪✪✪✪ £H
- **Gevrey-Chambertin** 1er Cru Lavaux-Saint-Jacques★★★★★ £G
- **Gevrey-Chambertin**★★★★ £F 1er Cru★★★★ £G
- **Bourgogne Rouge**★★ £D

153

BERNARD DUGAT-PY www.dugat-py.com

Bernard Dugat   Rue de Planteligone, BP 31, 21220 Gevrey-Chambertin
UK stockists: THt, BBR, Blx, Sec, JNi, F&R

Bernard Dugat has been making wine since 1975 but only bottling his own since 1989. His 7.2ha are planted exclusively to Pinot Noir. The concentration and richness of fruit, lush oak, silky textures and fine tannins make the wines irresistible. Nearly all the wines see 100% new oak but only rarely does this or the amount of extract or tannin seem overdone. These are big, dense wines but in the best sense. The Lavaux-Saint-Jacques and the *grands crus* have extra class and dimension as well as concentration. The Chambertin is distinguished by very, very concentrated black fruits that make the structure difficult to assess, a testament to very low-yielding and very old, very densely planted vines. Gevrey-Chambertin Coeur de Roy also comes from a selection of very old vines. Vieilles Vignes Vosne-Romanée (from 70-year-old vines) has only been made since 1999. Only tiny amounts of Mazis-Chambertin and Chambertin are made. (PW)

- Chambertin✪✪✪✪ £H ● Mazis-Chambertin✪✪✪✪ £H
- Charmes-Chambertin✪✪✪✪✪ £H
- Gevrey-Chambertin 1er Cru Petite Chapelle★★★★★ £G
- Gevrey-Chambertin 1er Cru Lavaux-Saint-Jacques★★★★★ £G
- Gevrey-Chambertin Évocelles★★★★ £F 1er Cru★★★★ £G
- Gevrey-Chambertin Vieilles-Vignes★★★★ £F Coeur de Roy★★★★ £F
- Vosne-Romanée Vieilles-Vignes★★★★ £F

DOM. DUJAC Morey-Saint-Denis www.dujac.com

Jacques Seysses   7 Rue de la Bussière, 21220 Morey-Saint-Denis
UK stockists: OWL, FMV, L&W, HRp, WSc, ABy, Las

Jacques Seysses is one of the best-known and most respected winemakers in Burgundy. His openness and generosity have helped many a fellow Burgundian and more than a few New World Pinot-phile winemakers along their way. Perhaps unsurprisingly the winemaking reflects modern influences as well as Burgundian traditions. There is great attention to detail, scrupulous hygiene and new oak is favoured for the top wines. A preference for clonal selection and cultured yeasts is offset by a desire for whole-bunch fermentation (no destemming). As a consequence the wines are never that deeply coloured but are intense, clean, elegant and perfumed. Now that Seysses is assisted by his son Jeremy, past criticisms of a lack of weight and occasionally too much oak have been countered with a slightly more flexible approach in recent vintages. At any rate the wines gain in richness and harmony with age, becoming ever more expressive of their *terroir*. Of the 5 *grands crus*, the Bonnes Mares is arguably the best, with remarkable breadth, power and flavour profile. An intense, vigorous Echezeaux and an expansive Clos de Roche are stylish examples of their respective appellations but all are fine and individual, as are the Chambolle and Gevrey *premiers crus*. The splendid regular Morey-Saint-Denis *premier cru* comes from Ruchots and some younger vines in Clos de la Roche. Some Vosne-Romanée Premier Cru Les Beaumonts is also made on a sharecropping basis. A little of the estate's 12-oddha is planted to Chardonnay for some white Morey-Saint-Denis, including some Monts Luisants since 2000. Wines made from bought-in grapes are sold under the label Dujac Fils et Père and include very good village level Gevrey-Chambertin, Morey-Saint-Denis and Chambolle-Musigny for red and Meursault and Puligny-Montrachet whites. (PW)

Domaine Dujac:
- Bonnes Mares✪✪✪✪✪ £H ● Clos de la Roche★★★★★ £H

● Echezeaux★★★★ £H ● Clos Saint-Denis★★★★★ £G
● Charmes-Chambertin★★★★ £G
● Gevrey-Chambertin 1er Cru Aux Combottes★★★★ £G
● Chambolle-Musigny★★★ £E 1er Cru Les Gruenchers★★★ £G
● Morey-Saint-Denis★★★ £E 1er Cru★★★★ £F
○ Morey-Saint-Denis★ £E

DOM. VINCENT DUREUIL-JANTHIAL   Rully

Vincent Dureuil 10 Rue de la Buisserolle, 71150 Rully
UK stockists: THt, CdP, OWL, Rae, Gau, CPp, Sel
Vincent Dureuil's 7-ha estate is planted to more red than white but the whites
are the better suit and among the best made by a local grower. Having
established his own domaine he is able to add to it bit by bit with plots
inherited from his father, Raymond, who also makes attractive red and white
Rully, albeit in a slightly less modern style. Greater use of new oak is apparent
but whites have a depth and fullish fruit character as well as decent acidity to
drink well with 2 or 3 years' ageing. The stars are *premiers crus* that come from
low-yielding old vines. Nuits-Saint-Georges Clos des Argillières was first made
in 1999 while new is Puligny-Montrachet Champs-Gain. Bourgogne Rouge is
good from vintages like 2002 (PW)
○ Rully 1er Cru Le Meix Cadot★★★ £C
○ Rully★★ £C 1er Cru Margotés★★★ £C
● Rully★★ £C Maizières★★★ £C ● Mercurey★★ £C
● Bourgogne Rouge★ £B
● Nuits-Saint-Georges 1er Cru Clos des Argillières★★★ £E

MAURICE ÉCARD ET FILS   Savigny-lès-Beaune

Maurice Écard et Fils 21420 Savigny-lès-Beaune
UK stockists: Las, Win, Dec
Here is a source of good-quality, full and concentrated red Burgundy at
reasonable prices. Maurice and Michel Écard have around 2ha in each of
several leading Savigny-lès-Beaune *premiers crus*. The wines don't have quite the
finesse of PAVELOT but consistently deliver plenty of fruit and style.
Serpentières is the most floral, Peuillet more solid if less expressive and
Narbantons has the richness and depth typical of this *cru*. Best is Jarrons which
comes from vines over 50 years old and offers still more concentration and
depth. It deserves to be kept for at least 5–6 years. A little white Savigny is also
made. (PW)
● Savigny-lès-Beaune 1er Cru Jarrons★★★ £D
● Savigny-lès-Beaune 1er Cru Narbantons★★★ £D
● Savigny-lès-Beaune 1er Cru Serpentières★★★ £D
● Savigny-lès-Beaune★★ £C 1er Cru Peuillets★★★ £D

DOM. RENÉ ENGEL   www.domaine-engel.com

Engel family 3 Place de la Mairie, 21700 Vosne-Romanée
UK stockists: FMV, Con, Gau, Gen, HRp, F&M
For more than 2 decades prior to his untimely death in May 2005, Philippe
Engel steadily revived the estate established by his industrious and learned
grandfather René. All 7ha are in the commune of Vosne and neighbouring
Flagey and Vougeot. The style is one of power, structure and richness and is
achieved in part through destemming, high fermentation temperatures, long
cuvaisons and a moderately high percentage of new oak. The wines are typically
deep coloured, full and structured with a dark fruit richness and impressive
depth and length. Older vintages had a tendency to be a bit too brutal but in
the 1990s the wines gained better balance and now show more of their intrinsic
quality and class, while retaining their muscular, concentrated stamp. Vosne-
Romanée Les Brulées comes from very old vines and shows tremendous fruit

155

quality and arguably represents the best value of this fabulous range. All the wines become ever richer and more luscious with age; the village Vosne-Romanée needs 5 years' ageing while the others are better with 10 years. Great 2002s, the hope is for more of the same under the new direction. (PW)

● **Grands-Echezeaux**✪✪✪✪ £G ● **Clos de Vougeot**★★★★★ £F
● **Echezeaux**★★★★ £F
●**Vosne-Romanée**★★★ £E 1er Cru Les Brulées★★★★★ £F

ARNAUD ENTE Meursault

Arnaud Ente 12 Rue de Mazeray, 21190 Meursault
UK stockists: FMV, Sec, Hrd

Arnaud Ente is a young grower able to make only a relatively small amount of wine but a lot of effort goes into each one. Yields are kept low and there is a good smattering of old vines. The wines are ripe, concentrated but not overdone with fine structures and good flavour intensity and depth. Of the 2 superior Meursaults, the Goutte d'Or has a more floral, exotic character in contrast to a citrusy but very concentrated Vieilles Vignes. The Puligny has a spicy intensity but less depth. Decent Bourgogne Blanc and Bourgogne Aligoté usually show good fruit too. (PW)

O **Meursault** 1er Cru Goutte d'Or★★★★ £F
O **Meursault**★★★ £E Vieilles Vignes★★★★ £F
O **Puligny-Montrachet** 1er Cru Les Referts★★★ £F
O **Bourgogne Chardonnay**★★ £C

FRÉDÉRIC ESMONIN Gevrey-Chambertin

Frédéric Esmonin 1 Rue de Curley, 21220 Gevrey-Chambertin
UK stockists: JAr, HRp, Hrd

This small estate only started bottling its own wines in the late 1980s after Frédéric's father, André, had established a reputation as a top grower. Most of the wines here are made from leased vineyards on a sharecropping basis; in addition some of the top *crus* are from bought-in grapes as this estate has also established a separate small *négociant* operation. Most significant is 1ha of the prized small *premier cru* Estournelles; the wine's concentration, depth and refinement do justice to the *cru's* cachet. The other estate wines show fine fruit and depth too. An intense, meaty, structured Ruchottes-Chambertin is rivalled by a very powerful, black-fruited and classy Mazis-Chambertin, made from the Esmonin's share of that which they cultivate for the Hospices de Beaune. A fine example of another *grand cru*, Griottes-Chambertin, was made here until 1999. Wines made to a high standard from purchased grapes (or wine) include Clos de Vougeot, Chambertin and Chambertin Clos-de-Bèze. Prices are very reasonable across the range. (PW)

● **Chambertin**★★★★★ £F ● **Chambertin Clos-de-Bèze**★★★★★ £F
● **Mazis-Chambertin**★★★★★ £F ● **Ruchottes Chambertin**★★★★ £F
● **Charmes-Chambertin**★★★★ £F
● **Gevrey-Chambertin** 1er Cru Lavaux Saint-Jacques★★★★ £E
● **Gevrey-Chambertin** 1er Cru Estournelles Saint-Jacques★★★★ £E
● **Gevrey-Chambertin** Clos Prieur★★★ £D

SYLVIE ESMONIN Gevrey-Chambertin

Sylvie Esmonin 1 Rue Neuve, 21220 Gevrey-Chambertin
UK stockists: FMV, HHB, C&R

This small 7-ha domaine, previously called Domaine Michel Esmonin et Fille (after Sylvie's father) makes some splendid Gevrey-Chambertin. Prior to 1987 most of the wine was sold to *négociants* but the highly trained Sylvie Esmonin has worked with her father for more than a decade and after making an immediate impact has continued to improve the wines. There is an extra vigour and concentration in the most recent vintages but this has been added whilst retaining their silky elegance. The wines can be drunk reasonably young but vintages like 99 or 2002 need more time. (PW)

- **Gevrey-Chambertin** Ier Cru Clos Saint-Jacques★★★★ £F
- **Gevrey-Chambertin**★★ £E Vieilles Vignes★★★ £E
- **Volnay** Santenots★★★ £E ● **Côte de Nuits-Villages**★★ £C
- **Bourgogne Rouge**★ £C

DOM. FAIVELEY www.bourgognes-faiveley.com

Faiveley 8 Rue de Tribourg, 21701 Nuits-Saint-Georges
UK stockists: MMD, BBR, HHC, HRp, JAr, L&W

Faiveley command more than 120ha of vines in the Côte d'Or and Côte Chalonnaise. Nearly all the wines of an extensive high-quality range come from their own vineyards, either owned or leased, and quality is closely supervised by François Faiveley. A long *cuvaison* is favoured and temperatures are kept well below the average for the red wine fermentation. The wines typically show fine perfumes combined with lots of depth and dimension on the palate. They also add richness with age and are proven keepers at every level. The character varies enormously from appellation to appellation, from intense, raspberryish Mercureys to burly, meaty Nuits-Saint-Georges *premiers crus* to deep, stylish Gevrey Cazetiers to splendid, classy Clos des Cortons. The wines can be a little slight in lighter years such as 1997 or 00, though they will still keep well. They are superb in the best years such as 99 and 02. Nuits-Saint-Georges *monopole* Clos de la Maréchale has been relinquished but newly acquired is another, Beaune Clos de L'Écu. Clos des Cortons and most of the Mercureys are also *monopoles*. All the leading domaine wines are listed below but there are others. (PW)

- **Chambertin Clos-de-Bèze**✪✪✪✪✪ £H
- **Corton** Clos des Cortons✪✪✪✪✪ £G
- **Mazis-Chambertin**★★★★★ £G ● **Echezeaux**★★★ £G
- **Latricières-Chambertin**★★★★ £G ● **Clos de Vougeot**★★★ £G
- **Gevrey-Chambertin** Ier Cru Cazetiers★★★★£F
- **Gevrey-Chambertin** Ier Cru Combe aux Moines★★★ £F
- **Gevrey-Chambertin** Les Marchais★★ £E
- **Chambolle-Musigny** Ier Cru La Combe d'Orveau★★★ £F
- **Chambolle-Musigny** Ier Cru Les Fuées★★★ £F
- **Nuits-Saint-Georges** Ier Cru Aux Chaignots★★★ £E
- **Nuits-Saint-Georges** Ier Cru Damodes★★★ £E
- **Nuits-Saint-Georges** Ier Cru Les Saint-Georges★★★ £F
- **Nuits-Saint-Georges** Ier Cru Porets Saint-Georges★★ £E
- **Nuits-Saint-Georges** Ier Cru Vignerondes★★ £E
- **Nuits-Saint-Georges** Ier Cru Lavières★★ £E
- **Nuits-Saint-Georges** Ier Cru Clos de la Maréchale★★ £E
- **Mercurey** Clos des Myglands★★ £C Clos du Roy★★ £C
- **Mercurey** La Framboisière★★ £C Les Mauvarennes★★ £C
- **Mercurey** Domaine de la Croix Jacquelet★ £C
- O **Corton-Charlemagne**★★★★ £H
- O **Mercurey** Les Mauvarennes★ £C Clos Rochette★ £C

JEAN-PHILIPPE FICHET Meursault

Jean-Philippe Fichet 21190 Meursault
UK stockists: **FMV**, BBR, Bal, HHB, Goe, WSc

Jean-Philippe Fichet produces ever better white wines from a range of different *climats* in the Côte de Beaune. Most come from vineyards managed on a sharecropping basis but he is able to supplement his production by buying back the vineyard owners' share of the crop. Though most of the Meursault is village-level wine, individual *lieux-dits* are bottled separately and show definite

157

stylistic differences from a ripe, typical Meursault Gruyaches through minerally Chevalières to a structured, classy Tessons that needs the greatest amount of time to show all its qualities. All contrast with a Puligny of real vigour and intensity. Without a superstar tag his wines are reasonably priced if made in fairly modest quantities. A little red wine is also made. (PW)

O **Meursault** Chevalières★★★ £E Tessons★★★★ £E
O **Meursault** Meix sous le Château★★★ £E Gruyaches★★★ £E
O **Meursault**★★★ £D Criots★★★ £E
O **Puligny-Montrachet** 1er Cru Les Referts★★★★ £F
O **Bourgogne Blanc**★★ £B O **Auxey-Duresses**★★ £B

RICHARD FONTAINE-GAGNARD Chassagne-Montrachet

Richard Fontaine 19 Route de Santenay, 21190 Chassagne-Montrachet
UK stockists: JAr, Dec, Maj

Richard Fontaine married 1 of Jacques Gagnard's daughters, Jean-Marc Blain the other (see BLAIN-GAGNARD). Both make fine wines. There are 3 *grands crus* and a host of Chassagne *premiers crus* made to increasingly high standards from a 9-ha estate. The wines are full and ripe, with lots of fruit, good breadth and balanced acidities, not heavy or overoaked. All the *premiers crus* show fine citrus and mineral intensity when young but generally drink best with between 4 and 8 years' age. The *grands crus* add more weight, breadth and class: the Criots has more finesse but the Bâtard more richness, while the Montrachet has both and then some. In addition to those listed, other fine *premier cru* Chassagne-Montrachet whites include La Grande Montagne, Les Murées, Chevenottes and Morgeots and new Clos Saint-Jean. Some Pommard is also made. (PW)

O **Montrachet**✪✪✪✪✪ £H O **Bâtard-Montrachet**★★★★★ £G
O **Criots-Bâtard-Montrachet**★★★★★ £G
O **Chassagne-Montrachet** 1er Cru La Boudriotte★★★★ £E
O **Chassagne-Montrachet** 1er Cru La Maltroie★★★★ £E
O **Chassagne-Montrachet** 1er Cru Caillerets★★★★ £F
O **Chassagne-Montrachet** 1er Cru Vergers★★★★ £E
O **Chassagne-Montrachet**★★★ £E 1er Cru La Romanée★★★★ £E
● **Volnay** 1er Cru Clos des Chênes★★★ £E
● **Chassagne-Montrachet** 1er Cru Morgeots★★ £D
● **Chassagne-Montrachet**★ £C 1er Cru Clos Saint-Jean★★ £D

DOM. FOURRIER Gevrey-Chambertin

Jean-Claude Fourrier 7 Route de Dijon, 21220 Gevrey-Chambertin
UK stockists: THt, JAr, Ben, Gau, Goe, HRp, Hrd, Sel

Since assuming control from his father in the mid-1990s, Jean-Marie Fourrier has determinedly pursued quality. Yields are kept low and while there is nothing unusual in a cold pre-fermentation maceration, minimal or no sulphur is utilised. A steady and gentle fermentation is sought in the pursuit of finer structures that allow the fruit to shine. To the same end, a relatively low percentage of new oak is used. He certainly has a good smattering of diverse *crus* from which subtle differences of *terroir* may be unearthed. All the wines are deep and ripe, with increasing concentration and complexity in the top wines. There is an excellent example of the would-be *grand cru*, Clos Saint-Jacques and very good Combe aux Moines too. All the wines are labelled 'Vieille Vigne' (sic). (PW)

● **Griotte-Chambertin**★★★★★ £G
● **Gevrey-Chambertin** 1er Cru Clos Saint-Jacques★★★★★ £F
● **Gevrey-Chambertin** 1er Cru Combe aux Moines★★★★ £E
● **Gevrey-Chambertin** 1er Cru Cherbaudes★★★★ £E
● **Gevrey-Chambertin** 1er Cru Champeaux★★★ £E

- **Gevrey-Chambertin** 1er Cru Goulots★★★ £E
- **Gevrey-Chambertin**★★★ £D Aux Echezeaux★★★ £D
- **Chambolle-Musigny**★★★ £E 1er Cru Les Gruenchers★★★★ £E

JEAN-NOËL GAGNARD Chassagne-Montrachet

Jean-Noël Gagnard and family 21190 Chassagne-Montrachet
UK stockists: GBa, JAr, Far, J&B, WSc

Caroline Lestimé has taken over the running of this domaine, one of the leading Chassagne estates, from her father, Jean-Noël Gagnard (whose brother is Jacques Gagnard – see BLAIN-GAGNARD). With half a dozen or so vintages to her credit, the wines have gained in both richness and finesse. As well as a fine village example, Les Masures, there are several *premiers crus*, from the lighter but elegant and more forward Chevenottes, through fuller Champgains, to rich, concentrated Blanchot-Dessus and Caillerets that need at least 5 or 6 years to reveal their full glory. The Bâtard-Montrachet adds more again but can usually be drunk from a similar age. The reds, including some Santenay Clos des Tavannes and Chassagnes Clos Saint-Jean and Morgeots, can be attractive but lack richness and depth, even in better years. In addition to those listed some Chaumées, Morgeots and La Maltroie white Chassagne *premiers crus* are made. (PW)

- O **Bâtard-Montrachet**★★★★★ £H
- O **Chassagne-Montrachet** 1er Cru Caillerets★★★★★ £F
- O **Chassagne-Montrachet** 1er Cru Champgains★★★★ £F
- O **Chassagne-Montrachet** 1er Cru Blanchots-Dessus★★★★ £F
- O **Chassagne-Montrachet** 1er Cru Chevenottes★★★★ £E
- O **Chassagne-Montrachet** 1er Cru Clos de la Maltroye★★★ £F
- O **Chassagne-Montrachet** Les Masures★★★ £E

JEAN-MICHEL GAUNOUX Meursault

Jean-Michel Gaunoux 1 Rue de Leignon, 21190 Meursault
UK stockists: C&C, Eno, FMV, HRp

Jean-Michel Gaunoux established his own label in 1990 (from this father's Domaine François Gaunoux) and produces fine examples of Meursault including good examples of Goutte d'Or and Perrières. The Goutte d'Or is usually very ripe and intense with spice and citrus while Perrières has much of the classic minerally complexity possible from this *cru*. Also tasted from the 2002 vintage (under the Gaunoux-Hudelot label) was a Genevrières with great intensity, structure and length. A little red from Pommard and Volnay also show excellent intensity and ripeness. The latter from the Clos des Chênes *premier cru* has impressive breadth and complexity and deserves at least 6–10 years' age. (PW)

- O **Meursault** 1er Cru Perrières★★★★ £E
- O **Meursault**★★★ £D 1er Cru Gouttes d'Or★★★★ £E
- ● **Volnay** 1er Cru Clos des Chênes★★★ £E

GEANTET-PANSIOT www.geantet-pansiot.com

Vincent Geantet 3 Route de Beaune, 21220 Gevrey-Chambertin
UK stockists: DDr, HRp, EoR, F&R, C&R

This 13-ha estate is a fine source for intense, concentrated and well-balanced northern Côte de Nuits reds. Vincent Geantet employs long macerations, but at a low temperature, prior to fermentation and has gone to great lengths to reduce yields and ensure optimum ripeness in his grapes. The very high average vine age shows in the wines, adding a succulence and intensity to the fruit. There are no poor wines here and they increasingly show well in lighter vintages as well the best years. The Charmes-Chambertin (from almost half a hectare) is a really fine example of how good this *grand cru* can be. Since taking

159

full control in 1989, Vincent Geantet has steadily built up the estate and from 1999 has had a new cellar and some new wines following the sale of the Vachet-Rousseau domaine. New Gevrey-Chambertin En Champ, from a small parcel of extremely old vines, has been made since 2000. There's good value here, too. (PW)

- **Charmes-Chambertin**★★★★★ £F
- **Gevrey-Chambertin** 1er Cru Le Poissenot★★★★ £E
- **Gevrey-Chambertin** En Champ★★★★ £E
- **Gevrey-Chambertin** Jeunes Rois★★★ £D Vieilles Vignes★★★★ £D
- **Chambolle-Musigny** Vieilles Vignes★★★ £E 1er Cru★★★★ £E
- **Marsannay** Champ-Perdrix★★ £C ● **Bourgogne Rouge**★ £C

GÉNOT-BOULANGER   Meursault

Génot-Delaby family   25 Rue de Cîteaux, 21190 Meursault
UK stockists: CTy, Jas, Eno

A large domaine with important vineyards in the Côte de Beaune but also a significant holding in Mercurey. Some 17ha of 27ha in total are in fact planted to Pinot but it is the whites, led by Meursault and Puligny *crus*, that provide the greatest interest. There is good concentration and intensity in village-level Meursault such as Clos du Cromin or from Puligny Les Levrons. There is a step-up with *premiers crus* La Garenne and a very good Folatières. They show good purity and intensity from 2002 and are also very good in 03 with better fruit intensity and structure than many examples in this difficult hot vintage. Those rated include several of the best wines but there are more besides worthy of investigation including some white Savigny-lès-Beaune. Mercurey Les Bacs, Meursault Clos du Cromin and Puligny Les Nosroyes stand out as particularly good value in a reasonably priced range. (PW)

- O **Puligny-Montrachet** 1er Cru Folatières★★★★ £E
- O **Puligny-Montrachet** 1er Cru La Garenne★★★★ £E
- O **Puligny-Montrachet** Les Levrons★★★ £D Les Nosroyes★★★ £D
- O **Meursault** Clos du Cromin★★★ £D 1er Cru Bouchères★★★ £E
- O **Chassagne-Montrachet** 1er Cru Chevenottes £E 1er Cru Vergers £E
- O **Mercurey** Les Bacs★★ £C

DOM. HENRI GERMAIN ET FILS   Meursault

Henri Germain   4 Rue des Forges, 21190 Meursault
UK stockists: DDr, L&S, Tan, Adm, HRp

Henri Germain possesses just 5ha, 2 of Pinot Noir and 3 of Chardonnay, but his son Jean-François continues the habit of making fine wines. Even the village Meursault is of good quality and exemplifies the efforts that go into every wine; its weight, structure and balance is particularly impressive so that it tastes attractive when fairly young, with pronounced citrus, spice and floral aspects, but it also has the capacity to keep far longer than average. Much is made of the importance of a cold cellar for the *élevage* and this does seem to be borne out here. The wines' slow development makes for late bottling. Reds are subject to both a cold maceration and long *cuvaisons*, evident in both the fine, complex, sappy but ripe, cherry, berry aromas and the real intensity and breadth on the palate. Both reds and whites are better with a little age and promise much more with 6 years or so. Some red Chassagne-Montrachet is also made, while more Meursault (Perrières) has been added as the estate expands a little. (PW)

- O **Meursault** Chevalières★★★ £E 1er Cru Charmes★★★★ £E
- O **Meursault**★★★ £D Limozin★★★ £E
- O **Chassagne-Montrachet** 1er Cru Morgeot★★★★ £E
- O **Bourgogne Blanc**★★ £B ● **Beaune** 1er Cru Bressandes★★★ £D

JEAN-JACQUES GIRARD Savigny-lès-Beaune

Jean-Jacques Girard   16 Rue de Cîteaux, 21420 Savigny-lès-Beaune
UK stockists: **CTy, FMV**, BBR

Any number of good Savigny-lès-Beaune reds are made here. The wines are
intense and expressive with good acidity. They are less rich, less sturdy than
some and oak plays no part in the flavour profile but all will fatten up with a
little age and each shows distinctive *terroir* and fruit characters. The best
premiers crus include elegant complex Les Lavières and Les Serpentières which
impress more when young than the more tannic and sturdy Les Fourneaux and
Les Peuillets, which are more gamey with age. At least as good as the Savignys
is a very intense and classy Pernand Vergelesses Les Vergelesses. The 99s have
lots of substance, 02s have particularly good fruit, 03s, energy and intensity.
Some white is also made with surprising sophistication to the village Pernand-
Vergelesses Les Belles Filles in 02. (PW)

- ● **Savigny-lès-Beaune** 1er Cru Serpentières★★★ £C
- ● **Savigny-lès-Beaune** 1er Cru Lavières★★★ £D
- ● **Savigny-lès-Beaune** 1er Cru Fourneaux★★★ £C
- ● **Savigny-lès-Beaune** 1er Cru Peuillets★★★ £D
- ● **Savigny-lès-Beaune**★★ £C 1er Cru Rouvrettes★★ £C
- ● **Pernand-Vergelesses** 1er Cru Vergelesses★★★ £C
- ● **Bourgogne Rouge**★ £B ○ **Savigny-lès-Beaune**★★ £C
- ○ **Pernand-Vergelesses** Belles Filles★★ £C

VINCENT GIRARDIN www.vincentgirardin.com

Vincent Girardin   4 Route de Chassagne-Montrachet, 21590 Santenay
UK stockists: THt, CTy, OWL, HRp, Tan, JNi, Las, Sel, WSc

This dynamic Santenay-based grower acquired a *négociant's* licence only in the
mid-1990s but has rapidly expanded, requiring a second move to larger
winemaking premises in 2002. From his own expanding estate he has made
some brilliant affordable red and white Santenay. The wines are modern, fruit-
rich and clean with a healthy but rarely excessive dose of new oak. There is an
energy and zip about most of the wines, a certain style and precision, yet they
are still indicative of their respective appellations. In his *négociant* role, only
grapes (rather than wine) are bought in, for while the sources are good this
allows for further sorting for quality. Girardin vinifies both red and white with
equal ease and is as sucessful in producing both more humble village wines as
grands crus, though some of the top wines fail to match the very best made.
There is real consistency too, important in an extensive and growing range of
wines. Despite the number of wines, most are made in relatively small
quantities and Girardin's total production is dwarfed by the likes of JADOT or
Louis LATOUR. The wines listed below are most of those that are regularly
made. (PW)

- ○ **Bienvenue-Bâtard-Montrachet**★★★★★ £H
- ○ **Bâtard-Montrachet**★★★★ £H ○ **Corton-Charlemagne**★★★★ £F
- ○ **Puligny-Montrachet** 1er Cru Folatières★★★★ £E
- ○ **Puligny-Montrachet** 1er Cru Les Referts★★★★ £E
- ○ **Puligny-Montrachet** 1er Cru Champs Gain★★★ £E
- ○ **Puligny-Montrachet** Vieilles Vignes★★★ £E
- ○ **Chassagne-Montrachet** 1er Cru Morgeots★★★★ £E
- ○ **Chassagne-Montrachet** 1er Cru Le Cailleret★★★ £E
- ○ **Meursault** 1er Cru Charmes★★★ £E 1er Cru Poruzots★★ £E
- ○ **Meursault** Narvaux★★★ £D
- ○ **Savigny-lès-Beaune** Vermots Dessus★★ £C
- ○ **Santenay** 1er Cru Clos de Tavannes★★ £C
- ○ **Santenay** 1er Cru Beaurepaire★★ £C
- ○ **Santenay** 1er Cru Clos du Beauregard★★ £C
- ● **Charmes-Chambertin**★★★★★ £G ● **Clos de la Roche**★★★★ £G

- Echezeaux★★★★ £G ● Corton Renardes★★★★ £F
- Gevrey-Chambertin Lavaux Saint-Jacques★★★★ £F
- Beaune 1er Cru Clos des Vignes Franches★★ £C
- Pommard 1er Cru Grands Epenots★★★ £E 1er Cru Rugiens★★★ £E
- Pommard Les Vignots★★ £E ● Volnay 1er Cru Santenots★★★★ £F
- Chassagne-Montrachet 1er Cru Clos de la Boudriotte★★★ £D
- Santenay 1er Cru Gravières Vieilles Vignes★★★ £C
- Maranges Clos des Loyères★★ £C

DOM. HENRI GOUGES www.gouges.com

Gouges family 7 Rue du Moulin, 21700 Nuits-Saint-Georges
UK stockists: OWL, Gen, HBJ, NYg, Sec, HRp, Las, Hrd

This famous 14.5-ha estate is run by 2 cousins. Pierre takes care of the vines, Christian the winemaking, but it was their grandfather, Henri, who first established the domaine and was one of the pioneers of domaine bottling in Burgundy. He amassed a full hand of some of Nuits' best *crus*, including Les Saint-Georges, Vaucrains and Pruliers as well as the 3.5-ha *monopole* of Clos des Porrets-Saint-Georges. The use of grasses to counter erosion has also made it possible to move slowly towards an essentially organic operation. The grapes are fully destemmed but the use of new oak is minimal (a maximum of 20%). Christian makes powerful, structured wines with excellent definition but most of all with an intensity and a quality to the fruit (particularly in the Vaucrains and the Les Saint-Georges) that sets them apart from most other Nuits. This core of quality is evident even when young and relatively tannic. Lush, soft and easy thankfully they are not; all the wines deserve (demand) at least 6–8 years' ageing. A further *premier cru*, Les Chaînes Carteaux is also made. The Nuits white (from a Pinot Noir mutation) is a treat with its spice, mineral and unusual exotic flavour intensity but benefits from a little age too. Prices are very good for the quality. (PW)

- Nuits-Saint-Georges 1er Cru Les Saint-Georges★★★★★ £F
- Nuits-Saint-Georges 1er Cru Les Vaucrains★★★★★ £E
- Nuits-Saint-Georges 1er Cru Les Pruliers★★★★ £E
- Nuits-Saint-Georges 1er Cru Clos des Porrets-Saint-Georges★★★★ £E
- Nuits-Saint-Georges★★★ £D 1er Cru Les Chaignots★★★★ £E
- Bourgogne Rouge★ £C ○ Bourgogne Pinot Blanc★★ £C
○ Nuits-Saint-Georges 1er Cru La Perrière★★★ £E

DOM. JEAN GRIVOT Vosne-Romanée www.grivot.com

Grivot family 6 Rue de la Croix Rameau, 21700 Vosne-Romanée
UK stockists: RsW, Bal, BBR, HRp, Sec

A brilliant 15-ha estate whose wines are much sought after. In 1987 Étienne took over the already successful family domaine built up by his grandfather, Gaston Grivot, in the first half of the 20th century. He immediately embraced some of the principles of the controversial consultant enologist Guy Accad. After a period of adjustment, the wines since the mid-1990s have been better than ever. The use of a cold pre-fermentation maceration seems to have been the main legacy of Accad's input but much thought and precision goes into every aspect of both viticulture and vinification. The wines are marvellous, combining great richness and concentration, and despite their size avoid any heaviness, with an excellent balance of acidity and fine tannins. The wines can sometimes show a reductive quality when tasted young but this doesn't persist. They all need at least 5 years' age and will be better with 10 or more. The top Vosnes and *grands crus* are an excellent cellaring prospect if you can afford them. Tiny amounts of Vosne *premiers crus* Les Chaumes and Les Reignots are also made to a very high standard. (PW)

- Richebourg✪✪✪✪✪ £H ● Echezeaux✪✪✪✪✪ £G

- **Clos de Vougeot**★★★★ £F
- **Vosne-Romanée** 1er Cru Les Beaux Monts✪✪✪✪✪ £F
- **Vosne-Romanée** 1er Cru Les Suchots✪✪✪✪✪ £F
- **Vosne-Romanée** 1er Cru Aux Brulées★★★★★ £F
- **Vosne-Romanée** 1er Cru Les Rouges★★★ £E
- **Vosne-Romanée**★★★ £D   Bossières★★★ £E
- **Nuits-Saint-Georges** 1er Cru Les Boudots★★★★ £F
- **Nuits-Saint-Georges** 1er Cru Les Pruliers★★★★ £F
- **Nuits-Saint-Georges** 1er Cru Les Roncières★★★★ £E
- **Nuits-Saint-Georges** Les Charmois★★★ £E   Les Lavières★★★ £E
- **Chambolle-Musigny** La Combe d'Orveaux★★★ £E

ROBERT GROFFIER   Morey-Saint-Denis

Robert Groffier   35 Route des Grands Crus, 21220 Morey-Saint-Denis
UK stockists: A&B, JAr, F&M, F&R, Blx, Las

Since the late 1990s the wines have become very rich and concentrated, adding to their already intense and classy character. With 8ha, Robert and his son Serge make a little wine across several different appellations. Most stunning are the *grands crus*; a small amount of Clos-de-Bèze and almost 1ha of Bonnes Mares are owned. There is also slightly over 1ha (the largest holding) of the excellent *premier cru* Les Amoureuses from Chambolle-Musigny. While new oak contributes to the wines' lush texture, low yields of first-rate fruit is the underlying reason behind the quality. The whole range is impressive and only rarely is the oak excessive, with real charm and style in the Hauts Doix and Les Sentiers and greater richness, dimension and complexity in the top trio. The wines can be drunk fairly young but bring further rewards to the patient; wait 8 years for the best. (PW)

- **Chambertin Clos-de-Bèze**✪✪✪✪✪ £H
- **Bonnes Mares**✪✪✪✪✪ £G
- **Chambolle-Musigny** 1er Cru Les Amoureuses★★★★★ £G
- **Chambolle-Musigny** 1er Cru Les Sentiers★★★★ £F
- **Chambolle-Musigny** 1er Cru Les Hauts Doix★★★★ £F
- **Gevrey-Chambertin**★★★ £E   ● **Bourgogne Rouge**★★ £C

A F GROS & FRANÇOIS PARENT   Beaune

Anne-Françoise Gros   La Garelle, 21630 Pommard
UK stockists: BSh, Dec, HHC

Anne-Françoise Gros is one of many family members involved in wine. Like brother Michel GROS she also includes some Vosne-Romanée in her range of wines. The wines are made by Anne-Françoise's husband, François Parent, and share the same cellar space as his wines, in Beaune. While the wines have very good depth and breadth, they had a tendency to be somewhat alike and indistinguishable. However, since 1999 there has been more finesse and flair, with particularly successful 2000s and 01s but fine 02s too. The Vosne-Romanée *lieux-dits* are reasonably priced, the Echezeaux rich and concentrated and the Richebourg really profound, intense and very powerful and long. François Parent, in addition to existing Beaune and Pommard vineyards, has recently acquired a further 12ha from Pommard-based Raymond Launay. Some fine solid Beaune and Pommard are made under his label. (PW)

A.F Gros:
- **Richebourg**✪✪✪✪✪ £H   ● **Echezeaux**★★★★★ £F
- **Vosne-Romanée** Aux Maizières★★★ £D   Aux Réas★★★ £D
- **Vosne-Romanée** Clos de la Fontaine★★★ £D
- **Chambolle-Musigny**★★★ £D
- **Savigny-lès-Beaune** 1er Cru Clos des Guettes★★★ £D
- **Bourgogne-Hautes Côtes de Nuits**★★ £B

163

F Parent:
- **Beaune** 1er Cru Les Boucherottes★★★ £D
- **Pommard** 1er Cru Les Arvelets★★★★ £E

ANNE GROS Vosne-Romanée www.anne-gros.fr

Anne Gros 11 Rue des Communes, 21700 Vosne-Romanée

UK stockists: Adm, Lay, L&W, HRp, JAr, Las

Anne's 6.5ha is the smallest of the various Gros estates but the wines are the most complete and refined of all. From Bourgogne Rouge to Richebourg, though deeply coloured with plenty of extract, there is a harmony and fruit quality that set the wines apart. A new cellar contains vats that can be adjusted in size according to the amount of wine to be vinified. Though only village-level, Chambolle-Musigny and Vosne-Romanée are lovely examples of their respective appellations. The outstanding Clos de Vougeot and Richebourg absorb the high percentage of new oak used and both have a wonderful, silky texture that belies an excellent structure. Not surprisingly the small quantities of wine are keenly sought after. In addition to some Bourgogne Blanc, a little Bourgogne-Hautes Côtes de Nuits Blanc has been made since 2000. Older wines will be labelled Domaine Anne et François Gros. (PW)

- **Richebourg**✪✪✪✪ £H
- **Clos de Vougeot** Grand Maupertuis★★★★★ £G
- **Vosne-Romanée** Les Barreaux★★★ £E
- **Chambolle-Musigny** La Combe d'Orveau★★★ £E
- **Bourgogne Rouge**★★ £C ● **Bourgogne Hautes-Côtes de Nuits**★ £C
- ○ **Bougogne Blanc**★★ £C ○ **Bourgogne Hautes-Côtes de Nuits**★★ £C

MICHEL GROS www.domaine-michel-gros.com

M Gros & J Gros family 7 Rue des Communes, 21700 Vosne-Romanée

UK stockists: THt, JNi, ABy, Tan, Hrd

For a time Michel Gros made wines both under his own name and those of his family's domain (Domaine Jean Gros). Now the estate of Michel Gros is, like those of his brother Bernard (Gros Frère et Soeur) and sister Anne-Françoise (A F GROS), a distinct entity. Michel has nearly 18ha but much of it lies in the Hautes-Côtes de Nuits and only a little in the top sites. The real exception is the 2.12-ha *monopole* Clos des Réas, a Vosne-Romanée *premier cru*. A dedicated and skilled *vigneron*, Michel avoids green-harvesting by careful pruning earlier in the growing season. Quite a lot of new oak is used, with 100% in the Clos de Vougeot. These are intense, elegant, very stylish wines, structured but not big or overpowering. Some Richebourg used to be made but this has now been relinquished. New is a Morey-Saint-Denis produced from young vines in En La Rue de Vergy. The Hautes Côtes de Nuits is a consistently good example. (PW)

- **Clos de Vougeot**★★★★ £F
- **Vosne-Romanée** 1er Cru Clos des Réas★★★★★ £F
- **Vosne-Romanée**★★★ £E 1er Cru Aux Brulées★★★★ £F
- **Morey-Saint-Denis** En la Rue de Vergy★★ £E
- **Nuits-Saint-Georges**★★ £E Chaliots★★★ £E 1er Cru★★★ £F
- **Chambolle-Musigny**★★★ £E ● **Bourgogne Rouge**★★ £C
- **Bourgogne Hautes-Côtes de Nuits**★★ £C
- ○ **Bourgogne Hautes-Côtes de Nuits**★★ £C

DOM. ANTONIN GUYON Savigny-lès-Beaune

M & D Guyon 2 Rue de Chorey, 21420 Savigny-lès-Beaune

UK stockists: **Frw**

Two brothers, Michel and Dominique Guyon oversee this relatively large (48ha), predominantly red wine domaine that has only recently moved up an extra notch or 2 in quality. They are now producing rich, clean, concentrated wines with an immediate appeal that is only partly due to a measure of new oak. While yields are high, wines since the late 1990s have shown an extra depth and intensity. The cellars are in Savigny but the extensive range of wines includes some of the best sites from the surrounding appellations, in some instances from old vines. If not of the very highest order, there are some very good medium-term reds and delicious whites. A little Corton Renardes is also made, as is some Gevrey-Chambertin and Chambolle-Musigny. (PW)

- ● **Corton** Bressandes★★★ £F ● **Corton** Clos du Roy★★★★ £F
- ● **Volnay** Clos des Chênes★★★ £E
- ● **Pernand-Vergelesses** 1er Cru Fichots★★ £D 1er Cru Vergelesses★★ £D
- ● **Aloxe-Corton** 1er Cru Fournières★★ £E 1er Cru Vercots★★★ £E
- ● **Savigny-lès-Beaune**★★ £D
- ● **Bourgogne Hautes-Côtes de Nuits** Dames de Vergy★ £C
- ○ **Corton-Charlemagne**★★★★ £G
- ○ **Meursault** 1er Cru Charmes Dessus★★★ £F
- ○ **Pernand-Vergelesses** 1er Cru Sous Frétille★★ £C

DOM. HERESZTYN Gevrey-Chambertin www.heresztyn.com

Bernard & Stanislas Heresztyn 21220 Gevrey-Chambertin
UK stockists: Goe, CdP, FWW, Las

This 11-ha Gevrey-based estate has been making steadily better wines over recent vintages. There is good ripe fruit, depth and plenty of expression, particularly with a little age. An extra harmony and finesse in the structures can be found in vintages like 2002. *Premiers crus* La Perrière and Les Goulots are perhaps less well-known but the latter in particular is deep, ripe and stylish. Les Champonnets is often the richest, fullest example. They rarely show their full potential with less than 6–8 years from the vintage. Also good are a regular Chambolle-Musigny and Morey-Saint-Denis Les Millandes which has a cool, refined red fruits expression and is expansive and long if more pricey. Clos Saint-Denis is a good example with lots of class, depth and length, best with 8–10 years age. (PW)

- ● **Clos Saint-Denis**★★★★ £F
- ● **Morey-Saint-Denis** 1er Cru Millandes★★★ £F
- ● **Gevrey-Chambertin** 1er Cru Champonnets★★★★ £E
- ● **Gevrey-Chambertin** 1er Cru Les Goulots★★★★ £E
- ● **Gevrey-Chambertin** 1er Cru Les Corbeaux★★★ £E
- ● **Gevrey-Chambertin** V.Vignes★★★ £D 1er Cru La Perrière★★★ £E
- ● **Chambolle-Musigny**★★★ £D

HUDELOT-NOËLLAT Chambolle-Musigny

Alain Hudelot-Noëllat 21220 Chambolle-Musigny
UK stockists: Dec, JAr, HRp, Col, Tur, F&R

Greater consistency has been a feature of this domaine in the 1990s and the latest vintages continue to endorse this view. The estate's 10ha is planted entirely to Pinot Noir and the constancy of the landholding makes it possible to track older vintages of many of the wines. Recent vintages have had input from Pierre Nawrocki who has helped to reduce yields whilst maintaining good balance in the vineyard. A light but responsive hand can be seen in the winemaking, along with an adeptness at bringing out the best in the grapes. A small proportion of the stems are usually retained and 100% new oak is used in the top wines. Some of the wines have a certain rigour and austerity when young but become supple, opulent, stylish wines with great depth and expression with the appropriate age; about 8 years for the Vosne *premiers crus* and the *grands crus* but closer to 5 for the other wines. Only a little Richebourg (the top wine) and Vosne Malconsorts is made. Village wines and *premiers crus*

165

are good value. (PW)

● **Romanée-Saint-Vivant**★★★★★ £H ● **Clos de Vougeot**★★★★ £G
● **Vosne-Romanée** 1er Cru Malconsorts★★★★★ £F
● **Vosne-Romanée** 1er Cru Petits Vougeots★★★★ £E
● **Vosne-Romanée** 1er Cru Beaux-Monts★★★★ £E
● **Vosne-Romanée** 1er Cru Suchots★★★★ £E
● **Vosne-Romanée**★★★ £E ● **Vougeot** 1er Cru★★★ £E
● **Chambolle-Musigny**★★★ £E 1er Cru Charmes★★★★ £E
● **Nuits-Saint-Georges** 1er Cru Murgers★★★★ £E

HENRI ET PAUL JACQUESON Rully

Henri & Paul Jacqueson 5-7 Rue de Chèvremont, 71150 Rully
UK stockists: THt, BWC, L&S, JNi, HHB

This small domaine run by Paul Jacqueson (son of Henri) makes superb Rully in both colours. The 9ha of vineyards are planted mostly to Pinot Noir and Chardonnay but also include a little Aligoté and Gamay. The wines are natural, pure and expressive, with delicious fruit. Of the whites a Pucelle is full and stylish, with a slightly floral, exotic character, while the Grésigny is more structured and minerally. Red Chaponnières has an enticing perfume and good depth but not the extra weight or class of Les Cloux. These delightful but not simple wines are also affordable, though due to a long-established reputation are not always that easy to find. Another white Rully, Raclot, is now also made, as is a rare, decent example of Bourgogne Passetoutgrains. (PW)

O **Rully** 1er Cru Grésigny★★ £C 1er Cru La Pucelle★★★ £C
O **Bourgogne** Aligoté★ £B
● **Rully** Chaponnières★★ £C 1er Cru Les Cloux★★ £C
● **Mercurey** 1er Cru Les Naugues★★ £C

LOUIS JADOT Beaune www.louisjadot.com

Kopf family 21 Rue Eugène Spuller, BP 117, 21203 Beaune
UK stockists: **HMA**, AAA

Under the direction of André Gagey, and more recently his son Pierre-Henry, and the winemaking mastery of Jacques Lardière, this giant (by Burgundian, not international standards) has made Burgundy of the highest order. Around half of the 144ha is in the Côte d'Or, the rest in Beaujolais (see CHÂTEAU DES JACQUES). As well as a string of *grands crus*, there are many of the leading *premiers crus* and most of the top wines come from their own vineyards, comprising 5 separate domaines. The Domaine des Héritiers Louis Jadot provides Corton, Corton-Charlemagne and Chevalier-Montrachet *grands crus* and other important Côte de Beaune *premiers crus*. Domaine Louis Jadot includes the superb Côte de Nuits *grands crus* and *premiers crus*, much of it from the original Clair-Däu domaine. Domaines André Gagey, Robert Tourlière and Duc de Magenta add further riches. The key is the know-how that ensures the highest possible quality from a diverse range of sources (including every village in the Côte d'Or) in every vintage, and the expert organisation of logistics. Destemming, a pre-fermentation maceration, high fermentation temperatures and long *cuvaisons* are important features of the red wine vinification. New oak, where it is used (up to 30%), never takes on more than a supporting role. A flexibile, responsive but generally non-interventionist approach can similarly seen in the white winemaking. Reds nearly always have good colour, excellent breadth and depth and plenty of structure but also marvellous concentration, complexity and class in the top wines. Not every bottle is a great one but most will provide a very good example of its appellation and if your only experience of Jadot is one of the humble generics then try one of the many fine domaine wines listed below. There are also several other outstanding wines, including whites Bâtard-Montrachet,

Bienvenues-Bâtard-Montrachet and Le Montrachet. (PW)
● **Musigny**✪✪✪✪✪ £H ● **Bonnes Mares**✪✪✪✪✪ £H
● **Chambertin Clos de Bèze**✪✪✪✪✪ £H
● **Clos Saint-Denis**★★★★ £G ● **Chapelle-Chambertin**★★★★ £G
● **Clos de Vougeot**★★★★ £G ● **Echezeaux**★★★★ £H
● **Gevrey-Chambertin** 1er Cru Clos Saint-Jacques✪✪✪✪✪£F
● **Gevrey-Chambertin** 1er Cru Estournelles-Saint-Jacques★★★★★ £F
● **Gevrey-Chambertin** 1er Cru Lavaux-Saint-Jacques★★★★★ £F
● **Gevrey-Chambertin** 1er Cru Cazetiers★★★★ £F
● **Chambolle-Musigny** 1er Cru Les Amoureuses★★★★ £F
● **Chambolle-Musigny** 1er Cru Les Baudes★★★ £F
● **Nuits-Saint-Georges** 1er Cru Boudots★★★★ £F
● **Corton** Pougets★★★★ £F ● **Beaune** 1er Cru Cent Vignes★★★ £E
● **Beaune** 1er Cru Teurons★★★ £E 1er Cru Clos des Ursules★★★ £E
● **Beaune** 1er Cru Clos de Couchereaux★★★ £E
● **Beaune** 1er Cru Avaux★★★ £E 1er Cru Bressandes★★★ £E
● **Beaune** 1er Cru Grèves★★★ £E ● **Santenay** Clos de Malte★★ £D
● **Savigny-lès-Beaune** 1er Cru La Dominode★★★ £D
○ **Chevalier-Montrachet** Les Demoiselles✪✪✪✪✪ £H
○ **Corton-Charlemagne**✪✪✪✪✪ £G ○ **Beaune** Grèves★★ £E
○ **Puligny-Montrachet** 1er Cru Champ Gain★★★ £G
○ **Puligny-Montrachet** 1er Cru Les Folatières★★★★ £G
○ **Santenay** Clos de la Malte★★ £D ○ **Marsannay**★ £C

Duc de Magenta:

○ **Puligny-Montrachet** 1er Cru Clos de la Garenne★★★★ £G
○ **Chassagne-Montrachet** Morgeots Clos de la Chapelle★★★★ £G

PATRICK JAVILLIER Meursault

Patrick Javillier 7 Impasse des Acacias, 21190 Meursault
UK stockists: FMV, BBR, L&W, OWL, Sel, N&P
Patrick Javillier produces a range of fine village Meursaults and bottles
individually several different *lieux-dits*. The best of these actually taste like
premiers crus and certainly offer better value than a top site from an
underperforming producer. The wines are rich and ripe, with surprising class
and depth for their origins. Though they can occasionally tend to be a bit too
broad and slightly clumsy, Les Clous, Les Tillets and Les Narvaux always show
a little more verve and racy minerality. Tête de Murgers is the richest, deepest
and most complex of all. Two Bourgogne Blancs are also treated like Meursault
– which the richer, more structured of the 2, Cuvée Oligocène, effectively is. A
village-level Puligny-Montrachet, in contrast, shows more of a Puligny style,
with more finesse and delineation, if less character, than the Meursaults. There's
good white Savigny-lès-Beaune, too. All the whites are now being vinified in 2
different ways before being blended back together prior to bottling. A little
grand cru Corton-Charlemagne has been made since the 1999 vintage and a
tiny amount of *premier cru* Meursault Charmes might also be found. An
increasing amount of red is also being produced; Savigny-lès-Beaune Grand
Liards and Premier Cru Serpentières are reasonable examples of their
appellation. (PW)
○ **Corton-Charlemagne**★★★★★ £G
○ **Meursault** Tête de Murgers★★★★ £F Les Tillets★★★★ £E
○ **Meursault** Clos du Cromin★★★ £E Les Clous★★★ £E
○ **Meursault** Les Narvaux★★★ £E
○ **Puligny-Montrachet** Levrons★★★ £E
○ **Savigny-lès-Beaune** Montchevenoy★★★ £D
○ **Bourgogne Blanc** Cuvée Oligocène★★★ £C
○ **Bourgogne Blanc** Cuvée des Forgets★★ £C

167

FRANÇOIS JOBARD   Meursault

François Jobard   2 Rue de Leignon, 21190 Meursault
UK stockists: RsW, A&B, Rae, Hrd, Sec

François Jobard makes somewhat tighter, more traditional wines than his nephew, Rémi JOBARD. Low yields are achieved through rigorous pruning, while vinification is a relatively hands-off affair. While favouring long oak-ageing with extended lees contact, the percentage of new wood is kept low. A rather old-fashioned, heavy sulphur treatment can show in the wines when tasted young but they are meant to be aged. More austere and minerally but with underlying intensity when young, a deep, ripe, leesy nuttiness and flavour complexity develops with extended cellaring. In general the Blagny is usually deep and minerally, Poruzots is also minerally but peachier, Genevrières the more honeyed and the Charmes the most refined. The Meursaults, particularly the *premiers crus,* deserve at least 5 years' ageing but even the Bourgogne Blanc needs 3 or more. A little Puligny-Montrachet and some red Blagny are also made. (PW)

O **Meursault** 1er Cru Charmes★★★★ £F 1er Cru Poruzots★★★★ £F
O **Meursault** 1er Cru Blagny★★★ £F 1er Cru Genevrières★★★★ £F
O **Meursault** En la Barre★★★ £E O **Bourgogne Blanc**★★ £C

RÉMI JOBARD   Meursault

Rémi Jobard   12 Rue Sudot, 21190 Meursault
UK stockists: L&S

Rémi Jobard has assumed the responsibility of running this 8-ha estate from his father, Charles (brother of François JOBARD). These are rich, ripe concentrated Meursaults with good depth and balance. The 3 *premiers crus* show more class and length but there is good style, too, in the village bottlings, even if the Sous la Velle and Chevalière tend to be broader and slightly heavy in warm years. The Charmes is consistently the finest Meursault with superb fruit, excellent balance and a long, intense finish. The most recent vintages, benefitting from later bottling after being refreshed in tank, show increasing finesse. Despite having so many different *cuvées* of Meursault, only around half the estate is planted to Chardonnay. Inexpensive Bourgogne Aligoté is regularly made and from 2.5ha of Pinot Noir there is good Bourgogne Rouge and some Monthelie and Volnay Santenots. (PW)

O **Meursault** 1er Cru Charmes★★★★ £F 1er Cru Genevrières★★★★ £F
O **Meursault** En Luraule★★★ £E 1er Cru Poruzots-Dessus★★★★ £F
O **Meursault** Sous la Velle★★ £D Chevalière★★★ £E
O **Bourgogne Blanc**★ £C

DOM. JOBLOT   Givry

Jean-Marc & Vincent Joblot   4 Rue Pasteur, 71640 Givry
UK stockists: **Hal**, F&R

Jean-Marc Joblot's 13.5-ha estate is one of Givry's most important owing to a demanding approach to both viticulture and winemaking. Yields are low, reflected in reds with intense, concentrated fruit and plenty of acidity. Powerful oak-enhanced structures ensure they are approachable young but capable of at least 5–6 years' age. This applies especially to both Grand Marole and Clos de la Servosine which are particularly rich with impressive depth and length. Now is the time to be opening the 99s. Alternatively try the intense and fruity Pied de Chaume or stylish, complex Cellier aux Moines from what were very successful 01, 02 and 03 vintages here. Whites have good intensity and precision too; Clos de la Servoisine is richer and more oaky in style than village *cuvées*. (PW)

● **Givry** 1er Cru Clos Grand Marole★★★ £C

● **Givry** 1er Cru Clos de la Servoisine★★★ £D
● **Givry** Pied de Chaume★★ £C Cellier aux Moines★★★ £C
○ **Givry** 1er Cru Clos de la Servoisine★★★ £C
○ **Givry** Pied de Chaume★★ £C

DOM. MICHEL JUILLOT Mercurey www.domaine-michel-juillot.fr

Juillot family   59 Grande Rue, BP 10, 71640 Mercurey
UK stockists: DDr, HHB

The Juillot vineyards comprise 21ha of Pinot Noir and 9ha of Chardonnay.
Laurent Juillot has taken over from his father and there are some very attractive
whites and excellent reds, including 4 *premiers crus* culminating in the well-sited
Clos des Barraults. The latter is the most forbidding and structured red but all
reveal good depth and richness with 3 years' age or more. Both pumping over
and punching down are employed, no doubt contributing to some youthful
austerity. As well as the reds listed below, some Combins and a few magnums
of the highly regarded Clos du Roi (both *premiers crus*) are also made. Other
than Mercurey, a little of the *grands crus* Corton Perrières (red) and Corton-
Charlemagne together with some village-level Aloxe-Corton are produced.
(PW)

● **Mercurey** 1er Cru Clos des Barraults★★★ £D
● **Mercurey** 1er Cru Champs-Martin★★★ £D
● **Mercurey**★★ £B 1er Cru Clos Tonnerre★★ £C
○ **Mercurey** 1er Cru Clos des Barraults★★★ £D
○ **Mercurey** 1er Cru Champs-Martin★★ £D
○ **Mercurey**★★ £B 1er Cru En Sazenay★★ £C

VINCENT & FRANÇOIS JOUARD Chassagne-Montrachet

Vincent & François Jouard   21190 Chassagne-Montrachet
UK stockists: FMV, HRp

Brothers Vincent and François Jouard produce only a part of what they grow
under their own label but the wines are increasingly good. There are top *crus*
but at better prices than more established names command. The 2002s follow
good 01s but have more potential: La Maltroie has ripe fruit and spice and a
certain elegance; Champs Gain reveals both concentration and structure;
Morgeot shows depth and vibrancy; and Les Chaumées (Clos de la Truffière)
has real class with lots more to come. The Bâtard-Montrachet has much of the
depth and intensity expected but not quite the extra class or richness of the best
examples. (PW)

○ **Bâtard-Montrachet**★★★★★ £G
○ **Chassagne-Montrachet** 1er Cru Champ Gain★★★★ £E
○ **Chassagne-Montrachet** 1er Cru Chaumées Clos de la Truffière★★★★ £E
○ **Chassagne-Montrachet** 1er Cru Maltroie★★★★ £E
○ **Chassagne-Montrachet** 1er Cru Morgeot Fairendes★★★★ £E

MICHEL LAFARGE Volnay

Lafarge family   Domaine Michel Lafarge, 21190 Volnay
UK stockists: BBR GFy, Gau, HRp, Sec

Michel and and his son Frédéric have an excellent and deserved reputation for
Volnay and are as good a source of fine Côte de Beaune reds as anybody. The
domaine is now farmed biodynamically and relatively old vines that give lowish
yields are picked at full physiological ripeness to provide the fine raw materials,
while care and consideration is evident at every step of the winemaking process.
There is much experience to draw on in order to adapt to the particular
conditions of each vintage. The wines are elegant and sophisticated, with
magical aromas and superb fruit together with good structure and
concentration; and vintages like 1993, 96, 99 or 02 show added intensity and

169

concentration. Most of the wines can be drunk fairly young but will only really start to open out after 5 years or more; in the case of the Clos des Chênes this is a minimum. Otherwise some of the class and complexity is tantalising but remains partially hidden. A Lafarge bottle always delivers fine quality wine that is balanced and complete and a lovely expression of where it comes from. Only 8ha of a total of 10 is planted to Pinot Noir and some Meursault is made. There's also a little Pommard Premier Cru Pézerolles. New is a small amount of Volnay Premier Cru Caillerets, which was purchased by Frédéric. Bourgogne Rouge is always a fine example. (PW)

- **Volnay** 1er Cru Clos des Chênes★★★★★ £F
- **Volnay** 1er Cru Clos du Château des Ducs★★★★ £F
- **Volnay** 1er Cru★★★★ £F 1er Cru Caillerets★★★★ £F
- **Volnay**★★★ £E Vendange Sélectionée★★★ £E
- **Beaune** 1er Cru Grèves★★★ £F ● **Côte de Beaune-Villages**★★ £C
- **Bourgogne Rouge**★★ £C

DOM. DES COMTES LAFON   Meursault

Lafon family   Clos de la Barre, 21190 Meursault
UK stockists: Adm, FMV, BBR, JAr, Far, Las, F&M

The finest domaine in Meursault and one of the very best in the Côte d'Or, with some excellent Volnay as well as outstanding Meursault. Dominique Lafon has had the mastery of this 14-ha estate for 2 decades now and in recent years has converted its viticulture to a biodynamic regime. In the Meursault *premiers crus* the fruit is intense, rich and pure and encased in a precise but seamless structure. An opulent Gouttes d'Or, wonderfully expressive Charmes and remarkably profound Genevrières are only surpassed by a peerless Perrières. Yet even the village wines, such as the Clos de la Barre, show good dimension and a touch of class. The fine Volnays are crowned by a rich Santenots du Milieu, with great finesse and length. The acclaim for these wines adds a premium and they need to be bought before changing hands too many times if prices are to be remotely proportionate to their quality. Most expensive, from just a few barrels, is a Montrachet of exalted reputation. A little Puligny-Montrachet Premier Cru Champ Gain is also made and some very good wines are now being produced in the Mâconnais under the Domaine des HERITIERS COMTES LAFON. (PW)

- O **Meursault** 1er Cru Perrières✪✪✪✪ £G
- O **Meursault** 1er Cru Charmes★★★★★ £G
- O **Meursault** 1er Cru Genevrières★★★★★ £G
- O **Meursault** 1er Cru Goutte d'Or★★★★ £G
- O **Meursault**★★★ £E Désirée★★★ £F Clos de la Barre★★★ £F
- **Volnay** 1er Cru Santenots du Milieu★★★★★ £F
- **Volnay** 1er Cru Clos des Chênes★★★★ £E
- **Volnay**★★★ £E 1er Cru Champans★★★★ £E
- **Monthelie** 1er Cru Les Duresses★★★ £D

DOM. FRANÇOIS LAMARCHE   www.domaine-lamarche.com

Lamarche family   9 Rue des Communes, 21700 Vosne-Romanée
UK stockists: Col, Rae, RsW, Sec

Only recently much improved, this estate has some prized possessions in its patchwork of 10ha, including all 1.65ha of that wedge of *grand cru*, La Grande Rue, lying between La Tâche and La Romanée-Conti. The wines previously showed a certain finesse but missed their real potential but have become more concentrated and classy under François's direction. Yields have been reduced, the grapes are now fully destemmed and up to 60% new oak is used but the wines still start out quite tight and tannic and this noble but at times slightly austere style demands patience. Deep and intense, La Croix Rameau and

Malconsorts are arguably the finest Vosne *premiers crus*, which is reflected in their marginally higher prices. Yet there are currently even better examples of most of the *crus* to be had from other producers. La Grande Rue however, is not only unique but very fine indeed. In addition to the 3 other *grands crus*, a small amount of Grands-Echezeaux is made. Only the most recent vintages should be bought for cellaring. A decent example of inexpensive Hautes-Côtes de Nuits red can be found here too. (PW)

- **La Grande Rue**✪✪✪✪✪ £G ● **Echezeaux**★★★★ £F
- **Clos de Vougeot**★★★★ £F
- **Vosne-Romanée** 1er Cru Suchots★★★★ £E
- **Vosne-Romanée** 1er Cru Malconsorts★★★★ £F
- **Vosne-Romanée** 1er Cru La Croix Rameau★★★★ £E
- **Vosne-Romanée**★★ £E 1er Cru Chaumes★★★ £E

DOM. DES LAMBRAYS Morey-Saint-Denis
Freund family   31 Rue Basse, 21220 Morey-Saint-Denis
UK stockists: OWL, HRp, BBR, HHC, Sel

The historic 8.8-ha Clos des Lambrays is almost entirely owned by Gunter Freund and, though relatively small, it is certainly a big chunk of *grand cru* under single ownership. After years of neglect, the Clos was partially replanted in 1981 and around the same time upgraded from *premier cru* to *grand cru*. Much effort and expense was poured into the estate under the guidance of winemaker Thierry Brouin, whose efforts have only really paid full dividends since 1996, coinciding with the most recent change of ownership. The wine is seductively plump and silky but with terrific class and complexity too, softer than adjoining Clos de Tart or indeed Bonnes Mares or Chambertin yet of true *grand cru* status. Morey-Saint-Denis (both in a village-level and a *premier cru* Les Loups bottling) shares the delicious fruit and superfine tannins if missing the depth and dimension of the *grand cru*. Small quantities of 2 very exciting whites are made from a few rows in top Puligny *premiers crus*. They have a depth, weight and structure allied to class, particularly the Clos du Cailleret which comes from a plot behind Les Pucelles adjoining Le Montrachet. (PW)

- **Clos des Lambrays**★★★★★ £F
- **Morey-Saint-Denis**★★★ £E 1er Cru Les Loups★★★★ £E
- O **Puligny-Montrachet** 1er Cru Clos du Cailleret★★★★★ £F
- O **Puligny-Montrachet** 1er Cru Les Folatières★★★★ £F

HUBERT LAMY Saint-Aubin
Lamy family   Le Paradis, 21190 Saint-Aubin
UK stockists: BBR, DDr,Gen, L&S, L&W

This is another estate where the input of a new generation has had a positive impact on quality. Already good Saint-Aubin whites have been honed into ripe, rich and stylish examples under the winemaking expertise of Hubert Lamy's son, Olivier. Only 5 of the 16.5ha of vineyard are planted to Pinot Noir but the reds are increasingly ripe and concentrated too, especially from good years like 1999 or 02. This is a good source of both red and white Burgundy without silly prices. The bottling of Puligny, Les Tremblots, for instance, could pass for a *premier cru* wine. A very small amount of Criots-Bâtard-Montrachet is also made. (PW)

- O **Chassagne-Montrachet** 1er Cru Macherelles★★★ £F
- O **Puligny-Montrachet** Les Tremblots★★★ £E
- O **Saint-Aubin** 1er Cru Murgers Dents de Chien★★★ £D
- O **Saint-Aubin** 1er Cru En Remilly★★★ £D
- O **Saint-Aubin** 1er Cru Clos de la Chatenière★★★ £D
- O **Saint-Aubin** Princée★★ £C 1er Cru Les Frionnes★★★ £C
- O **Bourgogne Blanc**★★ £B

171

● **Saint-Aubin** 1er Cru Derrière Chez Edouard★★★ £C
● **Saint-Aubin** 1er Cru Les Castets ★★ £C
● **Chassagne-Montrachet** Goujonne Vieilles Vignes★★ £C

LOUIS LATOUR   www.louislatour.com

Latour family   18 Rue des Tonneliers, 21200 Beaune
UK stockists: **LLt**, Hay, BBR, C&R, MCW, F&M, Maj

With an annual production of 5.5 million bottles, this historic Burgundy house (and domaine of 50ha) is one of the most widely seen labels outside of France. Not only are wines made from Chablis down through the Côte d'Or to the Chalonnaise, Mâconnais and Beaujolais, but beyond into the Ardèche and the Var. The continued use of flash-pasteurisation for the red wines (in order to kill bacteria) and filtration remain the most controversial aspects of their production. In addition a short *cuvaison* (8–10 days) has long been favoured – in search of greater finesse it is argued – but too often the reds lack vigour, depth and vibrancy as well as the flavour amplitude they surely otherwise have the potential for. White grapes are harvested late for optimum ripeness, yields are low and plenty of new oak is used in their *élevage*. While generally better quality and value can be found elsewhere, some of the top *crus* (including all 6 white *grands crus*) can be astonishingly good, with great concentration, complexity and power. A selection of the best white wines is listed below. (PW)

○ **Bâtard-Montrachet**★★★★ £H   ○ **Corton-Charlemagne**★★★★ £G
○ **Chevalier-Montrachet** Demoiselles★★★★ £H
○ **Meursault** 1er Cru Goutte d'Or★★★ £E
○ **Meursault** 1er Cru Château de Blagny★★★ £E
○ **Puligny-Montrachet** 1er Cru Truffières★★★ £E
○ **Puligny-Montrachet** 1er Cru Folatières★★★ £E
○ **Chassagne-Montrachet** 1er Cru Morgeot★★★ £E

LATOUR-GIRAUD   Meursault

Jean-Pierre Latour   21190 Meursault
UK stockists: Bib, THt

This previously underperforming domaine is now making whites of a quality expected of its impressive holdings. Of 10ha, 8ha planted to Chardonnay, arguably the most prized is that of a large, 2.4ha section of Genevrières. Recent vintages show great class and an elegant and intense expression that is true to its origins. Both this and the tiny production of a minerally Perrières shouldn't be rushed; the depth and intensity will slowly unfurl with up to 10 years' ageing. As well as some fine Charmes, 2 other *premiers crus*, Bouchères and Poruzots, are also made but there's also fine quality in Le Limozin and Cuvée Charles Maxine, which both give classic Meursault style and richness with less age and at a more affordable price. Besides a little Puligny some red is made, mostly from Maranges. (PW)

○ **Meursault** 1er Cru Perrières★★★★★ £F
○ **Meursault** 1er Cru Genevrières★★★★★ £F
○ **Meursault** 1er Cru Charmes★★★★ £F
○ **Meursault** Charles Maxime★★★ £E Le Limozin★★★ £E
○ **Puligny-Montrachet** Champs Canet★★★★ £F

DOMINIQUE LAURENT   Nuits-Saint-Georges

Dominique Laurent   2 Rue Jacques-Duret, 21700 Nuits-Saint-Georges
UK stockists: Far, HBJ, N&P, Las, HRp, Hrd

Ex-pastry chef Dominique Laurent buys only the best small lots of young red wine made from old low-yielding vines, ages them himself, then sells the many individual *cuvées* for very high prices. His considerable following in both France and other premium wine markets stems in part from the support of Michel

Bettane and *La Revue du Vin de France*. The wines are typically big, powerful and very concentrated, with lots of extract and tannin. Oak, and lots of it, was an early theme, resulting in some excessively oaky wines, though this is much less common in more recent releases. Now, in the same way that pastries can be butter-rich, many of the wines can be oak-rich (but without compromising the wine's structure with excessive oak tannins as is typical in a badly wooded wine) with the requisite balance of fruit richness and extract that is enriched and enhanced by the oak, resulting in a succulent creaminess. Quality is generally very high indeed but rare lapses can result in rather tough, chewy wines. Thanks, though, to the high prices obtained for other wines, even these can be declassified. Though all the wines are bought in, many of the exact same parcels can be acquired year after year. Some of the wines made fairly regularly include: (*grands crus*) Chambertin Clos de Bèze, Mazis-Chambertin, Le Musigny, Bonnes Mares, Clos de la Roche and Clos de Vougeot; (*premiers crus*) Vosne-Romanée Beaux Monts and Suchots, Chambolle-Musigny Charmes, Gevrey-Chambertin Clos Saint-Jacques, Nuits-Saint-Georges Les Saint-Georges, Vaucrains and Richemone, Volnay Clos des Chênes, Pommard Epenots, Beaune 1er Cru and Grèves as well as some excellent village examples designated Vieilles Vignes. If you like vibrant, rich, oaky Burgundy with often remarkable depth, length and intensity, never turn down the chance to taste any of the many varied offerings. Dominique applies some of the same methods in both the northern and southern Rhône (and beyond) where with Michel Tardieu he turns out small-volume, high-priced *cuvées* under the TARDIEU-LAURENT label. (PW)

OLIVIER LEFLAIVE   Puligny-Montrachet   www.olivier-leflaive.com
Olivier Leflaive (& others)   Place du Monument   21190 Puligny-Montrachet
UK stockists: C&B, HHC, L&W, WSc

Olivier Leflaive set up this merchant house in 1984 and continued to co-manage the family domaine (Domaine Leflaive) until 1994. The company now has a small 12-ha domaine of its own, though the lion's share of production (three-quarters of a million bottles) is made from bought-in grapes. Franck Grux, the winemaker for more than a decade, has provided a largely consistent and sometimes enviable range of white Burgundy. Leading *premiers crus* from Puligny-Montrachet, Chassagne-Montrachet and Meursault can be good if a little variable. In addition, examples of all 6 Côte de Beaune *grands crus* are made, including very fine Criots-Bâtard-Montrachet and Le Montrachet. If at a lower level the wines can be a little dull, occasionally even dilute in a lesser vintage, the Côte Chalonnaise whites, Rully and Montagny, can be also be very good. A increasing amount of fine Chablis is being made, including a range of fine *premiers crus*. While more than 90% of production is white, a relatively small range of reds is also made. The best, mostly Pommard and Volnays, are quite structured, with appreciable oak, but have the depth and richness to be very satisfying with 5 years' age or more. Bourgogne Blanc Les Sétilles is usually a good example of everyday white Burgundy. Listed are only some of the best wines that are regularly made. Franck Grux also makes some good Meursault Meix Chavaux under his own label. (PW)

O **Montrachet**✪✪✪✪✪ £H   O **Criots-Bâtard-Montrachet**★★★★★ £G
O **Puligny-Montrachet** I I er Cru Pucelles★★★★ £F
O **Puligny-Montrachet** I er Cru Champ Canet★★★ £F
O **Puligny-Montrachet** I er Cru Les Referts★★★ £F
O **Puligny-Montrachet** I er Cru Champs Gain★★★ £F
O **Chassagne-Montrachet** I er Cru Abbaye de Morgeot★★★ £F
O **Chassagne-Montrachet** I er Cru Les Chaumées★★★ £E
O **Chassagne-Montrachet** I er Cru Clos Saint-Marc★★★ £E
O **Meursault** I er Cru Perrières★★★★ £F

173

O **Meursault** Narvaux★★★ £E   1er Cru Poruzots★★★ £F
O **Saint-Aubin** 1er Cru Les Perrières★ £C   1er Cru En Remilly★★ £D
O **Rully** 1er Cru Rabourcé★★ £C   1er Cru Vauvry★★ £C
O **Rully** 1er Cru★ £C   1er Cru Les Clous★★ £C
O **Montagny** 1er Cru★ £B   1er Cru Bonneveaux★★ £C
O **Chablis Premier Cru** Montée de Tonnerre★★★ £D Vaillons★★★ £D
O **Chablis Premier Cru** Fourchaumes★★★ £D
● **Volnay** 1er Cru Champans★★★ £E   1er Cru Santenots★★★ £E
● **Volnay**★★ £D   1er Cru Clos des Angles★★★ £E
● **Pommard** 1er Cru Charmots★★★ £E   1er Cru Rugiens★★★ £E
● **Pommard**★★ £D   ● **Aloxe-Corton**★★ £D   ● **Santenay**★★ £C

DOM. LEFLAIVE   Puligny-Montrachet   www.leflaive.fr

Leflaive family   Place des Marronniers, 21190 Puligny-Montrachet
UK stockists: JAr, BBR, Goe, L&W, HRp, Tan, Las, Hrd

Under the direction of Vincent Leflaive this estate gained a fabulous reputation during the 1960s and 70s, so much so that the wines have been both sought-after and very expensive for as long as many wine enthusiasts can remember. Under the direction of his daughter Anne-Claude, who initially worked with her cousin Olivier (dedicated to his own business OLIVIER LEFLAIVE since 1994), the unsurpassed holding of prime white Burgundy vineyard has become progressively biodynamic, totally so since 1998. Of the 23.5ha, 11.5ha are of *premiers crus*, 5ha of *grands crus*, including nearly 2ha each of Chevalier-Montrachet and Bâtard-Montrachet. Pierre Morey has made the wines in recent years and brought to an end some of the criticism directed at wines from vintages between the mid-1980s and early 90s, when yields were high and the wines' considerable reputation for ageing was tarnished. With the balance and the health of the vineyards now paramount, wines from recent vintages look set to rival past glories. No end of descriptions of flavour nuances can do them justice. The wines have wonderful purity and clarity, great concentration and intensity but almost perfect precision and poise, together with compelling complexity, dimension and length in the *grands crus*. (PW)

O **Le Montrachet**✪✪✪✪✪ £H   O **Chevalier-Montrachet**✪✪✪✪✪£H
O **Bienvenues-Bâtard-Montrachet**✪✪✪✪✪ £H
O **Bâtard-Montrachet**✪✪✪✪✪ £H
O **Puligny-Montrachet** 1er Cru Les Pucelles★★★★★ £G
O **Puligny-Montrachet** 1er Cru Les Combottes★★★★★ £G
O **Puligny-Montrachet** 1er Cru Les Folatières★★★★ £G
O **Puligny-Montrachet**★★★ £F   1er Cru Clavoillon★★★★ £F
O **Bourgogne** Blanc★★ £D

DOM. LEROY   www.domaineleroy.com

Leroy and Bize families   Rue du Pont-Boillot, 21190 Auxey-Duresses
UK stockists: JAr, BBR, C&R, Far, HRp, Sec, Las, F&R

Madame Lalou Bize-Leroy, one of the most formidable and dynamic wine personalities on the planet, directs one of Burgundy's most prestigious domaines. Built around the former Domaine Charles Noëllat (Vosne-Romanée) purchased in 1988, it now boasts 22ha of some of the finest *crus* in the Côte d'Or. Lalou Bize has championed the cause of biodynamic viticulture and has built a domaine to rival the Domaine de la ROMANÉE-CONTI, which she co-managed until 1993. In terms of out and out quality there is arguably no finer estate. Yields are tiny (20–24 hl/ha is typical), and in common with Romanée-Conti there is no destemming, long *cuvaisons* and more than enough new oak to keep the *tonnelier* (barrelmaking) firms happy. The wines are distinguished by quite staggering concentration and richness, in some instances with almost overwhelming extract and structure, as well as great intensity, depth and length. Every wine needs the best part of a decade's age and they usually have the balance to keep for much longer. Due to insufficient repeated tastings of the wines they have not been rated individually but as an indication of their ratings generally the *grands crus* (8 red and 1 white) are 5 stars, leading *premiers crus* 4 or 5 stars, and others at least 3 stars. Reds include: (*grands crus*) Chambertin, Latricières-Chambertin, Clos de la Roche, Musigny, Clos de Vougeot, Richebourg, Romanée-Saint-Vivant and Corton Renardes; (*premiers crus*) Gevrey-Chambertin Combottes, Chambolle-Musigny Charmes, Vosne-Romanée Aux Brulées and Beaux Monts, Nuits-Saint-Georges Boudots and Vignerondes, Volnay Santenots and Savigny-lès-Beaune Narbantons; (village-level) Chambolle-Musigny Fremières, Vosne-Romanée Genevrières, Nuits-Saint-Georges Au Bas du Combe, Aux Allots and Lavières and Pommard Les Vignots. The only white is some Corton-Charlemagne. Bize-Leroy's own domaine is Domaine D'AUVENAY, while Leroy SA is the *négociant* and distribution operation. (PW)

VICOMTE LIGER-BELAIR   Vosne-Romanée

Vicomte Liger-Belair family   Ch. de Vosne-Romanée, 21700 Vosne-Romanée
UK stockists: **J&B, RsW**, Sec

Since 2002 Louis-Michel Liger-Belair has been enjoying (and exploiting) the fruits of a phased return of Burgundy's smallest *grand cru*, La Romanée. His family's vineyards have been leased to BOUCHARD Père et Fils for the best part of 30 years but come fully back under Liger-Belair control in 2006. Louis-Michel has recently trained as a winemaker but has also travelled widely so is able to harness the full potential of a little over 3ha of prime vineyards. La Romanée itself lies immediately above La Romanée-Conti but is even smaller at just 0.85ha. The first efforts together with the other wines, La Colombière, Clos du Château and *premiers crus* Les Chaumes and Les Reignots, will be rated after further tastings. (PW)

DOM. LORENZON   Mercurey

Bruno Lorenzon   Rue de Reu, 71640 Mercurey
UK stockists: **FMV**

Bruno Lorenzon is one of a number of young growers in Mercurey who are maximising the potential from the appellation's best sites. He has travelled widely thanks to his ongoing work with a cooperage company and his contact with other producers of Pinot Noir has enriched his own reds. He gets fully ripe fruit and the wines have shown lots of intensity and extract in recent vintages. There is not perhaps the elegance of others but the tannins are ripe and the wines, especially from 2002 and 03, promise much with 5 years' age. Cuvée Carline is particularly fine – suggestive of good village-level Vosne-Romanée. A small amount of white is also made from a part of the 5ha of vineyard, both Champs Martin and another *premier cru*, Croichots. Both are vibrant and intense but with better breadth and style in the finely oaked Champs Martin. (PW)

- ● **Mercurey** ler Cru Champs-Martin Cuvée Carline £D
- ● **Mercurey**★★ £C ler Cru Champs-Martin★★ £C
- O **Mercurey**ler Cru Croichots★★ £C ler Cru Champs Martin★★★ £C

HUBERT LIGNIER   Morey-Saint-Denis

Hubert Lignier   45 Grande Rue, 21220 Morey-Saint-Denis
UK stockists: **RRI, Eno, C&R, Far, Las**

Romain Lignier, Hubert's son, has gradually honed the quality of his family's wines over the last decade. Almost 8ha include a decent amount of Clos de la Roche and 5 *premier cru* bottlings. There is also a tiny amount of Charmes Chambertin. Moderately low yields are maintained and good extraction is

175

favoured; Romain aids the *pigéage* by entering the vats himself and physically agitating the grapes and pulp in what seems to be a family proclivity. The wines can start off quite tight but have real depth and intensity that more than covers their fine but abundant tannin. The wines don't lack for oak, particularly the Combottes, but this is generally better integrated than previously. The *premiers crus* are markedly more expensive than the village wines but this is where the real quality kicks in. The excellent Morey-Saint-Denis Premier Cru Vieilles Vignes combines the *crus* of Faconnières and Chenevery and is a little bolder and deeper than the other 2 Morey *premiers crus*. Chambolle-Musigny is the best of the 3 village-level wines. (PW)

- ● **Clos de la Roche**✪✪✪✪✪ £H
- ● **Morey-Saint-Denis** 1er Cru Vieilles Vignes★★★★ £F
- ● **Morey-Saint-Denis** 1er Cru La Riotte★★★ £F
- ● **Morey-Saint-Denis**★★ £E 1er Cru Les Chaffots★★★ £F
- ● **Gevrey-Chambertin**★★ £E 1er Cru Les Combottes★★★ £G
- ● **Chambolle-Musigny**★★★ £E 1er Cru Les Baudes★★★ £F

FRANÇOIS LUMPP Givry

Isabelle & François Lumpp 36 Avenue de Mortières, 71640 Givry
UK stockists: THt, L&S, N&P, JNi, Hrd

One of the best Givry producers (others include Joblot, René Bourgeon and Clos Salomon) with wines to match the best from the other Côte Chalonnaise appellations, too. From just 6.5ha (5 Pinot Noir) François Lumpp keeps yields low and shows a light hand in the winemaking that results in supple, harmonious and balanced reds, especially with a couple of years' bottle-age. The red from Crausot is particularly impressive. Whites are fine, too, ripe but not overripe, with good intensity and balanced acidities and an elegant minerality in the Petite Marole. (PW)

- O **Givry** 1er Cru Petit Marole★★★ £C Clos des Vignes Rondes★★ £C
- O **Givry** 1er Cru Crausot★★ £C
- ● **Givry** 1er Cru Clos Jus★★ £C 1er Cru Crausot★★★ £C
- ● **Givry** 1er Cru Clos du Gras Long★★ £C
- ● **Givry** Pied du Clou★★ £C 1er Cru Petite Marole★★ £C

DOM. MICHEL MAGNIEN ET FILS Morey-Saint-Denis

Michel & Frédéric Magnien 4 Rue Ribordot, 21200 Morey-Saint-Denis
UK stockists: JAr

Frédéric Magnien works with his father to make the wines on the family domaine but also makes a large number of *négociant* wines under his own label. The 11-ha domaine includes some excellent sites, mostly in the communes of Morey-Saint-Denis and Gevrey-Chambertin but they have only been bottling all of their production since 1994. The Magnien style is for richness and extract combined with lots of new oak. The wines are succulent, fleshy and richly fruity, with fine ripe tannins, at least in the best years. A lighter hand is needed in merely good years to avoid overly tannic, structured wines. The 1997s and 98s are not likely to be encountered due to their withdrawal following a bacterial contamination in the new cellars. With their own premises sealed off, Frédéric was fortunate to be offered winemaking facilities *chez* DUJAC in 1999. The resulting wines show a lot of new oak but have the fruit to match. While the top reds will keep, the hedonistic pleasure that just 5 or 6 years' age brings, will sway many wine drinkers. The balance in the 2000s and 01s is less satisfactory and shows a marked contrast though the style is more successful in 02. A little Charmes-Chambertin and other Morey-Saint-Denis are also made. (PW)

Domaine Michel Magnien et Fils:
- ● **Clos de la Roche**★★★ £F   ● **Clos Saint-Denis**★★★★ £G
- ● **Gevrey-Chambertin** 1er Cru Les Cazetiers★★★ £F
- ● **Gevrey-Chambertin** Seuvrées V.V★★★ £E   Aux Echezeaux★★★ £E
- ● **Morey-Saint-Denis** 1er Cru Les Chaffots★★★★ £E
- ● **Morey-Saint-Denis** 1er Cru Aux Charmes★★★ £E
- ● **Morey-Saint-Denis** 1er Cru Les Millandes★★★ £E
- ● **Morey-Saint-Denis** Mont Luisants★★★ £E

DOM. MATROT Meursault www.matrot.com
Matrot family   12 Rue de Matray, 21190 Meursault
UK stockists: C&B, BBR, Gau, GFy, Con, T&W

Thierry Matrot is a devoted *vigneron*, bestowing great care on his vines, ensuring low yields and harvesting as late as possible. He is not a huge fan of new oak and is not an advocate of *bâtonnage* but produces rich, powerful and structured whites, sometimes with more than a hint of sulphur when young. The wines can seem a little awkward at first, but all the *premiers crus* should have a minimum of 5 years' age before they are ready. Amongst the reds, both Volnay Santenots and Blagny are ripe, long and quite classy. The shape of this domaine is evolving as another Matrot estate, that of Thierry's sister, comes into existence. Domaine wines now appear under any of either of 2 labels (Pierre Matrot or Thierry Matrot). (PW)

- O **Meursault** 1er Cru Perrières★★★★★ £F   1er Cru Blagny★★★★ £E
- O **Meursault** 1er Cru Charmes★★★★ £F
- O **Meursault**★★★ £E   Chevalière★★★ £E
- O **Puligny-Montrachet** 1er Cru Les Chalumeaux★★★★ £F
- O **Puligny-Montrachet** 1er Cru Les Combettes★★★★ £F
- ● **Blagny** 1er Cru La Pièce sous le Bois★★★ £E
- ● **Volnay** 1er Cru Santenots★★★★ £E

MÉO-CAMUZET www.meo-camuzet.com
Jean Méo   11 Rue des Grands Crus, 21700 Vosne-Romanée
UK stockists: BBR, FMV, RsW, N&P, F&M, Las, F&R

One of Burgundy's great 20th-century winemakers, Henri Jayer, made the wines from this Domaine between 1945 and 1988. The rich legacy of prime vineyards that belonged to Étienne Camuzet provided Jayer with the opportunity to make some magnificient wines both for himself and others. The Méo-Camuzet label has only been around since the 1980s but most of that Camuzet legacy is now in the hands of the current generation, who have built up the holdings to 15ha. Jean-Nicolas Méo, son of Jean Méo, continues with the Jayer method, including total destemming, cold pre-fermentation maceration and an extended *cuvaison* and 100% new oak. The new oak is nearly always in evidence but there is a polish and a completeness that is the hallmark of these wines. At a lower level there is not the purity or intensity of others, especially at comparable prices, but the Cros Parentoux and Richebourg and increasingly the Corton and Echezeaux are very classy, very exciting wines. They have always been expensive and as good as some of them are, there's better value to be had. (PW)

- ● **Richebourg**✪✪✪✪ £H   ● **Clos de Vougeot**★★★★ £H
- ● **Echezeaux**★★★★ £H   ● **Corton**★★★★ £H
- ● **Vosne-Romanée** 1er Cru Cros Parentoux★★★★★ £H
- ● **Vosne-Romanée** 1er Cru Aux Brulées★★★★★ £H
- ● **Vosne-Romanée**★★★ £F   1er Cru Les Chaumes★★★ £G
- ● **Nuits-Saint-Georges** 1er Cru Aux Murgers★★★★ £G
- ● **Nuits-Saint-Georges**★★★ £F   1er Cru Aux Boudots★★★★ £G
- ● **Marsannay**★★★ £D   ● **Fixin**★★★ £E
- ● **Côtes de Nuits-Villages**★★ £D   ● **Bourgogne Rouge**★★ £C

177

PRINCE DE MÉRODE Ladoix

Prince de Mérode   Château de Serrigny, 21550 Ladoix-Serrigny
UK stockists: **L&W,** HRp

There have been ongoing improvements to this 11-ha Corton-based estate of Belgian origins. Yields have been lowered and there is improved fruit selection and better temperature control than previously. The wines, recently made by Didier Dubois, are now ripe and balanced with fine fruit expression and a measured use of oak. The Cortons in particular are very appealing with considerable refinement and style; Bressandes has impressive length and finesse if marginally less depth than Clos du Roi. There is more vigour and intensity from 2002 if still not quite the energy of the very best. Aloxe-Corton Les Maréchaudes is also a fine example in contrast to the sometimes lean and scarcely ripe reds from this appellation. Some Pommard Clos de la Platière is also made. (PW)

- **Corton Bressandes**★★★★ £F ● **Corton Clos du Roi**★★★★ £F
- **Corton Renardes**★★★ £F ● **Corton Maréchaudes**★★★★ £F
- **Aloxe-Corton** 1er Cru Les Maréchaudes★★★ £E
- **Ladoix** Les Chaillots★★ £C 1er Cru Hautes Mourottes★★ £D

ALAIN MICHELOT Nuits-Saint-Georges

Alain Michelot   6 Rue Camille-Rodier, 21700 Nuits-Saint-Georges
UK stockists: **L&W,** BWC, DDr, F&R

Alain Michelot, now assisted by his daughter Elodie, has almost 8ha of vineyards. This falls almost entirely in Nuits-Saint-Georges but also includes a little Morey-Saint-Denis (Les Charrières) and some Bourgogne Rouge. The wines are better defined, fuller and more expansive than previously. Yields are lower and the grapes are now 100% destemmed with a prolonged cuvaison of 3–5 weeks. A maximum of 30% new oak is used and the wines are bottled without filtration when possible. The 2002s are very good while the 03s promise to be the best yet. Most outstanding are Champs Perdrix, Les Chaignots, Les Porrets Saint-Georges and Vaucrains. All are deep with lots of dimension and intensity but need 8–10 years from the vintage to open out fully. Les Cailles and La Richemone also have plenty of depth and intensity as does a characterful, black-fruited Vieilles Vignes version. Very small quantities of Les Saint-Georges are also produced. (PW)

- **Nuits-Saint-Georges** 1er Cru Vaucrains★★★★ £E
- **Nuits-Saint-Georges** 1er Cru Champs Perdrix★★★★ £E
- **Nuits-Saint-Georges** 1er Cru Porrets-Saint-Georges★★★★ £E
- **Nuits-Saint-Georges** 1er Cru Chaignots★★★★ £E
- **Nuits-Saint-Georges** 1er Cru Richemone★★★ £E
- **Nuits-Saint-Georges** Vieilles Vignes★★★ £E 1er Cru Cailles★★★ £E
- **Morey-Saint-Denis** 1er Cru Charrières★★★ £E

FRANÇOIS MIKULSKI Meursault

François Mikulski   5 Rue de Leignon, 21190 Meursault
UK stockists: Eno, GFy, Han, N&P, Sec, Blx

François is one of the newest stars of the Côte de Beaune and makes the sort of wines that get noticed. He has 7ha and concentrates on Meursault. The wines are ripe and full-bodied and develop a creamy, honeyed richness with even a little age. Most convincing and complete of 3 *premiers crus* is the Genevrières, which has the structure to match the concentration. Yet a deeply flavoured, citrusy Poruzots and a floral, exotic old-vine Charmes are in much the same style. A regular Meursault is rich and ripe too but if you find the Meursaults out of reach then there's ripe, fruity Bourgogne Blanc and Aligoté that don't lack for flavour or character. Two reds, a Meursault and a Volnay, are also made but these don't as yet show the flair of the whites. (PW)

○ **Meursault** 1er Cru Genevrières★★★★ £F 1er Cru Poruzots★★★★ £F
○ **Meursault**★★★ £E 1er Cru Charmes★★★ £F
○ **Bourgogne Blanc**★★ £B ○ **Bourgogne Aligoté**★ £B

DEUX MONTILLE

Alix & Étienne de Montille Rue de Pied de la Vallée, 21190 Volnay
UK stockists: **Gen**

This brother-and-sister merchant operation is the enterprise of Étienne and Alix Montille (also see Domaine de MONTILLE). Despite the vintage conditions in 2003 they succeeded in producing intense, concentrated whites, often very ripe but in most cases with decent structure. Each one also manages to express something of the appellation character and there is good quality at both ends of the spectrum from Saint-Romain Les Jarrons with good breadth and weight to Corton-Charlemagne with classic minerality and depth. Red Corton-Renardes is minerally and classy with a cool undercurrent but has lots of extract and good promise. These seem certain to be a better bet than wines from some of the more established *négociant* operations, especially if the same vineyard sites are retained and quantities are kept small. (PW)

○ **Puligny-Montrachet** 1er Cru La Garenne★★★★ £F
○ **Puligny-Montrachet** 1er Cru Champgains★★★★ £F
○ **Meursault** 1er Cru Bouchères★★★ £F
○ **Meursault** Grands Charrons★★★ £E Rougeots★★★ £E
○ **Corton-Charlemagne**★★★★ £G ○ **Saint-Romain** Les Jarrons★★ £D
○ **Rully** 1er Cru Rabourcée★★ £D
○ **Montagny** 1er Cru Vieux Château★★ £D
● **Corton Renardes**★★★★ £F

DOM. DE MONTILLE Volnay

Hubert et Étienne de Montille Rue de Pied de la Vallée, 21190 Volnay
UK stockists: **Gen, FMV, OWL, HRp, CTy, GFy, Sel**

One of the leading producers of both Volnay and Pommard, Hubert de Montille (also star of film Mondovino) was well-known for his dislike of high alcohol wines and has always kept chaptalisation to an absolute minimum. He also favoured fermentation at high temperatures and an extended *cuvaison* followed by a low percentage of new oak. The wines? They showed great dimension and depth but also tended to have a lot of extract and tannin, only opening out with 10 years' age, but vintages since 1998 have been made by Hubert's son Étienne. The wines are now a little less formidable, with finer tannin yet without sacrificing their elegance and individuality. They are now also produced biodynamically. Of the Pommards, the brilliant Rugiens is the essence of Pommard but Pézerolles is scarcely any less intense and classy. Volnays are similarly fine and particularly full and concentrated in 1999, 02 and 03; the Taillepieds reveals great length, breadth and finesse. Also an extremely good Puligny Cailleret. (PW)

● **Pommard** 1er Cru Rugiens★★★★★ £F
● **Pommard** 1er Cru Grands Epenots★★★★ £F
● **Pommard** 1er Cru Pézerolles★★★★ £F
● **Volnay** 1er Cru Mitans★★★★ £F 1er Cru Taillepieds★★★★★ £F
● **Volnay** 1er Cru★★★ £E 1er Cru Champans★★★★ £F
● **Beaune** 1er Cru Perrières★★★ £E
○ **Puligny-Montrachet** 1er Cru Cailleret★★★★★ £F

BERNARD MOREY Chassagne-Montrachet

Bernard Morey 21190 Chassagne-Montrachet
UK stockists: **BWC, A&B, Las, DDr, Gen, CTy**

Bernard Morey is a true *vigneron* and takes great pride in his vineyards. Vines

179

are replaced individually and propagated from the best old vines rather than bought-in clones. As a result the average vine age is increasingly high as is the health and balance in the vineyards. He also favours late picking and produces ripe, ample and flavoursome whites with well-integrated oak. Of the consistently fine Chassagne-Montrachet, the Vieilles Vignes come from almost 80-year-old vines as does the Vide Bourse and both show very ripe fruit, with lots of depth and richness if not the definition and structure of the Caillerets or Morgeots. A rich powerful, minerally but stylish Puligny La Truffière can be even better. Several other Chassagne-Montrachets (including a good Premier Cru Les Macharelles) are made from grapes purchased as part of the *négociant* side of the business. A little Bâtard-Montrachet is also made. The reds, particularly both Chassagnes, can be good (promising in 2002) but suffered a little at the hands of the elements in 2000 and 01. (PW)

Domaine wines:

○ **Chassagne-Montrachet** 1er Cru Morgeot★★★★ £E
○ **Chassagne-Montrachet** 1er Cru Caillerets★★★★ £E
○ **Chassagne-Montrachet** 1er Cru Vide Bourse★★★ £E
○ **Chassagne-Montrachet** 1er Cru Embrazées★★★ £E
○ **Chassagne-Montrachet** 1er Cru Baudines★★★ £E
○ **Chassagne-Montrachet** Vieilles Vignes★★★ £E
○ **Puligny-Montrachet** 1er Cru La Truffière★★★★ £F
○ **Saint-Aubin** 1er Cru Charmois★★ £C
○ **Santenay** 1er Cru Passetemps★★ £D
● **Beaune** 1er Cru Grèves★★★ £E
● **Chassagne-Montrachet** 1er Cru Clos Saint-Jean★★★ £D
● **Chassagne-Montrachet** Vieilles Vignes★★★ £C
● **Santenay** Grand Clos Rousseau★★ £D
● **Santenay** Vieilles Vignes★★ £C 1er Cru Passetemps★★ £D
● **Maranges** 1er Cru La Fuissière★ £C

DOM. MARC MOREY Chassagne-Montrachet

Bernard Mollard 3 Rue Charles Paquelin, 21190 Chassagne-Montrachet
UK stockists: HHC, JAr, Gau, Las

Bernard Mollard, recently joined by his son Jerôme, makes outstanding whites from a small 9.5-ha domaine that has improved year-on-year under his direction. All the vineyards lie within or close to Chassagne-Montrachet. An excellent, minerally village-level example is structured, with good citrus intensity and can be drunk young or kept for 3 or 4 years. The *premiers crus* are all classy, with depth, intensity and fine structure. Les Vergers is tight and minerally in contrast to a more forward, fatter, more obvious Virondot. Cailleret and Morgeot are both rich and concentrated. The top wine is a powerful, classy and complex Bâtard-Montrachet. A very respectable Bourgogne Blanc is always attractive and fruity with decent acidity. Some Saint-Aubin comes from the Les Charmois *premier cru* adjacent to Chassagne-Montrachet. Good Puligny-Montrachet is also made, some Pucelles and Champ-Gain. Prices are reasonable for the quality, with excellent 2002s and 00s but generally very good since 98. A significant amount of red is made too. These are slightly austere when young but, while the regular version can lack for ripeness, Morgeot has attractive red fruit and good breadth. (PW)

○ **Bâtard-Montrachet**○○○○○ £G
○ **Chassagne-Montrachet** 1er Cru Cailleret★★★★ £E
○ **Chassagne-Montrachet** 1er Cru Morgeot★★★★ £E
○ **Chassagne-Montrachet** 1er Cru Les Vergers★★★★ £E
○ **Chassagne-Montrachet** 1er Cru En Virondot★★★★ £E
○ **Chassagne-Montrachet**★★★ £E 1er Cru Les Chenevottes★★★★ £E
○ **Puligny-Montrachet** 1er Cru Champ-Gain★★★★ £F
○ **Saint-Aubin** 1er Cru Charmois★★★ £E ○ **Bourgogne Blanc**★ £B

● **Chassagne-Montrachet** 1er Cru Morgeot★★ £C

PIERRE MOREY/MOREY BLANC Meursault

Pierre Morey   13 Rue Pierre Mouchoux, 21190 Meursault
UK stockists: HRp, L&W, MCW, Tan

Pierre Morey is one of Burgundy's most highly regarded white winemakers, making the wines for Domaine Leflaive as well as those of his own. He has nearly 3ha of Pinot Noir as well as 6 for whites, (predominantly Chardonnay but some Aligoté too). The wines build great richness and opulence with age, becoming nutty, buttery and peachy. Of his own estate wines there's intense minerally depth in the Meursault Perrières and indisputable class and complexity in the Bâtard-Montrachet. The wines can have quite a lot of sulphur and are generally quite closed when young. Buy these wines to cellar and give them at least 5–6 years from a good vintage. Good Bourgogne Blanc and Aligoté are usually better with a couple of years too. Reds include good Pommard Epenots and Monthelie. Morey Blanc is the label for the *négociant* wines, made to the same high standards but from bought-in grapes. (PW)

Pierre Morey:
O **Bâtard-Montrachet**✪✪✪✪✪ £H
O **Meursault**★★★ £E Tessons★★★★ £F 1er Cru Perrières★★★★★ £F
O **Bourgogne Blanc**★★ £B O **Bourgogne Aligoté**★ £B
● **Pommard** Grands Epenots★★★ £E ● **Monthelie**★★ £D

Morey Blanc:
O **Meursault**★★★ £E Navaux★★★ £E 1er Cru Genevrières★★★ £E
O **Saint-Aubin** 1er Cru★★ £C

DOM. MOREY-COFFINET Chassagne-Montrachet

Michel Morey   6 Place du Grand Four, 21190 Chassagne-Montrachet
UK stockists: RsW, BBR, L&W, A&B, UnC, SVS

Michel Morey makes increasingly fine Chassagne-Montrachet whites from almost 8ha of vineyards. Only the village-level example is a little disappointing as although it has plenty of fruit it is a little simple with modest structure. *Premiers crus* are of a different order with impressive intensity and concentration and are well defined with good structures. La Romanée has both class and complexity; Les Caillerets has impressive depth and richness; while En Remilly and Les Fairendes are typically well balanced and refined. All deserve to be drunk with at least 5–6 years' age. The 2000s are coming into their own now and the 03s should be drunk fairly young but the 02s deserve to be kept. Also excellent is Puligny-Montrachet Les Pucelles which has the great breadth and sheer style of this *cru*. Bâtard-Montrachet is big with typical richness and breadth if not the extra class and precision of the very best. (PW)

O **Bâtard-Montrachet**★★★★★ £H
O **Chassagne-Montrachet** 1er Cru En Remilly★★★★ £F
O **Chassagne-Montrachet** 1er Cru Romanée★★★★ £F
O **Chassagne-Montrachet** 1er Cru Caillerets★★★★ £F
O **Chassagne-Montrachet**★★ £E 1er Cru Fairendes★★★★ £F
O **Puligny-Montrachet** 1er Cru Les Pucelles★★★★ £F

DOM. ALBERT MOROT Beaune

Choppin family   Avenue Charles Jaffelin, 21200 Beaune
UK stockists: **Hal**, N&P

This 7-ha domaine, based on vineyards acquired in the 1890s, has until very recently been run by Mademoiselle Choppin, whose grandfather Albert Morot ran a *négociant* business. From the beginnning of the new millennium her nephew, Geoffroy Choppin de Janvry, has been in charge. The domaine is unusual in that it produces almost exclusively *premier cru* Beaune from the heart of the richest vein of *crus* on the slopes behind the town. The only exception is a sturdy but concentrated *premier cru* Savigny, with impressive depth and length for the appellation. All the wines see a percentage of new oak after an extended maceration, resulting in wines that can be quite robust and meaty when young but with a great propensity to age, especially in top vintages. All of the wines are of a high standard and all deserve at least 5 years' cellaring; a rich, concentrated and classy Teurons can be the most satisfying but is at least matched for complexity by an old-vine Bressandes. As well as 3 other *premiers crus*, a miniscule amount of Grèves is also made. New from the 2001 vintage is some Beaune Les Aigrots (white as well as red), sited closer to Pommard than the existing *premiers crus*. (PW)

- ● **Beaune** Ier Cru Bressandes★★★★ £E   Ier Cru Teurons★★★★ £E
- ● **Beaune** Ier Cru Cent Vignes★★★ £E   Ier Cru Marconnets★★★ £E
- ● **Beaune** Ier Cru Toussaints★★★ £E   er Cru Aigrots★★ £E
- ● **Savigny-lès-Beaune** Ier Cru Bataillère aux Vergelesses★★★ £E

DENIS MORTET   Gevrey-Chambertin   www.denis-mortet.com

Denis Mortet   22 Rue de l'Église, 21220 Gevrey-Chambertin
UK stockists: BBR, DDr, Sec, WSc, HHB, Las

One of the truly outstanding Gevrey estates, with 11ha of fine *premiers crus* and some of the best village *lieux-dits*. Denis Mortet's first vintage under his own name was as recent as 1992, after he and his brother Thierry (who also makes fine Gevrey and Chambolle-Musigny) split up the former Domaine Charles Mortet. After a flying start the wines have continued to improve. As with all the best *vignerons*, there is attention to each and every vine. What matters is the yield and health of each individual plant rather than an average low yield, which may disguise overbearing vines offset by poorly specimens. Rigorous selection, total destemming, a pre-fermentation maceration and a long *cuvaison* are important to the style, while the type and percentage of new oak is carefully adapted to each different *cuvée*. These are marvellously complete wines, full, ripe and rich and with everything in balance. The one criticism, that the oak and extraction were slightly overdone, has been countered in the most recent vintages, which show still greater refinement and harmony. Apart from the regular Gevrey-Chambertin and the Marsannay, all the wines should be drunk with 5 years' ageing or more, and closer to 10 from a vintage like 1999 or 02. Newish are a village Gevrey-Chambertin En Derée from very old vines and a straight Gevrey-Chambertin Premier Cru, a blend of several small *premiers crus* plots. A touch of reduction can be a problem if the reds are drunk very young. A little Aligoté and Bourgogne Blanc are also made. (PW)

- ● **Chambertin**✪✪✪✪ £H   ● **Clos de Vougeot**★★★★ £G
- ● **Gevrey-Chambertin** Ier Cru Lavaux Saint-Jacques★★★★★ £F
- ● **Gevrey-Chambertin** Ier Cru En Champeaux★★★★ £F
- ● **Gevrey-Chambertin** En Champs★★★ £E   En Motrot★★★ £E
- ● **Gevrey-Chambertin** Au Vellé★★★ £E   En Derée★★★ £E
- ● **Gevrey-Chambertin**★★★ £E   La Combe de Dessus★★★ £E
- ● **Chambolle-Musigny** Ier Cru Beaux Bruns★★★★ £F
- ● **Marsannay** Les Longeroies★★ £D   ● **Bourgogne Rouge**★★ £C

MUGNERET-GIBOURG/DR GEORGES MUGNERET

Mugneret family   5 Rue des Communes, 21700 Vosne-Romanée
UK stockists: BWC, HRp, L&S, OWL

Sisters Marie-Christine and Marie-Andrée, assisted by their mother, make consistently refined wines from this 8.8-ha estate. The original vineyards of the property are sold under the Mugneret-Gibourg label while those acquired by their widely respected late father, Dr Georges Mugneret, are sold under his name. Most of the vineyards are taken care of by others on a sharecropping basis. The grapes are now fully destemmed and the wine is given a maceration on the skins both before and after a fermentation at relatively high temperatures. Up to 80% new oak is used for the *grands crus*, each one being made in small quantities, but all the wines show a measure of oak. They also have a lovely ripe pure Pinot fruit within a firm structure and there is real class, style and definition to each. The village wines and the elegant, seductive Chambolle-Musigny need 5 years, the complex, refined Chaignots and the *grands crus* 8 or more. (PW)

● **Clos de Vougeot**★★★★ £F ● **Ruchottes-Chambertin**★★★★★ £F
● **Echezeaux**★★★★ £F ● **Vosne-Romanée**★★★ £D
● **Chambolle-Musigny** 1er Cru Les Feusselottes★★★★ £E
● **Nuits-Saint-Georges**★★★ £D 1er Cru Les Chaignots★★★★ £E
● **Bourgogne Rouge**★★ £C

JACQUES-FRÉDÉRIC MUGNIER www.mugnier.fr

Jacques-Frédéric Mugnier Ch de Chambolle-Musigny, 21220 Chambolle-Musigny
UK stockists: HHB, HRp, FMV, Sec, Las, F&R
The early 18th-century Château de Chambolle-Musigny is rather at odds with the style of the wines here. For me, the architecture of the building pales beside the elegance, finesse even grandeur of these, at times, sublime wines. Since taking charge in 1984, Frédéric Mugnier has not only refined the practices on this small 4-ha estate (grape quality and selection are paramount and high fermentation temperatures are a feature of the vinification) but he has also pursued his passion for flying as a commercial airline pilot (as an aerial photo on the website shows). Don't come looking for powerful blockbusters; not even the more robust Bonnes Mares, the most sturdy of these wines, offers that. And if it's masses of oak, extract and flesh you want in your glass, then again look elsewhere. Building in richness and complexity with age, these are beautiful wines true to their appellations and with wonderful finesse and harmony. The regular Chambolle-Musigny can sometimes be a little slight but there's a hint of nobility even here. (PW)

● **Musigny**✪✪✪✪✪ £H ● **Bonnes Mares**★★★★★ £G
● **Chambolle-Musigny** 1er Cru Les Amoureuses★★★★★ £G
● **Chambolle-Musigny**★★★ £E 1er Cru Les Fuées★★★★ £F

MICHEL NIELLON Chassagne-Montrachet

Niellon family 1 Rue du Nord, 21190 Chassagne-Montrachet
UK stockists: OWL, BBR, RRI, F&R, C&R, Sec
This domaine is remarkably small considering some of the plaudits it has received. The wines are made in quite a reductive manner (with minimal aeration), the oak is restrained and the wines tight and intense when young. The *grands crus* are usually brilliant but the *premiers crus*, while often very good, do not approach the same level in the way that that they do at other estates. At their best there is depth, fine fruit concentration and good style. When tasted young the wines can be a bit reduced but will usually come round with aeration. At any rate all the wines deserve at least 5–6 years' age. Some Chassagne-Montrachet Premier Cru Vergers used to be made but is currently being replanted. The *grands crus* are very expensive due to their scarcity and reputation; the *premiers crus* can be bought for prices more in line with their quality but don't offer better value than other examples. (PW)

O **Chevalier-Montrachet**✪✪✪✪✪ £H
O **Bâtard-Montrachet**✪✪✪✪✪ £H
O **Chassagne-Montrachet** 1er Cru Clos de la Maltroie★★★★ £F
O **Chassagne-Montrachet** 1er Cru Les Chaumées★★★★ £F
O **Chassagne-Montrachet** 1er Cru Champs Gain★★★ £F
O **Chassagne-Montrachet**★★ £E 1er Cru Clos Saint-Jean★★ £F

183

JEAN-MARC PAVELOT   Savigny-lès-Beaune

Pavelot family   1 Chemin des Guettottes, 21420 Savigny-lès-Beaune
UK stockists: DDr, L&W

A superior domaine in an appellation with a reputation for providing wines with plenty of fruit and body, though they can also be a bit coarse and simple too. Not so here. Jean-Marc Pavelot has *premiers crus* from Savigny's more northern band, where the wines are generally lighter and more elegant, but also in the southern group of *premiers crus* (nearer Beaune), where the wines are fuller but firmer yet all his wines have a grace and charm that sets them apart. From the northern band both a vigorous Guettes and a seductive Aux Gravains reveal delicious fruit and a stylish complexity with a little age; Narbantons and Peuillets from closer to Beaune are fuller, meatier but less stylish. La Dominode comes from very old vines and is the richest and most complete Savigny. Regular red and white Savigny have ample fruit and good structure and are great drinking with a little bottle-age. The *premiers crus* are capable of ageing for at least 8–10 years, though I doubt many are kept that long. Jean-Marc's son, Hughes, is now taking over the winemaking responsibility. (PW)

● **Savigny-lès-Beaune** Ier Cru La Dominode★★★★ £D
● **Savigny-lès-Beaune** Ier Cru Narbantons★★★ £D
● **Savigny-lès-Beaune** Ier Cru Aux Gravains★★★ £D
● **Savigny-lès-Beaune** Ier Cru Guettes★★★ £D
● **Savigny-lès-Beaune**★★ £C   Ier Cru Peuillets★★ £D
● **Pernand-Vergelesses** Ier Cru Les Vergelesses★★ £C
O **Savigny-lès-Beaune**★★ £C

DOM. PAUL PERNOT ET FILS   Puligny-Montrachet

Pernot family   7 Place du Monument, 21190 Puligny-Montrachet
UK stockists: JAr, Bal, L&S, HRp, Las, BWC, Sel

The owners of this relatively large estate of 19ha only bottle a portion of the grapes they grow, but it is very good. The remainder must be gratefully received by the merchants. Paul Pernot is assisted by 2 of his sons and makes concentrated, powerful whites that become increasingly rich and honeyed with age. There's arguably not the definition or poise of a Domaine Leflaive equivalent but there is wonderful proportion and balance despite the wines' size, and real finesse as well as great complexity in the *premiers* and *grands crus*. Reds have good intensity if not that much refinement. The *grands crus*, though hardly cheap, are better priced than most others and the village Puligny-Montrachet is remarkably good value. (PW)

O **Bâtard-Montrachet**✪✪✪✪✪ £G
O **Bienvenues-Bâtard-Montrachet**✪✪✪✪✪ £G
O **Puligny-Montrachet** Ier Cru Les Pucelles★★★★ £F
O **Puligny-Montrachet**★★★ £E   Ier Cru Folatières★★★★ £F
O **Bourgogne Blanc**★ £C   ● **Pommard** Noizons★★ £D
● **Volnay** Ier Cru Carelles★★★ £D
● **Beaune** Clos du Dessus des Marconnets★★ £C
● **Beaune** Ier Cru Teurons★★ £D   Ier Cru Renversées★★ £D

PERROT-MINOT   Morey-Saint-Denis   www.perrot-minot.com

Henri & Christophe Perrot-Minot   21220 Morey-Saint-Denis
UK stockists: BWC, Bal, Blx, F&R, HHB

Christophe Perrot works with his father to produce wines less extracted than previously but still with impressive power and intensity. The wines can still be quite austere and firm when young but nearly always have the fruit richness underneath to reveal great style and individuality with 7 or 8 years' age or more. Though all the wines are true to the general style, they are also true to their appellations and individual *terroirs*. The Chambolle-Musigny Premier Cru La Combe d'Orveau, adjacent to Le Musigny, is arguably the most classy and complex wine of all, though the *grands crus*, particularly the Chambertin, contrast with greater power and structure. The standard of the range is consistently high, with good Bourgogne Rouge at a lower level. The purchase of the Pernin-Rossin domaine in Vosne-Romanée has enlarged the family's holdings to 14ha. These exciting new wines include some old-vine Nuits-Saint-Georges La Richemone, some Vosne-Romanée Les Beaux-Monts and Gevrey-Chambertin Les Cazetiers. The first releases would seem to have already obtained the same balance, intensity and combination of elegance and vigour seen in the existing wines. Wines are now labelled either Henri Perrot-Minot or Christophe Perrot-Minot. (PW)

● **Chambertin**★★★★ £G ● **Charmes-Chambertin**★★★★ £G
● **Mazoyères-Chambertin**★★★★ £G
● **Morey-Saint-Denis** 1er Cru La Riotte Vieilles Vignes★★★★ £F
● **Morey-Saint-Denis** En la Rue de Vergy★★★ £E
● **Chambolle-Musigny** 1er Cru La Combe d'Orveau★★★★ £F
● **Chambolle-Musigny** Vieilles Vignes★★★ £E 1er Cru Les Fuées★★★★ £F
● **Vosne-Romanée** 1er Cru Les Beaux-Monts★★★★ £F
● **Nuits-Saint-Georges** 1er Cru La Richmone★★★★ £F
● **Gevrey-Chambertin**★★★ £E ● **Bourgogne Rouge**★★ £B

FERNAND ET LAURENT PILLOT   Chassagne-Montrachet

Laurent Pillot 13 Rue des Champgains, 21190 Chassagne-Montrachet
UK stockists: **THt**, L&S

This 14.5-ha estate had its beginnings in the late 19th century. Although it is Chassagne-based, the recent addition of several sites planted to Pinot Noir, mostly in Pommard, means slightly more red is now produced than white. Quality used to be a little uneven and the lesser reds in particular have struggled for ripeness and richness in cooler years. The current releases, however, are very good: 2003 whites are ripe and concentrated if relatively forward while the 02s have structure, intensity and complexity. *Premiers crus* Les Morgeots, Vide Bourse and Grandes-Ruchottes are particularly impressive. Also very good is Meursault Caillerets. The pick of the reds are the Pommard *premiers crus* although the village-level Tavannes shouldn't be overlooked. The 03 Clos des Vergers is elegant and refined while Rugiens (100% new oak) is richer, deeper and very classy. (PW)

O **Chassagne-Montrachet** 1er Cru Grandes Ruchottes★★★★ £E
O **Chassagne-Montrachet** 1er Cru Morgeots★★★★ £E
O **Chassagne-Montrachet** 1er Cru Vide Bourse★★★★ £E
O **Chassagne-Montrachet** 1er Cru Vergers★★★ £E
O **Meursault** 1er Cru Caillerets★★★★ £E
O **Puligny-Montrachet** Noyers Brets★★★ £D
● **Pommard** 1er Cru Rugiens★★★★★ £F
● **Pommard** 1er Cru Clos de Vergers★★★ £E
● **Pommard** Tavannes★★★ £D ● **Volnay**★★★ £D

JEAN PILLOT ET FILS   Chassagne-Montrachet

Pillot family Rue Combard, 21190 Chassagne-Montrachet
UK stockists: C&C, Eno, BBR, CTy, JNi, Hrd

Jean-Marc Pillot runs this family domaine of 10ha. The estate's reputation, like that of the commune (albeit only in modern times), is for whites, yet half the vines are Pinot Noir and this is an increasingly good source of red Chassagne. The whites have long been good but have become more consistent and richer, riper and oakier under Jean-Marc's hand. There is now marvellous concentration, breadth and depth in the top *premiers crus*. A bottle from a fine vintage is particularly rewarding. The reds show proper ripeness and richness too; a particularly oaky version (labelled L'Exception) of the otherwise very

185

good Morgeots was made in 1999. The range is continuing to expand and, as well as very good estate wines, some very fine Puligny-Montrachet Premier Cru Les Caillerets and Chevalier-Montrachet is made from bought-in wine. Good Saint-Romain white, red Santenay and Bourgogne red and white are made in most vintages too. The wines have been labelled both as Jean Pillot et Fils and Jean-Marc Pillot. (PW)

- O **Chassagne-Montrachet** 1er Cru Les Chevenottes★★★★ £E
- O **Chassagne-Montrachet** 1er Cru Caillerets★★★★ £E
- O **Chassagne-Montrachet** 1er Cru Morgeots★★★★ £E 1er Cru Les Vergers★★★★ £E
- O **Chassagne-Montrachet**★★★ £D 1er Cru Les Macherelles★★★ £E
- O **Chassagne-Montrachet** 1er Cru Les Champs Gain★★★ £E
- O **Puligny-Montrachet**★★★ £D ● **Santenay** Champs Claude★★ £C
- ● **Chassagne-Montrachet**★ £C 1er Cru Les Macherelles★★ £D
- ● **Chassagne-Montrachet**★ 1er Cru Morgeots★★★ £D

DOM. PONSOT www.domaine-ponsot.com

Ponsot family 17-21 Rue de la Montagne, 21220 Morey-Saint-Denis
UK stockists: L&W, BBR, Bal, Goe, Las, F&R, Sec

This is a very serious traditional and historic family estate that places huge importance on *terroir* and respect for the soil and the natural order. Laurent Ponsot has gradually assumed control from his father, Jean-Marie over the past decade or so. Several decades of expertise and refinement can be seen in the wines. The Ponsots undertake to pick the grapes as late as possible from vines with an average age of 40 years, though some individual parcels are as much as twice that age. Yields are very low, and naturally so without any green harvesting, which is abhorred. The Ponsots do not have a high tolerance for new oak or sulphur either and their use is kept to a minimum. No two wines are quite alike but there is a strength underpinning the truly marvellous expression and fine, silky textures that can be spellbinding. Though a charge of inconsistency has often been levelled at the domaine's wines, there seems little evidence of this in recent vintages, particularly since atypically good 1997s. The Morey-Saint-Denis white, made mostly from Aligoté in recent vintages, is very full and ripe but structured too, not remotely like most Aligoté. A very small amount of Chambertin is also made. Village Gevrey and Morey can be superb value. (PW)

- ● **Clos de la Roche** Vieilles Vignes✪✪✪✪✪ £H
- ● **Clos Saint-Denis** Vieilles Vignes✪✪✪✪✪ £H
- ● **Griotte-Chambertin**✪✪✪✪✪ £G
- ● **Chapelle-Chambertin**★★★★ £G
- ● **Morey-Saint-Denis** 1er Cru Alouettes★★★★ £E
- ● **Morey-Saint-Denis** Cuvée des Grives★★★ £E
- ● **Gevrey-Chambertin** Cuvée de l'Abeille★★★ £D
- ● **Chambolle-Musigny** 1er Cru Les Charmes★★★ £F
- O **Morey-Saint-Denis** Clos des Mont-Luisants★★★ £E

NICOLAS POTEL www.nicolas-potel.fr

Cottin Frères 21 Rue Thurot, 21700 Nuits-Saint-Georges
UK stockists: GFy, L&W, Bib, BBR, Tan, Gau, JNi, WSc

Nicolas Potel fashioned some seriously good reds with his late father, Gérard at the Domaine de la POUSSE D'OR until 1997 and since then has been employing his talents on an extensive range of bought-in wines. Volnay is still a strength but now he makes a host of others to a generally high standard, though there is some variability, more perhaps as a result of the disparate sources than anything else. Already well-established are some stylish, fragrant Volnays, concentrated Pommards and full, quite classy Nuits-Saint-Georges. His Clos de Vougeot is a fine example of this frustratingly uneven *grand cru*.

This is now an extensive range, only a selection are included below. It is to be hoped that the best sources become long-standing. Romanée Saint-Vivant and other Vosne-Romanée *premiers crus* are also made and still newer wines include Charmes-Chambertin, Chambertin and other northern Côte de Nuits *premiers* and *grands crus*. With Stéphane Aviron, Nicolas Potel applied Burgundian vinification practices to produce a series of cru Beaujolais (see POTEL-AVIRON) from mostly old vine fruit. (PW)

- **Clos de Vougeot**★★★★ £F ● **Grands Echezeaux**★★★★★ £G
- **Bonnes-Mares**★★★★★ £G ● **Echezeaux**★★★★ £F
- **Clos de la Roche**★★★★★ £F ● **Chapelle-Chambertin**★★★★ £F
- **Charmes-Chambertin**★★★★★ £G
- **Gevrey-Chambertin** Ier Cru Combe aux Moines★★★★ £F
- **Vosne-Romanée** Ier Cru Malconsorts★★★★ £F
- **Vosne-Romanée** Ier Cru Beaumonts★★★★ £F
- **Nuits-Saint-Georges** Ier Cru Vaucrains★★★ £E
- **Nuits-Saint-Georges** Ier Cru Roncières★★★ £E
- **Aloxe-Corton** Ier Cru Les Valozières★★★ £E
- **Volnay** Ier Cru Santenots★★★ £E Ier Cru Pitures★★★★ £E
- **Volnay** Vieilles Vignes★★★ £D Ier Cru Champans★★★ £E
- **Pommard** Ier Cru Epenots★★★ £E Ier Cru Rugiens★★★ £E
- **Beaune** Ier Cru Epenottes★★★ £D Ier Cru Grèves★★★ £D
- **Savigny-lès-Beaune** Vieilles Vignes★★★ £C
- **Bourgogne Rouge**★★ £B

DOM. DE LA POUSSE D'OR   Volnay   www.lapoussedor.fr

Patrick Landanger   Dom. de la Pousse d'Or, 21190 Volnay
UK stockists: DLW, HRp

After an initial dip in quality following the death of Gérard Potel (and its subsequent sale in 1997) this famous estate has been gradually revitalised. The 15ha include the *premier cru* Volnay *monopoles* of La Bousse d'Or (2.14ha) and celebrated 2.4-ha Clos des 60 Ouvrées (in the centre of Caillerets) as well as new purchases of parcels in Corton-Bressandes and Corton-Clos du Roi. New owner Patrick Landanger has overseen many changes including a further reduction in yields, extended maceration times and an increased percentage of new oak. The 2002s of both Volnays are impressively complex and meaty with lots of depth and style although it remains to be seen how well they will age. Also made is a very good Santenay from a leading site, Clos Tavannes. The Cortons will be rated with further tastings. (PW)

- **Volnay** Ier Cru Clos de la Bousse d'Or★★★★ £F
- **Volnay** Ier Cru Clos des 60 Ouvrées★★★★ £F
- **Santenay** Ier Cru Clos Tavannes★★★ £D

DOM. JACQUES PRIEUR

SCI Dom. Jacques Prieur   6 Rue des Santenots, 21190 Meursault
UK stockists: BBR, L&S, Blx, Las, F&R

This prestigious estate is run by Martin Prieur and Bertrand Devillard (of Antonin RODET). There are 21ha, two-thirds to Pinot Noir, one-third to Chardonnay including some of the finest *premier* and *grand cru* vineyards of the Côte d'Or. Its previously flagging reputation has been revived in the most recent vintages by Rodet's winemaker, Nadine Gublin. The Jacques Prieur whites are rich, ripe and powerful though sometimes at the expense of expression and finesse and include *grands crus* Le Montrachet, Chevalier-Montrachet and Corton-Charlemagne, and *premiers crus* Meursault Perrières and Puligny-Montrachet Les Combettes. Reds include *grands crus* Musigny, Echezeaux, Chambertin, Clos de Vougeot and Corton Bressandes; and *premiers crus* from Volnay (Santenots and *monopole* Clos des Santenots) and Beaune (Grèves, Champs Pimont and *monopole* Clos de la Féguine). Reds are more

187

consistently improved than whites. Further wines will be rated with more consistent notes. (PW)

● **Corton Bressandes★★★★** £G ● **Clos de Vougeot★★★★★** £G
● **Volnay** 1er Cru Clos des Santenots★★★ £F
● **Beaune** 1er Cru Champs Pimont★★★ £F
● **Beaune** 1er Cru Clos de la Féguine★★★ £F 1er Cru Grèves★★★★ £F
○ **Corton-Charlemagne★★★★** £G

RAMONET Chassagne-Montrachet

Ramonet family 21190 Chassagne-Montrachet
UK stockists: C&B, Far, OWL, HRp, Sel

Ramonet is another of the great white Burgundy estates. There is a division of responsibilities between brothers Jean-Claude and Noël Ramonet but it is Noël who makes the wines. There are 17ha of mostly first-rate Chassagne-Montrachet vineyard plus a little of 3 *grands crus* in Puligny, which makes for a fantastic array of wines. The winemaking is somewhat intuitive and responsive to the vintage conditions but usually results in wines that have an explosive concentration and breadth within a powerful structure. Only occasionally has anything less than very good wine been produced in the last couple of decades but there is some variability, with a tendency to be almost too structured and slightly hard in some instances. Others have lacked balance, with excess alcohol for the fruit concentration, and there can be a reductive quality in others. However these are the exceptions and can be avoided by taking the precaution of tasting and/or comparing notes of a specific wine and vintage before adding 1 or more of these great wines to a cellar (an approach advisable not just here but anywhere that involves the kind of sums the world's best wines now command). Reds play second fiddle to the whites but have been very good in recent good vintages including some Chassagne-Montrachet Premier Cru La Boudriotte (owned by Noël Ramonet and sold under his own label). A little Montrachet is made, as is some Puligny-Montrachet Premier Cru Champ Canet, while some Chevalier-Montrachet is produced from bought-in wine. (PW)

○ **Bâtard-Montrachet✪✪✪✪** £H
○ **Bienvenues-Bâtard-Montrachet★★★★★** £H
○ **Chassagne-Montrachet** 1er Cru Grandes Ruchottes★★★★★ £F
○ **Chassagne-Montrachet** 1er Cru Caillerets★★★★ £F
○ **Chassagne-Montrachet** 1er Cru Morgeots★★★★ £F
○ **Chassagne-Montrachet** 1er Cru Boudriottes★★★★ £F
○ **Chassagne-Montrachet** 1er Cru Les Vergers★★★ £F
○ **Chassagne-Montrachet★★** £E 1er Cru Les Chaumées★★★ £F
○ **Saint-Aubin** 1er Cru Le Charmois★★ £D ○ **Bourgogne Aligoté★** £B
● **Chassagne-Montrachet** 1er Cru Clos de la Boudriotte★★★ £E
● **Chassagne-Montrachet** 1er Cru Morgeots★★ £E
● **Chassagne-Montrachet★** £D 1er Cru Clos Saint Jean★★ £F

DOM. RAPET PÈRE ET FILS Pernand-Vergelesses

Rapet family Rue des Paulands, 21420 Pernand-Vergelesses
UK stockists: Anl, Goe, HRp

The input of Vincent Rapet over recent vintages has given a considerable boost to this long-established domaine. Though some two-thirds of the 18ha are planted to Pinot Noir, the reputation rests as much with the whites as reds. The core of the production is very good Pernand-Vergelesses but fine examples of Corton and Corton-Charlemagne are also made. There is now better grape selection, the whites have longer lees-contact than previously and show good depth, richness and restrained oak. Reds can be sturdy, occasionally with slightly coarse tannins, but generally show more refinement and depth in the most recent vintages, particularly in the very stylish Pernand-Vergelesses. All the better reds should be drunk with 5 years' or more, but whites can be drunk younger. New from 1999 is a second Beaune *premier cru*, Grèves. From the 2000 vintage white Pernand-Vergelesses is now being bottled as separate specified *premiers crus* (including Le Clos du Village, En Caradeux and Sous Frétille) following the recent promotion of some village land. (PW)

- ● **Corton**★★★★ £E ● **Corton Pougets**★★★★ £E
- ● **Pernand-Vergelesses** 1er Cru Île de Vergelesses★★★ £E
- ● **Pernand-Vergelesses** 1er Cru Les Vergelesses★★ £D
- ● **Beaune** 1er Cru Clos du Roi★★★ £D 1er Cru Grèves★★★ £D
- ● **Aloxe-Corton**★★ £D
- O **Corton-Charlemagne**★★★★ £F
- O **Pernand-Vergelesses** 1er Cru Sous Frétille★★★ £D
- O **Pernand-Vergelesses** 1er Cru En Caradeux★★ £D
- O **Pernand-Vergelesses** 1er Cru Clos du Village★★ £D

FRANÇOIS RAQUILLET Mercurey

François Raquillet 19 Rue de Jamproyes, 71640 Mercurey
UK stockists: THt, FMV, NYg, P&S, F&M, Sel

François Raquillet is a young vigneron who is turning his family's 11ha of vineyards into some of the most prized in Mercurey. A series of *premiers crus* reds benefit from being part aged in new oak resulting in wines of good colour, intensity but also accessibility. The purity of fruit is retained but the firmness of some Mercurey is usually avoided. Naugues is the most sophisticated but there is good intensity and character in all the reds. 2001s are good in the context of the vintage but 2002s are richer and more promising. As well as the wines listed below a small amount of Premier Cru Clos l'Eveque is also made. Most recently a small amount of grapes is also being bought-in to supplement the existing grape supply. (PW)

- ● **Mercurey** 1er Cru Puillets★★ £C 1er Cru Naugues★★★ £C
- ● **Mercurey** 1er Cru Vasées★★ £C 1er Cru Veleys★★ £C
- ● **Mercurey** Vieilles Vignes★★ £C O **Mercurey** 1er Cru Veleys★★ £C

DOM. DANIEL RION ET FILS www.domaine-daniel-rion.com

Rion family 21700 Prémeaux-Prissey
UK stockists: CTy, N&P, JNi, WSc

Christophe and Olivier are now making the wines here on their own after the departure of their brother, Patrice (Michèle & Patrice RION), following the 2000 vintage. Over the course of 2 decades Patrice had established a solid reputation for this estate created by his father. The 19ha is based primarily on Nuits-Saint-Georges and Vosne vineyards and includes some Chardonnay and Aligoté as well as Pinot Noir. The wines have long been characterised by their strength and a certain firmness allied to depth and intensity. In recent years there has been a gradual shift to finer tannins and more immediate richness and the wines are particularly successful in the best years, if sometimes a little harsh or tough in lighter vintages. Beaumonts, in particular is a classic old vine expression of Vosne-Romanée. Produced since the 1998 vintage are an Echezeaux as well as Clos de Vougeot from a different source to that previously made. The reds shouldn't be rushed, in fact they can be transformed with a little extra bottle age. The rich creamy white Nuits is produced from Pinot Blanc. (PW)

- ● **Clos de Vougeot**★★★★★ £F
- ● **Vosne-Romanée** 1er Cru Beaux-Monts★★★★★ £E
- ● **Vosne-Romanée**★★ £D 1er Cru Chaumes★★★★ £E
- ● **Nuits-Saint-Georges** 1er Cru Vignes Rondes★★★★ £E
- ● **Nuits-Saint-Georges** 1er Cru Hauts-Pruliers★★★ £E

189

- **Nuits-Saint-Georges** Grandes Vignes★★★ £D
- **Nuits-Saint-Georges** Lavières★★ £D Vieilles Vignes★★★ £E
- **Côte de Nuits-Villages** Le Vaucrain★★ £C
- O **Nuits-Saint-Georges** 1er Cru Terres Blanches★★★ £E

MICHÈLE & PATRICE RION   Nuits-Saint-Georges

Rion family   21700 Prémeaux-Prissey
UK stockists: FMV, NYg, UnC

Some very good wine was made by Patrice Rion for his own label even before he handed over the winemaking reins at the family domaine (Daniel RION ET FILS) to his 2 brothers. From 2000 the range here has been greatly expanded to include bought-in wines but these are labelled as simply Patrice Rion. Given an insistence on high-quality fruit, this promises to be a good quality range of *négociant* wines. The estate range has been expanded too with recent additions including an intense, full Chambolle-Musigny Les Charmes and very classy Nuits-Saint-Georges Clos des Argillières. 2002s are much superior to 2003s. (PW)

Dom. Michèle & Patrice Rion:
- **Chambolle-Musigny** Les Cras★★★ £E 1er Cru Charmes★★★★ £F
- **Nuits-Saint-Georges** 1er Cru Clos des Argillières★★★★ £F
- **Bourgogne Rouge** Bons Batons★★ £C

Patrice Rion:
- **Gevrey-Chambertin** Clos Prieur★★★★ £E
- **Nuits-Saint-Georges** Vieilles Vignes★★★ £E

ANTONIN RODET   Mercurey   www.rodet.com

Worms & Cie   Antonin Rodet, 71640 Mercurey
UK stockists: BBR, C&R, MCW, Las, N&P

Directed by Bertrand Devillard, this is a *négociant* house with substantial holdings in both the Côte d'Or and Côte Chalonnaise. The following estates are all either owned, partly owned or made and distributed by Antonin Rodet: Château de Rully (Rully), Château de Mercey (Maranges-based for Hautes Côtes de Beaune red and white, and Mercurey), Château de Chamirey (Mercurey), Domaine des Perdrix (Bertrand Devillard's own 12-ha property in Nuits-Saint-Georges) and the Meursault-based Domaine Jacques PRIEUR. The best wines under the Antonin Rodet label (many of them designated Cave Privée) are consistently very good indeed, at times quite oaky but rich and ripe, with great depth and complexity. Those listed include some of the best wines made on a regular basis. At a humbler level there are some remarkably good Côte Chalonnaise wines under the respective estate labels. In addition, as well as a range of Vin de Pays d'Oc varietals Antonin Rodet also owns the Domaine de l'AIGLE in Limoux, Languedoc-Roussillon. (PW)

Antonin Rodet:
- **Charmes-Chambertin**★★★★ £G ● **Clos de Vougeot**★★★★ £G
- **Gevrey-Chambertin** 1er Cru Estournelles★★★★ £F
- **Nuits-Saint-Georges** 1er Cru Les Saint-Georges★★★ £F
- **Nuits-Saint-Georges** 1er Cru Porêts-Saint-Georges★★★★ £F
- O **Meursault** 1er Cru Perrières★★★★ £F
- O **Bourgogne Blanc** Vieilles Vignes★★ £C

Domaine des Perdrix:
- **Echezeaux**★★★★ £G ● **Vosne-Romanée**★★★ £E
- **Nuits-Saint-Georges**★★★ £E 1er Cru Aux Perdrix★★★★★ £F

Château de Chamirey:
- O **Mercurey**★ £C 1er Cru La Mission★★ £D
- **Mercurey**★★ £C 1er Cru Les Ruelles★★★ £D

Château de Mercey:
O **Bourgogne Hautes-Côtes de Beaune**★ £B
O **Mercurey**★ £C ● **Mercurey** 1er Cru En Sazenay★★ £C
● **Bourgogne Hautes-Côtes de Beaune**★ £B

Château de Rully:
O **Rully**★★ £C ● **Rully**★ £C

DOM. DE LA ROMANÉE-CONTI Vosne-Romanée

de Vilaine and Leroy/Bize/Roch families   21700 Vosne-Romanée
UK stockists: **C&B**, BBR, F&M, Hrd, Las, F&R

DRC, as it referred to by both devotees and novices alike, is considered by many to be Burgundy's greatest domaine. The history and nobility of these famous *grand cru* vineyards make this a difficult assertion to refute, though over the past decade this domaine has been seriously challenged by part-owner Lalou Bize-Leroy's own estate, Domaine LEROY. Any serious text on Burgundy will provide background on both the estate and individual wines. Currently yields are lower than previously, the average vine age is now high across all the wines and the viticulture is now essentially biodynamic (in practice if not in name), making for healthier soils than previously. The most distinctive features of the vinification are that there is little or no destemming and automatic punching down is carried out. All the wines see 100% new oak. Individual wines seem to have had slight ups and downs but when on form they all rate 5 stars. Montrachet apart, all are made in decent quantities by Burgundian standards, assuming, that is, you can afford them. The holdings are: La Romanée Conti (1.81ha), La Tâche (6.06ha), Richebourg (3.51ha), Romanée-Saint-Vivant (5.28ha), Echezeaux (4.67ha), Grands-Echezeaux (3.53ha) and the solitary white, Le Montrachet (0.68ha). All the wines are £H. The first 2 are *monopoles* and are considered the brightest stars in the firmament, while the other reds account for a substantial proportion of the vineyard area of their respective appellations. A second selection, Cuvée Duvault-Blochet, sold as Vosne Romanée Premier Cru, was produced in 1999 and 2002. (PW)

ROSSIGNOL-TRAPET Gevrey-Chambertin

N & D Rossignol   4 Rue de la Petite Issue, 21220 Gevrey-Chambertin
UK stockists: **C&B, CTy**

The other half of the original Louis Trapet domaine. Jacques Rossignol, with his 2 sons, Nicolas and David, has been able to exploit the same impressive *crus* in Gevrey-Chambertin as Domaine TRAPET among 13ha of organically farmed vineyards. The wines have until recently been somewhat disappointing but are now beginning to make a more consistent and coherent range. As well as 1.6ha of Chambertin there are significant plots in Latricières-Chambertin and Chapelle-Chambertin. The wines show good dimension and fruit intensity with something of their origins and there is increased elegance in Petite Chapelle and more class in Chambertin. If there is anything still missing it is the extra depth and concentration that equivalent wines from other producers show. However, the 2003s are the best yet tasted and are much more reasonably priced than most. Savigny-lès-Beaune and Bourgogne Rouge are also made. (PW)

● **Chambertin**★★★★ £F
● **Gevrey-Chambertin** 1er Cru Petite Chapelle★★★ £E
● **Gevrey-Chambertin**★★★ £D 1er Cru Clos Prieur★★★ £E
● **Beaune** 1er Cru Teurons★★ £D

EMMANUEL ROUGET Vosne-Romanée

Emmanuel Rouget Flagey-Echezeaux, 21700 Vosne-Romanée
UK stockists: J&B, RsW, BBR, F&R, Sec

Emmanuel Rouget is the nephew of Henri Jayer and has retained a portion of the vineyards that Jayer, one of the great 20th-century figures in Burgundy, made famous. Jayer's use of a cold pre-fermentation maceration, 100% destemming, plenty of new oak, no filtration and rigorous attention to hygiene transformed the face of Burgundy as many others followed in his footsteps. Rouget's early efforts looked promising but some of the wines from vintages in the late 1990s and more recently seem to have lost a bit of the vigour and concentration of old. Yet quality is still good with no lack of style or class. Prices however are very high. (PW)

- **Echezeaux**★★★★ £H
- **Vosne-Romanée** 1er Cru Cros Parentoux★★★★ £H
- **Vosne-Romanée**★★ £G 1er Cru Les Beaumonts★★★ £H
- **Nuits-Saint-Georges**★★ £F ● **Bourgogne Rouge**★ £C

DOM. ROULOT Meursault www.domaineroulot.com

Roulot family 1 Rue Charles Giraud, 21190 Meursault
UK stockists: DDr, HHC, HRp, JAr, BWC

Since 1989 Jean-Marc Roulot has run this highly respected domaine with a hatful of Meursault *crus*, built up by his father Guy some 30 years earlier. The wines show something of a leesy character and and some new oak influence but neither dominate and the percentage of new oak is sometimes less than 20%. The *premiers crus* Charmes, Perrières (and more recently, Bouchères) are the top wines, the Perrières easily the most complex and complete of the 3, but this is reflected in their prices. The most significant proportion of the estate's 12ha comes from vineyards lying on higher slopes running towards Auxey-Duresses. Les Tessons and Les Tillets (from vines with a high average age) are arguably the pick of these and offer relatively good value for Meursault. Though majoring on Meursault, Roulot also produces an intense, vibrant, minerally Monthelie *premier cru* that adds richness with 2 or 3 years' age. Bourgogne Aligoté and a flavoursome, scented Bourgogne Blanc are more than dependable. (PW)

- O **Meursault** 1er Cru Charmes★★★★ £F 1er Cru Perrières★★★★★ £F
- O **Meursault** Les Tessons★★★★ £D 1er Cru Bouchères★★★★ £F
- O **Meursault** Les Luchets★★★ £D Les Tillets★★★★ £D
- O **Meursault** Les Vireuils★★★ £D Meix Chavaux★★★ £D
- O **Monthelie** 1er Cru Champs Fulliot★★ £C
- O **Bourgogne Blanc**★★ £B O **Bourgogne Aligoté**★ £B

DOM. ROUMIER www.roumier.com

Christophe Roumier Rue de Vergy, 21220 Chambolle-Musigny
UK stockists: JAr, HHC, DDr, HRp, FMV, Tan, Las

A fabulous domaine whose wines express the essence of Chambolle-Musigny. Christophe Roumier has now had 2 decades of input, achieving ever better balance in his vineyards and maximising the potential of each site. The vines are of a high average age and low-yielding, but naturally so without the need for the excessive pruning or green harvesting required elsewhere. Quality is consistently high but that is not to say the wines are the same year in, year out; rather each expresses something of the vintage without its defects. What is most impressive is the structure of the wines; always there's a dimension and depth without a trace of hardness, allied to harmony and persistence. The Chambolles, in particular, are fragrant and elegant with more power, depth and concentration in the *premiers crus*. In the *grands crus* the power and elegance of Le Musigny contrasts with the muscle, intensity and grip of Bonnes Mares. From outside Chambolle-Musigny, the 2.5-ha *monopole* Clos de la Bussière in

Morey-Saint-Denis produces a firmer, tighter wine, now showing more refinement and class than previously, and it can be very good value. Tiny amounts of very high quality Ruchottes-Chambertin and Charmes-Chambertin are also made, as is a little Corton-Charlemagne. (PW)

- ● Le Musigny✪✪✪✪✪ £H ● Bonnes Mares✪✪✪✪✪ £H
- ● Chambolle-Musigny 1er Cru Les Amoureuses✪✪✪✪✪ £G
- ● Chambolle-Musigny★★★ £D 1er Cru Les Cras★★★★★ £F
- ● Morey-Saint-Denis 1er Cru Clos de la Bussière★★★★ £E
- ● Bourgogne Rouge★★ £B

DOM. A ROUSSEAU www.domaine-rousseau.com

Charles Rousseau 1 Rue de l'Aumônerie, 21220 Gevrey-Chambertin
UK stockists: HRp, BBR, HBJ, OWL, Las, F&M, Hrd

Eric Rousseau and his sister, Corinne are gradually assuming control of this the most famous Gevrey-Chambertin domaine that has been directed by their father, Charles Rousseau, for more than 40 years. The estate was built up in the early part of the 20th century by their grandfather Armand but was further enlarged by Charles. A remarkable 8ha of the 14ha planted exclusively to Pinot Noir are *grands crus*. Only a small percentage of the stems are retained to assist a moderately long vinification complete with automatic *pigeage*. The top wines, Chambertin and Chambertin Clos-de-Bèze, show all the class and breed of great *grand cru* Burgundy, with a breadth and presence in the mouth that even the very best *premiers crus* lack. These and the Clos Saint-Jacques receive 100% new oak but the oak treatment is rarely, if ever, excessive, though shows more in the Clos-de-Bèze than the Chambertin. Other *crus* receive at most 30% new oak. In the Charmes-Chambertin and Mazy-Chambertin finesse and elegance are emphasised yet there is a vigour and intensity about all the wines. The textures of all the Rousseau wines are very impressive too, even if other wines may provide greater richness and extract. All the wines need 5 years, the top wines 10 or more. The Premier Cru Lavaux Saint-Jacques, previously part of the regular Gevrey, has been bottled separately since 1999. The 2002s are superlative with splendid Clos des Ruchottes and stunning Chambertin. (PW)

- ● Chambertin✪✪✪✪✪ £H ● Chambertin Clos-de-Bèze✪✪✪✪✪ £H
- ● Ruchottes-Chambertin Clos des Ruchottes✪✪✪✪✪ £G
- ● Mazy-Chambertin★★★★★ £F
- ● Charmes-Chambertin★★★★ £F ● Clos de la Roche★★★★★ £F
- ● Gevrey-Chambertin 1er Cru Clos Saint-Jacques✪✪✪✪✪ £F
- ● Gevrey-Chambertin 1er Cru Les Cazetiers★★★★★ £F
- ● Gevrey-Chambertin★★★ £E 1er Cru Lavaux-Saint-Jacques★★★★ £F

ETIENNE SAUZET www.etienne-sauzet.com

G & J Boudot 11 Rue de Poiseul, 21190 Puligny-Montrachet
UK stockists: HHC, L&W, OWL, BBR, Hrd, Tan, JAr Las, Maj

This estate has a fabulous reputation and highly respected winemaker in Gérard Boudot. However it is now significantly smaller than it once was. Gérard's wife, Jeanine Boudot, grand daughter of Étienne Sauzet, has retained only a third of the vines, though their company has another third under contract for some time to come (the rest of the legacy has gone to brother Jean-Marc BOILLOT). There are now 8ha (but much boosted by bought-in grapes) with small amounts of 4 *grands crus* (Bâtard-Montrachet, Bienvenues-Bâtard-Montrachet, Le Montrachet and Chevalier-Montrachet) and more significant amounts of some of Puligny's best *premiers crus*. Form in the 1990s was irregular, the winesometimes lean and slightly undistinguished - missing some of the class and finesse for which they are famous. Nor have they always aged as well as previously. High demand has of course contributed to high prices but some caution should be taken before investing heavily. Ratings are based on the best

193

recent vintages, 1999 and 2002. (PW)

○ **Le Montrachet**★★★★★ £H ○ **Bâtard-Montrachet**★★★★ £H
○ **Chevalier-Montrachet**★★★★★ £H
○ **Bienvenue-Bâtard-Montrachet**★★★★★ £H
○ **Puligny-Montrachet** 1er Cru Les Perrières★★★★ £F
○ **Puligny-Montrachet** 1er Cru Champ-Canet★★★★ £F
○ **Puligny-Montrachet** 1er Cru Les Referts★★★★ £F
○ **Puligny-Montrachet** 1er Cru Les Combettes★★★★ £F
○ **Puligny-Montrachet** 1er Cru La Garenne★★★ £F
○ **Puligny-Montrachet**★★★ £E 1er Cru Les Folatières★★★ £F

COMTE SENARD Aloxe-Corton www.domainesenard.com

Senard family 7 Rempart Saint-Jean, 21200 Aloxe-Corton
UK stockists: Anl, F&R

Philippe Senard was one of those to work with the controversial consultant
Guy Accad in the early 1990s, aiming for more colour and greater aroma and
fruit intensity, in part from an extended cold maceration on skins prior to
fermentation. Like other producers advised by Accad, he gradually incorporated
the best of his advice to make stylish, aromatic and intensely fruity red
Burgundies. More recently his daughter, Lorraine has assumed responsibility for
the winemaking. Some of the lesser wines can struggle for full ripeness but
typically there is a cool, pure vibrant fruit intensity to which is added more
breadth, length and elegance in the various Cortons. This is a good cellar from
which to compare several different Cortons including gentle but broad framed
monopole Clos des Meix with deep, intense Bressandes, and refined and
harmonious Clos du Roi. En Charlemagne has cool, classy fruit but the least of
these. All deserve at least 5 years' age. Good whites are also made, including an
Aloxe-Corton from old-vine Pinot Gris, while a Corton Blanc is gaining in
richness and complexity. Other reds include a Chorey-lès-Beaune and a *premier
cru* Beaune. Ratings apply only to top years. The Senards also make the wines
of Domaine des Terregelesses. (PW)

● **Corton** Bressandes★★★★ £F ● **Corton** Clos du Roi★★★★ £F
● **Corton** Clos des Meix★★★★ £F ● **Corton** En Charlemagne★★★ £F
● **Aloxe-Corton**★ £D 1er Cru Les Valozières★★ £E
○ **Corton** Blanc★★★★ £F ○ **Aloxe-Corton**★★ £D

CHRISTIAN SÉRAFIN Gevrey-Chambertin

Christian Sérafin 7 Place du Château, 21220 Gevrey-Chambertin
UK stockists: Eno, Goe, BBR F&R

Christian Sérafin has been quietly working away on his family's small 5-ha
estate, gradually refining his winemaking practices and producing ever more
satisfying and consistently good wines. His signature is the power that might be
expected from Gevrey together with plenty of oak and spice that embellish
wines that are lush and fruit-rich, with lots of obvious appeal. The top *crus* add
more class and breadth. The best wine made in any real quantity is the Vieilles
Vignes bottling, which is meaty and full of ripe fruit, with plenty of depth. All
the wines show very well with just 5 years' age. A tiny amount of top-quality
Charmes-Chambertin is also made but is likely to be hard to find. (PW)

● **Gevrey-Chambertin** 1er Cru Les Cazetiers★★★★★ £F
● **Gevrey-Chambertin** 1er Cru Les Corbeaux★★★★ £F
● **Gevrey-Chambertin** 1er Cru Fontenys★★★★ £F
● **Gevrey-Chambertin**★★★ £E Vieilles Vignes★★★★ £E
● **Chambolle-Musigny** 1er Cru Les Baudes★★★★ £F
● **Morey-Saint-Denis** 1er Cru Les Millandes★★★★ £F

TOLLOT-BEAUT   Chorey-lès-Beaune

Tollot families   Rue Alexandre Tollot, 21200 Chorey-lès-Beaune
UK stockists: DDr, Adm, L&W, OWL, Tan, HHB

Tollot-Beaut's 24-ha estate includes some of the northern Côte de Beaune's lesser but better-value appellations. With lots of new oak and ripe, forward fruit, the wines have had plenty of appeal in the past but also a tendency to lack a little structure despite some firm tannins and some have aged quite quickly. However since 1999 the wines have shown better definition and balance and, if less upfront, will have much more to offer with 4 or 5 years' age than previously. It has always been a team effort but the current members in charge, Nathalie, Jean-Paul and Olivier, look set to make better wines than ever before. Yields have been lowered, though they were never high. The Chorey-lès-Beaune is a very attractive, relatively inexpensive red Burgundy, even better in the La Pièce du Chapitre bottling. Only a little white is made but includes some Corton-Charlemagne. There are new labels but prices remain much the same. Ratings apply to the most recent vintages only. (PW)

- ● **Corton**★★★★ £F ● **Corton** Bressandes★★★★ £F
- ● **Aloxe-Corton** ler Cru Fournières★★★ £E
- ● **Aloxe-Corton**★★ £D ler Cru Vercots★★★ £E
- ● **Beaune** ler Cru Clos du Roi★★★ £E ler Cru Grèves★★★ £E
- ● **Chorey-lès-Beaune**★★ £C Pièce du Chapitre★★★ £D
- ● **Savigny-lès-Beaune** ler Cru Lavières★★★ £D
- ● **Savigny-lès-Beaune** ler Cru Champs Chevrey★★ £D

DOM. TORTOCHOT   Gevrey-Chambertin   www.tortochot.com

Chantal & Michel Tortochot   21220 Gevrey-Chambertin
UK stockists: **FMV**, BBR

Recently much improved Gevrey-Chambertin estate. After taking over from her father, Chantal Tortochot has produced wines with better restraint, balance and expression. The wines still have impressive colour and intensity with plenty of extract and from 2002 and 03 will be very good if given sufficient time. Village Gevrey *lieux-dits* need 5 years; a classy, pure but powerful Premier Cru Lavaux-Saint-Jacques needs 6–8 years; while *grands crus* Charmes-Chambertin (with impressive breadth and extract to match) and Mazy-Chambertin (powerful, concentrated and black-fruited) deserve a full 10 years' ageing. Regular Morey-Saint-Denis from 2003 is also well made with lots of extract, character and ripe tannins. Also made are a tiny amount of Chambertin and some Gevrey-Chambertin Premier Cru Les Champeaux. (PW)

- ● **Mazy-Chambertin**★★★★★ £F ● **Charmes-Chambertin**★★★★ £F
- ● **Gevrey-Chambertin** ler Cru Lavaux-Saint-Jacques★★★★ £F
- ● **Gevrey-Chambertin** Les Corvées★★★ £E
- ● **Gevrey-Chambertin** Champerrier Vieilles Vignes★★★ £E
- ● **Gevrey-Chambertin** Jeunes Rois★★ £D
- ● **Morey-Saint-Denis**★★★ £D

DOM. TRAPET PÈRE ET FILS   www.domaine-trapet.com

Jean et Jean-Louis Trapet   53 Route de Beaune, 21220 Gevrey-Chambertin
UK stockists: C&B, C&C, Hrd, F&R

The original Domaine Louis Trapet (source of some famous bottles from the 1950s and 60s) was built up from the late 19th century before being divided in 1990 between Jean and his sister (ROSSIGNOL-TRAPET). Jean's son, Jean-Louis, has revived their venerable vineyards, which include nearly 2ha of Chambertin and decent segments of Chapelle-Chambertin and Latricières-Chambertin. The raw material is now of much higher quality than previously, with reduced yields from higher than typical vine densities under a regime that

195

became progressively more biodynamic in the late 1990s. The 13ha also includes some excellent Premier Cru Petite Chapelle and Clos Prieur as well as village Gevrey-Chambertin and Marsannay. There is a measured use of new oak but the accent is on the quality of the fruit and producing wines of finesse and real class. There is great depth and dimension as well as a particular strength and definition characteristic to the wines, which require patience. Five years' is needed for Gevrey, 5–10 for the *premiers crus*, and a minimum of 10 for Chambertin. Given time these wines are some of the very best from Gevrey and are reasonably priced in that context. (PW)

● **Chambertin★★★★★** £G ● **Latricières-Chambertin★★★★★** £G
● **Gevrey-Chambertin** Ier Cru Clos Prieur★★★★ £F
● **Gevrey-Chambertin★★★** £D Ier Cru Petite Chapelle★★★★ £F
● **Marsannay★★** £C

VERGET www.verget-sa.com

Jean-Marie Guffens-Heynen & others 71960 Sologny
UK stockists: Far, L&S, L&W, BBR, Odd, F&R, Las, C&R

In just over a decade Jean-Marie Guffens has constructed a merchant house of remarkable constitution. It is not built around the great *crus* of the Côte de Beaune, though there are some of those, but rather the less hallowed vineyards of the Mâconnais and increasingly Chablis, where a new winemaking base has been established in conjunction with Olivier LEFLAIVE for their joint but independent use. The Mâconnais wines (including Pouilly-Fuissé, Saint-Veran and various Mâcon-Villages) are covered, together with the wines of his own private estate, GUFFENS-HEYNEN in the Mâconnais section. The wines from the Côte d'Or are true to the Verget style, which is one of great extract, concentration and richness, made from fully ripe grapes sourced from low-yielding vineyards. The wines from Chablis are also deep and concentrated but a little tighter, cooler and more minerally than his other wines (particularly in contrast to the Mâconnais wines). Largely eschewing the use of oak here, the wines are riper and fuller, if slightly less steely, than examples from other producers but nevertheless archetypal Chablis and very fine. Almost all of the Verget wines can be broached fairly young but should keep for a decade. (PW)

○ **Bâtard-Montrachet★★★★** £H ○ **Corton-Charlemagne★★★★** £E
○ **Meursault** Tillets★★★★ £E Rougeots★★★ £E
○ **Chassagne-Montrachet** Franchemont★★★ £E
○ **Puligny-Montrachet** Ier Cru Sous le Puits★★★ £F
○ **Puligny-Montrachet** Enseignières★★★ £F
○ **Chablis Grand Cru** Bougros Côte de Bougueyraud★★★★ £F
○ **Chablis Premier Cru** Montée de Tonnerre★★★ £E Vaillons★★★★ £D
○ **Chablis Premier Cru** Les Forêts★★★ £D

AUBERT ET PAMÉLA DE VILLAINE www.de-villaine.com

Aubert et Paméla de Villaine 2 Rue de la Fontaine, 71150 Bouzeron
UK stockists: **C&B**, ACh

Aubert de Villaine, co-director of the Côte d'Or's most prestigious estate (Domaine de la ROMANÉE-CONTI), and his wife Paméla continue to improve on their pure, natural expressions of the Côte Chalonnaise. More than half of 21ha is planted to Aligoté (the grape which dominates the appellation) and a fine characterful example - as good as any produced - is made along with Bourgogne red and white and some red Mercurey and white Rully. The wines are elegant and harmonious with definition and vibrancy in both reds. All are better with 2 or 3 years' age, including the Aligoté. (PW)

● **Mercurey** Les Montots★★ £C
● **Bourgogne Côte Chalonnaise** La Digoine★★ £C

O **Rully** Les Saint-Jacques★★ £C O **Bouzeron Aligoté**★★ £B
O **Bourgogne Côte Chalonnaise** Les Cloux★★ £C

DOM. COMTE GEORGES DE VOGÜÉ

Ladoucette family   Rue Sainte Barbe, 21220 Chambolle-Musigny
UK stockists: Men, DWS, JAr, BBR, F&M, Far, Sec, Las, Hrd, N&P

This estate is known for one of the single greatest red Burgundies made. The Musigny has an exalted reputation based in part on the on-going quality of the wine but also on some legendary old vintages (including 1945, 47, 59, 69 and 72). The domaine owns 7.2ha of the 10.7ha *grand cru*, though this includes 0.5ha of Musigny Blanc (recently sold as Bourgogne Blanc), the only place in the commune of Chambolle-Musigny where Chardonnay is permitted to be grown. François Millet has made the wines here since the Comte died in 1986 and his daughter took over the running of the estate. Vine age is high and yields vary but are kept low; adjustments are made where necessary in response to vintage conditions. The approach to vinification is also vintage-responsive, with individual parcels of vineyard treated in different ways, though a long *cuvaison* is favoured. Since 1990 few if any expert tasters have been left in any doubt about the true greatness of the Musigny Vieilles Vignes after some leaner offerings in the 1970s and 80s. The wine is now more deeply coloured than previously and its extraordinary aromatics, with preserved fruits and floral notes, precede a considerable structure that underpins the silky texture, wonderful definition and mouthfilling dimension on the palate that becomes increasingly opulent with age, the intense flavours being sustained long on the finish. Its remarkable longevity from top vintages make it a cellaring must for the few who can afford it. There is wonderful class, intensity and concentration in the Amoureuses too; and a rich, sturdy, darker fruit density to the Bonnes Mares. (PW)

● **Musigny** Vieilles Vignes✪✪✪✪✪ £H ● **Bonnes Mares**★★★★★ £H
● **Chambolle-Musigny**★★★ £F 1er Cru Les Amoureuses★★★★★ £H

DOM. DE LA VOUGERAIE   www.domainedelavougeraie.com

Boisset   Rue de l'Église, 21700 Premeaux-Prissey
UK stockists: Hay, FMV, L&W, BWC

This newcomer is a southern Côte de Nuits-based estate that comprises all of Boisset's (Burgundy's single biggest producer) own vineyards. Boisset recruited Pascal Marchand, the very highly regarded winemaker of the Clos des Epeneaux (Comte ARMAND) in Pommard, to direct operations. He made the wines in 1999 but has only assumed full responsibility for both viticulture and winemaking from 2000. The vineyards total an impressive 37ha, which are certified organic and now treated biodynamically, predominantly planted to Pinot Noir and much of it in the Côte de Nuits. Yields are low (less than 30 hl/ha in the reds), which is immediately apparent in wines of richness, depth and class. Gevrey-Chambertin and Nuits-Saint-Georges feature, including some *premier cru* sites, while *grands crus* run to Corton Clos du Roi, Clos de Vougeot, Bonnes Mares, Charmes-Chambertin and a third of a hectare of Musigny. Nearly all the wines are proving to be, at the very least, good examples of their respective appellations. Corton-Charlemagne and the solely-owned Vougeot *cru* are already very good whites. Some recent releases have been slightly marked by a cellar taint problem including Vougeot white. (PW)

● **Clos de Vougeot**★★★★ £F ● **Charmes-Chambertin**★★★★ £F
● **Vougeot** 1er Cru Les Cras★★★ £F
● **Vougeot** Clos du Prieuré★★★ £E ● **Chambolle-Musigny**★★★ £E
● **Gevrey-Chambertin** Les Evocelles★★★★ £F
● **Pommard** Les Petit Noizons★★★ £E
● **Côtes de Beaune** Les Pierres Blanches★★ £C

197

● **Bourgogne Rouge** Terres de Famille★★ £C
○ **Vougeot** 1er Cru Clos Blanc de Vougeot★★★★ £F
○ **Corton-Charlemagne**★★★★ £G

OTHER WINES OF NOTE

This list includes notable wines from a range of producers but is not intended to be a comprehensive list of a given producer's wines; just those that we have encountered. In some instances there may be several more good wines.

ROBERT AMPEAU ○ **Meursault** 1er Cru Perrières★★★★ £F
○ **Meursault**★★★ £E 1er Cru Pièce sous le Bois★★★ £F
○ **Puligny-Montrachet** 1er Cru Combettes★★★★ £F
○ **Auxey-Duresses** 1er Cru Ecusseaux★★★ £D
● **Volnay** 1er Cru Santenots★★★ £F
● **Savigny-lès-Beaune** 1er Cru Lavières★★ £D
DOM. D'ARDHUY ○ **Corton-Charlemagne**★★★ £F
○ **Meursault** Les Pellans★★★ £E ○ **Savigny-lès-Beaune**★★ £D
DOM. ARLAUD ● **Bourgogne Roncevie**★★ £C
● **Charmes-Chambertin**★★★★ £F
● **Morey-Saint-Denis** 1er Cru Millandes★★★★ £F
● **Morey-Saint-Denis**★★★ £E 1er Cru Ruchots★★★ £F
ARNOUX PÈRE ET FILS ● **Beaune** 1er Cru Cent Vignes★★★ £D
● **Savigny-lès-Beaune**★★ £C 1er Cru Vergelesses★★★ £D
● **Chorey-lès-Beaune** Confrelins★★ £C
JEAN-CLAUDE BACHELET ○ **Puligny-Montrachet**★★★ £E
○ **Puligny-Montrachet** 1er Cru Sous le Puits★★★ £E
○ **Saint-Aubin** 1er Cru Les Champlots★★ £D
BACHELET-RAMONET ○ **Chassagne-Montrachet**★★ £D
○ **Chassagne-Montrachet** 1er Cru Caillerets★★★★ £E
○ **Chassagne-Montrachet** 1er Cru Grde Montagne★★★ £E
● **Chassagne-Montrachet** 1er Cru Clos Saint-Jean★★ £D
PIERRE BERTHEAU ● **Chambolle-Musigny** 1er Cru★★★ £E
● **Chambolle-Musigny** 1er Cru Charmes★★★★ £F
BILLARD-GONNET ● **Pommard** 1er Cru Rugiens★★★★ £F
● **Pommard** 1er Cru Pezerolles★★★★ £E
● **Pommard**★★★ £D 1er Cru Chaponnières★★★ £E
JEAN-MARC BOULEY ● **Volnay** 1er Cru Clos des Chênes★★★ £E
● **Volnay** 1er Cru Caillerets★★★ £E
● **Volnay**★★ £D 1er Cru Clos de la Cave★★ £D
● **Pommard** 1er Cru Frémiets★★★ £E 1er Cru Rugiens★★★ £E
RENÉ BOURGEON ● **Givry**★ £B Baraude★★ £C
○ **Givry** Clos de la Brulée★★ £B
DENIS BOUSSEY ○ **Meursault** 1er Cru Charmes★★★ £E
JEAN-CLAUDE BRELIÈRE ○ **Rully** 1er Cru Margotée★★ £C
● **Rully** 1er Cru Préaux★★ £C 1er Cru Montpalais★★ £C
DOM. MICHEL BRIDAY ○ **Rully** 1er Cru Grésigny★★ £C
○ **Rully** Bergerie★ £B
● **Rully** Quatre Vignes★ £B 1er Cru Champs-Cloux★★ £C
CAVE DES VIGNERONS DE BUXY
○ **Montagny** Domaine des Pierres Blanches★★ £C
○ **Montagny** 1er Cru Cuvée Speciale★ £C 1er Cru Chaignots★★ £C
JACQUES CACHEUX ● **Echezeaux**★★★★ £F
● **Vosne-Romanée** 1er Cru Les Suchots★★★ £F
LUCIEN CAMUS-BRUCHON ● **Pommard** 1er Cru Arvelets★★★ £E
● **Savigny-lès-Beaune** Liards V. Vignes★★ £C 1er Cru Lavières★★ £D
● **Beaune** 1er Cru Clos du Roi★★★ £D
○ **Savigny-lès-Beaune** Goudelettes★★ £D
CHARTRON & TRÉBUCHET ○ **Bourgogne Blanc**★ £C

O **Puligny-Montrachet** 1er Cru Clos des Caillerets★★★ £F
O **Saint-Aubin** 1er Cru Murgers des Dents de Chien★★ £D
O **Saint-Aubin** 1er Cru Châtenière★★ £D
CHÂTEAU DE LA SAULE O **Montagny** 1er Cru★ £C
O **Montagny** 1er Cru Vignes sur les Cloux★★ £C
JEAN CHAUVENET ● **Nuits-Saint-Georges**★★★ £D
● **Nuits-Saint-Georges** 1er Cru Damodes★★★ £E
● **Nuits-Saint-Georges** 1er Cru Bousselots★★★ £E
● **Nuits-Saint-Georges** 1er Cru Vaucrains★★★★ £F
HUBERT CHAUVENET-CHOPIN ● **Nuits-Saint-Georges**★★★ £D
● **Nuits-Saint-Georges** 1er Cru Murgers★★★★ £E
● **Côte de Nuits-Villages**★★ £C
CHOFFLET-VALDENAIRE ● **Givry** 1er Cru Clos Jus★★ £C
● **Givry**★ £B 1er Cru Clos de Choué★★ £C O **Givry** Galaffres★ £B
DOMAINE DES CLOS ● **Beaune** 1er Cru Les Avaux★★★ £D
● **Nuits-Saint-Georges** Les Crots★★★ £D
DOM. ALAIN COCHE-BIZOUARD O **Meursault** Luchets★★ £D
O **Meursault** 1er Cru Gouttes d'Or★★★ £E
O **Meursault** 1er Cru Charmes★★★ £E
VINCENT DANCER O **Meursault** 1er Cru Perrières★★★★ £F
O **Meursault** Grands Charrons★★★ £E
O **Chassagne-Montrachet** 1er Cru Romanée★★★★ £F
DIGIOIA-ROYER ● **Chambolle-Musigny** Vieilles Vignes★★★ £E
● **Chambolle-Musigny** 1er Cru Groseilles★★★ £E
● **Chambolle-Musigny** 1er Cru Gruenchers★★★ £E
DAVID DUBAND ● **Nuits-Saint-Georges**★★★ £D
● **Nuits-Saint-Georges** 1er Cru Procès★★★★ £E
● **Nuits-Saint-Georges** 1er Cru Pruliers★★★★ £E
● **Bourgogne-Hautes Côtes de Nuits**★★ £B
BENOÎT ENTE O **Puligny-Montrachet** 1er Cru Les Folatières★★★ £F
O **Puligny-Montrachet**★★ £E 1er Cru Champ-Gain★★★ £F
DOM. FOREY PÈRE ET FILS ● **Echezeaux**★★★ £F
● **Vosne-Romanée** 1er Cru Gaudichots★★★★ £F
FOUGERAY DE BEAUCLAIR ● **Fixin** Clos Marion★★ £D
● **Marsannay** Saint Jacques★★ £C
DOMINIQUE GALLOIS ● **Gevrey-Chambertin**★★★ £E
● **Gevrey-Chambertin** 1er Cru Combe aux Moines★★★★ £E
ALEX GAMBAL O **Meursault** Clos du Cromin★★★ £E
O **Chassagne-Montrachet** 1er Cru La Maltroie★★★★ £F
O **Bourgogne Chardonnay**★★ £C O **Fixin Blanc**★★ £C
● **Gevrey-Chambertin** Vieilles Vignes★★★ £E ● **Vosne-Romanée**★★ £E
● **Bourgogne** Les Deux Papis★ £C
PAUL GARAUDET ● **Monthelie** 1er Cru Duresses★★★ £D
● **Monthelie**★★ £C 1er Cru Clos Gauthey★★ £C
● **Volnay**★★★ £D
CAMILLE GIROUD (from 2002) ● **Beaune** 1er Cru Avaux★★★ £D
● **Volnay** 1er Cru Carelles★★★ £E
● **Gevrey-Chambertin** 1er Cru Lavaux Saint-Jacques★★★★ £F
ALBERT GRIVAULT O **Meursault**★★★ £D
O **Meursault** 1er Cru Perrières★★★★ £F
GROS FRÈRE ET SOEUR ● **Clos de Vougeot** Musigni★★★★ £F
● **Vosne-Romanée**★★★ £E
● **Bourgogne-Hautes Côtes de Nuits**★★ £B
HUMBERT FRÈRES ● **Gevrey-Chambertin**★★★ £D
● **Gevrey-Chambertin** 1er Cru Poissenots★★★★ £E
● **Charmes-Chambertin**★★★★ £F
DOM. LUCIEN JACOB ● **Savigny-lès-Beaune**★★ £C
O **Savigny-lès-Beaune**★★ £C 1er Cru Les Vergelesses★★★ £D
DOM. JAYER-GILLES ● **Echezeaux**★★★★ £H
● **Côte de Nuits-Villages**★★★ £D
● **Bourgogne-Hautes Côtes de Nuits**★★ £D

199

● Bourgogne-Hautes Côtes de Beaune★★ £D
○ Bourgogne-Hautes Côtes de Beaune★★ £D
DOM. JEANNIN-NALTET
● Mercurey Clos des Grands Voyens★★★ £C
DOM. ÉMILE JUILLOT ● Mercurey★★ £B 1er Cru Cailloute★★ £C
● Mercurey 1er Cru Croichots★★ £C 1er Cru Combins★★★ £C
○ Mercurey 1er Cru★ £B 1er Cru Cailloute★★ £C
DOM. LAMY-PILLOT ○ Chassagne-Montrachet★★★ £D
○ Chassagne-Montrachet 1er Cru Morgeots★★★ £E
○ Chassagne-Montrachet 1er Cru Caillerets★★★★ £E
● Chassagne-Montrachet 1er Cru Clos Saint-Jean★★ £C
● Chassagne-Montrachet 1er Cru Morgeots★★ £C
DOM. LARUE ○ Saint-Aubin 1er Cru En Remilly★★ £D
○ Saint-Aubin 1er Cru Vieilles Vignes★★ £D
○ Saint-Aubin 1er Cru Murgers des Dents de Chien★★★ £D
○ Puligny-Montrachet 1er Cru La Garenne★★★ £E
○ Chassagne-Montrachet★★ £E
DOM. ALETH LE ROYER-GIRARDIN ● Pommard★★ £D
● Pommard 1er Cru Charmots★★ £E 1er Cru Rugiens-Bas★★★ £E
● Beaune Clos des Mouches★★ £D
DOM. LECHENAUT ● Morey-Saint-Denis★★★ £D
● Nuits-Saint-Georges★★ £D 1er Cru Pruliers★★★★ £F
● Vosne-Romanée★★★ £E
THIBAULT LIGER-BELAIR
● Bourgogne Les Grands Chaillots★★★ £C
● Nuits-Saint-Georges 1er Cru Les Saint-Georges★★★★ £F
LIGNIER-MICHELOT ● Chambolle-Musigny★★ £E
● Morey-Saint-Denis Vieilles Vignes★★ £E En la Rue de Vergy★★★ £E
MAROSLAVAC-LEGER
○ Puligny-Montrachet 1er Cru Champgains★★★★ £E
○ Puligny-Montrachet 1er Cru Combettes★★★★ £E
○ Saint-Aubin 1er Cru Murgers des Dents de Chien★★★ £D
BERTRAND MAUME ● Gevrey-Chambertin 1er Cru★★★ £D
● Gevrey-Chambertin 1er Cru Champeaux★★★ £E
● Gevrey-Chambertin 1er Cru Lavaux Saint-Jacques★★★★ £E
DOM. BERNARD MOREAU ET FILS
○ Chassagne-Montrachet 1er Cru Chevenottes★★★★ £E
○ Chassagne-Montrachet 1er Cru Maltroie★★★ £E
THIERRY MORTET ● Gevrey Chambertin★★ £D
● Gevrey Chambertin 1er Cru Clos Prieur★★★ £E
● Chambolle-Musigny★★ £D 1er Cru Beaux Bruns★★★ £E
GÉRARD MOUTON ● Givry 1er Cru Clos Jus★★ £C
GÉRARD MUGNERET ● Vosne-Romanée★★★ £D
● Nuits-Saint-Georges 1er Cru Boudots★★★★ £E
● Bourgogne Rouge★★ £B
DOM. LUCIEN MUZARD ET FILS
● Santenay 1er Cru Beauregard★★ £C 1er Cru Clos Faubard★★ £C
● Santenay 1er Cru Clos des Tavannes★★★ £D
PHILIPPE NADDEF ● Gevrey-Chambertin Vieilles Vignes★★★ £E
● Gevrey-Chambertin 1er Cru Cazetiers★★★★ £F
DOM. JEAN ET ANNICK PARENT
● Monthelie 1er Cru Duresses★★ £C
● Pommard 1er Cru Rugiens★★★ £E
DOM. PARIZE PÈRE ET FILS ● Givry 1er Cru Grandes Vignes★★ £C
○ Givry 1er Cru Grandes Vignes★★ £C
PAUL PILLOT ○ Chassagne-Montrachet 1er Cru Caillerets★★★ £F
○ Chassagne-Montrachet 1er Cru Clos Saint-Jean★★★ £E
○ Saint-Aubin 1er Cru Charmois★★ £D
HENRI PRUDHON ○ Puligny-Montrachet Les Enseignières★★★ £E
○ Saint-Aubin Murgers Dents de Chien★★ £C
MICHEL PRUNIER ○ Auxey-Duresses Vieilles Vignes★★ £C

DOM. RAGOT ● **Givry** 1er Cru Grande Berge★★ £C

HENRI ET GILLES REMORIQUET

● **Nuits-Saint-Georges** Allots★★ £D 1er Cru Damodes★★★ £E

● **Nuits-Saint-Georges** 1er Cru Les Saint-Georges★★★★ £E

JOSEPH ROTY ● **Charmes-Chambertin** Tres Vieilles Vignes★★★★ £G

● **Gevrey-Chambertin** 1er Cru Fontenys★★★★ £F

DOM. MICHEL SARRAZIN ET FILS ○ **Givry** Grognots★ £C

● **Givry** 1er Cru Grands Pretants★★ £C Clos de la Putin★★ £C

DOM. DE SUREMAIN ● **Rully** 1er Cru Préaux★★ £C

● **Monthelie** Ch. de Monthelie★★ £D 1er Cru Sur La Velle★★★ £E

H ET Y DE SUREMAIN ● **Mercurey** 1er Cru En Sazenay★★ £C

JEAN TARDY ● **Clos de Vougeot**★★★★ £G

● **Vosne-Romanée** 1er Cru Les Chaumes★★★ £F

DOM. CHARLES THOMAS ● **Romanée-Saint-Vivant**★★★★ £G

● **Chambertin Clos-de-Bèze**★★★★ £G

● **Vosne-Romanée** 1er Cru Les Malconsorts★★★★ £F

● **Nuits-Saint-Georges** 1er Cru Clos de Thorey★★★ £E

GÉRARD THOMAS ○ **Saint-Aubin**★★ £C

○ **Saint-Aubin** 1er Cru Murgers des Dents de Chien★★ £D

DOM. JOSEPH VOILLOT ● **Volnay**★★★ £D

● **Volnay** 1er Cru Champans★★★★ £E

● **Pommard** £D 1er Cru Rugiens★★★★ £E

Author's Choice for Côte d'Or & Côte Chalonnaise (PW)

30 classic red Burgundies

MARQUIS D'ANGERVILLE ● **Volnay** 1er Cru Clos des Ducs

DOM. DE L'ARLOT ● **Nuits-Saint-Georges** 1er Cru Clos des Forêts-Saint-Georges

COMTE ARMAND ● **Pommard** 1er Cru Clos des Epeneaux

DOM. ROBERT ARNOUX ● **Vosne-Romanée** 1er Cru Les Suchots

GHISLAINE BARTHOD ● **Chambolle-Musigny** 1er Cru Les Charmes

BOUCHARD PÈRE ET FILS ● **Pommard** 1er Cru Rugiens

SYLVAIN CATHIARD ● **Romanée-Saint-Vivant**

ROBERT CHEVILLON ● **Nuits-Saint-Georges** 1er Cru Les Saint-Georges

BRUNO CLAIR ● **Gevrey-Chambertin** 1er Cru Les Cazetiers

CLOS DE TART ● **Clos de Tart**

DOM. DE COURCEL ● **Pommard** 1er Cru Grand Clos des Epenots

DOM. DUJAC ● **Clos de la Roche**

DOM. RENÉ ENGEL ● **Clos de Vougeot**

DOM. FAIVELEY ● **Chambertin Clos-de-Bèze**

GEANTET-PANSIOT ● **Charmes-Chambertin**

DOM. HENRI GOUGES ● **Nuits-Saint-Georges** 1er Cru Les Vaucrains

DOM. JEAN GRIVOT ● **Vosne-Romanée** 1er Cru Les Beaux Monts

ANNE GROS ● **Richebourg**

LOUIS JADOT ● **Gevrey-Chambertin** 1er Cru Clos Saint-Jacques

MICHEL LAFARGE ● **Volnay** 1er Cru Clos des Chênes

DOM. DES LAMBRAYS ● **Clos des Lambrays**

MÉO-CAMUZET ● **Vosne-Romanée** 1er Cru Cros Parentoux

HUBERT DE MONTILLE ● **Volnay** 1er Cru Taillepieds

DENIS MORTET ● **Gevrey-Chambertin** 1er Cru Lavaux Saint-Jacques

JACQUES-FRÉDÉRIC MUGNIER ● **Musigny**

DOM. PONSOT ● **Griotte-Chambertin**

DOM. ROUMIER ● **Bonnes Mares**

DOM. ARMAND ROUSSEAU ● **Chambertin**

DOM. TRAPET PÈRE ET FILS ● **Gevrey-Chambertin** 1er Cru Petite Chapelle

DOM. COMTES GEORGES DE VOGÜÉ ● **Musigny** Vieilles Vignes

201

Consistently fine Côte de Beaune whites

DOM. GUY AMIOT ET FILS ○ Chassagne-Montrachet 1er Cru Les Caillerets

ROGER BELLAND ○ Chassagne-Montrachet 1er Cru Morgeot Clos Pitois

DOM. BONNEAU DU MARTRAY ○ Corton-Charlemagne

MICHEL BOUZEREAU ET FILS ○ Meursault 1er Cru Genevrières

LOUIS CARILLON ○ Puligny-Montrachet 1er Cru Perrières

GÉRARD CHAVY ET FILS ○ Puligny-Montrachet 1er Cru Folatières

JEAN-FRANÇOIS COCHE-DURY ○ Meursault 1er Cru Perrières

MICHEL COLIN-DELÉGER ET FILS ○ Puligny-Montrachet 1er Cru Les Demoiselles

JEAN-PHILIPPE FICHET ○ Meursault Tessons

VINCENT GIRARDIN ○ Chassagne-Montrachet 1er Cru Morgeot

PATRICK JAVILLIER ○ Meursault Les Tillets

DOM. DES COMTES LAFON ○ Meursault 1er Cru Charmes

DOM. LEFLAIVE ○ Puligny-Montrachet 1er Cru Les Pucelles

BERNARD MOREY ○ Chassagne-Montrachet 1er Cru Caillerets

DOM. ROULOT ○ Meursault 1er Cru Perrières

Value for money red Burgundy

DENIS BACHELET ● Côtes de Nuits-Villages

GHISLAINE BARTHOD ● Chambolle-Musigny

ROGER BELLAND ● Santenay 1er Cru Beauregard

DOM. CARRÉ-COURBIN ● Volnay Vieilles Vignes

SYLVAIN CATHIARD ● Bourgogne Rouge

JEAN-JACQUES CONFURON ● Côtes de Nuits-Villages Les Vignottes

DOM. DES COMTES LAFON ● Monthelie 1er Cru Les Duresses

THIBAULT LIGER-BELAIR ● Bourgogne Les Grands Chaillots

JEAN-MARC PAVELOT ● Savigny-lès-Beaune 1er Cru La Dominode

FRANÇOIS RAQUILLET ● Mercurey 1er Cru Les Naugues

MICHELE & PATRICE RION ● Bourgogne Rouge Bons Bâtons

TOLLOT-BEAUT ● Chorey-lès-Beaune Pièce du Chapitre

A & P DE VILLAINE ● Bourgogne Côte Chalonnaise Digoine

Value for money white Burgundy

ROGER BELLAND ○ Santenay 1er Cru Beauregard

BOUCHARD PERE ET FILS ○ Beaune 1er Cru Clos Saint-Landry

MICHEL COLIN-DELÉGER ○ Chassagne-Montrachet

VINCENT DUREUIL-JANTHIAL ○ Rully 1er Cru Les Margotés

JEAN-JACQUES GIRARD ○ Pernand-Vergelesses Les Belles Filles

HENRI ET PAUL JACQUESON ○ Rully 1er Cru La Pucelle

PATRICK JAVILLIER ○ Bourgogne Cuvée Oligocène

HUBERT LAMY ○ Bourgogne Blanc

OLIVIER LEFLAIVE ○ Rully 1er Cru Vauvry

FRANÇOIS LUMPP ○ Givry 1er Cru Petite Marole

RECOMMENDED HOTELS AND RESTAURANTS - BURGUNDY/CÔTE D'OR

Top Hotels

★★★★*Château de Gilly*   Gilly-les-Citeaux 21640
Tel. 03 80 62 89 98   Fax 03 80 62 82 34
Email gilly@grandesetapes.fr   39 rooms   £D/H

★★★★★*Le Relais Bernard Loiseau* 2 rue Argentine, Saulieu 21210
Tel. 03 80 90 53 53   Fax 03 80 64 08 92
Email. loiseau@relaischateau.com   22 rooms   £E/H

Top Restaurants

★★★★★*Lameloise*   Place d'Armes, Chagny 21150
Tel. 03 85 87 65 65   Fax 03 85 87 03 57
Email ot-chagny-bourgogne@wanadoo.fr   £G

★★★★*Le Relais Bernard Loiseau*   2 rue Argentine, Saulieu 21210
Tel. 03 80 90 53 53   Fax 03 80 64 08 92
Email. loiseau@relaischateau.com   £H

Value for money Hotels

★*Relais de la Sans Fond*   33 rte Dijon, Chevigny 21600
Tel. 03 80 36 61 35   Fax 03 80 36 94 89
No email address   17 rooms   £A/B

★★★★*Lameloise*   Place d'Armes, Chagny 21150
Tel. 03 85 87 65 65   Fax 03 85 87 03 57
Email ot-chagny-bourgogne@wanadoo.fr   16 rooms   £C/G

Value for money restaurants

★*Garaudière*   Levernois 21200
Tel. 03 80 22 47 70   Fax 03 80 22 64 01
No Email   £A

★*Les Terrasses de Corton*   Ladoix-Serrigny 21550
Tel. 03 80 26 42 37   Fax 03 80 26 42 13
Email patrice.sanchez3@wanadoo.fr   £A/B

BURGUNDY RECIPES

GOUGERES: *Ingredients:* 3.5 dl of water, 250gr. white flour, 200gr. Emmenthal or any other hard cheese or a mixture, roughly grated or chopped, 100 gr. butter, 4 to 5 eggs.

Bring the water and the butter to the boil, add the flour and a pinch of salt in one go; lower the heat to minimum and stir constantly with a wooden spoon until the bottom and sides of the pan are clean. Remove the pan from the fire and let the mixture cool so that the eggs do not cook as you are adding them.   Add them one at a time and beat (you can do this with an electric beater on slow speed) until the mixture becomes supple and holding so that you can pipe it if you want. If you want it in a ring mould as one gougère then the mixture can be softer and you can put all the eggs in at once. Mix the cheese well. You can either spoon it into a ring mould or pipe small individual gougères on silicone paper (like almond petits fours). You can freeze those and cook them from frozen when needed. They are delicious hot. Cook in quite a hot oven until golden brown; avoid opening the oven.

RECOMMENDED WINES

This is another little pre-dinner snackette which you could wash down with Champagne, or even Crémant de Bourgogne. It does require something that is a little austere and not too rich. Macon Solutré "Les Clos" from Domaine des Gerbeaux comes to mind as does the Bourgogne Aligoté from Robert Chevillon – much too good to waste in a Kir.

RABBIT OR CHICKEN, SAUCE DIJONNAISE

Ingredients: Rabbit or chicken cut in individual portions (for 4 people). 1/2dl. brandy or marc de Bourgogne, 3dl. white wine, 2dl. water, 2 small shallots, 1 clove of garlic, a pinch of thyme, a bay leaf, 1 tablespoon of Dijon mustard, a knob of butter, fresh tarragon, salt & pepper

Sauté the meat in a little butter or oil until golden, add chopped shallots, garlic, thyme and bay leaf, shake a little and flamber with the brandy or the marc. (Heat alcohol in a ladle, when it is alight, pour on the meat mix). Add wine and water, seasoning, (not too much salt, the sauce will be reduced) cover and cook on a very slow heat until cooked. Remove the meat and reduce the juices to 2 and half dl. Turn off the heat, beat in the mustard and the knob of butter, reheat without boiling; sprinkle a dessertspoon of chopped fresh tarragon and serve.

203

RECOMMENDED WINES

There's not a lot of white wine available in the Dijon area and as this a bit of a peasant dish, there's no need for wines with a lot of subtlety, which could rule out some of the grander crus from the Côte de Beaune. An interesting try would be the Nuits St. Georges Blanc from either Gouges, Arlot or Robert Chevillon which are Pinot Blanc rather than Chardonnay, but some good, mealy Meursault from someone like Javilier or Matrot should also do the trick.

EGGS EN MEURETTE

Ingredients: 100gr. bacon plus 100gr. mushrooms roughly chopped – 1 medium onion very finely chopped; a little thyme – 5dl. red wine (preferably Pinot Noir) – 1 dessertspoon of flour – 40gr. of butter - 4 very large eggs, some croutons. – chopped parsley.

Sauté onion, mushrooms and bacon in the butter; lower heat and add the flour – cook for a few minutes until golden and gradually add the wine, stirring all the time making it very smooth. Cook on a very slow heat for about 30 minutes stirring from time to time. Strain, reserve the bits. Poach one egg at a time in the sauce, covering the yolk with the white all the time. When set, put on plate; keep warm; put bits on top or around; finish all the eggs, and pour sauce on all 4 plates, with a few croutons (optional) and a sprinkle of parsley.

This sauce can also be used with entrecôte or any meat.

RECOMMENDED WINES

Well, eggs can often be a problem for matching food and wine, but the large dose of Pinot Noir needed for the sauce ensures compatibility with red Burgundies that are not too far up the quality scale. A Marsannay from Bruno Clair or a Santenay from Vincent Girardin should work here. With the meat, you can up the quality and whilst the choice is vast, you could do no better than exploring the large range from Bouchard Père et Fils who produce wines at all qualities and all prices right up to super 5 stars.

The Mâconnais is Burgundy's frontier region where the full potential of the Chardonnay grape is only just beginning to be realised. Thanks in part to a new wave of producers Pouilly-Fuissé is now at an unprecedented level of quality, increasingly expressed in individual climats that make this region so complex and fascinating. Not only is the trend swinging away from overblown high-octane examples but a handful of growers are also revitalising the soils of vineyard plots scattered wide across the Mâconnais.

Village secrets

The Mâconnais produces as much wine as the Côte d'Or and Côte Chalonnaise combined, though much of it is pretty ordinary. Red under the **Mâcon** and **Mâcon Supérieur** ACs is usually poor and Gamay-based; any better reds are likely to be sold as Bourgogne Rouge. Limestone soils are important to the increasing percentage of Chardonnay planted in the region and much of what is produced is sold as **Mâcon-Villages** or hyphenated with the name of the individual village (such as Uchizy or Chardonnay). From the best growers this is a source of inexpensive and increasingly good-quality white Burgundy. Since 1998, **Viré-Clessé** has been a separate appellation for a stretch of vineyards near the eastern edge of the Mâcon centred on the villages of Viré and Clessé.

Heart of the Mâconnais

For long the greatest interest has been centred around four communes in the very south of the Mâconnais. Chaintré, Fuissé, Solutré and Vergisson comprise **Pouilly-Fuissé**, the latter two famous for the rock bluffs that proved useful in prehistoric times for herding and killing wild animals. Now the slopes that run down from the foot of the cliffs are some of the best in the region for producing rich, ripe, full-bodied whites. There are still some heavy, alcoholic whites but radical improvement over the last decade or so has seen the emergence of wines to rival all but the most elegant, refined and complete Côte de Beaune. As well as displaying increasing balance and harmony there is definite refinement and elegance from the top sites. At a lower level the wines are more immediate and obvious than something from the Côte de Beaune. North of Chaintré at the eastern limit of these hills are the separate villages of **Pouilly-Loché** and **Pouilly-Vinzelles**. Bret Brothers/La Soufrandière show the quality that is possible here. **Saint-Véran** encompasses Chardonnay vineyards from villages to the north and south of Pouilly-Fuissé. Its quality is very producer-dependent, ranging from the lean and angular to a fine Pouilly-Fuissé substitute at considerably lower prices. Jean Rijckaert has shown what is possible both at Leynes and from further afield. More potential is also beginning to be exploited from other sites further along a north-west axis from Pouilly-Fuissé, including Merlin at La Roche Vineuse, Guffens-Heynen/Verget at Sologny and Héritiers du Comte Lafon at Milly Lamartine.

Mâconnais vintages

The ageing potential of the finest white Burgundy from the Mâconnais varies greatly, even within Pouilly-Fuissé. Most regular examples will only improve for two or three years' from the vintage date. Vineyard-designated or special *cuvées* however might improve for 5 to 10 years. However, not only does quality vary from producer to producer but so does style and the structure, and consequently it is difficult to generalize about ageing potential. The 2004 vintage looks very promsing, the first wines are fresh with good intensity and purity of fruit. Of other recent vintages, 2002 is the star. Despite changeable weather conditions healthy grapes were harvested with excellent balance

205

between ripeness and acidity. There are many good wines, vibrant with marvellous fruit and style. By contrast the extreme heat of 2003 meant producers had to battle to produce balanced, harmonious wines. Too many are overblown and will be short-lived. Conditions in 2001 were also much more difficult with an unsettled growing season and a struggle to achieve ripeness and avoid rot due to damp, warm conditions. Despite this the best 2001s, if sometimes leaner, can show good minerality and ripe fruit. There's plenty of excellent wine from 2000 due to a favourable growing season and harvest.

A-Z of producers

AUVIGUE Pouilly-Fuissé

Jean-Pierre Auvigue   Le Moulin du Pont, 71850 Charnay-lès-Mâcon
UK stockists: **WSS**, P&S

Based outside Pouilly-Fuissé at Charnay-lès-Mâcon, Auvigue produces less than 20,000 cases of a range of Mâcon whites. Top wines show particularly good structure. All the grapes are hand-harvested, with the estate vineyards supplemented by bought-in grapes for the lesser *cuvées*. Mâcon-Fuissé is a good example of round, plump, fruity white Burgundy, while the Les Chênes version of Saint-Véran has well-integrated oak with its lemony fruit. *Cru* Pouilly-Fuissé show good restraint if not the concentration of some examples but the most remarkable wines are the Vieilles Vignes and Hors Classé versions. The Vieilles Vignes adds much more depth and intensity and a structure that calls for at least 4 or 5 years' age. The Hors Classé is only made when conditions are right, and is late-picked – while in the rich blockbuster style, it is balanced by excellent strucure. (PW)

O **Pouilly-Fuissé** Vieilles Vignes★★★ £D   Hors Classé★★★★ £D
O **Pouilly-Fuissé** La Frairie★★ £C Les Chailloux★★ £C
O **Saint-Véran** Moulin du Pont★★ £B Les Chênes★★ £B
O **Mâcon-Solutré** Moulin du Pont★ £B   O **Mâcon-Fuissé** Moulin du Pont★★ £B

DANIEL ET MARTINE BARRAUD Pouilly-Fuissé

Daniel et Martine Barraud   Le Bourg, 71960 Vergisson
UK stockists: **L&S**, NYg

This couple are leaders in differentiating and better defining the various *terroirs* of Pouilly-Fuissé. This large appellation has a little over twice the vineyard area of Meursault and there are considerable differences in both quality and style across the 4 communes it covers. Most of the Barrauds' 7ha of vines are on the higher slopes of Vergisson, beneath the dramatic rock itself, where the grapes generally ripen a little later than in lower-lying vineyards. While new oak is employed, it is usually well-judged. Wines from vineyards with an average vine age in excess of 40 years are designated Vieilles Vignes. The En Buland is the richest, most full-bodied of the various *cuvées*, though the Les Crays shows great concentration, intensity and a mineral influence, La Roche more of a piercing mineral elegance. Of 2 Saint-Vérans, the lighter En Crèches shows more style than a fatter, more four-square Les Pommards. The Mâcon-Vergisson also comes from Vergisson vineyards but from just outside the Pouilly-Fuissé boundaries. The 2000s are particularly rich and powerful but with the fruit and structure to keep for the best part of a decade (in the top *cuvées*) while the 2001s are atypically good for the vintage and 2002s excellent. The wines remain reasonably priced for their quality. (PW)

O **Pouilly-Fuissé** En Bulands Vieilles Vignes★★★★ £D

O **Pouilly-Fuissé** La Roche★★★ £C Les Crays Vieilles Vignes★★★ £D
O **Pouilly-Fuissé** En France★★ £C La Verchère Vieilles Vignes★★ £C
O **Saint-Véran** En Crèches★★ £B Les Pommards★★ £C
O **Mâcon-Vergisson** La Roche★★ £B

ANDRÉ BONHOMME Viré-Clessé

André Bonhomme 71260 Viré
UK stockists: **DDr**, WSc

In an attempt to become profitable rather than just accepting what the *négociants* were prepared to pay, André Bonhomme was the first to bottle his own wines in the Mâcon-Villages area in 1957. He has long held a reputation as a reliable source for fine inexpensive white Burgundy. His 9ha are manually harvested and there has always been a willingness to wait until the grapes are fully ripe. The wines are now made by André's son, Pascal, but this domaine has been the one of the few steady alternatives to the lean, acidic wines that are still too prevalent in the Mâconnais. The regular *cuvée* is vinified solely in vats but oak is used in part for the Cuvée Speciale and Vieilles Vignes, around a quarter new for the latter. Older wines (they can keep for up to 5 years) made before the new Viré-Clessé appellation came into being, are labelled as Mâcon-Viré. (PW)

O **Viré-Clessé★** £B Cuvée Spéciale★★ £C Vieilles Vignes★★ £C

CH. DE BEAUREGARD/JOSEPH BURRIER Pouilly-Fuissé ,

Burrier family Château de Beauregard, 71960 Fuissé
UK stockists: DD

The Burrier family go back hundreds of year in southern Burgundy and have owned the Château de Beauregard estate since 1883. Frédéric-Marc Burrier of the current generation is increasingly realising the potential of a rich collection of some of Pouilly-Fuissé's finest *climats*. These form part of 36ha of estate vineyards, including 10ha in Beaujolais (see CH. DE BEAUREGARD in the Beaujolais section for these wines). Individual-*climat* Pouilly-Fuissé wines are fermented and aged in oak for 10–11 months with *bâtonnage*. The wines show good structure, fruit and depth if not quite the extra intensity and precision of the region's best. (Only a limited number of these *cuvées* have been tasted; more will be added with further tastings.) The Joseph Burrier wines (without Ch. de Beauregard on the label) are made from bought-in grapes but only represent around 15% of production. These can provide attractive if more everyday drinking. Much more interesting from a quality perspective is the fact that since 2003 wines from the 4-ha estate of Georges Burrier, on the high slopes of La Côte, have also been made here. The 2003s are atypically good for the vintage with better definition and fruit intensity than most. (PW)

Ch. de Beauregard:
O **Pouilly-Fuissé★★** £C Les Châtaigniers★★ £D Les Grands Champs★★★ £D
O **Pouilly-Fuissé** Les Cras★★★★ £D

Dom. Georges Burrier:
O **Pouilly-Fuissé★★** £C La Côte★★★ £D Les Champs★★★★ £D

CH. DE FUISSÉ Pouilly-Fuissé www.chateau-fuisse.fr

Vincent family Château de Fuissé, 71960 Fuissé
UK stockists: **ABy, OWL**, BBR, Hrd

Arguably Pouilly-Fuissé's most famous estate, if no longer one of the very best. It has been in the Vincent family since 1852 but has come to prominence under Jean-Jacques Vincent since he assumed control of the domaine in 1966. There are now 30ha, mostly in the commune of Fuissé from which a number of different Pouilly-Fuissé *cuvées* are made, including 3 separate *climats* (Le

207

Clos, Les Brûles, Les Combettes). All are vinified in oak followed by 9 months' ageing in barrel. At their best, the top wines combine a ripe fruit intensity with excellent structure and depth and usually come into their own with at least 5 years' age. Recent tastings reveal a slight lack of intensity, even hollowness, with the Vieilles Vignes easily the most convincing wine. Saint-Véran, Mâcon-Villages and Mâcon-Fuissé are also made under the Château-Fuissé label. A second range of wines is made under the Vincent label, in part from family domaines and in part from bought-in grapes. These include Pouilly-Fuissé, Saint-Véran (Domaine des Morats), Mâcon-Villages, Mâcon-Fuissé and 2 Beaujolais, Morgon Les Charmes and Juliénas Domaine le Cotoyon. (PW)

Château-Fuissé:
O **Pouilly-Fuissé** Les Brûles★★★ £E Vieilles Vignes★★★ £E
O **Pouilly-Fuissé**★★★ £D Les Combettes★★ £E Le Clos★★ £E
O **Saint-Véran**★ £C

CH. DES RONTETS Pouilly-Fuissé

Gazeau family Château des Rontets, 71960 Fuissé
UK stockists: VTr, C&R
Claire Gazeau and her Italian husband, Fabio Montrasi, have transformed the wines from this old family property since the mid-1990s. There are just 6ha but all are planted to Chardonnay. Being well-established, the average vine age is high (45 years in the Clos Varambon, 70 in Les Birbettes). The Clos Varambon is a fine example of Pouilly aged exclusively in large wood. Pierrefolle adds more depth and interest and a spicy component which derives in part from a small percentage of new oak. The top *cuvée*, Les Birbettes, has really superb fruit which easily takes up the new oak (30%) as well as excellent depth and is one of the most stylish examples of Pouilly-Fuissé. Though it is not inexpensive it outperforms many a more expensive village-level Chassagne or Puligny-Montrachet. Fine 2002s. (PW)
O **Pouilly-Fuissé** Clos Varambon★★ £C Pierrefolle★★★ £D Les Birbettes★★★ £D

DOM. CORDIER PÈRE ET FILS Pouilly-Fuissé

Cordier family Les Molards, 71960 Fuissé
UK stockists: **Gen**, HHB, L&S, Maj, WSc
Since Christophe Cordier joined his father Roger, this estate's inherent potential has been further realised. Their 14.5ha of vineyards are based in the commune of Fuissé but also includes some Saint-Véran. In addition some wine, including Viré-Clessé, Mâcon Milly Lamartine and Pouilly-Fuissé, is made from bought-in grapes and sold under the Christophe Cordier label. Domaine wines are very powerful, many of them high in alcohol – being made from very ripe, low-yielding fruit – but are still remarkably well-balanced. There is progressively more concentration and depth, as well as power, in the top *cuvées*. An intense minerality complements a preserved citrus character and oak-derived spiciness in many of the wines. Prices are now high, even in the context of the prices Pouilly-Fuissé now commands, but so is the quality. Most of the wines can be drunk young for their dramatic, exuberant richness, though the more structured and profound Vers Cras and Vers Pouilly, will be better with 4 or 5 years' age. In general the 2003s are concentrated with decent structures but lack the thrill and definition of 2002s. From the latter also look out particularly for some super special cuvées: an exotic Jean-Gustave, very intense and classy Fine Joséphine and powerful, ageworthy Juliette la Grande. (PW)

Dom. Cordier Père et Fils:
O **Pouilly-Fuissé**★★ £C Vieilles Vignes★★★ £E Au Metertière★★★ £E
O **Pouilly-Fuissé** Vignes Blanches★★★★ £E La Vigne de Monsieur Marguin★★★★ £E
O **Pouilly-Fuissé** Vers Pouilly★★★★ £E Vers Cras★★★★ £E Jean-Gustave★★★★ £E
O **Pouilly-Fuissé** Fine Joséphine★★★★ £E Juliette La Grande★★★★ £E
O **Saint-Véran** En Faux★★ £C Clos à la Côte★★★ £C Les Crais★★★★ £D
O **Pouilly-Loché**★★★ £C O **Mâcon-Fuissé**★★ £C O **Mâcon Blanc**★★ £B

Christophe Cordier:
O **Pouilly-Fuissé**★★ £C Vieilles Vignes★★★ £D

CORSIN Pouilly-Fuissé www.domaine-corsin.com

Corsin family Les Plantés, 71960 Davayé
UK stockists: **SsG, E&T**
Gilles and Jean-Jacques Corsin are the current generation making the wines at
this long-established Pouilly-Fuissé estate. The 12ha are split between Pouilly-
Fuissé and Saint-Véran. The wines are fermented and aged both partly in vats
and partly in oak, and typically show concentrated ripe fruit and a well-
integrated oak character. They can provide excellent, relatively inexpensive
drinking with 2 or 3 years' age. A Cuvée Précoce bottling of Saint-Véran comes
from younger vines, is bottled sooner and can be drunk earlier. (PW)
O **Pouilly-Fuissé**★★ £D O **Saint-Véran**★★ £C O **Mâcon-Villages**★ £B

DOM. DE LA CROIX SENAILLET Saint-Véran

Richard et Stéphane Martin En Coland, 71960 Davayé
UK stockists: OWL, CTy, B&T, Goe, P&S, CeB
The Martins have 22ha, the majority of which fall in Davayé (part of Saint-
Véran) but on the lower slopes of Vergisson and Solutré. The regular Saint-
Véran is an excellent example, ripe and intense with a refined floral and mineral
character – what more Saint-Véran should taste like. Les Rochats, 1 of 2 *crus*
(the other is La Grande Bruyère), shows more depth and a touch of class but
needs 3–4 years' age. A basic Mâcon Blanc is also attractive with a leesy, citrusy
character. As well as a little rich, ripe old-vines Pouilly Fuissé (from the *lieu-dit*
En Pommard), some red Mâcon is also produced. (PW)
O **Pouilly-Fuissé**★★★ £C O **Saint-Véran**★★ £B Les Rochats★★★ £C
O **Mâcon Blanc**★ £B

DOM. DES DEUX ROCHES Saint-Véran

Christian Collovray & Jean-Luc Terrier 71960 Davayé
UK stockists: **FMV**, BBR, ThP
Increasing amounts of very good whites are being made outside the quality
heart of Mâconnais, Pouilly-Fuissé. Saint-Véran lies both to the north and
south but this estate has long shown that high quality is possible here too.
While a number of Pouilly-Fuissé estates make fine Saint-Véran in addition to
their top whites, the 35-ha Deux Roches majors on Saint-Véran. As well as
attractive, fruity regular *cuvées*, a percentage of new oak is used for fermenting
and ageing the top wines. Generally there is good ripeness as well as a mineral
aspect to most of the wines, with a classic fruit/mineral intensity in Terres
Noires. There is also a little Pouilly-Fuissé La Roche. Owners Christian
Collovray and Jean-Luc Terrier also produce some very good wines from
Chardonnay at Domaine d'ANTUGNAC in the Limoux AC in the Languedoc-
Roussillon. (PW)

Dom. des Deux Roches:
O **Saint-Véran**★ £B Vieilles Vignes★★ £C Terres Noires★★★ £C Cras★★★ £D
O **Mâcon-Villages**★ £B O **Mâcon-Davayé**★ £B

209

Collovray & Terrier:
O **Saint-Véran** Tradition★ £B

CORINNE & THIERRY DROUIN   Pouilly-Fuissé

Corinne & Thierry Drouin   Le Grand Pré, 71960 Vergisson
UK stockists: GrD

Corinne and Thierry Drouin have 7.5ha in the southern Mâconnais, including 4.5ha in Pouilly-Fuissé. A lot of work goes into improving the quality of the fruit and each parcel is picked by hand before being vinified separately. Mostly 2003s have been tasted and these show concentrated ripe fruit, good minerality but only moderate structures. The fruit quality has also suffered slightly in Terres de Vergission but a 04 Mâcon-Bussières from Domaine du Vieux Puits suggests good promise from this vintage. Unusual is La Vieille Vigne du Bois D'Ayer (previously Vieilles Vignes) with very ripe exotic preserved peach, even guava and overripe quince and some residual sweetness in 2003 but lacking a corresponding structure. More convincing is a concentrated, minerally Mâcon-Vergisson La Roche. Also made is Mâcon Rouge in a fruity, juicy Beaujolais style for everyday drinking. (PW)

O **Pouilly-Fuissé** Terres de Vergisson★★ £C
O **Pouilly-Fuissé** Métertière★★ £C La Vieille Vigne du Bois d'Ayer★★ £C
O **Mâcon-Bussières** Dom. du Vieux Puits★★ £B
O **Mâcon-Vergisson** La Roche★★★ £C

DOM. J A FERRET   Pouilly-Fuissé

Colette Ferret   Le Plan, 71960 Fuissé
UK stockists: Bal, JAr, Lay, Rae

This domaine has been bottling its own wine for 60 years, though it had its beginnings more than 2 decades before the French Revolution. Colette Ferret's Pouilly-Fuissés, made famous by her mother before she died in 1993, have been compared not just to *premier cru* but also *grand cru* Côte de Beaune whites. They are certainly very full-bodied with remarkable concentration and extract and with added finesse and purity in the best examples. As might be expected, yields are low, the average vine age high and the grapes are manually harvested. The wines are barrel-fermented and aged with extended lees-contact for maximum enrichment. From 15ha are fashioned 4 great *crus*: Le Clos, Les Ménétrières, Les Perrières and Tournant de Pouilly. These are given the greatest amount of new oak and the longest period of ageing. Other bottlings are also made including 3 other *crus*, Les Sceles, Les Vernays and Les Moulins, which are sold only in the US. Rich and honeyed, the wines also display fine floral, mineral aspects as well as a classic grilled nuts character. The Hors Classé designation applies only to a selection of old vines in the best years and these wines are slightly more expensive than the Tête de Cru bottlings. (PW)

O **Pouilly-Fuissé** Ménétrières Hors Classé★★★★ £E
O **Pouilly-Fuissé** Tournant de Pouilly Hors Classé★★★★ £E
O **Pouilly-Fuissé** Le Clos Tête de Cru★★★ £E Perrières Tête de Cru★★★ £E

DOM. DES GERBEAUX   Pouilly-Fuissé

Beatrice et Jean-Michel Drouin   71960 Solutré
UK stockists: WTs, BBR

The husband-and-wife team of Beatrice and Jean-Michel Drouin make excellent examples of Mâcon, Saint-Véran and Pouilly-Fuissé whites which are not that widely seen on account of the production always selling out. The wines show excellent intensity, texture and structure and have balanced alcohol. There is attractive minerality even in Mâcon-Solutré, a lively intensity to ripe Saint-Véran and more depth and richness in Pouilly-Fuissé. The wines are also very reasonably priced without the premiums that the wines of more high-profile producers have acquired. All the wines can be drunk fairly young but the Pouilly-Fuissé in particular will also repay keeping. Two other special *cuvées* of Pouilly-Fuissé are also made, En Champs Roux and Jacques Charvet. (PW)

O **Pouilly-Fuissé** Terroir de Solutré Vieilles Vignes★★★ £C
O **Saint-Véran**★★ £B O **Mâcon-Solutré** Le Clos★★ £B
O **Mâcon-Chaintré**★★ £B

DOM. GUFFENS-HEYNEN www.verget-sa.com

Jean-Marie Guffens-Heynen Domaine Guffens-Heynen, 71960 Vergisson
UK stockists: **L&W, L&S, Far, C&R, Odd**
Jean-Marie Guffens is one of the wine world's larger-than-life characters but also one of its most exciting winemakers. Both through the substantial *négociant* VERGET operation and a small number of wines made at this, his own private 3-ha estate, he has made a significant impact on the fine wine scene. The grapes are picked very ripe from low-yielding vines that have been meticulously cared for, before being pressed very slowly in an old-fashioned vertical press. A mix of oak, both new and used, small and large, is used in their fermentation and ageing. Not only do the wines have fantastic richness, depth and substance but they also show finesse and elegance. They are not as consistent as some but neither is there uniformity; when these wines are particularly successful (there is brilliant quality in most 2002, 01 and 00s) they will provide memorable drinking for up to a decade. Guffens-Heynen *cru* bottlings of Pouilly-Fuissé have included Les Croux, Roche and Hauts de Vignes. The Verget Mâconnais wines are included below, for others see the Côte d'Or section. (PW)

Guffens-Heynen:
O **Pouilly-Fuissé**★★★★ £E O **Mâcon-Pierreclos**★★★ £C Le Chavigne★★★★ £D

Verget:
O **Pouilly-Fuissé** Terroir de Vergisson★★★ £D
O **Pouilly-Vinzelles** Les Quarts★★ £B
O **Saint-Véran** Terres Noires★★★ £C Vignes de Saint-Claude★★★ £C
O **Saint-Véran** Terroirs de Davayé★★ £C
O **Mâcon-Bussières** Vieilles Vignes de Montbrison★★★ £B Les Prusettes★★ £C
O **Mâcon-Burgy** Les Prusettes★★ £C En Chatelaine★★★ £C
O **Mâcon-Vergisson** La Roche★★★ £B O **Mâcon-Charnay** Clos Saint-Pierre★★ £B

HÉRITIERS DU COMTE LAFON Macon-Villages

Lafon family Cartelées, 71960 Milly Lamartine
Dominique Lafon's arrival in the Mâcon may not have aroused much interest amongst those who regularly jostle for his marvellous Meursaults (see Domaine des Comtes LAFON) but taste these wines and you'll see there is much more to this than a source of (somewhat) cheaper, more everyday white Burgundy. The wines have already improved considerably since the debut 1999s and now the potential quality that is possible in the Mâcon is increasingly apparent. The Mâcon Milly Lamartine shows a pure elegant minerally fruit and is very stylish and expressive. Clos du Four has more of everything – more depth, more mineral, more structure – and consequently needs more time. Mâcon-Bussières Le Monsard starts out austere but has real intensity of ripe citrus with a stony aspect, best with 4 or 5 years' age from a fine vintage like 2002. New vineyards from the villages of Chardonnay and Uchizy will augment production from the 2003 vintage. (PW)

O **Mâcon Milly Lamartine**★★★ £C Clos du Four★★★ £D
O **Mâcon-Bussières** Le Monsard★★★ £D O **Mâcon-Uchizy** Les Maranches★★ £C
O **Mâcon Villages**★★ £C

DOM. ROGER LASSARAT   Pouilly-Fuissé   www.roger-lassarat.com

Roger Lassarat   Le Martelet, 71960, Vergisson
UK stockists: **THt**, Mar, Sel

Roger Lassarat was inspired by quality pioneers CHÂTEAU DE FUISSÉ and J A
FERRET and set out to emulate them as he established his own estate more
than 30 years ago. Here as at so many of the best Pouilly-Fuissé estates the
secret to the quality of the fruit is manual picking of carefully maintained, low-
yielding old vines. The grapes receive a gentle pressing and partial barrel-
fermentation with prolonged lees-enrichment in barrel before the wines are
bottled unfiltered. The wines are ripe and richly textured, with increasing
definition and better balance and structure in the most recent vintages. The
range of wines has very recently been expanded to single out more individual
climats. Rich, concentrated Saint Véran Le Cras (Meursault-like) and Les
Mûres are of even better quality than the Pouilly-Fuissés. Fine 2003s as well as
2002s. (PW)

O **Pouilly-Fuissé** Clos de France★★★ £C Cuvée Prestige★★★ £D
O **Saint-Véran** Les Mûres★★★ £D Le Cras★★★★ £D
O **Saint-Véran** Fournaise★★ £C Cuvée Prestige★★★ £C Les Mûres★★★ £D
O **Mâcon-Vergisson** La Roche★★ £B

NICOLAS MAILLET   Pouilly-Fuissé   www.vins-nicolas-maillet.com

Nicolas Maillet   Domaine Nicolas Maillet, 71960 Verzé
UK stockists: TPg

Nicolas Maillet has 6ha in Verzé (some way north of La Roche Vineuse) in the
west of the southern Mâconnais. From vineyards which include a little Gamay,
Aligoté and Pinot Noir he makes excellent, inexpensive wines without any oak.
The wines have excellent fruit and purity, great character and expression with
fine minerality in Mâcon-Verzé. Even better, with more structure, depth and
intensity, is a Le Chemin Blanc version. Of other wines, well-made Bourgogne
Aligoté and Crémant de Bourgogne show good fruit but better is a stylish
Bourgogne Rouge with pure cherry and cassis fruit, a subtle minerality and fine
tannins. Mâcon-Verzé Rouge (100% Gamay) can show a green edge but is
sound, everyday drinking. Now if only there were more like him throughout
the scattered villages of the Mâconnais! (PW)

O **Mâcon-Verzé**★★ £B Le Chemin Blanc★★★ £B
O **Bourgogne Aligoté**★ £B O **Crémant de Bourgogne**★ £B
● **Bourgogne Rouge**★★ £B

OLIVIER MERLIN   Mâcon-Villages

Olivier Merlin   Domaine du Vieux Saint-Sorlin, 71960 La Roche Vineuse
UK stockists: **FMV**, P&S, Hrd, WSc

Olivier Merlin's Domaine du Vieux Saint-Sorlin has built a reputation since the
late 1980s as one of the Mâcon's most reliable as well as exciting producers. For
long this took the form of excellent white Mâcon-La Roche Vineuse but more
recently he has made wines to the same high standards from Pouilly-Fuissé. His
own 7.5ha includes a little Pinot Noir for some red Mâcon but is mostly
Chardonnay, from which he makes rich, full-bodied whites with deep ripe fruit
and a certain finesse and complexity, particularly in the very complete, old-vine
Les Cras. Three 'Terroir' designated Pouilly-Fuissé show good structures and in
Vergisson and Fuissé the capacity to age for at least 5 years. The Vergisson, with
a fine mineral streak, is most individual, Fuissé the most classic, and the creamy
Chaintré a good alternative to a fat village Meursault. 2003s are more modestly
structured than usual. A sophisticated Moulin-à-Vent is also made, as is
Bourgogne Rouge. (PW)

O **Mâcon-La Roche Vineuse**★★ £B Vieilles Vignes★★★ £C Les Cras★★★ £C

O **Pouilly-Fuissé** Terroir de Chaintré★★★ £D Terroir de Fuissé★★★ £D
O **Pouilly-Fuissé** Clos des Quarts★★ £D Terroir de Vergisson★★★ £D
O **Saint-Véran** Grand Bussière★★★ £C ● **Moulin-à-Vent**★★ £C

CAVE PRISSÉ Pouilly-Fuissé

'Co-operative' Les Grandes Vignes, 71960 Prissé
UK stockists: CTy, Maj, Wai

This is a grouping of 3 co-operatives, Prissé-Sologny-Verzé ,with some 500 growers and 1,000ha of vineyards. The large production encompasses all the major appellations in the Mâconnais, from Bourgogne and Bourgogne Aligoté through sparkling Crémant, Mâcon-Villages, Saint-Véran and Pouilly-Fuissé. Only a few wines have been regularly tasted but these have been consistently well-made. They also offer reasonable value and often far higher quality than generics produced by several of the large Burgundy *négociant* operations. (PW)

O **Pouilly-Fuissé**★★★ £C O **Saint-Véran** Les Pierres Blanches★★ £B
O **Mâcon Milly Lamartine**★★ £B O **Mâcon Prissé** Les Clochettes★ £B

DOM. RIJCKAERT Viré-Clessé

Jean Rijckaert En Correaux, 71570 Leynes
UK stockists: JAr, Far, BBR, Odd

Jean Rijckaert is one of the Mâconnais' most exciting new producers. He used to work with Jean-Marie Guffens (GUFFENS-HEYNEN) but he is now giving the Mâconnais a further boost with his own range of wines. Having helped mould the VERGET style, it is no surprise that the same principles of slow pressings, enhanced lees-enrichment and intelligent oak-ageing, are being continued here. Rijckaert also believes passionately in restoring life to the soils and the importance of promoting deep roots in the vines. He makes more than 2 dozen individual *cuvées*, mostly from 35–40-year-old vines, both from his own 4ha of vineyards and for other small growers. He seeks precision and minerality in his wines and achieves it with some superb aromatic, concentrated wines that show excellent definition and purity. Rarely is there any need to hurry to drink these wines, as most will be better with 3 or 4 years' age. A brown label indicate a grower's wine (and also includes their name), while a green label is used for the domaine wines. Only a selection are listed below. The 2002s are particularly fine. Also made are a number of excellent whites from the Jura where he has another 4ha of vineyard and a winery facility. Many are of an unprecedented level of quality for the region, both those based on Chardonnay and those from Savagnin. (PW)

Burgundy wines:
O **Pouilly-Fuissé** Vers Chânes Vieilles Vignes★★★ £C
O **Saint-Véran** En Avonne★★ £C L'Epinet★★ £C En Faux Vieilles Vignes★★★ £C
O **Viré-Clessé** En Thurissey Vieilles Vignes★★★ £C
O **Viré-Clessé** Les Vercherres Vieilles Vignes★★ £C
O **Saint-Aubin** En Monceau★★★ £D O **Mâcon Montbellet** En Pottes★★ £C

Jura wines:
O **Côtes de Jura Chardonnay** Vignes des Voises Vielles Vignes★★★ £C
O **Côtes de Jura Chardonnay** Les Sarres★★ £B
O **Côtes de Jura Savagnin** Les Sarres★★ £B
O **Arbois Chardonnay** Chantemerle★★★ £C En Paradis Vieilles Vignes★★★ £C

DOM. ROBERT-DENOGENT Pouilly-Fuissé

Jean-Jacques Robert Domaine Robert-Denogent, 71960 Fuissé
UK stockists: **Bib**, Gau

Jean-Jacques Robert has rapidly improved quality at this small 5-ha estate since taking over in 1988. There is a tremendous resource of old vines and yields are further reduced through careful pruning. Although new oak is used, all the

213

wines show lovely fruit intensity and fine structures with pronounced minerally, *terroir*-given definition; no 2 are quite alike. Mâcon-Solutré shows has lots of class for this level, with good depth and intensity. Of the Pouilly-Fuissé, La Croix has a striking mineral component due to more schistous soils while Les Reisses has more exotic fruit - both are excellent value. Cuvée Claude Denogent wine is an old-vine selection and has impressive weight, depth and dimension while powerful, complex Les Carrons comes from an exceptional site with a higher clay content and very old vines. All are superb in 2002 and will benefit from at least 3–4 years' ageing. As well as those listed below, another *cuvée*, Les Taches, is also made. (PW)

O **Pouilly-Fuissé** La Croix Vieilles Vignes★★★ £C Les Reisses Vieilles Vignes★★★ £C
O **Pouilly-Fuissé** Cuvée Claude Denogent★★★★ £D Les Carrons★★★★ £E
O **Mâcon-Solutré** Clos des Bertillonnes★★ £C

SAUMAIZE-MICHELIN Pouilly-Fuissé

Roger & Christine Saumaize   Le Martelet, 71960 Vergisson
UK stockists: **Eno**, **CTy**, Rae, SVS

Like the wines of Daniel et Martine BARRAUD and others, these wines show that Vergisson has the potential to equal Pouilly-Fuissé's more established and generally most highly regarded commune, Fuissé. The Saumaize estate extends to 9ha and as well as several different *cuvées* of Pouilly-Fuissé, some fine Saint-Véran and Mâcon-Villages are made. There is the utmost attention to detail and hygiene and the resulting consistency, both from year to year and across the range, is very impressive. The wines see some oak. They can be quite firm and steely when very young but they have good definition and added richness with age. The best Pouilly-Fuissé *cuvées* come from old vines. Clos sur la Roche has the class and depth of good Chassagne-Montrachet while the top wine, Ampelopsis is remarkably concentrated and proportioned. As well as 2 good Saint-Véran a well-structured and good value Mâcon-Villages is made. Very good 2002s, fatter, less well-defined 2003s. (PW)

O **Pouilly-Fuissé** Ampelopsis★★★★ £D Ronchevats★★★ £C
O **Pouilly-Fuissé** Vigne Blanche★★★ £C Clos sur la Roche★★★ £C
O **Saint-Véran** Crêches★★ £B Vieilles Vignes★★ £B
O **Mâcon-Villages** Les Sertaux★★ £B

DOM. DE LA SOUFRANDIÈRE Pouilly-Vinzelles

Jean-Guillaume & Jean-Philippe Bret   Domaine La Soufrandière, 71680 Vinzelles
UK stockists: **FMV**, BBR, F&M, WSc

These 2 young *vigneron* brothers have made the finest wines ever under the small Pouilly-Vinzelles AC, which together with the contiguous Pouilly-Loché AC has less than 100ha of vines. The Brets have less than 5ha but their rich, ripe, structured wines have finally shown that these separate zones at the south-eastern end of Pouilly-Fuissé have similar exciting potential to that being realised elsewhere in the region. The estate is now biodynamic and all the grapes are picked by hand. The wines are ripe and concentrated, verging on being overdone in both the regular bottling and Les Quarts, which comes from older vines. The top *cuvée* Millerandée show tremendous richness, coming from very small (*millerandé*) grapes from 70-year-old vines. While there is not the finesse of a top Côte de Beaune white it is well-proportioned and deserves to be drunk with 5 years' age. A series of wines is also are made from bought-in grapes and sold under the Bret Brothers label including Mâcon-Cruzilles and examples of Viré-Clessé, Saint-Véran and Pouilly-Fuissé. (PW)

Dom. de la Soufrandière:
O **Pouilly-Vinzelles**★★ £B Les Quarts★★★ £D Les Quarts Millerandée★★★ £E

Bret Brothers:
○ **Pouilly-Vinzelles** Les Remparts★★★ £D ○ **Saint-Véran** En Combe★★ £C

JEAN THÉVENET Macon-Villages www.bongran.com

Jean Thévenet Domaine de la Bongran, Quintaine, 71260 Clessé
UK stockists: L&S, GBa, Adm, HHB, JNi, T&W

Jean Thévenet's wines are like no one else's – atypically rich, very ripe and honeyed but with great structure and vibrancy. The wines from 15ha of vineyards are the products of 2 separate domaines, Domaine de la Bongran and Domaine Emilian Gillet. Yields are low and the grapes are harvested manually. The Emilian Gillet is more floral than the Bongran but similarly strikingly honeyed. Previously labelled Mâcon-Clessé and Mâcon-Viré, the wines are now simply labelled Mâcon-Villages as, with a degree of residual sugar, they were denied promotion to the new Viré-Clessé AC despite their evident quality. A Cuvée Levroutée is made from selected overripe grapes in certain years, while a little Cuvée Spéciale Botrytis (from botrytised grapes) is made when exceptional conditions permit (such as 2000 and 1995). This is a wine of exceptional richness and honeyed, preserved and tropical fruits but with excellent acidity and the ability to keep for more than a decade. Jean and his son Gautier now also run the Domaine de Roally. (PW)

○ **Mâcon-Villages** Tradition Sélection EJ Thévenet Domaine de la Bongran★★★★ £D
○ **Mâcon-Villages** Quintaine Domaine Emilian Gillet★★★ £C

DOM. THIBERT Pouilly-Fuissé

Thibert family Le Bourg, 71960 Fuissé
UK stockists: **ABy**, Dec, CRs, Wai

Christophe Thibert and his wife Catherine run this 16-ha estate, which has around half its vineyards in Pouilly-Fuissé. The wines show more finesse and less upfront richness than some but combine a minerally intensity with good concentration in the best years. Oak is used to enhance structure and is considerably less overt in most of the wines than in many a Pouilly-Fuissé. Though less immediate, the wines have excellent ageing potential, especially the top *cuvées*. Premium Vignes de la Côte is usually matched by the slightly cheaper Vieilles Vignes version. Ripe, peachy Pouilly-Vinzelles is also made. Recent releases have been a little uneven but always elegant. (PW)

○ **Pouilly-Fuissé**★★ £C Vieilles Vignes★★★ £C Vignes Blanches★★★ £D
○ **Pouilly-Fuissé** Vignes de la Côte★★★ £D ○ **Pouilly-Vinzelles** Longeays★★ £C
○ **Mâcon-Fuissé**★ £B ○ **Mâcon-Prissé** En Chailloux★ £B

DOM. VALETTE Pouilly-Fuissé

Valette family Vercheres, 71570 Chaintré
UK stockists: FMV, WSc

No list of the Mâconnais' best producers would be complete without Gérard Valette. Gérard and his son Philippe run what is effectively an organic estate of 17ha. Although more than half of it is in Mâcon-Chaintré, the rest is in Pouilly-Fuissé, producing full-bodied, very ripe-fruited blockbusters. The grapes are harvested very late from often very low-yielding old vines and a percentage of new oak is used for fermenting the 2 Réserve *cuvées*, resulting in very powerful oaky wines. Despite the rich, almost overwhelming fruit and lees-enriched character, the wines usually have the necessary balance to provide heady, complex drinking soon after their release and often for another 5 years' or more. The extended ageing of these *cuvées* before bottling means they become available a year or 2 later than other top Pouilly-Fuissé releases – but in the meantime you can enjoy the fresh, fruit-filled Mâcon-Chaintré made for relatively early drinking. A little Pouilly-Vinzelles is also made. (PW)

215

O **Pouilly-Fuissé** Tradition★★★ £D Clos Reyssie Réserve★★★★ £E
O **Pouilly-Fuissé** Clos de Monsieur Noly Vieilles Vignes Réserve★★★★ £F
O **Mâcon-Chaintré** Vieilles Vignes★★ £B

DOM. VESSIGAUD Pouilly-Fuissé www.domainevessigaud.com

Pierre Vessigaud Hameau de Pouilly, 71960 Solutré
UK stockists: **Anl, DLW,** Odd

This 11-ha domaine has risen rapidly to become one of the new stars of the
southern Mâconnais. Pierre Vessigaud transforms high-quality fruit into deep,
expressive and well-defined whites. Grapes are hand-picked and whole-bunch-
pressed. The wines are barrel-fermented without added yeast or temperature
control and aged in barrel, remaining on the lees for 12 months. Especially fine
are the individual-*climat* wines (in addition to those rated below is Vers
Asnières): no 2 are quite alike but they could easily pass for fine *premier cru*
Côte de Beaune Burgundies. The Vers Pouilly is both remarkably concentrated
and refined. Rich 2003s have far better structures than is typical in this vintage
while 04 promises elegance, purity and more mineral intensity. More will be
rated with further tastings. (PW)

O **Pouilly-Fuissé** Vieilles Vignes★★★ £C Vers Pouilly★★★★ £D
O **Mâcon-Fuissé**★★ £B Les Taches★★★ £B

For other Mâconnais wines see the following Burgundy producers with an
entry in the section *Côte D'Or & Côte Chalonnaise*:
BOUCHARD PERE ET FILS
as well as Beaujolais producers with an entry in the *Beaujolais* section:
GEORGES DUBOEUF

OTHER WINES OF NOTE

MICHEL FOREST O **Mâcon-Vergisson**★★ £B
O **Pouilly-Fuissé**★★ £C La Roche★★★ £C Les Crays★★★ £D
O **Pouilly-Fuissé** Vieilles Vignes★★★ £D
DOM. DE FUSSIACUS O **Mâcon-Fuissé**★★ £B
O **Pouilly-Fuissé** Vieilles Vignes★★★ £C
PIERETTE ET MARC GUILLEMOT-MICHEL
O **Mâcon-Villages** Quintaine★★ £B
MAURICE LAPALUS ET FILS O **Mâcon Pierreclos**★★ £B
JEAN MANCIAT O **Mâcon-Charnay**★★ £B
MANCIAT-PONCET O **Pouilly-Fuissé** La Roche Vieilles Vignes★★ £C
O **Pouilly-Fuissé** Les Crays Vieilles Vignes★★ £C
GILLES NOBLET O **Pouilly-Fuissé**★★ £C Vieilles Vignes Les Champs★★ £C
O **Mâcon-Fuissé**★ £B
DOM. ALAIN NORMAND O **Mâcon La Roche Vineuse**★★★ £B
JACQUES ET NATALIE SAUMAIZE O **Pouilly-Fuissé** Vieilles Vignes★★ £C
DOM. LA SOUFRANDISE/MELIN O **Pouilly-Fuissé** Vieilles Vignes★★★ £C
O **Mâcon-Fuissé**★★ £B
DOM. GÉRALD ET PHILIBERT TALMARD O **Mâcon-Uchizy**★ £B
O **Mâcon-Chardonnay**★ £B
DOM. PAUL ET MALLORY TALMARD O **Mâcon-Uchizy**★ £B
DOM. VERVIER ET FILS O **Pouilly-Fuissé**★★ £C

Author's Choice for Mâconnais (PW)
Great Mâcon whites

DANIEL ET MARTINE BARRAUD O **Pouilly-Fuissé** En Buland Vieilles Vignes

DOM. GEORGES BURRIER O **Pouilly-Fuissé** Les Champs

CH. DES RONTETS O **Pouilly-Fuissé** Les Birbettes

DOM. CORDIER PÈRE ET FILS O **Pouilly-Fuissé** Vignes Blanches

HÉRITIERS DU COMTE LAFON O **Mâcon Milly Lamartine** Clos du Four

DOM. DES DEUX ROCHES O **Saint-Véran** Cras

DOM. J A FERRET O **Pouilly-Fuissé** Ménétrières Hors Classé

DOM. GUFFENS-HEYNEN O **Pouilly-Fuissé**

OLIVIER MERLIN O **Pouilly-Fuissé** Terroir de Vergisson

DOM. RIJCKAERT O **Viré-Clessé** En Thurissey Vieilles Vignes

DOM. ROBERT-DENOGENT O **Pouilly-Fuissé** Cuvée Claude Denogent

DOM. LA SOUFRANDIÈRE O **Pouilly-Vinzelles** Les Quarts Millerandée

DOM. LA SOUFRANDISE/MELIN O **Pouilly-Fuissé** Vieilles Vignes

JEAN THÉVENET O **Mâcon-Villages** Quintaine Domaine Emilian Gillet

DOM. VALETTE O **Pouilly-Fuissé** Clos de M Noly Vieilles Vignes Réserve

Value for money Mâcon whites

AUVIGUE O **Mâcon-Fuissé** Moulin du Pont

ANDRÉ BONHOMME O **Viré-Clessé** Cuvée Speciale

DOM. DE LA CROIX SENAILLET O **Saint-Véran**

DOM. DES GERBEAUX O **Saint-Véran**

MAURICE LAPALUS & FILS O **Mâcon Pierreclos**

NICOLAS MAILLET O **Mâcon-Verzé**

OLIVIER MERLIN O **Mâcon-La Roche Vineuse** Vieilles Vignes

ALAIN NORMAND O **Mâcon-La Roche Vineuse**

DOM. ROBERT-DENOGENT O **Pouilly-Fuissé** La Croix Vieilles Vignes

SAUMAIZE-MICHELIN O **Mâcon-Villages** Les Sertaux

VERGET O **Mâcon-Charnay** Clos Saint-Pierre

RECOMMENDED HOTELS AND RESTAURANTS - CHALONNAISE, MÂCONNAIS AND BEAUJOLAIS

Top Hotels

★★★★*Georges Blanc*   place du Marché, Vonnas 01540
Tel. 04 74 50 90 90 Fax 04 74 50 08 80
Email blanc@relaischateau.com   35 rooms   £D/H

★★★★*Troisgros*   place Gare, Roanne 42300
Tel. 04 77 71 66 97 Fax 04 77 70 39 77
Email troisgros@avo.fr   13 rooms   £D/H

Top Restaurants

★★★★★*Georges Blanc*   place du Marché, Vonnas 01540
Tel. 04 74 50 90 90 Fax 04 74 50 08 80
Email blanc@relaischateau.com   £G/H

★★★★★*Troisgros*   place Gare, Roanne 42300
Tel. 04 77 71 66 97 Fax 04 77 70 39 77
Email. troisgros@avo.fr   £G/H

Value for money Hotels

★★*Raisin*   33 rte Dijon, Pont-de-Vaux 01190
Tel. 03 85 30 30 97 Fax 03 85 30 67 89
Email hotel.leraisin@wanadoo.fr   18 rooms   £B

217

★★*Chez la Rose*   Place Marché, Julienas 69840
Tel. 04 74 04 41 20   Fax   04 74 04 49 29
Email info@chez-la-rose.fr   10 rooms   £B

Value for money restaurants

★★*St. Loup*   on the N6, St-Loup-de-Varennes 71240
Tel. 03 85 44 21 58   Fax 03 85 94 85 27
Email sylparo@wanadoo.fr   £A

★★*Pouilly Fuissé*   Fuissé 71960
Tel. 03 85 35 60 68   Fax 03 85 35 60 68
No Email address   £A/B

Now that the cheap trick that was Beaujolais Nouveau seems pretty much played out the world over, more seems set to be made of the region's real strengths. Its crus, the Gamay grape, the old vines, its granite, schist and sandy soils, its many small estates and some dedicated vignerons are the fundamentals. Add improved vinification, breathe life back into the soils and promote a willingness to explore different interpretations of just what Beaujolais can be (both a quaffer and something more serious) and more wine lovers might just add it to their shopping lists.

Beaujolais by village

Burgundy's Mâconnais melts into Beaujolais where a few Chardonnay vines qualify to be sold as Beaujolais Blanc. But the real story concerns the Gamay grape and its predisposition for a radically different growing environment as granite, schist (and in places sand or clay) soils take over from the limestone-based soils of Burgundy proper. In these soils old vines seem to count for more than low yields and grapes must be hand-picked as they are subject (in most instances) to a vinification that involves semi-carbonic maceration of whole bunches of grapes. The quality of the fruit can leave much to be desired and too much Beaujolais finishes abruptly with a hard, green edge. Better examples are richly fruity but relatively short-lived with little real structure but easy drinkability. Different interpretations of style do exist however, and some producers get more structure into the wines without losing too much of their charm and quaffability. Jadot and one or two others make the wines in the style of red Burgundy with a similar vinification and oak-ageing as for Pinot Noir-based reds. Though it may not seem worth the effort the difference a dedicated progressive grower can make to the quality of Beaujolais can be a revelation.

The best Beaujolais comes from the northern or Haut-Beaujolais, with purer soils and better slopes. It is sold as **Beaujolais-Villages** or better still as one of ten recognised *crus* from within this area. There is a trend to increasing identification of individual *climats* within the *crus*. The vineyards of **Saint-Amour**, where Beaujolais takes over from Mâconnais, are on rather mixed soils and are generally a little unexciting. **Juliénas** in contrast, from well-positioned slopes and a significant clay component in its soils, is a consistent provider of wines with better depth and intensity than most. Lighter **Chénas** occupies higher ground than the adjoining **Moulin-à-Vent** and it is the latter that has the most strength, structure and longevity of all the *crus*. Its prices are matched only by **Fleurie**, the best examples of which are perfumed but also often unequalled for their density of fruit and lush texture. **Chiroubles** has some of the most elevated vineyards in the region; the best wines are light but as refined as they get. At the heart of **Morgon** is the Côte de Py with its distinctive *roches pourries* soils of friable schist, the wines are dense and intensely cherryish. **Regnié** is the most recent *cru* and rarely exciting. The large **Brouilly** *cru* surrounds the hill of Mont Brouilly whose slopes provide **Côte de Brouilly**. The best Brouilly can have attractive fruit but much of it is poor, while Côte de Brouilly is usually marginally better.

Beaujolais vintages

Do vintages in Beaujolais matter with most of the wines being drunk so young? As some of the better quality *cru* Beaujolais need at least 2 or 3 years' to open out, for these choosing one vintage over another can make a big difference to what's in your glass. Take 2003 and 2002. The latter was spoilt by late rains and many a supposedly better cru is marred by poor quality fruit. It has been recently shown that in some instances this was due to contamination of the grapes by Geosmin. Although harmless, it gives a distinctive unpleasant musty/vegetal character to the wine. However, even those wines produced from healthy ripe fruit tend to be a little dull and uninspiring. By contrast the hot dry 2003 vintage ensured healthy grapes and there are some super wines with thrilling vibrant fruit, in many instances without the low acidities (and the consequent need for acidification) that might have been expected. While some are over-ripe and others show green tannins, look out for some real gems. 2004 seems mostly free of the Geosmin taint and the best wines are intense, pure and elegant. Of older vintages, although 2001 has turned out better than first expected, some 2000s (those Geosmin free) and most 1999s are superior.

A-Z of producers

DOM. CALOT Morgon www.domaine-calot.com

François et Jean Calot   42 Place de la Pompe, 69910 Villié-Morgon
UK stockists: **HHB**, BBR, SVS
This 12-ha estate has long been an excellent source of ripe, concentrated and characterful Morgon. There are several *cuvées*, from a supple, fruity regular Cuvée Tradition to a deep, intense Vieilles Vignes that needs 3 years or so in order to soften a little. Vinification is traditional and not the semi-carbonic maceration favoured by most. An old-fashioned vertical press is employed and both small and large oak are used for ageing. A small amount of Tête de Cuvée and an intense, complex Cuvée Jeanne have also been made in recent vintages. All are very reasonably and honestly priced for the quality – there has been no attempt to sell any of the wines at a premium to enhance the domaine's status or cash flow as some growers in the region have done. (PW)
● **Morgon** Tradition★★ £B Vieilles Vignes★★★ £B Tête de Cuvée★★★ £B
● **Morgon** Cuvée Jeanne★★★ £B

NICOLE CHANRION/LA VOÛTE DES CROZES Côte de Brouilly

Nicole Chanrion   Domaine de la Voûte des Crozes, 69220 Cercié-en-Beaujolais
UK stockists: **THt**, L&W
This small estate produces one of the best examples of Côte de Brouilly from 6ha of well-established vines. It is consistently expressive and fruit-rich with plenty of intensity and depth and a profusion of mineral, raspberry and cherry is framed by good acidity and soft tannins. It can be drunk young or with 3–5 years' age. (PW)
● **Côte de Brouilly★★★** £B

DOM. DE LA CHAPONNE Morgon

Laurent Guillet   Domaine de la Chaponne, 69910 Villié-Morgon
UK stockists: **THt,** Tan
If you like soft, fruit-driven Beaujolais for immediate consumption then this is not the producer for you. From 11ha and some very old vines – up to 90 years old – come powerful, structured examples of Morgon that need to be drunk with some age. There is great intensity and fruit depth but sometimes the wines can be a little too extracted. The mineral, cherry and raspberry of good Morgon is always there but so too is the structure and strength. Cuvée Joseph, the oak-aged version, adds oak spice to a deep plum, cherry and mineral intensity. The 2004s have more charm and better balance than 03 or 02 but still should be drunk with 3 years' age or more. (PW)
● **Morgon** Vieilles Vignes★★ £B Cuvée Joseph Vieilles Vignes Fûts de Chêne★★★ £C

CH. DE BEAUREGARD/JOSEPH BURRIER Beaujolais

Burrier family Château de Beauregard, 71960 Fuissé
UK stockists: DDr

Château de Beauregard is more likely to be encountered in the shape of fine Pouilly-Fuissé or other Mâconnais whites (see Mâconnais section) but the family also have 10ha in Beaujolais, including 6ha in Fleurie and 3ha in Moulin-à-Vent. No *macération carbonique* is employed and for the *crus* around 50% of the fruit is destemmed before 10–15 days fermentation with *pigeage*. The wines can show a touch of reduction when young but are full and supple, with real density and flesh in Moulin-à-Vent. A Clos de Pérelles version from 2003 (25% new oak for 8 months) has rich, mineral-imbued fruit and both depth and breadth. With plenty of extract and fine, ripe tannins, it needs 4–5 years' age but promises to be both complex and classy. As well as another Moulin-à-Vent, La Salomine, a special version of Fleurie, Les Colonies de Rochgrès, is also produced. (PW)

● **Moulin-à-Vent**★★★ £C Clos de Pérelles★★★ £D ● **Fleurie**★★ £B

CH. DES JACQUES Moulin-à-Vent www.louis-jadot.com

Louis Jadot Château des Jacques, 71570 Romanèche-Thorins
UK stockists: **HMA,** Wai

Long before its recent purchase by Louis JADOT, this was the leading estate in the Beaujolais region. Singular in its approach to vinification, with a Pinot-like destemming followed by fermentation in open tanks and *pigeage*, the wines have been richer and fuller with none of the woodiness or greenness that the whole-bunch fermentation practised by others can bring. Following the arrival of Jadot's Jacques Lardière, maceration times have been extended and there is some use of automatic *pigeage*. In addition, 5 separate sites have been isolated from within the estate's 27ha of Gamay vines and each of these is aged in new oak (Clos du Grand Carquelin, Grand Clos de Rochegrès, Champ de Cour, La Roche and Clos des Thorins). So the Côte d'Or has come to Beaujolais and with some clout, in order to promote further efforts towards higher quality (and higher prices). The wines show a previously unseen sumptuous, velvety quality and in the case of the Grand Carquelin and the Rochegrès at least also show promising complexity and structure, while Champ de Cour is arguably the most refined. There are also 9ha of Chardonnay from which the white Beaujolais (stainless steel-vinified) and Bourgogne Blanc (barrel-fermented and aged) are made. Combe aux Jacques is a separate facility dedicated to producing high-quality Beaujolais-Villages in conjunction with local growers. In 2001 Jadot added Château Bellevue, one of Morgon's most prized estates, where a similar prestigious string of *crus* under the name Château des Lumières is being made along the same lines as at Château des Jacques. (PW)

Château des Jacques:
● **Moulin-à-Vent** Clos du Grand Carquelin★★★ £C Champ de Cour★★★ £C
● **Moulin-à-Vent**★★ £C Grand Clos des Rochegrès★★ £C
O **Beaujolais-Villages** Chardonnay★★ £B O **Bourgogne Blanc** Clos de Loyse★★ £B
Château des Lumières:
● **Morgon**★★ £C

CH. THIVIN Côte de Brouilly www.chateau-thivin.com

Claude & Evelyne Geoffray Château Thivin, 69460 Odenas
UK stockists: RHW, GWW,VTr,Wse

Château Thivin is renowned for its Côte de Brouilly and is one of Beaujolais' historic properties, with medieval origins. The top *cuvée*, Zaccharie Geoffray, is named for one of Claude Geoffray's ancestors who purchased the property in 1877. The 24ha include a second domaine, Manoir du Pavé (from his wife's

221

family), which is the source of a good Beaujolais-Villages. While ripe and supple with fine structures, the wines show real individual expression and distinctive fruit, with a mineral, floral and herbal quality that is unique to the local soils. Other *cuvées* now bottled separately and made to the same standards, include Clos Bertrand and La Croix Dessaigne. Prices are reasonable for the quality. (PW)

● **Côte de Brouilly**★★ £B La Chapelle★★★ £B Zaccharie Geoffray★★★ £B
● **Brouilly**★ £B ● **Beaujolais-Villages** Manoir du Pavé★ £B

MICHEL CHIGNARD Fleurie

Michel Chignard Domaine Michel Chignard, 69820 Fleurie
UK stockists: **FMV**
There probably isn't any better Fleurie than that from Michel Chignard. His wines manage to be ripe, full and intense with rich textures that offer some immediate gratification but have the structure and substance to improve for at least 3–5 years. Moriers is one of the best parts of Fleurie, close to both La Roilette and some of the best *climats* in Moulin-à-Vent, but the very composed and refined nature of the wines is also proof of a high degree of care and skill on the part of the producer. Most vintages will improve for at least 6–8 years' but it isn't necessary to wait. (PW)

● **Fleurie** Les Moriers★★★ £B Spéciale Vieilles Vignes★★★ £C

CLOS DE LA ROILETTE/COUDERT Fleurie

Coudert family Clos de la Roilette, La Roilette, 69820 Fleurie
UK stockists: **DDr**, L&W, Sav, L&S
Within their 9.5ha of vineyard, the Couderts possess the best part of La Roilette, the finest *climat* in Fleurie. The site gives Fleurie of more body, depth and complexity than is typical and theirs is a parcel of very old vines. The grapes are harvested very ripe and in the small amount of a special bottling called Cuvée Tardive there is more intensity and richness. The wines are sleek and supple, with a black fruit character and a subtle mineral streak. Both are consistently fine yet reasonably priced Beaujolais that drink well with anything from 1 –3 years' age, occasionally more. The newish Cuvée Christal is even more accessible. (PW)

● **Fleurie** Cuvée Christal★★ £B
● **Fleurie** Clos de la Roilette★★★ £C Cuvée Tardive★★★ £C

DOM. DE COLONAT Morgon

Christine & Bernard Collonge Dom. de Colonat, Saint-Joseph, 69910 Villié-Morgon
The Collonges have 12ha of vines and make Chiroubles, Regnié and Beaujolais-Villages but their prized possession is in Les Charmes in Morgon. The soils include friable schist and decomposed rock with typical dense planting of 10,000 vines per hectare. The wines are not of the pristine, fruit-driven style but more traditional in structure. The regular *cuvée* is aged in used wood and is quite closed when young, without any immediate fruit richness, and needs 3–4 years to unfurl. Cuvée Marguerite Montchanay comes from vines more than 50 years old and is aged in *barriques* but again starts out tight and closed. Yet there is real breadth with fruit intensity and depth underneath and with 5 years' age or more it begins to develop a Pinot-like complexity. The 99 still has much to give and will keep at least another 2–3 years. 2003 should be cellared for 5–6 years minimum. (PW)

● **Morgon** Les Charmes Cuvée Marguerite Montchanay★★★ £B
● **Morgon** Les Charmes★★ £B

DOM. LOUIS-CLAUDE DESVIGNES Morgon

Louis-Claude Desvignes   135 Rue de la Voûte, 69910 Villié-Morgon
UK stockists: **Sav**, BBR

Louis-Claude Desvignes was one of the first in Beaujolais to produce separate *cuvées* from the best parcels in his estate. From 1.5ha of Côte de Py and 2ha of Javernières (from different soils within the Côte de Py) are regularly produced 2 rich vibrant, aromatic and distinctly different Morgons that bear little resemblance to most of what comes out of the Beaujolais region. There is undoubted skill and care in their production; low yields and a cold pre-fermentation maceration are just 2 contributing factors. Though there are now several other versions of Côte de Py (including Jean FOILLARD'S), few rival this one and none at the price, which remains low. These are wines to drink with at least 3 or 4 years' age if their full potential is to be realised. (PW)

● **Morgon** La Voûte Saint-Vincent★★ £B Javernières★★ £B Côte de Py★★ £B

GEORGES DUBOEUF Beaujolais www.duboeuf.com

Georges Duboeuf   71570 Romanèche-Thorins
UK stockists: **BWC**, AAA

For many around the world Duboeuf represents Beaujolais, or at least the decent stuff. A production of 30 million bottles is one of the reasons why it can be found in local wine shops and supermarkets almost everywhere. Duboeuf has been admirably consistent despite the phenomenal growth over more than 3 decades. Many small domaines, including some in every *cru*, come under the Duboeuf umbrella and are marketed and bottled accordingly. Though some of the *cuvées*, especially the generic *crus*, are simple and rather short and firm on the finish, others show more expression, and more succulence and finesse in their structures. The individual *cuvées* (most from single domaines) are nearly always worth the small premium they command, particularly those from Moulin-à-Vent and Fleurie, when compared to regular examples of the more southerly Beaujolais *crus*, Brouilly or Régnié. Individual *crus* can be drunk with a couple of years' ageing but don't need it. Prices of fine wines around the globe may have escalated but those of most of these Beaujolais, like their quality, have remained steady. Some fresh, attractive whites with good substance are also made, as are many Rhône wines and vins de pays from the Languedoc-Roussillon. Below are some of the very best of Duboeuf's Beaujolais/Mâconnais wines. Some very good 2003s. (PW)

● **Moulin-à-Vent** Domaine des Rosiers★★ £B Prestige★★★ £B
● **Moulin-à-Vent**★★ £B Fût de Chêne★★ £B
● **Moulin-à-Vent** Domaine de la Tour de Bief★★★ £B
● **Fleurie** La Madone★★ £B Domaine des Quatre Vents★★ £B
● **Fleurie**★ £B Château des Déduits★ £B
● **Fleurie** Château des Bachelards★ £B ● **Chiroubles** Domaine des Tilleuls★★ £B
● **Saint-Amour** Domaine des Sablons★ £B Domaine du Paradis★★ £B
● **Morgon**★ £B Domaine Jean Descombes★★ £B
● **Juliénas** Domaine de la Seigneurie★ £B
● **Brouilly** Domaine de Combillaty★ £B
● **Beaujolais-Villages** Château de Varennes★★ £B
O **Pouilly-Fuissé** Fût de Chêne★ £B Prestige★★ £B
O **Saint-Véran** Domaine Saint-Martin★ £B
O **Mâcon-Villages** Prestige★ £B

HENRY FESSY Beaujolais www.vins-henry-fessy.com

Henry Fessy Bel Air, 69220 Saint-Jean d'Ardières
UK stockists: **Cib**, DDr, For, Frw

With both a domaine of 12ha and a *négociant* business, Henry and Serges Fessy make a number of ripe, vigorous, perfumed Beaujolais. The estate vineyards are confined to Brouilly and Beaujolais but some fine examples are made from other *crus*. The Brouilly wines are particularly good for this *cru*, with both intensity and length of flavour in a forward, supple Cuvée Georges Fessy and a richer Pur Sang. Other wines listed are those regularly encountered but the standard of Beaujolais seems good throughout. Prices are not excessive for the quality. Some white Beaujolais, Saint-Véran and Pouilly-Fuissé are also made but have not been tasted. (PW)

● **Brouilly** Cuvée Georges Fessy★★ £B   Domaine du Plateau de Bel Air★★ £B
● **Brouilly** Pur Sang★★ £B   ● **Morgon** Cuvée Luquet★★ £B
● **Fleurie**   La Roilette★★ £B   Mauriers★★ £B

JEAN FOILLARD Morgon

Jean Foillard   Le Clachet, 69910 Villié-Morgan
UK stockists: **HHB**

Jean Foillard is a disciple of Jules Chauvet, a noted enologist who believed in fashioning Beaujolais in an altogether different way from the modern standard of semi-carbonic maceration. Foillard's 8ha include one of the best sites in the whole Beaujolais region, Morgon's Côte du Py. Important to the style are low yields and very ripe grapes, which are subject to a long cool vinification, practically zero use of sulphur and minimal or no filtration. It's not what you would normally associate with Beaujolais; an intense, spice- and mineral-rich structured wine that needs 5 years or more before it is ready. Light years away from simple, fruity quaffing Beaujolais, it does achieve real harmony in the best years. (PW)

● **Morgon** Première★★ £B   Côte du Py★★★ £C

DOM. PAUL ET ERIC JANIN Moulin-à-Vent

Janin family   71570 Romanèche-Thorins
UK stockists: **DDr, L&S, CPp, Rae, SVS**

Eric Janin makes excellent Moulin-à-Vent to a biodynamic recipe. The domaine of 10ha of old vines are carefully nurtured by father and son and the result is a marvellous fruit quality and good concentration and depth in the wines. Occasionally the tannins can be a little firm in the finish but the Clos du Tremblay (which is a selection of the very best old vines) in particular benefits from a couple of years' age. Two-thirds of production is Moulin-à-Vent, the rest Beaujolais-Villages from the smaller Domaine des Vignes des Jumeaux. New from 2002 is another cuvée of Moulin-à-Vent, Cuvée Séduction. Prices, as so often from those most dedicated to the land, are very reasonable. (PW)

● **Moulin-à-Vent** Clos du Tremblay★★★ £C   Vignes du Tremblay★★ £B
● **Beaujolais-Villages** Domaine des Vignes du Jumeaux★ £B

JACKY JANODET/DOM. LES FINE GRAVES

Jacky Janodet   Les Garniers, 71570 Romanèche-Thorins
UK stockists: **THt,** BBR, Tan, UnC, Sel

Jacky Janodet is one of the best-known growers based in Moulin-à-Vent. He has just over 10ha, of which 6.5ha are in Moulin-à-Vent itself and much is planted to very old vines. The wine is classically powerful with good depth, its concentration, structure and texture owed in part to ageing in small barrels. The 2003 shows the intensity, vibrancy and ripeness of the vintage but as with other years will be at its best with 3–4 years' age. Some Chénas, Beaujolais-Villages and a tiny amount of white is also made. (PW)

● **Moulin-à-Vent** Vieilles Vignes★★★ £B

HUBERT LAPIERRE   Chénas   www.domaine-lapierre.com

Denise et Hubert Lapierre   Les Gandelins, 71570 La Chapelle de Guinchay
UK stockists: **L&W**

Chénas is not the most exciting *cru* in Beaujolais but those from Hubert
Lapierre can show good weight and ripe raspberryish fruit. As well as a Vieilles
Vignes version a small amount is aged in mostly used *barriques* for 10 months,
enriching both texture and flavour. The 7.5ha of vineyards also includes more
ample, riper, darker-fruited Moulin-à-Vent with good acidity that is better with
2–3 years and in the case of the Vieilles Vignes version usually keeps 5–6 years.
The wines show exceptionally well from warm vintages like 2003. (PW)

● **Chénas** Fût de Chêne★★ £B Vieilles Vignes★★ £B
● **Moulin-à-Vent** Tradition★★ £B Vieilles Vignes★★★ £B

DOM. DE LA MADONE   Fleurie

Despres family   La Madone, 69820 Fleurie
UK stockists: **OWL**, THt, Gen, Ear, RHW, NDb

Jean-Marc Despres and his son Arnaud consistently produce benchmark
Fleurie from almost 9ha of vines on south-west facing slopes. The regular *cuvée*
is supple and smooth with raspberry, cherry and refined floral characters. There
is no hardness or greenness even in a vintage like 2002, and there is depth and
breadth without being overdone. The Vieilles Vignes offers more complexity
and refinement (as well as density in the 2003 vintage). This ability to respond
to the vintage conditions marks these wines out; too many others are
overextracted and unbalanced in all but the best years. Another *cuvée* of old
vines, Grille Midi, comes from a particularly warm part of the vineyards and
can be more fleshy, more structured but displays a fine minerality. Also made
are a little Juliénas, an oak-aged Fleurie and some Beaujolais-Villages. (PW)

● **Fleurie**★★ £B Vieilles Vignes★★★ £C Grille Midi Vieilles Vignes★★★ £C

BERNARD MÉTRAT   Fleurie

Bernard Métrat   La Roilette, 69820 Fleurie

This is a typical small Beaujolais estate but with 6.5ha in Chiroubles and
Fleurie Bernard Métrat ensures that his are no run-of-the-mill examples. A very
perfumed, floral, berry-fruited Chiroubles has very good fruit intensity if not
the greatest depth, as is typical of the *cru*. Yet there is good structure to it and it
will flesh out nicely with at least 2–3 years' age so don't hurry to drink it. The
Fleurie vines in highly regarded La Roilette, contiguous with some of the best
lieux-dits in Moulin-à-Vent, produce even better wine – supple and
exceptionally smooth with real breadth and elegance. It wil benefit from at least
2–3 years' age in warmer vintages but was slightly marred by a vegetal,
geosmin-like taint (see Beaujolais Vintages) in 2004. (PW)

● **Fleurie** La Roilette Vieilles Vignes★★★ £B   ● **Chiroubles**★★★ £B

DOMAINES PIRON   Morgon   www.domaines-piron.fr

Dominique Piron   Domaines Piron, Morgon, 69910 Villié-Morgon
UK stockists: **MPe**, F&M

Descended from a long line of grape growers stretching back to the mid-17th
century, Dominique Piron has put much effort into improving viticulture and
the quality of his grapes. His 22ha of vineyard with an average vine age of 40
years are composed of the 17ha Domaine de la Chanaise and 5ha Domaine de
Combiaty. The best wines can show a minerality that, given the soils, ought to
be seen in more Beaujolais – yet most simply exhibit attractive fruit and floral
characters. This is most evident in the Morgon Côte de Py, the only 1 of 6
climats bottled separately. Given a relatively long maceration, this is usually the
top wine but Brouilly can also be very good, although quality of the sometimes

225

complex Moulin-à-Vent is a little more irregular. Good Beaujolais-Villages and a little Beaujolais Blanc (from Chardonnay) are also made. As well as the Domaines Piron wines, Dominique Piron acts as a *négociant* producing wines under his own name and own-label Beaujolais for Fortnum & Mason in London. (PW)

● **Morgon**★★ £B Côte du Py★★★ £B
● **Moulin-à-Vent** Les Vignes du Vieux Bourg★★★ £B
● **Brouilly** Château du Prieuré ★ £B   ● **Regnié**★ £B
● **Beaujolais-Villages** Les Vignes de Pierreux★ £B

DOM. DES TERRES DORÉES   Beaujolais

Jean-Paul Brun   Crière, 69380 Charnay-en-Beaujolais
UK stockists: **Sav**

Jean-Paul Brun's domaine is situated in the south of the Beaujolais region, known as the Pierres Doreés. His wines are the exception in what is otherwise a sea of inferior plonk (most of which appears under a simple 'Beaujolais' label). Soils in these parts are predominantly limestone, and that part of Brun's 20ha of vineyards with calcareous soils is planted not to Gamay but instead to Chardonnay and Pinot Noir. Therefore as well as producing pure, intense Beaujolais that really tastes of its origins there's both a light Bourgogne Grand Ordinaire (Pinot Noir) and Beaujolais Blanc (En Fût is a *barrique*-fermented version) that are intense and original. Late-harvested wines are also produced including Labeur d'Octobre and 'E sens de chardon né', from botrytis-affected Chardonnay grapes. Good Côte de Brouilly and Moulin-à-Vent are also made. (PW)

● **Beaujolais** Cuvée à l'Ancienne★★ £B   ● **Côte de Brouilly**★★ £B
● **Moulin-à-Vent**★★ £C
● **Bourgogne Grande Ordinaire**★ £B   O **Beaujolais Blanc**★ £B

MICHEL TÊTE/DOM. CLOS DU FIEF   Juliénas

Michel Tête   Les Gonnards, 69840 Juliénas
UK stockists: **L&W**

Michel Tête has 13ha of vineyard from which he produces a rare good example of Saint-Amour and 2 versions of Juliénas. Saint-Amour is silky, refined and harmonious particularly in good warm vintages. Regular Juliénas is full and chewy with good structure while a Prestige version from lower-yielding old vines is oak-aged. The latter is lush with better depth and breadth but can be kept at least 4–5 years, becoming more seductive and complex. Some 2003s can be overripe and jammy but not these. (PW)

● **Juliénas**★★ £B Cuvée Prestige★★★ £C   ● **Beaujolais-Villages**★ £B
● **Saint-Amour**★★★ £B

DOM. DU VISSOUX   Beaujolais

Pierre-Marie Chermette   Domaine du Vissoux, 69620 Saint-Vérand
UK stockists: **Eno,** Vne, Hrd

The wines from this 30-ha estate continue to improve and include excellent examples of both Fleurie and Moulin-à-Vent. Fleurie has lovely style and intensity, the Garants showing the lusher texture of the 2 bottlings. Moulin-à-Vent, both Rochegrès and slightly superior Rochelle, show more spice, mineral and greater breadth though have been slightly less consistent quality-wise. That said, in 2002 these were more successful than the Fleurie, which shone more in 2001. The regular Beaujolais Traditionelle, sourced from the southern Beaujolais, is not of the same ilk. Consitently high quality in 2003. (PW)

● **Fleurie** Poncié★★ £B Les Garants★★★ £C
● **Moulin-à-Vent** Rochegrès★★ £C Rochelle★★★ £C

BEAUJOLAIS/OTHER WINES OF NOTE

JEAN-MARC BURGAUD ● **Morgon** Côte du Py★★ £B Les Charmes★★ £B
CH. DE LA CHAIZE ● **Brouilly**★ £B
FERNAND CHARVET/DOM. DES VIEILLES CAVES
● **Chénas** Vieilles Vignes★★ £B
● **Moulin-à-Vent** Vieilles Vignes★★★ £B
GÉRARD CHARVET ● **Moulin-à-Vent** Vieilles Vignes★★ £B
CHÂTEAU DU MOULIN-À-VENT ● **Moulin-à-Vent** Cuvée Exceptionelle★★ £B
● **Moulin-à-Vent**★ £B
CH. DE PIERREUX ● **Brouilly**★★★ £C La Réserve du Château★★★ £C
CH. DES TOURS ● **Brouilly**★★ £C
DOM. ÉMILE CHEYSSON ● **Chiroubles**★★ £B Prestige★★ £B
ANDRÉ COLONGE ET FILS ● **Beaujolais-Villages**★ £B ● **Fleurie**★★ £B
JOELLE ET GÉRARD DESCOMBES ● **Beaujolais-Villages**★ £B
● **Juliénas**★★ £C
DOM. DIOCHON ● **Moulin-à-Vent** Vieilles Vignes★★ £B
DOM. DUBOST ● **Brouilly** La Bruyère Vieilles Vignes★★ £B
CAVE COOPÉRATIVE DE FLEURIE ● **Fleurie** Cuvée Millésimé★★ £B
DOM. MAURICE GAGET ● **Morgon** Côte du Py★★★ £C
JACKY GAUTHIER ● **Regnié** Domaine de Colette★ £B
DOM. GAY-COPERET ● **Moulin-à-Vent** Réserve Vieilles Vignes★★ £B
● **Moulin-à-Vent** Cuvée Prestige★★ £B
DOM. DE LA GRAND COUR ● **Fleurie** Clos de la Grand Cour★★ £B
● **Fleurie** Fût de Chêne V V★★★ £C
PASCAL GRANGER ● **Chénas**★ £B ● **Juliénas** Cuvée Speciale★★ £B
DOM. DE GRY-SABLON ● **Fleurie**★★ £B ● **Morgon**★★ £B
MARCEL LAPIERRE ● **Morgon**★★ £C
ALAIN MARGERAND ● **Moulin-à-Vent** Rochegrès★★ £B
JEAN-PIERRE MARGERAND ● **Juliénas**★★ £B
LAURENT MARTRAY ● **Brouilly** Vieilles Vignes★★ £B
ALAIN MICHAUD ● **Brouilly**★★ £B ● **Morgon**★★ £B
MONMESSIN ● **Beaujolais-Villages** Vieilles Vignes★ £B
● **Morgon** Les Griottes★★ £B ● **Fleurie** La Cerisaie★★ £B
ALBERT MOREL ● **Fleurie**★★ £B
ALAIN PASSOT/DOM. DE LA GROSSE PIERRE ● **Chiroubles**★★ £B
DOM. DES PINS/JEAN-FRANCOIS ECHALLIER ● **Saint-Amour**★★ £B
JEAN-CHARLES PIVOT ● **Beaujolais-Villages**★★ £B ● **Côte de Brouilly**★★ £B
POTEL-AVIRON ● **Morgon** Côte du Py Vieilles Vignes★★★ £C
● **Fleurie** Vieilles Vignes★★★ £C
● **Moulin-à-Vent** Vieilles Vignes★★★ £C
DOM. LES ROCHES BLEUES ● **Côte de Brouilly**★★ £B
BERNARD SANTÉ ● **Chénas**★★ £B ● **Juliénas**★★ £B
DOM. GEORGES VIORNERY ● **Côte de Brouilly**★★ £B

Author's Choice for Beaujolais (PW)

Some favourite Beaujolais

DOM. CALOT ● **Morgon** Tête de Cuvée
NICOLE CHANRION/IA VOUTE DES CROZES ● **Côte de Brouilly**
CH. DE BEAUREGARD ● **Moulin-à-Vent** Clos des Pérelles
CH. DES JACQUES ● **Moulin-à-Vent**
MICHEL CHIGNARD ● **Fleurie** Les Moriers
CLOS DE LA ROILETTE/COUDERT ● **Fleurie** Clos de la Roilette
DOM. DE COLONAT ● **Morgon** Les Charmes Cuvée Marguerite Montchanay
GEORGES DUBOEUF ● **Moulin-à-Vent** Prestige
DOM. PAUL ET ERIC JANIN ● **Moulin-à-Vent** Clos du Tremblay
DOM. DE LA MADONE ● **Fleurie** Vieilles Vignes
MICHEL TETE/DOM. CLOS DU FIEF ● **Saint-Amour**
DOM. DU VISSOUX ● **Fleurie** Les Garants

This is one of France's most unusual and exciting regions. Culturally it is as much German as it is French and twice during the last 130 years or so has been a part of the former. It is one of France's most spectacular regions to visit, with the splendour of the Vosges mountains complemented by the medieval architecture of many towns and villages. Unlike in other regions, the grape varietal plays a key element in wine labelling. The wines themselves can be piercingly aromatic and are quite unique in style. Although there are some substantial merchant operations and large co-ops the area is not a purveyor of bulk wine. However there is still a wide variation in quality and yields generally throughout the region are too high, with most wine still coming from over-productive sites on the plains. As elsewhere, who produced the wine is the key.

Geography

The region of Alsace is a narrow stretch of vineyards running north-south at the base of and nestled into the eastern foothills of the Vosges mountains. These, along with the Rhine just to the east of the *vignoble*, provide the region with an impressively favourable climate for such a northerly latitude. Sunshine hours are high during the growing season and rainfall low. The vineyard area stretches from just west of Strasbourg in the north to Mulhouse in the south, with the heart of the region centred around the town of Colmar. This is where the greatest concentration of top villages and vineyard sites, particularly *grands crus,* is to be found. These southern stretches are known as the **Haut Rhin**; the northern part is the **Bas Rhin.** There are fewer great sites in the Bas Rhin but some very fine wine is produced nonetheless. In some respects the region resembles the Côte d'Or. The finest sites are inevitably on the slopes of the Vosges, with well-drained, meagre soils. By contrast those vineyards planted on the fertile, heavy alluvial soils on the plains towards the Rhine are far less propitious for quality wine production.

Wine Styles

The generic appellation of the region is simply **Alsace** AC. The vast majority of wine is labelled by its grape variety. There is an ongoing debate in the region about the importance of the varieties themselves, as opposed to site and *terroir,* in determining style. There is just one permitted red grape, Pinot Noir, which can be good but is often light and insubstantial, needing a good vintage. The white varietals are the fairly neutral Pinot Blanc and Sylvaner (although there are some impressive old-vine examples) and the more aromatic Riesling, Muscat, Tokay Pinot Gris and Gewürztraminer. There is some Chasselas producing the odd varietal wine, as well as Auxerrois, but both will generally be used with Sylvaner and Pinot Blanc in generic blends. These are covered by the Alsace AC and are labelled either Edelzwicker or Gentil. An unusual rarity in the higher reaches of the Bas Rhin is the Klevner de Heilegenstein. No wines of real note have been produced from it. Confusingly, Auxerrois is often referred to as Klevner.

The 50 *grands crus* here were established in 1983. Wines produced from these are classified **Alsace Grand Cru** AC. The majority of these sites can be found in the heart of the Haut Rhin and were created to pinpoint the best vineyards. Much work still needs to be done with the region's labelling system and although there is talk of it, there is no further official classification. Many wines make reference to their *lieux-dits* in order to emphasise potential quality. A number of these sites produce wines that are comfortably a match for many *grands crus.* The vineyards of the latter must be planted to Gewürztraminer, Muscat, Riesling or Tokay Pinot Gris.

Almost all wines are varietal but there are experiments, particularly those by Jean-Michel Deiss, in establishing field blends.

Some of the region's greatest wines are the late-harvested wines, *Vendange Tardive* (VT) and *Sélection de Grains Nobles* (SGN). Being made from late-harvested grapes, these are generally sweet styles. Noble rot may occur, particularly in the SGNs, but not always. However, the classification is based on grape ripeness at harvest and some *Vendange Tardive* wines can be surprisingly dry. Indeed the whole question of levels of residual sugar can be confusing. Some producers tend towards a very steely, dry style, while others prefer to let nature take its course, with fermentation stopping naturally. The results in the latter case are wines with often surprising levels of sugar and extract. The best, though, are very well balanced with sometimes remarkable depth. In order to help with this confusion a scale has been established, indicating on the back label the degree of sweetness.

The final style is **Crémant d'Alsace** AC. These are made by the traditional method and are mostly produced from Pinot Blanc and Riesling, although Auxerrois, Pinot Noir and Tokay Pinot Gris are also permitted. The best examples have reasonable depth and structure, often with marked acidity.

Alsace vintages

The region is sunny and warm and, like many of the top areas of France, governed by a marginal climate. While this is important in the development of great wines, there will inevitably be some vintage variation. The lesser whites should be drunk young and certainly by the time they have had four or five years' ageing. Riesling is better in slightly cooler years, Gewürztraminer and Tokay Pinot Gris add dimension in warmer years. The chart below will provide a reliable guide as to what you should expect. The very best *grand cru* and late-harvest styles are remarkably ageworthy. Of the great earlier years to consider are 1983, 1976 and for very top wines 1971 and 1967.

Alsace vintage chart

	Riesling	Pinot Gris	Gewürztraminer	Late-Harvest Wines
	Grand or Top Cru	Grand or Top Cru	Grand or Top Cru	Vendange Tardive or SGN
2004	★★★/★★★★ A	★★★/★★★★ A	★★★/★★★★ A	★★★ A
2003	★★★★ A	★★★★ A	★★★★ A	★★★/★★★★ A
2002	★★★★ A	★★★★/★★★★★ A	★★★★/★★★★★ A	★★★★ A
2001	★★★★ A	★★★★ A	★★★★ A	★★★★ A
2000	★★★★ A	★★★★ A	★★★★ A	★★★★ A
1999	★★★★ A	★★★/★★★★ B	★★★/★★★★ B	★★★★ A
1998	★★★★/★★★★★ B	★★★★ B	★★★★ B	★★★★/★★★★★ A
1997	★★★★ B	★★★★/★★★★★ B	★★★★/★★★★★ B	★★★★/★★★★★ B
1996	★★★★/★★★★★ B	★★★★/★★★★★ B	★★★★ B	★★★★/★★★★★ B
1995	★★★★/★★★★★ B	★★★★/★★★★★ B	★★★★ C	★★★★/★★★★★ B
1994	★★★ C	★★★ C	★★★ C	★★★★ B
1990	★★★★/★★★★★ C	★★★★/★★★★★ C	★★★★/★★★★★ C	★★★★/★★★★★ B
1989	★★★★ C	★★★★/★★★★★ C	★★★★/★★★★★ C	★★★★/★★★★★ B
1988	★★★★/★★★★★ C	★★★★ C	★★★★ C	★★★★ C
1985	★★★★ C	★★★★/★★★★★ C	★★★★ C	★★★★ C

A-Z of producers

DOM. JEAN-BAPTISTE ADAM   Ammerschwihr   www.jb-adam.com

Jean-Baptiste Adam   5 Rue Aigle, 687700 Ammerschwihr
UK stockists: All

Long-established Alsace producer, founded in 1614. There are just 15ha of vineyards but fruit is bought in to produce no fewer than 80,000 cases a year, making this one of the largest operations in the region. The generic Sélection and Réserve wines offer reliable drinking but better are the Jean-Baptiste labels, including decent Pinot Noir in warmer years. The heart of the Adam estate is based on the *lieux-dits* Letzenberg and Kaefferkopf and Riesling also comes from the Grand Cru Winneck-Schlossberg. Letzenberg is just 2.5ha of mass-selected Riesling and Pinot Gris grown on mainly clay soils. The top site, the Kaefferkopf, has been cultivated by the Adam family since the early 1800s. Finely drained granite soils produce excellent Riesling and Gewürztraminer as well as the Traditional Kaefferkopf Cuvée, a blend of both varieties. Occasional Vendange Tardive and SGN bottlings are released as well as some sound Crémant d'Alsace, both Brut and Extra Brut. (DM)

O **Gewürztraminer** Kaefferkopf Jean-Baptiste★★★ £C Vendange Tadive★★★ £D
O **Riesling** Letzenberg★★ £B Kaefferkopf Vieilles Vignes★★★ £C
O **Riesling** Grand Cru Winneck-Schlossberg★★★ £C
O **Tokay Pinot Gris** Letzenberg★★★ £C
O **Muscat** Reserve★ £B

DOM. LUCIEN ALBRECHT   Orschwihr   www.lucien-albrecht.fr

Jean Albrecht   9 Grand-Rue, 68500 Orschwihr
UK stockists: **Eno**

There are just over 30ha of vineyards at this property. The regular wines are simple, straightforward and emphasise their varietal character well. The best wines are from Grand Cru Pfingstberg, particularly the special bottlings labelled Cuvée A de Albrecht. Vendange Tardive and SGN can be impressive as well. Top Pinot Gris and Gewürztraminer are quite opulent and reasonably approachable; Riesling is in a tighter, more structured mould – citrusy and intense with some age but relatively austere when young. Prices are very reasonable. (DM)

O **Gewürztraminer** Cuvée Martine Albrecht★★★ £B
O **Gewürztraminer** Pfingstberg Grand Cru Cuvée A de Albrecht★★★ £C
O **Riesling** Pfingstberg Grand Cru Cuvée A de Albrecht★★★ £C
O **Riesling** Vendange Tardive★★★ £C
O **Tokay Pinot Gris** Grand Cru Pfingstberg★★★ £C
O **Tokay Pinot Gris** Vendange Tardive★★★★ £D
O **Muscat** Bollenberg★★ £B

DOM. JEAN BECKER   Zellenberg   vinsbecker@aol.com

Marie-José Becker   4 route d'Ostheim, 68340 Zellenberg
Fine old family domaine established in 1610, which now has 18ha of vineyards in the villages of Zellenberg, Riquewihr, Beblenheim and Ribeauvillé. Of these, 4ha are *grand cru* and a small amount of fruit is bought in from other growers around Zellenberg. Among the *grands crus*, floral, elegant Riesling, Tokay Pinot Gris, Muscat and Gewürztraminer come from Froehn. Riesling and Gewürztraminer from the marl soils of Schoenenbourg can produce excellent late-harvest wines. Gewürztraminer is also grown at the Sporen, Sonnenglanz and Praelatenberg sites. Among the *lieux-dits*, fresh fruity Riesling comes from Hagenschlauf and Tokay Pinot Gris and Gewürztraminer, often produced as Vendange Tardive and occasionally as SGN, from Rimelsberg. Good fruit-driven Pinot Blanc and regular Tokay

Pinot Gris are produced organically. The style of the wines is traditional but they all show good fruit intensity. The top *crus* have a fine mineral complexity to them and you can expect them to age well. (DM)

O **Gewürztraminer** Grand Cru Sonnenglanz★★ £C Vendange Tardive★★★★ £D
O **Gewürztraminer** Grand Cru Schoenenbourg SGN★★★★ £E
O **Riesling** Hagenschlauf★★ £C Grand Cru Froehn★★★ £C
O **Tokay Pinot Gris**★★ £B Grand Cru Froehn★★★ £C
O **Muscat** Grand Cru Froehn★★★ £C
O **Pinot Blanc**★ £B

DOM. CÉCILE BERNHARD-RIEBEL Châtenois

Cécile Bernhard-Riebel 20 Rue de Lorraine, 67730 Châtenois
UK stockists:SVS

Small to medium-sized producer with an output of around 8–9,000 cases a year from 17ha of vineyards planted to Riesling, Tokay Pinot Gris, Gewürztraminer, Pinot Blanc and a little Sylvaner planted in well-drained granite soils. Unusually the domaine is run by mother Cécile and son Pierre. There are no *grand cru* vineyards but they have small holdings in the *lieux-dits* Weingarten, Hahnenberg and Rittesberg. The Rieslings are the best bets, very pure with classic varietal character, while the Tokay Pinot Gris are rich and weighty wines that go through malolactic fermentation. Vendanges Tardives are produced from Riesling, Gewürztraminer and Pinot Gris. Prices are very reasonable. (DM)

O **Riesling** Vieilles Vignes★★ £B Weingarten★★★ £C
O **Tokay Pinot Gris** Tradition★★ £B Hahnenberg★★★ £C
O **Pinot Blanc**★ £B

LÉON BEYER Eguisheim www.leonbeyer.fr

Léon Beyer 2 Rue de la Première-Arnée, 68420 Eguisheim
UK stockists: Hal, BBR

This is quite a substantial property producing wines from its own 20ha of vineyards and also buying in grapes for its *négociant* wines. Vineyard holdings include the Grands Crus Eichberg and Pfersigberg but as at HUGEL no wines are released as such. Output is around 60,000 cases a year. As one would expect, the generic bottlings do not set the world on fire but are generally well crafted and offer a particularly dry, almost austere style. They will develop well in bottle. Better are the Grandes Cuvées Comtes d'Eguisheim labels, which are rich and reasonably concentrated. Riesling Ecaillers and Gewürztraminer Réserve also stand out. Vendange Tardive Gewürztraminer is good but just lacks some of the weight one might hope for. Sélection de Grains Nobles from the same variety is very impressive. The Pinot Gris SGN is remarkable: structured, rich and very ageworthy. (DM)

O **Gewürztraminer** Comtes d'Eguisheim★★ £D Vendange Tardive★★★ £E
O **Gewürztraminer** SGN★★★★ £F
O **Riesling** Ecaillers★★ £C Comtes d'Eguisheim★★ £D
O **Tokay Pinot Gris** SGN✪✪✪✪✪ £F

DOM. PAUL BLANCK Kaysersberg www.blanck.com

Blanck family 32 Grand-Rue, 68240 Kientzheim
UK stockists: Lay

Medium-sized family producer with an output approaching 20,000 cases a year. Quality is generally good to very good across the board and the wines tend to be made in an opulent, rich vein. Often quite marked levels of residual sugar can be found in the drier styles. Generic labels including Riesling and Pinot Blanc are sound but can be a little simple. Very good is an intense, green-apple Sylvaner from old vines. There are a range of *vieilles vignes, grand cru*, VT

231

and SGN bottlings. You can expect almost all *grand cru* bottles to be at least ★★★. Very good examples are produced from the Grands Crus Furstentum, Sommerberg and Schlossberg and there are fine wines produced from other *lieux-dits* as well. Fine VT is almost invariably ★★★★ and there is an explosively rich and opulent Pinot Gris SGN. Make sure you get the right address; there is more than 1 Blanck in Kientzheim. (DM)

O **Pinot Auxerrois**★ £B
O **Gewürztraminer** Furstentum Grand Cru Vieilles Vignes★★★★ £E
O **Gewürztraminer** Furstentum Grand Cru Vendange Tardive★★★★★ £E
O **Riesling** Rosenbourg★★ £B Patergarten★★★ £C
O **Riesling** Furstentum Grand Cru★★★★ £D Schlossberg Grand Cru★★★★ £D
O **Tokay Pinot Gris** Patergarten★★ £B Furstentum Grand Cru★★★ £E
O **Tokay Pinot Gris** SGN✪✪✪✪✪ £G

DOM. BOTT-GEYL Beblenheim bottgeyl@libertysurf.fr

Bott-Geyl family 1 Rue du Petit-Château, 68980 Beblenheim
UK stockists: CTy

Impressive small family domaine that has some 12.5ha of estate vineyards producing close to 8,000 cases a year. The quality is nearly always very sound right across the range. The style is almost explosively rich and the wines will often have marked residual sugar. Harvesting as ripe as possible and letting nature and indigenous yeasts run their natural course produces such results. Good generic Pinot Auxerrois and Gewürztraminer Beblenheim as well as Muscat Riquewihr offer very good value. There are also considerable *grand cru* holdings. Gewürztraminer and Pinot Gris from Grands Crus Furstentum and Sonnenglanz are always ★★★, often better, and also come from the excellent *lieu-dit* of Schlosselreben. Riesling comes from Mandelberg, Schoenenbourg and Grafenreben. The Mandelberg tends to be fullest – rich and weighty with a marvellously pure mineral core. While the Gewürztraminer VT is quite tight and restrained in style, the Pinot Gris SGN from Sonnenglanz can be explosive, rich and sumptuous but with a marvellous fresh, structured backbone. The top wines will inevitably age extraordinarily well. Most offer very good value. (DM)

O **Pinot d'Alsace** Beblenheim★ £B   O **Muscat** Riquewihr★★ £B
O **Riesling** Mandelberg Grand Cru★★★★ £C
O **Gewürztraminer** Furstentum Grand Cru★★★ £C
O **Gewürztraminer** Sonnenglanz Grand Cru Vieilles Vignes★★★★ £D
O **Gewürztraminer** Sonnenglanz Grand Cru Vendange Tardive★★★★★ £E
O **Tokay Pinot Gris** de Beblenheim★★★ £B Furstentum Grand Cru★★★★ £C
O **Tokay Pinot Gris** Sonnenglanz Grand Cru Vendange Tardive★★★★★ £E
O **Tokay Pinot Gris** SGN✪✪✪✪✪ £F

ALBERT BOXLER Niedermorschwihr albert.boxler@9online.fr

Jean-Marc Boxler 78 Rue des Trois-Epis, 68230 Niedermorschwihr
UK stockists: Gau

Jean-Marc Boxler's small domaine, nearly 14ha, produces just over 4,000 cases across a small but well-made range. Generics including Riesling and Pinot Blanc are very good, but Gewürztraminer can occasionally disappoint. Top Gewürztraminer and Pinot Gris comes from the Brand vineyard, Riesling from Brand and Sommerberg. The Rieslings particularly stand out. The style is for very dry, almost austere wines with a restrained, youthful, green-apple and markedly mineral character. Pinot Gris and Gewürztraminer, even at *grand cru* level, do not have the formidable structure and depth of the Rieslings. They tend more towards a simpler, riper if more opulent style. Riesling VT and SGN can be stunning as can a very impressive Pinot Gris – all are ★★★★, often ★★★★★ or occasionally ✪✪✪✪✪. The top Rieslings will age magnificently and should not be broached without 6 or 7 years' ageing. (DM)

O **Riesling★★** £B Brand Grand Cru★★★ £D Sommerberg Grand Cru★★★★ £D
O **Gewürztraminer** Brand Grand Cru★★★ £D O **Tokay Pinot Gris★** £B
O **Gewürztraminer** Brand Grand Cru★★★ £C
O **Pinot Blanc★★** £B

ERNEST BURN Gueberschwihr www.domaine-burn.fr

Joseph et Francis Burn 8 Rue Basse, 68420 Gueberschwihr
UK stockists: Has, HHB, NYg, Gau

This is a very impressive small, traditional domaine with a holding of just 10ha.
The wholly owned *monopole* Clos Saint Imer is part of the Grand Cru Goldert
and this accounts for over half the vineyard holdings. A fine Pinot Blanc is
joined by some very well-crafted rich and stylish Muscat, Pinot Gris,
Gewürztraminer and Riesling. The style of the *grand cru* wines is for rich, very
late-harvested fruit with real density and imense depth. They can almost seem
overblown but always retain a fine, structured undercurrent. Riesling can be a
touch overwhelmed in this style when the vintage produces very ripe, soft
wines, as in 1997, and tends to be at its best in the cooler years. Some very fine,
sumptuous and honeyed VT is made from Gewürztraminer and Pinot Gris. (DM)

O **Pinot Blanc★★** £B
O **Gewürztraminer** Goldert Grand Cru Cuvée de la Chapelle★★★★ £E
O **Riesling** Goldert Grand Cru Cuvée de la Chapelle★★★ £D
O **Tokay Pinot Gris★★** £B Goldert Grand Cru Cuvée de la Chapelle★★★★ £D

CAVE DE CLEEBOURG Cleebourg www.cave-cleebourg.com

'Co-Operative' Route du Vin, 67160 Cleebourg
UK stockists: **C&B**

An extensive range is made at this sizeable co-op established in 1946. There are
192 member growers with a total of 180ha of vineyard holdings in the
extreme north of the Alsace region. The vineyard area was destroyed during the
Second World War but has been progressively built up since and some of the
plantings are now of considerable age. Some excellent, pure and intense single-
vineyard Gewürztraminer, Riesling and Tokay Pinot Gris are produced as well
as good examples of Muscat and Pinot Auxerrois and a clean, fresh Crémant
d'Alsace. Vendanges Tardives are released occasionally. They are sound but do
not offer the same value as the other wines. (DM)

O **Gewürztraminer★** £B Reiffenberg★★ £B O **Riesling** Hannesacker★★★ £B
O **Tokay Pinot Gris** Vieilles Vignes★★ £B Karchweg★★ £B O **Muscat** Sigille★ £B
O **Pinot Blanc/Auxerrois★** £B O **Crémant d'Alsace** Clerostein★ £B

MARCEL DEISS Bergheim www.marceldeiss.com

Deiss family 15 Route du Vin, 68750 Bergheim
UK stockists: Bal, L&S

The Deiss family has been producing wines here for over 50 years. Jean-Michel
Deiss is now in charge of the property and runs the domaine along biodynamic
lines. He is unquestionably now one of the 3 or 4 best producers in the entire
region. An exemplary range of wines is made from very low yields from a range
of sites including *grand cru* holdings at Altenberg, Mambourg and
Schoenenbourg. A very good generic Pinot Blanc is made, as well as Riesling
from Saint-Hippolyte and Pinot Gris and Gewürztraminer from Bergheim.
The *grands crus* are very fine. Riesling comes from Altenberg and
Schoenenbourg, Gewürztraminer and Pinot Gris from Altenberg. Deiss also
produces 3 remarkable and very rich *grands crus* from Altenberg, Mambourg
and Schoenenbourg that are field blends of the noble varieties. As well as these,
there is a very good Gentil from the Burg site. The intention is to increase the
complexity of the wines and emphasise their *terroir* rather than their varietal
character. The approach throughout is to achieve very ripe fruit and the wines

233

regularly have very marked sugar levels. Occasional super-rich VT and SGN are made. (DM)

O **Mambourg Grand Cru**★★★★★ £F   O **Schonenbourg Grand Cru**✪✪✪✪✪ £F
O **Altenberg Grand Cru**✪✪✪✪✪ £F   O **Pinot Blanc**★★★ £C
O **Gewürztraminer** Bergheim★★★★ £D   Altenberg Grand Cru★★★★ £F
O **Riesling** Saint-Hippolyte★★★ £C   Altenberg Grand Cru✪✪✪✪✪ £F
O **Tokay Pinot Gris** Bergheim★★★★ £E   Altenberg Grand Cru★★★★★ £F

DOM. DIRLER-CADÉ   Bergholz   jbdirler@terre-net.fr

Jean & Ludivine Dirler   5 Rue d'Issenheim, 68500 Bergholz

The Dirlers produce an excellent range of traditionally made wines from all the major Alsace varieties. The property was founded in 1871 and there are some 16ha of producing vineyards, which since 1998 have been farmed biodynamically. Over 40% of the family holding is *grand cru* with vines planted in the Saering, Spiegel, Kessler and Kitterlé sites. The Dirlers also have holdings in the *lieux-dits* Scwarzberg, Bux, Bollenberg, Schimberg and Belzbrunnen. While the wines are traditional in style, dry and tightly structured with a real mineral component running through them, vinification benefits from modern equipment, with temperature control for fermentation in *inox* as well as wood. Muscat in particular is very striking here and the Grand Cru Spiegel bottling is one of the very finest in the appellation. Some truly excellent *grand cru* Riesling and Gewürztraminer are produced as well as rich and pure VT and an exquisite Gewürztraminer Spiegel SGN. Expect the wines to develop very well in bottle, particularly the top *crus*. (DM)

O **Gewürztraminer** Grand Cru Kessler★★★★ £C
O **Gewürztraminer** Grand Cru Spiegel SGN★★★★★ £F
O **Riesling** Grand Cru Kessler★★★ £C   Grand Cru Spiegel★★★★ £C
O **Riesling** Grand Cru Saering★★★★ £C
O **Tokay Pinot Gris** Reserve★★★ £B Schwarzberg Vendanges Tardives★★★★ £E
O **Muscat**★★ £B   Grand Cru Spiegel★★★★ £C   O **Sylvaner** Vieilles Vignes★★ £B

FERNAND ENGEL   Rorschwihr   www.fernand-engel.fr

Engel family   1 route du Vin, 68750 Rorschwihr

This third-generation family-run domaine has 41ha of vineyards spread across 150 parcels and and 6 villages. As a result a vast array of soils, subsoils, vineyard sites and mesoclimates make up the varied *terroirs* of the wines. Output is over 30,000 cases a year although *grand cru*, late-harvested and selected-grape bottlings account for less than 1,000 cases of this total. The vineyards are cultivated organically and all harvesting is done by hand. The wines are all vinified in stainless steel with temperature control and some micro-oxygenation is used. The regular Alsace bottlings are labelled Les Classiques and will have a little residual sugar. The Cuvée Engel wines get a little more ageing on fine lees. The best wines are the Vins de Terroir, including the Clos des Anges bottlings and the late-harvest wines. The Clos des Anges has deep marly, limy soils and a clay subsoil. The wines have impressive depth and intensity, particularly a steely Riesling and toasty, nutty Pinot Gris. The Auxerrois is one of the better examples from the region and Pinot Noir impresses more than most. Of the late-harvest wines, there is a splendid and very concentrated full-blown Muscat SGN and best of all a superbly intense and pure Gewurztraminer SGN. These top whites will age well in bottle. (DM)

O **Gewürztraminer** Grand Cru Altenberg de Bergheim Vendanges Tardives★★★★ £C
O **Gewürztraminer** SGN★★★★★ £F   Clos des Anges★★ £C
O **Gewürztraminer** Grand Cru Altenberg de Bergheim★★★ £F
O **Riesling** Silberberg Rorschwihr★★ £C   Clos des Anges★★★ £C
O **Tokay Pinot Gris** Clos des Anges★★★ £B SGN★★★ £E
O **Muscat** Vendanges Tardive★★★ £B   SGN★★★★ £C

○ **Auxerrois** Vieilles Vignes Cuvée Saint-Michel★★ £B
● **Pinot Noir** Silberberg Rorschwihr★★ £C

DOM. PIERRE FRICK   Pfaffenheim   pierre.frick@wanadoo.fr

Chantal & Jean-Pierre Frick   5 Rue de Boer, 68250 Pfaffenheim
UK stockists: Vcs

An impressive and diverse range is produced by the Fricks at their biodynamically farmed 12-ha property, which they inevitably harvest solely by hand. In the winery chaptalisation is strictly avoided and fermentation is carried out naturally without interference. Ageing takes place in large cask. The resulting wines often have some degree of residual sugar but are rich, opulent and, crucially, always balanced. There is a range of good generic Cuvées Classiques but it is the single-vineyard and *grand cru* wines as well as the special Précieuse selections which really stand out here. The Pinot Blanc Précieuse is a benchmark for the variety in Alsace. The domaine possesses holdings in the *lieux-dits* Bergweingarten, Bihl, Rot Murle and Strangenberg as well as Grands Crus Steinert, Vorbourg and Eichberg. Both Vendange Tardive and SGN wines are released in propitious vintages. All the top wines here will develop very well in bottle. (DM)

○ **Gewürztraminer** Grand Cru Steinert★★★★ £C
○ **Riesling** Précieuse★★★ £C Vendange Tardive★★★★ £C
○ **Pinot Blanc** Précieuse★★★ £C
○ **Sylvaner** Bihl★★ £B Bergweingarten★★★ £D
● **Pinot Noir** Rot Murle★★★ £C

DOM. PAUL GINGLINGER   Eguisheim   ginglin@club-internet.fr

Paul Ginglinger   8 Place Charles de Gaulle, 68420 Eguisheim
This ancient domaine dates back to 1636. Paul Ginglinger, who heads the latest generation, now possesses some 12ha, 1.5ha being Pinot Noir, although it is his excellent whites that stand out. Decent enough Muscat and a Clevner are released but it is the classic Alsace varieties of Riesling, Gewürztraminer and Tokay Pinot Gris that impress most as well as a very good, piercing, finely structured, appley Pinot Blanc. Vinification is strictly non-interventionist and the wines often have a touch of residual sugar. The Rieslings have a penetrating mineral quality and demand cellaring, particularly the *grand cru* bottlings which come from Eichberg as well as Pfersigberg. Both the Tokay Pinot Gris and Gewürztraminer tend towards the opulent, again with that degree of residual sugar often apparent, but the Pinot Gris in particular is also tight and structured when young, with a marked mineral quality. The Gewürztraminer, notably the Pfersigberg, is opulent and classically full of lychee and spice – full, deep and very pure. Expect to age the top wines here for at least 5 or 6 years. (DM)

○ **Gewürztraminer** Wahlenbourg★★★ £C Grand Cru Pfersigberg★★★★ £C
○ **Riesling** Cuvée Drei Exa★★★ £C Grand Cru Pfersigberg★★★ £C
○ **Tokay Pinot Gris** Grand Cru Eichberg★★★ £C
○ **Pinot Blanc**★★ £B

DOM. ANDRÉ ET RÉMY GRESSER   Andlau   remy.gresser@wanadoo.fr

Rémy Gresser   2 Rue de l'Ecole, 67140 Andlau
UK stockists: **SVS**

Rémy Gresser produces an exemplary small range of wines, almost exclusively sourced from *grand cru* sites. The Gresser domaine is one of a number of ancient Alsace properties, dating from 1667, and now has a holding of just over 10ha, prodicing a total of 5,000 cases a year. Almost all is white but there is just 0.65ha of Pinot Noir as well. The vineyard is currently being converted to biodynamic farming. Andlau is in the centre of the Bas-Rhin, so is cooler than

235

most areas in the region and as such strongly favours the production of tight, minerally, pure Rieslings of classic structure and dimension. Inevitably they are relatively austere when young. The Grand Cru Kastelberg is notable for its slatey, schistous soils which encourage late-season ripening. Riesling also comes from the Grand Cru Moenchberg , with warmer years often producing wines of Vendange Tardive ripeness. Gewürztraminer and Tokay Pinot Gris will evolve well in bottle for at least 6 or 7 years, the Rieslings often longer. (DM)

O **Gewürztraminer** Duttenberg Vieilles Vignes★★★ £C
O **Riesling** Grand Cru Kastelberg Vieilles Vignes★★★★ £C
O **Riesling** Grand Cru Wiebelsberg★★★ £C
O **Tokay Pinot Gris** Brandhof Vieilles Vignes★★★★ £C

HUGEL ET FILS   Riquewihr   www.hugel.fr
Hugel family   3 Rue de la Première-Armee-Française, B.P. 32, 68340 Riquewihr
UK stockists: **Day**,OWL,BBR,PFx,WSc,Har

Along with TRIMBACH one of the best-known names in the region. As well as being a substantial merchant operation Hugel also has extensive vineyard holdings – some 127ha. The top wines here are good to exceptional and are excellent, structured examples of the region. What disappoints most is the very average, at times downright poor, quality of the generics. The Gentil basics and the Tradition *cuvées* struggle to stand up to much of their competition. Gewürztraminer Tradition is sound with good varietal character, as is Pinot Gris. The Jubilee wines and the VT and SGN *cuvées* are of an entirely different class. Riesling Jubilee is taut and intense, minerally with great structure; Pinot Gris is powerful with subtle, honeyed notes; the Jubilee Gewürztraminer floral and spicy with classic but youthfully restrained lychee character. These are wines that should be cellared for at least 4 or 5 years as they will continue to develop very well in bottle. Pinot Noir is less successful. VTs are very intense. The style tends towards the drier end of the spectrum but they have remarkable depth. Both Pinot Gris and Riesling SGN are quite splendid wines with remarkable depth and complexity. The Riesling is perhaps the finest, with astonishing toasty, citrus and mineral character. (DM)

O **Gewürztraminer** Tradition★★ £B Jubilee★★★ £F Vendange Tardive★★★★ £F
O **Riesling** Jubilee★★★ £C Vendange Tardive★★★★ £F SGN❀❀❀❀❀ £H
O **Tokay Pinot Gris** Tradition★ £B Jubilee★★★ £F Vendange Tardive★★★★ £F
O **Tokay Pinot Gris** SGN❀❀❀❀❀ £H

JOSMEYER   Wintzenheim   www.josmeyer.com
Jean Meyer   76 Rue Clemenceau, 68920 Wintzenheim
UK stockists: **Pol**, May, Vts

Long-established top-quality producer whose origins date back to 1854. Output at a little over 20,000 cases a year is sizeable for the region but dwarfed by some of the larger merchant houses. The Meyer family possess some 31ha of vineyard which form the base for an extensive collection of 6 small ranges. The Classic labels are straightforward and easy drinking, the Artist Label series a step up, of which the Riesling Kottabe, Pinot Gris Fromenteau and Gewürztraminer Folastries stand out. Muscat, Riesling and Pinot Noir are all produced from the Herrenweg site, the Riesling labelled Dragon. Of particular interest, though, are the prestige selections which include not only fine, pure Pinot Gris Foundation 1854 and opulent, spice-strewn Gewürztraminer Archenets but also very intense Pinot Blanc Les Lutins. *Grand cru* holdings include plots on both Brand and Hengst. Vendanges Tardives are produced from Pinot Gris and Riesling, SGN from Pinot Gris and Gewürztraminer. Particularly rare and unusual is the late-harvest Pinot Blanc Derrière La Chapelle, probably the best example of the variety in the region. All the top wines are very ageworthy. (DM)

O **Gewürztraminer** Grand Cru Hengst★★★★ £E Les Archenets★★★★ £E
O **Gewürztraminer** Les Folastries★★ £C O **Pinot Blanc** Les Lutins★★★ £C
O **Riesling** Le Kottabe★★ £C Grand Cru Hengst★★★★ £E
O **Tokay Pinot Gris** Le Fromenteau★★ £C Foundation 1854★★★★ £E
O **Pinot Auxerrois** H Vieilles Vignes★★★ £C

ANDRÉ KIENTZLER Ribeauvillé

André Kientzler 50 Route de Bergheim, 68150 Ribeauvillé
UK stockists: JAr, HHB
André Kientzler makes around 6,500 cases across a small but very impressive
range of wines. They are marked by their purity of fruit and elegant structure at
all levels. The top *grand cru* bottles are very ageworthy and require cellaring.
No varieties stand out but the Rieslings, particularly from the Grands Crus
Geisberg and Osterberg, are truly profound. On occasion Geisberg produces a
Riesling VT and SGN. These are wines of remarkable complexity: the latter is
astonishingly rich while the former is very structured, almost dry. You can
expect them to be ★★★★, often ★★★★★ or ○○○○○. Very good Muscat and
Pinot Gris is made from Kirchberg. Gewürztraminer is not *grand cru* but there
are occasional bottles of VT and SGN. Even the lesser Pinot Blanc, Auxerrois
and Chasselas offer excellent quality and value. (DM)

O **Chasselas**★ £B O **Auxerrois**★★ £B O **Pinot Blanc**★★ £B
O **Gewürztraminer**★★ £B Vendange Tardive★★★★ £E
O **Riesling** Réserve Particulière★★★ £B Geisberg Grand Cru★★★★ £D
O **Tokay Pinot Gris**★★ £B Kirchberg Grand Cru★★★★ £E

MARC KREYDENWEISS Andlau   marc.kreydenweiss@wanadoo.fr

Marc Kreydenweiss 12 Rue Deharbe, 67140 Andlau
UK stockists: C&C, Har
Marc Kreydenweiss's 12-ha domaine is in the north of the region in the Bas
Rhin. He produces around 5,000 cases using biodynamic principles in the
vineyard. In addition to the Alsace property, Marc and his wife Emmanuelle
own the Costières de Nîmes property Domaine des PERRIÈRES (see
Languedoc-Roussillon & Provence). The approach at both properties is the
same: to achieve elegance and refinement rather than weight and power. The
wines here are marked most by their intense fruit purity. Taut and with an
almost gripping structure the top wines should be cellared for 6 or 7 years,
sometimes more. Marc produces an unusual blend of mainly Riesling and
some Pinot Gris labelled Le Clos du Val d'Eléon, which technically is an
Edelzwicker but is unlike almost all you're likely to encounter elsewhere. Plots
are farmed in a considerable number of sites, both *lieux-dits* and *grands crus*.
Supreme examples include Tokay Pinot Gris from Moenchberg, and Riesling
from Kastelberg and Wiebelsberg. Among the great *lieux-dits* are
Gewürztraminer from Kritt and Pinot Gris from both Rebberg and
Lerchenberg. Fine Muscat Clos Rebgarten is intense, floral and musky and
there is also a most unusual, very impressive Klevner from the Kritt site. Very
stylish VT and SGN are produced from Gewürztraminer and VT Riesling
comes from Kastelberg. (DM)

O **Le Clos du Val d'Eléon**★★★ £D O **Klevner** Kritt★★★ £C
O **Gewürztraminer** Kritt★★★ £C
O **Riesling** Wiebelsberg Grand Cru★★★ £E Kastelberg Grand Cru★★★★ £E
O **Tokay Pinot Gris** Rebberg★★★ £C Lerchenberg★★★ £C
O **Tokay Pinot Gris** Moenchberg Grand Cru★★★★ £E

KUENTZ-BAS Husseren-les-Châteaux www.kuentz-bas.fr

Christian Bas 14 Route du Vin, 68420 Husseren-les-Châteaux
Solidly established old family merchant business with an output now

237

approaching 40,000 cases a year. There are 11ha of owned vineyards including plots in the Grands Crus Eichberg and Pfersigberg. As well as this a considerable volume of grapes are also bought in. Quality, particularly when contrasted with other *négociants*, is very good across the board, the best wines being rich, full and long-lived. The style can vary: some bottlings are relatively dry, while others can have a touch of residual sugar. The regular varietal bottlings are labelled Tradition, of which the Pinot Gris stands out. The Collection wines are a step up and made from the family's own vineyards. The Muscat and Gewürztraminer have impressive depth and substance. The Collection Rare wines come from a selection of the best plots and the Tokay Pinot Gris combines pungency with real intensity and finesse. A range of first-class wines is produced from the Eichberg and Pfersigberg. Riesling is minerally and finely structured, Pinot Gris more opulent. Riesling also comes from the Grand Cru Brand. Very good Cuvée Caroline Vendange Tardive is produced as Gewürztraminer, Riesling and Tokay Pinot Gris. Quite exceptional is the rich, fine and intense Cuvée Jérémy Tokay Pinot Gris. All the top wines will age well, the late-harvest bottlings for up to a couple of decades. (DM)

O **Gewürztraminer** Collection★★ £B Cuvée Caroline VT★★★★ £E
O **Riesling** Grand Cru Pfersigberg★★★ £D Cuvée Caroline VT★★★★ £E
O **Riesling** Collection★ £C Grand Cru Eichberg★★★ £D
O **Tokay Pinot Gris** Collection Rare★★★★ £D
O **Tokay Pinot Gris** Tradition★ £B Grand Cru Eichberg★★★ £D
O **Tokay Pinot Gris** Cuvée Jérémy SGN★★★★★ £G
O **Muscat** Collection★★ £B

DOM. SEPPI LANDMANN Soultzmatt www.seppi-landmann.fr

Seppi Landmann   20 Rue de la Vallée, 68570 Soultzmatt
UK stockists: **Tra**

With a total output of only a little over 5,000 cases a year and vineyard holdings of just 8.5ha, Seppi Landmann produces a bewildering array of wines of exemplary quality. Good examples are made from lowly varieties such as Sylvaner and Pinot Blanc and a range of Crémant d'Alsace is produced, the Brut Clos des Paiens being the top label. Sylvaner Z comes from the Grand Cru Zinnekoepflé like the best of Landmann's wines but this variety is not allowed *cru* status. The regular wines are labelled Vallée Noble and these range from good to very fine in the case of the Gewürztraminer Vendange Tardive. A number of special selections are released as Hospices de Strasbourg, where the wines are matured. Gewürztraminer, Riesling and Tokay Pinot Gris are produced from the Zinnekoepflé site and occasional Vendange Tardive and SGN are released. A real purity and character can be found in all the wines and you can expect the top wines to age very well. (DM)

O **Gewürztraminer** Vallée Noble Vendange Tardive★★★★ £E
O **Gewürztraminer** Grand Cru Zinnekoepflé Vendange Tardive★★★★★ £E
O **Gewürztraminer** Vallée Noble Sigilé★★ £C Grand Cru Zinnekoepflé★★★ £E
O **Riesling** Grand Cru Zinnekoepflé★★★ £C
O **Tokay Pinot Gris** Grand Cru Zinnekoepflé★★★ £C
O **Tokay Pinot Gris** Hospices de Strasbourg★★★ £C
O **Tokay Pinot Gris** Vallée Noble Sigilé★★ £C
O **Pinot Blanc** Vallée Noble★ £B O **Crémant d'Alsace** Brut★ £B

DOM. FRANÇOIS LICHTLÉ Husseren-les-Châteaux hlichtle@aol.com

Lichtlé family   17 Rue des Vignerons, 68420 Husseren-les-Châteaux
Hervé Lichtlé has progressively improved quality at this small family domaine and it is a property to watch. There are currently 6ha of vineyards spread across 33 separate plots. Sylvaner, Pinot Blanc, Gewürztraminer and Pinot Noir are grown in the *lieu-dit* of Horain and are some of the oldest vines of the property.

There is a small holding of Riesling in the Grand Cru Pfersigberg as well as a little Chardonnay which is used in the Crémant d'Alsace. The wines all display pure varietal characters with good depth and intensity, particularly in the Réserve and Vieilles Vignes bottlings. Pinot Gris Leo is rich and pungent, in marked contrast to the fine, minerally, steely Riesling Pfersigberg. Good to very good examples of both Vendange Tardive and SGN are produced from Gewürztraminer and Pinot Gris and there is a fine, elegant and intense Riesling SGN too. Expect the top wines here to develop well in bottle over the medium term. Prices are very reasonable. (DM)

O **Gewürztraminer**★★ £B Réserve★★★ £C Vieilles Vignes★★★ £C
O **Riesling** Grand Cru Pfersigberg★★★ £D SGN★★★★ £E
O **Riesling**★★ £B O **Pinot Blanc**★ £B
O **Tokay Pinot Gris**★ £B Réserve★★ £C Cuvée Leo★★★★ £D

DOM. ALBERT MANN Wettolsheim vins@mann-albert.com

Barthelmé family   13 Rue du Château, 68920 Wettolsheim
UK stockists: NYg

Very fine producer with a bewildering array of wines from just under 19ha of vineyards, which are now, like so many others, being tended organically. The style is for very ripe, full-bodied, traditional wines. Generics can be very good: Pinot Blanc/Auxerrois is one of the best in the region. Gewürztraminer at the generic level also impresses and the 2001 was ★★★. Rieslings have considerable weight and depth – more so than most – and they work best in a cooler vintage. The great Grand Cru Furstentum is a source not only of Riesling but of very rich and concentrated Gewürztraminer too, full of lychee and spice. Pinot Gris is very important and there is an excellent regular *cuvée* from old vines as well as first-class bottles from Altenbourg, Furstentum and Hengst. VT can be stunning and both the Grand Cru Hengst and Furstentum SGNs are remarkable wines, immensely rich and concentrated with substantial toffee, honey and peach. The style throughout is rich, opulent, almost extracted and the wines can be approached quite young, though the top examples age very well indeed. Prices are very fair. (DM)

O **Pinot Blanc /Auxerrois** Vieilles Vignes★★ £B O **Muscat**★★ £B
O **Gewürztraminer**★★ £B Steingrubler Grand Cru★★★★ £D
O **Gewürztraminer** Furstentum Grand Cru Vieilles Vignes★★★★ £D
O **Riesling** Schlossberg Grand Cru★★★ £C Furstentum Grand Cru★★★ £D
O **Riesling** Pfleck Vendange Tardive★★★ £D
O **Tokay Pinot Gris** Vieilles Vignes★★★ £C Hengst Grand Cru★★★★ £C
O **Tokay Pinot Gris** Altenbourg Vendange Tardive★★★★ £D
O **Tokay Pinot Gris** Hengst Grand Cru SGN❁❁❁❁❁ £E Furstentum Grand Cru
O **Tokay Pinot Gris** SGN❁❁❁❁❁ £E ● **Pinot Noir** Vieilles Vignes★★ £D

RENÉ MURÉ Rouffach www.mure.com

Muré family   Clos Saint Landelin, Route du Vin, 68250 Rouffach
UK stockists: BWC, Gau

René Muré's total production is not vast but sizeable for the area, at close to 25,000 cases per year. There are 2 distinct sides to the operation here. Domaine wines are labelled Clos Saint-Landelin and
produced from 20ha of estate vineyards at the Grand Cru Vorbourg and a number of neighbouring sites. The Muré family solely own the Clos Saint-Landelin vineyard, a *monopole* within the Vorbourg. The quality and prices of the wines are substantially above those of the *négoçiant* wines under the René Muré label. These are a range of generics which generally offer good value along with a decent Crémant d'Alsace. Superior bottlings of varieties go under the Côte de Rouffach label. Among the Domaine wines there is impressively steely Sylvaner from the *clos* which is full of ripe, green fruits and minerals and

239

one of the finest examples in the region. Intense, long-lived Riesling comes from Vorbourg and Clos Saint-Landelin, while rich, spicy and opulent Gewürztraminer hails from the *lieu-dit* Schultzengass as well as Vorbourg and Pinot Gris comes from Lutzeltal as well as the *clos*. Some better-than-average Pinot Noir is also produced, plus some very fine Muscat, as both VT and SGN, along with Riesling, Gewürztraminer and Tokay Pinot Gris. Clos Saint-Landelin is favoured by the regular occurrence of noble rot. The Gewürztraminer and Pinot Gris are more approachable than the Rieslings, which really will benefit from 6 or 7 years in bottle. The generic René Muré labels will be enjoyable on release, the Côte de Rouffach wines will be better for 2 or 3 years' ageing. (DM)

Domaine du Clos Saint-Landelin
O **Sylvaner** Cuvée Oscar★★ £B   O **Gewürztraminer** Schulzengass★★★ £C
O **Gewürztraminer** Vorbourg Grand Cru★★★ £D
O **Riesling** Vorbourg Grand Cru★★★ £C
O **Riesling** Clos Saint Landelin Vorbourg Grand Cru★★★★ £E
O **Tokay Pinot Gris** Lutzeltal★★ £D
O **Tokay Pinot Gris** Clos Saint Landelin Vorbourg Grand Cru★★★ £D
● **Pinot Noir** V★★ £D

René Muré
O **Muscat** Côte de Rouffach★★ £C
O **Gewürztraminer**★ £B   C te de Rouffach★★ £C
O **Riesling** Côte de Rouffach★★ £C   O **Tokay Pinot Gris** Côte de Rouffach★★ £D
O **Crémant d'Alsace**★★ £C   ● **Pinot Noir** Côte de Rouffach★★ £C

OSTERTAG   Epfig

André Ostertag   87 Rue Finckwiller, 67680 Epfig
UK stockists: **FMV**,BBR, Har

For more than 10 years André Ostertag has taken a radical approach to winemaking in the region. The vineyards are now farmed biodynamically but of greater significance has been the creation of wines that are given *barrique* treatment, including Pinot Blanc, Pinot Gris and Pinot Noir. Some of his experiments have brought him into open conflict with the appellation bureaucrats in the past. The generic labels he classifies as *vins du fruit*, the *lieux-dits* and *grands crus* as *vins du terroir*, and his late-harvest bottlings are *vins du temps*. In general the oak-handled wines work well. He also makes very good Rieslings with no recourse to wood, most notably from the Grand Cru Muenchberg, and some very fine Gewürztraminer. Ostertag favours producing a dry style but the Gewürztraminer will often have a touch of residual sugar for balance. Sylvaner from very old vines is arguably the best example in the region. Top wines are not only very ageworthy but require 5 or 6 years' cellaring at a minimum. (DM)

O **Sylvaner** Vieilles Vignes★★ £B   O **Pinot Blanc** Barriques★ £B
O **Gewürztraminer** d'Epfig★★★ £C   Fronholz Vendange Tardive★★★★ £E
O **Riesling** Fronholz★★★ £D   Muenchberg Grand Cru★★★★ £E
O **Riesling** Muenchberg Grand Cru Vendange Tardive★★★★ £F
O **Tokay Pinot Gris** Barriques★★ £C   Zellberg★★★ £E
O **Tokay Pinot Gris** Muenchberg Grand Cru★★★★ £E

GÉRARD NEUMEYER   Molsheim

Gabrielle & Gérard Neumeyer   29 Rue Ettore-Bugatti, 67120 Molsheim
This fine, small Molsheim domaine has 16ha of vineyards and an output of less than 8,000 cases a year. The vines are all cultivated organically and the core of the holding is on the Grand Cru Bruderthal. The regular labels are good and very well crafted with impressive varietal purity. The Pinot Gris here is particularly good, both the Coteau de Chartreux and the splendidly structured

and intense Bruderthal. Expect the top wines to develop very well with 4–5 years cellaring. As well as the wines rated here it would be well worth looking out for the Vengange Tardive and SGN bottlings of Gewürztraminer. (DM)

O **Gewürztraminer**★★ £B Bruderthal Grand Cru★★★ £D
O **Tokay Pinot Gris** Coteau des Chartreux★★★ £B
O **Tokay Pinot Gris** Bruderthal Grand Cru★★★★ £D
O **Riesling** Bruderthal Grand Cru★★★ £C O **Pinot Blanc** Vin de la Tulipe★★ £B

CAVE DE RIBEAUVILLÉ Ribeauvillé www.cave-ribeauville.com

'Co-operative' 2 Route de Colmar, 68150 Ribeauvillé
Founded in 1895, this is the oldest wine co-operative in France. Its 110 members provide up to 270ha of vineyards and output is sizeable for the region at upwards of 200,000 cases a year. As well as a good range of generic varietal wines the Ribeauville co-op has just released a series of exciting bio-dynamically producers wines which are quality benchmarks for large producers throughout the region. An extensive range of well-priced *grand cru* wines is available: Gewürztraminer comes from Gloekelberg and Osterberg, Pinot Gris from Gloekelberg and Riesling from Altenberg de Bergheim, Kirchberg, Osterberg and Rosacker. A range of wines is also released under the Collection d'Artistes label which supports local arts and culture, notably for blind people. The wines will develop well in the short to medium term, the *grand cru* labels keeping longer. (DM)

O **Gewürztraminer**★★ £B Weingarten Collection d'Artistes★★ £B
O **Riesling**★★ £B Steinacker Collection d'Artistes★★ £B Martin Zahn★★★ £B
O **Tokay Pinot Gris**★★ £B Weingarten Collection d'Artistes★★ £B
O **Tokay Pinot Gris**Martin Zahn★★★ £B
O **Pinot Blanc** Prestige★ £B Martin Zahn★★★ £B
O **Clos du Zahnacker**★★ £B

DOM. RIEFLÉ Pfaffenheim www.riefle.com

Rieflé family 7 Rue du Drottfeld, Pfaffenheim, 68250 Rouffach
UK stockists: **WTs**
The Rieflé estate has been handed down from father to son since the 15th century and Jean-Claude Rieflé is currently at the helm. The dry micro-climate of the family's vineyards helps to increase the concentration of fruit without making the wines too alcoholic. The generic bottlings represent superb value for money, whilst the special *cuvées* and single-vineyard wines show just how high a standard can be attained without going overboard on price. Tokay Pinot Gris has powerful fruit aromas reflected in intense autumnal flavours. The Gewürztraminer eschews the lychee for a touch of tamarind and is spicy and refreshing. The late-harvest wines are only made in exceptional years. (NB)

Late harvest range
O **Gewürztraminer** Vendange Tardive★★★★ £E SGN★★★★ £F
O **Tokay Pinot Gris** Vendange Tardive★★★★ £E SGN★★★★ £F

Grand Cru Steinert
O **Riesling**★★★ £D O **Tokay Pinot Gris**★★★★ £D O **Gewürztraminer**★★★ £D

Côtes du Rouffach range
O **Muscat** Bergweingarten★★★ £C O **Gewürztraminer** Bergweingarten★★★★ £C
O **Riesling** Gaentsbrunnen★★★ £C
O **Tokay Pinot Gris** Côtes du Rouffach★★★★ £C

Generic range
O **Silvaner**★ £B O **Pinot Blanc**★★ £B O **Muscat**★★ £B
O **Gewürztraminer**★★ £B
O **Riesling**★★ £B O **Tokay Pinot Gris**★★ £B O **Crémant d'Alsace**★★ £B

241

ROLLY-GASSMANN Rorschwihr rollygassmann@wanadoo.fr

Rolly-Gassmann family 2 Rue de l'Eglise, 68950 Rorschwihr
UK stockists: RsW, Bib, Rae, WSc

An extensive range of very good, traditionally produced wines emerges from this family domaine. There are no *grand cru* vineyards but a number of wines from some excellent *lieux-dits*. As well as the varietal and vineyard-labelled wines, including a good Edelzwicker, there are some particularly fine Vendange Tardive and SGN bottlings. The Muscat, Pinot Gris and Gewürztraminer are marked by pungent and concentrated varietal character. Riesling is intense and lightly mineral in style but with a piercing citrus character regularly showing through. The top wines need some cellaring to show at their best. Release dates can be confusing with a number of bottlings held back in the cellar and released with several years' age. This is however a rare source for purchasing top wines approaching their peak. (DM)

O **Pinot Blanc Auxerrois** Moenchreben★★ £B
O **Muscat** Moenchreben★★★ £C Moenchreben Vendange Tardive★★★★ £E
O **Gewürztraminer** SGN★★★★ £F
O **Riesling** Kappelweg★★★ £C Kappelweg Vendange Tardive★★★★ £E
O **Riesling** Pflaenzereben★★★ £C
O **Tokay Pinot Gris**★★ £B Réserve★★★ £C

DOM. SCHLUMBERGER Guebviller www.domaines-schlumberger.com

Sclumberger family 100 Rue Théodore-Deck, 68500 Guebviller
This is the largest domaine in the region in terms of vineyard holdings, which at some 140ha rival some of the larger co-ops. Of particular significant are the terroirs of the various plots spread across a 5km stretch of the southern Vosges. The vineyards are planted in sandstone at an altitude of 250–380m with a south-easterly aspect. Amongst the plots are holdings in the Grands Crus Kitterle, Kessler, Saering and Spiegel. Rich, perfumed and opulent Gewürztraminer and Tokay Pinot Gris from these sites are especially good. Riesling tends to impress less in this southerly location and among the regular Les Princes Abbés labels it is the Gewürztraminer which stands out. Some very fine late-harvest wines are also produced. In addition to the Cuvée Christine Vendange Tardive Gewürztraminer, SGNs Cuvée Anne (Gewürztraminer), Cuvée Clarisse (Pinot Gris) and Cuvée Ernest (Riesling) are also produced in exceptional vintages, generally only once or twice a decade. The top wines are firmly structured and require at least 5 or 6 years' cellaring. (DM)

O **Gewürztraminer** Grand Cru Kitterelé★★★★ £D
O **Gewürztraminer** Cuvée Christine Vendange Tardive★★★★ £E
O **Gewürztraminer** Grand Cru Kessler★★★ £D Grand Cru Saering★★★ £D
O **Gewürztraminer** Les Princes Abbés★★ £B
O **Riesling** Les Princes Abbés★ £B Grand Cru Kitterelé★★ £D
O **Gewürztraminer** Grand Cru Saering★★★ £D
O **Tokay Pinot Gris** Grand Cru Spiegel★★★ £D Grand Cru Kitterelé★★★ £D
O **Gewürztraminer** Cuvée Clarisse★★★★ £F
O **Tokay Pinot Gris** Les Princes Abbés★ £B

DOM. SCHOFFIT Colmar

Schoffit family 66-68 Nonnenholzweg, 6800 Colmar
UK stockists: HBJ, BBR, Gau, Har

There are some 16ha planted at this brilliant domaine based in Colmar, with production now running at around 8,000 cases a year. The regular bottlings are all very good. Pinot Blanc and particularly the humble Chasselas produced from venerable vines really stand out. A significant part of the Schoffits' vineyard holding is in lesser sites but quality is still admirable. The focal point of the domaine, though, is the fine volcanic soil of the Clos Saint-Théobald in the Grand Cru Rangen, which yields wines that are structured but with a remarkable array of exotic fruit aromas and always a pure mineral undercurrent. VT and SGN are very fine to exceptional. Given the extraordinary quality, the entire range represents excellent value for money. (DM)

O **Pinot Blanc** Cuvée Caroline★★ £B   O **Muscat** Tradition★★ £B
O **Gewürztraminer** Harth Cuvée Alexandre Vieilles Vignes★★★ £C
O **Gewürztraminer** Clos Saint-Théobald Rangen Grand Cru★★★★ £E
O **Gewürztraminer** Clos Saint-Théobald Rangen Grand Cru VT★★★★★ £F
O **Riesling** Harth Cuvée Alexandre★★ £B
O **Riesling** Clos Saint-Théobald Rangen Grand Cru★★★★ £E
O **Riesling** Clos Saint-Théobald Rangen Grand Cru Vendange Tardive✪✪✪✪✪ £F
O **Tokay Pinot Gris** Cuvée Alexandre Vieilles Vignes★★★ £C
O **Tokay Pinot Gris** Clos Saint-Théobald Rangen Grand Cru★★★★★ £E
O **Tokay Pinot Gris** Clos Saint-Théobald Rangen Grand Cru SGN✪✪✪✪✪ £F
O **Chasselas** Vieilles Vignes★★ £B

DOM. BRUNO SORG   Eguisheim

Sorg family   8 Rue Mgr-Stumpf, 68420 Eguisheim
UK stockists: **THt**,BBR

Very fine small grower, based just to the south of Colmar with 10ha of well-sited vineyards which include holdings in the Grands Crus Eichberg, Florimont and Pfersigberg. François Sorg is one of the best producers of Muscat in Alsace. The wines are always pure, musky and complex and the dry Pfersigberg is a benchmark example. Riesling is steely and minerally with a real intensity, particularly the finely structured and very ageworthy Vieilles Vignes. Pinot Gris and Gewürztraminer are richly textured and opulent, the latter full of concentrated lychee and tropical spices, but the wines always have great varietal purity and are impeccably balanced. The regular and old-vine bottlings will drink well with 2 or 3 years' age but will keep very well. Its best to leave the *grands crus* for 5 or 6 years, particularly the Rieslings. (DM)

O **Gewürztraminer** Vieilles Vignes★★★ £C
O **Riesling**★★ £B   Grand Cru Pfersigberg★★★ £C
O **Riesling** Grand Cru Pfersigberg Vieilles Vignes★★★★ £D
O **Tokay Pinot Gris** Vieilles Vignes★★★ £C   Grand Cru Florimont★★★★ £D
O **Muscat**★★ £B   Grand Cru Pfersigberg★★★ £C

TRIMBACH   Ribeauvillé   www.maison-trimbach.fr

Trimbach family   15 Route de Bergheim, 68150 Ribeauvillé
UK stockists: **Par**,BBR,WSc,Sel,Har

Large well-established merchant house producing close to 100,000 cases a year. As at HUGEL, the top wines are very impressive, although perhaps not quite the same dimension. This is with the exception of the remarkable Riesling Clos Sainte-Hune, arguably the greatest dry expression of the variety in the region and one of the greatest anywhere in the world. Indeed, the Rieslings are the most successful of the varietals. They are structured, very dry in style and have a pure and intense mineral depth. They age remarkably well. The Gewürztraminer Seigneurs de Ribeaupierre is in a similarly dry, structured style. Rich, aromatic, lychee notes and an increasingly honeyed character will emerge with 5 or 6 years' cellaring. VT and SGN bottlings are certainly impressive. They are structured and rich, just a little way short of the very best. The generics are less exciting than many equivalents you may find from smaller domaines and the prices for these are quite steep. (DM)

O **Gewürztraminer**★ £C   Seigneurs de Ribeaupierre★★★ £E
O **Gewürztraminer** Vendange Tardive★★★★ £F
O **Riesling**★★ £B   Réserve★★ £C   Clos Sainte-Hune✪✪✪✪✪ £G
O **Riesling** Cuvée Frédéric Émile★★★★ £E

243

○ **Tokay Pinot Gris** Réserve★★ £B   Réserve Personnelle★★★ £C   SGN★★★★ £G
○ **Muscat** Réserve★ £B

CAVE DE TURCKHEIM   Turckheim   www.cave-turckheim.com

'Co-operative'   16 Rue des Tuileries, 68230 Turckheim
UK stockists: **PBW**

Another fine co-op in a region that features an impressive number of such
quality-conscious operations. Turckheim's co-op is one of the more recently
established, dating from 1956. The Cave can call on 310ha of vineyards owned
by its members and output is sizeable, approaching 300,000 cases annually.
There are some sound generic wines under the Tradition label, in particular
Gewürztraminer and Tokay Pinot Gris. The Réserves are a step up. The best
part of the operation is a solid range of single-vineyard and *grand cru* wines
along with some excellent Vendange Tardive bottlings, particularly the
Gewürztraminer. Both Tokay Pinot Gris and Gewürztraminer from the great
Hengst and Brand sites stand out. Gewürztraminer is opulent and spicy with
real depth, the Hengst offering a subtle extra dimension, while Tokay Pinot
Gris is rich and honeyed with a fine mineral structure. Riesling tends to pale by
comparison and lacks the depth and intensity of the other varieties. The Brand
bottling is sound but you feel there should be more. Top Pinot Gris and
Gewürztraminer will develop very well in bottle. (DM)

○ **Gewürztraminer** Grand Cru Brand★★★ £C   Grand Cru Hengst★★★★ £C
○ **Gewürztraminer** Vendange Tardive★★★★★ £E
○ **Gewürztraminer** Tradition★ £B   Reserve★★ £B
○ **Riesling**   Grand Cru Brand★★ £C
○ **Tokay Pinot Gris** Grand Cru Hengst★★★ £D   Vendange Tardive★★★★ £E
○ **Tokay Pinot Gris** Tradition★ £B   Reserve★★ £B   Heimbourg★★ £C
○ **Crémant d'Alsace** Mayerling★ £B

DOMAINE WEINBACH   Kaysersberg   www.domaineweinbach.com

Mme Faller & family   25 route du Vin, 68240 Kaysersberg
UK stockists: J&B, Tan, NYg

Weinbach is one of the great names of Alsace. Madame Faller and her
daughters run an impressive 26-ha estate partly converted to biodynamic
cultivation since 1998. The wines are stylistically different from those of
Trimbach or Zind-Humbrecht, offering neither the elegance or reserve of the
former nor the same degree of definition and nuance of terroir seen in the
Zind-Humbrecht wines, yet they are rich, powerful and complex, particularly
concentrated and impressive in the top *cuvées*, and they are rarely
disappointing. The richest styles can be magnificent. The 2 most important
holdings are those of the 5-ha walled Clos des Capucins and 10ha in the Grand
Cru Schlossberg, but outstanding wines are also made from *lieu-dit* Altenbourg.
The number of bottlings is extensive and somewhat complicated with special
cuvées named after family members. Cuvée Theo Gewürztraminer and Riesling
(named after the late Theo Faller) come only from the Clos. Cuvée Sainte-
Catherine is a rich Riesling from the lower part of Schlossberg, usually
harvested in late November, but a more select bottling is additionally labelled
Grand Cru Schlossberg while L'Inédit represents the very best selection of this
vineyard. Regular Cuvée Laurence Tokay Pinot Gris and Gewürztraminer
comes from the foot of Altenbourg, while those additionally labelled
Altenbourg come from the vineyard itself. A small amount of Gewürztraminer
also comes from the Grand Cru Furstentum. VT and SGN styles add more
sweetness to the usual Weinbach concentration and depth whilst retaining good
balance. Cuvée d'Or Quintessence SGN is reserved for formidable rich and
sweet *cuvées* made when conditions allow it, such as an intensely sweet and
spicy botrytised Gewürztraminer. A scented, stylish Muscat Réserve Personelle

is also very good if drunk fairly young. (PW)

- ❍ **Riesling** Cuvée Theo★★★ £C
- ❍ **Riesling** Schlossberg Grand Cru Cuvée Sainte-Catherine★★★★★ £E
- ❍ **Riesling** Schlossberg Grand Cru Cuvée Sainte-Catherine l'Inédit★★★★★ £F
- ❍ **Riesling** Vendange Tardive★★★★★ £F
- ❍ **Gewürztraminer** Cuvée Theo★★★ £D Altenbourg Cuvée Laurence★★★★ £E
- ❍ **Gewürztraminer** Furstentum Vendange Tardive❁❁❁❁❁ £F
- ❍ **Gewürztraminer** Cuvée d'Or Quintessence SGN❁❁❁❁❁ £G
- ❍ **Tokay Pinot Gris** Cuvée Sainte-Catherine Fut II★★★★ £E
- ❍ **Pinot Blanc** Réserve★★ £C
- ❍ **Muscat** Réserve Personelle★★★ £D

ZIND-HUMBRECHT Turckheim   o.humbrecht@wanadoo.fr

Olivier Zind-Humbrecht 4 Route de Colmar, 68230 Turckheim
UK stockists: ABy,BBR,Har,Gau,Coe

It is very easy to eulogise both the wines and the winemaking ethos of Olivier Humbrecht. The family's 40ha of vineyards cultivated by Olivier's father Léonard (and biodynamic since 1997) offer an enviable resource from which individual *terroirs* have been given expression. In fact, from a combination of several different grape varieties and many excellent sites, one of France's, indeed the world's great white wine producers has created a miniature vinous wonderland. More than 30 wines are produced in every vintage – multiply that by the different vintage permutations that a non-interventionist winemaking approach emphasises and you might not ever find time to taste anything else. The wines, made only from fully ripe grapes, are full, concentrated and intense, each expressing something of the essence of their origins. Some of Zind-Humbrecht's *crus* are also produced in late-harvested VT and SGN styles and although even regular versions can vary in the degree of residual sugar there is almost always the necessary balance between sweetness and acidity. If the range and variable levels of sweetness can make it difficult to choose an individual bottle, the new scale of sweetness being introduced in Alsace will help make it a little less bewildering. Highlights include a fascinating array of fine Riesling: Clos Saint-Urbain combines breadth and a fine minerality; Brand has great structure and power that unfurls slowly with age; Clos Windsbuhl shows an intense fruit depth; while Clos Hauserer can be more classically crisp and stimulating. Fine Pinot Gris include a very rich, creamy Vieilles Vignes example, potent Rotenberg, vibrant and deeply fruity Clos Windsbuhl and the smoky, minerally Clos Saint-Urbain, all of which are surpassed by the Clos Jebsal for sheer richness and substance. Impressively rich and aromatic Gewürztraminers include fine, minerally Wintzerheim, broad and powerful Herrenweg, rich, almost overwhelming Heimbourg, exotic Goldert and marvellously deep and concentrated Clos Windsbuhl. There is also a very small amount of Grand Cru Rangen Clos Saint-Urbain. Fine Muscat is also made, both deeply grapey Herrenweg and a more expressive, floral Goldert. Muscat excepted, almost all the wines need a decent amount of bottle-age to show at their best. Regular bottlings should have at least 2 or 3 years' ageing; most *lieu-dits* or *grands crus* (whether in regular versions or either VT or SGN styles) deserve at least 5 or 6 years. The list below includes most but not all of the extensive range. VT and SGN bottlings add a considerable premium to prices, especially the latter style. (PW)

- ❍ **Riesling** Rangen Grand Cru Clos Saint-Urbain★★★★ £F
- ❍ **Riesling** Brand Grand Cru❁❁❁❁❁ £F
- ❍ **Riesling** Turckheim★ £B Clos Hauserer★★★★ £E Clos Windsbuhl★★★★ £E
- ❍ **Tokay Pinot Gris** Rangen Grand Cru Clos Saint-Urbain★★★★★ £F
- ❍ **Tokay Pinot Gris** Clos Windsbuhl★★★★★ £F
- ❍ **Tokay Pinot Gris** Vieilles Vignes★★★ £C Rotenberg★★★ £E Heimbourg★★★ £E

O **Tokay Pinot Gris** Clos Jebsal★★★★ £E
O **Gewürztraminer** Heimbourg★★★★ £E Goldert Grand Cru★★★★ £E
O **Gewürztraminer** Clos Windsbuhl★★★★ £E
O **Gewürztraminer** Herrenweg★★★ £D Wintzenheim★★★ £D
O **Gewürztraminer** Hengst Grand Cru★★★★★ £F
O **Muscat** Herrenweg★★★ £D Goldert Grand Cru★★★★ £D
O **Pinot d'Alsace** ★★ £C O **Sylvaner★** £B

OTHER WINES OF NOTE

ALLIMANT-LAUGNER O Muscat★ £B O Riesling★★ £B
O Gewürztraminer★★ £C
DOM. AUTHER O Muscat★ £B O Riesling★★ £B
DOM. BARMES-BUECHER O Gewürztraminer Wintzenheim★★ £D
JEAN-PIERRE BECHTOLD O Gewürztraminer Silberberg★★ £C
O Riesling Engelberg Grand Cru★★★ £C
LÉON BOESCH O Sylvaner★ £B
O Gewürztraminer Zinnkoepflé Grand Cru★★★ £C
DOM. FRANÇOIS BRAUN O Riesling Grand Cru Pfingtsberg★★★ £C
DOPFF & IRION O Tokay Pinot Gris Maquisards★ £B
O **Tokay Pinot Gris** Vorbourg Grand Cru★★ £F
DOPFF AU MOULIN O Gewürztraminer Brand Grand Cru★★ £D
DOM. JEAN-MARIE HAAG O Tokay Pinot Gris Vallee Noble★★ £B
CAVE DE HUNAWIHR O Muscat Réserve★ £B
O Gewürztraminer Rosacker Grand Cru★★ £C
O Riesling Rosacker Grand Cru★★ £C O **Tokay Pinot Gris** Réserve★★ £B
O **Tokay Pinot Gris** Rosacker Grand Cru★★★ £C
DOM. ROGER JUNG O Riesling Vieilles Vignes★★ £B
O Riesling Schoenenbourg Grand Cru★★★ £C
O **Tokay Pinot Gris** Schoenenbourg Grand Cru★★★ £C
DOM. CLEMENT KLUR O Crémant d'Alsace★ £B
O **Pinot Blanc** Grain d'Or★ £B
O **Tokay Pinot Gris** Vieilles Vignes★★ £C
O Riesling Sommerberg Grand Cru★★★ £C
O Gewürztraminer Grand Cru Sclossberg★★★ £C
JEAN-LUC MADER O Pinot Blanc★ £B O Gewürztraminer★★ £B
O Riesling★★ £B
DOM. JEAN-LOUIS & FABIENNE MANN O Sylvaner Vieilles Vignes★ £B
O Gewürztraminer Steinweg★★★ £C Pfersigberg Grand Cru★★★ £C
DOM. DES MARRONNIERS O Riesling Moenchberg Grand Cru★★ £C
O Riesling Kastelberg Grand Cru★★ £C
DOM. MATERNE-HAEGELIN O Gewürztraminer★ £B
O Riesling Bollenberg★★ £B
JEAN-LUC MEYER O Edelzwicker★ £B O Pinot Blanc★ £B
O Gewürztraminer Vieilles Vignes★★★ £B
MEYER-FONNÉ O Riesling Katzenthal★★ £B
O Riesling Winneck-Schlossberg Grand Cru★★★ £C
O Gewürztraminer Winneck-Schlossberg Grand Cru★★★ £C
DOM. MITTNACHT-KLACK O Riesling Muhlforst★★ £B
O Riesling Schoenenbourg Grand Cru★★★ £C
O Gewürztraminer Schoenenbourg Grand Cru★★★ £C
CAVE DE PFAFFENHEIM O Riesling Goldert Grand Cru★★ £C
O Riesling Zinnkoepflé Grand Cru★★ £C
DOMAINE MARTIN SCHAETZEL O Pinot Blanc Réserve★★ £B
O Riesling Réserve★★ £B
O **Tokay Pinot Gris** Réserve★★ £B O Gewürztraminer Kaefferkopf★★★ £C
ANDRÉ SCHERER O Riesling Pfersigberg Grand Cru★★★ £C
DOM. CHARLES SCHLERET O Sylvaner★ £B O Riesling Herrenweg★★★ £C
O **Tokay Pinot Gris** Herrenweg★★★ £C

DOM. ROLAND SCHMITT O Riesling Altenberg de Bergheim Grand Cru Cuvée

O **Riesling** Roland★★★ £C
GÉRARD SCHUELLER O **Muscat** Reserve★★ £B
O **Tokay Pinot Gris** Reserve★★ £B
DOM. JEAN SIPP O **Gewürztraminer** Vieilles Vignes★★★ £C
O **Tokay Pinot Gris** Trottacker★★ £C
LOUIS SIPP O **Gewürztraminer**★★ £B O **Riesling** Réserve Personelle★★ £C
O **Tokay Pinot Gris** Réserve Personelle★★ £C
PIERRE SPARR O **Gewürztraminer** GC Mambourg★★ £C
O **Tokay Pinot Gris** Réserve★★ £B
DOM. SYLVIE SPIELMANN O **Gewürztraminer** Blosenberg Bergheim★★ £C
O **Gewürztraminer** Grand Cru Altenberg de Bergheim ★★★ £D
DOM. STOEFFLER O **Tokay Pinot Gris**★★ £B O **Riesling** Kronenbourg★★ £B
PAUL ZINCK O **Riesling** Prestige £B Rangen Grand Cru £C
O **Tokay Pinot Gris** Prestige £B
O **Gewürztraminer** Prestige £B Eichberg Grand Cru £C

Work in progress!!

Producers under consideration for the next edition
AGATHE BURSIN
MARC TEMPÉ
DOM. PIERRE HERING
ROBERT FALLER
HUBER & BLÉGER
DOM. LOEW
DOM. ERIC ROMINGER

Author's choice (DM)

15 Alsace values
JEAN-BAPTISTE ADAM O **Tokay Pinot Gris** Letzenberg
DOM. BOTT-GEYL O **Muscat** Riquewihr
ERNEST BURN O **Pinot Blanc**
DIRLER-CADE O **Riesling** Saering Grand Cru
MARC KREYDENWEISS O **Klevner** Kritt
DOM. ALBERT MANN O **Pinot Blanc/Auxerrois** Vieilles Vignes
JOSMEYER O **Pinot Auxerrois** H Vieilles Vignes
OSTERTAG O **Sylvaner** Vieilles Vignes
DOM. SCHOFFIT O **Riesling** Harth Cuvée Alexandre
ANDRE KIENTZLER O **Gewürztraminer**
DOM. WEINBACH O **Riesling** Cuvée Theo
ZIND-HUMBRECHT O **Tokay Pinot Gris** Vieilles Vignes
PIERRE FRICK O **Pinot Blanc** Précieuse
BRUNO SORG O **Gewürztraminer** Vieilles Vignes
CAVE DE TURKHEIM O **Tokay Pinot Gris** Réserve

20 striking dry whites
DOM. PAUL BLANCK O **Gewürztraminer** Grand Cru Furstentum Vieilles Vignes
DOM. BOTT-GEYL O **Riesling** Mandelburg Grand Cru
ERNEST BURN O **Tokay Pinot Gris** Goldert Grand Cru Cuvée de la Chapelle
MARCEL DEISS O **Altenberg Grand Cru**
MARC KREYDENWEISS O **Le Clos du Val d'Eléon**
DOM. ALBERT MANN O **Pinot Blanc/Auxerrois** Vieilles Vignes
RENÉ MURÉ O **Riesling** Clos Saint Landelin Vorbourg Grand Cru
SEPPI LANDMANN O **Gewürztraminer** Zinnkoepfle Grand Cru
DOM. SCHOFFIT O **Gewürztraminer** Harth Cuvée Alexandre Vieilles Vignes
TRIMBACH O **Riesling** Clos Sainte-Hune
DOM. WEINBACH O **Muscat** Réserve Personelle
JEAN BECKER O **Riesling** Froehn Grand Cru
DIRLER-CADE O **Gewürztraminer** Kessler Grand Cru

247

A & R GRESSER O **Riesling** Kastelberg Grand Cru

DOM. SCHLUMBERGER O **Gewürztraminer** Grand Cru Kitterelé

BRUNO SORG O **Tokay Pinot Gris** Grand Cru Florimont

DOM. RIEFLÉ O **Tokay Pinot Gris** Grand Cru Steinert

GÉRARD NEUMAYER O **Tokay Pinot Gris** Grand Cru Bruderthal

FRANCOIS LICHTLÉ O **Tokay Pinot Gris** Cuvée Leo

ZIND-HUMBRECHT O **Riesling** Brand Grand Cru

An exciting selection of late harvest whites

DOM. JEAN BECKER O **Gewürztraminer** Schoenenbourg Grand Cru SGN

DOM. LÉON BEYER O **Tokay Pinot Gris** SGN

DOM. BOTT-GEYL O **Tokay Pinot Gris** Sonnenglanz Grand Cru SGN

HUGEL ET FILS O **Riesling** SGN

ANDRÉ KIENTZLER O **Gewürztraminer** Vendange Tardive

DOM. ALBERT MANN O **Tokay Pinot Gris** Hengst Grand Cru SGN

OSTERTAG O **Gewürztraminer** Fronholz Vendange Tardive

ROLLY-GASSMANN O **Muscat** Moenchreben Vendange Tardive

DOM. SCHOFFIT O **Riesling** Clos Saint Théobald Rangen Grand Cru Vendange Tardive

DOM. WEINBACH O **Gewürztraminer** Cuvée d'Or Quintessence SGN

DOM. SCHLUMBERGER O **Gewürztraminer** Christine Vendanges Tardives

KUENTZ-BAS O **Riesling** Caroline Vendange Tardive

CAVE DE TURKHEIM O **Tokay Pinot Gris** Vendange Tardive

DOM. RIEFLÉ O **Tokay Pinot Gris** SGN

FRANCOIS LICHTLÉ O **Riesling** SGN

RECOMMENDED HOTELS AND RESTAURANTS - ALSACE

Top Hotels

★★★★*Hotel des Berges*   2, Rue des Collognes, Illhaeusern 68970
Tel. 03 89 71 87 87 Fax 03 89 71 87 88
Email hotel-des-berges@wanadoo.fr   9 rooms   £G/H

★★★★*Château d'Isenbourg*   Rouffach 68250
Tel. 03 89 78 58 50 Fax 03 89 49 75 30
Email isenbourg@grandesetapes.fr 41 rooms   £C/H

Top Restaurants

★★★★★*Auberge de l'Ill*   2 Rue des Collognes, Illhaeusern 68970
Tel. 03 89 71 89 00 Fax 03 89 71 82 83
Email auberge-de-l-ill@auberge-de-l-ill.com   £H

★★★★★*Buerehiesel*   4 Parc de l'Orange, Strasbourg 6700
Tel. 03 88 45 56 65   Fax 03 88 61 32 00
Email westermann@buerehiesel.fr   £H

Value for money Hotels

★*Winzenberg*   58 Route des Vins, Blienschwiller 67650
Tel. 03 88 92 62 77 Fax 03 88 92 45 22
Email winzberg@visit-alsace.com   13 rooms   £A

★*Moschenross*   42 Rue Géneral de Gaulle, Thann 68880
Tel. 03 89 37 00 86 Fax 03 89 37 52 81
Email info@le-moschenross.com   23 rooms   £A

Value for money restaurants

★*Wistub du Sommelier*   51 Grande Rue, Bergheim 68750
Tel. 03 89 73 69 99 Fax 03 89 73 36 58
Email wistub.dusommelier@wanadoo.fr   £A

★★*Am Lindeplatzel*   71 Rue Principale, Mittelbergheim 67140
Tel. 03 88 08 10 69 Fax 03 88 08 45 08
No email address   £B

ALSACE RECIPES

TARTE FLAMBÉE:

Ingredients: 200gr. Bread dough- 150gr. Fromage Frais - 1dl. double cream-1 small onion - a teaspoon of flour -3 slices of bacon - A little olive or other oil.

Spread the dough as thinly as you can. Chop the onion and the bacon and cook in a little oil. Beat the fromage frais with the flour and the cream together, season with pepper and a little salt. Spread the cheese mix on the pastry and sprinkle the onion/bacon mix on top. Heat the oven to 200°C - and cook the tart between 15 to 20 minutes until golden.

RECOMMENDED WINES

This is a rich and somewhat filling dish which requires a wine of plentiful flavour to go with it. A single vineyard or Grand Cru Gewürztraminer would be ideal – Grand Cru Steinert from Domaine Rieflé in Pfaffenheim, if you prefer the wine to be on the dryer side, or Clos Windsbühl from Zind-Humbrecht if you prefer something richer and more concentrated.

SPAETZLE:

Ingredients: 250gr. flour or 200gr. flour and 80gr. semolina (lighter mix), 4 medium to large eggs and enough milk to make a mixture as thick as double cream. Fresh herbs (optional).

Mix the flour or flour and semolina with the 4 lightly beaten eggs until very smooth, and add enough milk to a consistency of double cream. Season to taste, adding fresh chopped herbs if you want. Boil a big pan of water to which you add some salt and oil. Rest a large colander with larger than normal holes on it and pour the mixture a little at a time scraping it with a spatula. When the spaetzle come to the surface they are done. Put then in a basin of cold water and carry on with the rest.

To serve, sauté them in a little butter or olive oil and leave them in the hot oven until very hot and slightly puffed.

RECOMMENDED WINES

Spaetzle are really the local type of sauté potatoes and so there isn't a specific wine that goes with them – you could literally have anything that is not too sweet. Spaetzle usually accompany veal or pork dishes which could be highly spiced, so a fine Tokay Pinot Gris could be the order of the day here. Again, the choice could be for either a dryer style, such as Brandhof Vieilles Vignes from Domaine Gresser, or a more opulent style, such as the Collection Rare from Kuentz-Bas, both wines having a good "rapport qualité/prix".

PARFAIT GLACÉ AU KIRSCH :

Ingredients: Crème anglaise made with 4dl.milk and 6 yolks - 250gr sugar - 4dl. double cream beaten in chantilly - 1dl. Kirsch.

Beat the 6 egg yolks (by hand) in a large bowl with half the sugar. Bring the milk to the boil and gradually add to the yolks beating all the time. Cook in a thick pan (large enough to half fill it with all the mix). Cook on a very small flame, scraping the bottom with a wooden spoon making a fast "8" movement. Do not boil, but the mixture must coat the reverse of the wooden spoon quite thickly. Cool right down to cold and add half dl. of Kirsch. Beat the cream with the rest of the Kirsch to light chantilly (soft peaks) and delicately add the crème anglaise to it. Line a mould with film, at the bottom you can put some griottines (wild cherries) which can be bought already marinated in Kirsch. Pour the mix and freeze for at least 24hrs. To serve, unmould.

RECOMMENDED WINES

Apart from drinking this with some of the excellent Kirsch liqueurs which abound in Alsace, you will need to have something which is pretty sweet to take this. It means, therefore that

249

you are going to have to get into the realms of Vendange Tardive or Séléction des Grains Nobles which are not going to be cheap. Tokay Pinot Gris SGN from Domaine Bott-Geyel is a well balanced, super 5 stars quality wine at a reasonable price, whilst if you prefer something with a little more concentration and depth then Colette Faller's Domaine Weinbach Gewürztraminer Cuvée d'Or Quintessance SGN – super 5 stars again, but a bit more expensive.

The name Champagne carries almost mystical properties for a vast number of people. However, there are a bewildering number of Champagne houses, co-operatives and growers bottling wine under their own labels and a further huge own-label business with wines of immensely variable quality all being bottled under the auspices of just one appellation. The great Champagne houses virtually invented the concept of the brand in winemaking and in most cases they do a very acceptable job. Nonetheless, in the absence of a better classification system the area remains a minefield for consumers. There are some 30,000-plus ha under vine with many of the 19,000 growers cultivating no more than a hectare or two. Both in the cellars of the region and in the vineyards there are inevitably substantial variations in quality.

The appellation and its districts

Making sparkling wine is realistically the only consistent vinegrowing activity that can be undertaken here, among the windswept rolling hills of the most northerly of France's wine regions. Alsace may be on a not dissimilar latitude but crucially it is protected by the Vosges Mountains. Ripening the three varieties Pinot Meunier, Pinot Noir and Chardonnay is by no means easy. Pinot Noir and Chardonnay are at their optimum in the production of the great wines of the Côte d'Or some 240 km (150 miles) to the south. The vital requirement here is to provide grapes that are physiologically ripe and of sufficient intensity to produce at least good wine. That means controlling yields and harvesting properly ripened fruit, which remains a problem.

Within the appellation the communes have been classified as Grand Cru, Premier Cru or Deuxième Cru. This does not however give an indication of quality or the potential of a given *terroir* as it does in Burgundy but works more as a means by which to establish the price a grower gets for his harvest. You may have an outstanding performer in a second-classed village and a moderate grower in a *grand cru*.

The appellation falls into five main districts, which account for some two-thirds of the working vineyard area. These five districts may yet become their own sub-appellations in a desired move to establish better regional identity within this geographically extensive AC. The rest of the appellation is spread across a vast area. Indeed the idea that all Champagne comes from fabled chalk soils is not the case. Much of the *vignoble* is clay, sand or marl. The **Montagne de Reims** is just to the south of that city and the aspect of the vineyards improves as it extends southwards. Pinot Noir and Pinot Meunier are the predominant varieties here and are famed for producing rich, full-bodied Champagnes. The village of **Bouzy** is as well known for producing the best still Coteaux Champenois reds as it is sparkling wines.

The **Vallée de la Marne** to the north-west of the Montagne de Reims stretches east along the River Marne. The centre of the district is the town of Épernay and the best vineyard sites are to the east. Red grapes are predominant here and the wines tend to be a touch lighter than those from the Montagne de Reims, with more elegance and refinement. The **Côte des Blancs** is, as the name suggests, white wine territory. Chardonnay is virtually the exclusive grape here with very few red plantings. The vineyards are largely sited with an easterly aspect. The great Chardonnay villages of Avize, Le Mesnil-sur-Oger and Vertus are found here.

In the far south-west of the main Champagne area, north of Troyes, is the **Côte**

251

de Sézanne, with the small town of the same name at its heart. The vineyards are dominated by Chardonnay, which accounts for some seven out of every 10 vines. As in the Côte des Blancs there is extensive chalk in the soil but not to the same degree. Way to the south of Troyes and away from the main Champagne appellation boundaries is the **Aube**. The area is one hundred miles from Reims. The soil is different, there is no chalk but more of the Kimmeridgian clay and limestone soils of Sancerre and Chablis. The latter is in fact a good deal closer to the Aube than any of the other Champagne vineyards.

At present the Aube is largely planted to Pinot Noir. There is a case for a considerable increase in Chardonnay. The area could potentially make extremely rich and powerful Blanc de Blancs.

The styles

The range of different styles available takes in sparkling white and rosé along with the still red wines which use the Coteaux Champenois appellation. While the role of the master blender in Champagne remains as significant as ever, the development of wines that come from single *terroirs* or from the same, very specific sources when vintage conditions favour – like the great Salon wines – seems likely to accelerate as time goes on. The sheer quality of many of the emerging small growers is a signal of things to come.

The styles and method outlined below should only be used as a very general guide; there can be significant variation within these. It is quite possible to find deluxe super-premium *cuvées* that are non-vintage, Blanc de Blancs that may be from a single vineyard or a blend of many, or Blanc de Noirs in vintage and non-vintage versions.

Most common and providing the bulk of the output of the great Champagne houses are the regular **non-vintage** blends. The use of reserve wine stocks is an undoubted asset, but a huge variation in quality exists. Available vineyard resources (and consequent fruit quality) and the length of time on lees in bottle are just two of the factors that affect the style of these wines. You should expect **vintage** *cuvées* to be a significant step up. They should be denser and richer with significantly greater structure. Inevitably there will be more variation in style with these as they reflect the nature of the year. Generally they should only be released after good harvests.

Blanc de Blancs is produced solely from Chardonnay while **Blanc de Noirs** is produced from Pinot Noir and/or Pinot Meunier, to the complete exclusion of Chardonnay. Blanc de Blancs is more refined and elegant and often has a tighter structure when young, whereas a Blanc de Noirs is fuller, with richer, more opulent flavours. The pink **Rosés** can be made either by blending in a little red wine (the only AC where this is permitted) or, and generally with better results, by the normal manner of a short maceration on skins. The best rosé generally comes from pure Pinot Noir.

The most expensive Champagnes are the deluxe bottlings. There is a wide range of styles but the best are among the finest white or rosé wines in the world. The latter are generally more expensive and made in minute quantities.

Champagne vintages

Because of the variable and challenging climate there is much vintage variation. Vintage wines are only produced when conditions permit. Among recent years 2004 produced a good crop and some good wines are likely to emerge. 2003 may also produce some excellent vintage bottles but balance will be a problem with many wines after a very hot summer. Volume too was very low. 2002 looks to be very promising. 2001, though, was a disaster with unprecedented rainfall. From 1995 to 2000 the Champenois were very lucky, having a string of good to very good vintages. 1996 and 1998 were outstanding. 1996 was uniformly good, very warm and sunny with ideal ripening conditions. There was some variation in 1998. 1996 and 1997 are now emerging on the market. Prior to 1995 the only really halfway presentable year was 1993. There were an alarming number of 1992s which were green and hard. 1990 is a classic. There are fine wines on release now, like the Bollinger RD 1995. 1989 and 1988 were both very good but not quite on a par with 1990. 1989 has less structure and should be drunk now. 1985, 1983 and 1982 are all great earlier years and top wines encountered from these will be worth considering, although 1985 and 1983 particularly do need drinking now.

A-Z of producers

AGRAPART   www.champagne-agrapart.com
Agrapart family   57 Ave Jean Jaures, 51190 Avize
Impressive small family-owned producer run by brothers Pascal and Fabrice with 9.6 ha of vineyards on the Côte des Blancs, almost half of which are at Avize. Other plots are in the *grand cru* villages of Oger, Cramant and Oiry. The Agraparts' holding is exclusively Chardonnay, traditionally established by mass selection and crucially the vines are of significant age: the oldest parcels over 55 years. This is clearly perceptible in the wines which have great purity and intensity. The non-vintage Brut Réserve is partly wood-aged and gets four years on its lees. The Brut Millésime is vinified in *demi-muids* and comes from calcareous soils at Avize and argilo-calcareous soils at Cramant. Both richness and complexity are gained from six years on lees. The top wine, the marvellously intense, citrus and mineral-laden L'Avizoise gets a similar period of lees-ageing and comes from the oldest vines. It will age very well in bottle. (DM)

O **Brut Réserve Grand Cru** Non-Vintage★★ £C O **Brut Grand Cru** Vintage★★★ £D
O **L'Avizoise Brut Grand Cru** Vintage★★★★ £E

AYALA   www.champagne-ayala.fr
Ducellier family   2 Boulevard du Nord, 51160 Aÿ
UK stockists: **Lib**
Jean-Michel Ducellier owns this recently improved small house as well as the Haut-Médoc classed growth Château LA LAGUNE. Recent releases have been showing greater richness, weight and concentration than a decade ago. These are very ripe, almost rustic styles of Champagne. The non-vintage Brut is dominated by Pinot Noir with a fair proportion of Pinot Meunier as well. The vintage Brut is again dominated by Pinot Noir with sufficient Chardonnay to provide additional complexity and intensity. The Blanc de Blancs is rich and weighty for the style with surprising opulence. There is also a light, fruit-driven rosé and also a special prestige bottling Grand Cuvée. (DM)

O **Brut** Non-Vintage★★ £D O **Brut** Vintage★★★ £E
O **Brut Blanc de Blancs** Vintage★★★ £E
◉ **Brut** Non-Vintage★ £D

PAUL BARA
Bara family   4 Rue Yvonnet, 51150 Bouzy
UK stockists: **OWL**
Very good small and traditional producer with vineyard holdings in the *grand*

253

cru village of Bouzy. The wines have a high level of Pinot Noir in the blend and this tends to show through with weight and substance. The Grand Cru Vintage is rich and bready, the Vintage Club shows extra depth and there is a very impressive, intense rosé. The Comtesse Marie de France is lighter and more elegant. The wines are all good value. (DM)

○ **Brut Réserve Grand Cru** Non-Vintage★★ £C   ○ **Brut Grand Cru** Vintage★★★ £D
○ **Brut Grand Cru Comtesse Marie de France** Vintage★★★★ £E
○ **Grand Cru Vintage Club** Vintage★★★★ £E
◉ **Brut Grand Cru Grand** Rosé de Bouzy★★★ £D

EDMOND BARNAUT   www.champagne-barnaut.com

Philippe Secondé   2 Rue Gambetta, BP 19, 51150 Bouzy
UK stockists: L&S, GFy

The 14 ha of vineyards are, like those of the Bara family, planted around the village of Bouzy. Unlike the Bara vineyards, though, they contain a high proportion of Chardonnay. This gives an added finesse and grip although the wines are of an impressively weighty, substantial style. There are two fine non-vintage wines: the Sélection-Extra and Grand Réserve. The former has a higher proportion of Pinot Noir which is evident, as it is in a rich, bready Blanc de Noirs. The Authentique Rosé gains its colour from the Pinot Noir skins rather than from blending with red base wine. There is also a limited-production special Cuvée Edmond Brut (1995 is the latest release), a Cuvée Douceur Sec and a fruity Bouzy Rouge. (DM)

○ **Brut Sélection-Extra** Non-Vintage★★★ £D   ○ **Grand Réserve** Non-Vintage★★★ £D
○ **Blanc de Noirs** Non-Vintage★★★ £D
◉ **Brut Authentique** Non-Vintage★★ £D

BEAUMONT DES CRAYÈRES   www.champagne-beaumont.com

Co-operative   BP 103, 51318 Epernay
UK stockists:Tan

This small, quality-concious co-op has over 200 growers who between them have only 80 ha of vineyards. Output for a co-op is also fairly low at just 50,000 cases a year and prices are generally very fair. The Grande Réserve is a soft, forward and fruity non-vintage blend dominated by Pinot Meunier and including a fair dollop of reserve wine. The Grand Prestige is again fruit-driven in style, but subtler and more elegant with a light citrus and bready character from 40 per cent Chardonnay as well as the Pinots. The Fleur de Prestige is particularly good value, with 60 per cent Chardonnay adding intensity and elegance. The top cuvée, Nostalgie, again has 60 per cent Chardonnay and 40 per cent Pinot Noir and is richer and fuller with surprising opulence for such a blend. The 1996 was rich and softly structured. (DM)

○ **Brut Grande Réserve** Non-Vintage★ £C   ○ **Brut Grand Prestige** Non-Vintage★★ £C
○ **Fleur de Prestige** Vintage★★★ £D   ○ **Nostalgie** Vintage★★★ £E

BILLECART-SALMON   www.champagne-billecart.fr

Billecart family   40 Rue Carnot, 51160 Mareuil-sur-Aÿ
UK stockists: **B-S**

A medium-sized and very impressive house, family-owned Billecart-Salmon produces 100,000 cases a year. The house was founded in 1818. The Brut Réserve non-vintage is classy stuff at this level and the top wines are very intense and marvellously refined. A sizeable proportion of Chardonnay is used and this helps the wines' balance and classic Champagne structure. The elegant non-vintage Blanc de Blancs is sourced from Le Mesnil-sur-Oger and is normally a blend of two vintages. The super Cuvée Nicolas-François Billecart is a very complex and elegant blend of 40 per cent Chardonnay and 60 per cent Pinot Noir. A vintage Blanc de Blancs is also produced along with a vintage

Grande Cuvée, the current release of which is 1990. There is also a tiny amount of prestige rosé Cuvée Elisabeth Salmon. (DM)

○ **Brut Réserve** Non-Vintage★★★ £E
○ **Blancs de Blancs Grand Cru** Non-Vintage★★★★ £F
○ **Brut Cuvée Nicolas-François Billecart** Vintage★★★★★ £F
◉ **Brut Rosé**★★★ £F

BOLLINGER www.champagne-bollinger.fr
Bollinger family 16 Rue Jules-Lobet, BP4, 51160 Aÿ
UK stockists: **Men**

One of the greatest names in sparkling wine production. Bollinger produces around 150,000 cases a year. It is one of just a handful of producers here to still ferment base wines in wood. A high proportion of Pinot Noir is used and the non-vintaged Special Cuvée is always full and rich in style. The vintage Grande Année can almost take on a hint of Burgundian gaminess with age, as can the remarkable RD *(récemment dégorgé)*. This wine is kept in bottle on its yeast sediment for up to 10 years and possesses a rich toastiness; it is both concentrated and exceptionally well balanced. 1995 is the current release. A tiny amount of a 100 per cent Pinot Noir *cuvée,* Vieilles Vignes, is made from ungrafted, very low-yielding old vines and there is a decent Coteaux Champenois red, Côte aux Enfants. (DM)

○ **Brut Spécial Cuvée** Non-Vintage★★★ £E
○ **Brut Grande Année** Vintage★★★★★ £G ○ **RD**✪✪✪✪✪ £H
◉ **Brut Grande Année** Rosé Vintage★★★ £G

RAYMOND BOULARD www.champagne-boulard.com
Boulard family 43 Rue Paul Douce, 51480 Damery
UK stockists: **IdG**

This small grower has just over 10 ha of impressively aged vineyards averaging around 30 years, older than most in the region. The holding is spread across 7 villages which helps in providing a range of diverse *terroirs* and champagnes. Red dominates the plantings with Pinot Meunier accounting for nearly half the vignoble. The wines are none the worse for this though. The Brut Réserve non-vintage is ripe and forward the vintage Brut Millesime bottling offering a rich biscuity texture and real depth and intensity. The Blancs de Blancs is tighter and more restrained, as one would expect and gains added depth from old vines. The splendidly rich and opulent Petraea comes from three different vintages and is bottled unfined and unfiltered. (DM)

○ **Blanc de Blancs Brut** Non-Vintage★★★ £D
○ **Brut Réserve** Non-Vintage★★ £C ○ **Brut Millésimé** Vintage★★★ £D
○ **Petraea Brut** Vintage★★★★ £E

DEUTZ www.champagne-deutz.com
Louis Roederer 16 Rue Jeanson, BP 9, 51160 Aÿ
UK stockists: BWC, Lay

Now owned by Louis Roederer, Deutz also has a successful sparkling wine partnership in New Zealand with Montana. By comparison with many of the other great houses the annual production here is relatively modest at some 80,000 cases or so. Quality is generally good to very good indeed and the wines are well priced, perhaps with the exception of the luxury *cuvées* William Deutz and Blanc de Blancs Amour de Deutz. The non-vintage Brut Classic is a good and well-structured, yeasty style; the vintage wines are tighter, more refined. (DM)

○ **Brut Classic** Non-Vintage★★★ £E
○ **Brut** Vintage★★★★ £F ○ **William Deutz** Vintage★★★★★ £G
○ **Blanc de Blancs** Vintage★★★★ £F
◉ **Brut** Rosé Vintage★★★★ £F

255

DOQUET-JEANMAIRE

Pascal Doquet   44 Chemin de Moulin de la Cense Bizet, 51130 Vertus

Relatively small family-owned domaine with 10 ha of vineyards on the Côte des Blancs, as well as a further 5.6 ha at Epernay and Perthois. There are 2.5 ha of *grand cru* vineyards at Le Mesnil-sur-Oger and a further 7.5 ha of *premier cru* vineyards. The huge majority of the plantings (99 per cent) are Chardonnay and the wines surprisingly show quite a forward opulent character. The best bottles, though, do show a real propensity to age. This is one of the rare cellars in the region where you can acquire very old bottles. There are vintage releases of both Premier Cru and the more expensive Premier Cru Coeur de Terroir. At the time of writing vintages available included Premier Cru 1990, 1985 and a surprisingly fresh but not terribly complex 1970. Coeur de Terroir releases currently available are 1993, probably the best structured, as well as 1989, 1988 and 1985. The Brut rosé is also exuberantly fruity and forward. A Coteaux Champenois is also produced. (DM)

O **Blanc de Blancs Premier Cru Coeur de Terroir** Vintage★★★ £D
O **Blanc de Blancs Premier Cru** Vintage★★ £D
O **Blanc de Blancs Premier Cru Sélection** Non-Vintage★★ £C
O **Blanc de Blancs Carte d'Or** Non-Vintage★★ £C
◉ **Brut Premier Cru** Rosé Non-Vintage★★ £C

EGLY-OURIET

Michel et Francis Egly-Ouriet   9-15. Rue de Trépail, 51150 Ambonnay

Very impressive, small family-run property with some 7 ha of Pinot Noir and 2 ha of Chardonnay. Production is tiny at some 5,500 cases a year. Quality is high, with well-aged vineyards that are over 30 years old and a dedicated, generally organic approach to viticulture. Yields are carefully tempered and a partial *vendange vert* is practised. In the cellar minimal handling extends to an absence of both fining and filtration for the base wines. The result is wonderfully pure, full-bodied wines of great character. A very good example of Coteaux Champenois is also produced but available only in very limited quantities. (DM)

O **Brut Tradition** Non-Vintage★★★ £D   O **Grand Cru** Vintage★★★★★ £E
O **Blanc de Noirs Vieilles Vignes** Non-Vintage★★★★ £E
◉ **Brut** Rosé Non-Vintage★★★ £D

PIERRE GIMONNET ET FILS   www.champagne-gimmonet.com

Gimonnet family   1 Rue de la République, 51530 Cuis
UK stockists: Odd

Family domaine that possesses 26 ha of very well-sited vineyards in the Côte des Blancs populated exclusively with old Chardonnay vines. Part of the vineyard holding is *premier cru* and part *grand cru*. This provides the property with a superb resource of base wine material. The style varies from the fresh, taut and lightly toasty Cuis Premier Cru to the weightier and richer Fleuron and Club Premier Cru labels. The Extra-Brut Oenophile, bottled without *dosage*, is very tight and lean but elegant. (DM)

O **Blanc de Blancs Cuis** Premier Cru Non-Vintage★★ £D
O **Brut Fleuron** Premier Cru Vintage★★★ £E
O **Brut Club** Premier Cru Vintage★★★ £E
O **Brut Gastronome** Vintage★★ £D
O **Extra-Brut Oenophile** Vintage★★★ £E

GOSSET   www.champagne-gosset.com

Cointreau family   69 Rue Jules-Blondeau, 51160 Aÿ
UK stockists: McK

This is among the very oldest of the Champagne houses, its commercial origins going back to 1584. The regular non-vintage Excellence is generally very reliable. The Grande Réserve and Grand Rosé, both non-vintage, and the vintage offerings here are a step up. The style is one of weight and a rich toastiness in the top wines but unfortunately a lack of elegance can creep in as well. Celebris is clearly a cut above the rest. (DM)

O **Brut Excellence** Non-Vintage★★ £D
O **Grande Réserve** Non-Vintage★★★ £F **Grande Millésime** Vintage★★★ £F
O **Celebris** Vintage★★★★ £G
◉ **Grand Rosé** Non-Vintage★★★ £F

ALFRED GRATIEN www.alfredgratien.com

Henkell and Sohnlein 30 Rue Maurice Cerveaux, BP 3, 51201 Épernay
UK stockists: Wit, WSc

Very good, small, traditional house which produces barely 15,000 cases a year. The base wines are vinified in wood and all cellar operations are still carried out by hand. The malolactic fermentation is blocked and this provides the taut, structured style. The wines, even the non-vintage, are ageworthy. The purchase by German *sekt* producer Henkell and Sohnlein is a recent development and it remains to be seen whether the house style will remain faithful and equally whether production will soar. (DM)

O **Brut** Réserve Non-Vintage★★★ £E O **Paradis** Non-Vintage★★★★ £F
O **Brut** Vintage★★★★★ £F
◉ **Brut Rosé Paradis** Non-Vintage★★★ £F

CHARLES HEIDSIECK www.charlesheidsieck.com

Remy Cointreau 4 Boulevard Henri-Vasnier, 51100 Reims
UK stockists: **Max**

Under the ownersip of Remy-Cointreau, the quality of the wine at this house over the past 15 years has been very impressive. The non-vintaged Brut Réserve Mis-en-Cave is arguably the best of its style in the appellation. The wine draws on a considerable amount of reserve wine and unusually gives the date of bottling so that the consumer has some idea of the age of the wine. Much of the consummate skill in creating this wine was achieved by the late Daniel Thibaut, one of the great modern master blenders of Champagne. There are two first-class vintage reserves: the elegant, superbly-crafted Blanc des Millénaires made from Chardonnay and the Pinot-dominated Charlie, a powerful, concentrated, weighty but very refined wine. (DM)

O **Brut Réserve Mis-en-Cave** Non-Vintage★★★★ £E
O **Charlie** Vintage★★★★★ £G O **Blanc des Millénaires** Vintage★★★★★ £G
◉ **Brut** Rosé Vintage★★★★ £G

HENRIOT contact@champagne-henriot.com

Joseph Henriot 81 Rue Coquebert, 51100 Reims
UK stockists: **JEF**

Medium-sized producer accounting for some 80,000 cases a year of moderately priced Champagne. The price reflects the quality here but the top vintage wines are reasonably impressive. The wines, including the straightforward Brut Souverain non-vintage, are weighty enough but lack a certain amount of refinement. The Cuvée des Enchanteleurs is a marked step up in both elegance and depth. (DM)

O **Blanc de Blancs** Non-Vintage★★ £D O **Brut Souverain** Non-Vintage★★★ £E
O **Brut** Vintage★★★ £E
O **Cuvée des Enchanteleurs**★★★★ £F ◉ **Brut** Rosé Vintage★★★★ £E

JACQUESSON champagne.jacquesson@wanadoo.fr

Chiquet family 68 Rue du Colonel-Fabien, 51530 Dizy
UK stockists: **May**

This is a good small-scale, family-run operation producing around 25,000 cases a year of good to very good quality. Barrel-fermentation is used for the base wine and the resulting Champagnes are characterful and refined. The style is rich, full-bodied and harmonious. The Non vintage bottlings are labelled Cuvée No, the current release 729. The Brut Signature vintage bottlings are very serious and structured and there is a very impressive vintage Blanc de Blancs as well. A complex and very pricey Dégorgement Tardif is now being produced, which is given extended ageing on lees. (DM)

O **Cuvée No** Non-Vintage★★ £E   O **Grand Cru** Vintage★★★ £E
O **Grand Vin Signature** Vintage★★★★ £G
O **Blanc de Blancs Vintage**★★★★ £G
◉ **Brut Perfection Rosé** Non-Vintage★★ £E
◉ **Grand Vin Signature** Vintage★★★ £E

KRUG krug@krug.fr

LMVH 5 Rue Coquebert, 51100 Reims
UK stockists: **Par**

Still run by Rémy Krug, this is arguably the most prestigious of all the great Champagne houses. However, production remains quite small at just over 40,000 cases a year. It is to be hoped that the exceptional quality standards here will remain under LMVH ownership and that volume will not escalate. These are quite remarkably impressive and structured wines. Tight and very restrained, perhaps more so than all other Champagnes, they demand cellaring. Even the non-vintage Grande Cuvée, a wine often on the cusp of a super-five rating, will benefit from at least five years after release. The Clos du Mesnil is that rare breed in this appellation, a wine from a small single vineyard. The range is completed by the tiny-production and undoubtedly very fine non-vintage Rosé. (DM)

O **Grande Cuvée** Non-Vintage★★★★★ £H   O **Clos du Mesnil** Vintage✪✪✪✪✪ £H
O **Vintage**✪✪✪✪✪ £H

LANSON www.lanson.fr

Marne et Champagne 12 Boulevard Lundy, 51100 Reims
UK stockists: **MCD**

Production here is vast at close to some 600,000 cases a year. In the light of that, quality has been at least solid. The Black Label Brut is probably the best-known Champagne brand after the MOËT ET CHANDON Brut Impérial; recent releases have shown a sound upturn in form – by no means where it could be, but a marked improvement. As well as the big brand a non-vintage rosé is fairly unexciting but there is a stylish Blanc de Blancs vintage and a decent enough Ivory Label Demi-Sec. The Brut Gold Label vintage was good rather than spectacular in 1995 but the quality of the current wines does seem to indicate real progress. The Noble Cuvée is a seriously structured and impressive Champagne. (DM)

O **Brut Black Label** Non-Vintage★ £D   O **Gold Label** Vintage★★ £E
O **Blanc de Blancs** Vintage★★★ £F
O **Noble Cuvée** Vintage★★★★ £G

LARMANDIER-BERNIER larmandier@terre-net.fr

Larmandier-Bernier family 43 Rue de 28 Août, 51130 Vertus
UK stockists: VTr

Small, top-class grower based in the Côte des Blancs, with an understandably large proportion of Chardonnay plantings. Like most really quality-conscious winemakers around the world, Pierre Larmandier keeps the human input to a minimum. The style is for very structured, minerally, intense Champagnes that have been given extra weight and depth through cask-ageing (no new wood is used) prior to bottling and further cellaring prior to release. Very low *dosage* is the approach here, with the Né d'Un Terre de Vertus being bone dry. The wines have the depth and texture to support the style but will reward cellaring, the vintage wines for many years. A very small amount of red Coteaux Champenois is also produced and is among the very best examples of the style. The fact that the wines are excellent value is another plus. (DM)

O **Brut Tradition** Non-Vintage★★★ £D   O **Blanc de Blancs** Non-Vintage★★★ £D
O **Extra Brut Vieille Vignes de Cramant** Vintage★★★★★ £E
O **Né d'Un Terre de Vertus Non Dosé** Non-Vintage★★★★ £D
◉ **Brut Rosé** Non-Vintage★★ £D

LAURENT-PERRIER   www.laurent-perrier.co.uk
De Nonancourt family   151150 Tour-sur-Marne
UK stockists: **L-P**

Still very much a family-run operation, although interests also include the other Champagne houses of DE CASTELLANE, DELAMOTTE and the super-prestige SALON. The great wines here are the Grand Siècle labels, which are all immensely refined. The two whites have a rich, powerful, bready character underpinned by a pure mineral structure. The rosé is very complex with a remarkable array of berry fruit aromas. The regular Brut non-vintage is sound with quite a heavy *dosage* but lacks a bit of grip. The non-vintaged rosé, though, is stylish and fresh, with attractive fruit. The Ultra Brut is impressively piercing and will develop well with some bottle-age. (DM)

O **Brut LP** Non-Vintage★ £E   O **Vintage**★★ £F   O **Ultra Brut** Non-Vintage★★★ £F
O **Grand Siècle La Cuvée** Non-Vintage★★★★ £G
O **Grand Siècle** Vintage★★★★★ £H
◉ **Brut Rosé** Non-Vintage★★★ £H
◉ **Grand Siècle Alexandra Rosé** Vintage★★★ £H

A.R. LENOBLE   www.champagne-lenoble.com
Jean-Marie Malassagne   43 Rue Paul Douce, 51480 Damery
UK stockists: **EoR**

This small house was founded in 1915 and possesses 18 ha of vineyards, with some fine Grand Cru holdings. Output is currently just under 30,000 cases a year. There is a decent, fresh and a tightly structured Brut Réserve which shows a large proportion of Chardonnay. The vintage Blanc de Noirs comes from 100% Pinot Noir and is the softest of the wines. Rosé is good, better than many and vintaged with real persistence. Unusually it is a blend of 85% Chardonnay, the balance Pinot Noir vinified as a red. The real excitement here though are the varietal Chardonnay wines from six Grand Cru villages on the Côte des Blancs. The non-vintage gets around 25% reserve wine and is nicely structured. The vintage is tighter with a purer mineral structure and impressive depth. Particularly striking is the luxury cuvée Les Aventures which comes from the terroir of the same name in the village of Chouilly. Some of the base wine is barrel-fermented to lend extra structure and the wine has a slightly lower dosage than the other bottlings. Give it two or three years after release. (DM)

O **Brut Réserve** Non-Vintage★ £C
O **Blanc de Blancs Grand Cru** Non-Vintage★★ £D   Vintage★★★ £E
O **Blancs de Noirs Premier Cru** Vintage★★ £D
O **Cuvée Les Aventure Grand Cru Blanc de Blancs** Vintage★★★★ £F
◉ **Brut Millésimé Rosé** Vintage★★ £D

259

SERGE MATHIEU www.champagne-serge-mathieu.fr

Mathieu family   6 Rue des Vignes, 10340 Avirey-Lingey
UK stockists: **SVS**

Small but very good property based in the Aube. Pinot Noir is the key
component here and the wines certainly display a real weight and
concentration. However, what marks them out is their elegance and
refinement, something that a great many of the family's near neighbours
struggle to achieve. The vintage Brut is impressively concentrated, rich, bready
and toasty but with a fine mineral backbone. The Tête de Cuvée is subtler,
more refined, with a higher proportion of Chardonnay and a shorter period on
lees. Both are ageworthy. (DM)

O **Brut Tradition** Non-Vintage★★ £C   O **Brut Prestige** Non-Vintage★★ £D
O **Brut Millésime** Vintage★★★ £E   O **Tête de Cuvée** Non-Vintage★★★ £E
O **Blanc de Noirs** Non-Vintage★★★ £D   ◉ **Brut Rosé** Non-Vintage★★ £D

MOËT ET CHANDON www.moet.com

LMVH   20 Rue avenue de Champagne, 51220 Épernay
UK stockists: **MHn**, AAA

Of all the Champagne houses this is the one that most readily comes to most
consumers' minds. The tendency among the majority of occasional wine
drinkers is to think of Moët as a brand rather than understanding it as a great
Champagne house. Production is considerable, around 2,500,000 cases a year.
Brut Impérial can be a lot more impressive than it is often given credit for. The
White Star is marketed in the US and contains a higher *dosage*. The vintage
Brut is well made with reasonable yeasty complexity and will age well over the
medium term. Like the house itself, Dom Pérignon is the most established of
the region's luxury *cuvées* and production is not small. The wine is very good
and consistent, becoming increasingly complex and harmonious with age.
There is a fine vintage rosé and a very small amount of the Dom Perignon
Rosé, every bit as impressive as the white. Three expensive additions have also
been made from *grand cru* villages: Champs de Romont is based on Pinot
Meunier, Vignes de Saran is from Chardonnay and Sarment d'Aÿ is a Pinot
Noir. All are non-vintage. There is also now a non-vintage *premier cru* bottling
blended from all three Champagne varieties. (DM)

O **Brut Impérial** Non-Vintage★★ £E   O **Brut White Star** Non-Vintage★ £E
O **Brut Impérial** Vintage★★★ £E
O **Dom Pérignon** Vintage★★★★★ £E
◉ **Brut Rosé** Vintage★★ £H

PIERRE MONCUIT

Nicole & Yves Moncuit   11 Rue Persault-Maheu, 51190 Le Mesnil-sur-Oger
UK stockists: **HHB**, SVS

The Moncuits produce two very fine Blanc de Blancs at their 20-ha property at
Le Mesnil-sur-Oger. The Grand Cru Vintage bottling is superbly crafted,
intense and refined with not a hint of austerity, rather a rich, biscuity
approachability. The Vieilles Vignes is a very fine expression of Champagne
hand-crafted from Chardonnay – intense, refined and very ageworthy. Sadly
very little is made. What makes these wines all the more remarkable is the
reasonable prices. (DM)

O **Blanc de Blancs** Grand Cru Vintage★★★ £D
O **Nicole Moncuit Vieilles Vignes** Vintage★★★★ £E

MONTAUDON

Luc Montaudon   6 Rue Ponsardin, 51061 Reims
UK stockists: **GPW**, ACh

Small and reasonably long-established Champagne house originally founded in

1891 and with a sizeable vineyard holding of some 45ha. The wines are all very well crafted in a showy and opulent style. The non-vintage Réserve is tight and citrussy, with a nice mineral undercurrent and fine biscuity persistence. The vintage is richer and fuller with surprising flesh and mid palate weight. The elegant Classe M is the houses luxury cuvée and offers real breadth as well as persistence with very complex candied, citrus and toasted aromas opening out on the palate. The wines all drink very well on release. (DM)

O **Réserve Première** Non-Vintage★★ £E O **Millésimé** Vintage★★★ £E
O **Classe M** Non-Vintage★★★★ £F

G H MUMM www.mumm.com

Allied Domecq 29 Rue du Champs-de-Mar, 51100 Reims
UK stockists: **ADo, AAA**

Allied Domecq purchased this old house in 2001 and it now joins PERRIER-JOUËT in the same stable. It will be interesting to see how the operations perform. The main brand, Cordon Rouge, was for a long time a serious underperformer. However during the late 1990s the quality has been altogether sounder. The wine is not complex but has a good core of appley fruit and is bottled with quite a high *dosage*. The vintage bottling is really only marginally better but the Grand Cordon vintage is a classier proposition. There is also now a vintage Grand Cru, a decent Brut Rosé and of course the prestige, non-vintaged Mumm de Cramant. (DM)

O **Cordon Rouge** Non-Vintage★ £E O **Cordon Rouge** Vintage★ £E
O **Grand Cordon** Vintage★★★ £F O **Grand Cru** Vintage★★ £E
O **Mumm de Cramant** Non-Vintage★★★★ £G ◉ **Brut Rosé** Non-Vintage★ £E

BRUNO PAILLARD www.champagnebrunopaillard.com

Bruno Paillard Avenue de Champagne, 51100 Reims
UK stockists: **Bib**

Bruno Paillard runs a modern, well-organised cellar producing nearly 45,000 cases a year. The style is relatively austere but these are wines, particularly the vintage *cuvées*, that should develop well in bottle. The prestige NPU (Nec Plus Ultra) is undoubtedly a serious step up from the rest of the range but is also very pricey. The wines are labelled with a date of disgorging which gives a clear idea about when to drink the non-vintaged wines. (DM)

O **Brut Première Cuvée** Non-Vintage★ £E O **Brut Millésime** Vintage★★★ £F
O **Chardonnay** Réserve Privée★★ £E O **Nec Plus Ultra** Vintage★★★★ £H
◉ **Brut Rosé Première Cuvée** Non-Vintage★ £E

JOSEPH PERRIER josephperrier@wanadoo.fr

Thienot 69 Avenue de Paris, 51016 Châlons-en-Champagne
UK stockists: **CHk, SsG, GWW**

Relatively small among the big Champagne houses, Joseph Perrier is noted for traditional, medium- to full-bodied wines. The Brut Royale non-vintage has roughly equal proportions of Chardonnay, Pinot Meunier and Pinot Noir in the blend, resulting in a full, fruity style. The vintage Royale is more complex. There is no Pinot Meunier and the wine is tighter, more structured. The Joséphine vintage is of a different order. The concentrated Pinot fruit is beautifully balanced by a refined, nutty quality with its Chardonnay component providing finesse and a real depth and mineral purity. This will cellar well. (DM)

O **Cuvée Royale Brut** Non-Vintage★★ £E O **Cuvée Royale Brut** Vintage★★★ £F
O **Joséphine** Vintage★★★★ £G ◉ **Brut Royale** Non-Vintage★★ £E

PERRIER-JOUËT www.perrier-jouet.com

Allied Domecq   51201 Epernay
UK stockists: **ADo**, AAA

Like G H MUMM this house, nearly 200 years old, has only been under the
Allied Domecq banner since 2001. The wines have a relatively high proportion
of Chardonnay but at the lower level they struggle to offer a great deal. The
basic non-vintage Brut is a straightforward and simple offering with more green
apple than complex, yeast-developed flavours. The Brut Rosé is a touch more
impressive and there is a non-vintaged Blason white which provides a hint of
bready complexity with a little time in bottle. The Blason Rosé is marked by
very simple, straightforward fruit, no more. The vintage Brut has better depth
than the regular and a hint of toastiness but there should be greater dimension.
The prestige *cuvée* La Belle Époque has a stylish bottle design and impressively
tight, Chardonnay-based fruit. It achieves good to very good complex
characters with age. There's a very good Belle Époque rosé as well. (DM)

O **Brut Blason de France** Non-Vintage★ £E   O **Grand Brut** Vintage★ £F
O **La Belle Époque** Vintage★★★★ £G
◉ **Grand Brut** Non-Vintage★★ £E

PHILIPPONNAT www.champagnephilipponnat.com

Bruno Paillard   13 Rue du Pont, 51160 Mareuil-sur-Aÿ
UK stockists: Fte, Las

This is a relatively small *négociant-manipulant* with an output of just 50,000
cases a year. Until its acquisition by Bruno PAILLARD, the range was decidedly
ordinary – with the exception of the great prestige *cuvée* Brut Clos de Goisses, a
wine of super-five quality in extravagant vintages like 1990. However things
appear to be taking a turn for the better. A good, attractive, strawberry-fruited
rosé is joined by the Royale Réserve, which has reasonable depth and a light
nutty, biscuity character. The vintage is clearly a step up, more complete and
complex, while the impressive Grand Blanc is a tight and structured Blanc de
Blancs that needs time. The Clos des Goisses should be given additional
cellaring – up to five years' ageing after release. (DM)

O **Brut Royale Réserve** Non-Vintage★ £E   O **Brut Réserve Spécial** Vintage★★ £F
O **Grand Blanc** Vintage★★★ £F   O **Clos des Goisses** Vintage★★★★★ £H
◉ **Brut Réserve** Non-Vintage★ £E

PIPER-HEIDSIECK www.piper-heidsieck.com

Remy Cointreau   52 Boulevard Henry-Vasnier, 51100 Reims
UK stockists: **Max**, AAA

Under the same ownership as Charles HEIDSIECK but the Champagne here is
a very different proposition. The non-vintage Brut is a simple, fruit-driven
style, now produced without malolactic fermentation to retain its fresh, forward
character. In recent years it has been better than of old – some releases used to
be basically dilute. The Brut Rosé is simple and straightforward, with some
pleasant red berry fruit showing through. The Brut vintage is a good deal better
– the wine has structure and depth with some complex toasty, yeasty notes
evolving – while the Rare prestige *cuvée* is tight, structured and displays some
real class. (DM)

O **Brut** Vintage★★ £F   O **Rare** Vintage★★★★ £G

POL ROGER www.polroger.co.uk

Pol Roger family   1 Rue Henri-de-Large, 51206 Epernay
UK stockists: **Pol**

Family-owned, sizeable house with production approaching some 125,000
cases a year. The non-vintage White Foil is now consistently good, a style with

real depth and a refined biscuity character but, like all the wines here, elegance and intensity is displayed more than weight. The vintage is just that little bit more complex and structured, very good and intense. There is a first class Blanc de Blancs Chardonnay vintage offering which is lighter still in style but impeccably balanced. Sir Winston Churchill is a very impressive prestige *cuvée* which demands to be cellared. (DM)

O **Brut White Foil** Non-Vintage★★★ £E O **Brut** Vintage★★★★ £F
O **Brut Chardonnay** Vintage★★★ £F O **Sir Winston Churchill** Vintage★★★★★ £H
◉ **Brut** Vintage★★★ £F

POMMERY www.pommery.fr

Vranken 5. Place du Général Gouraud, 51100 Reims
UK stockists: Eve, PFx

Production is considerable at this large house, with a volume of some 500,000 cases a year. However the LMVH group has sold its interest to Vranken who, while commercially successful throughout the appellation, have not so far established themselves as a beacon of top quality. Under LMVH ownership the quality throughout the range has been at least sound. There is a straightforward non-vintage Brut Royal – biscuity with a slightly raw edge to it – a better non-vintage Apanage and a sound rosé. The Blanc de Blancs Summertime is tight and structured, really quite elegant, while the Blanc de Noirs Wintertime is fuller and weightier. The vintage Grand Cru is refined and very well balanced in the best years, not overly weighty but long and intense. The Cuvée Louise is very impressive, not a full style but very long, harmonious and ageworthy. There is also a very fine Louise Rosé. Time will tell how the style and quality of the house will develop as a part of the Vranken empire. (DM)

O **Brut Royal** Non-Vintage★★ £E O **Brut Apanage** Non-Vintage★★ £E
O **Blanc de Blancs Summertime** Non-Vintage★★★ £E
O **Blanc de Noirs Wintertime** Non-Vintage★★★ £E
O **Brut Grand Cru** Vintage★★★ £F O **Louise** Vintage★★★★ £G
◉ **Brut** Non-Vintage★ £E

LOUIS ROEDERER www.champagne-roederer.com

Champagne Louis Roederer 21 Boulevard Lundy, 51100 Reims
UK stockists: **MMD**, AAA

This has long been established as one of the great Champagne houses. It is still family-owned and the company has invested heavily in other projects. As well as the Roederer Estate venture in California's Anderson Valley (see California North Coast), much closer to home it has acquired DEUTZ, along with Château de PEZ in the Médoc and in Portugal the Port house Ramos Pinto. The style here is weighty and rich with a considerable Pinot Noir influence. The Blanc de Blancs is the most obviously restrained style and has its malolactic blocked for freshness and to achieve balance and harmony. A considerable holding of reserve wine helps the non-vintage Brut Premier, while the Cristal prestige *cuvée* is one of the greatest and most refined sparkling wines in the world. It needs time. (DM)

O **Brut Premier** Non-Vintage★★★ £E O **Brut** Vintage★★★★ £F
O **Blanc de Blancs** Vintage★★★ £F
O **Cristal** Vintage❂❂❂❂❂ £H
◉ **Brut** Vintage★★★ £F

RUINART www.ruinart.com

LMVH 4 Rue des Crayères, BP 85, 51053 Reims-Cedex
UK stockists: **Rui**, AAA

Among the big houses Ruinart has maintained a relatively low profile in recent years despite being under the same ownership as MOËT ET CHANDON and more recently KRUG. Surprisingly its production is relatively large at close to 200,000 cases a year. The wines, though, are good to excellent, with the prestige *cuvées* (both Blanc de Blancs Dom Ruinart and the Rosé) worthy of a super-five rating on occasion. Chardonnay is an important part of the blending equation here and the wines are both refined and powerful, particularly the vintage *cuvées,* due to some extended ageing of the base wines. The non-vintage Brut is consistently one of the best of its kind. Newly added is a luxury blend of six *grands crus* and five vintages all from Chardonnay, the rare and pricey l'Exclusive de Ruinart. (DM)

○ **Brut R de Ruinart** Non-Vintage★★★ £E ○ **Brut R de Ruinart** Vintage★★★★ £F
○ **Blanc de Blancs** Non-Vintage★★★ £F ○ **Dom Ruinart** Vintage★★★★★ £H
◉ **Brut R de Ruinart** Non-Vintage★★ £F ◉ **Dom Ruinart** Vintage★★★★★ £H

SALON

Laurent-Perrier   5 Rue de la Brèche-d'Oger, 51190 Le Mesnil-sur-Oger
UK stockists: **C&B**, Las
Now owned by Laurent-Perrier. Just one exceptional wine is produced here: a Blanc de Blancs, in fact the first created, sourced entirely from selected vineyard plots in the village of Le Mesnil. Only bottled in the very best vintage years (the average through the last century was just over one year in four), an exceptional 1995 is the current release. Surprisingly rich and intense, but of course as well structured as one would expect, the wine should be cellared for at least a decade after release. (DM)

○ **Salon** Vintage✪✪✪✪✪ £H

FRANÇOIS SECONDÉ

François Secondé   6 Rue des Galipes, 51500 Sillery
Based in the Marne village of Sillery, François Secondé produces very well-priced and finely structured Champagne from just 5 ha. Around three-quarters of the vineyard is planted to Pinot Noir with the balance Chardonnay, but the style is for tight, restrained, wines which need a little time to show at their best. The vineyards are farmed organically and the vines are approaching 35 years age, all of which helps in providing excellent raw material. The wines are traditionally made with manual *remuage.* They offer very good value. (DM)

○ **Brut** Non-Vintage★★★ £C ○ **Brut Clavier** Non-Vintage★★★ £D
◉ **Brut Rosé** Non-Vintage★★ £C

JACQUES SELOSSE

Corinne & Anselme Selosse   22 Rue Ernest-Vallé, 51190 Avize
Remarkable small producer. Anselme Selosse bottles less than 4,000 cases of very impressive Champagne every year. The approach in the vineyard is biodynamic and yields are severely resticted to provide the purest, greatest intensity of fruit possible. What makes the approach here radical is the use of new as well as old oak to barrel-ferment the base wine. Extensively aged prior to release, these are massive and powerful wines for Champagne but no less impressive for that. On occasion the presence of oak can almost overwhelm, particularly in young or newly released wines, but there is no doubt that they are some of the most exciting and original wines of the appellation. (DM)

○ **Blanc de Blancs Tradition** Non-Vintage★★★ £E
○ **Originale** Extra-Brut Non-Vintage★★★★ £E
○ **Grand Cru Substance** Non-Vintage★★★★ £E
○ **Blanc de Noirs Contraste** Non-Vintage★★★★ £E
○ **Blanc de Blancs** Vintage★★★★★ £F

TAITTINGER   www.taittinger.com

Taittinger family   9 Place Saint-Nicaise, 51100 Reims
UK stockists: **HMA**, AAA

A large house producing around 400,000 cases a year of generally reliable if
rather unexciting non-vintage Brut Réserve. Better are some really very fine
vintage wines and an exceptional Blanc de Blancs prestige *cuvée* Comtes de
Champagne, matched by an equally exquisite and very rare rosé. Taittinger also
owns the Loire Valley sparkling wine house BOUVET-LADUBAY and Domaine
Carneros in California. (DM)

O **Brut Réserve** Non-Vintage★ £E   O **Brut Millésime** Vintage★★★ £F
O **Blanc de Blanc Comtes de Champagne** Vintage✪✪✪✪✪ £H
◉ **Brut Prestige** Non-Vintage★ £E   ◉ **Comtes de Champagne** Vintage★★★★★ £H

VEUVE CLICQUOT   www.veuve-clicquot.fr

LVMH   12 Rue du Temple, 51100 Reims
UK stockists: **Par**, AAA

Second to MOËT ET CHANDON in the LVMH hierarchy in terms of volume
but most certainly ahead in terms of quality. Throughout the last five or six
years the quality here has always been good, even for the regular Carte Jaune
(Yellow Label). The vintage wines have weight and structure and are full of
rich, toasty character. La Grande Dame is an exceptional wine, both the more
easily available white and the scarce rosé. Both are rich, heady blends of Pinot
Noir and Chardonnay. A number of prestige wineries around the world
originally purchased by Veuve Clicquot now fall within the LVMH banner.
These include Cloudy Bay in New Zealand, Cape Mentelle in Western
Australia and Newton in the Napa Valley. The house of Canard-Duchêne,
which continues to disappoint of late, has long been under the Clicquot wing.
(DM)

O **Brut Carte Jaune** Non-Vintage★★★ £E   O **Vintage Réserve**★★★ £F
O **Rich Réserve** Vintage★★★ £F   O **La Grande Dame** Vintage✪✪✪✪✪ £H
◉ **Rosé Réserve** Vintage★★★ £F

OTHER WINES OF NOTE

HENRI ABELE O **Brut Traditionelle** Non-Vintage★ £C
H BLIN O **Brut** Vintage★★ £E
BOIZEL O **Brut Réserve** Non-Vintage★★ £C   O **Brut Grand** Vintage★★★ £E
◉ **Brut Rosé** Non-Vintage★★ £D
ALEXANDRE BONNET O **Blanc de Blancs** Vintage★★ £E
O **Blanc de Noirs** Non-Vintage★ £D
PHILIPPE BRUGNON O **Brut** Non-Vintage★★ £D
ROGER BRUN O **Brut Réserve** Non-Vintage★★ £D
O **Brut Réserve Grand Cru** Non-Vintage★★ £D
O **Cuvée des Sires Grand Cru** Non-Vintage★★★ £E
CHARLES DE CAZENOVE O **Brut Azur Premier Cru** Non-Vintage★ £D
O **Brut Azur Premier Cru** Vintage★★ £E
GUY CADEL O **Carte-Blanche** Non-Vintage★★ £C   O **Brut** Vintage★★ £E
◉ **Brut Rosé** Non-Vintage★ £D
GUY CHARLEMAGNE O **Blanc de Blancs Grand Cru** Vintage★★★ £E
JACKY CHARPENTIER O **Brut Prestige** Non-Vintage★★ £D
O **Brut** Vintage★★★ £E   ◉ **Brut Rosé** Non-Vintage★★ £E
DE CASTELLANE O **Cuvée Florens** Vintage★★ £F
DELAMOTTE O **Brut** Non-Vintage★ £C   O **Brut** Vintage★★★ £E
DE SOUSA O **Blanc de Blancs** Réserve★★★ £E
PAUL DÉTHUNE O **Grand Cru** Non-Vintage★ £C
O **Grand Cru** Vintage★★ £D
DE VENOGE O **Cordon Bleu** Non-Vintage★ £D

265

O **Blanc de Blancs** Vintage★★ £E

DRAPPIER O **Brut Carte d'Or** Non-Vintage★ £D

O **Brut Carte d'Or** Vintage★★ £E   O **Grande Sendrée** Vintage★★★ £F

J. DUMANGIN O **Brut Grande Réserve** Non-Vintage★★ £D

◉ **Brut Rosé de Saignée** Non-Vintage★★ £E   O **Brut** Vintage★★★ £E

O **Extra Brut** Non-Vintage★★★ £E

DUVAL-LEROY O **Fleur de Champagne 1er Cru** Non-Vintage★ £D

O **Fleur de Champagne Blanc de Chardonnay** Vintage★★ £E

◉ **Fleur de Champagne Rosé de Saignée** Non-Vintage★★ £E

GALLIMARD O **Cuvée Réserve** Non-Vintage★★ £D

GARDET O **Brut Special** Non-Vintage★★ £E

O **Brut Cuvée Charles Gardet** Vintage★★ £E

GATINOIS O **Réserve Grand Cru** Non-Vintage★★ £E

O **Grand Cru** Non-Vintage★★ £D

RENE GEOFFROY O **Brut Réserve** Non-Vintage★★ £D

HENRI GIRAUD O **Brut Grand Cru Tradition** Non-Vintage★★ £D

MICHEL GONET O **Brut Réserve** Non-Vintage★★ £D

O **Cuvée Prestige** Vintage★★ £E

GEORGES GOULET O **Brut** Non-Vintage★★ £D

HENRI GOUTORBE O **Brut Cuvée Tradition** Non-Vintage★★ £D

JACQUART O **Blanc de Blancs Mosaïque** Vintage★★ £E

A. JACQUART O **Blanc de Blancs** Vintage★★★ £E

JEAN-LUC LALLEMENT O **Brut Réserve** Non-Vintage★★ £D

J. LASSALLE O **Cuvée Imperial Préférence** Non-Vintage★★ £D

O **Cuvée Special Club** Vintage★★★ £E

◉ **Premier Cru** Non-Vintage★★ £D

LE MESNIL O **Blanc de Blancs Grand Cru** Non-Vintage★★★ £D

O **Blanc de Blancs Grand Cru** Vintage★★★ £E

LILBERT O **Blanc de Blancs Grand Cru** Non-Vintage★★★ £D

MAILLY GRAND CRU O **Brut Réserve** Non-Vintage★★ £D

O **Brut Grand Cru** Vintage★★★ £E   O **Echansons** Vintage★★★★ £G

◉ **Grand Cru** Non-Vintage★★ £E

A. MARGAINE O **Brut Premier Cru** Non-Vintage★★ £C

O **Special Cuvée Club** Vintage★★★ £E   ◉ **Brut** Non-Vintage★★ £D

HENRI MANDOIS O **Brut** Non-Vintage★★ £C

O **Brut Cuvée Victor Vieilles Vignes** Vintage★★★ £E

◉ **Brut Premier Cru** Non-Vintage★ £D

MOUTARD O **Carte d'Or Blanc de Blancs** Non-Vintage★ £C

O **Cuvée Prestige** Non-Vintage★★ £E   ◉ **Cuvée Prestige** Non-Vintage★★ £E

JEAN MOUTARDIER O **Brut Carte d'Or** Non-Vintage★★ £C

O **Brut Sélection** Non-Vintage★★ £D

NICOLAS FEUILLATTE O **Brut Réserve Particulière** Vintage★ £D

O **Brut** Vintage★★ £E   O **Cuvée Spéciale** Vintage★★★ £F

PALMER O **Amazone de Palmer** Non-Vintage★★ £D

PANNIER O **Brut** Non-Vintage★ £C   O **Blanc de Noirs** Vintage★★★ £E

◉ **Egérie Rosé** Non-Vintage★★ £D

ROGER POUILLON O **Brut Réserve** Non-Vintage★★ £C

O **Fleur de Mareuil** Non-Vintage★★★ £C

J.P. ROBERT O **Cuvée Réserve** Non-Vintage★★ £C

J.P. SECONDÉ O **Brut Grand Cru** Non-Vintage★★ £C   O **Brut** Vintage★★★ £E

◉ **Brut Rosé** Non-Vintage★★ £D

SOUTIRAN-PELLETIER O **Blanc de Blancs Grand Cru** Non-Vintage★★ £E

TARLANT O **Brut Réserve** Non-Vintage★★ £D **Brut** Vintage★★ £E

PIERRE VAUDON O **Brut Premier Cru** Non-Vintage★★ £C

O **Brut Premier Cru** Vintage★★★ £D

◉ **Brut Premier Cru** Non-Vintage★ £D

JEAN VESSELLE O **Brut Réserve** Non-Vintage★★ £D

VEUVE A DEVAUX O **Blanc de Noirs** Non-Vintage★★ £E

VEUVE FOURNY O **Blanc de Blancs 1er Cru** Non-Vintage★★★ £E

VILMART O **Grand Cellier** Non-Vintage★★★ £E

O **Grand Cellier d'Or** Vintage★★★ £E

○ Coeur de Cuvée Vintage★★★★ £F

Work in progress!!

Producers under consideration for the next edition
MICHEL ARNOULD
BARON FUENTÉ
CÉDRIC BOUCHARD
PIERRE CALOT
COLIN
LAMIABLE
GUY LARMANDIER
LECLERC-BRIANT
MARIE-NOËLLE LEDRU
JÉRÔME PRÉVOST
ALAIN ROBERT
SADI MALOT
SANT-GALL
WARIS LARMANDIER

Author's Choice (DM)

Good value Champagnes
AGRAPART ○ **Brut Grand Cru** Vintage
EDMOND BARNAUT ○ **Brut Sélection-Extra** Non-Vintage
BEAUMONT DE CRAYERES ○ **Fleur de Prestige** Vintage
RAYMOND BOULARD ○ **Brut Millésimé** Vintage
DEUTZ ○ **Brut Classic** Non-Vintage
DOQUET_JEANMAIRE ○ **Blanc de Blancs Premier Cru Coeur de Terroir** Vintage
SERGE MATHIEU ○ **Brut Millésime** Vintage
PIERRE MONCUIT ○ **Blanc de Blancs** Grand Cru Vintage
FRANÇOIS SECONDÉ ○ **Brut Clavier** Non-Vintage
JOSEPH PERRIER ○ **Cuvée Royale Brut** Non-Vintage

A selection of lesser known Champagnes
PAUL BARA ○ **Brut Grand Cru** Vintage
PHILIPONAT ○ **Clos des Goisses** Vintage
EGLY-OURIET ○ **Brut Tradition** Non-Vintage
PIERRE GIMONNET ET FILS ○ **Blanc de Blancs Cuis** Premier Cru Non-Vintage
ALFRED GRATIEN ○ **Paradis** Non-Vintage
LARMANDIER-BERNIER ○ **Extra Brut Vieille Vignes de Cramant** Vintage
SERGE MATHIEU ○ **Brut Millésime** Vintage
GOSSET ○ **Celebris** Vintage
BRUNO PAILLARD ○ **Nec Plus Ultra** Vintage
JACQUES SELOSSE ○ **Blanc de Blancs Tradition** Non-Vintage

Pick of the luxury cuvée's
BILLECART-SALMON ○ **Brut Cuvée Nicolas-François Billecart** Vintage
BOLLINGER ○ **RD** Vintage
CHARLES HEIDSIECK ○ **Charlie** Vintage
KRUG ○ **Clos du Mesnil** Vintage
LAURENT-PERRIER ○ **Grand Siécle** Vintage
MOËT ET CHANDON ○ **Dom Pérignon** Vintage
POL ROGER ○ **Sir Winston Churchill** Vintage
LOUIS ROEDERER ○ **Cristal** Vintage
SALON ○ **Salon** Vintage
VEUVE CLICQUOT ○ **La Grande Dame** Vintage

RECOMMENDED HOTELS AND RESTAURANTS - CHAMPAGNE

Top Hotels

★★★★★*Les Crayères*   64 bvd. Vasnier, Reims 51100
Tel. 03 26 82 80 80   Fax 03 26 82 65 52
Email crayeres@relaischateaux.com   16 rooms   £H

★★★★*Hostellerie La Briqueterie*   Route de Sézanne, Vinay 51530
Tel. 03 26 59 99 99   Fax 03 26 59 92 10
Email. info@labriqueterie.fr   42 rooms   £E/G

Top Restaurants

★★★★★*Les Crayères*   64 bvd. Vasnier, Reims 51100
Tel. 03 26 82 80 80   Fax 03 26 82 65 52
Email crayeres@relaischateaux.com   £H

★★★*Le Foch*   37 Bvd. Foch, Reims 51100
Tel. 03 26 47 48 22   Fax 03 26 88 78 22
Email. mjackylouaze@aol.com   £B/E

Value for money Hotels

★★*Auberge St-Vincent*   1 rue St Vincent, Ambonnay 51150
Tel. 03 26 57 01 98   Fax 03 26 57 81 48
Email info@auberge-st-vincent.com   10 rooms   £ A

★*Cathédrale*   20 rue Libergier, Reims 51100
Tel. 03 26 47 28 46   Fax 03 26 88 65 81
No email address   17 rooms   £A

Value for money restaurants

★★★*Le Foch*   37 Bvd. Foch, Reims 51100
Tel. 03 26 47 48 22   Fax 03 26 88 78 22
Email. mjackylouaze@aol.com   £B/E

★★*Pré St-Alpin*   2bis rue Abbé Lambert, Châlons-en-Champagne 51000
Tel. 03 26 70 20 26   Fax 03 26 68 52 20
Email pre.st.alpin@wanadoo.fr   £A

CHAMPAGNE RECIPES

FONDUE AU FROMAGE

Ingredients: 250gr. rich gruyère or emmenthal - one and half dl. double cream – 2tblspns. white wine – 30gr. of butter, a scratch of nutmeg and a pinch of cinnamon – three egg yolks – enough short pastry to line 4 individual ramekin dishes.

Bring the cream to the boil; add the grated cheese and stir with a wooden spoon until melted and very hot. Beat egg yolks with wine and add to the cheese mix with seasoning and butter; carry on cooking on very small heat, stirring all the time until thick but never boiling, line the ramekins with pastry and cook blind until golden. Add cheese mix and put in a very hot oven or under the grill until surface is golden. The inside must remain very soft, the consistency of thick cream.

RECOMMENDED WINES

Despite the assertions from the Champenois that you can drink Champagne throughout the meal, I don't always find this a good idea – too monotonous, so this little fondue is going to go best with a still Côteaux Champenois such as Ch. de Saran from Moët & Chandon (if you can find it). If you must stick to Champagne then choose one with a bit of weight such as Gosset or Joseph Perrier.

CÔTES DE PORC À L'ARDENNAISE:

Ingredients; 4 boneless thick, best quality pork cutlets, 300gr. wild mushrooms (girolles are best, but any would do), 2 small shallots, enough butter to sauté the mushrooms, half dl. white port, salt, pepper, 4 dessertspoons of thick cream, very finely chopped parsley; 4 slices of ham - greaseproof or silicone paper to make 4 papillottes .

Grill the cutlets on a griddle just to mark them and seal them (3mns). Cool down - slit them. Season the inside. Melt the butter until golden and sautÈ the mushrooms and shallots, add the white port, and cook for about 12 minutes. Add a spoonful of cream; the mixture must be quite tight and hold. Lay down the 4 pieces of paper large enough to make papillottes , put a cutlet on each, opened, put on each a coat of mushrooms, slice of ham cut to size, another coat of mushrooms; shut the cutlet and put a tablespoon of cream, chopped parsley on top and close the papillottes tightly, but leaving some air inside. Cook in a medium oven between 18 to 20 mns.

RECOMMENDED WINES

This dish will suit the earthy style of a red Côteaux Champenois and good ones are made by Bollinger and Larmandier-Bernier although they may be difficult to track down. A weightier rosé Champagne such as from Roederer or Laurent-Perrier will also do the trick.

CRÊPES SOUFFLÈES AU CHAMPAGNE

Ingredients: 4 pancakes – 150gr. glacé fruit (pineapple, cherries, orange peel - good quality, not in syrup) – one and half dl. Champagne, 1 dessertspoon sugar. Mix those ingredients and put in a tight jar and leave for at least a week to macerate. 150gr. of fromage frais – 1.5 dl. fresh double cream, 100gr. sugar. 3 yolks and 5 whites of egg - 2 tablespoons of Kirsch.

Beat the fresh cream into soft peaks, add the fromage frais gradually beating all the time and keeping the same consistency. Stop beating as soon as you reach same consistency as before you added the fromage frais. Beat the 3 egg yolks with 50gr. of the sugar until light and fluffy. Mix to the cream and cheese mix. When you are ready to serve, beat the 5 whites to soft peaks with the rest of the sugar, fold in the cheese and cream mix. Stuff each pancake, fold in half, cook in a medium to hot oven until puffed up. Meanwhile heat the Champagne and fruit mix, flambÈ with the Kirsch – share between the pancakes and serve immediately.

RECOMMENDED WINES

This dish will need a Champagne that is either rich or old (not unlike many of the drinkers!). Rich Champagne is a bit out of fashion now – everyone likes to have it 'Brut' (at least, on the label), so it may be hard to find. Clicquot do a very passable Rich Reserve, but any fine vintage Champagne with as much bottle age as possible in order to get that slightly maderised taste, should also work.

The Loire is perhaps the most diverse and certainly geographically the most extensive of all France's classic wine regions. Inevitably there is a vast difference in styles from Nantes on the Atlantic coast to the heart of the Auvergne. Much of the region is steeped in tradition but, while you won't find the wave of new developments that is happening in the Midi for instance, there are new high-quality producers emerging in almost all appellations. A number of them are committed to either organic farming practices or indeed biodynamic viticulture. Applying these principles in this northerly climate is a far taller order than in, say, dry and sunny Provence.

Pays Nantais

The Pays Nantais generally means just one wine to the majority of people: Muscadet. Generic **Muscadet** can be pretty dire stuff, but there are a number of beacons of quality; names like Domaine de l'Ecu and Louis Métaireau. From a quality perspective the most important appellation is **Muscadet de Sèvre-et-Maine** with the best wines bottled *sur lie*. This means the wine spends a period of time on its lees for added richness. There are two other superior ACs, **Muscadet-Coteaux de la Loire** and **Muscadet Côtes de Grandlieu**. Covering the same area is the **Gros Plant VDQS**, producing simple, austere wines and to the south is the **Fiefs Vendéens VDQS** – you are most likely to encounter these on holiday in the area and the odd exciting example is emerging. Further east and stretching towards the south of Anjou and Saumur is the heart of the **Vin de Pays du Jardin de la France,** although this covers the whole of the valley; the odd fine white is appearing here. To the south is the VDQS of **Haut-Poitou**, where there are some relatively interesting whites and reds in vineyards surrounding the town of Poitiers. Good Muscadet can be crisp, minerally and with a real green-fruited depth, not dissimilar to sound village Chablis.

Anjou and Saumur

The **Anjou** appellation includes red, rosé and white wines. It covers a vast area north and south of the River Loire, from the west of Angers east to beyond Saumur. The quality can range from dire to very impressive, with some stylish barrel-fermented whites from the major white variety of the region, Chenin Blanc. Reds tend to be light, but the best are ripe and juicy with the odd more serious example and can be made from Gamay, Cabernets Sauvignon and Franc and Pineau d'Aunis. The medium to sweet rosé is generally very average, but well-made examples occasionally turn up under the Cabernet d'Anjou AC. The best red now has its own AC, **Anjou-Villages** and some very good wines are being made from Cabernet Franc and Cabernet Sauvignon. New oak is increasingly favoured.

The great wines here, though, are the steely, intense dry whites of **Savennières** and the sweet botrytised wines of the **Coteaux du Layon**. Those from the **Coteaux de l'Aubance** are less impressive but there are good examples. Within the Coteaux du Layon are the ACs of **Quarts de Chaume** and **Bonnezeaux** along with a number of communes which may append their names. These sweet wines tend to be traditional, quite restrained and very ageworthy or, increasingly, wines of immense extract and honeyed richness. Producers of the latter have become known as the sugar hunters. The best of these wines are marvellously rich and refined but some seem overblown and not entirely balanced and you have to wonder how they will age. A small amount of fine sweet Chenin Blanc is also made at Saumur and labelled as **Coteaux de Saumur**.

The vineyards of Saumur are also a haven for sparkling wine production. As well as sparkling Saumur there is also the catch-all appellation of **Crémant de Loire**. The attraction in making sparkling Chenin, as opposed to still, is the option it offers in poor vintages like those of the late 1990s. Many small producers take this route and there are some sizeable merchant houses and commercial offshoots of the big Champagne houses in Saumur. Quality can be quite good. The wines are generally more green apple in character than rich and biscuity in the manner of Champagne.

The best wines from Saumur, though, are the impressive barrel-fermented still white Chenin Blancs of the **Saumur** AC and the rich, ripe and supple reds of **Saumur-Champigny** produced from Cabernet Franc and Cabernet Sauvignon. These tend to be softer and lusher in texture than the equally impressive reds from Bourgueil, Chinon and Saint-Nicolas-de-Bourgueil. Chinon is produced exclusively from Cabernet Franc and tends to be tighter and leaner. However, that said, there is still an alarming amount of dull, over-sulphured white and under-ripe, green-flavoured red throughout Anjou. The producer rather than the appellation is all-important.

Touraine

As in Anjou there is a catch-all **Touraine** AC that encompasses most of the region. Sauvignon Blanc is as important for whites here as Chenin and is common under the Touraine banner. In the far west of the region are the red wine appellations of **Bourgueil** and **Saint-Nicolas-de-Bourgueil** north of the river Loire and **Chinon** just to the south. The best of these wines are very good indeed and new oak is increasingly favoured. Bourgueil tends to be the fullest, while Saint-Nicolas often shows greater elegance and Chinon grown on the limestone *coteaux* is equally refined.

Just to the east of the city of Tours are the vineyards of **Vouvray** amd **Mountlouis**. Vouvray is found on the north of the river, Montlouis just to the south. Depending on the vintage conditions – and there have been some very moderate recent years although 2002 and particularly 2003 have been favourable – dry, *demi-sec* and *moelleux* styles are all created. The latter can be some of the greatest and longest-lived sweet wines in the world. Green and minerally in their youth, the dry and medium styles become increasingly rich and honeyed with age. The dry styles can be very austere when young and the searing acidity can be almost overwhelming. This can be the same with the *moelleux* wines – it's just better disguised by the residual sugar. Like many of the sweet wines along the valley the dependence on liberal sulphur additions is beginning to wane and you don't need to wait 20 years now for it to dissipate.

There are a number of lesser Touraine appellations. To the west of Tours can be found **Touraine Azay-le-Rideau** and to the immediate east of Vouvray and Montlouis **Touraine-Amboise** and **Touraine-Mesland**. Gamay, Cabernet Franc and Cabernet Sauvignon feature for the reds and Chenin Blanc for the whites. There are a few good examples. To the south of Blois are the regions of **Cheverny** and **Cour-Cheverny**. Similar reds are planted at Cheverny but the whites include Sauvignon Blanc and the unusual Romorantin. Cour-Cheverny is a white-only appellation planted to Romorantin.

To the north of Tours and the Touraine appellation are the regions of the **Coteaux du Loir** and its sub-region of **Jasnières**. The climate here is extremely marginal. The best wines – dry and late-havested Chenin Blancs – are Jasnières from vines planted on south-facing aspects with a protected mesoclimate. A handful of very good wines are made.

Central Vineyards and the South

The main wines of consequence are the Sauvignon Blancs from **Quincy**, **Reuilly**, **Menetou-Salon**, **Sancerre** and **Poully-Fumé**. Good Pinot Noir is also

271

made at Sancerre and to a lesser extent at Menetou-Salon. While a considerable amount of very average white wine is made from these appellations there are some seriously good wines too. Those whites that are barrel-fermented and kept on lees are capable of considerable age and bottle development.

To the south is the Auvergne. The best wines come from the **Côte Roannaise**, where the odd decent example of Gamay is produced. Indeed the vineyards are nearer to and have more similarity geographically with Beaujolais than the rest of the Loire. Gamay is also produced in the **Côtes du Forez**.

A-Z of producers by appellation/region

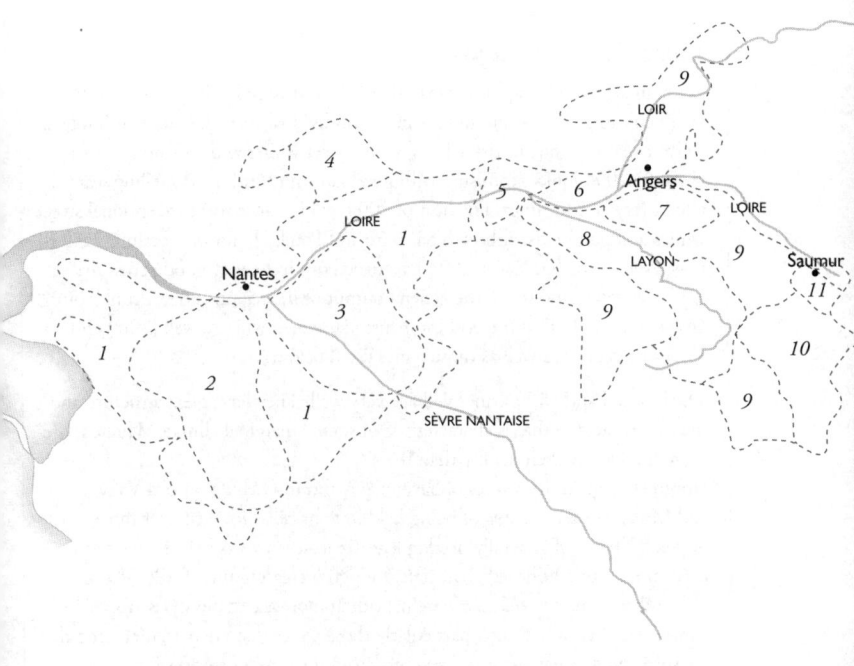

1 Muscadet	13 Coteaux du Loir
2 Muscadet Côtes de Grand Lieu	14 Saint-Nicolas-de-Bourgeuil
3 Muscadet de Sèvre-et-Maine	15 Bourgeuil
4 Muscadet des Coteaux de la Loire	16 Chinon
5 Anjou Coteaux de la Loire	17 Vouvray
6 Savennières	18 Montlouis
7 Coteaux de l'Aubance	19 Touraine
8 Coteaux du Layon	20 Cheverny, Cour Cheverny
9 Anjou	21 Reuilly
10 Saumur	22 Quincy
11 Saumur-Champigny	23 Menetou-Salon
12 Jasnières	24 Sancerre
	25 Pouilly-Fumé

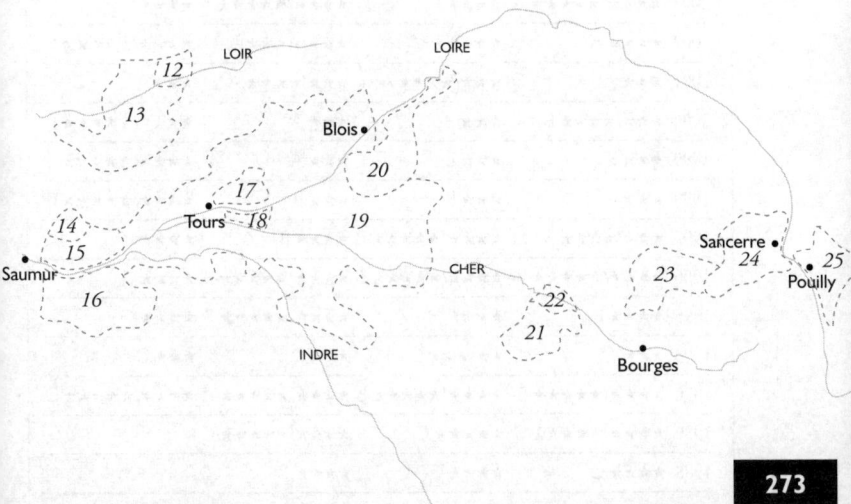

Loire Valley vintages

With an area as geographically extensive and as diverse in climate as the Loire it is difficult to generalise about its wines or individual years. Cooler conditions in a given year may favour dry whites, while sweet whites and reds need warm vintages. 2004 looks promising with good autumn sunshine dispelling fears after a very wet summer. The heat of 2003 will produce some exceptional sweet whites and good reds, although Sancerre and Pouilly Fume will be fully evolved now, even in the best cases. 2002 has turned out to be very good across the region. A huge amount of the general output of the region is best drunk young. You will, though, find the odd top Muscadet which will age well (2000 and 1997 were good) as well as those wines listed below.

The best red and white wines will age very well. They have great structure and the intense acidity that is characteristic of such a marginal climate. The reds are more marked by their acidity than their tannin. The great dry whites of Savennières and top *demi-secs* from Vouvray and Montlouis are capable of being held in your cellar for well over three decades. They will generally need at least six to seven years before they show their more exotic honeyed characters, though increasing use of oak, new and old, and *macération pellicullaire* are providing more accessible styles. Top Sancerre and Pouilly-Fumé, particularly those wines that are barrel-fermented, are surprisingly ageworthy and a far cry from the kind of tropical, gooseberry-laden examples of Sauvignon Blanc from the southern hemisphere that will barely make it past their first birthday.

Of the great earlier vintages Savennières was particularly impressive in 1985, 1983, 1982, 1978 and 1976. The great sweet wine vintages to consider were 1985, 1983, 1982, 1976, 1971, 1959, 1949, 1947 and 1921. Top reds were made in 1986, 1985, 1983, 1982, 1978 and 1976.

Loire Valley vintage chart

	Anjou & Touraine Top Dry Whites inc Savennières	Anjou & Touraine Sweet Whites	Saumur & Touraine Top Red Cuvées	Sancerre & Pouilly- Fume Whites
2004	★★★★ A	★★★★ A	★★★★ A	★★★★ A
2003	★★★★/★★★★★ A	★★★★★ A	★★★★/★★★★★ A	★★★ C
2002	★★★★ A	★★★★ A	★★★/★★★★ A	★★★★/★★★★★ B
2001	★★★ A	★★★/★★★★ A	★★★/★★★★ A	★★★ C
2000	★★★/★★★★ B	★★★ B	★★★ A	★★★★/★★★★★ B
1999	★★★ B	★★★ B	★★★ A	★★★★/★★★★★ B
1998	★★★ B	★★★ B	★★★ B	★★★★/★★★★★ C
1997	★★★/★★★★ B	★★★★/★★★★★ B	★★★★ B	★★★★ C
1996	★★★★/★★★★★ B	★★★★/★★★★★ B	★★★★/★★★★★ B	★★★★ C
1995	★★★★ B	★★★★ B	★★★★/★★★★★ B	★★★★ C
1993	★★★ C	★★/★★★ C	★★★ D	★★★ D
1990	★★★★/★★★★★ B	★★★★/★★★★★ B	★★★★/★★★★★ C	★★★★/★★★★★ D
1989	★★★★/★★★★★ C	★★★★★ C	★★★★/★★★★★ C –	
1988	★★★★ C	★★★★ C	★★★★ C	–

A-Z of producers

PHILIPPE ALLIET   Chinon

Philippe Alliet   L'Ouche Monde, 37500 Cravant-les-Coteaux
UK stockists: Lay
One of the very best producers in Chinon with 9ha of Cabernet Franc planted on the *coteaux* at Cravant. In the vineyard Alliet severely restricts his yields and looks to produce a full, powerful style with an extended fermentation and maceration. The resulting wines possess marvellously pure blackcurrant and cedar fruit all underpinned by supple, velvety tannins. New oak is avoided as are fining and filtration. The top wines possess additional depth and weight. The Coteau de Noiré and Vieilles Vignes are the sturdiest and longest-lived. (DM)
● **Chinon**★★ £B Coteau de Noiré★★★★ £C Vieilles Vignes★★★★ £C

YANNICK AMIRAULT   Bourgueil

Yannick Amirault   5 Pavillon du Grand Clos, 37140 Bourgueil
UK stockists: L&S, SVS
The Amirault family domaine possesses some 17ha spread throughout both Bourgueil and Saint-Nicolas-de-Bourgueil. The wines are among the very best produced in either appellation. The Bourgueils are marginally deeper, more brawny wines, the Saint-Nicolas bottlings a touch more elegant and tightly structured. La Petite Cave is a splendid, dark and complex wine produced from old vines. Malgagnes is the denser, more tannic of the 2 Saint-Nicolas-de-Bourgueils. Young-vine *cuvées* of both are also produced. The top wines are very ageworthy and will improve in bottle for 10 years or more. (DM)
● **Bourgueil** Quartiers★★★ £B La Petite Cave★★★ £C
● **Saint Nicolas-de-Bourgueil** Graviers★★★ £B Malgagnes★★★★ £C

AMPELIDÆ   Haut-Poitou

Frédéric Brochet   Manoir de Lavauguyot, 86380 Marigny-Brizay
Domaine located south of the Loire towards Poitiers with a fairly extensive range of wines. Basic fruit-driven reds and whites under the Marigny label include a crisp Sauvignon Blanc, a zesty new Sauvignon bottling called Château de Roches and a Pinot Noir. A clean, fresh, fruit-driven sparkler Armance B is also produced. It is, though, the striking *vins de pays* varietals that really stand out here. These are all marketed under the Ampelida label, as opposed to the Latin plural used for the domaine's full range. Le S is a barrel-vinified Sauvignon Blanc of some depth and concentration, fatter and fuller than most Touraine examples from further north. Le X is a barrel-aged rosé which will stand a little age. Le C is an old-vine Chardonnay with impressive weight and quite marked toasty, nutty, barrel-ferment character. Three reds are also produced under this label. Le Y is a Gamay that will stand a little age in the same way as a decent *cru* Beaujolais. Le K is produced from old-vine Cabernet Sauvignon and aged in small oak, some new, and is rich, cedary and impressively concentrated for the region. The range is completed by a sound, berry-laden Pinot Noir PN 1328 which is sourced from a specific numbered limestone-based parcel. The top reds in particular will develop well for 3 or 4 years. (DM)
● **Vin de Pays de la Vienne** PN 1328★★★ £C Le K★★ £C
● **Vin de Table** Le Y★★ £C
○ **Vin de Pays de la Vienne** Le C★★★ £C Le S★★ £C
◉ **Vin de Pays de la Vienne** Le X★ £B

275

AUBERT LA CHAPELLE Jasnières

Jean-Michel Aubert   La Roche, 73240 Marçon

One of just a handful of top domaines in these most northerly of vineyards. Like the wines from neighbours Joël GIGOU and Domaine de BELLIVIÈRE these examples are marked by their extreme minerality as well as their marvellous depth and intensity. From just 12ha of vineyards Jean-Michel Aubert makes both Coteaux du Loir (including red and rosé) and Jasnières. The white Coteaux du Loir is, like the 3 Jasnières, produced from Chenin Blanc, offering a hint of minerality as well as lightly peachy fruit. It is mostly produced in a slightly off-dry style. The regular Jasnières is intensely mineral and very structured. In the ripest years like 2003, there is often a hint of peachy botrytis apparent as well. The Cuvée Anne-Mathilde is generally produced in a *demi-sec* style from later-harvested fruit. That extra weight and texture makes the wine more accessible in its youth, although still somewhat more austere than you are likely to find in Vouvray or Mountlouis. The rich and concentrated Cuvée Prestige is a pure *vendange tardive* style. As ever from this region it is far tighter and more firmly structured than more southerly Loire examples. As well as that mineral backbone there is a marvellous array of honey, peach, toast and citrus aromas. All the wines will benefit from 4 or 5 years' patience and the top Jasnierès bottlings will keep for decades. (DM)

O **Jasnières★★** £B Cuvée Anne-Mathilde★★★ £C Cuvée Prestige★★★ £C
O **Coteaux du Loir★★** £B

DOM. DES AUBUISIÈRES Vouvray www.vouvrayfouquet.com

Bernard Fouquet   Rue de la Vallée-de-Nouy, 37210 Vouvray
UK stockists: C&R

Very good Vouvray from bone dry to lusciously sweet is made at this 22-ha domaine. Production is relatively small at around 9,000 cases a year and an extensive range is produced when conditions are favourable. Silex is dry, almost austere and very pure, while the stylish Marigny Sec is barrel-fermented. The Girardières shows a sweet citrus and mineral style and is refined and well balanced. Currently available vintages haven't favoured the production of any sweet Moelleux. When the right conditions do occur, as in 2003, the magnificent top bottling is the Cuvée Alexandre. All of the wines will age very well. (DM)

O **Vouvray** Silex Sec★★ £B Marigny Sec★★★ £C
O **Vouvray** Girardières Demi-Sec★★★ £B
O **Vouvray** Brut★★ £C

PATRICK BAUDOUIN Coteaux du Layon

Patrick Baudouin   Princé, 49290 Chaudefonds-sur-Layon
UK stockists: WTs

Baudouin is one of the Layon's "sugar hunters", and the style here is rich, heady and unctuously sweet. What impresses, though, is the balance and elegance achieved at the same time. He also produces 2 very decent reds. The Anjou is solely from Cabernet Franc and displays some attractive berry and leafy notes. The Anjou-Villages is more serious and structured; a blend of both Cabernets, it is part oak-aged. Neither is filtered. Of the great sweet wines the regular Bruandières is intense and honeyed and it just needs a little extra dimension for true class. The Grains Nobles and Maria Juby are seriously impressive. Both are honeyed with marked botrytis and the Maria Juby has a marvellously fresh mineral balance. Aprés Minuit, made in tiny quantities, is an astonishing wine. Selected berry by berry it is very opulent, concentrated and complex. It should not only age well but is surprisingly approachable when young. (DM)

● **Anjou★** £B ● **Anjou-Villages★★** £B

○ **Coteaux du Layon** Les Bruandières★★★ £D Grains Nobles★★★★ £F
○ **Coteaux du Layon** Maria Juby★★★★★ £F Aprés Minuit✪✪✪✪ £G

BERNARD BAUDRY Chinon www.bernard-baudry@chinon.com

Bernard Baudry 13 Coteau de Sonnay, Cravant-les-Coteaux, 37500 Chinon
UK stockists: **L&S**

Bernard Baudry has 25ha under vine at Chinon with a tiny amount planted to
Chenin Blanc, from which he makes an impressive white Chinon Croix Boisée.
Good regular red Chinon is marked by approachable leafy, berry fruit and a
hint of spiciness. Les Granges is soft, vibrant and forward. The 3 top *cuvées* that
stand out. Clos Guillot is sturdy and dense, Grézeaux deep and extracted but
supple and sufficiently soft too. The top red Croix Boisée is dark, dense and
complex and needs 3 to 4 years' ageing. (DM)

● **Chinon**★★ £B Les Granges★★ £B Clos Guillot★★★ £C Grézeaux★★★ £C
● **Chinon**Croix Boisée★★★★ £C

DOM. DES BAUMARD Anjou-Saumur www.baumard.fr

Florent Baumard 8 Rue de l'Abbaye, 49190 Rochefort-sur-Loire

One of the Loire Valley's great and noble properties and among Anjou's best
producers of dry and sweet wines. The range is fairly extensive despite a
production of barely more than 10,000 cases a year. Anjou red and white, Rosé
de Loire, Cabernet d'Anjou rosé and Crémant de Loire are all produced. The
latter can be good but on the whole are somewhat unexciting. The real gems
here are the Layon sweet wines and the various *cuvées* of Savennières. The latter
are impressively steely and formidably structured in great years. Top years also
see the release of a Trie Spéciale. Among the sweet whites there are 4 Layons,
including the impressive Cuvée Le Paon and Clos Sainte-Catherine bottlings,
as well as the unquestioned star, the magnificent Quarts de Chaumes – a
sublime, restrained and extraordinarily subtle sweet wine, ✪✪✪✪✪ in great
years. (DM)

○ **Savennières**★★ £B Clos du Papillon★★★★ £C
○ **Coteaux du Layon** Carte d'Or★★ £B Clos Sainte-Catherine★★★★ £D
○ **Quarts de Chaume**★★★★★ £E

DOM. DE BELLIVIÈRE Coteaux du Loir www.belliviere.com

Eric Nicolas 72340 Lhomme
UK stockists: **RsW**

Brilliantly styled, mineral whites are made at this 11-ha domaine. Reds from
the Coteaux du Loir are also worth looking at. Very intense red berry fruit can
be found in the Rouge Gorge which is dominated by Pineau d'Aunis with just
a touch of Gamay to add a little extra fruit. The acidity and tight structure
require at least 4 or 5 years patience and it is not easy young, but expect an
increased smoky complexity with time. A special, very old-vine red *cuvée*,
Hommage à Louis Derré, is also made in great years. The main focus here,
though, is on steely, piercingly mineral dry whites from the 7ha or so of
Chenin Blanc. The Coteaux du Loir L'Effraie comes from younger vines, which
here means less than 50 years of age. It has marvellous poise and intensity;
more classically tight and lean in 2002, richer and fuller in 2003. The old-vine
Eparses comes from vines of 50 to 80 years of age and is a wine of marvellous
depth and persistence. Subtle honeyed notes will emerge in time. A relatively
young-vine *cuvée*, Haute-Rasné, is made from a late-harvested *lieu-dit* that
regularly develops noble rot. The Jasnières Les Rosiers is very tight, intensely
mineral and backward young. Its intense, peachy and honeyed fruit is more
immediately apparent in opulent years like 2003. A wine of serious depth and
class, it will develop well with a decade or more of age. An old-vine *cuvée*

277

Calligramme is also produced as well as 2 late-harvest wines, Discours de Tuf and a *vin liquoreux* Elixir de Tuf. These will undoubtedly be very well worth considering. (DM)

○ **Jasnières** Les Rosiers★★★★ £D   ○ **Coteaux du Loir** L'Effraie★★★ £C
○ **Coteaux du Loir** Eparses Vieilles Vignes★★★★ £D
● **Coteaux du Loir** e Rouge-Gorge★★★ £C

DOM. HENRI BOURGEOIS   Sancerre   www.bourgeois-sancerre.com

Jean-Marie Bourgeois   Chavignol, 18300 Sancerre
UK stockists: WSS

This is a reasonably substantial but very impressive Sancerre producer and *négociant*. The domaine covers a total of some 60ha with 50ha planted to Sauvignon Blanc, the balance Pinot Noir. The Bonnes Bouches and Grande Réserve are the regular *cuvées* of Sancerre, while the MD de Bourgeois (named after the local Monts Damnés slopes) and Bourgeoise are a level up. There is a good Pouilly-Fumé as well. Among the top *cuvées* d'Antan is very concentrated, made from 65-year-old vines, while Jadis is intense and minerally from vines planted in Kimmeridgian marl. The top wine, produced in extremely small quantities, is the very intense, flinty and lightly nutty Étienne Henri, vinified in oak for 12 months on fine lees. The red Sancerre Bourgeoise can be good but needs the benefit of a warm, sunny vintage. (DM)

● **Sancerre** Bourgeoise★★ £C
○ **Pouilly Fumé**★★ £B Demoiselle de Bourgeoise★★★ £C
○ **Sancerre** Grande Réserve★★ £B Bonne Bouches★★ £B
○ **Sancerre** La Côte des Monts Damnés★★★ £C
○ **Sancerre** Bourgeoise★★★ £C Jadis★★★★ £D d'Antan★★★★ £E

DOM. BOURILLON-DORLÉANS   Vouvray   www.bourillon.com

Frédéric Bourillon-Dorléans   4 Rue de Chalateau, 37210 Rochcordon
UK stockists: TWS, FMV

There are some 18ha at this Vouvray property where the emphasis is on dry and *demi-sec* Chenin wines. Two *moelleux* bottlings are made when the vintage conditions allow, most recently in 2003. Art'ronia is produced in reasonable volume and the top wine La Coulée d'Or is much rarer. The range is also buoyed up by a regularly produced sparkling Brut. The dry styles are very tight and minerally in their youth with piercing green-apple aromas. The Coulée d'Argent gets a touch more oak during vinification, some of it new. The Demi-Sec is minerally and honeyed; it will become rich and profound with age. Handling is kept to a minimum and there is just a light filtration prior to bottling. (DM)

○ **Vouvray** Argilo Sec★★ £B Coulée d'Argent Sec★★★ £C
○ **Vouvray** Cuvée Gaston Dorléans Demi-Sec★★★ £C

DOM. DE LA BUTTE   Bourgueil   www.jackyblot.com

Jacky Blot   37140 Bourgueil
UK stockists: J&B,JAr,Far

As well as making some brilliant Montlouis and, more recently, Vouvray bottlings, Jacky Blot now owns this fine 14-ha Bourgueil property from which he is producing some of the best reds of the appellation. The property is solely planted to Cabernet Franc and a firm, elegant leafiness is apparent in the wines. The regular Pied de la Butte, aged in *inox*, is good if a touch light and leafy. Perrières is aged in *foudres* and offers impressive depth and concentration; it is a clear step up. The Haute de la Butte is rich, dense and full of dark, cedary fruit. It is partly aged in new oak which is seamlessly handled. Top *cuvée* Mi-Pente is rich dense and very ripe and opulent in top years like 2003. Youthfully firm and powerful tannins suggest 5 years' patience will be rewarded. (DM)

● **Bourgueil** Le Pied de la Butte★ £B Perrières★★ £C Le Haut de la Butte★★★ £C
● **Bourgueil** Mi-Pente★★★★ £D

ALAIN CAILBOURDIN Pouilly-Fumé

Alain Cailbourdin Maltaverne, 58150 Tracy-sur-Loire
UK stockists: THT

Alain Cailbourdin has 16ha under vine at Pouilly Fumé from which he
produces around 8,000 cases a year of fine, tight, minerally white. The
vineyards, some up to 65 years old, are tended as naturally as possible and there
are varied soils including limestone and flint. Temperature control is used
during fermentation and the wines are very lightly filtered before bottling. The
Cuvée de Boisfleury is the lightest and most floral of the 3 bottlings; Les Cris is
fuller and more structured, becoming lightly tropical and richer with 2 or 3
years' age. Les Cornets, grown in clay-limestone is the sturdiest and most
backward when young. All will evolve well over 5 years or more.

O **Pouilly Fumé** Les Cris★★★ £C Cuvée de Boisfleury★★★ £C Les Cornets★★★ £C

DIDIER CHAMPALOU Vouvray champalou@wanadoo.fr

Didier et Cathérine Champalou 7 Rue du Grand Ormeau, 37210 Vouvray
UK stockists:GWW,Tan,Sel

The Champalous run a model Vouvray property with 20ha of vineyards. Total
output is around 8,000 to 8,500 cases a year. The regular Vouvray and the
Fondraux are vinified in stainless steel and aged in old wooden casks. They are
generally *sec* in style but can have a fair level of residual sugar depending on the
nature and conditions of the vintage. In cooler years such as 2000 a stylish
sparkling Brut is produced and in great years for sweet wines, such as 1995,
1997 and most recently 2002, a *moelleux* style labelled La Moelleuse is
produced. Very occasionally a very sweet and late-harvested Trie de Vendange is
released. Both of these sweet wines are rich, honeyed and extremely long-lived.
(DM)

O **Vouvray**★★ £B Fondraux★★★ £B

LAURENT CHATENAY Montlouis www.laurentchatenay.com

Laurent Chatenay 41 route de Montlouis, 37270 Saint-Martin-le-Beau

Laurent Chatenay has been farming his family's vineyards since 1996. Their
holdings have now grown to a total of 13ha of which the great majority are
planted to very old vines ranging from 40 to 80 years of age. This priceless raw
material allied to low yields of less than 35 hl/ha is resulting in some of the
finest wines of the Mountlouis appellation. Les Maisonnettes is a tight, steely
dry style with classic Chenin Blanc varietal character. The La Vallée is *demi-sec*
but the piercing fruit and high acidity tend to mask the sweetness. Backward
and restrained, the wine ideally needs 6 or 7 years to add some flesh; expect it
to become increasingly honeyed with time. In the cellar SO_2 additions are kept
to a minimum and the wines are never chaptalised. The propitious conditions
of 2001 and 02 have yielded a *moelleux* La Vallée aux Prêtres and 01 and 03
will see the release of the *liquoreux* Clos Michet. (DM)

O **Montlouis** Les Maisonnettes★★ £B La Vallée★★★ £B

JEAN-CLAUDE CHATELAIN Pouilly-Fumé

Jean-Claude Chatelain Les Berthiers, 58150 Saint-Andelain
UK stockists:CTy

Father and son Jean-Claude and Vincent have 20ha of vines in the Pouilly-
Fumé AC and act as small-scale *négociants,* buying in fruit to supplement their

279

needs. They are now producing a regular Sancerre as well as the Pouilly and if anything it's the better of the 2. Les Charmes is a level up, richer and with a hint of oak (10% is barrel-fermented), while the top *cuvée*, the Prestige, from old vines is tight and structured and very classy. It is vinified in stainless steel but gets 6 to 7 months on lees. Pilou, an unusual and concentrated barrel-fermented style, is occasionally produced from late-harvest dried grapes if vintage conditions permit. (DM)

O **Pouilly Fumé**★★ £B Les Charmes★★★ £C Préstige★★★★ £D
O **Sancerre**★★ £B

CH. DE COULAINE Chinon

Etienne & Pascal de Bonnaventure 37420 Beaumont-en-Véron

A number of excellent wines are now being made by the Bonnaventures. They have a holding of 14ha, just 0.5ha of which is Chenin Blanc from which a little white Chinon is made. They also have a few parcels in Bourgueil from which they produce a single *cuvée* Bonnaventure which, like the Chinon reds, is marked by its elegant, stylish fruit and well-defined supple tannic structure. Fuller than the Chinon of the same label, this is less extracted than a number of other Bourgueils. The regular Chinon is produced from young vines and is more obviously fruit-driven with a hint of leafiness but good brambly upfront fruit dominating. The 3 top *cuvées* are impressively structured wines of real dimension and depth. The Diablesses is tighter and more intense than the Clos de Turpenay, while Les Picasses has been added for the first time with the 2003 vintage and offers great potential. (DM)

● **Chinon** Clos de Turpenay★★★ £C La Diablesse★★★ £D Les Picasses★★★ £D
● **Chinon**★★ £C Bonnaventure★★★ £C ● **Bourgueil** Bonnaventure★★★ £C

CH. D'EPIRÉ Savennières www.chateau-epire.com

Luc Bizard 49170 Savennières
UK stockists:Gau

Luc Bizard produces only Savennières, around 4,000 to 5,000 cases a year, from his 11ha of vineyards. Viticulture is traditional and the harvest is hand-picked with up to 3 *tries*. The wines are vinified in *inox* and aged on lees in barrel. A small-production bottling, Hu-Boyau, is sourced from the oldest parcel in the vineyard and is barrel-aged for 9 months. Cuvée Spéciale is usually just 15% of the harvest and is generally sourced from parcels that are closest to COULÉE DE SERRANT. These are fine, tightly structured, minerally examples and all show impressive depth and intensity. They are also very fairly priced. (DM)

O **Savennières**★★ £B Cuvéé Spéciale★★★ £C Moëlleux★★★ £C

CH. DE FESLES Bonnezeaux www.chateaux-partners.com

Bernard Germain Château de Festes, 49380 Thouarcé
UK stockists:Bsh, BBR, WTs

Bordeaux producer Bernard Germain who owns YON-FIGEAC purchased Château de Fesles in 1996. At that time the property had been through a period of serious decline. In the 1970s and 1980s the top Bonnezeaux had been labelled La Chapelle and if you encounter any old vintages prior to 1985 they can be superb. The Bonnezeaux is now just labelled as such and is very good once more in top recent vintages for sweet wines here. The wine possesses a mineral intensity and structure as well as piercingly subtle botrytis character rarely found even in the most exalted of Germains' neighbours. One other property is also owned, the Château de la Roulerie, a source of impressive Coteaux du Layon and there are some classy reds from Anjou, particularly the dense and chunky Fesles Anjou-Villages. (DM)

Château de Fesles
● **Anjou** Vieilles Vignes★★ £B ● **Anjou-Villages**★★★ £C ○ **Bonnezeaux**★★★★ £F

Château de la Roulerie
● **Anjou**★ £B ○ **Coteaux du Layon Chaume** Aunis★★★★ £E

CH. DE FOSSE-SÈCHE Saumur www.chateaudefosseseche.com
EARL Keller 49700 Brossay
This small, Swiss-owned property has 16ha under vine planted in argile-siliceous soils. Both reds and whites of impressive depth come from 30–50-year-old vines picked as ripe as possible. The regular white Saumur is vinified in stainless steel to emphasise its rich, forward, honeyed fruit but it has good acidity to maintain balance as well. The Tris de La Chapelle is sourced from very late-harvested fruit, often picked as late as November, and is vinified in small oak, a proportion of which is new. In 2002 the fruit had 100% botrytis resulting in an extraordinarily low yield of just 8–10hl/ha yet the wine was fermented fully dry. These are impressively ripe and concentrated wines but they will not be to all tastes. The cedary and elegant regular red Saumur is two-thirds Cabernet Franc, the balance Sauvignon. The Clef de Voûte is a similar blend although deeper and fuller and aged in used small oak. The top red, the Réserve de Pigeonnier, is one of the best examples in the region. Rich and very concentrated, with lovely dark, smoky, cedary fruit, it is a vineyard selection from yields of barely more than 20hl/ha. The wine is aged in 50/50 new and 1-year-old oak. Minimal handling is employed throughout and the wines are bottled unfined and unfiltered. (DM)
● **Saumur**★★ £B La Clef de Voûte★★★ £D Réserve de Pigeonnier★★★ £E
○ **Saumur**★★★ £C Les Tris de La Chapelle★★★★ £D

CH. DU HUREAU Saumur-Champigny www.domaine-hureau.fr
Philippe Vatan Dampierre-sur-Loire, 49400 Saumur
UK stockists: GWW
Philippe Vatan produces excellent Saumur Blanc and sumptuous and supple Saumur-Champigny. He possesses 21ha planted in tufa/limestone soils, which are particularly suitable for producing first-rate Cabernet Franc. As well as the regular red *cuvée* there are 2 very fine wines produced from old vines. Cuvée des Fevettes gets new wood treatment, whereas the Lisgathe has more exuberant, fleshy dark berry fruit and is aged in old barrels. The white is everything that good dry Chenin Blanc should be. Minerals, citrus and honey are all in evidence. These are approachable but ageworthy wines, keeping well for 10 years and more in the best vintages. (DM)
● **Saumur-Champigny** Grande Cuvée★★ £B Fevettes★★★ £C Lisgathe★★★★£C
○ **Saumur**★★★£B

CH. PIERRE-BISE Coteaux du Layon
Claude Papin 49750 Beaulieu-sur-Layon
UK stockists: L&S
Based in sleepy Beaulieu-sur-Layon, Claude Papin possesses 53ha of vines spread across the Anjou-Villages, Coteaux du Layon and Savennières appellations. He is one of the best-established quality producers in the region. The wines are well-crafted and offer great value for money. The reds are full of rich blackberry and mulberry fruit and are aged in a small proportion of new oak. The Coteaux du Layon *cuvées* are full of peach, honey and nutmeg in the best years and are always well structured, refined and ageworthy. The Quarts de Chaume is richer still, with formidable depth. The intense, ageworthy, Clos de Coulaine Savennières is not only remarkably well-priced but it has marvellous citrus and mineral aromas. It will be better with 5 or 6 years' cellaring. (DM)

281

- ● Anjou-Villages Clos de Coulaine★★ £B Sur Spilite★★★ £B
- O Anjou Haut de la Garde★★ £B O Savennières Clos de Coulaine★★★ £B
- O Coteaux du Layon-Beaulieu Rouannières★★★★£D
- O Coteaux du Layon-Rochefort Rayelles★★★★ £D
- O Quarts de Chaume★★★★★ £F

CH. DE TRACY Pouilly-Fumé tracy@wanadoo.fr

Comtesse Alain d'Estutt d'Assay Château de Tracy, 58150 Tracy-sur-Loire
UK stockists: JBa, Lay
Historic property with a Renaissance château whose origins date back to 1396.
There are approximately 31ha under vine, all of which are Sauvignon Blanc.
Just the 1 wine is made and output is by no means small, approaching 20,000
cases a year. Despite this the wine has been consistently good in recent vintages.
It is a steely, flinty style with surprisingly exotic fruit emerging with age.
Structured and refined it needs at least a year or 2 in your cellar. (DM)
- ● Pouilly-Fumé★★★ £D

CH. LA VARIÈRE Anjou

Jacques Beaujeau 49320 Brissac
UK stockists: L&S
Good-quality Anjou, both red and white, is made at this sizeable 90ha
property. The various red *cuvées* from Brissac stand out among the dry wines
and red plantings account for around three-quarters of the domaine. The top
red *cuvée* is the Grande Chevalerie, an impressively dense example dominated
by Cabernet Sauvignon. Other red labels include J. Beaujeau and Prestige. The
really striking wines, though, are the late-harvest whites which are some of the
best of the region, particularly in great vintages like 2003. Various parcels are
held in the Coteaux du Layon, Bonnezeaux and Quarts de Chaume. The richly
concentrated 2003s all show intensely complex botrytis character and
impressive depth. The Bonnezeaux Melleresses has an intensely honeyed,
peachy concentration but with a citrus undercurrent that gives it exceptional
balance. Best of all, the Quarts de Chaume Les Querches offers similar depth
with a piercing undercurrent of quince. These wines offer more structure and
grip than other 'sugar-hunter' examples and should age very well. (DM)
- ● Anjou-Villages Brissac La Grande Chevalerie★★★ £C O Anjou Clos Division★★ £B
- O Bonnezeaux Melleresses★★★★£E O Quarts de Chaume Les Querches★★★★★ £F

CH. DE VILLENEUVE Saumur-Champigny

Jean-Pierre Chevallier Château de Villeneuve, 49400 Souzay-Champigny
UK stockists: THt
Very good property producing red and white from the Saumur-Champigny
and Saumur ACs. The vineyards are run organically and partly on biodynamic
principles. The focus here is the quality of the fruit, its intensity and
concentration achieved through careful viticulture, a tight control on yields and
minimal handling in the cellar. The white Cormiers is subtly oaked and barrel-
fermented with a period on lees. The reds are concentrated, dark and spicy
examples of the very best Loire Cabernet Franc. A special *cuvée*, Grand Clos, is
a super-rich special bottling made in the greatest years only. These are all very
ageworthy, improving in bottle for 5 to 10 years. (DM)
- ● Saumur-Champigny★★ £B Vieille Vignes★★★ £C
- O Saumur★★★ £B Cormiers★★★ £C

DOM. FRANÇOIS CHIDAINE Montlouis

M & F Chidaine, N Martin 5 Grande-Rue, 37270 Montlouis-sur-Loire
During recent vintages this domaine has emerged as one of the very finest in

the appellation, producing wines of real class and finesse. There are currently 20ha in Montlouis and a further 10ha in Vouvray. An extensive range includes a number of single-plot wines as well as *cuvées* at different sweetness levels and in 2003 exceptional wines were made across the board. In addition to Vouvray and Montlouis, a straightforward, clean and varietally pure Sauvignon de Touraine and a Crémant de Loire are regularly produced. Among the dry bottlings, Vouvray Les Argiles is very tight and stuctured while Vouvray Clos Baudoin and Montlouis Clos du Breuil carry a little more residual sugar, with a hint of new oak in the latter. The Montlouis Clos Habert and Les Tuffeaux are both *demi-sec*, the latter tighter and more mineral. Good *moelleux* bottlings are produced in both appellations. The Vouvray Le Bouchet, *demi-sec* in 2002, was richer and later-harvested in 2003 and offers exemplary depth and concentration. The top of the tree here is the exceptional Le Lys, a *vin liquoreux* produced only in exceptional years and with naturally very high sugar and marked botrytis. All the Vouvrays and Montlouis bottlings will age gloriously. As is often the case, the *sec* wines will be the most austere in their youth. (DM)

O **Montlouis** Les Tuffeaux★★★★ £C Moelleux★★★★ £C Le Lys★★★★★ £F
O **Montlouis** Clos des Breuil★★★ £B Clos Habert★★★ £C
O **Vovray** Moelleux★★★ £C Le Bouchet★★★★ £C
O **Vovray** Les Argiles★★ £B Clos Baudoin★★★ £B
O **Touraine** Sauvignon★ £B O **Crémant de Loire**★ £B

CLOS DE LA COULÉE DE SERRANT Savennières

Nicolas Joly   Château de la Roche-aux-Moines, 49170 Savennières
UK stockists: Yap

Nicolas Joly has 14.5ha of Chenin Blanc which is tended biodynamically. Indeed, Joly is one of the most outspoken proponents of this concept of organic farming. In the past he has been criticised for being more concerned with the application of biodynamic principles than in his wines. This would appear to be unjustified because these are some of the finest expressions of dry Chenin to be found anywhere. The supremely structured and refined Coulée de Serrant is loaded with subtle citrus, mineral and flint. This is a very fine wine with a remarkable capacity to age: it is not really ready for 10 years and will keep with ease for more than twice that time. The Clos de la Bergerie is also impressive and more accessible although it still ages very well. When vintage conditions allow, there is a small amount of Moelleux. (DM)

O **Savennières**★★★ £D
O **Savennières Coulée de Serrant**✪✪✪✪✪ £F
O **Savennières Roches aux Moines** Clos de la Bergerie★★★★ £E

DOM. DU CLOS NAUDIN Vouvray

Philippe Foreau   14 Rue de la Croix Buisée, 37210 Vouvray
UK stockists: Gau, SVS

A marvellous traditional producer of the some of the greatest Vouvrays made in recent decades. Only the wines of HUËT L'ECHANSONNE bear comparison. Intense and very well-crafted *sec* and *demi-sec* wines are tight, very minerally and superbly structured. They need time to emerge from their shell and will age for decades. Very good sparkling Méthode Traditionelle Réserve and a limited amount of a vintage sparkler are also made. When the gods are favourable in this most marginal of climates for great sweet wines, Foreau produces precisely that: magnificent Moelleux, as he did in 2002, and Moelleux Réserve. (DM)

O **Vouvray** Sec★★★ £B Demi-Sec★★★ £B Méthode Traditionelle Réserve★★★ £C

283

CLOS ROUGEARD Saumur-Champigny

Foucault family   15 Rue de l'Église, 49400 Chacé
UK stockists: HHB

There are 10ha under vine and just one of those is planted with Chenin Blanc, the balance being Cabernet Franc. Inevitably the impressive Saumur Blanc Brezé is very rarely encountered. It is a subtly barrel-fermented style and strikingly intense. There is a very good regular Saumur-Champigny with ripe, dark fruit and soft and supple tannins. The 2 superior *cuvées*, Bourg and Poyeux, are equally velvety in texture but with greater depth and power. Le Bourg offers slightly darker and more overt notes of cassis while the Poyeux is the more elegant with classic leafy, Loire spice. (DM)

● **Saumur-Champigny**★★★ £B Bourg★★★★ £C Poyeux★★★★ £C

DOM. DU CLOSEL Savennières   www.savennieres-closel.com

De Jessey family   Château des Vaults, 1 Place du Mail, 49170 Savennières
UK stockists: Yap, BBR

The de Jessey family produce decent, solid, fruity Anjou-Villages red and more importantly some impressive, rich, and mineral-laden Savennières. The regular Savennières is good if lacking real depth; the Caillardières is a solid step up. The Clos du Papillon is very impressive indeed; intense and minerally but with a remarkable depth of citrus and rich honeyed aromas emerging with age. These are cellarworthy, particularly the Clos du Papillon. An occasional Vieilles Vignes bottling is produced in the best years as well as a *moelleux* labelled Cuvée Isa. (DM)

● **Savennières** Les Vaults★★ £B Caillardières★★★ £C Clos du Papillon★★★★ £C

PASCAL COTAT Sancerre

Pascal/Francis Cotat   98 Chemin de Grous, 18300 Sancerre
UK stockists: Bal, Gau, Rae, SVS

The Cotats make some of the very finest Sancerre. Their production is tiny at just 1,200 to 1,300 cases a year with minimal intervention in both vineyard and cellar. Their sites are superb and naturally low-yielding and all that is required is to ensure that the vines stay in balance. The wine is fermented naturally and no fining or filtration is undertaken. These are rich, explosive Sauvignon Blancs which need at least a year or 2 to show at their best. Remarkable Cuvée Spéciale is produced in the greatest years for both wines. (DM)

O **Sancerre** Grande Côte★★★★ £C Monts Damnés★★★★ £D

DOM. DE LA COTELLERIE Saint-Nicolas-de-Bourgueil

Claude & Gérald Vallée   37140 Saint-Nicolas-de-Bourgueil
This fine Saint-Nicolas property now has 25ha of vineyards producing an impressive small range of reds. The *vignoble* is dominated by Cabernet Franc, which accounts for 90% of the planting, and the balancing 10% is Cabernet Sauvignon. Vinification for all the wines is modern with stainless steel vats used to keep temperatures under control and ageing in small oak barrels. Les Perruches is the lightest of the wines, with attractive, bright, red-berry fruit and soft, easy tannins. The fine Cuvée Domaine is sourced from throughout the Vallées' holding. It is soft, forward and vibrant with impressive intensity. Le Vau Jaumier comes from a sloping southerly aspect on clay and limestone soils and is thicker, sturdier and aged in used oak. The L'Envol is rich, full and very intense and offers real grip and structure. The L'Envol and Vau Jaumier will both develop with a little bottle age. (DM)

● **Saint-Nicolas-de-Bourgueil** Cuvée Domaine★★★ £C L'Envol★★★ £C
● **Saint-Nicolas-de-Bourgueil** Les Perruches★★ £B Le Vau Jaumier★★★ £C

LUCIEN CROCHET Sancerre lcrochet@terres-net.fr

Gilles Crochet Place de l'Église, 18300 Bué
UK stockists: BSh, EoR

The Crochets have 35ha of their own vineyards in Sancerre and also act as *négociants*. Inevitably the best wines here are from their own vineyards. As well as the white Sancerre, which is vinified without new oak, the reds are also noteworthy. So often Pinot Noir fails to perform in this climate and red Sancerre is frequently light and insubstantial, but not here. Late harvesting and ripe fruit is always the key to quality. The Cuvée Prestige white and red are both old-vine bottlings and most impressive. The white Le Chêne Marchand is lighter but very intense and minerally. The Prestige labels will be better given 4 or 5 years' ageing. (DM)

O **Sancerre** Le Chêne Marchand★★★ £C Cuvée Prestige★★★ £D
● **Sancerre** Le Croix du Roy★★ £C Cuvée Prestige★★★ £D

DIDIER DAGUENEAU Pouilly-Fumé silex@wanadoo.fr

Didier Dagueneau Le Bourg, 58150 Saint-Andelain
UK stockists: HHB, Tan, BBR

Didier Dagueneau is the finest producer in Pouilly Fumé and while he has a few rivals in Sancerre he stands out as the region's standard bearer for magnificent, complex and very ageworthy Sauvignon Blanc. These wines are light years away from the simple gooseberry and tropical flavours many associate with the variety. Immense care is taken in the vineyard, yields are low, harvesting is only at peak maturity with several passes through the vines and handling in the cellar is kept to an absolute minimum. Buisson Renard, Pur-Sang and the magnificent Silex are all barrel-fermented but in no way does the oak become intrusive. What you are left with is an intense and very complex mix of green fruits and minerals. Superbly structured, these are wines that demand cellaring for half a dozen years or more. (DM)

O **Pouilly-Fumé** En Chailloux★★★★ £E Buisson Renard★★★★★ £E
O **Pouilly-Fumé** Pur-Sang★★★★★ £E Silex✪✪✪✪✪ £F

PHILIPPE DELESVAUX Coteaux du Layon

Philippe et Catherine Delesvaux 49190 Saint-Aubin-de-Luigné
UK stockists: Gau

Philippe Delesvaux is one of a small new group of dedicated and quality-conscious wine producers in the sleepy Coteaux du Layon. Recent vintages have not been kind to sweet wine makers here but Delesvaux continues to handcraft intense, stylish examples. The Anjou reds are deeper and with better grip and structure than most. The Anjou bottling is Cabernet Franc; the more substantial Anjou-Villages is Cabernet Sauvignon. Both are vinified in *inox*. In whites there is a very stylish barrel-fermented Anjou Blanc as well as the sweet Layons. What marks these wines out is not just their rich, honeyed botrytised character but their intensity, refinement and balance. In exceptional vintages 2 remarkable special *cuvées*, Anthologie and Carbonifera, are produced, both comfortably ★★★★★. The former is just that touch more unctuous and heady. (DM)

● **Anjou**★★ £B ● **Anjou-Villages**★★ £B
O **Anjou** Feuille d'Or★★★ £B O **Coteaux du Layon**★★★ £C
O **Coteaux du Layon-Saint-Aubin** Clos de la Guiberderie★★★★ £D
O **Coteaux du Layon** Grains Nobles★★★★ £E

OLIVIER DELÉTANG Montlouis www.domaine-deletang.com

Olivier Delétang 19 Rue d'Amboise, 37270 Saint-Martin-Beau
Olivier Delétang produces very good Montlouis from 3 different sites – his

285

own 20ha vineyard, Les Batisses and Les Petits Boulay. The vineyard and the climate conditions are the key here rather than individual wines. He produces *sec* and often *demi-sec* regularly from each site. Some very special sweet wines have been made in great years but none since 1997, when great Moelleux, Moelleux Réserve and Garde Réserve of very fine quality indeed were produced. As well as the Montlouis bottlings there are some simple straightforward Touraines, a white from Sauvignon Blanc and a red from Cabernet Franc. There is also a regular sparkling Brut, called Effervescent, which is clean, appley and fresh. (DM)

O **Montlouis** Sec★★ £B   Demi-Sec★★★ £B   Les Batisses Sec★★★ £B
O **Montlouis** Les Batisses Demi-Sec★★★ £B   Les Petits Boulay Sec★★ £B

PIERRE-JACQUES DRUET   Bourgueil

Pierre-Jacques Druet   7 Rue de la Croix-Rouge, 37140 Benais
UK stockists: J&B, Bal, HHB, ABy, Har

A brilliant source of top Cabernet Franc. The Bourgueil rosé is delicious and fruity, far better than most of its kind. There are 3 *cuvées* of Bourgueil as well as the marvellously elegant and pure Chinon Clos de Danzay, which is aged in *demi-muids*. The Bourgueil Cent Boisselées is handled entirely in stainless steel and displays classic blackcurrant fruit and just a subtle hint of leafiness. The Grand Mont is refined and elegant with hints of cassis and cedar. Produced from chalk vineyards the tannin is supple and well balanced. The top red Vaumoreau comes from nearly 100-year-old vines. It is an unfiltered, dense, very powerful and concentrated red, full of ripe intense cassis and cedar. A wine of immense class and finesse, it is only produced in top years. (DM)

● **Bourgueil** Cent Boisselées★★ £B   Grand Mont★★★ £C   Vaumoreau★★★★ £E
● **Chinon** Clos de Danzay★★★ £C   ◉ **Bourgueil**★ £B

DOM. DE L'ECU   Muscadet Sèvre-et-Maine

Guy Bossard   La Bretonnière, 44430 Le Landreau
UK stockists: VRt

This 20.5ha domaine produces arguably the finest of all Muscadet and light years away from most examples generally encountered. The age of the vines for the top wines varies between 40 and 50 years and the 3 special Expression cuvées are all sourced from different soils and making strikingly different wines. Bossard also produces a regular bottling, "Guy Bossard" which while it does'nt have quite the piercing mineral depth of the Expression wines is impressively intense and smoky. The 3 top labels are, as one would expect from Melon de Bourgogne, relatively austere in style but each has a rich, deep mineral character and an intensity lacking in most Chablis. The most austerely mineral and stony is the Gneiss. The Granit, perhaps the best of the 3 has a citrus and melon undercurrent to its stony fruit. All possess impressive weight and substance. They should develop well in bottle for 5 to 7 years. (DM)

O **Muscadet Sèvre-et-Maine** Expression de Orthogneiss★★ £B
O **Muscadet Sèvre-et-Maine** Expression de Granit★★★ £B
O **Muscadet Sèvre-et-Maine** Cuvée Guy Bossard★★ £B   Expression de Gneiss★★ £B

DOM. DES FORGES   Coteaux du Layon

Branchereau family   Vignoble Branchereau, 49190 Saint-Aubin-de-Luigné
UK stockists: FMV, Tan, SVS

A wide range of Anjou wines are made at this underrated property: good straightforward Sauvignon Blanc and Chardonnay Vin de Pays de la Jardin de France along with supple, fruity Anjou reds and some decent Anjou white. But best of all are the impressive sweet whites – stylish, rich but restrained Coteaux du Layon and Quarts de Chaume. The top wines are the Quarts de Chaume and Coteaux du Layon-Chaume. There is also a good well-crafted Savennières which is tight and flinty. Recent moderate vintages have prevented the domaine from producing great sweet wines. (DM)

O **Coteaux du Layon**★★ £C Coteaux du Layon-Saint-Aubin★★★ £C
O **Coteaux du Layon-Chaume**★★★★ £D Les Onnis★★★★ £E
O **Quarts de Chaume**★★★ £F O **Savennières** Clos des Mauriers★★ £B

JOËL GIGOU/DOM. DE LA CHARRIÈRE Jasnières

Joël Gigou   4 Rue des Caves, 72340 La Chartre-sur-le-Loir
UK stockists: Yap

Joël Gigou is an immensely dedicated grower in this most marginal and extreme of Loire Valley climates. The vineyard is close to organic, yields are kept in check and balanced vines mean no *vendange vert*. There are 2 intense and almost austere dry whites. A real mineral backbone runs through the wines and they have piercing acidity but are very ageworthy. The Clos Saint-Jacques will take on a marvellously rich citrus and honeyed character with age. Also produced is a very fine late-harvest white which is far removed from a Bonnezeaux or a Quarts de Chaume. The wine is tightly structured, lightly honeyed but very long and intense. It is extraordinarily long-lived. (DM)

O **Jasnières** Cuvée Trois Clos★★ £B Cuvée Clos Saint-Jacques Vieilles-Vignes★★★ £C
O **Jasnières** Sélection de Grains Nobles★★★★ £D

VIGNOBLES GITTON Sancerre www.gitton.fr

Gitton family   Chemin de Lavaud, 18300 Menetreol-sous-Sancerre
UK stockists: **Wai**

Pascal Gitton's family-owned domaine covers some 27ha with vineyard parcels spread across various sites. All the wines are from separate vineyards and display the characteristics of their individual *terroirs*. The Pouilly-Fumé Clos Joanne d'Orion differs from the Sancerres in that it is not vinified as a separate parcel. It is still good, if lacking the depth and definition of the best Sancerre bottlings. Rosé comes from Les Romains and is lighter in style than most but offers good depth and grip. Red also comes from the same site as well as a subtle minerally white of impressive intensity. Both the softer fruit-driven Montachins and the more structured and mineral older-vine L'Amiral come from chalky soils. Les Belles Dames is from silex (flint) soils and is classically mineral in style. Les Herses, also from flinty soils, is even more ferociously mineral. A selection from Les Herses, Herses d'Or, is barrel-fermented in a proportion of new oak and a slight citrus element creeps in as well as smoky, toasty notes. La Vigne du Larrey is the family's oldest vineyard holding, planted in 1953 from a mass selection. The wine is vinified in used 600-litre barrels and has a rich and concentrated texture and real depth. Galinot is vinified in new oak, again of 600-litre size, and is more obviously citrusy and opulent. The top wines here should develop very well in bottle for 4 or 5 years. (DM)

O **Sancerre** Galinot★★★ £D Vigne du Larrey★★★ £D Les Herses d'Or★★★ £C
O **Sancerre** Les Romains★★ £B Les Belles Dames★★ £B L'Amiral★★ £C
O **Sancerre** Les Herses★★ £C Les Montachins★★ £B
O **Pouilly Fume** Clos Joanne d'Orion★★ £D ◉ **Sancerre** Les Romains★ £B

DOM. GUIBERTEAU Saumur

Roman Guiberteau   3 Impasse du Cabernet, 49260 Saint-Just-sur-Dive
UK stockists: **Sav**

Roman Guiberteau established this excellent small domaine in 1996 and was joined in the early vintages by partner, Englishman Stephen Eggerton. The property consists of 2.5ha of Chenin Blanc and just under 6ha of Cabernet Franc. Output is small, barely more than 2,500 cases a year, but quality is very

287

impressive. The low-yielding vineyards are now handled organically and great pains are taken to work the soil effectively to ensure deep-rooting vines and top-quality fruit, even in difficult years. In the winery minimal handling is the order of the day, although some micro-oxygenation is used to help ensure rich, supple wines. The regular red Saumur is elegant and intense with classic Cabernet Franc fruit. The Motelles is aged in used wood for up to 30 months and has that extra dimension with piercingly intense red berry fruit and the firm structure to develop very well in bottle for 6 or 7 years. The top red, Les Arbois, is similarly given long oak-ageing in one-third new wood. Rich and really intense, the 2002 was right on the cusp of ★★★★. Two whites are now produced and both are vinified and aged in *barriques*. The Saumur is lightly opulent with a real citrus undercurrent. Les Clos, a *cru*, is really intense and offers great fruit persistence with honey and citrus notes as well as a hint of toastiness from one-third new oak. These wines will all develop very well in the medium term. (DM)

● **Saumur**★★ £B Motelles★★★ £C Les Arboises★★★ £D
O **Saumur**★★ £B Le Clos★★★ £C

HUET L'ECHANSONNE Vouvray www.huet-echansonne.com

Huet family/Antony Hwang   11–13 Rue de la Croix Buisée, 37210 Vouvray
UK stockists: **RsW**,WSc,Sel,Har

There may be a rising tide of new quality-conscious producers in Vouvray but this biodynamically farmed domaine remains the standard-bearer for the appellation. The property has a total of 40ha and sources its fruit from 3 different sites; Clos du Bourg, Haut-Lieu and Le Mont. Some 80% of the domaine has now been purchased by the partnership of Istvan SZEPSY and American financier Antony Hwang, who are helping to revolutionise sweet-wine production in Hungary's Tokaji region. The wines are made as *sec, demi-sec* and when conditions allow, like those in 1997, some magnificent *moelleux* including the extraordinary Cuvée Constance. The dry wines are intense, minerally and very backward when young. They will, though, evolve into superb, complex, honeyed masterpieces with time, but you have to be patient. The *demi-sec* and *moelleux* are more immediately approachable, drinking with 3 or 4 years' ageing but very fine indeed. (DM)

O **Vouvray** Clos du Bourg Sec★★★ £B Clos du Bourg Demi-Sec★★★ £C
O **Vouvray** Clos du Bourg Moelleux★★★★★ £E
O **Vouvray** Haut-Lieu Sec★★★ £B Haut-Lieu Demi-Sec★★★★ £C
O **Vouvray** Haut-Lieu Moelleux★★★★★ £E
O **Vouvray** Le Mont Sec★★★ £B Le Mont Demi-Sec★★★ £C
O **Vouvray** Le Mont Moelleux★★★★★ £E
O **Vouvray** Cuvée Constance✪✪✪✪✪ £F

DOM. CHARLES JOGUET Chinon

Jacques Genet   La Dioterie, 37220 Sazilly
UK stockists: FMV,SVS,OWL

The Joguet domaine is mainly planted to Cabernet Franc with 37ha under vine and just 3ha of Chenin Blanc. Jacques Genet now owns the estate and he is ably assisted by Alain Delaunay and cellarmaster Michel Pinarde. Seven and sometimes 8 different *cuvées* are made each year and these are based on both vine age and soil type. The Terroir and Clos de la Cure bottlings are relatively soft and forward, the most approachable of these most traditional of Chinons. The Varennes du Grand Clos is grown in limestone soils and produced from a yield of 40 hl/ha. The top 2 wines the Clos du Chene Vert and Clos de la Dioterie come from lower-yielding plots, barely 30 hl/ha. The wines are marked by their traditional vinification with fermentation being instigated in the high 30s celsius, and are correspondingly backward when young. Even the lesser *cuvées* can seem angular and awkward before gaining richness with age. Chenin Blanc was planted in the early to mid-1990s and now makes a decent Touraine white Clos de la Plante Martin. (DM)

● **Chinon** Clos du Chêne Vert★★★ £C Clos de la Dioterie★★★ £C
● **Chinon** Terroir★★ £B Clos de la Cure★★ £B Les Varennes du Grand Clos★★★ £C

DOM. DE JUCHEPIE Coteaux du Layon www.juchepie.com

E & M-M Oosterlinck-Bracke Les Quarts, 49380 Faye d'Anjou

Eddy Oosterlinck's tiny Layon property is making some increasingly good dry and late-harvested whites. He currently has 6ha under vine and his output is a mere 800 to 850 cases a year so the wines won't be that easy to find. However, they are good value for money and will be worth the hunt. The vineyard faces south to south-west and there are 2 parcels – Les Churelles, with carboniferous soils, and Les Quarts, which has slatey soils on a clay bedrock. The vines average 40 years and the oldest are close to 100 years. The sweet Layons are harvested in 6–8 tries and yields are low at 30 hl/ha for the dry Anjou and just 10hl/ha for the Layons. The Anjou, vinified in used oak, has a pronounced citrus character and gets weight from ageing on fine lees. Both the Quarts and the Quintessence, particularly the latter, are marked by their rich and unctuously sweet fruit. The wines have good grip and sufficient acidity but will drink well young. Expect them to develop nicely over the medium term . (DM)

O **Coteaux du Layon** Les Quarts de Juchepie★★★ £D
O **Coteaux du Layon** La Quintessence de Juchepie★★★★ £E
O **Anjou** Le Sec de Juchepie★★ £B

DOM. LA TOUR SAINT-MARTIN Menetou-Salon

Bertrand Minchin 18340 Crosses

Fast emerging as one of the very leading lights in Menetou-Salon. Unlike a number of his neighbours, Bertrand Minchin only makes reds and whites from his own appellation. He has a total of some 15ha and the vineyards all have a south to south-east exposure and the soils are a mix of argile, limestone and Kimmeridgian marl. The wines are modern, stylish, vibrant and essentially fruit-driven. The Morogues white is vinified in *inox*, the red a mix of *cuve* and *inox*. The red Celestin gets 12 months ageing in a mix of *barriques* and *tonneaux* and is rich and savoury with a hint of new oak; it was comfortably ★★★ in 2003. The Honorine is aged on fine lees with *bâttonage* and offers greater depth and intensity than the Morogues. All the wines drink well young although the reds will benefit from a couple of years' patience. (DM)

● **Menetou-Salon** Morogues★★ £B Celestin★★ £C
O **Menetou-Salon** Morogues★★ £B Honorine★★★ £C

DOM. RENÉ-NOËL LEGRAND Saumur-Champigny

René-Noël Legrand 13 Rue des Rogelins, 49400 Varrains

Well-established and very impressive Saumur-Champigny producer. Legrand has 15ha and produces around 5,000 cases a year. The reds are very traditional but have a great purity and real style. He has just 1ha of Chenin Blanc from which he produces a very acceptable, ripe and full Saumur white from fruit harvested late – sometimes, like in 2003, almost overly so. Four reds are produced. Les Lizières is the softest and most accesible of the wines. Les Terrages is denser and fuller with ageing in *cuve*. La Chaintre is aged in *foudres* and offers altogether more complexity and intensity. Les Togelins, the top label, is aged in part new oak, which is in no way overdone as the depth and purity of fruit comfortably absorbs the new wood. Give the top 2 wines at least 3 or 4 years to fully unfurl. (DM)

● **Saumur** Les Lizières★★ £B Les Terrages★★ £B

289

● **Saumur** La Chaintre★★★ £B Les Rogelins★★★ £C
○ **Saumur**★★ £B

DOM. FRÉDÉRIC MABILEAU   Saint-Nicolas-de-Bourgueil

F & N Mabileau   17-19 Rue de la Treille, 37140 Saint-Nicolas-de-Bourgueil
UK stockists: Cam

Frédéric Mabileau has been running his small domaine with his wife Nathalie
since the early 1990s. He now has some 9ha under vine planted to a
combination of Cabernet Franc (90%) and Cabernet Sauvignon. There is a
softly fruity Cabernet Sauvignon Anjou made from younger vines and a
Bourgueil, Les Racines, has also been added. Saint-Nicolas-de-Bourgueil stands
out and there are 3 good to very good and pure bottlings, marked more by
their elegance and refinement than by their weight. The Mabileaus possess plots
across the AC in a range of *terroirs*. Les Rouillères is the softest of the trio,
sourced from sandy/gravel soils where the vines are relatively young. Les
Coutures is fuller and firmer, sourced from older vines (over 40 years) grown in
gravel. The wine gets a brief cold soak, 20 day maceration and is aged for 12
months in oak. The brilliant, piercingly intense top wine, Éclipse, comes from
the lowest-yielding plots of clay/gravel over limestone. The wine gets 12
months in oak, a proportion new, and malolactic takes place in barrel. The top
2 wines in particular will benefit from 5 or 6 years' ageing. (DM)

● **Saint-Nicolas-de-Bourgueil** Les Coutures★★★ £C Éclipse★★★★ £C
● **Saint-Nicolas-de-Bourgueil** Rouillères★★ £B

DOM. HENRI MARIONNET   Touraine

Henri Marionnet   La Charmoise, 41230 Soings
This substantial operation has long been regarded as a benchmark for Touraine
AC wines and still continues to be so, although quality is now rivalled by some
smaller domaines. The 2 key varieties here are Gamay and Sauvignon. There is
also a little Cot, Chenin Blanc and Romorantin planted. Output is now
around 33–34,000 cases a year. Of the whites, the regular Touraine Sauvignon
is fresh and grassy with reasonable varietal character. The Vinifera bottling, like
all those under this label, is produced from ungrafted vines and is a clear step
up with greater depth, structure and intensity. Other bottlings include M de
Marionnet and a special *vin de pays* bottling from very old vines, Provinage. Of
the reds, the Touraine Gamay is soft and forward while the Première Vendange,
from Gamay plots of around 35–40 years of age, is vibrant and deeper with
great fruit intensity. The Cépages Oubliés is a rarity, from an almost obsolete
clone of the Gamay, de Bouze, which is darker in colour and surprisingly firm
in structure. The Vinifera Gamay is subtler and lighter but offers impressive
intensity. Best of the Vinifera bottlings is the Cot. Full of dark berries and
spices, it has impressive depth and concentration. All will drink well with a
couple of years of age except the regular Touraines which should be drunk
young. (DM)

● **Touraine** Gamay★ £C 1ère Vendange★★ £B Gamay Cépages Oubliés★★ £B
● **Touraine** Gamay Vinifera★★ £B Cot Vinifera★★★ £C
○ **Touraine** Sauvignon★ £B Sauvignon Vinifera★★★ £C

ALEX MATHUR/DOM. LEVASSEUR   Montlouis

Eric Gougeat   38. Rue des Bouvineries, 37270 Husseau
This excellent 10-ha domaine makes a small range of Montlouis as well as a
little Touraine Sauvignon, Cabernet and some Crémant de Loire. It is the
Montlouis Chenins which really stand out and above all they represent
extraordinarily good value for money. Both Les Perruches and the marginally
richer, more intense Lumen are dry. Dionysus is a fine and well-structured

demi-sec, tight and minerally with a hint of youthful honey and peach. There are also 2 very impressive sweet wines of which Rive Gauche is the tighter and less obviously honeyed although even when young the weight and dimension on the palate are particularly luscious. The Cuvée des Pruides is a particularly interesting blend of Chenin Blanc, Sauvignon Blanc as well as a little Chardonnay. Full, rich and very intense with marked botrytis, this offers marvellous fruit definition and and a fine mineral structure. Unlike the other wines, vinification is in *barrique*. Expect these wines to evolve well for a decade or more and the Montlouis to keep for much longer. (DM)

O **Montlouis** Rive Gauche★★★★ £D Dionysus★★★★ £B
O **Montlouis** Lumen★★★ £B Les Perruches★★ £C
O **Touraine** Cuvée des Pruides★★★★ £D

ALPHONSE MELLOT Sancerre mellot@sifiedi.fr

Alphonse Mellot La Moussière, 18300 Sancerre
UK stockists: **Hal**, GVF

Mellot is one of the leading producers in Sancerre. There are *négociant* wines including good Menetou-Salon and Pouilly-Fumé but the domaine wines are of a different order, particularly the top *cuvées*. The white Edmond and Génération XIX, made from very old vines and vinified in oak, are wines of real dimension, the latter often on the cusp of ★★★★★ The Pinot Noirs are increasingly impressive, displaying considerable depth and a round, supple texture, especially the brilliant, subtly oaked Génération XIX. The top wines will undoubtedly develop very well in bottle. (DM)

O **Sancerre** La Moussière★★★ £C Edmond★★★★ £E Génération XIX★★★★ £E
● **Sancerre** Génération XIX★★★★ £F

MOLLET-MAUDRY Sancerre

J-P Mollet & Florian Mollet-Maudry 84 Avenue de Fontenay, 18300 Saint Satur
UK stockists: **WTs**

Now that Florian has taken over the reins from his father Jean-Paul he is the 10th generation of his family at the long-established Mollet domaine. Between the 2 sides of his family he nows looks after holdings in both Sancerre and Pouilly-sur-Loire. The regular Sancerre and Pouilly-Fumé are good, rather than spectacular. The vine age of 35–40 years enables a fairly sound commercial yield of 60 hl/ha. The Sancerre is more marked by citrus and has a fuller, fleshier texture. A clear level up are the Pouilly-Fumé Les Sables and Sancerre Roc de l'Abbaye from older vines, around 45 years old. Les Sables comes from Kimmeridgian marl soils and displays raw gooseberry and blackcurrant aromas. Roc de l'Abbaye, in marked contrast, is from silex (flint) soils and is much less obviously fruity, tighter and more piercingly mineral in style. L'Antique is the top label. Again the Pouilly-Fumé comes from Kimmeridgian marl and is fuller and more opulent in style than the Sancerre from a combination of limestone and clay. These are the oldest vines of the domaine, around 55 years, and the depth and intensity of the wines is apparent, with the Sancerre on the cusp of ★★★★. The top labels will develop very well for 5 to 7 years. There is also a wood-aged Sancerre but this lacks the priercingly mineral quality of l'Antique. (DM)

O **Sancerre**★★ £C Roc de l'Abbaye★★★ £C Futs de Chene★★★ £D
O **Sancerre** L'Antique★★★ £D
O **Pouilly Fume**★★ £C Les Sables★★ £C L'Antique★★★ £D

GÉRARD MORIN Sancerre

Gérard Morin 18300 Bué
UK stockists: **WTs**

Gérard Morin epitomises the image of a French *vigneron* who holds sway in his candlelit *cave*. His domaine is based in the commune of Bué, a hamlet just 3 kilometres from Sancerre, which has a reputation for making the fullest and fattest wines of the appellation. His son Pierre, who developed his winemaking craft in Australia, has been taking on more and more responsibility and is now making the wine. The white is typically fat and richly aromatic. The red is a little less consistent, being more subject to the vagaries of the climate, but in a good vintage the depth and colour can reach Burgundian proportions. (NB)

O **Sancerre** PMG★★★ £C ● **Sancerre**★★ £C

DOM. RENÉ MOSSE Anjou www.domaine-mosse.com

René Mosse 4 Rue de la Chauvière, 49750 Saint-Lambert-du-Lattay
The Mosse domaine consists of 13ha planted to Chenin Blanc, Chardonnay, Cabernets Sauvignon and Franc, Gamay and Grolleau. There is a soft, easy, fruit-driven Rosé d'Anjou which is made using *pressurage direct* and a more serious red Anjou, a good example of the style aged in oak for 12 months with malolactic in barrel. All the Anjou dry whites are vinified and aged in oak for a year. The special bottlings, Rouchefer and Bonnes Blanches, offer more depth and intensity. Both wines offer subtle use of oak and a lightly honeyed and citrus character with great purity. A bottling from 60-year-old vines, Marie-Besnard, is also produced. The top wine is the Coteaux du Layon Bonnes Blanches, made in the best vintages and strikingly impressive in 2003. The Anjou whites and red will develop well in the medium term; the Coteaux du Layon is finely structured and will develop well over a decade. (DM)

● **Anjou** Le Gros★★ £C
O **Coteaux du Layon-Saint-Lambert** Bonnes Blanches★★★★ £E
O **Anjou**★★ £C Les Bonnes Blanches★★★ £C Rouchefer★★★ £C

DOM. HENRY NATTER Sancerre www.henrynatter.com

Henry Natter Place de l'Eglise, 18250 Montigny
UK stockists: **L&W**
Established in 1974, this domaine based in the top village of Montigny is now one of the best for fine-quality white Sancerre. As well as the regular white there is a small-volume special bottling, Cuvée François de la Grange de Montigny, and a fruity red and rosé. Vinification of the whites is traditional with fermentation in large oak vats. The regular version is then aged in stainless steel, while François de la Grange de Montigny sees 12 months in oak. The wines have been consistently good in recent years and will develop well with short bottle age. (DM)

O **Sancerre**★★★ £C Cuvée François de La Grange★★★ £C

DOM. OGEREAU Anjou

Vincent Ogereau 44 Rue de la Belle-Angevine, 49750 Saint-Lambert-du-Lattay
UK stockists: **CdP**
Vincent Ogereau produces very good Anjou-Villages reds, decent minerally dry white Anjou and rich, well-crafted Coteaux du Layon. The regular Anjou-Villages is a blend of Cabernet Franc and Cabernet Sauvignon, whereas the Côte de la Houssaye is a dense and powerful, brambly Cabernet Sauvignon. Both will be the better for 5 years' ageing. The Coteaux du Layon is powerful, sweet and unctuous and achieves a really intense botrytised peachy character in the very best years. A special selection, Clos de Bonnes Blanches, is also produced. (DM)

● **Anjou**★★ £B ● **Anjou-Villages**★★★ £B Côte de la Houssaye★★★ £C
O **Anjou** Prestige Sec★★ £B
O **Coteaux du Layon-Saint-Lambert-du-Lattay** Prestige★★★★ £C

DOM. DES OUCHES Bourgueil perso.wanadoo.fr/gambier
Denis Gambier 3 Rue des Ouches, 37140 Ingrandes-de-Touraine
UK stockists: THT
First class Bourgueil producer offering classic, restrained and ageworthy examples of the appellation at very keen prices indeed. The style is tighter and more backward than many, even from this cool-climate region. All the wines have an angular character in their youth, as much from their high acidity as from their tannin, and require a few years' ageing to add flesh. The top 2 *cuvées* in particular should be cellared for at least 4 to 5 years. Cabernet Franc is the main variety but there is a little (10%) Cabernet Sauvignon in the Grande Réserve. Some of the vines are remarkably old here, up to 100 years, and this undoubtedly contributes to quality. With the exception of the Grande Réserve, which is aged in new oak (50%) with malolactic in barrel, the wines are traditionally vinified and aged in *foudres*. (DM)
● **Bourgueil**★★ £B Clos Prince★★ £B Vieilles Vignes★★★ £B
● **Bourgueil** Grande Réserve★★★★ £C

HENRY PELLÉ Menetou-Salon www.henry-pelle.com
Pellé family 18220 Morogues
UK stockists: PBW,FMV,HHB,GVF,Sel
The leading estate in Menetou-Salon and a producer of Sancerre as well. There are some 40ha under vine and these split roughly two-thirds to one-third Sauvignon Blanc to Pinot Noir. The vineyards in Menetou-Salon are planted on Kimmeridgian clay and tended organically, and green harvesting is practised. Straightforward Menetou-Salon and Sancerre white and red now come from a mix of estate and bought-in grapes. Of the estate-grown wines, the white Menetou-Salon tends to impress more than the Sancerre, the vineyards of which are younger, although the Sancerre is increasingly improving as the vines mature. 2002 was very good here. White Clos de Ratier is from a single parcel as is the rich and intense Clos des Blanchais, which is from the domaine's oldest vines and possesses an impressive depth of ripe gooseberry fruit and a fine, mineral structure. The reds, while fruity enough, can be insubstantial. (DM)
● **Menetou-Salon** Les Cris★ £B ● **Sancerre** La Croix au Garde★ £C
O **Menetou-Salon** Morogues★★ £B Clos de Ratier★★ £B Clos des Blanchais★★★ £C
O **Sancerre** La Croix au Garde★★ £C

DOM. JO PITHON Coteaux du Layon
Jo Pithon 44 Rue de la Belle-Angevine, 49750 Saint-Lambert-du-Lattay
UK stockists: BBR,Gau,HHC
Jo, like his bother Olivier PITHON in the Côtes du Roussillon, makes wine without compromise and with a dedication solely to high quality. On occasion this has resulted in some of the wines pushing the boundaries, particularly his astonishingly rich and concentrated sweet wines. As well as these there are some very well crafted dry Chenins. There are 3 Anjou whites and a Savennières La Croix Pocot from young vines – the first harvest was in 2002 – and vinified in older wood. Of the Anjou bottlings, Les Pépinières and Les Bergères see around 10% new wood and both show subtle barrel-ferment character. Les Bergères is the richer and more honeyed of the 2. The rich, long and intense Bonnes Blanches is very fine with subtle citrus and honeyed fruit and smoky barrel-fermented oak from 80% new wood, which is beautifully integrated. The regular Coteaux du Layon comes from plots in 4 different villages. It is relatively lightly influenced by botrytis, just 50% of the fruit, and is elegant and finely structured with a marked mineral component providing backbone. Both the Coteaux du Layon and the Quarts de Chaume come from 100%

293

botrytised fruit. They have up to 150gms of residual sugar and both see plenty of new oak. The Quarts de Chaume has particularly striking aromas of nutmeg and honey as well as a peachy, citrus character. The wines will all drink well with 2 or 3 years' ageing and the opulent sweeties will keep in the medium term although they don't appear to have the grip and structure to make very old bones. (DM)

O **Anjou** Les Pépinières★★★ £C Les Bergères★★★ £C
O **Anjou** Les Bonnes Blanches★★★★ £D
O **Savennières** La Croix Picot★★ £C O **Coteaux du Layon** Les 4 Villages★★★★ £E
O **Coteaux du Layon-Saint-Lambert** Les Bonnes Blanches★★★★ £E
O **Quarts de Chaume** Les Varennes★★★★ £F

VINCENT PINARD Sancerre

Vincent Pinard 42 Rue Saint-Vincent, 18300 Bué
UK stockists: GWW, HHB, Han
There are some 15ha at this model Sancerre domaine where Vincent Pinard produces good to very good white and red Sancerre. The regular red is good, light but exuberantly fruity with attractive berry fruit. Charlouise is denser, richer. Of the whites the Cuvée Florès emphasises ripe classic gooseberry fruit. The 2 top whites are fuller and more complex, and both are vinified in wood. Harmonie in particular is spicy and toasty in its youth, needing 3 or 4 years to achieve a balance of fruit and oak. (DM)

● **Sancerre**★★ £C Charlouise★★★ £D
O **Sancerre** Cuvée Florés★★£D Nuance★★★ £C Harmonie★★★ £D

DOM. DES ROCHES NEUVES Saumur-Champigny

Thierry Germain 56 Boulevard Saint-Vincent, 49400 Varrains
Thierry Germain's father Bernard has owned CHÂTEAU DE FESLES in Bonnezeaux since 1996 but his son has been established in Anjou for longer. He produces opulent, powerful, ripely extracted reds from Cabernet Franc. The wines are deeply coloured, dense and oaky. Vinification is aimed at maximum extraction, with the fruit getting a pre-fermentation cold soak and the wine staying on its skins in order to achieve rounded, supple tannins. He notably succeeds in reducing some of the austere youthful characteristics that can often show in other Loire Cabernets. He also makes a very good barrel-fermented white Saumur which is stylish and refined with a nice balance of toasty, citrus fruit and a fresh mineral structure. The Terres Chaudes and the Marginale are the 2 top reds. The latter is marked by new oak in its youth and needs time. (DM)

● **Saumur-Champigny**★★ £B Terres Chaudes★★★ £C Marginale★★★ £C
O **Saumur** Insolite★★★ £C

DOM. SAINT NICOLAS Fiefs Vendéens

Thierry Michon 11 Rue des Vallées, 85470 Brem-sur-Mer
This property is a real benchmark for this unheralded region on the Atlantic coast south of Nantes. The domaine has been run on biodynamic lines since 1995 and the vineyard holding covers 32ha. Chenin, Chardonnay and a little Groslot are planted for whites and Gamay and Pinot Noir are the dominant red grapes. A little Cabernet Franc is also grown. Of the whites, Les Clous is a full, fat and lightly mineral blend of Chenin Blanc and Chardonnay. Le Haut de Clous is solely Chenin Blanc from lower yields on argile and schist soils. It is very intense and a subtle lees and barrel-ferment character shows through. The Soleil de Chine *cuvée* is again 100% Chenin from old vines and a yield of just 15–20hl/ha. It has around 20 grams of residual sugar adding a little sweetness to its rich texture. There is a good, light Reflets rosé from Pinot Noir and a red

from mainly Pinot Noir with a little Gamay. Softer and less structured is the ripe and strawberry-fruited Gamay Gammes en May. The Cuvée Jacques is the top Pinot Noir bottling. It offers subtle, finely structured fruit and quite a marked youthful oak character. The fascinating Le Poiré is produced solely from the small holding of Negrette. It has an intensely piercing, bright cool-climate berry character as well as impressive depth. The top wines will evolve well with a little age. (DM)

- ● **Fiefs Vendéens** Gammes en May★ £B Reflets★★ £B Cuvée Jacques★★★ £D
- ● **Fiefs Vendéens** Le Poiré★★★ £D
- O **Fiefs Vendéens** Les Clous★★ £B Le Haut des Clous★★★ £D
- O **Cuvée Soleil de Chine** Vin de Table★★★ £D
- ◉ **Fiefs Vendéens** Reflets★ £B

DOM. DE LA SANSONNIÈRE Anjou

Marc Angeli   49380 Thouarcé
UK stockists: Har

Marc Angeli farms his 7ha biodynamically and he makes some of the very finest examples of the humble Anjou AC. He has also produced tiny amounts (from less than a hectare) of exquisite Bonnezeaux that are released as Les Blanderies and Le Coteau du Houet. The largest volume here is saved for his Anjou La Lune which accounts for nearly half his holding at 3.1ha. The wine is produced from low yields and is vinified in 400- to 600-litre barrels. It is remarkably pure with an intense mineral quality amidst complex, very subtly tropical fruit. It is occasionally bottled with just a hint of residual sugar. Les Fouchardes and Les Vieilles Vignes des Blanderies are produced from much smaller holdings and therefore very hard to find. The range is completed by a Cabernet Sauvignon Les Gelinettes and a Rosé d'Anjou, Coteau du Houet. (DM)

- O **Anjou** La Lune★★★★ £E

SILICES DE QUINCY Quincy

Jacques Sallé   Place de L'Echuzeau, 18120 Quincy
UK stockists: Gau,Har,THT

From his tiny holding of 5.5ha, Jacques Sallé produces around 1,000 cases of Quincy which is the benchmark for the appellation. In order to ensure the integrity of the main wine a second label Silicette is also made. The vineyard is tended biodynamically and the vines are very old. The wine possesses an intense mineral, green-fruit character underpinned by tight gripping acidity. The depth and structure here suggest the top wine will develop surprisingly well over at least 4 or 5 years. (DM)

- O **Quincy**★★★ £C

YVES SOULEZ/CH. DE LA GENAISERIE Coteaux du Layon

Yves Soulez   Ch. de la Genaiserie, 49190 Saint-Aubin-de-Luigné
UK stockists: GVF

Yves Soulez makes very good, stylish and refined Coteaux du Layon in a more restrained style than most of his peers. His wines are quite different from the new wave of super-ripe and unctuous styles achieved elsewhere by the likes of Patrick BAUDOUIN or Jo PITHON. They are tight and often quite backward when young but have a real intensity and finesse also. There are 3 very fine special *cuvées* in addition to the regular bottling. Les Simonelles is elegant and minerally with subtle botrytis and comes from vines grown on volcanic, schistous soils. La Roche is from a vineyard with a high charcoal content and is very restrained. Les Tetuères is the fullest and most obviously honeyed of the 3 and generally has more marked botrytis character. There are also good Anjou

295

reds from Gamay and Cabernet Franc and a fruity, fresh medium-sweet Cabernet d'Anjou; a revelation in comparison with so many wines sold under this label. (DM)

● **Anjou★** £B ● **Anjou-Villages★★** £B ○ **Coteaux du Layon-Chaume★★★** £C
○ **Coteaux du Layon-Chaume** Les Simonelles★★★★ £D La Roche★★★★ £D
○ **Coteaux du Layon-Chaume** Les Tetuères★★★★ £D

TAILLE AUX LOUPS   Montlouis

Jacky Blot   8 Rue des Aitres, Husseau, 37270 Montlouis-sur-Loire
UK stockists: FMV, BBR

One of the best domaines in Montlouis. A varying small range of *sec, demi-sec* and sweet wines are made both in Montlouis and Vouvray. Recent vintages have seen the production of mainly dry and medium styles along with good sparkling wines including Brut Tradition and a very dry Pétillant, although some brilliant late-harvest wines emerged in 2002. The Montlouis Remus *sec* is barrel-fermented in new oak and aged on lees with *bâtonnage*. The impressive *demi-sec* is not oversweet and when nature is kind *moelleux* are very impressive indeed. The Montlouis Cuvée des Loups and particularly Montlouis Cuvée Romulus can be explosively rich. Vouvray is also now produced from Clos de Venise as well as some fine bottlings of Bourgueil. (DM)

○ **Montlouis** Brut Tradition★★ £B Pétillant★★ £B Sec★★ £B Demi-Sec★★★ £C
○ **Montlouis** Moelleux★★★ £D Cuvée des Loups★★★★ £E
○ **Vouvray** Clos de Venise Sec★★★ £C

DOM. VACHERON   Sancerre

Vacheron family   1 Rue du Puis Poulton, 18300 Sancerre
UK stockists: E&T, SsG, TWS

The Vacherons have some 37ha under vine with no less than 11ha planted to Pinot Noir. They are one of only a handful of growers in Sancerre to make impressive red wines. There are regular red and white Sancerres and 2 very impressive reserve *cuvées*; the white Romains and the dense and surprisingly powerfully structured red Belle Dame. Good rosé is also produced. The white Sancerre has fine grass and mineral notes and the Romains an impressive depth with subtle, nutty, oak-derived notes and real finesse. Both the top wines have the structure to develop well with 5 years' cellaring. (DM)

● **Sancerre★★** £C Belle Dame★★★ £C
○ **Sancerre★★** £C Romains★★★ £D

OTHER WINES OF NOTE

Pays Nantais

SERGE BATARD ○ **Muscadet** Les Hautes Noëlles★ £B
○ **Muscadet Côtes de Grandlieu sur-lie★** £B Les Granges★★ £B
CH. LA RAGOTIÈRE ○ **Muscadet-de-Sèvre-et-Maine** Clos Petit Chateau★ £B
○ **Muscadet-de-Sèvre-et-Maine** Collection Privée M★★ £B
CHÉREAU-CARRÉ ○ **Muscadet-de-Sèvre-et-Maine** Château Chasseloir £B
BRUNO CORMERAIS ○ **Muscadet-de-Sèvre-et-Maine** Sur-lie★ £B
MICHEL DAVID ○ **Muscadet-de-Sèvre-et-Maine** Sur Lie Clos du Ferré★ £B
DOM DES DORICES ○ **Muscadet-de-Sèvre-et-Maine** Sur Lie★ £B
DOM. GADAIS ○ **Muscadet-de-Sèvre-et-Maine** La Grande Reseve du Moulin★ £B
○ **Muscadet-de-Sèvre-et-Maine** Vieilles Vignes★★ £B
DOM. GUINDON ○ **Muscadet-Coteaux de la Loire** Sur Lie Tradition★★ £B ○
Muscadet-Coteaux de la Loire Prestige★★ £B
DOM. DES HAUTES PEMIONS ○ **Muscadet-de-Sèvre-et-Maine** £B
DOM. LA ROCHE RENARD ○ **Muscadet-de-Sèvre-et-Maine** £B
DOM. DE LA LOUVETRIE ○ **Muscadet-de-Sèvre-et-Maine★** £B
○ **Muscadet-de-Sèvre-et-Maine** Hermine d'Or★★ £B

O Muscadet-de-Sèvre-et-Maine Cuvée Gneiss★★ £B Elevé en Barrique★ £B
PIERRE LUNEAU O Muscadet-de-Sèvre-et-Maine Le L d'Or★ £B
LOUIS MÉTAIREAU O Muscadet-de-Sèvre-et-Maine Cuvée LM★★ £B

Anjou

PIERRE AGUILAS O Coteaux du Layon Cuvée Claire★★★ £D
DOM. DE BABLUT O Coteaux de l'Aubance Séléction★★★ £D
O Coteaux de l'Aubance Grand Pierre★★★★ £D
O Coteaux de l'Aubance Vin Noble★★★★ £D
DOM. DE LA BERGERIE O Chaume 1rt Cru★★★ £E
DOM. MICHEL BLOUIN O Chaume 1er Cru★★★ £E
DOM. CADY O Coteaux-du-Layon Saint-Aubin Cuvée Voluptué★★★ £D
CH. DE BROSSAY O Coteaux-du-Layon Vieilles-Vignes Eparses★★★ £C
CH. DE LA GUIMONIÈRE ● Anjou★ £B
O Coteaux du Layon Chaume Julines★★★ £E
CH. DES NOYERS O Anjou-Villages★★ £B
O Coteaux-du-Layon Réserve Vieilles Vignes★★★★ £C
CH. DE PASSAVANT O Anjou-Villages★★ £B
O Coteaux-du-Layon Les Greffiers★★★ £C
CH. PRINCE O Coteaux l'Aubance★★★ £C
CH. DE SOUCHERIE O Savennières Cuvée Anais★★ £C
O Coteaux du Layon-Beaulieu★★★ £E
CH. DE SURONDE O Quarts de Chaume £E
CH. DE TIGNÉ ● Anjou-Villages Mozart★★★ £C Cyrano★★★ £C
CH. DE VARENNE O Savennières★★ £C
DOM. DES CHESNAIES ● Anjou-Villages La Musse★★ £B
CLOS DE VARENNES O Savennières★★★ £C
DOM. DE HAUTE PERCHE O Coteaux de l'Aubance Les Fontanelles★★★ £D
DOM. LAUREAU DU CLOS FREMUR O Anjou★ £C
O Savennières★★ £B Les Genêts★★★ £C Bel Ouvrage★★★ £C Demi-Sec★★ £C
J-Y LEBRETON ● Anjou-Villages-Brissac★★ £B La Croix de Mission★★★ £B
● Anjou-Villages-Brissac Les Millerifs★★★ £C
O Coteaux de L'Aubance Ambre de Roche★★★ £D
DOM. LES GRANDES VIGNES O Anjou Varenne de Combre★★★ £C **O Coteaux de Layon**★★★ £C
O Coteaux de Layon Noble Selection★★★ £D
O Bonnezeaux★★★ £C Noble Selection★★★★ £E
DOM. DE MONTGILET O Coteaux de l'Aubance★★ £B Les Trois Schistes★★★ £C
O Coteaux de l'Aubance Le Tertereaux★★★★ £E Clos des Huittières★★★★ £E
DOM. AUX MOINES O Savennières Roches-aux-Moines★★★ £C
DOM. DE LA MONNAIE O Savennières £C
DOM. DU PETIT VAL O Coteaux du Layon Cuvée Simon★★★ £D
O Bonnezeaux La Montagne★★★★ £E
DOM. DES PETITS QUARTS O Bonnezeaux ★★★ £C Malabé★★★★ £D
DOM. DES QUARRES ● Anjou-Villages Les Métifs★ £B
O Coteaux de Layon-Faye Le Magdelaine Prestige★★★ £D
DOM. ROY RENÉ O Coteaux du Layon-Lambert Le Cormier★★★ £C
RENÉ RENOU O Bonnezeaux Les Mellereses★★★ £D
DOM. RICHOU O Anjou Chavigné★★ £B
O Coteaux de l'Aubance Cuvée Les Trois Desmoiselles★★★ £C
DOM. DE RICHAMBEAU O Coteaux du L'Aubance★★★ £C
DOM. DES SABLONNETTES ● Anjou★★ £B **O Anjou** Genêts★★★ £C
O Coteaux du Layon Champ du Cygne★★★★ £E
PIERRE SOULEZ O Savennières Château de Chamboreau Cuvée d'Avant★★★ £C

Saumur

BOUVET-LADUBAY O Saumur Mousseux Crémant Excellence★★ £B
O Saumur Mousseux Brut Saphir Vintage★ £B
O Saumur Mousseux Brut Trésor★★ £B **● Saumur Mousseux** Brut Rubis★★ £C
CHAPIN & LANDAIS O Saumur Mousseux Brut Le Grand Saumur Vintage★ £B

DOM. DE CH. GAILLARD ● **Saumur**★★ £B
CH. DE TARGÉ ○ **Saumur** Les Fresnelles★★ £B
● **Saumur-Champigny** Traditionelle★★ £B
● **Saumur-Champigny** Cuvée Ferry★★ £C
FILLIATREAU ● **Saumur-Champigny**★ £B Vieilles-Vignes★★ £C
GRATIEN & MEYER ○ **Crémant de Loire**★ £B
LANGLOIS-CHÂTEAU ● **Saumur**★ £B
● **Saumur-Champigny** Château de Varrains★★ £B
○ **Saumur** Vieilles-Vignes★★ £B
DOM. LA PERRUCHE ● **Saumur-Champigny** Clos de Chaumont Prestige★★ £C
○ **Coteaux de Saumur**★★ £C
DOM. DU PETIT SAINT-VINCENT ● **Saumur-Champigny**★★ £B
DOM. DE NERLEUX ● **Saumur-Champigny**★ £B ○ **Saumur**★ £B
DOM. SAINT-JUST ● **Saumur** Tradition★★ £B
● **Saumur-Champigny** Les Terres Rouge★★ £B Montée des Roches★★★ £C
● **Saumur-Champigny** Le Clos Moleton★★★ £C
○ **Saumur** Tradition★★ £C Le Coulée de Saint-Cyr★★ £C
○ **Crémant de Loire**★ £B ● **Saumur Mousseux**★ £B
PATRICK VADE ● **Saumur-Champigny** Les Trezeillieres★★ £B Les Echalys★★ £B
● **Saumur-Champigny** Lea★★★ £C ○ **Saumur** La Papareille★★★ £C
DOM. DES VARINELLES ● **Saumur-Champigny**★★ £B Vieilles Vignes★★ £B
● **Saumur-Champigny**Larrivale★★ £C Laurenride★★★ £C
○ **Saumur**★★ £B

Touraine

THIERRY AMIRAULT ● **Saint-Nicolas-de-Bourgueil**★ £B
DOM. DE L'AUMONIER ○ **Touraine** Sauvignon★ £B
DOM. J & C BAUDRY ● **Chinon**★★ £B
DOM. DE BEAUSÉJOUR ● **Chinon**★★ £B L'Ancelot★★ £B
DOM. BRETON ● **Bourgueil** Les Galichets★★ £B Clos Senechal★★★ £C
DOM. BRISEBARRE ○ **Vouvray** Cuvée Amédée★★ £B Réserve Personnelle
○ **Vouvray** Moelleux★★★ £C
CH. DE L'AULÉE ● **Chinon** Cèdre★ £B
CH. GAILLARD ○ **Touraine-Mesland**★★ £B
CH. GAUDRELLE ○ **Vouvray**★★ £B Réserve Spéciale★★★ £C
CH. DE SAINTE-LOUAND ● **Chinon** Réserve des Trompegueux★ £B
DOM DE LA CHEVALERIE ● **Bourgueil** Les Galichets★★ £B
● **Bourgueil** Vieilles Vignes★★ £B Busardières★★★ £B
CLOS BAUDOIN ○ **Vouvray** Aigle Sec £B
CLOS DE LA BRIDERIE ○ **Touraine-Meslands** Vieilles-Vignes★★ £B
CLOS DU CHÂTEAU DE MOSNYS ○ **Montlouis** Moelleux★ £B
CLOS ROCHE BLANCHE ● **Touraine** Closerie★★★ £B
○ **Touraine** Sauvignon No 5★★ £B
DOM. DU CLOS ROUSSELY ○ **Touraine** Le Clos★ £B
MAX COGNARD ● **Bourgueil** Les Tuffes★★ £B
● **Saint-Nicolas-de-Bourgueil** Estelle★★ £B
● **Saint-Nicolas-de-Bourgueil** Malgagnes★★ £B
DOM. DU COLOMBIER ● **Chinon** Vieilles Vignes★ £B
DOM. DE CORBILLÈRES ○ **Touraine** Sauvignon★★ £B
COULY-DUTHEIL ● **Chinon** Clos de l'Echo £B
DOM. DELAUNAY ● **Bourgueil** Prestige★ £B
JOEL DELAUNAY ○ **Touraine** Sauvignon★ £B
DOM. DOZON ● **Chinon** Les Lysons★★ £B Clos du Saint-au-Loup★★ £B
● **Chinon** Le Bois Joubert★★ £B
BENOIT GAUTIER ○ **Vouvray** Argiles★★ £B
DOM. DE LA HAUTE BORNE ○ **Vouvray** Sec★★ £B Tendre★★★ £B
○ **Vouvray** Moelleux★★★ £B
DOM. DES HUARDS ● **Cour-Cheverny**★★ £B
○ **Cour-Cheverny** Cuvée François 1er★★ £B
DOM. HUBERT ● **Bourgueil**★ £B

LAMÉ DELISLE BOUCARD ● **Bourgueil** Prestige★★ £B Vieilles Vignes★★ £B
DOM. DES LIARDS ○ **Montlouis** Demi-Sec Vieilles-Vignes★★ £B
LOGIS DE LA BOUCHARDIÈRE ● **Chinon**★ £B Le Chêne Vert★★ £B
● **Chinon** Logis de La Bouchardière★★ £B Le Clos Vieilles Vignes★★★ £C
● **Chinon** Les Cornuelles★★ £C
ALAIN MARCADET ○ **Touraine** Sauvignon★ £B
DOM. JEAN-FRANÇOIS MÉRIEAU ○ **Touraine** Sauvignon Blanc★ £B
PHILIPPE PICHARD ● **Chinon** l'Ancestral★ £B
DOM. PICHOT ○ **Vouvray** Sec Coteau de la Biche £B
○ **Vouvray** Demi-Sec Peu de la Moriette £B
DOM. PINON ○ **Vouvray** Sec Tradtion £B
DOM. DE LA PRESLE ○ **Touraine** Sauvignon Blanc★ £B
DOM. DES RAGUENIERES ● **Bourgueil**★ £B Les Haies★ £B
DOM. RAIFAULT ● **Chinon** £B Allets £B
DOM. RICARD ○ **Touraine** Le Petiot★ £A Les Trois Chênes★★ £B
○ **Touraine** Cuvée Armand★★★ £B L'Effrontée★★★ £C
DOM. DU RONCÉE ● **Chinon** Clos des Marronniers★★ £B
DOM. WILFRID ROUSSE ● **Chinon** Cuvée Terroir★★ £B Vieilles Vignes★★ £B
DOM. LA SAUVETE ○ **Touraine** Sauvignon★ £B
TALUAU & FOLTZENLOGEL ● **Saint-Nicolas-de-Bourgueil** Jeunes Vignes★ £B
● **Saint-Nicolas-de-Bourgueil** Vieilles Vignes★★ £C Le Vau Jaumier★★ £C
DOM. VIGNEAU-CHEVREAU ○ **Vouvray** Sec★★ £B
○ **Vouvray** Sec Clos de Rougemont★★ £C Demi-Sec★★ £B
○ **Vouvray** Moelleux★★★ £D

Central Vineyards

DOM. MICHEL BAILLY ○ **Pouilly-Fumé** Les Vallons★★★ £C
DOM. JEAN-PAUL BALLAND ○ **Sancerre**★★ £B Grand Cuvée★★★ £C
● **Sancerre**★ £B
BALLAND-CHAPUIS ○ **Sancerre** Le Chêne Marchand★★ £B
DOM. FRANCIS BLANCHET ○ **Pouilly-Fumé** Les Pernets★★ £B
○ **Pouilly-Fumé** Cuvée Silice★★★ £C
DOM. HUBERT BROCHARD ● **Sancerre** Tradition★★ £C Vieilles Vignes★★ £C
○ **Pouilly-Fumé**★★ £B ○ **Saancerre** Tradition★★ £ Terroir de Silex★★★ £C
○ **Saancerre** Vieille Vignes★★★ £C
DOM. DES CAVES ○ **Quincy**★★ £B
DOM. CHAMPAULT ○ **Sancerre** Clos du Roy★★★ £C ● **Sancerre** Les Pierris★★ £B
DOM. DE CHATENOY ● **Menetou-Salon**★★ £B ○ **Menetou-Salon**★★ £B
DOM. CHAVET ○ **Menetou-Salon**★★ £B
PAUL CHERRIER ○ **Sancerre** Vieilles-Vignes★★ £B
DOM. DE CHEVILLY ○ **Quincy**★★ £B
DOM. DE LA COMMANDERIE ○ **Quincy**★ £B
JEAN-CLAUDE DAGUENEAU ○ **Pouilly-Fumé**★★★ £C
VINCENT DELAPORTE ○ **Sancerre**★★★ £C
ANDRE DÉZAT ○ **Sancerre**★★★ £C ◉ **Sancerre**★★ £C
● **Sancerre**★★ £C Vieilles-Vignes★★ £C Fûts de Chêne★★ £C
PIERRE & ALAIN DÉZAT ○ **Sancerre**★★★ £B ◉ **Sancerre**★★ £C
DOM. FOURNIER ○ **Menetou-Salon**★ £B
PIERRE GIRAULT ○ **Sancerre** Chêne du Roy★★ £C
DOM. JEAN-CLAUDE GUYOT ○ **Pouilly-Fumé** Les Loges★★ £C
DE LADOUCETTE ○ **Pouilly-Fumé**★ £C Baron de L★★★ £E
SERGE LALOUE ○ **Sancerre**★★ £C ● **Sancerre**★★ £C
DOM. MARTIN ○ **Sancerre** Chavignol★★★ £C L'Indigène★★★ £C
● **Sancerre** Chavignol★★★ £C
MASSON-BLONDELET ○ **Pouilly-Fumé** Angelots £C Villa Paulus★★★ £C
DOM. MERLIN CHERRIER ○ **Sancerre** £B
ROGER NEVEU ○ **Sancerre**★★ £B
DOM. JEAN PABIOT ○ **Pouilly-Fumé** £C
DOM. PHILIPPE PORTIER ○ **Quincy**★★ £B
DOM. PAUL PRIEUR ○ **Sancerre**★ £B ● **Sancerre**★ £B

DOM. MICHEL REDDE O **Sancerre** Les Tuilières★★ £C

O **Pouilly-Fumé** La Moynerie★★ £C

PASCAL ET NICOLAS REVERDY O **Sancerre** Vieille-Vignes★★★ £C

CLAUDE RIFFAULT O **Sancerre** Cuvée Antique★★★ £C

MATTHIAS ROBLIN ● **Sancerre**★ £C   O **Sancerre**★★ £C

JEAN-MAX ROGER O **Sancerre** Cuvée CM★★ £C   O **Menetou-Salon**★★ £B

DOM. DE LA ROSSIGNOL O **Sancerre**★★ £B

DOM. SAUTEREAU O **Sancerre** Vieilles Vignes★★ £C

DOM. HERVÉ SEGUIN O **Pouilly-Fumé** Cuvée Prestige★★ £C

DOM. THIBAULT O **Pouilly-Fumé**★★ £C

DOM. ANNICK TINEL O **Pouilly-Fumé**★★ £C

DOM. ANDRE VATAN O **Sancerre** Saint-François★ £C

Work in progress!!

Producers under consideration for the next edition
ADÉÂ CONSULES (VIN DE PAYS - LOIRE)
CH. DE PASSAVANT (ANJOU)
CH. YVONNE (SAUMUR)
DOM. DU COLLIER (SAUMUR)
DOM. DAVIAU (ANJOU-VILLAGES)
DOM DE LA GARRELIÈRE (TOURAINE)
DOM. DES GRIOTTES (ANJOU)
DOM. RICHARD LEROY (ANJOU/COTEAUX-DU-LAYON)

Author's choice (DM)
A diverse selection of sweet whites
PATRICK BAUDOUIN O **Coteaux du Layon** Aprés Minuit

DOM. DES BAUMARD O **Quarts de Chaume**

CH. DE FESLES O **Bonnezeaux**

DOM. DU CLOS NAUDIN O **Vouvray** Moelleux

PHILIPPE DELESVAUX O **Coteaux du Layon** Grains Nobles

OLIVIER DELÉTANG O **Montlouis** Les Petits Boulay Garde Réserve

JOËL GIGOU O **Jasnières** Sélection de Grains Nobles

HUET L'ECHANSONNE O **Vouvray** Haut-Lieu Moelleux

YVES SOULEZ O **Coteaux du Layon** Les Tetuères

TAILLE AUX LOUPS O **Montlouis** Cuvée Romulus

DOM. DES FORGES O **Quarts de Chaume**

CH. LA VARIÈRE O **Quarts de Chaume** Les Querches

RENÉ MOSSÉ O **Coteaux du Layon-Saint-Lambert** Bonnes Blanches

JO PITHON O **Quarts de Chaume** Les Varennes

DOM. FRANÇOIS CHIDAINE O **Montlouis** Le Lys

A choice of individual dry whites
DOM. HENRI BOURGEOIS O **Sancerre La** Bourgeoise

CH. D'EPIRÉ O **Savennières** Cuveé Spéciale

CH. DE VILLENEUVE O **Saumur** Cormiers

JEAN-CLAUDE CHATELAINE O **Pouilly Fumé** Prestige

CLOS DE LA COULÉE DE SERRANT O **Savennières Coulée de Serrant**

PASCAL COTAT O **Sancerre** Monts Damnés

DIDIER DAGUENEAU O **Pouilly Fumé** Silex

HENRY PELLÉ O **Menetou-Salon** Clos des Blanchais

DOM. DE LA SANSONNIÈRE O **Anjou** La Lune

SILICES DE QUINCY O **Quincy**

DOM. DE BELLIVIÈRE O **Coteaux du Loir** Eparses Vieilles Vignes

DOM. SAINT-NICOLAS O **Fiefs Vendéens** Le Haut des Clous

The best of the reds

PHILIPPE ALLIET ● **Chinon** Vieilles-Vignes

YANNICK AMIRAULT ● **Saint-Nicolas-de-Bourgueil** Malgagnes

BERNARD BAUDRY ● **Chinon** Croix Boisée

CH. DU HUREAU ● **Saumur-Champigny** Lisgathe

CLOS ROUGEARD ● **Saumur-Champigny** Poyeux

PIERRE-JACQUES DRUET ● **Bourgueil** Vaumoreau

DOM. OGEREAU ● **Anjou-Villages** Côte de la Houssaye

DOM. DES OUCHES ● **Bourgueil** Grande Réserve

DOM. DES ROCHES NEUVES ● **Saumur-Champigny** Marginale

DOM. DE LA COTELLERAIE ● **Saint-Nicolas-de-Bourgueil** L'Envol

CH. DE COULAINE ● **Chinon** Les Picasses

DOM. FRÉDÉRIC MABILEAU ● **Saint-Nicolas-de-Bourgueil** Éclipse

A selection of great Loire values

AMPELIDAE ○ **Vin de Pays de la Vienne** Le C

AUBERT LA CHAPELLE ○ **Jasnières**

DOM. DE LA BUTTE ● **Bourgueil** Perrières

ALAIN CAILBOURDIN ○ **Pouilly Fumé** Les Cris

CH. DE VILLENEUVE ○ **Saumur**

DOM. FRANÇOIS CHIDAINE ○ **Montlouis** Clos des Breuil

DOM. LAURENT CHATENAY ○ **Montlouis** La Vallée

DOM. DU CLOS NAUDIN ○ **Vouvray** Sec

DOM. DU CLOSEL ○ **Savennières** Clos du Papillon

DOM DE L'ECU ○ **Muscadet Sèvre-et-Maine** Expression de Granit

DOM. GUIBERTEAU ○ **Saumur** Le Clos

DOM. LA TOUR SAINT MARTIN ○ **Menetou-Salon** Morogues

DOM. RENÉ-NOEL LEGRAND ● **Saumur** La Chaintre

ALEX MATHUR ○ **Touraine** Cuvée des Pruides

DOM. GÉRARD MORIN ○ **Sancerre** PMG

RECOMMENDED HOTELS AND RESTAURANTS - LOIRE

Top Hotels

★★★★*Jean Bardet*   57 rue Groison, Tours 37000
Tel. 02 47 41 41 11 Fax 02 47 51 68 72
Email sophie@jeanbardet.com   16 rooms   £ C/G

★★★★★*Château d'Artigny*   D 17, Montbazon 37250
Tel. 02 47 34 30 30 Fax 02 47 54 30 39
Email. artigny@grandesetapes.fr   59 rooms   £D/H

Top Restaurants

★★★★★*Jean Bardet*   57 rue Groison, Tours 37000
Tel. 02 47 41 41 11 Fax 02 47 51 68 72
Email sophie@jeanbardet.com   £ D/G

★★★★*Le Relais de Bracieux*   1 Ave. de Chambord, Bracieux 41250
Tel. 02 54 46 41 22 Fax 02 54 46 03 69
Email. relaisbracieux.robin@wanadoo.fr   £D/G

Value for money Hotels

★*Bonnheure*   9bis rue René Masson, Bracieux 41250
Tel. 02 54 46 41 57 Fax 02 54 46 05 90
No email address   14 rooms   £A

★★*de l'École*   12 rte de Montrichard, Pontlevoy 41400
Tel. 02 54 32 50 30 Fax 02 54 32 33 58
No email address   11 rooms   £A

Value for money restaurants

★★*de l'École*   12 rte de Montrichard, Pontlevoy 41400
Tel. 02 54 32 50 30 Fax 02 54 32 33 58
No email address   £A/B

★★*Côte des Monts Damnés*   Chavignol 18300
Tel. 02 48 54 01 72 Fax 02 48 54 14 24
Email restaurantcmd@wanadoo.fr   £A/B

TOURAINE RECIPES
RILLETTES DE TOURS

Rillettes can be made with any meat that can be shredded into filaments; the
process is the same. The classic one is : 500 gr. of pork belly that has 65% meat
35% fat, and 500gr. of duck legs with same proportion of fat to meat, a large
bouquet garni : 2 bay leaves, thyme, sage, rosemary and marjoram, one clove and 4
crushed juniper berries.

Cut some of the fat and melt it in a very large sauté pan; add the meats, sauté
lightly and cover with water, and cook for at least three hours until meat falls off
the bone and the water is almost evaporated. Cool enough so you can handle the
meats, which must be boned and shredded with a fork; mix with the rest of
cooking liquids and fat, season to taste and put in storage jars filling them to the
top. Keep on stirring the meat in the jars until the mixture is almost cold and set.
Those rillettes last for a long time. My favourite one is using oxtail and duck legs,
increasing the duck fat a little to make up for the lack of fat in the oxtail.

RECOMMENDED WINES

*We would be looking for some BIG Chenin here, preferably sec, to cut the greasiness
of the rillettes. The wines of Gaston Huët come to mind, of course, but the Coulée de
Serrant Savennières is equally appropriate.*

Recipes for 4 people

FRICASSÉE DE POULET À L'ANGEVINE:

Ingredients; 1.5 kg. very good quality chicken (free range, maize fed or Poulet de
Bresse) cut in 8 pieces, 50gr. butter; 200gr. tiny white baby onions, 250gr. button
mushrooms cut in quarter, 1 bottle Anjou white wine, 2,5 dl. cream, 2 yolks of
egg.

Garnish: Asparagus, carrots, new potatoes.

Melt the butter and sauté the pieces of meat in a heavy pan; add the mushrooms,
the little onions and the white wine, and cook for at least 35 minutes until the
meat is very tender. Take out the meat, onions and mushroom, put on a serving
dish and keep covered and warm. Cook the asparagus, carrots and potatoes
separately, set around the meat. Reduce the remaining cooking juices from the
meat by half: beat the two egg yolks, add to the juices gradually whilst stirring
constantly over a slow heat and until thick but do not boil, add the cream, season
to taste, and pour on the meat and the cooked garnish and vegetables.

RECOMMENDED WINES

*Red or white would suit here, but not Pinot Noir from the eastern part of the region.
Pierre-Jacques Druet's top Bourgeuil "Vaumoreau" has some biting Cabernet Franc to
cope with the asparagus, which would also go equally well with a "fat" Sancerre Blanc
such as that produced by Gérard Morin. Chicken is a versatile meat to go with wine
and a dry Chenin, perhaps not quite as heavy and intense as that which would go
with the rillettes, would also suit. The Saumur from Ch. de Hureau comes to mind as a
good value choice.*

PÊCHES DE TOURAINES À LA ROYALE:

Ingredients; Four very large and very ripe peaches, dropped in boiling water for 30
seconds to peel them. Half a bottle of Anjou Rosé, 150gr. of sugar, 250gr. of fraises
des bois or small very tasty strawberries, 2dl. of thick cream to make a chantilly,
one good tablespoon of fine de Champagne.

Make a syrup with the wine and 125gr. of sugar in a saucepan just big enough to
contain the peaches (no bigger), bring to the boil and cook the peaches. Cool the

peaches in their juices and chill very well. Meanwhile, purée the strawberries, beat the cream to soft peaks with the 25gr. of sugar remaining, and mix to the purée of strawberries. Before serving (very cold) add the fine de Champagne to the peaches. Serve peaches with the juices, and coat with the strawberry chantilly.

RECOMMENDED WINES

Well, there's bags of choice in the Loire to go with this dish, from a medium-sweet Anjou rosé from Yves Soulez through the honeyed Jasnières SGN from Joël Gigou, right up to the Côteaux de Layon wines from one of the "sugar hunters" – Patrick Baudouin.

The vineyards of the Jura in particular and Savoie produce some of the most strikingly original wines in France. They are steeped in tradition and relatively unknown outside of their homeland but some fine and very diverse styles are produced. The Jura is more marked by rolling hills than high mountains. The Savoie by contrast offers a magnificent backdrop with the Alps in the background. With the proximity of the ski fields and their thirsty winter tourists, much of what Savoie produces is disappointingly light and dilute. As in all regions though there are instances of really characterful wines being made. To enjoy the best both regions have to offer you are likely to have to visit in person.

Jura

Located to the west of Burgundy's Côte d'Or, the vineyard area is situated at altitude on the western slopes of the Jura mountains. There are a number of appellations here. The **Côte du Jura** AC encompasses the whole region and produces red, rosé and white wine. Reds and rosés are produced from the local Poulsard and Trousseau as well as Pinot Noir. Those produced from Pinot and the sturdy and structured Trousseau are the best bets. Among the whites, Chardonnay is good and can be very elegant and structured with great fruit purity. Equally interesting are the nutty, characterful Savagnin-based wines. Some oak is used but it tends to be subtle and restrained. The speciality of the region is *vin jaune*. This is not dissimilar to fino sherry in character as it is aged under a yeast film, yet it remains unfortified. Many regular Savagnin wines are also produced in a similar style but generally spend less time under the flor yeast. *Vin jaune* is remarkably ageworthy.

There are also three smaller ACs. **Arbois** produces good red and white (from the same varieties as in the Côte du Jura), *vin de paille* and sparkling wines are also produced. At **L'Étoile** dry whites from Chardonnay and Savagnin and some moderate sparkling wine are produced as well as *vin jaune*. The spectacularly sited vineyards of **Château Chalon** are solely for the production of *vin jaune*. Another speciality found throughout the region is the rare *vin de paille*. It is, like examples in the northern Rhône, a late-harvested sweet white with a hint of nutty oxidation. Both whote and red varieties are used and some examples can be very sweet indeed. Most sparkling wine is made by the traditional method and is labelled as **Crémant de Jura**. There is the odd decent example. Most growers also offer Macvin du Jura, a *vin de liqueur* which has *marc* added to fermenting grape juice. There are some characterfully nutty examples.

Savoie

This high alpine vineyard area is located to the south-west of Geneva and covers a large area. The backdrop of the Alps provdes for some of the most spectularly sited vineyards in France. The regional AC is **Vin de Savoie**. There are some good whites from the Altesse and Bergeron (Roussanne) grapes which are fresh and floral and reds mainly from Pinot Noir and Mondeuse. The latter particularly are worth considering, the wines at best are sturdy, structured and very characterful. Altesse is also known as Roussette and has its own AC, **Roussette de Savoie**. Good light, fresh, dry whites from Altesse and sparkling wines from Molette (with some Altesse) are produced under the **Seyssel AC**. The Chasselas-based whites at **Crepy AC** are generally unexciting.

Jura & Savoie vintages

With the large variation in styles throughout the two regions providing detailed vintage assessments is nigh on impossible. Most Savoie whites and reds should be drunk young and fresh. Mondeuse will though stand a little age. Of recent available vintages, 2004 offers some good well structured wines, whereas 2003 was marked as elsewhere by the summer heat and some very big sturdy wines have been produced. In the Jura Trousseau and Pinot Noir will both develop with three or four years cellaring, as will the structured, minerally Chardonnay. Savagnin is very ageworthy particularly Vin Jaune which will keep for decades. 2002 and 2000 are both showing well at the moment for Chardonnay and Savagnin and the best recent vintages to look for *Vin Jaunes* are 1995 and 1996.

A-Z of producers

Jura

DOM. PAUL BENOIT   Arbois-Pupillin

Paul Benoit La Chenevrière, Rue du Chardonnay, 39600 Pupillin
Among the very best of the small producers based in the sleepy little village of Pupillin to the south of Arbois. Paul Benoit has a number of very well-sited vineyard holdings in some of the best *terroirs* in the appellation. He has a total of some 13ha under vine and makes a full range of reds and whites as well as some intriguing Macvin, both white and, more unusually, rosé. Chardonnay is crisp and fresh in style and is vinified in *inox*. La Loge is a Savagnin vinified in oak with *bâtonnage*. It offers very impressive depth and intensity and the very characterful 2003 was nudging towards ★★★★. The Savagnin is more traditional and vinified in the same oxidative manner as the *vin jaune*, which itself has really piercing citrus and lightly nutty fruit underpinned by a marked *flor* character. The reds don't quite have the same substance. The Ploussard (the local synonym for Poulsard) is soft and fruit-driven and typically light in colour. Pinot Noir offers a little more depth and structure. The Trousseau from Arbois vineyards is firm and needs time. The top red, La Grande Chenevrière, was made for the first time in 2003 and is solely Pinot Noir. Subtle and elegant, it offers really good depth and intensity. The *vin de paille* is a blend of Savagnin, Chardonnay and Poulsard which offers better acidity and structure than many of the style as well as unctuously sweet fruit. The range is completed by a fresh, well-crafted Crémant du Jura. (DM)

● **Arbois-Pupillin** Ploussard★★ £B Pinot Noir★★ £C
● **Arbois-Pupillin** La Grande Chenevrière★★ £C
● **Arbois** Trousseau★★ £C   O **Arbois-Pupillin** La Loge★★★ £E
O **Arbois-Pupillin** Vin de Paille★★★★ £E Vin Jaune★★★★ £E
O **Arbois-Pupillin** Chardonnay★★ £B Savagnin★★★ £C   O **Crémant du Jura**★ £C

DOM. BERTHET-BONDET   Château-Chalon

Jean Berthet-Bondet 39210 Château-Chalon
First-class traditional Jura producer, making top-quality whites from Chardonnay and the local white Savagnin. Of the 2 Côtes du Jura dry whites, Alliance is produced from Chardonnay, the more complex and structured Tradition from a blend of Savagnin and Chardonnay. Both wines offer marvellously pure and intense mineral and light citrus fruit characters. In the Tradition an almost salty tang underpins the wine. The Château-Chalon, a *vin jaune*, is not dissimilar to a top level Fino sherry and has an earthy, salty character derived from the layer of *flor* yeast under which it is aged in cask. Unlike Fino, these wines have a piercing acidity, lending them the structure for very long ageing. The wines require time to show at their best. (DM)

O **Côtes du Jura** Alliance★★★ £B Tradition★★★★ £C

305

O **Château-Chalon**★★★★ £E

CH. D'ARLAY   Côtes du Jura   www.arlay.com

Alain de Laguiche   Route de Saint-Germain, 39140 Arlay

This château and historic monument dates back to the 1700s. The vineyards are planted to a mix of 17ha of red varieties and just 10ha of Chardonnay and Savagnin. Annual output is around 10,000 cases a year. The unusual red Cuvée Corail is a blend of all 5 Jura varieties. Maceration is around one and a half weeks and the wine is in a light style, very pale in colour, but offers good intensity nonetheless. The Vin Rouge is solely from Pinot Noir and is structured and quite backward for the variety. It should add more flesh with age. Chardonnay is aged for 3 years on lees and is likewise very traditional in style. It will open out splendidly with time. The Blanc Tradition is richer and fuller. A blend of Savagnin and two-thirds Chardonnay there is just a hint of oxidation from the Savagnin. The *vin jaune* is marked by a piercing citrus quality and quite different to the wines of nearby Château-Chalon. Like the Corail, the *vin de paille* is characterised by the number of varieties in the blend, 4 in this case. The residual sugar varies considerably from year to year; 2000 was much sweeter than 99, which was surprisingly dry. These are good, if somewhat traditional and austere wines which need time. Good Macvin and a Vieille Fine Réserve Marc are worth considering. (DM)

● **Côtes du Jura** Cuvée Corail★★ £B Le Vin Rouge★★ £C
O **Côtes du Jura** Chardonnay a la Reine★★ £B Tradition★★★ £C
O **Côtes du Jura** Le Vin Jaune de Garde★★★★ £E
O **Côtes du Jura** Le Vin de Paille★★★★ £F

DOM. GANEVAT   Côtes du Jura

Jean-François Ganevat   Route du Pont, La Combe, 39190 Rotalier
UK stockists:CdP

Good white and red are made here. Jean François Ganevat worked for René Monnier in Burgundy and this influence comes through in his wines. As well as a lightly citrusy and nutty Chardonnay there is a fine old-vine bottling and a dry Savagnin. These are good, if somewhat traditional and austere wines which need time. The red Poulsard is light but exuberant and has impressive intensity. The Trousseau is big, firm and structured; it demands 5 years' cellaring at least. Pinot Noir of subtle but piercing depth is found in the Cuvée Julien Ganevat. Low yields are key and the Pinot crops at barely more than 20hl/ha. The Poulsard will drink well young; the other wines will improve with age and will keep for a decade. (DM)

● **Côtes du Jura** Poulsard Vieilles Vignes★★ £C Trousseau Sous La Roche★★★ £D
● **Côtes du Jura** Cuvée Julienne Ganevat★★★ £C
O **Côtes du Jura** Cuvée Florine Ganevat★★ £C

DOM. ROLET   Arbois   www.rolet-arbois.com

Rolet family   Route de Dole, 39600 Arbois
UK stockists: SVS

This is a sizeable producer for the region but also one of the very best. The Rolets now have a total vineyard holding of 61ha: 36ha in Arbois, 21ha in the Côtes du Jura and the remaining 4ha in L'Étoile. The Arbois rosé has more structure than most. It is vinified like a red with 8 days maceration and is just a touch austere. The Poulsard Vieilles Vignes is soft and fruit-driven albeit with the complexity of old vines and the natural acidity found in all the region's wines. Trousseau is firm and structured but possesses an elegance and subtlety not found elsewhere. Pinot Noir is strawberry scented, light and elegant with good intensity. It too is edging ★★★. The top red, Memorial, is a very impressive 80/20 blend of Trousseau and Pinot Noir. Aged in oak for 15–18 months, this not only has depth and intensely striking red berry fruit but a richer texture than many other reds from the region. There are 3 fine Chardonnays, of which the Arbois is a little more tropical than the others and the L'Étoile is the most mineral and structured. All are barrel fermented in one-third new wood. The Côtes du Jura white comes from vineyards very close to Château-Chalon. It is a rich and concentrated blend of 50/50 Chardonnay and Savagnin from untopped barrels and consequently has a light *flor* character. The Arbois Tradition is a similar blend and aged in wood for 30–36 months. It offers a little more structure and intensity. The *vin jaune* is one of the very best in the region with a very subtle yeast character and intensely nutty, citrusy fruit and superb length. *Vin de paille* is rich and intense although not as sweet as some. It is a very fine, piercing blend of Poulsard, Savagnin and Chardonnay full of dried-fruit character. The Crémant du Jura is clean and fresh with a little complexity from 21 months on lees. (DM)

● **Arbois** Poulsard Vieilles Vignes★★ £B Pinot Noir★★ £C Trousseau★★★ £C
● **Arbois** Memorial★★★ £C O **Arbois** Chardonnay★★ £B
O **Côtes du Jura** Chardonnay★★ £B O **Côtes du Jura**★★★ £C
O **Arbois** Tradition★★★ £C Vin Jaune★★★★★ £E
O **Arbois** Vin de Paille★★★★★ £F O **Crémant du Jura**★★★ £C
◉ **Arbois** Poulsard★ £B

DOM. ANDRÉ & MIREILLE TISSOT   Arbois

André & Mireille Tissot   39600 Montigny-les-Arsures
UK stockists: SVS

Like the Quénards in the Savoie, there a number of Tissots in the Jura so take care to avoid confusion. André and Mireille Tissot produce some of the most outstanding wines in the region and in a very pure, fruit-driven style quite unlike many of their neighbours. This is in no small part down to the involvement of their son Stéphane who has had experience in Australia and South Africa and now handles all the winemaking. He also runs a small *négoce* business, Caves de la REINE JEANNE. There are 3 very good Chardonnays, all striking, intense and pure wines vinified in one-third new oak. Les Bruyeres is the tightest and most mineral, Les Graviers the most opulent. The fascinating Sélection is a nutty, citrusy blend of 70% Chardonnay with Savagnin, and it's the latter that really drives the wine. The varietal Savagnin is in a reductive style – the casks are kept filled and *flor* is not allowed to develop. Rich and pure, it offers great concentration with ripe lemon and grilled nut character. The *vin jaune* is of course traditional and is lightly citrusy with subtler yeast character than others as well as marvellous piercing depth and intensity of flavour. The most extraordinary wine is the Spirale *vin de paille*, a rare example from fruit genuinely aged on straw mats. The 2002 achieved just 8% alcohol with 300 grams of residual sugar and as a result it is classified as *vin de pays*. Reds are good, although not quite of the same order. Poulsard is bright with strawberry fruit, Trousseau impressively structured without hard or dried tannins. The unfiltered Pinot Noir en Barberon comes from Côtes du Jura vineyards yielding barely 20hl/ha and is aged in 60% new wood. (DM)

● **Arbois** Poulsard Vieilles Vignes★★ £B Trousseau★★★ £C
● **Côtes du Jura** Pinot Noir En Barberan★★★ £C
O **Arbois** Chardonnay la Mailloche★★★ £C Chardonnay les Bruyeres★★★ £C
O **Arbois** Chardonnay les Graviers★★★ £C Sélection★★★ £B
O **Arbois** Savagnin★★★★ £C Vin Jaune★★★★ £E
O **Spirale** Vin de Pays★★★★★ £F

DOM. JACQUES TISSOT   Arbois

Jacques Tissot   30. Rue de Courcelles, 39600 Arbois
Jacques Tissot has been running his family domaine just outside Arbois since

1962. He has a total of 32ha spread across the Arbois, Arbois-Pupillin and Côtes du Jura ACs. An extensive range is made including dry white and red, *vin jaune, vin de paille,* some Crémant du Jura and characterful local Macvin. There is a good fresh, forward Chardonnay as well as a richer Grande Réserve. The Arbois Nature from young-vine Savaginin is young and fresh with some depth and intensity and a nice citrus undercurrent. The Blanc-Typé is a more seriously structured 50/50 blend of Savagnin and Chardonnay. The varietal Arbois Savagnin is regularly topped up in barrel, resulting in a rich and characterful style with loads of nutty, citrus character. There are 2 *vin jaune* bottlings. The Côtes du Jura is rich and intense with piercing fruit but it is the splendid Arbois bottling that stands out. It has a marvellous citrus depth to its fruit and magnificent intensity. Of the reds, the Poulsard La Ronde from a *lieu-dit* is soft and approachable, as is the Tradition, which blends in a little Pinot Noir. The very good and well-structured Trousseau Grande Réserve is a real *vin de gard* that needs time to shed a touch of youthfully hard tannin. The Côtes du Jura Pinot Grande Réserve is bright and elegant with a firm and fresh undercurrent and should develop well with 5 years' age. The top whites all demand up to 10 years' patience and the *vin jaune* labels will keep for decades. (DM)

- **Arbois** Trousseau Grande Reserve★★★ £C
- **Côtes du Jura** Pinot Noir Grande Reserve★★★ £C
- **Arbois-Pupillin** Poulsard La Ronde★★ £B ● **Arbois** Tradition★★ £B
- O **Arbois** Chardonnay★★ £B Naturé★★ £C Blanc-Typé★★★ £C Savagnin★★★ £C
- O **Côtes du Jura** Vin Jaune★★★★ £E O **Arbois** Vin Jaune★★★★★ £E

Savoie

DOM. BELLUARD Vin de Savoie

Patrick & Dominique Belluard 74130 Ayze
UK stockists:**CdP**

This 13-ha domaine south of Crépy in the Haute-Savoie is run organically and is in the process of being converted to full biodynamic cultivation. The *terroir* has real potential with vineyards planted at a significant altitude of some 450m on slopes with well-drained glacial soils and a southerly aspect. As elsewhere, these Alpine vineyards benefit from warm summer days and cool nights, which ensure good acidity and structure in the fruit. The Gringet white is a piercing, fruit-driven style which is not put through malolactic, fresh acidity being the key to its style. The variety is thought to be related to the Jura's Savagnin and although it is less obviously weighty it shares some of the characteristic citrus and lightly peachy character found in that variety. The Mondeuse is darkly coloured with a classic dark cherry twist to its fruit and is well structured with youthfully firm but supple tannins. It will benefit from 3 or 4 years' patience. A good Ayze Mousseux is also produced. (DM)

- **Vin de Savoie** Mondeuse★★ £B O **Vin de Savoie** Gringet★★ £B

DOM. G & G BOUVET Vin de Savoie

Henriette Bouvet 73250 Frétérive

An extensive range of both red and white is made at this 13-ha domaine just to the east of Chignin. These are spectacularly sited vineyards, sloping down from the rock wall behind the village, the Massif des Bauges. Argile-calcareous soils and a south-south-east exposure provide an excellent *terroir*, where those international favourites Chardonnay and Cabernet Sauvignon are planted as well as the more established local varieties. There is a soft, forward, fruit-driven Roussette de Savoie. Chardonnay is in a quite cool-climate style with some oak. Chignin-Bergeron is from Roussanne and is lightly floral with a subtle nutty undercurrent. A step up is the Le B de Bouvet, also a Chignin-Bergeron, which is aged in oak. The white Grand Savoie is a blend of Chardonnay, Jacquère and Altesse (Roussette) also aged in oak, but it doesn't quite have the same depth and fruit definition. Reds are the main focus here. Gamay Le Vignoble and Pinot Noir Le Beau Chêne are both soft and full of berry fruit. The Mondeuse La Persanne offers greater depth of both flavour and colour. The L de Bouvet Mondeuse Prestige is fuller and richer as a result of a longer *cuvaison* and ageing for 3–6 months in oak. The Grand Savoie red is a blend of Mondeuse, Pinot Noir and Gamay. Round and supple with good berry fruit, this is a little softer than the Mondeuse Prestige. There are 2 top reds. Amariva is a fascinating blend of Cabernet Sauvignon and Persan, an old variety that has virtually disappeared in Savoie. It is aged in new wood and the Cabernet dominates the blend with a pronounced minty, cool-climate character but sufficient blackcurrant and cedar fruit behind, while the Persan adds a slightly rustic quality. The Mondeuse Cuée Guillaume Charles is one of the best examples of the variety in the region. The concentrated dark cherry and bramble fruit comfortably absorbs the oak, some of it new. The top reds in particular will benefit from 4 or 5 years' ageing. (DM)

● **Vin de Savoie** Grand Savoie★★ £B Amariva★★★ £B
● **Vin de Savoie** Cuvée Guillaume Charles Mondeuse★★★ £D
● **Vin de Savoie** Mondeuse La Persanne★ £B L de Bouvet Mondeuse★★ £B
● **Vin de Savoie** Gamay Le Vignoble★ £B Pinot Noir Le Beau Chêne★ £B
○ **Vin de Savoie** Chardonnay Prestige★★ £B Grand Savoie★★ £B
○ **Vin de Savoie Chignin-Bergeron**★★ £B Le B de Bouvet★★ £B
○ **Roussette de Savoie**★★ £B

DOM. ANDRÉ & MICHEL QUÉNARD   Vin de Savoie

André & Michel Quénard Tonnéry, 73800 Chignin
UK stockists:
Perhaps the best known of the various branches of the Quénards in Chignin. There are 21ha of vineyards and whites are the main plantings with 16ha of Jacquère, Bergeron and Altesse. The regular Vin de Savoie and Roussette de Savoie whites are floral and fruit-driven, while the Chignin has a touch of minerality. The Chignin-Bergeron Les Terasses is honeyed, nutty and intensely mineral in character. A fine old-vine Chignin is also made. Among reds from the small holding of Gamay, Mondeuse and Pinot Noir the Chignin Mondeuse Vieilles Vignes is particularly striking, with concentrated black cherry fruit and a real old-vine quality. It will benefit from 5 or so years of ageing. (DM)

● **Vin de Savoie** Mondeuse Vieilles Vignes★★★ £C
○ **Vin de Savoie Chignin-Bergeron** Les Terrasses★★★ £B
○ **Roussette de Savoie**★★ £B ○ **Vin de Savoie Chignin**★ £B

DOM. J-P & J-F QUÉNARD   Vin de Savoie

Jean-Pierre & Jean-François Quénard Le Villard, 73800 Chignin
This domaine is quite a bit larger than very near neighbour and namesake Raymond QUÉNARD but quality is similarly impressive. Gamay is simple and straightforward. Mondeuse is altogether more serious. The regular bottling is deep and spicy, full of dark berry fruit and spices with not inconsiderable tannin; 2003 was very ripe and classy. The Séléction de Terroir is a vineyard selection aged in used oak, which gives the wine extra weight and dimension on the palate. Both will benefit from 5 years' ageing. Of 2 Chignin whites made from Jacquère, the Anne de la Biguerne comes from 65-year-old vines and is richer and more intense. The Chignin-Bergeron Les Demoiselles comes from a 3-ha south-west-facing plot grown on calcareous soils and is cool-fermented to emphasise its floral, lightly tropical and minerally fruit. All 3 should be drunk young. An old-vine bottling, Tradition, is produced from a specific 0.6-ha plot. This is made from Roussanne and vinification and ageing

are in used small oak. It comes from the last pass through the vineyard and should develop well with 2 or 3 years. (DM)

● **Vin de Savoie** Gamay★ £B   Mondeuse★★★ £C
● **Vin de Savoie** Mondeuse Cuvée Séléction de Terroir★★★ £C
○ **Vin de Savoie Chignin**★★ £B   Anne de la Biguerne★★ £B
○ **Vin de Savoie Chignin-Bergeron** Les Demoiselles★★ £C
○ **Vin de Savoie** Cepage Tradition★★★ £C

DOM. RAYMOND QUÉNARD   Vin de Savoie

Raymond Quénard   Le Villard, 73800 Chignin

Raymond Quénard makes a small range of good to very good red and white from his holding, a mere 4ha in the village of Chignin. The larger part of his domaine he recently handed over to his son Pascal who now makes his own wine separately. The 3ha of whites are evenly split between Jacquère and Bergeron, while the red plantings comprise Gamay and Mondeuse. The Gamay is a good example – full, fruit-driven and plush, to be drunk young. The structured but sufficiently supple Mondeuse is more serious, full of dark berry, spice and cherry fruit. It is almost rustic but in the best sense. The Chignin Cépage Jacquère is made from very old vines. Vinified in *inox* with no malolactic, it is very pure, deep and minerally with great intensity. The Chignin-Bergeron (100% Roussanne) is fuller and more opulent in style with a touch of oak. Old vines again contribute to the style and quality. A late-harvest Chignin-Bergeron is also produced. (DM)

● **Vin de Savoie** Gamay★ £B   Mondeuse★★★ £C
○ **Vin de Savoie Chignin** Cepage Jacquere Vieilles Vignes★★★ £C
○ **Vin de Savoie Chignin-Bergeron**★★★ £C

OTHER WINES OF NOTE

Jura
FRUITIÈRE VINICOLE D'ARBOIS ○ **Arbois** Chardonnay★ £B
○ **Arbois** Cuvée Bethanie★★ £B   ○ **Arbois** Savagnin Grand Sélection★★★ £B
○ **Arbois** Vin Jaune★★★★ £E
DOM. JEAN MACLE ○ **Côtes du Jura**★★★ £B   ○ **Château-Chalon**★★★★ £E
DOM. JACQUES PUFFENEY ○ **Arbois** Chardonnay★★★ £B
CAVES DE LA REINNE JEANNE ○ **Côtes du Jura** Chardonnay★★ £B
○ **Arbois** Trousseau★★ £B

Savoie
PIERRE BONIFACE ○ **Vin de Savoie** Jacquère★ £B
PATRICK CHARLIN ○ **Bugey** Montagnieu Altesse★★ £B
CH. DE RIPAILLE ○ **Vin de Savoie**★★ £B
DOM. MICHEL GRISARD ○ **Roussette de Savoie**★★ £B
DOM. EDMOND JACQUIN ○ **Vin de Savoie** Chardonnay★★ £B
○ **Roussette de Savoie**★★ £B
BRUNO LUPIN ○ **Roussette de Savoie** Frangy★★ £B
DOM. LOUIS MAGNIN ○ **Roussette de Savoie**★★ £B
● **Vin de Savoie** Mondeuse Vieilles Vignes★★★ £C
DOM. VULLIEN ○ **Roussette de Savoie**★★ £B

Work in progress!!

Producers under consideration for the next edition
LUCIEN AVIET (CÔTES DU JURA)
DOM. DUPASQUIER (VIN DE SAVOIE)

DOM. DURAND-PERRON (CHATEAU-CHALON)
DOM. LABET (CÔTES DU JURA)
DOM. LIGIER (ARBOIS)
DOM. DE LA PINTE (ARBOIS)

Author's choice (DM)

A dozen good value reds and whites

DOM. PAUL BENOIT ● Arbois-Pupillin Ploussard
DOM. BERTHET-BONDET O Côtes du Jura Alliance
CH. D'ARLAY O Côtes du Jura Chardonnay a la Reine
DOM. GANEVAT O Côtes du Jura Cuvée Florine Ganevat
DOM. ROLET O Arbois Chardonnay
ANDRE & MIREILLE TISSOT O Arbois Séléction
JACQUES TISSOT O Arbois Chardonnay
DOM. RIJCKAERT O Bandol Tradition
DOM. BELLUARD ● Vin de Savoie Mondeuse
ANDRÉ & MICHEL QUÉNARD O Roussette de Savoie
DOM. RAYMOND QUÉNARD O Vin de Savoie Chignin-Bergeron Les Terrasses
DOM. J-P & J-F QUÉNARD O Vin de Savoie Chignin

A selection of classics from the Jura

DOM. BERTHET-BONDET O Château-Chalon
CH. D'ARLAY O Côtes du Jura Tradition
DOM. GANEVAT ● Côtes de Jura Julienne Ganevat
DOM. PAUL BENOIT ● Arbois-Pupillin La Loge
DOM. ROLET O Arbois Tradition
DOM. ROLET O Arbois Vin Jaune
ANDRE & MIREILLE TISSOT O Arbois Savagnin
ANDRE & MIREILLE TISSOT O Spirale Von de Pays
JACQUES TISSOT O Arbois Savagnin
JACQUES PUFFENEY O Arbois Chardonnay

Some of the best of Savoie

DOM. BELLUARD O Vin de Savoie Gringet
G & G BOUVET ● Vin de Savoie Amariva
BRUNO LUPIN O Roussette de Savoie Frangy
MICHEL GRISARD O Roussette de Savoie
ANDRÉ & MICHEL QUÉNARD O Vin de Savoie Chignin-Bergeron Les Terrasses
DOM. J-P & J-F QUÉNARD ● Vin de Savoie Mondeuse Cuvée Sélection de Terroir
DOM. RAYMOND QUÉNARD ● Vin de Savoie Mondeuse
DOM. LOUIS MAGNIN ● Vin de Savoie Mondeuse Vieilles Vignes

RECOMMENDED HOTELS AND RESTAURANTS - JURA & SAVOIE

Top Hotels

★★★★★*La Maison du Marc Veyrat* 13 Vieille rte des Pensières, Veyrier-du-Lac 74290
Tel. 04 50 60 24 00 Fax 04 50 60 23 63
Email reservation@marcveyrat.fr 11 rooms　　　　£H

★★★★*Grand Hotel* ave. des Thermes, Divonne-les-Bains 01220
Tel. 04 50 40 34 34 Fax 04 50 40 34 24
Email stmartin@relaischateau.com 116 rooms　　　£E/H

Top Restaurants

★★★★★*La Maison du Marc Veyrat* 13 Vieille rte des Pensières, Veyrier-du-Lac 74290
Tel. 04 50 60 24 00 Fax 04 50 60 23 63
Email reservation@marcveyrat.fr　　　　£H

311

★★★*Jean-Paul Jeunet*   rue de l'Hôtel de Ville, Arbois 39600
Tel. 03 84 66 05 67 Fax 03 84 66 24 20
Email jpjeunet@wanadoo,.fr   £F/H

Value for money Hotels

★*Auberge St-Simond*   130 ave. St-Simond, Aix-les-Bains 73100
Tel. 04 79 88 35 02 Fax 04 79 88 38 45
Email auberge@saintsimond.com   28 rooms   £A

★*Nouvel Hotel*   50 rue Lecourbe, Lons-le-Saunier 39000
Tel. 03 84 47 20 67 Fax 03 84 43 27 49
Email nouvel.hotel@wanadoo.fr   26 rooms   £A

Value for money restaurants

★*Le Comtois*   Doucier 39130
Tel. 03 84 25 71 21 Fax 03 84 25 71 21
Email restaurant.comtois2wanadoo.fr   £A/E

★*Le Cordonant*   Cordon 74700
Tel. 04 50 58 34 56 Fax 04 50 47 95 57
Email lecordonant@wanadoo.fr   £A

SAVOIE/DAUPHINE RECIPES

GRATIN SAVOYARD: for 4 people: *Ingredients:* 500gr. of large baking potatoes, 2.5dl. of milk mixed with 2.5dl. cream, salt and pepper, a pinch of nutmeg, two cloves of garlic (optional), 200gr of Comté or Gruyère cheese (or any hard cheese).

Cook the potatoes in their skins until almost done but firm. Peel and slice thinly. Bring the cream and milk to the boil, add salt and pepper and nutmeg; delicately mix the potatoes and milk and cream mix, and cook, stirring from time to time to prevent from sticking for about 5 mns. Take a large baking tray, butter it and rub a clove of garlic generously. Put a layer of the potato mix and a layer of grated cheese, repeat twice, finishing with cheese, and put in the oven until cooked and golden. Serve immediately.

RECOMMENDED WINES

This dish could either be a meal in its own or an accompaniment to meat dishes such as the one below. On its own, a light, creamy white would go best, such as a Chignin from Domaine Quénard. If accompanied by meat, then Quénard's Mondeuse, a softly structured red would be best.

ESCALOPE SAVOYARDE: for 4 people: *Ingredients:* 4 escallops weighing 100 to 150 gr. each, you can use veal, turkey or chicken breasts. 60 gr of dried cêpes, morilles or any other dried mushrooms. (You can also use 150gr. fresh Paris mushrooms); butter, 3 spoonfuls each of Cognac and Madeira, a dash of fresh cream, four very thin slices of ham, and some grated Comté or Gruyère cheese.

Soak the dried mushrooms in just enough water to soften them. Sauté the escallops in a little butter. Butter an oven dish large enough to take the escallops, put the escallops, a slice of ham on each; sprinkle a nice coat of grated cheese and leave on the side until the last minute. Strain the mushrooms and sauté in the same pan as the meat; flambé with Cognac, add Madeira and the soaking juice of the mushrooms (must not exceed 2dl.) Reduce a little. At the last minute, glaze the meat in the oven until golden, and finish the sauce with a dash of cream, salt and pepper

RECOMMENDED WINES

The Mondeuse above would go perfectly well here as would "Memorial", an 80/20 blend of Trousseau and Pinot Noir from Domaine Rolet in the Jura. A white Vin de Savoie Cépage

Tradition, made with Roussanne, would also go well.

FLOGNARDES AUX POIRES. For 6 people: *Ingredients:* 500gr. of ripe pears, 100gr. flour, 100gr. sugar, 3 eggs, 2dl. milk and 2dl. cream or 4dl. of milk and 50gr. of butter, a liqueur glass of Cognac. Peal the pears and cut very thinly lengthwise. Butter a round oven dish big enough to put the pears in a daisy shape. Caramelise the sugar, add the milk, cream and/or butter and the Cognac. Cool the mixture. Put the flour in a basin, break the eggs in the middle, start mixing, adding the milk mix a little at a time. Pour the lot on the pears, sprinkle a little more sugar and bake until pears are cooked and set.

RECOMMENDED WINES

Some Vin de Paille from the Jura would be the order of the day here and Domaine Tissot's extraordinary "Spirale" fits the bill with the 2002 vintage achieving just 8% alcohol and 300 grams of residual sugar.

No longer undiscovered gems of French wine, the top vineyards of the Rhône are producing increasingly widely distributed wines of world class. The established and increasing number of Rhône super-cuvées are now some of the most exciting as well as expensive wines in the world. However, there remains a vast sea of simple, sometimes disappointingly poor wine at the bottom end of the market. Two-thirds of all wine made throughout the Rhône Valley is generic AC Côtes du Rhône, although the region is improving fast and smart and slick generic marketing is being allied to generally higher quality standards. It is worth seeking out the ever-increasing number of young growers, mainly in the south, who are endeavouring to produce wines of quality and style at still very fair prices, rather than selling to the co-ops or large négociants.

The Northern Rhône

The northern and southern parts of the valley are very different geographically. The Northern Rhône stretches south down the narrow valley of the River Rhône, from Vienne in the north to Valence in the south. The vineyards of **Côte-Rôtie** are on steep, precipitous terraces and provide some of the world's most challenging viticultural conditions. The name Côte-Rôtie means 'roasted slope'. This may be the most northerly of the Rhône appellations, but the vineyards have a superb aspect facing south-east and the soils are ideal for viticulture – high in minerals, relatively infertile and very well drained.

There are only some 200 ha under vine, with a number of *cru* sections identified. The best quality wine comes from the centre of the appellation. Côte Brune to the north of Ampuis produces wines of fuller body, the Côte Blonde to the south lighter more elegant wines often with Viognier blended in, which is permitted here. The style of Côte-Rôtie is perhaps less overtly muscular than the wines of Hermitage and Cornas and its climate can be very marginal in achieving full ripeness. In great years, when everything comes together at vintage, these wines at their best are quite sublime.

Immediately south of Côte-Rôtie, the vineyards of **Condrieu** continue on the western bank of the river. They are planted on granite and sandstone rather than on the schistous soils to the north. The slope becomes less precipitous and the conditions are more suitable for that uniquely perfumed, aromatic variety Viognier. Widely planted now further afield, from the Languedoc to California, the variety has only come into vogue in the last decade or so. While the weight and aromatic power of the wines can be almost overwhelming, Viognier is a difficult variety to grow and Condrieu lacks the structure of other great French whites. The majority are best drunk in their first two or three years. An increasing number are now barrel-fermented on lees with *bâtonnage* and a few more are produced as late-harvest and very occasionally botrytis-affected wines. The best of these can be stunning.

The most extensive appellation in the north is **Saint-Joseph**. It encompasses the southern part of Condrieu and runs right down the western bank of the river to the borders of Cornas, just to the north of Valence. The reds are produced from Syrah, while the whites are a blend of Marsanne and Roussanne. The best wines are produced from the gravel-based soils close to the river. An impressive number of very good wines, both red and white, have been made in recent years and prices are rising. The best sites have real potential.

The great hill of **Hermitage** and its wines, dark, brooding and powerful, are perhaps the quintessential expression of classic northern Rhône reds. There are many fewer producers here than at Côte-Rôtie and a mere 131 ha of vineyards. The hill is split up into seven different *crus* or *lieux-dits* with varying soil types. One grower, Jean-Louis Chave, is able to draw on all seven in blending his reds. The Syrah is joined by whites based on Marsanne with some Roussanne. These can be remarkably long lived, often more so than the reds. New oak and destemming in the cellar are playing an increasing role and the whites often see barrel-fermentation. More often than not here though, the oak is used rather than new. Red Hermitage should be cellared, as it is slow-developing. The white, too, needs years to show at its best. It can be approachable for a couple of years and then mysteriously close up, so if you plan to drink it young, do so within a year or two or else you will be very disappointed.

Surrounding the hill of Hermitage are the vineyards of **Crozes-Hermitage**. The same grapes are used but the vineyard area is much larger and encompasses some 1,238 ha of vines. The better wines are made on isolated outcrops of granite and there can be a wide variation in quality. The best are very good and generally well-priced and there are an increasing number of relatively highly priced special *cuvées*.

To the south and on the west bank of the river opposite Valence, are the appellations of **Cornas,** which borders southern Saint-Joseph, and immediately to its south Saint-Péray. Cornas is dense and muscular Syrah. It shares more in common with Hermitage than Côte-Rôtie, which is not surprising given its near proximity. A wide range of styles are produced, from the modern oak-influenced wines of Jean-Luc Colombo to the fiercely traditional style of Auguste and Pierre-Marie Clape. At their finest, these are dark-fruited, intense and splendidly long-lived expressions of Syrah.

Many of the Cornas growers also produce the still and sparkling wines of **Saint-Péray**; the still having greater potential on the whole. They are blended from Marsanne and Roussanne, like their white counterparts to the north. A further sparkling wine comes from a little further south-east under the **Clairette de Die** AC, which produces lighter semi-sweet sparkling Muscats. **Crémant de Die** is now the AC for dry sparklers from Clairette. At best they are crisp and fresh. There also some dry white still wines produced under the **Châtillon-en-Diois** appellation, from cool-planted Chardonnay and Aligoté in the same area.

The Southern Rhône

While the north meanders down a narrow river valley, giving it its unique viticultural environment, the southern Rhône covers a much greater area, and is extensively planted with vines. The total vineyard area planted in the north is just under 2,700 ha, whereas the total for the whole region is some 75,000 ha and nearly 42,000 ha of that Côtes du Rhône. The climate is altogether warmer in the south and Grenache is the mainstay variety. There can be a significant influence on the region from the cold Mistral wind, which blows down out of the Alps. While it has some influence in the north, it can cause devastation in the south, with not only physical damage to vineyards but stressing of the vines, causing them to shut down. The same Mistral can on occasion help in ripening fruit close to *vendange* and keeping cellars free of humidity.

The most important quality region in the south is **Châteauneuf-du-Pape**. This is a sizeable appellation with some 3,084 ha of vineyards. Quality has soared in recent very good vintages and an increasing number of growers are now bottling their own wine. The main Châteauneuf variety is Grenache, but there are 13 permitted varieties in the red blend, a number of them white. Syrah and Mourvèdre are also very important in lending structure and grip. The

315

Châteauneuf soils are varied with clay, gravel and stone all playing a role. The larger *galets roulés*, the famous round stones that store up heat and reflect it onto the vines at night are not universally found throughout the appellation and many consider the clay to be the key component in controlling moisture supply.

Among current trends an increasing number of growers are making limited-production special *cuvées* from old vines. While some of these are very splendid wines, there is some question as to whether the quality of the regular bottlings suffers as a consequence. The best red Châteauneuf is rich, heady, almost exotic and very ageworthy. The best will easily continue to improve for a decade or more. The white can be good, floral and nutty and there are some more serious structured wines as well, with oak playing a limited role. In general the whites should be drunk young.

To the north and west of Châteauneuf-du-Pape and the ancient Roman town of Orange are the **Côtes du Rhône-Villages** and the separate appellations of **Gigondas** and **Vacqueyras**. The best vineyards of Gigondas are planted on the slopes of the Dentelles de Montmirail, the small range that merges into the hills of the Vaucluse. The wines are dense, massive and brooding. They tend to lack the refinement of the very greatest Châteauneufs, but they can offer not only excellent quality but also value for money. Like Gigondas, Grenache is the most important variety in Vacqueyras, which was awarded its own AC in 1990. The wines are generally lighter than Gigondas and an increasing amount of Syrah is now being used. There are even some varietal wines being produced. The best have an intoxicating combination of ripe dark berry fruit and a marked *garrigues* character.

There are 16 villages which can append their names after the Côtes du Rhône-Villages name. Among these are **Cairanne**, **Rasteau**, **Sablet** and **Beaumes-de-Venise** to the south and **Valréas**, **Vinsobres** and **Saint-Maurice** further north where, unsurprisingly, the Syrah is planted with greater success. It is the southern villages, though, and particularly Cairanne, which are producing the greatest number of stylish wines. At their best these express vibrant and complex dark fruit and subtle herbal notes. Those wines produced from old vines can be both excellent value and remarkably impressive. Outside these 16 villages there are several thousand hectares of vines producing straight Côtes du Rhône-Villages. A number of very good wines under both this appellation and the humble **Côtes du Rhône** label are now being produced. The latter tend to emphasise their forward fruit, but there are also some very serious and ageworthy wines being produced. Some of the better Rhône-Villages domaines may also have vineyards outside the appellation boundaries, or may chose to label younger-vine *cuvées* as Côtes du Rhône.

There are also two regional specialities, which have their own appellations. **Muscat de Beaumes de Venise** is a floral, grapey fortified Muscat. It is not late-harvested and tends to lack the quality found in the Muscat de Rivesaltes wines of the Roussillon. **Rasteau** is a fortified red *vin doux naturel* produced from Grenache that can develop marked *rancio* notes with cask age. This AC should not be confused with Côtes du Rhône-Villages Rasteau, where some of the best modern southern reds are being made.

To the west of Châteauneuf-du-Pape are the appellations of **Lirac** and **Tavel**. The latter is for rosé only, Lirac for both rosé and, of greater importance from a quality point of view, some very good Grenache-based reds planted in the limestone-rich soils. The rosé can often be excessively high in alcohol and dull. Further to the east is the newly developed appellation of the Costières de Nîmes

Towards the outer extremities of the Rhône are four other appellations. To the north of the Côtes du Rhône-Villages sector, west and east respectively of the River Rhône, are the **Côtes du Vivarais** and the **Coteaux du Tricastin**. To the south in the Vaucluse are the vineyards of the **Côtes du Ventoux**, where encouraging progress is being made by a number of domaines and reds of some substance are being produced. Immediately south again, on the borders of Provence, is the **Côtes du Lubéron**. The odd exciting red is beginning to emerge and there are some stylish whites as well. To the far east towards the Alpes some good reds and whites are also emerging from the **Coteaux de Pierrvert**.

There are a number of *vin de pays* classifications. In the northern Rhône the important one is the **Vin de Pays des Collines Rhodaniennes**, under which some impressive red and white is produced. Two important southern *vins de pays* offering wines largely based on Grenache (but also Cabernet Sauvignon in the case of the former) are the **Vin de Pays de la Principauté d'Orange** and further south the **Vin de Pays de Vaucluse**.

Just to the west of the River Rhône is the emerging region of the **Costières de Nîmes**. Not surprisingly the wine here has more in common with the blends of the southern Rhône than the rest of the Languedoc and for this reason is covered here. Intense, strawberry-scented, Grenache-based reds are being produced by a number of good domaines and increasing use is being made of Mourvèdre. Many of these properties are also making rich, stylish blends of Cabernet Sauvignon and Syrah, generally labelled as **Vin de Pays du Gard**.

A-Z of producers by appellation/commune

Northern Rhône

317

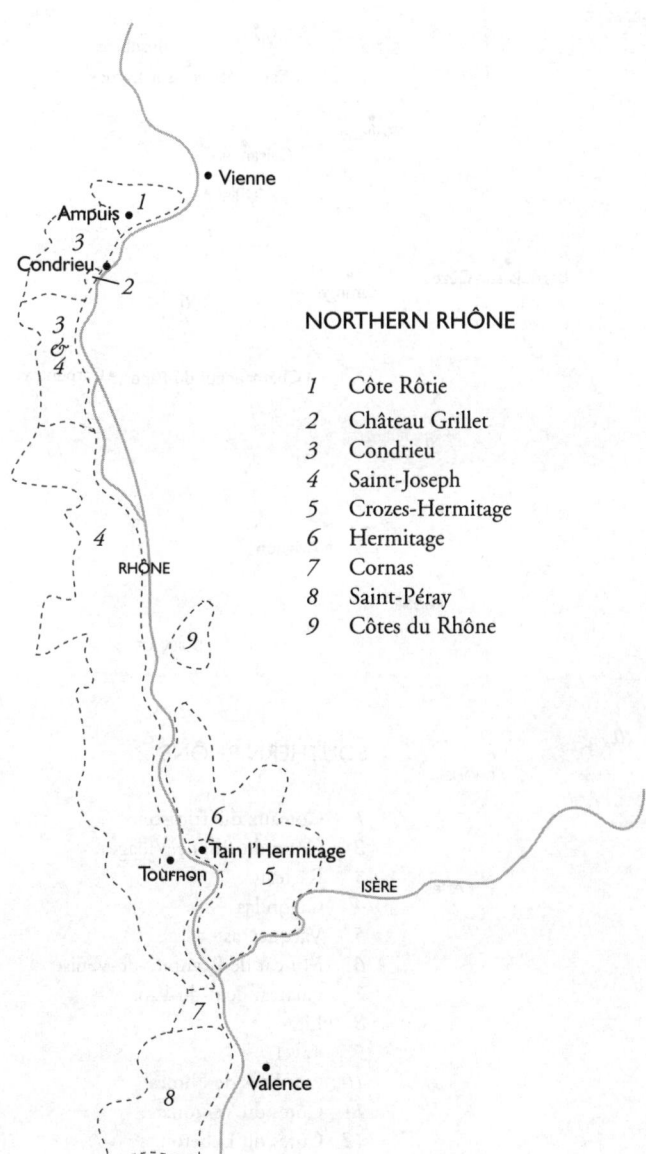

NORTHERN RHÔNE

1 Côte Rôtie
2 Château Grillet
3 Condrieu
4 Saint-Joseph
5 Crozes-Hermitage
6 Hermitage
7 Cornas
8 Saint-Péray
9 Côtes du Rhône

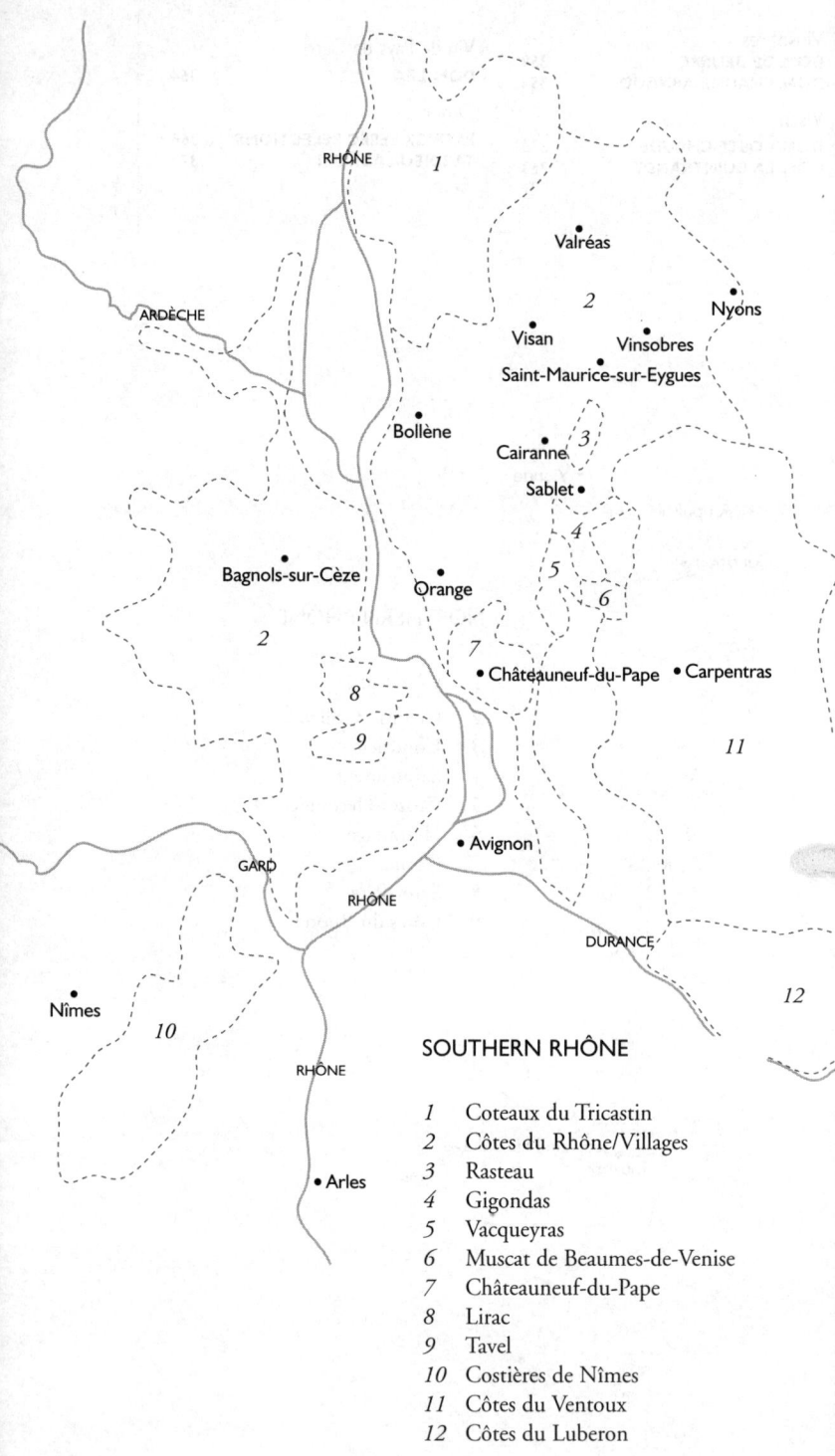

RHÔNE

1

Valréas

2

Nyons

Visan   Vinsobres

ARDÈCHE

Saint-Maurice-sur-Eygues

Bollène

Cairanne   *3*

Sablet

4

5

Bagnols-sur-Cèze   Orange   *6*

2   *7*

8   Châteauneuf-du-Pape   Carpentras

9   *11*

Avignon

GARD

RHÔNE

DURANCE

12

Nîmes

10

RHÔNE

SOUTHERN RHÔNE

1   Coteaux du Tricastin
2   Côtes du Rhône/Villages
3   Rasteau
4   Gigondas
5   Vacqueyras
6   Muscat de Beaumes-de-Venise
7   Châteauneuf-du-Pape
8   Lirac
9   Tavel
10 Costières de Nîmes
11 Côtes du Ventoux
12 Côtes du Luberon

Arles

Rhône Valley vintages

The run of vintages from 1998 to 2001 was remarkable in both the north and south of the Rhône Valley. The wines were either very good or excellent. The best wines from these years are becoming extraordinarily scarce but it is still well worth your while to hunt around for them. 2004 is likely to be worth following as well. Over the same period, the lesser Rhône-Villages wines have performed in a similarly impressive manner to those at Châteauneuf-du-Pape. The top wines will keep very well, 10 even 20 years in the best examples. The lesser wines from recent years will last comfortably for five years or more.

2004: A much easier year for growers in both the north and south of the region. The best reds look like they have good depth with deep colours and form and in the main well ripened tannins. Likely to be of a similar level to 2001 in the north and 1999 in the south.

2003: The super warm summer of resulted in some good wines from this vintage in the north. The key was who had harnessed the ripening of their grape tannins best, a difficult feat. Potentially good in the south, some wines are very alcoholic though and achieving balance with Grenache will be the key.

2002: After the previous four bountiful vintages this was a disappointment. There was very heavy rain in the north requiring extreme care and selectivity by growers to achieve any real quality. In the south it was a similar tale of woe with heavy flooding. The wines are likely to be for early drinking.

2001: This was very good throughout the valley, if not quite hitting the heights of 1999 for the northern appellations or 2000 for the south. Nevertheless these are impressive and cellarworthy examples, a smaller than normal yield helping to ensure this. White Hermitage is very ageworthy.

2000: A generally very good year, particularly in the south with good crop levels and some very rich, profound and complex wines being made. The best are ripe, very full and approachable. Not quite the same quality in the north, but good and very ageworthy wines were produced. Côte-Rôtie is the most successful among the reds.

1999: A very good year throughout the north, with well-structured, opulent and heady wines being produced in all the major appellations. Conditions were excellent with a balmy and dry summer and adequate rainfall. The wines are surprisingly forward and approachable but should be long-lived. The south was good to very good but lacked the sheer quality of 1998 and 2000. The wines will be a little lighter but the best will age very well.

1998: The northern appellations fared well, producing very good results after a solid 1997. The wines are generally sizeable and and masculine in structure. They should turn out to be very good cellaring prospects but without the opulence or elegance of 1999. In the south the vintage was spectacularly good. The wines are immensely opulent, ripe and exotic but have a fine balance and structure. They will be enjoyable in their relative youth but are excellent cellaring prospects.

1997: A generally average year at best in the south after spring frost damage. The summer was very hot and the wines have neither perfect balance nor ripeness. Almost all should be drunk now. The north fared better, with good quality. Saint-Joseph and Crozes-Hermitage are drinking well now.

1996: A pretty moderate year with the best results in the north, where the top wines have higher than normal acidity after a cold wet summer and windy ripening period. Some good wines were produced in a relatively austere style.

321

The south produced soft, forward reds somewhat lacking in structure. They should now be drunk.

1995: Generally the best year since 1990 for reds with the exception of the magnificent 1991 Côte-Rôties. Yields were low but a warm and propitious summer and favourable harvest produced wines of impressive density and extract both in the north and the south. Whites were somewhat less impressive and will be surprisingly short-lived. They should be drunk very soon except for the best white Hermitage.

1994: These wines are marked more by their soft tannins and elegance than their power and are for the mid-term. Many are drinking well now.

1993: For much of the north this was a disastrous vintage. Côte-Rôtie was a little better but not much. Châteauneuf-du-Pape produced some soft agreeable reds which need finishing up.

1992: Sadly the vintage was badly affected by rain in September and most wines were light and soft. Most should have been drunk by now.

1991: This was a good to very good year in the northern Rhône and in Côte-Rôtie in particular. There was quite marked variation and some producers were more successful than others, particularly in Cornas and Hermitage. The south was disappointing and the wines should by now have been drunk.

1990: A superb year for great long-lived Hermitage. These will need more time to achieve their full potential. Côte-Rôtie did not quite match the superb 91s. Cornas and Côte-Rôtie are both drinking well now, as are some of the excellent wines produced at Châteauneuf-du-Pape.

1989: A good to very good vintage, particularly at Hermitage and Cornas and in the south for top reds. White Hermitage was also good and is drinking well now as are the generally fleshy reds. These are not the great structured wines of 1990 but are perfect now if you have them cellared or come across them.

1988: This was a very good year for classic northern Rhône reds; the best Hermitage will probably benefit from a little more time. Also tremendous exotic white Hermitage which is drinking well now. Impressive in the south but only the top wines will still be at their best.

Earlier Years: 1985 was good in both the north and the south. 1983 produced some excellent long-lived Hermitage. Châteauneuf-du-Pape in 1981 is worth considering from very top producers. A few good 1979s from both north and south are still drinking well. 1978 was a truly great year in the north, with some very fine Châteauneuf also. Other very good earlier years for the north were 1971, 1970, 1969, 1966, 1964 and 1961.

Rhône Valley vintage chart

	Côte-Rôtie	Red Hermitage	White Hermitage	Châteauneuf -du-Pape
2004	★★★★ A	★★★★ A	★★★★ A	★★★★ A
2003	★★★/★★★★ A	★★★/★★★★ A	★★★★ A	★★★/★★★★ A
2002	★★ B	★★ A	★★/★★★★ A	★★ A
2001	★★★★ A	★★★★ A	★★★★/★★★★★ A	★★★★ A
2000	★★★★/★★★★★ A	★★★★ A	★★★★ A	★★★★/★★★★★ A
1999	★★★★/★★★★★ A	★★★★/★★★★★ A	★★★★/★★★★★ A	★★★★ B
1998	★★★★ A	★★★★ A	★★★★ A	★★★★★ B
1997	★★★/★★★★ B	★★★/★★★★ A	★★★/★★★★ A	★★★ C
1996	★★★ C	★★★ C	★★★/★★★★ B	★★/★★★ C
1995	★★★★CB	★★★★ B	★★★/★★★★ C	★★★★ C
1994	★★★/★★★★ C	★★★/★★★★ C	★★★/★★★★ C	★★★ C
1991	★★★★★ B	★★★★ C	★★★★ C	★/★★ D
1990	★★★★ C	★★★★★ B	★★★★/★★★★★ C	★★★★/★★★★★ C
1989	★★★★ C	★★★★/★★★★★ C	★★★★ C	★★★★/★★★★★ C
1988	★★★★ C	★★★★ C	★★★★/★★★★★ C	★★★★ C

A-Z of producers

Northern Rhône

THIERRY ALLEMAND   Cornas

Thierry Allemand   22 Impasse des Granges, 07130 Cornas
UK stockists:**RsW**,Sec,Rae

Small Cornas domaine with just over 3ha, producing 2 rich, sturdy and powerful Syrah wines. Total production is tiny at a mere 1,000 cases a year but the quality is very good to exceptional and among the best in the appellation. Vinification is traditional with a long *cuvaison* at high temperatures to extract both flavour and supple, well-rounded tannins. The resulting wines are impressive, concentrated and very elegant. They are both bottled unfiltered. Reynard, made from vines that are over 80 years old, is very ageworthy and will continue to improve for up to a decade, sometimes longer in the best years. (DM).

● **Cornas** Chaillot★★★★ £E   Reynard★★★★★ £F

DOM. BALTHAZAR   Cornas

René Balthazar   07130 Cornas
UK stockists:**Has**,SVS

Balthazar produces traditionally vinified and aged Cornas that is generally very good. 2002, 01 and 00 are all ripe and structured, with the depth and complexity of dark berry fruit that can only be coaxed from a vineyard planted with very old vines. Aged in large old wood the wine is nevertheless surprisingly ripe, forward and approachable with just 4 or 5 years' ageing. Like many producers in this village Balthazar offers very good value. (DM)

● **Cornas**★★★ £D

323

GILLES BARGE Côte-Rôtie

Gilles Barge 8 Boulevard des Allées, 69420 Ampuis
UK stockists: C&B,Bib,Tan,SVS,Rae,Sec

Gilles Barge took over from his father Pierre in the mid-1990s and is now producing excellent Côte-Rôtie, if not in the absolute top flight. He has not only reduced yields from his holdings of around 7ha but has refined the approach in the cellar as well. The wines are still vinified with stems but the tannins are riper and suppler. They are characterised by elegance and finesse rather than by raw power and are bottled unfiltered. The Cuvée du Plessy is the lighter, more forward of the 2, elegant and approachable. Both wines are impressively ageworthy and will improve in bottle for 7–10 years. Enjoy his peachy Condrieu and straightforward spicy, berry-fruited Saint-Joseph young. (DM)

● **Côte-Rôtie** Cuvée du Plessy★★★ £E Côte Brune★★★★ £F

ALBERT BELLE Hermitage

Albert Belle Quartier les Marsuriaux, 26600 Larnage
UK stockists: **Ear**,Cdp

This young domaine which has been producing good red and white for upwards of a decade. Total vineyard holdings are now close to 18ha, almost all in Crozes-Hermitage. Reds are made traditionally and destemming is avoided. Good, structured, ageworthy wines result in the best years but there can be an occasional green hint in cooler vintages. The key here is to get the stems as well as the fruit fully ripe at harvest. The white is fully or part-fermented in oak and the Hermitage is fat and toasty with real depth and concentration. The top wines will be all the better for 5 or 6 years' cellaring. (DM)

● **Hermitage**★★★ £E
● **Crozes-Hermitage** Les Pierelles★★ £B Cuvée Louis Belle★★★ £C
O **Hermitage**★★★ £D O **Crozes-Hermitage**★ £B

DOM. BONNEFOND Côte-Rôtie

Patrick & Christophe Bonnefond Mornas, 69420 Ampuis
UK stockists:Goe,GWWSVS,Odd,N&P,WAe

From their small holding of 6ha, the Bonnefond brothers produce very good Condrieu and – in their top bottling, Les Rochains – one of the finest of all Côte-Rôties. The style of the reds is modern, with destemming and new oak in the top *cuvée,* and a really elegant spicy, mineral character shows through in all the wines. The regular bottling is a little light in comparison to Côte Rozier and Les Rochains but is nonetheless ripe and well-structured with the slightest hint of green pepper. Côte Rozier, with 10% Viognier has a characteristic floral undercurrent but with depth and real dimension. Les Rochains is rich, opulent and firmly structured, needing 2 3 years longer in bottle than the other reds, and should not be broached without 5 or 6 years' ageing. Condrieu is opulent, peachy and immediately accessible. (DM)

● **Côte-Rôtie**★★★ £E Côte Rozier★★★★ £E Les Rochains★★★★★ £F
O **Condrieu**★★★ £D

DOM. DE BONSERINE Côte-Rôtie

Richard Dommerc Verenay, 69420 Ampuis
UK stockists:Ear

This is a large property for the appellation, which has been developed with considerable outside investment from Georges DUBOEUF among others. It is now the second-largest vineyard owner after GUIGAL with a total of just under 10ha of Syrah (95%) and Viognier (5%) spread across 17 different parcels. Vinification is modern and the fruit is all destemmed before ageing in barrel.

The regular *cuvée,* La Sarrasine, has 5% Viognier blended in whereas the 2 top wines, Les Moutonnes and La Garde, are both 100% Syrah and are aged in new oak for 24 months, which tends to show through when the wine is very young. These are impressive, modern and opulent examples of the appellation which should be aged for 5, even as much as 7, years. (DM)

● **Côte-Rôtie★★★** £D   Les Moutonnes★★★ £E La Garde★★★★ £E

BERNARD BURGAUD   Côte-Rôtie

Bernard Burgaud   Le Champin, 69420 Ampuis
UK stockists: J&B, BBR, Yap, SVS

Just 1 wine is produced here but it is among the better examples in the appellation. It is made from a number of different sites that are always vinified separately to maximise the wine's complexity. Bernard Burgaud maintains strict control of yields, and a portion of the harvest is regularly sold off after careful sorting. Finally a *saignée* of up to 20% of the juice prior to fermentation results in a wine that is both concentrated and full of character, and which benefits from 4–5 years' ageing. It always offers good value. (DM)

● **Côte-Rôtie★★★★** £E

DOM. DE CHAMPAL   Saint-Joseph   www.domaine-champal.com

Eric Rocher   Quartier Champal, 07370 Sarras
Eric Rocher has 18ha of red grapes planted in Saint-Joseph and Crozes-Hermitage as well as 6ha of white varieties, mostly Viognier in Condrieu along with a little Roussanne and Marsanne. He produces a *vin de pays* Viognier as well as his Condrieu but it is the reds that offer the greatest interest and value. The Crozes-Hermitage, from the northern stretches of the appellation, is marked by firm tannin and fresh acidity and delivers more poise and balance than many. The Terroir de Champal is now emerging as one of the best Saint-Joseph reds, with great purity of fruit and just a hint of new oak. It has been on the cusp of ★★★★, not only in 2000 and 01 but also 03, and will develop very well in the medium term. (DM)

● **Crozes-Hermitage** Chaubayou★★★ £B ● **Saint-Joseph** Terroir de Champal★★★ £C

M CHAPOUTIER   Hermitage   www.chapoutier.com

Chapoutier family   18 Avenue Dr Paul Durand, 26600 Tain-l'Hermitage
UK stockists: **Men**, Tan, Sel, BBR, F&M, Las

One of the most important *négociants* in the northern Rhône, with the largest vineyard holding on the great Hermitage hill. Interests are not restricted to the Rhône and include M CHAPOUTIER AUSTRALIA at Mount Benson in South Australia, as well as some fine, chunky Collioure, rich Banyuls and Muscat de Rivesaltes from Roussillon. Côtes du Roussillon is also the source of new reds from Domaine de Bila Haut, with a top label Occultum Lapidem, as the Chapoutiers have not been slow to realise the potential of the Agly Valley. Amidst the vast array of Rhône labels the top wines are superbly crafted examples of their appellations. New benchmarks have been set in both Crozes-Hermitage – with the dense, muscular and very concentrated Les Varonniers – and Saint-Joseph, with both red and white Les Granits. These are not cheap but have established new standards that others are following. Côte-Rôtie La Mordorée is a magnificent example of the appellation; even though not quite of the order of the 3 GUIGAL *super-cuvées* it is still very impressive. Hermitage red and white now comes in a number of guises. Pavillon and L'Ermite are perhaps the finest among the reds and the former is the weightiest and most powerful of the trio. Of the whites Cuvée de l'Orée is now joined by Le Méal. There is no doubting the supreme quality at this level. The wines are remarkably plush, even when relatively young, and very different to a Jean-Louis CHAVE

325

Hermitage. The regular Hermitage Monier de la Sizeranne and Chante Alouette white pale a little in comparison, but at least won't break the bank. In the south, Châteauneuf-du-Pape is good to very good and Barbe Rac is 100% Grenache. New is the Coteaux du Tricastin Château des Estubiers,with a very good red example of that appellation. At a lower level the wines from lesser appellations can be disappointing. The generic Côtes du Rhône Belleruche labels are light and insubstantial. The top Hermitage wines are labelled with the traditional spelling, Ermitage. (DM)

- ● **Côte-Rôtie** Les Bécasses★★★ £E La Mordorée✪✪✪✪✪ £H
- ● **Hermitage** Monier de la Sizeranne★★★★ £E Le Meal✪✪✪✪✪ £H
- ● **Hermitage** L'Ermite✪✪✪✪✪ £H Le Pavillon✪✪✪✪✪ £H
- O **Hermitage** Chante Alouette★★★★ £E Cuvée de l'Orée✪✪✪✪✪ £H
- O **Hermitage** Le Meal✪✪✪✪✪ £H
- O **Hermitage Vin de Paille**✪✪✪✪✪ £H O **Condrieu**★★ £D
- ● **Crozes-Hermitage** La Petite-Ruche★★ £B Les Meysonniers★★ £C
- ● **Crozes-Hermitage** Les Varonniers★★★★ £E
- O **Crozes-Hermitage** La Petite-Ruche★ £B Les Meysonniers★ £B
- ● **Cornas**★★★ £D ● **Saint-Joseph** Deschants★★ £C Les Granits★★★★ £E
- O **Saint-Joseph** Deschants★★ £C Les Granits★★★ £D
- ● **Chateauneuf-du-Pâpe** La Bernadine★★★ £D Croix de Bois★★★★ £E
- ● **Chateauneuf-du-Pâpe** Barbe Rac★★★★★ £G
- O **Chateauneuf-du-Pâpe** La Bernadine★★ £D
- ● **Côtes-du-Rhône Villages Rasteau**★ £B ● **Côtes-du-Rhône Villages Valréas**★ £B
- ● **Coteaux du Tricastin** Ch. des Estubiers★★ £B
- ● **Collioure**★★ £B ● **Banyuls**★★★ £C Terra Vinya★★★★ £D
- ● **Côtes du Roussillon-Villages** Dom. de Bila-Haut★★ £B
- ● **Côtes du Roussillon-Villages** Occultum Lapidem★★★ £C
- O **Muscat de Beaumes-de-Venise**★★ £C O **Muscat de Rivesaltes**★★★ £C

CH. D'AMPUIS Côte-Rôtie www.guigal.com

Marcel Guigal Château d'Ampuis, 69420 Ampuis
UK stockists: **JEF**,BBR,C&B

Guigal is rightly famed for the resurrection of the wines of Côte-Rôtie during the 1970s and 80s. His top 3 red *cuvées*, La Mouline, La Landonne and La Turque, are now sold under the Château d'Ampuis rather than E. GUIGAL label. Super-rich, very extracted and with loads of new oak, they are produced in very limited quantities and not surprisingly sell for stratospheric prices. However, their balance and extraordinary finesse is more important still. All 3 are truly profound wines with that extra dimension and depth found in only a handful of truly great wines. Perhaps La Turque is the finest. The vinification of each is quite unique. The Côte-Rôtie Château d'Ampuis and Condrieu La Doriane are very good but not of the same order. In 2001 Marcel Guigal purchased the domaine and vineyards of Jean-Louis GRIPPAT, embellishing his estate with top-class sites in both Saint-Joseph and Hermitage. These wines are now labelled Lieu-Dit Saint Joseph and are released under the d'Ampuis label. The Vignes de l'Hospice red remains particularly striking under the new ownership. (DM)

- ● **Côte-Rôtie** Ch. d'Ampuis★★★★★ £E La Mouline✪✪✪✪✪ £H
- ● **Côte-Rôtie** La Turque✪✪✪✪✪ £H La Landonne✪✪✪✪✪ £H
- O **Condrieu** La Doriane★★★★★ £F

CH. GRILLET Château Grillet

Neyret-Gachet family 42410 Vérin
UK stockists: **Yap**, BBR,Sel,F&M

This is in fact a tiny appellation as well as a single estate and one of the smallest in France at around 3ha. Like Condrieu the wine is produced solely from Viognier and has always been vinified in barrel on its *lees*. Unlike many

Viogniers, at its best this wine can be aged. After a period in the doldrums the quality at Grillet has improved somewhat. However there is some way to go before the wine offers the same quality and dimension of the best examples in Condrieu. (DM)

O **Château Grillet★★★** £F

DOM. YANN CHAVE Hermitage

Yann Chave La Burge, 26600 Mercurol
UK stockists: **GrD**,HHB,L&W,SVS,Gau

Fine, improving small domaine with 16ha of Syrah and a tiny amount of Marsanne and Roussanne producing increasingly impressive supple and structured red wines. Vinification is modern and more new wood is being used both for red and white. These are now wines of finesse and depth and the top reds need cellaring. The Crozes-Hermitage Tête de Cuvée and Hermitage will improve in bottle for up to 10 years, the latter for even longer in great years. (DM)

● **Hermitage★★★★** £E
● **Crozes-Hermitage★★** £B Tête de Cuvée★★★ £C
O **Crozes-Hermitage★★** £B Le Rouvre★★★ £C

JEAN-LOUIS CHAVE Hermitage

Gérard et Jean-Louis Chave 37 Avenue de St-Joseph, 07300 Mauves
UK stockists: Yap,Adm,BBR,WSc,C&BTan,Sel,F&M, Las

Utterly splendid ancient domaine, perhaps the finest in the northern Rhône and among the best in France. The Chave family own plots in all 7 *lieux-dits* on the Hermitage hill, which contributes to the marvellous complexity and finesse of their wines. Any of the components felt to be below standard will be sold off in order to protect the integrity of the wine. Cuvée Cathelin is a special selection which sees more new wood and is produced only in top years. Both red and white are extraordinarily ageworthy and are not wines to approach in their youth. Also produced are a very good Saint-Joseph and an extraordinary *vin de paille*, the latter only in tiny quantities. (DM)

● **Hermitage**✪✪✪✪✪ £F Ermitage Cuvée Cathelin ✪✪✪✪✪ £H
O **Hermitage**✪✪✪✪✪ £F ● **Saint-Joseph★★★** £C

DOM. DU CHÊNE Côte-Rôtie

Marc & Dominique Rouvière Le Pêcher, 42410 Chavanay
UK stockists: Rev,F&M

Marc Rouvière makes small but impressive quantities of both red and white Saint-Joseph, as well as a striking and intensely peachy, honeyed Condrieu. Medium- rather than full-bodied, with a fine lightly mineral structure, this will drink well over 3–4 years. 2002 was impressively concentrated despite the vintage. In addition to the regular Saint-Joseph bottlings – a good fruit-driven white produced from Marsanne and a medium-weight, spicy, strawberry-scented red – there is a much deeper special Cuvée Anais. Firm and structured in its youth, with rich, dark berry fruit and spicy oak, it should be aged for 3 or 4 years to show at its best. (DM)

O **Condrieu★★★** £E O **Saint-Joseph★★** £C
● **Saint-Joseph★★** £C Cuvée Anais★★★ £D

DOM. LOUIS CHÈZE Condrieu

Louis Chèze Les Chênes Verts, 26600 Pont-de-l'Isère
UK stockists: **C&C**,N&P

Louis Chèze has gradually built up a small domaine of some 20ha, with the largest plots planted to Syrah in Saint-Joseph. His holding of Viognier in

Condrieu is mainly young vines but the wines are stylish and well-crafted with good, nicely integrated oak. The Coteau de Brèze in particular is very fine with rich, peachy, opulent fruit. The white Saint-Joseph emphasises Marsanne's broad, nutty character. The top reds are supple and sufficiently structured to provide excellent drinking with a few years' cellaring. (DM)

O **Condrieu**★★★ £D Coteau de Brèze★★★★ £E
● **Saint-Joseph** Ro-Rée★★ £C Cuvée des Anges★★★ £C Caroline★★★ £C
O **Saint-Joseph**★★ £B Ro-Rée★★ £C

AUGUSTE CLAPE Cornas

Auguste et Pierre-Marie Clape RN 146, 07130 Cornas
UK stockists: **Yap**,Sel,F&M,Las
Pierre-Marie now makes the wine at this domaine, an established leader in the appellation. The winemaking is fiercely traditional and no new wood is used whatsoever. However, any stems retained during vinification are always fully ripened and the the wines are supple with harmonious tannin and fruit, balanced and very refined. Vines that date from the 1890s contribute to the impressive quality. Cuvée Renaissance is a second wine, made to help maintain the quality of the Cornas. Inevitably from younger vines, it lacks the weight and power of the *grand vin*. Both the spicy Côtes du Rhône red and Saint-Péray offer good value. (DM)

● **Cornas**★★★★★ £D Cuvée Renaissance★★ £C
O **Saint-Péray**★★ £B ● **Côtes du Rhône**★★ £B

CLUSEL ROCH Côte-Rôtie

Gilbert Clusel et Brigitte Roch 15 Route du Lacat, Verenay, 69420 Ampuis
UK stockists: **L&S**,VTr
Among the leading handful of small domaines in Côte-Rôtie, this tiny operation with just 4ha of Syrah and Viognier produces barely more than 1,000 cases a year. The Côte-Rôties are powerful and structured for the long haul, particularly Les Grandes Places, made from 65- to 70-year-old vines and occasionally ✪✪✪✪✪. Neither is for drinking young. The Condrieu is good, with attractive peachy Viognier fruit, but lacks the intensity and depth of the reds. (DM)

● **Côte-Rôtie**★★★★ £D Les Grandes Places★★★★★ £F O **Condrieu**★★★ £D

DOM. DU COLOMBIER Hermitage

Florent Viale 2 Route de Chantemerle, 26600 Tain L'Hermitage
UK stockists: Bib, Gau, J&B,Tan,HHB,BBR, Bal,SVS
Another small, improving northern Rhône domaine. The Viale family own just over 15ha of vineyards, some with very old vines on the Hermitage hill. They produce around 6,000 cases of wine including a cool-fermented white Crozes-Hermitage, vinified with a touch of oak, and 3 stylish, complex reds. The Crozes-Hermitage Cuvée Gaby and in particular the Hermitage are powerful, structured reds that benefit from 5 or 6 years' cellaring. The Hermitage keeps extremely well. Prices are very fair indeed. (DM)

● **Crozes-Hermitage**★★★ £B Cuvée Gaby★★★ £C ● **Hermitage**★★★★ £D
O **Crozes-Hermitage**★★ £B

JEAN-LUC COLOMBO Cornas

Jean-Luc Colombo Chemin Pied la Vigne, 07130 Cornas
UK stockists: **L&W**, HHB,N&P
This operation is essentially split into 2. Domaine Jean-Luc Colombo produces wines from vineyards in and around Cornas and Saint-Péray, whereas the Jean-Luc Colombo label is reserved for an extensive range of *négociant* wines. There are also 2 separate domaines in the Midi. Domaine de Salente in the

Languedoc produces red and white Vins de Pays d'Oc from Syrah and Viognier as well as a Coteaux du Languedoc red, L'Ame de Salente, a structured blend of Syrah, Carignan, Grenache and a smattering of Mourvèdre. Good red Côtes du Roussillon and Muscat de Rivesaltes are produced at Domaine de Saint-Luc and a premium red, La Mission Saint-Luc, has been added here. New reds are also now produced from vineyards in Provence's Coteaux d'Aix-en-Provence and there is a good white Vin de Pays des Bouches-du-Rhône, Les Pins Couchés. The wines are labelled Domaine de la Côte Bleue. Of the Rhône *négociant* wines, which range from ordinary to very good, the Châteauneuf-du-Pape Bartavelles stands out, a powerful, dense, Grenache-based red. Top Cornas *cuvées* Les Ruchets and La Louvée are most impressive. Aged in new oak, the wines are always well-balanced and are some of the best in the appellation.(DM)

Domaine Jean-Luc Colombo
● **Cornas** Les Mejeans★★★ £E Terres Brûlées★★★ £E Les Ruchets★★★★ £F
● **Cornas** La Louvée★★★★★ £F
Jean-Luc Colombo
● **Hermitage** Le Louet★★★ £E O **Hermitage** Le Louet★★★ £E
● **Saint-Joseph** Le Prieuré★★★ £C Les Lauves★★ £C
O **Condrieu**★★★ £E O **Vin de Pays Viognier** Les Ramilles Blanche★★ £B
● **Crozes-Hermitage** La Tuilière★★ £B O **Crozes-Hermitage**★ £B
● **Vin de Pays des Collines Rhodaniennes** Collines de Laure★ £B
● **Vin de Pays des Collines Rhodaniennes** Syrah la Serine Pointue★★ £B
● **Chateauneuf-du-Pape** Les Bartavelles★★★★ £D
● **Côtes du Rhône** Abeilles★★ £B Les Forots★★★ £C
O **Côtes du Rhône** Les Figuières★★ £B
● **Vin de Pays Syrah** Les Ramilles★★ £B
Domaine de Saint-Luc
● **Côtes du Roussillon** La Chance de Saint-Luc ★★ £B
O **Muscat de Rivesaltes** Les Saintes★★★ £C

DOM. COMBIER Crozes-Hermitage
Maurice et Laurent Combier RN 7, 26600 Pont de l'Isère
UK stockists: Eno
Good stylish and concentrated wines are made at this recently established domaine. The regular red and white wines are well crafted and see some new wood during maturation. The Clos des Grives is altogether more serious and amongst the best in the appellation. The red, which is macerated for around 30 days on skins, is dense and muscular, with refined fruit and supple, balanced tannins. The wine is aged in new oak and requires a little patience before it is ready. The whites are mainly Roussanne, barrel-fermented and kept on their lees with *bâtonnage*. Both will develop well in the medium term. (DM)

● **Crozes-Hermitage**★★ £B Clos des Grives★★★ £C
O **Crozes-Hermitage**★★ £B Clos des Grives★★★ £C
● **Saint-Joseph**★★ £C

DOM. DE COULET Cornas
Mathieu Baret 07130 Cornas
UK stockists: J&B
Newly emerging 4.5-ha domaine at present producing no more than 400 or so cases a year. Mathieu Baret's vineyards are biodynamic with cover crops grown and he uses no pumps in the winery and an absolute minimum of sulphur dioxide. Just 2 wines are produced, both of which will benefit from 5 years' ageing. Les Belles des Serre is the softer and more accessible of the 2; top wine Les Belles Nom is just that bit deeper and more structured, made with fruit from higher-altitude vineyards and from 70–90-year-old vines. A wine of tremendous potential. (DM)

329

● **Cornas** Les Belles des Serre★★★★ £E Les Belles Nom★★★★ £E

DOM. COURBIS Saint-Joseph

Dominique Courbis   Les Ravières, 07130 Chateaubourg
UK stockists: **Ege**, HHB, SVS

The bulk of this estate's 26ha is in Saint-Joseph, with 5ha planted to white varieties. The average vine age is fairly young. This is to some extent illustrated in the wines, which as yet do not have quite the density or complexity of the best in the appellation. The Cornas bottlings, though, are of a different order. Les Eygats and La Sabarotte are wines of dense muscular power. The latter comes from old vine plantings and is very ageworthy. It is close to ★★★★★ in top years like 2001. Both top Cornas will improve for up to a decade with ease. (DM)

- ● **Saint-Joseph**★★ £B Domaine Les Royes★★★ £C ○ **Saint-Joseph**★★ £B
- ● **Cornas** Champelrose★★★ £C Les Eygats★★★★ £E La Sabarotte★★★★ £E

DOM. PIERRE COURSODON Saint-Joseph

Pierre et Gilbert Coursodon   3 place du Marché, 07300 Mauves
UK stockists: **Win**,WSc,BRW

During the early to mid-1990s the Coursodon wines were sound enough but often possessed a raw, harsh undercurrent. Destemming was not practised and old *foudres* were the order of the day. Jérôme Coursodon has now taken over the winemaking and the results in the late 90s have been impressive, particularly with the top red *cuvées*. The wines have concentrated dark fruit but are more refined and better balanced than of old. The very fine bottling of La Sensonne is produced in association with Patrick LESEC. (DM)

- ● **Saint-Joseph**★★ £B L'Olivaie★★★ £C Le Paradis St-Pierre★★★ £C
- ● **Saint-Joseph** La Sensonne★★★★ £D
- ○ **Saint-Joseph**★ £B Le Paradis St-Pierre★★ £C

YVES CUILLERON Condrieu www.cuilleron.com

Yves Cuilleron   Verlieu, 42140 Chavanay
UK stockists: **Eno**,A&B,BBR,Swg,P&S,Las,But

One of the new younger superstars of the northern Rhône, Cuilleron is best known for superb Condrieu made in a number of guises including Fleur d'Automne, a very intense and distinctive sweet botrytised example that spends 8 months in wood. A new dry wine labelled Vertige was added to the range of Condrieus with the 2001 vintage, which like the others is barrel-fermented and aged on lees. He also produces a small range of first-class Saint-Joseph, both red and white. The whites are barrel-fermented and aged and the reds macerated for 3–4 weeks and aged in oak. He is also working with François VILLARD and Pierre GAILLARD in a new small-scale *négociant* venture, Les VINS DE VIENNE. An additional Côte-Rôtie and a small range of *vins de pays* are the latest additions. The wines offer generally very good value. (DM)

- ● **Côte-Rôtie** Coteau de Bassenon★★★★ £E Terres Sombres★★★★★ £F
- ○ **Vin de Pays Marsanne**★ £B
- ○ **Condrieu** La Petite Côte★★★★ £D Chaillets Vieilles Vignes★★★★★ £E
- ○ **Condrieu** Les Ayguets○○○○○ £F Fleur d'Automne○○○○○ £G
- ● **Saint-Joseph** Les Pierres Sèches★★ £C Les Serines★★★ £C L'Amarybelle★★★ £C
- ○ **Saint-Joseph** Coteaux Saint-Pierre★★★ £C Le Lombard★★★★ £C Lyseras★★★ £C

DELAS FRÈRES Hermitage

Maison Louis Roederer   2 Allée de l'Olivet, 07300 Saint-Jean-de-Muzols
UK stockists: **BWC**, BBR, Las

Once one of the northern Rhône's under-performers, Delas is now a serious player among the top Rhône *négociants*. With the purchase by leading Champagne house Louis ROEDERER and the arrival of Jacques Grange as winemaking chief, the wines have radically improved. The range is comprehensive and even the humbler wines are now sound and well-crafted. Far better fruit quality and well-handled new oak in the better wines are just 2 of the keys here to the transformation in fortune and quality. Star turns are the top *cuvées*, which are densely textured and explosively rich and concentrated. The outstanding Hermitage Les Bessards and Côte-Rôtie La Landonne are remarkably ageworthy propositions now, demanding at least 6–7 years' cellaring. The other top reds and white Hermitage also deserve cellaring. (DM)

● **Côte-Rôtie** Seigneur de Maugiron★★★★ £E La Landonne★★★★★ £G
○ **Condrieu** Galopine★★★ £D Clos Boucher★★★★ £F
○ **Condrieu** Vendange Tardive Brumaire de Bruyère★★★★ £F
● **Hermitage** Marquise de la Tourette★★★ £E Les Bessards✪✪✪✪✪ £H
○ **Hermitage** Marquise de la Tourette★★★ £E
● **Crozes-Hermitage** Les Launes★★ £B Tour d'Albon★★★ £D Le Clos★★★★ £E
○ **Crozes-Hermitage** Les Launes★★ £B
● **Saint-Joseph** François de Tournon★★★ £C Les Challeys★★★ £C
● **Saint-Joseph** Sainte-Épine★★★ £D
○ **Saint-Joseph** François de Tournon★★ £B Les Challeys★★★ £C
● **Cornas** Chante Perdrix★★★ £D
● **Châteauneuf-du-Pape**★★ £C ● **Gigondas**★★★ £C
● **Vacqueyras** Domaine des Genêts★ £B ● **Côtes du Ventoux**★ £A
● **Côtes du Rhône** Saint-Esprit★ £B
○ **Côtes du Rhône** Saint-Esprit★ £A

PIERRE DUMAZET Condrieu

Pierre Dumazet RN 86, 07340 Limony
UK stockists: **Bib**

Somewhat controversial among Condrieu producers, Dumazet produces wines which are rich, dense and full of classic Viognier dried peaches, spices and minerals. Don't expect modern squeaky-clean fruit-driven wines here. The *vin de pays* and Cuvée du Zenith offer a similar style at a lower level than the Condrieus. Old-fashioned and quite heavily oaked, the Condrieus are at times almost rustic. However they are also characterful, powerful and structured. This is an excellent source of traditional wines from the appellation. (DM)

○ **Condrieu**★★★ £D Côte de Fournet★★★★ £E
○ **Vin de Pays Viognier**★★ £B ○ **Côtes du Rhône** Cuvée du Zenith★★ £B

ERIC ET JOËL DURAND Cornas

Eric et Joël Durand 07130 Châteaubourg
UK stockists: **N&P, NYg**

Just 2 reds are made here from a small holding of some 7ha. They are traditionally vinified and are bottled unfiltered. Ageing at present is in older barrels and, while the wines are dense and impressively concentrated, they are not quite in the first division. However, the vineyard is still relatively young and the best has probably yet to emerge. Both wines are firmly structured and will age well in the medium term. The Cornas requires 4–5 years at a minimum. (DM)

● **Cornas**★★★ £C ● **Saint-Joseph** Les Coteaux★★★ £C

DOM. DES ENTREFAUX Crozes-Hermitage

Charles & François Tardy Quartier de la Beaume, 26600 Chanos-Curson
UK stockists: **GSe, Fal, Evg, RGr**

The Tardys are now very well established in the appellation and make an exemplary range of both red and white wines. They possess a total of 20ha of Syrah and a further 6ha of white varieties, mainly Marsanne with a little Roussanne. Both the regular red and white are sound. The white is vinified solely in *inox* to emphasise its fruit while the red is aged in *cuve* and used small wood. Under the Coteau des Pends label the white is a blend of Marsanne and

331

Roussanne (which adds a floral fragrance) vinified in small oak, while the red, which also sees some oak during ageing, is rich and reasonably concentrated with good varietal fruit and a hint of oak spice. The Cuvée des Machonnières is sourced from a selection of *terroirs* characterised by their argile-calcaire soils and, while certainly oaky, this has great fruit substance and class. By contrast the Cuvée des Champs Fournée, from a single parcel of vines, is marked by its fruit but also an impressive purity and depth. (DM)

- ● **Crozes-Hermitage**★★ £B Coteau des Pends★★ £C
- ● **Crozes-Hermitage** La Cuvée des Machonnières★★★ £C
- ● **Crozes-Hermitage** La Cuvée des Champs Fournée★★★ £C
- ○ **Crozes-Hermitage**★ £B Coteau des Pends★★ £C

BERNARD FAURIE Hermitage

Bernard Faurie 27 Avenue Hélène de Tournon, 07300 Tournon
UK stockists: **THt,**J&B,HHC

Producer of old-style Hermitage and Saint-Joseph from a tiny holding of just 3ha of vines. The wines are at their best in great years, when they are both ripe and powerful. In lesser vintages the odd green note can creep in. The Hermitage Le Méal packs a real punch of complex old-vine fruit. They demand cellaring for 10 years or more. (DM)

- ● **Hermitage**★★★ £D Le Méal★★★★ £E ○ **Hermitage**★★★ £D
- ● **Saint-Joseph**★★ £B Cuvée Vieilles-Vignes★★★ £D

DOM. DE FAUTERIE Cornas

Sylvain Bernard 07130 Saint-Péray
UK stockists: **FMV**, BBR,Yap

This is a recently established domaine but assuredly traditional in its approach to viticulture. Sylvain Bernard trained with Jean-Louis CHAVE before establishing his own small holding of vineyards in Saint-Peray, Saint-Joseph and now of most interest in Cornas. The vines in the latter, leased from Guy de Barjac, are around 100 years old and are grown in ideal sandy granite soils with an exceptional and very sunny mesoclimate. The result is a wine with considerable depth, complexity and some power. It will be all the better for 5 years' ageing. Top recent vintages are particularly impressive. (DM)

- ● **Cornas**★★★★ £D ● **Saint-Joseph**★★★ £C Les Combaud★★★ £C
- ○ **Saint-Péray** Les Hauts de Fauterie★★ £B

PIERRE GAILLARD Saint-Joseph

Pierre Gaillard Chez Favier, 42520 Malleval
UK stockists: **HHB,**Cav,J&B,L&S,Sel

A diverse range of wines from a scattered 17ha in Saint-Joseph, Côte-Rôtie and Condrieu. Gaillard also runs to a good Côtes du Rhône Viognier and, when conditions permit, an excellent late-harvest Condrieu and a rare *vin de paille* Jean-Elise. Though small, this is an expanding domaine. The wines are modern and stylish and, given the relative youth of the vines, it is clear that the best is yet to come. New oak is present but not overdone in the best reds. The regular Côte-Rôtie is lighter and more elegant, with the inclusion of Viognier. It like the Saint-Joseph Les Pierres and Clos du Cuminaille is a good medium-term cellaring prospect. The Rose Pourpre is altogether denser and more firmly structured. It requires 5 or 6 years' cellaring at a minimum. Gaillard is also the inspiration and one of the partners behind the excellent range at LES VINS DE VIENNE. (DM)

- ● **Côte-Rôtie**★★★ £D Rose Pourpre★★★★ £E
- ○ **Condrieu**★★★★ £E
- ● **Saint-Joseph**★★★ £C Les Pierres★★★ £C Clos du Cuminaille★★★★ £C
- ○ **Saint-Joseph**★★★ £C ○ **Côtes du Rhône** Viognier★★★ £C

DOM. YVES GANGLOFF Condrieu

Mathilde & Yves Gangloff 2 Rue de la Garenne, 69420 Condrieu
UK stockists: **Rae**, FMV BBR, F&M

Yves Gangloff has been established here for nearly 20 years and has gradually
built up a small holding in the same way as many of his neighbours. He now
has 3.5ha. The rich and opulent Condrieu is sourced from 2 separate parcels,
La Bonnette and Chéry, adding to the wine's complexity. For Viognier it is
finely structured with sufficient grip to develop well over 4 or 5 years. There are
2 Côte-Rôties, Barbarine, which is blended with a little Viognier and produced
from younger vines, and the sturdier Sereine Noir, which is partly aged in new
wood. Both are very impressive, with the Sereine Noir requiring 5 years or so to
show at its best. (DM)

● **Côte-Rôtie** Barbarine★★★★ £D Sereine Noir★★★★★ £E
○ **Condrieu**★★★★ £E

JEAN-MICHEL GERIN Côte-Rôtie

Jean-Michel Gerin 19 Rue de Montmain, Verenay, 69420 Ampuis
UK stockists: **C&C**, IVV, Blx, Las

Jean-Michel Gerin's 9ha are the source of some fine rich and modern Côte-
Rôtie with an emphasis on dark, brambly and chocolaty fruit. New oak is not
used sparingly either. Champin Junior and Champin Le Seigneur are a little
light but La Landonne and Les Grandes Places, which is produced from vines
that are over 80 years old, are very good indeed. Modern and oaky they may be
but the wines are superbly crafted and display a fine balance of complex fruit
and firm but supple rounded tannins. These top *cuvées* need 5 years or so of
ageing at a minimum and will keep much longer. (DM)

● **Côte-Rôtie** Champin Junior★★ £C Champin Le Seigneur★★★ £E
● **Côte-Rôtie** Les Grandes Places★★★★★ £F La Landonne★★★★★ £F
○ **Condrieu** Coteau de la Loye★★ £D ● **Côtes du Rhône**★ £B

DOM. PIERRE GONON Saint-Joseph

Gonon family 3 place du Marché, 07300 Mauves
UK stockists: VTr

Pierre and Jean Gonon are now producing some of the best reds in the Saint-
Joseph appellation. They have 5.5 ha of Syrah and a couple of Roussanne and
Marsanne. The white is produced in a very firm, structured style but
nevertheless offers good fruit and real intensity. The red is full, savoury and
concentrated with dark, blackberry and black pepper spices. It is vinified and
aged traditionally in *foudre* and will be all the better for 5 years' ageing. The
2004 shows real potential, but the 03 has just a hint of green pepper. (DM)

● **Saint-Joseph**★★★ £C ○ **Saint-Joseph** Les Oliviers★★ £C

ALAIN GRAILLOT Crozes-Hermitage

Alain Graillot Les Chênes Verts, 26600 Pont-de-l'Isère
UK stockists: Yap, L&W, ABy, Sel

In barely 2 decades Alain Graillot has become a benchmark, if not *the*
benchmark, producer of Crozes-Hermitage, both white and red. Others are
now emerging and new special bottlings from the likes of CHAPOUTIER
may challenge him but he has been the inspiration for an appellation that for
too long represented mediocrity. Yields are kept in check but green harvesting is
not practised. Graillot considers winter pruning sufficient to set the yield for
the year, the productivity of his vineyard being fully in balance. The white is
vinified in wood and *inox* and kept on lees and the reds given an extended
maceration of up to 21 days. The special *cuvée* La Guiraude is a very impressive

333

barrel selection. The reds, particularly La Guiraude, will age very well. (DM)

● **Crozes-Hermitage★★★** £B La Guiraude★★★★ £C   O **Crozes-Hermitage★★** £B
● **Hermitage★★★** £D   ● **Saint-Joseph★★★** £C

DOM. BERNARD GRIPA   Saint-Joseph

Bernard Gripa   5 avenue Ozier, 07300 Mauves
UK stockists: VTr, F&R, Las

Long-established grower and a real benchmark for characterful white Saint-Peray, arguably the best producer of the appellation. Fine Saint-Joseph, both red and white, is also produced from a total of a mere 12ha of vineyards. The regular Saint-Joseph labels are good and characterful but it is the Les Berceau bottlings that stand out. The regular white Saint-Peray is rich and characterful, showing Marsanne at its best, while the densely textured Les Figuières is surely the best wine here – long, persistent and ageworthy. (DM)

● **Saint-Joseph★★** £C Les Berceau★★★ £C
O **Saint-Joseph★★** £C Les Berceau★★★ £C
O **Saint-Peray★★★** £B Les Figuières★★★ £C

E GUIGAL   Côte-Rôtie   www.guigal.com

Marcel Guigal   Château d'Ampuis, 69420 Ampuis
UK stockists: **JEF**,AAA

The E. Guigal label covers an extensive range produced from the length and breadth of the Rhône Valley. The firm is far and away the largest producer of Côte-Rôtie and also owns Domaine de VALLOUIT as well as the merchant house of VIDAL FLEURY. The vibrant red Côtes du Rhône, if not quite of the quality of a decade ago, remains a model of consistency. The Côte-Rôtie Brune et Blonde, which is sourced mainly from bought-in fruit, is good rather than great. More impressive is the Hermitage, which is dense and concentrated. It generally offers very fair value for the appellation. The southern Rhône wines in general lack the quality and refinement of their northern counterparts. The top Guigal wines appear under the separate CHÂTEAU D'AMPUIS label. (DM)

● **Côte-Rôtie** Brune et Blonde★★★ £D   O **Condrieu★★★** £D
● **Hermitage★★★★** £D   O **Hermitage★★★** £D
● **Châteauneuf-du-Pape★★★** £D   ● **Gigondas★★** £C
● **Côtes du Rhône★** £B   O **Côtes du Rhône★** £B

PAUL JABOULET AINÉ   Hermitage   www.jaboulet.com

Jaboulet family   Les Jalets, La Roche-sur-Glun, 26600 Tain-l'Hermitage
UK stockists: **DAy**,Tan,BBR,WSc,F&M, Las

Large *négociant* operation with some 100ha of their own vineyards, 84 of which are planted to Syrah. As such they have the largest holding of vineyards producing under their own label of the big Rhône merchant houses. An extensive range is produced but the main focus is the northern Rhône appellations. The Jaboulet name is most famous for 1 massive and very ageworthy *cuvée* of red Hermitage, La Chapelle. With dense and dark fruit, the wine is more approachable than, say, a Jean-Louis CHAVE but not as modern and opulent as a top CHAPOUTIER. Recent vintages have not been quite so good, although 2000 looks to be back on fine form. There is also a much lighter second red Hermitage, Le Pied de la Côte, produced from younger vines. During the 1990s the Raymond Roure property was added to the portfolio and with the dense and chocolaty Thalabert offers good to very good quality in Crozes-Hermitage. Domaine de Saint-Pierre Cornas is powerful and tannic in its youth and the Châteauneuf-du-Pape Les Cèdres has been better of late. Top wines are ageworthy but the lesser appellations should be approached young. (DM)

● **Côte-Rôtie** Les Jumelles★★ £E   O **Condrieu** Les Cassines★★ £D
● **Hermitage** La Chapelle✪✪✪✪✪ £G
O **Hermitage** Chevalier de Sterimberg★★★★ £E
● **Crozes-Hermitage** Les Jalets★ £B   Raymond Roure★★★ £C   Thalabert★★★ £C
O **Crozes-Hermitage**★ £B   Raymond Roure★★ £C   Mules Blanche★★ £C
● **Cornas** Les Grandes Terrasses★★ £C   Domaine de St Pierre★★★ £D
● **Saint-Joseph** La Grand Pompée★ £B   O **Saint-Joseph** La Grand Pompée★★ £B
● **Châteauneuf-du-Pape** Les Cèdres★★★ £D   ● **Vacqueyras**★★ £B
● **Gigondas** Pierre Aiguille★★ £C
O **Muscat de Beaumes-de-Venise**★★★ £C

DOM. JAMET   Côte-Rôtie

Jean-Paul et Jean-Luc Jamet   Le Vallin, 69420 Ampuis
UK stockists: **Bib**,C&B,IVV,Las
Brothers Jean-Luc and Jean-Paul Jamet own 6.5ha of Syrah and a tiny amount
of Viognier. They make a sumptuous, almost opulent Côte-Rôtie which has
marvellous balance and poise. The oak is seamlessly handled and the wine is
bottled unfiltered. Not only is this one of the finest examples of the appellation
but it also represents excellent value for money. 1999 was ✪✪✪✪✪. An
attractive light and vibrant Syrah is also produced from young vines and
classified as Vin de Pays des Collines Rhodaniennes. (DM)
● **Côte-Rôtie**★★★★★ £E

DOM. JASMIN   Côte-Rôtie

Patrick Jasmin   14 Rue des Maraîchers, 69420 Ampuis
UK stockists:**Yap**,F&M
Patrick Jasmin took over the running of this fine, traditional domaine after his
late father Robert's early death. Patrick continues to make the wines in a
traditional and elegant style. However destemming is now employed, which
helps in lesser years, and the wine is aged for around 2 years in mainly old
wood. Never blockbusters, there is always great purity of fruit and impressive
intensity and depth in these wines. Top years like 2001 and 00 require 7–10
years' ageing. (DM)
● **Côte-Rôtie**★★★★ £

DOM. DU MONTEILLET   Condrieu

Antoine et Stéphane Montez   Le Montelier, 42140 Chavanay
UK stockists: Cdp,Goe,GWW,Gau,SVS
Stéphane Montez runs this small family domaine in Condrieu. The property
consists of some 7ha in Condrieu, Côte-Rôtie and Saint-Joseph. Vinification is
modern and plenty of new oak is used in the top *cuvées*. The Condrieu is rich
and peachy but has a fine minerally backbone. The top *cuvée* Les Grandes
Chaillées is particularly impressive. Both should develop well over 3 or 4 years.
A late-harvest label, Tries Grains de Folie, is also produced when conditions
permit. The reds are ripe and spicy; both the Cuvée Papy and Côte-Rôtie are
wines of considerable dimension and should be cellared for a good 4 or 5 years.
(DM)
● **Côte-Rôtie** Fortis★★★★ £E
O **Condrieu**★★★★ £D   Les Grands Chaillees★★★★★ £E
O **Condrieu** Tries Grains de Folie★★★★★ £F
● **Saint-Joseph** Fortior★★★ £C   Cuvée Papy★★★ £C   O **Saint-Joseph**★★ £C

DOM. DU MURINAIS   Crozes-Hermitage

Catherine & Luc Tardy   Quartier Champ Bernard, 26600 Beaumont-Monteux
UK stockists: OWL,GVV
This is an impressive producer of well priced Crozes-Hermitage with 12.5ha of

335

Syrah and a mere 0.5ha planted to Marsanne. The Tardys produce a little under 4,000 cases a year. The white is good and lightly nutty with moderate depth and intensity. The 2001 was particularly successful. The reds are a step up, particularly the densely structured Vieilles Vignes bottling from vines that are over 30 years old. A special selection Cuvée Valentin will also now be produced in exceptional years. (DM)

- ● **Crozes-Hermitage** Cuvée Amandier★★ £B   Vieilles Vignes★★★ £C
- ● **Crozes-Hermitage** Cuvée Valentin★★★ £C
- O **Crozes-Hermitage** Cuvée Marine★★ £B

DOM. NIERO-PINCHON   Condrieu

Robert Niero   20 Rue Cuvillère, 69420 Condrieu
UK stockists: **FMV**,BBR, SVS,PWa

Robert Niero has been in charge of this fine domaine since the 1980s. The vineyard holding is typically small, with some 3ha in Condrieu and a small parcel within Les Viaillères in Côte-Rôtie. Insecticides are never used and the vines tended as naturally as possible. Les Ravines is part vinified in *inox* and part in old wood and is elegant and lightly mineral with less overt peachy, honeyed character than others. The Coteau de Chéry comes from old vines, some approaching 60 years, and the wine is fuller and more opulent with an added dimension and greater weight and concentration. The Côte-Rôtie is lighter than some of his neighbours' examples but very elegant, not least because of the 10% Viognier in the blend. Both Condrieus should be drunk young but the Côte-Rôtie will benefit from 5 years' cellaring. (DM)

- ● **Côte-Rôtie**★★★★ £E
- O **Condrieu** Les Ravines★★★ £E   Coteau de Chéry★★★★ £E

DOM. MICHEL OGIER   Côte-Rôtie   sogier@club-internet.fr

Michel & Stéphane Ogier   3 Chemin du Bac, 69420 Ampuis
UK stockists: **CTy**, BBR, N&P, Las

Some exceptional Côte-Rôtie is made at this 3.5ha property as well as very good *vin de pays* La Rosine from vineyards just to the south of Ampuis towards Condrieu. Winemaking is modern and the fruit is always destemmed prior to fermentation. New oak is used both for the regular Côte-Rôtie as well as for the limited-release special bottlings, Belle Hélène, Les Embruns and Lancement, the latter 2 released for the first time with the 2001 vintage. The wines are supple and velvety, with a real dimension to the fruit. The Belle Hélène has become established as one of the *super-cuvées* of the appellation and as such is very pricey. (DM)

- ● **Côte-Rôtie** Embruns★★★★★ £F   Belle Hélène✪✪✪✪✪ £H
- ● **Côte-Rôtie**★★★★ £E   Lancement★★★★★ £F
- ● **Vin de Pays des Collines Rhodaniennes** La Rosine★★★ £C

DOM. ALAIN PARET   Saint-Joseph

Alain Paret   Place du lEglise, 42520 Saint-Pierre-du-Boeuf

Some excellent Condrieu and very good Saint-Joseph red are made here. As well as this, Alain Paret makes an extensive range of red and white *vins de pays* and an unusual late-harvest *vin de table*, Cuvée Marie-Josée, which is a blend of Syrah, Grenache and Viognier. The white Saint-Joseph Larmes du Père is a typically full, fat Marsanne with reasonable depth and a touch of Roussanne blended in. Of the reds, the Larmes du Père is the softest with bright, forward berry fruit and a hint of new oak. The Domaine Bertrand is aged solely in 600-litre vats and is just a touch leaner and tighter. The top red is the 420 Nuits, which is aged in 100% new wood and offers really formidable depth and intensity. Ceps du Nebadon is the lighter and less intense of 2 Condrieu bottlings, although showing a fimer edge than many from the AC. The Lys de

Volan is more seriously structured with hints of both minerals and rich apricot and peach – a wine with real style and class. When conditions permit a late-harvest bottling, Sortilèges d'Automne, is produced. (DM)

● **Saint-Joseph** Domaine Bertrand★★ £C Larmes du Père★★★ £C
● **Saint-Joseph** 420 Nuits★★★ £D
O **Condrieu** Ceps du Nebadon★★★ £E Lys de Volan★★★★ £E
O **Saint-Joseph** Larmes du Père★★ £C

DOM. ANDRÉ PERRET Côte-Rôtie

André Perret Verlieu, 42410 Chavanay
UK stockists: VTr, L&W, CTy, WTs, FMV

André Perret took over the family domaine in 1982 and now has some 10ha of vines from which he produces Condrieu, Saint-Joseph, Côtes du Rhône and varietals. The Condrieus are some of the finest of the AC. These and the white Saint-Joseph are vinified in a combination of *inox* and oak, some of it new and kept on lees. The reds are fully destemmed and spend 2–3 weeks on their skins. Some late-harvest grapes are also included in the blend, adding greater complexity. Les Grissières is dense and dark with ripe, black pepper notes. It will age well. Varietal Syrah and Marsanne are produced as *vins de pays* and offer attractive early drinking. (DM)

O **Condrieu**★★★ £D Clos Chanson★★★★ £E Coteau du Chéry★★★★★ £F
● **Saint-Joseph**★★ £B Les Grissières★★★ £C O **Saint-Joseph**★★ £B

DOM. ÉTIENNE POCHON Crozes-Hermitage

Etienne Pochon Château de Curson, 26600 Chanos Curson
UK stockists: J&B, GBa, L&W, WSc, Las

Étienne Pochon makes straightforward, attractively fruity regular red and white Crozes-Hermitage and a special Château de Curson bottling of each. Theses are vinified using more oak and are a significant step up in quality. The property consists of a total of 18ha with 14 planted to Syrah plus around 3ha of Roussanne and a single hectare of Marsanne. The Curson white is dominated by Roussanne and is enticingly floral as well as lightly toasty and spicy. The red Curson is weighty but supple and will benefit from 2 or 3 years' cellaring. (DM)

● **Crozes-Hermitage**★★ £B Cuvée Château de Curson★★★ £C
O **Crozes-Hermitage**★ £B Cuvée Château de Curson★★★ £C

DOM. DES REMIZIÈRES Crozes-Hermitage

Philippe Desmeure Route de Romans, 26600 Mercurol
UK stockists: Bib, SVS

This 27-ha property has greatly improved in recent vintages. At best the wines used to be no more than middle-ranking examples of their appellations. The reds are now deep and intense. The Hermitage Émilie is powerful and structured with considerable grip but there is also real concentration and old-vine complexity here. Patrick LESEC also produces his own *cuvée* of the same wine in association with Philippe Desmeure. The Cuvée Christophe red is ripe and full of dark fruit, needing 3 or 4 years' ageing, while the whites display all the nutty, pure character of Marsanne at its best. The wines also represent very good value. (DM)

● **Hermitage** Cuvée Émilie★★★★ £E O **Hermitage** Cuvée Émilie★★★★ £E
● **Crozes-Hermitage** Cuvée Christophe★★★ £C
O **Crozes-Hermitage** Cuvée Christophe★★★ £B ● **Saint-Joseph**★★ £C

DOM. GILLES ROBIN Crozes-Hermitage

Gilles Robin Les Chassis-Sud, 26600 Mercurol
UK stockists: L&S

Gilles Robin has emerged as one of the leading lights among red Crozes

337

producers during the last 5 years. His wines have a depth and purity of Syrah fruit rarely found among his neighbours. He now has 12ha under vine and his output has reached between 4,500 and 5,000 cases a year. The regular Crozes, Papillon, has impressive and very pure varietal fruit while the Albéric Bouchet shows real depth, structure and character. Both wines will develop well and the Bouchet needs 5 years to achieve perfect harmony. A red Saint-Joseph, Andre Péalat, has now been added to this small range. (DM)

● **Crozes-Hermitage** Papillon★★ £C Albéric Bouchet★★★ £C

RENÉ ROSTAING   Côte-Rôtie

René Rostaing   69420 Ampuis
UK stockists: **Mis**, BBR, J&B, HHB, GBa, SVS, Las

Rostaing is now one of the very best producers of great Côte-Rôtie. He is continually seeking to keep yields in check, to harvest at optimum ripeness and to minimize handling in the cellar. The wines are uniformly bottled without filtration. He has tremendous vineyards to draw upon, having taken over the running of those of Albert Dervieux-Thaize as well as Marius Gentaz-Dervieux. The wines are deep and extracted but always refined and with supple, finely crafted, velvety tannins. The top *cuvées* are very ageworthy. They will improve in bottle for a decade or more. La Landonne is dense, massive in its youth, while the Côte Blonde is lighter and typically more elegant as one might expect from vines planted in these soils. The Condrieu is marked by glorious ripe, peachy varietal fruit and should be drunk young. (DM)

● **Côte-Rôtie**★★★ £D Classique★★★ £E La Viallières★★★★ £E
● **Côte-Rôtie** La Landonne★★★★★ £F Côte Blonde✪✪✪✪✪ £G
○ **Condrieu** La Bonnette★★★★ £E

MARC SORREL   Hermitage   marc.sorrel@wanadoo.fr

Marc Sorrel   Avenue Jean-Jaurès, 26600 Tain-l'Hermitage
UK stockists: CTy, Gau, NYg, Las

The top *cuvées*, both red and white, are some of the finest expressions of the great wines of the Hermitage hill. The regular bottlings, in particular the red, can be a touch disappointing and should often have more depth and substance. 2001, though, looks to be more impressive and Le Gréal potentially exceptional. The red Crozes-Hermitage is a reasonable example with moderately intense, dark berry fruit in a lighter style than some but stylish for what it is. What marks out Le Gréal is its powerful, dense and complex fruit and backward structure. If you give it 7 or 8 years at least you'll be rewarded with a great example of the appellation. In exceptional years, among them 1998, 91 and 90, this can be legendary. Les Rocoules is an equally fine, but equally backward example of great Marsanne. Honeyed, nutty and complex with age, this really needs at least 10 years. (DM)

● **Hermitage**★★★ £D Le Gréal★★★★★ £F
○ **Hermitage**★★★ £D Les Rocoules★★★★★ £F
● **Crozes-Hermitage**★★ £B ○ **Crozes-Hermitage**★ £B

CAVE DE TAIN L'HERMITAGE   Hermitage

Co-operative members 22 Route de Larnage, 26601 Tain-l'Hermitage Cedex
UK stockists: **PBW**,AAA

The growers belonging to this co-operative have a considerable holding, in total some 1,000ha, planted throughout the region and production is around 475,000 cases a year. The range is fairly extensive and there are varietal *vins de pays* as well as AC bottlings. These are sound but relatively unexciting. It is the top bottlings within each appellation, labelled as Nobles Rives, which particularly stand out. There are also special superior *cuvées* of Hermitage and

Crozes-Hermitage red. The former, Gambert de Loche, is from an individual plot of old vines. It is dense, rich and very complex, impressive indeed for a co-op wine. A further special bottling from Saint-Joseph, Esprit de Granit, has also been added to the range and this should enhance the quality of the somewhat disappointing regular Saint-Joseph. Occasionally a little *vin de paille* is also produced, which is rich, intense and nutty. (DM)

- ● **Hermitage** Les Nobles Rives★★ £D Gambert de Loche★★★ £E
- ○ **Hermitage** Les Nobles Rives★★★ £D
- ● **Crozes-Hermitage** Les Nobles Rives★ £B Les Hauts du Fief★★ £C
- ○ **Crozes-Hermitage** Les Nobles Rives★ £B
- ● **Cornas** Les Nobles Rives★★ £C
- ● **Saint-Joseph** Les Nobles Rives★ £B

DOM. DU TUNNEL Saint-Péray

Stéphane Robert 20 Rue de la République, 07130 Saint-Péray
UK stockists:HHB,Gau,Lib,FCA

Very good Saint-Péray as well as Cornas are made at this 3.5-ha property which was established as recently as 1996. The regular Saint-Péray is fresh, forward and attractively nutty, while the Prestige is denser and altogether more concentrated. The 2 Cornas are both splendid wines made from ancient vineyard plantings; the Prestige comes from a parcel of 80-year-old vines originally farmed by Marcel JUGE. The wines are dense, sumptuous and full of classic dark fruit, spice and black pepper, the Prestige characterised by complex old-viney fruit. The 2001 was particularly impressive. A small amount of well-crafted Saint-Joseph is also made. (DM)

- ● **Cornas**★★★ £D Prestige★★★★ £E ● **Saint-Joseph**★★★ £C
- ○ **Saint-Péray**★★ £B Prestige★★★ £C

DOM. GEORGES VERNAY Condrieu

Georges Vernay 1 Route National, Condrieu 69420
UK stockists: Yap, Win, Cco

Vernay is one of the great Condrieu producers. His daughter Christine now runs the domaine and they possess some 9ha of Viognier and a further 7ha of Syrah from which they are making increasingly impressive Côte-Rôtie, an appellation they used to struggle with. There has been some consultancy for the reds from Jean-Luc COLOMBO. Other reds are a simple red *vin de pays*, a sound fruit-driven Côtes du Rhône and a Saint-Joseph that as yet lacks the depth of the Côte-Rôties. Good white *vin de pays* Viognier is made from the youngest vines but it is the 3 Condrieus that are the main focus here. Terasses de l'Empire, the regular bottling, is well-crafted but lacks a little depth. The other 2 wines are part barrel-fermented and of serious depth and weight; Chaillées de L'Enfer is just a little more opulent and heady. Both will develop well in the short term. (DM)

- ● **Côte-Rôtie** Blonde du Seigneur★★★ £E Cuvée Maison Rouge★★★★ £E
- ○ **Condrieu** Les Terrasses de L'Empire★★★ £D Les Chaillées de L'Enfer★★★★ £E
- ○ **Condrieu** Coteau du Vernon★★★★ £E
- ○ **Vin de Pays** Viognier Le Pied de Samson★★ £C
- ● **Saint-Joseph**★ £B

FRANÇOIS VILLARD Condrieu

François Villard Montjoux, 42410 Saint-Michel-sur-Rhône
UK stockists: **HHB**

Out of a total of 9ha of vineyards, 3.5ha are in Condrieu, where 3 fine dry examples of the appellation are produced. Vinified in new oak on their lees with careful *bâtonnage*, they have considerable depth and structure for Viognier

339

and age uncharacteristically well. A sweet Condrieu, Quintessence, is also made as are very good Côte-Rôtie and red and white Saint-Joseph. The range is completed by *vin de pays* bottlings of impressive quality. A Merlot has been introduced to join the Syrah and Viognier. François is involved with Pierre GAILLARD and Yves CUILLERON in Les VINS DE VIENNE. (DM)

- ● **Côte-Rôtie** la Brocarde★★★★★ £E
- ● **Vin de Pays des Collines Rhodaniennes** Syrah★★ £B
- ○ **Vin de Pays des Collines Rhodaniennes** Viognier Contours de Deponcins★★★ £C
- ○ **Condrieu** Grand Vallon★★★ £E Les Terrasses du Palat★★★★ £E
- ○ **Condrieu** Coteaux de Poncin★★★★★ £E
- ○ **Condrieu** Quintessence✪✪✪✪✪ £G
- ● **Saint-Joseph** Côtes de Mairlant★★★ £C Reflet★★★★ £D
- ○ **Saint-Joseph** Côtes de Mairlant★★★★ £C

LES VINS DE VIENNE Côte-Rôtie

Y Cuilleron, P Gaillard & F Villard Le Bas de Seyssuel, 38200 Seyssuel
UK stockists: **Goe**,C&B,BBR,Lay

A recently established small-scale operation that is part domaine and part *négociant*. The 3 partners are re-establishing the pre-phylloxera vineyards of the Côteaux du Seyssuel to the west of Vienne. This once famous area, known to Pliny and Plutarch, produces the red Sotanum, a wine of real potential, and a partially barrel-aged Viognier, Taburnum. The vines are as yet very young at 6 years and the wines are likely to improve considerably as they age. The *négociant* offerings range from good to exciting. New oak is evident in all the wines but is well handled. One criticism might be that the character of the individual appellations can struggle to show through. The Côte-Rôtie Les Essartailles and Condrieu La Chambée particularly stand out. The best are undoubtedly very ageworthy. (DM)

- ● **Vin de Pays des Collines Rhodaniennes** Sotanum★★★★ £C
- ○ **Vin de Pays des Collines Rhodaniennes** Taburnum★★★ £C
- ● **Côte-Rôtie** Les Essartailles★★★★★ £E
- ○ **Condrieu** La Chambée★★★★ £E
- ● **Hermitage** Les Chirats de Saint-Christophe★★★ £E
- ○ **Hermitage** La Bachole★★★ £E
- ● **Crozes-Hermitage** Palignons★★ £C ○ **Crozes Hermiotage** Chaponnières★★ £C
- ● **Cornas** Les Barcillants★★★ £D
- ● **Saint-Joseph** L'Arzelle★★ £C ○ **Saint-Joseph** L'Elouède★★ £C
- ○ **Saint-Péray** Les Bialères★★★ £B
- ● **Châteauneuf du Pape** Les Oteliées★★★ £C
- ● **Gigondas** Les Pimpignoles★★★ £D ● **Vacqueyras** La Sillote★★ £B
- ● **Côtes du Rhône-Villages Visan** Tine★★★ £B ● **Cairanne** Perpendaille★★★ £B
- ● **Côtes du Rhône** Les Cranilles★★ £B ○ **Côtes du Rhône** Les Laurelles★★ £B

ALAIN VOGE Cornas

Alain Voge 4 Rue de l'Equerre, 07130 Cornas
UK stockists: GWW,VTr, SVS

As well as his very powerful and muscular Cornas, Alain Voge also produces some of the best Saint-Péray, both dry and sparkling. The Mélodie William and Harmonie are unoaked and marked by impressive nutty Marsanne fruit, while the Cuvée Boisée sees some new oak. The top Fleur du Crussol is amongst the very finest in the appellation. His Cornas vineyards are of increasingly venerable age and this is showing through in the wines with immensely complex smoky dark fruits and black spices emerging in the Vieilles Vignes and Vieille Fontaines bottlings. A very small amount of new oak is used to barrel-age the wines, which you should expect to cellar for 5 years or more. (DM)

● **Cornas**★★★ £D Vieilles Vignes★★★★ £E Vieilles Fontaines★★★★★ £E
O **Saint-Péray** Cuvée Mélodie William★★ £B Cuvée Harmonie★★ £B
O **Saint-Péray** Cuvée Boisée★★★ £B Fleur du Crussol★★★ £B Dry Vintage★ £B

OTHER WINES OF NOTE

GUY DE BARJAC ● **Cornas**★★ £D
DOM. BAROU O **Condrieu**★★ £D
DOM. GUY BERNARD ● **Côte-Rôtie**★★★ £E O **Condrieu**★★★ £E
DOM. DE BIGUET ● **Cornas**★★★ £D O **Saint-Péray**★★ £B
DOM. BOISSEYT-CHOL ● **Côte-Rôtie**★★★ £E
DOM. FRÉDÉRIC BOISSONET O **Condrieu**★★ £E Les Rochains★★★ £E
DOM. STÉPHANE CHABOUD ● **Cornas**★★★ £D O **Saint-Péray**★★ £B
JOEL CHAMPET ● **Côte-Rôtie**★★★ £E
CH. MONTLYS ● **Côte-Rôtie**★★ £E
CH. DU ROZAY O **Condrieu**★★ £D
CAVE DES CLAIRMONTS ● **Crozes-Hermitage**★ £B O **Crozes-Hermitage**★ £B
DOM. COLLONGE ● **Crozes-Hermitage**★ £B
EMMANUEL DARNAUD ● **Crozes-Hermitage** Mise en Bouche★★ £B
● **Crozes-Hermitage** Les Trois Chênes★★★ £C
MARTIN DAUBRÉE ● **Côte-Rôtie** Côte Brune★ £D
EDMOND ET DAVID DUCLAUX ● **Côte-Rôtie**★★★ £E
OLIVIER DUMAINE ● **Crozes-Hermitage**★★ £B O **Crozes-Hermitage**★ £B
DOM. DUMIEN-SURETTE ● **Cornas** Patou★★★ £D
CHRISTIAN FACCHIN O **Condrieu** Les Grands-Maison★★★ £E
DOM. FARJON ● **Saint-Joseph**★★ £C Ma Sélection★★★ £D
O **Condrieu**★★★ £D Les Grains Dorée★★★★ £E O **Saint-Joseph**★★ £C
PHILIPPE FAURY ● **Saint-Joseph**★★ £C Les Glorieuses★★★ £D
● **Côte-Rôtie**★★ £E O **Condrieu** La Berne★★ £E O **Saint-Joseph**★★ £C
CAVE FAYOLLE ● **Crozes-Hermitage** Les Pontaix★★ £B ● **Hermitage**★★ £D
O **Hermitage**★★ £D
DOM. FERRATON ● **Hermitage** Les Miaux★★★ £E Le Méal★★★★ £F O
Hermitage Le Reverdy★★★★ £F ● **Crozes-Hermitage** La Matinière★ £B
GILLES FLACHER ● **Saint-Joseph** Prestige★★ £C
O **Condrieu**★★ £D Cuvée Lea★★★ £E
DOM. GACHON ● **Saint-Joseph**★★ £C
HENRI GALLET ● **Côte-Rôtie**★★★ £E
DOM. GARON ● **Côte-Rôtie**★ £D Côte Blonde★★ £E
VINCENT GASSE ● **Saint-Joseph**★★ £C
● **Côte-Rôtie**★★ £D Vieilles Vignes★★★ £E
DOM. DES HAUTS CHASSIS ● **Crozes-Hermitage**★ £B
DOM. MICHEL JOHANN ● **Cornas** Cuvée SC★★ £D
DOM. MARCEL JUGE ● **Cornas**★ £D
DOM. LA BATELLERIE ● **Crozes-Hermitage**★ £B
DOM. YVES LAFOY ● **Côte-Rôtie**★★★ £D O **Condrieu** Moelleux★★★ £E
JACQUES LEMENCIER ● **Cornas**★★★ £D
DOM. LES BRUYÈRES ● **Crozes-Hermitage**★★ £D
BERNARD LEVET ● **Côte-Rôtie**★★ £D La Chavaroche★★★ £E
DOM. JEAN LIONNET ● **Cornas**★★ £C Rochepertuis★★★ £E
DOM. DES MARTINELLES ● **Crozes-Hermitage**★ £B
O **Crozes-Hermitage**★ £B
DOM. FRANÇOIS MERLIN O **Condrieu**★★ £D Cuvée Jeancaude★★★ £E
ROBERT MICHEL ● **Cornas** Cuvée de Coteaux★★ £C La Geynale★★★ £D
DOM. DIDIER MORION O **Condrieu**★★★ £E
DOM. MOUTON ● **Côte-Rôtie**★★★ £E
O **Condrieu** Côte Bonnette★★ £E Côte Chatillon★★★ £E
VINCENT PARIS ● **Cornas** Granit 30★★★ £D Granit 60★★★★ £E
DOM. PAVILLON-MERCUROL ● **Crozes-Hermitage**★★ £B
DOM. PICHAT ● **Côte-Rôtie**★★★ £D
CHRISTOPHE PICHON ● **Côte-Rôtie**★★★ £E ● **Saint-Joseph**★★ £C
O **Condrieu**★★★ £D

341

PHILIPPE PICHON ● Saint-Joseph★★ £C   O Condrieu★★ £D
JEAN-PAUL REMILLIER ● Côte-Rôtie £E
HERVÉ RICHARD O Condrieu★★ £D L'Amarage★★★ £E
O Saint-Joseph★★ £C ● Saint-Joseph★★★ £C
CAVE CO-OPÉRATIVE DE SAINT DÉSIRAT   ● Saint-Joseph★ £B
JEAN-MICHEL STEPHAN ● Côte-Rôtie★★ £D Coteau de Tupin★★★ £E
● Côte-Rôtie Vieilles Vignes En Coteau★★★ £F
TERROIRS DE FAMILLE ● Crozes-Hermitage★★ £B
JEAN-LOUIS THIERS ● Cornas £D
DOM. DE VALLOUIT ● Côte-Rôtie Les Roziers★★★ £E
● Hermitage Les Greffières★★★★ £F
DANIEL VERNAY ● Côte-Rôtie★★★ £D
NOËL VERSET ● Cornas★★★ £E
VIDAL FLEURY ● Côte-Rôtie★★★ £E La Chatillon★★★ £F
O Condrieu★★★ £E

Author's choice (DM)

10 of the Northern Rhône's most distinguished reds
THIERRY ALLEMAND ● Cornas Reynard
M CHAPOUTIER ● Hermitage Le Pavillon
CH. D' AMPUIS ● Côte-Rôtie La Turque
JEAN-LOUIS CHAVE ● Hermitage Ermitage Cuvée Cathelin
AUGUSTE CLAPE ● Cornas
CLUSEL ROCH ● Côte-Rôtie Les Grandes Places
PAUL JABOULET AINÉ ● Hermitage La Chapelle
DOM. JAMET ● Côte-Rôtie
RENÉ ROSTAING ● Côte-Rôtie Côte Blonde
MARC SORREL ● Hermitage Le Gréal

A choice of opulent dry whites
M CHAPOUTIER O Hermitage Cuveé de l'Orée
JEAN-LOUIS CHAVE O Hermitage
DOM. DU CHENE O Condrieu
YVES CUILLERON O Condrieu Chaillets Vieilles Vignes
DOM. YVES GANGLOFF O Condrieu
DOM. DU MURINAIS O Crozes Hermitage Vieilles Vignes
ANDRÉ PERRET O Condrieu Coteaux du Chéry
GEORGES VERNAY O Condrieu Les Chaillées de L'Enfer
FRANÇOIS VILLARD O Saint-Joseph Côtes de Mairlant
ALAIN VOGE O Saint-Péray Cuvée Fleur du Crussol

A selection of up and coming reds and whites
ALBERT BELLE ● Crozes-Hermitage Cuvée Louis Belle
M CHAPOUTIER ● Saint-Joseph Les Granits
YANN CHAVE ● Crozes-Hermitage Tête de Cuvée
JEAN-LUC COLOMBO O Hermitage Le Louet
DOM. COMBIER O Crozes-Hermitage Clos des Grives
YVES CUILLERON O Saint-Joseph Le Lombard
DELAS FRÈRES ● Crozes-Hermitage Le Clos
PIERRE GAILLARD O Côtes du Rhône Viognier
DOM. MICHEL OGIER ● Vin de Pays des Collines Rhodaniennes La Rosine
DOM. DU TUNNEL O Saint-Peray Prestige

Southern Rhône

DANIEL ET DENIS ALARY   Cairanne

Daniel & Denis Alary   Font d'Estevenas, Route de Rasteau, 84290 Cairanne
UK stockists: HHB, Sel

A comprehensive and impressive range of Côtes du Rhône and Cairanne village wines are made here from the Alarys' 25ha. Nearly 90% of the vineyard is planted to red varieties, with some of the plantings now of notable age. The floral, forward white Côtes du Rhône blends Clairette with Bourboulenc. The Font d'Estevenas white is a step up, a rich, nutty and complex blend of Roussanne with some Viognier. The reds are unfiltered, full of dense and aromatic *garrigue* scents and complex, heady, berry fruit. The Font d'Estevenas and Jean de Verde are among the best expressions of old-vine Grenache outside Châteauneuf-du-Pape. The former usually has a proportion of Syrah, whereas La Jean de Verde is 100% Grenache. The overall quality across all the wines is very good indeed as are the prices. The top 2 reds will age well. (DM)

- ● **Côtes du Rhône**★ £B ● **Côtes du Rhône-Villages Cairanne**★★ £B
- ● **Côtes du Rhône-Villages Cairanne** Réserve du Vigneron★★★ £B
- ● **Côtes du Rhône-Villages Cairanne** La Jean de Verde★★★ £C
- ● **Côtes du Rhône-Villages Cairanne** La Font d'Estevenas★★★★ £C
- O **Côtes du Rhône** La Chevre d'Or★★ £B
- O **Côtes du Rhône-Villages Cairanne** La Font d'Estevenas★★★ £C
- ◉ **Côtes du Rhône**★ £A

DOM. DES AMADIEU   Cairanne   www.achiary.com

Marylène & Michel Achiary   Quartier Beauregard, 84290 Cairanne
UK stockists: P-F

Small 7-ha domaine established in 1984 which produces some excellent-value Cairanne. The property is planted to Grenache, Syrah and Mourvèdre and the Grenache vines now average 50 years of age. Yields are restricted to an average of 35 hl/ha and *pigeage* is employed during vinification. With output a mere 1,500 cases or so the wines will not be the easiest to find. The small range consists of 2 wines which are labelled Vitalis and Vieilles Vignes. Vitalis generally blends all 3 of the varieties planted and is the softer, more vibrantly fruit-driven example of the 2. The Vieilles Vignes is usually crafted from an equal amount of Syrah and Grenache. It is denser and firmer and will age well in the medium term. The 2001 was nudging ★★★. (DM)

- ● **Côtes du Rhône-Villages Cairanne** Vitalis★★ £B
- ● **Côtes du Rhône-Villages Cairanne** Vieilles Vignes★★ £B

DOM. AMIDO   Tavel

Christian Amido   Rue des Carrières, 30126 Tavel

This is the most significant domaine in Tavel from a quality point of view, producing one of the best examples of the appellation. The wine undergoes a 36 hour pre-fermentation maceration and is fermented cool to preserve its attractive fresh berry fruit, something many in the AC fail to achieve. More important from a quality perspective are a fine Côtes du Rhône-Villages blended from Grenache (70%) and Syrah (30%) and a benchmark red Lirac. This is produced from 50-year-old Grenache (just over 50%) plus Syrah and Mourvèdre. It is aged first in cement tanks and then transferred to used oak. The wine shows rich dark berry fruit and classic southern herbal spice and will benefit from a year or 2 of bottle age. (DM)

- ● **Lirac**★★★ £B ● **Côtes du Rhône-Villages**★★ £B
- ◉ **Tavel** Les Amandines★★ £B

343

DOM. DES AMOURIERS   Vacqueyras

Patrick Gras   Les Garrigues, 84260 Sarrians
UK stockists: EoR, HHB

First-class operation run by Patrick Gras, producing very stylish, balanced wines. There are 34 ha all planted to reds, half Grenache with the balance a mix of Mourvèdre, Syrah and Carignan. Up until the mid-1990s the estate fruit was sold on but in only a few years this has become one of the finest sources in the AC. The Vacqueyras are wines of depth and rich savoury fruit and considerable structure, with new oak playing a large part in the style. The 1998, 99, 2000 and now 01 Genestes are benchmarks for the appellation and will age very well. Both Les Hautes Terasses and Les Genestes are ageworthy, the latter rising ★★★★ in recent vintages. (DM)

● **Vin de Pays du Vaucluse**★ £A   ● **Côtes du Rhône**★ £B
● **Vacqueyras**★★ £B Signature★★ £B Les Hautes Terrasses★★★ £C
● **Vacqueyras**Les Genestes★★★ £C

DOM. PAUL AUTARD   Châteauneuf-du-Pape

Autard family   Route de Châteauneuf-du-Pape, 84350 Courthézon
UK stockists: **Las**

A small but impressive range of wines is made by Jean-Paul Autard at his 12-ha family domaine. The winemaking style has become more modern over the last decade: the fruit is not only carefully sorted at harvested but the reds are now fully destemmed as well. The good, sound, forward Côtes du Rhône red blended from Syrah and Counoise should be drunk young. More serious are the red Châteauneuf-du-Papes. The Traditionelle *cuvée* blends 70% Grenache with Syrah, Counoise and Mourvèdre and is aged in a mix of *foudres* and *barriques*. It is marked by its peppery, herbal *garrigue* notes and approachable berry fruit. The Côte Ronde is considerably fuller and richer with a firmer structure. It demands 5 years' ageing, particularly in top years like 2000 and 01. A blend of Grenache and Syrah, it is aged in part new and part used *barriques* for up to 18 months. 2 whites are produced, a nicely concentrated, nutty and toasty barrel-fermented white Châteauneuf-du-Pape from Grenache Blanc, Clairette and Roussanne and a late-harvest *vin de pays*, Je ne Souvione, produced solely from Viognier. Rich, sweet and not at all cloying, it has sufficient fresh acidity to offer a fine balance of honey, peach and citrus flavours and should be drunk young. (DM)

● **Châteauneuf du Pape** Traditionelle★★★ £D La Côte Ronde★★★★ £E
○ **Châteauneuf du Pape**★★★ £D   ○ **Vin de Pays** Je ne Souvione★★★ £D

DOM. LUCIEN BARROT   Châteauneuf-du-Pape

Barrot family   Chemin du Clos, 84230 Châteauneuf-du-Pape
UK stockists: FMV, BBR, Maj, Bal

This is a small family-run operation with 20ha of vineyards spread across the Châteauneuf-du-Pape appellation. The Barrots have been established as winemakers here since the late 17th century. The vines are old, approaching 50 years, planted on limestones soils with a *galets roulés* stone topsoil. The resulting wine is dense, complex and stylish and possesses a classic rich, savoury, *garrigue*-scented character. It is blended from Grenache, Syrah, Mourvèdre and Cinsault and vinification is traditional: the grapes are not destemmed and maceration lasts up to 4 weeks in top years. The wine is then aged in *foudres* for around 18 months. Firmly structured when young, it will drink well at 5 years or so. Excellent value for the appellation. (DM)

● **Châteauneuf du Pape**★★★ £C

DOM. DE BEAURENARD   Châteauneuf-du-Pape   www.beaurenard.fr

Paul Coulon   Avenue Pierre-de-Luxembourg, 84231 Châteauneuf-du-Pape
UK stockists: BWC, Las

The Coulon family make an impressive range of stylish reds and whites in modern, well-equipped cellars. The lighter reds and white Châteauneuf-du-Pape are forward and full of fruit, the latter enjoying some lees-enrichment. The Côtes du Rhône Rasteau has 20% Syrah blended into the Grenache, to add to the wine's structure. The regular Châteauneuf-du-Pape red is supple, rich and forward, whereas the Boisrenard is a dense, powerful wine produced from very low yields of 15–20 hl/ha. It requires 6 or 7 years' ageing in years such as 1998, 99 and 2000. The fortified Rasteau is one of the better examples. (DM)

- **Châteauneuf du Pape★★★** £D Boisrenard★★★★★ £F
- **Côtes du Rhône★** £A ● **Côtes du Rhône-Villages Rasteau★★** £B
- **Rasteau★** £B O **Châteauneuf du Pape★★★** £C

DOM. LE BÉRANE   Côtes du Ventoux

Anne-Claire Rabatel & Bertrand Férary   Route de Flassan, 84570 Mormoiron
A very recently established 12-ha Ventoux property. The vines, though, are very old, particularly the Grenache that makes up 80% of the holding, and the *terroir* is excellent, south-east facing with a combination of finely drained argile and schist soils. Just 2 *cuvées* of red are currently produced and both have real potential. Les Agapes is a blend of 80/20 Grenache and Syrah, while top label Les Blaques is Syrah-dominated (80%). Care is taken not to over-extract the wines and the Grenache gets 18 days' vatting, the Syrah just 12. The wines are aged in *cuve* for 6 months and are marked by the quality and purity of fruit. Les Blaques will stand a bit of bottle-ageing, although the wines will be attractive young. (DM)

- **Côtes du Ventoux** Les Agapes★★ £B Les Blaques★★★ £C

DOM. BERTHET-RAYNE   Châteauneuf-du-Pape

Berthet-Rayne family   2334 Route de Caderousse, 84350 Courthézon
The Berthet-Rayne family produce a small range of good middle-grade Châteauneuf-du-Pape and sound red and white Côtes du Rhône from their property in the north of the appellation, where the limestone soils are covered by the famous *galet* stones. Of the Rhônes, the white offers straightforward light, nutty fruit, while the red is more intense, a blend dominated by Grenache and sourced from vineyards just on the Châteauneuf appellation boundary. Among the Châteauneuf labels, the white is in a clean fresh, fruit-driven style and should be drunk within a couple of years of release. The regular red is in a modern, fleshy mould with bright berry fruit and soft, easy tannins. It will drink well young. Vieilli en Fûts de Chêne was added with the successful 2000 vintage and produced again in 01. It will only be released in similarly good vintages and blends Grenache with Mourvèdre and Syrah. Cadiac is the most structured and dense of the wines, rich and impressively concentrated. Produced from equal proportions of Grenache and Mourvèdre it is relatively backward and firm young and will benefit from 4 or 5 years' cellaring. (DM)

- **Châteauneuf du Pape★★★** £D Vieilli en Fûts de Chêne★★★★ £E
- **Châteauneuf du Pape** Cuvée Cadiac★★★★ £F ● **Côtes du Rhône★** £B
- O **Châteauneuf du Pape★★** £C

BOIS DE BOURSAN   Châteauneuf-du-Pape

Jean et Jean-Paul Versino   Quartier Saint-Pierre, 84230 Châteauneuf-du-Pape
UK stockists: Tur

Small, extremely quality-conscious Châteauneuf producer, located just on the edge of the village itself, with around 15ha planted mainly to Grenache, Syrah and Mourvèdre. The white is relatively unexciting but both the reds are dense, powerful wines needing time to soften their youthful tannins and fiery character. Both are bottled without filtration. The Cuvée Felix is aged in part in smaller oak and offers more opulent and exotic characters. Both wines are finely structured and notably ageworthy. (DM)

● **Châteauneuf du Pape★★★★** £D Cuvée des Felix★★★★★ £E

HENRI BONNEAU Châteauneuf-du-Pape

Henri Bonneau 35 Rue Joseph-Ducos, 84230 Châteauneuf-du-Pape
UK stockists: HHB, BBR, Sec, Las

A somewhat controversial producer, M. Bonneau is, as was the late Jacques Reynaud at CH. RAYAS, one of Châteauneufs more interesting characters. The 2 special *cuvées*, which are produced from a high proportion of Grenache, are generally only bottled if the vintage justifies it – otherwise a regular Châteauneuf-du-Pape is produced – and he sells to *négociants* to maintain quality. Both the Marie Beurrier and Réserve des Célestins wines will improve with a decade or more in bottle. (DM)

● **Châteauneuf du Pape★★** £C Marie Beurrier★★★★★ £F
● **Châteauneuf du Pape** Réserve des Célestins✪✪✪✪✪ £G

BOSQUETS DES PAPES Châteauneuf-du-Pape

Boiron Family 18 Route d'Orange, BP 50, 84232 Châteauneuf-du-Pape
UK stockists: Cty, HHB, SVS, OWL, Las

The Boiron family own 8ha of vineyards but also lease from other properties, working with close to 30ha in total. There is a relatively dull white as well as 3 potentially classic dense and rich reds. Vinification is traditional and the fruit is not destemmed. They can be some of the most impressive traditional Châteauneufs, particularly the old-vine Cuvée Chantemerle. Bottling is carried out according to demand, so beware, there can be considerable variation. Tasting can reveal wines of extraordinary richness and also others bottled later that show excessive oxidation. The best advice is to buy as close to the vintage as possible. (DM)

● **Châteauneuf -du-Pape★★★** £C Cuvée Grenache★★★★ £E
● **Châteauneuf -du-Pape** Cuvée Chantemerle★★★★★ £F

DOM. BRESSY-MASSON Rasteau

Marie-France & Thierry Masson grange Neuve, 84110 Rasteau
First class Rasteau-based property with 30ha of vineyards. Although Viognier and Clairette are planted it is the red Côtes du Rhône Rasteau bottlings that stand out here. The regular red is a soft, brambly and immediately approachable blend of Grenache, Syrah, Mourvèdre and Cinsault. The Cuvée Paul Emile is fuller and richer and gets the benefit of some Grenache from vines that are over 80 years old. It is aged in small oak as is the A La Gloire de Mon Père, although in the case of this wine the oak is mostly new and the Syrah and Mourvèdre are also 45 years old. Expect to age the top 2 reds for at least 4–5 years. Also produced is a classic *rancio* Rasteau made in the traditional manner. (DM)

● **Côtes du Rhône-Villages Rasteau★★** £B Cuvée Paul Emile★★★ £C
● **Côtes du Rhône-Villages Rasteau** A La Gloire de Mon Père★★★ £C

DOM. BRUSSET Cairanne www.domaine brusset.fr

Daniel & Laurent Brusset Le Village, 84290 Cairanne
UK stockists: Eno, NYg, Sel, Las

The Brusset family make an excellent range of wines, producing some 30,000 cases annually from a sizeable vineyard holding of 84ha. The top wines are modern in style with pre-fermentation maceration, ageing on lees and no filtration. They are marked by rich, concentrated fruit and ripe but powerful tannins; they need to be cellared to show of their best but are less backward than some, particularly in Gigondas. Les Hauts de Montmirail is a magnificent, complex old-vine *cuvée* mainly from Grenache. In contrast lesser *cuvées* exhibit vibrant juicy fruit and are great youthful gluggers. (DM)

- **Gigondas** Le Grand Montmirail★★★ £C   Les Hauts de Montmirail★★★★ £D
- **Côtes du Rhône-Villages Cairanne** Travers★★ £B Vendange Chabrille★★★ £C
- **Côtes du Rhône-Villages Cairanne** Hommage à André Brusset★★★★ £D
- O **Côtes du Rhône-Villages Cairanne**★ £B
- **Côtes du Rhône** Laurent Brusset★ £A   O **Côtes du Rhône** Viognier★★ £C
- **Côtes du Ventoux** La Boudale★ £A

DOM. DE CABASSE Seguret www.domaine-de-cabasse.fr
Alfred Haeni   84110 Séguret
UK stockists: JNi

Alfred Haeni and his son Nicolas make an impressive small range of Rhône wines and have now added a small property in Banyuls where they are making some exciting Collioure. A total of 20ha are spread across Séguret, Sablet and Gigondas with white varieties accounting for just 2.3 hectares. A fine, juicy rosé is made by the *saignée* method and a white Séguret, Les Primevères, comes from 50% Grenache Blanc, 20% each of Roussanne and Viognier and a little Clairette, cool-fermented to emphasise its fresh floral fruit. Among the reds, Les Deux Anges comes from Sablet and is the most obviously fruit-driven; Grenache dominates, with a little Syrah and Carignan added. The Cuvée Garnacho, not surprisingly dominated by Grenache but with a little Carignan, Counoise and Syrah, is richer and more complex with a marked old-vine character showing through. The dense and structured Casa Bassa, a blend of Grenache (55%) and Syrah, is aged in *barriques* for 12 months and comes from vines up to 50 years old. It has perhaps more overt muscle than the piercingly intense Gigondas, which is aged in *foudres*. The top wine, the D'Eux, is a blend two-thirds Syrah and one-third Grenache aged in barrel for 18 months. Rich, dense and concentrated, it needs time to throw off the marked new oak character. At Vignoble de Terrimbio they are producing an extremely impressive red Collioure from very old Grenache and Carignan aged traditionally in *cuve*. A barrel-fermented white from Grenache Gris is also produced. (DM)

Domaine de Cabasse
- **Côtes du Rhône-Villages Séguret** Cuvée de La Casa Bassa★★★ £C
- **Côtes du Rhône-Villages Séguret** Cuvée D'Eux★★★ £C
- **Côtes du Rhône-Villages Séguret** Cuvée Garnacho★★★ £C
- **Côtes du Rhône-Villages Sablet** Les Deux Anges★★ £B   ● **Gigondas**★★★ £C
- O **Côtes du Rhône-Villages Séguret** Les Primevères★★ £B
- ◉ **Côtes du Rhône-Villages Séguret** Le Rose de Marie-Antoinette★ £B

Vignoble de Terrimbo
- **Collioure** Primo★★★ £C

CAVE DE CAIRANNE Cairanne
Co-operative members   84290 Cairanne
UK stockists: RSo

Very good modern co-op producing an extensive range of wines from this important southern Rhône village as well as decent straightforward Côtes du Rhône. The basic *cuvées* represent good value with attractive berry fruit and are best drunk young, while the top wines are a notch up in quality. The Réserve des Voconces is made from 40-year-old vines. The red Cuvée Salyens sees 30% new oak while the Cuvée Antique is quite firmly structured and will benefit

347

from 3 or 4 years of ageing. The top reds are bottled unfiltered and represent very fair value for money. (DM)

- ● **Côtes du Rhône-Villages Cairanne** Temptation★ £B Grand Réserve★ £B
- ● **Côtes du Rhône-Villages Cairanne** Réserve des Voconces★★ £B
- ● **Côtes du Rhône-Villages Cairanne** Cuvée Antique★★ £B Cuvée Salyens★★ £B
- ○ **Côtes du Rhône-Villages Cairanne** Cuvée Salyens★★ £B

DOM. DE CASSAN Beaunes-de-Venise

Marie-Odile Paillet 84190 Beaumes-de-Venise
UK stockists: **SVS**
This fine Beaumes-de-Venise property is equally well known for the quality of its fine, sturdy, classic Gigondas. This is a dark, structured wine of great depth and persistence, so far at very reasonable price for the AC. The Beaumes-de-Venise bottles are really no less impressive. The white is floral and lightly honeyed with an enticing herbal edge and offers good concentration and depth at this level. The regular red is soft and lightly structured but with sufficient depth to stand a little age. The Saint-Christophe benefits from some of the domaine's older vineyard holdings, some up to 45 years, which add greater depth and complexity. Expect both this and the Gigondas to evolve for 8–10 years. (DM)

- ● **Côtes du Rhône-Villages Beaumes-de-Venise**★★ £B
- ● **Côtes du Rhône-Villages Beaumes-de-Venise** Cuvée Saint-Christophe★★★ £C
- ● **Gigondas**★★★ £C ○ **Côtes du Rhône-Villages Beaumes de Venise**★★ £B

DOM. DU CAYRON Gigondas

Michel Faraud 84190 Gigondas
UK stockists: JAr
Just 1 wine is made at this traditional estate, and very good it is in most years. The vineyard holding is not small at 15ha, split between Grenache (70%) and an equal amount of Cinsault and Syrah, and yields 5,000 cases a year. With vines close to 50 years old and very well-drained stony soils producing fruit of exceptional quality, this is one of the best estates in the appellation. Odd years like 1998 can be a bit disappointing, but most recent vintages have been on good form. 2002 has yet to be tasted. (DM)

- ● **Gigondas**★★★ £C

DOM. DE LA CHARBONNIÈRE Châteauneuf-du-Pape

Michel Maret 84230 Châteauneuf-du-Pape
UK stockists: GWW,VWs, BBR
Generally good, if not in the top division. The wines are produced from a total of 21ha of vines. Michel Maret avoids filtration and in the best years the results are very impressive. The Mourre de Perdrix is partially aged in new wood, but it is the impressively concentrated Haut Brusquières (blending a proportion of Syrah with Grenache) and Vieilles Vignes bottlings that really stand out. The Vacqueyras is a good chunky, earthy example and represents good value for money. (DM)

- ● **Vacqueyras**★★ £B
- ● **Châteauneuf-du-Pape**★★£C Mourre des Perdrix★★★ £D
- ● **Châteauneuf-du-Pape** Haut Brusquières★★★★ £E Vieilles Vignes★★★★ £E
- ○ **Châteauneuf-du-Pape**★ £C

GÉRARD CHARVIN Châteauneuf-du-Pape

Gérard Charvin Quartier Maucoil, 84100 Orange
UK stockists: **Las**,VTr
Small, high-quality domaine now run by Laurent Charvin, producing full-

blown, rich spicy reds. Both the Côtes du Rhône and the Châteauneuf-du-Pape offer quality and value. The latter is a blend of Grenache with a little Syrah, Mourvèdre and Vaccarese adding both definition and a firm youthful structure. The wine has been particularly impressive in the current run of fine vintages – a real blockbuster style, it will age very well. (DM)

● **Côtes du Rhône**★★ £B   ● **Châteauneuf-du-Pape**★★★★ £D

CH. DE BEAUCASTEL   Châteauneuf-du-Pape

Perrin family   84350 Courthezon
UK stockists: Mis,Far,Tan,Rae,F&M

Among the very top echelon of producers in the southern Rhône. Notable for the organic approach in their 131ha estate vineyards, where all 13 permitted varieties are planted, the Perrins also employ a process called *vinification à chaud* for their red Châteauneuf, which extracts good colour and fruit and guards against bacteria and oxidation. The very finest quality is achieved in both red and white, the former unusually dominated by Mourvèdre and Syrah, and there is a good second label Coudoulet de Beaucastel. The red is not filtered but is given a light fining to help soften the very firm structure of the wine in its youth. Also produced are a range of *négociant* wines under the Domaines PERRIN label, while the Côtes du Rhône property Château du Grand Prebois is a recent acquisition. Further afield the Perrins have a partnership in the Californian Paso Robles winery TABLAS CREEK. Both the Châteauneuf red and white must be cellared, up to 8–10 years in top vintages. (DM)

● **Châteauneuf-du-Pape**★★★★★ £E   Homage à Jacques Perrin✪✪✪✪✪ £H
O **Châteauneuf-du-Pape**★★★★ £E   Vieilles Vignes✪✪✪✪✪ £G
● **Côtes du Rhône** Coudoulet du Beaucastel★★★ £C
O **Côtes du Rhône** Coudoulet du Beaucastel★★ £C

CH. DU CAMPUGET   Costières de Nîmes   www.campuget.com

Dalle family   30129 Manduel
UK stockists: N&P

Sizeable Nîmes property with 160ha under vine. As well as producing a range of Costières de Nîmes under the Campuget label, the Dalle family also own Château de l'AMARINE. A good nutty white blend from Grenache Blanc and Roussanne, a Vin du Pays du Gard Viognier and a rosé from Grenache and Syrah are produced in addition to the reds. Vineyard age now averages around 25 years. The soft, forward and lightly herb-scented Tradition red is a blend of Syrah (65%), Grenache (30%) and a little Mourvèdre. The Prestige (Syrah and Grenache) and the new 1753 (mainly Syrah) offer more depth and concentration. The 1753 is in a very modern, vibrant and fleshy style. Both are edging ★★★. (DM)

● **Costières de Nîmes** Tradition★★ £B   Reserve★★ £C   1753★★ £C

CH. DE FONSALETTE   Côtes du Rhône

Reynaud family   84290 Lagarde-Pareol
UK stockists: Sec, Blx, Las

Benchmark 11-ha Côtes du Rhône property owned by the Reynaud family of CHÂTEAU RAYAS. Emmanuel Reynaud now also undertakes vinification here as well as at Rayas and his own Vacqueyras property, CHÂTEAU DES TOURS. The regular bottling is a blend of Grenache with a sizeable dollop of Cinsault. The Syrah is a varietal bottling. These fine, intense and firmly structured wines are long-lived albeit expensive examples of the AC. (DM)

● **Côtes du Rhône**★★★ £C   Syrah★★★★ £D   O **Côtes du Rhône**★★★ £C

349

CH. DE FONTSÉGUGNE Côtes du Rhône

Geren family 84470 Chateauneuf de Gadagne

Impressive, small Côtes du Rhône property which produced its own wines for the first time in 2000. The vineyard, planted on well-drained gravel-pebble soils, is tended with minimal use of fertilisers and the resulting wines are all bottled unfiltered. Three *cuvées* are produced. The Tradition, from 20-year-old vines, is a blend of Grenache, Syrah, Mourvèdre, Cinsault and Carignan, while Santo Estello comes from 30-year-old vines and is a blend of Grenache (70%) and Syrah (20%) with the balance Mourvèdre. It is aged for 10 months in 500-litre *tonneaux*. The Li Felibre differs in that it is aged in smaller oak, all used. All the wines are marked by impressive fruit purity and the top 2 labels will develop well with 5 years' ageing. (DM)

● **Côtes du Rhône** Tradition★★ £B Santo Estello★★★ £B Li Felibre★★★ £C

CH. LA GARDINE Châteauneuf-du-Pape www.gardine.com

Brunel family Route de Roquemaure, BP 35, 84231 Châteauneuf-du-Pape
UK stockists: T&W

A modern approach to vinification here allied to a dedication to terroir results in an impressive range of wines. The reds are dense and deeply coloured when young but supple and impeccably balanced. In their youth they are sturdy and firm and they require several years' ageing. Temperature control is used in producing fruity, gloriously nutty whites, with new oak in abundance in the top cuvées. The Brunels purchased the Lirac property Château Saint-Roch in 1998 and have started to bring about considerable improvements. The reds in particular have a fine, subtle garrigue-laden intensity. (DM)

Château La Gardine

● **Côtes du Rhône-Villages**★ £B
● **Châteauneuf-du-Pape** Tradition★★★★ £D
● **Châteauneuf-du-Pape** Cuvée des Générations Gaston Philippe★★★★★ £F
○ **Châteauneuf-du-Pape** Tradition★★★ £D
○ **Châteauneuf-du-Pape** Cuvée des Generations Marie-Léoncie★★★★ £E

Château Saint-Roch

● **Lirac** Tradition★★ £C Cuvée Confidentielle★★★ £D
○ **Lirac** Tradition★ £C

CH. LA NERTHE Châteauneuf-du-Pape

LVMH Route de Sourgues, 84230 Châteauneuf-d-Pape
UK stockists: BBR, C&C

This large (for Châteauneuf) property has been performing at a high level since it was purchased by the Richard family in the mid-1980s. Annual production is now around 25,000 cases. There tends to be less Grenache in the reds here than elsewhere. The Cadettes, a sturdy blend of 100-year-old Grenache and Mourvèdre, is right on the edge of ★★★★★ and was undoubtedly so in 2000. Throughout the small range a modern, sophisticated approach to vinification has produced excellent results, with destemming and extended vatting for reds and increasing use of *barriques* for both reds and whites. (DM)

● **Châteauneuf-du-Pape**★★★★ £D Cuvée des Cadettes★★★★ £E
○ **Châteauneuf-du-Pape**★★★ £C Clos de Beauvenir★★★★ £D

CH. MAS NEUF Costières de Nîmes www.chateaumasneuf.com

Luc Baudet 30600 Gallician
UK stockists: VTr, Vnf

Luc Baudet has a sizeable property of 60ha, 53ha of which are planted to red varieties. Of the whites the regular Costières de Nîmes is straightforward and fruity with some nutty, spicy tones. Richer and fuller are the Compostelle Blanc, a blend of Grenache Blanc and Roussanne which is lent some additional weight from ageing in oak, and the *vin de pays* Chardonnay/Viognier blend which is leaner but more aromatic. The regular red is a sturdy, forward blend of Syrah, Grenache and Mourvèdre with a hint of Carignan adding some herbal spice notes. The Compostelle red, a blend of Syrah, Grenache and Mourvèdre, is a serious step up. There are 3 very good *vin de pays* varietal reds, the Si Rare is 100% Syrah, La Mourvache a 50/50 blend of Mourvedre and Grenache. There is also a limited-production red *super-cuvée*, Armonio, made in association with Louis Mitjavile of CH.TERTRE-RÔTEBOEUF in Saint-Emilion. None of the top wines is either fined or filtered after a long 30-day maceration and ageing is in *barriques* for 8–12 months, in the case of the Armonio 20 months and in 100% new wood. These wines will benefit from at least 2 or 3 years' further cellaring after release. (DM)

- ● **Vin de Pays d'Oc** Armonio★★★★ £E Si Rare★★★★ £D La Mourvache★★★ £C
- ● **Vin de Pays d'Oc** Merlot★★★ £C Syrah★★★ £C
- ● **Costières de Nîmes**★★ £B Compostelle★★★ £C
- O **Costières de Nîmes** Compostelle★★ £B
- O **Vin de Pays d'Oc** Chardonnay/Viognier★★ £B

CH. MONT-REDON   Châteauneuf-du-Pape   www.chateaumontredon.fr

Abeille-Fabre family   BP 10, 84321 Châteauneuf-du-Pape
UK stockists: **PFx**,Sel

By the standards of the appellation this is a large property producing good to very good rather than exceptional wines. Vinification is now modern, using a mix of *inox* and some *barriques* for the Châteauneuf bottlings. A Lirac property, Château Cantegril, has recently been purchased and these wines are now to be marketed under the Mont-Redon label. Expect quality at Cantegril to improve. The red Châteauneuf ages well over the medium term, acquiring additional depth and finesse. These are very fairly priced wines. (DM)

- ● **Côtes du Rhône**★★ £B ● **Châteauneuf-du-Pape**★★★ £D ● **Lirac**★★ £B
- O **Châteauneuf-du-Pape**★★★ £C O **Côtes du Rhône**★ £B Viognier★ £B

CH. MOURGUES DU GRÈS   Costières de Nîmes

François Collard   Route de Bellegarde, 30300 Beaucaire
UK stockists:Bal

Some 20,000 cases of red, white and rosé are now made here each year. As one would expect the majority of the planting is to red varieties, which make up 34ha of the 40ha. Of these Syrah accounts for 70%, the balance being mainly Grenache with a small amount of Carignan and Mourvèdre. Whites consist of Grenache (40%), Roussanne (40%) and Viognier. Galets is the label for the basic red, white and rosé and these are straightforward wines characterised by their approachable, forward fruit. The second tier Terre d'Argence wines are more serious. There is a nutty, floral white dominated by Roussanne and a dense, powerful red. The top wine is Capitelles des Mourgues, which spends a year in barrel. There is also a premium rosé under the same label. The top reds will improve with short ageing. (DM)

- ● **Costières de Nîmes** Galets Rouge★★ £B Terre d'Argence★★★ £B
- ● Capitelles des Mourgues★★★ £C
- O **Costières de Nîmes** Terre d'Argence★★ £B

CH. D'OR ET DE GUEULES   Costières de Nîmes

Diane de Puymorin   Chemin des Cassagnes, Route de Générac, 30800 Saint-Gilles
UK stockists:Maj

This property was very recently established (in 1998) and the wines appear to

351

be improving with every vintage. The vineyards have an excellent south to south-east exposure and its large pebbles and stones retain heat well, aiding ripening. A couple of rosés are produced including a Cuvée Trassegum which is part barrel-fermented. The Cep de Diane Chardonnay is full, rich and toasty, with an almost toffeed character. It is vinified in barrel on lees. There are 2 lower-level Costières de Nîmes reds, of which the Tradition, a blend of Grenache, Carignan and Mourvèdre, has more dimension than the Classique. Some of the Carignan is very old and adds dark and spicy complexity. Les Cimels is a blend of Syrah with very old Carignan with yields restricted to 35 hl/ha. The wine is dark, spicy and full of old-viney character. Top of the line are the Cuvée Trassegum red (formerly Cuvée Prestige) and La Bolida. Trassegum is now aged in less oak than in the debut 1998 vintage and is the better for it. La Bolida is a blend of 90% very old Mourvèdre and 10% Syrah. Rich and supple it could do with just a little more refinement but is a wine of great potential. (DM)

● **Costières de Nîmes** Tradition★★ £B Les Cimels★★ £B Cuvée Trassegum★★★ £C
● **Costières de Nîmes** La Bolida★★★ £D
O **Vin de Pays d'Oc** Le Ceps de Diane★★★ £C

CH. PESQUIÉ Côtes du Ventoux

Chaudière Bastide family 84570 Mormoiron
UK stockists: VWs, OWL

Medium-sized property with over 70ha of vineyards producing some 25,000 cases a year. Quality is generally good across the board, with attractive forward, fruit-driven styles being the order of the day. The Terrasses labels are simple and straightforward and there is a very decent fresh and characterful rosé, Perle de Roses. The real stars here, though, are the Prestige and Quintessence. These are a serious step up and are among the best examples of the appellation. Prestige is dominated by Syrah with some old-vine Grenache lending opulence and complexity. Quintessence is 80% Syrah but the small proportion of Grenache is 70 years old. The wines are aged in small barrels, around 30–35% new. Both are impressively cellarworthy. Ageing for 4 or 5 years is advisable. (DM)

● **Côtes du Ventoux** Terre Précieuse★ £B Prestige★★★ £B Quintessence★★★ £B
◉ **Côtes du Ventoux** Perle de Roses★ £A
O **Vin de Pays** Chardonnay du Pesquié★ £B Viognier du Pesquié★ £B

CH. RAYAS Châteauneuf-du-Pape

Reynaud family Route de Courthézon, 84230 Châteauneuf-du-Pape
UK stockists: OWL, BBR, Las

Legendary estate, which produced stunning red and white Châteauneuf for decades under the late Jacques Reynaud. The second label, Pignan, is also very impressive and comes from a separate plot rather than a selection. The property consists of just under 14ha with old vines planted on sand and clay/limestone soils, rather than on *galets roulés*. The red is made solely from Grenache while an even split of Clairette and Grenache Blanc contribute to the very ageworthy white. The wines are now vinified by Jacques' nephew, Emmanuel Reynaud of CHATEAU DES TOURS, who also produces the wines at the Rayas sister property CHATEAU DE FONSALETTE. They have unquestionably been very fine in the late 1990s but lack some of the sublime quality of earlier years. (DM)

● **Châteauneuf-du-Pape**◉◉◉◉ £F Pignan★★★★★ £E
O **Châteauneuf-du-Pape**★★★★★ £E

CH. REDORTIER Gigondas

Étienne & Sabine de Menthon 84190 Suzette
UK stockists: BRW

Although a little white is produced it is the reds that show real refinement and class at this excellent property. As yet the overall vine age, at around 25 years, is younger than at some other estates, so there should be more to to look forward to. The blend for the Gigondas is dominated by Grenache but there is a hefty dollop of Syrah as well. The wine is firmer and more structured than some of its neighbours. It undergoes extended cask-ageing and requires a few years of patience. The Beaumes-de-Venise Cuvée Prestige is an undoubted star of that village. (DM)

● **Côtes du Rhône-Villages Beaumes-de-Venise★★** £B Cuvée Prestige★★ £C
● **Gigondas★★★** £C

CH. SAINT-COSME Gigondas louis@chateau-st-cosme.com

Louis Barruol 84190 Gigondas
UK stockists: Dec, NYg, Han

Louis Barruol owns vines only in Gigondas but in recent years he has made an excellent small range of *négociant* wines as well. The Côtes du Rhône offerings represent excellent value, notably the reds, whereas the Gigondas Cuvée Valbelle, Châteauneuf-du-Pape and Côte-Rôtie are all impressively concentrated and ageworthy. The Gigondas bottlings are dense and powerful and quite marked by youthful new oak. At their best they are both intense and complex. There is also decent if not yet top-flight Condrieu but the potential here is exciting and current releases are very fairly priced. (DM)

● **Côtes du Rhône★★** £B Les Deux Albions★★ £B
○ **Côtes du Rhône★** £A ● **Gigondas★★** £C Cuvée Valbelle★★★ £D
● **Châteauneuf-du-Pape★★★** £E ● **Côte-Rôtie★★★** £E ○ **Condrieu★★** £E

CH. SAINT-ESTÈVE D'UCHAUX Côtes du Rhône-Villages

Marc Français Route de Sérignan, 84100 Uchaux
UK stockists:HBJ

Some very good reds and whites are made at this sizeable 60-ha property in the northern Vaucluse, at the southern limit of the Côtes du Rhône-Villages appellation. There are 3 regular reds and the same number of whites. The straightforward white Côtes du Rhône is a blend of mainly Grenache Blanc and Roussanne. There are also 2 fine Viognier-based whites, one from young vines which is blended with a little Grenache Blanc and a very striking top *cuvée*, Dionysos, which is 100% varietal. In reds, there is a good straightforward fruit-driven Côtes du Rhône as well as 2 more serious Côtes du Rhône-Villages. Grande Réserve is 60% Grenache and 40% Syrah whereas the dense and impressively structured Vieilles Vignes is the reverse blend. The range is completed by a straightforward juicy rosé and a Méthode Traditionelle Blanc de Blancs sparkler. There is also a very limited production pricey oak-aged Viognier Cuvée Thérèse. Top reds will benefit from 2 or 3 years' ageing. (DM)

● **Côtes du Rhône** Tradition★ £B
● **Côtes du Rhône-Villages** Grande Réserve★★ £C Vieilles Vignes★★★ £C
○ **Côtes du Rhône★** £B Viognier Jeune Vignes★★ £B
○ **Côtes du Rhône-Villages** Dionysos★★★ £C

CH. DES TOURS Vacqueyras

Emmanuel Reynaud Quartier des Sablons, 84260 Sarrians
UK stockists: Yap, Bib, Rae

As well as owning this excellent 40-ha property, Emmanuel Reynaud, the nephew of the late Jacques Reynaud, is now vinifying the wines at Château

353

RAYAS and Château de FONSALETTE. His Vacqueyras has long been a
yardstick example for the AC and is produced from mainly Grenache from
very low-yielding old vines. Always emphasising classic *garrigue* aromas, these
are complex, even refined wines, in marked contrast to some of the more
extracted examples of some of his neighbours. A ripe and fruit-laden red and
nutty white *vin de pays* complete the small range. (DM)

● **Côtes du Rhône**★★ £B ● ▼**Vacqueyras**★★★ £C O **Côtes du Rhône**★ £B

DOM. CHAUME-ARNAUD Vinsobres

Valérie & Philippe Chaume-Arnaud 26110 Vinsobres
UK stockists:**FMV**, BBR

This is a good source of well-priced southern Rhône red and white. The
domaine is small with 13.5ha situated around the lesser-known village of
Vinsobres. Reds are dominated by Grenache and Syrah and there is a little
Viognier and Marsanne for the white. Quality is key, yields are kept low and no
artificial fertilizers are used on the soil. The property also benefits from some
very old vines. The small amount of Carignan used in the Vinsobres red is now
over 60 years old. Both the Vinsobres reds will develop well in bottle with 3 or
4 years' age. (DM)

● **Côtes du Rhône**★★ £B
● **Côtes du Rhône-Villages Vinsobres**★★ £B La Cadene★★★ £C
O **Côtes du Rhône-Villages Vinsobres**★★ £B

DOM. DE LA CITADELLE Côtes du Lubéron

Yves & Alexis Rousset-Rouard Route de Cavaillan, 84560 Ménerbes
UK stockists:HHB,Vnf

Among the absolute top flight of producers in the Lubéron appellation. The
Rousset-Rouards have 44ha of vineyards spread across no fewer than 65
separate parcels. The soils are highly varied and they possess some very fine
terroirs. The winery is completely gravity-fed and stainless steel, temperature
control and new oak are all used. Of the *vins de pays*, the Cabernet Sauvignon
is sound if a touch leafy, the Viognier more interesting with some vibrant
honey and peach character. La Châtaignier is the basic Lubéron label and red,
white and rosé are all produced. The red is soft and berry-laden, immediately
drinkable. Les Artèmes white is an enticing floral, nutty blend of Roussanne,
Clairette, Grenache Blanc, very old Ugni Blanc and a smattering of Marsanne
and Bourboulenc which is aged in *inox* on fine lees. The red Les Artèmes
comes from Syrah (65%), and Grenache (30%) with the remainder Mourvèdre
and Carignan. Ageing is for 12 months in a mix of *barriques* and *foudres*. The
top wine, Le Gouverneur, is an impressively dense and concentrated blend of
Syrah, Grenache and Mourvèdre with a little very old Carignan adding a dark,
spicy complexity. Ageing for this is 12 months in small oak, 20% new. 2 tiny-
volume *cuvées* from single parcels of old vines can be obtained from the winery:
Noé comes from Syrah, Paul from Mourvèdre. (DM)

● **Côtes du Luberon** Les Artèmes★★★ £B Le Gouverneur Saint-Auban★★★ £C
● **Côtes du Luberon** La Châtaignier★★ £B ● **Vin de Pays** Cabernet Sauvignon★ £B
O **Côtes du Luberon** Les Artèmes★★ £B O **Vin de Pays** Viognier★ £B

CLOS DU CAILLOU Châteauneuf-du-Pape

Jean-Denis Vacheron 84350 Courthezon
UK stockists: HHB, BBR, NYg, Las

Jean-Denis Vacheron (related to the VACHERONS of Sancerre) has been in
charge of the winemaking at this domaine since the late 1990s and quality has
gone from strength to strength. Careful vineyard management, modern
vinification with some malolactic in cask and a tight control of yields are

producing excellent results. Les Quartz is tight and firmly structured, the Réserve bottling richer and more opulent with added dimension from a large dollop of Mourvèdre. The top 2 *cuvées* will age very well. (DM)

● **Côtes du Rhône** Bouquet des Garrigues★ £B
● **Châteauneuf-du-Pape**★★★ £D Les Quartz★★★★ £E
● **Châteauneuf-du-Pape** Réserve Clos du Caillou★★★★★ £F

CLOS DE CAVEAU Vacqueyras

EARL Le Clos de Caveau 84190 Vacqueyras

Manager Jérôme Guimberteau has run this small estate with great skill for the past 10 years. Indeed the Lao Muse is one of the signature wines of the appellation. The 12-ha vineyard consists of a single plot on the slopes of the Dentelles de Montmirail. With organically tended vineyards planted at some altititude on excellent limestone subsoils the potential for high quality is there and yields from Grenache, Syrah, Cinsault and Mourvèdre are also restricted to a maximum of 35 hl/ha. The Côtes du Rhône is soft, juicy and forward and the regular Vacqueyras is produced in a similarly fruit-driven style but offers a firm grip and structure. The Lao Muse is deeper with darker spicy berry fruit and a real old-vine quality and depth. The oldest vines here are now up to 70 years. The Vacqueyras needs a little age, the Lao Muse ideally 5 years or so. (DM)

● **Vacqueyras**★★ £B Lao Muse★★★ £C ● **Côtes du Rhône**★★ £B

CLOS DES CAZAUX Vacqueyras

Jean-Michel & Frédéric Archimbaud-Vache 84190 Vacqueyras
UK stockists: CBg, Lay, VWs, Tan

The Archimbaud-Vache family make a surprisingly diverse range of wines from their holdings in Vacqueyras and Gigondas. There is a very good nutty white Vacqueyras, a blend of Clairette, Roussane and Grenache Blanc which is aged in *cuve* to emphasise its fruit. The Blanc Barrique is vinified in wood and has a small portion of Viognier to add fragrance. A very small amount of a 100% Grenache Blanc Quintessence is also made. The red Cuvées Saint-Roche and Reservé are mainly Grenache with some Syrah. The former has 5% Mourvèdre and comes from marginally older vines. The Templiers is dominated by Syrah whereas the Prestige is solely Syrah. Green harvesting is practised and there is minimal intervention in the cellar. Particularly unusual and generally successful is a late-harvest Vacqueyras produced from Grenache infected by noble rot. It has great depth and intensity. Expect the reds to develop well in the medium term, particularly the Syrah based *cuvées*. (DM)

● **Vacqueyras** Cuvée des Templiers★★★ £B Réserve★★★ £C
● **Vacqueyras** Grénat Noble★★★★ £C
● **Vacqueyras** Cuvée St Roche★★★ £B Réserve★★★ £B
O **Vacqueyras** Cuvée des Clefs d'Or★★ £B Blanc Barrique★★ £B
● **Gigondas** La Tour Sarrazine★★★ £C

CLOS DU MONT OLIVET Châteauneuf-du-Pape

Sabon family Chemin Bois la Ville, 84230 Châteauneuf-du-Pape
UK stockists: Hal, Rae

These are very traditional, old fashioned examples of the appellation. The regular bottling is moderately dense with some marked dark fruit and herbal scents and reasonable depth. The Cuvée du Papet is bigger and fuller. The fruit is not destemmed, which works very well in the best years, but occasionally the wines can show a marked rusticity and some hard and green tannin in more challenging years. Bottling occurs in several stages, so the fruit will not be consistent. Buy as soon after the vintage as you can. (DM)

● **Châteauneuf-du-Pape**★★★ £C Cuvée du Papet★★★★ £E
O **Châteauneuf-du-Pape**★★ £C

CLOS DES PAPES   Châteauneuf-du-Pape

Avril family 13 Avenue Pierre-de-Luxembourg, BP 8, 84231 Châteauneuf-du-Pape
UK stockists: RsW, Rae, SVS, BBR

One of the great benchmark names in Châteauneuf-du-Pape, producing just 1 white and 1 red. The Avrils have 32ha of which 29ha are planted to reds. Considerable investment in the cellar during the 1990s has enabled the property to go from strength to strength. The red is a very structured, ageworthy example of the AC. It is always destemmed and the different varieties are fermented together, which the Avrils feel adds complexity. The red needs 5 or 6 years' patience and the white will also age well, which is unusual for a white Châteauneuf. Vincent has now taken over the winemaking from his father Paul. (DM)

● **Châteauneuf-du-Pape★★★★★** £E   O **Châteauneuf-du-Pape★★★★** £D

CLOS PETITE BELLANE   Valréas

Olivier Peuchot   Chemin de Sainte-Croix, 84600 Valréas
UK stockists:Odd

Impressive property producing modern, stylish wines with classic Rhône fruit. The vineyard covers an area of 44ha and some of the vines, particularly the Grenache, are up to 65 years old. The white Côtes du Rhône is half Roussanne and half Viognier and like all the whites is given a period of *macération pelliculaire*. The white Les Echalas is finer and purer, produced from 100% Roussanne. The red Côtes du Rhône is ripe, forward and brambly, the Valréas bottlings fuller and more concentrated. The top 2 reds have real depth and concentration. Les Echalas is 100% Syrah and can show a hint of reduction when young. Vieilles Vignes is very fine and complex, full of old-viney character and spicy, herbal scents. Both will age well. (DM)

● **Côtes du Rhône★★** £B   ● **Côtes du Rhône Valréas★★** £B
● **Côtes du Rhône Valréas** Les Echalas★★★ £D Vieilles Vignes★★★★ £D
O **Côtes du Rhône★★** £B   O **Côtes du RhôneValréas** Les Echalas★★★ £D

DOM. COSTE CHAUDE   Visan   ww.domaine-coste-chaude.com

Marianne Fues   84820 Visan

Small hillside estate with 21ha under vine. The vineyards are planted on a mix of gravel and clay soils with a large pebble topsoil providing excellent drainage – ideal conditions for producing excellent fruit. Grenache, Syrah, Mourvèdre and Carignan are all planted. The Côtes du Rhône and Côtes du Rhône-Villages are both soft, forward and brambly. The Rocaille and l'Argentière bottlings are altogether more serious and sourced from the plots at higher altitude. Rocaille is vinified from Grenache and Syrah and aged in *cuve*, offering an impressive depth of dark, spicy, lightly plummy fruit. L'Argentière by contrast is aged in small oak for 12 months, which is well integrated and complements the sweet and spicy berry-fruit character of the wine.   (DM)

● **Côtes du Rhône★** £B   ● **Côtes du Rhône Visan★★** £B
● **Côtes du Rhône Visan** Rocaille★★ £C L'Argentière★★★ £C

DOM. COTEAUX DES TRAVERS   Rasteau

Robert Charavin   84110 Rasteau

Robert Charavin produces some of the best examples from this Rhône village, which is now a candidate for its own appellation for dry wines as well as for the fortifieds that the Rasteau AC currently covers. He has 20ha under vine, including a sizeable planting of old vines, and produces around 5,000 cases a year. In the vineyard everything is as natural as possible and no fertilizers are used on the soil. There is a good, nutty white which blends equal parts of Marsanne, Grenache Blanc, Roussanne and Viognier. The soft, forward red

Côtes du Rhône is produced from young vines and is mainly Grenache with some Carignan. More serious are the Rasteau reds. Prestige is made from 60-year-old vines, a blend of Grenache, Syrah and Mourvèdre which gets 12 months in wood. The top wine is the complex, structured Cuvée Paul, full of old-vine character and very ageworthy. Produced from 50- to 100-year-old vines it blends Syrah with a little Mourvèdre and Grenache. It needs a year or 2 of bottle-ageing to integrate the 24 months spent in oak. (DM)

● **Côtes du Rhône**★ £B   ● **Côtes du Rhône Rasteau**★★ £B   Prestige★★★ £C
● **Côtes du Rhône Rasteau**Cuvée Paul★★★ £C
O **Côtes du Rhône Rasteau** Cuvée Marie★★ £D

DOM. DE CRISTIA   Châteauneuf-du-Pape

Grangeon family   84350 Courthézon
UK stockists: Las
Baptiste Grangeon makes very good red Côtes du Rhône and Châteauneuf-du-Pape in a modern accessible style. The Côtes du Rhône is aged in *cuve* and is light, soft and fruit-driven, whereas the Côtes du Rhône Villages is richer and sturdier. A blend of mainly Grenache with 20% Syrah, it is aged in a combination of *cuve* and used barrels. The white Châteauneuf-du-Pape is a fairly even blend of Grenache Blanc, Clairette, Bourboulenc and Roussanne. Vinified in stainless steel it possesses very fresh fruit, full of citrus, nutmeg and herbs. Drink it young. The regular red Châteauneuf is mainly Grenache but has 15% Syrah and just 5% Mourvèdre blended in. Finely crafted, with attractive bright berry fruit, it has a firm but supple structure which will enable it to develop well over 5–7 years and to keep for longer. The 2001 was right on the edge of ★★★★ and the 2003 looks to have similar potential. The top wine, Cuvée Renaissance, is mainly sourced from a 100-year-old vineyard of Grenache with a small amount of Mourvèdre and Syrah added. Aged in old oak to preserve the remarkable intensity and character of the fruit it needs a minimum of 8–10 years to show at its best. In 2003 Baptiste also experimented with a 50/50 blend of Syrah and Grenache, vinified with no sulphur. It will have minimal handling and exposure to oxygen and it will be very interesting to see how it develops. (DM)

● **Châteauneuf du Pape**★★★ £D   Cuvée Renaissance★★★★★ £E
● **Côtes du Rhône**★ £B   ● **Côtes du Rhône-Villages**★★ £B

CROS DE LA MÛRE   Côtes du Rhône

Eric Michel   Hameau de Derboux, 84430 Mondragon
UK stockists: JAr, CBg
Small estate making stylish, elegant Côtes du Rhône, Côtes du Rhône-Villages and denser fuller Gigondas. These wines are not blockbusters but display very good classic *garrigue*-scented red berry fruit. The Côtes du Rhône has a high proportion of old-vine Grenache and will drink well in the short to medium term. The Villages bottling has a higher proportion of Syrah and a touch more density and structure. The Gigondas is the sturdiest of the wines and will benefit from tucking away for 4 or 5 years. All the wines offer good value. (DM)

● **Côtes du Rhône**★★ £B   ● **Côtes du Rhône-Villages**★★★ £B
● **Gigondas**★★★ £B

CUVÉE DU VATICAN   Châteauneuf-du-Pape

Jean-Marc Diffonty   10 Route de Courthézon, 84321 Châteauneuf-du-Pape
UK stockists: BBR, Far, Las
There are a total of 23ha planted at this property, just 2ha of which are white. These are planted to Clairette, Grenache, Roussanne and a little Bourboulenc

357

which successfully adds acidity and grip to the lightly floral wine. There is a decent *vin de pays* red, Domaine de Bres-Casenove, which offers more than most wines of this style from the area. It is a blend of Merlot (50%) and Carignan (25%) with some Syrah and Grenache. The regular red Châteauneuf is an impressively dense, powerful and structured example that offers more depth than most of the so-called *classique* offerings from others in the AC. The dark and smoky Reserve Sixteen is one of the great wines of the appellation, a blend of old Grenache, Syrah and Mourvèdre partially aged in small oak and partially in *foudres*. Formidable depth and concentration are allied to great complexity. Both Châteauneuf reds should be cellared for 6 or 7 years and upwards. (DM)

● **Châteauneuf-du-Pape**★★★★ £D   Réserve Sixteen★★★★★ £D
● **Vin de Pays** Domaine de Bres-Casenove★★★★ £D   O **Châteauneuf-du-Pape**★★ £D

DOM. DE DEURRE   Vinsobres

Hubert Valayer   26110 Vinsobres
UK stockists: MtC, SVS

Hubert Valayer's property is newly established but the results are very promising and the wines show increasing potential with every vintage. The 2001s and 00s are all stunning and a marked step up on earlier vintages. As well as the southern Rhône wines a Cornas is produced thanks to a leasehold agreement with a cousin. As yet it does not show the same potential as Valayer's other wines. The Saint-Maurice is supple and well-structured, with around 30% Syrah in the blend, and the Vinsobres richer, more savoury, with a touch of Mourvèdre. Both are edging towards ★★★. There are 2 splendid Côtes du Rhônes. Les Oliviers is 100% Syrah and the brilliant Les Rabasses 100% Grenache. In 2000 the Rabasses was right on the edge of ★★★★. Newly added Cuvée J.M. Valayer, which is aged in used barriques, resembles a very good Châteuneuf-du-Pape. (DM)

● **Côtes du Rhône**★ £B   Les Oliviers★★★ £C   Les Rabasses★★★ £C
● **Côtes du Rhône-Villages Saint-Maurice**★★ £B
● **Côtes du Rhône-Villages Vinsobres**★★ £B   Cuvée JM Valayer★★★★ £C
● **Cornas**★★ £C

DOM. DURBAN   Beaumes-de-Venise

Jean-Pierre Leydier   84190 Beaumes-de-Venise
UK stockists: Yap, BBR

The Beaumes-de-Venise Vieilles Vignes at this sizeable 57-ha property is a good, spicy, nicely intense red dominated by Grenache, with some Syrah and Mourvèdre. Made from 50-year-old vines, it is traditionally vinified and aged in *cuve*. However, it is the fortified Muscat de Beaumes-de-Venise that marks out this estate. One of the very best examples made, it is richly intense and gloriously honeyed but has a real finesse and elegance very rarely encountered in these wines. It should, though, in the style of the appellation, be drunk young and fresh. (DM)

● **Côtes du Rhône-Villages Beaumes-de-Venise** Vieille Vignes★★ £B
O **Muscat de Beaumes-de-Venise**★★★ £C

DOM. DES ESPIERS   Vacqueyras

Philippe Cartoux   84190 Vacqueyras
UK stockists: Bal

With cellars based in the village of Vacqueyras, Philippe Cartoux crafts his excellent wines from parcels totalling some 10ha around Gigondas and Sablet. A little white and rosé Côtes du Rhône is produced but it is the top reds that particularly impress. The Cuvée des Blâches is wonderfully dense and gamey with some attractive herbal *garrigue* notes. It is produced from 35-year-old vines. Both Gigondas *cuvées* will be the better for 4 or 5 years' cellaring; the Sablet too will benefit from short ageing. (DM)

● **Côtes du Rhône**★ £B   ● **Côtes du Rhône-Villages Sablet**★★ £B
● **Gigondas**★★★ £B Cuvée des Blâches★★★★ £C

FERAUD-BRUNEL   Châteauneuf-du-Pape
Feraud/Brunel families   84230 Châteauneuf-du-Pape
Fine quality small *négociant* operation run by Laurence Feraud of Domaine du PEGAÜ and André Brunel of LES CAILLOUX in Châteauneuf-du-Pape. The traditional-style wines are vinified by the Brunel *oenologue*, Philippe Cambie, in a manner similar to that at Pegaü and Les Cailloux. Results are impressive across the board. The *vin de table*, Images du Sud, is an attractive, spicy, forward red blend. All represent good value. (DM)

● **Vin de Table** Image du Sud★★ £B
● **Côtes du Rhône-Villages Cairanne**★★★ £B
● **Côtes du Rhône-Villages Rasteau**★★ £B   ● **Vacqueyras**★★ £B
● **Gigondas**★★★ £C   ● **Châteauneuf-du-Pape**★★★ £C

DOM. FOND CROZE   Côtes du Rhône-Villages
Long family   84290 Saint Roman de Malegarde
There are 65ha at this long-established property. Father Raymond and sons Daniel, who tends the vineyards, and Bruno, who runs the cellar, have between them moved the quality at this estate to a new level in recent vintages. A faily extensive range includes *vin de pays* Merlot and Chardonnay as well as straightforward Côtes du Rhône white and rosé. The white Cuvée Analys, a Viognier from very low-yielding, late-harvested vines, is of a different order. The spicy, berry-fruited regular red Côtes du Rhône blends Grenache (70%) with Syrah. The warmly spicy Côtes du Rhône-Villages Vincent de Catari is mainly Grenache with Carignan and just a smattering of Syrah and Mourvèdre. The top labels now also come under the Côtes du Rhône umbrella. The Saint-Romanaise, originally a blend of Grenache and Syrah, is now solely Grenache. Ageing is in 400-litre used *barriques* and there is now a real depth and style to the fruit. The Cuvée Fond Croze is dominated by Syrah with just a small proportion of Viognier. Again new oak is avoided and the wine is aged in used *tonneaux*. Rich and concentrated, this in particular will age well for up to a decade. Newly added in 2004 is an impressively dark and spicy Cuvée Shyros. (DM)

● **Côtes du Rhône-Villages** Cuvée Vincent de Catari★★ £B
● **Côtes du Rhône** Cuvée Fond Croze★★★ £C Cuvée Shyros★★★ £C
● **Côtes du Rhône**★★ £B Cuvée Saint-Romanaise★★★ £B
○ **Côtes du Rhône** Cuvée Analys★★ £B

DOM. DE FONDRÈCHE   Côtes du Ventoux
Sébastien Barthélémy   Quartier Fondrèche, 84380 Mazan
UK stockists: **N&P**
With their 30-oddha Sébastien and Nanou Barthélémy are rivals to CHÂTEAU PESQUIÉ – both are making benchmark wines for the appellation. Careful viticulture with increasingly old vines (now averaging 40 years) and minimal interference throughout vinification and *élévage* is paying off with an impressive range. The regular red, blended from Grenache, Syrah and Cinsault, is silky and forward. The Fayard, similarly aged in tank, adds Carignan to Grenache and Syrah. The Persia red is mainly Syrah and aged in *barriques*, some new. Nadal is roughly equal proportions of Syrah and Grenache, a blockbuster style

often marked by alcohol but generally well-balanced. A number of single varietal bottlings of reds have also been produced in recent vintages. Roussanne is an important component of the 2 whites. The regular bottling blends in some Clairette as well, whereas the Persia is almost exclusively Rousanne aged in barrel on its lees. The wines are well worth seeking out and very good value. (DM)

- ● **Côtes du Ventoux**★ £A   Cuvée Fayard★★ £B   Cuvée Persia★★★ £B
- ● **Côtes du Ventoux** Cuvée Carles Nadal★★★ £B
- ○ **Côtes du Ventoux**★ £A   Cuvée Persia★★ £B

FONT DE MICHELLE   Châteauneuf-du-Pape

Gonnet family   14 Impasse de Vignerons, 84370 Bedarrides
UK stockists: JAr, Yng, Tan, WSS

There has been a marked step up in quality here since the late 1990s, not least because of considerable investment in the cellar. The Côtes du Rhône and Rhône-Villages reds are fruity and approachable. Les Promesses is dominated by Grenache with some Carignan and Cinsault, while Notre Passion blends Syrah and Grenache in equal parts. It is understandably denser and fuller but ripe and forward too. Both are 80% destemmed and get a 2 week maceration. A small portion Notre Passion is aged in oak. The Font de Viognier is 100% varietal, cool-fermented and marked by clean, lightly perfumed peach fruit. It should be drunk young and fresh. White Châteauneuf-du-Pape is also for early drinking, although the stylish Cuvée Etienne Gonnet, vinified with a high proportion of Rousanne, will develop well over the short term. The regular red Châteauneuf used to lack real depth and substance, with part being vinified by carbonic maceration. The style now, though, is for sturdier, longer-lived wines and the Gonnets have produced serious wines in recent vintages. Part of the key is some very old Grenache: 50-year-old vines go into the regular wine and 90-year-olds into the *barrique*-aged (part new) Etienne Gonnet, which is now very cellarworthy and will improve for a decade or more. (DM)

- ● **Côtes du Rhône** Font du Vent Les Promesses★★ £B
- ● **Côtes du Rhône-Villages** La Font du Vent Notre Passion★★ £B
- ○ **Côtes du Rhône** F de Font Viognier★★ £B
- ● **Châteauneuf-du-Pape**★★★ £D   Cuvée Etienne Gonnet★★★★★ £F
- ○ **Châteauneuf-du-Pape**★★ £C   Cuvée Etienne Gonnet★★★★ £E

DOM. DE FONT SANE   Gigondas

Peysson family   Route Sablet, 84190 Gigondas
UK stockists: Bib, GBa

First-class producer of both Gigondas and Côtes du Ventoux with 14ha of very low-yielding vineyards. The Ventoux is among the better examples in that AC and excellent value for money. The vineyards are planted on the lower slopes of the Dentelles and the climate is warmer than most in the appellation. The regular Gigondas is a spicy herb-laden blend of Grenache, Syrah, Mourvèdre and Cinsault, while the oak-aged barrel selection Cuvée Futée is dense, powerful and very ageworthy. It is generally made from the oldest vines on the property and requires 5 years' patience to show at its best. (DM)

- ● **Côtes du Ventoux**★ £A   ● **Gigondas**★★★ £C   Cuvée Futée★★★★ £C

DOM. LA GARRIGUE   Vacqueyras

Bernard family   84190 Vacqueyras

Very good traditional domaine with 65ha of vineyard spread across Vacqueyras and Gigondas and additional holdings simply classified as Côtes du Rhône. Clairette and Grenache Blanc make up the blend of the white Vacqueyras but the main focus of the property is on red Vacqueyras and Gigondas from plantings dominated by Grenache with a smattering of Syrah, Mourvèdre and

Cinsault. Vinification is traditional, with no destemming and no fining or filtration. There is a 20 day *cuvaison* and the resulting wines are sturdy and powerful. The Cuvée de Hostellerie is particularly fine and in 2001 was close to ★★★★. (DM)

● **Vacqueyras**★★★ £B Cuvée de Hostellerie★★★ £C ● **Gigondas**★★★ £C

GOURT DE MAUTENS Rasteau

Jérôme Bressy   84110 Rasteau
UK stockists: Rae, SVS

Enormously impressive producer with some 14ha planted almost exclusively to red varieties: Grenache, Carignan, Syrah, Mourvèdre and a few others. The rich, dense and ageworthy red is produced from vines that are up to 80 years old. The Bressy style is to create wines with considerable extraction, producing fiery almost ferocious examples which always not only show concentration but are complex, dark and spicy too. In recent vintages it has been quite as good as many a top Châteauneuf. The white, a blend of Bourboulenc and Grenache Blanc, doesn't quite hit the same stellar heights but is still among the most interesting and structured examples of the region. In keeping with the approach, the wines are bottled unfiltered. (DM)

● **Côtes du Rhône-Villages Rasteau**★★★★ £D
O **Côtes du Rhône-Villages Rasteau**★★★★ £D

DOM. GRAMENON Côtes du Rhône

Laurent family   26770 Monbrison-sur-Lez
UK stockists: BRW, HHB, Rae, SVS

Long established as one of the great producers in the lesser area of the Côtes du Rhône. Michèle Laurent has now taken over the running of this domaine from her late husband. The vineyard is planted to Grenache and Syrah with a little Cinsault and Carignan for the reds and a little Clairette and Viognier for the whites. Yields are very low and minimal handling and an absence of filtration in the cellar produces wines of density, concentration and finesse. The remarkable Ceps Centenaires Cuvée Mémé, produced from very old vines, is as fine as the very best from the southern Rhône. Prices are very reasonable as well. (DM)

● **Côtes du Rhône** Le Gramenon★★ £B Les Laurentides★★★ £B
● **Côtes du Rhône** La Sagesse★★★ £B La Sierra du Sud★★ £B
● **Côtes du Rhône** Ceps Centenaires Cuvée Mémé★★★★ £C
● **Côtes du Rhône-Villages** Les Hauts de Gramenon★★★ £C
O **Côtes du Rhône** Vie on y est★ £B

DOM. DE GRAND TINEL Châteauneuf-du-Pape

Jeune family   Route de Bedarrides, 84230 Châteauneuf-du-Pape
UK stockists: NoG, EoR, OWL, WSc

Fine, traditional old Châteauneuf property producing earthy, robust reds, albeit without the power of their counterparts a decade ago. Alexis Establet is produced from the family's parcels of particularly old vines and shows greater complexity. Bottling here is staged and it's worth trying to purchase as close to the vintage as possible. (DM)

● **Châteauneuf-du-Pape Traditionelle**★★★ £C Cuvée Alexis Establet★★★ £D

DOM. GRAPILLON D'OR Gigondas

Bernard Chauvet   84190 Gigondas
UK stockists: CTy

Bernard Chauvet produces good traditional wines from around 15ha in

361

Gigondas, including several different parcels, and a further 9ha in Vacqueyras. Plantings are dominated by Grenache but also include Syrah and Cinsault and, as is the practice in a number of properties, they are vinified together. The fruit is not destemmed and there is a long *cuvaison* of up to 20 days for the Gigondas. The Vacqueyras is the lighter of the wines and will drink well with 2 or 3 years age, while the Gigondas is sturdy and masculine, and will add increasing complexity with up to 10 years' age. The wines are bottled without filtration after ageing in old *foudres*. (DM)

● **Gigondas★★★** £C ● **Vacqueyras★★** £B

DOM. DE LA JANASSE Châteauneuf-du-Pape

Aimé Sabon 27 Chemin de Moulin, 84350 Courthezon
UK stockists: Eno, N&P, NYg, WSc, Las

Splendid, medium-sized domaine producing good to excellent wines across the board. A total of some 12,500 cases are produced annually from 50ha of vines. The Châteauneuf vines are planted on ideal, free-draining stony soils and this, together with a vine age averaging over 60 years, results in lovely supple, dense and powerful wines. Vinification is a good deal more modern than at some properties in the region. Jean-Luc COLOMBO has consulted here and part of the red crop is always destemmed. Ageing is in an assortment of vessels with some new oak being used for the red and white Châteauneuf-du-Pape. The Chaupin and Vieilles-Vignes reds develop very well in bottle and should be given at least 4 or 5 years. (DM)

● **Côtes du Rhône** Tradition★ £B Les Garrigues★★ £B
O **Côtes du Rhône★** £B
● **Châteauneuf-du-Pape★★★★** £D Cuvée Chaupin★★★★★ £E
● **Châteauneuf-du-Pape** Vieilles Vignes★★★★★ £F
O **Châteauneuf-du-Pape** Tradition★★★ £C Prestige★★★★ £F
● **Vin de Pays de la Principaute d'Orange** Terre de Buissière★★ £B
O **Vin de Pays de la Principaute d'Orange** Viognier★★ £B

DOM. LA BLAQUE Coteaux de Pierrevert

M. Pampus Route de la Bastides-des-Jourdans, 04860 Pierrevert

As well as being the leading property in size at 62 ha, Domaine la Blaque is also the beacon for quality in this small (450 ha), little-known but potentially fine appellation. A range of AC wines are joined by a couple of *vin de pays* labels, a fresh fragrant Viognier and a Pinot Noir. The vineyards are planted at altitude, 450–550m up in the Alpes de Haute Provence, and the Alps proper can be seen in the distance from the vineyards. The climate, though, is very benign for wine-growing. There are up 320 sunny days a year and during the summer the diurnal swing in temperature between day and night ensures good acidity in the fruit. The regular AC labels are vinified to emphasise their fruit, although the red has the structure to stand a little age. Both the red and white Reserves will develop well in bottle. The white, a blend of Grenache Blanc, Vermentino and Roussanne is barrel-fermented with rich, concentrated honey, citrus and nutmeg aromas and impressive structure. It will develop well over 5 years or so. The dense and structured Réserve red is mainly Syrah with carefully selected Grenache. Aged in oak for 12 months, it is dense and structured, full of black pepper and rich blackberry fruit and just a hint of herb spice. The top wine, Cuvée Collection, is dominated by old-vine Syrah. Vinified with whole bunches and macerated for 4 weeks before ageing in new oak, it is rich, pure and ageworthy. (DM)

● **Coteaux de Pierrevert★★** £B Reserve★★★ £C
O **Coteaux de Pierrevert★★** £B Reserve★★★ £C
◎ **Coteaux de Pierrevert★** £B

DOM. LA BOUISSIERE   Gigondas
Gilles & Thierry Faravel   84190 Gigondas
UK stockists: Las

The Faravels make particularly striking and intense Gigondas from a small holding of just 8ha. The regular red is a blend of Grenache (70%) and Syrah. Ageing is in a mix of barrels and *cuve*, with all the oak having been used previously. Old vines of close to 40 years and no fining or filtration all contribute to the quality. The rich, and dense Font de Tonin is from even older vines and gets around one-third new wood. The blend here is roughly half Grenache and a quarter each of Mourvèdre and Syrah. The 2003 came in at a whopping 15.8% alcohol but retained reasonable balance. (DM)

● **Gigondas** Traditionelle★★★ £C La Font de Tonin★★★ £C

DOM. LAFOND-ROC-EPINE   Tavel   www.lafond.roc-epine.com
Jean-Pierre & Pascal Lafond   Route des Vignobles, 30126 Tavel
UK stockists: CTy, BBR

Excellent-value wines produced from Lirac, Châteauneuf-du-Pape and the Côtes du Rhône as well as one of the better Tavels, which shows some vibrant fresh fruit. The Lirac and Châteauneuf-du-Pape are blended from a mix of Grenache, Syrah and Mourvèdre, while the Côtes du Rhône is just Grenache and Syrah. Vinification of the reds is modern with fermentation in stainless steel before ageing in a mix of large and small oak. In addition, the Lafonds produce a straightforward, pleasant white Lirac from a blend of Grenache Blanc, Viognier and Roussanne and a sumptuously rich special *cuvée* La Ferme Romaine, which is aged in small oak for a year. The Liracs and Châteauneuf-du-Pape will evolve well in the medium term. (DM)

● **Lirac**★★ £B La Ferme Romaine★★★ £C
● **Châteauneuf-du-Pape**★★★ £D ● **Côtes du Rhône**★★ £B O **Lirac**★ £B

DOM. LA GUINTRANDY   Visan
Olivier Cuilleras   84820 Visan

Olivier Cuilleras is emerging as one of the new stars of the southern Rhône. His family possesses 28ha of vineyards, all but 1ha being planted to reds, and produces 4–5,000 cases a year. The domaine is characterised by the extent of its old-vine plantings, which contribute greatly to the quality of the wines. As well as the 3 fine bottlings from Visan there is an improving Côtes du Rhône, which includes 70 % of 30-year-old Grenache and some very old Carignan. The *vin de pays* red, generally 50/50 Grenache and Syrah, is produced from some of the youngest vines on the property. The Visan Vieilles Vignes is a blend of mainly 50-year-old Grenache with a little Carignan and Syrah. The Cuvée Les Devès and top Cuvée Louise Amelie are both aged in oak, the Louise Amelie seeing some new wood. These wines are marked out by pure, rich and complex old-vine character. Expect all the Visan bottlings to develop well over 5 years or more. (DM)

● **Côtes du Rhône-Villages Visan** Les Devès★★★ £B Vieilles Vignes★★★ £B
● **Côtes du Rhône**★★ £B ● **Côtes du Rhône-Villages Visan** Louise Amelie★★★ £C
● **Vin de Pays de Comté de Grignan**★ £A

DOM. LA ROQUETTE   Châteauneuf-du-Pape   www.vignoblesbrunier.fr
Brunier family   Avenue Louis Pasteur, 84230 Châteauneuf-du-Pape
UK stockists: L&W, BBR

While this property is owned by the Bruniers it is quite separate from VIEUX-TÉLÉGRAPHE. Produced from vineyard parcels spread throughout the appellation, these are unfiltered modern wines of some class and finesse. The average vine age is now around 40 years and this undoubtedly helps quality.

363

The white should be broached young, the red with a little age. It is marked particularly by its vibrant, attractive, dark, spicy fruit character, supple velvety tannin and approachable style. (DM)

● **Châteauneuf-du-Pape★★★** £D ○ **Châteauneuf-du-Pape★★★** £D

DOM. LA SOUMADE   Rasteau

Andre Romero   84110 Rasteau
UK stockists: BBR, HHB, NYg, Hal

A great range of wines, especially the impressive red Côtes du Rhône, Rasteau and Gigondas. These are vinified as true *vins de garde*. Romero goes for maximum extraction but the results are almost always very good indeed. Even the lesser wines have an abundance of vibrant, crunchy fruit. With the best *cuvées* the lengthy vatting, allied to extensive parcels of old vines (some up to 100 years), provides for dense, chewy, powerful reds in need of 5 years' cellaring. Romero also produces fine *vins doux naturels* under the Rasteau AC. (DM)

● **Vin de Pays de la Principauté d'Orange** Prestige★★ £B
● **Vin de Pays** Cabernet Sauvignon★ £B ● **Côtes du Rhône** Les Violettes★★★ £C
● **Côtes du Rhône-Villages Rasteau** Prestige★★★ £C Confiance★★★★ £D
● **Côtes du Rhône-Villages Rasteau** Fleur de Confiance★★★★★ £E
● **Gigondas★★★★** £C ● **Rasteau★★** £C

DOM. LEA   Vin de Pays de Gard   www.domaine-lea.com

Vincent Auquier   30260 Cannes et Clairan
UK stockists: Vne

Very new small property of some 18ha planted to a range of varieties including Cabernet Sauvignon, Syrah, Grenache, Cinsault and Carignan among the reds, along with Sauvignon Blanc, Chardonnay and Ugni Blanc. At present 2 wines are produced. The excellent-value domaine wine is a blend of Merlot and Syrah. Broad, fleshy and approachable with black fruits, pepper and spice, it is marked by its fruit more than anything. The Terres Blanches is dominated by old-vine Carignan with a little Syrah. Vinification is carefully controlled and temperature during the maceration is restricted to ensure a rich but fruit-driven style. (DM)

● **Vin de Pays d'Oc★★** £B Terres Blanches★★ £B

DOM. LE MURMURIUM   Côtes du Ventoux

Jean Marot   Route de Flassan, 84570 Mormoiron

An emerging Ventoux star, Murmurium is joining the ranks of the very best from the appellation including FONDRÈCHE. There are 19ha of vines here and Jean Marot has consistently invested in and updated his cellar since 1995. The vineyards are cultivated organically and yields are deliberately restricted to 15–25 hl/ha. White, rosé and 4 red *cuvées* are produced. The rosé is ripe and full of fruit with a light stucture which suggests it will keep a year or so. The white is a blend of mainly Clairette with a little Roussanne, Bourboulenc and Grenache Blanc providing both fragarance and grip. The regular red is smoky with characterful berry fruit. The Opéra, which is 90% old-vine Grenache and a little Syrah, is a dense, powerful and very firmly structured red that sees no oak. By contrast the Carpe Diem, a 50/50 blend of Grenache and Syrah, sees the Syrah component aged in 40% new wood and is rich, dense and very complex. There is also a further limited production *cuvée* called Florence. All the reds are bottled unfined and unfiltered and the top *cuvées* will evolve very well with 4–5 years' cellaring. (DM)

● **Côtes du Ventoux★★★** £B Opéra★★★★ £C Carpe Diem★★★★ £D
○ **Côtes du Ventoux★★** £B ◉ **Côtes du Ventoux★** £B

DOM. LES APHILLANTHES   Travaillan

Daniel Boulle   Quartier Saint Jean, 84850 Travaillan
*UK stockists:*Sec, Las

This is one of the new rising stars of the southern Rhône based in the village of Travaillan. R & R is the most accesible of the wines but Les Galets, which is mainly Grenache, is similarly open and approachable. The more seriously structured Trois Cepages blends Grenache, Syrah and Mourvèdre. The Cuvée du Cros is produced solely from Syrah, while the Vieilles Vignes is made from very old Grenache with around 20% Mourvèdre. Bottled with neither fining nor filtration all the wines show real depth and impressive concentration and will develop very well in bottle. A Côtes du Rhône-Villages made from pure low-yielding Mourvèdre is also now produced. (DM)

● **Côtes du Rhône-Villages** Vieilles Vignes★★★★ £C
● **Côtes du Rhône** Mourvèdre★★★★ £D
● **Côtes du Rhône-Villages** Trois Cépages★★★ £C Cuvée du Cros★★★ £C
● **Côtes du Rhône-Villages** Les Galets★★ £C ● **Côtes du Rhône**★★ £B

LES CAILLOUX   Châteauneuf-du-Pape

André Brunel   84230 Châteauneuf-du-Pape
UK stockists: Hal, SVS, Las

Very fine traditional producer of Côtes du Rhône and Châteauneuf-du-Pape. The Côtes du Rhônes are produced at the Brunel family property Domaine de l'Enclos. The profound Cuvée Centenaire produced from 100-year-old vines is one of the great wines of the appellation, while the regular red Châteauneuf is dense and powerful and lacks just a little of the depth of the centenarian. The Brunel family are also involved with the Feraud family of Domaine du PEGAÜ in an excellent small-scale *négociant* venture, FERAUD-BRUNEL. (DM)

Domaine de l'Enclos

● **Côtes du Rhône**★★£B Cuvée Sommelongue★★★ £B

Les Cailloux

● **Châteauneuf-du-Pape**★★★★ £C Cuvée Centenaire✪✪✪✪✪ £E

DOM. LES GRANDS BOIS   Côtes du Rhône-Villages

Mireille & Marc Besnardeau   84290 Sainte-Cecile-les-Vignes
UK stockists: Gau

The Besnardeau family have a vineyard holding of 46ha spread across a number of villages, among them Rasteau and Cairanne. The majority of their vines now have considerable age with the oldest now over 70 years. The white Malorie is a cool-fermented fruit-driven blend of Viognier (80%), Grenache Blanc and Gris (15%) and a little Clairette. There is an attractive berry-scented rosé, Les Trois Soeurs, and a more serious spicy red version. The Villages wines, Gabrielle and Philippine, come from a number of sources and include fruit from some of the oldest vines. Both are aged in oak for 6 months, with the Philippine more berry scented, the Gabrielle more overtly oaky in its youth. The 3 Cairanne *cuvées* come from vines that range from 10–50 years and all are a blend of Grenache (55%), Mourvèdre (35%), and 5% each of Syrah and Carignan. The Maximilien is perhaps the most exciting with minimal oak influence – only the Mourvèdre sees any wood – providing a style of rich, spicy fruit and impressive complexity. The Eloise and Mireille bottlings both see up to 6 months oak ageing but it is very well handled. The Mireille is a touch more elegant, the Eloise denser and fuller. Expect all the Villages wines to develop well with 5 years' age or more. (DM)

● **Côtes du Rhône-Villages Cairanne** Cuvée Eloise★★★ £C Cuvée Mireille★★★ £C

365

● **Côtes du Rhône-Villages Cairanne** Cuvée Maximilien★★★ £C
● **Côtes du Rhône-Villages** Cuvée Gabrielle★★ £C Cuvée Philippine★★ £C
● **Côtes du Rhône** Les Trois Soeurs★★ £B ◎ **Côtes du Rhône** Les Trois Soeurs★ £B
○ **Malorie** Vin de Table★★ £B

PATRICK LESEC SELECTIONS

Patrick Lesec   15 bis, Rue Hégésippe Moreau, 75018 Paris
UK stockists: **Gau**,NYg

As well as a portfolio that now covers Alsace, Bordeaux, Burgundy, the Rhône, Languedoc and Roussillon, the Loire, the South-West and Italy, wine broker Patrick Lesec also works in association with fine quality-conscious domaines in Languedoc and Roussillon and particularly in the Rhône Valley to produce wines which are released under his own label. As a part of his portfolio he produces top *cuvées* from a number of properties, such as Dom. des Remizières with their Cuvée Emilie and Dom. Coursodon with the La Sensonne. His approach is to vary these slightly to match his own style of ripe, elegant and above all approachable wines. Some of the Rhône *cuvées* are very, very good indeed and there is real potential here at all levels. Excellent results were produced throughout his range for the 2001 vintage and it remains to be seen how well the difficult 02s will fare. (DM)

● **Coteaux du Languedoc** Château Roumanière Tonneaux★★ £C
● **Coteaux du Languedoc** Domaine de Granoupiac★★★ £C
● **Saint-Chinian** Domaine Rouanet Tonneaux★★ £C
● **Faugères** J.C. Estève Tonneaux★★★ £C
● **Hermitage** Domaine des Remizières Cuvée Émilie★★★★★ £E
● **Saint-Joseph** Domaine Coursodon La Sensonne★★★★ £C
● **Cornas** Domaine Michel Perraud Sarah★★★ £D
● **Cornas** Domaine Michel Perraud Le Vignon★★★★ £E
● **Châteauneuf-du-Pape** Marquis★★★★ £E Marquis Tonneaux★★★★★ £E
● **Châteauneuf-du-Pape** Chasse-Temps★★★★ £E Les Galets Ronds★★★★★ £F
● **Gigondas** Cuvée l'Estrale★★★ £C Les Blaches★★★★ £C
● **Côtes du Rhône-Villages Cairanne** Vieilles Vignes★★★ £C
● **Côtes du Rhône-Villages Rasteau**Vieilles Vignes★★ £B
● **Côtes du Rhône** Bouquet★★ £B

DOM. LES GOUBERT   Gigondas

Jean-Pierre Cartier   84190 Gigondas
UK stockists: BRW

An extensive range of Côtes du Rhône and Rhône-Villages wines is made by this domaine and the quality is generally good, sometimes very good. There are 23ha under vine, of which 20 or so are red, with the majority Grenache but a decent planting of Syrah as well. Barrel-fermentation is used to produce the Viognier, which has real depth and some gloriously ripe, peachy fruit. It is best drunk young. Vinification of the reds is modern without a hint of rusticity emerging in the wines and new oak is used to age the Gigondas Cuvée Florence. Both Gigondas wines are good cellaring prospects. (DM)

● **Gigondas**★★ £C Cuvée Florence★★★ £C
● **Côtes du Rhône-Villages Sablet**★★ £B
● **Côtes du Rhône-Villages Beaumes de Venise**★★ £B
● **Côtes du Rhône**★ £B ○ **Côtes du Rhône-Villages Sablet**★ £B
○ **Côtes du Rhône**★ £B Viognier Cuvée de V★★ £C

LES PALLIÈRES   Gigondas   www.vignoblesbrunier.fr

Brunier family/Kermit Lynch   84190 Gigondas
UK stockists: **THt**,F&M

Now owned as a joint venture between the Bruniers of VIEUX-TÉLÉGRAPHE and US wine merchant Kermit Lynch. The potential of the *terroir* is beginning to be fully explored – the 25ha of vineyards are ideally located in limestone soils on the precipitous slopes of the Dentelles de Montmirail. The 50-year-old vines produce wines which are now less rustic and increasingly impressive. Some destemming has been introduced and there is careful control in the cellar. The wines are bottled without filtration after 15 months in *cuve* and *foudres*. (DM)

● **Gigondas★★★** £C

DOM. DE MARCOUX   Châteauneuf-du-Pape

Armenier family   Chemin de la Gironde, 84100 Orange
UK stockists: HHB, CCC, Alo, Las

Model 24-ha property run on biodynamic lines since 1990. There are 16ha of red grapes planted and just 1ha of Roussanne and Bourboulenc, which adds a refreshing grip to the white Châteauneuf. The main purpose of the viticultural approach is to optimise the fruit quality of the late-ripening Grenache and Mourvèdre in particular. There can be no question about the results. Vieilles Vignes has for a decade been one of the benchmark wines of the appellation: very ageworthy and extraordinarily complex. (DM)

● **Châteauneuf-du-Pape★★★★** £E Vieilles Vignes✪✪✪✪✪ £F
O **Châteauneuf-du-Pape★★★** £D

MAS DE BOISLAUZON   Châteauneuf-du-Pape

Christine & Daniel Chaussy   Quartier Bois Lauzon, 84100 Orange
UK stockists: SVS

Good small producer with 24ha for red and white Châteauneuf and a little Côtes du Rhône-Villages. The vineyards are planted in argile and calcareous soils and have the famous *galets roulés* stony topsoil. The red Châteauneuf vineyard is planted to a mix of 70% Grenache and 15% each of Syrah and Mourvèdre. The white is equal parts of Grenache, Clairette, Roussanne and Bourboulenc. The red Châteauneuf is classically berry scented with an intense, herby character but is not a bit rustic. It will drink well at 4 or 5 years. A limited-production Cuvée du Quet is made from a selection of the oldest vines on the property. (DM)

● **Châteauneuf-du-Pape★★★** £C

DOM. MATHIEU   Châteauneuf-du-Pape

Mathieu family   Route de Courthézon, 84230 Châteauneuf-du-Pape
Good, small, family-run domaine with 22ha divided into no fewer than 50 separate plots. Of these, 4ha are in the Côtes du Rhône appellation. The reds here are traditionally vinified and are not destemmed. The white, by contrast, is vinified cool at 16–17°C to emphasise its bright, nutty, floral fruit and should be drunk young. The regular red is dominated by Grenache and offers bright berry fruit with a slight herbal edge. The rich and well-structured Vin de Felibre is dominated by Mourvèdre (80%) and is aged in 60% new oak which needs a year or 2 to integrate. The top wine, Marquis Anselme Mathieu, comes from some of the oldest Grenache on the property, from a vineyard originally planted in 1890. Dense and complex with a real old-vine fruit quality, this impressively structured red needs at least 6 or 7 years. (DM)

● **Châteauneuf-du-Pape★★★** £D Vin de Felibre★★★ £E
● **Châteauneuf-du-Pape** Marquis Anselme Mathieu★★★★ £E
O **Châteauneuf-du-Pape★★** £D

DOM. DE LA MILLIÈRE   Châteauneuf-du-Pape

Aimé & Michel Arnaud   Route de Courthézon, 84230 Châteauneuf-du-Pape
UK stockists: RsW
The Arnauds possess some 27ha in Châteauneuf-du-Pape as well as the Côtes

du Rhône. Their vineyards vary from 25 years to close to 100 years of age. This gives them tremendous raw material which, combined with organic farming and a general minimalist approach, results in some excellent wines. The regular Côtes du Rhône is a herb-scented, strawberry-laden blend of Grenache, Syrah and Mourvèdre. The Vieilles Vignes bottling offers considerably more grip and structure but has very impressive depth. The Côtes du Rhône-Villages, from Grenache, Cinsault and Mourvèdre, is from vines very close to the Châteauneuf border and has a real old-vine complexity. The regular Châteauneuf is a blend of Grenache, Syrah, Mourvèdre, Cinsault and Counoise. Firm and structured in its youth, it needs 5 or 6 years to express its subtle violet and herb-scented aromas to the full. The Vieilles Vignes bottling is bigger, sturdier and loaded with chewy, opulent old-vine character. (DM)

● **Châteauneuf-du-Pape**★★★ £D Vieilles-Vignes★★★★ £E
● **Côtes du Rhône-Villages**★★ £B ● **Côtes du Rhône**★ £B Vieilles Vignes★★★ £B
● **Côtes du Rhône**★★ £B

DOM. DE LA MONARDIÈRE   Vacqueyras

Martine & Christian Vache   Les Grès, 84190 Vacqueyras

A good, small range of wines is produced by Christian Vache at this well-established Vacqueyras property. Volume is accounted for by the reds but a small amount of a fairly pricey and oaky white Vacqueyras is produced from less than 1ha of Grenache Blanc, Roussanne and Viognier. The regular red, Les Calades, is soft, forward and approachable, whereas the Réserve des Deux Monardes and in particular the dense and complex Vieilles Vignes are wines of greater depth, substance and structure. The Monardes is full of dark cherry character and hints of *garrigue;* the Vieilles Vignes, dense and more imposingly structured, is a wine of real depth and intensity. Both the top reds will benefit from 4 or 5 years' patience. (DM)

● **Vacqueyras** Calades★★ £B Réserve des Deux Monardes★★ £C
● **Vacqueyras** Vieilles Vignes★★★ £C   O **Vacqueyras**★★ £C

DOM. MONTIRIUS   Vacqueyras

Christine & Eric Saurel   Le Devés, 84260 Sarrians

One of the better properties in Vacqueyras, Montirius has been run on biodynamic lines since the 1999 vintage and is operating from a new winery since 2002. The Saurels have over 50ha of vineyard of which 35ha are in Vacqueyras. The white Vacqueyras blends Grenache Blanc, Roussanne and Bourboulenc, which adds a refreshing acidity, and should be drunk within a year or 2. The Côtes du Rhône is sourced from vineyards just outside the village of Sablet. Soft and accesible it too should be broached when young and full of fruit. The Gigondas comes from a 16-ha plot of which 12ha date from 1925 and which is planted in 5 different soil types. Rich and complex at best, the wine has impressive substance even in a difficult year like 2002. Of the 2 red Vacqueyras, the regular bottling comes from vines which average 40 years. It is a blend of 70% Grenache and 30% Syrah. The Clos Montirius comes from a particular 8.5ha sector of the Vacqueyras vineyard which enjoys a very localised drier mesoclimate. From a blend of 50/50 Grenache and Syrah it undoubtably has an extra level of depth and complexity. (DM)

● **Vacqueyras**★★ £B Clos Montirius★★★ £C   ● **Gigondas**★★★ £C
● **Côtes du Rhône**★★ £B   O **Vacqueyras**★ £B

DOM. DE MONTPERTUIS   Châteauneuf-du-Pape

Paul Jeune   84230 Châteauneuf-du-Pape
UK stockists: L&W, SVS

Paul Jeune produces impressively deep and concentrated red Châteauneuf-du-Pape, which is occasionally labelled Domaine de Croze. The wine, a blend of

Grenache, Mourvèdre, Syrah and Cinsault, is a powerful, structured example with intense dark berry fruit and spicy, herbal *garrigue* scents. A white Châteauneuf produced from Clairette, Bourboulenc, Grenache Blanc and Roussanne is full, weighty and soft. It should be drunk relatively young. Forward, fruit-driven Côtes du Rhône and *vin de pays* are also produced. Paul Jeune now has an interest in the Côtes du Ventoux property Château de Valcombe, where some increasingly impressive dense and structured examples of this lesser appellation are being made. The Cuvée Genevrières is very good. Montpertuis's winemaker, Gilles Basq, is also making a dense, richly concentrated new Côtes du Rhône under his own label, Domaine La Manarine. (DM)

Domaine de Montpertuis
● **Châteauneuf-du-Pape★★★** £D ● **Vin de Pays du Gard** Counoise★ £B
● **Côtes du Rhône★** £B
O **Châteauneuf-du-Pape★★** £C O **Côtes du Rhône★** £B

Château de Valcombe
● **Côtes du Ventoux** Signature★ £B Cuvée Genevrières★★ £B

Domaine La Manarine
● **Côtes du Rhône★★** £B

DOM. DE LA MORDORÉE Tavel

Christophe Delorme Chemin des Oliviers, 30126 Tavel
UK stockists: L&S, Bal, Box, Rae, HHB, Las

Christophe Delorme produces an extensive and impressive range of wines from his fully biodynamic domaine in Tavel. A total of over 55ha spread across Lirac, Tavel and Châteauneuf-du-Pape yields an excellent range of wines. An impressive number of varieties are planted, particularly white. The Tavel is a benchmark wine, arguably the best of the appellation, and the various Reine des Bois *cuvées* are very refined and characterful and will improve in bottle for 5–10 years, the Châteauneuf almost certainly longer. A superb source of very well-priced wines, although some recent very high scores from a well-known American wine critic are bound to put inflationery pressure on them. (DM)

● **Côtes du Rhône★★** £B O **Côtes du Rhône★** £B
● **Lirac★★★** £C Reine des Bois★★★★ £C O **Lirac** Reine des Bois★★★ £C
● **Châteauneuf-du-Pape★★★★** £D Reine des Bois★★★★★ £F
◉ **Tavel★★** £B

MOULIN DE LA GARDETTE Gigondas

Jean-Baptiste Meunier Place de la Mairie, 84190 Gigondas
UK stockists: A&B

These are powerful, traditionally slightly rustic styles of Gigondas. Grenache (90%) and Mourvèdre comprise the blend of the regular *cuvée,* whereas Syrah is blended with Grenache and Cinsault in the Ventabren, which is also aged in *barrique* rather than the larger vats used for the regular bottling. Only a relatively small proportion is new and the wine is not overwhelmed by the wood, although some vintages need time for the fruit to show through. There is a general dedication to quality – the wines are neither fined nor filtered and are produced from vines that are over 50 years old. Fine and very intense, they drink very well over the medium term. (DM)

● **Gigondas★★** £C Cuvée Ventabren★★★ £C

DOM. DE MOURCHON Seguret www.domainedemourchon.com

Walter McKinlay 84110 Séguret
UK stockists: L&W

This property was purchased by Scotsman Walter McKinlay in 1998 and quality is moving forward very impressively. He has 24ha and an imposing *mas*, or farmhouse. The soft, fruity, easygoing rosé, Pié Loubié, blends Cinsault, Grenache and Syrah from 40-year-old vines but it is the Séguret reds which now mark this property out among the better producers in the region. The Tradition is a blend of Grenache (60%), Syrah (25%), Cinsault (10%) and Carignan. The vineyard is 40 years old and the wine is aged in *cuve* to emphasise its vibrant dark, spicy fruit. The Grande Réserve, a blend of Grenache in the main with 35% Syrah, is dense, powerful and concentrated with a marvellous old-vine purity. The 60-year-old vines are no doubt a major contributing element. Both wines will evolve well in the medium-term. (DM)

● **Côtes du Rhône-Villages Séguret** Tradition★★★ £B Grande Reserve★★★ £C
◉ **Côtes du Rhône** Pié Loubié★ £B

DOM. DE L'ORATOIRE SAINT-MARTIN Cairanne

Frédéric and François Alary   Route de Saint-Roman, 84290 Cairanne
UK stockists: Car

Frédéric and François are cousins of Daniel and Denis ALARY and produce equally exciting results in this outperforming Rhône village. The main Rhône varieties are planted and there are various blends. All the Cairanne bottlings are very impressive. The white Haut Coustias is a rich, nutty, almost honeyed blend of Marsanne, Roussanne and Viognier. The lesser reds have a high proportion of Grenache but are intense and heady. The Haut Coustias red is lent considerable depth and structure by its large Mourvèdre/Syrah component (60 and 20% respectively). It can hold its own against top-quality Châteauneuf-du-Pape and is rich, concentrated, powerful and very ageworthy. (DM)

● **Côtes du Rhône-Villages Cairanne** Haut Coustias★★★★ £C
● **Côtes du Rhône-Villages Cairanne** Prestige★★★ £B Réserve des Seigneurs★★★ £C
● **Côtes du Rhône**★★ £B   O **Côtes du Rhône**★ £B
O **Côtes du Rhône-Villages Cairanne** Haut Coustias★★★ £C

DOM. DU PEGAÜ Châteauneuf-du-Pape www.pegau.com

Feraud family   Avenue Impériale, 84230 Châteauneuf-du-Pape
UK stockists: Gau, GrD,SVS, NYg, Las

Very fine traditional domaine now run largely by Laurence Feraud. The *vin de table* Plan Pegaü is good, if a little light, but in the traditional style of the property. The white Châteauneuf-du-Pape is honeyed, nutty and concentrated. The reds are classic, formidably structured wines. Cuvée Réservée is in fact the regular red bottling but is full of impressive super-ripe, dark berry Grenache character and loaded with muscular tannin in its youth. The immensely concentrated Cuvée da Capo has emerged as one of the Rhône Valley's great reds – dense, massively powerful but refined and very pure as well. The Ferauds are also involved with André Brunel of LES CAILLOUX in a fine new *négociant* venture (FERAUD-BRUNEL). (DM)

● **Vin de Table** Plan Pegau Non-Filtré★★ £B
● **Châteauneuf-du-Pape** Cuvée Réservée★★★★★ £E Cuvée da Capo✪✪✪✪✪ £G
O **Châteauneuf-du-Pape** Cuvée Réservée★★★ £D

DOM. DES PERRIÈRES Costières de Nîmes

Emmanuelle & Marc Kreydenweiss   30129 Manduel
Marc Kreydenweiss and his wife Emmanuelle are better known for their stylish Alsace domaine but here in the Costières de Nîmes they produce 2 good to very good elegant reds in quite marked contrast to many of their neighbours. The approach is one of refinement not muscle. Marc Kreydenweiss feels many of the current new wave of Mediterranean reds are over-extracted and alcoholic.

How will they age? The Domaine de Grimaud bottling is Emmanuelle's baby and comes from its own 7-ha vineyard. Blended from 50% Carignan, 25 Cinsault and 25 Grenache, it is full of upfront brambly fruit. Domaine des Perrières is a refined and harmonious blend of Carignan, Syrah and Grenache with vines ranging from 25–70 years. It has more depth and a firmer structure and will age well for 5 or 6 years. (DM)

● **Costières de Nîmes** Domaine des Perrières★★★ £C Domaine de Grimaud★★ £B

DOM. PERRIN Côtes du Rhône www.beaucastel.com

Perrin Brothers 84350 Courthezon
UK stockists:Bib, JAr, Mis, BRW, BBR, Las

This is the *négociant* arm of the Perrin brothers of CHÂTEAU DE BEAUCASTEL. Production is now considerable at over 300,000 cases a year. Most famous among the wines is the long-established brand, La Vieille Ferme, an original trendsetter for quality in the Côtes du Ventoux, although other producers have now taken quality there to higher levels. They also now produce reliable to good examples from a number of southern Rhône ACs along with a sound Crozes-Hermitage. The wines offer an attractive, approachable style with forward, juicy fruit but fail to sing in the way that some of the best small growers in these appellations now do. (DM)

● **Crozes-Hermitage★** £B ● **Vacqueyras★★** £B ● **Gigondas★★** £C
● **Châteauneuf-du-Pape** Les Sinards★★ £C
● **Côtes du Rhône★** £B ● **Côtes du Rhône-Villages** Réserve★ £B
O **Côtes du Rhône-Villages** Réserve★ £B

DOM. DE PIAUGIER Sablet piaugier@wanadoo.fr

Jean-Marc Autran 3 Route de Gigondas, 84110 Sablet
UK stockists: GVF

Jean-Marc Autran possesses some 30ha of vineyards in Sablet and Gigondas, almost all of which are planted to red varieties. A very small amount of very good, nutty and lightly herbal white Sablet is made from Grenache Blanc, Roussanne, Viognier and Clairette, which lends a fresh grip to the wine. Among the reds the real star turns are the special *cuvées* from Sablet. All of these are dense, rich, powerful and very impressive for the appellation. Ténébi is an unusual 100% Counoise, Réserve de Maude 100% Syrah. The other Sablets blend Grenache with Mourvèdre. The approach to vinification is traditional and the fruit is not destemmed. The result, though, is never rustic. In the lesser regular Sablet, Côtes du Rhône and even the Gigondas – which are all lighter – a green undercurrent can occur in poorer vintages. However the Gigondas was very good in 2001. The top Sablet reds and the Gigondas all improve with 3 or 4 years' ageing. (DM)

● **Côtes du Rhône★** £A ● **Côtes du Rhône-Villages Sablet★★** £B
● **Côtes du Rhône-Villages Sablet** Montmartel★★★ £C Ténébi★★★ £C
● **Côtes du Rhône-Villages Sablet** Les Briquières★★★★ £C
● **Côtes du Rhône-Villages Sablet** Réserve de Maude★★★★ £D
● **Côtes du Rhône-Villages Sablet** Réserve Alphonse Vautour★★★★★ £E
● **Gigondas★★** £C O **Côtes du Rhône-Villages Sablet★★** £B

DOM. RABASSE-CHARAVIN Cairanne

Corinne Couturier La Font d'Estevenas, 84290 Cairanne
UK stockists: THt

A good small range here with fairly extensive vineyards (over 65 ha) and a surprisingly large annual production of around 15,000 cases. All but 2ha are planted to red varieties. The average vine age is now over 50 years, which no doubt ably assists in maintaining wine quality. The approach to vinifying the reds is traditional, with no destemming and ageing in vat. The wines are well made, with good dark berry fruit and a typically intense herbal component. Cuvée Estevenas has impressive depth and firm tannin in its youth. It is a good medium-term cellar prospect. (DM)

- ● **Côtes du Rhône-Villages Cairanne★★** £B Estevenas★★★ £B
- ● **Côtes du Rhône-Villages Rasteau★★** £B
- ○ **Côtes du Rhône-Villages Cairanne★** £B

DOM. RASPAIL-AY Gigondas

Dominique Ay   Le Colombier, 84190 Gigondas
UK stockists: Has

Dominique Ay produces just 2 wines from his 18ha in Gigondas. There is a little rosé but the real interest here is the burly, powerful but elegant and very ageworthy Gigondas. The fruit is all destemmed and the result is not at all rustic. The wine is aged in large vats rather than in *barrique* but is none the worse for that. On occasion the wine can lack the intensity and power of the very best. 2000 lacked a touch of ripeness whereas 01 was very impressive indeed, clearly ★★★★. (DM)

- ● **Gigondas★★★** £C

DOM. DES RELAGNES Châteauneuf-du-Pape

Henri Boiron & Olivier Hillaire   Route de Bédarrides, 84232 Châteauneuf-du-Pape
The Boiron family have been established in the appellation since 1716 and this relatively small estate with 16 ha benefits greatly from vines which average 60 years of age. The Côtes du Rhône is a soft, easy, forward style and should be drunk young, as should the white Châteauneuf. The Tradition is a blend of Grenache, Syrah and Mourvèdre marked by bright berry fruit and a hint of *garrigue* in the background. The Cuvée Vigneronne is unusually a blend of 6 varieties – Grenache, Syrah, Mourvèdre, Cinsault, Counoise and Terret Noir – and comes from the oldest vines on the property. The Petits Pieds d'Armande comes mainly from a century-old plot of Grenache in the La Crau sector of the appellation, blended with a little Syrah. This is aged in new oak and is richer, fleshier and more opulent than the more traditionally stuctured Vigneronne. Both wines demand at least 6 or 7 years' patience. (DM)

- ● **Châteauneuf-du-Pape** Tradition★★★ £D Cuvée Vigneronne★★★★ £E
- ● **Châteauneuf-du-Pape** Les Petits Pieds d'Armand★★★★ £E
- ● **Côtes du Rhone★** £B

DOM. RÉMÉJEANNE Côtes du Rhône-Villages

Remy Klein   Cadignac, 30200 Sabran
UK stockists: CTy

A real benchmark for other Côtes du Rhône properties. This medium-sized domaine makes some 12,500 cases annually, 90% of it red, from 35ha of vineyards. Les Arbousiers red and white are classic southern Rhône blends – the red is vibrant and spicy, the white subtly nutty. Les Chevrefeuilles adds Carignan and Counoise from old vines to Syrah and Grenache. The top 2 *cuvées* are Les Églantiers(100% Syrah) and Les Génevriers, a blend of Grenache, Syrah and Mourvèdre. Vinification is high-tech and modern and micro-oygenation is used during *élevage*. The top wines are rich, concentrated and develop well in bottle after 3–5 years' ageing. A powerful white Les Eglantiers, currently labelled as a *vin de table*, has recently been added. (DM)

- ● **Côtes du Rhône** Les Arbousiers★★ £B Les Chèvrefeuilles★★★ £B Les ● **Côtes**
- ● **Côtes du Rhône** Églantiers★★★★ £C
- ○ **Côtes du Rhône** Les Arbousiers★ £B
- ● **Côtes du Rhône-Villages** Les Génevriers★★★ £B

DOM. DE RENJARDE Côtes du Rhône www.chateau-la-nerthe.com

LVMH Route d'Uchaux, 84830 Serignan du Comtat
UK stockists: BBR, C&C

Good, well-priced reds from a sister property to CHÂTEAU LA NERTHE. There are 50ha under vine so this is quite a substantial operation with an annual output of around 20,000 cases in all. The vineyard is planted to a blend of Grenache, Syrah, Cinsault, Carignan and Mourvèdre. Alain Dugas, the director of Château La Nerthe, also guides operations here. Unlike at its sister property, vinification of each variety is separate, emphasising the quality of the fruit, with *assemblage* prior to bottling. Undoubtedly the quality stamp of the Richard family shows through, with a good, medium-weight, attractive fruit-driven Côtes du Rhône of some style and the Réserve de Cassagne, which is a particularly well-priced concentrated and structured red. (DM)

● **Côtes du Rhône**★★ £B
● **Côtes du Rhône-Villages** Réserve de Cassagne★★★ £B

MARCEL RICHAUD Cairanne

Marcel Richaud Route de Rasteau, 84290 Cairanne
UK stockists: Lib

Marcel Richaud is one of a number of excellent producers from this top-performing village. He has a reasonably sizeable vineyard holding of over 40 ha, some of which dates back over 100 years, so the potential of his raw material is remarkable and this shows through in his wines. All have impressive, spicy berry fruit with intense notes of thyme and the classic scent of *garrigues* from a range offering very fair prices. The top 2 *cuvées* are impressively structured; the Estrambords is aged in *barriques*, while the Côtes du Rhône Les Garrigues is particularly good value. In the difficult 2002 vintage only the Côtes du Rhône labels were released – no Cairanne – with quality holding up reasonably well. (DM)

● **Côtes du Rhône**★ £B Terres d'Aigues★★ £B Les Garrigues★★★ £B
○ **Côtes du Rhône**★ £B
● **Côtes du Rhône-Villages Cairanne**★★★ £B L'Ebrescade★★★★ £C
● **Côtes du Rhône-Villages Cairanne**Les Estrambords★★★★ £C
○ **Côtes du Rhône-Villages Cairanne**★★ £B

DOM. ROUGE GARANCE Côtes du Rhône-Villages

J-L Trintignant/Claudie et Bertrand Cortellini 30210 Saint-Hilaire d'Ozhilan
This is a small 5ha estate run by the Cortellinis and jointly owned with the French comedy film actor Jean-Louis Trintignant. They own a total of 28ha spread across various vineyards in the communes of Castillon du Gard and Saint-Hilaire d'Ozilhan. Feuille de Garance is from young vines, Garances comes from mainly old vine Carignan. Only a relatively small part of the harvest each year is vinified as Rouge Garance, a blend of 60/20/20 Syrah, Grenache and Mourvedre. The top red is the splendid Les Saintpierre from the oldest and lowest yielding Syrah vines and aged for 18 months in cask. The top reds will age well over the short to medium term. There is also a ripe and spicy fruit-driven Côtes du Rhône rosé and a well-priced nutty and forward easy-drinking white. (DM)

● **Côtes du Rhône-Villages** Les Saintpierre★★★★ £C Rouge Garance★★★ £C
● **Côtes du Rhône-Villages** Garances★★ £B
● **Côtes du Rhône** Feuille de Garance★ £B
○ **Côtes du Rhône** Blanc de Garance★ £B
◎ **Côtes du Rhône** Rosée de Garance★ £B

373

DOM. ROCHE-AUDRAN Côtes du Rhône

Vincent Rochette   Route de Saint Roman de Malegarde, 84110 Buisson
UK stockists: Gau

Some extraordinary and very complex Côtes du Rhône red is now made at this small domaine. The white is a blend of Grenache and Viognier and is fermented in barrel with *bâtonnage*. Subtle and nutty, it shows only minimal oak character. The regular Côtes du Rhône is bright and forward: berry fruit and a supple style is the approach. The Visan red is a clear step up. Deeply coloured, dark and structured, it blends Grenache and Syrah. But the brilliant wines here are the 3 Côtes du Rhône *cuvées*, sourced from a range of *terroirs*, some with vines older than 100 years. Père Mayeaux is a blend of Syrah and Grenache and is aged in new oak, which is very well judged. Smoky black fruits and a hint of *garrigue* are the prominent characters. The richly-textured and very concentrated Cesar is Grenache (50%), Syrah (46%) and a tiny hint of Mourvèdre (4%) showing great depth and fruit purity. Perhaps the most striking is the Caillou, 100% Grenache from very old vines, which has a depth and intensity only matched by some of the very best examples elsewhere. (DM)

● **Côtes du Rhône**★★ £B Père Mayeaux★★★ £B Cesar★★★★ £B
● **Côtes du Rhône**Le Caillou★★★★ £B ● **Côtes du Rhône-Villages Visan**★★★ £B
O **Côtes du Rhône**★★★ £B

DOM. JEAN ROYER Châteauneuf-du-Pape

Jean Royer   Avenue Saint-Joseph, 84230 Châteauneuf-du-Pape
UK stockists: Idg

Very good, traditionally made Châteauneuf is produced by Jean Royer. As well as producing his own labels he is also a source for TARDIEU-LAURENT. The wines all get a lengthy vatting and are in a dense, full-bodied style. The regular Tradition red is a touch less muscular than the other 2 *cuvées*, a blend of Grenache and Syrah that will drink well with 4 or 5 years' ageing. The Prestige is blended from Grenache, Syrah and Mourvèdre and is a selection of older vines. It is impressively deep and structured in both 2003 and 04, surprisingly a touch more so than the 01. Give it at least 6 or 7 years. The top wine, made only in great vintages, is the Hommage à Mon Père. Dense and chewy with formidable depth, it demands 7 or 8 years and will keep well for a decade and beyond. (DM)

● **Châteauneuf-du-Pape** Tradition★★★ £D Prestige★★★★ £E
● **Châteauneuf-du-Pape** Hommage à Mon Père★★★★ £E

ROGER SABON Châteauneuf-du-Pape

Roger Sabon   Avenue Impérial, BP 57, 84230 Châteauneuf-du-Pape
UK stockists: Gau, Rae, BBR, Bal, Sel

While there is good to very good regular Lirac and Châteauneuf-du-Pape here it is the marvellous old-vine Cuvée Prestige and Le Secret de Sabon that show real intensity and sheer class. They are produced from very low-yielding, superbly sited, venerable vines. The latter is one of the great wines of the appellation. The wines are all bottled without filtration. (DM)

● **Châteauneuf-du-Pape** Les Olivets★★ £D Cuvée Réservée★★★ £D
● **Châteauneuf-du-Pape** Cuvée Prestige★★★★ £E Le Secret de Sabon★★★★★ £F
● **Lirac**★★ £B

SAINT JEAN DU BARROUX Côtes du Ventoux

Philippe Gimel & Associés   Chemin de Saint Jean, 84330 Le Barroux
This newly established small property has the potential to become one of the shining lights in this aspiring appellation. Winemaker Philippe Gimel is widely experienced, having worked with such luminaries as PIERRE-BISE in the Loire and more locally BEAUCASTEL and JANASSE. There are 15ha here planted at

an altitude of 300–400m and a total of 7 varieties are being cultivated. The rich and nutty white is a blend of Grenache Blanc with Clairette and Bourboulenc adding stucture and backbone, aged in old wood. The dense and very concentrated red is a blend of Grenache, Syrah, Carignan and Cinsault, again vinified in *cuve*. It was on the edge of ★★★★ in 2003 and 04 looks like it may have even more potential. A domaine to watch. (DM)

● **Côtes du Ventoux**★★★ £C ○ **Côtes du Ventoux**★★★ £B

SANG DES CAILLOUX Vacqueyras

Serge Férigoule 84260 Sarrians
UK stockists: CPp

The performance at this estate represents one of the region's notable turnarounds in recent years. Quality in the early to mid-1990s was acceptable but only just. The wines were light, lacked dimension and appeared heavily processed. Now, though, they have minimal manipulation and are all the better for it. A barrel-fermented white is made from Grenache Blanc, Bourboulenc, Clairette and Roussanne but in tiny quantities, fewer than 200 cases a year. It is the 2 excellent-value reds which demand attention, particularly for their availability. They are now rich, dense and loaded with black fruit and spicy *garrigue* scents. The Classique has been variously named Doucinello, Azalais and Floureto over recent vintages (since 1995). It is blended from Grenache, Syrah, Mourvèdre and Cinsault and is the mainstay of the domaine. The Cuvée Lopy is produced from the oldest vines of Grenache (75 years) and Syrah. It is firmly structured and requires 3 or 4 years. Both reds keep very well. (DM)

● **Vacqueyras** Classique★★★ £B Cuvée Lopy Vieilles Vignes★★★★ £C

DOM. SANTA DUC Gigondas

Yves Gras 84190 Gigondas
UK stockists: Bib,Rae,HHB,F&M

For the past decade or more Santa Duc has been one of the finest and most reliable names in Gigondas. Even in some of the lesser vintages of the 1990s the wines showed impressively well. Just over half of Yves Gras's holding is in Gigondas and of other wines the red *vin de pays* is attractively fruity with crunchy strawberry and dark cherry flavours to the fore, while the Côtes du Rhône is lighter than some but has intensity and a marked scent of *garrigues*. The wines are given a cold soak prior to fermentation and are bottled unfined and unfiltered after being aged on lees. In Gigondas there is a solid *negociant* wine, La Garancières, but it is the 2 domaine wines which really stand out. The regular *cuvée* is the softer, more forward of the 2, with the more structured and very, very fine Les Hautes Garrigues seeing around one-third new oak. The balance is aged in *foudres*. A small range of *negociant* offerings from the southern Rhône is also now being offered, labelled Santa Duc Selections. (DM)

● **Vin de Pays de la Principauté d'Orange**★ £B ● **Côtes du Rhône**★★ £B
● **Gigondas**★★★ £C La Garancières★★ £B Les Hautes Garrigues★★★★ £D

DOM. SAINTE-ANNE Côtes du Rhône

Steinmaier family Les Cellettes, 30200 Saint-Gervais
UK stockists: OWL, Tan, SVS, BBR

Quality has been of a high order here throughout the 1990s but the wines still remain very good value. There are some 33ha under vine and Syrah and Mourvèdre as well as Grenache are important in shaping the style of the reds. These are full-bodied and dense; the top 2 *cuvées* in particular will benefit from medium-term ageing. The Viognier is important here and is one of the better southern Rhône examples. It should always be enjoyed young and fresh, when

375

it will be both exotic and peachy. (DM)

- **Côtes du Rhône-Villages**★★ £B Cuvée St Gervais★★★ £B
- **Côtes du Rhône-Villages**Cuvée Notre-Dame des Celettes★★★ £B
- O **Côtes du Rhône** Viognier★★ £C

DOM. SAINT BENOIT   Châteauneuf-du-Pape

Jacumin & Cellier families   Route de Sourgues, 84230 Châteauneuf-du-Pape
UK stockists:**WTs**

This property was established in 1989 and all 13 grapes permitted for reds in
the appellation are planted. Varieties for the red Châteauneuf are vinified
separately and blending takes place after ageing. A number of different *cuvées*
are produced. Elise includes most of the permitted varieties and is lightly toasty
(20% sees new French oak). The deep and reasonably concentrated Laureline
comes from 60-year-old vines. The 2000 was overly chocolaty but better poise
and elegance are consistently showed by the Soleil et Festins, which is mainly
Grenache with some Syrah and Mourvèdre, and the more densely structured
Grande Garde, mainly Mourvèdre with some old-vine Grenache. Of the whites
Elegance is an unusual blend of Bourboulenc, Picpoul and Grenache Blanc and
offers more depth and fresh acidity than many examples from the region. The
Roussane (spelt this way on the label) is more typically nutty and floral and is
100% varietal. Côtes du Rhône and Rhône-Villages are both produced here as
well as some impressive Côtes du Ventoux and Gigondas. The range is
completed by a number of *vin de pays* labels. (DM)

- **Châteauneuf-du-Pape** Soleil et Festins★★★ £C Grande Garde★★★ £C
- **Châteauneuf-du-Pape** Elise★★ £C Laureline★★ £D
- O **Châteauneuf-du-Pape** Elégance★★ £C Cuvée de Roussane Vieille Vignes★★ £D
- **Côtes du Rhône-Villages Cairanne** Cuvée du Belvédère★★ £B
- **Côtes du Rhône-Villages** Le Puy de Maupas★ £B
- **Côtes du Ventoux** Clos Fayard★★ £B

DOM. SAINT DAMIEN   Gigondas

Joël Saurel   84190 Gigondas
With vineyards located in one of the warmest sectors of the appellation and
galets roulés stony soils, Joël Saurel produces very full, rich and concentrated
Gigondas. He is helped in this endeavour by vines which are in some cases over
100 years old. Even the vines for the subtle, berry-scented Classique are on
average over 70 years old. No new oak is used and the wines are all bottled
without fining or filtration. Les Souteyrades is much more backward, darkly
spicy and mineral in character. The *terroir* is largely limestone and the wine has
a very fine piercing intensity. La Louisiane comes from pure *garrigues*.
Mourvèdre is blended with Grenache: there is no Syrah. Rich, heady and full,
this like the Souteyrades demands 5 or 6 years' patience. (DM)

- **Gigondas**★★★ £C Les Souteyrades★★★★ £D La Louisiane★★★★ £D

DOM. DE LA SOLITUDE   Châteauneuf-du-Pape

EARL Domaines Pierre Lançon   84231 Châteauneuf-du-Pape
UK stockists: **Las**
Decent red and white Côtes du Rhône as well as some impressive
Châteauneuf-du-Pape are made at this ancient estate. Indeed one of the family
ancestors, Maffeo Barberini, became Pope Urbain VIII in the early 1600s.
There are a total of 38ha planted in Châteauneuf-du-Pape of which 30ha are
red varieties and a further 48ha are covered by the Côtes du Rhône AC. The
richly juicy Côtes du Rhône red comes from 2 separate low-yielding vineyards
where just 30 hl/ha are cropped. Two modern-style white Châteauneufs see the
Roussanne component barrel-fermented. Ageing on lees produces a nutty,

floral, almost mineral character and in the case of the Barberini great intensity.
The spicy, berry-fruited Tradition red is a blend of Grenache, Syrah, Mourvèdre
and a little Cinsault. The richer, fuller and denser Barberini is a mix of
40/30/30 Grenache, Syrah and Mourvèdre aged in 60% new small oak. The
top wine is the remarkably complex, richly textured Réserve Secret, aged in
80% new oak. This is only made in the best years and is sourced from the best
plots. Expect the Tradition to evolve well for up to decade, the top 2 reds for
twice that. (DM)

● **Châteauneuf-du-Pape** Tradition★★★ £D   Cuvée Barbarini★★★★ £F
● **Châteauneuf-du-Pape** Réserve Secret★★★★★ £G
○ **Châteauneuf-du-Pape** Tradition★★ £D   Cuvée Barbarini★★★★ £F
● **Côtes du Rhône**★★ £B   ○ **Côtes du Rhône**★ £B

TARDIEU-LAURENT

Michel Tardieu/Dominique Laurent Route de Cucuron, 84160 Lourmarin
UK stockists: HBJ, Gcw, Rae, BBR, Las

An exceptional range of wines from throughout the Rhône Valley is produced
by the partnership of Michel Tardieu and Dominique LAURENT of Burgundy.
Along with wines from the Rhône there are selected bottlings from the
Costières de Nimes, Provence and the Languedoc. Almost everything is of at
least ★★ or ★★★ quality. Top wines from Hermitage, Côte-Rôtie and Cornas
in the north and Châteauneuf-du-Pape, Gigondas and Vacqueyras in the south
invariably rate at least ★★★ and often ★★★★, particularly the Vieilles Vignes
labels. (DM)

● **Côtes du Rhône** Guy Louis★★★ £C   ● **Saint-Joseph** Vieilles Vignes★★★ £D
● **Côtes du Rhône-Villages Rasteau** Vieilles-Vignes★★★ £C
● **Costières de Nimes**★★★ £B   ● **Corbières** Roquefort★★★ £B

DOM. DE LA TOURADE Gigondas

André Richard & Frédéric Haut 84190 Gogondas

This 15-ha property is now responsible for some of the most exciting Gigondas
of all. Also produced is a little spicy, forward Côtes du Rhône and 2
Vacqueyras, of which the old-vine Cuvée de l'Euse is much the more serious.
The regular Gigondas bottling is full of characterful dark, spicy Grenache fruit.
The Font des Aieux is fuller and more structured and shows real old-vine
complexity. The top wine, Cuvée Morgan, blends some Syrah and Mourvèdre
with Grenache and is aged in *barrique* for 12 months. One-third is new and
the wood is fairly prominent in the wine's youth. Ageing for 4 or 5 years should
ensure greater harmony. (DM)

● **Gigondas** Traditionelle★★★ £B Font des Aieux★★★★ £C   Cuvée Morgan★★★★ £C
● **Vacqueyras**★ £B   Cuvée de l'Euse★★★ £C

DOM. DU TRAPADIS Rasteau

Michèle Charavin & Helen Durand Route d'Orange, 84110 Rasteau
UK stockists: GrD, VTr,SVS

Helen Durand has been in charge here since 1994 and the estate is now run
with minimal interference in vineyard or cellar. Les Adrès is a classic, Grenache-
based southern Rhône blend while Harys is produced from Syrah. Traditional
vinification (no destemming) produces wines which are both rich and
structured. Even the Côtes du Rhône will benefit from short cellaring. In short
these are powerful and complex wines. (DM)

● **Côtes du Rhône**★★ £B
● **Côtes du Rhône-Villages Rasteau**★★★ £B   Les Adrès★★★ £C   Harys★★★ £C

377

PIERRE USSEGLIO Châteauneuf-du-Pape

Jean-Pierre & Thierry Usseglio   Route d'Orange, 84230 Châteauneuf-du-Pape
UK stockists: Gau, BBR, Las

Jean-Pierre and Thierry are now running their father's property of some 23 ha, where they produce around 4,500 cases a year. The white is sound but it is the reds which excel. They include very good regular red Châteauneuf as well as the super-dense and rich old-vine Mon Aïeul and an exceptional Cuvée Cinquantenaire which was produced in 1999. Réserve des Deux-Frères, an expensive special bottling that replaces the Cinquantenaire as the top label, was made in 2000 and 01. (DM)

● **Châteauneuf-du-Pape** Tradition★★★ £C Cuvée de Mon Aïeul★★★★ £E
O **Châteauneuf-du-Pape** Tradition★★ £C

RAYMOND USSEGLIO Châteauneuf-du-Pape

R & S Usseglio   16. Route de Courthézon, 84230 Châteauneuf-du-Pape
UK stockists: F&R

The Usseglios' vineyard is planted to 15ha of Grenache, Syrah, Mourvèdre, Cinsault and Counoise, while there is also just 1.5ha of the white varieties Clairette, Bourboulenc, Roussanne and Grenache Blanc. The white is produced in an approachable forward style with attractive floral, citrus and nutty fruit. Drink it young. The reds are sturdy and traditional. The Tradition is firmly structured in its youth while the Impériale, sourced from a plot planted in 1902, understandably offers greater depth and complexity and is a wine of real substance and power. The reds are bottled unfiltered and offer great value. A Côtes du Rhône red is also produced (DM)

● **Châteauneuf-du-Pape** Tradition★★★ £D Cuvée Impériale★★★★ £E
O **Châteauneuf-du-Pape** Tradition★★★ £D

DOM. DE LA VIEILLE-JULIENNE Châteauneuf-du-Pape

Jean-Paul Daumen   84100 Orange
UK stockists: OWL,Sel

The wines here are now of a different order to those of a few years back. The *vin de pays* is still from relatively young vines but for the Côtes du Rhône and Châteauneuf-du-Pape bottlings the vines are old to very old. The Vieilles Vignes Côtes du Rhône is produced from 60-year-old plantings and is a blend of Grenache, Syrah and Mourvèdre. It is very intense and complex. The regular Châteauneuf-du-Pape is sweet, spicy and intense, full of *garrigue* and super-ripe dark berry fruit – the 2000 rated ★★★★. The top 2 *cuvées* are remarkable. The Vieilles Vignes is immensely powerful and structured and it needs time. The Vieilles Vignes Réservé is extraordinary – 95% Grenache, heady and super-rich, it's the more open and approachable of the 2 but immensely ageworthy. (DM)

● **Châteauneuf-du-Pape** Vieilles Vignes★★★★★ £F Vieilles Vignes Réservé✪✪✪✪✪ £H
● **Châteauneuf-du-Pape**★★★ £C ● **Côtes du Rhone**★★ £B Vieilles Vignes★★★ £B
● **Vin de Pays de la Principauté d'Orange**★ £B

DOM. DU VIEUX-TÉLÉGRAPHE Châteauneuf-du-Pape

Brunier family   3 Route de Châteauneuf-du-Pape, 84370 Bedarrides
UK stockists: J&B,BBR,THt,Sel,Tan,SVS,F&M, Las

The Bruniers have been benchmark producers here for 2 decades. They now own the Domaine LA ROQUETTE also in Châteauneuf, and have an interest in the revitalised LES PALLIÈRES in Gigondas. The 70-ha estate is planted largely to reds, understandably, with a little Clairette, Grenache Blanc, Bourboulenc and Roussanne, which are used to produce a spicy, intensely nutty and surprisingly refined white Châteauneuf. The Vieux Mas des Papes is a very impressive second wine. The approach is to maximise the potential of the *grand vin*, rather than bottling small plots as special individual *cuvées*. The Châteauneuf-du-Pape red is now denser and more powerful than of old but with marvellous depth and refinement. There have been significant improvements at many properties throughout the appellation in recent years but few of these wines can achieve the balance and harmony of those of the Bruniers. (DM)

● **Châteauneuf-du-Pape**✪✪✪✪✪ £E   Le Vieux Mas des Papes★★★ £C
O **Châteauneuf-du-Pape**★★★★ £E
● **Vin de Pays de Vaucluse** Le Pigeoulet★★ £B

DOM. DE VILLENEUVE   Châteauneuf-du-Pape

Marie-Christine du Roy de Blicquey   Route de Courthézon, 84100 Orange
*UK stockists:*SVS
There are just 8.5ha of red varieties planted here and output is small at around 3,000 cases a year. A recently added white, blended from roughly equal parts of Grenache Blanc, Clairette and Roussanne, has impressive depth and intensity. The red Vieilles Vignes bottling is one of the best-value wines in the appellation, a blend of Grenache, Syrah, Mourvèdre and Cinsault with dark, peppery, spicy fruit, a hint of *garrigue* scent and real persistence on the palate. It offers loads of ripe, concentrated fruit along with firm youthful tannin and real old-vine complexity and ageing for 5 or 6 years is advisable. (DM)

● **Châteauneuf-du-Pape** Vieilles Vignes★★★★ £D
O **Châteauneuf-du-Pape**★★★ £D

DOM. VIRET   Côtes du Rhône-Villages

Philippe & Alain Viret   26110 Saint-Maurice-sur Eygues
Very impressive 30-ha domaine planted almost exclusively to red varieties. Just 1.5ha are accounted for by whites and the main focus of these is the Coudée d'Or. A tiny amount of a special *cuvée* MM and a red equivalent MIM were produced to celebrate the millenium. The estate is particularly noteworthy for its dedication to organic farming and what the Virets refer to as their 'cosmoculture'. Sharing some of the principles of biodynamics, cosmoculture is based on farming principles dating back to the Mayan and Inca civilisations. The key is an absolute desire to avoid any unnatural practices which may affect the growing conditions in the vineyards. The reds here are particularly striking: all come from low yields, are vinified without recourse to sulphur dioxide and are bottled without filtration. The softer and vibrant Renaissance blends Grenache, Syrah and Mourvèdre and is aged in cement. More structured are Les Colonnades, which includes Carignan rather than Syrah and is aged for 24 months with the Mourvèdre in *barrique*. The Emergence, a blend of Grenache, Syrah and Carignan, is similarly aged for 24 months but in a mix of *barriques* and vat. The densely structured and very characterful top 2 wines will undoubtedly benefit from 5 years' ageing. (DM)

● **Côtes du Rhône-Villages Saint-Maurice** Les Colonnades★★★ £C
● **Côtes du Rhône-Villages Saint-Maurice** Emergence★★★★ £C
● **Côtes du Rhône-Villages Saint-Maurice** Renaissance★★★ £B
O **Côtes du Rhône** La Coudée d'Or★★ £C

OTHER WINES OF NOTE

DOM. D'AÉRIA ● **Côtes du Rhône★** £B
● **Côtes du Rhône-Villages Cairanne** Tradition★★ £B
● **Côtes du Rhône-Villages Cairanne** Prestige★★ £C
● **Côtes du Rhône-Villages Rasteau★★** £B
DOM. DE L'AMEILLAUD ● **Côtes du Rhône-Villages Cairanne★★** £B
DOM. DES ANGES ● **Côtes du Ventoux★★** £B Clos de l'Archange★★★ £C
LES DOMAINES BERNARD ● **Châteauneuf-du-Pape** Louis Bernard★★ £C
DOM. DES BERNARDINS ○ **Muscat de Beaumes-de-Venise★★** £C
BOIS DAUPHIN ● **Châteauneuf-du-Pape★★★** £C
DOM. DES BOSQUETS ● **Gigondas★★** £C
DOM. BOUCHASSY ● **Lirac★** £B
DOMAINES BOUR ● **Coteaux du Tricastin** Vieilles Vignes★ £B La Truffière★★ £B
DOM. DE LA BRUNELY ● **Châteauneuf-du-Pape★★** £C
DOM. DES BUISSERONS ● **Côtes du Rhône-Villages Cairanne★★** £B
DOM. DE CHANABAS ● **Châteauneuf-du-Pape★★** £C
CHANTE PERDRIX ● **Châteauneuf-du-Pape★★** £C
DOM. CHAPOTON ● **Côtes du Rhône★★** £B
● **Côtes du Rhône-Villages Rochegude★★** £B
● **Côtes du Rhône-Villages Rochegude** Géodaisia★★ £C
○ **Côtes du Rhône** Géodaisia★★ £B
DIDIER CHARAVIN ● **Côtes du Rhône Villages Rasteau★★** £B Prestige★★ £B
CH. D'ACQUERIA ● **Lirac★** £B ◉ **Lirac★** £B ◉ **Tavel★** £B
CH. DE L'AMARINE ● **Costières de Nîmes** Cuvée de Bernis★★ £B
CH. BEAUBOIS ● **Costières de Nîmes★★** £B Elégance★★ £B
○ **Costières de Nîmes** Elégance★★ £B
CH. CABRIÈRES ● **Châteauneuf-du-Pape★★** £C Tête de Cru★★★ £E
CH. FORTIA ● **Châteauneuf-du-Pape★★★** £C
CH. GIGOGNAN ● **Châteauneuf-du-Pape** Clos du Roi★★ £C
CH. DE GRAND MOULAS ● **Côtes du Rhône★** £B
● **Côtes du Rhône-Villages★★** £B
CH. GRANDE-CASSAGNE ● **Costières de Nîmes** La Civette★★ £B
● **Costières de Nîmes** Les Rameaux★★ £B Hippolyte★★ £B
● **Costières de Nîmes** Tradition★ £B ○ **Costières de Nîmes** Tradition★ £B
○ **Costières de Nîmes** Hippolyte★★ £B
CH. LA CANORGUE ● **Côtes du Luberon★★** £B ● **Côtes du Rhône★★** £B
● **Côtes du Rhône-Villages Laudun★★** £B
CH. LA DECELLE ● **Côtes du Rhône-Villages★★** £B ● **Coteaux du Tricastin★** £B
CH. MAUCOIL ● **Châteauneuf-du-Pape★★** £C Cuvée Privilège★★★ £D
CH. LA TUILERIE ● **Costières de Nîmes** Cuvée Eole★★ £B
CH. DE MARJOLET ● **Côtes du Rhône-Villages Laudun★★★** £C
● **Côtes du Rhône-Villages★★** £B ● **Côtes du Rhône★** £B
○ **Côtes du Rhône★** £B ◉ **Côtes du Rhône★** £B
CH. DE MONTMIRAIL ● **Vacqueyras** l'Ermite★★ £B Saint Papes★★ £B
● **Gigondas** Beauchamp★★ £B
CH. DE NAGES ● **Costières de Nîmes★** £B Vieilles Vignes★★ £C
○ **Costières de Nîmes** Vieilles Vignes★★ £B
CH. DE ROUANNE ● **Côtes du Rhône-Villages Vinsobres★★** £B
CH. DES ROQUES ● **Vacqueyras★** £B
CH. SAINT-CYRGUES ○ **Costières de Nîmes★** £B
CH. SAINT LOUIS LA PERDRIX ● **Costières de Nîmes** Cuvée Marianne★★ £B
● **Vin de Pays du Gard** Cabernet/Carignan★ £B
CH. DE SEGRIES ● **Côtes du Rhône** Clos de l'Hermitage★ £B
● **Lirac** Cuvée Reservée★★ £C ○ **Lirac★** £C
CH. SIGNAC ● **Côtes du Rhône-Villages★** £B Combe d'Enfer★★ £B
● **Côtes du Rhône-Villages** Terra Amata★★ £B
CH. DU TRIGNON ● **Côtes du Rhône-Villages Sablet★** £B ● **Gigondas★★** £C
CH. VAL JOANIS ● **Côtes du Luberon** Réserve Les Griottes★★ £B
CH. DE VALCOMBE ● **Costières de Nîmes** Tradition★★ £B Prestige★★ £B
● **Costières de Nîmes** Garance★★★ £C

CH. DE LA VERRERIE ● **Côtes du Luberon**★ £B

CH. VIRGILE ● **Costières de Nîmes**★★ £B

CLOS DU JONCUAS ● **Gigondas** Esprit de Grenache★★ £B

CLOS DE L'ORATOIRE DES PAPES ● **Châteauneuf-du-Pape**★★★ £C

CLOS SAINT-MICHEL ● **Châteauneuf-du-Pape**★★ £C Cuvée Réservée★★★ £D

DOM. DES CORIANCON ● **Côtes du Rhône-Villages Vinsobres**★ £B

● **Côtes du Rhône-Villages Vinsobres** Cuvée Claude Vallot ★★ £B

DOM DU CORNE-LOUP ● **Lirac**★★ £B

DOM. DE LA DAYSSE ● **Gigondas**★★ £B

DOM. BRUNO DELUBAC ● **Côtes du Rhône-Villages Cairanne** Les Bruneau★★ £B

● **Côtes du Rhône-Villages Cairanne** L'Authentique★★★ £C

O **Côtes du Rhône**★★ £B

DOMAINE DUCLAUX ● **Châteauneuf-du-Pape**★★ £C

CAVE D'ESTÉZARGUES ● **Côtes du Rhône** Dom. d'Andezon★ £B

● **Côtes du Rhône-Villages** Dom. d'Andezon Vieilles Vignes★★ £B

DOM. DE FERRAND ● **Châteauneuf-du-Pape**★★ £C

DOM. DE FONTENILLE ● **Côtes du Luberon**★ £B Vieilles Vignes★★ £B

● **Côtes du Luberon**Prestige★★ £B

DOM. LOU FREJAU ● **Châteauneuf-du-Pape**★★★ £C

GALET DES PAPES ● **Châteauneuf-du-Pape** Tradition★★ £C Vieilles Vignes★★★ £E

O **Châteauneuf-du-Pape**★★ £C

DOM. GRAND BOURJASSOT ● **Gigondas**★★★ £B

DOM. DES GRAND DEVERS ● **Côtes du Rhône** Enclave des Papes★ £B

● **Côtes du Rhône** La Syrah★★ £C ● **Côtes du Rhône-Villages Valreas**★★ £B

● **Côtes du Rhône-Villages Visan**★★ £B O **Côtes du Rhône-Villages Visan**★ £B

DOM. GRAND VENEUR ● **Châteauneuf-du-Pape**★★ £C

● **Châteauneuf-du-Pape** Cuvée Les Origines★★★ £D

DOM. DE GRANGENEUVE ● **Coteaux du Tricastin** Vieilles Vignes★★ £B

● **Coteaux du Tricastin** La Truffière★★ £B

DOM. DU JONCIER ● **Lirac**★★ £B

DOM. LA BASTIDE SAINT DOMINIQUE ● **Châteauneuf-du-Pape**★★★ £C

DOM. LA CABOTTE ● **Côtes du Rhône-Villages**★ £B

● **Côtes du Rhône-Villages** Élevé en Futs de Chene★★ £B

DOM. LA FOURMONE ● **Vacqueyras**★★ £B ● **Gigondas** l'Oustau Fauquet★★★ £B

DOM. LA MAVETTE ● **Gigondas**★★★ £C

DOM. LA ROCALIÈRE ● **Lirac** Cuvée Prestige★★ £B

DOM. LE COLOMBIER ● **Côtes du Ventoux**★ £B ● **Vacqueyras** Cuvée G★★ £B

DOM. LE COUROULU ● **Vacqueyras**★★ £B Vieilles Vignes★★★ £B

DOM. CATHERINE LEGOEUIL ● **Côtes du Rhône-Cairanne** Lea Felsch★★ £B

● **Côtes du Rhône-Villages Cairanne** Cuvée Marie Rouvière★★ £B

● **Côtes du Rhône-Villages Cairanne** Les Beauchières★★★ £C

DOM. LES CLEFS D'OR ● **Châteauneuf-du-Pape**★★★ £C

DOM. LES HAUTES CANCES ● **Côtes du Rhône**★ £B

● **Côtes du Rhône-Villages Cairanne**★★ £B

● **Côtes du Rhône-Villages Cairanne** Vieilles Vignes★★ £B Col du Débat★★★ £B

O **Côtes du Rhône-Villages Cairanne**★ £B

DOM. LES TERRASSES D'EOLE ● **Côtes du Ventoux** Lou Mistrano★ £B

LE VIEUX DONJON ● **Châteauneuf-du-Pape**★★★ £E

DOM. LONGUE TOQUE ● **Gigondas**★★★ £C

MAS DES BRESSADES ● **Costières de Nîmes** Tradition★★ £B Excéllence★★ £B

● **Vin de Pays du Gard** Cabernet/Syrah★★ £B

O **Costières de Nîmes** Tradition★£B Excéllence★★ £B

◉ **Costières de Nîmes** Tradition★ £B

DOM. DU MAS CARLOT ● **Costières de Nîmes** Château Paul Blanc★ £B

O **Costières de Nîmes** Château Paul Blanc★ £B

MAS DE GUIOT ● **Vin de Pays du Gard** Cabernet Syrah★ £B

MAS DE LIBIAN ● **Côtes du Rhône**★ £B ● **Côtes du Rhône-Villages**★★ £B

DOM. DE MONTVAC ● **Vacqueyras**★★ £B Cuvée Vincilan★★★ £C

● **Gigondas**★★ £C O **Vacqueyras**★★ £B

DOM. DU MOULIN ● **Côtes du Rhône-Villages Vinsobres**★★ £B

● **Côtes du Rhône-Villages Vinsobres**Charles Joseph★★ £B

381

● **Côtes du Rhône**★ £B   O **Côtes du Rhône-Villages Vinsobres**★ £B
DOM. MOULIN-TACUSSEL ● **Châteauneuf-du-Pape**★★★ £C
DOM. DE NALYS ● **Châteauneuf-du-Pape**★★★ £C
NOTRE DAME DE COUSIGNAC ● **Côtes du Rhône**★ £B
● **Côtes du Rhône** Hommage à Léon Pommier★★ £B   O **Côtes du Rhône**★ £B
DOM. PÉLAQUIÉ ● **Lirac**★★ £B   O **Côtes du Rhône-Villages Laudun**★ £B
DOM. L'OUSTAU FAUQUET ● **Gigondas**★★★ £C
DOM. PÈRE CABOCHE ● **Châteauneuf-du-Pape**★★ £C
● **Châteauneuf-du-Pape** Cuvée Elisabeth Chambellan★★★ £D
DOM. DU PÈRE PAPE ● **Châteauneuf-du-Pape**★★ £C
● **Châteauneuf-du-Pape**La Crau de Ma Mère★★★ £D
ROGER PERRIN ● **Côtes du Rhône**★★ £B Prestige★★ £B
● **Châteauneuf-du-Pape**★★★ £C Vieilles Vignes★★★★ £E
DOM. PESQUIER ● **Gigondas**★★★ £C
DOM. RIGOT ● **Côtes du Rhône**★★ £B Prestige des Garrigues★★ £B
DOMINIQUE. ROCHER ● **Côtes du Rhône-Villages Cairanne**★★ £B
● **Côtes du Rhône-Villages Cairanne** Cuvée Monsieur Paul★★ £B
● **Côtes du Rhône**★ £B   O **Côtes du Rhône**★ £B
DOM SAINT-AMANT ● **Côtes du Rhône** Les Clapas★★ £B
● **Côtes du Rhône-Villages Beaumes-de-Venise** Grangeneuve★★★ £C
O **Côtes du Rhône** La Borry★★ £B
O **Côtes du Rhône-Villages Beaumes-de-Venise** La Tabardonne★★ £C
DOM. SAINT-ANTOINE ● **Costières de Nîmes** Cuvée des Oliviers★ £B
DOM. SAINT-GAYAN ● **Côtes du Rhône-Villages Rasteau**★★ £B
● **Gigondas**★★ £C Fontmaria★★★ £C
DOM. DE SAINT-LUC ● **Coteaux du Tricastin** Syrah★ £B
● **Côtes du Rhône-Villages**★★ £B
DOM. DE SAINT-SIFFREIN   ● **Côtes du Rhône**★ £B
● **Châteauneuf-du-Pape**★★★ £C
DOM. TARA ● **Côtes du Ventoux** Terre d'Ocre★ £B Hautes Pierres★★ £B
O **Côtes du Ventoux** Hautes Pierres★★ £B
DOM. DU TERME ● **Gigondas**★★★ £C
ERIC TEXIER ● **Côtes du Rhône-Villages Cairanne**★★ £B
● **Côtes du Rhône-Villages Seguret**★★★ £C
● **Côtes du Rhône-Villages Saint-Gervais** Vieilles Vignes★★★ £C
DOM. LES TEYSSONIERES ● **Gigondas** Vendange Manuelle★★ £B
● **Gigondas** Cuvée Alexandre★★★ £C
DOM. LES TOURELLES ● **Gigondas**★★★ £C
DOM. DE VERQUIERE ● **Côtes du Rhône-Villages Sablet**★ £B
DOM VERDA ● **Lirac** Cuvée Prestige★ £B
DOM. DE LA VERRIÈRE ● **Côtes du Ventoux**★ £B
DOM. DU VIEUX RELAIS ● **Costières de Nîmes** Tradition★ £B Sélection★★ £B

Work in progress!!

Producers under consideration for the next edition
ALAIN GALLETY (COTES DU VIVARAIS)
CH. DE BECK (COSTIERES DE NIMES)

Author's choice (DM)

12 benchmark Châteauneuf-du-Papes
DOM. DE BEAURENARD ● **Châteauneuf du Pape** Boisrenard
M CHAPOUTIER ● **Châteauneuf du Pape** Barbe Rac
CH. DE BEAUCASTEL ● **Châteauneuf du Pape** Hommage à Jacques`Perrin
CH. LA NERTHE ● **Châteauneuf du Pape** Cuvée des Cadettes
CH. RAYAS ● **Châteauneuf du Pape**
CLOS DES CAILLOU ● **Châteauneuf du Pape** Réserve
CLOS DES PAPES ● **Châteauneuf du Pape**

DOM DE LA JANASSE ● **Châteauneuf du Pape** Vieilles Vignes
DOM. DE MARCOUX ● **Châteauneuf du Pape** Vieilles Vignes
DOM. DE LA MORDORÉE ● **Châteauneuf du Pape** Reine des Bois
DOM. DE LA VIEILLE-JULIENNE ● **Châteauneuf du Pape** Vieilles Vignes Réservé
DOM. DU VIEUX TÉLÉGRAPHE ● **Châteauneuf du Pape**

A diverse selection of a dozen emerging reds

DANIEL ET DENIS ALARY ● **Côtes du Rhône-Villages Cairanne** La Font d'Estevenas
DOM. BRUSSET ● **Gigondas** Les Hauts de Montmirail
CLOS DES CAZAUX ● **Vacqueyras** Grénat Noble
CLOS PETITE BELLANE ● **Côtes du Rhône Valréas** Vieilles Vignes
DOM. DE DEURRE ● **Côtes du Rhône** Les Rabasses
GOURT DE MAUTENS ● **Côtes du Rhône-Villages Rasteau**
DOM. LA SOUMADE ● **Côtes du Rhône-Villages Rasteau** Fleur de Confiance
DOM. LES APHILLANTHES ● **Côtes du Rhône-Villages** Vieilles Vignes
DOM. DE L'ORATOIRE SAINT-MARTIN ● **Côtes du Rhône-Villages Cairanne** Haut Coustias
DOM. DE PIAUGIER ● **Côtes du Rhône-Villages Sablet** Réserve Alphonse Vautour
MARCEL RICHAUD ● **Côtes du Rhône-Villages Cairanne** Les Estrambords
DOM. SANTA-DUC ● **Gigondas** Les Hautes Garrigues

A selection of good value reds and whites

CH. SAINT-COSME ● **Côtes du Rhône** Les Deux Albions
DOM. CHAUME-ARNAUD O **Côtes du Rhône-Villages Vinsobres**
CROS DE LA MÛRE ● **Côtes du Rhône-Villages**
DOM. DE FONDRÈCHE ● **Côtes du Ventoux** Cuvée Persia
FONT DE MICHELLE O **Côtes du Rhône** F de Font de Michelle
DOM. LA GARRIGUE ● **Vacqueyras**
DOM. GRAMENON O **Côtes du Rhône** Vie on y est
DOM. GRAPILLON D'OR ● **Gigondas**
DOM. RABASSE-CHARAVIN ● **Côtes du Rhône-Villages Cairanne** Estevenas
DOM. DE RÉMÉJEANNE ● **Côtes du Rhône** Les Génevriers
SANG DES CAILLOUX ● **Vacqueyras** Classique
DOM. SAINTE-ANNE O **Côtes du Rhône** Viognier

RECOMMENDED HOTELS AND RESTAURANTS - RHÔNE VALLEY - NORTH

Top Hotels

★★★★★*Villa Florentine*   25, Montée St-Barthélémy, Lyon 69005
Tel. 04 72 56 56 56 Fax 04 72 40 90 56
Email florentine@relaischâteau.com   20 rooms   £ H

★★★★*Pyramide*   14 bvd. F. Point, Vienne 38200
Tel. 04 74 53 01 96 Fax 04 74 85 69 73
Email. pyramide.f.point@wanadoo.fr   21 rooms   £F/G

Top Restaurants

★★★★★*Auberge et Clos des Cimes*   St-Bonnet-le-Froid
Tel. 04 71 59 93 72 Fax 04 71 59 93 40
Email contact@regismarcon.fr   £E/G

★★★★★*Pyramide*   14 bvd. F. Point, Vienne 38200
Tel. 04 74 53 01 96 Fax 04 74 85 69 73
Email. pyramide.f.point@wanadoo.fr   £F/H

Value for money Hotels

★★*Schaeffer*   Quai Jules Roche (N 86), Serrières 07340
Tel. 04 75 34 00 07 Fax 04 75 34 08 79
Email mathe@hotel-schaeffer.com   11 rooms   £A

383

★★*Hostellerie St-Laurant* St-Laurent-de-Mure 69720
Tel. 04 78 40 91 44 Fax 04 78 40 45 41
Email le-stlaurant@wanadoo.fr   12 rooms   £A/C

Value for money restaurants

★★★*Schaeffer* Quai Jules Roche (N 86), Serrières 07340
Tel. 04 75 34 00 07 Fax 04 75 34 08 79
Email mathe@hotel-schaeffer.com   £B/D

★*Bistrot 'Albert* 116 ave. J. Jaurès, St-Vallier 26240
Tel. 04 75 23 01 12 Fax 04 75 23 38 82
Email bistrot.albert@wanadoo.fr   £A

RHÔNE VALLEY - SOUTH

Top Hotels

★★★★★*Oustau de Baumanière* val d'Enfer, Les Baux-de-Provence 13520
Tel. 04 90 54 33 07 Fax 04 90 54 40 46
Email baumaniere@relaischateaux.fr   13 rooms   £G/H

★★★★★*La Mirande* 4 place Amirande, Avignon 84000
Tel. 04 90 85 93 93 Fax 04 90 86 26 85
Email. mirande@la-mirande.fr   21 rooms   £H

Top Restaurants

★★★★★*Oustau de Baumanière* val d'Enfer, Les Baux-de-Provence 13520
Tel. 04 90 54 33 07 Fax 04 90 54 40 46
Email baumaniere@relaischateaux.fr   £G/H

★★★★*Moulin de Lourmarin* rue Temple, Lourmarin 84160
Tel. 04 90 68 06 69 Fax 04 90 68 31 76
Email. info@moulindelourmarin.com   £ H

Value for money Hotels

★★*Auberge de Carcarille* route d'Apt, Gordes 84220
Tel. 04 90 72 02 63 Fax 04 90 72 05 74
Email carcaril@club-internet.fr   11 rooms   £A

★★*La Ferme* Ile de Barthelasse, Avignon 84000
Tel. 04 90 32 42 91 Fax 04 90 32 08 29
Email info@hotel-lafernme.com   20 rooms   £A/B

Value for money restaurants

★*La Table du Meunier* 42 cours Hyacinthe Bellon, Fontvieille 13990
Tel. 04 90 54 61 05 Fax 04 90 54 77 24
No email address   £A

★★*Mas de Bouvau* rte. de Cairanne, Violés 84150
Tel. 04 90 70 94 08 Fax 04 90 70 95 99
No email address   £A

LYONNAIS RECIPES

QUENELLES DE BROCHET A LA LYONNAISE
(any other fish can be used)

Ingredients: For 6 people: 300gr. of pike filets or any other fish; 100gr. of choux pastry (see below) 2dl. of double cream, 3 whites of eggs.

Mix the fish, white of eggs and choux pastry **very well in a food processor**. Put in freezer with the cream but separately. Chill very well until some ice crystals are showing. Take out of freezer and put fish mixture back in food processor and slowly add the very chilled cream. Mix very quickly and stop as soon as it becomes thick and smooth. Make quenelle shapes by rolling two spoons, and drop in boiling water until they come to the surface and are cooked. Serve in fish soup or with a very thin béchamel, *made in advance*, as the quenelles must remain really swollen. If they go flat, put quenelles in the broth, and cook covered until they are big. With béchamel sauce put into a medium to hot oven, covered in béchamel until swollen.

Choux pastry:

Ingredients: 4 dl of water, 250gr. white flour, 100 gr. butter, 4 to 5 large eggs or 6/7 medium to small.

Bring the water and the butter to the boil, add the flour and a pinch of salt in one go; lower the heat to minimum and stir constantly with a wooden spoon until the bottom and sides of the pan are clean. Remove from the fire and the pan, and let the mixture cool so that the eggs do not cook as you are mixing them! (You can beat in the eggs with an electric beater on slow speed) The mixture must be supple and hold so you can pipe it if you want. This mixture is more than 100gr. so you can make so many things with choux pastry: éclairs, cream puffs, or gougères adding 200gr. of cheese. Cook in quite a hot oven until golden brown; avoid opening the oven.

RECOMMENDED WINES

This dish probably needs something a little more delicate than some of the Marsanne/Roussanne blends that abound in the Rhône Valley. So it's probably best to go for some top Condrieus from the likes of Yves Cuilleron or André Perret, or even a more modestly priced Côtes du Rhône Viognier from Domaine Sainte-Anne in the south.

POULET GRILLE A LA LYONNAISE:

Ingredients; 4 breasts of chicken or a whole chicken cut up in portions. 2 shallots, 4 tablespoons white wine, salt and pepper, breadcrumbs, melted butter.

Marinate the chicken pieces in a little white wine, very finely chopped shallots, salt and pepper and some melted butter. Grill the chicken first and put in a dish with more melted butter, and cook until almost done. Cover each portion with a slice of ham, breadcrumbs and pommes lyonnaises, and finish cooking in the oven. Serve with a sauce lyonnaise.

Pommes lyonnaises: two medium size potatoes, one medium size onion, duck fat or butter. Cook the potatoes with the skin on. Peel and slice the potatoes and sauté in the hot butter or duck fat. Slice the onion very thinly, sauté in butter or duck fat until cooked. Toss onions and potatoes together delicately and put on the chicken as indicated.

Sauce lyonnaise: chop very finely 2 medium size onions and cook slowly in duck fat or butter until almost melting. Add 1dl. wine vinegar and reduce almost totally; add 2dl. of good white wine and reduce by half. Add 2dl. of strong stock, reduce a little; season to taste and serve with the chicken. If you prefer it, you can liquidise the sauce before serving.

RECOMMENDED WINES

Anything goes here, either red or white, but you need wines with structure and finesse, not any old clumsy cheapo. A Châteauneuf-du-pape red or white from the likes of Beaucastel or Vieux Télégraphe would certainly do the trick here and from the north, anything from Guigal's range would be suitable for all pockets. At the top end of the spectrum, Jean-Louis Chave's red or white Hermitage would go splendidly if you could find some with enough bottle age and are still affordable. A more down to earth choice may be one of the Crozes-Hermitages from Alain Graillot

BUGNES LYONNAISES ET COMPOTE DE FRUITBUGNES;

FOR 6 PEOPLE: *Ingredients:* 260gr. flour; 60gr. melted butter; 2 whole eggs, 60gr. caster sugar; pinch of salt. 1 Tablespoon cognac, 1 Tablespoon rum.

Put sieved flour into a bowl; make a well in the centre and break in the eggs and add melted butter and the sugar. Slowly work the flour into the well, mixing thoroughly until a very smooth dough is obtained. Let it rest for a couple of hours wrapped in a cloth. Roll out the pastry down to the thickness of a pound coin and cut out lozenges of about 4 to 5 cms long. Fry a few at a time in hot but

385

not smoking oil until they become puffed up and golden. Place on absorbent paper and sprinkle with icing sugar. Serve warm with fruit compôte.

RECOMMENDED WINES

There's a bit of a shortage of dessert wines in the Rhône Valley to go with this dish except for Muscat de Beaumes de Venise where the wine from Domaine Durban has a great deal more finesse than most of them. The other alternative would be to try the botrytised Condrieus from either Yves Cuilleron or André Perret, but these are not made in every year and are relatively pricey.

The focus here is on established pioneers, as well as the many new small domaines now placing Languedoc-Roussillon solidly on the country's quality wine map. Although many appellations here are of long standing only recently have widespread improvements been made in the standard of the wines. While many high quality domaines are emerging, in the Languedoc in particular many of the wines are over-extracted. There are many fewer new names in the Roussillon but these have been producing wines of a uniformly impressive quality. Many vineyards originally used for fortifieds are now providing some great reds in particular. While prices generally remain very fair some are creeping up significantly. The transformation here is unique in France.

Languedoc

Some truly great wine is now being made in the Languedoc. Most but by no means all of this is produced under a number of different appellations. For reasons of practicality and location a number of splendid new-wave wines, particularly red, are being produced as *vins de pays*. A number are **Vins de Pays d'Oc** but **Vin de Pays de l'Hérault** also features, including two of the greatest properties in the Languedoc, Mas de Daumas Gassac and Domaine de La Grange des Pères.

To the west of the Costières de Nîmes (see Rhône Valley) is the giant spread of the **Coteaux du Languedoc** AC. Vast and sprawling, it stretches from Nîmes in the east around the coastline to Narbonne and a considerable distance into the hills of the Gard and Hérault *départements*. There are twelve communes which are allowed to add their village names as *crus* and these include **La Clape**, **Picpoul de Pinet**, **Cabrières**, **Montpeyroux**, **Pic-Saint-Loup** and **Saint-Drézéry**. At best there are some splendid wines, generally blends of Syrah, Grenache and Mourvèdre for the reds with whites from a host of varieties including Roussanne, Grenache Blanc and Clairette. Sadly, you are also likely to encounter a great many moderate to average bottles, so always try to buy from a good source.

Just to the north of Béziers and to the west of the Coteaux du Languedoc are the small appellations of **Faugères** and **Saint-Chinian**. Some very fine small properties are now producing great reds, the most important variety being Syrah (which performs superbly in the schistous soils of Faugères) although Grenache, Mourvèdre and old-vine Carignan all play an important role in the local viticulture. There are a number of Muscat-based *vins doux naturels* as well but none are comparable to their peers from Muscat de Rivesaltes in the Roussillon. They include **Muscat de Frontignan**, **Muscat de Mireval** and **Muscat de Lunel**.

South of Narbonne and stretching down to the hills of the Roussillon are a number of key appellations. **Minervois**, **Corbières** and **Fitou** had for a long time been regarded as little more than Midi workhorse wines, vinified by unambitious local co-ops or volume *négociants*. This has to a large extent changed for the better. The wines of Minervois have shown the most potential and within that appellation is the new *cru* sub-zone of **La Livinière**, the source of generally the densest and most substantial wines of the AC. Old-vine Carignan plays an important role here although plantings of the Rhône *cépages améliorateurs* continue apace with some vineyards now possessing some increasingly old Syrah, Grenache and Mourvèdre. Carbonic maceration is widely used for Carignan, particularly in Corbières.

To the west of Minervois, the smaller new AC of **Cabardès** has real potential

387

and the Bordeaux varieties Cabernet Sauvignon, Merlot and Cabernet Franc are important here. The biggest disappointment over the past decade has been the performance of Fitou, one of the first ACs established in the region. The co-op at Mont-Tauch has always been a solid source but other promising new producers are emerging.

To the west of Fitou, in the hills around the town of **Limoux**, cool hillside vineyards are planted to Chardonnay and Mauzac. Good sparkling wine is made here, both **Blanquette de Limoux** and **Crémant de Limoux**, but it is the barrel-fermented Chardonnays that have come to prominence in recent years that impress most.

Roussillon

Until recently the vineyards in the Pyrenées-Orientales *département* were best known in quality wine terms for the production of fine *vins doux naturels*. This situation is changing apace though, and there seems perhaps even more potential here than in the Languedoc. Some stunning reds have appeared over the past decade and the emergence of exciting new small producers continues unabated. One of the region's great strengths is the extensive hillside vineyards planted to both old-vine Carignan and equally importantly Grenache. This is because of the traditional importance of fortified Rivesaltes and Maury, from north of Perpignan, and of Banyuls-sur-Mer, another fortified wine further south on the coast.

Exciting wines are being made throughout the **Côtes du Roussillon** and the **Côtes du Roussillon-Villages** ACs. As well as Grenache, the other Rhône varieties are important too, and a number of top *cuvées* vinified largely from Syrah and aged in high-quality new oak are also emerging, along with the occasional exceptional blend dominated by Mourvèdre. On the coast around the village of Banyuls-sur-Mer the **Collioure** appellation shares the same vineyard area as **Banyuls**. Syrah, Carignan, Mourvèdre and Cinsault are all cultivated here but interestingly it is Mourvèdre planted in close proximity to the sea that has performed particularly well, as it does in Bandol. The **Vin de Pays des Côtes Catalanes** is also increasingly important for red blends and these include Cabernet Sauvignon and Merlot. A new and very exciting region that covers much of the physical area shared by the Maury sweet wine appellation is the newly established **Vin de Pays des Coteaux de Fenouillèdes** in the Agly Valley in the north western section of the Côtes du Roussillon. There is a tremendous resource of old vine Grenache and Carignan. A number of top producers have emerged, although not all use the Vin de Pays classification.

The great traditional wines of the Roussillon are the fortified **Maury**, **Rivesaltes** and **Banyuls**, which in their most exquisite and aged manifestations are characterised by an intense baked, raisiny, *rancio* character. A whole range of styles are produced, with small differences between the appellations. Almost all these wines depend on Grenache as the backbone of the blend; indeed, many are produced solely from the variety. There are youthful, fruit-driven styles that spend only a limited time in cask, wines that are aged for an extended time and wines that are made from a blend of vintages very much in a *solera*-style system. The wines of Maury tend to be more overtly tannic when young and those earlier-released vintages will need more cellaring. Most wines are aged in cool cellars but in Rivesaltes they are also left out for a period in the summer sun in large glass containers – *bonbonnes* – to encourage the development of those complex *rancio* aromas.

As well as the Grenache-based wines there is some very impressive **Muscat de**

LANGUEDOC & ROUSSILLON

Rivesaltes, which is markedly different in style. At their best these wines emphasise Muscat's rich grapy character, and are heady and impressively perfumed. Indeed, the best examples are better generally than their equivalents in the Languedoc and the Rhône Valley at Beaumes-de-Venise.

A-Z of producers by appellation

LANGUEDOC & ROUSSILLON

1   Muscat de Lunel
2   Coteaux du Languedoc
3   Coteaux du Languedoc Pic Saint-Loup
4   Coteaux du Languedoc Montpeyroux
5   Muscat de Mireval
6   Muscat de Frontignan
7   Coteaux du Languedoc Picpoul de Pinet
8   Faugères
9   Saint-Chinian
10 Muscat de Saint-Jean de Minervois
11 Minervois
12 Coteaux du Languedoc La Clape

13 Cabardès
14 Côtes de la Malepère
15 Limoux
16 Corbières
17 Fitou
18 Maury
19 Côtes du Roussillon-Villages
20 Côtes du Roussillon
21 Rivesaltes, Muscat de Rivesaltes
22 Banyuls, Collioure

Languedoc & Roussillon vintages

It is extremely difficult in a vast region such as this to make specific vintage assessments. Also much of the development that has been made in recent years makes a longer term assessment of the wines more erratic. However, there have been significant changes in vintage conditions from one year to another throughout the region. These variations are more pronounced as you move further inland. Vineyards nearer the coast benefit from a benign maritime climate and are more consistent.

In terms of the wines, the best red examples from year to year have the potential to age. Some red Languedoc wines have shown a recent tendency to fade prematurely, particularly those from the Coteaux du Languedoc. As producers become more successful in unleashing the best character from their grapes this should improve. The *cépages améliorateurs* varieties planted in the Languedoc are also generally still young and the wines made from them can easily be over-extracted. There is no question that as these vines age and the Midi's keen young producers develop their craft the wines will become increasingly refined and cellarworthy.

Languedoc & Roussillon vintage chart

	Corbieres & Minervois	Coteaux du Languedoc	Côtes du Roussillon-Villages including Collioure
2004	★★★★ A	★★★★ A	★★★★ A
2003	★★★★ A	★★★★ A	★★★★ A
2003	★★★/★★★★ A	★★★/★★★★ A	★★★★ A
2002	★★★ B	★★★ A	★★★/★★★★ A
2001	★★★★/★★★★★ B	★★★★/★★★★★ A	★★★★/★★★★★ A
2000	★★★★/★★★★★ B	★★★★/★★★★★ B	★★★★ B
1999	★★★/★★★★ B	★★★/★★★★ B	★★★★ B
1998	★★★★/★★★★★ B	★★★★/★★★★★ B	★★★★★ B
1997	★★/★★★ D	★★/★★★C	★★★ C
1996	★★★ C	★★★ C	★★★ C
1995	★★★★ C	★★★★ C	★★★★ C
1994	★★★ D	★★★ D	★★★/★★★★ C
1993	★★★/★★★★ D	★★★/★★★★ C	★★★/★★★★ C
1991	★★/★★★ D	★★/★★★ D	★★/★★★ D
1990	★★★★★ D	★★★★ D	★★★★ C

A-Z of producers

Languedoc

JEAN-MICHEL ALQUIER   Faugères

Alquier family   4 Route de Pézenes-les-Mines, 34600 Faugères
UK stockists: Rae

Long-established quality producer in this appellation. These are impressive wines, almost rustic in the case of the reds – but in the best sense. There are some 12ha under vine with the vast majority of this planted to red varieties. Syrah accounts for 40% of the *vignoble* and does very well in the meagre, well-drained, soils. The average vine age of the *cépages ameliorateurs* is increasing and this along with a healthy planting of very old Carignan provides tremendous raw material. The regular red Faugères Les Premières, a blend of Syrah, Grenache and Carignan, is good if austere when very young, while there is an extra dimension in the 2 top reds. La Réserve La Maison Jaune is a mix of Syrah and Mourvèdre whereas Les Bastides is aged in some new oak and has a smattering of Grenache adding a touch of red-berry character. These 2 wines will age well over 6 or 7 years. The basic white *vin de pays* Roussanne/Marsanne is attractively fruity while the Domaine Jean-Michel Alquier bottling is a gloriously nutty and complex southern-style white. Both of these should be drunk young. (DM)

● **Faugères** Les Premières★★ £B   La Réserve La Maison Jaune★★★ £C
● **Faugères** Les Bastides★★★ £C
○ **Vin de Pays de l'Hérault** Roussanne/Marsanne★ £B   Jean-Michel Alquier★★★ £C

DOM. L'AIGUELIÈRE   Coteaux du Languedoc Montpeyroux

Aimé Commeyras   2 Place du Square, 34150 Montpeyroux
UK stockists: GVF, N&P

One of the finest properties in the Languedoc, producing top class reds of impressive depth and raw power. Even in the tricky 2002 vintage the wines are of very sound quality. There are 25ha planted, nearly 90% being Syrah. A small parcel of Viognier and Sauvignon Blanc results in a fresh, fruit driven white Sarments, produced for the first time in 1999. Fermented and vinified in tank, the wine is best enjoyed within a couple of years of the vintage. Tradition, which blends around 40% Grenache with Syrah, is aged in *cuve* and offers ripe, vibrant upfront dark berry fruit supported by soft youthfully accesible tannins. The 2 100% Syrah *cuvées* are of an entirely different order, dense and powerful, with an underlying elegance and refinement often missing in the region. Produced from yields of barely 20hl/ha the opulent Côte Dorée comes from gravel soils, the more structured and backward Côte Rousse from limestone. Both will benefit from 5 years' ageing. (DM)

● **Coteeaux du Languedoc Montpeyroux** Côte Rousse★★★★★ £E
● **Coteeaux du Languedoc Montpeyroux** Côte Dorée★★★★ £E
● **Coteeaux du Languedoc Montpeyroux** Tradition★★ £B
○ **Vin de Pays d'Oc** Sarments★★ £B

DOM. DES AIRES HAUTES   Minervois

Gilles Chabbert   34210 Siran
UK stockists: Gau, Maj

This property stands out in an appellation that often disappoints more than it should. Gilles Chabbert produces just over 12,000 cases a year from his 30ha of organically farmed vines, the vast majority of which are planted to red varieties. As well as the regular forward, fruit-driven Minervois Tradition there is a spicy Vin de Pays d'Oc Malbec and a little Chardonnay. The top 2 reds are from the sub-appellation of La Livinière and both are blended from Syrah, Grenache and Carignan. Vinification is traditional with an extended *cuvaison* and for the Carignan carbonic maceration is employed to emphasise the fruit. The La Livinière is aged partly in used oak and partly in *cuve*; the Clos de l'Escandil sees around one-third new wood. These are impressive and finely structured examples. The l'Escandil in particular will be all the better for 3 or 4 years' cellaring. (DM)

● **Minervois La Livinière**★★ £B Clos de l'Escandil★★★ £C
● **Minervois** Tradition★ £B

DOM. D'ANTUGNAC   Limoux

Jean-Luc Terrier & Christian Collovray   4 Rue du Château, 11190 Antugnac
UK stockists: BBR
Jean-Luc Terrier and Christian Collovray also own the Mâconnais property DOMAINE DES DEUX ROCHES and Chardonnay is their most successful variety at Limoux. They have a substantial holding of 60ha, half of which is planted to Chardonnay, Mauzac, Sauvignon and Chenin among white varieties and half to Pinot Noir, Merlot, Cabernet Franc, Syrah, Cabernet Sauvignon and a smattering of lesser-known red grapes. The vineyard is planted at altitude and warm summer days and cool nights contribute to the fresh style. There is a decent vibrant, fruit-driven Merlot, a light and relatively simple Pinot Noir and a red blend Planal but the whites, particularly the Limoux bottlings, are the wines to go for. Rich and very Burgundian in style, they are traditionally vinified, offering opulent citrus and nutmeg character with subtle creamy vanilla oak in the background. The Gravas bottling is a step up from the standard wine but both will develop well in the short term. (DM)

○ **Limoux**★★ £B Gravas★★★ £B ○ **Chardonnay** Vin de Pays d'Oc★ £B
○ **Vin de Pays de la Hautee Vallée de l'Aude** Les Grands Penchants★ £B
● **Pinot Noir** Vin de Pays de la Haute Vallée de l'Aude★ £C
● **Merlot** Vin de Pays d'Oc★ £B

DOM. LES AURELLES   Coteaux du Languedoc

Karl Mauguin et Basil Saint-Germain   34720 Caux
UK stockists:Bal, Han
Although this property was only established in 1994 some of the vines are up to 70 years old. The vines are planted in ancient sand and gravel terraces providing for a meagre yield of around 25 hl/ha. The owners were both classically trained in Bordeaux and this seems to come through in wines which are tight, well-structured and elegant. Varieties are vinified separately and the vatting for the reds lasts between 3 and 5 weeks. They get a light egg-white fining but filtration is avoided. The Deella, a blend of Carignan, Grenache, Mourvèdre and Syrah is soft, forward and fruit-driven. Solen and Aurel are much more seriously structured and will develop well over 5 or more years. Solen is 65% Carignan with the balance Grenache, rich and full with complex old-vine character. Aurel is a blend of Grenache, Mourvèdre and Syrah. Very fine, elegant and pure, it is tight and closed in its youth and will open up and add real complexity and depth with age. The Aurel Blanc, which is 100% Roussanne, is barrel-fermented but not in new wood and is loaded with subtle, complex spicy, nutty southern fruit. Drink it young or with a little age. (DM)

● **Coteaux du Languedoc** Déella★★ £B Solen★★★ £C Aurel★★★★ £D
○ **Coteaux du Languedoc** Aurel★★★★ £D

BARON' ARQUES   Limoux

Baron Philippe de Rothschild SA/Vignerons du Sieur d'Arques   11250 Gardie
UK stockists:Par, FWC,PWa, B&B

393

Newly established joint venture producing just 1 red wine from vineyards planted in the Limoux region. Early releases have been labelled Vin de Pays until Limoux gained its own red wine appellation in 2003. Currently produced from just under 35ha of vineyard the partnership has identified 150ha which should be suitable for producing top-quality red wine. Baron'Arques is a blend of 60–70% Bordeaux varieties Merlot, Cabernets Sauvignon and Franc and 30–40% Grenache, Syrah and Malbec. The wine currently shows much more in common with Bordeaux than with other Languedoc reds. The first vintage was 1998, which was relatively light but there was a marked increase in quality with both the 1999 and 2000 on which the rating is based. It is to be hoped that the wine will improve further to correspond with its price tag. Cellaring for 5 or more years will add weight and complexity. (DM)

● **Baron'arques** Vin de Pays de la Haute Vallée de l'Aude★★★ £E

DOM. LEON BARRAL Faugères

Didier Barral Rue de la Sellele, 34210 Felines-Minervois
UK stockists: WTr, A&B, P&S

Impressive, small Faugères domaine producing wines with all the raw, spicy, meaty character of the appellation. The regular bottling is a blend of mainly Carignan along with Grenache and Cinsault. The Cuvée Jadis is a step up in quality and is a supple, structured and enticingly perfumed blend of Carignan (50%), Syrah (40%) and a smattering of Grenache. Barral's top red Valinière is outside appellation regulations and is simply labelled, like the wines of TERRE INCONNUE, *vin de table.* A heady, rich, ripe and powerful blend of 80% of Mourvèdre plus Syrah, it is by no means cheap. The wines are structured and ageworthy. (DM)

● **Faugères**★★ £C Cuvée Jadis★★★ £D ● **Valinière** Vin de Table★★★★ £F

DOM. BORIE DE MAUREL Minervois

Michel Escande Rue de la Sellele, 34210 Felines-Minervois
UK stockists: Odd, CdP

Sizeable Minervois property producing close to 12,000 cases a year across the appellation. There are 30ha under vine with just 2 planted to whites Marsanne and Muscat à Petits Grains. The white Aude is broad and fat with rich nutty fruit. Esprit d'Automne is a straightforward fruit-driven blend of Grenache, Syrah and Carignan, whereas Belle de Nuit is solely Grenache which should also be enjoyed young for its vibrant fruit but has added weight and concentration. More seriously structured is the La Livinière bottling, La Féline. Spicy dark berry fruit and a dense, rich texture are provided from 70% Syrah. The Cuvée Léopold is 100% Cabernet Sauvignon. Ripe and elegant it avoids some of the green notes found in other Languedoc examples. Of the top 2 Minervois reds, Maxim is 100% Mourvèdre, Sylla 100% Syrah. Both are finely structured and will develop well with 4 or 5 years in bottle. Exclusive to the UK is a varietal Carignan, La Rêve de Carignan, dark, dense and with an attractive spicy edge to the fruit. (DM)

● **Minervois** Cuvée Maxim★★★ £C Cuvée Sylla★★★★ £D
● **Minervois** Esprit d'Automne★ £B Belle de Nuit★★ £C
● **Minervois** La Rêve de Carignan★★ £C
● **Minervois La Livinière** La Féline★★★ £B
● **Vin de Pays d'Oc** Cuvée Léopold★★★ £C
O **Minervois** Aude★★ £B

DOM. BORIE LA VITARÈLE Saint-Chinian

Jean-François Izarn & Cathy Izarn Plane 34490 Saint-Nazaire de Ladarez
UK stockists: GVF, Por

The Izarns have some 30ha under vine now, of which a mere 2ha are planted with white varieties. Most are in Saint-Chinian but some extend into the Coteaux du Languedoc. Powerful, dense and muscular reds are the order of the day, achieved through controlling yields, which rarely exceed 30 hl/ha. Coteaux du Languedoc Les Terres Blanches is supple, approachable and full of spicy dark fruit, whereas the *vin de pays* bottlings, including Cabernet Sauvignon and Merlot, are softer and show more overt fruit character. La Combe is the more serious and structured of the 2. Of the 2 Saint-Chinians Les Schistes, mainly Grenache with Syrah and a touch of Carignan, has depth and a firm structure. Give it 2 or 3 years. The top wine Les Crès, like all the wines here, is named after the soil in which the vines are grown; in this case it is formed of the *galet*-type stones found at Châteauneuf-du-Pape. The wine is a blend of Syrah, Grenache and Mourvèdre and comes from vines yielding less than 20 hl/ha. No new wood is used and it is all the better for it, emphasising its dark, brooding, spicy fruit character. There is real depth and concentration with the structure to ensure ageing for up to a decade or more. (DM)

● **Saint-Chinian** Les Schistes★★★ £C Les Crès★★★★ £C
● **Coteaux du Languedoc** Les Terres Blanches★★ £B
● **Vin de Pays Coteaux de Murviel** Bouïsset★ £B La Combe★★ £B

DOM. CANET-VALETTE Saint-Chinian
Marc Valette Route de Causses-et-Veyran, 34460 Cessenon
UK stockists: C&C, SVS

There are 18ha under vine here, all of it planted to red varieties. Along with BORIE LA VITARÈLE this is a benchmark for Saint-Chinian and the top red here, Le Vin Maghani, is arguably the finest in the AC. Minimal handling in the cellar with neither fining nor filtration helps to achieve this. No new oak is used and as a result the character of the impressively intense fruit really shines through in the wines. Une et Mille Nuits is a blend of Grenache, Mourvèdre, Syrah, Carignan and Cinsault. Aged in a mix of *inox* and older oak it is vibrant and approachable, but with sufficient structure to develop well over 4 or 5 years. Le Vin Maghani is more serious; dense, rich and very complex, the wine is full of dark fruits, spice and black pepper. Cellaring for 5 years is a must to enjoy this at its best. (DM)

● **Saint-Chinian** Une et Mille Nuits★★ £B Le Vin Maghani★★★★ £D

CH. CAPITOUL Coteaux du Languedoc www.chateau-capitoul.com
Charles Hock Route de Gruissan, 11000 Narbonne
UK stockists: BFs

The bulk of the production at this organically farmed 65-ha property is red and white Coteaux du Languedoc La Clape, with some rosé produced as well under the same appellation. The Lavandines white blends Marsanne and Roussanne while the more complex barrel-aged Rocailles adds Viognier, to mostly Roussanne. The Les Lavandines red is almost equal proportions of Grenache, Syrah and Carignan whereas the striking and very good-value Les Rocailles is 40% Grenache and 40% Mourvèdre with 20% Carignan adding some peppery spice. Richly concentrated, the wine is given a very lengthy period on skins for up to 45 days and is aged in *cuve* using micro-oxygenation rather than racking during *élevage*. A small-volume red, Maelma, is produced from mainly Mourvèdre and Carignan and there are 2 luscious late-harvest Viogniers, Les Oubliées and Les Tardives. The yield for Les Oubliées is barely more than 5 hl/ha. Not surprisingly fewer than 60 cases are produced. (DM)

● **Coteaux du Languedoc Pic Saint-Loup** Les Lavandines★ £B Les Rocailles★★★ £C
O **Coteaux du Languedoc** Les Rocailles★★ £B

395

CH. DE CAZENEUVE   Coteaux du Languedoc Pic Saint-Loup

André Leenhardt   34270 Lauret
UK stockists: CBg,Bal,Lay,BBR,SVS

First class Languedoc property with some 20ha under vine. Since acquiring
Cazeneuve in the late 1980s André Leenhardt has been actively planting the
top red Rhône varieties which are now dominated by Syrah. Output is still low
for the area at just over 4,000 cases a year. His reds come in a number of guises.
Syrah features strongly in the blend of Les Calcaires and the oak-aged Le Roc
des Mates. Le Sang du Calcaire, now the top red, is an individual selection of
the best the harvest has to offer. It too is aged in oak. The white is a stylish,
nutty barrel-fermented blend of Roussanne, Grenache Blanc and Viognier. Top
reds are ageworthy. (DM)

● **Coteaux du Languedoc Pic Saint-Loup** Roc des Mates★★★ £C
● **Coteaux du Languedoc Pic Saint-Loup** Sang du Calvaire★★★ £D
● **Coteaux du Languedoc Pic Saint-Loup** Les Calcaires★★ £B
● **Coteaux du Languedoc Pic Saint-Loup** Les Terres Rouges★ £B
O **Coteaux du Languedoc Pic Saint-Loup**★★ £B

CH. CAZAL VIEL   Saint-Chinian

Miquel Family   34460 Cessenon-sur-Orb
UK stockists: HWC,Wai

Large Saint-Chinian domaine producing around 75,000 cases of sturdily
traditional Saint-Chinian under the Château Cazal Viel label and a range of
mainly varietal Vin de Pays d'Oc under the Laurent Miquel label. Of the latter
look out for simple, attractively fruity and well-priced Nord Sud Syrah and
Viognier, as well as a Chardonnay/Viognier. Of a completely different order
though is a fine, opulently rich, fleshy and spicy Saint-Chinian, Bardou,
sourced from a single block of the finest Syrah on the Cazal Viel estate. Aged in
new and 1-year-old oak, all seamlessly integrated, the wine offers both density
and finesse. The Château Cazal Viel Saint-Chinians are more traditional in
style, although Syrah is an important component at 65% of the estate
vineyards. Both the l'Antenne and pricey Larmes des Fées are dense, structured
and capable of developing well in bottle with 5 or more years of age. The 2000
Larmes des Fées was right on the cusp of ★★★★. (DM)

Château Cazal Viel
● **Saint-Chinian** l'Antenne★★ £C Larmes des Fées★★★ £E
● **Saint-Chinian** Vielles Vignes★★ £B Cuvée des Fées★★ £B
Laurent Miquel
● **Saint-Chinian** Bardou★★★ £E

CH. COUPE-ROSES   Minervois

de Calvez family   34210 La Caunette
UK stockists:RsW

A quite extensive range is made at this fine Minervois producer, beginning with
a simple fruit-driven white *vin de pays* from Grenache Blanc, Marsanne and
Muscat. Better is the *vin de pays* Viognier, which is floral and lightly peachy,
gaining weight from ageing on lees in tank. The white Minervois, wholly
produced from Roussanne has a floral, nutty complexity and impressive
intensity with 20% aged in small oak. The rosé is soft and fruit-driven for early
drinking. La Bastide is the softest and most approachable of the Minervois reds,
a 50/50 blend of Grenache and Carignan, the latter vinified by *macération-
carbonique*. Les Plots offers considerably more depth and concentration. This is
60% Syrah blended with Grenache and Carignan aged in tank and regularly on
the cusp of ★★★. The top 2 reds are among the best examples in the
appellation. Richly textured and impressively concentrated Orience is 90%
Syrah with a little Grenache; 50% is aged in new oak and 50% in 1-year-old

barrels and the oak in no way intrudes on the dark, smoky fruit. The smoky, herb/spice-edged Granaxa is largely old-vine Grenache aged in small oak with around 10% Syrah blended in before bottling. The fascinating Rancio is a blend of Viognier, Grenache Blanc and Roussanne aged in barrel for between 10 and 14 years. Great intensity and rich, nutty, citrus intensity are apparent. The top 2 reds will benefit from 5 years' ageing. (DM)

● **Minervois** Cuvée Orience★★★ £B Granaxa★★★ £C
● **Minervois** La Bastide★★ £B Les Plots★★ £C
● **Rancio** Vin de Table★★★ £B ◯ **Vin de Pays d'Oc** Viognier★★ £B
◯ **Minervois**★★ £B ◉ **Minervois**★ £B

CH. DES CRES RICARDS   Coteaux du Languedoc

Gérrard Foltran 34800 Ceyras
UK stockists:ldg
Syrah is the important variety at this small domaine in the Terrasses de Larzac. The summers are particularly hot and arid and the winters cold here and the wines are marked by a ripe, smoky, warm-climate character but nevertheless possess a fine, elegant backbone, no doubt aided by cooler ripening conditions and the excellent drainage afforded by the Villafranchien stony soils. The Stécia is the more obviously fruit-driven wine, a blend of around 60% Syrah with Grenache and Carignan aged in tank. Les Hauts de Milesi is richer and fuller with more meaty concentration and just a hint of black pepper underpinning the fruit. Expect the wines to evolve well for 3 or 4 years or so. (DM)

● **Coteaux du Languedoc** Cuvée Stecia★★ £B Les Hauts de Milesi★★★ £C

CH. DES L'ENGARRAN   Coteaux du Languedoc

Diane Losfelt-Grill & Constance Rérolle-Grill 34270 Fontanes
This 18th-century château has been in the Grill family since 1923. Most of the output from their 55ha under vine is red (70%); rosé accounts for 20% and white just 10%. A decent range of bag-in-box *vins de pays* is made. The bottled Vin de Pays d'Oc red and white are soft, straightforward and fruit-driven, if a touch simple. The key wines here are the Coteaux du Languedoc reds and the Domaine de l'Engarran Adelys white, arguably the best wine in the range and nudging ★★★ in quality. It is a ripe, tropical, piercing varietal Sauvignon Blanc, barrel-fermented for 9 months in oak that has been seasoned unusually by steam rather than the normal flame-charring. The Languedoc Cuvée Sainte-Cécile is soft and berry-laden, the Tradition sturdier and denser. The top red is the Cuvée Quetton Saint-Georges, a blend of Syrah (70%), Grenache and old-vine Carignan aged in small French oak and larger vats for up to 16 months. Like the white Adelys, it is on the cusp of ★★★. (DM)

● **Coteaux du Languedoc** Cuvée Querton Saint-Georges★★★ £C
● **Coteaux du Languedoc** Cuvée Sainte-Cécile★★ £B Tradition★★ £B
◯ **Vin de Pays d'Oc** Adelys★★ £B

CH. DES ESTANILLES   Faugères

Michel Louison Lenthéric, 34480 Caberolles
UK stockists: THt,Ter,C&R
Michel Louison produces upwards of 15,000 cases of Faugères and a white Coteaux du Languedoc each year, a sizeable production for a high-quality Midi property. Syrah now dominates the plantings and, as with the wines of Jean-Michel ALQUIER, the variety is notably successful here. Grenache and Mourvèdre are also important among the reds and the white is a blend of Marsanne, Roussanne and Viognier. The Préstige and Syrah *cuvées*, the latter seeing around a year in oak, will both stand some age, while the other wines are best approached young. (DM)

397

● **Faugères** Tradition★ £B Préstige★★★ £B Cuvée Syrah★★★ £C
○ **Coteaux du Languedoc★★** £B
◉ **Faugères★** £B

CH. L'EUZIÈRE   Coteaux du Languedoc Pic Saint-Loup

Michel & Marcel Causse   34270 Fontanes
UK stockists: Lib,Gar,But

The Causse siblings are, in fact, the fourth generation of vinegrowers at this impressive Languedoc property but it is only much more recently that they have established themselves as quality wine producers. They have some 22ha under vine and produce around 5,000 cases a year. A good nutty, lightly floral white, Grains de Lune, is an unusual blend of Roussanne, Vermentino, Rolle and Grenache Blanc produced from young vines – the average age is still only 8 years. After *macération pelliculaire* it is cool-fermented with limited lees-ageing. Of the 3 reds, Cuvée Tourmaline is a blend of Syrah and Grenache, whereas the more serious and structured Cuvées l'Almandin and Les Escarboucles are neither fined nor filtered and have a small dollop of Mourvèdre. They are both marvellously expressive with a fine balance of herb, spice and complex berry fruits and each will benefit from 3 or 4 years' ageing. (DM)

● **Coteaux du Languedoc Pic Saint-Loup** Cuvée Les Escarboucles★★★ £C
● **Coteaux du Languedoc Pic Saint-Loup** Cuvée l'Almandin★★★ £B
● **Coteaux du Languedoc** La Tourmaline★★ £B
○ **Coteaux du Languedoc** Grains de Lune★★ £B

CH. GRÈS SAINT-PAUL   www.gres-saint-paul.com

Jean-Philippe Servière   Route de Restinclières, 34400 Lunel
UK stockists: FCA,Gar,ldg

Small to medium-sized property with 24ha of vineyards farmed along organic lines. Total production is now around 10,000 cases a year. An extensive range of wines is produced including some straightforward well-priced, fruit-driven *vin de pays* Chardonnay, Sauvignon Blanc and Merlot. It is the red Coteaux du Languedoc wines that are most important though from a quality point of view. Of the 4 *cuvées* La Grange Philippe is 90% Syrah and 10% Grenache and is vinified with some *macération carbonique* for the Syrah. It is soft, brambly and forward. Romanis, like all the red Languedocs, is dominated by Syrah with Grenache and Mourvèdre. Aged for 12 months in *cuve*, it is denser, more structured. The excellent-value Antonin is between 80 and 90% Syrah, the balance Grenache and Mourvèdre, produced from yields of 25–30 hl/ha. It is dark, concentrated and spicy with subtle hints of black pepper and just a touch of oak spice from the 16 months spent in one-third new barrels. The top wine is the impressive Syrhus, a varietal Syrah produced from a yield of less than 20 hl/ha. It needs 2 or 3 years' cellaring to integrate the 100% new oak. Of the sweet white Muscats the Bohémienne has moderate depth, the Sévillane greater weight and intensity. These are well made but lack the depth of a good Muscat de Rivesaltes. (DM)

● **Coteaux du Languedoc** Syrhus★★★★ £D Antonin★★★ £C
● **Coteaux du Languedoc** Romanis★★ £B La Grange Phlippe★★ £B
○ **Muscat de Lunel** Sévillane★★ £B ○ **Muscat Moelleux** Bohémienne★ £B

CH. DE JONQUIÈRES   Coteaux du Languedoc

Isabelle & François de Cabissole   34725 Jonquières
UK stockists:Vne,Vnf

This 23-ha property located in the foothills of the Plateau de Gassac now has 19ha planted to vines. The small range includes a good straightforward white, which is barrel-fermented and aged with *bâtonnage* and has the malolactic blocked to preserve freshness. It is a blend of Grenache Blanc, Chenin Blanc,

Roussanne and Viognier. its red partner is a juicy, soft, easygoing Vin de Pays de l'Hérault red Domaine de Jonquières dominated by Cinsault and Carignan. More serious are the red Coteaux du Languedoc which blends Mourvèdre with lesser amounts of Syrah, Carignan and Grenache and the Syrah-dominated Renaissance. These top 2 red labels are dark, powerful and supple wines with a sufficiently firm structure and depth to ensure limited bottle-development with age, while at the same time retaining their core vibrant fruit quality. (DM)

● **Vin de Pays de l'Hérault** Domaine de Jonquières★★ £B
● **Coteaux du Languedoc★★★** £C ○ **Coteaux du Languedoc★** £B

CH. LA BARONNE Corbières

Andre Lignères   11700 Fontcouverte
UK stockists:Lib, AoW

A source of good well-priced examples of the Corbières appellation, this 80-ha domaine is in the Montagne d'Alaric sub-zone, arguably the best in this sizeable AC. The fine, ripe and supple standard Corbières is produced from a blend of 50% Carignan, 20% each of Grenache and Mourvèdre and 10% Syrah. Low yields of 25–35 hl/ha and vineyards planted at an altitude of 150 metres help to contribute to quality and carbonic maceration emphasises the fruit of the Carignan without compromising the wine's depth and intensity. The unfiltered bottling is a step up and will keep for a year or 2. (DM)

● **Corbières** Montagne d'Alaric★★ £B Montagne d'Alaric Unfiltered★★ £B

CH. LA DOURNIE Saint-Chinian

Annick & Henri Étienne   34360 Saint-Chinian
UK stockists:Idg

Fine small Saint-Chinian property where daughter Valérie is now in charge of the winemaking and quality has been consistently good across the last 5 years or so. She is producing wines which reflect the *terroir* and character of the appellation but also with a great exuberance of fruit. There is a soft, vibrant and easygoing rosé but it is the 2 reds which stand out. The regular bottling, a blend of Syrah, Grenache and Carignan, is ripe, forward and brambly with a fine mineral undercurrent to its fruit. The more seriously structured and denser Elise is just Syrah and Grenache. Complex and offering great fruit purity this should continue to develop well for 4 or 5 years. (DM)

● **Saint-Chinian★★** £B Cuveé Elise★★★ £C ○ **Saint-Chinian★** £B

CH. LA LIQUIÈRE Coteaux du Languedoc

Vidal-Dumoulin family   34480 Cabrerolles
UK stockists:SVS

This sizeable domaine with 55ha of red varieties and 7ha of whites under vine produces good quality in both the Coteaux du Languedoc and Faugères. The vineyard holding is largely at altitude and planted in the schistous soils prevalent in the best *terroirs* of Faugères. The white Coteaux du Languedoc Schistes is a barrel-fermented blend of Grenache Blanc, Roussanne and Viognier offering hints of oak and lightly nutty tropical fruit. Aged on fine lees, which add weight and a richer texture, it will nevertheless drink well young. Of the 2 red bottlings from Faugères, the Vieilles Vignes comes from 40–100-year-old plots. It is a blend of Carignan, Grenache and small proportions of Syrah and Mourvèdre. Its dark, peppery character partly comes from carbonic maceration, by which over half the fruit is vinified. The Cistus is quite a step up in quality and as elsewhere in the appellation Syrah is very important (45% of the blend), with the balance made up of Grenache, Mourvèdre and Syrah. This richly textured, dark, spicy red is aged in oak for 12 months and needs 4 or 5 years to show at its best. (DM)

399

● **Faugères** Vieilles Vignes★★ £B Cistus★★★ £C
○ **Coteaux du Languedoc** Schistes★★★ £B

CH. DE LASCAUX   Coteaux du Languedoc

Jean-Benoit Cavalier   34270 Valflaunès
UK stockists: BBR,Gar,L&S

Jean-Benoit Cavalier established his Languedoc domaine located between
Montpellier and Nîmes as long ago as 1984. The vineyards are planted at an
altitude of 150 metres on a mix of gravel and limestone, ensuring some
excellent growing conditions for the 26ha of red varieties and 9ha of whites.
Syrah dominates the red plantings with a balanace of 30% Grenache. Whites
consist of Roussanne, Marsanne, Viognier and Rolle and tend to be cropped at
a lower yield of 25–30 hl/ha. A good regular white Coteaux du Languedoc
blended from Roussanne, Marsanne and Rolle is joined by a stylish, subtly
oaked, nutty white Pierres d'Argent which also includes Viognier. Both should
be enjoyed young. The Coteaux du Languedoc red is a soft approachable blend
of Syrah and Grenache, while the top 2 reds are largely Syrah and aged in oak.
All of the wines offer a marked *garrigue* character that underpins their dark
berry fruit. Both richly sumptuous Les Secrets and the leaner Nobles Pierres
will benefit from 3 or 4 years' age. (DM)

● **Coteaux du Languedoc**★★ £B Nobles Pierres★★ £C Les Secrets★★★★ £D
○ **Coteaux du Languedoc**★ £B Pierres d'Argent★★ £C
◉ **Coteaux du Languedoc**★ £B

CH. LA VOULTE-GASPARETS   Corbières

Patrick Reverdy   11200 Boutenac
UK stockists:C&C

One of the longer-established quality producers in Corbières, whose wine is
distributed and marketed by VAL D'ORBIEU. There are 42ha under vine and
decent regular red and white are produced along with 2 special *cuvées,* Réservée
and Romain Pauc. The Réservée is good, stylish and shows some class and
refinement but the Romain Pauc is clearly the benchmark wine here. Quality is
helped by some very old vines, and the wine displays a rich, savoury
concentration with marked vanilla oak and real complexity: a powerful spicy
red that will age well in the medium term. (DM)

● **Corbières** Cuvée Réservée★★ £B Cuvée Romain Pauc★★★ £C

CH. LE THOU   Coteaux du Languedoc

Comtesse de Ferrier de Montal 34410 Sauviau
UK stockists: A&B

This 24-ha estate on the outskirts of Béziers is planted largely to Syrah.
Significant improvements have been seen in the wines since the 2000 vintage,
particularly the top *cuvée* Georges et Clem. Blended from Syrah(at least 70%)
with the balance Grenache, Mourvèdre and a little spicy Carignan, the wine is
rich, fleshy and opulent. Ageing takes place in both *barrique* and tank. Even
the 2002 vintage which was far from ideal looks highly promising thanks to
very rigorous selection in both vineyard and winery. (DM)

● **Coteaux du Languedoc**★★ £B Georges et Clem★★★ £C

CH. MANSENOBLE   Corbières   mansenoble@wanadoo.fr

Jansegers et De Witte 11700 Moux
UK stockists:RMe

Fine, modern Corbières property with 20ha planted to Carignan, Grenache,
Syrah and a small amount of Mourvèdre. Production runs at just under 10,000
cases a year. Three red Corbières are produced. In addition to those rated below

a small amount of a special limited *cuvée* Marie-Annick (named after one of the owners, Marie-Annick de Witte) is produced. The Montagne d'Alaric bottling is ripe, spicy and forward. The Réserve is rich and opulent, with creamy new oak underpinning the wine's dark and spicy berry fruit. Both wines are approachable on release although the Réserve has a sufficiently firm structure to enable short-term ageing. (DM)

● **Corbières** Montagne d'Alaric★★ £B Réserve★★★£C

CH. MASSAMIER LA MIGNARDE   Minervois

Jacques Venes   11700 Pépieux
UK stockists:ldg,BBR

This relatively sizeable Minervois property with 60ha under vine produces wines from both the Minervois and Minervois La Livinière ACs as well as under various *vin de pays* labels. The basic wines are labelled Cuvée des Oliviers. The red includes Cabernet Sauvignon along with southern varieties and there is also a rosé and a Sauvignon-dominated white. The Tradition reds are all Minervois AC, including a Cuvée Aubin. There are 2 wines under the Expression label, a Cinsault and a particularly striking varietal Carignan from very old vines. Vinified traditionally with no carbonic maceration, it is a wine of real density and dark-fruited spicy concentration. The top wines are the Minervois La Livinière, a dense and impressively structured Domus Maximus (80/20 Syrah and Grenache) and Tenement des Garouilas, a limited-production *cuvée* blended from Syrah, Grenache and Carignan. Both are aged in new oak and the Garouilas bottling is very modern with malolactic in barrel. These top wines will develop well with 4 or 5 years' age. (DM)

● **Minervois La Livinière** Domus Maximus★★★ £C
● **Vin de Pays des Coteaux de Peyriac** Expression de Carignan★★ £B
● **Vin de Pays des Coteaux de Peyriac** Cuvée des Oliviers★ £B

CH. DE MONTPEZAT   Coteaux du Languedoc

Christophe Blanc   34120 Pezenas
UK stockists:Vnf

Vineyards have been planted at this estate to the west of Montpellier for over 100 years. The stone and clay/limestone soils provide the successful growing conditions for both AC Coteaux du Languedoc as well as *vin de pays* reds and some Sauvignon Blanc. Future plans include a vineyard Les Epines from which a traditional Carignan/Grenache red blend and a white mix of Grenache Blanc and Marsanne will be produced. The Domaine de Montpezat-labelled *vin de pays* bottles are as striking as their Coteaux du Languedoc stablemates. Les Enclos is a soft, vibrant lightly plummy blend of mainly Merlot with some Cabernet Sauvignon, which gets 12 months in cask. The Cuvée Prestige is bigger, and considerably more concentrated. Blending Cabernet Sauvignon (60%) with Syrah, the wine posseses both depth and surprising finesse. The Palombières is an approachable blend of Grenache, Syrah and Mourvèdre. Pharaonne is big, firm and impressively structured. A mix of Mourvèdre and Grenache, it needs 4 or 5 years to bring out all its rich brambly fruit potential. The top wines get a light fining but are not filtered. (DM)

● **Coteaux du Languedoc** Les Palombières★★ £B La Pharaonne★★★ £C
● **Vin de Pays d'Oc** Domaine de Montpezat Les Enclos★★ £B
● **Vin de Pays d'Oc** Domaine de Montpezat Cuvée Prestige★★★ £C

CH. DE LA NÉGLY   Coteaux du Languedoc La Clape

Jean Paux-Rosset   11560 Fleury d'Aude
UK stockists: THt

Medium-sized but consistently excellent Languedoc domaine producing sound

401

quality at all price levels. Since taking over the family property in 1992 Jean Paux-Rosset has single-mindedly dedicated himself to producing wines of interest and excitement. He is aided by consultant Claude Gros and produces the *super-cuvée* Clos du Truffière from a small plot of exceptional Syrah near Pezenas, which is part owned by Bordeaux wine merchant Jeffrey Davies. The white Brise Marine blends Bourboulenc with Marsanne and Roussanne and has a fresh cutting edge to its nutty fruit. Les Embruns is ripe and full flavoured with hints of strawberry and spice, Palazy, a *vin de pays*, is the lighter of the 2 rosés. Two wines are released under the Domaine de Boède label. Le Pavillon is a soft fruit-driven blend of Carignan and Grenache, whereas Le Grès is a firmer richer blend of Syrah and Grenache. It gets a 45-day vatting and is aged in *cuve* for 14 months. La Côte is mainly Carignan. It has a fine, spicy, dark-berried character and drinks well young. La Falaise is sourced from south-east limestone slopes on the Massif de la Clape. A blend of Syrah, Grenache and Mourvèdre, it is aged in a mix of new and 1-year-old oak and needs a year or 2 to find its equilibrium. All of these wines are excellent value. Less so, perhaps understandably given their small production and meagre yields, are the top 3 reds. L'Ancely is a rich, powerful and highly characterful blend of 95% Mourvèdre with Grenache. You'll struggle to find a Bandol sold at this price but similarly it is rare to find wines of this quality in that appellation. Finally there are 2 remarkably pure, powerful and very intense 100% Syrahs. Porte au Ciel is marked by its density and sheer power. The Clos du Truffière is finer, with greater elegance and sheer harmony. It vies for the title of finest red in the Languedoc. Both require cellaring for upwards of 6 or 7 years and will age gracefully. All the reds here are bottled unfined and unfiltered. (DM)

- ● **Coteaux du Languedoc** Porte au Ciel★★★★★ £G Clos du Truffière★★★★★ £G
- ● **Coteaux du Languedoc** La Falaise★★★ £C L'Ancely★★★★ £F
- ● **Coteaux du Languedoc** La Côte★★ £B Domaine de Boède Le Grès★★★ £C
- ◗ **Vin de Pays des Côtes de Perpignan** Domaine de Boède Le Pavillon★ £B
- ◎ **Coteaux du Languedoc** Les Embruns★★ £B
- O **Coteaux du Languedoc** La Brise Marine★ £B

CH. SAINT-JACQUES D'ALBAS www.chateaustjacques.com
Graham Nutter   11800 Laure Minervois
UK stockists:Han,Goe

The harvest at this small Minervois domaine used to be sold to the co-op. However, since the 2001 vintage new owner Graham Nutter has been releasing 2 impressive examples of the appellation. Winemaking expertise is provided by Australian Chester Osborne and the wines clearly have real potential. The Domaine wine is a blend of Syrah with older vines Grenache and Carignan. The grapes are all destemmed and carbonic maceration is not employed but the must gets a short cold soak prior to fermentation to ensure some attractive bright dark fruit character. The Château label has a higher proportion of Syrah, part of which is vinified without a pre-fermentation maceration. Sturdier, deeper and more firmly structured the wine is aged for around a year in a mix of new, 1- and 2-year-old barrels of Russian and American as well as French origin. The Château label will keep well for 4 or 5 years; the Domaine label should be drunk young. (DM)

- ● **Minervois** Château Saint-Jacques d'Albas★★★ £C
- ● **Minervois** Domaine Saint-Jacques d'Albas★★ £B

CHEVALIER VINS Minervois www.chevaliervins.fr
Brigitte Chevalier   Route de Pèzènes, La Papeterie 34600 Bédarieux
For 10 years Brigitte Chevalier was the export manager for Jean-Luc Thunevin of Ch. VALANDRAUD in Saint-Emilion, but in 2003 she decided to go it

alone in her native Languedoc to fulfil a dream and create some exceptional wines from her own area. Without a vineyard of her own, she has initially sourced 3 properties where the vineyard owners have allowed her to select the best parcels and to vinify and age the wines in their cellars. A maximum of 500 cases of each wine are produced and then only in the best vintages. The Laure Saint-Martin (Minervois) is mainly Grenache, with a little Syrah, and bags of appealing upfront fruit. The subtle and fine Clos du Causse (Minervois La Livinière) is mainly Syrah with a little Grenache, while the organic Saint-Chinian, Château La Bousquette, is from Syrah and Grenache and is a little more restrained. Concertino, a blend of Grenache and Syrah from Château Fabas in Minervois, showed excellent balance and concentration of fruit. Additionally, Brigitte has produced a string of single-varietal entry-level wines under the Stricto Senso label at an astonishingly low price for the quality. For the moment you will have to go to France to find these wines, either through herself, or the *négociant* house of Jean-Luc Thunevin. A promising start which should only get better. (NB)

Chevalier Vins
- ● **Minervois** Laure Saint★★★ £B ● **Minervois** Concertino★★★ £B
- ● **Minervois La Livinière** Clos du Causse★★★ £B
- ● **Saint Chinian** Château La Bousquette★★★ £C

Stricto Senso
- ● **Vin de Pays d'Oc** Cinsault★★★ £B Grenache★★ £B Syrah★★ £B
- O **Vin de Pays d'Oc** Chardonnay★★★ £B

DOM. CLAVEL Coteaux du Languedoc

Pierre Clavel 34160 Saint-Bauzilles de Montmes
UK stockists: CBg,N&P, Odd,Tan,Adm,NYg

This property is situated just beyond the suburbs of the city of Montpellier. Some 40ha are planted to Syrah, Grenache, Mourvèdre and Carignan among the reds, along with white varieties Roussanne, Grenache Blanc and Rolle. The latter are blended into a lightly herb-scented, nutty, fruit-driven white. It is the reds, though, that stand out here. Both Le Mas and Les Garrigues are ripe and sturdy with well-integrated, dark blackberry and herb-spiced fruit and supple tannins, while the old-vine Copa Santa, regularly on the cusp of ★★★★, is a splendid ageworthy blend of Syrah, Grenache and Mourvèdre. (DM)

- ● **Coteaux du Languedoc** Le Mas★★ £B Les Garrigues★★ £B
- ● **Coteaux du Languedoc** Copa Santa★★★★£C

CLOS DE L'ANHEL Corbières www.anhel.fr

Sophie Guiraudon et Philippe Mathias 11220 Lagrasse
UK stockists: L&W,SVS

Small 7-ha property making some of the very best wine in Corbières. Planted at an altitude of over 200 metres the vineyard comprises 2ha each of Carignan and Grenache planted in clay/limestone soils and small 0.4ha plots of both Syrah and Cinsault planted in a more gravelly/limestone soil which provides good water retention for the Syrah. Cultivation follows organic principles and harvesting is by hand. Characterful, supple, spicy and approachable red Les Terrassettes blends 60-year-old Carignan with Grenache, Syrah and Cinsault and is aged in cask with micro-oxygenation employed prior to the malolactic. Les Dimanches is a serious and more backward blend of just Carignan and Grenache. It gets a vatting of up to 3 weeks and is aged in a portion of new wood, again with micro-oxygenation rather than racking employed during *élevage*. Rich and concentrated with dark fruit and black pepper notes, it will benefit from 4 or 5 years' patience.   (DM)

- ● **Corbières** Les Terrassettes★★ £B Les Dimanches★★★£C

403

CLOS BAGATELLE Saint-Chinian closbagatelle@libertysurf.fr

Luc & Christine Simon 34360 Saint-Chinian
UK stockists: Han,ACH,Ter

With over 50ha, the Simons are one of the larger Saint-Chinian growers but also one of the best. 47ha is planted to Carignan, Grenache, Mourvèdre and Cinsault. For white they have a small holding of just 7ha of Muscat. Production is now around 20,000 cases a year. There are 4 straightforward fruit-driven Vin de Pays d'Oc bottlings: a Sauvignon and a Chardonnay along with a red blend La Tuilière and a Merlot. It is though the Saint-Chinians that mark out this estate. A characterful rosé, Donnadieu Camille et Juliette, is produced from young vines and there are no fewer than 5 red labels. The Tradition is crafted from some of the younger Carignan vines along with Grenache, Syrah and Cinsault. No carbonic maceration is used and the wine shows some really attractive and vibrant spicy, brambly fruit. The Donnadieu labels are sourced from some of the higher-altitude plots and are harvested a little later. Camille et Juliette is 50% Carignan put through carbonic maceration, with Grenache, Syrah and a further small proportion of Carignan vinified traditionally. Vibrant and powerful but with a firm structure, it should develop well in the short term. In the Marie et Mathieu, a small (15%) portion of Syrah goes through *macération carbonique*, with the balancing Syrah, Grenache and Mourvèdre vinified traditionally. Yields of less than 30 hl/ha ensure a rich, stylish but accessible red. The Veillée d'Automne and premium *cuvée* La Gloire de Mon Père are more seriously structured and ageworthy examples. Both blend Mourvèdre, Syrah and Grenache, the Mourvèdre being the more important component of La Gloire Mon Père. The former is refined, well structured and intense with hint of new oak showing through; the latter is richer, purer and finer and is very intense and complex. Both need 4–5 years but the Gloire Mon Père will benefit from further age. An excellent range is completed by a honeyed and grapey sweet Muscat of impressive poise and class. (DM)

- ● **Saint-Chinian** Veillée d'Automne★★★ £B La Gloire de Mon Père★★★★ £D
- ● **Saint-Chinian** Tradition★ £B Donnadiieu Camille et Juliette★★ £B
- ● **Saint-Chinian** Donnadieu Mathieu et Marie★★ £B
- O **Muscat de Saint-Jean de Minervois**★★ £B
- ◉ **Saint-Chinian** Donnadiieu Camille et Juliette★ £B

CLOS DES CAMUZEILLES Fitou

Laurent Tibes Allee des Jardins, 11360 Cascatel
UK stockists: SVS

Fitou was the first of the Languedoc appellations to gain full AC status way back in 1948. It has however produced fewer domaines of real style than many neighbouring ACs. Laurent Tibes' Clos des Camuzeilles is very much an exception to this rule with 2 very fine reds and a Muscat de Rivesaltes as well. He only took over his family's 3.5ha in 1998 but the quality here is immediately apparent. From finely drained schistous soils he produces a very fine varietal Carignan which is aged in *cuve* and shows great intensity of fruit and a well-defined mineral edge. La Grangette Fitou is dominated by 80-year-old Carignan with a touch of 35-year-old Grenache. Aged in one-third new oak *demi-muids*, the wine is richer and fuller than the varietal Carignan with marked oak and dark, spicy berry fruit offering real depth and purity. Expect both wines to develop well with a little age, particularly the Grangette. (DM)

- ● **Vin de Pays de l'Aude** Carignan★★★ £B ● **Fitou** La Grangette★★★★ £D

CLOS CENTEILLES   Minervois

Daniel & Patricia Domergue   34210 Siran
UK stockists: Ter

Stylish Minervois has been produced at this property for a decade and the Domergues have been established considerably longer than some of their competitors who opt, not often wisely, for a much fuller and more extracted style. There is a minimum of new wood here and the wines are restrained, intentionally so, but are good and well-crafted, with elegant fruit and well-honed, ripened tannins. A number of *cuvées* are produced. Carignanissime is made from 100% old-vine Carignan vinified in part by *macération carbonique*. It shows just what old-vine Carignan properly ripened can achieve. Capitelle de Centeilles is a juicy, vibrant 100%t Cinsault that, like Carignanissime, is aged for a couple of years in *cuve* before bottling. Campagne de Centeilles is a straightforward soft, fruit-driven blend of Cinsault and a little Syrah. The top wine is the Minervois La Livinière which is structured and refined and needs 3–4 years. The Guigniers de Centeilles Pinot Noir is less impressive and a touch one dimensional, possessing relatively simple red-berry fruit. (DM)

● **Minervois** Carignanissime★★ £B Capitelle de Centeilles★★ £B
● **Minervois** Campagne de Centeilles★ £B ● **Minervois** La Livinière★★ £C

CLOS MARIE   Coteaux du Languedoc Pic Saint-Loup

Françoise Julien et Christophe Peyrus   34230 Saint-Pargoire

Some of the best and priciest wines in the Coteaux du Languedoc are now emerging from this 17ha property which has 15.5ha planted to mainly Grenache and Mourvèdre with some Carignan and a little Syrah. There is also a small white holding of Grenache, Roussanne and Clairette which is used to produce a fine nutty white Manon. The 4 reds take pride of place and all are serious, dense and powerful examples. Vinification is traditional, with no carbonic maceration and only a small amount of new oak in the top wines. L'Olivette is ripe and forward, Simon and Métairie du Clos more structured and firm. The top label Les Glorieuses is rich and concentrated but like all the wines refined with an elegance and purity rarely encountered in the Languedoc. L'Olivette will drink well young but the other *cuvées*, particularly Les Glorieuses, should be given 5 years or so of ageing. (DM)

● **Coteaux du Languedoc Pic Saint-Loup** Glorieuses★★★★£F
● **Coteaux du Languedoc Pic Saint-Loup** Métairie du Clos★★★★ £E
● **Coteaux du Languedoc Pic Saint-Loup** L'Olivette★★★ £C Simon★★★£D
O **Coteaux du Languedoc Pic Saint-Loup** Manon★★ £C

DOM. DE LA CROIX-BELLE   Vin de Pays des Côtes de Thongue

Jacques et Françoise Boyer   34480 Puissalicon
UK stockists: SVS, Gar, L&S

The fairly extensive range of wines made at this property all offer good value for money. The mix of clay, limestone, silt and gravel soils have excellent drainage and assist in keeping yields down to around 45 hl/ha, helped by a green harvest. Although most of the vineyard is machine-harvested this is generally done at night to keep the fruit, particularly from the white varieties, as fresh as possible. The straightforward varietal wines are soft and fruity but it is the Champs, No 7 and Cascaillou wines that stand out here. Les Champs are fruit-driven styles which see no wood. Les Champ du Lys is blended from Grenache, Viognier and Sauvignon Blanc and is aged on lees for 6 months to add weight to its spicy, floral fruit. The red Champ du Coq combines Syrah, Grenache and Merlot and works better than Les Calades, which is Syrah, Mourvèdre and Carignan aged in oak for a year. The No 7 red and white are a clear step up, the former an unusual barrel-fermented blend of Viognier,

405

Chardonnay, Grenache Blanc, Sauvignon Blanc, Carignan Blanc and Muscat à Petits Grains; the latter, comprising a varied mix of Syrah, Grenache, Mourvèdre, Cinsault, Merlot and Cabernet Sauvignon, is bottled unfiltered after 12 months in oak. Top of the range Cascaillou, an elegant blend of Grenache, Syrah and Mourvèdre, is bottled after just 8 months in cask in order to emphasise its fruit. (DM)

● **Vin de Pays des Côtes de Thongue** no 7★★ £B Cascaillou★★★ £C
● **Vin de Pays des Côtes de Thongue** Le Champ du Coq★ £B Les Calades★ £B
○ **Vin de Pays des Côtes de Thongue** Les Champ des Lys★ £B no 7★★ £B
○ **Vin de Pays des Côtes de Thongue** Chardonnay★ £B Caringole★ £B

DOM. JEAN-LOUIS DENOIS   Vin de Pays d'Oc jl.denois@wanadoo.fr
Jean-louis Denois Borde Longue,   11300 Roquetaillade
UK stockists: BBR, Gar

Jean-Louis Denois formerly owned the Limoux property DOMAINE DE L'AIGLE but sold up in frustration at the intransigent bureaucracy of the appellation authorities. He now cultivates 4 hectares of red and 4 hectares of white varieties from which he produces a range of *vins de pays* as well as Limoux wines of good to excellent quality. He blends traditional southern varieties with those from Bordeaux for his reds. The more forward of the 2 is a finely structured, supple, lightly cedary blend of Merlot, Cabernet Sauvignon and Grenache which will benfit from 3 or 4 years' patience. Richer and fuller is the *cuvée* Chloé, a full-blown Right Bank blend of Merlot and Cabernet Sauvignon, aged in oak. Taut and firmly structured when young but with impressive weight and concentration it will benefit from 5 years' ageing. Neither of the wines is fined or filtered. He also makes a fine sparkling white Tradition Brut. Fermented in small oak, it is a blend of Pinot Noir and Chardonnay and rivals any of the current offerings from Limoux as well as many lesser Champagnes. Of perhaps greatest interest though are 2 excellent barrel-fermented still whites. La Rivière is a taut mineral-scented Chenin Blanc, Sainte-Marie an elegant and finely structured Chardonnay. Both possess a piercing intensity rare in this southerly region. Expect them to evolve well with 3 or 4 years' age. A very pricey late-harvest Limoux Vendanges d'Octobre Vieilles Vignes is sold at the domaine. (DM)

● **Vin de Pays d'Oc** Grande Cuvée★★ £B Chloé★★★ £C
○ **Vin de Pays d'Oc** Sainte Marie★★★ £C
○ **Limoux** La Rivière★★★ £C
○ **Tradition Brut**★★ £B

DOM. ALAIN CHABANON   Coteaux du Languedoc Montpeyroux
Alain Chabanon 34150 Lagamas
UK stockists:N&P,Ter

From his small Montpeyroux property, formerly known as Domaine Font Caude, Alain Chabanon produces somewhat less than 3,000 cases a year of 3 very good reds and a tiny amount of a white labelled Trelans, which is classified as *vin de table*. The reds are vinified with long macerations, often over a month, and are aged in wood, not all new. The Vin de Pays d'Oc Merle aux Alouettes is a fleshy, vibrant Merlot loaded with ripe plum and blackberry fruit, nicely supported by fine, supple, well-rounded tannins. The more powerfully structured Les Boissières is produced from Grenache. It is ripe and bold with an impressive depth of fruit. The third red is L'Esprit de Font Caude. Generally produced from a blend of Syrah and Mourvèdre this is a marvellously rich, dense red, full of smoky dark berry fruit and just a subtle hint of oak. In some vintages the wine has had more Mourvèdre than Syrah, when it tends to show more elegance and less overt concentration and extract. It will be interesting to see how the style develops here. (DM)

- ● **Coteaux du Languedoc Montpeyroux** Les Boissières★★★★ £E
- ● **Coteaux du Languedoc Montpeyroux** L'Esprit de Font Caude★★★★ £E
- ● **Vin de Pays d'Oc** Merle aux Alouettes★★★ £E

DOM. DE LA GARANCE   Vin de Pays de l'Hérault

Murielle & Pierre Quinonero   34720 Caux
UK stockists:ldg,GCW

This 11ha property is the source of a number of fine, very traditional wines. Key here are some very old plantings of Carignan as well as the lowly Ugni Blanc allied to very low yields of around 15–20 hl/ha, not to mention an excellent *terroir* just to the north of Pézenas with vines planted in a mix of limestone, basalt and clay soils. Les Armières, fully old-vine Carignan, is given a very long *cuvaison* of up to a month and demands 4 or 5 years to shed its ealy mineral austerity. It offers great depth and purity, though. The white Les Claviers blends Ugni Blanc with Sauvignon Blanc and a little Terret. The Sauvignon just adds a crisp freshness to this ripe, full and nutty wine, which will evolve well over 5 years or so. The Bruixas is made from Grenache. Fermentation is halted at around 13 degrees by fortification to leave a lightly sweet, fascinatingly pruney and figgy late-harvest red. (DM)

- ● **Vin de Pays de l'Hérault** Les Armières★★★ £C
- ● **Bruixas** Vin de Liqueur★★★ £D
- O **Vin de Pays des l'Hérault** Les Claviers ★★ £C

DOM. DU GRAND ARC   Corbieres

Bruno Schenk   Rue Tranquille, 11350 Paderne
UK stockists:SVS

Fine quality red emerges from this small domaine in the Hautes Corbières with 13.5ha of vineyard planted on south-facing slopes on clay-limestone soils close to the famous Cathar castle of Peyrepertuse. The vines are tended as naturally as possible with minimal use of fertilisers and yields are resticted to between 35 and 45hl/ha to maximise quality. There is a good, richly berry-fruited rosé but it is the reds that stand out. The Réserve is approximately two-thirds Carignan and one-third Grenache with the merest hint of Syrah. It is pure, minerally and very elegant for the AC. Fuller and more opulent, with a hint of toasty, almost chocolaty oak, the Cuvée de Quarante has more Grenache and Syrah. This wine is on the edge of ★★★ and excellent value for money. The reds will drink well with a year or 2 in bottle but have the depth and supple structure to develop well in the medium term. (DM)

- ● **Corbières** Réserve★★ £B Cuvée de Quarante★★ £B   ⊙ **Corbières** ★ £B

DOM. DE LA GRANGE DES PÈRES   Vin de Pays de l'Hérault

Laurent Vaillé   34150 Aniane
UK stockists: Gun

The wine here now rivals the long-established leader among Languedoc-Roussillon producers, MAS DE DAUMAS GASSAC. There is no doubt that Grange des Pères is every bit as impressive as its near neighbour. The production is much smaller, though, and Laurent Vaillé has just 10ha under vine, the majority planted to Mourvèdre, Syrah and Cabernet Sauvignon farmed to almost organic standards. The wine is surprisingly approachable in its youth but has all the density, velvety tannin and class to age gracefully. Although matured in 100% new oak this is very well integrated and the wine is, of course, bottled without fining or filtration. There is a tiny amount of a very fine Roussanne-based white with equally deftly handled oak. (DM)

- ● **Vin de Pays de l'Hérault**★★★★★ £F

407

DOM. DE L'HORTUS Coteaux du Languedoc Pic Saint-Loup

Jean Orliac 34270 Valflaunes
UK stockists: CdP, L&S, HHB, Ter

Jean Orliac established this 54-ha property in the late 1970s but only began producing wine himself in 1990. This is now one of the benchmark producers for Pic Saint-Loup, an appellation with a depressingly large number of average wines that should be better. The red Grande Cuvée, blended mainly from Syrah and Mourvèdre, is aged in two-thirds new wood but is surprisingly tight and restrained in its youth. The Grande Cuvée white is ripe, almost tropical and produced from barrel-fermented and aged Viognier and Chardonnay. There is a second label, Bergerie de l'Hortus which offers decent value with an approachable straightforward red and white. (DM)

● **Coteaux du Languedoc Pic Saint-Loup** Grande Cuvée★★★ £C
○ **Vin de Pays Val de Montferrand** Grande Cuvée★★★ £C

DOM. VIRGILE JOLY Coteaux du Languedoc

Virgile Joly 22 Rue de Portail, 34725 Saint Saturnin de Lucian
UK stockists: GCW

This very recently established domaine, started in 2000, has around 10ha under vine spread across a number of plots in the communes of Jonquières and Saint Saturnin. The *terroir* is excellent, with meagre argile-calcareous and gravel soils providing naturally moderate yields of a mere 20hl/ha or so. Two reds are produced and the vinification is traditional with 4–5 weeks maceration on skins and hand plunging. The Saturne is a blend of 30% each of Carignan, Grenache and Cinsault with 10% Syrah. Full of impressive dark, spicy fruit with a subtle mineral edge it will evolve well with 4–5 years' ageing. The Virgile bottling is denser and fuller. The texture is rich and concentrated but the tannin is sufficiently firm to demand at least 5 years' patience. The blend is Carignan (30%) and Grenache (40%) with a further 30% of Syrah adding a darker, richer character. The white *vin de pays* bottling is 100% Grenache Blanc. Barrel-fermented and aged for 9 months in 500-litre oak to minimise the wood influence, it is gloriously rich and full with nutty, lightly citrus-edged fruit and a rich texture on the palate. It will drink very well with 3 or 4 years' age. A *vin de liqueur*, Carthagene, is an unusual blend of Chasselas, Servan and Syrah. (DM)

● **Coteaux du Languedoc** Saturne★★★ £C Virgile★★★ £D
○ **Vin de Pays de l'Hérault**★★★ £C

DOM. DES JOUGLA Saint-Chinian

Alain Jougla 34360 Prades-sur-Vernazobre
UK stockists: THt, BBR, But

Alain Jougla has a reasonable holding of 40ha from which he produces good earthy examples of Saint-Chinian. The vineyards are partly comprised of clay/limestone soils and partly more schistous. The Classique is the regular bottling, a blend of Grenache, Syrah, Mourvèdre, Carignan and Cinsault. It is soft, supple and immediately approachable, with aromas of dark fruits and spicy herbs. Les Tradition is Grenache, Mourvèdre and Syrah. It is a clear step up in quality, with an almost *sauvage* quality with a mineral undercurrent and firmly structured, well-rounded tannins. Best of all is the oak aged Cuvée Signée which has a rich and concentrated old-vine character. It is produced from Grenache, Syrah and Carignan grown on some the property's higher schistous slopes. A Vin de Pays d'Oc Viognier and white Coteaux du Languedoc are also produced. All of the wines offer very good value. The top 2 reds will keep well in the short term. (DM)

● **Saint-Chinian** Classique★★ £B Les Tradition★★★ £B Cuvée Signée★★★ £B

DOM. LACOSTE   Muscat de Lunel
Francis Lacoste   Mas de Bellevue 34400 Lunel
This domaine is very unusual in being planted solely to Muscat à Petits Grains. Sweet and late-harvest wines are the speciality here although a dry Vin de Pays d'Oc Muscat is produced from the estate's youger vines and cool-fermented for immediate appeal. Of the 2 Muscat de Lunel bottlings, the Lacoste is forward and richly grapey, full of simple luscious fruit but with a finesse often absent in such wines. Yields of less than 30 hl/ha no doubt help in achieving this. The Clos Bellevue is rich and very intense with great poise and refinement. Produced from a yield of less than 20 hl/ha and from some of the estate's oldest vines it is a beguiling example of sweet fortified Muscat. A small quantity of a very late-harvested white is also produced. This Muscat Passerillé Vendange d'Octobre is simply labelled *vin de table*. Produced from a microscopic yield of barely 6 hl/ha from both botrytis-affected and very late-harvested grapes it is aged solely in new oak. (DM)
O **Muscat de Lunel** Lacoste★★ £B Clos Bellevue★★★£B

DOM. LACROIX-VANEL   Coteaux du Languedoc
Jean-Pierre Vanel   46 bd du Puits-Allier, 34720 Lunel
Fine, newly established small domaine with just over 8ha of Grenache, Syrah, Carignan and Cinsault and a tiny holding of Grenache Blanc near Pezenas. Two reds are produced at present. The Clos Fine Amor is soft, round and forward: an immediately appealing red. The Clos Melanie is fuller, richer and more opulent. Principally from Syrah, with Grenache and old-vine Carignan, the wine is a full, rich, fleshy and quite extracted style with sufficiently firm and supple tannins to develop in the short term. Both wines will drink well young. (DM)
● **Coteaux du Languedoc** Clos Fine Amor★★ £B Clos Mélanie★★★£C

LA GRANGE DE QUATRE SOUS   Vin de Pays d'Oc
Hildegard Horat   34360 Assignan
The first vineyards at this property were established in the early 1980s and the age of the vines is beginning to show through in the quality of the wines. The holding is small with 6ha of red and just 2ha of white varieties. The viticultural approach is essentially organic and no herbicides are used. As well as the Jeu du Mail, a little Chardonnay is also made. Jeu du Mail is an aromatic blend of Viognier and Marsanne, lent additional structure from ageing in oak. Les Serrottes is a southern-style blend of Syrah and Malbec, whereas the Lo Molin is a fine and elegant Bordeaux blend of Cabernet Sauvignon and Cabernet Franc. Both reds will evolve well with 3 or 4 years' age. (DM)
● **Vin de Pays d'Oc** Lo Molin★★★ £C Les Serrottes★★★£C
O **Vin de Pays d'Oc** Jeu du Mail★★ £B

DOM. LA TOUR BOISÉE   Minervois
Jean-Louis Poudou   11800 Laure-Minervois
UK stockists: The,HKW,Wat,SVS
This is among the very best estates in Minervois, producing wines of density and real class. Production is sizeable for the appellation at 40,000 cases a year from 80ha of estate vineyards. In addition to the top Minervois labels there is some decent regular white and rosé Minervois as well as Merlot, Cabernet Sauvignon and Chardonnay Vin de Pays d'Oc and a straightforward range of wines under the Domaine de Subremont label. The white Minervois Marie-Claude is dominated by Marsanne, with some Maccabeo and a little Muscat adding a touch of perfume to the wine's youthful oak. The regular red Minervois is a blend of Carignan, Grenache, Syrah and Cinsault. Fully de-

409

stemmed prior to fermentation it is soft and rounded with lively blackberry fruit. The top Minervois *cuvées* are more seriously structured. Marie-Claude blends Syrah with Grenache and Carignan; Marielle et Frédérique adds in some Mourvèdre. Marie-Claude is a little firmer with some press wine and a touch of oak. The top wine Jardin Secret is an opulently rich Grenache aged in new oak. Expect all the top reds to develop well with short to mid-term ageing. The range is now completed by the 1905 which is produced from some of the very oldest vines in the appellation. (DM)

- **Minervois** Marielle et Frédérique★★★ £B Jardin Secret★★★★ £D
- **Minervois**★★ £B La Marie-Claude★★★ £B
- O **Minervois** La Marie-Claude★★ £B

DOM. LE CONTE DE FLORIS   Coteaux du Languedoc

Daniel Le Conte des Floris   9. Avenue de Mougeres, 34720 Caux
UK stockists: Idg

Just 1,250 cases are made at this tiny domaine with 4.9ha of red varieties and a mere 1.1ha of white varieties under vine. There are 3 red *cuvées*: La Lena, Villafranchien and the top wine Carbonifère. The relatively high Syrah component here (40%) is apparent, although in the Villafranchien there is a higher proportion of Grenache in soils not disimilar to those in Châteauneuf-du-Pape. The white Lune Blanche, marked by its rich, nutty, spicy, herbal southern fruit, is a fascinating blend of old-vine Carignan Blanc and Grenache Blanc with Roussanne lending a real floral quality. The top 2 reds will stand a little age. (DM)

- **Coteaux du Languedoc** Villafranchien★★★ £C
- O **Vin de Pays de Cassan** Lune Blanche★★★ £C

DOM. LES CREISSES   Vin de Pays de l'Hérault

Philippe Chesnelong   34290 Valros
UK stockists: **GCW**

Recently established domaine just outside the village of Valros, inland to the north-east of Béziers. Just 2 reds are produced here. The regular Domaine Les Creisses bottling is a blend of Syrah, Grenache and Cabernet Sauvignon. Produced from grapes grown in calcareous soils, the wine has excellent definition and structure with just a slight raw edge to its youthful tannin. It will be better with 2 or 3 years' ageing. Les Brunes is a considerable step up in quality and has a price tag to match. This richly textured dense, and cedary blend of Cabernet Sauvignon and Syrah should age well. As yet there is a feeling that the structure overpowers the wine. Great potential here, though.(DM)

- **Vin de Pays d'Oc** Les Creisses★★ £B Les Brunes★★★★ £D

DOM. DE LA MARFÉE   Coteaux du Languedoc

Thierry Hasard   34570 Murviel-lès-Montpellier
UK stockists: **GCW**, Han

Very small new property: the first vintage was in 1997, with just 6-ha of vines. The wines are sturdy, powerful and very extracted in style, with a really characterful, almost earthy component. There is no doubt that there is real depth and power and an absolute commitment to quality but on occasion the tannin can play a very significant role. Les Champs Murmurés is a southern Rhône-style blend with some Cabernet Sauvignon thrown in, while Les Vignes qu'on Abat is dominated by old-vine Carignan. There is the potential here for these to be very classy wines indeed. (DM)

- **Coteaux du Languedoc** Les Champs Murmurés★★★★ £E
- **Coteaux du Languedoc** Les Vignes qu'on Abat★★★ £D

DOM. LA MAURERIE   Saint-Chinian

Michel Depaule   34360 Vernazobres
UK stockists: SVS

The Depaule family have been *vignerons* at Saint-Chinian for around 200 years. As well as their excellent-value AC red they also make a soft and juicy bag-in-box wine which is an excellent alternative to many of the often depressingly flavourless, slightly sweet and confected offerings from the big brands. The Esprit du Terroir is a blend of Syrah, Grenache and Carignan. The wine is aged for 1 year in used small oak and is soft, vibrant and immediately accessible. Dark red berry fruit, spicy undertones and the characteristic minerality of the appellation are all apparent. (DM)

● **Saint-Chinian** Esprit du Terroir★★ £B

LA REGALONA   Cabardès

A Escourrou & E Soulat   6 Avenue de la Viale, 11610 Ventenac-Cabardes
This tiny new operation of just 2ha was established in 1999, the same year the region of Cabardès itself became AC. The 2 partners have plantings of Syrah, Merlot and Cabernet Sauvignon. Yields are kept below 30hl/ha and this is helped by carrying out a green harvest. Winemaking is modern with pre-fermentation cold maceration of the fruit to extract colour. The fruit is all destemmed and the varieties are vinified and aged separately. Both *pigeage* and *remontage* are employed during a 30 day vatting. Malolactic is carried out in barrel, new and 1-year-old, and the wine is aged in wood for 15–18 months. The 2003 was a blend of just Cabernet Sauvignon (75%) and Syrah, but it is felt that Merlot will be a vital component of future blends. The individual components of the 2004 all point towards ★★★★ in the future. A new small domaine to watch. (DM)

● **Cabardès** La Regalona★★★ £C

MAS DES BROUSSES   Coteaux du Languedoc

Géraldine Combes & Xavier Peyraud   34150 Puéchabon
UK stockists: **SVS**

This couple make a Coteaux du Languedoc red of impressive potential and real style. Xavier, who looks after the winemaking, is the grandson of Lucien Peyraud of the Peyraud family of Domaine TEMPIER in Bandol (see Provence and Corsica). The vineyards are tended organically and an absolute minimum of sulphur dioxide is employed during vinification. As well as the impressively dense and concentrated Coteaux du Languedoc a Vin de Pays d'Oc red is also produced from Merlot, Grenache and a little Cinsault. (DM)

● **Coteaux du Languedoc**★★★ £C

MAS BRUGUIÈRE   Coteaux du Languedoc Pic Saint-Loup

Guilhem Bruguière   La Plaine, 34270 Valflaunes
UK stockists: HHB

Guilhem Bruguière is one of the best producers in the Pic Saint-Loup sub-region. This is a small property of around 13ha and Guilhem now produces close to 6,000 cases a year. Syrah, Grenache and Mourvèdre are grown, along with Roussanne for the white Les Muriers; a nutty, floral, medium-weight spicy white. The basic Cuvée Calcadiz is well-priced but can be raw with some aggressive green notes creeping through. L'Arbouse though is round, suppler and fuller while the flagship La Grenadière is a blockbuster red: spicy and dense, with a solid chunk of vanilla oak. The top wine will keep well over 5 or 6 years. (DM)

● **Coteaux du Languedoc Pic Saint-Loup** L'Arbouse★★ £B La Grenadière★★★ £C

411

● **Coteaux du Languedoc Pic Saint-Loup** Cuvée Calcadiz★ £B
○ **Coteaux du Languedoc Pic Saint -Loup** Les Muriers★★ £B

MAS CAL DEMOURA Coteaux du Languedoc

Vincent Goumard Chemin du Mas Jullien, 34725 Jonquières
UK stockists: GVF

A very good red and a simple, vibrant, berry-fruited rosé are produced here from 6ha or so, which are all planted to red varieties. It is the *cuvée* L'Infidèle, though, that is the serious business here, a blend of Syrah, Mourvèdre, Grenache, Cinsault and Carignan, of which the Syrah, Grenache and Mourvèdre see some new oak during the 12 months of ageing. The wine is full, rich and quite extracted, with supple tannins and real depth. The 1999 and 2001 were particularly good and 2002 was simnilarly promising. It will be interesting to see how they develop with age. (DM)

● **Coteaux du Languedoc** L'Infidèle★★★ £D
◉ **Coteaux du Languedoc** Qu'es Aquo★★ £B

MAS CHAMPART Saint-Chinian

Isabelle & Matthieu Champart 34360 Saint-Chinian
*UK stockists:*RsW, SVS,Ter

There are now 16ha planted at this fine Saint-Chinian property where the Champarts produce a fruity rosé and a rich, lightly oaked white from Roussanne, Marsanne, Viognier, Bourboulenc and Grenache, as well as 4 reds. Up until 1988 they sold their crop to the local co-op and a small proportion of the harvest is still sold on. The 4 reds are blends of different *terroirs* across the property. The wines are only lightly fined with egg whites and the top 2 reds are bottled without filtration. The Vin de Pays d'Oc is an unusual blend of 80% Cabernet Franc with the balance Syrah. It is lightly leafy with attractive ripe berry fruit. The brambly, forward Côte d'Arbo comprises Syrah, old vine Carignan, young Grenache and a tiny amount of Graciano. The top 2 wines are more serious and firmly structured. Causse du Bouquet blends Syrah with Mourvèdre, Grenache and, in certain vintages, some Carignan. It is aged for a year in barrel and then 6 months in vat. The impressively dense and concentrated Clos de la Simonette is mainly Mourvèdre with some Grenache. It is aged in oak, some new, for around 18 months. The top 2 reds will develop well for a decade at least. (DM)

● **Saint-Chinian** Causse de Bousque★★★ £B Clos de La Simonette★★★★ £C
● **Saint-Chinian** Côte d'Arbo★★ £B ● **Vin de Pays d'Oc**★ £B

MAS DE DAUMAS GASSAC Vin de Pays de l'Hérault

Aimé & Véronique Guibert Guibert de la Vaissière, 34150 Aniane
UK stockists: Adm

Undoubtedly the most famous property in the Midi and the inspiration for the many high-quality winemakers now spread throughout Languedoc and Roussillon. There are some 26ha of red varieties and 12ha of white. The vineyard potential here in the upper Gassac Valley was discovered in 1970. The key is soil that is mineral-rich, superbly drained and that stresses the vines just sufficiently to produce grapes of remarkable flavour, the key to all great wine. The red is a dense and immensely powerful but refined blend of mainly Cabernet Sauvignon (80%) blended with a plethora of other varieties. Very backward and even austere when young this is best left for a decade or more. The white is an intense, nutty, complex blend dominated by Viognier, Petit Manseng and Chardonnay. Finely structured with a piercing mineral core the wine needs 3 or 4 years and will keep comfortably for a great deal longer. A tiny amount of a limited red *cuvée* Emile Peynaud, in honour of the great

Bordeaux enology professor, was produced in 2001. Aimé Guibert also produces an additional range of wines under the Moulin de Gassac label. The Cuvée Elise is a structured and firm Merlot based red, the other two wines are softer and more approachable. (DM)

- ● **Vin de Pays de l'Hérault** Mas de Daumas Gassac★★★★★ £F
- ● **Vin de Pays de l'Hérault** Moulin de Gassac Elise★★★ £C Moulin de Gassac★ £B
- O **Vin de Pays de l'Hérault** Mas de Daumas Gassac★★★★★ £F
- O **Vin de Pays de l'Hérault** Moulin de Gassac★ £B

MAS D'ESPANET   Vin de Pays d'Oc

Agnès & Denys Armand   30730 Saint-Mamert-du-Gard

The Armand property is located just inland between Picpoul de Pinet and Nîmes. Production is spread across 2 reds and a white, all of which take the Vin de Pays d'Oc classification. The white Eolienne is a part tank- and part barrel-fermented blend of Sauvignon Blanc, Grenache Blanc and Viognier. The vines are grown in calcareous soils and from a yield of just 25 hl/ha the wine has a fine grassy, nutty intensity and is best enjoyed young. Les Lens is an exuberant, fruit-driven blend of Cinsault, Grenache and Syrah. It displays a marvellous pure strawberry character and will drink well over 3–4 years. The top red, Bois du Roi, is a Syrah-based oak-aged red. The blend has varied including Grenache, and on occasion some Carignan providing a real black pepper and spice character. It is an impressive wine with complexity, a fine balance of dark berry fruit and herbs, subtly oaked with a supple tannic structure. The Carignan adds a greater depth to the wine. (DM)

- ● **Vin de Pays d'Oc** Les Lens★★ £B Bois du Roi★★★ £C
- O **Vin de Pays d'Oc** Eolienne★★ £B

MAS DE L'ECRITURE   Coteaux du Languedoc   www.masdelecriture.fr

Pascal Fulla   Rue de la Font du Loup, 34725 Jonquières
UK stockists:**GCW**, Han,Ter

Top-quality small Languedoc domaine producing around 2,000 cases of some of the finest red wines in the appellation. Located in the commune of Jonquières, the vineyards are planted on elevated limestone and gravel terraces providing the property with an excellent *terroir*. Yields are purposely restricted below 20 hl/ha and both leaf-thinning and a limited green harvest are carried out to optimise the balance of the vineyard. Just 2 wines are produced. Les Pensées is the more approachable and forward of the 2. A blend of Grenache with smaller proportions of Syrah, Cinsault and Carignan. L'Ecriture is a denser, firmer blend of mainly Syrah with some Grenache and Mourvèdre. Both wines are given a lengthy vatting and aged in new and 1-year-old oak of differing sizes for up to 12 months. The wines complete their *élevage* in *cuve* for a further 3 months before final blending. Neither is fined nor filtered. Both will age well, with L'Ecriture gaining further complexity for up to a decade. (DM)

- ● **Coteaux du Languedoc** Les Pensées★★★ £D L'Ecriture★★★★ £E

MAS FOULAQUIER   Coteaux du Languedoc Pic Saint Loup

Jequier, Stolt, Fallot   34270 Claret
UK stockists:THt,BBR

Another top-quality small Languedoc producer with 8ha planted equally to Syrah and Grenache. The operation is very new with the first vintage emerging in 1999. Swiss winemaker Pierre Jequier makes wines which are richly concentrated and well crafted with great fruit definition and purity. They are marked by the composition of their blends. L'Orphée is the most approachable and is dominated by Grenache, with powerful scents of ripe berries and spice. Le Rollier is a roughly equal blend of the 2 varieties, full of licorice and dark

413

cherry character. Les Calades is mainly Syrah with a touch of oak ageing, it is the most firmly structured of the trio, it needs a minimum of 4–5 years to evolve. The wine has a marvellous mineral purity. Handling is kept to a minimum and inevitably filtration avoided. (DM)

● **Coteaux du Languedoc Pic Saint-Loup** L'Orphée★★★ £B Le Rollier★★★ £C
● **Coteaux du Languedoc Pic Saint-Loup** Les Calades★★★★ £C

MAS DE FOURNEL   Coteaux du Languedoc Pic Saint Loup

Gerard Jeanjean   34270 Valflaunès
UK stockists: Han

Gerard Jeanjean has only been bottling his own wine since 1997 but he produces 2 of the more striking examples in Pic Saint-Loup. The soils are a combination of gravel/pebbles and some clay/limestone particularly suitable for Syrah. He has just 8ha and only 3ha of Syrah and some old Grenache vines are currently in production, with 5ha having recently been replanted with Syrah and Grenache as well as Mourvèdre. Harvesting is by parcel rather than by variety to ensure maximum ripeness and all the fruit is destemmed before fermentation. The Pic Saint-Loup is 70% Syrah and 30% Grenache, ripe and supple with richly concentrated dark berry, mint, herb and spice-scented fruit and a sufficiently firm structure to suggest further development with 4 or 5 years in bottle. The Cuvée Pierre is a post-fermentation vat selection aged in small oak, a proportion of it new, and adds some rich creamy vanilla notes to the excellent fruit of the regular bottling. (DM)

● **Coteaux du Languedoc**★★ £B Pierre★★★ £B

MAS HAUT BUIS   Coteaux du Languedoc

Olivier Jeantet   34520 Lavacquerie-et-Saint-Martin

The production at Olivier Jeantet's property is tiny, barely more than 1,200 cases a year for just one wine. It is, though, among the better examples in the appellation. Costa Caoude is a blend of Syrah, Grenache and Cabernet Sauvignon, of which 70% is aged in barrique and 30% in *cuve* for up to 12 months. It is then aged for a further year in *demi-muids* before bottling. Deep, dense and powerful but with well-judged oak and supple, well-rounded tannins, this is balanced and surprisingly refined wine. (DM)

● **Coteaux du Languedoc** Costa Caoude★★★ £D

MAS JULLIEN   Coteaux du Languedoc

Olivier Jullien   34725 Jonquières
UK stockists: Ter,Gun,Han

Now one of the most established properties in the Coteaux du Languedoc. The wine style and indeed the labels have changed over the years. Olivier Jullien's vineyards are now farmed biodynamically and the oldest vines are approaching 50 years of age, which will improve his potential further. Two reds and a floral white Vin de Pays de l'Hérault are produced and the approach is one of restraint, in quite marked contrast to some of the extracted wines of his neighbours. The top Coteaux du Languedoc is tight and restrained, with a refined, intense mineral quality, whereas the États d'Âme is in a supple and forward fruit-driven style. The reds, particularly the Coteaux du Languedoc, should age very well. (DM)

● **Coteaux du Languedoc**★★★ £D États d' Âme★★★£C
O **Vin de Pay de l'Hérault**★★ £C

MAS LUMEN   Coteaux du Languedoc

Pascal Perret   34120 Pezenas

Tiny and newly established 6-ha domaine which has just over 3.5ha planted, mainly to Syrah, Carignan and Grenache. There is also half a hectare planted to the white Terret variety. Two reds are produced, the first vintage being in 2001. The organically handled terroir appears to be potentially exceptional and Pascal Perret also believes in minimal handling in the cellar. The wines are rich, concentrated and very pure. Although possessing immediate appeal, the exceptional La Sylve is firm but supple and will develop greater complexity with 5 years or so of cellaring. (DM)

● Coteaux du Languedoc★★★ £B La Sylve★★★★ £C

MAS DE MORTIÈS Coteaux du Languedoc

Isabelle & Rémi Duchemin Route de Cazevieille, 34270 Saint-Jean-de-Cuculles
UK stockists: HHB

This is a very good property with some 20ha under vine in the southern sector of the Pic Saint-Loup sub-region. The estate has been continually improved over the last 6 or 7 years with a careful replanting programme to improve quality in the vineyard. Good white as well as vibrant dark and chunky Coteaux du Languedoc are produced and Syrah Que Sera Sera is first class. The wines here are very reasonably priced. (DM)

● Coteaux du Languedoc Pic Saint-Loup Que Sera Sera★★★ £B

MAS MOURIES Coteaux du Languedoc

Solange & Eric Bouet 30260 Vic le Fesq
UK stockists: Vne

Fine new property located 25 km north-west of Nîmes with organically tended vineyards planted in well-drained calcareous soils. Two wines are produced, both red. Mas Mouries Coteaux du Languedoc is a blend of Syrah and Grenache. The varieties are vinified separately before blending and ageing in *cuve*. The fruit is forward and accessible, but the tannin is just a touch hard – perhaps 30 days vatting is too much here. The top *cuvée* Les Myrthes, which is aged in part new wood, is again a blend of Syrah and Grenache but at a lower yield – some 25 hl/ha rather than 40. The wine displays excellent black fruits with nicely handled vanilla oak; in short plenty of depth and class. (DM)

● Coteaux du Languedoc★★ £B Les Myrthes★★★ £C

MAS PLAN DE L'OM Coteaux du Languedoc

Joël Foucou 34700 Saint-Jean-de-la-Blaquière

Another fine emerging Languedoc domaine producing 3 reds and a white of impressive class and style. The estate's vineyards are planted at an altitude of 200 metres and benefit from a swing in temperature during the summer months which promotes acidity and freshness in the fruit. Well-drained schistous soils with interspersed *galets roulés* (similar to Châteauneuf-du-Pape) along with controlled yields of 15–25 hl/ha ensure excellent-quality fruit. The white Feuillage, blending Roussanne with Grenache Blanc and fermented partly in new barrels, is really refined with well-judged oak underpinning an intense nutty, citrus character. Vinification for the reds is traditional with a long maceration of 30–40 days. Œillade is sufficiently firmly structured for a little age and development but has immediate forward blackberry and bramble fruit. Aged partly in *cuve* and partly in old oak it is a mix of Cinsault, Grenache, Carignan and Syrah. The top 2 reds both require a little patience. Miéjour combines Grenache, Syrah and Carignan and the low-yielding fruit offers firm but supple youthful tannins and a mineral undercurrent to its dark, spicy, herbal character. The wine is solely aged in tank. Roucan, by contrast, sees only oak for ageing, part of which is new, and offers a rich, almost creamy, character to the fruit which is a blend of Syrah, Grenache and Carignan. Ageing both the Miéjour and Roucan for 4 or 5 years will be rewarded with bottles of greater

415

depth and complexity. (DM)

● **Coteaux du Languedoc** Œillade★★ £B Miéjour★★★ £C Roucan★★★ £D
○ **Coteaux du Languedoc** Feuillage★★★ £B

DOM. DU MÉTEORE   Faugères

Geneviève Libes   34
UK stockists: SVS

Fine Faugères white as well as red is produced at this small domaine, and a good-quality Viognier is made here too. Two red cuvées are produced. The Tradition is unoaked, a very classic blend of Syrah, Grenache, Mourvèdre and Carignan. Full of dark berry and mineral notes this offers great character and style. Deeper and fuller is the oak aged Les Orionides. Blended from Syrah, Grenache and Mourvèdre, it is more obviously modern and fleshy in style but offers great depth of fruit and perfectly judged spicy, smoky oak. Both will drink well with 2 or 3 years' age. (DM)

● **Faugères** Tradition★★ £B Les Orionides★★★ £B
○ **Faugères** Tradition★★ £B

DOM. DE MONTCALMES   Coteaux du Languedoc

Frederic Poutalie   34150 Puechabon
UK stockists: THt

This very impressive new Languedoc red by Frederic Poutalie is produced from a mere 2.8ha. The vineyards are now established by mass-selection and exceptionally well-drained calcareous topsoils with *galets roulés* provide the base for raw material of outstanding quality. Green harvesting is practiced and yields are resticted to barely more than 20 hl/ha. Just 1 wine is made here, a dense, fleshy modern blend of Syrah, Grenache and Mourvèdre. In the winery all operations are carried out by gravity and individual plots are vinified separately. The wine possesses real depth and intensity as well as a piercing mineral purity to its fruit. There is a balance and harmony here so often lacking in the appellation. Deep and concentrated dark berry fruit is subtly underpinned by a grip of creamy new wood and supple, well-rounded tannins. There is no doubt that 5 or so years' patience will provide both weight and additional complexity. (DM)

● **Coteaux du Languedoc**★★★★ £D

MOULIN DE CIFFRE   Saint-Chinian   www.moulindeciffre.com

Bernadette & Jacques Lesineau   34480 Autignac
UK stockists: BBR, OddL&W, WSc, Ter

Small to medium-sized estate producing around 10,000 cases a year from 30ha across a number of appellations. The vineyards are dominated by red varieties with just 1.5ha planted to Viognier, from which a good spicy barrel-fermented *vin de pays* is produced. Ageing on lees with *bâtonnage* adds extra richness. Reds are produced under 3 appellations, Coteaux du Languedoc, Saint-Chinian and Faugères. A richly textured *vin de pays* red Val Taurou is also produced from a blend of Cabernet Sauvignon, Syrah and Grenache. The oak aged Saint-Chinian and Faugères *cuvées* add a rounder, suppler character, while the Eole is a step up. Firmly structured when young, this blend of Syrah, Grenache and Mourvèdre from the best parcels the estate has in the AC is aged in a mix of new and old barriques. The wines offer good value and the Eole and Val Taurou will develop well with 3–5 years' ageing. (DM)

● **Faugères**★★ £B Élevé en Fûts de Chêne★★ £B Eole★★★ £C
● **Saint-Chinian**★★ £B Élevé en Fûts de Chêne★★ £B
● **Coteaux du Languedoc**★★ £B
● **Vin de Pays des Coteaux de Murviel** Val Taurou★★★ £C
○ **Vin de Pays des Coteaux de Murviel** Viognier★★ £C

DOM. GUY MOULINIER Saint-Chinian

Moulinier Family Pierrerue, 34360 Saint-Chinian

Among a wave of new domaines being established, the Moulinier family continue to produce some of the better wines in this potentially great appellation at their new winery completed in 1999. Their 24ha of vineyards are spread across 3 communes and planted on a mix of clay/limestone, schist and sandstone soils to provide a diverse array of raw material. The bulk of the vineyards are planted at altitudes of 100–200 metres and low yields of 15–25 hl/ha are easy to achieve. Tradition, a blend of Grenache, Syrah and Mourvèdre aged in *cuve* is the most accessible of the wines, fruit-driven but traditionally firm. Les Sigillaires, an unusual blend of 70% Mourvèdre with Syrah aged in used barrels, is rich and full of dark, spicy herb-strewn fruit. The top wine Les Terrasses Grillées gets full oak ageing (40% new). A blend of 95% Syrah and a tiny proportion of Grenache and Mourvèdre, it positively demands 5 or so years to pull it all into balance. (DM)

● **Saint-Chinian** Les Sigillaires★★★ £B Les Terrasses Grillées★★★ £B
● **Saint-Chinian** Tradition★★ £B

DOM. THIERRY NAVARRE Saint-Chinian

Thierry Navarre Ave de Balaussan, 34460 Roquebrun
UK stockists: **SVS**

Thierry Navarre took over from his father in the late 1980s and now has 12ha of biodynamically farmed vines from which he produces around 3,000 cases of 2 fine Saint-Chinians and a straightforward third wine, a *vin de table* called Œillades. His *terroir* is excellent with deep, very well-drained schist soils providing an ideally stressed environment during ripening. The Saint-Chinians are among the more striking wines of the appellation. Le Lazouil is aged in large old vats and is dominated by Carignan with a further 30% of Grenache and 10% of Syrah and others. It is sturdy and characterful with dark and spicy fruit and a hint of minerality. The Olivier, blended from roughly equal parts of Grenache, Syrah and Carignan, is by contrast aged in some new small wood and is rounder and fleshier with impressive depth and intensity. It should develop very well with 3 or 4 years' age. (DM)

● **Saint-Chinian** Le Laouzil★★ £B Olivier★★★ £C

DOM. DE NIZAS Coteaux du Languedoc www.domainedenizas.com

SCEA Domaine de Nizas et Sallèles Hameau de Sallèles, 34720 Caux
UK stockists: **May**

This well-equipped, modern domaine now has 38ha under vine and output is around 15,000 cases a year. The style is very modern and approachable with temperature control in the cellars and new-wave techniques including micro-oxygenation used to maximise the fruit-driven character of the wines. The vineyards are run on a sustainable agricultural basis to maximise the potential of the *terroir*. A number of wines are produced. There is a crisp, ripely tropical and zesty Sauvignon Blanc as well as 2 red *vin de pays* bottlings. The old-vine Carignan, the vines for which are over 35 years, is particularly fine with rich brambly, mineral fruit. The Mas Sallèles blends Cabernet Sauvignon with Merlot and Syrah and is a lighter style. Quite minty and leafy, it won't be to everyone's taste. The densely textured Coteaux du Languedoc is not only excellent value but very sound too. It blends Syrah (65%), Mourvèdre (35%) and a little Grenache. The Coteaux du Languedoc rosé is soft, forward and fruity. (DM)

● **Vin de Pays d'Oc** Carignan Vieilles Vignes★★★ £B Mas Sallèles★ £C
● **Coteaux du Languedoc**★★★ £B O **Vin de Pays d'Oc** Sauvignon Blanc★ £B

DOM. DE PEYRE ROSE   Coteaux du Languedoc
Marlène Soria   34230 Saint-Pargoire
UK stockists: Ter

This 25-ha property is responsible for 2 of the most renowned reds in the
Languedoc and they certainly have a price tag to match their reputation. The
vineyard is planted in ideal sparse, rocky soils and there is a commitment to
low-yielding fruit of the highest quality. Of the 2 reds Clos des Cistes has a hint
of Grenache and is the more forward of the 2. It is supple and full of piercing
spicy, black fruit. Clos Syrah Léone is the more structured, denser, darker and
on occasion shows real animal aromas. The wines are certainly very impressive
in their youth, although it has to be said very marked by oak and highly
extracted in style. It remains to be seen how they will develop. Some earlier
bottles seemed prematurely evolved with 5 or 6 years' age. A stylish, nutty
white is also now produced from Rolle, Roussanne and Viognier. (DM)

● **Coteaux du Languedoc** Clos de Cistes★★★ £E Clos Syrah Léone★★★★ £E

PRIEURÉ DE SAINT-JEAN-DE-BÉBIAN   www.bebian.com
Chantal Lecouty & Jean-Claude Lebrun   Route de Nizas, 34120 Pezenas
UK stockists: Rs W, Ter

This has long been one of the esteemed names of the Languedoc but it is only
in the last few years, under the stewardship of Chantal Lecouty and Jean-
Claude Lebrun, that quality has been back to where it was in the mid- to late
1980s. The early 90s were vintages to avoid here. The current bottlings of both
red from Syrah, Grenache and Mourvèdre and white from mainly Roussanne
are very rich and stylish, especially the white. Perhaps the real disappointment is
the Chapelle de Bébian, a second wine that has on occasion shown a fierce
angular austerity. (DM)

● **Coteaux du Languedoc**★★★ £D Chapelle de Bébian★ £B
○ **Coteaux du Languedoc**★★★★ £D

DOM. DES RAVANES   Vin de Pays des Coteaux de Murviel
Guy & Marc Benin   34490 Thezan Les Beziers
UK stockists: **GCW**

This small 54-ha family domaine is based to the north of Pézenas.
Unusually they are mainly focused on the Bordeaux varieties and their
terroir supports this with a mix of argile-calcareous and gravel soils. There
is a straightforward fruit-driven Merlot/Cabernet blend which is aged in
cuve. The Diogène is more serious and structured. It blends mainly Merlot
(70%) with 20% Petit Verdot and some Cabernet Sauvignon. Les
Gravières du Taurou is a richly textured 50/50 Merlot and Petit Verdot
blend which is lent additional structure from 26 months in small used
oak. The top wine among the reds is the splendid Le Prime Verd, a pure
Petit Verdot of great intensity and depth. Dark, spicy and tarry, this
should develop very well with 5 or 6 years' ageing. There are also 2
fascinating and unusual late-harvest wines. The Cinq Seaux d'Oeillade is
produced solely from Cinsault. The wine is harvested berry by berry but
without any botrytis. It has an extraordinary, light raspberry flavour. The
Cuvée de l'Ille is a very sweet, richly textured Ugni Blanc with marked
botrytis, harvested in November and December. From microscopic yields
of less than 10hl/ha, this is not dissimilar to good Sauternes and also has a
subtle floral quality. The wines are bottled unfined and unfiltered. (DM)

● **Vin de Pays de Coteaux de Murviel** Les Gravières du Taurou★★★★ £D
● **Vin de Pays de Coteaux de Murviel** Prime Verd★★★★ £E
● **Vin de Pays de Coteaux de Murviel** Cuvée Diogène★★★ £C
● **Vin de Pays de Coteaux de Murviel** Merlot/Cabernet Sauvignon★★ £B

● **Vin de Pays de Coteaux de Murviel** Cinq Seaux d'Oeillade★★★ £E
○ **Vin de Pays de Coteaux de Murviel** L'Ille★★★★ £E

DOM. RIMBERT   Saint-Chinian   www.domainerimbert.com

Jean-Marie Rimbert   4 Avenue des Mimosas, 34360 Berlou
UK stockists: FWW, Gar, SVS, Ter

Jean-Marie Rimbert's domaine was only established in 1997 but he is proving
to be one of the really exciting producers of the appellation. He now has 20ha
under vine and is producing between 7,000 and 8,000 cases per year. He has
some very well sited vineyards with impoverished schistous soils planted to
Carignan, Syrah, Grenache, Cinsault and Mourvèdre. Most of the vines are
over 40 years old and some Carignan is extremely venerable. 3 wines are made.
The good regular Saint-Chinian Les Travers de Marceau is blended from 40%
each of Carignan and Cinsault, 15% Syrah and 5% Grenache. It is a finely
structured, elegant example, not at all over-extracted and with a pure mineral
undercurrent running through it. There are also 2 very fine pure Carignan
wines which are simply labelled as *vin de table*. Le Chant de Marjolaine comes
from old vines in some of the best parcels, whereas the extraordinary
Carignator, blended from 2 vintages, is sourced from 50- to 70-year-old vines
and fermented in *barriques*. Heady and exotic it is one of the most characterful
wines of the region. (DM)

● **Carignator**★★★★ £D   ● **Le Chant de Marjolaine**★★★ £C
● **Saint Chinian** Les Travers de Marceau★★ £B

ROC D'ANGLADE   Coteaux du Languedoc

Remy Pedreno & René Rostaing   30980 Langlade
UK stockists : RsW, GCW

One of the finest reds in the Languedoc is produced at this small domaine co-
owned by René Rostaing from Côte-Rôtie. The porperty is 10 km to the west
of Nîmes and planted on limestone based soils. The red is produced from a
blend of 50% Syrah and equal proportions of Grenache and old-vine
Carignan. Yields are kept very low, generally below 25 hl/ha, and the wine is
traditionally vinified with no destemming and a lengthy vatting of around 3
weeks. Ageing in the cellar is for up to 18 months in one-third new wood. This
is dark, spicy and very intense wine with sumptuous tannins and an elegant
hint of black pepper and herbs in the background. Expect it to evolve very well
in bottle with 5 or more years' age. A barrel-fermented white from Chenin
Blanc and Grenache Blanc is also produced and Pedreno owns a tiny 0.3ha
vineyard in the Costières de Nîmes from which he produces a very low-yielding
Syrah (with a hint of Grenache) labelled Clos de la Belle. (DM)

● **Coteaux du Languedoc**★★★★ £E

SIEUR D'ARQUES   Limoux

'Co-operative' Avenue de Mauzac, 11303 Limoux
UK stockists: PVF

A very sizeable but well-organized co-op that produces close to a million cases a
year. Its membership controls around 3,000ha of vineyards, the vast majority of
the whole Limoux appellation. Good, well-made Blanquette de Limoux is
produced as well as Crémant de Limoux. There is a good lightly oaked regular
Chardonnay but the top wines are 4 well-crafted Toques et Clochers bottlings,
which are barrel-fermented and aged partly in new wood, on lees and with
bâtonnage. With a number of decidedly cool mesoclimates within the AC these
are surprisingly elegant and tight, with a fine piercing mineral undercurrent to
the fruit. (DM)

Toques et Clochers
O **Chardonnay** Terroir Océanique★★★ £B Terroir d'Autan★★ £B
O **Chardonnay** Terroir Méditerranéen★★ £B Terroir Haute Vallée★★ £B

DOM. DE TABATAU Saint-Chinian

Beuno & Jean-Paul Gracia   Rue du Bal, 34360 Assignan

The Gracia brothers have a small holding of just over 10ha of vineyards, the
majority of which are planted to Syrah, Grenache and Carignan with a little
Mourvèdre. There is also around 1ha of Chardonnay, Roussanne and Clairette.
At present 2 red Saint-Chinians, a rosé and a *vin de pays* Cuvée Geneviève from
the white holdings are produced. The Camprigou is the softer and more
accessible of the reds, being aged in *cuve* for 10 months without any recourse to
new oak. The more sturdy Le Tabataire is aged for just over a year and in a mix
of *demi-muids* and *barriques*. New oak is avoided because the brothers wish to
emphasise the quality and character of their old vines. Bottling is without
filtration.(DM)

● **Saint-Chinian** Élevé en Fûts de Chêne★★ £B Élevé en Fûts de Chêne★★★ £B

DOM. TERRE INCONNUE Gard

Robert Creus   62 Rue des Albizzias, 34400 Saint Séries

Robert Creus is based in the eastern borders of the Coteaux du Languedoc but
has little interest in the bureaucracy of appellation regulations. As a result his
garage-style wines are simply labelled as *vin de table*. His production is still very
small but jumped dramatically in 2003, rising to 1,000 cases from the previous
vintage of a mere 300 or so. He now has 4ha of vines and these are handled as
naturally as possible although he has no truck with biodynamism. The wines
are vinified with a minimum of sulphur and aged in *barriques* for 16–18
months. Handling is by gravity, fining is avoided and the wines are bottled
without filtration. There are 3 main *cuvées* as well as a second wine, Les
Bruyères, for lots which are not felt to be up to scratch. Léonie is an
astonishingly heady and rich 100% Carignan, in many ways the most exciting
and shocking of Creus's wines. Los Abuelos is 100% Grenache, rich and
characterful, always super-ripe. Alcohol levels for any of the top *cuvées* can easily
be 15% or more but balance and purity are always maintained. Sylvie is
dominated by Syrah with 12% Grenache and 5% Carignan blended in. More
opulent than the wines of the northern Rhône and loaded with super-ripe fruit,
perhaps a slightly firmer structure would add a further dimension. The wines
are very good value. (DM)

● **Los Abuelos**★★★★ £E ● **Léonie**★★★★★ £E ● **Sylvie**★★★★★ £E

VAL D'ORBIEU Narbonne

Les Vignerons du Val d'Orbieu   11100 Narbonne

This vast organisation has among its membership many of the major co-ops of
the Midi as well as a number of individual growers. Interests spread as far as
Bordeaux, where Val d'Orbieu now owns GRAND-PUY-DUCASSE and RAYNE-
VIGNEAU among others. It is responsible as well for the marketing and
distribution of a number of small quality domaines. These include the CH. DE
JAU in the Roussillon, CLOS DE PAULLILES in Collioure and fine Corbières
produced at CH. LA VOULTE GASPARETS. The prestige Val d'Orbieu label is
the Cuvée Mythique, a red blend from varying sources and varieties. It is
inevitably labelled as Vin de Pays d'Oc. Good stylish and moderately fleshy, it
has reasonable depth for drinking over the short to medium term. (DM)

Val d'Orbieu

● **Vin de Pays d'Oc** Cuvée Mythique★★ £B
O **Vin de Pays d'Oc Chardonnay** Réserve Saint-Martin Vin de Pays d'Oc★ £B

Also see the following Rhône *négociants* with an entry in the section *Rhône Valley:*

M CHAPOUTIER
JEAN-LUC COLOMBO
TARDIEU-LAURENT

OTHER WINES OF NOTE

ABBAYE DE SYLVA PLANA ● **Faugères** La Closeraie★★ £B

ABBAYE DE THOLOMIES ● **Minervois** £B ● **Minervois La Livinière** £C

ABBOTTS WINES ● **Minervois** Cumulo Nimbus★ £B

DOM. DE L'AIGLE O **Limoux** les Aigles★★ £C

DOM. DE L'ARJOLLE ● **Vin de Pays Côtes de Thongue** Cabernet★★ £B
● **Vin de Pays Côtes de Thongue** Paradoxe★★★ £C

DOM. D'AUPILHAC ● **Coteaux du Languedoc-Montpeyroux**★★★ £C
● **Vin de Pays des Gorges de l'Hérault** Les Plos de Baumes★★★ £D

DOM. DE BARROUBIO ● **Minervois**★★ £B Jean Miquel★★ £C

DOM. DE BARUEL ● **Vin de Pays des Cevennes** Syrah/Cabernet★★ £C

GÉRARD BERTRAND ● **Vin de Pays d'Oc** Cigalus★★★ £D

DOM. BERTRAND BERGÉ ● **Fitou**★ £B Ancestrale★★ £B

DOM. JEAN-MARC BOILLOT ● **Vin de Pays d'Oc** Domaine de La Truffière★★ £C
● **Vin de Pays d'Oc** Les Roques★★ £C

DOM. DE CABROL ● **Cabardès** Vent d'Est★★ £C Vent d'Ouest★★ £C

DOM. CAPION ● **Syrah** Vin de Pays de l'Hérault★ £B
O **Chardonnay** Vin de Pays de l'Hérault★ £B

CAVES DE CASTELMAURE ● **Corbières** Cuvée No 3★★★ £D

CH. BONHOMME ● **Minervois** Les Amandiers★ £B Les Oliviers★★ £C

CH. BOUISSET ● **Coteaux du Languedoc La Clape** Eugénie★ £B

CH. CABEZAC ● **Minervois** Belvèze Grand Cuvée★★ £C Arthur Cuvée★ £B

CH. CAMPLAZENS ● **Coteaux du Languedoc La Clape** La Reserve★ £B

CH. CASCADAIS ● **Corbières**★ £B

CH. CESSERAS ● **Minervois La Livinière**★★ £B

CH. DE COMBEBELLE ● **Saint-Chinian** Tradition★ £B Réserve★★ £C

CH. D'EXINDRE ● **Coteaux du Languedoc** Magdalia★★ £B

CH. FLAUGERGUES ● **Coteaux du Languedoc**★★ £B

CH. GLÉON MONTANIE ● **Corbières** Gaston Bonnes★★ £C
● **Corbières** Combe de Berre★★ £B

CH. DE GOURGAZAUD ● **Minervois** Quintus MMI★★ £B
● **Minervois La Livinière** Réserve★★ £B

CH. GRAND MOULIN ● **Corbières** Vieilles Vignes★ £B

CH. GRÉZAN ● **Faugères** Cuvée Arnaud Lubac★ £B

CH. HAUT-BLANVILLE ● **Coteaux du Languedoc**★★ £C

CH. HAUT-GLÉON..● **Corbières**★★ £B O **Corbières**★★ £B

CH. LA BASTIDE ● **Corbières** Optimé★★ £B

CH. LA CLOTTE FONTAINE ● **Coteaux du Languedoc**★★ £B

CH. DE LANCYRE ● **Coteaux du Languedoc** La Coste d'Aleyrac★★ £B
● **Coteaux du Languedoc** Vieilles Vignes★★★ £C Grande Cuvée★★★ £C
● **Coteaux du Languedoc** Clos des Combes★★★ £C
O **Coteaux du Languedoc** La Rouvière★★ £B

CH. LA ROQUE ● **Coteaux du Languedoc Pic Saint-Loup**★★ £C
● **Coteaux du Languedoc Pic Saint-Loup** Cupa Numismae★★ £C

CH. LA SAUVAGEONNE ● **Coteaux du Languedoc** Cuvée Prestige★★ £C

CH. DE LASTOURS ● **Corbières** Cuvée Simon Descamps★★ £B
● **Corbières** Fûts de Chêne★★ £B

CH. LES PALAIS ● **Corbières** Tradition★★ £B Randolin Vieille Vignes★★ £B

CH. MARIS ● **Minervois La Livinière**★★ £C Vieilles Vignes★★ £C

CH. DE NOUVELLES ● **Fitou** Vieilles Vignes★★ £B

CH. OLLIEUX ROMANIS ● **Corbières** CuvéeClassique★★ £B

421

CH. D'OUPIA ● **Minervois**★ £B Les Barons★★ £B

CH. PECH-CELEYRAN ● **Coteaux du Languedoc La Clape** Réserve★★ £C

CH. PECH-LATT ● **Corbières** Cuvée Vieille Vignes★ £B Cuvée Alix★★ £C

CH. PUECH-HAUT ● **Coteaux du Languedoc** Prestige★★ £C
● **Coteaux du Languedoc** Tête de Cuvée★★★ £D

CH. DE RIEUX ● **Minervois**★★ £B

CH. ROUMANIÈRES ● **Coteaux du Languedoc**★ £B

CH. SAINT-AURIOL ● **Corbières** Les Terrassettes★ £B

CH. SAINTE-EULALIE ● **Minervois La Livinière**★★ £B

CH. VEYRAN ● **Saint-Chinian** Cuvée Henri★★ £B

CH. VILLERAMBERT-JULIEN ● **Minervois**★★ £C ○ **Minervois**★ £B

CLOS DU GRAVILLAS ● **Vin de Pays d'Oc** Le Rendez-Vous du Soleil★★ £B
● **Vin de Pays d'Oc** Lo Viehl★★ £B

DOM. DE CLOVALLON ● **Vin de Pays d'Oc** Pinot Noir★★ £B
● **Vin de Pays d'Oc** Mas d'Alezin★★★ £D ○ **Vin de Pays d'Oc** Viognier★★ £B

DOM. DE LA COMBE-BLANCHE ● **Minervois** La Chandelière★★ £B
● **Vin de Pays d'Oc** Le Dessous de l'Enfer★★ £B

DOM. DE COURTILLES ● **Corbières**★★ £C Côte 125★ £B

DOM. DES CREYSELS ○ **Picpoul de Pinet**★ £B

ERMITAGE DU PIC SAINT LOUP ● **Pic Saint-Loup** Cuvée Saint-Agnes★ £C

FÉLINES-JOURDAN ○ **Picpoul de Pinet**★ £B

DOM. FONTEDICTO ● **Coteaux du Languedoc** Coulisses★★ £C Promise★★★ £D

DOM. JEAN-MARIE FOURRIER ● **Faugères** Élegance★★ £B Finesse★★ £B

DOM. DU GRAND CRÈS ● **Corbières**★★ £B

DOM. DE GRANOUPIAC ● **Coteaux du Languedoc**★★ £B

DOM. DES GRECAUX ● **Coteaux du Languedoc** Hemera★★ £D

DOM. HENRY ● **Coteaux du Languedoc** Les Chailles★★ £D

JEANJEAN ● **Faugères** Domaine de Fenouillet★★ £B

LA JASSE CASTEL ● **Coteaux du Languedoc**★★ £C

DOM. LA MADURA ● **Saint-Chinian**★★ £B Grand Vin★★★ £C

DOM. LA ROUVIOLE ● **Minervois** Sélection★★ £B
● **Minervois La Livinière**★★★ £C

DOM. DE LAVABRE ● **Coteaux du Languedoc Pic Saint-Loup**★★ £B

LE BIEN DECOUVERTIS ● **Coteaux du Languedoc**★★★★ £E

LES TROIS TOMATES ● **Vin de Pays d'Oc** Classic★★ £B Barrique★★ £C

DOM. LUC LAPEYRE ● **Minervois** L'Amourier★★ £B

MA REFERENCE ● **Vin de Pays d'Oc**★★★ £D

DOM. MARIA FITA ● **Fitou**★★ £D

MAS DES CHIMÈRES ● **Vin de Pays du Salagou** Oeillades★★ £B
● **Vin de Pays du Salagou** Marie et Joseph★★ £B

MAS GRANIER ● **Coteaux du Languedoc** Les Gres★★ £B

MAS LA CHEVALIÈRE ● **Vin de Pays d'Oc**★★ £C

MAS DE MARTIN ● **Coteaux du Languedoc** Cinarca★★ £B Ultreia★★★ £C

MAUREL-VEDEAU ● **Coteaux du Languedoc** Clos de Fontedit★★ £C

CAVES DU MONT TAUCH ● **Fitou** Les Crouzels★★ £B   Les Quatre★★ £B
● **Fitou** Terroir de Tuchan★★ £C

LES DOMAINES PAUL MAS ● **Coteaux du Languedoc** Vinus★★ £B Faisses★★ £D
● **Vin de Pays d'Oc** La Forge Merlot★ £B La Forge Cabernet Sauvignon★ £B
○ **Vin de Pays d'Oc** La Forge Chardonnay★ £B

DOM PERDIGUIER ● **Vin de Pays des Coteaux d'Ensérune** Oeillades★★ £B
● **Vin de Pays des Coteaux d'Ensérune** Marie et Joseph★★ £B

DOM. PICCININI ● **Minervois La Livinière** Line et Laetitia★★ £B

DOM. DU POUJOL ● **Coteaux du Languedoc** Podio Alto★★★ £C
○ **Vin de Pays de l'Hérault** Pico★★ £B Tèras★★★ £C

DOM. DE LA PROSE ● **Coteaux du Languedoc** Cuvée Prestige★★ £B
● **Coteaux du Languedoc** Les Embruns★★ £B

DOM. PUJOL-IZARD ● **Minervois** Cuvée Saint-Fructueux★★ £C

DOM SAINT-ANDRIEU ● **Coteaux du Languedoc** Noel★★★ £C
● **Coteaux du Languedoc** Les Roches Blanches★★ £B

DOM. ST-MARTIN LA GARRIGUE ● **Coteaux du Languedoc** St-Martin★★★ £C
● **Coteaux du Languedoc** Bronzinelle★★ £B
○ **Coteaux du Languedoc**★★ £B ○ **Picpoul de Pinet**★ £B

CAVE DE SAINT-SATURNIN ● Coteaux du Languedoc Lucian★ £B
● Coteaux du Languedoc Seigneur des Deux Vierges★★ £B
DOM. SERRES MAZARD ● Corbières Cuvée Henri Serres £B
DOM. DU SILÈNE DES PEYRALS ● Coteaux du Languedoc★★ £C
SKALLI-FORTANT DE FRANCE ● Cabernet Sauvignon Édition Limité F★★ £C
VILLA SYMPOSIA ● Coteaux du Languedoc L'Equilibrium★★★ £C
● Vin de Pays d'Oc Merlot★★ £B

Work in progress!!

Producers under consideration for the next edition
HECHT & BANNIER (COTEAUX DU LANGUEDOC)
LA TERASSE D'ELISE (VIN DE PAYS D'OC)
DOM. DU CHAMP DES SOEURS (FITOU)
LE PETIT DOMAINE DE GIMIOS (MUSCAT ST-JEAN-DE-MINERVOIS)
DOM LES GRANDES COSTES (COTEAUX DU LANGUEDOC)
LAURAIRE DE LYS (MINERVOIS)
DOM. DE L'OUSTAL BLANC (MINERVOIS)
DOM. JEAN-BAPTISTE SENAT (MINERVOIS)

Author's choice (DM)

New wave Languedoc whites
DOM. LES AURELLES O Coteaux du Languedoc Aurel
STRICTO SENSO O Vin de Pays d'Oc Chardonnay
DOM. JEAN-LOUIS DENOIS O Vin de Pays d'Oc Sainte Marie
DOM. VIRGILE JOLY O Vin de Pays de l'Hérault
DOM. LACOSTE O Muscat de Lunel Clos Bellevue
DOM. LE CONTE DE FLORIS O Vin de Pays de Cassan Lune Blanche
MAS PLAN DE L'OM O Coteaux du Languedoc Feuillage
DOM. DE L'HORTUS O Vin de Pays Val de Montferrand Grande Cuvée
MAS JULLIEN O Vin de Pay de l'Hérault
MAS DE DAUMAS GASSAC O Vin de Pays de l'Hérault
PRIEURÉ DE SAINT-JEAN-DE-BÉBIAN O Coteaux du Languedoc
DOM. DE LA GARANCE O Vin de Pays des l'Hérault Les Claviers

15 top Languedoc reds
DOM. CANET-VALETTE ● Saint-Chinian Le Vin Maghani
CH. GRÈS SAINT-.PAUL ● Coteaux du Languedoc Syrhus
CH. DES ESTANILLES ● Faugères Cuvée Syrah
MAS DE l'ECRITURE ● Coteaux du Languedoc l'Ecriture
DOM. CLAVEL ● Coteaux du Languedoc Copa Santa
DOM. FONT CAUDE ● Coteaux du Languedoc Montpeyroux L'Esprit de Font Caude
DOM. DE LA GRANGE DES PÈRES ● Vin de Pays de l'Hérault
CH. DE LA NÉGLY ● Coteaux du Languedoc Clos du Truffière
MAS CHAMPART ● Saint-Chinian Clos de La Simonette
MAS DE DAUMAS GASSAC ● Vin de Pays de l'Hérault
PRIEURÉ DE SAINT-JEAN-DE-BÉBIAN ● Coteaux du Languedoc
DOM. RIMBERT ● Carignator
DOM. TERRE INCONNUE ● Sylvie
BORIE DE MAUREL ● Minervois Cuvée Sylla
CH. DE CAZENEUVE ● Coteaux du Languedoc Le Sang du Calvaire

Great Languedoc values
DOM. BORIE LA VITARELLE ● Saint-Chinian Les Cres
CH. DES ESTANILLES ● Faugères Prestige
CH. DE JONQUIERES ● Coteaux du Languedoc
CH. CAPITOUL O Coteaux du Languedoc Les Rocailles
CLOS BAGATELLE ● Saint-Chinian La Gloire de Mon Pere
MAS PLAN DE L'OM ● Coteaux du Languedoc Roucan

423

CH. CAZAL VIEL ● **Saint-Chinian** Cuvée des Fées
CH. LA BARONNE ● **Corbières** Montagne d'Alaric Unfiltered
GUY MOULINIER ● **Saint-Chinian** Les Terasses Grillées
CH. SAINT-JACQUES D'ALBAS ● **Minervois** Château Saint-Jacques d'Albas
CLOS DES CAMUZEILLES ● **Vin de Pays de l'Aude** Carignan
DOM. LA MAURERIE ● **Saint-Chinian** Esprit du Terroir
LA REGALONA ● **Cabardès** La Regalona
MAS DE FOURNEL ● **Coteaux du Languedoc** Pierre

Roussillon

DOM. CALVET-THUNEVIN Maury

Jean Roger Calvet & Jean-Luc Thunevin 66000 Maury
This partnership, Jean-Luc Thunevin is the owner of Château de
VALANDRAUD in Saint-Emilion, purchased their small property in Maury in
2000 and the first vintages were 2001. The terroir is ideal for producing red
wines of the highest calibre from the naturally low yielding vines. Early yields
from the vineyards have been just 18 hl/ha. The soils are very finely drained
black schist which produce a real piercing minerality in the wines. You are
struck as with some top Priorats by the mineral character of the wines rather
than by their fruit. Constance is a blend of 70% Grenache and 30% Carignan
aged in *cuve*. The Côtes du Roussillon-Villages Les Dentelles blends 60% of
Carignan with 30% of Grenache and 10% Syrah; whereas the Hugo is 50%
Grenache, 40% Syrah and the balance Carignan. Both are aged in new wood.
Hugo in particular offers an extraordinarily complex mineral character to its
fruit. These are wines that will evolve very well with 5 or 6 years cellaring. (DM)
● **Côtes du Roussillon-Villages** Les Dentelles★★★★ £E Hugo★★★★★ £E
● **Vin de Pays des Côtes Catalanes** Constance★★★ £D

DOM. DE CASENOVE Côtes du Roussillon

Etienne Montes Mas Sabole, 66300 Trouillas
An ancient estate which, unlike many in the Midi, has been in the same family
for generations. However, impressive modern fruit-driven wines are now being
made at this fine property, where owner Etienne Montes has enjoyed
consultancy input from Jean-Luc COLOMBO. A total of some 50ha of vines are
planted, including 16ha of whites comprising Grenache Blanc, Maccabeo,
Muscat and the rare Torbat. Rich, honeyed Muscat de Rivesaltes and raisiny
Rivesaltes are produced as well as a rather dull Côtes du Roussillon white. The
red Commandant François Jaubert, produced from mainly Syrah and partly
aged in new oak, is powerful, dense and smoky. The Garrigue bottling is spicy
and approachable. Newly added are a rich and spicy red Torrespeyes and a very
limited production *super-cuvée* Domaine Saint-Luc Pla del Rei, which is
extremely expensive. (DM)
● **Côtes du Roussillon** Garrigue★★ £B Commandant François Jaubert★★★★ £E

DOM. CAZES Rivesaltes www.cazes-rivesaltes.com

André & Bernard Cazes 4 Rue Francisco-Ferrer, BP 61, 66602 Rivesaltes
UK stockists:Eno,Luv
In a region marked by new arrivals and vinegrowers becoming winemakers, this
venerable and substantial property with some 160ha of vineyards produces
close to 70,000 cases of both table and fortified wines a year and has done so
consistently for decades. An extensive range is produced here, including good
red Vin de Pays des Côtes Catalanes. Le Credo is a decent blend of Cabernet
Sauvignon and Merlot. There are red and white Côtes du Roussillons, red

Côtes du Roussillon-Villages and Muscat de Rivesaltes, with some splendid aged examples, along with very good Rivesaltes. These have an intense nutty complexity and will keep very well. There are some remarkable and expensive limited-release old vintages available under the Aimé Cazes label. (DM)

● **Côtes du Roussillon-Villages** Alter★★ £B Trilogy★★ £C
● **Vin de Pays des Côtes Catalanes** Le Credo★★ £C ● **Côtes du Roussillon**★ £B
● **Rivesaltes** Tuilé★★★ £C Ambré★★★ £C ○ **Muscat de Rivesaltes**★★★ £B

CELLIER DES TEMPLIERS Banyuls & Collioure

Co-operative' Route du Mas-Reig, 66650 Banyuls-sur-Mer
This is the largest co-operative in the Banyuls and Collioure regions, producing traditional Collioure and some impressive fortifieds. The ownership consists of over 750 growers who between them farm close to 900ha in Banyuls and Collioure, producing wines under both appellations along with a *vin de pays* white. The majority of the fortified production is relatively ordinary and the Collioure bottlings are sound rather than really inspiring, although the domaine wines are altogether more serious. The top Banyuls Grand Cru *cuvées,* though, are a big step up in quality and are labelled Cuvées de Prestige. These are wines with a real nutty complexity and often marked by a dry tangy finish. The Henri Caris is a *demi-sec* style. (DM)

● **Collioure** Château des Abelles★★ £C Abbaye de Valbonne★★ £C
● **Banyuls Grand Cru** Henri Caris★★★ £E Henri Vidal★★★★ £E
● **Banyuls Grand Cru** Vivianne Leroy★★★ £E

CH. DE CALADROY Côtes du Roussillon-Villages

Michel Mezerette 66720 Belesta-de-la-Frontière
Sizeable well established Roussillon property with a fine range of dry reds, a Muscat de Rivesaltes, a relatively light red Rivesaltes and a barrel-fermented white dominated by Chardonnay. It is a vin de pays and has a balance of Maccabeu and Muscat in the blend. Indeed there is a surprisingly forceful floral, grapey character to the wine. The reds are particularly impressive and very fairly priced. Les Schistes, the lightest and softest is a blend of Syrah, Carignan and Grenache. Les Grenats is more densely structured, a blend of mainly Syrah with Mourvèdre and Grenache. La Juliane is of a similar blend with just 5% of Carignan as well and adding flesh through maturation in *barrique*. Particularly dark, spicy and characterful is the Cour Carrée which is an equal blend of Carignan (its dark, peppery character very evident), Syrah, Mourvèdre and Grenache. There is also a small quantity of a Mourvèdre dominant top *cru*, Cuvée Saint Michel. With the exception of the forward Les Schistes the reds will all benefit from a little age. (DM)

● **Côtes du Roussillon-Villages** Les Grenats★★★ £C La Juliane★★★ £C
● **Côtes du Roussillon-Villages** Les Schistes★★ £B La Cour Carrée★★★ £B
● **Rivesaltes** Tuilé★★ £B ○ **Muscat de Rivesaltes**★★ £B
○ **Vin de Pays des Côtes Catalanes** Expression de Caladroy★★ £B

CH. DE JAU Côtes du Roussillon-Villages

Estelle Dauré 20 Rue du Colombier, 66600 Case-de-Pene
UK stockists: GVF
This is one of the largest properties in the Roussillon, just to the south of Corbières in the heart of the increasingly important Agly Valley. The origins of the château date back to the 12th century and one of the original towers remains today. The estate covers a massive 500ha of *garrigue*-strewn landscape with 134ha planted to vines in clay/limestone, marl and schistous soils, 110ha being red and 24ha white varieties. Production is considerable for the area at almost 80,000 cases a year and to some extent this is reflected in the regular red

425

Tradition bottling which although relatively characterful is lighter than many other examples from the region. Talon Rouge, though, is a serious step up in quality, full of black fruits, licorice and dark tar flavours. Blended mainly from Syrah, along with Mourvèdre and Grenache it is dense, rich and very powerful. It should continue to develop well in bottle for 4 or 5 years. A white Côtes du Roussillon is also produced along with a Muscat de Rivesaltes. The Daure family also own the Collioure property CLOS DES PAULILLES and Mas Cristine in the Rivesaltes. (DM)

● **Côtes du Roussillon-Villages** Tradition★ £B Talon Rouge★★★ £D

DOM. DES CHÊNES Côtes du Roussillon-Villages

Razungles & Fils   7 Rue de Maréchal-Joffre, 66600 Vingrau
UK stockists: L&S

The 38ha under vine here is fairly evenly divided between red and white and 8,000 or so cases are produced. Sturdy Côtes du Roussillon-Villages red Alzines is a blend of varieties, Grands Mères is vinified from Carignan and the rich and spicy Tautavel is Syrah and Mourvèdre. A limited-release Carissa is produced from the latter variety. Stylish barrel-fermented white *vin de pays* is joined by an impressive white Côtes du Roussillon Magdaleniens. The range is completed by a Muscat and 2 well-priced Rivesaltes fortifieds. (DM)

● **Côtes du Roussillon-Villages** Alzines★★ £B Tautavel★★★ £C
● **Côtes du Roussillon-Villages** Grands Mères★ £B ● **Rivesaltes** Ambré★★ £B
● **Rivesaltes** Tuilé★★★ £C O **Vin de Pays** Val d'Agly Sorbiers★★ £B
O **Muscat de Rivesaltes**★★★ £B

CLOS DEL REY Maury

Jacques Montagné   7 Rue Barbusse, 66460 Maury
UK stockists: GCW

The first vintage at this excellent Agly Valley domaine was only in 2001. However quality has been consistently exciting and Clos del Rey is among the finest producers in the Roussillon. There are a total of 12ha now and the vineyards consist of 60% Grenache and 40% Carignan from old vines. The Mas del Rey *vin de pays* bottling is from a blend of equal parts of Grenache and Carignan. Dark, spicy fruit and an almost ferocious minerality underpin the wine. Long, intense and fine, it needs at least 5 years. More edgy, nervy and intense in style is the brilliant Clos del Rey Côtes du Roussillon. Produced from 100% Carignan grown on schist soils, this has superb depth and intensity. (DM)

● **Côtes du Roussillon-Villages** Clos del Rey★★★★ £E
● **Vin de Pays d'Oc** Mas del Tey★★★★ £D

DOM. DU CLOS DES FÉES www.closdesfees.com

Claudine & Hervé Bizeul   69 Rue du Maréchal-Joffre, 66600 Vingrau
UK stockists: Odd

Very impressive newly established domaine producing good to stunning red Roussillons from 11ha of Carignan, Grenache, Syrah, Mourvèdre and Lladoner Pelut; the latter is not exactly a regular point of discussion around most dinner tables. Even the entry level Les Sorcières is full of dark, spicy bramble and herbs. Approachable and supple, it is mainly aged in *cuve* with a small portion put in new oak. The Vieilles Vignes, a blend produced from very old vines, many 50–100 years old, is not racked; instead micro-oxygenation is used, as it is with Le Clos des Fées, the domaine's flagship wine. The latter is a blend of Syrah, Mourvèdre, Grenache and Carignan aged in oak for 18 months. A tiny amount of a remarkable 100% Grenache, La Petite Sibérie, is also produced. Very intense and concentrated, it displays more piercing pure berry-fruit intensity than a top Châteauneuf-du-Pape but is softer and more approachable and is very stylish indeed. The vineyard plot of some 1ha and 17 ares yields a mere 175 cases of this wine a year. Not surprisingly the price has now gone through the roof. (DM)

● **Côtes du Roussillon-Villages** Les Sorcières★★ £B Vieilles Vignes★★★★ £E
● **Côtes du Roussillon-Villages** Clos des Fées★★★★ £F La Petite Sibérie★★★★★ £H

CLOT DE L'OUM Côtes du Roussillon-Villages

Eric Monne & Leia Obara 66720 Belesta

This is among the new wave of exciting new arrivals in the Agly Valley. The original vineyard owners here, like many before, were happy to sell the fruit from their overcropped vines to the local co-op, unaware of the tremedous potential of the area. The 3 reds now produced at Clot de l'Oum are wines of great finesse and real style and purity, not in any way over-extracted or overdone. The high altitude vineyards are planted at between 200 and 500 metres on a mix of granite, gneiss and schistous soils. Drainage is excellent and the potential of the *terroir* is now being handled entirely naturally with no recourse to chemicals or fertilizers. The excellent-value La Compagnie des Papillons is produced from Grenache and Carignan with some of the vines up to 50 years old. Fruit is vinified by the parcel to ensure maximum ripeness and ageing is in used oak. The Saint-Bart Vieilles Vignes is produced from equal proportions Syrah (known here as Shiraz), Grenache Velu (known as Lladoner Pelut and closely related to Grenache Noir) and Carignan from the highest parcels on the property. The wine is given a cold-maceration prior to fermentation resulting in a dense and opulent red that nevertheless retains a fine, elegant mineral core to its fruit. Numero Uno is named after the famous Berlin restaurant. Dominated by Syrah it is also blended with the best barrel of Carignan. Once again used oak is preferred to age the wine for 15 months and there is a remarkable depth, purity and complexity. It is certainly likely to be ★★★★★ in a great vintage. All the wines have the structure and refinement to evolve very well in bottle. Numero Uno particularly will reward the patient. (DM)

● **Côtes du Roussillon-Villages** Numero Uno★★★★ £D
● **Côtes du Roussillon-Villages** Saint-Bart Vieilles Vignes★★★★ £C
● **Côtes du Roussillon-Villages** Las Compagnie des Papillons★★★ £C

CLOS DE PAULILLES Banyuls & Collioure

Estelle Dauré 66660 Port-Vendres
UK stockists:GVF, P&S

Like CHÂTEAU DE JAU this domaine is owned by the Dauré family. There are 90ha of vineyards planted in slate soils with the climate moderated by regular sea breezes. Both Collioure and Banyuls are produced. Among the Collioures there is a soft fruity rosé and a barrel fermented white. It is the red though that stands out. Quality has improved significantly in recent vintages and despite the size of the estate this is one of the better examples of the appellation. It is dominated by Mourvèdre with the balance Syrah. Fermentation and maceration is lengthy at 3 weeks before ageing in one-third new oak, one-third used oak and one-third in larger vats. The wine gets a light egg-white fining before bottling. Dense and finely structured, it will develop further with 4 or 5 years' age. Three Banyuls are produced solely from Grenache, of which the Rimage Mise Tardive and Cap Bear stand out. Mise Tardive gets up to 30 months' ageing to add structure and depth. The Cap Bear is aged traditionally in glass demijohns for 18 months before spending a final 3 months in in barrel in the cellars. The Mas Cristine Rivesaltes is produced from fruit grown on a separate property also with slate soils. Yields are easily kept naturally at less than

427

30 hl/ha and the wine is produced from 100% Grenache Blanc. Vinification is halted at 9% alcohol and fortified before being aged for 30 months. It is rich, full of dark honeyed aromas and impressively complex on release. (DM)

Clos des Paulilles
- **Collioure**★★★ £C
- **Banyuls** Rimage Mise Tardive★★★ £E Cap Bear★★★ £E

Mas Christine
- **Rivesaltes**★★★ £E

COUME DEL MAS   Banyuls & Collioure

Philippe Gard   3 Rue Alphonse Daudet, 66650 Banyuls
UK stockists: GCW, FWW

This 10-ha domaine is fast emerging as one of the leading lights of both the Banyuls and Collioure appellations. The majority of the vineyard holding is in the site of Coume del Mas, with south-facing slopes and deep, well-drained clay soils with sufficient water to provide a perfect equilibrium during the hot summer months. A number of *cuvées* are produced from both appellations. The Folio Collioure Blanc is 90% Grenache Gris, the balance Grenache Blanc and Vermentino. Barrel-fermented in new oak, this has real style from fruit grown on schist soils. A yield of just 20hl/ha ensures a wine of impressive nutty, citrus concentration. The red Schistes is very much in a lighter, fruit-driven style. Produced solely from Grenache, it is aged in *cuve*. The top red Collioure, Quadratur, is a blend 50% Grenache with Mourvèdre and Carignan. Aged in one-third new oak for 12 months on lees, this is dense and characterful. The Banyuls Galateo is a blend of Grenache Noir, Gris and Blanc and like all the fortifieds here is made in a non-oxidative style. The top Banyuls, the Quintessence, is solely Grenache Noir and is given a long maceration and aged on lees in new oak. Coming from the oldest Grenache vines, it offers very impressive depth and concentration and in 2004 had just 18 grams of residual sugar, in an off-dry style. (DM)

- **Banyuls** Galateo★★★ £C Quintessence★★★★ £E
- **Collioure** Schistes★★ £B Quadratur★★★ £C O **Collioure** Folio★★★ £C

DOM. DEPEYRE   Côtes du Roussillon

Brigitte Bile & Serge Depeyre   1 Rue Pasteur, 66600 Cases-de-Pène
UK stockists: SVS

Small emerging Roussillon property with 7ha under vine, 6ha of which are red. The first vineyard was purchased in 1997 and Serge Depeyre has used his winemaking experience gained at first MAS AMIEL and then CLOS DES FÉES to very good effect. The white *vin de pays* is a blend of both Grenache Gris and Blanc as well as Muscat à Petits Grains. It is barrel-fermented and aged in oak, a small portion of which is new, and the wine absorbs it easily. Both reds are traditionally vinified getting a maceration of up to a month. The regular Roussillon is dominated by Carignan, with a little Syrah and Grenache whereas the Sainte-Colombe is mainly Grenache and aged in a combination of *cuve* and small oak. Although both will cellar well, the Sainte-Colombe just has that extra dimension. (DM)

- **Côtes du Roussillon-Villages**★★★ £B Sainte-Colombe★★★★ £C
- O **Vin de Pays Côtes Catalanes** Eleve en Futs de Chene★★ £B

DOM. FONTANEL   Côtes du Roussillon-Villages

Pierre Fontanel   25 avenue Jean-Jaurés, 66720 Tautavel
UK stockists: SVS, ldg

A good small range of wine is produced in the commune of Tautavel by the

Fontanels, who have a total of some 35ha from which they produce approaching 15,000 cases a year. Rich and heady fortifieds are fine examples and good value for money, as are the 3 Roussillon reds. The regular Roussillon is soft, forward and juicy, while Cistes is rich and opulent with upfront, nicely ripe brambly, spicy fruit. The Prieuré is denser and more powerful, a real medium-term cellaring prospect. However it shows remarkably well in its youth, with opulent dark-berry fruit and a velvety, rounded, supple texture. (DM)

● **Côtes du Roussillon-Villages**★★ £B Cistes★★★ £B Prieuré★★★★ £C
● **Rivesaltes** ★★★ £C O **Muscat de Rivesaltes**★★★ £B

DOM. GARDIES Côtes du Roussillon-Villages

Jean Gardies 1 Rue Millères, 66600 Vingrau
UK stockists: GVF, Bal, Jer

A really first-class 30-ha property among a seemingly ever increasing number in this exciting appellation. Some good Muscat de Rivesaltes is produced here and now 2 excellent dry whites from the 5ha of mainly Grenache Blanc and a little Roussanne. It is however the reds that are particularly noteworthy. There are 25ha of Grenache, Syrah, Mourvèdre and Carignan and the property has superbly drained limestone and schistous soils and these provide ideal growing conditions. The Millères, a blend of all 4 red varieties, is vibrant and approachable. The Vieilles Vignes has a high proportion of Grenache from old vines while La Torre is a massive and dense dark, brooding mix of Mourvèdre and Carignan. The most expensive wine, La Falaise is an extremely ageworthy and powerful expression of Syrah. (DM)

● **Côtes du Roussillon-Villages** La Torre★★★★ £E Falaises★★★★★ £E
● **Côtes du Roussillon-Villages** Millères★★★ £B Vieilles Vignes★★★ £C
O **Côtes du Roussillon** Glacières★★ £B Vieilles Vignes★★★ £C

DOM. GAUBY Côtes du Roussillon-Villages

Gérard Gauby La Faradjal, 66600 Calce
UK stockists: A&B, F&R, Rae

Gérard Gauby and his wife Ghislaine produce a stunning range of reds and whites from the Roussillon. They are also now involved with the equally thrilling wines of DOM. LE SOULA in the high-altitude vineyards of the Agly Valley and are a source of inspiration for the remarkable new domaines emerging from those vineyards. The white Gauby La Jasse is a crisp, piercing dry Muscat, while the Vieilles Vignes is a powerful nutty blend of southern varieties including Grenache Blanc, Maccabeo and Viognier, a wine of depth and great value for money. The top white Coume Gineste is sourced from a single vineyard and is produced from Grenache Blanc. Among the reds Les Calcinaires is a juicy, vibrant red made from Grenache, Syrah and Carignan and laden with sumptuous raspberry fruit, while the marvellous Vieilles Vignes is a structured, dense, powerful expression of intensely complex old-vine Grenache and Carignan with a smattering of Syrah, Mourvèdre and Cinsault. The top red, and among the most expensive wines in the South of France, is the magnificent Muntada. This is a superbly crafted Syrah, very rich, concentrated and powerful but increasingly refined and no doubt very long lived. (DM)

● **Côtes du Roussillon** Les Calcinaires★★ £B
● **Côtes du Roussillon-Villages** Vieilles Vignes★★★★ £D Muntada★★★★★ £F
O **Vin de Pays de Côtes Catalanes** Coume Gineste★★★★ £E Vieille Vignes★★★ £C
O **Vin de Pays de Côtes Catalanes** La Jasse★★ £B

DOM. JOREL   Vin de Pays d'Oc

Manuel Jorel   66220 Saint-Paul de Fenouillet
UK stockists: **SVS**

This is another small domaine from the Roussillon offering exciting fruit-driven wines at exceptional value for money. The tiny cellar here is underneath Manuel's house in Saint-Paul de Fenouillet. He now has 11ha of vineyards in several plots in and around the village. There are various parcels of old-vine Carignan as well as Grenache and further exciting reds are likely to emerge here. The regular *vin de pays* Grenache red is soft, forward and juicy, the Pesquies bottling offering more depth and structure. Both wines will drink well young and expect the the Pesquies to develop with a little age. (DM)

● **Vin de Pays d'Oc** Grenache Pesquies★★ £B
● **Vin de Pays d'Oc** Grenache★★ £B

DOM. LAGUERRE   Côtes du Roussillon

Eric Laguerre   66220 Saint-Martin-de-Fenouillet
UK stockists:RSW

Eric Laguerre, the former head of the Saint-Martin de Fenouillet co-op, is also involved with Gérard GAUBY at DOM. LE SOULA but has his own small 15-ha domaine with high-altitude biodynamically farmed vineyards where he produces both red and white Côtes du Roussillon. The dark and spicy red has real potential as does the richly complex, nutty, mineral-scented white. The style here is influenced not only by the 600m vineyards but also by vines that range from 20–50 years of age and the well-drained granite soils. The white Le Ciste blends Marsanne, Roussanne and Grenache Gris; the red is Grenache, Syrah and unusually Cabernet Sauvignon. The wines offer both excellent quality and very good value for money. (DM)

● **Côtes du Roussillon** Le Ciste★★★ £B   O **Côtes du Roussillon** Le Ciste★★★ £B

LA PASSION D'UNE VIE   Côtes du Roussillon-Villages

Henri Despeaux   c/o Terroirs d'Exception, 33330 Saint-Christophe des Bardes
First class Roussillon property owned by Henri Despeaux and Bernard Magrez in Bordeaux, the owner of PAPE-CLEMENT and much else besides. With consultancy advice from Michel Rolland as in all of the wines marketed under the Terroirs d'Exception banner this is a rich, opulent, fruit-driven red but of impressive grip and structure also. The vineyards are planted at an altitude of 180–250 metres above sea level on free-draining shale slopes. With an average vine age of over 30 years and some vines up to 100 years there is great potential here. Yields are naturally low, barely more than 20 hl/ha and a green harvest is also practised. In the winery everything is handled by gravity with a traditional vinification and ageing in 400-litre casks. Expect to be able to age the wine for 5 or more years and gain additional complexity. (DM)

● **Côtes du Roussillon-Villages**★★★★ £D

DOM. LE SOULA   Vin de Pays des Côteaux des Fenouillèdes

G Gauby, E Leguerre, R Richard   66220 Saint-Martin-de-Fenouillet
UK stockists:RSW,BBR

The white and the red here are labelled under the new Vin de Pays des Fenouillèdes in the Agly Valley. Both wines are excellent and are indicative of the long-term potential of these high-altitude vineyards. The property has been developed by Gérard GAUBY, Eric Laguerre, who has his own property at DOM. LAGUERRE, and UK wine importer Roy Richards. The key to quality is the 600m elevation of the vineyards, at the limit of ripening but where the south-facing aspect creates a sun trap. The red Le Soula blends Grenache and Syrah and the wine is extraordinarily dense, very backward young but with the potential to add layers of complex dark mineral fruit with age. The brilliantly intense, mineral and citrus white is a blend of Roussanne and Grenache Gris. It is a benchmark Roussillon white. The vineyards are all farmed biodynamically. (DM)

● **Vin de Pays des Côteaux des Fenouillèdes** Le Soula★★★★★ £E
○ **Vin de Pays des Côteaux des Fenouillèdes** Le Soula★★★★ £E

DOM. LA TOUR VIEILLE Banyuls & Collioure

Vincent Cantié & Christine Campadieu 66190 Collioure
UK stockists: Yap

Well-established producer of both Collioure and Banyuls, the quality of which is consistently good. There are 3 red labels as well as a nutty honeyed white, Les Canadells, blended from Grenache Gris and Blanc as well as some Maccabeo. The red La Pinède, from Grenache, Carignan and Mourvèdre is a full, dense, spicy black-fruit style, while the Puig Oriol, which is 70% Grenache and the balance Syrah, is more fragrant with a marvellous *garrigue* scent to the deep berry fruit, the Grenache very prominent. A further red Collioure, Puig Ambeille has recently been added. Good Banyuls comes in 2 guises: the Cuvée Francis Cantié is the more serious with sophisticated nutty *rancio* characters from extended time in cask. (DM)

● **Collioure** La Pinède★★ £B Puig Oriol★★★ £C
● **Banyuls** Cuvée Francis Cantié★★★ £C
○ **Vin de Pays de la Côte Vermeille** Les Canadells★★★ £C

MAS AMIEL Maury

Olivier Decelle 66460 Maury
UK stockists: L&S,HHB

A historic 155-ha property that is understandably best known for its remarkable range of Maury *vins doux naturels*. Two stylish and impressive red Côtes du Roussillons are also produced here in addition to a well-priced, vibrant *vin de pays*, Plaisir, and a white Côtes du Roussillon. The 2 Roussillon reds are impressively large, structured wines. The range of fortified Maury is extensive, from young minimally aged current vintages through to old vintage bottles. The top *cuvées* are Réserve, Privilège and the immensely rich Charles Dupuy. The wines are marked by a classic burnt raisiny, toffeed *rancio* character. The top wines are extraordinarily intense. Olivier Decelle now has a number of interests in Bordeaux. (DM)

● **Côtes du Roussillon-Villages** Carrerades★★★ £C
● **Côtes du Roussillon** Hautes Terres★★★ £B
● **Vin de Pays des Côtes Catalanes** Plaisir★★ £B
● **Maury** 10 Ans d'Age★★★ £C 15 Ans d'Age★★★★ £E
● **Maury** Privilège★★★★ £E Charles Dupuy★★★★★ £E
● **Maury** Vintage★★ £C Vintage Réserve★★★ £D
○ **Côtes du Roussillon** Altaïr★★★ £D

MAS DES BAUX Côtes du Roussillon

Serge et Marie-Pierre Baux Chemin du Mas Durand, 66140 Canet-en-Roussillon
Small Roussillon property producing a comprehensive range of *vin de pays* red, white and rosé as well as a fine, pure and complex Côtes du Roussillon red. There are just over 12ha under vine and output is around 2,500 cases a year, with the objective being to reach 4,000 cases. The first *vendange* was only in 1999. There is a minimalist approach here in the best sense: all vineyard work is carried out as naturally as possible and handling is kept to a minimum in the cellar. Growing conditions are ideal, with sunny days, just sufficient rainfall and superbly drained soils with a layer of *galets roulés* helping to check yields on average at 25–35 hl/ha. Fermentation is traditional and the reds are fully

431

destemmed. The white Baux Blond, from Muscat à Petit Grains, is cool-fermented and aged for 4 months in *inox* with *bâtonnage*. Like the rosé Rouge à Levres it should be drunk young and fresh. The red Velours Rouge is the softest and most immediately accessible of the reds. A blend of Grenache and Syrah, it gets a short ageing in *inox* and because of this is bottled after a light fining and earth filtration. Rouge Gorge blends Syrah and Mourvèdre with some old Grenache (over 35 years) and is aged in old oak for 12 months. The top *vin de pays* Rouge Baux is a rich and opulent blend which adds Cabernet Sauvignon to the Rhône red varietals and gets 12 months in new oak. The Côtes du Roussillon Soleil Rouge is tighter, more restrained and elegant. Low-yielding younger Syrah and Mourvèdre are blended with some of the oldest Grenache. It is aged in a combination of *inox* and older oak. The top reds will comfortably improve for 5 years or more. (DM)

- **Vin de Pays des Côtes Catalanes** Rouge Gorge★★★ £B Rouge Baux★★★ £C
- **Vin de Pays des Côtes Catalanes** Velours Rouge★★ £B
- **Côtes du Roussillon** Soleil★★★ £C
- ◉ **Vin de Pays des Côtes Catalanes** Rouge à lèvres★★ £B
- O **Vin de Pays des Côtes Catalanes** Baux Blond★★ £B

DOM. DU MAS BLANC   Banyuls & Collioure

Jean-Michel Parcé   9 Avenue du Général-de-Gaulle, 66650 Banyuls-sur-Mer
UK stockists: VTr, C&R

Splendid 21-ha Banyuls and Collioure property developed by the late Dr André Parcé and now run by his son Jean-Michel. There are 4 Collioures. La Llose is the regular bottling while there are 3 very fine single-vineyard wines: the Cosprons Levant is an old-vine blend of Mourvèdre, Syrah and Counoise, Clos du Moulin is produced from Mourvèdre and Counoise and Les Junquets is from Syrah with a hint of Roussanne and Marsanne for fragrance. Production of these 3 is small but they are very impressive, refined reds. Some of the very best Banyuls is also created here. There are 2 Rimage bottlings that have spent less time in cask, the sumptuous Cuvée de la Saint-Martin, which has intense, nutty, *rancio* notes and the Hors d'Age de Solera, resembling a great old Oloroso. These are expensive. (DM)

- **Collioure** Cosprons Levant★★★ £C Les Junquets★★★★ £D
- **Collioure** La Llose★★ £B Clos du Moulin★★★ £C
- **Banyuls** Rimage★★★★ £E La Coume★★★★ £F

MAS DE LA DEVÈZE   Côtes du Roussillon-Villages

Anne-Lise & Olivier Bernstein   66720 Tautavel
UK stockists: L&S

This is a recently established property in the Roussillon village of Tautavel producing both red and white. The Bernsteins originate from Burgundy but like others have realised the great potential of the Agly Valley for making light rather than fortified wines of considerable flair and intensity. At their old restored Mas they have installed a brand new winery. The vineyards are planted in a mix of limestone, clay and schistous marl, providing excellent drainage to optimise the intensity of the fruit and provide adequate mineral nourishment. The top red Roussillon a 70/30 blend of Grenache and Syrah is typically intense and minerally while the 66 is a soft, forward brambly red dominated by Grenache. Matured in tank there is just a small portion of Syrah in the blend. The Mas red is aged in oak. The very characterful, barrel-fermented nutty Mas white blends Maccabeu and Grenache Gris in equal amounts. These are well priced wines to watch. (DM)

- **Côtes du Roussillon-Villages**★★★★ £D La 66★★★ £C
- O **Vin de Pays des Pyrénées Orientales**★★★ £C

MAS KAROLINA   Côtes du Roussillon-Villages

Caroline Bonville   29. Bld de 'Agly, 66220 Saint-Paul de Fenouillet
Newly established domaine adding further evidence of the splendid potential of
the wines of the Agly Valley. The vineyards are spread across a number of plots
with soils that include black marls, granite and schist. Vinification is modern
with a pre-fermentation cold soak for the reds, vatting of 3–4 weeks and
malolactic in new oak for the Syrah components. The white is fermented
relatively cool at less than 20°C and both reds and whites are aged on fine lees.
The white comes from 50-year-old Grenache Gris and Maccabeu and from
yields of no more than 20hl/ha. Rich, tropical and quite oaky, it should drink
well young. The Vin de Pays des Côtes Catalanes red is a blend of Carignan
(66%) and Grenache from the black marls of Maury. Ripe and forward, the
wine is full of dark, spicy and brambly fruit. The more backward and seriously
structured Côtes du Roussillon-Villages is a blend of Grenache (56%), Syrah
(34%) and Carignan. The old-vine character of the fruit really shines through
here, with a powerful mineral undercurrent and a hint of the new wood in
which the Syrah is aged. The debut 2003 vintage was right on the edge of
★★★★. Clearly a domaine with great potential. (DM)
- ● **Côtes du Roussillon-Villages**★★★ £D
- ● **Vin de Pays des Côtes Catalanes**★★★ £C
- O **Vin de Pays des Côtes Catalanes**★★ £C

DOM. MATASSA   Vin de Pays des Côtes Catalanes

Tom Lubbe & Sam Harrop   66600 Calce
UK stockists: Adm
Just over 300 cases are made a year at this excellent high altitude property near
the village of Calce in the Agly Valley. A white and red are produced. Tom
Lubbe is also a partner at The OBSERVATORY in South Africa with his sister
Catherine. Much care is lavished on the vineyards and teas are used to treat the
soil helping guard against fungal disease and aid full early ripening. The
Matassa wines like those at the Observatory are marked by their surprisingly
firm, gripping acidity and should develop well in bottle. The white is
dominated by Grenache Gris and is barrel-fermented and aged for around 9
months but without *batonnage*. The red is currently just classified as Vin de
Table because of the tedious bureaucracy of the area and is dominated by
highly characterful very old vine Carignan, full of dark pepper and herbal
spices. Unusually there is around 5% of Grenache Noir, Blanc and Gris
interspersed in the vineyard. Reserved and youthfully tight the red particularly
requires 3 or 4 years at a minimum. (DM)
- ● **Vin de Table** Matassa★★★★ £E
- O **Vin de Pays des Côtes Catalanes** Matassa★★★ £D

DOM. PIÉTRI-GÉRAUD   Banyuls & Collioure

Piétri-Géraud Family   66190 Collioure
UK stockists: **FMV**, BBR
This is a very fine mother-and-daughter domaine producing benchmark
Collioure and Banyuls. As well as an excellent Collioure – one of the best in the
appellation – a white Banyuls and dense Cuvée Joseph Geraud are produced.
The vineyards are planted on steep terraced, schistous slopes, to a combination
of old Grenache and Carignan (the vines are generally above 50 years of age)
and younger Syrah and Mourvèdre. Yields are naturally low, barely 30 hl/ha,
and the wines are generally marked by their style and refinement. In the
Collioure, a blend of Grenache (60%) with Syrah and Mourvèdre, filtration is
avoided. The Banyuls Blanc gets a year in large vats, while the Cuvée Joseph
Geraud sees an extended ageing period of 7 years to bring out more

433

complex, smoky *rancio* characters. The red Collioure will benefit from 4 or 5 years' cellaring. (DM)

● **Collioure**★★★ £C

OLIVIER PITHON   Côtes du Roussillon-Villages

Laurence & Olivier Pithon   66600 Calce
UK stockists:CdP

The Pithons have 9ha of organically tended vineyards spread around the village of Calce, close to Gérard GAUBY. From these they produce 2 reds and 2 whites of impressive style and intensity. Olivier is the brother of Jo PITHON, who is producing similarly exciting results with very different wines in the Coteaux du Layon. The white Lais is a blend of Maccabeu as well as Grenache Blanc and Gris. The D18 differs, being just the 2 Grenache varieties. Both are vinified and aged in a mix of new and used oak from very low yields of barely more than 15hl/ha. The D18 has greater depth and intensity but both offer tremendously stylish nutty southern fruit and impressive structure. The intensely dark and spicy Coulée blends old-vine Carignan and Grenache in equal parts; the more intense and minerally Les Vignes de Saturne has some Syrah as well. Both reds are vinified traditionally with a long 25–30 day maceration and ageing in a mix of small oak and *foudres*. All the wines will evolve well for 4 or 5 years and the Saturne will benefit from a little longer. (DM)

● **Côtes du Roussillon** La Coulée★★★ £C Les Vignes de Saturne★★★★ £D
○ **Côtes du Roussillon** Cuvée Lais★★★ £C Cuvée D18★★★★ £D

DOM. POUDEROUX   Maury

Robert Pouderoux   2 Rue Emile Zola, 66460 Maury
UK stockists: THt

Splendid producer, with a range of not only excellent Côtes du Roussillon reds but some very fine fortified wines as well. Although among the finest of the new wave of red wine producers in the Roussillon, the Poudereaux domaine is no flash in the pan. The family have been involved in Maury viticulture since 1826. Indeed it is this continuity across the last century in particular that is responsible for the splendid raw material available to Robert Poudereaux. His vineyards are planted to Grenache, Syrah, Mourvèdre and Carignan grown on finely drained soils of black and white schist and limestone. There is a first-class barrel-fermented white of real density produced from Grenache Blanc, even in a marginal vintage like 2002 on the edge of ★★★. Among the dry reds Latour de Grès is dense and powerful, marked by the characteristic dark berry and spice complexity of old-vine Carignan. Terre Brune blends Grenache, Syrah and Mourvèdre and gets an extra week of vatting to add depth. Like Latour de Grès it is aged in older barrels. The premium, richly opulent and complex Mouriane also blends Grenache, Syrah and Mourvèdre. Macerated on its skins for a month or more and aged in new oak for a year, it demands 5 years' patience. There is a splendid range of Maury all produced solely from Grenache Noir. Vendange is aged in a combination of *cuve* and bottle until release, The Mise Tardive gets 3 years in barrel, which adds complexity and more tertiary aromas. The top 2 wines are a serious step up. The Hors d'Age gets twelve years in small oak, the Grande Réserve 4 years in a combination of *foudres* and *bonbonnes*. There is also an excellent fortified Muscat, grown on schistous soils. Rich and opulent it is in complete contrast to the Maury reds with ripe, fresh grapey character. (DM)

● **Côtes du Roussillon-Villages** Terre Brune★★★ £C Mouriane★★★★ £E
● **Côtes du Roussillon-Villages** Latour de Grès★★★ £B
● **Maury** Vendange★★★ £C Mise Tardive★★★ £C Hors d'Age★★★★ £D

● **Maury** Grande Reserve★★★★ £E   O **Côtes du Roussillon-Villages★★** £C
O **Muscat de Rivesaltes★★★** £D

DOM. PUIG-PARAHŸ   Côtes du Roussillon

Georges Puig-Parahÿ   Le Fort de Saint-Pierre, 66300 Passa

Georges Puig-Parahÿ's domaine is sizeable in comparison to those of his like-minded, quality-conscious neighbours. This however is relative, certainly in comparison to the New World because Georges produces a vast total of some 8,000–9,000 cases a year! The Puig family have been involved in Roussillon viticulture since the phylloxera crisis in France in 1878 and as a result own some remarkable old-vine holdings. Grenache is up to 80 years old, Carignan as much as 130. Syrah and Mourvèdre are also now planted to produce modern-style wines. There is a good, clean and fresh, impressively grapey Muscat Vin de Pays but more serious are the Sant Lluc and Miserys whites blended from Grenache Blanc and Gris. The former is vinified *en cuve;* the latter in a combination of tank and new oak. With low yields in well-drained argilo-calcaire soils the 3 Côtes du Roussillon reds are of good to very good quality. Mes Amis is mainly Carignan and Grenache but has marvellous old-vine character – not complex but exciting. Georges is similarly aged in *cuve* but is more serious and structured, containing Grenache, Syrah and Mourvèdre as well as Carignan. The top 2 *cuvées*, Le Fort de Saint-Pierre and Ballides, are both ageworthy. The former is aged in *cuve,* the latter in *barrique*. The Saint-Pierre is the better balanced, its beguiling fruit offering great class and purity. A range of exciting fortifieds are available to taste at the domaine. (DM)

● **Côtes du Roussillon** Le Fort Saint-Pierre★★★ £C Ballides★★★ £D
● **Côtes du Roussillon** Mes Amis★★ £B Georges★★★ £B
O **Vin de Pays d'Oc** Sant Lluc★★ £B Miserys★★ £B
O **Vin de Pays d'Oc** Muscat Sec★ £B

DOM. DE LA RECTORIE   Banyuls & Collioure

Parcé Frères   54 Avenue du Puig-Delmas, 66650 Banyuls-sur-Mer
UK stockists: A&B,Bal,Cam

One of the finest producers of Collioure and Banyuls. There are 3 *cuvées* of red Collioure and a presentable rosé. Of the reds Col de Bast is the lightest and made from 100% Grenache, whereas the denser and more structured La Coume Pascole is a blend of Grenache, Syrah and Carignan. The sturdiest of the 3, Le Seris is produced from very old Carignan and Grenache vines. Even the latter 2 are not in any way overblown; they are more wines of refinement and elegance. These are complemented by a white *vin de pays*, L'Argile, a powerfully oaked Grenache Gris. Very good Banyuls includes 2 regular *cuvées* – the best is Cuvée Léon Parcé, which is aged for around a year in cask and an altogether different, less evolved style to that found at MAS BLANC – and an aged wine, L'Oublée, which is understandably pricey. (DM)

● **Collioure** Col de Bast★★ £B La Coume Pascole★★★ £D Le Seris★★★ £C
● **Banyuls** Cuvée Léon Parcé★★★ £C
O **Vin de Pays de la Côte Vermeille** L'Argile★★★ £C

DOM. DES SCHISTES   Côtes du Roussillon-Villages

Jacques Sire   1 Avenue Jean-Lurçat, 66310 Estagel
UK stockists: FMV, BBR, P&S, ACh

A small, first-class range of both table and fortified wines is produced at this 44-ha property. The reds are characterised by the old-vine quality of the fruit, which adds an extra dimension. Indeed some of the oldest vines are approaching 80 years. Tradition is a forward, fruit-driven style blended from Syrah, Grenache and Carignan and vinified both traditionally and with some carbonic maceration. Les Terrasses is produced from the same varieties but with

435

a higher proportion of Syrah aged in 1-year-old oak, the balance in *cuve*. Stylish and intense, there is a real mineral quality running through the wine. La Coumeille, the top red, is 100% Syrah, aged in oak of which only a small portion is new and the wine is very fine with a really spicy, dark, intense fruit quality. There's a lovely nutty and raisiny Maury and a very good floral yet powerful and concentrated Muscat de Rivesaltes. (DM)

- ● **Côtes du Roussillon-Villages** Les Terrasses★★★ £C   La Coumeille★★★ £C
- ● **Côtes du Roussillon-Villages** Tradition★★ £B
- ● **Maury** Cerisaie★★★ £C   O **Muscat de Rivesaltes**★★★ £B

DOM. SEGUELA   Côtes du Roussillon-Villages

Trinidad & Jean-Pierre Seguela   12 Avenue de Caramany, 66720 Rasiguères
UK stockists:GVF,May

Production is small at this dedicated Roussillon producer, with a total of less than 3,000 cases made annually. Yields are kept very low, fruit is carefully sorted prior to vinification and in the cellar filtration is avoided. What marks these wines out is the depth and purity of their fruit. Increasingly they are matching the structure of the very best. Les Condalies is a blend mainly of Carignan but with some Syrah and Grenache also. Soft easy tannins and spicy brambly fruit mark the style of the wine, which is excellent value. Cuvée Jean-Julien is a dense old-vine blend of Syrah and Carignan partly aged in new oak (but this is seamlessly handled), while the Planète-Seguela is an astonishingly low-yielding (as low as 12 hl/ha) *assemblage* of Carignan, Syrah, Grenache and Cinsault and is refined, long and well-structured. (DM)

- ● **Côtes du Roussillon-Villages** Planète-Seguela★★★★ £E
- ● **Côtes du Roussillon-Villages** Les Condalies★★★£B   Cuvée Jean-Julien★★★ £C

DOM. DE LA SERRE   Maury

Jean-Louis Vera & Yves Blanc   66460 Maury

Among the larger of the new wave of domaines in the Agly Valley. There are 20ha planted at Maury and a further 10ha of Syrah around the village of Cassagnes. The vines range from 25–120 years of age and the complex old-vine character of the Grenache and Carignan at Maury is reflected in the wines. Quality is key here. Consultant Bordeaux winemaker Daniel Bonnet (who advises various domaines in the region) ensures that all the grapes are sorted prior to fermentation and 100% new oak is being used for ageing all 3 wines. Each is blended from Grenache, Carignan and Syrah. The 2002 Serre Longue came in at a whopping 16% alcohol but such is the ripeness and firm mineral structure that the wine remains balanced. Hypogée posseses that extra depth and dimension. Firmly, structured and very complex. Most expensive is the tiny production Cuvée Pierre Levée. Expect the wines to develop well in bottle over at least 5–7 years. (DM)

- ● **Côtes du Roussillon-Villages** Serre Longue★★★★ £C   Hypogee★★★★ £D

DOM. SERRELONGUE   Maury

Julien Fournier   149 Avenue Jean Jaurès, 66460 Maury

Tiny domaine producing exquisite wines from a small holding of just 5ha. The vineyards are planted to a combination of Mourvèdre, Syrah, Carignan and Grenache and vine age ranges from 20–120 years. This combined with high-altitude vineyards and a committed approach to reducing yields results in wines of remarkable depth and purity. Do not expect fruit bombs, the overriding character here is minerality, with subtle deeply spicy black fruits and an intensity rarely found in the Midi. The Extrait de Passion blends Grenache with Mourvèdre and is aged in *demi-muids*. The Esprit de Vin also has a proportion of Syrah and seems to have that small extra dimension on the palate. These are beguiling wines, full-bodied and rampantly alcoholic but balanced too. (DM)

● **Côtes du Roussillon-Villages** Extrait de Passion★★★★ £D Esprit de Vin★★★★★ £E

DOM. DES SOULANES   Maury

Cathy & Daniel Laffite   Mas de Las Fredas, 66720 Tautavel

This is another recently established operation in the vineyards of the Roussillon. Based at Tautavel in the heart of Côtes du Roussillon, 2 of the the wines here take the Vin de Pays des Côtes Catalanes classification. They will also be producing Côtes du Roussillon-Villages and Maury fortifieds. The Laffites have 17 hectares spread across 18 diverse parcels with their Grenache and Carignan planted in a mix of schistous soils. The red Jean Pull is a soft, ripe and brambly style with 35% Carignan as well as Grenache. A rich opulent character to the fruit is ensured through low yields and old vines. The Cuvée Bastoul-Laffite is sturdier, firmer and will develop extremely well in bottle. The spicy and exotic Sarrat del Mas is aged in new oak. Yields here are barely 20 hl/ha and the wines are bottled unfiltered. The Maury is one of the best in the AC. A domaine to watch.(DM)

● **Vin de Pays des Côtes Catalanes** Cuvée Bastoul-Laffite★★★★ £C
● **Vin de Pays des Côtes Catalanes** Cuvée Jean Pull★★★ £B
● **Côtes du Roussillon-Villages** Cuvée Sarrat del Mas★★★★ £D

DOM. DU TRAGINER   Banyuls & Collioure

Jean-François Deu   56 Avenue du Puig del Mas, 66650 Banyuls-sur-Mer
UK stockists: **SVS**

A fine range of Banyuls and improving Collioures are produced at this small 9ha property. Red varieties Mourvèdre, Syrah, Grenache and Carignan are planted along with Grenache Blanc and Gris as well as Muscat. The vineyards are planted on schistous soils and since 1997 have been farmed organically. Jean-François Deu is the only remaining Banyuls grower to plough his vineyards by mule; indeed his name means mule driver in Catalan. There is a very good white Collioure which is fermented relatively cool and aged in *cuve*, with piercing spicy, citrus fruit. The red Collioures are traditionally vinified with a maceration on the skins of 25 days. The Traditionelle is aged in *foudre*, Al Riberal in 1- to 5-year-old *barriques* and the Octobre and the top label Cuvée de Capitas in new and 1-year-old barrels. The wines took a real step up in the 2001 vintage. Full of dark spicy fruit the Octobre and Cuvée de Capitas are impressively structured and ageworthy. Like PIÉTRI-GÉRAUD, Traginer is one of the few remaining producers of a Banyuls Blanc. Blended from Grenache Blanc, Grenache Gris and Muscat à Petit Blancs, the wine has a marked floral as well as grapey character with considerably more intensity than you would generally find in white Port. Of the red Banyuls the Rimage is marked by its fresh berry fruit and is bottled after 7 months. Mise Tardive is aged in *foudre* for 30 months and has a notably evolved nutty character. Best of all though, the Grand Cru Hors d'Age is aged for at least 10 years in *demi-muid*. It is rich and toffeed with real depth and intensity. (DM)

● **Collioure** Octobre★★★ £C Cuvée de Capitas★★★ £C
● **Collioure** Traditionelle★★ £B Al Riberal★★ £B
● **Banyuls** Mise Tardive★★★ £C Rimage★★★ £C Grand Cru Hors d'Age★★★★ £E
○ **Collioure**★★ £B ○ **Banyuls** Mise Tardive★★ £C

DOM. VAQUER   Vin de Pays des Côtes Catalanes

Vaquer family   1. rue des Écoles, 66300 Tresserre
UK stockists: **GCW**

Some fine traditional wines, often radically different from many of the region's

437

new wave wines, are made at this long-established domaine, including outstanding Rivesaltes. Vinification is traditional and the red wines are aged in *cuve* with no use of new oak. Of the whites the Esquisse is an attractively floral, lightly nutty 100% Roussanne. More serious is the white l'Exception, a blend of Grenache Blanc and Maccabeu, just over a third of which is vinified in new oak. The oak is just a touch raw in the wine's youth, so give it a couple of years. The rosé L'Éphimère is a blend of Carignan and Syrah. Fuller and richer than most of its kind, it is marked by concentrated bright crushed berries. Of the reds the Cuvée Bernard Vaquer is the softest, a supple and forward Carignan-dominated wine. The denser, more structured Exigence is 100% Grenache. Arguably the most characterful of the reds is L'Expression, a Carignan from old vines of very impressive density and structure. It smacks of rich, dark, spicy, minerally varietal fruit with great complexity. The L'Exception red is Grenache and Syrah blend. While rich and reasonably concentrated it lacks the sheer character of the L'Expression. Of the fortifieds there is a fine Muscat de Rivesaltes as well as 2 fine Rivesaltes. L'Extrait is the more fruit forward, while the Tuilé Post Scriptum is aged for around 6 years in *cuve* and has a classic nutty *rancio* character. A Vieux Rivesaltes is also produced in very limited quantities. (DM)

- ● **Vin de Pays des Côtes Catalanes** L'Expression★★★ £D L'Exception★★★ £D
- ● **Vin de Pays des Côtes Catalanes** Exigence★★★ £C Bernard Vaquer★★ £B
- O **Vin de Pays des Côtes Catalanes** L'Exception★★★ £C Esquisse★★ £B
- ◉ **Vin de Pays des Côtes Catalanes** L'Éphimère★★ £B
- ● **Rivesaltes** L'Extrait★★ £C Tuilé Post Scriptum★★★ £C
- O **Muscat de Rivesaltes**★★ £C

Also see the following Rhône *négociants* with an entry in the section *Rhône Valley:*

M CHAPOUTIER
JEAN-LUC COLOMBO
TARDIEU-LAURENT

ROUSSILLON OTHER WINES OF NOTE

DOM. ARGUTI ● **Vin de Pays des Côtes de Catalanes**★★★ £C
O **Vin de Pays des Côtes de Catalanes**★★★ £C
CH. AYMERICH ● **Côtes du Roussillon** Jean Aymerich★★ £B
● **Côtes du Roussillon** Général Aymerich★★ £C
● **Côtes du Roussillon** Estang Poulée★★ £C Tradition★★ £B
O **Muscat de Rivesaltes**★★ £C
CH. PLANÈRES ● **Côtes du Roussillon**★★ £B
DOM. DE L'ETERNEL ● **Côtes du Roussillon** Cuvée Elsa★★★ £D
DOM. FERRER-RIBIÈRE ● **Côtes du Roussillon** Cana★★★ £D Sélénae★★★ £C
DOM. FORÇA-REAL ● **Côtes du Roussillon-Villages**★★ £B
● **Rivesaltes** Hors d'Age★★ £B
DOM. JOLIETTE ● **Côtes du Roussillon-Villages** André Mercier★★ £B
DOM. LAPORTE ● **Côtes du Roussillon** Domitia★★ £B
LA PRÉCEPTORIE DE CENTERNACH ● **Vin de Pays** Terre Promise★★ £B
L'ETOILE ● **Banyuls** Extra Vieux★★★ £D
DOM. L'HÉRITIER ● **Côtes du Roussillon** Romani★★★ £C
DOM MARCEVOL ● **Côtes du Roussillon**★★ £B Prestige★★★ £C
MAS CRÉMAT ● **Côtes du Roussillon**★★ £B Fût de Chêne★★★ £C
MAS JANEIL ● **Côtes du Roussillon-Villages**★★★ £C
DOM. DE LA PERTUISANE ● **Côtes du Roussillon** La Pertuisane★★★ £D
ROC DES ANGES ● **Côtes du Roussillon-Villages**★★★ £C
● **Vin de Pays des Pyrenées Orientales** Carignan 1903★★★ £C

DOM. SARDA-MALET ● **Côtes du Roussillon** Réserve★★★ £C
● **Côtes du Roussillon** Terroir Mailloles★★★ £D
DOM. VIAL-MAGNÈRES ● **Banyuls** Vintage★★★ £C

Work in progress!!

Producers under consideration for the next edition
DOM. D'ARFEUILLE (VIN DE PAYS DES CÔTEAUX DES FENOUILLÈDES)
DOM. GRAIN D'ORIENT (V DE P DES CÔTEAUX DES FENOUILLÈDES)
DOM. TERRE ROUSSE (MAURY)

Author's choice (DM)
A selection of fortifieds
CELLIER DES TEMPLIERS ● **Banyuls Grand Cru** Henri Vidal
DOM. CAZES ● **Rivesaltes** Ambré
COUME DEL MAS ● **Banyuls** Quintessence
LES CLOS DE PAULILLES ● **Banyuls** Rimage Mise Tardive
DOM. FONTANEL ● **Rivesaltes**
DOM. LA TOUR VIEILLE ● **Banyuls** Cuvée Francis Cantié
MAS AMIEL ● **Maury** Charles Dupuy
DOM. DU MAS BLANC ● **Banyuls** La Coume
DOM. DES SCHISTES O **Muscat de Rivesaltes**

Classic Rousillon reds
DOM. CALVET-THUNEVIN ● **Côtes du Roussillon-Villages** Hugo
DOM. DE CASENOVE ● **Côtes du Roussillon** Commandant François Jaubert
CLOS DEL REY ● **Côtes du Roussillon-Villages** Clos del Rey
DOM. DU CLOS DES FÉES ● **Côtes du Roussillon-Villages** La Petite Sibérie
DOM. FONTANEL ● **Côtes du Roussillon-Villages** Prieuré
DOM. GARDIES ● **Côtes du Roussillon-Villages** La Torre
DOM. GAUBY O **Vin de Pays de Côtes Catalanes** Coume Gineste
DOM. LA TOUR VIEILLE ● **Collioure** Puig Oriol
CLOT DE L'OUM ● **Côtes du Roussillon-Villages** Numero Uno
DOM. DEPEYRE ● **Côtes du Roussillon-Villages** Sainte-Colombe
DOM. DE LA RECTORIE ● **Collioure** La Coume Pascole
DOM. LE SOULA ● **Vin de Pays des Côteaux des Fenouillèdes** Le Soula
DOM. MATASSA ● **Vin de Table** Matassa
MAS DE LA DEVEZE ● **Côtes du Roussillon-Villages**
DOM. POUDEROUX ● **Côtes du Roussillon-Villages** Mouriane

A value for money selection
CH. DE CALADROY ● **Côtes du Roussillon-Villages** La Cour Carrée
DOM. DE CASENOVE ● **Côtes du Roussillon** Garrigue
CLOS DEL REY ● **Vin de Pays d'Oc** Mas del Tey
CH. DE JAU ● **Côtes du Roussillon-Villages** Talon Rouge
DOM. FONTANEL ● **Côtes du Roussillon-Villages** Cistes
LES CLOS DE PAULILLES ● **Côllioure**
DOM. JOREL ● **Vin de Pays d'Oc** Grenache Pesquies
DOM. LA TOUR VIEILLE ● **Collioure** Puig Oriol
DOM. LAGUERRE ● **Côtes du Roussillon** Le Ciste
MAS DES BAUX ● **Vin de Pays des Côtes Catalanes** Rouge Gorge
DOM. PIETRI-GERAUD ● **Collioure**
MAS KAROLINA ● **Vin de Pays des Côtes Catalanes**

LANGUEDOC & ROUSSILLON

RECOMMENDED HOTELS AND RESTAURANTS - LANGUEDOC_ROUSSILLON

Top Hotels

★★★★★*Le Jardin des Sens*   11 ave. St-Lazare, Montpellier 34000
Tel. 04 99 58 38 38 Fax 04 99 58 38 39
Email contact@jardindessens.com   14 rooms   £D/G

★★★★★*Hôtel de la Cité*   pl. Église, Carcassonne 11000
Tel. 04 68 71 98 71 Fax 04 68 71 50 15
Email reservations@hoteldelacite.com   32 rooms   £H

Top Restaurants

★★★★★*Le Jardin des Sens*   11 ave. St-Lazare, Montpellier 34000
Tel. 04 99 58 38 38 Fax 04 99 58 38 39
Email contact@jardindessens.com   £H

★★★★*Auberge du Vieux Puits*   Fontjoncouse 11360
Tel. 04 68 44 07 37 Fax 04 68 44 08 31
Email aubergeduvieuxpuyits@wanadoo.fr   £E/G

Value for money Hotels

★★★*Renaissance*   17 rue Victor Hugo, Castres 81100
Tel. 05 63 59 30 42 Fax 05 63 72 11 57
No email address   20 rooms   £A/B

★*Ribes*   Prats-de-Mollo-la-Preste 66230
Tel. 04 68 39 71 04 Fax 04 68 39 78 02
Email hotel.ribers@free.fr   24 rooms   £A

Value for money restaurants

★*Banyols et Banyols*   7, rue Cardeurs, Perpignan 66000
Tel. 04 68 34 48 40 Fax 04 68 51 25 99
No email address   £A/B

★*L'Os à Moelle*   route Salles d'Aude, Coursan 11110
Tel. 04 68 33 55 72 Fax 04 68 33 35 39
No email address   £A/B

LANGUEDOC-ROUSILLON RECIPES

CRABE A LA LANGUEDOCIENNE

For 4 people, you need either a large crab weighing 1kg. or 300gr. of white crab meat, and 100gr. of crab soft brown meat. 3 eggs, a coffee spoon of mustard, salt and pepper. 2 cloves of garlic, a teaspoon of tomato purée, a squeeze of lemon juice (to taste) 2dl. of olive oil, two tablespoon of boiling water, salt and pepper to taste.

If you are using an uncooked crab, cook it in a *court bouillon* made with one large onion, 2 carrots, celery leaves, 5 cloves of garlic a **bouquet garni**, (parsley, a bay leaf, a sprig of thyme, a zest of lemon), 1dl. of wine vinegar; 2dl. of white wine and enough water to cover the crab.

Cook the *court bouillon* for at least 20mn. until vegetables are quite cooked and plunge the crab into it. Bring to the boil and cook for 10 to 15mns. Turn off the heat and let the crab cool in the court bouillon. Soft boil the eggs but the white must be hard. Cool down and peel. Extract all the white meat from the claws Open the hard shell on top by separating the carcass from the clawless body (the clawless body also contains a lot of white meat if you have the patience to extract it!) Extract all the soft roe and brown meat. Put the brown meat and roe in a blender or in a bowl, add two of the eggs and the yolk of the third. Keep the white. Add the mustard, tomato purée, the crushed cloves of garlic and start beating or blending like a mayonnaise by adding the olive oil little by little. Half way through, add salt and pepper, and a squeeze of lemon; carry on adding oil and right at the end add the two spoons of boiling water, mix once more and leave. Mix the white meat with this mayonnaise, leaving a few spoonfuls to coat the surface once you put it in a nice bowl to serve. Sprinkle the shredded remaining white of egg and chopped parsley on top and you can also sprinkle a pinch of paprika to give it colour.

RECOMMENDED WINES

This is a chance to get to grips with some of the intensely flavoured whites of the far south, although it's best to avoid the dry Muscats with this dish and the Chardonnays from the area are generally a little too lightweight. The Vin de Pays des Pyranées Orientales from Mas de la Devèze in the Agly Valley, a blend of Maccabeau and Grenache Gris would suit this dish very well and is very reasonably priced and for (quite) a bit more money, you could go for the Vin de Pays de l'Hérault from Mas de Daumas Gassac - a 5 star blend of enormous structure.

CASSOULET

For 4 people: *Ingredients:* 500gr. of white beans: soaked over night. 300gr. Toulouse sausages, 300gr. unsmoked streaky bacon in one piece if possible, with the rind on, 500gr. of duck or goose **confit,** 500gr. of boned shoulder of lamb, one large carrot peeled and sliced, 3 cloves of chopped garlic, two big onions studded with a clove, one **bouquet garni** (bay leaf, sprig of thyme, parsley marjoram and/or rosemary), 2 dessertspoons of tomato purée, breadcrumbs, salt & pepper.

Drain the beans, put in a large saucepan with the onion studded with cloves, the sliced carrots, **bouquet garni,** 2 chopped cloves of garlic, and the streaky bacon. Cover with water and cook on a very low flame for two hours or until cooked, seasoning with salt and pepper half way through. You can make the **confit** and cook the lamb together at the same time. To make the **confit**, chop the last onion, clove of garlic and carrot, sauté them in duck fat, lard or butter, and add the pieces of duck or goose (the best part for the **confit** are the legs and thighs with skin and fat attached); add the lamb and just cover with half white wine and half water, season well, add some thyme and a bay leaf and simmer well covered until almost cooked. Slice the Toulouse sausages and sauté them as well, and add to the meat; cook together for the last 30 minutes. When the beans are cooked, add the tomato purée, rectify seasoning and roughly cut the streaky bacon. To serve, put a layer of beans in an earthenware dish, followed by a layers of meat and beans alternately. Finish with breadcrumbs and glaze.

RECOMMENDED WINES

This is a big flavoured dish that needs a big flavoured red wine and these days there are enough producers in the Languedoc to provide that with a large dose of class. A small caveat, however, is to find wines with sufficient bottle age to really enjoy, as many of them are so well structured, they may need at least five years to come round. That said, the Vin de Pays de l'Hérault from the Domaine de la Grange des Pères is surprisingly approachable in its youth, possibly because of the element of Cabernet Sauvignon therein. The Domaine Terre Inconnue, in the Gard, produces three stunning Vins de Table with super ripe fruit in tiny quantities – it's a real "garagiste" operation which is certainly worth seeking out.

COCA FOUGASSE

For 6 people: *Ingredients:* 250gr cake flour, 250gr. caster sugar, 1 teaspoon baking powder (or use self-raising flour), 2 teaspoons of cinnamon, 2 large eggs, 2.5dl milk, half dl. oil, 2 small lemons. Break the eggs in a bowl, add sugar and oil and the zests of the two lemons; beat well then gradually add the sieved flour with baking powder then very slowly the milk to obtain a very smooth almost liquid paste. Butter a round cake tin and butter a greaseproof paper on both sides with which you line the mould. Pour the mixture in the mould; sprinkle the cinnamon over the top. Cook on a medium heat for approx. 30 minutes, let the cake rest for 10ms. before unmoulding. Serve cool.

RECOMMENDED WINES

This is just the job for a Muscat de Rivesaltes or a Banyuls. There is good value Muscat de Rivesaltes to be had from Domaine Cazes, whilst the top quality (and price) Banyuls from Domaine de Mas Blanc will take a lot of beating.

441

Provence has emerged in recent years with a number of exciting high quality small domaines from most of her appellations. The change has been less dramatic than in the Midi, but here too many quality-minded individuals are bringing a new focus to viticulture and expressing the potential of their terroirs. The role of Provence as a purveyor of easy-drinking pink plonk to sun-seeking tourists is gradually changing and indeed many of the examples are much improved. However the overall importance of moderate quality rosé in the region's wine production is still depressingly high. Some interesting wines and fortified styles are emerging from Corsica although the wines remain hard to find outside France. In the main they continue to be traditional and fairly rustic.

Provence and Corsica

While rosé remains the mainstay of Provençal wine production, exciting reds and some very well-made whites have emerged over the last fifteen years or so. In the foothills of the Alpes-Maritimes inland of Nice the tiny appellation of **Bellet,** with a total of a mere 39ha under vine, offers some unusual albeit pricey, well-structured reds and lightly floral nutty whites and fruity rosés. The proximity of neighbouring Italy shows itself with the Braquet (Brachetto) among the varieties that make up the permitted red blend, along with Folle Noir and the more usual Grenache and Cinsault. The vineyards are planted at altitude of some 300m, moderating the climate.This provides an unusual opportunity in ripening Chardonnay in such a southerly maritime climate, which in the whites is blended with Rolle.

The vast bulk of central Provence is covered by the appellations of **Côtes de Provence** and **Coteaux Varois**. While both produce vast amounts of glugging rosé, some very impressive reds are being produced from blends of Rhône varieties, some with the addition of Cabernet Sauvignon. The **Coteaux d'Aix en Provence** and the spectacularly sited vineyards of **Les Baux de Provence** produce similar wines. Domaine de Trevallon, now forced to label its wine as Vin de Pays des Bouches du Rhône, set the trend with a stunning blend of Cabernet and Syrah. There are a number of other such blends now; some like Trevallon use more traditional ageing in large vats while others are seduced by new oak. Whatever the approach an exciting array of different styles is emerging.

Palette is another tiny AC of just 40ha for both red and white and with only two established producers, although others are emerging. Château Crémade has yet to challenge Château Simone, thus far the only producer of wines of real quality. An extensive number of varieties can be planted but increasingly replanting is concentrated on Syrah, Grenache and Mourvèdre.

The two coastal appellations of **Cassis** and **Bandol** between Marseilles and Toulon are sources of red, white and rosé. Generally Cassis tends to be pretty dull fare but there is the odd impressive white. The best whites and rosés from Bandol are good but it is the reds that you should look out for. The appellation is situated in the foothills just inland of the port of Bandol in a natural coastal amphitheatre. The vineyards stretch from La Ciotat in the east to Sanary-sur-Mer in the west and enjoy a unique warm, dry maritime climate. The style of the wine itself varies surprisingly due to differing calcareous, gravel and clay soils and varying levels of Mourvèdre, the main grape variety. Established Bandol leaders Domaine Tempier and Château Pibarnon are now being joined by a new wave of small, high-quality growers. This is an exciting area to follow. Remember, though, that these wines need cellaring, often for up to a decade.

There are three main appellations on the island of Corsica; **Vin de Corse**, **Patrimonio** and **Ajaccio**. Almost all viticulture is carried out around the coast. The forested, mountainous interior is far too extreme for viticulture. There are also a number of *crus* within the Vin de Corse appellation: **Calvi**, **Sartène**, **Figari**, **Porto-Vecchio** and **Coteaux du Cap Corse**. Both Coteaux du Cap Corse and Patrimonio are entitled to the Muscat du Cap Corse appellation and it is some of these good to very good rich fortified Muscats which offer the greatest excitement here. Some good reds, albeit somewhat rustic, are also produced from the native Nielluccio along with Grenache, Carignan and Cinsault.

Provence & Corsica vintages

It is extremely difficult in a large region such as Provence to make specific vintage assessments. However, there have been significant changes in vintage conditions from one year to another throughout the region. These variations are more pronounced as you move further inland. Bandol, particularly, has a very benign maritime climate and is reasonably consistent.

The more established Provençal red appellations have consistently produced wines that develop well with age. Bandol, particularly, with its high percentage of the structured and noble Mourvèdre, is a very ageworthy red. Among the top older years for premium Provençal reds (mainly Bandol) are 1989, 1988, 1985, 1982, 1978, 1975 and 1970.

The whites throughout the area are generally intended for drinking young, although the best traditional examples from the likes of Château Simone in Palette will keep for a decade.

Provence vintage chart

	Bandol	Côtes de Provence Top Reds	Les Baux de Provence Top Reds
2004	★★★/★★★★ A	★★★/★★★★ A	★★★/★★★★ A
2003	★★★★ A	★★★/★★★★ A	★★★/★★★★ A
2002	★★★ A	★★★ A	★★★ A
2001	★★★★ A	★★★★ A	★★★★ A
2000	★★★★/★★★★★ A	★★★★/★★★★★ B	★★★★/★★★★★ A
1999	★★★★ A	★★★★ B	★★★★ B
1998	★★★★/★★★★★ A	★★★★/★★★★★ B	★★★★/★★★★★ B
1997	★★★/★★★★ B	★★★ C	★★★ C
1996	★★★/★★★★ B	★★★/★★★★ C	★★★/★★★★ C
1995	★★★/★★★★ C	★★★/★★★★ C	★★★/★★★★ C
1994	★★★ C	★★★ D	★★★ C
1993	★★★/★★★★ C	★★/★★★ D	★★/★★★ D
1991	★★★/★★★★ C	★★★ D	★★★ D
1990	★★★★★ B	★★★★★ D	★★★★★ C

443

A-Z of producers by appellation

Provence

1	Les Baux de Provence
2	Coteaux d'Aix en Provence
3	Palette
4	Côtes de Provence
5	Coteaux Varois
6	Cassis
7	Bandol
8	Bellet

A-Z of producers

DOM. DES BÉATES   Coteaux d'Aix-en-Provence

Pierre-François Terrat   Route de Caireval, 13410 Lambesc
UK stockists: Men

Biodynamic operation that attracted the interest of Michel CHAPOUTIER of the Rhône Valley in the late 1990s, although that interest was sold in 2002. Three labels are now produced here. The soft, fruity Les Béatines red, white and rosé are easygoing, drink-me-now styles. The superior Domaines des Béates and Terra d'Or labels are blends of Cabernet Sauvignon, Syrah and Grenache. The Domaine label is structured, dense and powerful but with supple, well-rounded, ripe tannin. It will develop well in the medium term. The fruit from the oldest vines, which are around 45 years old, is reserved for the top *cru*, Terra d'Or, which is a serious step up. Vinified and aged in new oak, it is surprisingly approachable but rich and concentrated with a velvety texture. Complex dark berry fruit, herbal spice and subtle oak are all seamlessly integrated. (DM)

- **Coteaux d'Aix-en-Provence** Béates★★★ £C Terra d'Or★★★★ £E
- **Coteaux d'Aix-en-Provence** Les Béatines★ £B

DOM. DE LA BÉGUDE   Bandol   domainestari@wanadoo.fr

Guillaume Tari   83330 Le Camp du Castellet
UK stockists: GCW

This dramatically improving Bandol domaine is now producing some of the more exciting wines in the appellation. It is ideally situated at the highest point of the AC at an altitude of 430 metres. The estate itself is substantial but a mere 16ha are planted to vines as olive groves are also an important constituent. The vineyard is now around 30 years of age and this helps in keeping yields naturally down to 30h/ha or less. A red, a white and a rosé are produced. The rosé is a blend of all the red varieties here, namely Mourvèdre, Cinsault, Grenache and Carignan. It is one of the very best examples of the style and has the structure to develop well for 2 or 3 years. Quality has improved dramatically over the last 3 years. The white Bandol is a barrel-fermented blend of Clairette, Ugni Blanc and Rolle. The red is dominated by Mourvèdre (90%), with the balance Grenache. The wine is now less extracted during maceration and the fruit is increasingly stylish and well defined. It is bottled unfiltered and will evolve well for 7–10 years. (DM)

- **Bandol★★★★** £D   **O Bandol★★★** £C   **◉ Bandol★★** £C

DOMAINES BUNAN   Bandol   www.bunan.com

Bunan Family   83740 La Cadière-d'Azur
UK stockists: Yap

One of the longest-established producers in the appellation, the Bunan family arrived in Bandol in 1961. The family business is run to this day by Paul Bunan and his son Laurent, who has gained an international perspective having worked in California. The focal point of production here is Bandol from 3 estates. Along with the reds, both white and rosé are produced at all 3 estates and these are sound examples of the appellation, the whites fermented cool in stainless steel to emphasise their fruit. In addition to this there is a Côtes de Provence property, Domaine Belouve, producing solid red, white and rosé. Three generic Bandols are produced under the Domaines Bunan label but it is the estate reds that are the real excitement. The Mas de La Rouvière and Moulin des Costes regular bottling are the lighter wines. Moulin des Costes gets a slightly longer vatting and has Grenache as well as Mourvèdre, Cinsault and Syrah, which comprise the Mas de La Rouvière blend. The Moulin des Costes offers slightly more spicy, peppery characters but both will develop well

445

with 5 years' ageing. The Château de la Rouvière is richer, more complete, sourced from a single plot of just over 2.5ha. Dense, spicy dark fruit and truffles are defined in its impressive fruit. Firmly tannic in its youth, it demands 6 or 7 years' patience. The top wine, Cuvée Charriage, is the richest and lushest of the wines. Vinified with cold maceration and extended maceration of up to a month, it is structured but supple and should be very fine with 8–10 years' cellaring. (DM)

Château de La Rouvière
● **Bandol★★★★** £D

Moulin des Costes
● **Bandol★★★** £C Cuvée Charriage★★★★ £E
Mas de la Rouvière
● **Bandol★★★** £C

CH. BAS Coteaux d'Aix-en-Provence

Georges de Blanquet   13116 Vernègues
Sizeable property producing sound to very good red, white and rosé under the Coteaux d'Aix-en-Provence appellation. There are 72ha of vines on the estate with 64ha planted to reds and production is now over 30,000 cases a year. Three separate ranges, L'Alvernègue, Pierre du Sud and Cuvée du Temple, all include a red, a white and a rosé. The L'Alvernègue wines are soft, forward and fruit-driven. The red offers a little structure and grip, although it should be drunk young. The Pierre du Sud wines are a step up in quality, with well-defined fruit character, and are also for drinking young – although the red will stand short ageing. The Cuvée du Temple wines are of a different order. The rosé is part barrel-fermented and has surprising depth and structure for the style. The red, a blend of Syrah, Cabernet Sauvignon and Grenache, has impressive depth. Richly texured with subtle spicy undertones, it should be aged for 3 or 4 years at least. Perhaps the standout wine here is the barrel-fermented white, blended from Sauvignon Blanc, Rolle and Grenache Blanc. Subtle use of oak and very pure citrus and herb spice fruit are supported by a rich creamy finish. While the wine drinks very well young it will also stand a little age. (DM)

● **Coteaux d'Aix-en-Provence** Pierre du Sud★★ £B Cuvée du Temple★★★ £C
● **Coteaux d'Aix-en-Provence** L'Alvernègue★ £B
○ **Coteaux d'Aix-en-Provence** Pierre du Sud★ £B Cuvée du Temple★★★ £B
◉ **Coteaux d'Aix-en-Provence** Pierre du Sud★ £B Cuvée du Temple★★ £B

CH. DE BELLET Bellet chateaudebellet@aol.com

Ghislain de Charnacé   Quartier Saint-Roman, 440 Route de Saquier, 06200 Nice
One of a handful of properties in the tiny appellation of Bellet in the Provençal hills inland of Nice. As at neighbouring CHATEAU DE CRÉMAT, a red, white and rosé are produced. Because the vineyards are in a protected *mesoclimate* and planted at altitude, they are cooler than their southerly location would suggest. This enables Chardonnay to ripen successfully as well as the local Rolle that completes the white blend. The red and rosé are produced from Folle Noire, Bracquet, Cinsault and Grenache. The Bracquet variety can also be found further east in Piedmont in Italy, where it is known as Brachetto. The wines are good; the red perfumed, supple and approachable and the white lightly floral and aromatic with an underlying nutty character. They may be approached young but will benefit from a year or 2 in the cellar. The rosé should be drunk young. (DM)

● **Bellet★★★** £D   ○ **Bellet★★** £D   ◉ **Bellet★** £C

CH. LES VALENTINES   Côtes de Provence   gilles@lesvalentines.com

Gilles Pons   83250 La Londe-les-Maures

From just over 20ha of biodynamically farmed vineyards, Les Valentines, like a number of other Côtes de Provence properties, is showing what this appellation is capable of achieving. As well as the Côtes de Provence bottlings, soft, easy-drinking red, white and rosé are produced under the Caprice de Clementine label. The rosé Les Valentines blends Cinsault with Grenache, Syrah, Mourvèdre and Tibouren. It has better definition and intensity than most Provençale examples. Les Valentines Blanc is dominated by very old Ugni Blanc and is vinified from a combination of fruit picked early for freshness and late for increased richness, which adds both weight and complexity. Of the 2 reds, Les Valentines is vibrant, pure and accessible young, a blend of Grenache, Syrah and a little Cabernet Sauvignon and Mourvèdre. Particularly impressive is the small-production Cuvée Bagnard, which is sourced from the best parcels of Syrah, Mourvèdre and Cabernet Sauvignon and aged for 12 months in *demi-muids*. Richly textured, with hints of dark berry fruit, oriental spice and mocha, it will add further complexity with 5 or so years of   cellaring. (DM)

● **Côtes de Provence**★★ £B Bagnard★★★★ £D
◉ **Côtes de Provence**★★ £B

CH. DE PIBARNON   Bandol   pibarnon@wanadoo.fr

Eric de Saint-Victor   83740 La Cadière d'Azur

UK stockists: **CdP**, Bal, ABy, N&P, P&S, F&M

One of the 2 best and most established properties in the appellation, the other being Domaine TEMPIER. The style of wine is quite different, though. The red here is powerful and structured, very backward in its youth, requiring up to a decade to fully develop. A very large proportion of Mourvèdre (90–95%) accounts for the dark, brambly and mineral style of its wine, dense but very refined as well. The site is ideal for ripening the variety: well-drained limestone-based soils and vineyards that are cooled by elevation as well as being very sunny ensure fruit loaded with intense flavour and fine, well-ripened but sturdy tannins. The 2001 looks to be quite exceptional. While the red excels, the white and rosé are a touch less exciting but good nonetheless. (DM)

● **Bandol**★★★★ £D   O **Bandol**★★ £C
◉ **Bandol**★ £C

CH. PRADEAUX   Bandol

Cyrille Portallis   676 Chemin des Pradeaux, 83270 Saint-Cyr-sur-Mer

UK stockists: HHB, Lay

Just over 4,000 cases of red are made here from 20ha of prime Bandol vineyard that is permanently being encroached upon by urban planners. A small amount of rosé is also produced. The blend is almost exclusively Mourvèdre with a little Grenache. Traditionally vinified, the fruit is not destemmed, and the wine is aged in large wooden *foudres* for over 3 years which helps in softening its raw youthful tannic edge. It is a wine that demands a minimum of 6–7 years in the cellar. Anything less would be to miss the point of it. (DM)

● **Bandol**★★★★ £D

CH. REVELETTE   Coteaux d'Aix-en-Provence

Peter Fischer   13490 Jouques

UK stockists: N&P

This 25ha domaine produces a very good *vin de pays* Chardonnay, Le Grand Blanc, as well as one of the very best reds in the region. The vineyards, located inland of the Mont Saint-Victoire, are some of the highest in the Coteaux d'Aix-en-Provence at around 400 metres. This is reflected in the style and

447

elegance of the wines. The regular red, white and rosé Coteaux d'Aix-en-Provence are well-priced although relatively simple by comparison. The red Grand Rouge is a blend dominated by Syrah and Cabernet Sauvignon. It is given a long vatting and aged in small oak. Very finely crafted and with great purity of fruit, it requires a minimum of 5–6 years to reveal its full complexity and rich intensity. (DM)

● **Coteaux d'Aix-en-Provence** Le Grand Rouge★★★★ £E

CH. ROMANIN   Les Baux   www.romanin.com

Jean-Pierre Peyraud   13210 Saint-Remy-de-Provence

Sizeable, biodynamically farmed property of 250ha. Currently 58ha are planted to vines with the older vines in sandy, loamy, calcareous soils whereas the newer plantings are in calcareous, stony soils. The climate is not only warm, dry and sunny but during the growing season there is sufficient wind to help rather than hinder balanced growth. Production is gradually increasing and is currently just under 17,000 cases a year, 80% of which is red. The rosé Les Baux is soft and easy drinking, the white more serious with pronounced fresh, lightly herbal fruit character and good intensity, in part achieved through blocking the malolactic. It is a blend of Rolle, Ugni Blanc and Bourboulenc. Jean le Troubador is a light, easy-drinking red made from the youngest vines, which are just over 10 years old. La Chapelle de Romanin is in effect the second wine of the property, made from an extensive blend of young-vine Syrah, Grenache, Cabernet Sauvignon and Mourvèdre along with older Carignan, Cinsault and Counoise. Lightly spicy and herbal with ripe berry fruit, the wine is aged for around a year in *inox* and cement. The Romanin red blends Grenache, Syrah, Cabernet Sauvignon and Mourvèdre. As yet although good it lacks the weight and depth of the best examples of the region, in part because the Syrah and Mourvèdre are still young. The top wine, the Coeur Tertius is sourced from Syrah, Mourvèdre, Cabernet Sauvignon and Grenache from the best site on the property. Vine age ranges from 8–40 years so the best should be yet to come. Finely structured with medium weight, it has a nice balance of dark fruits, cedar and herb spice, with subtle and well-judged oak. The 2000, which was an excellent year here, is right on the edge of ★★★★. (DM)

● **Les Baux-de-Provence**★★ £C Coeur Tertius★★★ £E
● **Les Baux-de-Provence** La Chapelle de Romanin★ £B
○ **Les Baux-de-Provence**★★ £B

CH. DE ROQUEFORT   Côtes de Provence

Raimond de Villeneuve   13830 Roquefort-la-Bedoule

UK stockists: Vex

Raimond de Villeneuve now runs one of the most exciting domaines in Provence, with a firm emphasis on high quality. The property is just inland of the Bandol appellation and benefits from vineyards planted at an altitude of over 300 metres. The first vintage to be bottled here was as recent as 1995; prior to this the fruit was sold off in bulk. The estate is farmed on biodynamic principles, not because its trendy but because de Villeneuve believes this approach will provide the best balance for his vineyard. Of the whites a straightforward *vin de pays* produced from Clairette is joined by the more serious, minerally Genêts, which also has Rolle in the blend and is partially barrel-fermented. The Corail rosé is soft and easygoing. It is, though, the 3 reds that stand out here. The very well-priced Mûres blends Grenache, Syrah, Carignan, Cinsault and Cabernet Sauvignon. Pure, elegant and intense, it will keep well. The Rubrum Obscurum is rich, dense and powerful. Loaded with dark old-vine character, it blends Grenache, Mourvèdre and Carignan. It was very good indeed in 1999, 2000 and 01, and 03 may well be of similar calibre.

In exceptional years Raimond also produces a similarly dense blend of Syrah and Carignan called La Pourpre. The top reds here should be given 5–7 years. (DM)

- ● **Côtes de Provence** Corail★ £B Mûres★★★ £C
- ● **Côtes de Provence** Rubrum Obscurum★★★★ £E
- O **Côtes de Provence** Genêts★★ £B

CH. DU ROUËT   Côtes de Provence

Savatier family   Route de Bagnols-en-Foret, 83490 Le Muy

The Savatier family have been at this property close to Fréjus in the foothills of the Estérel range since the 19th century. Rosé, white and red Côtes de Provence are produced under 3 labels. The l'Estérel wines are the softest and fruitiest; the Réservée range, marketed in traditional Provençale bottles, are sturdier and more structured; Belle Pouelle is the label for the top wines. Rosé is made by cold maceration and the l'Estérel is soft and straightfoward, the Réservée fuller, with a little structure from Grenache and Syrah. The Belle Pouelle is from the same grapes and made solely from first run juice. The white Réservée is cold-fermented after a period of skin maceration. It is aged on lees for 2–3 months and is a nutty, spicy blend of Ugni Blanc and Rolle. The Belle Pouelle white has more Rolle in the blend and a touch of Sémillon. Fermented and aged in barrel with lees-stirring, it offers a richer, creamier texture. The l'Estérel red is soft and vibrant, blending Carignan vinified by carbonic maceration with Grenache and Syrah. The Réservée is a traditionally vinified blend of Grenache, Syrah and Mourvèdre. It is aged for 3–4 months in *foudres* and is marked by its elegant berry and spice fruit. The Belle Pouelle is Grenache (65%), Syrah (35%) and just 5% of Cabernet Sauvignon. This is firmer and more structured and needs 3 or 4 years' patience at least. The 2002 was nudging ★★★. The Savatiers also have a small holding of very old Alicante Bouschet from which they make a splendidly dense and characterful varietal *vin de garde*, Severac. Rich, dark and smoky, it is aged in 500-litre barrels to emphasise its splendid fruit. Just 500 cases or so are produced each year and you'll probably have to visit to get this one, but there are *gîtes* available so it shouldn't be a hardship. (DM)

- ● **Côtes de Provence** Belle Pouelle★★ £C   ● **Severac** Vin de Pays★★★ £D
- ● **Côtes de Provence** Cuvée de l'Estérel★ £B Réservée★★ £C
- O **Côtes de Provence** Réservée★ £B Belle Pouelle★★ £C
- ◉ **Côtes de Provence** Réservée★ £B Belle Pouelle★ £B

CH. ROUTAS   Coteaux Varois   www.routas.com

David Murray   Chateauvert, 83149 Bras

UK stockists: **Col**,BBR

Established for upwards of a decade, Routas is located in the wild inland Provençale hills of the Coteaux Varois and has vineyards that are just that bit cooler than its neighbours'. Former owner Philippe Bieler invested considerably in both the vineyard and the cellar, with state-of-the-art vinification equipment. Production runs at around 20,000 cases and the wines, particularly the top reds and the white Coquelicot, are good to very good. The reds, fashioned in a full but approachable style, will nevertheless improve with some cellar time. Le Trou de Infernet is a blend of Grenache, Syrah and Cabernet Sauvignon whereas Agrippa d'Aubigne is just Syrah and Cabernet Sauvignon. There is an easy-drinking white blend of southern French grapes, the Wild Boar white. The 2 best wines truly stand out: Cyrano, a spicy, smoky 100% Syrah, and Coquelicot, a nutty, subtly oaked, herb-scented blend of Viognier and Chardonnay. (DM)

- ● **Coteaux Varois** Carignane★★ £B Wild Boar Cabernet Sauvignon★★ £B
- ● **Coteaux Varois** Cuvée Le Trou de Infernet★★★ £C
- ● **Coteaux Varois** Cuvée Agrippa d'Aubigne★★★ £C

449

● **Vin de Pays du Var** Cuvée Cyrano★★★ £C
○ **Vin de Pays du Var** Cuvée Coquelicot★★★ £C

CH. SIMONE Palette

Rougier family   13590 Meyreuil
UK stockists: **Yap**

This is the benchmark property in the tiny appellation of Palette just outside
Aix-en-Provence. The property has around 17ha of vineyard and there are a
bewildering number of permitted red varieties under the appellation
regulations. Small quantities of some of the rarer ones are still planted but the
emphasis is increasingly on Grenache, Mourvèdre and Syrah. White varieties
are dominated by Clairette and it is the white which is the most exciting of the
wines. Full, rich and decidedly old fashioned, it nevertheless possesses some
marvellous nutty, spicy and honeyed notes which increase with age. The red is
good but can be somewhat rustic and four-square. There's a small amount of
decent but pricy rosé. (DM)

● **Palette**★★★ £E   ○ **Palette**★★★★ £E

CH. VANNIÈRES Bandol www.chateauvannieres.com

Colette & Eric Boisseaux   83740 La Cadière d'Azur
UK stockists: C&O

One of the best of the current generation of Bandol producers. Along with the
likes of CHATEAU PRADEAUX and Domaine du GROS NORÉ this is a
property that's knocking on the door of PIBARNON and TEMPIER. The wine
is a powerful but stylish example of the appellation. All its intense, dark-berry
Mourvèdre character and intense herbal, garrigue scents will shine through
when the tannin has had time to soften and the wine achieves real balance and
harmony. Good floral white Bandol is produced along with a good rosé and
recently a red Côtes de Provence, an increasingly impressive junior version of
the *grand vin*. (DM)

● **Bandol**★★★★ £E

CH. VIGNELAURE Coteaux d'Aix-en-Provence www.vignelaure.com

Catherine & David O'Brien   13116 Vernègues
The O'Briens took over Vignelaure in 1994 in partnership and gained sole
control of the domaine in the late 90s. Vignelaure was one of the early
benchmark properties of the AC in the 1980s and the O'Briens have been
successfully returning it to Provence's first division. Work in the vineyard is key,
with canopy management and a tight control on yields ensuring top-quality
fruit from well-drained limestone, gravel and clay soils. The estate is solely
planted to red varieties and there are some 60ha under vine. Investment and
modernisation in the cellar is ongoing and vinification is now very modern
with malolactic carried out in barrel. The rosé is soft and vibrant with a little
structure and grip and will keep a year or 2. The Coteaux d'Aix-en-Provence
rarely comes from a yield much above 30hl/ha and is a blend of Cabernet
Sauvignon, Syrah and Grenache. Ageing is in one-third new oak and the wine
is a fine mix of elegant cedar and spicy herbal *garrigue* scents. Surprisingly it is
Merlot not Cabernet that's king here. The La Colline red comes from Merlot
and a little Cabernet Sauvignon planted on the stony hillside parcels of the
same name. These naturally low-yielding vines provide a rich, opulent and
spicy red that benefits from 24 months ageing in new oak. Unfined and bottled
with minimal filtration, it will certainly benefit from 4 or 5 years' patience. (DM)

● **La Colline de Vignelaure** Vin de Pays du Coteaux du Verdon★★★ £D
● **Coteaux d'Aix-en-Provence**★★★ £C   ◉ **Coteaux d'Aix-en-Provence** ★ £B

DOM. DU CLOS D'ALARI   Côtes de Provence   leclosdalari@noos.fr
Anne-Marie & Nathalie Vancoillie   83510 Saint-Antonin-du-Var
Small 20-ha estate with just 8ha under vine. Olives are also grown. The
vineyard comprises 6ha of Côtes de Provence and a further 2ha are *vin de pays*.
A minimalist approach is taken in both vineyard and cellar, although a
vendange vert is practised to control crop yields. Harvesting is by hand and
vinification is traditional. The fresh and lightly herb-scented rosé is made from
a blend of Cinsault, Syrah, Grenache and unusually Rolle as well as a little
Mourvèdre. The *vin de pays* Syrah and Merlot blend is soft and fruit-driven and
there is also a regular Côtes de Provence red. Pride of place goes to the prestige
red which has variously been labelled Manon in 2001, Lola in 02 and Alix in
03. As with the other wines here, this oak-aged blend of Syrah, Grenache and
Cabernet is marked by its elegance as well as a supple texture and great depth
and persistence of flavour. It will develop very well for 4 or 5 years. (DM)
● **Côtes de Provence** Cuvée Alix★★★ £C   ● **Vin de Pays de Var** Syrah/Merlot★ £B
◉ **Côtes de Provence** Grand Clos★ £B

DOM. DE LA COURTADE   Côtes de Provence
Henri Vidal   83400 Ile-de-Porquerolles
UK stockists:GBa
The Ile-de-Porquerolles is best known as a secluded destination for holidaying
Mediterranean yachtsmen. The island lies off the coast of Provence between
Bandol and Saint-Tropez. There are some 30ha of vines, 13ha of them the
white Rolle. This is used exclusively to vinify the white Côtes de Provence,
which is lightly oaked and displays some ripe tropical notes as well as a more
typically southern nutty character. It will stand a little age as will the red
Alycastre, which is the second wine here, produced to ensure the integrity of
the top red. The *grand vin* is a rich, brambly, spicy blend of Mourvèdre,
Grenache and Syrah and is impressive, concentrated and worth seeking out. (DM)
● **Côtes de Provence**★★★ £D Alycastre★★ £B
○ **Côtes de Provence**★★ £D

DUPÉRÉ BARRERA   Côtes de Provence
Emmanuelle & Laurent Barrera   122 Rue de Dakar, 83100 Toulon
This small operation with a total output of less than 3,000 cases a year is part
micro-négociant and part producer. Red and a tiny amount of white Côtes de
Provence come from the Barreras' own Domaine du Clos de la Procure
vineyard, which was purchased in 2003. As well as this they have also produced
so far Côtes du Rhône-Villages, Coteaux du Languedoc and Rivesaltes as well
as Côtes de Provence from bought-in fruit. Their most established label, and
one of the most opulent and stylish of the appellation, is the Bandol India. This
rich, concentrated, dark and smoky red is sourced from an argile-calcareous
terroir, 90% of the grapes are destemmed and the wine is vatted for as much as
4–6 weeks. Ageing in the cellar is in a combination of *foudres* and small oak.
The Clos de la Procure comes from old vines. The vineyard is at the limit of
the Mediterranean influence on the local climate and the argile-calcareous soils
are ideally water-stressed during ripening. A rich, spicy and lightly herb-scented
blend of Grenache and Mourvèdre, the wine has real depth and intensity.
Handling for all the wines is kept to a minimum and the wines are bottled
unfined and unfiltered. (DM)
Domaine du Clos de la Procure
● **Côtes de Provence**★★★★ £E
Dupéré-Barrera
● **Bandol** India★★★★ £D

451

DOM. DU GRAND CROS   Côtes de Provence   www.grandcros.fr

Faulkner Family   83660 Carnoules

A fairly extensive range of red, white and rosé is made at this 22-ha property situated in the foothills of the Massif des Maures in the centre of the Var. Vineyard development here is ongoing and new planting is at a density of 4–5,000 vines per hectare with a cover crop of grass to stress the vines sufficiently to optimise fruit ripening. Farming is as natural as possible with minimal use of pesticides and fungicides. Fruit-driven, forward wines are released under the Domaine label. Of more interest are a cool-fermented Chardonnay and a Carignan that are both *vin de pays*. The Carignan gets some pre-fermentation maceration to highlight its dark blackberry, spicy, peppery fruit. The regular Côtes de Provence wines are labelled L'Esprit de Provence and include a red blended from Cabernet Sauvignon and Syrah and a soft, forward rosé produced from Grenache and Cinsault along with a little Syrah and Rolle to add depth. Just 5% of the 8,000-case production is accounted for by the 2 Nectar wines. The white is a barrel-fermented Chardonnay, whereas the red is a rich, powerful and impressively concentrated Cabernet Sauvignon, with just a touch of Syrah and Grenache, produced from yields of just 20 hl/ha. A 48-hour cold soak is undertaken prior to a temperature-controlled vinification which emphasises the dark, cedary fruit. Ageing is for 12 months in small oak with micro-oxygenation rather than conventional racking. In general the wines should be drunk young but the Nectar red will develop very well in bottle for 5 years or more. (DM)

● **Côtes de Provence** L'Esprit de Provence★★ £B Nectar★★★ £C
● **Vin de Pays des Maures** Carignan★★ £B
○ **Vin de Pays des Maures** Chardonnay★★ £B
◉ **Côtes de Provence** L'Esprit de Provence★ £B

DOM. DU GROS NORÉ   Bandol   www.gros-nore.com

Alain Pascal   675 Chemin de l'Argile, 83740 La Cadière d'Azur
UK stockists:**Han**

The first vintage at this newly established Bandol producer was as recent as 1997, but it was still one of real class and style. Almost all of the 11.5ha are planted to red varieties but a small amount of white is also produced – a typically fat wine with broad, warm, nutty fruit – as well as a reasonable rosé. The improtant wine is the red Bandol, a big, brooding unfiltered blend of Mourvèdre, Grenache and Cinsault full of dark, savoury, roasted aromas with real intensity and purity. A complex, spicy, herbal undercurrent adds interest to the beefy fruit. Backward in its youth it needs time. Very characterful and likely to improve in bottle for up to a decade or more. (DM)

● **Bandol**★★★★ £C ○ **Bandol**★★ £C

DOM. HAUVETTE   Les Baux

Dominique Hauvette   13210 Saint-Rémy-de-Provence
UK stockists:**CdP**

Dominique Hauvette's small 13-ha property is fast emerging as one of the finest, not only in Les Baux but in Provence. A small range of 3 reds and one white of uniformly excellent quality is produced. The white Blanc de Blancs – a blend of Marsanne, Roussanne and Clairette, and as such labelled as *vin de pays* – is part barrel-fermented and aged on lees with *bâtonnage*. There is a piercing, nutty, citrus intensity here with finely judged oak and a rich creamy texture. It should develop very nicely in the medium term. The red Amethyste is based unusually around Cinsault, with varying amounts of Carignan, Grenache, Syrah and occasionally Cabernet Sauvignon. It is the softest, lushest of the Hauvette reds but there is sufficient structure, elegance and refinement to enable short-term development. The Cornaline is bigger, with a raw almost *sauvage* character from a blend driven by Carignan (60%) with equal proportions of Cinsault and Grenache. The top red, the Domaine Hauvette, blends 50% Grenache with 30% Syrah and a balance of Cabernet Sauvignon. Two years in *foudres* and small oak are comfortably absorbed. The wine is rich, powerful and seriously structured. Expect to age it for at least 5–7 years to get the best out of it. (DM)

● **Coteaux d'Aix-en-Provence** Améthyste★★★ £D Cornaline★★★ £D
● **Les Baux-de-Provence★★★★** £D
O **Vin de Pays des Bouches du Rhône** Blanc de Blancs★★★ £D

DOM. LA BASTIDE BLANCHE Bandol bastide.blanche@libertysurf.fr

EARL Bronzo   367 Route des Oratoires, 83330 Sainte-Anne-du-Castellet
UK stockists:BRW

Red, white and rosé are produced under the Bandol AC at this 28ha property, established by the Bronzo family over 30 years ago. The vineyards are cultivated largely organically and great care is taken at harvest to select the best fruit. The 3 reds here inevitably stand out. The sturdy Longue Garde is around three-quarters Grenache with the balance Mourvèdre. Both the Fontanieu and Estagnol are Mourvèdre bottlings. These last 2 wines are produced from vines grown on different soils. The reds will all develop very well for a decade or longer and require cellaring for at least 4–5 years. (DM)

● **Bandol** Longue Garde★★★ £C Fontanieu★★★★£D Estagnol★★★★ £D

DOM. LAFRAN VEYROLLES Bandol

Mme Jouve-Férec   2115 Route de l'Aigle, 83740 La Cadière-d'Azur
UK stockists: **PBW**

Very impressive red Bandol is now being made at this 10-ha property, with production small at less than 4,000 cases per year. Mourvèdre dominates the red plantings, while the whites are a mix of Clairette and Ugni Blanc. The vineyards are farmed organically and the argilo-calcareous soils provide an excellent base for growing fruit of the highest quality. The white is one of the better examples produced in the appellation, as is the softly strawberry-scented rosé. The 2 reds with their sizeable Mourvèdre component stand out. Both are dense, powerful and finely structured. Firm youthful tannin will be seamlessly integrated with 5 or 6 years' ageing. The 2001 reds were quite exceptional, effortlessly ★★★★★. (DM)

● **Bandol** Tradition★★★★ £D Spéciale★★★★ £D ◉ **Bandol** ★ £C

DOM. DE LA LAIDIÈRE Bandol

Freddy Estienne   426 Chemin du Font-Vive, Sainte-Anne-d'Evenos, 83330 Evenos
Well-crafted and good-value red, white and rosé are produced at this Bandol property of some 24ha. The bulk of the vineyard is planted to red varieties, with 60% Mourvèdre and 20% each of Cinsault and Grenache. The rosé is ripe and forward, while the white, from a blend of Clairette and Ugni Blanc, has a light nutty elegance and a hint of herb spice. The red, as is the case at most Bandol properties, is the key wine. Firmly structured in its youth with a savoury, almost meaty character to its fruit it will gain an extra dimension with 5 years' age.(DM)

● **Bandol★★★** £C

DOM. LA SUFFRENE Bandol

Cédric Gravier   1066 Chemin du Cuges, 83740 La Cadière d'Azur
Up until the 1996 vintage Cédric Gravier sold his harvest to the co-op. His

welcome decision to vinify under his own label has resulted in some of the best wines to emerge from what is arguably the top Provençale appellation. A fresh *vin de pays* red and soft, easy rosé are produced but it is the Bandols that stand out. There is a sound rosé produced from Mourvèdre, Cinsault, Grenache and Carignan. The white blends 75% Clairette with the balance Ugni Blanc. Vinified and aged in *inox* it has impressive depth and intensity, with a mix of floral, spice and citrus aromas. The regular Bandol is a blend of Mourvèdre, Grenache, Cinsault and just a little Carignan. Sturdy and structured with traditional, dark berry fruit and meaty characters, it shows all the potential to improve with 5 or 6 years' cellaring. The very rich, supple and concentrated top wine, Cuvée des Lauves, is dominated by Mourvèdre with just 5% of old Carignan adding dark pepper notes to the sumptuous dark fruit. (DM)

● **Bandol**★★★ £C Cuvée des Lauves★★★★★ £E
O **Bandol**★★ £C

DOM. DE LAUZIÈRES Les Baux

Jean-Daniekl Schlaepfer & Gérard Pitton Le Destet, 13890 Mouriès
Jean-Daniel Schlaepfer discovered this superbly located property at the heart of the Baux-de-Provence appellation in 1992. The vineyards are planted to a varied mix of Grenache, Syrah, Mourvèdre, Carignan, Cinsault and Petit Verdot among the reds and Grenache Blanc with a tiny amount of Clairette for the whites. Two very fair reds are produced as Baux-de-Provence, the lighter Equinoxe and the denser and more structured Solstice, but the owners believe that the conventional varieties authorised by the appellation authorities here are not capable of expressing the greatest potential of the estate and the top wines are labelled as *vin de table*. The white Astérie is a pure and very intense barrel-fermented varietal Grenache Blanc. The oak is superbly handled with the piercing citrus and creamy, nutty fruit dominating the wine. The red Sine Nomine very unusually blends 75% Petit Verdot with the balance Grenache. Rich, powerful and very concentrated, this muscular red needs at least 5 or 6 years. (DM)

● **Les Baux-de-Provence** Solstice★★ £C **Sine Nomine** Vin de Table★★★★ £E
O **Astérie** Vin de Table★★★★ £D

MAS DE CADENET Côtes de Provence www.masdecadenet.fr

Guy Négrel 13530 Trets-en-Provence
This estate with vineyards only a few miles as the crow flies from Palette has been in the Négrel family since 1813. It is now entitled (since 2004) to add the Sainte-Victoire sub appellation to the AC name for its reds. There are 40ha, most planted to red varieties, and the *terroir* consists of well-drained gravel, clay and sand. Yields are purposely restricted. The range consists of 2 labels, Mas de Cadenet and the more serious Mas Négrel. The Mas de Cadenet rosé and white are soft, forward and attractively fruit-driven. The red is a blend of Syrah, Grenache and Cabernet Sauvignon aged in *foudres* for 8 months and offers some depth and substance. The Mas Négrel Prestige is the top white, made from 100% Rolle. Aged in wood for 6–8 months on fine lees, it is nutty and characterful. The Mas Négrel Cadenet rosé is more structured than most, being aged in oak. The Mas Négrel Cadenet red is a blend of Grenache, Syrah and Cabernet Sauvignon, vatted for over 20 days to add extract and flesh and aged in oak for 12–15 months. Dark, spicy and concentrated, it requires 4 years at a minimum. (DM)

● **Côtes de Provence Sainte-Victoire** Mas de Cadenet★★ £B
● **Côtes de Provence Sainte-Victoire** Mas Négrel Cadenet★★★ £D
O **Côtes de Provence** Mas de Cadenet★ £B Mas Négrel Prestige★★★ £C
◉ **Côtes de Provence** Mas de Cadenet★ £B Mas Négrel Cadenet★★ £C

MAS DE LA DAME   Les Baux   www.masdeladame.com

Anne Ponitowski & Caroline Missoffe   13520 Les Baux-de-Provence
UK stockists: L&W, HHB, AVn

Good-quality producer from Les Baux-de-Provence with 57ha of vineyards.
The property was immortalised by Vincent Van Gogh when he painted it in
1889. As one would expect the great majority of vines are red varieties but there
are 5ha of whites including some Sémillon. Very good olive oils are also
produced from the estate's 25ha of olive groves. A relatively extensive range of
wines is made here with consultancy provided by Jean-Luc COLOMBO. The
red Réserve and white Cuvée de la Stèle offer reasonable value and
straightforward drinking. The Coin Caché white is very stylish, floral, nutty
and perfumed, the Cuvée de la Stèle red rich and chunky with hints of garrigue
and smoke. The Coin Caché red is a supple, smoky, powerful, old-vine blend
of Grenache and Syrah. (DM)

● **Les Baux-de-Provence** Cuvée de la Stèle★★★ £C Coin Caché★★★ £D
● **Les Baux-de-Provence** Réserve★★ £B
O **Les Baux-de-Provence** Coin Caché★★★ £D
◎ **Coteaux d'Aix-en-Provence** Cuvée de la Stèle★★ £B
◎ **Les Baux-de-Provence** Rosé Mas★ £B ◎ **Côtes de Provence**★ £B

DOM. RABIEGA   Côtes de Provence   www.rabiega.com

Vin & Spirit AB Sweden   Clos d'Ière Méridional, 83300 Draguinan
UK stockists: L&S

Owned by the Swedish Vin & Spirit operation since 1988, this property,
produces good to very good red and white under both the Domaine Rabiega
label and Rabiega Vin, the recently established *negoçiant* label for a range of
very good well priced reds and whites. Of these the low yielding Carignan,
Carbase aged in a mix of new and used oak and the elegant brambly Mourbase,
produced from Mourvedre and aged in new French, Slovenian and Hungarian
oak stand out among the reds. Whites are not ignored either. The Roussanne,
Rouxanne is elegant and aromatic, the Svala produced from Rolle is barrel-
fermented and aged on lees for up to 9 months, it offers weight, extract and
subtle nut and citrus character. It has the structure to develop for a few years.
The Domaine Rabiega vineyards are planted on limestone and clay soils near
Draguignan. The property is farmed organically and there are some 9ha under
vine, with productiona mere 1,600–1,700 cases a year. A fine ripe, tropically
scented, barrel-fermented white, Clos d'Ière Blanc, produced from Sauvignon
Blanc, Chardonnay and Viognier, is impressive, as is the Clos d'Ière I, a
powerful, dense, oak-aged Syrah. The Clos d'Ière II was produced for the last
time in the 2001 vintage. The wine blended Carignan, Grenache and Cabernet
Sauvignon. (DM)

● **Côtes de Provence** Carbase★★ £C Mourbase★★ £C Clos Dière I★★★★ £E
O **Vin de Pays du Var** Clos Dière★★★ £E
O **Côtes de Provence** Rouxanne★★ £C Svala★★ £C

DOM. RICHEAUME   Côtes de Provence

Henning Hoesch   13114 Puyloubier
UK stockists: BGL

Very good estate that has been producing consistently excellent wine under the
Côtes de Provence appellation for years. The property consists of some 25ha
planted largely to Cabernet Sauvignon, Syrah, Grenache and Merlot. There is
also a little Viognier, from which a decent white is made. The Tradition
includes all 4 red varieties, complemented by fine varietal Cabernet and Syrah
bottlings and a splendid *grand vin,* Cuvée Columelle. This massive, dense and

455

very concentrated wine is one of the best reds in Provence. (DM)

● **Côtes de Provence** Tradition★★★ £C Cuvée Columelle★★★★ £E

DOM. RIMAURESQ   Côtes de Provence   www.rimauresq.fr

Wemyss Family   83970 Pignans
UK stockists:**May**

This fine 36-ha Scottish-owned property is notable for making some of the
best examples of rosé in the Côtes de Provence. They are fine and pure with
subtle, elegant red berry fruit and like all the wines here have a persistent
mineral character which lends a tight, firm structure. This is particularly
notable in the reds and in part may be attributable to the soils which are
crystalline rock with sandstone and gravel. Average vine age is now 40 years and
some are up to 70 years. Replacement planting is now ensuring an increased
vine density of up to 5,000 vines per hectare in an ongoing drive to improve
quality. A superior range labelled Cuvée R has been introduced for red, white
and rosé. The red R blends solely Syrah and Cabernet Savignon, whereas the
regular red is mainly Cabernet with much smaller proportions of Syrah,
Mourvèdre and Carignan. Both whites are blended from Ugni Blanc and Rolle
and ageing is in *demi-muids*. The Cuvée R rosé is produced from older
plantings of Cinsault, Grenache and Mourvèdre, which gives it extra depth and
that piercing mineral and red berry fruit intensity. Both the reds are firmly
structured with a herb spice character, the Cuvée R being fuller and deeper but
with a background touch of austerity in its youth. Give it 5 years or so to
soften. (DM)

● **Côtes de Provence**★★ £B Cuvée R★★★ £D
◉ **Côtes de Provence**★ £B Cuvée R★★ £C

DOM. SAINT-ANDRÉ DE FIGUIÈRE   Côtes de Provence

Alain & François Combard   83250 La Londe-les-Maures
This 19-ha property located just inland between Toulon and Saint-Tropez, with
the Massif des Maures immediately to the north, benefits from a benign, sunny
maritime climate. As a result the Combards tend to enjoy better growing
conditions than other Provençale properties in difficult years like 2002. Quality
is characterised here by a range of excellent old-vine and reserve *cuvées*. As well
as the premium wines there are both a red and white released as Vin du Pays
du Var and a regular bottling of red, white and rosé, respectively labelled *cuvées*
François, Magali and Valérie, all of which offer good everyday drinking. The 3
Côtes de Provence wines are a step up. The rosé Vieilles Vignes is blended from
30- to 35-year-old Mourvèdre, Cinsault and Grenache, a wine of impressive
intensity for the style. The white Vieilles Vignes is a cool-fermented blend of
Ugni Blanc, Rolle and Sémillon, whereas the splendidly pure and intense
Cuvée Delphine is barrel-fermented and aged on lees. It is 100% Rolle. The 2
top reds are impressively structured with real depth and concentration. The
Vieilles Vignes is blended from Mourvèdre, 100-year-old Carignan (unusually
vinified together) and Syrah. The Réserve is 90% Mourvèdre with the balance
Syrah. Both get an extended maceration of 1 month before ageing for up to a
year in used oak. Cellaring for 5 years or so will bring added complexity in
both wines. (DM)

● **Côtes de Provence** Grande Cuvée Vieilles Vignes Réserve★★★ £D
● **Côtes de Provence** Vieilles Vignes★★★ £C
O **Côtes de Provence** Grande Cuvée Delphine Réserve★★★ £D
O **Côtes de Provence** Vieilles Vignes★★ £D
◉ **Côtes de Provence** Vieilles Vignes★★ £D

DOM. SORIN   Bandol   luc.sorin@wanadoo.fr

Luc Sorin   83270 Saint Cyr-sur-Mer

The Burgundian Luc Sorin took over this small Bandol property in 1994 after having been the winemaker at Château ROUTAS in the Coteaux Varois. He has plots in the Côtes de Provence AC as well as Bandol and produces red wines of impressive density and depth. As well as the Tradition *rouge* a limited Côtes de Provence Cuvée Privée is also produced which has 50% Syrah. There is also a white Côtes de Provence Cuvée Sergine. The rosé is soft and fruit-driven and will drink well young or with a very little age. The reds are destemmed then fermented and macerated in large rotating oak vats which provide an even plunging process for the fermenting skins. The wines certainly have a soft, supple texture and in the Bandol real density and persistence. (DM)

● **Bandol** Longue Garde★★★ £D ● **Côtes de Provence** Tradition★★ £C
◉ **Côtes de Provence** Terra Amata★ £D

DOM. TEMPIER   Bandol

Peyraud family   Le Plan du Castellet, 83330 Le Castellet
UK stockists: Sav,SVS

This is one of the great Bandol producers and has remained so for the past 2 decades despite the emergence of newer names such as PIBARNON and more recently GROS NORÉ. More than anything these wines are characterised by their elegance and refinement as opposed to the sheer power and density often achieved elsewhere. There are around 28ha planted to red varieties but a mere 1ha to white. Along with the 5 reds there is also a very decent rosé. The regular *cuvée* produced from the youngest vines on the property is somewhat light in comparison to the other wines. Cuvée Spéciale is denser and richer, with altogether greater concentration. It is, though, the 3 single vineyard wines, La Tourtine, Migoua and Cabassou, that stand out. The latter, with the highest proportion of Mourvèdre, is the sturdiest of the trio, the Migoua the most stylish and elegant. All will age gracefully for well over a decade. (DM)

● **Bandol** Cuvée Classique★★ £C Cuvée Spéciale★★★ £D
● **Bandol** La Tourtine★★★★ £E Migoua★★★★ £E Cabassou★★★★★ £E
◉ **Bandol**★★ £C

DOM. DE TERREBRUNE   Bandol

Georges Delille   724 Chemin de la Tourelle, 83190 Ollioulles
The red Bandol produced by Georges Delille from his 25-ha vineyard is a massive, muscular and brooding example of the appellation. The vineyards have an ideal aspect with finely drained calcareous soils and the average vine age is now moving towards 30 years, adding intensity, depth and character to the fruit. This is a true *vin de garde*: a dense smoky, spicy Mourvèdre requiring 7 or 8 years at a minimum to achieve true balance and harmony. The small amount of rosé and white produced is of a reasonable quality, the latter capable of some age. (DM)

● **Bandol**★★★★ £D
◉ **Bandol**★★ £C ○ **Bandol**★★ £C

DOM. DE LA TOUR DU BON   Bandol

Claude Hocquard   714 Chemin des Olivettes, 83330 Le Brûlat-du-Castellet
A small property with just 12ha planted to vines. Production is small at some 3,500 cases but the quality of the red Bandols is very good indeed. These are stylish, supple and very well crafted and the Saint-Ferréol is finely structured, refined and very long-lived – a wine of not only weight and concentration but wonderful herbal intensity. As with so many properties in the appellation, though, the rosé and white are decent and well enough made but lack the

interest of the reds. (DM)

● **Bandol★★★** £D   Saint-Ferréol★★★★ £E
O **Bandol★★** £C

DOM. DE TREVALLON   Les Baux-de-Provence   www.trevallon.fr

Eloi Dürrbach   13103 Saint-Étienne-du-Grès
UK stockists: Yap, Har

It remains one of the ludicrous features of the *appellation contrôlée* regulations
that this benchmark Provençale red is now only entitled to *vin de pays* status.
Theoretically there should be some Grenache planted but the vineyard with
north-facing calcareous slopes will not ripen the variety adequately. The
mesoclimate here is remarkably cool, much more so than one would imagine.
The resulting red blend of Cabernet and Syrah and the tiny amount of white
produced (barely more than a couple of barrels) are very impressive and
remarkably refined wines. Cask-aging of the red is in large older wood and it
needs at least 5 years to unfurl. The wine is a classic Provençale example of the
blend with floral *garrigue* scents underpinning the concentrated, dark, cedary
fruit. The white is a barrel-fermented blend of Marsanne, Roussanne and
Chardonnay, very fine and intense with concentrated, lightly floral, nutty fruit.
(DM)

● **Vin de Pays des Bouches-du-Rhône★★★★★** £F
O **Vin de Pays des Bouches-du-Rhône★★★★★** £G

Also see the following Rhône *négociant* with an entry in the section *Rhône
Valley:*

JEAN-LUC COLOMBO

OTHER WINES OF NOTE
Provence

DOM. DES ALYSSES ● Coteaux Varois £C
CH. BARBANAU ● Côtes de Provence★★ £B
CH. DE BEAUPRÉ ● Coteaux d'Aix-en-Provence Clos Victoire★★ £D
CH. CALISSANNE ● Coteaux d'Aix-en-Provence Clos Victoire★★ £D
CH. DU GALOUPET ● Côtes de Provence★★ £B   O Côtes de Provence★ £B
CH. LA CALISSE ● Coteaux Varois Patricia Ortelli★★ £C
CH. LA MOUTÈTE ● Côtes de Provence Vieilles Vignes★★ £C
CH. MINUTY ● Côtes de Provence Prestige★★ £C
◉ Côtes de Provence Prestige★ £C
CH. REAL MARTIN ● Côtes de Provence★★ £C   Optimum★★★ £D
CH. SAINTE-ROSELINE ● Côtes de Provence Prieuré★★ £D
CH. SALETTES ● Bandol★★ £D
CH. DES SARRINS ● Côtes de Provence★★ £B
CLOS SAINTE-MAGDELEINE O Cassis★★ £C
COMMANDERIE DE PEYRASSOL ● Côtes de Provence Cuvée Marie-Estelle★★ £C
O Côtes de Provence Cuvée Marie-Estelle★★ £C
DOM. DU DEFFENDS ● Coteaux Varois Marie Liesse★★ £B
● Coteaux Varois Clos de La Truffière★★ £B
DOM. DE LA FRÉGATE ● Bandol★★ £B
DOM. DE L'HERMITAGE ● Bandol★★ £C
DOM. DE JALE ● Côtes de Provence La Bouisse★★ £C   La Nible★★★ £C
O Côtes de Provence La Garde★★ £C   ◉ Côtes de Provence La Garde★★ £C
LA FERME BLANCHE O Cassis★★ £C
DOM. LA GALANTIN ● Bandol★★ £C
DOM. GAVOTY ● Côtes de Provence Cuvée Clarendon★★ £C
O Côtes de Provence Cuvée Clarendon★★ £C
MAÎTRES VIGNERONNES DE SAINT-TROPEZ ● Bandol La Roque★★ £C
MAS DE GOURGONNIER ● Les Baux-de-Provence Réserve★★ £D
MAS SAINTE-BERTHE ● Les Baux-de-Provence Louis David★★ £C

DOMAINES OTT - CLOS MIREILLE ○ **Côtes de Provence** Blanc de Côte★★ £C
○ **Côtes de Provence** L'Insolent★★ £E
DOMAINES OTT - CH. ROMASSAN ● **Côtes de Provence** Longue Garde★★★ £E
○ **Côtes de Provence**★★ £D
DOMAINES OTT - CH. DE SELLE ● **Bandol**★★ £E
DOM. SAINT-ESTÈVE ● **Coteaux d'Aix-en-Provence**★ £B
DOM. DE TRIENNES ● **Vin de Pays des Var** Les Auréliens★★ £B

Corsica

DOM. CULOMBU ○ **Calvi**★★ £B
CLOS CANARELLI ● **Vin de Corse-Figari**★★ £C   ○ **Vin de Corse-Figari**★★ £C
DOM. LECCIA ● **Patrimonio**★★ £B Petra Bianca★★ £C ○ **Patrimonio**★★ £B
ORENGA DE GAFFORY ● **Patrimonio**★★ £B ○ **Muscat de Cap Corse**★★★ £C
DOM. DE TORRACCIA ● **Vin de Corse Porto-Vecchio** Oriu★★ £C

Work in progress!!

Producers under consideration for the next edition

ANTOINE ARENA (PATRIMONIO)
CH. ROCHE REDONNE (BANDOL)
JEAN-PIERRE GAUSSEN (BANDOL)
DOM. GENTILE (PATRIMONIO)

Author's choice (DM)

15 Emerging classics from Provence
DOM. DES BÉATES ● **Coteaux d'Aix-en-Provence** Terra d'Or
CH. DE PIBARNON ● **Bandol**
CH. PRADEAUX ● **Bandol**
CH. ROUTAS ○ **Vin de Pays du Var** Cuvée Coquelicot
CH. SIMONE ○ **Palette**
DOM. DE LA TOUR DU BON ● **Bandol**
DOM. DU GROS NORÉ ● **Bandol**
DOM. LAFRAN-VEYROLLES ● **Bandol** Tradition
DOM. RABIEGA ● **Côtes de Provence** Clos Dière I
DOM. RICHEAUME ● **Côtes de Provence** Cuvée Columelle
DOM. TEMPIER ● **Bandol** Cabassou
DOM. DE TREVALLON ● **Vin de Pays des Bouches-du-Rhône**
CH. DE ROQUEFORT ● **Côtes de Provence** Rubrum Obscurum
DOM. HAUVETTE ● **Les Baux de Provence**
DOM. DE LAUZIERES ● **Sine Nomine**

Some great value choices from Provence and Corsica
CH. VIGNELAURE ● **Coteaux d'Aix-en-Provence**
DUPERE-BARRERA ● **Bandol** India
DOM. DES BÉATES ● **Coteaux d'Aix-en-Provence** Béates
DOM. SORIN ● **Bandol**
DOM. RIMAURESQ ● **Côtes de Provence**
DOM. DE LA COURTADE ● **Côtes de Provence**
CH. BAS ● **Coteaux d'Aix-en-Provence** Cuvée du Temple
CH. DU ROUET ● **Côtes de Provence** Réservée
DOM. DU GRAND CROS ● **Côtes de Provence** Nectar
DOM. LECCIA ● **Patrimonio**
DOM. DE TORRACCIA ● **Vin de Corse Porto-Vecchio** Oriu
DOM. CULOMBU ○ **Calvi**

RECOMMENDED HOTELS AND RESTAURANTS - PROVENCE & CORSICA

Top Hotels

★★★★★*Hotel de Paris*   place Casino, Monte Carlo 98000
Tel. 00 377 92 16 30 00 Fax 00 377 92 16 38 50
Email hp@sbm.mc   145 rooms   £H

★★★★★*Château du Domaine St-Martin*   route de Coursegoules, Vence 06140
Tel. 04 93 58 02 02 Fax 04 93 24 08 91
Email stmartin@relaischateau.com   32 rooms   £H

Top Restaurants

★★★★★*La Terrace Hotel Juana*   ave. G. Gallici, Juan-les-Pins 06160
Tel. 04 93 61 08 70 Fax 04 93 61 76 60
Email. info@hotel-juana.com   £F/H

★★★★★*Hotel de Paris - Le Louis XV*   Monte Carlo 98000
Tel. 00 377 92 16 30 00 Fax 00 377 92 16 38 50
Email hp@sbm.mc   £H

Value for money Hotels

★*L'Avenue*   ave. de la Gare, Annot 04240
Tel. 04 92 83 22 07 Fax 04 92 83 33 13
Email hot.avenue@wanadoo.fr   11 rooms   £A

★*Bosquet*   Chemin de Périssols, Pégomas   06580
Tel. 04 92 60 21 20 Fax 04 92 60 21 49
Email hotel.lebosquet@wanadoo.fr   16 rooms   £A

Value for money restaurants

★*L'Avenue*   ave. de la Gare, Annot 04240
Tel. 04 92 83 22 07 Fax 04 92 83 33 13
Email hot.avenue@wanadoo.fr   £A/B

★*L'Oustaou*, 5 pl. Brémond, Flayosc 83780
Tel. 04 94 70 42 69   Fax 04 94 84 64 92
No email address   £A/C

PROVENCALE RECIPES

TAPENADE: for 6 people

Ingredients: 250gr. stoneless fat black olives; 75gr. anchovy fillets; 75 gr. capers, 3 cloves of garlic (4 if you like garlic); 2.5dl olive oil, a dash of balsamic vinegar, a dash of boiling water at the end; pepper, and salt if needed.

Soak the anchovy fillets in cold water for half an hour to take the salt away; then put garlic (with the germ out) the olives, anchovies, capers in a mixer and gradually add the olive oil. Then add a dash of balsamic vinegar and a dash of boiling water. Taste and season accordingly. Tapenade lasts a long time in the fridge and is wonderful on crostini with a little basil and half a cherry tomato!

RECOMMENDED WINES

Another aperitif dish which would go splendidly with fine Bandol rosés from either Domaine Tempier or Domaine de Terrebrune

BRANDADE DE MORUE for 4 people:

Ingredients: 500gr. salted cod: 3dl of good olive oil, half dl. of cream, 2 cloves of garlic very finely chopped, the germ removed; pepper. A court bouillon made with 2 litres of water, one large onion with a clove stuck to it, half a carrot, a celery stick, a sprig of parsley and a bay leaf.

Put the salted cod in a colander, and soak the lot in plenty of cold water overnight to remove the salt. The salt will then fall to the bottom of the water. Rinse the fish very, very well; if still salty change the water and soak again. Squeeze all water from the fish and cook in the boiling court bouillon on a very small heat for ten minutes removing the scum constantly. Place the fish on a board, remove skin and bones leaving a little of the white gelatinous skin attached to the fish. Warm the olive oil and the cream separately. Put the hot cod and garlic in a mixer and gradually add olive oil and cream alternatively. If you are doing it by hand, mash the cod with the garlic first, put it in a pan over very slow heat and gradually add oil and cream stirring all the time. Rectify seasoning at the end. Should be served very hot with grilled bread. Tapenade should go very well with it as well.

RECOMMENDED WINES

A really flavoursome white is needed here to take this dish, although the above rosés would do just as well. Ch. Simone white from Palette has the right kind of flavours as do a trio from the les Baux area, Mas de la Dame "Coin Caché", Domaine de Lauzières "Astérie" and, of course, Domaine de Trevallon's Vin de Pays des Bouches-du-Rhône.

DAUBE DE BOEUF À LA PROVENÇALE

For 4 people: *Ingredients:* 1kg of skirt, feather blade or very good quality braising steak cut up in large pieces: 250gr. of streaky bacon, 150gr. of mushrooms, 4 carrots, 3 medium size onions, 1 bouquet garni (bay leaf, thyme, rosemary, marjoram, or any combination), a sprig of parsley, and two cloves of garlic with the germ out, a bottle of strong red wine, one dl. of cognac, water to cover the meat.

Marinate the meat in the wine and cognac for two hours. Cut the mushrooms in small pieces, chop two onions and stick two cloves in the third one, slice the carrots 1cm. thick, Cut the garlic in thin slices. Line a dish (preferably earthenware)with a good lid with the streaky bacon, strain the meat and put a layer of meat on the bacon and then a layer of vegetables, then another layer of meat, then vegetables, garlic and bouquet garni. Bring the wine and cognac marinade to the boil and pour on the meat pouring enough boiling water to cover the meat. Fit the lid very tightly and cook for 5 hours in a very slow oven. To serve: rectify the seasoning, let the meat rest in its juices keeping it hot then try to remove as much fat as possible from the surface of the dish (you can remove some of the meat to do this and then put it back). Sprinkle a lot of parsley on top mixed with finely chopped garlic and breadcrumbs.

RECOMMENDED WINES

The red Bandols really come into their own with this dish and whilst the traditional producers such as Domaine Tempier and Ch. de Pibarnon still hold sway, you would do well to look at some of the up and coming producers like Domaine Lafran Veyrolles and Domaine de Gros Noré, which are better value. Of course, there is always Domaine de Trevallon as the Provence benchmark red.

POIRES FARCIES DES SANTONS: for 4 people

Ingredients: 4 nice Poires Williams: peeled, cut in half and cored: Syrup for cooking the pears: 125gr. sugar and 4dl. water, 150 gr. of fruits confits (glacé fruit like pineapple, orange skins, a few cherries etc.), 30gr. of raisins, 1.5dl. of Kirsch, 2dl of fresh cream, 150gr. raspberry, 50gr. sugar for the sauce; 4 scoops of vanilla ice cream (optional).

Macerate the glacé fruit and raisins in the Kirsch overnight. Cook the pears in a syrup made of 125gr. sugar and 4dl water until soft but slightly firm. Remove from syrup and cool; meanwhile sieve the glace fruit, chop finely and stuff each half pear with this mix. Reconstitute the pears, wrap each individually with cling film and chill. Meanwhile make the sauce with the fresh cream, the rest of the sugar, the raspberries (mashed), and the kirsch marinade and beat a little to thicken, Put a layer off vanilla ice cream at the bottom of a chilled bowl, place the unwrapped pears on top, pour the raspberry sauce over them.

RECOMMENDED WINES

There's no Provence dessert wine of real quality – the nearest being the Beaumes de Venise from the southern Rhône Valley, so perhaps you should slip out and grab a bottle of Ch. d'Yquem to go with this excellent dessert

This section of the guide covers south-western France. A number of the regions in the south-west are close neighbours of Bordeaux and the style inevitably mirrors that of the Bordelais. Further south, both in the Lot Valley at Cahors and south towards the Pyrenees at Madiran and Jurançon, first-class dry and sweet whites and rich, stylish reds are becoming justifiably known to a wider audience.

South-West France

Immediately to the east of Bordeaux on the river Dordogne is Bergerac. There are a number of ACs north and south of the river, but the large, generic **Bergerac AC** encompasses all the smaller sub-regions. Red, white and rosé are produced from the Bordeaux varieties. Quality is fairly pedestrian with high yields and widespread mechanical harvesting. The number of good reds and whites being produced here is, however, increasing. Lees-enrichment and *bâtonnage* are now being used for whites and new oak is increasingly common for both reds and whites. The **Côtes de Bergerac** and **Pécharmant** are immediately to the north of the town of Bergerac. The former is a source of some good reds and sweet whites (labelled as Côtes de Bergerac Moelleux). Pécharmant should do better than it does with its well-drained sandy, limestone soils. To the south of the river are the sweet-white ACs of **Monbazillac** and **Saussignac**. The former is worth considering as an alternative to Sauternes. The wines can be remarkably rich and complex with heady levels of botrytis. Be aware though that they are becoming more established and prices are rising. Both ACs are a blend of Sémillon and Sauvignon Blanc. Some good red and dry white is made at **Montravel** in vineyards bordering the Côtes de Castillon in Bordeaux. Sweet styles are also produced here and in the small ACs of **Côtes de Montravel** and **Haut-Montravel**. Thus far they lack the richness and depth found in Monbazillac.

South of Bergerac are the appellations of the **Côtes de Duras**, **Côtes du Marmandais** and **Buzet**. Both red and white are produced in the vineyards around Duras, with an occasional late-harvest white. As at Bergerac, Bordeaux varieties are planted. The reds tend towards a vegetal character and the whites are at best fresh and grassy. More new oak is being used, with varying success. Marmandais and Buzet appellations are red only, with more interest in the Côtes du Marmandais, where as well as Bordeaux grapes some indigenous south-western varieties are also permitted.

To the south-east of Bergerac along a 30-mile stretch of the river Lot are the vineyards of **Cahors**. Some of the finest red wines of the south-west are now produced here. Auxerrois (Malbec) dominates plantings, with some Merlot and Tannat. Expect anything from light, plummy, easy-drinking wines (occasionally with a green vegetal note) to serious and very structured ageworthy reds. Prices of the best examples seem to be surging upwards. West of Cahors the AC of **Marcillac** produces spicy reds from Fer-Servadou, while to the south the VDQS of the **Coteaux du Quercy** produces reds of some potential. further south, towards Toulouse, are the VDQS of both the **Côtes du Brulhois** and **Lavilledieu**; and the **Côtes du Frontonnais** AC. The latter has turned out a number of interesting reds based on the Negrette grape. The wines are both perfumed and spicy, the best impressively structured. To the north-east of Toulouse, **Gaillac** AC offers some unusual and diverse styles; Mauzac is the key white variety, although Muscadelle and Ondenc are also important. Good dry and sweet wines are produced along with *perlé* (a white bottled some residual CO_2) and Gaillac Mousseux, produced by the *méthode rural*. The majority of the red is light although there are an increasing number of significant examples.

463

To the south are the great red and white wines of Gascony. This is also bulk-white **Vin de Pays des Côtes de Gasgogne** country. The **Madiran** and **Pacherenc du Vic-Bilh** ACs share the same geographical area and many growers produce both. Pacherenc can be dry or sweet and is produced from Gros and Petit Manseng, Petit Courbu and Arrufiac, with the odd touch of Sémillon and Sauvignon Blanc (for *moelleux*) blended in. The best are very good. Madiran itself produces powerful, dense and ageworthy reds based on Tannat and often blended with a bit of Cabernets Franc and Sauvignon and Fer-Servadou. It was here that the technique of micro-oxygenation was developed to harness and soften the Tannat's often aggressive and sturdy tannins. Some of the wines are world-class and provide very good value. **Jurançon** is without doubt the finest white-wine appellation of the south-west. Gros and Petit Manseng as well as Petit Courbu are planted. The wines can be sublime, particularly the sweet styles. Yields are low and inevitably prices are rising. The reds of nearby **Béarn** are generally light and insubstantial. To the south-west of Jurançon, nestled into the foothills of the Pyrenees, **Irouléguy** provides some good reds and whites from the same varieties as at Madiran and Jurançon.

South-West France vintages

In general most red and white should be drunk young and only a number of appellations provide wines with the substance for real ageing. Top Cahors needs several years in bottle and evolves well. Jurançon, both dry and sweet, will improve over half a decade or more and keep much longer. Top Madiran, more approachable than in the past, needs five years at least, particularly the top cuvées. Throughout the south-west 2004, 2003, 2002, 2001, 2000, 1999, 1998, 1996 and 1995 were good. 1993, 1990 and 1988 are worth considering for top Jurançon and the trio of 1990, 1989 and 1988 for top Madiran.

		7	Monbazillac
		8	Côtes de Duras
		9	Côtes du Marmandais
		10	Cahors
1	Bergerac	11	Buzet
2	Côtes de Montravel	12	Côtes du Frontonnais
3	Montravel, Haut-Montravel	13	Gaillac
4	Rosette	14	Madiran
5	Pécharmant	15	Béarn
6	Saussignac	16	Jurançon
		17	Irouléguy

A-Z of producers

DOM. BERTHOUMIEU Madiran barre.didier@wanadoo.fr

Didier Barré Dutour, 32400 Viella

UK stockists: CdP, AVn

Impressive 25-ha Madiran property producing around 15,000 cases a year. The main focus of the property and, it has to be said, the best wines are the 2 Madiran *cuvées*. Vinification is traditional and the wines have considerable extract and youthful tannin after a maceration of 3 weeks or so. The Tradition is spicy, dense and structured with an earthy, mineral core. A blend of Tannat, Cabernet Sauvignon, Cabernet Franc and Fer-Servadou, it is aged partly in wood and partly in *cuve*. The old-vine Charles de Batz is a rich, brooding wine with sweet, chocolaty notes. It sees a large portion of new oak. The wines here are extensively racked as opposed to using micro-oxygenation to minimise those burly, aggressive Tannat tannins. The result is uniformly ripe and supple. The Pacherenc Sec is crisp and fresh, while the sweet Symphonie d'Automne is weighty, rich and more aromatic. (DM)

● **Madiran** Tradition★★ £B Charles de Batz★★★★ £C
○ **Pacherenc de Vic-Bilh** Sec★ £B Cuvée Symphonie d'Automne Doux★★ £C

ALAIN BRUMONT Madiran www.montus-madiran.com

Alain Brumont Château Bouscassé, 32400 Maumusson

UK stockists: THt, CdP, HHB, N&P

With a large vineyard holding of some 140ha and a total production of 65,000 to 70,000 cases, Alain Brumont makes impressively structured, rich and very concentrated Madiran under the Montus and Bouscassé labels as well as a softer, more immediately appealing example labelled Torus. He also produces good dry Pacherenc de Vic Bilh under the Montus label. Mainly Petit Courbu, the wine is barrel-fermented and aged and is rich, nutty and intensely honeyed in character. There is also a Bouscassé white that is not vinified in oak and is understandably more aromatic in nature. A number of very good late-harvest Pacherencs are produced as well. Bouscassé is the secondary property, producing a well-priced regular Madiran and a dense and powerful Vieilles Vignes. The approach to vinification emphasises power and extraction. Maceration lasts for over 4 weeks and no micro-oxygentation is employed during maturation. The regular Château Montus is full of firm, dark-fruited Tannat character. The Cuvée Prestige is pricey but a serious step up. Very, powerful and structured, it demands 7 or 8 years' ageing to achieve a harmonious balance of fruit and tannin. It will show great refinement with time. Three special *cuvées* have now been introduced, Argile, Les Menhirs and La Tyre. All offer real weight, power and structure. La Tyre, undoubtedly the finest, offers extraordinary depth and richness but at a very heavy price.(DM)

Alain Brumont
● **Madiran** Torus★★ £B

Château Montus
● **Madiran**★★★ £C Cuvée Prestige★★★★ £F La Tyre★★★★ £F
● **Madiran** La Tyre★★★★★ £G ○ **Pacherenc de Vic-Bilh**★★★ £C

Château Bouscassé
● **Madiran**★★ £B Vieilles Vignes★★★★ £D Argile★★★★ £D
○ **Pacherenc de Vic-Bilh**★★ £B

CAMIN LARREDYA Jurançon jm.grussaute@wandoo.fr

Jean-Marc Grussaute Chapelle de Rousse, 64110 Jurançon

Small domaine producing just 4 wines from 10ha of vineyards. Output is currently around 3,500 cases a year and the wines are very favourably priced.

The vineyards are cultivated along organic principles and Jean-Marc follows an approach of minimal intervention. There is a crisp, well-crafted dry Jurançon, mainly from Gros Manseng, which is floral and lightly aromatic with fine persistence and good fresh acidity lending grip. A later-harvested *doux* is also produced. The top wines are the 2 Petit Manseng-based sweet wines, Les Terasses and Cuvée Simon. Both will age very well and the Simon in particular will continue to develop over 10 years or more. (DM)

O **Jurançon** Sec★★ £B Les Terasses★★★ £C Cuvée Simon★★★★ £E

DOM. CAUHAPÉ Jurançon domainecauhape@wanadoo.fr
Henri Ramonteu   Quartier Castet, 64360 Monein
UK stockists: SsG, FMV, BBR, N&P

Henri Ramonteu's domaine is sizeable for the region at some 40ha but he is arguably the finest exponent of the appellation. He makes an extensive range with 2 dry and 4 sweet wines from very low-yielding vineyards. The sweet wines are classified according the harvesting date of the grapes. The dry styles are produced mainly from Gros Manseng and vinified with some skin contact, with the Sève d'Automne being barrel-fermented, and all the wines are kept on their lees. The sweet wines, with a high proportion of Petit Manseng are increasingly luscious and richly concentrated but with a fine, fresh backbone of acidity. They are structured and very ageworthy. Rare and only produced when conditions favour it from Petit Manseng fruit harvested close to the year's end, Quintessence is among the great wines not only of Jurançon but of France as well. (DM)

O **Jurançon** Chant des Vignes★★ £B Sève d'Automne★★★ £C
O **Jurançon** Ballet d'Octobre★★★ £C Symphonie de Novembre★★★★ £C
O **Jurançon** Noblesse du Temps★★★★ £E

CHAPELLE LENCLOS Madiran
Patrick Ducournau   32400 Maumusson Laguian
UK stockists: THt, CdP

Patrick Ducournau has 18ha of vineyards of which a mere 2.5ha are planted to white varieties, from which he produces decent, lightly honeyed and intense Pacherenc de Vic-Bilh, occasionally as a *moelleux*. The main focus is on the Madiran reds. There are 2 wines here. The Domaine Mouréou is supple and surprisingly approachable for the appellation. The wine is mainly aged in tank and requires a little time to take the hard edge off its tannins. La Chapelle Lenclos is denser and more structured; it will be better with 4 or 5 years' ageing. The wine is partly aged in *cuve* and partly in large 400-litre barrels. Winemaker Damiens Sartori is trying to emphasise fruit and underplay the oak influence that is increasingly evident in some of his neighbours' wines. Much of the style is achieved by the process of micro-oxygenation, which was developed by Ducournau. (DM)

● **Madiran** Domaine Mouréou★★ £B la Chapelle Lenclos★★★ £C
O **Pacherenc de Vic-Bilh** Moelleux★★ £B

CH. D'AYDIE Madiran
Laplace family   64330 Aydie
UK stockists: GBa, AVn

A small but fine range of Madirans and Pacherenc de Vic-Bilhs is produced at this sizeable property. There are 45ha of vineyards of which 35ha are devoted to producing Madiran. Decent, straightforward red Madiran is released as Fleury-Laplace, which is produced from bought-in fruit and offers a soft, accessible example of the appellation. Odé d'Aydie is the second label and is reasonably dense and powerful. The Château d'Aydie is a serious step up, full of dark fruit, well-judged oak and firm, youthful tannin – 5 or 6 years' ageing is needed. The wine is kept on its lees in barrel and micro-oxygenation is employed. Pacherenc is produced in a dry style under the Frédéric Laplace label, which is both aromatic and intense, with piercing green, nettly fruit. Rich and impressively concentrated *moelleux* is also made. (DM)

● **Madiran** Odé d'Aydie★★ £B Château d'Aydie★★★ £C
O **Pacherenc de Vic-Bilh** Frédéric Laplace★★ £B

CH. BARRÉJAT   Madiran
Denis Capmartin 32400 Maumusson
Good to very good Madiran is made by Denis Capmartin at his 22-ha domaine. One of the important keys to quality here is the impressive age of some of the vineyards, which are farmed along organic principles. For the remarkable top label, Vieux Ceps, some of the vines are an astounding 200 years of age. The regular Madiran Tradition is as forward as Madiran manages to be but it still needs a year or 2 to soften its hard youthful edge, which is promoted by a lengthy 21-day *cuvaison* and ageing in *cuve*. Richer and lusher in texture is the Séduction, a blend of 60% Tannat and 40% Cabernets Sauvignon and Franc. Aged in small oak *barriques*, a small proportion new, it is ripe and full of deep, dark, cedary fruit and subtle spicy oak. The Vieux Ceps has just 20% of the Cabernets blended with Tannat. It is both rich and understandably very complex. The top 2 wines will benefit from at leasts 5 years, ageing. (DM)

● **Madiran** Tradition★★ £B Séduction★★★ £C Vieux Ceps★★★★ £C

CH. BEAULIEU   Côtes du Marmandais
Robert Schulte 32400 Maumusson
Robert Schulte is among a small handful of producers independently striving for fine quality in this lesser-known appellation. Most of his neighbours choose to sell to the local co-op. Beaulieu's 26.5ha of vineyards have great potential and are planted on a mix of gravel and calcareous soils. The vineyard is also being replanted to achieve a density of up to 6,000 vines per hectare, which will improve quality further. Three reds are made here and the style is traditional, particularly for the Côtes du Marmandais and top Cuvée de l'Oratoire. You need to give them at least 4 or 5 years' ageing to soften their firm youthful edge. These latter 2 wines are about structure rather than fruit. The Galapian de Beaulieu, produced from young vines, is softer and more obviously fruit-driven. The Cuvée de l'Oratoire comes from vines up to 40 years old and is produced from a yield of just 18 to 20 hl/ha. It is impressively dense, rich and concentrated. (DM).

● **Côtes du Marmandais**★★ £B l'Oratoire★★★ £C Galapian de Beaulieu★ £B

CH. BELLEVUE SUR VALLÉE   Bergerac
Robert and Claire Adler 24240 Thénac
Yet another dream fulfilled, this time by ex-New York banker Robert Adler and his Korean-born wife, Claire. In 2002, they bought this run-down property in the Dordogne, grubbed out all the vines except for a block of old venerable Cabernet Franc and Cabernet Sauvignon and replanted at high density. Buildings and equipment were also upgraded and 2002 was their first vintage. 2003 produced a fresh and fruity Sémillon and Sauvignon Blanc - both vinified and bottled separately and both showing upfront tropical fruit characteristics. The red blend (60% Merlot, 30% Cabernet Sauvignon, 10% Cabernet Franc) is a big, fruity, supple wine, which will drink well young. The 2003 Saussignac (none made in 2004 - conditions not right) is very classy with intense botrytised and biscuity sweetness. (NB).

467

● **Bergerac** Le Vin du Bob★★★ £B   O **Saussignac** Le Vin du Bob★★★★ £C
O **Bergerac** Le Vin du Bob Semillon★★ £B   Le Vin du Bob Sauvignon★★★ £B

CH. DU CÈDRE   Cahors   chateauducedre@wanadoo.fr

Pascal et Jean-Marc Verhaeghe   46700 Vire-sur-Lot
UK stockists: CdP, GWW

The Verhaegue family possess some 25ha of vineyards and produce 3 good to very good reds. The regular Cahors is made from the youngest vines. It is a ripe, brambly, forward style for drinking young. The Prestige *cuvée* is altogether sturdier and denser. The top wine, Le Cèdre, is now fairly pricey, particularly for the appellation. Produced entirely from old Malbec vines and aged in 100% new oak, it is powerful, structured and very ageworthy – best with 5 years in the cellar or more. There are also ongoing experiments here with lees-ageing for reds and the use of micro-oxygenation. (DM)

● **Cahors**★ £B   Prestige★★ £C   Le Cèdre★★★★ £E

CH. JONC BLANC   Montravel

Isabelle Carles & Franck Pascal   Le Jonc Blanc, 24230 Velines
UK stockists: Imperial

Newly emerged Montravel property producing wines of real style and substance from 12ha of vineyards run on organic principles and planted solely to red varieties. As well as the reds there is a straightforward, bright, fresh, fruit-driven rosé, Isabelle. The vineyards are planted on argile-calcareous soils with a very high gravel component in the topsoil which provides an ideal base for the wines. The regular bottling, the Blanches Pierres is traditionally vinified without recourse to new oak. The Automnale and Rubis are both fuller and denser and see a touch of small oak. These are good, well-priced examples of an often disappointing appellation. (DM)

● **Bergerac** Blanches Pierres★★ £B   Cuvée Autumnale★★★ £B
● **Montravel** Rubis★★★ £C

CH. LAFFITTE-TESTON   Madiran

Jean-Marc Laffitte   32400 Maumusson
UK stockists: CdP, GWW

Jean-Marc Laffitte producers not only good Madiran but also some of the most striking examples of Pacherenc du Vic-Bilh. His output of over 20,000 cases is not inconsiderable for the region but fine quality is maintained throughout. He has just over 34ha of red varieties, 70% of which are Tannat, as well 5.5ha of white Petit and Gros Manseng and a smattering of Courbu. The stylish Ericka is barrel-fermented, with a fair proportion of new wood being used, and offers impressively piercing floral, nutty, spicy fruit. The Moelleux is opulent and richly textured. Both will evolve well in the short term. The Madiran Tradition is good if a touch angular in its youth, while the Vieilles Vignes is altogether rounder and fuller and is capable of adding real complexity with 6 or 7 years' ageing. (DM)

● **Madiran** Tradition★★ £B   Vieilles Vignes★★★ £C
O **Pacherenc du Vic-Bilh** Ericka★★★ £B   Moelleux★★★ £C

CH. LAGREZETTE   Cahors   www.chateau-lagrezette.tm.fr

Alain-Dominique Perrin   46140 Caillac
UK stockists: CCC

Another recent top-quality performer in Cahors, Alain-Dominique Perrin is a wealthy entrepreneur whose portfolio includes prestige jewellery operation Cartier. No expense is spared at this 65-ha property and roving consultant Michel Rolland provides guidance over vinification. Classic Rolland techniques are all evident including pre-fermentation maceration, extended vatting, malolactic in barrel and judicious use of new oak. A number a soft fruity Cahors are made under the *négociant* Domaine de Lagrezette label: Grezette, Expression de Grezette and Chevalier-Lagrezette. Grezette is a straightforward commune wine, while Expression and Chevalier get a touch of used oak for ageing. The rich and impressively concentrated Château Lagrezette is a regular Cahors given an extended maceration of up to 4 weeks. The 2 prestige *cuvées*, Dame Honneur and the very pricey Pigeonnier, are a step up, particularly the deep and saturated Pigeonnier. It is 100% Malbec sourced from the property's oldest vines and produced from a yield of barely more than 15 hl/ha. The Dame Honneur will benefit from 5 years or so, the Pigeonnier a year or 2 longer. (DM)

● **Cahors**★★★ £C Chevaliers★★ £C Lagrezette Dame Honneur★★★★ £E
● **Cahors** Pigeonnier★★★★★ £G

CH. LAMARTINE   Cahors

Alain Gayraud   46700 Soturac
UK stockists: Imperial

This is emerging as a consistently good source of Cahors. The property is relatively sizeable with 30ha (28ha Cahors AC) under vine. Auxerrois (Malbec) is much the most important variety, accounting for 90% of the land under cultivation. Output now totals around 16–18,000 cases a year. Much of the quality here is down to the aspect of the vineyards and the *terroir*, with south-facing slopes on the calcareous soils of the Cahors *coteaux*. The regular bottling is sound and characterful with some spicy tobacco as well as dark fruit notes. The Cuvée Particulière comes from older vines; it is denser and fuller and is lent weight from ageing in oak. The L'Expression is one of the appellation's new-wave wines, produced solely from old-vine Auxerrois and aged for 20 months in new *barriques*. Rich, dense and very serious, this requires 5 years' patience. (DM)

● **Cahors**★ £B Cuvée Particulière★★ £C L'Expression★★★ £D

CH. TIRECUL-LA-GRAVIÈRE   Monbazillac

Claudie et Bruno Billancini   24240 Monbazillac
UK stockists:L&S

Arguably the top property for sweet Monbazillac. The Billancinis have just 9ha or so planted and produce a tiny amount – some 1,500 cases in total every year. The style is radically different from their neighbours' with intensely honeyed wines full of rich fruit, quince, toast and very marked botrytis. They achieve this by controlling yields and conducting a succession of *tris* as extensive as any top Sauternes property. The regular bottling is very impressive with rich fruit and spicy, vanilla notes from new oak. There is also a tiny volume of the special and very pricey Cuvée Madame. The wines may be enjoyed young but will keep very well. (DM)

● **Monbazillac**★★★★ £E Cuvée Madame★★★★★ £F

CH. TOUR DES GENDRES   Bergerac

De Conti family   Les Gendres, 24240 Ribagnac
UK stockists:CdP,GWW,HHB

Very impressive Bergerac property with a range of reds and whites produced as Bergerac as well as a red Côtes de Bergerac, the stylish and concentrated Gloire de Mon Père. There are a total of some 43ha of vineyards with more than half planted to red varieties. Production is now over 25,000 cases a year, which is in no way detrimental to quality. White planting is typically Bordelais, mainly Sémillon with Sauvignon Blanc and around 10% Muscadelle; reds are

469

dominated by Merlot and full of rich, plummy fruit. In addition to the regular range, Casanova des Conti wines – a simple fruit-driven white blend of Sémillon, Sauvignon and Muscadelle and a red comprising mainly Merlot with some Cabernet Sauvignon – are produced exclusively for the UK market. The top *cuvées* have real dimension and class. The Anthologia bottlings are as impressive as anything yet produced from the region, the red adding a round, supple character through partial barrel-fermentation. The white is marvellously intense and pure with beautifully balanced oak. It has only been released in 1996 and 2001. Some of the vineyards are now being farmed biodynamically. (DM)

● **Bergerac**★ £B Moulin des Dames★★★ £D Cuvée Anthologia★★★★ £E
● **Côtes de Bergerac** Gloire de Mon Père★★★ £B
O **Bergerac** Cuvée des Conti★★ £B Moulin des Dames★★★ £C
O **Bergerac** Cuvée Anthologia★★★★ £E ◎ **Bergerac**★ £B

CH.VIELLA Madiran

Alain Bortolussi Route de Maumusson, 32400 Viella
UK stockists: Ben

The Bortolussi family is in the course of renovating the splendid old château at this property. They make a simple, very straightforward Bearn rosé but of more importance is a good barrel-fermented dry Pacherenc du Vic-Bilh from mainly Arrufiac, as well as a little Gros and Petit Manseng, and a very fine late-harvest Pacherenc which is 100% Petit Manseng. The latter is luscious but very finely structured, with a glorious ripe citrus and mineral character. The good regular Madiran is aged in *cuve* with 40% Cabernets Franc and Sauvignon blended with Tannat. It needs a year or 2 to add some flesh. The Cuvée Prestige is rich, dense and powerfully structured. It is 100% Tannat and aged in new wood. A minimum of 4 to 5 years is needed to achieve an equilibrium of fruit and oak. The wines are all very fairly priced. (DM)

● **Madiran**★★ £B Cuvée Prestige★★★ £C
O **Pacherenc du Vic-Bilh**★★ £B Moelleux★★★ £C

CLOS LA COUTALE Cahors pro.wanadoo.fr/philippebernede

Bernède family La Coutale, 46700 Vire-sur-Lot
UK stockists: **WTs**

Philippe Bernède is the current winemaker at this long-established family property. His top wine, Clos la Coutale, is a little more easygoing than the traditional 'black wine' of Cahors but a long way from a fruit-forward modern style. It has beautiful floral and spice characters on the nose with hints of tobacco and oak on the palate and a firm, long finish. The composition of the wine is generally 70% Malbec, 15% Merlot and 15% Tannat. (NB)

● **Cahors**★★ £B

CLOS LAPEYRE Jurançon jean-bernard.larrieu@wanadoo.fr

Jean-Bernard Larrieu La Chapelle de Rousse, 64110 Jurançon
UK stockists: **CdP, HHB**

There are 12ha under vine here and both dry and sweet styles are produced. The regular Jurançon Sec is fermented in stainless steel and kept on its lees for added depth. The old-vine Vitatge Vielh is barrel-fermented, which gives greater weight. Three sweet wines are made. The regular Moelleux is full and spicy with nicely balanced acidity; the barrel-fermented Sélection is richer and more intensely citrusy with subtle oak in the background. The top late-harvested wine, Vent Balaguer, is produced solely from Petit Manseng grapes that are marked by *passerillage*. Remarkably rich and concentrated, it is only produced in the most exceptional years. (DM)

○ **Jurançon** Sec★ £B Vitatge Vielh★★ £B Moelleux★★ £B
○ **Jurançon** Sélection Petit Manseng★★★ £C

CLOS TRIGUEDINA   Cahors   www.clos-triguedina.com

Jean-Luc Baldés   46700 Puy l'Evêque
UK stockists: CdP, HHB

The Baldés family have been in the region for nearly 2 centuries and in the Prince Probus *cuvée* they established one of the benchmark wines of the appellation long before some of the more recently famous names. To this they have added a massive, dark new *cuvée*, New Black Wine, named after the fabled Cahors of old. There are 57ha of reds and just 2ha of whites. From the latter they produce a good barrel-fermented *vin de pays* white blended from Chardonnay and Viognier and a small amount of late-harvest Chenin Blanc. Some rosé is also produced but it is the red Cahors which defines quality here. In order to maintain the standard of the top wines, 2 forward and fruit-driven secondary labels are also released. Of these, Domaine Labrande comes from a separate property, while Balmont de Cahors is produced at Clos Triguedina. The estate red is a structured and impressively ageworthy example of the appellation. Aged in used oak, it is full of spicy tobacco and red berry fruit. Prince Probus is fuller and darker with a marked vanilla undercurrent from new wood. (DM)

● **Cahors**★★ £C Prince Probus★★★ £D New Black Wine★★★★ £E

CLOS UROULAT   Jurançon

Charles Hours   Quartier Trouilh, 64360 Monein
UK stockists: HHB

Charles Hours possesses a small holding of some 7ha with the bulk planted to Petit Manseng and the balancing 25% Gros Manseng with a bit of Courbu. Just 2 wines are produced here and very good and attractively priced they are too. Both wines are barrel-fermented. The dry Cuvée Marie is full of intense, citrus character and subtle, vanilla oak. The sweet Clos Uroulat is unctuous and rich with a few years in bottle but has marvellously fresh acidity cutting through it. Both will develop well with time. (DM)

○ **Jurançon** Cuvée Marie★★ £B Clos Uroulat★★★ £C

ROBERT PLAGEOLES   Gaillac

Robert & Bernard Plageoles   Domaine de Tres-Cantous, 81140 Cahuzac-sur-Vère
UK stockists: CdP

The Plageoles produce some of the most striking and original of all Gaillac with a firm commitment to the region's indigenous varieties. Syrah is the most obvious interloper and there is a little Muscadelle as well. There are a total of 20ha under vine with 13ha accounted for by white varieties. The reds are very much in a traditional style. No oak is used and they emphasise fruit and are pure and well crafted. They are generally light in colour and extract, particularly the Mauzac Noir, and the Syrah is the darkest of the trio with a hint of black pepper. It is the whites which are particularly important. The Mauzac Nature is a light, fresh sparkler and the Mauzac Vert is a dry style marked by a fascinating array of green fruits. The Mauzac Doux by contrast is a late-harvest white with hints of peach and a slight undercurrent of white pepper and mineral. The Plageoles also make their own version of a *vin jaune*, Vin de Voile, which is also from Mauzac. The dry Ondenc is rich and impressively concentrated with hints of honey, peach and quince just underpinned by a subtle green fruit character. The great wine here and surely the finest white in Gaillac is the superbly rich and concentrated Vin d'Autan, produced from Ondenc. The vines are pinched to encourage dehydration of the fruit by the *Autan* wind and

471

the grapes are then further dried after harvesting in the manner of a *vin de paille*. The 2001 was produced from a microscopic yield of just 6hl/ha. (DM)

● **Gaillac** Braucol★★ £B Mauzac Noir★★ £B Syrah★★ £B
○ **Gaillac** Mauzac Vert★★ £B Mauzac Nature★ £B Ondenc★★★ £B
○ **Gaillac Doux** Mauzac Doux★★★ £C Vin d'Autan★★★★★ £F

PRIMO PALATUM Vin de Pays d'Oc xavier.copel@primo-palatum.fr

Xavier Copel 1 Cirette, 33190 Morizes
UK stockists: N&P

Xavier Copel has now established himself as a very successful small-scale merchant and *négociant*, specialising in limited-production bottlings from the important South-West appellations as well as as in Languedoc and Roussillon. He sources fruit from some of the best growers in each of the appellations he works in. Overall production is less than 6,000 cases a year and some wines are barely more than *micro-cuvées*. Apart from the wines rated below, his considerable range includes bottlings from Bordeaux, Graves, Sauternes and in the Midi, Minervois and the Côtes du Roussillon. The regular or lesser bottlings are labelled Classica and the top *cuvées* within an appellation are usually labelled Mythologia. The wines are very impressive: modern and stylish, with an emphasis on *terroir*, and always impeccably made in the various growers' own cellars. (DM)

● **Cahors** Classica★★★ £C Mythologia★★★★ £D
● **Vin de Pays d'Oc** Classica★★ £C Mythologia★★★ £C
○ **Limoux** Anthologie★★★ £D **Jurançon** Classica★★★ £D Mythologia★★★★ £E

DOM. ROTIER Gaillac

Alain Rotier & Francis Marre Petit Nareye, 81600 Cadalen
UK stockists: GWW

Good-quality small Gaillac grower with an output of around 14,000 cases a year. Alain Rotier has been vinifying his own wines since 1985 and has now been joined by his brother-in-law Francis Marre. They farm 31ha of vines, 70% of which are red. The vines are now approaching an average age of 30 years and in an ongoing drive to improve quality vine density is being increased from 4,000 to over 6,000 vines per hectare. Regular red, white and rosé are labelled Initiales and a *perlé* is included in the range. More significant wines appear under the Gravels and Renaissance labels and the reds both stand out. The Renaissance is structured and dense and shows impressive dark fruit and cedary complexity. The dry whites don't have quite the same depth but are good examples nonetheless. The sweet white Renaissance Doux shows good, rich peachy fruit with a fine, piercing citrus structure. Most of the wines are forward and approachable but expect the Renaissance wines to develop well in the medium term, particularly the sweet white and the red. (DM)

● **Gaillac** Gravels★★ £B Renaissance★★★ £B
○ **Gaillac** Gravels★ £B Renaissance★★ £B Renaissance Doux★★★ £C

OTHER WINES OF NOTE

DOM. ABOTIA ● **Irouléguy**★★ £B
DOM. DE L'ANCIENNE CURE ● **Bergerac** Abbaye★★ £B L'Extrase★★★ £D
○ **Monbazillac**★★ £B Cuvée de l'Abbaye★★★★ £E
DOM. ARRETXIA ● **Irouléguy**★★ £B Haitza★★★ £C
DOM. BELLEGARDE ○ **Jurançon**★★ £B Cuvée Thibaut★★★ £C
DOM. BRANA ● **Irouléguy**★★ £C Ohitza★ £B Harri Gorri★★ £B
DOM. BRU-BACHÉ ○ **Jurançon** Casterrasses★★ £B Quintessence★★★ £C
DOM. GUY CAPMARTIN ● **Madiran** Tradition★★ £B Cuvée de Couvent★★ £B
DOM. CASTERA ○ **Jurançon**★★ £B

DOM. DE CAUSSE-MARINES ○ **Gaillac** Greilles★★ £B Délires d'Automne★★★ £D

CH. BAUDARE ● **Côtes du Frontonnais** Tradition★ £B

CH. BEAUPORTAIL ● **Pécharmant** Fûts de Chêne★★ £B

CH. BÉLINGARD ○ **Bergerac** Blanche de Bosredon★ £B
○ **Monbazillac** Blanche de Bosredon★★★ £D

CH. BELLEVUE-LA-FORÊT ● **Côtes du Frontonnais**★ £B Préstige★★ £B
● **Côtes du Frontonnais**Optimum★★ £C

CH. BOUISSEL ● **Côtes du Frontonnais**★ £B Cuvée d'Or★ £B
● **Côtes du Frontonnais** Cuvée Sélection★★ £B

CH. CLEMENT TERMES ○ **Gaillac** Sec★ £B

CH. HAUT-MONPLAISIR ● **Cahors**★ £B Prestige★★ £B Pur Plaisir★★★ £C

CH. JOLYS ○ **Jurançon** ★★ £B Cuvée Jean★★★ £B

CH. LA CAMINADE ● **Cahors**★★ £B Esprit★★★ £B

CH. LES HAUTS D'AGLAN ● **Cahors**★ £B Cuvée A★★ £B

CH. LE ROC ● **Côtes du Frontonnais**★ £B Cuvée Reservée★★ £B
● **Côtes du Frontonnais** Cuvée Don Quichotte★★ £C

CH. MASBUREL ○ **Montravel**★★ £C ● **Côtes de Bergerac**★★ £C

CH. LES MIAUDOUX ● **Bergerac**★★ £B ○ **Bergerac**★★ £B
○ **Saussignac**★★★ £C

CH. MOULIN CARESSE ● **Bergerac**★★ £B ○ **Montravel** Fûts de Chêne★★ £B

CH. PEYROS ● **Madiran**★ £B Greenwich 43 N★★ £C

CH. PLAISANCE ● **Côtes du Frontonnais**★ £B Cuvée Thibaut★★ £B

CH. LES RIGALETS ● **Cahors** Cuvée Prestige★ £B Cuvée Quintessence★★ £C

CH. THEULET ● **Bergerac**★★ £B ○ **Monbazillac**★★ £C

CH. DE TIREGAND ● **Pécharmant**★★ £C

CLOS DE GAMOT ● **Cahors**★★ £C

CLOS THOU ○ **Jurançon** Guilhouret Sec★★ £C

CAVE DE COCUMONT ● **Côtes du Marmandais** Béroy★ £B

DOM. DU CRAMPILH ● **Madiran** Vieilles Vignes★★ £B Cuvée Baron★★ £C

CAVE DE CROUSEILLES ● **Madiran**★ £B

DOM. D'ESCAUSSES ● **Gaillac** La Croix Petite★★ £B
○ **Gaillac** La Vigne de l'Oubli★★ £B

DOM. ETXEGARAYA ● **Irouléguy**★ £B

DOM. DE GINESTE ○ **Gaillac** Grande Cuvée★ £C
● **Gaillac** Grande Cuvée★★ £C

DOM. DU HAUT-MONTLONG ● **Côtes de Bergerac** Vents d'Anges £C

DOM. ILARRIA ● **Irouléguy**★★ £B

DOM. LABRANCHE-LAFFONT ● **Madiran** Tradition★★ £B
● **Madiran** Vieilles Vignes★★ £C

DOM. LAFFONT ● **Madiran** Cuvée Erigone★★ £C Cuvée Hecaté★★★ £D

DOM. DE LAULAN ○ **Côtes de Duras**★ £B

LES VERDOTS ○ **Bergerac** Clos des Verdots★★ £B
○ **Bergerac** Grand Vin Les Verdots★★★ £D
● **Côtes de Bergerac** Clos des Verdots★★ £B Grand Vin Les Verdots★★★ £E

DOM. MONTAURIOL ● **Côtes du Frontonnais** Tradition★ £B
● **Côtes du Frontonnais** Mons Aureolus★★ £B

DOM. PINERAIE ● **Cahors** Château Pineraie★★ £B

DOM. DE LA MÉTAIRIE ● **Pécharmant**★★ £B

PRODUCTEURS PLAIMONT ● **Côtes de Saint-Mont** Château de Sabazan★★ £B

Work in progress!!

Producers under consideration for the next edition
CH. DU BLOY (MONBAZILLAC)
CH. LA ROBERTIE (BERGERAC)
CH. LES MARNIÈRES (BERGERAC)
CLOS GUIROUILH (JURANÇON)
DOM. COSSE MAISONNEUVE (CAHORS)
DOM. ELIAN DA ROS (CÔTES DU MARMANDAIS)
DOM. DE SOUCH (JURANÇON)

Author's choice (DM)
A dozen values from the South West

DOM. BERTHOUMIEU ● **Madiran** Tradition
ALAIN BRUMONT ● **Madiran** Torus
CAMIN LARREDYA O **Jurançon** Sec
DOM. CAUHAPÉ O **Jurançon** Chant des Vignes
CH. D'AYDIE O **Pacherenc de Vic-Bilh** Frédéric Laplace
CHAPELLE LENCLOS ● **Madiran** Domaine Mouréou
CH. DU CÈDRE ● **Cahors** Prestige
CH. JONC BLANC ● **Bergerac** Cuvée Autumnale
CH. TOUR DES GENDRES O **Bergerac** Cuvée des Conti
CH. VIELLA ● **Madiran**
CLOS UROULAT O **Jurançon** Cuvée Marie
ROBERT PLAGEOLES O **Gaillac** Ondenc

Cellarworthy South West reds

DOM. BERTHOUMIEU ● **Madiran** Charles de Batz
ALAIN BRUMONT ● **Madiran** Château Montus Cuvée Prestige
CHAPELLE LENCLOS ● **Madiran** la Chapelle Lenclos
CH. D'AYDIE ● **Madiran** Château d'Aydie
CH. BARREJAT ● **Madiran** Vieux ceps
CH. BEAULIEU ● **Côtes du Marmandais** L'Oratoire
CH. DU CÈDRE ● **Cahors** Le Cèdre
CH. LAGREZETTE ● **Cahors** Pigeonnier
CH. TOUR DES GENDRES ● **Bergerac** Moulin des Dames
CH. VIELLA ● **Madiran** Cuvée Prestige
CLOS TRIGUEDINA ● **Cahors** Prince Probus
PRIMO PALATUM ● **Cahors** Mythologia

Diverse regional whites

ROBERT PLAGEOLES O **Jurançon** Noblesse du Temps
CH. TIRECUL-LA-GRAVIÈRE O **Monbazillac** Cuvée Madame
CH. TOUR DES GENDRES O **Bergerac** Cuvée Anthologia
CH. VIELLA O **Pacherenc du Vic-Bilh** Moelleux
CLOS UROULAT O **Jurançon** Clos Uroulat
CH. LAFFITTE-TESTON O **Pacherenc du Vic-Bilh** Ericka
DOM. CAUHAPÉ O **Jurançon** Noblesse du Temps
CAMIN LARREDYA O **Jurançon** Cuvée Simon
CH. BELLEVUE SUR VALLEE O **Bergerac** Le Vin du Bob Sauvignon
PRIMO PALATUM O **Jurançon** Mythologia
DOM. ROTIER O **Gaillac** Renaissance Doux
CH. LAFFITTE-TESTON O **Pacherenc du Vic-Bilh** Moelleux

RECOMMENDED HOTELS AND RESTAURANTS - SOUTH WEST FRANCE

Top Hotels

★★★★★*Les Prés d'Eugénie*   Eugénie-les-Bains 40320
Tel. 05 58 05 06 07 Fax 05 58 51 10 10
Email guerard@relaischateau.fr   22 rooms   £H

★★★★★*Hôtel du Palais*   pl. Église, Biarritz 64200
Tel. 05 59 41 64 00 Fax 05 59 41 67 99
Email reception2hotel-du-palais.com   132 rooms   £H

Top Restaurants

★★★★★*Les Prés d'Eugénie*   Eugénie-les-Bains 40320
Tel. 05 58 05 06 07   Fax 05 58 51 10 10
Email guerard@relaischateau.fr   £H

★★★★*Les Pyrénées*   St-Jean-Pied-de-Port 64220
Tel. 05 59 37 01 01   Fax 05 59 37 18 97
Email pyrenees@relaischateaux.fr   £D/G

Alicante Bouschet   Characterful red-fleshed crossing (that claims Grenache as a parent) once heavily planted in southern France.

Aligoté   Decent examples of Aligoté can be found the length and breadth of Burgundy but relatively few have the verve and subtle spice (without green or hard edges) that make it interesting.

Cabernet Franc   Parent variety of the more famous Cabernet Sauvignon, it is more successful in cooler soils. Only in the Anjou and Touraine in the Loire Valley does it thrive as a varietal as despite its importance on Bordeaux's Right Bank it is almost invariably blended with Merlot and some Cabernet Sauvignon. Its importance as a component in Bordeaux style blends is undeniable. Though it can emulate the flavours of its off-spring, it can miss its extra richness and depth and also show more of a raspberry-like fruit and a more leafy, herbal or even floral component.

Cabernet Sauvignon   Now grown with great success in many parts of the world, Bordeaux is still seen as the mother country. A grape of forceful and easily recognisable personality, it is much more fussy in showing at its best. Though capable of great richness, depth and structure, a lack of full ripeness in both fruit and tannin tends to detract from so many examples. A long growing season and well-drained soils are two prerequisites to producing the greatest elegance and classic telltale blackcurrant but also black cherry or blackberry flavours that mesh so well with new French oak. On Bordeaux's left bank Cabernet Sauvignon nearly always dominates blends but is complemented in the main by Merlot or Cabernet Franc which contribute to both complexity and structure. On the right bank Cabernet Sauvignon is typically in the supporting role but percentages vary considerably. It also contributes to top reds from Languedoc-Roussillon and Provence.

Carignan   Infamous red grape of the Languedoc-Roussillon still widely planted and often very high- yielding resulting in dilute, astringent wine. However from low yields and fully ripe fruit its a different beast. Deeply coloured, robust but characterful reds have been on the increase in the past decade or so.

Carmenère   Old Bordeaux variety now of only minor importance in France despite recent success in Chile.

Chardonnay   The great white grape of Burgundy has a great affinity for oak and can produce whites of marvellous texture, depth and richness but will also render a wonderful expression of its origins where yields are low. Some of the top mineral-imbued examples of Chablis are aged only in large used oak while others see no oak whatsoever. High quality grapes allied to winemaking sophistication is essential – too many examples, wherever they are made, show a clumsy winemaking fingerprint (excessive leesy, skin contact or oak flavours) or inferior fruit (under-ripe, over-ripe) or are simply unclean, acidified or lacking balance. Top quality is not restricted to Burgundy and the best examples from the Jura or southern France can provide good value for money. Chardonnay also forms a part of almost all Champagne. When varietal and sparkling it is known as Blanc de Blancs. Rich botrytised versions are unusual but have been made to a high standard in the Mâconnais.

Chasselas   Relatively neutral white grape also known as Fendant in Switzerland where it assumes greater importance and produces whites of higher quality than anywhere else in the world. The best examples reflect something of the specific *terroirs* with good structure and minerality in Dézaley and Calamin. From the opposite, southern shore of Lac Léman in Savoie come the best French examples (including Crépy). Rare decent examples are also made in the Loire (Pouilly-sur-Loire) and Alsace.

Chenin Blanc   High quality white grape of Touraine and Anjou in the Loire Valley. Outstanding long-lived wines ranging from dry to sweet are made and owe much to the grape's high acidity. Apple and citrus flavours within a firm, demanding texture are usually complemented by floral, honey and mineral characters with quince, peach even apricot in sweeter styles. Also an important base for some good quality sparkling wines, particularly Crémant de Loire.

Cinsaut/Cinsault   Characterful Rhône variety where taken seriously. Can add perfume and complexity both to southern Rhône blends and wines from the Languedoc and Corsica, especially when yields are low.

Gamay   The grape of the Beaujolais region and well-suited to its granitic soils. Examples range from the dilute and insipid to the impressively deep and fruity. Most but not all of it is produced by semi- carbonic maceration producing a supple texture but partly compromising its cherry fruit perfume and flavour. Plantings extend into the Mâconnais to the north where it generally performs poorly. It is also grown in the scattered wine districts of the Auvergne but is of greater significance in Touraine in the Loire Valley.

Gewürztraminer   A remarkably aromatic distinctive grape variety. Redolent in scents from the floral and musky to rosé petal, lychee and spices, styles range from the light and fresh to rich, oily textured wines, and from dry to off-dry through late-harvested to sweet, botrytised wines. Weaker efforts lack definition and a certain coarseness, particularly on the finish, is only avoided in top quality examples. Alsace still produces the greatest range of styles and highest quality of anywhere in the world.

Grenache   Leading grape variety in the southern Rhône where it forms the backbone wines from the leading appellations, including Châteauneuf-du-Pape and Gigondas. Quality and style vary enormously but is capable of great longevity when produced from low-yielding fruit. Grenache also forms a component of many of Languedoc-Roussillon's reds including Banyuls and Collioure near the border with Spain.

Grenache Blanc   Previously undistinguished grape particularly important in southern Rhône and Languedoc whites. Low yields and better winemaking have given it much more personality and it is sometimes made varietally.

Gros Manseng   Important grape of South-West France, particularly for the production of the dry wines of Jurançon with an exotic fruit character. Also used for the sweet wines, often together with the related but finer Petit Manseng.

Malbec   Essentially another of Bordeaux's rejects, the peppery, black-fruited Malbec has found favour as the major constituent of Cahors in South-West France where much effort has gone into tamer its potentially formidable tannins. There is high quality if from a relatively small number of producers. It is of minor importance in the Loire Valley where it is known as Cot.

Marsanne   At its best this is an intensely flavoured white with succulent peach and apricot fruit and often a tell-tale honeysuckle character. It is particularly important in northern Rhône whites, sometimes in partnership with Roussanne. It is also produced in Hermitage as *Vin de Paille*. It crops up again in blends in Côtes du Rhône whites (but not white Châteauneuf-du-Pape), Languedoc-Roussillon and even in Provence.

Melon de Bourgogne   The grape responsible for the many bland dry

477

whites of Muscadet. The best examples however can be both refreshing and flavoursome, usually owed, at least in part, to ageing *sur lie*.

Merlot This grape is as international as Chardonnay or Cabernet Sauvignon but its home is Bordeaux where it can range from a few per cent within a blend to almost being almost varietal (as in Château Pétrus). Few of France's other Merlot-dominated wines (mostly from the Midi) come remotely close to the best from Bordeaux's Right Bank. At its best it is rich, ripe, deep and plummy; both pure and seductive and capable of great complexity with age. Too many Merlot-based reds are, however lean, weedy and under-ripe and this includes much of that produced from Bordeaux's lesser appellations. Choosing one from recommended producer is essential.

Mondeuse Characterful French grape from Savoie. High in acidity but capable of intense beetroot, plum and cherry flavours and an attractive floral scent.

Mourvèdre High quality grape found in southern France at the very limits of ripening. It is most important incarnation is as powerful, tannic and ageworthy Bandol but some in Châteauneuf-du-Pape use it for blending as do producers in the Languedoc-Roussillon.

Muscadelle Relatively unsung grape of Bordeaux where it is used sparingly in sweet wines (including Sauternes) and in some of the dry whites.

Muscadet see Melon de Bourgogne

Muscat There is a whole family of Muscat grapes and it comes in many guises however there three principal grapes: Muscat Blanc à Petits Grains, Muscat of Alexandria and Muscat Ottonel. It can be dry, medium-dry or sweet – whether from dried grapes or fortified or a combination of the two. It is also made sparkling. What all the best examples have in common is the intense, heady grapiness – that taste of the grape itself. Only occasionally is it a wine for ageing. Alsace makes it both dry and intensely sweet, in southern France there are the *Vins Doux Naturel* of Beaumes de Venises and Rivesaltes (amongst others).

Négrette Grape of South-West France of greatest importance in Côtes du Frontonnais where it forms the major part of the blend. It gives supple, perfumed berryish wines with a slightly wild edge.

Petit Manseng Quality grape producing sometimes exquisite dry and sweet wines of Jurançon in South-West France. Increasingly used by growers in the Languedoc for its exotic, floral and spice character that is supported by good acidity.

Petit Verdot Sometimes an important minor component in Bordeaux, especially the Médoc but increasingly too in similar blends made in other regions where Cabernet Sauvignon is successful. Late ripening, it can show more than hint of violet in aroma as well as intense blackberry fruit.

Pinot Blanc Variety most associated with Alsace. Old low yielding vines give it good character though is often blended with the delightfully scented Auxerrois which can make the better wine. It is also the basis of most Crémant d'Alsace. One or two high quality examples are also produced in Burgundy's Côte d'Or.

Pinot Gris Excellent white grape most associated with Alsace where it produces distinctively flavoured whites of intense spice, pear and quince flavours. Late-harvested it takes on an almost exotic, honeyed richness and nobly-rotted *Sélection des Grains Nobles* can be superb.

Pinot Meunier Very important component in most Champagne blends if rarely used for anything else. Early ripening and as a wine, early developing, it complements both Chardonnay and Pinot Noir.

Pinot Noir   Burgundy continues to be the standard by which all Pinot Noir-based reds from around the world are judged. Although more examples now emulate the fabulous flavour complexityof top red Burgundy few display the same structural profile and supreme texture. Flavours include cherry, raspberry, strawberry and plum but can also include sappy, undergrowth characters or become more gamey in response to both origin and wine making. The expressions of *terroir* and differing winemaking interpretations in Burgundy are almost endless. Pinot Noir is also very important as a component of most Champagne and Crémant de Bourgogne.

Poulsard   Variety of France's Jura giving relatively light coloured reds and rosés. Most wines are for everyday drinking being soft and fruity yet with an acid sinew. Can also form a part of Vin de Paille with Savagnin and Chardonnay.

Riesling   This outstanding white grape has an almost infinite number of expressions. Styles vary from bone dry to intensely sweet, from low alcohol to powerful and full-bodied. Its impressive range of flavours including apple, citrus, peach and apricot, are complemented by a minerality that subtle differences of place or *terroir* bring. It is nearly almost made varietally and aged in stainless steel or large old wood. Obtaining full ripeness and the right balance between sugar and acidity is crucial to quality. Alsace provides the fullest, most powerful examples from anywhere in the world.

Roussette   Fine white grape found in Savoie in eastern France where it is also known as Altesse. The best wines with good structure and weight have a mineral, herb and citrus intensity as well as more exotic nuances when produced from low yielding vines on the best steep slopes.

Roussanne   High quality white grape that is difficult to grow. Roussanne's impressive texture and depth can be seen in wines from both the northern and southern Rhône, sometimes on its own but other times complementing Marsanne. It is also favoured by some of the leading quality producers in Languedoc-Roussillon and Provence, if mostly in blends. Also the grape used for fine perfumed Chignin-Bergeron whites in Savoie.

Sauvignon Blanc   Aromatic white grape capable of a wide range of expression and quality. The most structured and ageworthy examples come from France whether the classic mineral-laced wines of Sancerre and Pouilly-Fumé (now richer and riper than previously) or the more oak-influenced, peachy examples from Bordeaux (some blended with Sémillon) that will age for more than a decade. Sauvignon Blanc is also important in combination with Sémillon for Bordeaux's sweet wines.

Savagnin   A top quality grape used in the production of Vin Jaune, the speciality of the Jura, as well as other dry whites from the region.

Sémillon   Great French Sémillon comes from Bordeaux. Sémillon is made both dry, in usually oak-aged blends with Sauvignon Blanc (as it is in Bergerac), or sweet where it is typically the dominant component in all its great sweet wines. Botrytis enrichment is the key to the power, flavour richness and complexity of the best long-lived Sauternes and Barsac. Lesser appellations can also make attractive sweet wines and some good examples come from neighbouring Monbazillac.

Sylvaner   While better known as Silvaner, a leading variety in

479

Germany's Franken region, good examples are also produced in Alsace. A relatively neutral grape it can take on real richness and and a smoky, spicy flavour when produced from old vines.

Syrah   The home of Syrah is in the northern Rhône where a range of appellations give the most classic expression to one of the most exciting red grapes in the world. Those showing the most aromatic, smoky, white pepper and herbs expression come from Côte Rôtie (where they often include a little Viognier); broader, more powerful, minerally versions come from the hill of Hermitage. Many good examples also come from the surrounding appellations of Crozes-Hermitage, Cornas and Saint-Joseph. Syrah is also made varietally in the southern Rhône but more often is used to complement Grenache. As well as being important in Provence many of the best wines from the Languedoc-Roussillon are either based on it or include a significant percentage.

Tannat   Vine from the basque country, most important in Madiran where its powerful tannins need to be softened. Also an important component in other reds from the South-West such as Irouléguy.

Trousseau   Important variety in the Jura, particularly Arbois for red wines. Produced both varietally and in blends it is often firm and structured with a tendency to being too tough but the best examples need to be kept.

Viognier   There is no other Viognier quite like the best Condrieu (in the northern Rhône). From this small appellation the wine is opulent, lush and superbly aromatic – rich in apricot and peach with floral, blossom, honeysuckle and spice. Most are dry and best drunk young though a few age quite well, especially when they have acquired an enhanced structure from delicate oak treatment. One or two examples are made from late-harvested grapes. Viognier has become increasingly important in the southern Rhône, Languedoc-Roussillon and Provence, sometimes made varietally but as often injecting some perfume and fruit into a blend.

A

AC Appellation Controlée is the top category of French wine regulations and guarantees origin, grape varieties and style.

Acidification Addition of acid to must or wine if the wine has either naturally low acidity or is from a particularly warm grown climate. Usually in the form of tartaric acid.

Assemblage This is the final blend of a wine prior to its bottling. Many fine wines are assembled from different components after ageing. This process will determine the final selection for wines such as those from top Bordeaux Châteaux.

Autolysis Enzymatic process in sparkling wine whereby dead yeast cells add increased flavour to wine. The longer the period the richer and more complex the characteristic becomes. Sparkling wines with less than 18 months on their yeast sediment will have little or no autolysis character.

B

Bâtonnage Stirring of a wines fine lees to provide additional flavour and texture. Commonplace among top white Burgundies and other premium barrel fermented whites and also now lesser whites as well. Lees also need stirring to provide limited aeration and to avoid the development of off smelling sulphides.

Barriques The most well-known barrel type of 225 litre capacity. The Burgundian Pièce is fractionally larger with thicker staves than the classic Bordeaux barrique.

Biodynamic Method of organic farming that seeks to promote the natural balance of the land. This includes both soil and plants. Natural treatments are used to protect the vineyard and applications carried out in line with lunar and planetary activity. Many first class wine producers now farm biodynamically.

Botrytis Botrytis or Botrytis Cinerea is a fungal infection of the vine which is particularly harmful to red grapes. In certain unique conditions though it provides for the development of Noble Rot in areas such as Sauternes, the Mosel and the Loire Valleys Coteaux du Layon. In late warm harvests with early morning humidity and sunny days the grapes will dehydrate concentrating their sugar and flavour. Wines produced from such grapes have a uniquely intense, peachy character.

Botrytised Wine produced from grapes effected by noble rot.

C

Canopy Management Vineyard management techniques designed to improve yield and quality as well as minimizing risk of vine disease. Utilises a number of trellising/training systems to better expose the vines foliage and fruit to sunlight, resulting in improved photosynthesis and grape ripening.

Carbonic maceration Method used prior to conventional fermentation of red wine whereby colour rather than tannin is extracted. This occurs during a limited fermentation which takes place within grapes kept in anaerobic conditions. The berries will gradually split and fermentation will proceed as normal. Red winemaking particularly of Pinot Noir but also other varieties may involve using whole uncrushed grape bunches and partial carbonic maceration will occur. Greater colour and flavour complexity can be achieved. The flavours are forward and vibrant often resembling bubble gum and can have a hint of green pepper from the grape stems. The process has long been used in Beaujolais but increasingly elsewhere.

481

Cépage French term for grape variety.

Cépage ameliorateurs This means an improving variety. The term has been widely used in Languedoc-Roussillon where there have been increasing amounts of Syrah, Grenache and Mourvedre planted in addition to the widely distributed Carignan.

Champagne method Method for the production of sparkling wine originating in Champagne. A secondary fermentation takes place in bottle and the wine is left on the resulting yeast lees.

Chaptalisation The addition of sugar to grape must to increase its alcoholic strength. If added during fermentation has the added effect of prolonging the process. Some winemakers feel this can add complexity.

Clonal Selection see Clones

Clones Vines reproduced by taking cuttings of original plants. Vines reproduced by clonal selection. Vines reproduced by taking cuttings of original plants. Vines reproduced by clonal selection provide for uniformity of yield and flavour but wines produced from whole vineyards of the same clone can lack complexity. Many fine winegrowers instead use mass selection (see Sélection Massale) establishing vineyards from a range of original vinecuttings.

Cold maceration Period prior to fermentation where crushed red grapes are kept in solution with the juice at a cool temperature to extract both colour and primary fruit flavours.

Cold soaking See Cold maceration

Cork taint See TCA

Coulure Incomplete fruit set after flowering caused by cool or wet conditions. Some fruit loss can be positive to quality.

Crossing The result of a cross between two different grape varieties of the same vine species, almost always Vinifera. While some crossings have been commercially and qualitatively successful they rarely approach the best of what nature has produced (i.e all the most highly regarded varieties).

Cru Classé (CC) Classification of Bordeaux wines. Those from the Médoc (from 1er to 5ème Cru Classé/ first to fifth growth) and Barsac/Sauternes (1er or 2ème Cru Classé/ first and second growths) are covered by a famous classification of 1855. Graves (1959) and Saint-Emilion (Grand Cru Classé or Premier Grand Cru Classé) are also classified, the latter is now subject to revision every ten years (the last in 1996).

Cryo-Extraction Process used during sweet wine production where a must is frozen in order to concentrate the wine. Used in particular in Sauternes in poorer vintages with low botrytis levels. (also see Must Concentration).

Cuvaison This is the period during red wine vinification where the grape skins and other solid matter are kept in solution in the grape juice and then finished wine. This may include a period cold maceration to extract more colour, followed by fermentation and in some cases continued contact post-fermentation to round the wines tannins and provide greater harmony.

Cuve French term for a wine vat or tank. Can be used for fermentation or storage/ageing and is made from wood, stainless steel or concrete.

D

482

Débourbage Period where white grape juice or wine is left in order for solid matter to settle. Lighter aromatic and fruity whites will require all solids settling whereas a top white Burgundy or Chardonnay is more likely to be vinified from only partially settled must. Straightforward commercial whites may also be fined and even filtered as well prior to fermentation.

Demi-muid A wooden barrel of, generally 600 litre capacity. Although sometimes used to refer to smaller sizes they are always considerably larger than a barrique. (also see Tonneaux)

De-stemmed Most wine must is crushed and de-stemmed prior to fermentation. Some whites however, particularly Chardonnay may be whole bunch pressed and reds may include whole bunches added to the fermentation vat. Wine produced by carbonic maceration will also retain its stems. Traditionally made reds may also be vinified with some of their stems in order to add additional tannin and structure. In the case of the latter aggressive green tannins can be extracted if the stems as well as the grapes are not fully ripe.

Dosage Sparkling wine produced from the Champagne method will be topped up after disgorging with a mix of wine and sugar and this dosage determines the style and sweetness of the final wine.

E

Élévage The handling of wine from fermentation to bottling.

En Primeur Sale of wine while still in barrel. Commonplace now in Bordeaux and becoming so in Burgundy and other regions.

Enology The science of winemaking.

Enologist A winemaker.

Extraction Process where tannins, colour and other matter is extracted during Maceration. (also see Cuvaison).

F

Field blend Wine produced from vineyards planted to a mix of grape varieties. The practice is increasingly rare.

Filtration The removal of solid particles by means of a filter prior to bottling. While it saves the time required for a natural settling it may also rob a wine of flavour and character. Where the wine is healthy both filtration and fining (see below) have proved to be unnecessary.

Fining Process used to clarify grape juice or wine by removing the smallest (soluble) microscopic particles which attach themselves to the fining agents added. Great care should be used to avoid stripping the must or wine of flavour.

Foudres French term for large wooden vats used to age wine in.

G

Grand cru French wine classification. In Burgundy and Alsace this refers to specific vineyard sites. In Champagne to villages with vineyards of the best potential. For Bordeaux see Cru Classé.

Grand Vin Refers to a producers top wine. Commonly used in Bordeaux.

Green harvesting Crop thinning by cutting down the number of grape bunches in order to promote ripening and reduce yields. There will be a greater impact on yield and fruit quality if this is done after veraison (when the berries change colour). Popular among some growers, others maintain a well balanced vineyard with sufficient winter pruning produces the best results.

Guyot Old and very well established French vine training system. One or two fruiting canes are trained along wires with the new seasons shoots

483

trained above on a second wire.

I

Inox French for stainless steel. In wine terms generally refers to fermenting and ageing in stainless steel vessels.

L

Lees The sediment left after fermentation, including the dead yeast cells. White wine will often be racked off the gross lees but some sediment will remain which is known as the fine lees. This is important in providing additional flavour and texture as well as acting as an anti-oxidant during early barrel maturation. Lees stirring (see Bâtonnage) is regularly practiced at the same time. An increasing number of top quality reds are also now being aged on lees, some with micro-oxygenation.

Lieu-dit A specific vineyard or climat which has no official classification but identified on a label when that site has been bottled separately from other village-level wine. Regularly found on Alsace and Burgundy labels.

M

Maceration The period during which flavour, colour, tannins and other components are leeched from the grape skins before, during and after fermentation. Temperature plays an important role with primary fruit aromas and colour extracted at cooler temperatures whereas more tannin is released with heat. The cap of grape skins formed during fermentation needs to be kept in solution with the fermenting must and various methods are used which also aid extraction (see Pigeage).
Pre-fermentation maceration (see Cold maceration) is regularly practiced as well as extended post fermentation maceration which helps to polymerise the wines tannins, making them rounder and softer in texture. Some skin contact prior to fermentation is also practiced by a number of producers of white wines (see Macération Pelliculaire).

Macération carbonique See Carbonic Maceration

Macération pelliculaire French expression meaning skin contact. In effect it refers to the period of just a few hours where white wine must is macerated with its skins prior to fermentation. Semillon and Sauvignon Blanc in Bordeaux and Chenin Blanc in the Loire as well as more aromatic varieties like Muscat have all successfully been vinified using this technique. Excessive skin contact will result in coarseness and very early oxidation.

Malolactic fermentation Chemical process whereby malic acid is transferred into softer lactic acid. All red wine is put through malolactic but for whites it depends on the variety and style. For aromatic varieties such as Sauvignon Blanc and Riesling the process is avoided. For cool climate top quality Chardonnay it will add weight and texture. It may often be blocked with warmer grown Chardonnay to preserve acidity. Top reds including those based on Cabernet Sauvignon and other similarly structured and tannic blends are increasingly having the malolactic conducted in new oak. The wines are lusher and more softly textured, when young but the consequences for long-term ageing are less certain.

Mass Selection See Sélection Massale.

Mesoclimate The localised climate found generally within a vineyard or small specific area and responsible for particular characteristics found in the resulting wines. Often incorrectly referred to as a microclimate. The latter is in fact the very specific climate of the vine canopy.

Méthode Traditionelle The classic method of Champagne production (see Champagne method) as it is referred to in other regions for sparkling wines made in this way.

Micro-oxygenation Cellar operation devised by Patrick Ducournau in Madiran (South-West France) to assist in softening the often aggressively tannic wines produced from the local Tannat. Now increasingly practiced around the globe, small quantities of oxygen are regularly pumped into the ageing wine avoiding the need to rack the wine from one container to another, minimising handling and providing better balanced, finer tannins.

Millerandage Irregular fruit development after flowering caused by cool weather. Yield is reduced because some berries are smaller. Quality though is likely to improve. This characteristic of smaller and larger berries in the same grape bunch is often referred to as hen and chickens.

Moelleux French term meaning medium-sweet.

Monopole French for a solely owned vineyard site, particularly relevant in Burgundy.

Mousseux French for sparkling.

Must Can refer to either unfermented grape juice or the mix of grape juice, skins, pulp and seeds prior to or at the onset of fermentation. *Moût* in French.

Must concentration Any of a series of techniques for removing water from grape juice in order to make more concentrated wine. As well as evaporation under vacuum, freeze concentration (see Cyro-Extraction), which simulates eiswein/icewine production, can be used to remove water. Reverse Osmosis is a sophisticated process that allows the water content in finished wine to be reduced.

N

Négociant French term for a wine merchant. They may buy grapes as well as finished wine and also have their own vineyards and properties. While there has been a trend in Burgundy and other areas to more wines being Domaine-bottled an increasing number of small producers are also now acting as négociants as well.

Négociant-manipulant In Champagne, a merchant who also makes wine. Includes all the great Champagne houses.

Noble Rot See Botrytis.

O

Oenologue French term for an enologist.

Organic An increasing number of winegrowers around the world are now producing wines without recourse to chemical treatments in the vineyard and with a minimum of chemical additives during vinification. (also see Biodynamic).

Oxidation Exposure of must or wine to air. Controlled oxidation is important in the maturation of wine before bottling and can add complexity to fortified wines aiding the production of rancio character. Oxidation of grape juice is also popular in producing barrel fermented white wine particularly premium Chardonnay. Reduction is the opposite of oxidation.

P

Phenolics Compounds found in grapes and extracted during vinification. These include tannins, flavour compounds and anthocyanins (responsible for the colour in red wines). See also Cuvaison, Extraction and Maceration.

485

Phylloxera Vine aphid which was the great scourge of the world's vineyards in the 19th century. It can be resisted by planting vinifera varieties on resistant American species rootstocks.

Pigeage Method of plunging down the cap produced during red wine fermentation. This can be done by hand plunging with a number of devices or even by foot. A number of specialist automatic machine driven methods have also been developed. Particularly common and successful among the latter is the Rotofermenter. Pigeage can be gentler and less aggressively extractive than remontage or pumping the must back over itself.

Propagated Meaning reproduced. In viticultural terms this most commonly refers to vegetative propagation using cuttings taken from other vines.

R

Racked Winery procedure where must or wine is pumped or transferred under gravity from one container to another. This is both to remove the wine from solids but also to provide adequate aeration during maturation.

Rancio Maderised character with burnt, toffee like aromas produced in the development of aged fortified wines through a combination of controlled oxidation and exposure to heat. Banyuls, Maury and Rivesaltes in the Roussillon all show classic rancio character.

Récemment dégorgé French term meaning recently disgorged. This can either relate specifically to the actual disgorging of a Champagne method sparkling wine from its bottle sediment but also to the style of wine. These tend to have spent an extended period on there yeast lees. The quintessential example of this style is Bollinger RD.

Reduced This is the opposite of oxidised. Excessive reduction can result in the development foul smelling sulphides during cask ageing and so wines need to be exposed to controlled aeration during this phase, this can be achieved by either racking or more recently the use of micro-oxygenation.

Reductive Refers to wines that are in a reduced state.

Residual Sugar There is always a small portion of unfermentable sugar in wine even those that are technically classified as dry. It is commonplace in some whites particularly straightforward fruit driven styles to purposely leave a hint of residual sugar. More serious wines from cooler regions like Alsace may well be completed with some sugar left naturally. Late harvested wines are deliberately left on the vine to accumulate sufficient sugar to ensure considerable sweetness after vinification. (also see Botrytis)

Rootstock The plant formed from the root system of the vine to which the scion (fruiting part) is grafted. Most vinifera vines (the european species to which most quality grape varieties belong) are grafted on to rootstocks of American vines (or hybrids of them) due to its resistance to phylloxera.

S

Saignée Running off some free run juice prior to fermentation in order to increase the ratio of skins and solids in the must and therefore flavour and tannin. Regularly practiced in the production of top quality Pinot Noir.

Sélection Massale Mass Selection – the propagation of new plants from existing vines rather than the use of a single clone. Typically only the best vines are used in order to enhance the overall quality within a plot.

Stelvin/Stelvin Cap Closure used instead of cork to avoid any possible contamination of the wine by TCA, oxidation or other potential spoilage from external sources.

T

TCA Chemical compound, its full name is 2,4,6-trichloroanisole, responsible for most of the off flavours in wine caused by contaminated corks. Chlorine reacts with the cork to produce the contamination and the aroma can be picked up in minute quantities. Cork taint remains a major problem in spoilt wine and alternative methods of closure are on the increase. The chemical or variants of it can also be found elsewhere and has been a cause of contamination in some wine cellars.

Terroir French concept which considers the unique physical environment of a site or vineyard. Also refers to the character in a wine that is derived from its origins rather than the grape variety.

Tonneaux A bordeaux barrel size of 900 litres but can often be used to refer to considerably smaller vessels.

Triage Selective sorting of grapes prior to fermentation order to remove inferior quality fruit.

Tris Multiple passages through a vineyard to selectively pick late harvested or botrytis effected grapes. In order to produce great wines it may be necessary to make many such passes. In Bordeaux Tri also refers to the sorting of grapes generally after harvest. This selection process is vital in all wineries to ensure top quality wines.

U

Unfiltered See filtration

Unirrigated See Irrigation

V

Vatting Period where wine is macerated and fermented prior to ageing. See also Cuvaison.

Vendange vert See Green Harvesting

Vin Doux Naturels French term for fortified wines. These are sweet, achieved by adding fortifying spirit part way through fermentation in much the same way as is practiced in producing Port.

Vin De Paille 'Straw Wine' is a rare type of white wine (of varying sweetness) produced from dried grapes. Traditionally laid out on straw mats, grapes are now more usually hung and dried in the Jura where it is of the greatest importance. It has also undergone a small revival in the Rhône.

Vin de Pays French category of regional identification for wines that fall outside either the boundaries or regulations of an AC.

Vin Jaune Jura wine made from Savagnin grapes aged in old casks under a *voile* (a film of yeast not unlike Flor that covers Fino sherry) that results in a distinctive oxidised nutty character.

Vinifera Vitis Vinifera is the European species of vine to which nearly all the grape varieties used in global wine production belong.

Vignoble A vineyard or close grouping of vineyards.

Voile The thin yeast film that develops on Vin Jaune, the speciality of the Jura, is not dissimilar to the Flor that grows on dry Fino and Manzanilla sherries. The powerful tangy wines take on a nutty, oxidised complexity with age.

Volatile Acidity The volatile acids in wine are those that are unstable and chief among these is acetic acid. Excessive exposure of a wine with high volatile acidity to air will encourage a bacterial reaction that causes off volatile aromas (similar to nail varnish) and will eventually convert wine to vinegar.

Y

Yield The size of crop yielded from a vineyard. Yield is fundamental to wine quality. In general the smaller the yield the greater the wine quality. There are though many additional influences. If yield is reduced too much then the vines balance and equilibrium will be disturbed and quality will suffer. Increasingly yields are measured per vine rather than per acre or hectare because of the variable conditions within a vineyard and the density of planting. Older vines are naturally less productive and when their crop is reduced the resulting grapes can be of exceptional quality. In all cases the yield of a vine should be sufficiently restricted in order to achieve complete physiological ripeness.

Buying guide A code is provided in most A-Z producer entries and these can be found listed alphabetically on the pages that follow. In the first instance these are intended to give the most direct link with that producer in the UK. When the first code given appears in bold this indicates the agent or direct importer of the wines. In some instances such an agent sells only to the trade or acts purely a producers representative in the UK but all should still be able to suggest retail stockists of a given wine. Additional codes (not in bold) indicate a retailer (or regional agent) who are regular stockists of these wines. In a few cases where we have found there to be no UK agent or retailer we have suggested a broker who has traded some vintages of the wine. Where there is no code at all we hope that producers inclusion will prompt someone in the UK to sell these wines. Many of these codes refer to a leading independent merchant/retailer who sell much of the best or most interesting wine in this country – often very competitively priced against the bigger, better known brands. While we haven't profiled individual merchants, a glance through the codes within any regional section is likely to give a good idea as to which ones have a particular strength there.

In Bordeaux most wine from the leading châteaux is sold through a Bordeaux broker (*courtier*) or agent and then to retailers and merchants in different countries. While the system is elaborate it is not so difficult to obtain many of the wines. Both independent UK merchants, such as one of 'The Bunch' (a group of six leading merchants - Adm, Tan, JAr, C&B, L&W, Yap) and leading broker/shippers (such as Farr Vintners - Far) are the best place to start. These contacts also provide the opportunity to buy wine en primeur or ex-cellars. This requires paying for the cost of the wine before it is shipped with the additional costs (freight, VAT and duty) paid on its arrival in the UK. Purchasing wine in this way was once seen as an investment opportunity for would be speculators, but it is now increasingly important as the only means of obtaining the best, not only from Bordeaux but also from Burgundy or the Rhône. It also usually means that the wine hasn't changed hands several times already. Leading merchants will also prove useful when buying older vintages as will auction houses and brokers (additional contacts have been provided at the end of the list of codes). Bordeaux wines stocked by a large number of merchants have been coded AAA.

This same code (AAA) is also used for wines that are that are easily found in supermarkets or on the high street. Supermarkets account for the bulk of wine sold in the UK. To an extent their ranges tend to be dominated by the ubiquitous big volume brands – much of it outside of the scope of this book. The small production of many high quality estates remains outside their reach whether as part of a deliberate decision on the part of the producer or due to logistical reasons. Nonetheless the best supermarkets include those producers who combine quality and quantity. In addition there is an increasing trend toward the inclusion of a selection of fine wines of more limited availability in their flagship stores or through an on-line facility. Although the national supermarkets chains have not been included as agents or leading stockists, a search on their internet sites can be used as a quick check for availability. There are also an increasing number of Internet-only retailers whose search engines provide a further aid to tracking down a hard to find wine, the best known being www.everywine.co.uk.

It is also worth noting that a growing number of producers now sell their wine direct via a mailing list or over the internet. Such is the demand for their wines there is no need for them to use an agent and the cost saving is effectively passed on to the wine drinker. Individual producers websites are worth checking for information about buying their wines.

489

AAA
Widely available
In supermarkets or the high street
OR
in the case of Bordeaux or Port available
through any number of wine merchants.
also see Buying Guide

A&B – A & B Vintners
Little Tawsden, Spout Lane,
Brenchley, Kent TN12 7AS
Tel 01892 724977
Fax 01892 722673
info@abvintners.co.uk
www.abvintners.co.uk

ABy – Anthony Byrne
Ramsey Business Park,
Stocking Fen Road,
Ramsey, Cambridgeshire PE26 2UR
Tel 01487 814555
Fax 01487 814962
admin@abfw.co.Uk
www.abfw.co.uk

ACh – Andrew Chapman Fine Wines
14 Haywards Road, Abingdon,
Oxfordshire OX14 4LB
Tel 01235 550707
Fax 0870 136 6335
info@surf4wine.co.uk
www.surf4wine.co.uk

Add – Addison Wines
165 Battersea Rise, London SW11 1HP
Tel 020 7924 2416
Fax 020 7924 2417
sales@addisonwines.co.uk
www.addisonwines.co.uk

Adm – Adnams
Sole Bay Brewery, Southwold,
Suffolk IP18 6JW
Tel 01502 727222
Fax 01502 727223
wines@adnams.co.uk
www.adnams.co.uk

ADo – Allied Domecq Wine UK
Argentum, 2 Queen Caroline Street,
London W6 9DX
Tel 020 8323 8196
Fax 020 8323 8313
www.allieddomecqplc.com

AHW – AH Wines
Back Street, West Camel, Yeovil,
Somerset BA22 7QB
Tel 01935 850166
Fax 01935 851264

All – Alliance Wine Co
7 Beechfield Road, Willowyard Estate,
Beith, Ayrshire KA15 1LN
Tel 01505 506060
Fax 01505 506066
sales@alliancewine.co.uk
www.alliancewine.co.uk

Alo – Alouette Wines
Prenton Way, North Cheshire Trading
Estate, Prenton, Wirral CH43 3DU
Tel 0151 6089900
Fax 0151 608 8844
info@alouettewines.co.uk
www.alouettewines.co.uk

Amp – Amps Fine Wines
6 Market Place, Oundle,
Peterborough PE8 4BQ
Tel 01832 273502
Fax 01832 273611
info@ampsfinewines.co.uk
www.ampsfinewines.co.uk

AnI – Anglo International Wine Shippers
Chantarella House, 25 New Road,
Esher, Surrey KT10 9PG
Tel 01372 469841
Fax 01372 469816

AoW – Architects of Wine
Grange Park Unit 1, Cheaney Drive,
Northampton NN4 5FB
Tel 0870 121 3610
Fax 0870 121 3655
sales@aow-uk.com
www.aow-uk.com

ARe – Arthur Rackham Emporia
216 London Road, Burpham,
Guildford GU4 7JS
Tel 0870 870 1110
Fax 0870 870 1120
cellars@ar-emporia.com
www.ar-emporia.com

AVn – Allez Vins!
PO Box 1019, Long Itchington,
Southam, Warwickshire CV47 9ZU
Tel 01926 811969
Fax 01926 815840
wine@allezvins.co.uk
www.allezvins.co.uk

AWW – Andrew Wilson Wines
Little Acre, Hall Lane, Cotes Heath,
Staffordshire ST21 6RT
Tel 01782 791798
Fax 01782 791787
andrew@awwines.co.uk
www.awwines.co.uk

B&B – Barrels & Bottles
3 Oak Street, Sheffield S8 9UB
Tel 0114 255 6611
Fax 0114 255 1010
sales@barrelsandbottles.co.uk
www.barrelsandbottles.co.uk

B&T – C G Bull & Taylor
6G Hewlett House, Havelock Terrace,
London SW8 4AS
Tel 020 7498 8022
Fax 020 7498 7851
info@cgbull.co.uk
www.cgbull.co.uk

Bal – Ballantynes of Cowbridge
3 Westgate, Cowbridge,
Glamorgan CF71 7AQ
Tel 01446 774840
Fax 01446 775253
sales@ballantynes.co.uk
www.ballantynes.co.uk

Bat – Bat & Bottle
9 Ashwell Road, Oakham,
Rutland LE15 6QG
Tel 0845 108 4407
Fax 0870 458 2505
post@batwine.co.uk
www.batwine.co.uk

BBR – Berry Bros & Rudd
3 St James Street,
London SW1A 1EG
Tel 020 7396 9600
Fax 020 7396 9611
orders@bbr.com
www.bbr.com

Bel – Bella Wines Limited
Beaufort House, 28 Lisburn Road,
Newmarket, Suffolk CB8 8HS
Tel 01638 604899
Fax 01638 604901
sales@bellawines.co.uk
www.bellawines.co.uk

Ben – Bennetts
High Street, Chipping Campden,
Gloucestershire GL55 6AG
Tel 01386 840392
Fax 01386 840974
enquiries@bennettsfinewines.com
www.bennettsfinewines.com

BFs – Bonhote Foster
The Mews, Broadgate House,
Steeple Bumpstead, Suffolk CB9 7DG
Tel 01440 730779
Fax 01440 730789
info@bonhotefoster.co.uk
www.bonhotefoster.co.uk

Bib – Bibendum
113 Regents Park Road,
London NW1 8UR
Tel 020 7449 4120
Fax 020 7722 7354
sales@bibendum-wine.co.uk
www.bibendum-wine.co.uk

BIx – Bordeaux Index
6th Floor, 159 - 173 St John's Street,
London, EC1V 4QJ
Tel 020 7253 2110
Fax 020 7490 1955
sales@bordeauxindex.com
www.bordeauxindex.com

Box – Boxford Wine Co
Spring Cottage, Butchers Lane, Boxford,
Sudbury, Suffolk, C010 5EA
Tel 01787 210187
Fax 01787 211391
boxfordwine@aol.com

BRW – Big Red Wine Company
Baron Coach House, The Street,
Barton Mills, Suffolk IP28 6AA
Tel 01638 510803
Fax 01638 510803
sales@bigredwine.co,uk
www.bigredwine.co.uk

B-S – Billecart-Salmon UK
Thornton House, Thornton Road,
London, SW19 4NG
Tel 020 8405 6345
Fax 020 8405 6346
info@billecart-salmon.co.uk
www.billecart-salmon.co.uk

BSh – Burgundy Shuttle
168 Ifield Road, London, SW10 9AF
Tel 020 7341 4053
Fax 020 7244 0618
mail@burgundyshuttle.ltd.uk
www.burgundyshuttle.co.uk

Bur – Burridges of Arlington St
Burridge House, Priestley Way, Crawley,
West Sussex RH10 9NT
Tel 01293 530151
Fax 01293 530104
sales@burridgewine.com
www.burridgewine.com

But – Butler's Wine Cellar
247 Queen's Park Road, Brighton,
East Sussex BN2 9XJ
Tel 01273 698724
Fax 01273 622761
henry@butlers-winecellar.co.uk
www.butlers-winecellar.co.uk

491

BWC – Berkmann Wine Cellars
10/12 Brewery Road, London, N7 9NH
Tel   020 7609 4711
Fax   020 7607 0018
info@berkmann.co.uk
www.berkmann.co.uk

C&B – Corney & Barrow
No.1 Thomas More Street,
London E1W 1YZ
Tel   020 7265 2400
Fax   020 7265 2539
wine@corbar.co.uk
www.corneyandbarrow.com

C&C – Champagnes & Châteaux
11 Calico House, Plantation Wharf,
London SW11 3TN
Tel   020 7326 9655
Fax   020 7326 9656
info@champagnesandchateaux.co.uk

C&O – C & O Wines
Unit 14 Park Road Estate, Park Road,
Timperley, Altrincham WA14 5QH
Tel   0161 976 3696
Fax   0161 962 4525
info@cowines.com

C&R – Classic & Rare
The Famous Old Brewery,
Springfield Road,
Crawley, West Sussex RH10 6AL
Tel   01293 525777
Fax   01293 528144
sales@classicrarewines.com
www.classicrarewines.com

Cad – Cadman Fine Wines
Encon House, Owl Close,
Moulton Park,
Northamptonshire NN3 6HZ
Tel   0845 121 4011
Fax   0845 121 4014
sales@cadmanfinewines.co.uk
www.cadmanfinewines.co.uk

Cam – Cambridge Wine Merchants
2 Mill Road, Cambridge CB1 2AD
Tel   01223 568991
Fax   01223 568992
info@cambridgewine.com
www.cambridgewine.com

Cas – Castang Wine Shippers
Belhay Farm, Pelyent, Looe PL13 2JX
Tel   01503 220359
Fax   01503 220650
sales@castang-wines.co.uk
www.castang-wines.co.uk

Cav – Cavavin/Le Bon Vin
340 Brightside Lane, Sheffield S9 2SP
Tel   0114 256 0090
Fax   0114 256 0092
cavavin@lebonvin.co.uk
www.lebonvin.co.uk

CBg – Charles Blagden
135 Avenue Joseph Lioter,
84740 Velleron, France
Tel   0033 4 90 20 07 07
Fax   0033 4 90 20 05 77
blagwin@aol.com

CCC – Cave Cru Classé
Unit 13 Leathermarket, Weston Street,
London, SE1 3ER
Tel   020 7378 8579
Fax   020 7378 8544
enquiries@ccc.co.uk
www.cave-cru-classe.com

Cco – Champagne Company
26 Astwood Mews, London, SW7 4DE
Tel   020 7373 5578
Fax   020 7373 4777
ukchampagne@aol.com
www.champagnecompany.co.uk

CdP – Les Caves de Pyrene
Pew Corner, Old Portsmouth Road,
Arlington,
Guildford, Surrey, GU3 1LP
Tel   01483 538820
Fax   01483 455068
sales@lescaves.co.uk
www.lescaves.co.uk

CeB – Croque-en-Bouche
Col House Road, Walwyn Road,
Upper Colwall, Malvern WR13 6PR
Tel   01684 540011
Fax   0870 706 6282
mail@croque.co.uk
www.croque-en-bouche.co.uk

Che – Cheviot UK / WM Morton
137 Shawbridge Street, Glasgow G43 1QQ
Tel   0141 649 9881
Fax   0141 649 7074
cheviot@w-m.co.uk

CHk – Charles Hawkins
The Offices, Glaston Road, Uppingham,
Rutland, LE15 9EU
Tel   01572 823030
Fax   01572 823040
info@charleshawkinsandpartners.com
www.charleshawkins-wines.com

Cht– Charterhouse Wine Co Ltd
Spalding Common, Spalding,
Lincolnshire PE11 3JZ
Tel 01775 720300
Fax 01775 722271
info@charterhousewine.co.uk
www.charterhousewine.co.uk

ChV – Château Vintners
121 Beaufort Street, London, SW3 6BS
Tel 020 7376 8828
Fax 020 7376 8818
chateauvintners@yahoo.co.uk

Cib – Ciborio
Ciborio House, 74 Long Drive,
Greenford, Middlesex, UB6 8XH
Tel 020 8578 4388
Fax 020 8575 2758
www.ciborio.com

Coe – Coe Vintners
53 Redbridge Lane East, Ilford,
Essex IG4 5EY
Tel 020 8551 4966
Fax 020 8550 6312
enquiries@coevintners.com
www.coevintners.com

Col - Colombier Vins Fins
Colombier House, Ryder Close,
Cadley Hill Industrial Estate,
Swadlincote, Derbyshire, DE11 9EU
Tel 01283 552552
Fax 01283 550675
colombier@colombierwines.co.uk
www.colombierwines.co.uk

Con – Connolly's Wine Merchants
Arch 13, 220 Livery Street,
Birmingham, B3 1EU
Tel 0121 236 9269
Fax 0121 233 2339
sales@connollyswine.co.uk
www.connollyswine.co.uk

CPp – Christopher Piper Wines
1 Silver Street, Ottery St Mary,
Devon, EX11 1DB
Tel 01404 814139
Fax 01404 812100
sales@christopherpiperwines.co.uk

CRs – Chalié Richards
Unit 7 Mulberry Trading Estate,
Foundry Lane,
Horsham, West Sussex, RH13 5PX
Tel 01403 250500
Fax 01403 250123
admin@chalie-richards.co.uk

CTy – Charles Taylor / Montrachet Fine Wine
59 Kennington Road, London, SE1 7PZ
Tel 020 7928 1990
Fax 020 7928 3415
www.montrachetwine.com

**CWF – CWF Ltd
(Continental Wine & Food)**
Trafalgar Winery, Leeds Road,
Huddersfield HD2 1YY
Tel 01484 538333
Fax 01484 544734
info@continental-wine.co.uk
www.continental-wine.co.uk

DAy – Dreyfus Ashby & Co
143a High Street, Tonbridge, Kent, TN9 1DH
Tel 01732 361639
Fax 01732 367834
office@dreyfusashby.co.uk

DDr – Domaine Direct
6-9 Cynthia Street, London, N1 9JF
Tel 020 7837 1142
Fax 020 7837 8605
mail@domainedircct.co.uk
www.domainedirect.co.uk

Dec – Decorum Vintners
Unit 12, Grand Union Centre,
West Row, London W10 5AS
Tel 020 8969 6581
Fax 020 8960 7693
admin@decvin.com
www.decvin.com

DLW – Daniel Lambert Wines Ltd
8 Rhodfas Ceirios, Pen-y-Fai,
Bridgend CF31 4GG
Tel 01656 661010
Fax 01656 668088
www.daniellambertwines.co.uk
info@daniellambertwines.co.uk

Dou – Dourthe UK
The Old Imperial Laundry,
71 Warriner Gardens,
London SW11 4XW
Tel 020 7720 6611
Fax 020 7720 2670
uk@cvbg.com
www.cvbg.com

DWS – Direct Wine Shipments (NI)
5/7 Corporation Square, Belfast,
BT1 3AJ
Tel 028 9050 8000
Fax 028 9050 8004
enquiry@directwine.co.uk
www.directwine.co.uk

E&T – Elliot & Tatham
c/- Larroque Haut, 47370 Bourlens,
France
Tel 0870 762 0900
Fax 0870 762 0901
wine@elliot-tatham.com

Ear – Earle Wines
Applegarth, Wormald Green, Harrogate,
North Yorkshire, HG3 3PS
Tel 01765 677296
Fax 01765 677839
sales@earlewines.com
www.earlewines.com

EGe – Ernst Gorge
73 High Street, Dorchester-on-Thames,
Oxon OX14 3LF
Tel 01865 341817
Fax 01865 343184

Eno – Enotria Winecellars
4-8 Chandos Park Estate, Chandos
Road,
London NW10 6NF
Tel 020 8961 4411
Fax 020 8961 8773
info@winecellars.co.uk
www.winecellars.co.uk

EoR – Ellis of Richmond
Unit 1, Richmond House, The Links,
Popham Close, Hanworth, Middlesex,
TW13 6JE
Tel 020 8744 5550
Fax 020 8744 5581
www.ellisofrichmond.co.uk

Eur – Eurowines
93 Bollo Lane, Chiswick, London
W4 5LU
Tel 020 8747 2100
Fax 020 8994 8054
enquiries@eurowines.co.uk
www.eurowines.co.uk

Eve – Evertons
Worsley Estates, Bark Lane, Abberley,
Worcestershire WR6 6BQ
Tel 01299 890113
Fax 01299 890114
sales@evertonswines.co.uk
www.evertonswines.co.uk

Evg – Evington's Wines
120 Evington Road, Leicester LE2 1HH
Tel 0116 254 2702
Fax 0116 254 2702
info@evingtons-wines.com
www.evingtons-wines.com

EWG – EWGA (European Wine Growers Associates)
Challan Hall, Silverdale, Lancashire
LA5 0UH
Tel 01524 701723
Fax 01524 701189
sales@ewga.net

ExC – Ex Cellar
20 Craddocks Parade, Ashtead
KT21 1QJ
Tel 01372 275247
Fax 01372 813937
charles@excellar.co.uk
www.excellar.net

F&R – Fine & Rare Wines Ltd
Pall Mall Deposit, 124-128 Barlby Road,
North Kensington, London W10 6BL
Tel 020 8960 1995
Fax 020 8960 1911
wine@frw.co.uk
www.frw.co.uk

F&M – Fortnum & Mason
181 Piccadilly, London W1A 1ER
Tel 020 7734 8040
Fax 020 7437 3278
info@fortnumandmason.co.uk
www.fortnumandmason.com

Fal – Falcon Vintners
Trident Business Centre, 89 Bickersteth
Road, London SW17 9SH
Tel 020 8516 7780
Fax 020 8516 7781
info@falconvintners.co.uk

Far – Farr Vintners
220 Queenstown Road, London
SW8 4LP
Tel 020 7821 2000
Fax 020 7821 2020
sales@farr-vintners.com
www.farr-vintners.com

FCA – Fraser Crameri Associates
The Stable, Cottenden View, Stonegate,
Wadhurst, East Sussex TN5 7DX
Tel 01580 200304
Fax 01580 200308
fraser@frasercrameri.com
www.frasercrameri.com

FFW – Food & Fine Wine
760 Eccleshall Road, Sheffield S11 8TB
Tel 01142 668747
Fax 0870 8912376
www.foodandfinewine.com

Fin – The Fine Wine Company Ltd
145 North High Street, Musselburgh EH21 6AN
Tel 0131 665 0088
Fax 0131 665 0098
mail@thefinewinecompany.co.uk
www.thefinewinecompany.co.uk

FMV – Fields, Morris & Verdin
Unit 2, Bankside Industrial Estate, Sumner Street, London SE1 9JZ
Tel 020 7921 5300
Fax 020 7921 5333
info@fmvwines.com
www.fmvwines.com

For – Forth Wines
Crawford Place, Milnathort, Kinross-Shire KY13 9XF
Tel 01577 866001
Fax 01577 866020
enquiries@forthwines.com
www.forthwines.com

Frw – Friarwood
26 New Kings Road, Fulham, London SW6 4ST
Tel 020 7736 2628
Fax 020 7731 0411
sales@friarwood.com
www.friarwood.com

Fsp – Flagship Wines Ltd
39 Rowan Close, St Albans AL4 0ST
Tel 01727 841968
Fax 01727 841968
info@flagshipwines.co.uk
www.flagshipwines.co.uk

FSt – Frank Stainton Wines
3 Berry's Yard, Finkle Street, Kendal, Cumbria LA9 4AB
Tel 01539 731886
Fax 01539 730396
admin@stainton-wines.co.uk
www.stainton-wines.co.uk

Fte – Fortitude Wines Ltd
5 Purley Oaks Road, Sanderstead, Surrey CR2 0NU
Tel 020 8660 8456
Fax 020 8660 6686
info@fortitudewines.com
www.fortitudewines.com

FWC – Fareham Wine Cellar
55 High Street, Fareham, Hampshire PO16 7BG
Tel 01329 822733
Fax 01329 282355
dominic@farehamwinecellar.co.uk
www.farehamwinecellar.co.uk

FWW – FWW Wines UK Ltd
15 South Ealing Road, London W5 4QT
Tel 020 8567 1589
Fax 020 8567 3731
sales@fwwwines.demon.co.uk

Gar – Garrigue Wines
8 Castle Court, Bankside, Falkirk FK2 7UU
Tel 0845 8886677
Fax 0845 8886678
themacaloneys@garriguewines.com
www.garriguewines.com

Gau – Gauntleys
4 High Street, Exchange Arcade, Nottingham NG1 2ET
Tel 0115 911 0555
Fax 0115 911 0557
rhone@gauntleywine.com
www.gauntleywine.com

GBa – Georges Barbier
267 Lee High Road, London SE12 8RU
Tel 020 8852 5801
Fax 020 8463 0398
georgesbarbier@f2s.com

GCW – Grand Cru Wines
Mas de Moussier, 1100-5 Avenue des Alpilles,
13310 Saint-Martin de Crau, France
Tel 0871 474 0635
Fax 0033 49047 13 21
gcw@wanadoo.fr
www.grandcruwinesltd.net

Gen – Genesis Wines
14 Denbeigh Road, London SW1V 2ER
Tel 020 7963 9060
Fax 020 7963 9069
sales@genesiswines.com
www.genesiswines.com

GFy – Folly Wines
Chestnut Road, London Road, Chalford,
Gloucestershire GL6 8NR
Tel 01453 731509
Fax 01453 731134
info@follywines.co.uk
www.follywines.co.uk

495

GGW – Great Gaddesden Wines/ The Flying Corkscrew
Leighton Buzzard Road, Water End,
Hertfordshire HP1 3BD
Tel 01442 412312
Fax 01442 412313
info@flyingcorkscrew.com

GGg – Great Grog
33-41 Ratcliffe Terrace, Edinburgh
EH9 1SU
Tel 0131 662 4777
Fax 0131 662 4983
richard@greatgrog.co.uk
www.greatgrog.co.uk

Goe – Goedhuis & Co
6 Rudolf Place, Miles Street,
London SW8 1RP
Tel 020 7793 7900
Fax 020 7793 7170
enquiries@goedhuis.com
www.goedhuis.com

GPW – GP Wines
Beedcote, Brighton Road,
Lower Beeding, West Sussex RH13 6PP
Tel 01403 891163
Fax 01403 892590
info@gpwines.com
www.gpwines.com

GrD – Winegrowers Direct
2 Station Road, Swavesey,
Cambridge CB4 5QJ
Tel 01954 230176
Fax 01954 231822

GSe – Gerrard Seel
31 Melford Court, Hardwick Grange,
Woolston, Warrington, Cheshire
WA1 4RZ
Tel 01925 819695
Fax 01925 818192
wine@gerrardseel.co.uk
www.gerrardseel.co.uk

Gun – Gunson Fine Wines
29 Emmanuel Road, Hastings
TN34 3LB
Tel 07979 861026
Fax 01342 843955
dion@gunsonfinewines.co.uk

GVF – Grand Vins de France
Carrayol Arch, 8 Church Crescent,
London, N10 3ND
Tel 020 8442 1088
Fax 020 8444 4288

GWW – Great Western Wine
The Wine Warehouse, Wells Road,
Bath, Somerset BA2 3AP
Tel 01225 322800
Fax 01225 442139
post@greatwesternwine.co.uk
www.greatwesternwine.co.uk

Hal – Hallgarten
Dallow Road, Luton, Bedfordshire
LU11UR
Tel 01582 722538
Fax 01582 723240
sales@hallgarten.co,uk
www.hallgarten.co.uk

Han – Handford Fine Wine
12 Portland Road, Holland Park,
London W11 4LE
Tel 020 7221 9614
Fax 020 7221 9613
wine@handford.net
www.handford.net

Har – Harris Fine Wine
4 Albion Way, Kelvin Industrial Estate,
East Kilbride G75 0YN
Tel 01355 571157
Fax 01355 571158

Has – Haslemere Cellar
16 West Street, Haslemere,
Surrey GU27 2AB
Tel 01428 645081
Fax 01428 645108
info@haslemerecellar.co.uk
www.haslemerecellar.co.uk

Hay – Hayward Bros Ltd
44 Willow Walk, London SE1 5SF
Tel 020 7237 0576
Fax 020 7237 6212
wine@haybrowine.co.uk
www.haybrowine.co.uk

HBJ – Hayman Barwell Jones Ltd
24 Fore Street, Ipswich, Suffolk IP4 1JU
Tel 01473 232322
Fax 01473 280381
www.hbjwines.co.uk

Hfx – Halifax Wine Company
18 Prescott Street, Halifax,
West Yorkshire HX1 2LG
Tel 01422 256333
andy@halifaxwinecompany.com
www.halifaxwinecompany.com

HHB – H & H Bancroft
1 China Wharf, Mill Street, London,
SE1 2BQ
Tel 020 7232 5440
Fax 020 7232 5451
sales@handhbancroftwines.com
www.bancroftwines.com

HHC – Haynes, Hanson & Clark
25 Eccleston Street, London,
SW1W 9NP
Tel 020 7259 0102
Fax 020 7259 0103
london@hhandc.co.uk
www.hhandc.co.uk

HMA – Hatch Mansfield Agencies
New Bank House, 1 Brockenhurst Road,
Ascot, Berks, SL5 9DJ
Tel 01344 871800
Fax 01344 871871
sales@hatch.co.uk
www.hatchmansfield.co.uk

HoK – Hammonds of Knutsford
Warford Grange Farm,
Pedley House Lane,
Great Warford, Knutsford, Cheshire
WA16 7SP
Tel 01565 872872
Fax 01565 872900
wine@hammondsofknutsford.co.uk

Hrd – Harrods
Knightsbridge, London SW1X 7XL
Tel 020 7730 1234
Fax 020 7225 5872
www.harrods.com

HRp – Howard Ripley
25 Dingwall Road, London, SW18 3AZ
Tel 020 8877 3065
Fax 020 8877 0029
info@howardripley.com
www.howardripley.com

HrV – Harrison Vintners
23 Alliance Court, Alliance Road,
London W3 0RB
Tel 020 8752 1400
Fax 020 8993 9720
sales@harrisonvintners.co.uk
www.harrisonvintners.co.uk

HSA – HS Wine Agencies
76 Impington Lane, Impington,
Cambridge CB4 9NJ
Tel 01223 234604
Fax 01223 234604
hswineagencies@ntlworld.com

HWC – HWCG
Threm Hall, Start Hill,
Bishop's Stortford, Hertfordshire,
CM22 7TD
Tel 01279 873500
Fax 01279 873501
wine@hwcg.co.uk
www.hwcg.co.uk

Idg – Indigo Wine
7 Beverstone Road, London SW2 5AL
Tel 020 7733 8391
Fax 020 7733 8391
info@indigowine.com
www.indigowine.com

IGH – Ian G Howe
35 Appletongate, Newark,
Nottinghamshire, NG24 1JR
Tel 01636 704366
Fax 01636 610502
howe@chablis-burgundy.co.uk
www.chablis-burgundy.co.uk

IRW – Irvine Robertson Wines
10-11 North Leith Sands, Edinburgh
EH6 4ER
Tel 0131 553 3521
Fax 0131 553 5465
irviner@nildram.co.uk
www.irwines.co.uk

IVi – I Vini
Unit 2, The Old Kennels,
Cirencester Park,
Cirencester, Gloucestershire GL7 1UR
Tel 01285 655595
Fax 01285 650684
enquiries@ivini.co.uk
www.ivini.co.uk

IVV – In Vino Veritas
3 Wessex Court, Main Road,
Shuttington, Staffs, B79 0DS
Tel 01827 899449
Fax 01827 899936
webmaster@ivvltd.com
www.ivvltd.com

J&B – Justerini & Brooks
61 St James Street, London, SW1A 1LZ
Tel 020 7484 6400
Fax 020 7484 6499
www.justerinis.com

497

JAr – John Armit
5 Royalty Studios, 105 Lancaster Road,
London, W11 1QF
Tel 020 7908 0600
Fax 020 7908 0601
info@armit.co.uk
www.armit.co.uk

Jas – Jascots Wine Merchants Ltd
The Observatory, Pinnacle House,
260 Old Oak Common Lane, London
NW10 6DX
Tel 020 8965 2000
Fax 020 8965 9500
team@jascots.co.uk
www.jascots.co.uk

JBa – Julian Baker
Pound House, Bures Road, Wissington,
Nayland, Colchester, CO6 4LU
Tel 01206 262538
Fax 01206 263574
julianbaker@supranet.com

JEF – John E Fells
Fells House, Prince Edwards Street,
Berkhamstead, HP4 3EZ
Tel 01442 870900
Fax 01442 878555
info@fells.co.uk
www.fells.co.uk

JFW – James Fearon Wines
Centenary Buildings, Cleveland Avenue,
Holyhead LL65 2LB
Tel 01407 765200
Fax 01407 765620
enquiries@jamesfearonwines.co.uk
www.jamesfearonwines.co.uk

JIC – Just In Case
Symes Corner, Bank Street,
Bishops Waltham,
Hampshire SO32 1AN
Tel 01489 892969
Fax 01489 892969

JNi – James Nicholson
27a Killyleagh Street, Crossgar,
County Down, BT30 9DQ
Tel 028 4483 0091
Fax 028 4483 0028
info@jnwine.com
www.jnwine.com

JNV – Jackson Nugent Vintners
30 Homefield Road, Wimbledon
Village,
London SW19 4QF
Tel 020 8947 9722
Fax 020 8944 1048
www.jnv.co.uk

JTD – J T Davies & Son
7 Aberdeen Road, Croydon, CR0 1EQ
Tel 020 8681 3222
Fax 020 8681 5931
postbox@jtdavies.co.uk
www.jtdavies.co.uk

L&S – Lea & Sandeman
170 Fulham Road, Chelsea,
London, SW10 9PR
Tel 020 7244 0522
Fax 020 7244 0533
info@leaandsandeman.co.uk
www.londonfinewine.co.uk

L&T – Lane & Tatham
12 Market Place, Devizes SN10 1HT
Tel 01380 720123
Fax 01380 720111
wines@lanetat.demon.co.uk

L&W – Lay & Wheeler
Holton Park, Holton St Mary,
Suffolk CO7 6NN
Tel 0845 330 1855
Fax 0845 330 4095
sales@laywheeler.com
www.laywheeler.com

Las – L'Assemblage
Pallant Court, West Pallant, Chichester,
West Sussex PO19 1TG
Tel 01243 537775
Fax 01243 538644
sales@lassemblage.co.uk
www.lassemblage.co.uk

Lay – Jeroboams / Laytons
7-9 Elliot's Place, London N1 8HX
Tel 020 7259 6716
Fax 020 7495 3314
sales@jeroboams.co.uk
www.jeroboams.co.uk

Lib – Liberty Wines
Unit D18-23, The Food Market,
New Covent Garden, London SW8 5LL
Tel 020 7720 5350
Fax 020 7720 6158
info@libertywine.co.uk
www.libertywine.co.uk

LLt – Louis Latour UK
PO Box 4286, London W1A 7WL
Tel 020 7409 7276
Fax 020 7409 7092
enquiries@louislatour.co.uk
www.louislatour.com

L-P – Laurent Perrier UK
66-68 Chapel Street, Marlow,
Buckinghamshire SL7 1DE
Tel 01628 475404
Fax 01628 471891
enquiries@laurent-perrier.co.uk
www.laurent-perrier.co.uk

Luv – Luvians Bottleshop
93 Bonnygate, Cupar, Fife SL7 1DE
Tel 01334 654820
Fax 01334 654820
info@luvians.com
www.luvians.com

**Lwt – Laithwaites /
Direct Wines Ltd**
New Aquitaine House, Exeter Way,
Theale, Reading, Berkshire RG7 4PL
Tel 0870 444 8282
Fax 0870 444 8182
www.laithwaites.co.uk

Maj – Majestic Wine Warehouses
Majestic House, Otterspool Way,
Watford WD25 8WW
Tel 01923 298200
Fax 01923 819105
info@majestic.co.uk
www.majestic.co.uk

Mar – Martinez Wines
35 The Grove, Ilkley,
West Yorkshire LS29 9NJ
Tel 01943 603241
Fax 0870 9223940
julian@martinez.co.uk
www.martinez.co.uk

Max – Maxxium
Maxxium House, Castle Business Park,
Stirling FK9 4RT
Tel 01786 430500
Fax 01786 430600

May – Mayfair Cellars
Unit 3b, Farm Lane Trading Centre,
101 Farm Lane, London SW6 1QJ
Tel 020 7386 7999
Fax 020 7386 0202
sales@mayfaircellars.co.uk
www.mayfaircellars.co.uk

**MCD – Marne & Champagne
Diffusion**
18 Bolton Street, London W1J 8BJ
Tel 020 7499 0070
Fax 020 7408 0841
sales@mcduk.com

McK – McKinley Vintners
14 Kennington Road, London SE1 7BL
Tel 020 7928 7300
Fax 020 7928 4447
info@mckinleyvintners.co.uk
www.mckinleyvintners.co.uk

MCl – Matthew Clark
Whitchurch Lane, Whitchurch,
Bristol BS14 0JZ
Tel 01275 891400
Fax 01275 890595
www.mclark.co.uk

MCW – Morgan Classic Wines
Crown House, 4 Market Lane, Lewes,
East Sussex 7BN 2NT
Tel 01273 487000
Fax 01273 487700
sales@morganclassics.com
www.morganclassicwines.com

Men – Mentzendorff
8th Floor, Prince Consort House,
27-29 Albert Embankment, London
SE1 7TJ
Tel 020 7840 3600
Fax 020 7840 3601
www.mentzendorff.co.uk

MHn – Moët Hennessey UK
13 Grosvenor Crescent, London
SW1X 7EE
Tel 020 7235 9411
Fax 020 7235 6937

Mis – Mistral Wines
5 Junction Mews, Sale Place, London
W2 1PN
Tel 020 7262 5437
Fax 020 7402 7957
info@mistralwines.co.uk

**MMD – Maison Marques &
Domaines**
4 College Mews, St Ann's Hill,
London SW18 2SJ
Tel 020 8812 3380
Fax 020 8812 3390
maison@mmdltd.co.uk
www.mmdltd.com

Mor – Moreno Wines
26 Macroom Road, Maida Vale,
London W9 3HY
Tel 020 8960 7161
Fax 020 8960 7165
sales@moreno-wines.co.uk

499

UK STOCKISTS

MPe – Michael Peace MW
24 Drayson Mews, London W8 4LY
Tel 020 7937 9345
Fax 020 7937 7884
info@michaelpeace.com

MtC – Morgenrot-Chevaliers
Olde Forge, Bent Street Estate, Kearsley,
Bolton, BL4 9DH
Tel 01204 573093
Fax 01204 466259
sales@morgenrot.co.uk
www.morgenrot-chevaliers.co.uk

MVs – Merchant Vintners
Red Duster House, York Street, Hull,
East Yorkshire, HU2 0QX
Tel 01482 329443
Fax 01482 213616
sam@merchantvintners.co.uk

N&P – Nickolls & Perks
37 High Street, Stourbridge,
West Midlands, DY8 1TA
Tel 01384 394518
Fax 01384 440786
sales@nickollsandperks.co.uk
www.nickollsandperks.co.uk

NDb – Nick Dobson Wines
38 Crail Close, Wokingham, Berkshire
RG41 2PZ
Tel 0800 849 3078
Fax: 0870 460 2358
sales@nickdobsonwines.co.uk
www.nickdobsonwines.co.uk

Nid – Nidderdale Fine Wines
2a High Street, Pateley Bridge,
North Yorkshire HG3 5AW
Tel 01423 711703
Fax 01423 712239
info@southaustralianwines.com
www.southaustralianwines.com

NoG – Noble Grape
21-27 Brandon Terrace, Edinburgh,
EH3 5DZ
Tel 0131 556 3133
Fax 0131 556 8766
info@thenoble-grape.co.uk
www.thenoble-grape.co.uk

Nov – Novum Wines
166 Sail Street, Vauxhall, London
SE11 6NQ
Tel 020 7820 6720
Fax 020 7091 0878
info@novumwines.com
www.novumwines.com

NYg – Noel Young Wines
56 High Street, Trumpington,
Cambridgeshire, CB2 2LS
Tel 01223 844744
Fax 01223 844736
admin@nywines.co.uk
www.nywines.co.uk

Oak – Oakley Wine Agencies
PO Box 3234, Earls Colne,
Colchester, CO6 2SU
Tel 01787 220070
Fax 01787 224734
oakleywine@btconnect.com

Ock – Ockse Wines
28 Gloucester Circus, London SE10
8RY
Tel 020 8858 8636
Fax 020 8333 8889
office@ocksewines.net
www.ocksewines.net

Odd – Oddbins
31-33 Weir Road, London, SW19 8UG
Tel 0800 328 2323
Fax 0800 328 3848
customer.services@oddbinsmail.com
www.oddbins.com

OWL – O W Loeb
3 Archie Street, London SE1 3JT
Tel 020 7234 0385
Fax 020 7357 0440
finewine@owloeb.com
www.owloeb

OxW – Oxford Wine Company
The Wine Warehouse, Witney Road,
Standlake,
Oxfordshire OX29 7PR
Tel 01865 301144
Fax 01865 301155
info@oxfordwine.co.uk
www.oxfordwine.co.uk

P&S – Philglas & Swiggot
21 Northcote Road, London SW11
1NG
Tel 020 7924 4494
Fax 020 7924 4736
info@philglas-swiggot.co.uk
www.philglas-swiggot.co.uk

Par – Paragon Vintners
Regent Gate, 21 Dartmouth Street,
London, SW1H 9BP
Tel 020 7887 1800
Fax 020 7887 1810
welcome@paragonvintners.co.uk

Pat – Patriarche Wine Agencies
7 Rickett Street, Fulham, London,
SW6 1RU
Tel 020 7381 4016
Fax 020 7381 2023
sales@patriarchewines.com

PBW – Paul Boutinot Agencies
Brook House, 4 Northenden Road,
Gatley, Cheshire, SK8 4DN
Tel 0161 908 1371
Fax 0161 908 1375
marketing@boutinot.com
www.boutinot.com

PDn – Pimlico Dozen / Vintage Cellars
33 Churton Street, London, SW1V 2LT
Tel 020 7834 3647
Fax 020 7233 7536
pimlico@winecellarsales.co.uk
www.winecellarsales.co.uk

PFx – Percy Fox & Co
Unit C Woodside, Dunmow Road,
Bishop's Stortford CM23 5RG
Tel 01279 756200
Fax 01279 757022
percyfoxmarketing@diageo.com

PLB – PLB Group Ltd
Dorset House, 64 High Street,
East Grinstead, RH19 3DE
Tel 01342 318282
Fax 01342 314023
general@plb.co.uk
www.plb.co.uk

Pic – Pic Wines
3, rue Basse, 34380 Viols le Fort, France
Tel 0033 499 62 09 27
Fax 0033 467 55 81 28
contact@picwines.co.uk
www.picwines.co.uk

Pol – Pol Roger Ltd
Shelton House, 4 Conningsby Street,
Hereford, HR1 2DY
Tel 01432 262800
Fax 01432 262806
wineshops@polroger.co.uk
www.polroger.co.uk

Por – Portland Wine
152a Ashley Road, Hale, Altrincham,
Cheshire
Tel 0161 928 0357
Fax 0161 905 1291
portwineco@aol.com
www.portlandwine.co.uk

POs – Peter Osborne & Co
Watcombe Manor Farm, Ingham Lane,
Watlington, Oxfordshire OX9 5EJ
Tel 01491 612311
Fax 01491 613322
info@peterosbornewine.co.uk
www.peterosbornewine.co.uk

Pre – Premier Vintners
Tel 020 8870 3550
Fax 020 8870 3559
info@premiervintners.co.uk
www.premiervintners.co.uk

PVF – Producteurs et Vignerons de France
Toad Hall, Wilbury Road, Hove,
East Sussex BN3 3JJ
Tel 01273 730277
Fax 01273 328691
admin@vigneronsdefrance.co.uk

PWa – Peter Watkins Wine
2 Manor Road, Pitsford, Northampton
NN2 9AR
Tel 01604 882370
Fax 01604 889465
sales@peterwatkinswine.co.uk
www.peterwatkinswine.co.uk

PWt – Peter Watts Wines
Wisdom's Barn, Colne Road,
Coggeshall, Essex CO6 1TD
Tel 01376 561130
Fax 01376 562925
sales@peterwattswines.co.uk
www.peterwattswines.co.uk

PWy – Peter Wylie Fine Wines
Plymtree Manor, Plymtree,
Cullompton, Devon EX15 2LE
Tel 01884 277555
Fax 01884 277557
peter@wylie-fine-wines.demon.co.uk
www.wyliefinewines.co.uk

Rae – Raeburn Fine Wines
The Vaults, 4 Giles Street, Leith,
Edinburgh EH6 6DJ
Tel 0131 343 1159
Fax 0131 332 5166
sales@raeburnfinewines.com
www.raeburnfinewines.com

Rec – Recount Wines
44 Lower Sloane Street,
London SW1W 8BP
Tel 020 7730 6377
Fax 020 7730 6377

501

en – Renvic Wines
2 School Cottages, Abington Pigotts,
Nr Royston, Herts SG8 0SQ
Tel 01763 852470
Fax 01763 852470

Rev – Revelstoke Wine Co
Unit 8 Saxon Business Centre, Windsor
Avenue,
London SW19 2RR
Tel 020 8545 0077
Fax 020 8545 0044
info@revelstoke.co.uk
www.revelstoke.co.uk

RGr – Richard Granger Fine Wine
West Jesmond Station, Lyndhurst
Avenue,
Newcastle NE2 3HH
Tel 0191 281 5000
Fax 0191 281 8141
sales@richardgrangerwines.co.uk
www.richardgrangerwines.co.uk

RHW – Roger Harris Wines
Loke Farm, Weston Longville,
Norfolk NR9 5LG
Tel 01603 880171
Fax 01603 880291
sales@rogerharriswines.co.uk
www.rogerharriswines.co.uk

RMe – Richard Marlowe
187 Tarlton, Cirencester GL7 6PN
Tel 01285 770401
Fax 01285 771211

RRl – Robert Rolls
36-37 Charterhouse Square,
London EC1M 6EA
Tel 020 7606 1166
Fax 020 7606 1144
mail@rollswine.com
www.rollswine.com

RSJ – RSJ Wine
33 Coin Street, London SE1 9NR
Tel 020 7928 4554
Fax 020 7928 9768
tom.king@rsj.uk.com
www.rsj.uk.com

RSL – RS Wines Ltd
Upper Littleton Mills, Chew Road,
Winford BS40 8HJ
Tel 01275 331444
Fax 01275 332444
info@rswines.co.uk
www.rswines.co.uk

RSo – Raisin Social
Linden House, 34 Crowhurst Mead,
Godstone, Surrey RH9 8BF
Tel 01883 731173
Fax 01883 731174
info@raisin-social.com
www.raisin-social.com

RsW – Richards Walford
Hales Lodge, Pickworth,
Nr Stamford, Lincolnshire PE9 4DJ
Tel 01780 460451
Fax 01780 460276
sales@r-w.co.uk

Rui – Ruinart UK
13 Grovesnor Crescent,
London SW1X 7EE
Tel 020 7416 0592
Fax 020 7416 0593
www.ruinart.com

RWs – Reid Wines
The Mill, Marsh Lane, Hallatrow,
Bristol BS39 6EB
Tel 01761 452645
Fax 01761 452642
reidwines@aol.com

Sav – Savage Selection
The Ox House, Market Place,
Northleach,
Gloucestershire GL54 3EG
Tel 01451 860896
Fax 01451 860996
wine@savageselection.co.uk
www.savageselection.co.uk

Sec – Seckford Wines
Dock Lane, Melton, Ipswich, Suffolk
IP12 1PE
Tel 01394 446622
Fax 01394 446633
sales@seckfordwines.co.uk
www.seckfordwines.co.uk

Sel – Selfridges & Co
400 Oxford Street, London W1A 1AB
Tel 020 7318 3730
Fax 020 7491 1880
www.selfridges.co.uk

SFW – Stokes Fine Wines
41 Trewint Street, London SW18 4HB
Tel 020 8944 5979
Fax 020 8944 5935
sales@stokesfinewines.com

SsG – Stevens Garnier & FSA
47 West Way, Botley, Oxford OX2 0JF
Tel 01865 263300
Fax 01865 791594
info@stevensgarnier.co.uk
www.stevensgarnier.co.uk

SVS – Stone, Vine & Sun
No.13 Humphrey Farms, Hazeley Road,
Twyford, Winchester SO21 1QA
Tel 01962 712351
Fax 01962 717545
sales@stonevine.co.uk
www.stonevine.co.uk

Swg – Swig
188 Sutton Court Road, London
W4 3HR
Tel 08000 272 272
Fax 020 8995 7069
imbibe@swig.co.uk
www.swig.co.uk

T&W – T & W Wines
5 Station Way, Brandon, Suffolk
IP27 0BH
Tel 01842 814414
Fax 01842 819967
contact@tw-wines.com
www.tw-wines.com

Tan – Tanners Wine Merchants
26 Wyle Cop, Shrewsbury, Shropshire,
SY11XD
Tel 01743 234500
Fax 01743 234501
sales@tanners-wines.co.uk
www.tanners-wines.co.uk

Ter – Terroir Limited
Treetops, Grassington Road, Skipton,
North Yorkshire BD23 1LL
Tel 01756 700512
Fax 01756 797856
enquiries@terroirlanguedoc.co.uk
www.terroirlanguedoc.co.uk

The – Theatre of Wine
75 Trafalgar Road, Greenwich,
London SE10 9TS
Tel 020 8858 6363
Fax 020 8305 1936
info@theatreofwine.com
www.theatreofwine.com

ThP – Thomas Panton
The Wine Warehouse,
Hampton Street, Tetbury,
Gloucestershire GL8 8JN
Tel 01666 503088
Fax 01666 503113
sales@wineimporter.co.uk
www.wineimporter.co.uk

THt – Thorman Hunt
4 Pratt Walk, Lambeth, London,
SE11 6AR
Tel 020 7735 6511
Fax 020 7735 9779
info@thormanhunt.co.uk

TPg – Thos Peatling
Westgate House, Westgate Street,
Bury St Edmunds, Suffolk IP33 1QS
Tel 01284 755948
Fax 01284 714483
sales@thospeatling.co.uk
www.thospeatling.co.uk

TPt – Terry Platt
Council Street West, Llandudno,
LL30 1ED
Tel 01492 874099
Fax 01492 874722

Tra – Transatlantic Wines
The Magpies, Eye Kettleby Drive,
Eye Kettleby,
Melton Mowbray LE14 2TD
Tel 01664 565013
Fax 01664 564938
patrick@transatlantic-wines.co.uk

Tur – Turville Valley Wines
The Firs, Potter Row, Great Missenden,
Buckinghamshire, HP16 9LT
Tel 01494 868818
Fax 01494 868832
info@turville-valley-wines.com
www.turville-valley-wines.com

TWS – Thierry's Wine Services
Horsefair House, The Horsefair,
Romsey,
Hampshire, SO51 8EZ
Tel 01794 507100
Fax 01794 516856
info@thierrys.co.uk
www.thierrys.co.uk

UnC – Uncorked
Exchange Arcade, Broadgate,
London EC2M 3WA
Tel   020 7638 5998
Fax   020 7638 6028
drink@uncorked.co.uk
www.uncorked.co.uk

V&C – Valvona & Crolla
19 Elm Road, Edinburgh EH7 4AA
Tel   0131 556 6066
Fax   0131 556 1668
wine@valvonacrolla.co.uk
www.valvonacrolla.co.uk

Vbr – Vickbar
25 Patshull Road, London NW5 2JX
Tel   020 7267 3324
gjdlemos@btinternet.com

VCq – Veuve Clicquot
Third Floor, 15 St George's Street,
London, W1S 1FH
Tel   020 7408 7430
Fax   020 7408 7457
yellow@veuve-clicquot.co.uk
www.veuveclicquot.fr

Vcs – Vinceremos Organic Wines
74 Kirkgate, Leeds LS2 7DJ
Tel   0113 244 0002
Fax   0113 288 4566
info@vinceremos.co.uk
www.vinceremos.co.uk

VDu – Van Duuren Wines Ltd
3 Framfield Road, Hanwell, London
W7 1NG
Tel   020 8567 4428
Fax   020 8567 4428
svanduuren@aol.com

VdV – Vin du Van
Colthups, The Street, Appledore,
Ashford, Kent TN26 2BX
Tel   01233 758727
Fax   01233 758389

Ver - Veritaus & Co
Unit 7, Caker Stream Road, Alton,
Hampshire GU34 2QA
Tel   0870 7704112
Fax   0870 7704113
info@veritaus.com
www.veritaus.com

Vex - Vinexcel Ltd
121 Crossefield Road, Cheadle Hulme
SK8 5PF
Tel   0161 485 4592
Fax   0161 485 4892

Vic - Vickery Wines
Vickery House, 3 Ridgewood Drive,
Harpenden, Herts AL5 3NL
Tel   01582 469930
Fax   01582 462039
info@vickerywines.co.uk
www.vickerywines.co.uk

Vim – Vinum
1 Barrow Walk, Brentford, Middlesex
TW8 0RA
Tel   020 8847 4699
Fax   020 8847 4771
vinum@vinum.co.uk
www.vinum.co.uk

Vin – Vineyard Cellars
The Bindery, Wantage Road,
Hungerford, Berkshire, RG17 0PL
Tel   01488 681313
Fax   01488 681411
jameshocking@vineyardcellars.com
www.vineyardcellars.com

Vir – Virgin Wines Online Ltd
St James' Mill, Whitefriars, Norwich
NR3 1TN
Tel   0870 164 9593
Fax   01603 619277
help@virginwines.com
www.virginwines.com

ViV – Vitis Vinifera
33 Godfrey Way, Great Dunmow,
Essex, CM6 2AY
Tel   01371 873383
Fax   01371 873383

VKg - The Vine King
16 Steerforth Street, London
SW18 4HH
Tel   020 8879 3030
Fax   020 8946 6474
erik@thevineking.com
www.thevineking.com

Vne - Villeneuve Wines Ltd
1 Venlaw Court, Peebles EH45 8AE
Tel   01721 722500
Fax   01721 729922
wines@villeneuvewines.com
www.villeneuvewines.com

Vnf - Vin Neuf
Stratford upon Avon, Warwickshire
Tel   01789 261747
Fax   01789 261749
info@vinneuf.co.uk
www.vinneuf.co.uk

Vni – Vinites UK
37 Montholme Road, London
SW11 6HX
Tel 020 7924 4974
Fax 020 7228 6109

Vns – Vinoceros
Stanley Way, Cardrew, Redruth,
Cornwall, TR15 1SP
Tel 01209 314711
Fax 01209 314712
enquiries@vinoceros.com
www.vinoceros.com

Vnt – The Vintner Ltd
The Church, 172 London Road,
Guildford, Surrey GU1 1XR
Tel 01483 458700
Fax 01483 454677
info@thevintner.co.uk
www.thevintner.co.uk

VRt – Vintage Roots
Farley Farms, Bridge Farm,
Reading Road,
Arborfield, Berkshire RG2 9HT
Tel 0118 976 1999
Fax 0118 976 1998
info@vintageroots.co.uk
www.vintageroots.co.uk

VTr – Vine Trail
266 Hotwell Road, Hotwells, Bristol
BS8 4NG
Tel 0117 921 1770
Fax 0117 921 1772
enquiries@vinetrail.co.uk
www.vinetrail.co.uk

Vts – Veritas Wines
103 Cherry Hinton Road, Cambridge
CB1 7BS
Tel 01223 212500
info@veritaswines.co.uk
www.veritaswines.co.uk

Vxs – Vinexus
34 Islington Green, London N1 8DU
Tel 020 7704 6313
Fax 020 7704 6318
vinexus.ltd@virgin.net

WAe – WineAlive.com
37 The Tything, Worcester WR1 1JL
Tel 01905 731730
Fax 01905 731443
info@winealive.com
www.winealive.com

Wai – Waitrose/John Lewis
Doncastle Road,
Southern Industrial Area,
Bracknell, Berkshire RG12 8YA
Tel 01344 424680
Fax 01344 825255
www.waitrose.com

Wat – Waterloo Wine Co.
6 Vine Yard, London, SE1 1QL
Tel 020 7403 7967
Fax 020 7357 6976
sales@waterloowine.co.uk
www.waterloowine.co.uk

Wav – Waverley TBS
Punchbowl Park, Cherry Tree Lane,
Hemel Hempstead, Herts HP1 7EU
Tel 01442 293000
Fax 01442 293006
iws@intwine.co.uk
www.waverley-group.co.uk

WBn – Wine Barn
2 Stable Cottages, Church Barns,
East Stratton,
Winchester, Hampshire SO21 3XA
Tel 01962 774102
Fax 01962 774102
info@thewinebarn.co.uk
www.thewinebarn.co.uk

WEx – Winexcel
5 Avebury Close, Horsham,
West Sussex RH12 5JY

WhW – Whittaker Wines
35 Chatsworth Road, High Lane,
Bredbury
Cheshire, SK6 8DA
Tel 01663 764497
Fax 01663 765910
sales@whittakerwines.com
www.whittakerwines.com

WIE – Wine Importers Edinburgh
Unit 7, Beaverhall House,
27 Beaverhall Road,
Edinburgh EH7 4JE
Tel 0131 556 3601
Fax 0131 557 8493
www.wine-importers.net

Win – The Winery
4 Clifton Road, Maida Vale, London,
W9 1SS
Tel 020 7286 6475
Fax 020 7286 2733

Wit – Withers Agencies
1 South Street, Lewes, East Sussex,
BN7 2BT
Tel 01273 477132
Fax 01273 476612

WKe – The Wine Keller
Little Orchard, Cox Green Lane,
Maidenhead, Berkshire SL6 3EL
Tel 01628 620143
Fax 01628 620143
info@thewinekeller.co.uk
www.thewinekeller.co.uk

WRk – Wine Raks
21 Springfield Road, Aberdeen
AB15 7RJ
Tel 01224 311460
Fax 01224 312186
enq@wineraks.com
www.wineraks.com

WsB – Wills-Burgundy
200 Brook Drive, Green Park,
Reading RG2 6UB
Tel 0845 057 3218
Fax 0870 755 9722
will@wills-burgundy.com
www.wills-burgundy.com

WSc – The Wine Society
Gunnels Wood Road, Stevenage,
SG1 2BG
Tel 01483 741177
Fax 01483 741392
memberservices@thewinesociety.com
www.thewinesociety.com

WSe – Wineservice
Semper Fidelis Mews, Wire Mill Lane,
Lingfield, Surrey RH7 6HJ
Tel 01342 837333
Fax 01342 837444
sales@wineservice.co.uk

WSo – Winesource
393 Ham Green, Holt, Trowbridge,
Wiltshire, BA14 6PX
Tel 01225 783007
Fax 01225 783504
winesource@saqnet.co.uk

WSS – Siegel Wine Agencies
Regent House, 123 High Street,
Odiham,
Hampshire, RG29 1LA
Tel 01256 701101
Fax 01256 701518
wine@walter-siegel.co.uk
www.walter-siegel.co.uk

WTs – The Wine Treasury
69 - 71 Bondway, London, SW8 1SQ
Tel 020 7793 9999
Fax 020 7793 8080
www.winetreasury.com

Wvr – Weavers of Nottingham
Vintners House, 1 Castle Gate,
Nottingham NG1 7AQ
Tel 0115 958 0922
Fax 0115 950 8076
weavers@weaverswines.com
www.weaverswines.com

WWC – Wimbledon Wine Cellar
1 Gladstone Road, Wimbledon,
London SW19 1QU
Tel 020 8540 9979
Fax 020 8540 9399
enquiries@wimbledonwinecellar.com
www.wimbledonwinecellar.com

Yap – Yapp Brothers
The Old Brewery, Mere, Wiltshire,
BA12 6DY
Tel 01747 860423
Fax 01747 860929
sales@yapp.co.uk
www.yapp.co.uk

Yng – Young and Company
The Ram Brewery, Wandsworth,
London,
SW18 4JD
Tel 020 8875 7007
Fax 020 8875 7197
winedirect@youngs.co.uk
www.youngswinedirect.co.uk

3DW – 3D Wines Ltd
1-2 North End, Swineshead,
Lincolnshire PE20 3LR
Tel 01205 820745
Fax 01205 821042
info@3dwines.com
www.3dwines.com

Other wine traders of note

Bonhams
101 New Bond Street, London W1S
1SR
Tel 020 7447 7447
Fax 020 7447 7400
wine@bonhams.com
www.bonhams.com

Christie's
8 King Street, St James's, London SW1Y
6QT
Tel 020 7752 3295
Fax 020 7752 3023
delswood@christies.com
www.christies.com

LIV-ex
Unit 147, Battersea Business Centre,
99-109 Lavender Hill, London SW11
5QL
Tel 020 7228 2233
admin@live-ex.co.uk
www.liv-ex.com

Sotheby's
34/35 New Bond Street, London
W1A 2AA
Tel 020 7293 6423
Fax 020 7293 5961
wine.london@sothebys.com
www.sothebys.com

Uvine (Universal Wine Exchange)
Swan Court, 9 Tanner Street, London
SE1 3LE
Tel 020 7089 2200
Fax 020 7089 2211
enquiries@uvine.com
www.uvine.com

Wilkinson Vintners
38 Chagford Street, London NW1 6EB
Tel 020 7616 0404
Fax 020 7616 0400
wine@wilkinsonvintners.com

This producer index is ordered according to the name by which an estate is most commonly referred. There is priority to surnames but otherwise they appear as they are written. 'Domaine' is ignored but 'Château', 'Clos', 'Mas' etc are respected as is the definite article when implicitly part of the name (eg Mas de Daumas Gassac appears under 'M'). The only exception is in Bordeaux where 'Château' is also ignored and the name of the château or estate takes precedent.

INDEX

511

INDEX

INDEX

515

INDEX

Bring the Book Alive - live links to producer websites at **www.winebehindthelabel.com**

Bring the Book Alive - live links to producer websites at www.winebehindthelabel.com

INDEX

Bring the Book Alive - live links to producer websites at www.winebehindthelabel.com

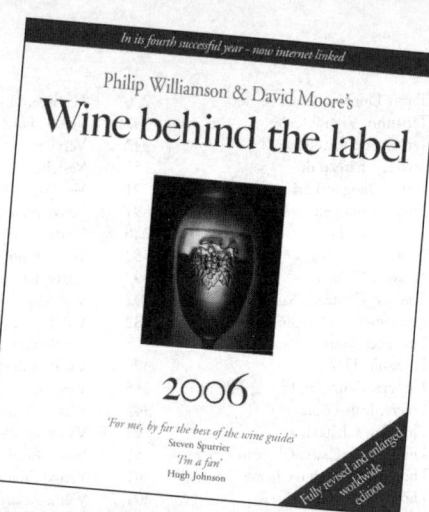

We hope you have enjoyed this book as much as we enjoyed compiling it. You may like to know that we have produced three other books for 2006 - *Wine behind the label*, now in its fourth year, an in-depth guide to the world's leading wine producers and their wines; *Wine Wizards*, a compact guide to the world's wines and *The Top 100 UK Restaurant Wine Lists* by Neville Blech. For more information go to *www.williamson-moore.co.uk*

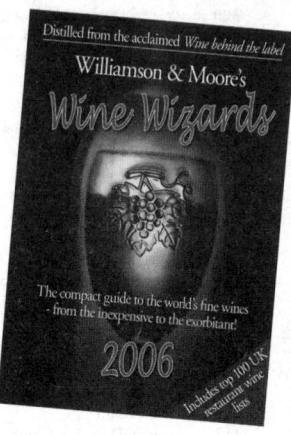